W9-BZR-386

SYSTEMS ANALYSIS AND DESIGN

Fourth Edition

SYSTEMS ANALYSIS AND DESIGN

Kenneth E. Kendall

Rutgers University
School of Business-Camden
Camden, New Jersey
USA

Julie E. Kendall

Rutgers University
School of Business-Camden
Camden, New Jersey
USA

Prentice Hall, Upper Saddle River, New Jersey 07458

Acquisitions Editor: David Alexander
Editorial Assistant: Shane Gemza
Editor-in-Chief: PJ Boardman
Marketing Manager: Nancy Evans
Production Editor: Susan Rifkin
Permissions Coordinator: Jennifer Rella
Manufacturing Supervisor: Paul Smolenski
Manufacturing Manager: Vincent Scelta
Design Manager: Patricia Smythe
Cover Design: John Romer
Composition/Illustrator (Interior): The Clarinda Company
Cover Art: Michael Tunney, *S.J., Buffalo No. 6 (Ross' Critique),* 1996

Microsoft and Windows are registered trademarks of the Microscoft Corporation in the U.S.A. and other countries. Screen shots and icons reprinted with permission from Microsoft Corporation. This book is not sponsored or endorsed by or affiliated with the Microsoft Corporation.

 Copyright ©1999, 1995, 1992, 1988 by Prentice-Hall, Inc.
A Simon & Schuster Company
Upper Saddle River, New Jersey 07458

All rights reserved. No part of this book may be reproduced, in any form or by any means, without written permission from the Publisher.

Library of Congress Cataloging-in-Publication Data

Kendall, Kenneth E.,
    Systems analysis and design / Kenneth E. Kendall, Julie E.
Kendall. — 4th ed.
        p.   cm.
    Includes index.
    ISBN 0–13–646621–4
    1. System design.   2. System analysis.   I. Kendall, Julie E.
    II. Title.
QA76.9.S88K45   1998
004.2'1—dc21   99-36001
                                                                          CIP

Prentice-Hall International (UK) Limited, London
Prentice-Hall of Australia Pty. Limited, Sydney
Prentice-Hall Canada, Inc., Toronto
Prentice-Hall Hispanoamericana, S.A., Mexico
Prentice-Hall of India Private Limited, New Delhi
Prentice-Hall of Japan, Inc., Tokyo
Simon & Schuster Asia Pte. Ltd., Singapore
Editora Prentice-Hall do Brasil, Ltda., Rio de Janeiro

Printed in the United States of America

10   9   8   7   6   5   4   3

To Edward J. Kendall and Julia A. Kendall,
whose lifelong example of working together will inspire us forever

COMPANY TRADEMARKS

Apple and Macintosh are registered trademarks of Apple Computer. Dragon Dictate is a registered trademark of Dragon Systems, Inc. Ecco is a registered trademark of NetManage, Inc. Excelerator is a registered trademark of INTERSOLV. FormFlow is a registered trademark of JetForm Corporation. HyperCase is a registered trademark of Raymond J. Barnes, Richard L. Baskerville, Julie E. Kendall, and Kenneth E. Kendall. Lotus 1-2-3, Freelance Graphics, Organizer, and Smartmasters are registered trademarks of Lotus Corporation. Micrografx Designer, Flowcharter, WebCharter, and Graphics Suite are registered trademarks of Micrografx Corporation. Microsoft Windows, Microsoft Access, Microsoft Word, Microsoft FrontPage, Microsoft PowerPoint, Microsoft Project, and Microsoft Excel are registered trademarks of Microsoft Corporation. Netscape Communicator and Netscape Navigator are registered trademarks of Netscape Communications Corp. Palm Pilot is a trademark of 3COM Corporation. ProModel, ProcessModel, and Service Model are registered trademarks of PROMODEL Corporation. Visible Analyst Workbench is a registered trademark of Visible Systems Corporation. Visio Professional is a registered trademark of Visio Corpoartion. Visual Page and Visual Cafe' Pro for Java are registered trademarks of Symantec Corporation. XperCase is a registered trademark of Siemens AG Osterreich. Other product and company names mentioned herein may be the trademarks of their respectful owners. Companies, names, and/or data used in screens and sample output are fictitious unless otherwise noted.

BRIEF CONTENTS

CONTENTS

ix

CONTENTS

CONTENTS

XV

PREFACE

The Year 2000 is almost upon us, and that means that we are faced with both problems (such as the Year 2000 Crisis) and opportunities (such as using the World Wide Web). These challenges were in our minds when we undertook this revision .

The fourth edition of *Systems Analysis and Design* includes many **New Features**. In particular:

- **Year 2000** compliance
- **Year 2000** problem examples and Consulting Opportunities
- **Web-based design**
- Expanded coverage of **graphical user interface (GUI) design**
- **Client/server** system design and **Intranet and Extranet** concepts
- Re-engineered ongoing case for use with **Visible Analyst Workbench**
- New **Consulting Opportunities**
- **Improved symbols** and notation for **Entity-Relationship** diagrams

DESIGN FEATURES

Figures take on a stylized look in order to help students more easily grasp the subject matter.

Paper forms are used throughout to show input and output design as well as the design of questionnaires. Blue is always used to show writing or data input, thereby making it easier to identify what was filled in by users. Much data capture is still done through the use of paper forms. Improved forms design enables analysts to ensure accurate and complete input and output. This example from Chapter 6 shows how to design scales for a questionnaire:

Computer display screens (enclosed by a blue box) demonstrate important features of software that are useful to the analyst. Actual screen shots show important aspects of design. This example shows Visio Professional, a drawing package useful to the systems analyst:

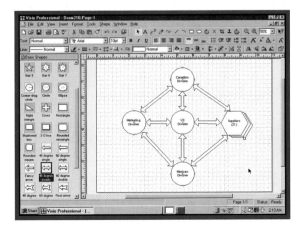

Conceptual diagrams are used to introduce the many tools systems analysts have at their disposal. This example shows how to label or read an entity-relationship diagram

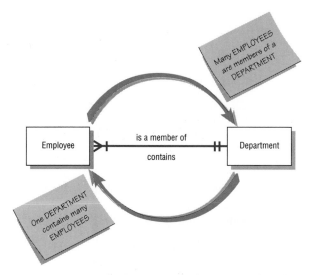

Tables are used when an important list needs special attention, or when information needs to be organized or classified. This example from Chapter 12 shows the different classes of services that gather information directly from the Web. The underlying philosophy of our book is that systems analysis and design is a process that integrates the use of many tools to systematically

Type of Service	Product	Web Site
Push technologies	BackWeb	www.backweb.com
	Marimba Castanet	www.marimba.com
	PointCast	www.pointcast.com
	Webcaster	www.microsoft.com/ie/ie40
	Netcaster	www.netscape.com/communicator
Personalized home pages	My Yahoo!	www.my.yahoo.com
	Personal Front Page	www.msnbc.com
On-line Newspapers	CNN Interactive	www.cnn.com
	London Times	www.the-times.co.uk
	New York Times	www.nytimes.com
	USA Today	www.usatoday.com
Intelligent Agents	Farcast	www.farcast.com
	Headliner	www.headliner.com
	Press Agent	www.agentware.com

accomplish its goals of improving business through the implementation or modification of computerized information systems.

The text is divided into five major parts: Systems Analysis Fundamentals (Part One), Information Requirements Analysis (Part Two), The Analysis Process (Part Three), The Essentials of Design (Part Four), and Software Engineering and Implementation (Part Five).

Part One (Chapters 1-3) stresses the basics that students need to know about what an analyst does; and how information systems fit into them; how to

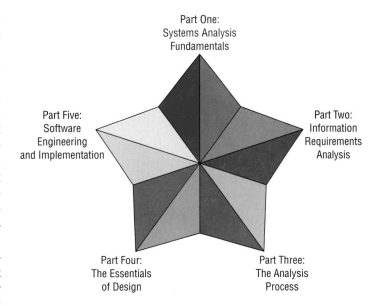

Part One:
Systems Analysis
Fundamentals

Part Two:
Information
Requirements
Analysis

Part Three:
The Analysis
Process

Part Four:
The Essentials
of Design

Part Five:
Software
Engineering
and Implementation

determine whether a systems project is worthy of commitment; and how to manage a systems project using special software tools. Improved techniques for drawing entity-relationship diagrams and context level data flow diagrams when first entering the organization are introduced. Alternative systems analysis and design methods such as ETHICS are introduced. The three roles of the systems analyst as consultant, supporting expert, and agent of change are also introduced and the ethical issues of serving as a consultant are raised.

Part Two (Chapters 4-8) emphasizes the use of systematic and structured methodologies. Attention to analysis helps analysts ensure that they are addressing the correct problem before designing the system. The presentation of each methodology (sampling, investigating hard data, interviewing, questionnaires, and observation) moves students clear to understand what information users need and how those needs can best be ascertained. Chapter 5 includes material on joint application design (JAD) for ascertaining information requirements in concert with users. Chapter 7 is especially innovative and goes well beyond the typical text in showing how to accomplish systematic observation of decision-makers. Chapter 8 is unique in its treatment of prototyping as another data gathering technique that enables the analyst to solve the right problem by getting users involved from the start.

Part Three (Chapters 9-14) details the analysis process. It builds on the previous two parts to move students into analysis of data flows as well as structured and semistructured decisions. It provides step-by-step details on how to use structured techniques to draw data flow diagrams. Chapter 9 provides coverage of how to create child diagrams; how to develop both logical and physical data flow diagrams; and how to partition data flow diagrams. Chapter 10 features new material on the data repository and vertical balancing of data flow diagrams. Chapter 11 includes material on developing process specifications. A discussion of both logical and physical process specifications shows how to use process specifications for horizontal balancing.

Part Three also covers how to diagram structured decisions with the use of structured English, decision tables, and decision trees. Students then progress to a consideration of semistructured decisions that are featured in decision support systems. New material in Chapter 12 gives practical guidelines about choosing decision support system methods and software. New approaches include the analytic hierarchy process (AHP), the use of recommendation systems, Web-based systems, and the use of simulations such as Promodel and ServiceModel to aid in decision-making.

After analysis of decisions is accomplished, students learn how to ascertain the hardware and software needs of the organization. In addition, students are taught several methods for forecasting costs and benefits, which is necessary to the discussion of software and hardware. Next, students are supplied with the quantitative and qualitative techniques needed to compare costs and benefits of a proposed system. Chapter 14 features material giving the guidelines for using graphics presentation packages to present the systems proposal. It stresses the importance of a professionally prepared, written and oral presentation of the systems proposal. The proposal is viewed as a persuasive document that is extremely important to the future acceptance and success of the system.

Part Four (Chapter 15-19) covers the essentials of design. It begins with designing output, since many practitioners believe systems to be output driven. The design of Web-based forms has been added. Particular attention is paid to relating output method to content, the effect of output on users, and designing good forms and screen. Chapter 15 features new material comparing advantages and disadvantages of output including Web screens, audio, micro forms, CD-ROM, DVD, and electronic output such as e-mail, faxes and bulletin boards. Chapter 16 includes innovative material on designing Web-based input forms as well as other electronic forms design. Also included is computer-assisted form design. Chapter 16 also covers new approaches to designing Web pages and Web sites. Other sections cover differences between mainframe and PC screen design; using icons in screen design; and GUI design. Input design stresses the importance of the systematic approach to the design of screens and forms and the influence of analysts in persuading users to use the system. How the user interacts with the computer and how to design an appropriate interface are also covered. The importance of user feedback and correct ergonomic design of computer workstations are also found in Part Four. How to design accurate data-entry procedures that take full advantage of computer and human capabilities to assure entry of quality data is the key here.

Chapter 17 includes improved notation for drawing entity-relationship diagrams. In also demonstrates how to use the entity-relationship diagram to determine record keys, as well as providing guidelines for file/database relation design. Students are shown the relevance of database design for the overall usefulness of the system, and how users actually use databases. Chapter 18 adds new material on important aspects of data mining and data warehousing. Innovative approaches to searching on the Web are also presented. Also highlighted is material on GUI design as well as providing innovative approaches to designing dialogs. Chapter 19 includes new material on solving the Year 2000 problem.

Finally, Part Five (Chapters 20, 21, and 22) introduces students to structured software engineering and documentation techniques as ways to implement a quality system. Chapter 20 includes a section on the important concepts of code generation and design re-engineering. We also cover developments in structured techniques while also teaching students which techniques are appropriate for which situations. The material on structure charts includes details on how to use data flow diagrams to draw structure charts. In addition, material on system security and firewalls is included. Testing, auditing, and maintenance of systems are discussed in the context of total quality management (TQM). Also, in Part Five, Chapter 21 introduces innovative tools for modeling networks, which can be done with popular tools such as Visio. A discussion of groupware is also included. Part Five also introduces the student to designing client/server systems and designing distributed systems. New material on security and in particular the use of firewalls has been added. Techniques for evaluating the completed information systems project are covered systematically as well.

Part Five concludes with Chapter 22 on Object-Oriented systems Analysis and Design. This chapter demonstrates, through several examples and Consulting Opportunities how to use an object-oriented approach. An example of problems associated with running a six-train semi-automated monorail in a small theme park is used to make key concepts come alive. Material on new proposals to standardize object-oriented notation is introduced.

Once again, Kendall & Kendall, *Systems Analysis and Design* fourth edition, includes the **CPU Case**, which is included in every chapter. In response to user feedback, the CPU case has been rewritten to use the popular CASE tool Visible Analyst Workbench by Visible Systems, Inc., as well as Microsoft Access for the example screen shots and the student exercises.

The fourth edition presents over 60 **Consulting Opportunities**, many of which have been rewritten to make them more challenging to solve; and the questions have been refined and made more specific in order to make them easier to respond to and consequently to grade. New Consulting Opportunities address new topics that have arisen in the field including the Year 2000 Problem and issues relating to data mining and data warehousing. Consulting Opportunities can be used for stimulating in-class discussions or assigned as homework or take-home exam questions. Since not all systems are huge two-year or three-year projects, our book contains many Consulting Opportunities that can be solved quickly in 20 to 30 minutes of group discussion or individual writing. These minicases, written in a humorous manner to enliven the material, require students to synthesize what they have learned up that point in the course, ask students to mature in their professional and ethical judgment, and expect students to articulate the reasoning that led to their systems decisions.

Each of the 22 chapters provides an end-of-the chapter summary that ties together the salient points of each chapter while providing an excellent review source for exams. Group projects are placed at the end of most chapters. Group Projects help students to learn to work together in a systems team to solve important problems that can best be solved through group interaction.

Systems analysis and design is typically taught in one or two semesters. Our book may be used in either situation. The text is appropriate for undergraduate (junior or senior) curricula at a four-year university, graduate school, or community college. The level and length of the course can be varied and supplemented by using real-world projects, HyperCase or other materials available on the instructor's portion of our Web site.

CONSULTING OPPORTUNITY 19.1

The Time Bomb

As you enter the IS groups' coffee room at Premium Airlines headquarters in Philadelphia, two of your systems teammates barely acknowledge your presence as they continue a lively discussion about a problem they're experiencing. Wanting to help out, you finally ask, "What's up guys?"

Kara Sell looks up briefly, gesturing for you to join them at the table. As you sit down next to her, Kara continues her conversation. "When we first started entering information about the date in our 'Flying for Prizes' mileage club, nobody ever imagined that there would *be* a year 2000 problem!"

Fresh from college and new to the team, Miles Garner is sitting across from you at the table. Miles asks, "What is a year 2000 problem anyway?"

After you and Kara exchange looks of slight surprise, Kara patiently explains. "The year 2000 problem refers to the crisis we will have with our database when the year 2000 comes around. When we entered data, we used a two-digit code for the year. For 1993 we entered 93; for 1994 we entered 94."

Miles replies quickly, "Well, I was still in school then. That's what we always did. But why does it matter that you entered '93 or '94? That was the right year, right?"

Kara tries to clarify her concern by giving an example. "Well, someone born in 1970 is 27 in the year 1997."

Miles interrupts. "Of course."

Kara continues. "That is, 97 − 70 = 27. But when the year 2000 comes, that person is 00 − 70 or −70 years old."

Replying swiftly, Miles counters, "Can't you just add 100 years when the year 2000 comes, so 100 + 00 −70 = 30? Wouldn't that solve it?"

You know from working with Kara for many years that she has been thinking about this for some time, as she tells Miles, "Well, that may work for awhile, but don't forget that we reward people who have been in our mileage program for five years. If someone joins in 1998, it will work, but what about our customers in the year 2000? In five years, that calculation would lead to 100 + 05 − 00 = 105 years."

Before you have a chance to contribute your own suggestion, Miles eagerly says, "Maybe we can fix that, too."

Kara looks up at the door as Douglas McDonnell, a long-time team member, enters. It's apparent he has been listening to the discussion from the hall and already has formulated a comment. After pouring himself a cup of coffee, he addresses Miles, saying, "I know you'll solve the year 2000 problem if you think about it long enough, but I am more concerned about the 1999 problem. Whenever our data entry people didn't know a person's date of birth, we instructed them to enter in a code of "99"—and our software recognized this as 'year unknown.' This was a common practice in computing for many, many years—and it made a lot of sense at the time. I am afraid that decision is going to explode in our faces."

How would you solve the year 2000 problem? (*Hint:* For more background on Premium Airlines, see Consulting Opportunity 11.4.) Suggest to your systems team in three paragraphs how you could solve it. Draw a data entry screen (or screens) for keeping track of customer frequent flier miles, birth dates, length of time in the program, and any other relevant data that shows your solution will work. Would your proposed solution to the year 2000 problem fix the 1999 problem as well? Respond in a paragraph. If not, propose what you would do in another paragraph-long response.

PEDAGOGICAL FEATURES

Chapters in the Fourth Edition contain:
- *Summary*
- **Keywords and Phrases**
- **Review Questions**
- **Problems**
- **Group Projects**
- **Over 60 Consulting Opportunities**

- **HyperCase Experiences** that pose challenging student exercises are present in each chapter. HyperCase version 2.0 is now available on the Web. HyperCase now has updated organizational problems featuring state of the art technological systems as well. HyperCase is an original, virtual organization that allows students who access it to become immediately immersed in organizational life. Students will interview people, observe office environments, analyze their prototypes, and review the documentation of their existing systems. HyperCase version 2.0 is Web-based, interactive software that presents an organization called Maple Ridge Engineering in a colorful, three-dimensional graphics environment. HyperCase permits professors to begin approaching the systems analysis and design class with exciting multimedia material. Carefully watching their use of time and managing multiple methods, students use the hypertext characteristics of HyperCase on the Web to create their own individual paths through the organization.

Maple Ridge Engineering (MRE) is drawn from the actual consulting experiences of the authors of the original version (Raymond Barnes, Richard Baskerville, Julie E. Kendall, and Kenneth E. Kendall). Allen Schmidt joined the project for Version 2.0. Peter Schmidt was the HTML programmer and Jason Reed created the images for this new Web version.

In each chapter there are special HyperCase Experiences that include assignments (and even some clues) to help students solve the difficult organizational problems they encounter at MRE. HyperCase has been fully classroom tested, and was also an award winner in the Decision Sciences Institute Innovative Instruction competition.

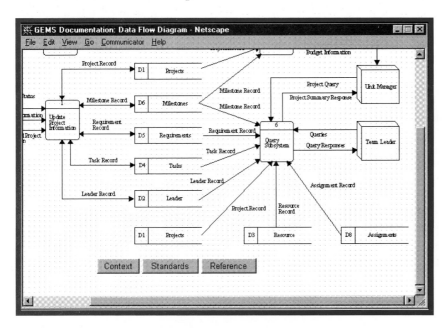

- **CPU Case Episodes**
  In keeping with our belief that a variety of approaches is important, we have once again integrated the Central Pacific University (CPU) Case into every chapter of the fourth edition. The CPU Case takes students through all phases of the systems development life cycle, demonstrating the capabilities of the popular CASE tool, Visible Analyst Workbench by Visible Systems, Inc. a student edition of which can be bundled with our book. This CASE tool gives students an opportunity to solve problems on their own, using Visible Analyst Workbench and data that users of the book can download from the Web containing Visible Analyst exercises specifically keyed to each chapter of the book. Additionally, partially-completed exercises in Microsoft Access files are also available for student use on the Web. The CPU Case has been fully classroom tested with a variety of students over numerous terms. The case is detailed, rigorous, and rich enough to stand alone as a systems analysis and design project spanning one or two terms. Alternatively, the CPU Case can be used as a way to teach the use of CASE tools in conjunction with the assignment of a one-term or two-term, real-worlds project outside the classroom.

9 *Episode* CPU *Case*

JUST FLOWING ALONG

After the results of interviews, questionnaires, and prototyping are gathered and analyzed, Anna and Chip move to the next step—modeling the system. Their strategy is to create a layered set of data flow diagrams and then describe the components.

Modeling starts with analyzing the context diagram of the current microcomputer system. This diagram is simple to create and is the foundation for successive levels because it describes the external entities and the major data flow.

"Shall we create a physical data flow diagram of the current system?" asks Chip.

Anna replies, "No, it's fairly simple to understand, and we wouldn't gain any significant new knowledge of how the system operates. Let's start by creating a logical model of the current system."

INTRODUCING WEB SUPPORT

Kendall & Kendall's *Systems Analysis and Design* fourth edition breaks new ground by adding Web-based support to solid yet lively pedagogical techniques in the information systems field.

The Web site, located at **www.prenhall.com/kendall/** contains a wealth of critical learning and support tools which keep class discussions exciting.

- **HyperCase** version 2.0, an award-winning, virtually interactive organization game. Students are encouraged to interview people in the organization, analyze problems, modify data flow diagrams and data dictionaries, react to prototypes, and design new input and output. HyperCase now has a new 3-D look.

- **Student Exercises** based on the ongoing CPU Case, with partially solved problems and examples stored in **Visible Analyst Workbench** files.

• **Student Exercises** based on the ongoing CPU Case, with partially solved problems and examples stored in **Microsoft Access** files.

A secure Faculty Section contains special downloadable supplemental resources including:

• **Instructor Manual** with answers to problems, solutions to cases, and suggestions for approaching the subject matter.
• **Sample Course Outlines** for one or two semester or quarter courses
• **Solutions to Student Exercises** based on the ongoing CPU Case, with solutions and examples stored in **Visible Analyst Workbench** files.
• **Solutions to Student Exercises** based on the ongoing CPU Case, with solutions and examples stored in **Microsoft Access** files.
• The **HyperCase Users Guide to the Corporation**, an instructor's guide to interpreting HyperCase and suggested approaches for classroom use.

ACKNOWLEDGMENTS

When we began writing the fourth edition of *Systems Analysis and Design*, we were amazed at the speed with which the Web has revolutionized the way our work as analysts is understood by others and even ourselves. More people than ever before are expected to be systems designers, and even more people are supposed to be sophisticated consumers of Web-based systems and information. Users interact, critique, and respond to what they see and hear. Good systems analysts and designers use both art and science to reply to the feedback they receive in order to develop systems that are in tune with their users, their environments, and even society at large.

Our cover artist tells us that his painting, Buffalo No. 6 (Ross' Critique), which is featured on the front of our book, was a result of just such a cycle of creation, feedback, analysis, refinement and resolution. The analysis and critiques his painting instructor provided over a period of time served as powerful guidance to designing a painting wherein the problems encountered with composition and color eventually "resolved themselves;" but only after much reflection, many new brush strokes and some inspired all-night sessions. So it goes with much of the information systems work that you will encounter. As you respond to user feedback and your own reflections on what you are learning, you will bring to bear the technical skills you learn in this book to resolve new systems problems.

As with any new edition, our students deserve great praise for helping us to improve. We thank them all for all of their comments and insights. We want to thank our co-author Allen Schmidt for all of the talent, enthusiasm, and joy he brings to our collaborations. He is a rare human being. Our hearty thanks also go to Peter Schmidt and Jason Reed for their dedication to the HyperCase project. Their potential seems to know no bounds. We also want to thank the other two original authors of HyperCase, Richard Baskerville and Raymond Barnes, who contributed so much.

We would like to thank our editor David Alexander who understands us and our dreams. His input has made this project exciting and fresh. Susan Rifkin, our production editor, also deserves praise for maintaining a calm presence and helping us focus on the work at hand. Our cover artist Michael Tunney has inspired us and helped us connect a variety of disparate interests into a meaningful whole. We are also appreciative of the support and encouragement of our provost at Rutgers-Camden, Roger J. Dennis.

Many of our reviewers, colleagues, and friends have encouraged us through the process of writing this book. We thank them for their comments on our work. They include: Bob Benjamin, Charles J. Coleman, Melissa Covelli, Gordon Davis, Dorothy Dologite, Phillip Ein-Dor, Jim Evans, Bruce Fanning, Rich Gates, Paul Gray, Mathew Greenfield, Varun Grover, Nancy V. Gulick, Frank Kaminski, Ken and Nancy Kopecky, Art and Joan Kraft, Lee Krajewski, Ken and Jane Laudon, Robert Mockler, Nancy Omaha Boy, M. Owen Lee, Bill Perkins, Caryn Schmidt, Marc Schniederjans, Don Sherwood, Eric and Tisha Stahl, Detmar Straub, Gary Toste, Malcolm Warner, Jane Webster, Carol Wong, Shaker and Patricia Zahra, and all of our friends and colleagues in the Decision Sciences Institute and IFIP Working Group 8.2.

Our heartfelt thanks go to our father Edward J. Kendall who always encouraged us to "finish the book," and our mother Julia Kendall whose love and spirit still nurture us in every endeavor.

1

ASSUMING THE ROLE OF THE SYSTEMS ANALYST

INFORMATION AS AN ORGANIZATIONAL RESOURCE

Organizations have long recognized the importance of managing key resources such as labor and raw materials. Information has now moved to its rightful place as a key resource. Decision makers now understand that information is not just a byproduct of conducting business; rather, it fuels business and can be the critical factor in determining the success or failure of a business.

Managing Information as a Resource

To maximize the usefulness of information, a business must manage it correctly, just as it manages other resources. Managers need to understand that costs are associated with the production, distribution, security, storage, and retrieval of all information. Although information is all around us, it is not free, and its strategic use for positioning a business competitively should not be taken for granted.

Managing Computer-Generated Information

The ready availability of networked computers, along with access to the Internet and the World Wide Web, has created an information explosion throughout society in general and business in particular. Managing computer-generated information differs in significant ways from handling manually produced data. Usually there is a greater quantity of computer information to administer. Costs of organizing and maintaining it can increase at alarming rates, and users often treat it less skeptically than information obtained in different ways. This chapter examines the fundamentals of different kinds of information systems, the varied roles of systems analysts, and the phases in the systems development life cycle; it also introduces Computer-Aided Software Engineering (CASE) tools.

1

SYSTEMS ANALYSIS AND DESIGN CONCEPTS

Information systems are developed for different purposes, depending on the needs of the business. Transaction processing systems (TPS) function at the operational level of the organization; office automation systems (OAS) and knowledge work systems (KWS) support work at the knowledge level. Higher-level systems include management information systems (MIS) and decision support systems (DSS). Expert systems apply the expertise of decision makers to solve specific, structured problems. On the strategic level of management we find executive support systems (ESS). Group decision support systems (GDSS) and the more generally described computer supported collaborative work (CSCW) systems aid group-level decision making of a semistructured or unstructured variety.

Transaction Processing Systems

Transaction processing systems (TPS) are computerized information systems that were developed to process large amounts of data for routine business transactions such as payroll and inventory. A TPS eliminates the tedium of necessary operational transactions and reduces the time once required to perform them manually, although people must still input data to computerized systems.

Transaction processing systems are boundary-spanning systems that permit the organization to interact with external environments. Because managers look to the data generated by the TPS for up-to-the-minute information about what is happening in their companies, it is essential to the day-to-day operations of business that these systems function smoothly and without interruption.

Office Automation Systems and Knowledge Work Systems

At the knowledge level of the organization are two classes of systems. Office automation systems (OAS) support data workers, who do not usually create new knowledge but rather analyze information in order to transform data or manipulate it in some way before sharing it with, or formally disseminating it throughout, the organization and, sometimes, beyond. Familiar aspects of OAS include word processing, spreadsheets, desktop publishing, electronic scheduling, and communication through voice mail, e-mail (electronic mail), and video conferencing.

Knowledge work systems (KWS) support professional workers such as scientists, engineers, and doctors by aiding them in their efforts to create new knowledge and by allowing them to contribute it to their organization or to society at large.

Management Information Systems

Management information systems (MIS) do not replace transaction processing systems—rather, all MIS include transaction processing. MIS are computerized information systems that work because of the purposeful interaction between people and computers. By requiring people, software (computer programs), and hardware (computers, printers, etc.) to function in concert, management information systems support a broader spectrum of organizational tasks than transaction processing systems, including decision analysis and decision making.

In order to access information, users of the management information system share a common database. The database stores both data and models that help the user interpret and apply that data. Management information systems output information that is used in decision making. A management information system can also help unite some of the computerized information functions of a business, although it does not exist as a singular structure anywhere in the business.

Decision Support Systems

A higher-level class of computerized information systems is the decision support system (DSS). The DSS is similar to the traditional management information system because they both depend on a database as a source of data. A decision support system departs from the traditional management information system because it emphasizes the *support* of decision making in all of its phases, although the actual decision is still the exclusive province of the decision maker. Decision support systems are more closely tailored to the person or group using them than is a traditional management information system.

Expert Systems and Artificial Intelligence

Artificial intelligence (AI) can be considered the overarching field for expert systems. The general thrust of AI has been to develop machines that behave intelligently. Two avenues of research of AI are understanding natural language and analyzing the ability to reason through a problem to its logical conclusion. Expert systems use the approaches of AI reasoning to solve the problems put to them by business (and other) users.

Expert systems are a very special class of information system that have been made practicable for use by business as a result of widespread availability of hardware and software such as microcomputers and expert system shells. An expert system (also called a knowledge-based system) effectively captures and uses the knowledge of an expert for solving a particular problem experienced in an organization. Notice that unlike the DSS, which leaves the ultimate judgment to the decision maker, an expert system selects the best solution to a problem or a specific class of problems.

The basic components of an expert system are the knowledge base, an inference engine connecting the user with the system by processing queries via languages such as SQL (structured query language), and the user interface. People called knowledge engineers capture the expertise of experts, build a computer system which includes this expert knowledge, and then implement it. It is entirely possible that building and implementing expert systems will be the future work of many systems analysts.

The variety of information systems that analysts may develop are shown in Figure 1.1. Notice that the figure presents these systems from the bottom up, indicating that the operational, or lowest level of the organization, is supported by TPS, and the highest, or strategic level of semistructured and unstructured decisions, is supported by ESS at the top. This text uses the terms *management information system, information system* (IS), *computerized information system,* and *computerized business information system* interchangeably to denote computerized information systems that support the broadest range of business activities through the information they produce.

FIGURE 1.1
A systems analyst may be involved with any or all of these
systems.

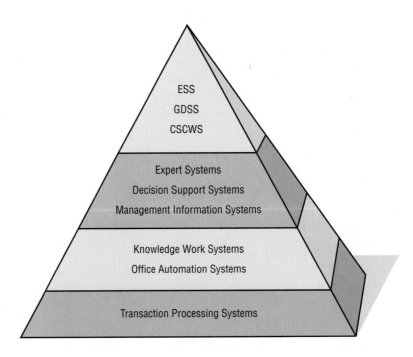

ESS
GDSS
CSCWS

Expert Systems
Decision Support Systems
Management Information Systems

Knowledge Work Systems
Office Automation Systems

Transaction Processing Systems

Group Decision Support Systems and Computer-Supported Collaborative Work Systems

When groups need to work together to make semistructured or unstructured decisions, a group decision support system may afford a solution. Group decision support systems (GDSS), which are used in special rooms equipped in a number of different configurations, permit group members to interact with electronic support—often in the form of specialized software—and a special group facilitator. Group decision support systems are intended to bring a group together to solve a problem with the help of various supports such as polling, questionnaires, brainstorming, and scenario creation. GDSS software can be designed to minimize typical negative group behaviors such as lack of participation due to fear of reprisal for expressing an unpopular or contested viewpoint, domination by vocal group members, and "group think" decision making. Sometimes GDSS are discussed under the more general term computer supported collaborative work (CSCW), which might include software support called "groupware" for team collaboration via networked computers.

Executive Support Systems

When executives turn to the computer, they are often looking for ways to help them make decisions on the strategic level. An executive support system (ESS) helps executives to organize their interactions with the external environment by providing graphics and communications support in accessible places such as boardrooms or personal corporate offices. Although ESS rely on the information generated by TPS and MIS, executive support systems help their users address unstructured decision problems, which are not application-specific, by creating an environment that is conducive to thinking about strategic problems in an informed way. ESS extend and support the capabilities of executives, permitting them to make sense of their environments.

Need for Systems Analysis and Design

Systems analysis and design, as performed by systems analysts, seeks to systematically analyze data input or data flow, processing or transforming data, data storage, and information output within the context of a particular business. Furthermore, systems analysis and design is used to analyze, design, and implement improvements in the functioning of businesses that can be accomplished through the use of computerized information systems.

Installing a system without proper planning leads to great dissatisfaction and frequently causes the system to fall into disuse. Systems analysis and design lends structure to the analysis and design of information systems, a costly endeavor that might otherwise have been done in a haphazard way. It can be thought of as a series of processes systematically undertaken to improve a business through the use of computerized information systems. A large part of systems analysis and design involves working with current and eventual users of information systems.

End Users

Anyone who interacts with an information system in the context of his or her work in the organization can be called an *end user*. Over the years the distinctions among users have become blurred. Further, any categories of users employed should not be thought of as exclusive.

However end users are classified, one fact about them remains pertinent to the systems analyst: Some kind of user involvement throughout the systems project is critical to the successful development of computerized information systems. Systems analysts, whose roles in the organization are discussed next, are the other essential component in developing useful information systems.

ROLE OF THE SYSTEMS ANALYST

The systems analyst systematically assesses how businesses function by examining the inputting and processing of data and the outputting of information with the intent of improving organizational processes. Many improvements involve better support of business functions through the use of computerized information systems. This definition emphasizes a systematic, methodical approach to analyzing—and potentially improving—what is occurring in the specific context created by a business.

Our definition of a systems analyst is necessarily broad. The analyst must be able to work with people of all descriptions and be experienced in working with computers. The analyst plays many roles, sometimes balancing several at the same time. The three primary roles of the systems analyst are: consultant, supporting expert, and agent of change.

Systems Analyst as a Consultant

The systems analyst frequently acts as a systems consultant to a business and thus may be hired specifically to address information systems issues within a business. This can be an advantage since outside consultants can bring with them a fresh perspective that other members of an organization do not possess. It also means that outside analysts are at a disadvantage because the true organizational culture can never be known to an outsider.

As an outside consultant, you will rely heavily on the systematic methods discussed throughout this text in order to analyze and design appropriate information systems for a particular business. Additionally, you will rely on information system users to help you understand the organizational culture from their viewpoints.

Systems Analyst as Supporting Expert

Another role that you may be required to play is that of supporting expert within a business where you are regularly employed in some systems capacity. In this role the analyst draws on professional expertise concerning computer hardware and software and their uses in the business. This work is often not a full-blown systems project, but rather it entails a small modification or decision affecting a single department.

As the support expert, you are not managing the project; you are merely serving as a resource for those who are. If you are a systems analyst employed by a manufacturing or service organization, many of your daily activities may be encompassed by this role.

Systems Analyst as Agent of Change

The most comprehensive and responsible role that the systems analyst takes on is that of agent of change, whether internal or external to the business. As an analyst, you are an agent of change whenever you perform any of the activities in the systems development life cycle (discussed in the next section) and are present in the business for an extended period of time (from two weeks all the way to more than a year). An agent of change can be defined as a person who serves as a catalyst for change, develops a plan for change, and works with others in facilitating that change.

Your presence in the business changes it. As a systems analyst, you must recognize this fact and use it as a starting point for your analysis. This is why you must interact with users and management (if they are not one and the same) from the very beginning of your project. Without their help you cannot understand what is happening in an organization, and real change cannot take place.

If change (that is, improvements to the business that can be realized through information systems) seems warranted after analysis, the next step is to develop a plan for change along with the people who must enact the changes. Once a consensus is reached on the change that is to be made, you must constantly interact with those who are changing. You facilitate change by using your expertise with humans as well as with computers to bring about their integration in a human–machine information system.

As a systems analyst acting as an agent of change, you advocate a particular avenue of change involving the use of information systems. Additionally, you teach users the process of change, because you are aware that changes in the information system do not occur independently but cause changes in the rest of the organization as well.

Qualities of the Systems Analyst

From the foregoing descriptions of the roles the systems analyst plays, it is easy to see that the successful systems analyst must possess a wide range of qualities. Many different kinds of people are systems analysts, so any description is destined to fall short in some way. However, there are some qualities that most systems analysts seem to display.

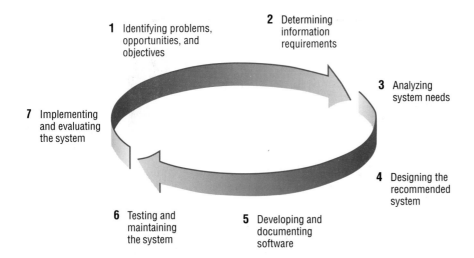

FIGURE 1.2
The seven phases of the systems development life cycle.

1 Identifying problems, opportunities, and objectives

2 Determining information requirements

3 Analyzing system needs

4 Designing the recommended system

5 Developing and documenting software

6 Testing and maintaining the system

7 Implementing and evaluating the system

Above all, the analyst is a problem solver. He or she is a person who views the analysis of problems as a challenge and who enjoys devising workable solutions. When necessary, the analyst must be able to systematically tackle the situation at hand through skillful application of tools, techniques, and experience. The analyst must also be a communicator capable of relating meaningfully to other people over extended periods of time. Systems analysts need enough computer experience to program, to understand the capabilities of computers, to glean information requirements from users, and to communicate what is needed to programmers.

It is appropriate at this time for you to reflect on the personal and professional ethics you bring to a consulting relationship. Most probably your values have been shaped by your parents, your education, and perhaps formal spiritual training. When you begin interacting with and advising others, you must be aware of the ethical framework that will shape your responses. Work to clarify the values that you embrace as you build relationships (and create actual and psychological contracts) with users and team members. Self-knowledge can help you to become a better analyst, and the codes of conduct of professional groups such as the ACM (The Association for Computing Machinery) provide a reasonable context for examining your ethical beliefs.

The systems analyst must be a self-disciplined, self-motivated individual who is able to manage and coordinate innumerable project resources, including other people. Systems analysis is a demanding career but, in compensation, an ever-changing and always challenging one.

THE SYSTEMS DEVELOPMENT LIFE CYCLE

Throughout this chapter we have referred to the systematic approach analysts take to the analysis and design of information systems. Much of this is embodied in what is called the *systems development life cycle* (SDLC). The SDLC is a phased approach to analysis and design which holds that systems are best developed through the use of a specific cycle of analyst and user activities.

Analysts disagree on exactly how many phases there are in the systems development life cycle, but they generally laud its organized approach. Here we have divided the cycle into seven phases, as shown in Figure 1.2. Although each phase is presented discretely, it is never accomplished as a separate step. Instead, several activities can occur simultaneously, and activities may be repeated. That is why it is more useful to think of the SDLC as accomplished in phases (with activities in full swing overlapping with others, and then tapering off) and not in separate steps.

Identifying Problems, Opportunities, and Objectives

In this first phase of the systems development life cycle, the analyst is concerned with identifying problems, opportunities, and objectives. This stage is critical to the success of the rest of the project, since no one wants to waste subsequent time addressing the wrong problem.

The first phase requires that the analyst look honestly at what is occurring in a business. Then, together with other organizational members, the analyst pinpoints problems. Often, these will be brought up by others, and they are the reason the analyst was initially called in.

Opportunities are situations that the analyst believes can be improved upon through the use of computerized information systems. Seizing opportunities may allow the business to gain a competitive edge or set an industry standard.

Identifying objectives is also an important component of the first phase. First, the analyst must discover what the business is trying to do. Then the analyst will be able to see if some aspect of information systems applications can help the business reach its objectives by addressing specific problems or opportunities.

The people involved in the first phase are the users, analysts, and systems managers coordinating the project. Activities in this phase consist of interviewing user management, summarizing the knowledge obtained, estimating the scope of the project, and documenting the results. The output of this phase is a feasibility report containing a problem definition and summarizing the objectives. Management must then make a decision on whether to proceed with the proposed project. If the user group does not have sufficient funds in its budget or wishes to tackle unrelated problems, or if the problems do not require a computer system, a manual solution may be recommended, and the systems project does not proceed any further.

Determining Information Requirements

The next phase that the analyst enters is that of determining information requirements for the particular users involved. Among the tools used to define information requirements in the business are: sampling and investigating hard data, interviewing, questionnaires, observing decision makers' behavior and office environments, and even prototyping.

In this phase the analyst is striving to understand what information users need to perform their jobs. You can see that several of the methods for determining information requirements involve interacting directly with users. This phase serves to fill in the picture that the analyst has of the organization and its objectives. Sometimes only the first two phases of the systems development life cycle are completed. This kind of study may have a different purpose and is typically carried out by a specialist called an information analyst (IA).

The people involved in this phase are the analysts and users, typically operations managers and operations workers. The systems analyst needs to know the details of current system functions: the who (the people who are involved), what (the business activity), where (the environment in which the work takes place), when (the timing), and how (how the current procedures are performed) of the business under study. The analyst must then ask why the business uses the current system. There may be good reasons for doing business using the current methods, and these should be considered when designing any new system.

However, if the reason for current operations is that "It's always been done that way," the analyst may wish to improve on the procedures. Business process reengineering may be of help in framing an approach for rethinking the business in a creative way. At the completion of this phase, the analyst should understand how the business functions and have complete information on the people, goals, data, and procedures involved.

Analyzing System Needs

The next phase that the systems analyst undertakes involves analyzing system needs. Again, special tools and techniques help the analyst make requirements determinations. One such tool is the use of data flow diagrams to chart the input, processes, and output of the business's functions in a structured graphical form. From the data flow diagrams, a data dictionary is developed that lists all of the data items used in the system, as well as their specifications—whether they are alphanumeric or text, and how much space they take up when printed.

During this phase the systems analyst also analyzes the structured decisions made. Structured decisions are those for which the conditions, condition alternatives, actions, and action rules can be determined. There are three major methods for analysis of structured decisions: structured English, decision tables, and decision trees.

Not all decisions in organizations are structured, but it is still important for the systems analyst to understand them. Semistructured decisions (decisions made under risk) are often supported by decision support systems. When analyzing semistructured decisions, the analyst examines the decisions based on the degree of decision-making skill required, the degree of problem complexity, and the number of criteria considered when the decision is made.

Analysis of multiple-criteria decisions (decisions where many factors must be balanced) is also part of this phase. Many techniques are available for analyzing multiple-criteria decisions, including the tradeoff process and the use of weighting methods.

At this point in the systems development life cycle, the systems analyst prepares a systems proposal that summarizes what has been found, provides cost/benefit analyses of alternatives, and makes recommendations on what (if anything) should be done. If one of the recommendations is acceptable to management, the analyst proceeds along that course. Each systems problem is unique, and there is never just one correct solution. The manner in which a recommendation or solution is formulated depends on the individual qualities and professional training of each analyst.

Designing the Recommended System

In this phase of the systems development life cycle, the systems analyst uses the information collected earlier to accomplish the logical design of the information system. The analyst designs accurate data-entry procedures so that data going into the information system are correct. In addition the analyst provides for effective input to the information system by using techniques of good form and screen design.

Part of the logical design of the information system is devising the user interface. The interface connects the user with the system and is thus extremely important. Examples of user interfaces include a keyboard (to type in questions and answers), on-screen menus (to elicit user commands), and a variety of Graphical User Interfaces (GUIs), that use a mouse or touch screen.

The design phase also includes designing files or databases that will store much of the data needed by decision makers in the organization. A well-organized database is the basis for all information systems. In this phase the analyst also works with users to design output (either on-screen or printed) that meets their information needs.

Finally, the analyst must design controls and backup procedures to protect the system and the data and to produce program specification packets for programmers. Each packet should contain input and output layouts, file specifications, and processing details; and it may also include decision trees or tables, data-flow diagrams, a system flowchart, and the names and functions of any prewritten code routines.

Developing and Documenting Software

In the fifth phase of the systems development life cycle, the analyst works with programmers to develop any original software that is needed. Some of the structured techniques for designing and documenting software include structure charts, Nassi-Shneiderman charts, and pseudocode. The systems analyst uses one or more of these devices to communicate to the programmer what needs to be programmed.

During this phase the analyst also works with users to develop effective documentation for software, including procedure manuals, online help, Web sites featuring Frequently Asked Questions (FAQ), on "Read Me" files shipped with new software. Documentation tells users how to use software and also what to do if software problems occur.

Programmers have a key role in this phase because they design, code, and remove syntactical errors from computer programs. If the program is to run in a mainframe environment, job control language (JCL) must be created. To ensure quality, a programmer may conduct either a design or a code walkthrough, explaining complex portions of the program to a team of other programmers.

Testing and Maintaining the System

Before the information system can be used, it must be tested. It is much less costly to catch problems before the system is signed over to users. Some of the testing is completed by programmers alone, some of it by systems analysts in conjunction with programmers. A series of tests to pinpoint problems is run first with sample data and eventually with actual data from the current system.

Maintenance of the system and its documentation begins in this phase and is carried out routinely throughout the life of the information system. Much of the programmer's routine work consists of maintenance, and businesses spend a great deal of money on maintenance. Some maintenance, such as program updates, can be done automatically via a vendor site on the World Wide Web. Many of the systematic procedures the analyst employs throughout the systems development life cycle can help ensure that maintenance is kept to a minimum.

Implementing and Evaluating the System

In this last phase of system development, the analyst helps implement the information system. This involves training users to handle the system. Some training is done by vendors, but oversight of training is the responsibility of the systems analyst. Additionally, the analyst needs to plan for a smooth conversion from the old system to the new one. This process includes converting files from old formats to new ones or building a database, installing equipment, and bringing the new system into production.

Evaluation is shown as part of this final phase of the systems development life cycle mostly for the sake of discussion. Actually, evaluation takes place during every phase. A key criterion that must be satisfied is whether the intended users are indeed using the system.

It should be noted that systems work is often cyclical. When an analyst finishes one phase of system development and proceeds to the next, the discovery of a problem may force the analyst to return to the previous phase and modify the work done there. For example, during the testing phase, the programmer may discover that the program does not work correctly, either because code was not written to support certain portions of the system design or the design was incomplete. In either event the programs must be modified, and the analyst may have to change some of the system design materials. In turn, this may necessitate that the analyst meet with the user and reinvestigate how a specific business activity functions.

The Impact of Maintenance

After the system is installed, it must be maintained, meaning that the computer programs must be modified and kept up-to-date. Figure 1.3 illustrates the average amount of time spent on maintenance at a typical MIS installation. Estimates of the time spent by departments on maintenance have ranged from 48 to 60 percent of the total time spent developing systems.[1] Very little time remains for new system development. As the number of programs written increases, so does the amount of maintenance they require.

Maintenance is performed for two reasons. The first of these is to correct software errors. No matter how thoroughly the system is tested, bugs or errors creep into computer programs. Bugs in commercial microcomputer software are often documented as "known anomalies" and corrected when new versions of the software are released or in an interim release. In customized software, bugs must be corrected as they are detected.

The other reason for performing system maintenance is to enhance the software's capabilities in response to changing organizational needs, generally involving one of the following three situations:

1. *Users often request additional features after they become familiar with the computer system and its capabilities.* These requested features may be as simple as displaying additional totals on a report or as complicated as developing new software.

2. *The business changes over time.* Software must be modified to encompass changes as new government or corporate reporting requirements arise, as new client information needs to be produced, and so on.

---

[1] S. Yoo and K. E. Kendall. "Pseudocode-Box Diagrams: An Approach to More Understandable, Productive, and Adaptable Software Design and Coding," *International Journal on Policy and Information,* Vol. 12, No. 1, June, 1988, pp. 39–51.

FIGURE 1.3
Some researchers estimate
that the amount of time spent
on system maintenance may
be as much as 60% of the total
time spent on systems projects.

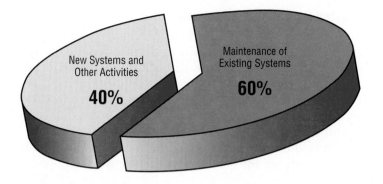

3. *Hardware and software are changing at an accelerated pace.* A system that uses older technology may be modified to use the capabilities of newer technology. An example of such a change is replacing a mainframe with a client/server system where client PCs house some data and processing and servers provide data and applications; splitting up tasks efficiently via a local area network (LAN).

Figure 1.4 illustrates the amount of resources—usually time and money— spent on system development and maintenance. The area under the curve represents the total dollar amount spent. You can see that over time the total cost of maintenance is likely to exceed that of system development. At a certain point it becomes more feasible to perform a new systems study, since the cost of continued maintenance is clearly greater than that of creating an entirely new information system.

In summary, maintenance is an ongoing process over the life cycle of an information system. After the information system is installed, maintenance usually takes the form of correcting previously undetected program errors. Once these are corrected, the system approaches a steady state, providing dependable service to its users. Maintenance during this period may consist of removing a few previously undetected bugs and updating the system with a few minor enhancements. However, as time goes on and the business and technology change, the maintenance effort increases dramatically.

FIGURE 1.4
Resource consumption over
the system life.

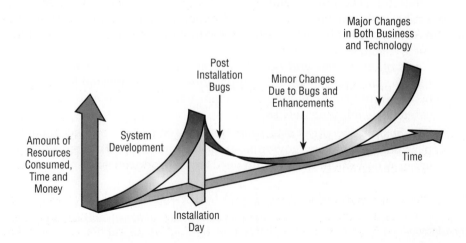

USING CASE TOOLS

Throughout this book we emphasize the need for a systematic, thorough approach to the analysis, design, and implementation of information systems. We recognize that in order to be productive, systems analysts must be organized, accurate, and complete in what they set out to do. Within the last ten years, analysts have begun to benefit from productivity tools that have been created explicitly to improve their routine work through the use of automated support. These are called CASE tools for Computer Aided Software Engineering tools.

Analysts rely on CASE tools to increase productivity, communicate more effectively with users, and integrate the work that they do on the system from the beginning to the end of the life cycle.

Increasing Analyst Productivity

Excelerator allows its users to draw and modify diagrams easily. By our definition the analyst can thus become more productive simply by reducing the considerable time typically spent in manually drawing and redrawing data flow diagrams until they are acceptable.

A tools package such as Visible Analyst Workbench, Excelerator, or XperCASE also enhances group productivity by allowing analysts to share work easily with other team members, who can simply access the file on their PC and review or modify what has been done. This reduces the time necessary to reproduce and distribute data flow diagrams among team members. Thus, rather than mandating a strict distribution and feedback response schedule, such a tools package further allows members of the systems analysis team to work with the diagrams whenever they have the time.

CASE tools also facilitate interaction among team members by making diagramming a dynamic, iterative process rather than one in which changes are cumbersome and therefore tend to become a drain on productivity. In this instance the CASE tool for drawing and recording data flow diagrams affords a record of the team's changing thinking regarding data flows.

Improving Analyst–User Communication

In order for the proposed system to come into being and actually be used, excellent communication among analysts and users throughout the systems development life cycle is essential. The success of the eventual system implementation rests on the capability of analysts and users to communicate in a meaningful way. So far, it has been the experience of analysts currently using CASE tools that their use fosters greater, more meaningful communication among users and analysts.

PROVIDING A MEANS OF COMMUNICATION. Analysts and users alike report that CASE tools afford them a means of communication about the system during its conceptualization, as shown in Figure 1.5. Through the use of automated support featuring on-screen output, clients can readily see how data flows and other system concepts are depicted, and they can then request corrections or changes that would have taken too much time with a manual system.

Whether a particular diagram will be adjudged useful by users or analysts at the end of the project is questionable. What is important is that such automated support for many life cycle design activities serves as a means to

FIGURE 1.5
Analysts can improve their
communication with users
with the help of computer-
generated diagrams.

an end by acting as a catalyst for analyst–user interaction. The same arguments used to support CASE tools' role in increasing productivity are equally valid in this arena: That is, the manual tasks of drawing, reproducing, and distributing take much less time, and so work in progress can be shared more easily with users.

Integrating Life Cycle Activities

The third reason for using CASE tools is to integrate activities and provide continuity from one phase to the next throughout the systems development life cycle.

CASE tools are especially useful when a particular phase of the life cycle requires several iterations of feedback and modification. Recall that user involvement can be important in each of the phases. Integration of activities through the underlying use of workbench technologies makes it easier for users to understand how all of the life cycle phases are interrelated and interdependent.

Accurately Assessing Maintenance Changes

The fourth and possibly one of the most important reasons for using CASE tools is that they enable users to analyze and assess the impact of maintenance changes. For example, the size of an element such as a customer number may need to be made larger. The CASE tool will cross-reference every screen, report, and file within which the element is used, leading to a comprehensive maintenance plan.

UPPER AND LOWER CASE

CASE tools are classified as lower CASE, upper CASE, and integrated CASE, which combines both upper and lower CASE in one toolset. Although experts disagree about what precisely constitutes an upper CASE tool versus a

FIGURE 1.6
Selected CASE tools.

Corporation	Product Name	Type of CASE Tool
AI Lee & Associates	Magec	Lower CASE
Anderson Consulting	Foundation	Integrated CASE
Cadre Technologies, Inc.	Teamwork	Upper CASE
CGI Systems, Inc.	PacBase	Integrated CASE
Computer Systems Advisers Inc.	POSE	Upper CASE
Intersolv	Excelerator	Upper CASE
	APS	Lower CASE
KnowledgeWare, Inc.	Application Development Workbench (ADW)	Integrated CASE
	Information Engineering Workbench (IEW)	Integrated CASE
Siemens AG	XperCASE	Integrated CASE
Synon, Inc.	Synon	Integrated CASE
System Software Associates, Inc.	AS/SET	Lower CASE
Texas Instruments	Information Engineering Facility (IEF)	Integrated CASE
Visible Systems Corp.	Visible Analyst	Upper CASE
Yourdon, Inc.	Analyst/Designer Toolkit	Upper CASE

lower CASE tool, it might be helpful to conceptualize upper CASE tools on the basis of whom they support. Upper CASE tools primarily help analysts and designers. Lower CASE tools are used more often by programmers and workers who must implement the systems designed via upper CASE tools. Figure 1.6 lists some of the more popular CASE tools.

Upper CASE Tools

An upper CASE tool allows the analyst to create and modify the system design. All the information about the project is stored in an encyclopedia called the CASE repository, a large collection of records, elements, diagrams, screens, reports, and other information. (See Figure 1.7.) Analysis reports may be produced using the repository information to show where the design is incomplete or contains errors.

Upper CASE tools can also help support the modeling of an organization's functional requirements, assist analysts and users in drawing the boundaries for a given project, and help them visualize how the project meshes with other parts of the organization. Additionally, some upper CASE tools can support prototyping of screen and report designs.

Lower CASE Tools

Lower CASE tools are used to generate computer source code, eliminating the need for programming the system. Code generation has several advantages:

1. The system may be produced more quickly than by writing computer programs. However, becoming familiar with the methodology used by the code generator often takes a great deal of time, so program generation may initially be slower. Additionally, the design must be thoroughly entered into the toolset, which may require a lengthy period of time.

FIGURE 1.7
The repository concept.

```
        ADD CUSTOMER

   NUMBER   XXXXXX

   NAME     XXXXXXXXXXX
   STREET   XXXXXXXXXXX
   CITY     XXXXXXXXXXX
   STATE    XX
   ZIP      XXXXX-XXXX
```

```
        SALES ANALYSIS REPORT
          ITEM           TOTAL
       DESCRIPTION        SALES
   XXXXXXXXXXXXX        ZZ,ZZ9
   XXXXXXXXXXXXX        ZZ,ZZ9
   XXXXXXXXXXXXX        ZZ,ZZ9
   XXXXXXXXXXXXX        ZZ,ZZ9
   XXXXXXXXXXXXX        ZZ,ZZ9
   XXXXXXXXXXXXX        ZZ,ZZ9
```

Screen and Report Design

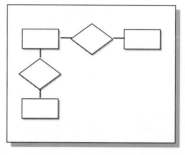

System Diagrams and Models

```
Item = Number +
       Description +
       Cost +
       Price +
       Quantity on hand +
       Quantity on order +
       Reorder point +
       Monthly sales +
       Year to date sales
```

```
DO WHILE NOT End of file
   Read Item record
   IF Item is low in stock
      Print Purchase Order
      Update Item record
   ENDIF
ENDDO
```

Data Dictionary and Process Logic

System Requirements
• Add new customers
• Identify fast and slow selling items
• Enter customer orders
• Look up customer credit balance
• Maintain adequate inventory

Deliverables
• Add customer screen
• Item Analysis Report
• Customer order entry screen
• Customer inquiry screen
• Vendor purchase order program
• Seasonal forecasting

Project Management

2. The amount of time spent on maintenance decreases with code genera-
    tion. There is no need to modify, test, and debug computer programs.
    Instead, the CASE design is modified, and the code is regenerated. De-
    creased time spent on maintenance results in more time to develop
    new systems and helps to relieve a backlog of projects under consider-
    ation for development.

3. Code may be generated in more than one computer language, so it is
    easier to migrate systems from one platform, such as a mainframe, to
    another, perhaps a microcomputer. For example, VAW Corporate Edi-
    tion, Version 6.1, can generate full ANSI, COBOL, or C-language 3 GL
    source code.

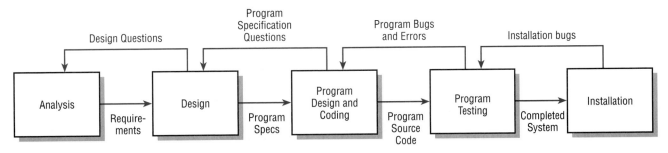

Traditional Systems Development Life Cycle

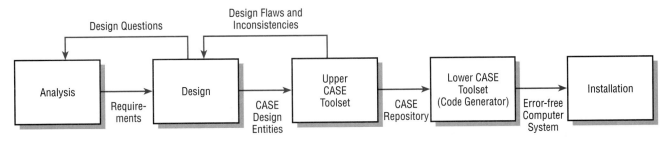

CASE Systems Development Life Cycle

FIGURE 1.8
Traditional versus CASE systems development life cycles.

4. Code generation provides a cost-effective way of tailoring systems purchased from third-party vendors to the needs of the organization. Often, modifying purchased software requires such great effort that the cost of doing so exceeds that of the software. With code generation software, purchasing CASE design and repository for the application enables the analyst to modify the design and generate the revised computer system.

5. Generated code is free of computer program errors. The only potential errors are design errors, which may be minimized by running CASE analysis reports to ensure that the system design is complete and correct.

Figure 1.8 illustrates the traditional systems development life cycle and the CASE life cycle. Notice that the program coding, testing, and debugging portions of the cycle are eliminated from the CASE life cycle.

SOFTWARE REVERSE ENGINEERING AND REENGINEERING

Software reverse engineering and reengineering are methods for extending the life of older programs, called legacy software. Both approaches use CARE (Computer Assisted Reengineering) software to analyze and restructure existing computer code. Several reverse engineering toolsets are available. They are summarized in Figure 1.9.

FIGURE 1.9
Selected reverse engineering
tools.

Corporation	Product Name
Bachman Information Systems, Inc.	Analyst Capture
Cadre Technologies, Inc.	Teamwork
CGI Systems, Inc.	PacReverse
Intersolv	XL Recover
	Design Recovery
Siemens AG	XperCASE

Note the term *reengineering* is used in a number of different engineering, programming, and business contexts. Often, it is used to mean "business process reengineering," which is a way of reorienting an organization around key processes. Systems analysts can play an important role in business process reengineering, since many of the necessary changes are possible only because of the availability of innovative information technology. Many analysts are now being educated in ways to facilitate organizational change.

Reverse engineering is the opposite of code generation. The computer source code is examined, analyzed, and converted into repository entities, as illustrated in Figure 1.10. The first step in software reverse engineering is to load existing computer programs' code (as written in COBOL, C, or another high-level language) into the toolset. Depending on the reverse engineering toolset used, the code is analyzed and the toolset produces some or all of the following:

1. Data structures and elements, describing the files and records stored by the system
2. Screen designs, if the program is on line
3. Report layouts for batch programs
4. A structure chart showing the hierarchy of the modules in the program
5. Database design and relationships

The design stored in the repository may be modified or incorporated into other CASE project information. When all the modifications are complete, the new system code may be regenerated. Reengineering refers to the complete process of converting program code to the CASE design, modifying the design, and regenerating the new program code.

FIGURE 1.10
Reverse engineering concepts.

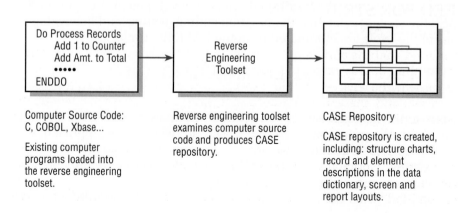

Computer Source Code:
C, COBOL, Xbase...

Existing computer
programs loaded into
the reverse engineering
toolset.

Reverse engineering toolset
examines computer source
code and produces CASE
repository.

CASE Repository

CASE repository is created,
including: structure charts,
record and element
descriptions in the data
dictionary, screen and
report layouts.

The advantages of using a reverse engineering toolset are numerous:

1. The time required for system maintenance is reduced, freeing up time for new development.
2. Documentation, which may have been nonexistent or minimal for older programs, is produced.
3. Structured programs are created from unstructured or loosely structured computer code.
4. Future maintenance changes are easier to make, since changes may be made at the design level rather than at the code level.
5. Analysis may be performed on the system to eliminate unused portions of computer code, code that may still exist in older programs even though it was made obsolete by revisions of the program throughout the years.

OBJECT-ORIENTED SYSTEMS ANALYSIS AND DESIGN

A very different approach to systems development is object-oriented (O-O) systems analysis and design. Object-oriented techniques, which are based on object-oriented programming concepts, can help analysts respond to organizational demands for new systems that must undergo continuous maintenance, adaptation, and redesign. Basically, in object-oriented programming, objects are created that include not only code about data, but also instructions about the operations to be performed on it.

Using the Coad and Yourdon approach to O-O analysis, we employ a five-layer model consisting of: (1) the class/object layer, (2) the structure layer, (3) the attribute layer, (4) the service layer, and (5) the subject layer. Object-oriented analysis and design can be thought of as the development and assembly of these five layers into one all-encompassing design package. The design activities are grouped into the four major components of the final system: the problem component, the human interface component, the data management component, and the task management component.

Operational prototypes (discussed in Chapter 8) are frequently used during the design phase. Chapter 22 provides a practical explanation of object-oriented analysis and design which takes the structured analysis and design presented in the preceding twenty-one chapters as its point of departure.

NEED FOR STRUCTURED ANALYSIS AND DESIGN

Structured analysis and design provides a systematic approach to designing and building quality computer systems. Throughout the phases of analysis and design, the analyst should proceed step by step, obtaining feedback from users and analyzing the design for omissions and errors. Moving too quickly to the next phase may require that the analyst return to rework portions of the design that were produced earlier.

Figure 1.11 illustrates the cost of correcting an error detected in each of the phases. Notice that considerably more effort is required to correct an error in each succeeding phase. For example, suppose several elements were omitted when the analyst was examining the details of the data used

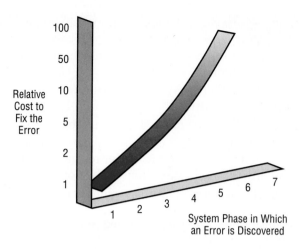

within the system. If the analyst learned that these elements were missing after programs were written, the file, report, and screen layouts would have to be modified, as would the test data files, programs, and documentation. These corrections might take 100 hours, whereas if the elements had been part of the original design, it might have taken only four hours at the outset to add them to the design materials and programs. Look for suggestions throughout the following chapters that indicate where analysis should take place and how to determine whether the systems design is accurate and complete.

Analysts have at their disposal a number of microcomputer software tools that may be used to assist them in the development of systems. In addition to CASE and reverse engineering tools, the following may be used at various parts of the analysis and design life cycle: management software to optimize the allocation of people and project resources; prototyping software to rapidly create screens and reports that users can review and modify; form design tools to help design forms or source documents; and graphics and presentation software to assist in creating illustrations and producing a professional presentation to users.

ALTERNATIVE METHODOLOGIES

Although this text focuses on the most widely used approach in practice, there will be times when the analyst recognizes that the organization could benefit from the use of an alternative approach. Perhaps a systems project using a structured approach has recently failed, or perhaps the organizational subcultures, comprised of several different user groups, seem more in step with an alternative method. We cannot do justice to these methods in a small space; each deserves and has inspired its own books and research. However, by mentioning these approaches here we hope to help you become aware that under certain circumstances, your organization may want to consider an alternative or supplement to structured analysis and design and to the systems development life cycle.

Among the most popular alternatives are: prototyping (distinct from the prototyping we discuss in Chapter 8), ETHICS, the project champion approach, Soft Systems Methodology, and Multiview. Prototyping, established in other disciplines and applied to IS (information systems), was offered as a response to the long development times associated with the systems devel-

CONSULTING OPPORTUNITY 1.1

Y2K: *Racing Towards the New Millennium*

"We have a crisis!" exclaims Al Falfa, a systems analyst for the multi-outlet, international chain of Marathon Vitamin Shops. He is meeting with a large team of systems analysts and functional vice presidents who have been convened to consider planning the company's systems priorities for the next two years. Al continues saying, "Year 2000, or Y2K problems are going to show up in places we haven't dreamed of. We have products that expire, inventory based on ordering dates, special promotions based on dates, and so on. Why even dealing with our suppliers who aren't Y2K compliant could create major headaches."

Ginger Rute, another analyst, injects a healthy dose of practicality into the discussion by saying, "In general, your assessment is correct. But let's take a specific example of what the Year 2000 problem means for us. When we make a sale our system checks the expiration date on customer credit cards. Suppose the transaction date is June 12, 1998 or 06/12/98 and the customer's credit card expires in 06/99, our computer is programmed to compare the dates as 98-06-12 and 99-06-30 (because the card is good through the end of the month). When we compare the dates we find that 99-06-30 > 98-06-12 and the charge is accepted. But if the expiration date is June 30, 2000 or 06/00, the computer determines that 00-06-30 is < 98-06-12 and rejects the charge. Our old bad habits of saving space by using two-digit dates means that we're going to have some sick systems. I'd prescribe a change, and soon."

"When you stop to think about it, we use an enormous amount of date logic in our programs," Al maintains. "How are we going to find all of the potential trouble spots? How will we choose a software tool to fix the problems we identify? And remember we need to increase our IT budget so that we have adequate resources to address these problems. I've read estimates that range from a dollar up to a $1.70 to change one line of code. Some of our systems have almost a million lines of code. The increased expense of fixing code in our legacy systems could be a bitter pill to swallow," Al cautions.

How would Marathon Vitamin Shops improve their overall fitness by involving users such as store managers and suppliers in the systems development life cycle? How does the Y2K problem confirm what you have learned about program maintenance? At what point in the SDLC might an analyst be faced with solving a Y2K problem? Discuss how reengineering might help find potential Y2K problems that exist in a company.

---

opment life cycle approach and to the uncertainty often surrounding user requirements. ETHICS was introduced as a sociotechnical methodology combining social and technical solutions. The project champion approach, a concept borrowed from marketing, adopts the strategy of involving one key person from each area affected by the system to ensure the system's success. Soft Systems Methodology was envisioned as a way to model a world that is often chaotic by using "rich pictures," ideographs that capture characteristic organizational narratives. Multiview was proposed as a way to organize and use elements of several competing methodologies.

SUMMARY

Information can be viewed as an organizational resource. As such, it must be managed carefully, just as other resources are. The availability of affordable computer power to organizations has meant an explosion of information, and consequently, more attention must be paid to coping with the information generated.

All computerized information systems have as their basis a database that stores the data necessary to support business functions. A transaction processing system (TPS) supports large-volume, routine business transactions such as payroll and inventory. Office automation systems (OAS) support data workers who use word processing, spreadsheets, and so on to analyze, transform, or manipulate data. Knowledge work systems (KWS) support professionals such as scientists and engineers who create new knowledge. Management information systems (MIS) are computerized information systems that support a broader range of business functions than do transaction processing systems. Most often, MIS output reports to decision makers. Decision support systems (DSS) are information systems whose output is tailored to their users' needs and which help support decision makers in making semistructured decisions. Expert systems capture the expertise of decision makers for use in solving a problem or a class of problems. Group decision support systems (GDSS) and computer supported collaborative work (CSCW) systems bring together group members in special electronic ways to help groups solve semistructured or unstructured problems. Executive support systems (ESS) help executives organize their interactions with the external environment by providing graphics and communications support in accessible locations.

Systems analysis and design is a systematic approach to identifying problems, opportunities, and objectives; to analyzing the information flows in organizations; and to designing computerized information systems to solve a problem. As information proliferates, a systematic, planned approach to the introduction, modification, and maintenance of information systems is essential. Systems analysis and design provide this.

Systems analysts are required to take on many roles in the course of their work. Some of these roles are: (1) outside consultant to business, (2) supporting expert within a business, and (3) agent of change in both internal and external situations.

Analysts possess a wide range of skills. First and foremost, the analyst is a problem solver, someone who enjoys the challenge of analyzing a problem and devising a workable solution. Systems analysts require communication skills that allow them to relate meaningfully to many different kinds of people on a daily basis, as well as computer skills. End-user involvement is critical to their success.

Analysts proceed systematically. The framework for their systematic approach is provided in what is called the systems development life cycle (SDLC). This can be divided into seven sequential phases, although in reality the phases are interrelated and often are accomplished simultaneously. The seven phases are: identifying problems, opportunities, and objectives; determining information requirements; analyzing system needs; designing the recommended system; developing and documenting software; testing and maintaining the system; and implementing and evaluating the system.

Automated, microcomputer-based software packages for systems analysis and design are called CASE (Computer Aided Software Engineering) tools. The four reasons for adopting CASE tools are increasing analyst productivity, improving communication among analysts and users, integrating life cycle activities, and analyzing and assessing the impact of maintenance changes.

Analysts also use CARE (Computer Assisted Reengineering) approaches to do software reverse engineering and reengineering to extend the life of legacy software.

A different approach to systems development is object-oriented (O-O) systems analysis and design. These techniques are based on object-oriented programming concepts in which objects that are created include not only code about data, but also instructions about the operations to be performed on it.

When the organizational situation demands it, the analyst may depart from the SDLC to try an alternative methodology such as prototyping,

"Welcome to Maple Ridge Engineering, what we call MRE. We hope you'll enjoy serving as a systems consultant for us. Although I've worked here five years in different capacities, I've just been reassigned to serve as an administrative aide to Snowden Evans, the head of the new Training and Management Systems Department. We're certainly a diverse group. As you make your way through the company, be sure to use all of your skills, both technical and people-oriented, to understand who we are and to identify the problems and conflicts that you think should be solved regarding our information systems.

"To bring you up to date, let me say that Maple Ridge Engineering is a medium-sized medical engineering company. Last year, our revenues exceeded $287 million. We employ about 335 people. There are about 150 administrative employees, as well as management and clerical staff like myself; approximately 75 professional employees, including engineers, physicians, and systems analysts; and about 110 trade employees, such as draftsmen and technicians.

"There are four offices: You will visit us through HyperCase in our home office in Maple Ridge, Tennessee. We have three other branches in the southern United States as well: Atlanta, Georgia; Charlotte, North Carolina; and New Orleans, Louisiana. We'd love to have you visit when you're in the area.

"For now, you should explore HyperCase using either Netscape Navigator or Microsoft Internet Explorer

"To learn more about Maple Ridge Engineering as a company, or to find out how to interview our employees, who will use the systems you design, and how to observe their offices in our company, you may want to start by going to the World Wide Web Internet site found at the location:

www.prenhall.com/kendall

This page contains useful information about the project as well as files that may be downloaded to your computer. One of the files is a set of Visible Analyst data files that match HyperCase. These files contain a partially constructed series of data flow diagrams, entity-relationship diagrams and repository information. The HyperCase Web site also contains additional exercises that may be assigned. HyperCase is designed to be explored and you should not overlook any object or clue on a Web page. To start consulting immediately, click the mouse on the MRE Reception area link and read more about HyperCase in Chapter 2."

ETHICS, the project champion approach, Soft Systems Methodology, or Multiview.

KEYWORDS AND PHRASES

computer-generated information
transaction processing
  systems (TPS)
office automation systems (OAS)

analyst's ethical framework
systems development life
  cycle (SDLC)
CASE tools

knowledge work systems (KWS)
management information
  systems (MIS)
decision support systems (DSS)
expert systems
executive support systems (ESS)
group decision support
  systems (GDSS)
computer supported
  collaborative work (CSCW)
artificial intelligence (AI)
groupware
systems analysis and design
systems analyst
systems consultant
supporting expert
agent of change

CASE repository
code generation
maintenance
migrate systems
software reverse engineering
reengineering
legacy software
CARE (Computer Assisted
  Reengineering)
object-oriented (O-O) systems
  analysis and design
prototyping
ETHICS
Soft Systems Methodology
Multiview
project champions

REVIEW QUESTIONS

1. Describe why information is most usefully thought of as an organizational resource rather than as an organizational byproduct.
2. Define what is meant by a transaction processing system.
3. Explain the difference between office automation systems (OAS) and knowledge work systems (KWS).
4. Compare the definition of a management information system (MIS) to the definition of a decision support system (DSS).
5. Define the term *expert systems.* How do expert systems differ from decision support systems?
6. List the problems of group interaction that group decision support systems (GDSS) and computer supported collaborative work (CSCW) systems were designed to address.
7. Which is the more general term—CSCW or GDSS? Explain.
8. List the advantages of using systems analysis and design techniques in approaching computerized information systems for business.
9. List three roles that the systems analyst is called upon to play. Provide a definition for each one.
10. What personal qualities are helpful to the systems analyst? List them.
11. List and briefly define the seven phases of the systems development life cycle (SDLC).
12. Define software reverse engineering and reengineering as they apply to CARE (Computer Assisted Reengineering).
13. List the four reasons for adopting CASE tools.
14. Define the term *object-oriented systems analysis and design.*

SELECTED BIBLIOGRAPHY

Alavi, M. "An Assessment of the Prototyping Approach to Information Systems." *Communications of the ACM,* Vol. 26, No. 6, June 1984, pp. 556–563.

Avison, D. E., and A. T. Wood-Harper. *Multiview: An Exploration in Information Systems Development.* Oxford: Blackwell Scientific Publications, 1990.

Beath, C. M. "Supporting the Information Technology Champion." *MIS Quarterly,* Vol. 15, No. 3, September 1991, pp. 355–372.

Checkland, P. B. "Soft Systems Methodology." *Human Systems Management,* Vol. 8, No. 4, 1989, pp. 271–289.

Checkland, P. B. *Systems Thinking, Systems Practice.* Chichester, U.K.: John Wiley, 1981.

Coad, P., and E. Yourdon. *Object-Oriented Analysis,* 2nd ed. Englewood Cliffs, NJ: Prentice-Hall, 1991.

Davis, G. B., and M. H. Olson. *Management Information Systems: Conceptual Foundation, Structure, and Development,* 2nd ed. New York: McGraw-Hill Book Company, 1985.

Holsapple, C. W., and A. B. Whinston. *Business Expert Systems.* Homewood, IL: Irwin, 1987.

Jackson, M. A. *Systems Development.* Englewood Cliffs, NJ: Prentice-Hall, 1983.

Kendall, J. E., and K. E. Kendall. "Systems Analysis and Designs," in M. Warner (ed.), *International Encyclopedia of Business and Management,* Vol. 5; pp. 4749–4759. London: Routledge, 1996.

Kendall, J. E., K. E. Kendall, R. Baskerville, and R. Barnes. "An Empirical Comparison of a Hypertext-based Systems Analysis Case with Conventional Cases and Role Playing." *The DATA BASE for Advances in Information Systems,* Vol. 27, No. 1, Winter 1996, pp. 58–77.

Kendall, K. E. "Behavioral Implications for Systems Analysis and Design: Prospects for the Nineties." *Journal of Management Systems,* Vol. 3, No. 1, 1991, pp. 1–4.

Laudon, K. C., and J. P. Laudon. *Management Information Systems,* 4th ed. Upper Saddle River, NJ: Prentice Hall, 1996.

Mumford, E., and M. Weir. *Computer Systems in Work Design—the ETHICS Method.* London: Associated Business Press, 1979.

Naumann, J. D., and A. M. Jenkins. "Prototyping The New Paradigm for Systems Development." *MIS Quarterly,* Vol. 6, No. 3, September 1982, pp. 29–44.

Schmidt, A. *Working with Visible Analyst Workbench for Windows.* Upper Saddle River, NJ: Prentice Hall, 1996.

Visible Analyst Workbench (VAW), Corporate Edition, Version 6.1 *Product and Pricing Information.* Waltham, MA: Visible Systems Corporation, 1997.

Whitten, J. L., L. D. Bentley, and V. M. Barlow. *Systems Analysis & Design Methods,* 3rd ed. Homewood, IL: Irwin, 1994.

Yourdon, E. *Modern Structured Analysis.* Englewood Cliffs, NJ: Prentice-Hall, 1989.

THE CASE OPENS

On a warm, sunny day in late October, Chip Puller parks his car and walks into his office at Central Pacific University. It felt good to be starting as a systems analyst, and he was looking forward to meeting the other staff.

In the office, Anna Liszt introduces herself. "We've been assigned to work as a team on a new project. Why don't I fill you in with the details, and then we can take a tour of the facilities."

"That sounds good to me," Chip replies. "How long have you been working here?"

"About five years," answers Anna. "I started as a programmer analyst, but the last few years have been dedicated to analysis and design. I'm hoping we'll find some ways to increase our productivity," Anna continues.

"Tell me about the new project," Chip says.

"Well, like so many organizations, we have a large number of micro-computers with different software packages installed on them. In the 1980s there were few microcomputers and a scattered collection of software, but there has been a rapid increase in recent years. The current system used to maintain software and hardware has been overwhelmed."

"What about the users? Who should I know? Who do you think will be important in helping us with the new system?" Chip asks.

"You'll meet everyone, but there are key people I've recently met, and I'll tell you what I've learned so you'll remember them when you meet them.

"Dot Matricks is manager of all microcomputer systems at Central Pacific. We seem to be able to work together well. She's very competent. She'd really like to be able to improve communication among users and analysts."

"It will be a pleasure to meet her," Chip speculates.

"Then there's Mike Crowe, the micro-maintenance expert. Really seems to be the nicest guy. But too busy. We need to help lighten his load. The software counterpart to Mike is Cher Ware. She's a free spirit, but don't get me wrong, she knows her job," Anna says.

"She could be fun to work with," Chip says.

"Could be," Anna agrees. "You'll meet the financial analyst, Paige Prynter, too. I haven't figured her out yet."

"Maybe I can help," Chip says.

"Lastly, you should—I mean, you will—meet Hy Perteks, who does a great job running the Information Center. He'd like to see us be able to integrate our life cycle activities."

"It sounds promising," Chip says. "I think I'm going to like it here."

Exercise

E-1. From the introductory conversation Chip and Anna shared, which elements mentioned might suggest the use of CASE tools?

Allen Schmidt,
Julie E. Kendall, and
Kenneth E. Kendall

2

UNDERSTANDING ORGANIZATIONAL STYLE AND ITS IMPACT ON INFORMATION SYSTEMS

ORGANIZATIONAL FUNDAMENTALS

In order to analyze and design appropriate information systems, systems analysts need to comprehend the organizations they work in as systems shaped through the interactions of three main forces: the levels of management, design of organizations, and organizational cultures.

Organizations are large systems composed of interrelated subsystems. The subsystems are influenced by three broad levels of management decision makers (operations, middle management, and strategic management) that cut horizontally across the organizational system. Organizational cultures and subcultures all influence the way people in subsystems interrelate. The foregoing topics and their implications for information systems development are considered in this chapter.

ORGANIZATIONS AS SYSTEMS

Organizations are usefully conceptualized as systems designed to accomplish predetermined goals and objectives through people and other resources that they employ. Organizations are composed of smaller, interrelated systems (departments, units, divisions, etc.) serving specialized functions. Typical functions include accounting, marketing, production, data processing, and management. Specialized functions (smaller systems) are eventually reintegrated through various mechanisms to form an effective organizational whole.

The significance of conceptualizing organizations as complex systems is that systems principles allow insight into how organizations work. It is of primary importance to understand the organization as a whole in order to ascertain information requirements properly and to design appropriate information systems. All systems are composed of subsystems (which include information systems); therefore, when studying an organization, we also examine how smaller systems are involved and how they function.

Source: ©1996 Robert Mankoff from the Cartoon Bank, Inc. All Rights Reserved.

"The E-Mail isn't functioning - pass it on."

Interrelatedness and Interdependence of Systems

All systems and subsystems are interrelated and interdependent. This fact has important implications both for organizations and for those systems analysts who seek to help them better achieve their goals. When any element of a system is changed or eliminated, the rest of the system's elements and subsystems are also impacted.

For example, suppose that the administrators of an organization decide not to hire personal secretaries any longer and to replace their functions with networked PCs. This decision has the potential to impact not only the secretaries and the administrators but also all of the organizational members who built up communications networks with the now-departed secretaries, the secretaries remaining in other organizational positions, and those in the organization already using microprocessors to handle secretarial functions.

Systems Processes

All systems process inputs from their environments. By definition, processes change or transform inputs into outputs. Whenever you examine a system, check to see what is being changed or processed. If nothing is changed, then you may not be identifying a process. Typical processes in systems include verifying, updating, printing, and so on.

Organizational Boundaries

Another aspect of organizations as systems is that all systems are contained by boundaries separating them from their environments. Organizational boundaries exist on a continuum ranging from extremely permeable to almost impermeable. In order to continue to adapt and survive, organizations must be able first to import people, raw materials, and information through their boundaries (inputs), and then to exchange their finished products, services, or information with the outside world (outputs). However, if boundaries become too lax, the organization's competitive edge is endangered, and control over performance is diminished.

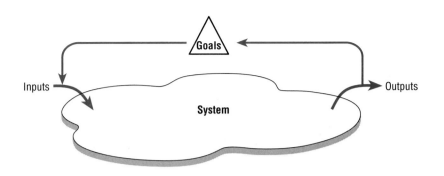

System Feedback for Planning and Control

Feedback is one form of system control. As systems, all organizations use planning and control to manage their resources effectively. Figure 2.1 shows how system outputs are used as feedback with which to compare performance to goals. This comparison in turn helps administrators formulate more specific goals as inputs. An instance of this is a manufacturing company that produces red, white, and blue weight-training sets as well as gunmetal–colored sets. The company finds that one year after the Olympics, very few red, white, and blue sets are purchased. Production managers use that information as feedback to make decisions about what quantities of each color to produce. Feedback in this instance is useful for planning and control.

However, the ideal system is one that self-corrects or self-regulates in such a way that decisions on typical occurrences are not required. An example is a computerized information system for production planning that takes into account current and projected demand and formulates a proposed solution as output. An Italian knitwear manufacturer that markets its clothing in the United States has just such a system. This company produces most of its sweaters in white, uses its computerized inventory information system to find out what colors are selling best, and then dyes sweaters in hot-selling colors immediately before shipping them. With a self-regulating information system, a manager can review the proposed production figures and make interventions only when exceptional factors, not accounted for in the computer's software formulation of the problem, are present.

Environments for Organizational Systems

Feedback is received from within the organization and from the outside environments around it. Anything external to an organization's boundaries is considered to be an environment. Numerous environments, with varying degrees of stability, constitute the milieu in which organizations exist.

Among these are: (1) the environment of the community where the organization is physically located, which is shaped by the size of its population and its demographic profile, including factors such as education and average income; (2) the economic environment, influenced by market factors, including competition; and (3) the political environment, controlled through state and local governments. Although changes in environmental status can be planned for, they often cannot be directly controlled by the organization.

Openness and Closedness in Organizations

Related and similar to the concept of external boundary permeability is the concept of internal openness or closedness of organizations. Openness and closedness also exist on a continuum, since there is no such thing as an absolutely open or completely closed organization.

Openness refers to the free flow of information within the organization. Subsystems such as creative or art departments often are characterized as open, with a free flow of ideas among participants and very few restrictions on who gets what information at what time when a creative project is in its infancy.

At the opposite end of the continuum might be a defense department unit assigned to work on top-secret defense planning affecting national security. Each person needs to receive clearance, timely information is a necessity, and access to information is only on a "need to know" basis. This sort of unit is limited by numerous rules.

Using a systems overlay to understand organizations allows us to acknowledge the idea of systems composed of subsystems; their interrelatedness and their interdependence; the existence of boundaries that allow or prevent interaction between various departments and elements of other subsystems and environments; and the existence of internal environments characterized by degrees of openness and closedness, which might differ across departments, units, or even projects.

Taking a Systems Perspective

Taking a systems perspective allows systems analysts to start broadly clarifying and understanding the various businesses with which they will come into contact. It is important that members of subsystems realize that their work is interrelated. Notice in Figure 2.2 that the outputs from the production subsystems serve as inputs for marketing, and that the outputs of marketing serve as new inputs for production. Neither subsystem can properly accomplish its goals without the other.

Problems occur when each manager possesses a different picture of the importance of his or her own functional subsystem. In Figure 2.3 you can see that the marketing manager's personal perspective shows the business as driven by marketing, with all other functional areas interrelated but not of central importance. By the same token the perspective of a production manager positions production at the center of the business, with all other functional areas driven by it.

FIGURE 2.2
Outputs from one department serve as inputs for another such that subsystems are interrelated.

How a marketing manager may view the organization

FIGURE 2.3
A depiction of the personal perspective of functional managers shows that they feature their own functional area as central to the organization.

How a production manager may see the organization

The relative importance of functional areas as revealed in the personal perspectives of managers takes on added significance when managers rise to the top through the ranks, becoming strategic managers. They can create problems if they overemphasize their prior functional information requirements in relation to the broader needs of the strategic manager.

For example, if a production manager continues to stress production scheduling and performance of line workers, the broader aspects of forecasting and policy making may suffer. This tendency is a danger in all sorts of businesses—where engineers work their way up to become administrators of aerospace firms, college professors move from their departments to become deans, or programmers advance to become executives of software firms. Their tunnel vision often creates problems for the systems analyst trying to separate actual information requirements from desires for a particular kind of information.

DEPICTING SYSTEMS GRAPHICALLY

A system or subsystem as it exists within the corporate organization may be graphically depicted in several ways. The various graphical models show the boundaries of the system and the information used within the system.

FIGURE 2.4
The basic symbols of a data
flow diagram.

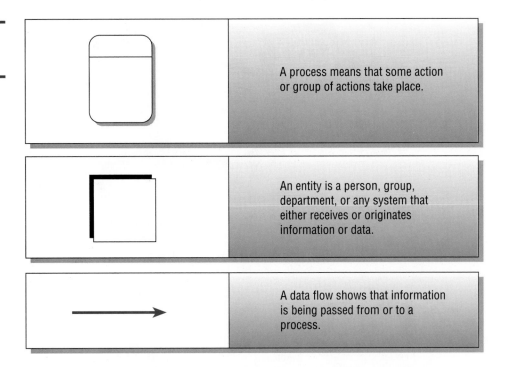

A process means that some action or group of actions take place.

An entity is a person, group, department, or any system that either receives or originates information or data.

A data flow shows that information is being passed from or to a process.

Systems and the Context Level Data Flow Diagram

The first model is the context level data flow diagram (also called an environmental model). Data flow diagrams focus on the data flowing into and out of the system and the processing of the data. These basic components of every computer program may be described in detail and used to analyze the system for accuracy and completeness.

The context level diagram employs only three symbols: (1) a rectangle with rounded corners, (2) a square with two shaded edges, and (3) an arrow, as shown in Figure 2.4. Processes transform incoming data into outgoing information, and the content level has only one process, representing the entire system. The external entity represents any entity that supplies or receives information from the system but is not a part of the system. This entity may be a person, a group of people, a corporate position or department, or other systems. The lines that connect the external entities to the process are called data flows, and they represent data.

An example of a context level data flow diagram is found in Figure 2.5. In this example the most basic elements of an airline reservation system are represented.

The passenger (an entity) initiates a travel request (data flow). The context level diagram doesn't show enough detail to indicate exactly what happens (it isn't supposed to), but we can see that the passenger's preferences and the available flights are sent to the travel agent, who sends ticketing information back to the process. We can also see that the passenger reservation is sent to the airline.

In Chapter 9 we will see that a data flow contains much information. For example, the passenger reservation contains the passenger's name, airline, flight number(s), date(s) of travel, price, seating preference, etc. For now, however, we are concerned mainly with how a context level defines the boundaries of the system. In the preceding example only reservations are part of the process. Other decisions that the airline would make (e.g., pur-

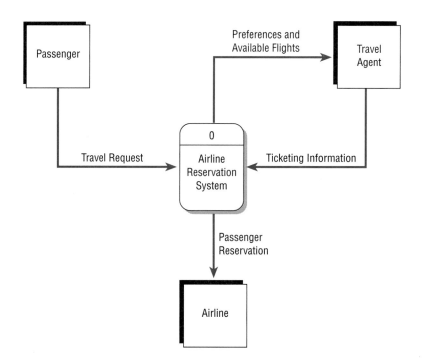

FIGURE 2.5
A context level flow diagram
for an airline reservation
system.

chasing airplanes, changing schedules, pricing, etc.) are not part of *this* system.

Systems and the Entity-Relationship Model

One way a systems analyst can define proper system boundaries is to use an entity-relationship model. The elements that make up an organizational system can be referred to as entities. An entity may be a person, a place, or a thing, such as a passenger on an airline, a destination, or a plane. Alternatively, an entity may be an event, such as the end of the month, a sales period, or a machine breakdown. A relationship is the association that describes the interaction among the entities.

There are many different conventions for drawing entity-relationship, or E-R, diagrams (with names like Crow's Foot, Arrow, or Bachman notation). In this book we will use Crow's Foot notation. For now we will assume that an entity is a plain rectangular box.

Figure 2.6 shows what a simple entity-relationship diagram would look like. Two entities are linked together by a line. In this example the end of the line is marked with two short parallel marks (I I), signifying that this relationship is one-to-one. That means that exactly one employee is assigned to one phone extension. No one shares the phone extension in this office.

The colored arrows are not part of the entity-relationship diagram. They are present to demonstrate how to read the entity-relationship diagram. The phrase on the right side of the line is read from top to bottom as follows: "One EMPLOYEE is assigned to one PHONE EXTENSION." On the left side, as you read from bottom to top, the arrow says, "One PHONE EXTENSION is listed for one EMPLOYEE."

Similarly, Figure 2.7 shows another relationship. The crow's foot (>—+) is obvious on this diagram, and this particular example is a many-to-one example. As you read from left to right, the arrow signifies that "Many EMPLOYEES are members of a DEPARTMENT." As you read

FIGURE 2.6
An entity relationship diagram showing a one-to-one
relationship.

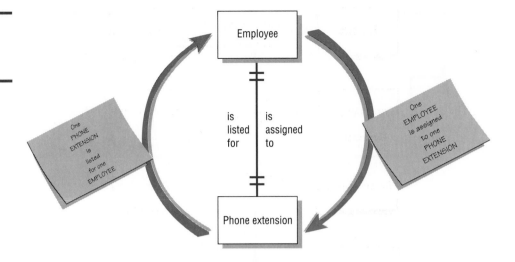

from right to left, it implies that "One DEPARTMENT contains many EMPLOYEES."

Notice that when a many-to-one relationship is present, the grammar changes from "is" to "are" even though the singular "is" is written on the line. The crow's foot and the single mark does not literally mean that this end of the relationship must be a mandatory "many." Instead, it implies that this end could be anything from one to many.

Figure 2.8 elaborates on this scheme. Here we have listed a number of typical entity relationships. The first, "An EMPLOYEE is assigned to an OFFICE," is a one-to-one relationship. The second one is a one-to-many relationship: "One CARGO AIRCRAFT will serve one or more DISTRIBUTION CENTERs."

The third one is slightly different because it has a circle at one end. It can be read as "A SYSTEMS ANALYST may be assigned to MANY PROJECTS," meaning that the analyst can be assigned to no projects [that is what

FIGURE 2.7
An entity relationship diagram showing a many-to-one
relationship.

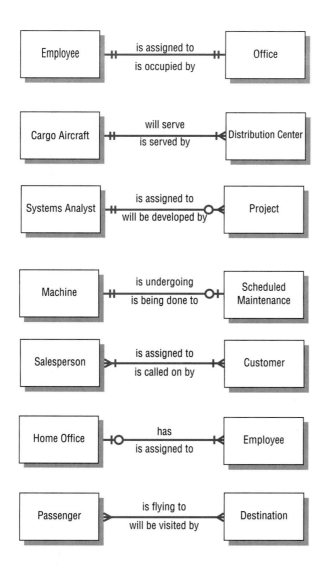

FIGURE 2.8
Examples of different types of
relationships in E-R diagrams.

the circle (**O**) or zero is for], one, or many projects. Likewise the circle (**O**) indicates that none is possible in the next relationship. Recall that the short mark means one. Therefore, we can read it as follows: "A MACHINE may or may not be undergoing SCHEDULED MAINTENANCE." Notice that the line is written as "*is* undergoing," but the end marks on the line indicate that either no maintenance (**O**) or maintenance (**I**) is actually going on.

The next relationship states that "One or many SALESPEOPLE (plural of SALESPERSON) are assigned to one or more CUSTOMERs." It is the classic many-to-many relationship. The next relationahip can be read as follows: "The HOME OFFICE can have one or many EMPLOYEEs," or "One or more EMPLOYEEs may or may not be assigned to the HOME OFFICE." Once again the **I** and **O** together imply a Boolean situation—in other words, zero or one.

The final relationship shown here can be read as "Many PASSENGERs are flying to many DESTINATIONs." This symbol, —< is preferred by some to indicate a mandatory "many" condition. (Would it ever be possible to have only one passenger or only one destination?) Even so, some CASE tools like Visible Analyst Workbench do not offer this as a possibility, because the optional one-or-more condition as shown in the SALESPERSON–CUSTOMER relationship above will do.

FIGURE 2.9
Three different types of entities used in E-R diagrams.

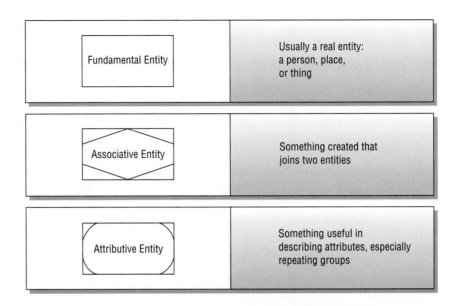

Up to now we have modeled all of our relationships using just one simple rectangle and a line. This works well when we are examining the relationships of real things like real people, places, and things. But sometimes we create new items in the process of developing an information system. Some examples are invoices, receipts, files, and databases. When we want to describe how a person relates to a receipt, for example, it becomes convenient to indicate the receipt in a different way. This is shown in Figure 2.9 as an associative entity.

An associative entity can only exist if it connected to at least two other entities. For that reason, some call it a gerund, a junction, an intersection, or a concatenated entity. This makes sense because a receipt wouldn't be necessary unless there were a customer and a salesperson making the transaction.

Another type of entity is the attributive. When an analyst wants to show data that are completely dependent on the existence of a fundamental entity, an attributive entity should be used. For example, if a video store had

FIGURE 2.10
Starting to draw an E-R diagram; the first attempt.

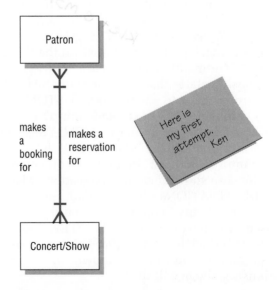

multiple copies of the same video title, an attributive entity could be used to designate which copy of the tape is being checked out. The attributive entity is useful for showing repeating groups of data. For example, suppose we are going to model the relationships that exist when a patron gets tickets to a concert or show. The entities seem obvious at first; "a PATRON and a CONCERT/SHOW," as shown in Figure 2.10. What sort of relationship exists? At first glance the PATRON gets a reservation for a CONCERT/SHOW, and the CONCERT/SHOW can be said to have made a booking for a PATRON.

The process isn't that simple of course, and the E-R diagram need not be that simple either. The PATRON actually makes a RESERVATION, as shown in Figure 2.11. The RESERVATION is for a CONCERT/SHOW. The CONCERT/SHOW holds the RESERVATION and the RESERVATION is in the name of the PATRON. We added an associative entity here because a RESERVATION was created due to the information system required to relate the PATRON and the CONCERT/SHOW.

Again this is quite simple, but because concerts and shows have many performances, the entity relationship diagram is drawn once more in Figure 2.12. Here we add an attributive entity to handle the many performances of the CONCERT/SHOW. In this case, the RESERVATION is made for a particular PERFORMANCE, and the PERFORMANCE is one of many that belong to a specific CONCERT/SHOW. In turn the CONCERT/SHOW has many per-

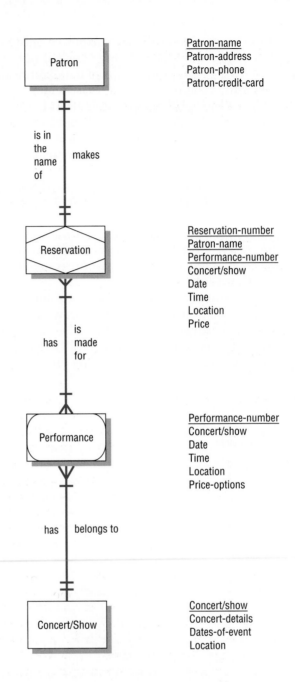

FIGURE 2.12
A more complete E-R diagram showing data attributes of the entities.

Patron

Patron-name
Patron-address
Patron-phone
Patron-credit-card

is in the name of   makes

Reservation

Reservation-number
Patron-name
Performance-number
Concert/show
Date
Time
Location
Price

has   is made for

Performance

Performance-number
Concert/show
Date
Time
Location
Price-options

has   belongs to

Concert/Show

Concert/show
Concert-details
Dates-of-event
Location

formances, and one PERFORMANCE has a RESERVATION which is in the name of a particular PATRON.

To the right of this E-R diagram is a set of data attributes that make up each of the entities in this E-R diagram. Some entities may have attributes in common. The attributes that are underlined can be searched for. The attributes are referred to as keys and will be discussed in Chapter 17.

Entity-relationship diagrams are often used by systems designers to help model the file or database. However, it is even more important that the systems analyst understand early on both the entities and relationships in the organizational system. In sketching out some basic E-R diagrams, the analyst needs to:

1. List the entities in the organization in order to gain a better understanding of the organization.

2. Choose key entities in order to narrow the scope of the problem to a manageable and meaningful dimension.

3. Identify what the primary entity should be.

4. Confirm the results of steps 1–3 through other data-gathering methods (investigation, interviewing, administering questionnaires, observation, and prototyping), as discussed in Chapters 4–8.

It is critical that the systems analyst begin to draw E-R diagrams upon entering the organization rather than waiting until the database needs to be designed, because E-R diagrams help the analyst understand what business the organization is actually in, help determine the size of the problem, and help discern whether the right problem is being addressed. The E-R diagrams need to be confirmed or revised as the data-gathering process takes place.

Organizational factors that influence the analysis and design of information systems include levels of management and organizational culture. We discuss each one of these factors and their implications for the analysis and design of information systems in the remaining sections of this chapter.

LEVELS OF MANAGEMENT

Management in organizations exists on three broad, horizontal levels: operational control, managerial planning and control (middle management), and strategic management, as shown in Figure 2.13. Each level carries its own responsibilities, and all work toward achieving organizational goals and objectives in their own ways.

Operations Management

Operational control forms the bottom tier of three-tiered management. Operations managers make decisions using predetermined rules that have predictable outcomes when implemented correctly.

Operations managers are the decision makers whose work is the most clear-cut because of the high degree of certainty in their decision-making environment. They make decisions that affect implementation in work sched-

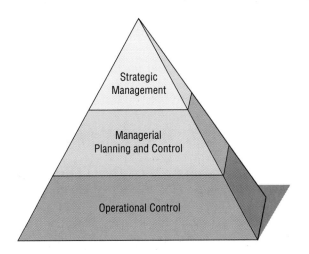

CHAPTER 2:
UNDERSTANDING
ORGANIZATIONAL STYLE
AND ITS IMPACT ON
INFORMATION SYSTEMS

CONSULTING OPPORTUNITY 2.1

Where There's Carbon, There's a Copy

"I don't know what we do with the pink ones yet," Richard Russell admitted. "They're part of a quadruplicate form that rips apart. All I know is that we keep them for the filing clerk, and he files them when he has time."

Richard is a newly hired junior account executive for Carbon, Carbon & Rippy, a brokerage house. You are walking through the steps he takes in making a stock purchase "official," since his boss has asked you to streamline the process whereby stock purchase information is stored in the computer and retrieved.

After you leave, Richard continues thinking about the pink forms. He tells his clerk, Harry Schultz, "In my two months here, I haven't seen anyone use those. They take up my time and yours, not to mention all the filing space. Let's pitch them."

Richard and Harry proceed to open all of the old files kept by Richard's predecessor and to throw out the filed pink forms, along with those accumulated but not yet filed. It takes hours, but they make a lot of room. "Definitely worth the time," Richard reassures Harry.

Three weeks later, an assistant to Richard's boss, Carol Vaness, appears. Richard is happy to see a familiar face, greeting her with, "Hi, Carol. What's new?"

"Same old thing," Carol sighs. "Well, I guess it isn't old to you, since you're the newcomer. But I need all those pesky pink forms."

Almost in shock, Richard exchanges looks with Harry, then mumbles, "You're kidding, of course."

Carol looks more serious than Richard ever thought possible, replying, "No joke. I summarize all the pink forms from all the brokers, and then my totals are compared with computerized stock purchase information. It's part of our routine, three-month audit for transaction accuracy. My work depends on yours. Didn't Ms. McCue explain that to you when you started?"

What systems concept did Richard and Harry ignore in tossing out the pink forms? What are the possible ramifications for systems analysts if general systems concepts are ignored?

uling, inventory control, shipping, receiving, and control of processes such as production. Operations managers oversee the operating details of the organization, ensuring that the basic tasks of the organization are accomplished on time and in accordance with organizational constraints.

Middle Management

Middle management forms the second, or intermediate, tier of the three-tiered management system. Middle managers make short-term planning and control decisions about how resources may best be allocated to meet organizational objectives.

Middle managers experience very little certainty in their decision-making environment. Their decisions range all the way from forecasting future resource requirements to solving employee problems that threaten productivity. Few of the decisions that middle managers make are as structured as those made by operations managers. The decision-making domain of middle managers can usefully be characterized as partly operational and partly strategic, with constant fluctuations.

Strategic Management

Strategic management composes the third level of three-tiered management control. Strategic managers look outward from the organization to the future, making decisions that will guide middle and operations managers in the months and years ahead.

Strategic managers work in a highly uncertain decision-making environment. Through statements of goals and the determination of strategies and policies to achieve them, strategic managers actually define the organization as a whole. Theirs is the broad picture, wherein the company decides to develop new product lines, divest itself of unprofitable ventures, acquire other compatible companies, or even allow itself to be sold.

There are sharp contrasts among the decision makers on many dimensions. For instance, strategic planners have multiple decision objectives while operations managers have single ones, and it often is difficult for high-level managers to identify problems, but it is easy for operations managers to do so. Strategic planners are faced with semistructured problems, whereas lower-level managers deal mostly with structured problems. The alternative solutions to a problem facing the strategic managers are often difficult to articulate, but the alternatives that operations managers work with are usually easy to enumerate. The nature of the decisions made by the various levels of management is entirely different. Strategic managers most often make one-time decisions, whereas the decisions made by operations managers tend to be repetitive. Finally, the decision style of strategic managers tends toward the heuristic, while operations managers tend to be mainly analytic in their style.

Implications for Information Systems Development

Each of the three management levels holds differing implications for developing management information systems. Some of the information requirements for managers are clear-cut, while others are fuzzy and overlap.

Operations managers need internal information that is of a repetitive, low-level nature. They are highly dependent on information that captures current performance, and they are large users of on-line, real-time information resources. The need of operations managers for past performance information and periodic information is only moderate. They have little use for external information that allows future projections or creation of "what-if" scenarios.

Information systems designed for operations managers are valuable if they can provide information to help in controlling operations in a timely manner. Much of the information needed for operations is already being generated or can be easily pinpointed, but it would be more useful if it were accessible from an on-line system.

On the next management level, middle managers, who both plan and control, are in need of both short- and longer-term information. Due to the troubleshooting nature of their jobs, middle managers experience extremely high needs for information in real time. In order to control properly, they also need current information on performance as measured against set standards.

Middle managers are highly dependent on internal information. In contrast to operations managers, they have a high need for historical information, along with information that allows prediction of future events and simulation of numerous possible scenarios.

Strategic managers differ somewhat from both middle and operations managers in their information requirements. They are highly dependent on information from external sources that supply news of market trends and the strategies of competing corporations.

Since the task of strategic managing demands projections into the uncertain future, strategic managers have a high need for information of a predictive nature and information that allows creation of many different "what-if" scenarios. Strategic managers also exhibit strong needs for periodically reported information as they seek to adapt to fast-moving changes.

CONSULTING OPPORTUNITY 2.2

Pyramid Power

"We really look up to you," says Paul LeGon. As a systems analyst, you have been invited to help Pyramid, Inc., a small, independent book publishing firm that specializes in paperback books outside of the publishing mainstream.

Paul continues, "We deal with what some folks think are fringe topics. You know, pyramid power, end-of-the-world prophecies, and healthier living by thinking of the color pink. Sometimes when people see our books, they just shake their heads and say, 'Tut—uncommon topic.' But we're not slaves to any particular philosophy, and we've been very successful. So much so that because I'm 24, people call me the 'boy king'." Paul pauses to decipher your reaction.

Paul continues, "I'm at the top as president, and functional areas such as editorial, accounting, production, and marketing are under me."

Paul's assistant, Ceil Toom, who has been listening quietly up to now, barges in with her comments: "The last systems experts that did a project for us recommended the creation of liaison committees of employees between accounting, production, and marketing so that we could share newly computerized inventory and sales figures across the organization. They claimed that committees like that would cut down on needless duplication of output, and each functional area would be better integrated with all the rest."

Paul picks up the story, saying, "It was fair—oh, for a while—and the employees shared information, but the reason you're here is that the employees said they didn't have time for committee meetings and were uncomfortable sharing information with people from other departments who were further up the ladder than they were here at Pyramid."

According to Paul and Ceil, what were the effects of installing a management information system at Pyramid, Inc., that required people to share information in ways that were not consistent with their structure? Propose some general ways to resolve this problem so that Pyramid employees can still get the sales and inventory figures they need.

Strategic planners need general, summarized information rather than the highly detailed, raw data required by low-level managers. Information for strategic planners may be older and estimated, whereas operational managers need current, accurate information. Finally, the strategic planner needs qualitative information, mainly from external sources, rather than the quantitative information from internal sources required by the operations manager.

ORGANIZATIONAL CULTURE

Organizational culture is a burgeoning area of research that has grown remarkably in the past fifteen years. Just as it is appropriate to think of organizations as including many technologies, it is similarly appropriate to see them as hosts to multiple, often competing subcultures.

Since the area is relatively new, there is little agreement on what precisely constitutes an organizational subculture. It is agreed, however, that competing subcultures may be in conflict, attempting to gain adherents to their vision of what the organization should be.

Rather than thinking about culture as a whole, it is more useful to think about the researchable determinants of subcultures, such as shared verbal and nonverbal symbolism. Verbal symbolism includes shared language used to construct, convey, and preserve subcultural myths, metaphors, visions, and humor. Nonverbal symbolism includes shared artifacts, rites, and ceremonies such as clothing; the use, placement, and decoration of offices; and rituals for celebrating members' birthdays, promotions, and retirements.

Subcultures coexist within "official" organizational cultures. The officially sanctioned culture may prescribe a dress code, suitable ways to address superiors and co-workers, and proper ways to deal with the outside public. Subcultures may be powerful determinants of information requirements, availability, and use.

Organizational members may belong to one or more subcultures within the organization. Subcultures may exert a powerful influence on member behavior, including sanctions for or against the use of information systems.

Understanding and recognizing predominant organizational subcultures may help the systems analyst overcome the resistance to change that arises when a new information system is installed. For example, the analyst might devise user training to address specific concerns of organizational subcultures. Identifying subcultures may also help in the design of decision support systems that are tailored for interaction with specific user groups.

SUMMARY

There are three broad organizational fundamentals to consider when analyzing and designing information systems. These are the concept of organizations as systems, the various levels of management, and the overall organizational culture.

Organizations are complex systems composed of interrelated and interdependent subsystems. Additionally, systems and subsystems are characterized by their internal environments on a continuum from open to closed. An open system allows free passage of resources (people, information, materials) through its boundaries; closed systems do not permit free flow of input or output.

Entity relationship diagrams help the systems analyst understand the entities and relationships that comprise the organizational system. The four different kinds of E-R diagrams are: a one-to-one relationship, a one-to-many relationship, a many-to-one, and a many-to-many relationship.

The three levels of managerial control are: operational, middle management, and strategic. The time horizon of decision making is different for each level.

Organizational cultures and subcultures are important determinants of how people use information and information systems. By grounding information systems in the context of the organization as a larger system, it is possible to realize that numerous factors are important and should be taken into account when ascertaining information requirements and designing and implementing information systems.

KEYWORDS AND PHRASES

systems	Crow's Foot notation
interrelatedness	entity (fundamental entity)
interdependent	associative entity
organizational boundaries	attributive entity
feedback	operations management
environment	middle management
openness	strategic management
closedness	organizational culture
entity-relationship (ER) diagrams	

"You seem to have already made a good start at MRE. Even though I can tell you a lot about the company, remember that there are a number of ways to orient yourself within it. You will want to interview users, observe their decision-making settings, and look at archival reports, charts, and diagrams. In order to do so, you can click on the telephone directory to get an appointment with an interviewee, click on the building map to go to a particular location, or click on organizational charts that show you the functional areas and formal hierarchical relationships at MRE.

"Many of the rules of corporate life apply within the MRE HyperCase. For instance, there are many public areas in which you are free to walk. However, if you want to tour a private corporate office, you must first book an appointment with one of our employees. Some secure areas are strictly off limits to you, just because you are an outsider and could pose a security risk.

"I don't think you'll find us excessively secretive, however, since you may assume that any employee who grants you an interview will also grant you access to the archival material in his or her files, as well as to current work. You'll be able to go about your consulting freely in most cases. If you get too curious or invade our privacy in some way, we'll let you know. We're not afraid to tell you what the limits are.

"Unfortunately, some people in the company never seem to make themselves available to consultants. If you need to know more about these hard-to-get interviewees, I suggest you be persistent. There are lots of ways to find out about the people and the systems of MRE, but much of the time creativity is what pays off. You will notice that the systems consultants who follow their

FIGURE 2.HC1
Click on key words in Hyper-Case and find out more detail.

hunches, sharpen their technical skills, and never stop thinking about piecing together the puzzles here at MRE are the ones who are the best.

"Remember to use multiple methods—interviewing, observation, and investigation—to understand what we at MRE are trying to tell you. Sometimes actions, documents, and offices actually speak louder than words!"

HYPERCASE QUESTIONS

1. What major organizational change recently took place at MRE? What department(s) were involved, and why was the change made?
2. What does the Management Systems Unit at MRE do? Who are its clients?
3. What are the goals and strategies of the Engineering and Systems division at MRE? What are the goals of the Training and Management Systems Department?
4. Would you categorize MRE as a service industry, a manufacturer, or both? What kind of "products" does MRE "produce" (i.e., does it offer material goods, services, or both)? Suggest how the type of industry MRE is in affects the information systems it uses.
5. What type of organizational structure does MRE have? What are the implications of this structure for MIS?
6. Describe in a paragraph the "politics" of the Training and Management Systems Department at MRE. Who is involved and what are some of the main issues?

REVIEW QUESTIONS

1. What are the three groups of organizational fundamentals that carry implications for the development of information systems?
2. What is meant by saying that organizational subsystems are interrelated and interdependent?
3. Define the term *organizational boundary*.
4. What are the two main purposes for feedback in organizations?
5. Define *openness* in an organizational environment.
6. Define *closedness* in an organizational environment.
7. What is meant by the term *entity-relationship diagram*?
8. What symbols are used to draw E-R diagrams?
9. List the types of E-R diagrams.
10. How do an entity, an associative entity, and an attributive entity differ?
11. List the three broad, horizontal levels of management in organizations.
12. How can understanding organizational subcultures help in the design of information systems?

PROBLEMS

1. "It's hard to focus on what we want to achieve. I look at what our real competitors, the convenience stores, are doing and think we should

copy that. Then a hundred customers come in, and I listen to each of them, and they say we should keep our little store the same, with friendly clerks and old-fashioned cash registers. Then, when I pick up a copy of *SuperMarket News,* they say that the wave of the future is super grocery stores, with no individual prices marked and UPC scanners replacing clerks. I'm pulled in so many directions I can't really settle on a strategy for our grocery store," admits Geoff Walsham, owner and manager of Jiffy Geoff's Grocery Store.

In a paragraph, apply the concept of permeable organizational boundaries to analyze Geoff's problem in focusing on organizational objectives.

2. Write seven sentences explaining the right-to-left relationships in Figure 2.8.

3. Draw an entity-relationship diagram of a patient–doctor relationship.
   a. Which of the types of E-R diagrams is it?
   b. In a sentence or two, explain why the patient–doctor relationship is diagrammed in this way.

4. You began drawing E-R diagrams soon after your entry into the health maintenance organization for which you're designing a system. Your team member is skeptical about using E-R diagrams before design of the database is begun.

   In a paragraph, persuade your team member that early use of E-R diagrams is worthwhile.

5. Sandy works as a manager for Arf-Arf Dog Food Company. Since there are several different suppliers of ingredients and their prices fluctuate, she has come up with several different formulations for the same dog food product, depending on the availability of particular ingredients from particular suppliers. She then orders ingredients accordingly. Even though she cannot predict when ingredients will become available at a particular price, her ordering of supplies can be considered routine.
   a. On what level of management is Sandy working? Explain in a paragraph.
   b. What attributes of her job would have to change before you would categorize her as working on a different level of management? List them.

6. Many of the people who work at Arf-Arf Dog Food Company laugh about Arf-Arf and about how silly it is that making dog food is such an important enterprise in the United States. However, other groups in the company are extremely proud of Arf-Arf's products and reputation for producing quality dog chow, and they happily display industry awards they have received.
   a. In a paragraph, identify and give descriptive names to organizational subcultures that seem apparent at Arf-Arf.

GROUP PROJECT

1. With your group, draw a context level diagram of your school's or university's registration system. Label each entity and process. Discuss why there appear to be different ways to draw the diagram. Reach consensus as a group about the best way to draw the diagram and defend your choice in a paragraph. Now, working with your group's members, follow the appropriate steps for developing an E-R diagram and create

one for your school or university registration system. Make sure your group indicates whether the relationship you depict are one-to-one, one-to-many, many-to-one, or many-to-many.

SELECTED BIBLIOGRAPHY

Burch, J. G., F. R. Strater, and G. Grudnitski. *Information Systems: Theory and Practice,* 3rd ed. New York: John Wiley & Sons, 1983.

Chen, P. "The Entity-Relationship Model—Towards a Unified View of Data." *ACM Transactions on Database Systems 1,* March 1976, pp. 9–36.

Davis, G. B., and M. H. Olson. *Management Information Systems, Conceptual Foundations, Structure, and Development,* 2nd ed. New York: McGraw-Hill Book Company, 1985.

Galbraith, J. R. *Organizational Design.* Reading, MA: Addison-Wesley, 1977.

Kendall, K. E., J. R. Buffington, and J. E. Kendall. "The Relationship of Organizational Subcultures to DSS User Satisfaction." *Human Systems Management,* March 1987, pp. 31–39.

PICTURING THE RELATIONSHIPS

"So the project involves more than simply performing maintenance work on the current programs," Chip says.

"Are we using a formal methodology for analyzing and designing the new system?"

"Yes," replies Anna. "We are also using a CASE tool, Visible Analyst Workbench, to analyze and design the system.[1,2] We've recently installed the product on our microcomputer in the office." Anna motions to a large computer work area containing a microcomputer with attached laser printer and mainframe terminal.

"That's great!" exclaims Chip. "Have you used Visible Analyst on other projects?"

"No," Anna says. "This is the pilot project involving Visible Analyst. I've attended training sessions and I'm somewhat familiar with its operation. Are you familiar with Visible Analyst?"

"I've had some experience with it at school. I understand that's one of the reasons that I was hired for this position," answers Chip. "Let me see what you've done so far."

They both move to the microcomputer area, where Anna loads Visible Analyst. With a few easy mouse clicks she comes to a context level data-flow diagram (see Figure E2.1). "It's very useful to begin thinking of the system this way," Anna says as they look at the diagram on the screen.

Chip agrees, saying, "I can very easily see what you think is happening with the system. For instance, I see that the external entity Management supplies hardware and software inquiries and receives the corresponding response in return. It shows the system within the larger organization."

"I've also drawn an E-R diagram of the system (see Figure E2.2), so I could start understanding the relationships between the data structures," Anna says as she brings up the entity-relationship diagram on the screen.

"Yes, the many-to-many and one-to-many relationships are very clear when you look at this," Chip says, viewing the screen. "You've got a good start here," Chip continues. "Let's get to work and see what needs to be done next."

Allen Schmidt,
Julie E. Kendall, and
Kenneth E. Kendall

---

[1] For more details on how to begin using Visible Analyst Workbench, see *Working with Visible Analyst Workbench for Windows,* by Allen Schmidt (Prentice Hall, 1996).

[2] The Central Pacific University case can be adapted to other CASE tools. Other tools include Excelerator and Visio. Alternatively, many of the exercises can be accomplished manually if CASE tools are unavailable.

FIGURE E2.1
Context level data flow diagram, Current System.

Exercises*

E-1. Use Visible Analyst to view and print the context level data-flow diagram for the microcomputer systems, as Chip and Anna did.

E-2. Use the Repository feature to view the entry for the central process.

E-3. Use Visible Analyst to view and print the entity-relationship diagram for the microcomputer system.

E-4. Explain why the external entities on the context level diagram are not found on the entity-relationship diagram.

E-5. Explain why the entities MANAGEMENT and FACULTY are found on both sides of the process on the context level diagram.

---

* Exercises preceded by a disk icon require the program Visible Analyst Workbench or another CASE tool. A disk is provided free of charge to any professor adopting this book. The examples on the disk may be imported into Visible Analyst and then used by students.

FIGURE E2.2
Entity-relationship diagram, Microcomputer System.

REFERENCE TEXTS

Schmidt, A. *Working with Visible Analyst Workbench for Windows.* Upper Saddle River, NJ: Prentice Hall, 1996.

3

DETERMINING FEASIBILITY AND MANAGING ANALYSIS AND DESIGN ACTIVITIES

PROJECT FUNDAMENTALS

Initiating projects, determining project feasibility, scheduling projects, planning and then managing activities and team members for productivity are all important capabilities for the systems analyst to master. As such, they are considered project fundamentals.

A systems project begins with problems or with opportunities for improvement within a business that often come up as the organization adapts to change. Changes that require a systems solution occur in the legal environment as well as in the industry's environment. Once a project is suggested, the systems analyst works quickly with decision makers to determine whether it is feasible. If a project is approved for a full systems study, the project activities are scheduled through the use of tools such as Gantt charts and PERT diagrams, so that the project can be completed on time. Part of assuring the productivity of systems analysis team members is effectively managing their scheduled activities. This chapter is devoted to a discussion of these project fundamentals.

PROJECT INITIATION

Systems projects are initiated by many different sources for many reasons. Some of the projects suggested will survive various stages of evaluation to be worked on by you (or you and your team); others will not and/or should not get that far. Businesspeople suggest systems projects for two broad reasons: (1) to experience problems that lend themselves to systems solutions and (2) to recognize opportunities for improvement through upgrading, altering, or installing new systems when they occur. Both of these situations can arise as the organization adapts to and copes with natural, evolutionary change.

PROBLEMS WITHIN THE ORGANIZATION

Managers do not like to conceive of their organization as having problems, let alone talk about them or share them with someone from outside. However, good managers realize that recognizing symptoms of problems or, at a later stage, diagnosing the problems themselves and then confronting them is imperative if the business is to keep functioning at its highest potential.

Problems surface in many different ways. One way of conceptualizing what problems are and how they arise is to think of them as situations where goals have never been met or are no longer being met. Useful feedback gives information about the gap between actual and intended performance. In this way feedback spotlights problems.

In some instances problems that require the services of systems analysts are uncovered because performance measures are not being met. Problems (or symptoms of problems) with processes that are visible in output and that could require the help of a systems analyst include excessive errors and work performed too slowly, incompletely, incorrectly, or not at all.

Other symptoms of problems become evident when people do not meet baseline performance goals. Changes in employee behavior such as unusually high absenteeism, high job dissatisfaction, or high worker turnover should serve to alert managers to potential problems. Any of these, alone or in combination, might be sufficient reason to request the help of a systems analyst.

Although difficulties such as those just described occur within the organization, feedback on how well the organization is meeting intended goals may come from outside, in the form of complaints or suggestions from customers, vendors, or suppliers, and lost or unexpectedly lower sales. This feedback from the external environment is extremely important and should not be ignored.

A summary of symptoms of problems and approaches useful in problem detection is provided in Figure 3.1. Notice that checking output, observing or researching employee behavior, and listening to feedback from external sources are all valuable in problem finding.

FIGURE 3.1
Checking output, observing employee behavior, and listening to feedback are all ways to help the analyst pinpoint systems problems and opportunities.

To Identify Problems	Look for These Specific Signs:
Check output against performance criteria	• Too many errors • Work completed slowly • Work done incorrectly • Work done incompletely • Work not done at all
Observe behavior of employees	• High absenteeism • High job dissatisfaction • High job turnover

Listen to external feedback from:
  Vendors
  Customers
  Suppliers
	• Complaints
	• Suggestions for improvement
	• Loss of sales
	• Lower sales

When reacting to accounts of problems within the organization, the systems analyst plays the roles of consultant, supporting expert, and as agent of change, as discussed in Chapter 1. As you might expect, roles for the systems analyst shift subtly when projects are initiated because the focus is on opportunities for improvement rather than on the need to solve problems.

OPPORTUNITIES FOR IMPROVEMENT

The systems analyst serves as catalyst and supporting expert primarily by being able to see where processes can be improved. Optimistically, opportunities can be conceived of as the obverse of problems; yet in some cultures, crisis also means opportunity. What looms as a disturbing problem for a manager might be turned into an opportunity for improvement by an alert systems analyst.

Improvements to systems can be defined as changes that will result in incremental yet worthwhile benefits. There are many possibilities for improvements, including:

1. Speeding up a process.
2. Streamlining a process through the elimination of unnecessary or duplicated steps.
3. Combining processes.
4. Reducing errors in input through changes of forms and display screens.
5. Reducing redundant output.
6. Improving integration of systems and subsystems.
7. Improving worker satisfaction with the system.
8. Improving ease of customer, supplier, and vendor interaction with the system.

It is well within the systems analyst's capabilities to notice opportunities for improvements. However, people who come into daily contact with the system may be even better sources of information about improvements that should be made. If improvements have already been suggested, your expertise is needed to help determine whether the improvement is worthwhile and how it can be implemented.

Although the list of improvements given above is long, it is not an exhaustive one. The difficult part of suggesting and implementing improvements is that they must be worth the discomfiture and cost of change.

SELECTION OF PROJECTS

Projects come from many different sources and for many reasons. Not all of them should be selected for further study. You must be clear in your own mind about the reasons for recommending a systems study on a project that seems to address a problem or could bring about improvement. Consider the motivation that prompts a proposal on the project. You need to be sure that the project under consideration is not being proposed simply to enhance your own political reputation or power or that of the person or group proposing it, since there is a high probability that such a project will be ill-conceived and eventually ill-accepted.

CONSULTING OPPORTUNITY 3.1

The Sweetest Sound I've Ever Sipped

Felix Straw, who represents one of the many U.S. distributors of the European soft drink Sipps[1], gazes unhappily at a newspaper weather map, which is saturated with a dark red color, indicating that most of the United States is experiencing an early spring heat wave with no signs of a let-up. Pointing to the paper as he speaks, he tells your systems group, "It's the best thing that could happen to us, or at least it should be. But when we had to place our orders three months ago, we had no idea that this spring monster heat wave was going to devour the country this way! We need to be able to tell them (nodding his head toward a picture of their European plant on the wall) when things are hot over here so we can get enough product. Otherwise, we'll miss out every time. This happened two years ago and it just about killed us.

"Each of us distributors meets with our district managers to do three-month planning. When we agree, we fax our orders into European headquarters. They make their own adjustments, bottle the drinks, and then we get our modified orders about 9–15 weeks later. But we need ways to tell them what's going on now. Why, we even have some new superstores that are opening up here. They should know we have extra-high demand."

Corky, his assistant agrees, saying, "Yeah, they should at least look at our past sales around this time of year. Some springs are hot, others are just average."

Straw concurs, saying, "It would be music to my ears, it would be really sweet, if they would work with us to spot trends and changes—and then respond quickly."

Stern's, based in Blackpool, England, is a European beverage maker and the developer and producer of Sipps. Sipps is a sweet, fruit flavored, nonalcoholic, noncarbonated drink, which is served chilled or with ice, and it is particularly popular when the weather is hot. Selling briskly in Europe and growing in popularity in the United States since its introduction five years ago, Sipps has had a difficult time adequately managing inventory and keeping up with U.S. customer demand, which is impacted by seasonal temperature fluctuations. Places with year-round temperature climates and lots of tourists (such as Florida and California) have large standing orders, but the other areas of the country could benefit from a less cumbersome, more responsive order-placing process. Sipps is distributed by a network of local distributors located throughout the United States and Canada.

As one of the systems analysts assigned to work with the U.S. distributors of Sipps, begin your analysis by listing some of the key symptoms and problems you have identified after studying the information flows, ordering process, and inventory management and after interviewing Mr. Straw and his assistant. In a paragraph describe which might indicate the need for a systems solution.

---

[1] This consulting opportunity is loosely based on J.C. Perez, "Heineken's HOPS Software Keeps A-Head on Inventory," *PC Week,* Vol. 14, Number 2, January 13, 1997, pp. 31 and 34.

As outlined in Chapter 2, prospective projects need to be examined from a systems perspective, in such a way that you are considering the impact of the proposed change on the entire organization. Recall that the various subsystems of the organization are interrelated and interdependent, so that a change to one subsystem might affect all of the others. Even though the decision makers directly involved ultimately set the boundaries for the systems project, a systems project cannot be contemplated or selected in isolation from the rest of the organization.

Beyond these general considerations are the five specific criteria for project selection listed in Figure 3.2. The first and foremost is backing from management. Absolutely nothing can be accomplished without the endorsement of the people who eventually will foot the bill. This does not mean that you lack influence in directing the project or that people other

Criteria for Selection of Systems Projects
• Backing from management • Appropriate timing of project commitment • Possibility of improving attainment of organizational goals • Practical in terms of resources for systems analyst and organization • Project is worthwhile compared to other ways organization could invest resources

FIGURE 3.2
Selecting systems projects
based on five criteria.

than management can't be included. However, management backing is essential.

Another important criterion for project selection includes timing for you and the organization. Ask yourself and the others who are involved if the business is presently capable of making a time commitment for installation of new systems or improvement to existing ones. You must also be able to commit all or a portion of your time for the duration.

A third criterion is the possibility of improving attainment of organizational goals. The project should put the organization on target, not deter it from its ultimate goals.

A fourth criterion is selecting a project that is practicable in terms of your resources and capabilities, as well as those of the business. Some projects will not fall within your realm of expertise, and you must be able to recognize them.

Finally, you need to come to a basic agreement with the organization about the worthiness of the systems project relative to any other possible project being considered. Remember that when a business commits to one project, it is committing resources that thereby become unavailable for other projects. It is useful to view all possible projects as competing for the business resources of time, money, and people.

DETERMINING FEASIBILITY

Once the number of projects has been narrowed according to the criteria discussed previously, it is still necessary to determine if the selected projects are feasible. Our definition of feasibility goes much deeper than common usage of the term. For systems projects *feasibility* is assessed in three principal ways: operationally, technically, and economically. A project must be feasible in all three ways to merit further development, as shown in Figure 3.3.

The feasibility study is not a full-blown systems study. Rather, the feasibility study is used to gather broad data for the members of management that in turn enables them to make a decision on whether to proceed with a systems study.

Data for the feasibility study can be gathered through interviews, which are covered in detail in Chapter 5. The kind of interview required is directly related to the problem or opportunity being suggested. The systems analyst typically interviews those requesting help and those directly concerned with the decision-making process—typically, management.

While it is important to address the correct problem, the systems analyst should not spend too much time doing feasibility studies, since many

FIGURE 3.3
Determining feasibility of a
systems project by judging
how it meets organizational
objectives.

FEASIBILITY Means That the Proposed Project:
• Helps the organization attain overall objectives
• Is possible to accomplish with present organizational resources in the following three areas:

Technical Feasibility
  Add on to present system
  Technology available to meet users' needs
Economic Feasibility
  Systems analysts' time
  Cost of systems study
  Cost of employees' time for study
  Estimated cost of hardware
  Cost of packaged software/software development
Operational Feasibility
  Whether the system will operate when installed
  Whether the system will be used

projects will be requested and only a few can or should be executed. The feasibility study must be highly time-compressed, encompassing several activities in a short span of time.

Defining Objectives

Ascertaining the overall feasibility of a requested project means finding out what the organizational objectives are and then determining if the project serves to move the business toward its objectives in some way. The objectives of the project should be clarified through interviews with the person, group, or department proposing it. Additionally, a review of written work related to the requested project is also useful.

There are several acceptable objectives for systems projects. These include, but are not limited to:

1. Reducing errors and improving the accuracy of data input.
2. Reducing the cost of the system output by streamlining and eliminating duplicate or unnecessary reports.
3. Integrating business subsystems.
4. Upgrading customer services to gain a competitive edge.
5. Speeding up input.
6. Shortening data-processing time.
7. Automating manual procedures to improve them in some way (reduce errors, increase speed or accuracy, cut down on employee time required, etc.).

There also are some unacceptable objectives for systems projects. As mentioned before, these include undertaking a project solely to prove the prowess of the systems analysis team or purely to assert the superiority of one department over another in terms of its power to command internal resources. Without a consideration of its true contribution to the achievement of the organization's goals, it is also unacceptable to automate manual procedures for the sake of automation alone or to invest in new technology because of infatuation with the "bells and whistles" it provides over and above what the present system offers.

The objectives of the project need to be cleared formally on paper as well as informally by talking to people in the business. Find out what problem they believe the systems project would solve or what situation it would improve and what their expectations are for the proposed system.

Determining Resources

Resource determination for the feasibility study follows the same broad pattern discussed previously and will be revised and reevaluated if and when a formal systems study is commissioned. Resources will be discussed in relationship to three areas of feasibility: technical, economic, and operational.

TECHNICAL FEASIBILITY. A large part of determining resources has to do with assessing technical feasibility. The analyst must find out whether current technical resources can be upgraded or added to in a manner that fulfills the request under consideration. However, sometimes "add-ons" to existing systems are costly and not worthwhile, simply because they meet needs inefficiently. If existing systems cannot be added onto, then the next question becomes whether there is technology in existence that meets the specifications.

This is where the expertise of systems analysts is beneficial, since by using their own experience and their contact with vendors, they will be able to answer the question of technical feasibility. Usually the response to whether a particular technology is available and capable of meeting the users' requests is "yes," and then the question becomes an economic one.

ECONOMIC FEASIBILITY. Economic feasibility is the second part of resource determination. The basic resources to consider are: your time and that of the systems analysis team, the cost of doing a full systems study (including time of employees you will be working with), the cost of the business employee time, the estimated cost of hardware, and the estimated cost of software and/or software development.

The concerned business must be able to see the value of the investment it is pondering before committing to an entire systems study. If short-term costs are not overshadowed by long-term gains or produce no immediate reduction in operating costs, then the system is not economically feasible, and the project should not proceed any further.

OPERATIONAL FEASIBILITY. Suppose for a moment that technical and economic resources are both judged adequate. The systems analyst must still consider the operational feasibility of the requested project. Operational feasibility is dependent on the human resources available for the project and involves projecting whether the system will operate and be used once it is installed.

If users are virtually wed to the present system, see no problems with it, and generally are not involved in requesting a new system, resistance to implementing the new system will be strong. Chances for it ever becoming operational are low.

Alternatively, if users themselves have expressed a need for a system that is operational more of the time, in a more efficient and accessible manner, chances are better that the requested system will eventually be used. Much of the art of determining operational feasibility rests with the user interfaces that are chosen, as we shall see in Chapter 18.

At this point, determining operational feasibility requires creative imagination on the part of the systems analyst, as well as the powers of persuasion to let users know which interfaces are possible and which will satisfy their needs. The systems analyst must also carefully listen to what users really want and what it seems they will use. Ultimately, however, assessing operational feasibility to a large extent involves educated guesswork.

Judging Feasibility

From the foregoing discussion, it is evident that judging the feasibility of systems projects is never a clear-cut or easy task. Furthermore, project feasibility is a decision to be made not by the systems analyst but instead by management. Decisions are based on feasibility data expertly and professionally gathered and presented by the analyst.

The systems analyst needs to be sure that all three areas of technical, economic, and operational feasibility are addressed in the preliminary study. The study of a requested systems project must be accomplished quickly so that the resources devoted to it are minimal, the information output from the study is solid, and any existing interest in the project remains high. Remember that this is a preliminary study, which precedes the system study, and it must be executed rapidly and competently.

Projects that meet the criteria discussed in the project selection subsection earlier in the chapter, as well as the three criteria of technical, economic, and operational feasibility, should be chosen for a detailed systems study. At this point the systems analyst must act as a supporting expert, advising management that the requested systems project meets all of the selection criteria and has thus qualified as an excellent candidate for further study. Remember that a commitment from management at this juncture means only that a systems study may proceed, not that a proposed system is accepted. Generally, the process of feasibility assessment is effective in screening out projects that are inconsistent with the business's objectives, technically impossible, or economically unprofitable. While it is painstaking, studying feasibility is worthwhile and saves businesses and systems analysts a good deal of time and money in the long run.

ACTIVITY PLANNING AND CONTROL

Systems analysis and design involves many different types of activities that together make up a project. The systems analyst must manage the project carefully if the project is to be a successful one. Project management involves the general tasks of planning and control.

Planning includes all of the activities required to select a systems analysis team, assign members of the team to appropriate projects, estimate the time required to complete each task, and schedule the project so that tasks are completed in a timely fashion. Control means using feedback to monitor the project. This includes comparing the plan for the project with

CONSULTING OPPORTUNITY 3.2

Food for Thought

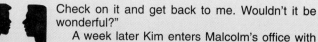

"We could really make some changes. Shake up some people. Let them know we're with it. Technologically, I mean," said Malcolm Warner, vice president for AllFine Foods, a wholesale dairy products distributor. "That old system should be overhauled. I think we should just tell the staff that it's time to change."

"Yes, but what would we actually be improving?" Kim Han, assistant to the vice president, asks. "I mean, there aren't any substantial problems with the system input or output that I can see."

Malcolm snaps, "Kim, you're purposely not seeing my point. People out there see us as a stodgy firm. A new computer system could help change that. Change the look of our invoices. Send jazzier reports to the food store owners. Get some people excited about us as leaders in wholesale food distributing *and* computers."

"Well, from what I've seen over the years," Kim replies evenly, "a new system is very disruptive, even when the business really needs it. People dislike change, and if the system is performing the way it should, maybe there are other things we could do to update our image that wouldn't drive everyone nuts in the process. Besides, you're talking big bucks for a new gimmick."

Malcolm says, "I don't think just tossing it around here between the two of us is going to solve anything.

Check on it and get back to me. Wouldn't it be wonderful?"

A week later Kim enters Malcolm's office with several pages of interview notes in hand. "I've talked with most of the people who have extensive contact with the system. They're happy, Malcolm. And they're not just talking through their hats. They know what they're doing."

"I'm sure the managers would like to have a newer system than the guys at Quality Foods," Malcolm replies. "Did you talk to them?"

Kim says, "Yes. They're satisfied."

"And how about the people in systems? Did they say the technology to update our system is out there?" Malcolm inquires insistently.

"Yes. It can be done. That doesn't mean it should be," Kim says firmly.

As the systems analyst for AllFine Foods, how would you assess the feasibility of the systems project Malcolm is proposing? Based on what Kim has said about the managers, users, and systems people, what seems to be the operational feasibility of the proposed project? What about the economic feasibility? What about the technological feasibility? Based on what Kim and Malcolm have discussed, would you recommend that a full-blown systems study be done?

its actual evolution. Control additionally means taking appropriate action to expedite or reschedule activities to finish on time, while motivating team members to complete the job properly.

Estimating Time Required

The systems analyst's first decision is to determine the amount of detail that goes into defining activities. The lowest level of detail is the systems development life cycle itself, while the highest extreme is to include every detailed step. The optimal answer to planning and scheduling lies somewhere in between.

A structured approach is useful here. In Figure 3.4 the systems analyst beginning a project has broken the process into three major phases: analysis, design, and implementation. Then the analysis phase is further broken down into data gathering, data flow and decision analysis, and proposal preparation. Design is broken down into data entry design, input and output design, and data organization. The implementation phase is divided into implementation and evaluation.

In subsequent steps the systems analyst needs to consider each of these tasks and break them down further, so planning and scheduling can take place. Figure 3.5 shows how the analysis phase is described in more detail.

FIGURE 3.4
Beginning to plan a project by
breaking it into three major
activities.

Analysis	Data Gathering Data Flow and Decision Analysis Proposal Preparation
Design	Data Entry Design Input Design Output Design Data Organization
Implementation	Implementation Evaluation

Break apart the major activities into smaller ones.

For example, data gathering is broken down into five activities, from conducting interviews to observing reactions to the prototype. This particular project requires data flow analysis but not decision analysis, so the systems analyst has penciled in "analyze data flow" as the single step in the middle phase. Finally, proposal preparation is broken down into three steps: perform cost/benefit analysis, prepare proposal, and present proposal.

The systems analyst, of course, has the option to break down steps further. For instance, the analyst could specify each of the persons to be interviewed. The amount of detail necessary depends on the project, but all critical steps need to appear in the plans.

Sometimes the most difficult part of project planning is the crucial step of estimating the time it takes to complete each task or activity. There is no substitute for experience in estimating time requirements, and systems analysts who have had the opportunity of an apprenticeship are fortunate in this regard.

Planners have attempted to reduce the inherent uncertainty in determining time estimates by projecting most likely, pessimistic, and optimistic

FIGURE 3.5
Refining the planning and
scheduling of analysis activities by adding detailed tasks
and establishing the time required to complete these
tasks.

	Detailed Activity	Weeks Required
Data Gathering	Conduct Interviews	3
	Administer Questionnaires	4
	Read Company Reports	4
	Introduce Prototype	5
	Observe Reactions to Prototype	3
Data Flow and Decision Analysis	Analyze Data Flow	8
Proposal Preparation	Perform Cost/Benefit Analysis	3
	Prepare Proposal	2
	Present Proposal	2

Break these down further,

then estimate time required.

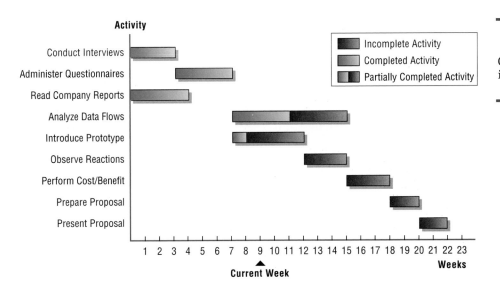

FIGURE 3.6
Using a two-dimensional
Gantt chart for planning activities that can be accomplished
in parallel.

estimates and then using a weighted average formula to determine the expected time an activity will take. This approach offers little more in the way of confidence, however. Perhaps the best strategy for the systems analyst is to adhere to a structured approach in identifying activities and describing these activities in sufficient detail. In this manner the systems analyst will at least be able to limit unpleasant surprises.

Using Gantt Charts for Project Scheduling

A Gantt chart is an easy way to schedule tasks. It is essentially a chart on which bars represent each task or activity. The length of each bar represents the relative length of the task.

Figure 3.6 is an example of a two-dimensional Gantt chart where time is indicated on the horizontal dimension and a description of activities makes up the vertical dimension.

In this example the Gantt chart shows the analysis or information-gathering phase of the project. Notice on the Gantt chart that conducting interviews will take three weeks, administering the questionnaire will take four weeks, and so on. These activities overlap part of the time.

Special graphical devices described in the key can help the developer of the chart control the project. Figure 3.6 depicts the current state of the data-gathering project in the ninth week. The ▲ symbol signifies that it is week 9. The bars with color shading represent projects or parts of projects that have been completed. This tells us that the systems analyst is behind in introducing prototypes but ahead in analyzing data flows. Action must be taken on introducing prototypes soon so that other activities or even the project itself will not be delayed as a result.

The main advantage of the Gantt chart is its simplicity. The systems analyst will find not only that this technique is easy to use but also that it lends itself to worthwhile communication with end users. Another advantage of using a Gantt chart is that the bars representing activities or tasks are drawn to scale; that is, the size of the bar indicates the relative length of time it will take to complete each task.

FIGURE 3.7
Gantt charts compared with
PERT diagrams for scheduling
activities.

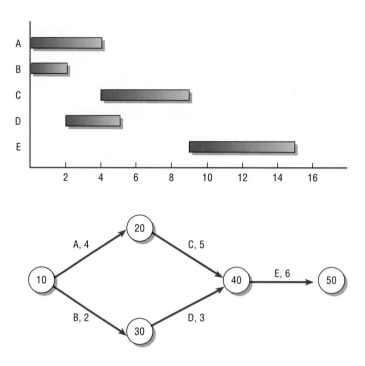

Using PERT Diagrams

PERT is an acronym for Program Evaluation and Review Techniques. A *program* (a synonym for a project) is represented by a network of nodes and arrows that are then evaluated to determine the critical activities, improve the schedule if necessary, and review progress once the project is undertaken. PERT was developed in the late 1950s for use in the U.S. Navy's Polaris nuclear submarine project. It reportedly saved the U.S. Navy two years' development time.

PERT is useful when activities can be done in parallel rather than in sequence. The systems analyst can benefit from PERT by applying it to systems projects on a smaller scale, especially when some team members can be working on certain activities at the same time that fellow members are working on other tasks.

Figure 3.7 compares a simple Gantt chart with a PERT diagram. The activities expressed as bars in the Gantt chart are represented by arrows in the PERT diagram. The length of the arrows has no direct relationship with the activity durations. Circles on the PERT diagram are called *events* and can be identified by numbers, letters, or any other arbitrary form of designation. The circular nodes are present to (1) recognize that an activity is completed and (2) indicate which activities need to be completed before a new activity may be undertaken (precedence).

In reality activity C may not be started until activity A is completed. Precedence is not indicated at all in the Gantt chart, so it is not possible to tell whether activity C is scheduled to start on day 4 on purpose or by coincidence.

A project has a beginning, a middle, and an end; the beginning is event 10 and the end is event 50. In order to find the length of the project, each path from beginning to end is identified, and the length of each path is calculated. In this example path 10-20-40-50 has a length of 15 days, while path 10-30-40-50 has a length of 11 days. Even though one person may be working on path 10-20-40-50 and another on path 10-30-40-50, the project is not

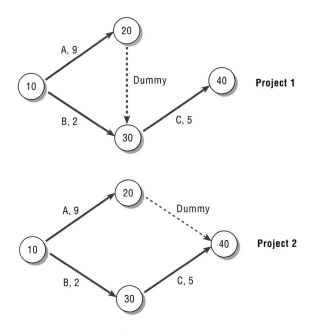

a race. The project requires that both sets of activities (or paths) be completed; consequently, the project takes 15 days to complete.

The longest path is referred to as the *critical path.* Although the critical path is determined by calculating the longest path, it is defined as the path that will cause the whole project to fall behind if even one day's delay is encountered on it. Note that if you are delayed one day on path 10-20-40-50, the entire project will take longer, but if you are delayed one day on path 10-30-40-50, the entire project will not suffer. The leeway to fall behind somewhat on noncritical paths is called slack time.

Occasionally, PERT diagrams need pseudo-activities, referred to as dummy activities, to preserve the logic of or clarify the diagram. Figure 3.8 shows two PERT diagrams with dummies. Project 1 and project 2 are quite different, and the way the dummy is drawn makes the difference clear. In project 1 activity C can only be started if *both* A and B are finished, since all arrows coming into a node must be completed before leaving the node. In project 2, however, activity C requires only activity B's completion and can therefore be underway while activity A is still taking place.

Project 1 takes 14 days to complete, while project 2 takes only 9 days. The dummy in project 1 is necessary, of course, since it indicates a crucial precedence relationship. The dummy in project 2, on the other hand, is not required, and activity A could have been drawn from 10 to 40 and event 20 may be eliminated completely.

Therefore, there are many reasons for using a PERT diagram over a Gantt chart. The PERT diagram allows:

1. Easy identification of the order of precedence.
2. Easy identification of the critical path and thus critical activities.
3. Easy determination of slack time.

A PERT EXAMPLE. Suppose a systems analyst is trying to set up a realistic schedule for the data-gathering and proposal phases of the *systems analysis and design life cycle.* The systems analyst looks over the situation

FIGURE 3.9
Listing activities for use in
drawing a PERT diagram.

Activity	Predecessor	Duration
A Conduct Interviews	None	3
B Administer Questionnaires	A	4
C Read Company Reports	None	4
D Analyze Data Flow	B, C	8
E Introduce Prototype	B, C	5
F Observe Reactions to Prototype	E	3
G Perform Cost/Benefit Analysis	D	3
H Prepare Proposal	G	2
I Present Proposal	H	2

and lists activities that need to be accomplished along the way. This list, which appears in Figure 3.9, also shows that some activities must precede other activities. The time estimates were determined as discussed in an earlier section of this chapter.

DRAWING THE PERT DIAGRAM. In constructing the PERT diagram, the analyst looks first at those activities requiring no predecessor activities—in this case, A (conduct interviews) and C (read company reports). In the example in Figure 3.10, the analyst chose to number the nodes 10, 20, 30, and so on, and he or she drew two arrows out of the beginning node 10. These arrows represent activities A and C and are labeled as such. Nodes numbered 20 and 30 are drawn at the end of these respective arrows. The next step is to look for any activity requiring only A as a predecessor; task B (administer questionnaires) is the only one, so it can be represented by an arrow drawn from node 20 to node 30.

Since activities D (analyze data flow) and E (introduce prototype) require both activities B and C to be finished before they are started, arrows labeled D and E are drawn from node 30, the event that recognizes the completion of both B and C. This process is continued until the entire PERT diagram is completed. Notice that the entire project ends at an event called "node 80."

IDENTIFYING THE CRITICAL PATH. Once the PERT diagram is drawn, it is possible to identify the critical path by calculating the sum of the activity times on each path and choosing the longest path. In this example, there are four paths: 10-20-30-50-60-70-80; 10-20-30-40-60-70-80; 10-30-50-60-70-80;

FIGURE 3.10
A completed PERT diagram
for the analysis phase of a systems project.

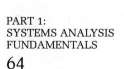

FIGURE 3.11
This screen from Microsoft
Project illustrates a Gantt
chart.

and 10-30-40-60-70-80. The longest path is 10-20-30-50-60-70-80, which takes 22 days. It is essential that the systems analyst carefully monitor the activities on the critical path in order to keep the entire project on time or even shorten the project length if warranted.

COMPUTER-BASED PROJECT SCHEDULING

Using microcomputers for project scheduling has now become practical. DOS-based scheduling programs were unwieldy because of the number of keystrokes, the time needed to memorize those keystrokes, and the steep learning curve proved to be barriers to everyday computerized scheduling by the typical end user. Under a GUI (Graphical User Interface) environment, using project management software is less of a problem. Microsoft Project, Symantec's Timeline, and Computer Associates' CA-Super Project are three good examples of powerful programs.

An example of project management from Microsoft Project can be found in Figure 3.11. Here you can see that the expediting problem completed earlier in this chapter is entered into Microsoft Project. New tasks can be entered into either the top or the bottom part of the screen, whichever is easier for the user. Let's assume that we want to enter the task "Analyze data flow" on the bottom half of the screen. First we enter the name of the activity, then its duration, 8d (including a qualifier: d for day, w for week, etc.), and the ID for any predecessors (in this case there are two). The ID, or identifier, is simply the number of the task. We don't have to enter a start date if we want the computer program to schedule it for us (as soon as possible, given the predecessors). The upper part of the table lists the activities in the order in which we entered them. Following is a Gantt chart. The lighter bars appear in orange on the screen and indicate the critical path. The darker bars are shaded blue and are noncritical.

Figure 3.12 is another screen from Microsoft Project. The bottom half of the screen is essentially the same, but the top half now shows a PERT diagram. Computer programs take the liberty of representing the tasks or activities with rectangles rather than with arrows. Although this goes against the traditional conventions used in PERT diagrams, the software authors feel that it is easier to read tasks in rectangular boxes than to read them on arrows. A darker line, shown in red on the actual screen, indicates the critical path. Once activities are drawn on the screen, they can be repositioned using a mouse in order to enhance readability and communication with others. The dark box indicates that we are looking at that activity at the moment. The dotted vertical line on the right side of the screen shows the user where the page break will occur. The icons at the top of the page are familiar to anyone who uses Word for Windows, Excel, or PowerPoint, three other Microsoft products.

Other approaches to scheduling include integrated personal information managers, or PIMs. Some examples of a PIM include ECCO by NetManage, and Organizer by Lotus Corporation. These PIMs are useful because they are a repository for phone and fax numbers of business associates; for daily, weekly, or monthly planners; and for to-do lists. Some PIMs are designed to be shells that enable you to launch other programs and even allow you to store similar data from word processing and spreadsheet programs in "folders" organized around a particular topic. Some, like ECCO, are good at sharing data with other programs, while others include Gantt charts to aid in project management.

MANAGING ANALYSIS AND DESIGN ACTIVITIES

Along with managing time and resources, systems analysts must also manage people. Management is accomplished primarily by communicating accurately to team members who have been selected for their competency and compatibility. Goals for project productivity must be set, and members of systems analysis teams must be motivated to achieve them.

Communication Strategies for Managing Teams

Teams have their own personalities, a result of combining each individual team member with every other in a way that creates a totally new network of interactions. A way to organize your thinking about teams is to visualize them as always seeking a balance between accomplishing the work at hand and maintaining the relationships among team members.

In fact, teams will often have two leaders, not just one. Usually one person will emerge who leads members to accomplish tasks, and another person will emerge who is concerned with the social relationships among group members. Both are necessary for the team. These individuals have been labeled by other researchers as, respectively, task leader and socioemotional leader. Every team is subject to tensions that are an outgrowth of seeking a balance between accomplishing tasks and maintaining relationships among team members.

For the team to continue its effectiveness, tensions must be continually resolved. Minimizing or ignoring tensions will lead to ineffectiveness and eventual disintegration of the team. Much of the tension release necessary can be gained through skillful use of feedback by all team members. However, all members need to agree that the way they interact (i.e., process) is important enough to merit some time. Productivity goals for processes are discussed in a later section.

Securing agreement on appropriate member interaction involves creating explicit and implicit team norms (collective expectations, values, and ways of behaving) that guide members in their relationships. A team's norms belong to it and will not necessarily transfer from one team to another. These norms change over time and are better thought of as a team process of interaction rather than a product.

Norms can be functional or dysfunctional. Just because a particular behavior is a norm for a team does not mean it is helping the team to achieve its goals. For example, an expectation that junior team members should do all project scheduling may be a team norm. By adhering to this norm, the team is putting extreme pressure on new members and not taking full advantage of the experience of the team. It is a norm that, if continued, could make team members waste precious resources.

Team members need to make norms explicit and periodically assess whether norms are functional or dysfunctional in helping the team achieve its goals. The overriding expectation for your team must be that change is the norm. Ask yourself whether team norms are helping or hindering the team's progress.

Setting Project Productivity Goals

When you have worked with your team members on various kinds of projects, you or your team leader will acquire an acumen for projecting what the team can achieve within a specific amount of time. Using the hints discussed in the earlier section in this chapter on methods for estimating time required and coupling them with experience will enable the team to set worthwhile productivity goals.

Systems analysts are accustomed to thinking about productivity goals for employees who show tangible outputs such as the number of bluejeans

Goal Tending

"Here's what I think we can accomplish in the next five weeks," says Hy, the leader of your systems analysis team as he confidently pulls out a schedule listing each team member's name alongside a list of short-term goals. Just a week ago, your systems analysis team went through an intense meeting on expediting their project schedule for the Kitchener, Ontario Redwings, a hockey organization whose management is pressuring you to produce a prototype.

The three other members of the team look at the chart in surprise. Finally, one of the members, Rip, speaks: "I'm in shock. We each have so much to do as it is, and now this."

Hy replies defensively, "We've got to aim high, Rip. They're in the off-season. It's the only time to get them. If we set our goals too low, we won't finish the systems prototype, let alone the system itself, before another hockey season passes. The idea is to give the Kitchener Redwings the fighting edge through the use of their new system."

Fiona, another team member, enters the discussion, saying, "Goodness knows their players can't give

them that!" She pauses for the customary groan from the assembled group, then continues. "But seriously, these goals are killers. You could have at least asked us what we thought, Hy. We may even know *better* than you what's possible."

"This is a pressing problem, not a tea party, Fiona," Hy replies. "Polite polling of team members was out of the question. Something had to be done quickly. So I went ahead with these. I say we submit our schedule to management based on this. We can push back deadlines later if we have to. But this way they'll know we're committed to accomplishing a lot during the off-season."

As a fourth team member listening to the foregoing exchange, formulate three suggestions that would help Hy improve his approach to goal formation and presentation. How well-motivated do you think the team will be if they share Fiona's view of Hy's goals? What are the possible ramifications of supplying management with overly optimistic goals? Write one paragraph devoted to short-term effects and another one discussing the long-term effects of setting unrealistically high goals.

---

sewn per hour, the number of entries keyed in per minute, or the number of items scanned per second. However, as manufacturing productivity rises, it is becoming clear that managerial productivity must keep pace. It is with this aim in mind that productivity goals for the systems analysis team are set.

Goals need to be formulated and agreed to by the team, and they should be based on team members' expertise, former performance, and the nature of the specific project. Goals will vary somewhat for each project undertaken, since sometimes an entire system will be installed, while other projects might involve limited modifications to a portion of an existing system.

Motivating Project Team Members

Although motivation is an extremely complex topic, it is a good one to consider, even if briefly, at this point. To oversimplify, recall that people join organizations to provide for some of their basic needs such as food, clothing, and shelter. But all humans also have higher-level needs that include affiliation, control, independence, and creativity. People are motivated to fulfill unmet needs on several levels.

Team members can be motivated, at least partially, through participation in goal setting, as described in the previous section. The very act of setting a challenging but achievable goal and then periodically measuring performance against the goal seems to work in motivating people. Goals act almost as magnets in attracting people to achievement.

Part of the reason goal setting motivates people is that team members know prior to any performance review exactly what is expected of them. The success of goal setting for motivating can also be ascribed to the fact that it affords each team member some autonomy in achieving the goals. While a goal is predetermined, the means to achieve it may not be. In this instance team members are free to use their own expertise and experience to meet their goals.

Setting goals can also motivate team members by clarifying for them and others what must be done in order to get results. Team members are also motivated by goals because goals define the level of achievement that is expected of them. This simplifies the working atmosphere, but it also electrifies it with the possibility that what is expected can indeed be done.

Avoiding Project Failures

The early discussions that you have with management and others requesting a project, along with the feasibility studies you do, are usually the best defenses possible against taking on projects that have a high probability of failure. Your training and experience will improve your ability to judge the worthiness of projects and the motivations that prompt others to request projects. If you are part of an in-house systems analysis team, you must keep current with the political climate of the organization, as well as with financial and competitive situations.

Remember that you are not alone in the decision to begin a project. Although apprised of your team's recommendations, management will have the final say about whether a proposed project is worthy of further study (that is, further investment of resources). The decision process of your team must be open and stand up to scrutiny from those outside of it. The team members should consider that their reputation and standing in the organization are inseparable from the projects they accept.

SUMMARY

The five major project fundamentals that the systems analyst must handle are: (1) project initiation, (2) determining project feasibility, (3) project scheduling, (4) activity planning and control, and (5) managing systems analysis team members. Projects may be requested by many different people within the business or by systems analysts themselves.

Selecting a project is a difficult decision, since more projects will be requested than can actually be done. Five important criteria for project selection are: (1) that the requested project be backed by management, (2) that it be timed appropriately for a commitment of resources, (3) that it move the business toward attainment of its goals, (4) that it be practicable, and (5) that it be important enough to be considered over other possible projects.

If a requested project meets these criteria, then a feasibility study of its operational, technical, and economic merits can be done. Through the feasibility study, systems analysts gather data that enable management to decide whether to proceed with a full systems study.

Project planning includes the estimation of time required for each of the analyst's activities, scheduling them, and expediting them if necessary to ensure a project is completed on time. One technique available to the systems analyst for scheduling tasks is the Gantt chart, which displays activities as bars on a graph.

Another technique, called PERT (for Program Evaluation and Review Techniques), displays activities as arrows on a network. PERT helps the analyst determine the critical path and slack time, which is the information required for effective project control.

Computer-based project scheduling using microcomputers is now practical, due largely to the use of graphical user interfaces. Additionally, personal information managers (PIMs) can be used by analysts to do planning, create repositories for phone and fax numbers, or even launch other programs.

Once a project has been judged feasible, the systems analyst must manage the team members, their activities, time, and resources. Most of this is accomplished by communicating with team members. Teams are constantly seeking a balance between working on tasks and maintaining relationships within the team. Tensions arising from attempting to achieve this balance must be addressed. Often two leaders of a team will emerge—a task leader and a socioemotional leader. Members must periodically assess team norms in order to assure that the norms are functional rather than dysfunctional for the attainment of team goals.

It is important that the systems analysis team set reasonable productivity goals for tangible outputs and process activities. Project failures can usually be avoided by examining the motivations for requested projects, as well as your team's motives for recommending or avoiding a particular project.

KEYWORDS AND PHRASES

technical feasibility	personal information
economic feasibility	managers (PIMs)
operational feasibility	task leader
Gantt chart	socioemotional leader
PERT diagrams	team norms
critical path	team process
computer-based project	productivity goals
scheduling	team motivation

REVIEW QUESTIONS

1. What are the five major project fundamentals?
2. List three ways to find out about problems or opportunities that might call for a systems solution.
3. List the five criteria for systems project selection.
4. Define *technical feasibility*.
5. Define *economic feasibility*.
6. Define *operational feasibility*.
7. When is a two-dimensional Gantt chart more appropriate than a one-dimensional Gantt chart?
8. When is a PERT diagram useful for systems projects?
9. List three advantages of a PERT diagram over a Gantt chart for scheduling systems projects.
10. Define the term *critical path*.
11. List the functions of PC-based project scheduling that are available in common software packages.
12. List the functions of some commonly used personal information manager (PIM) software.
13. List the two types of team leaders.

"I hope everyone you've encountered at MRE has treated you well. Here's a short review of some of the ways you can access our organization through HyperCase. The reception area at MRE contains the key links to the rest of our organization. Perhaps you've already discovered these on your own, but I wanted to remind you of them now, since I don't want to get so engrossed in the rest of our organizational problems that I forget to mention them.

"The telephone on the receptionist's desk has instructions about how to answer the phone in the rest of the organization. You have my permission to pick up the phone if it is ringing and no one else answers it.

The empty doorway that you see is a link to the next room, which we call the East Atrium. You have probably noticed that all open doorways are links to adjacent rooms. Notice that the building map displayed in the reception area is dynamic, in that it is linked to all public rooms. As you know, you must have an employee escort you into a private office. You cannot go there on your own.

"By now you have probably noticed the two documents and the computer on the small table in the reception area. The little one is the MRE internal phone directory. Just click on an employee name, and if that person is in, he or she will grant you an interview and a tour of the office. I leave you to your own devices in figuring out what the other document is.

FIGURE 3.HC1
The reception room resembles a typical corporation. While you are in this HyperCase screen, find the directory if you want to visit someone.

"The computer on the table is on and displays the World Wide Web home page for MRE. You should take a look at the corporate page and visit all of the links. It tells the story of our company and the people that work here. We're quite proud of it and have gotten positive feedback about it from visitors.

"If you have had a chance to interview a few people and see how our company works, I'm sure you are becoming aware of some of the politics involved. But we are also worried about more technical issues, such as what constitutes feasibility for a training project and what does not."

HyperCase Questions

1. What criteria does the Training Unit use to judge the feasibility of a new project? List them.
2. List any changes or modifications to these criteria which you would recommend.
3. Snowden Evans has asked you to help prepare a proposal for a new project tracking system for the Training Unit. Briefly discuss the technical, economic, and operational feasibility of each alternative for a proposed project tracking system for the Training Unit.
4. Which option would you recommend? Use evidence from HyperCase to support your decision.

14. What is meant by *dysfunctional team norm*?
15. What is meant by *team process*?
16. What are three reasons that goal setting seems to motivate systems analysis team members?

PROBLEMS

1. Dressman's Chocolates of St. Louis makes an assortment of chocolate candy and candy novelties. The company has six in-city stores, five stores in major metropolitan airports, and a small mail-order branch. Dressman's has a small, computerized information system that tracks inventory in its plant, helps schedule production, and so on, but this system is not tied directly into any of its retail outlets. The mail-order system is handled manually. Recently, several Dressman's stores experienced a rash of complaints from mail-order customers that the candy was spoiled upon arrival, that it did not come when promised, or that it never arrived; the company also received several letters complaining that candy in various airports tasted stale. Finally, a few sales clerks in company stores reported being asked whether the firm would be willing to market a new, dietetic form of chocolate made with aspartame.

   You had been working for two weeks with Dressman's on some minor modifications for its inventory information system when you overheard two managers discussing these occurrences. List the possible opportunities or problems among them that might lend themselves to systems projects.

Description	Task	Must Follow	Expected Time (Days)
Draw data flow	P	None	9
Draw decision tree	Q	P	12
Revise tree	R	Q	3
Write up project	S	R,Z	7
Organize data dictionary	T	P	11
Do output prototype	X	None	8
Revise output design	Y	X	14
Design database	Z	T,Y	5

2. Where is most of the feedback on problems with Dressman's products coming from in problem 1? How reliable are the sources? Explain in a paragraph.

3. After getting to know them better, you have approached Dressman's management people with some of your ideas on possible systems improvements that could address some of the problems or opportunities given in problem 1.

   a. In two paragraphs, provide your suggestions for systems projects. Make any realistic assumptions necessary.

   b. Are there any problems or opportunities discussed in problem 1 that are *not* suitable? Explain your response.

4. The systems analysis consulting firm of Flow Associates is working on a systems design project for Wind and Waves Waterbeds, Inc.

   a. Using the data from the table above, draw a Gantt chart to help Flow Associates organize its design project.

   b. When is it appropriate to use a Gantt chart? What are the disadvantages? Explain in a paragraph.

5. Figure 3.EX1 is a PERT diagram based on the data from problem 4. List *all* paths and calculate and identify the critical path.

6. Recently, two analysts fresh out of college have joined your systems analyst group at the newly formed company, Mega Phone. When talking to you about the group, they mention that some things strike them as odd. One is that group members seem to look up to two group leaders, Bill and Penny, not just one.

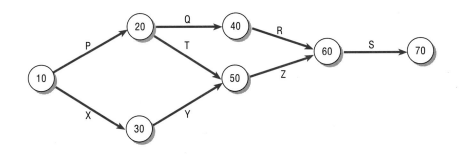

FIGURE 3.EX1
The PERT diagram from Flow Associates.

CHAPTER 3:
DETERMINING FEASIBILITY
AND MANAGING ANALYSIS
AND DESIGN ACTIVITIES

73

Their observation is that Bill seems pretty relaxed, while Penny is always planning and scheduling activities. They have also observed that everyone "just seems to know what to do" when they get into a meeting, even though no instructions are given. Finally they have remarked on the openness of the group in addressing problems as they arise, instead of letting things get out of hand.

   a. By way of explanation to the new team members, label the types of leaders Bill and Penny appear to be, respectively.

   b. Explain the statement that "everyone just seems to know what to do." What is guiding their behavior?

   c. What concept best describes the openness of the group that the new team members commented on?

GROUP PROJECT

  1. With your group members, explore a computerized project manager such as Microsoft Project or Lotus Organizer. What features are available? Work with your group to list them. Have your group evaluate the usefulness of the software for managing a systems analysis and design team project. In a paragraph, state whether the software you are evaluating facilitates team member communication and management of team activities, time, and resources. State which particular features support these aspects of any project. Note whether the software falls short of these criteria in any regard.

SELECTED BIBLIOGRAPHY

Adam, E. E., Jr., and R. J. Ebert. *Production and Operations Management,* 3rd ed. Englewood Cliffs, NJ: Prentice-Hall, Inc., 1986.

Bales, R. F. *Personality and Interpersonal Behavior.* New York: Holt, Rinehart and Winston, 1970.

Gildersleeve, T. R. *Successful Data Processing for Systems Analysis.* Englewood Cliffs, NJ: Prentice-Hall, Inc., 1977.

Merry, U., and M. E. Allerhand. *Developing Teams and Organizations.* Reading, MA: Addison-Wesley, 1977.

Schein, E. H. *Process Consultation: Its Role in Organization Development.* Reading, MA: Addison-Wesley, 1969.

Weinberg, G. M. *Rethinking Systems Analysis and Design.* Boston: Little, Brown and Company, Inc., 1982.

GETTING TO KNOW U

Chip enters Anna's office one day saying, "I think the project will be a good one, even though it's taking some long hours to get started."

Anna looks up from her screen and smiles. "I like what you've done in getting us organized," she says. "I hadn't realized Visible Analyst could help us this much with project management. I've decided to do a PERT diagram for the data gathering portion of the project. It should help us plan our time and work as a team on parallel activities."

"Can I take a look at the PERT diagram," replies Chip.

Anna shows him a screen with a PERT diagram on it (see Figure E3.1) and remarks, "This will help immensely. It is much easier than planning haphazardly."

"I notice that you have Gather Reports, Gather Records and Data Capture Forms, and Gather Qualitative Documents as parallel tasks," notes Chip, gazing at the screen.

"Yes," replies Anna. "I thought that we would split up the time that it takes to gather the information."

"We can also divide up the task of analyzing what we have learned," Anna continues.

"I notice that you have a rather large number of days allocated for interviewing the users," notes Chip.

"Yes," replies Anna. "This activity also includes creating questions, sequencing them, and other tasks, such as taking notes of the office environment and analyzing them. I've also assumed a standard of six productive hours per day."

Anna glances at her watch. "But now it's getting late. I think we've made a lot of progress in setting up our project. Let's call it a day, or should I say evening? Remember, I got us tickets for the football game."

Chip replies, "I haven't forgotten. Let me get my coat, and we'll walk over to the stadium together."

Walking across campus later, Chip says, "I'm excited. It's my first game here at CPU. What's the team mascot, anyway?"

"Chipmunks, of course," says Anna.

"And the team colors?" Chip asks, as they enter the stadium.

"Blue and white," Anna replies.

"Oh, *that's* why everyone's yelling, 'Go Big Blue!'" Chip says, listening to the roar of the crowd.

"Precisely," says Anna.

Exercises*

Use Visible Analyst to define the following User entities and User Requirements.

🖫 **E-1.** Use Visible Analyst to view the Gathering Information PERT diagram.

---

* Exercises preceded by a disk icon require the program Visible Analyst Workbench or another CASE tool. A disk is provided free of charge to any professor adopting this book. The examples on the disk may be imported into Visible Analyst Workbench and then used by students.

*Allen Schmidt,
Julie E. Kendall, and
Kenneth E. Kendall*

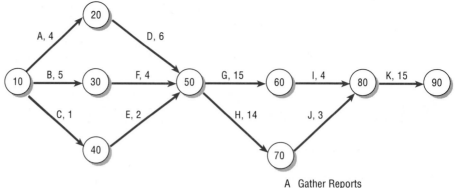

A Gather Reports
B Gather Records and Data Capture Forms
C Gather Qualitative Documents
D Analyze Reports
E Understand Corporate Culture
F Analyze Records and Forms
G Interview Users
H Administer Questionnaires
I Summarize Interviews
J Summarize Survey Results
K Prototype System

FIGURE E3.1
PERT diagram, the gathering information phase.

E-2. List all paths and calculate and determine the critical path for the Gathering Information PERT diagram.

⌸ **E-3.** Use Visible Analyst to create the PERT diagram shown in Figure E3.2. It represents the activities involved in interviewing the users and observing their offices.

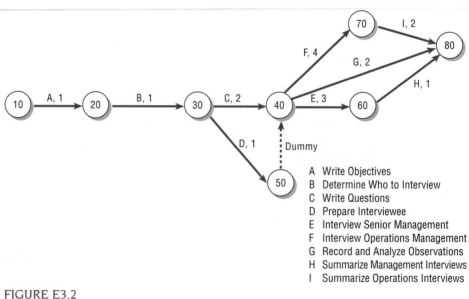

A Write Objectives
B Determine Who to Interview
C Write Questions
D Prepare Interviewee
E Interview Senior Management
F Interview Operations Management
G Record and Analyze Observations
H Summarize Management Interviews
I Summarize Operations Interviews

FIGURE E3.2
PERT diagram, interviewing users.

E-4. List all paths and calculate and determine the critical path for the Interviewing Users PERT diagram.

E-5. Use Visible Analyst to create a PERT diagram for creating system prototypes. The activity information is show in the table below.

Activity	Predecessor	Duration
A Determine Overall Prototype Screens and Reports	None	2
B Determine Report and Screen Contents	A	4
C Create Report Prototypes	B	3
D Create Screen Prototypes	B	4
E Obtain Report Prototype Feedback	C	1
F Obtain Screen Prototype Feedback	D	2
G Modify Report Prototypes	E	2
H Modify Screen Prototypes	F	4
I Obtain Final Approval	G, H	2

4

SAMPLING AND INVESTIGATING HARD DATA

Underlying all of the data-gathering methods of investigation, interviewing, and observing are the crucial decisions regarding what to examine and who to question or observe. The systems analyst can make these decisions based on a structured approach called sampling.

SAMPLING

Sampling is the process of systematically selecting representative elements of a population. When these selected elements are examined closely, it is assumed that the analysis will reveal useful information about the population as a whole.

The systems analyst has to make a decision on two key issues. First, there are many reports, forms, output documents, and memos that have been generated by members of the organization. Which of these should the systems analyst pay attention to and which should the systems analyst ignore?

Second, a great many employees can be affected by the proposed information system. Which people should the systems analyst interview, seek information from via questionnaires, or observe in the process of carrying out their decision-making roles?

The Need for Sampling

There are many reasons why a systems analyst would want to select either a representative sample of data to examine or representative people to interview, question, or observe. They include:

1. Containing costs
2. Speeding up the data gathering
3. Improving effectiveness
4. Reducing bias

Examining every scrap of paper and talking with everyone in the organization would be far too costly for the systems analyst. Copying reports, asking employees for valuable time, and duplicating unnecessary surveys would result in much needless expense.

Sampling helps accelerate the process by gathering selected data rather than all data for the entire population. In addition the systems analyst is spared the burden of analyzing data from the entire population.

Effectiveness in data gathering is an important consideration as well. Sampling can help improve effectiveness if more accurate information can be obtained. This is accomplished, for example, by talking to fewer employees but asking them more detailed questions. Additionally, if fewer people are interviewed, the systems analyst can afford the time to follow up on missing or incomplete data, thus improving the effectiveness of data gathering.

Finally, data-gathering bias can be reduced by sampling. When the systems analyst interviews an executive of the corporation, for example, the executive is involved with the project, since this person has already given a certain amount of time to the project and would like it to succeed. When the systems analyst asks an opinion about a permanent feature of the installed information system, the executive interviewed may provide a biased evaluation, since there is little possibility of changing it.

Sampling Design

The four steps that a systems analyst must follow to design a good sample are:

1. Determine the data to be collected or described.
2. Determine the population to be sampled.
3. Choose the type of sample.
4. Decide on the sample size.

These steps are described in detail in the following subsections.

DETERMINING THE DATA TO BE COLLECTED OR DESCRIBED. The systems analyst needs a realistic plan about what will be done with the data once it is collected. If irrelevant data is gathered, then time and money are wasted in the collection, storage, and analysis of useless data.

The duties and responsibilities of the systems analyst at this point are to identify the variables, attributes, and associated data items that need to be gathered in the sample. The objectives of the study must be considered, as well as the type of data-gathering method (investigation, interviews, questionnaires, observation) to be used. The kinds of information sought when using each of these methods will be discussed in more detail in this and subsequent chapters.

DETERMINING THE POPULATION TO BE SAMPLED. Next, the systems analyst must determine what the population is. In the case of hard data, the systems analyst needs to decide, for example, if the last two months are sufficient, or if an entire year's worth of reports are needed for analysis.

Similarly, when deciding who to interview, the systems analyst has to determine whether the population should include only one level in the organization, or all of the levels—or maybe he or she should even go outside of the sys-

	Not Based on Probability	Based on Probability
Sample elements are selected directly without restrictions	Convenience	Simple random
Sample elements are selected according to specific criteria	Purposive	Complex random (systematic, stratified, and cluster)

The systems analyst should use a complex random sample if possible.

FIGURE 4.1
Four main types of samples the analyst has available.

tem to include the reactions of customers. These decisions will be explored further in the chapters on interviewing, questionnaires, and observation.

CHOOSING THE TYPE OF SAMPLE. The systems analyst can use one of four main types of samples, as pictured in Figure 4.1. They are convenience, purposive, simple, and complex. **Convenience samples** are unrestricted, non-probability samples. A sample could be called a convenience sample if, for example, the systems analyst put a notice in the company newsletter asking for everyone interested in the new sales performance reports to come to a meeting at 1:00 P.M. on Tuesday the 12th. Obviously, this sample is the easiest to arrange, but it is also the most unreliable. A **purposive sample** is based on judgment. A systems analyst can choose a group of individuals who appear knowledgeable and who are interested in the new information system. Here the systems analyst bases the sample on criteria (knowledge about and interest in the new system), but it is still a nonprobability sample. Thus purposive sampling is only moderately reliable. If you choose to perform a **simple random sample,** you need to obtain a numbered list of the population to ensure that each document or person in the population has an equal chance of being selected. This often is not practical, especially when sampling involves documents and reports. The **complex random samples** that are most appropriate for the systems analyst are: (1) systematic sampling, (2) stratified sampling, and (3) cluster sampling.

In the simplest method of probability sampling, systematic sampling, the systems analyst would, for example, choose to interview every kth person on a list of company employees. However, this method has certain disadvantages. You would not want to use it to select every kth day for a sample because of the potential periodicity problem. Furthermore, a systems analyst would not use this approach if the list were ordered (for example, a list of banks from the smallest to the largest) because bias would be introduced.

Stratified samples are perhaps the most important to the systems analyst. Stratification is the process of identifying subpopulations, or strata, and then selecting objects or people for sampling within these subpopulations. Stratification is often essential if the systems analyst is to gather data efficiently. For example, if you want to seek opinions from a wide range of employees on different levels of the organization, systematic sampling would select a disproportionate number of employees from the operational control level. A stratified sample would compensate for this. Stratification is also called for when the systems analyst wants to use different methods to collect data from different subgroups. For example, you may want to use a survey to gather data from middle managers, but you might prefer to use personal interviews to gather similar data from executives.

Sometimes the systems analyst must select a group of documents or people to study. This is referred to as cluster sampling. Suppose an organization had twenty warehouses scattered across the country. You may want to select one or two of these warehouses under the assumption that they are typical of the remaining warehouses.

DECIDING ON THE SAMPLE SIZE. Obviously, if everyone in the population viewed the world the same way or if each of the documents in a population contained exactly the same information as every other document, a sample size of one would be sufficient. Since this is not the case, it is necessary to set a sample size greater than one but less than the size of the population itself.

It is important to remember that the absolute number is more important in sampling than the percentage of the population. We can obtain satisfactory results sampling 20 people in 200 or 20 people in 2,000,000.

The sample size depends on many things, some set by the systems analyst, some determined by what we know about the population itself, and other important factors. The systems analyst can choose the acceptable interval estimate (i.e., the degree of precision desired) and the standard error (by choosing the degree of confidence).

Furthermore, the characteristics of the population may change the sample size. If the sales figures in a report range from $10,000 to $15,000, a small sample size would be sufficient to give you an accurate estimate of average sales. However, if the sales ranged from $1,000 to $100,000, then a much larger sample size would be required. Sample size is discussed in greater detail in the following section.

The Sample Size Decision

The sample size often depends on the cost involved or the time required by the systems analyst—or even the time available by people in the organization. This subsection gives the systems analyst some guidelines for determining the required sample size under ideal conditions.

DETERMINING SAMPLE SIZE WHEN SAMPLING DATA ON ATTRIBUTES. Sometimes the systems analyst might want to find out what proportion of people in an organization think a certain way or have certain characteristics. Other times the analyst may need to know what percentage of input forms have mistakes. This type of data can be referred to as attribute data.

The systems analyst needs to follow a series of steps, some of which are subjective judgments, to determine the required sample size. The following is the list of seven steps:

1. Determine the attribute you will be sampling.
2. Locate the database or reports where the attribute can be found.
3. Examine the attribute. Estimate p, the proportion of the population having the attribute.
4. Make the subjective decision regarding the acceptable interval estimate, i.

Confidence Level	Confidence Coefficient (z-value)
99%	2.58
98	2.33
97	2.17
96	2.05
95	1.96
90	1.65
80	1.28
50	0.67

First decide on the confidence level,

then look up the z value.

5. Choose the confidence level and look up the confidence coefficient (z value) in a table.

6. Calculate σ_P, the standard error of the proportion as follows:

$$\sigma_P = \frac{i}{z}$$

7. Determine the necessary sample size, n, using the following formula:

$$n = \frac{p(1 - p)}{\sigma_P^2} + 1$$

The first step, of course, is to determine which attribute you will be sampling. Once this is done, you can find out where this data is stored—perhaps in a database, on a form, or in a report.

It is important to estimate p, the proportion of the population having the attribute so that you set the appropriate sample size. Many textbooks on systems analysis suggest using a heuristic of 0.25 for $p(1 - p)$. This almost always results in a sample size larger than necessary because 0.25 is the maximum value of $p(1 - p)$, which occurs only when $p = 0.50$. When $p = 0.10$, as is more often the case, $p(1 - p)$ becomes 0.09, resulting in a much smaller sample size.

Steps 4 and 5 are subjective decisions. The acceptable interval estimate of ± 0.10 means that you are willing to accept an error of no more than 0.10 in either direction from the actual proportion, p. The confidence level is the desired degree of certainty—say, for example, 95 percent. Once the confidence level is chosen, the confidence coefficient (also called a z value) can be looked up in a table like the one found in Figure 4.2.

Steps 6 and 7 complete the process by taking the parameters found or set in steps 3 through 5 and entering them into two equations to eventually solve for the required sample size.

EXAMPLE

The foregoing steps can best be illustrated by an example. Suppose the A. Sembly Company, a large manufacturer of shelving products, asks you to determine what percentage of orders contain mistakes. You agree to do this job and perform the following steps. You:

1. Determine that you will be looking for orders that contain mistakes in names, addresses, quantities, or model numbers.

2. Locate copies of order forms from the past six months.
3. Examine some of the order forms and conclude that only about 5 percent (0.05) contain errors.
4. Make a subjective decision that the acceptable interval estimate will be ±0.02.
5. Choose a confidence level of 95 percent. Look up the confidence coefficient (z value) in Figure 4.2. The z value equals 1.96.
6. Calculate σ_P as follows:

$$\sigma_P = \frac{i}{z}$$

$$= \frac{0.02}{1.96} = 0.0102$$

7. Determine the necessary sample size, n, as follows:

$$n = \frac{p(1-p)}{\sigma_P^2} + 1$$

$$= \frac{0.05(0.95)}{(0.0102)(0.0102)} + 1 = 458$$

The conclusion, then, is to set the sample size at 458. Obviously, a greater confidence level or a smaller acceptable interval estimate would require a larger sample size as shown below. If we keep the acceptable interval estimate the same but increase the confidence level to 99 percent (with a z value of 2.58), the standard error of the proportion is:

$$\sigma_P = \frac{i}{z}$$

$$= \frac{0.02}{2.58} = 0.0078$$

and the necessary sample size is:

$$n = \frac{p(1-p)}{\sigma_P^2} + 1$$

$$= \frac{(0.05)(0.95)}{(0.0078)(0.0078)} + 1 = 782$$

If the confidence level stays at 95 percent (z value = 1.96) but the acceptable interval estimate is set to 0.01, then the standard error of the proportion is:

$$\sigma_P = \frac{i}{z}$$

$$= \frac{0.01}{1.96} = 0.0051$$

and the necessary sample size is:

$$n = \frac{p\,(1 - p)}{\sigma_P^2} + 1$$

$$= \frac{(0.05)(0.95)}{(0.0051)(0.0051)} + 1 = 1827$$

DETERMINING SAMPLE SIZE WHEN SAMPLING DATA ON VARIABLES. A systems analyst may sometimes need to gather information on actual numbers such as gross sales, amount of items returned, or number of mistakes keyed in. Data of this type are referred to as variables.

The steps in determining the necessary sample size for variables is similar to the steps for attribute data. The steps are:

1. Determine the variable you will be sampling.
2. Locate the database or reports where the variable can be found.
3. Examine the variable to gain some idea about its magnitude and dispersion. Ideally, it would be useful to know the mean to determine a more appropriate acceptable interval estimate and the standard deviation, s, to determine sample size (in step 7).
4. Make a subjective decision regarding the acceptable interval estimate, i.
5. Choose a confidence level and look up the confidence coefficient (z value) in a table.
6. Calculate $\sigma_{\bar{x}}$ the standard error of the mean as follows:

$$\sigma_{\bar{x}} = \frac{i}{z}$$

7. Determine the necessary sample size, n, using the following formula:

$$n = \left(\frac{s}{\sigma_{\bar{x}}}\right)^2 + 1$$

Step 3 is difficult to do precisely. In order to estimate the mean and standard deviation accurately, you would actually have to sample the population. This is, of course, a chicken-or-egg problem because the systems analyst does not know which comes first. Consequently, it is not necessary to know precisely the mean and standard deviation. A reasonable estimate will do.

The importance of estimating the mean and standard deviation becomes obvious when you attempt to set the acceptable interval estimate. Suppose you were asked to determine the average gross sales for a small greeting card store ($3,500 per week) and a large grocery store ($70,000 per week). A desired interval estimate of $350 for the small greeting card store would be inappropriate for the large grocery store.

Furthermore, the estimated dispersion is important because the smaller the dispersion (as measured by the standard deviation), the smaller the necessary sample size. For example, suppose you were trying to determine the average age of purchasers of music on CDs (compact discs). If you make the assumption that anyone from 10 to 100 years of age purchases CDs, you would need a very large sample size. If, however, you estimate that generally the ages of CD purchasers are between 13 and 23, you can get by with a much smaller sample size.

The formulas for determining the necessary sample size for variables are different from the formulas for attribute data. Since the systems analyst must take more care in estimating the magnitude and dispersion of a variable, determining the sample size for a variable is slightly more difficult than determining the sample size for attribute data.

EXAMPLE

Another example from the A. Semble Company can be used to illustrate how to find the necessary sample size for variables. Now you are asked to determine the average dollar amount for an order. You agree to do this task and perform the following steps:

1. Determine that you will be looking for the mean dollar amount for orders on shelving.
2. Locate copies of order forms from the past six months.
3. Examine some of the order forms and conclude that orders average about $1,500, with a standard deviation, s, of about $100.
4. Make a subjective decision that the acceptable interval estimate will be $5.00.
5. Chose a confidence level of 96 percent. Look up the confidence coefficient (z value) in Figure 4.2. The z value equals 2.05.
6. Calculate $\sigma_{\bar{x}}$ as follows:

$$\sigma_{\bar{x}} = \frac{i}{z}$$

$$= \frac{5.00}{2.05} = 2.44$$

7. Determine the necessary sample size, n, as follows:

$$n = \left(\frac{s}{\sigma_{\bar{x}}}\right)^2 + 1$$

$$= \left(\frac{100}{2.44}\right)^2 + 1$$

$$= 1680 + 1$$

$$= 1681$$

You therefore would want to sample 1681 orders to determine the mean dollar amount of orders.

As with sampling attribute data, a greater confidence level or a smaller acceptable interval estimate would require a larger sample size. If we keep the acceptable interval estimate the same but increase the confidence level to 99 percent (with a z value of 2.58), the standard error of the mean is:

$$\sigma_{\bar{x}} = \frac{i}{z}$$

$$= \frac{5.00}{2.58} = 1.94$$

and the necessary sample size is:

$$n = \left(\frac{s}{\sigma_{\bar{x}}}\right)^2 + 1$$

$$= \left(\frac{100}{1.94}\right)^2 + 1$$

$$= 2{,}658$$

If the confidence level stays at 96 percent (z value = 2.05) but the acceptable interval estimate is set to \$1.00, the standard error of the mean is:

$$\sigma_{\bar{x}} = \frac{i}{z}$$

$$= \frac{1.00}{2.05} = 0.488$$

and the necessary sample size is:

$$n = \left(\frac{s}{\sigma_{\bar{x}}}\right)^2 + 1$$

$$= \left(\frac{100}{0.488}\right)^2 + 1$$

$$= 41{,}992$$

This implies that accuracy to the nearest dollar would be far too costly in sampling, because sampling over 41,000 of anything is excessive.

DETERMINING SAMPLE SIZE WHEN SAMPLING QUALITATIVE DATA. A good deal of information cannot be obtained by searching through files. That information can best be obtained by interviewing people in the organization.

There are no magic formulas to help the systems analyst set the sample size for interviewing. The overriding variable that determines how many people the systems analyst should interview in depth is the time an interview takes. A true in-depth interview and follow-up interview is very time-consuming for both the interviewer and the participant.

A good rule of thumb is to interview at least three people on every level of the organization and at least one from each of the organization's functional areas (as described in Chapter 2) who will be directly involved with a new or updated system. Remember also that one does not have to interview more people just because it is a larger organization. If the stratified sample is done properly, a small number of people will adequately represent the entire organization.

KINDS OF INFORMATION
SOUGHT IN INVESTIGATION

The systems analyst seeks facts and figures, financial information, organizational contexts, and document types and problems through the sampling and investigation of hard data, as shown in Figure 4.3. Hard data accumu-

Trapping a Sample

"Real or fake? Fake or real? Who would have thought it, even five years ago?" howls Sam Pelt, a furrier who owns stores in New York, Washington, D.C., Beverly Hills, and Copenhagen. Sylva Foxx, a systems analyst with her own consulting firm, is talking with Sam for the first time. Currently, P & P, Ltd. (which stands for Pelt and Pelt's son) is using a PC that supports package software for a select customer mailing list, accounts payable and accounts receivable, and payroll.

Sam is interested in making some strategic decisions that will ultimately effect the purchasing of goods for his four fur stores. He feels that while the computer might help, there are also other approaches to be considered.

Sam continues, "I think we should talk to each of the customers when they come in the door. Get their opinion. You know some of them are getting very upset about wearing fur from endangered species. They're very environment-minded. They prefer fake to real, if they can save a baby animal. Some even like fake better—call them 'fun furs.' And I can charge almost the same for a good look-alike.

"But it's a very fuzzy proposition. If I get too far away from my suppliers of pelts, I may not get what I want when I need it. They see the fake fur people as worms—worse then moths! If I deal with them, the real fur men might not talk to me. They can be animals. On the other hand, I feel strange showing fakes in my stores. All these years, we've prided ourselves on having only the genuine article."

Sam continues, in a nearly seamless monologue, "I want to talk to each and every employee, too."

Sylva glances at him furtively and begins to interrupt. "But that will take months, and purchasing may come apart at the seams unless they know soon what—"

Pelt continues. "I don't care how long it takes, if we get the right answers. But they have to be right. Not knowing how to solve this dilemma about fake furs is making me feel like a leopard without its spots."

Sylva talks to Sam Pelt for a while longer and then ends the interview by saying, "I'll talk it all over with the other analysts at the office and let you know what we come up with. I think we can outfox the other furriers if we use the computer to help us sample opinions, rather than trapping unsuspecting customers into giving an opinion. But I'll let you know what they say. This much is for sure: If we can sample and not talk to everybody before making a decision, every coat you sell will have a silver lining."

As one of the systems analysts who is part of Sylva Foxx's firm, suggest some ways that Sam Pelt can use the PC he has to sample adequately the opinions of his customers, store managers, buyers, and any others you feel will be instrumental in making the strategic decision regarding the stocking of fake furs in what has always been a real fur store. Suggest a type of sample for each group and justify it. The constraints you are subject to include the need to act quickly so as to remain competitive, the need to retain a low profile so that competing furriers are unaware of your fact-gathering, and the need to keep costs of the data gathering to a reasonable level.

---

lated in records supply information that cannot be obtained through other methods such as interviewing or observation.

Although hard data are produced by the organization as a generic product (much like "to whom it may concern" material), the analyst needs to remember that meanings taken from hard data are constructed personally by organizational members. So it becomes important to ask: Who were the documents produced for originally, and why they have been kept? In other words the role of the document in the organization needs to be understood. Generally, well-documented organizations may be more rigid than businesses with less documentation, since documentation may function to create one-way centralized control.

The analyst also needs to be aware that documents in an organization can serve as persuasive messages, since they offer information about how people are expected to behave. It also follows that organizational change is facilitated through the changing of documents.

FIGURE 4.3
Kinds of information sought
in investigation.

Types of Hard Data

As the systems analyst works to understand the organization and its information requirements, it will become important to examine different types of hard data, which offer information unavailable through any other method of data gathering. Hard data reveal where the organization has been and where its members believe it is going. The analyst needs to examine both quantitative and qualitative hard data in order to piece together an accurate picture.

ANALYZING QUANTITATIVE DOCUMENTS. A variety of quantitative documents is available for interpretation in any business, and they include reports used for decision making, performance reports, records, and a variety of forms. All of these documents have a specific purpose and audience for which they are targeted.

Reports used for decision making. A systems analyst needs to obtain some of the documents that are used in running the business. These documents are often paper reports regarding the status of inventory, sales, or production. Many of these reports are not complex, but they serve mainly as feedback for quick action. For example, a sales report may summarize the amount sold and the type of sales. Additionally, sales reports might include graphical output comparing revenue and income over a set number of periods. This enables the decision maker to readily spot trends.

Production reports include recent costs, current inventory, recent labor, and plant information. Beyond these key reports, many summary reports are used by decision makers to provide background information, spot exceptions to normal occurrences, and afford strategic overviews of organizational plans.

Performance reports. Most performance reports take on the general form of actual versus intended performance. One important function of performance reports is to assess the size of the gap between actual and intended performance. It is also important to be able to determine if that gap is widening or narrowing as an overall trend in whatever performance is being measured. Figure 4.4 shows a clear improvement in sales performance over 2–3

FIGURE 4.4
A performance report showing improvement.

Week	Number of Batches Produced	Number of Batches Rejected	Percentage Rejected	Amount Away from 5% Goal
2/2	245	19	7.8	2.8
2/9	229	19	8.3	3.3
2/16	219	14	6.3	1.4
2/23	252	13	5.2	0.2
3/2	245	13	5.3	0.3
3/9	260	13	5.0	* * *
3/16	275	14	5.1	0.1
3/23	260	13	5.0	* * *
3/30	260	13	5.0	* * *
4/6	244	12	4.9	* * *
4/13	242	11	4.5	* * *
4/20	249	11	4.4	* * *
4/27	249	11	4.4	* * *

* * * indicates met or exceeded the < 5% goal

Performance reports show goals...

and trends.

months. The analyst will want to note if performance measurement is available and adequate for key organizational areas.

Records. Records provide periodic updates of what is occurring in the business. If the record is updated in a timely fashion by a careful recorder, it can provide much useful information to the analyst. Figure 4.5 is a manually completed payment record for apartment rental. Notice that there are several ways that the analyst can inspect a record, including:

1. Checking for errors in amounts and totals.
2. Looking for opportunities for improving the recording form design.
3. Observing the number and type of transactions.
4. Watching for instances where the computer can simplify the work (that is, calculations and other data manipulation).

Data capture forms. Before you set out to change the information flows in the organization, you need to be able to understand the system that is currently in place. You or one of your team members may want to collect and catalog a blank copy of each form (official or unofficial) that is in use. (Sometimes businesses have a person already charged with forms management, who would be your first source for forms in use.)

Blank forms, along with their instructions for completion and distribution, can be compared to filled-in forms to see if any data items are consistently left blank on the forms, whether the people who are supposed to receive the forms actually do get them, and if they follow standard procedures for using, storing, and discarding them.

Here is how to proceed when creating a catalog of forms to help you understand the information flow currently in use in the business:

FIGURE 4.5
A manually completed payment record.

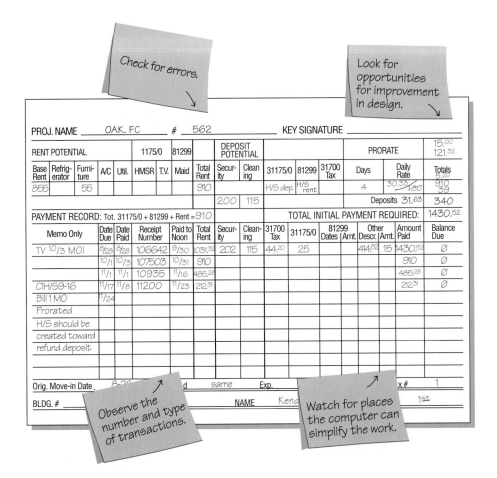

1. Collect examples of all of the forms in use, whether officially sanctioned by the business or not (official versus bootleg forms).

2. Note the type of form (whether printed in-house, handwritten, computer-generated in-house on-line forms, printed externally and purchased, etc.).

3. Document the intended distribution pattern.

4. Compare the intended distribution pattern with who actually receives the form.

Although this procedure is time-consuming, it is useful. Another approach is to sample data capture forms that have already been completed. The analyst must keep in mind many particular questions, as illustrated in Figure 4.6. They include:

1. Is the form filled out in its entirety? If not, what items have been omitted, and are they consistently omitted? Why?

2. Are there forms that are never used? Why? (Check the design and appropriateness of the form for its purported function.)

3. Are *all* copies of forms circulated to the proper people or filed appropriately? If not, why not?

4. Can people who must access on-line forms do so?

FIGURE 4.6
Questions to ask about official
and bootleg forms that are already filled out.

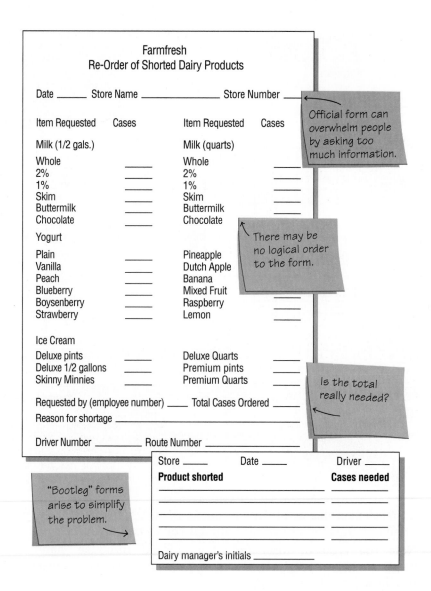

Farmfresh
Re-Order of Shorted Dairy Products

Date _____ Store Name _____ Store Number _____

Official form can overwhelm people by asking too much information.

Item Requested	Cases	Item Requested	Cases
Milk (1/2 gals.)		Milk (quarts)	
Whole	_____	Whole	_____
2%	_____	2%	_____
1%	_____	1%	_____
Skim	_____	Skim	_____
Buttermilk	_____	Buttermilk	_____
Chocolate	_____	Chocolate	

Yogurt

There may be no logical order to the form.

Plain	_____	Pineapple	
Vanilla	_____	Dutch Apple	
Peach	_____	Banana	
Blueberry	_____	Mixed Fruit	
Boysenberry	_____	Raspberry	_____
Strawberry	_____	Lemon	

Ice Cream

Deluxe pints	_____	Deluxe Quarts	_____
Deluxe 1/2 gallons	_____	Premium pints	_____
Skinny Minnies	_____	Premium Quarts	_____

Requested by (employee number) _____ Total Cases Ordered _____

Is the total really needed?

Reason for shortage _____

Driver Number _____ Route Number _____

"Bootleg" forms arise to simplify the problem.

Store _____ Date _____ Driver _____
Product shorted   **Cases needed**
_____   _____
_____   _____
_____   _____
_____   _____
Dairy manager's initials _____

5. Are "unofficial" forms being used on a regular basis? (Their use might indicate a problem in standard procedures or may indicate political battles within the organization.)

You can learn many things about an organization's information flow through examination of the forms it uses. Some of the signs to watch for that may be symptomatic of larger problems include:

1. Data or information doesn't flow as intended (too many people, too few people, or the wrong people receive it).
2. Bottlenecks in the processing of forms result in slowed or stopped work.
3. Access to on-line forms is cumbersome.
4. Unnecessary duplication of work occurs because employees are unaware that information is already in existence on another form that they do not receive.

CONSULTING OPPORTUNITY 4.2

A Rose by Any Other Name . . . or Quality not Quantities

"I think we have everything we need. I've sampled financial statements, sales figures for each branch, wastage for each shop—we have it all. With all of these numbers, we should be able to figure out how to keep Fields in the green, or at least at the forefront of the flower business. We can even show Seymour Fields himself how his new computer system can make it all happen," says Rod Golden, a junior systems analyst working for a medium-sized consulting group.

The firm, under the supervision of its head systems analyst, Clay Potts, has been working on a systems project for the entire chain of fifteen successful florist shops and indoor floral markets called Fields. Each of three Midwestern cities has five Fields outlets.

"Although it's just a budding enterprise now, eventually we want to grow with offshoots to half a dozen states," says Seymour Fields, the owner. "I want to reap the benefits of all the happiness we've sown so far. I think we can do it by playing my hunches about what is the best time to purchase flowers at each European market we buy from and then we should prune back our purchases."

"Over the past three years, I've written lots of memos to our managers about this. They've written some good ones back, too. I think we're ready to stake out some territory on this soon," continues Seymour, painting a rosy picture of Fields' future.

"I agree," says Rod. "When I come back from my analysis of these figures," he says, indicating a large stack of material he has unearthed from Fields field offices, "we'll be able to deliver."

Three weeks later, Rod returns to Clay with wilting confidence. "I don't know what to make of all this. I can't seem to get at what's causing the company's growth, or how it's managed. They've been expanding, but I've been through all of the figures, and nothing really seems to make sense yet."

Clay listens empathetically, then says, "You've given me a germ of an idea. What we need is some cross-pollination, a breath of fresh air. We need to dig a little deeper. Did you examine anything but their bottom line?"

Rod looks startled and replies, "No, I—uh—what do you mean?"

How can Clay Potts tactfully explain to Rod Golden that examination of qualitative as well as quantitative documents could be important to delivering an accurate assessment of Fields' potential to be a more fruitful enterprise? In a paragraph, recommend some specific documents that should be read. List the specific steps Rod should follow in evaluating qualitative documents obtained from Fields. Write a paragraph to explain how qualitative documents help in presenting an overall account of Fields' success.

---

5. Employees lack understanding about the interrelatedness of information flow (that is, they do not know that their output work serves as input for another person).

ANALYZING QUALITATIVE DOCUMENTS. Many documents circulating within organizations are not quantitative. Although qualitative documents may not follow a predetermined form, analysis of them is critical to understanding how the organizational members engage in the process of organizing. Qualitative documents include memos, signs on bulletin boards and in work areas, procedure manuals, and policy handbooks. Many of these documents are rich in details revealing the expectations for behavior of others that their writers hold.

Although many systems analysts are apprehensive about analyzing qualitative documents, they need not be. Several guidelines that can help analysts to take a systematic approach to this sort of analysis are:

1. Examine documents for key or guiding metaphors.
2. Look for insiders versus outsiders or an "us against them" mentality in documents.

FIGURE 4.7
Analysis of memos provides
insights into the metaphors
that guide the organization's
thinking.

MEMO

To: All Night Shift Computer Operators
From: S. Leep, Night Manager
Date: 2/15/97
Re: Get Acquainted Party Tonight

It's a pleasure to welcome 2 new 11-7 computer operators,
Twyla Tine and Al Knight. I'm sure they'll enjoy working
here. Being together in the wee hours makes us feel like
one big happy family. Remember for your breaks tonight
that some of the crew has brought in food. Help yourself
to the spread you find in the break room, and welcome to
the clan, Twyla and Al.

3. List terms that characterize good or evil and appear repeatedly in documents.

4. Recognize a sense of humor, if present.

Each guideline is explained briefly in the following paragraphs. Guidelines should be viewed as a way to begin interpreting qualitative documents. Certainly there are other approaches that go much further in analysis than necessary for the systems analyst's purposes.

Examining documents for key or guiding metaphors is done because language shapes behavior, and thus the metaphors we employ are critical. For example, an organization that discusses employees as "part of a great machine" or "cogs in a wheel" might be taking a mechanistic view of the organization. Notice that the guiding metaphor in the memo in Figure 4.7 is "We're one big happy family." The analyst can use this information to predict the kinds of metaphors that will be persuasive in the organization as well as to understand how a new system might be characterized metaphorically.

When the analyst finds language that pits one group or department against another or sets the business as a whole against competitors, it is possible to understand more clearly the "us against them" politics that exist. Obviously, if one department is battling another, it may be impossible to gain any cooperation on a systems project until the politics are resolved in a satisfactory manner. By the same token, if the business is fiercely competitive in its remarks about other businesses in the industry, part of the thrust for the systems project may come from wanting to hold the competitive edge.

Listing the terms found in qualitative documents that characterize actions, groups, or events as good or evil allows the analyst to see what is considered good in the business and what is deemed bad or wrong. This knowledge allows insights into what group values are being espoused. For

FIGURE 4.8
Analysis of memos reveals
values, attitudes, and beliefs
of organizational members regarding use of information.

MEMO

To: All department managers
From: Phil Baskett, General Manager
Subject: Collecting paper

At our last store-wide meeting the sensitive topic of 'what to save' came up. Many of you openly admitted to being 'pack rats', squirreling away every scrap of output just in case you ever need it. The word from now on is that you should think before you save. The paper monster has taken over many of your offices and more storage is too expensive. I refuse to authorize any additional money for file cabinets. Most department secretaries maintain files of important correspondence, reports, and official memos; more is on the computer. So don't be a pack rat. If your secretary saves it, you should toss it.

instance, if accumulating information without apparent reason is described in negative terms (as depicted in Figure 4.8), then the analyst will want to ensure that system output is actually used and is not being accumulated "just in case."

The fourth guideline encourages the analyst to recognize the existence of a sense or senses of humor in the qualitative documents of the organization. Assessing the use of humor provides a quick and accurate barometer of many organizational variables, including which subculture a person belongs to and what kind of morale exists. For example, conservative, traditionalist organizational members tend to relate formula jokes, with a beginning, a middle, and an ending punchline. People who are sensitive to others' communication needs tend to relate anecdotal, humorous stories that are self-deprecating. Additionally, if morale is low, "black" or "gallows" humor tends to be a common way of coping with organizational uncertainties. Cartoons that are posted in work spaces, coffee rooms, and corridors also are helpful in revealing a sense of humor and some areas of frustration or tension among organizational members.

Memos. When possible, analysts should sample memos sent throughout the business. However, sometimes memos are not kept or they are made available only to those who have "a need to know," as defined in organizational policy. Along with the four preceding guidelines, the analyst should also consider who sends memos and who receives them. Typically, most information flows downward and horizontally rather than upward in organizations, and extensive e-mail systems mean messages are sent to many work groups and individuals, too. Memos in print or on e-mail reveal a lively, continuing dialogue in the organization. Analysis of memo content will provide you with a clear idea of the values, attitudes, and beliefs of organizational members.

FIGURE 4.9
Posted signs reveal the official
organizational culture.

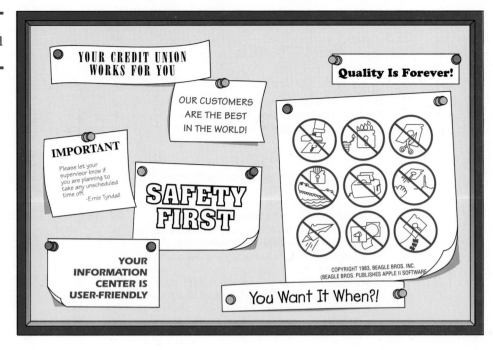

Signs on bulletin boards or in work areas. Although signs may seem incidental to what is happening in the organization, they serve as subtle reinforcers of values to those who read them, as depicted in Figure 4.9. Signs such as "Quality Is Forever" or "SAFETY FIRST" give the analyst a feel for the official organizational culture. It is also instructive to note whom signs are intended for and to find out through interviews whether organizational members are held accountable for acting on the information posted.

Corporate Web sites. Web sites accessible to the public should also be viewed by the analyst. (Indeed, sometimes your design work will take advantage of Web technologies.) Examine the contents for metaphors, humor, use of design features (such as color), and the meaning and clarity of any messages provided. Are there discrepancies between the stated goals of the organization and what is presented to the public? How does this impact the systems you are investigating? Remember to note the level of interactivity of the Web site or sites, the accessibility of the messages, as well as the apparent security.

Manuals. Other qualitative documents the analyst should examine are organizational manuals, including manuals for computer operating procedures and on-line manuals. Manuals should be analyzed following the four guidelines spelled out previously. Writers of manuals are allowed more elaboration in making a point than is typically accorded to those writing memos or posting signs. Remember that manuals present the "ideal"—the way machines and people are *expected* to behave. Examining manuals, both printed and on-line, systematically will give you a picture of the way things ought to happen. It is important to recall that printed manuals are rarely kept current and are sometimes relegated to a shelf, unused. Check to see if the manuals you are looking at are current and whether they are followed or forgotten.

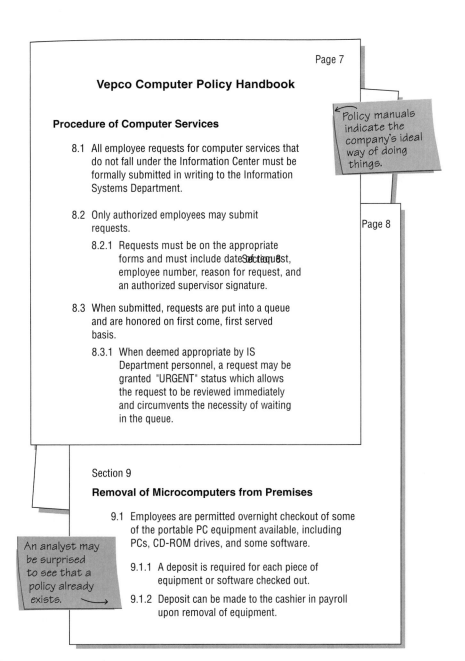

Policy handbooks. The last type of qualitative document that we consider is the policy handbook. While these documents typically cover broad areas of employee and corporate behavior, you can be primarily concerned with those that address policies about computer services, use, access, and charges. Some computer policies may appear on screen whenever a particular program is run.

Policies are larger guidelines that spell out the organization's ideal of how members should conduct themselves in order to achieve strategic goals, as depicted in Figure 4.10. Once again, members may not even be aware of particular policies, or policies may be purposely sidestepped in the name of efficiency or simplicity. However, examining policies allows the systems analyst to gain an awareness of the values, attitudes, and beliefs that are guiding the corporation.

Advantages of Using Archival Data	Disadvantages of Using Archival Data
• Archival documents are already paid for—by someone else • Data are not changed since the producer is unaware of being studied	• Uncertainty exists if the data are only a subset of original data • The records that survive may not be the most important or meaningful • May be biased because someone originally decided what to file • New data are difficult to obtain from equivalent samples

Abstracting Data from Archival Documents

Much of the data, both quantitative and qualitative, that you will need will not be in current use. Rather they will be stored in archives of some sort. Some material is kept because of government regulations, some because of accounting practices, and some because the business may have formerly been called upon to produce historical information.

Examples of archival data that may be of interest to the systems analyst include actuarial records, budgets, and sales reports. One common characteristic that all archival data share is that their collection was paid for by someone other than the systems analyst. This may or may not influence the content, but as a result archival data is a relatively low-cost informational source. Another advantage of archival data is that there is no overt changing of data, since its producer is unaware that he or she is being studied.

One disadvantage of using archival data is that the analyst may be uncertain about their meaning if only a limited subset of the data originally created exists. Another disadvantage of using archival data is that the records that survive (or that someone decided to keep) may *not* be the most important or meaningful. A third disadvantage of using archival data is that there is a large degree of built-in bias because someone has decided, for whatever reasons, to file the original data as well as to preserve some data and not others. Additionally, new data are difficult to obtain from the same or equivalent samples. Advantages and disadvantages of using archival data are summarized in Figure 4.11.

Even with all of the preceding cautions, there are some guidelines that can make abstracting data from archives and archival databases worthwhile. They are:

1. Fragment the data into subclasses and make cross checks to reduce errors.
2. Compare reports on the same phenomenon by different analysts (or maybe even someone within the organization).
3. Realize the inherent bias associated with original decisions to file, keep, and/or destroy reports.
4. Use other methods such as interviewing and observation to fill out your organizational picture and supply a cross check.

SUMMARY

The process of systematically selecting representative elements of a population is called sampling. The purpose of sampling is to select and study documents such as invoices, sales reports, and memos; or perhaps to select and

One of the drawbacks of using archival data is that the data may be important only to the one who originally saved it. "Not So Vital Statisitics" from *Unscientific Americans* by Roz Chast. Copyright 1978, 1979, 1980, 1981, 1982 by Roz Chast. Reprinted by permission of Doubleday & Company, Inc.

interview, give questionnaires to, or observe members of the organization. Sampling can reduce cost, speed data gathering, potentially make the study more effective, and possibly reduce the bias in the study.

A systems analyst must follow four steps in designing a good sample. First, there is a need for determining the population itself. Second, the type of sample must be decided upon. Third, the sample size is calculated. Finally, the data that need to be collected or described must be planned.

The types of samples useful to a systems analyst are: convenience samples, purposive samples, simple random samples, and complex random samples. The last type includes the subcategories of systematic sampling and stratified sampling. There are several guidelines to follow when determining sample size. The systems analyst can make a subjective decision regarding acceptable interval estimates. Then a confidence level is chosen, and the necessary sample size can be calculated.

Systems analysts need to investigate current and archival data and forms, including reports, documents, financial statements, corporate Web sites (on-line and printed), procedure manuals, and e-mail content and memos. Current and archival data and forms reveal where the organization has been and where its members believe it is going. Both quantitative and qualitative documents need to be analyzed. Since documents are persuasive messages, it must be recognized that changing them might well change the organization.

There are many ways to analyze both quantitative and qualitative documents. However, it is important to remember that the investigation of archival data has drawbacks as well as advantages. Because many of these drawbacks can be overcome, archival investigation is worthwhile.

We're glad that you find MRE an interesting place to consult. According to the grapevine, you've been busy exploring the home office. I know, there's so much going on. We find it hard to keep track of everything ourselves. One thing we've made sure of over the years is that we try to use the methods that we believe in. Have you seen any of our reports? How about the data that was collected on one of Snowden's questionnaires? (He seems to favor questionnaires over any other method. Some people resent them, but I think you can learn a lot from the results.) Some people have been good about cooperating on these projects. Have you met Kathy Blandford yet?"

HyperCase Questions

1. Use clues from the case to evaluate the Training Unit's computer experience and its staff's feeling about a computerized project tracking system. What do you think the consensus is in the Training Unit toward a computerized tracking system?
2. What reports and statements are generated by the Training Unit during project development? List each with a brief description.
3. According to the interview results, what are the problems with the present project tracking system in the Training Unit?
4. Describe the "project management conflict" at MRE. Who is involved? Why is there a conflict?
5. How does the Management Systems Unit keep track of project progress? Briefly describe the method or system.

KEYWORDS AND PHRASES

sampling	attribute data
sample population	acceptable interval estimate
convenience sample	confidence level
purposive sample	variables
simple random sample	dispersion
complex random sample	hard data
systematic sampling	quantitative data
stratified sampling	qualitative data
cluster sampling	archival data

REVIEW QUESTIONS

1. Define what is meant by sampling.
2. List four reasons why the systems analyst would want to sample data or select representative people to interview.
3. What are the four steps to follow in order to design a good sample?
4. Give an example of a convenience sample.
5. Define what is meant by taking a purposive sample.
6. Why is it often impractical to use a simple random sample for sampling documents and reports?

7. List the three approaches to complex random sampling.
8. Define what is meant by stratification of samples.
9. Give an example of attribute data.
10. What two changes can cause the analyst to use a larger sample size when sampling for attributes?
11. In what way does determining the sample size for variables differ from determining the sample size for attribute data?
12. What effect on sample size does using a greater confidence level have when sampling attribute data?
13. What is the overriding variable that determines how many people the systems analyst should interview in depth?
14. List three of the quantitative documents that the analyst should analyze when attempting to understand the organization.
15. List five qualitative sources that the analyst should analyze when attempting to understand the organization.
16. What are four guidelines for the systematic analysis of qualitative documents?
17. What are two advantages of using archival data as a source for understanding the organization?
18. What are four disadvantages of using archival data as a source for understanding the organization?

PROBLEMS

1. Dee Fektiv is concerned that too many forms are being filled out incorrectly. She feels that about 10 percent of all of the forms have an error.
   a. How large a sample size should Dee use to be 99 percent certain she will be within 0.02?
   b. Suppose Dee will accept a confidence level of 95 percent that she will be within 0.02. What will the sample size of forms be now?
2. Rhea Fund has asked you to determine the average number of rebates mailed on a daily basis. You examine some records and believe the average to be about 200, with a standard deviation of 20. You want to be more certain, so you decide to sample.
   a. How large should the sample size be if you want to be 99 percent certain that the number will be within 5 of the mean?
   b. How large should the sample size be if you change the confidence limit to 95 percent?
3. Phil Ittup, a member of your systems analysis group, has been assigned the task of interviewing organizational members for your systems study. The business, Fall Back Industries, has five layers of management. Also, production, accounting, marketing, systems, logistics, and top management are the functional areas that will be affected by the proposed system. Each level has about 40 people. Production has 80 people total, accounting has 35, marketing has 42, systems has 10, and logistics has 28. There are 5 people in top management.
   a. Draw up an interviewing sample for Phil to follow in choosing who to interview. Justify why you have recommended that he interview the number of people you have chosen. What factors influenced your decision?

b. While waiting for you to make up your sample, Phil Ittup decided that, just to be on the safe side, he would skip sampling and interview each person. In a paragraph, explain to him why it is unwise for your systems analysis team not to follow a sampling strategy.

c. Phil has finally asked you for a hard-and-fast rule for how many people to interview in the organization. If you know of one, state it. If there isn't one, explain why one does not exist.

4. "I see that you have quite a few papers there. What all do you have in there?" asks Betty Kant, head of the MIS task force that is the liaison group between your systems group and Sawder's Furniture Company. You are shuffling a large bundle of papers as you prepare to leave the building.

"Well, I've got some financial statements, production reports from the last six months, and some performance reports that Sharon got me that cover goals and work performance over the last six months," you reply as some of the papers fall to the floor. "Why do you ask?" Betty Kant takes the papers from you and puts them on the nearest desk. "Because you don't need all this junk. You're here to do one thing, and that's talk to us, the users. Bet you can't read one thing in there that'll make a difference."

a. The only way to convince Betty Kant of the importance of each document is to tell her what you are looking for in each one. Use a paragraph to explain what each kind of document contributes to the systems analyst's understanding of the business.

b. While you are speaking with Betty, you realize that you actually need other quantitative documents as well. List any that you are missing.

5. Figure 4.EX1 and 4.EX2 are two filled-in pages that compose a larger computer usage log that the administrator of the information center has been using:

a. Analyze the way the log has been completed. Compare the data collected with the data the information center administrator intended to get from the form. List the omissions or errors users are making.

b. To what do you attribute the problems that people are having with filling out the log? Explain in a sentence or two the reason for each problem you found in 5a.

c. In a paragraph, explain why it is important to examine forms that have been completed, as well as blank ones that are in use.

6. You've sampled the e-mail messages that have been sent to several middle managers of Sawder's Furniture Company, which ships build-your-own particle board furniture across the country. Here is one that repeats a message found in several other memos.

To: Sid, Ernie, Carl
From: Imogene
Re: computer/printer supplies
Date: 11/10/97

It has come to my attention that I have been waging a war against requests for computer and printer supplies (disks, toner, paper, etc.) that are all out of proportion to what has been negotiated for

Form AB1-iDB Log of Employee Computer Use
Note: to aid our staff, use military time to report
all sign in and sign offs

Today's Date
6/12

Sign On Sign Off
2:00 - 4:20 PM
Project Name:
ZEBRA
Reason for Project:
Assignment
Project Authorized by: *JEK*

Your Name: *JEK*

Your Password:
MYOB

• •

FIGURE 4.EX1
One user's idea of how to
complete the computer usage
log.

Form AB1-iDB Log of Employee Computer Use
Note: to aid our staff, use military time to report
all sign in and sign offs

Today's Date
FEB. 4

Sign On Sign Off
9:15 - 9:40
Project Name:
2378
Reason for Project:
?
Project Authorized by: _____

Your Name:
MIKE H.
Your Password:
TOIL-ON

• •

FIGURE 4.EX2
A second user's idea of how to
complete the computer usage
log.

in the current budget. Since we're all good soldiers here, I hope you will take whatever our supply sergeant says is standard issue. Please, no "midnight requisitioning" to make up for shortages. Thanks for being GI in this regard; it makes the battle easier for all of us.

    a. What metaphor(s) is (are) being used? List the predominant metaphor and other phrases that play on that theme.

    b. If you found repeated evidence of this idea in other e-mail messages, what interpretation would you have? Use a paragraph to explain.

    c. In a paragraph, describe how the people in your systems analysis group can use the information from the e-mail messages to shape their systems project for Sawder's.

    d. In interviews with Sid, Ernie, and Carl, there has been no mention of problems with obtaining enough computer and printer supplies. In a paragraph, discuss why such problems may not come up in interviews and the value of examining e-mail messages and other memos in addition to interviewing.

7. "Here's the main policy manual we've put together over the years for system users," says Al Bookbinder, as he blows the dust off it and hands the manual to you. Al is a document keeper for the systems department of Prechter and Gumbel, a large manufacturer of health and beauty aids. "Everything any user of any part of the system needs to know is in what I call the Blue Book. I mean it's chock a block with policies. It's so big, I'm the only one with a complete copy. It costs too much to reproduce it." You thank Al and take the manual with you. When you read through it, you are astonished at what it contains. Most pages begin with a message such as: "This page supersedes page 23.1 in manual Vol. II. Discard previous inserts; do not use."

    a. List your observations about the frequency of use of the "Blue Book."

    b. How user-friendly are the updates in the manual? Write a sentence explaining your answer.

    c. Write a paragraph commenting on the wisdom of having all-important policies for all systems users in one book.

    d. Suggest a solution that incorporates the use of on-line policy manuals for some users.

8. Arch Ives, a newly hired and rather shy systems analyst with your systems group, has come to you with an idea that he assures you will save the team time—and hence the business you're consulting with will save money. Arch proposes that, rather than doing time-consuming interviews or collecting current quantitative and qualitative documents, the team should rely primarily on what it discovers in an archival database. "They've kept everything. They even have their old reports from earlier systems projects. We don't have to talk with anyone; we can access the database all day, without seeing a soul."

    a. List the merits of what Arch is proposing.

    b. List the problems with what Arch is proposing.

    c. In a paragraph, explain tactfully to Arch why the systems team uses many different approaches to gathering data.

GROUP PROJECT

1. Assume that your group will serve as a systems analysis and design team for a project designed to computerize or enhance the computerization of all business aspects of a 15-year-old, national U.S. truck-ing firm called Maverick Transport. Maverick is an LTL (less-than-a-truckload) carrier. The people in management work from the philosophy of JIT (just in time), in which they have created a partnership that includes the shipper, the receiver, and the carrier (Maverick Transport) for the purpose of transporting and delivering the materials required just in time for their use on the production line. Maverick maintains 626 tractors for hauling freight and has 45,000 square feet of warehouse space and 21,000 square feet of office space.

   a. Along with your group members, develop a list of sources of archival data that should be checked when analyzing the information requirements of Maverick.

   b. When this list is complete, devise a sampling scheme that would permit your group to get a clear picture of the company without having to read each document generated in its 15-year history.

SELECTED BIBLIOGRAPHY

Babbie, R. R. *Survey Research Methods.* Belmont, CA: Wadsworth Publishing Company, Inc., 1973.

Bormann, E. G. *Discussion and Group Methods: Theory and Practice,* 2nd ed. New York: Harper and Row, 1975.

Emory, C. W. *Business Research Methods,* 3rd ed. Homewood, IL: Richard D. Irwin, Inc., 1985.

Johnson, B. M. *Communication—The Process of Organizing.* Boston: Allyn and Bacon, 1977.

Kendall, J. E., and K. E. Kendall. "Metaphors and Methodologies: Living Beyond the Systems Machine." *MIS Quarterly,* Vol. 17, No. 2, June 1993, pp. 149–171.

Kendall, J. E., and K. E. Kendall. "Metaphors and Their Meaning for Information Systems Development." *European Journal of Information Systems,* 1994, pp. 37–47.

Sano, D. *Designing Large-Scale Web Sites: A Visual Methodology.* New York: Wiley Computer Publishing, 1996.

Webb, E. J., D. T. Campbell, R. D. Schwartz, and L. Sechrest. *Unobtrusive Measures: Nonreactive Research in the Social Sciences.* Chicago: Rand McNally College Publishing Company, 1966.

MINDING THE MEMOS

"Anna, I've been busy gathering some memos to help us understand what's behind some of the changes people have requested to the system," says Chip as he hands over a sheaf of papers to Anna.

Central Pacific University

MEMO

To: Cher Ware
From: Ed U. Cater *EUC*
CC:
Date: July 23, 1997
Re: PowerBuilder in the CIS lab

I would like to request that PowerBuilder (Powersoft Corporation) be installed in the new microcomputer lab. We have recently acquired the software at a great academic price and are excited to be using it.

This should be ready for the fall semester since we are planning to use the product for 9 programming classes, including several sections of 331, 335, and 336.

FIGURE E4.1
July 23rd memo from Ed U. Cater.

"Good idea," she replies, "but do you have any way to make them meaningful to us?"

Chip carefully rereads the memos shown in Figures E4.1, E4.2, E4.3, and E4.4.

"They tell an interesting story," Chip replies. "I can't wait for you to take a look."

Exercises

E-1. Analyze the four memos depicted in Figures E4.1–E4.4. Discuss how you analyzed them and, in a paragraph, describe what you have found.

Central Pacific University

MEMO

To: Cher Ware
From: Ed U. Cater   *EUC*
CC: Dot Matricks
Date: July 30, 1997
Re: PowerBuilder install problems

Thanks for your recent memo. I went into the new lab to check out PowerBuilder and found out that it does not run correctly and that many of the features are not installed.

I tried to re-install PowerBuilder on one of the machines and apparently there is not enough hard drive space to include the full product. In addition, the amount of main memory is not enough to work smoothly with the product. Is there a means of adding more memory and increasing the amount of hard drive space? Time is running short for us to set up projects and make student handouts.

Extreme urgency is needed in fixing the problem!!

FIGURE E4.2
July 30th memo from Ed U. Cater.

Central Pacific University

MEMO

To: Ed U. Cater
From: Cher Ware   CW
CC: Dot Matricks, Mike Crowe
Date: August 1, 1997
Re: PowerBuilder install problems

I have checked with Mike on the problem with main memory and additional hard drive space. He has informed me that there are many other requests for hardware installation prior to the start of the semester and doubts that the machines will be upgraded until the middle of October.

You may still use PowerBuilder with the minimal configuration, but the help system and other features will not be available.

We are evaluating budgetary concerns and looking for options to obtain the funds to upgrade the machines.

Another potential solution is to run some of the software from the installation CD. Let us know what you decide.

FIGURE E4.3
August 1st memo from Cher Ware.

E-2.   In a paragraph, answer the following question: Is any information missing from the memos? What is it? Where would you get it?

E-3.   In a paragraph, discuss who you would contact to better understand the memos. Additionally, discuss how you would bring up the content of the memos so that they can be incorporated into the requirements determination phase.

Central Pacific University

MEMO

To: Cher Ware
From: Ed U. Cater *EUC*
CC: Dot Matricks, Mike Crowe
Date: August 5, 1997
Re: PowerBuilder install problems

Thanks for your recent memo on the PowerBuilder installation problems. I have thought over your suggestions and considered using CD ROM drives; however, these are slow, being double speed. Further, we feel that the CD ROMs may be mishandled, causing read problems, or may become lost.

The help system is essential for students who will be writing programs, and therefore it must be installed. Is there any other computer lab that has the available hard drive space and main memory? These labs should be on the main campus — hopefully in the Computer Sciences building or one nearby.

Another solution is to delete all unnecessary software from the machines that are in the CIS lab. I realize that this will severely impact other instructors and courses, but perhaps their software is also installed in other labs.

I don't mean to sound panicked, but time is running short. The students need this to complete the course. Please respond quickly.

FIGURE E4.4
August 5th memo from Ed U. Cater.

5
INTERVIEWING

Before you interview someone else, you must in effect interview yourself. You need to know your biases and how they will affect your perceptions. Your education, intellect, upbringing, emotions and ethical framework all serve as powerful filters for what you will be hearing in your interviews.

You need to think out the interview thoroughly before you go. Visualize why you are going, what you will ask, and what will make it a successful interview in your eyes. The other half of all this is the individual you will interview. You must anticipate how to make the interview fulfilling for him or her as well.

KINDS OF INFORMATION SOUGHT

An information-gathering interview is a directed conversation with a specific purpose that uses a question-and-answer format. In the interview you want to get the opinions of the interviewee and his or her feelings about the current state of the system, organizational and personal goals, and informal procedures, as shown in Figure 5.1.

Above all, seek the opinions of the person you are interviewing. Opinions may be more important and more revealing than facts. For example, imagine asking the owner of a store how many customer refunds she typically gives each week. She replies, "About 20 to 25 a week." When you search the records and discover that the average is only 10.5 per week, you might conclude that the owner is overstating the facts and the problem.

Imagine instead that you ask the owner what her major concerns are and that she replies, "In my opinion, customer refunds are way too high. We must strive to get it right the first time." By seeking opinions rather than facts, you discover a key problem that the owner wants addressed.

In addition to opinions, you should try to capture the feelings of the interviewee. Remember that the interviewee knows the organization better than you do. You can understand the organization's culture more fully by listening to the feelings of the respondent. You can also determine the existing degree of optimism.

111

FIGURE 5.1
Kinds of information sought
in interviewing.

Expressed feelings help capture emotion and attitudes. If the owner of the store tells you, "I feel encouraged that you are working on this project," then you can take it as a positive sign that the project will go well. This information is available only through asking about feelings.

Goals are important information that can be gleaned from interviewing. Facts that you obtain from hard data may explain past performance, but goals project the organization's future. Try to find out as many of its goals as possible from interviewing. You may not be able to determine goals through any other data-gathering methods.

In the interview you are setting up a relationship with someone who is probably a stranger to you. You need to build trust and understanding quickly, but at the same time you must maintain control of the interview. You also need to sell the system by providing needed information to your interviewee. The way to begin doing this is by planning for the interview before you go, so that conducting it is second nature to you. Fortunately, effective interviewing can be learned. As you practice, you will see yourself improving. Later in the chapter we discuss Joint Application Design (JAD), which can serve as an alternative to one-on-one interviewing in certain situations.

PLANNING THE INTERVIEW

Five Steps in Interview Preparation

The five major steps in interview preparation are shown in Figure 5.2. These steps include a range of activities from gathering basic background material to deciding who to interview.

READ BACKGROUND MATERIAL. Read and understand as much background information about the interviewees and their organization as possible. This material can often be obtained by a quick call to your contact person to ask for a corporate Web site, a current annual report, a corporate newsletter, and any publications sent out to explain the organization to the public. Check the Internet for any corporate information such as that in *Standard and Poor's*.

As you read through this material, be particularly sensitive to the *language* the organizational members use in describing themselves and their or-

FIGURE 5.2
Steps the systems analyst follows in planning the interview.

Steps in Planning the Interview

1   Read Background Material

2   Establish Interviewing Objectives

3   Decide Whom to Interview

4   Prepare the Interviewee

5   Decide on Question Types and Structure

ganization. What you are trying to do is build up a common vocabulary that will eventually enable you to phrase interview questions in a way that is understandable to your interviewee. Another benefit of researching your organization is to maximize the time you spend in interviews; without such preparation you may wind up wasting time asking general background questions.

ESTABLISH INTERVIEWING OBJECTIVES. Use the background information you gathered as well as your own experience to establish interview objectives. There should be four to six key areas concerning information-processing and decision-making behavior about which you will want to ask questions. These areas include: information sources, information formats, decision-making frequency, qualities of information, and decision-making style.

DECIDE WHO TO INTERVIEW. When deciding who to interview, include key people at all levels who will be affected by the system in some manner. As discussed in Chapter 4, it is important to sample organizational members. Strive for balance so that as many user's needs are addressed as possible. Your organizational contact will also have some ideas about who should be interviewed.

PREPARE THE INTERVIEWEE. Prepare the person to be interviewed by calling ahead or sending an e-mail message and allowing the interviewee time to think about the interview. Arrange time for phone calls and meetings. Interviews should be kept at 45 minutes to an hour at the most. No matter how much your interviewees seem to want to extend the interview beyond this limit, remember that when they spend time with you, they are not doing their work. If interviews go over an hour, it is likely that the interviewees will resent the intrusion, whether or not they articulate their resentment.

DECIDE ON QUESTION TYPES AND STRUCTURE. Write questions to cover the key areas of decision making that you discovered when you ascertained interview objectives. Proper questioning techniques are the heart of interview-

Open-Ended Interview Questions
• What's your opinion of the present computer system?
• How do you view the goals of this department?
• How does this form relate to the work you do?
• What are some of the problems you experience in receiving information on time?
• What are some of the common errors made in data entry in this department?
• Describe the most frustrating computer system you've worked with.

ing. Questions have some basic forms that you need to know. The two basic question types are open-ended and closed. Each question type can accomplish something a little different from the other, and each has benefits and drawbacks. You need to think about the effect each question type will have.

It is possible to structure your interview in three different patterns: a pyramid structure, a funnel structure, or a diamond structure. Each is appropriate under different conditions and serves a different function, and each one will be discussed later in the chapter.

The following discussion describes in detail some of the important decisions the interviewer must make. These include which questions to ask and how, whether to structure the interview, and how to document the interview.

Question Types

OPEN-ENDED QUESTIONS. Open-ended questions include those such as "What do you think about putting all of the managers on an intranet ?" and "Please explain how you make a scheduling decision." Consider the word *open-ended.* "Open" actually describes the interviewee's options for responding. They are open. The response can be two words or two paragraphs. Some examples of open-ended questions can be found in Figure 5.3.

The benefits of using open-ended questions are numerous and include:

1. Putting the interviewee at ease.
2. Allowing the interviewer to pick up on the interviewee's vocabulary, which reflects his or her education, values, attitudes, and beliefs.
3. Providing richness of detail.
4. Revealing avenues of further questioning that may have gone untapped.
5. Making it more interesting for the interviewee.
6. Allowing more spontaneity.
7. Making phrasing easier for the interviewer.
8. Using them in a pinch if the interviewer is caught unprepared.

As you can see, there are several advantages to using open-ended questions. However, there are also many drawbacks, which include:

1. Asking questions that may result in too much irrelevant detail.
2. Possibly losing control of the interview.
3. Allowing responses that may take too much time for the amount of useful information gained.

FIGURE 5.4
Closed interview questions
limit the options the respondent has for responding. The
examples were selected from
different interviews and are
not shown in any particular
order.

Closed Interview Questions

- How many reports do you generate in a month?
- How long have you worked for Bakerloo Brothers?
- Which of the following sources of information is most valuable to you:
  fill-out customer complaint forms
  face-to-face interaction with the customer
  returned merchandise itself
- List your top two priorities for the marketing department.
- Who receives this output?

---

4. Potentially seeming that the interviewer is unprepared.

5. Possibly giving the impression that the interviewer is on a "fishing ex-
pedition" with no real objective for the interview.

You must carefully consider the implications of using open-ended questions
for interviewing.

CLOSED QUESTIONS. The alternative to open-ended questions is found in
the other basic question type: closed questions. Such questions are of the basic form: "How many subordinates do you have?" The possible responses
are closed to the interviewees, since they can only reply with a finite number such as "None," "One," or "Fifteen." Some examples of closed questions
can be found in Figure 5.4.

A closed question limits the response available to the interviewee. You
may be familiar with closed questions through multiple-choice exams in
college. You are given a question and five responses, but you are not allowed
to write down your own response and still be counted as having correctly
answered the question.

A special kind of closed question is the bipolar question. This limits
the interviewee even further by only allowing a choice on either pole, such
as yes or no, true or false, agree or disagree. Examples of bipolar questions
can be found in Figure 5.5.

The benefits of using closed questions of either type include:

1. Saving time.
2. Easily comparing interviews.
3. Getting to the point.
4. Keeping control over the interview.

FIGURE 5.5
Bipolar interview questions
are a special kind of closed
question. The examples were
selected from different interviews and are not shown in
any particular order.

Bipolar Interview Questions

- Do you use the Internet to locate customers?
- Do you agree or disagree that commerce on the Web lacks security?
- Do you want to receive a printout of your account status every month?
- Does your accounting department offer on-line assistance for employee payroll
  questions?
- Is this form complete?

FIGURE 5.6
Attributes of open-ended and closed questions.

Open-ended		Closed
Low	Reliability of Data	High
Low	Efficient Use of Time	High
Low	Precision of Data	High
Much	Breadth and Depth	Little
Much	Interviewer Skill Required	Little
Difficult	Ease of Analysis	Easy

5. Covering lots of ground quickly.
6. Getting to relevant data.

The drawbacks of using closed questions are substantial, however. They include:

1. Being boring for the interviewee.
2. Failing to obtain rich detail (due to the fact that the interviewer supplies the frame of reference for the interviewee).
3. Missing main ideas for the preceding reason.
4. Failing to build rapport between interviewer and interviewee.

So as the interviewer, you must think carefully about the question types you will use.

Both open-ended and closed questions have advantages and drawbacks, as shown in Figure 5.6. Notice that choosing one question type over the other actually involves a trade-off; while an open-ended question affords breadth and depth of reply, responses to open-ended questions are difficult to analyze.

PROBES. A third type of question is the "probe" or "follow-up." The strongest probe is the simplest: the question "Why?" Other probes are "Can you give me an example?" and "Will you elaborate on that for me?" Some examples of probing questions can be found in Figure 5.7. The purpose of the probe is to go beyond the initial answer to get more meaning, to clarify, and to draw out and expand on the interviewee's point. Probes may be either open-ended or closed questions.

It is essential to probe. Most beginning interviewers are reticent about probing and consequently accept superficial answers. They are usually grateful that employees have granted interviews and feel somewhat obligated to accept unqualified statements politely.

If done in a systematic and determined manner, your probing will be acknowledged as a sign that you are listening to what's being said, thinking

Probes
• Why? • Give an example of your decision-making process. • Please provide an illustration of the performance measures you mentioned earlier. • You mentioned both an intranet solution and an extranet solution. Please give an example of how you think each differs from the other. • What makes you feel that way? • Tell me what happens step by step to the form the patient fills out.

FIGURE 5.7
Probes allow the systems analyst to follow up questions to get more detailed responses. The examples were selected from different interviews and are not shown in any particular order.

it through, and responding appropriately. This can only help the situation. Rather than using a tough "investigative-reporter" type of approach, you should probe in a way that exhibits your thoroughness and your desire to comprehend the interviewee's responses. Formulating a sound probe indicates that you are listening.

Question Pitfalls

By wording your questions beforehand, you are able to correct any poor questions that you have written. Watch for troublesome question types that can ruin your data. They are called "leading questions" and "double-barreled questions."

AVOIDING LEADING QUESTIONS. Leading questions tend to lead the interviewee into a response that you seem to want. The response is then biased since you are setting up a kind of trap. Here is an example: "You agree with other managers that inventory control should be computerized, don't you?" You have made it very uncomfortable to disagree. An alternative, preferred phrasing could be: "What do you think of computerizing inventory control?" Your data will be more reliable and more valid, hence easier to understand and more useful.

AVOIDING DOUBLE-BARRELED QUESTIONS. Double-barreled questions are those that use only one question mark for what are actually two separate questions. A question such as "What decisions are made during a typical day and how do you make them?" is an example of a double-barreled question. If your interviewee responds to this type of question, your data may suffer.

A double-barreled question is a poor choice because interviewees may answer only one question (purposely or not), or you may mistake which question they are answering and draw the wrong conclusion. If you are lucky enough to discover your error, it still means orally retracing steps and straightening out the misunderstanding, a process which takes extra time. Most of this can be avoided by phrasing questions carefully beforehand.

Arranging Questions in a Logical Sequence

Just as there are two generally recognized ways of reasoning—inductive and deductive—there are two similar ways of organizing your interviews. A third way combines both inductive and deductive patterns.

CONSULTING OPPORTUNITY 5.1

Strengthening Your Question Types

Strongbodies, a large, local chain of sports clubs, has experienced phenomenal growth in the past 5 years. Management would like to refine its decision-making process for purchasing new body-building equipment. Currently, managers listen to customers, attend trade shows, look at advertisements, and put in requests for new equipment purchases based on their subjective perceptions. These are then approved or denied by Harry Mussels.

Harry is the first person you will interview. He is a 37-year-old division manager who runs five area clubs. He travels all over the city to their widespread locations. He keeps an office at the East location, although he is there less than a quarter of the time.

Additionally, when Harry is present at a club, he is busy answering business-related phone calls, solving on-the-spot problems presented by managers, and interacting with club members. His time is short, and to compensate for that he has become an extremely well-organized, efficient divisional manager. He cannot grant you a lot of interview time. Yet his input is important, and he feels he would be the main beneficiary of the proposed system.

What types of interview questions might be most suitable for your interview with Harry? Why are they most appropriate? How will your choice of question type affect the amount of time you spend in preparation for interviewing Harry? Write 5–10 questions of this type. What other techniques might you use to supplement information unavailable through that type of question? Write a paragraph to explain.

USING A PYRAMID STRUCTURE. Inductive organization of interview questions can be visualized as having a pyramid shape. Using this form, the interviewer begins with very detailed, often closed, questions. The interviewer then expands the topics by allowing open-ended questions and more generalized responses, as shown in Figure 5.8.

A pyramid structure should be used if you believe your interviewee needs to warm up to the topic. It is also useful if the interviewee seems reluctant to address the topic. For example, if you are interviewing someone who has told you over the phone that he or she does not need to talk with

FIGURE 5.8
Pyramid structure for interviewing goes from specific to general questions.

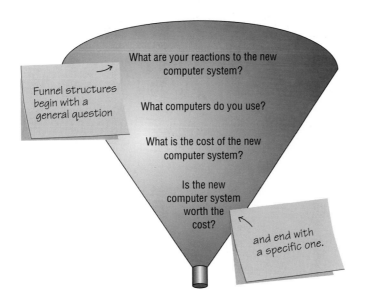

FIGURE 5.9
Funnel structure for interviewing begins with broad
questions, then funnels to
specific questions.

you because that person already knows what is wrong with the forecasting model, you should probably structure the interview as a pyramid.

Utilizing a pyramid structure for question sequencing is also useful when you want an ending determination about the topic. Such is the case in the final question: "In general, how do you feel about forecasting?"

USING A FUNNEL STRUCTURE. In the second kind of structure, the interviewer takes a deductive approach by beginning with generalized, open-ended questions and then narrowing the possible responses by using closed questions. This interview structure can be thought of as funnel-shaped, like that depicted in Figure 5.9.

Using the funnel structure method provides an easy, nonthreatening way to begin an interview. Respondents will not feel pressured that they are giving a "wrong" response to an open-ended question. A funnel-shaped question sequence is also useful when the interviewee feels emotional about the topic and needs freedom to express those emotions. A benefit of using a funnel structure is that organizing the interview in such a manner may elicit so much detailed information that long sequences of closed questions and probes are unnecessary.

USING A DIAMOND-SHAPED STRUCTURE. Often a combination of the two above structures, one resulting in a diamond-shaped interview structure, is best. This entails beginning in a very specific way, then examining general issues, and finally coming to a very specific conclusion, as shown in Figure 5.10.

The interviewer begins with easy, closed questions that provide a warmup to the interview process. In the middle of the interview, the interviewee is asked for opinions on broad topics that obviously have no "right" answer. The interviewer then narrows the questions again to get specific questions answered, thus providing closure for both the interviewee and the interviewer.

The diamond structure combines the strengths of the other two approaches but has the disadvantage of taking longer. The chief advantage of

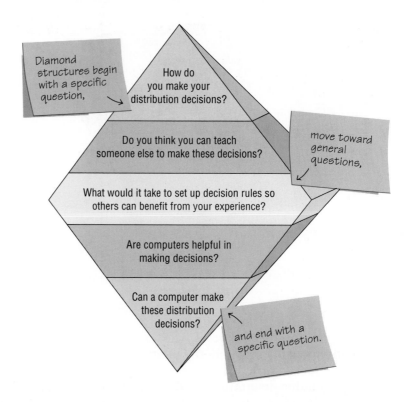

FIGURE 5.10
Diamond-shaped structure for interviewing combines the pyramid and funnel structures.

using a diamond-shaped structure is keeping your interviewee's interest and attention through a variety of questions. Remember that once you know how to ask the right questions at the right time, you have many options for sequencing them.

Structured Versus Unstructured Interviews

Many beginning interviewers believe that, because interviews are similar to conversations, they would be better off not structuring the questions or question sequences in their interviews. For a completely structured interview, everything is planned out and the plan is strictly adhered to. Closed questions are at the core of a completely structured interview.

There are explicit trade-offs involved for each of ten variables, as shown in Figure 5.11. Notice that while it is difficult to evaluate an unstructured interview, it is easier to evaluate one that is structured; greater contact time is required to conduct an unstructured interview than a structured one; much training is needed to conduct a successful unstructured interview, limited training is required to conduct a completely structured interview; and so on.

Awareness of the trade-offs between structured and unstructured interviews will enable you to make a better decision about which kind of interview is more appropriate for a particular situation. If you decide to follow the unstructured route, you should still prepare for the interview as discussed in the previous steps. For the unstructured approach we advocate, at minimum, a brief outline (including many questions worded as precisely as they will be asked). Remember that *unstructured* here refers only to the order in which the questions are asked and does not imply a lack of other preparation.

The only way to tell if your question is appropriate is to word it precisely beforehand, then anticipate possible responses and how you will fol-

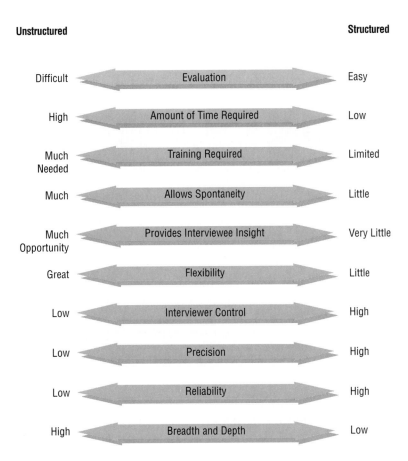

Unstructured		Structured
Difficult	Evaluation	Easy
High	Amount of Time Required	Low
Much Needed	Training Required	Limited
Much	Allows Spontaneity	Little
Much Opportunity	Provides Interviewee Insight	Very Little
Great	Flexibility	Little
Low	Interviewer Control	High
Low	Precision	High
Low	Reliability	High
High	Breadth and Depth	Low

FIGURE 5.11
Attributes of unstructured and structured interviews to consider when deciding on an interview format.

low up on them. It is necessary for you to project what the other person might say. This takes considerable time and thought and is in itself an excellent argument for preparing several questions which will allow you to take various avenues during the course of the interview. This approach is actually a branching program—if the answer is "yes," you proceed one way; if "no," you take the other path of questioning.

Making a Record of the Interview

Record the most important aspects of your interview. Either you can use a tape recorder, or you can rely on pen and paper notetaking, but it is important to make a permanent record during the actual interview.

Whether you take notes or make an audio recording depends in part on who you are interviewing and what you will do with the information once the interview is over. Additionally, there are advantages and disadvantages inherent in each of the recording methods.

MAKING AN AUDIO RECORDING. Consider your interviewee when deciding how to record your interview. When you make an appointment, tell the interviewee that you would like to make an audio recording of the interview. Mention what you will do with the tape: Either it will be listened to by you and by the other team members and then destroyed, or it will be transcribed and used as information for system development. Be truthful about your intentions and reassuring about the confi-

Skimming the Surface

You are about to leave SureCheck Dairy after a preliminary tour, when another member of your systems analysis team calls you at the dairy to say he cannot make his interview appointment with the plant manager because of illness. The plant manager is extremely busy, and you want to keep his enthusiasm for the project going by doing things as scheduled. You also realize that without the initial interview data, the rest of your data gathering will be slowed. Although you have no interview questions prepared, you make the decision to go ahead and interview the plant manager on the spot.

You have learned that SureCheck is interested in processing its own data on quantities and kinds of dairy products sold, so that its people can use that information to better control production of the company's large product line (it includes whole, skim, 2 percent, and 1 percent milk, half-and-half, cottage cheese, yogurt, and frozen novelties). Sales managers are currently sending their sales figures to corporate headquarters, 600 miles away, and processing turnaround seems slow. You will base your ad-libbed questions on what you have just found out on the tour.

In the few minutes before your interview begins, decide on a structure for it: funnel-shaped, pyramid-shaped, or diamond-shaped. In a paragraph, justify why you would proceed with the interview structure you have chosen based on the unusual context of this interview. Write a series of questions and organize them in the structure you have chosen.

dentiality of any of the interviewee's remarks. If your interviewee refuses to allow you permission to make an audio recording, graciously accept that constraint.

Audio recording has advantages and disadvantages. The advantages are that such recording accomplishes the following:

1. It provides a completely accurate record of what each person said.
2. It frees the interviewer to listen to what is said and to respond more rapidly.
3. It allows better eye contact and hence better development of rapport between interviewer and interviewee.
4. It allows a replay of the interview for other team members.

The disadvantages of audio recording are also numerous. They include:

1. Possibly making the interviewee nervous and less apt to respond freely.
2. Possibly making the interviewer less apt to listen, since it's all being recorded.
3. The difficulty in locating important passages on a long tape.
4. The increasing costs of data gathering because of the need to transcribe tapes.

The decision to make an audio recording of interviews is a professional one that you will have to make based on what you know about interviewing, the interviewee's outlook on taping, and the particular project. Evaluate audio recording each time it is chosen, just as you would evaluate any other procedure.

Hitting the High Note

Late in the afternoon, you see Gabriel García, manager of Chumco's infant toy line, turning a corner in the corridor to return to his office. Gabriel, who is walking rather slowly, looks baffled. Your team member, Arthur Brown, just completed an interview with him about the possibility of having your systems analysis team design a decision support system to support Gabriel's process of deciding which new toys to produce. As project leader, you are curious about uncharacteristic behavior and want to learn his impression of the interview.

You easily catch up with Gabriel and ask if everything went all right in the interview. This is his reply:

"Yes, it was okay, I guess. We covered a lot of territory. It was a little strange, though. I'm not even sure I'll recognize the guy who interviewed me if I see him again. All I saw was the top of his head, his pad, and his pencil. He wrote down every word I spoke! I felt like I was in court. What are you going to do with all that information? Publish quotations? I hope it doesn't get back to the wrong people."

What important notetaking guidelines did Arthur apparently forget to follow? Make a list. As project team leader, what assurances can you give Gabriel now that this has happened? Respond in a paragraph.

NOTETAKING. Notetaking may be your only way to record the interview if your interviewee refuses your request to make an audio tape. It is important that you somehow record the interview as it takes place. The advantages of notetaking include:

1. Keeping the interviewer alert.
2. Aiding recall of important questions.
3. Helping recall of important interview trends.
4. Showing interviewer interest in the interview.
5. Demonstrating the interviewer's preparedness.

There are some very good reasons for notetaking, but it is not without drawbacks. The disadvantages include:

1. Losing vital eye contact (and therefore rapport) between the interviewer and interviewee.
2. Losing the train of the conversation.
3. Making the interviewee hesitant to speak when notes are being made.
4. Causing excessive attention to facts and too little attention to feelings and opinions.

Even though the technology (and temptation) exists to take notes on your laptop or notebook computer during the interview, we do not recommend it. Our experience shows that while your accuracy of reporting may increase, your rapport with interviewees and your general concentration decrease. Focus on listening to the interviewee.

In order to prepare for your interview properly, you must understand yourself, your own biases, and your values. Then research your interviewee and his or her organization, sketch out key areas for questioning, contact interviewees, write interview questions, and formulate an interview plan.

Before the Interview

The day preceding your interview, contact your interviewees via phone or e-mail to reconfirm times and places of interviews. Coordinate appointments with any other team members and gather necessary materials.

When you conduct interviews, dress appropriately, perhaps wearing what you would wear to interview for a job in the same organization. Since you will be controlling the interview, you must dress in a credible manner. Failing to dress appropriately could result in poor data gathering. Interviewee's responses to you are geared to their initial perceptions.

Arrive a little early for your interview. You can use the extra time to review your notes or start making observations about the organization. (See Chapter 7 for observation techniques.) Affirm with the interviewee that you are present and ready to begin the interview.

CONDUCTING THE ACTUAL INTERVIEW

Beginning the Interview

As you enter, firmly shake your interviewee's hand. This applies whether you are male or female. As in any other business situation, a handshake helps establish your credibility and trustworthiness. Remind the interviewee of your name and briefly outline once more why you are there and why you chose to interview him or her.

As you sit down, immediately take out your cassette recorder and/or note pad. Remind your interviewee that you will record important points. Tell the interviewee what you will do with the data you collect and be reassuring about its confidentiality.

Now is the time to check whether your audio recorder and microphone are working properly. Some beginning interviewers are too embarrassed to take the time to check equipment, but the result of assuming that you're taping when you're not is disastrous. Your interviewee will respect your professionalism in guaranteeing that everything is in working order before you begin.

Depending on the structure you are following in your interview, you may begin with some very general, nonthreatening, open-ended questions. Opening an interview this way helps to relax you and your interviewee. It also provides a frame of reference for you that is helpful in tailoring your later questions. By listening closely to early responses, you can pick up on vocabulary and jargon (maybe the organization doesn't have "departments," for example, but instead it calls them "units") and the relevant metaphors such as, "The EDP department is a zoo," "Our scheduling system works like a well-oiled machine," or "We're one big happy family here." Recall from Chapters 2 and 4 that metaphors help reveal membership in organizational subcultures.

Early open-ended responses can also reveal the attitudes, values, and beliefs of the interviewee that will help you understand how he or she uses information and how he or she feels toward others in the organization. You must listen and respond appropriately to what your interviewee is saying.

As you proceed through your interview schedule, mention to your respondent what sort of detail you would like to receive in answers. For instance, if you feel you need depth on a question, encourage your interviewee to provide an example. If you have only passing interest in a topic, tell your

A Systems Analyst, I Presume?

"Know what I think of the work the last systems analyst team did? The printouts they created are a jungle. In order to figure out the cost of raw materials to us, I have to cut my way through the overgrowth of data, hacking my path with a pen. I cross out everything that's irrelevant. Sometimes I physically rip out the excess vegetation until I reach the numbers I need," says Henry Stanley, accounting supervisor for Zenith Glass Company. As you interview him, he points unhappily to an untidy

stack of mutilated printouts sprouting beside his desk.

Identify the overriding metaphor Henry is using to describe the printouts he is receiving and the accessibility of information in them. In a paragraph, describe how this helps you understand Henry's attitude toward any work proposed by *your* systems analysis team. In a paragraph, adopt Henry's metaphor and extend it in a more positive sense during your interview with him.

respondent a "yes" or "no" is sufficient. You are in control of time usage in this kind of interview, and providing guidelines for length of response is helpful in maintaining interview balance.

All interview material should be covered in 45 minutes to an hour, and by now you are well aware of the planning and managing necessary to accomplish this goal. Closing the interview appropriately is just as important as opening it well.

During the interview, reflect back to some of your interviewee's responses through paraphrasing or summarizing in order to double-check that you understand his or her meaning. If at any time you are unsure, you must ask for definitions or other clarification. Feigning knowledge only works against your ultimate objectives. The close of the interview is not the place to bring up all of these concerns. Rather, they are more naturally handled as they arise.

However, the end of the interview is a natural place to ask one key question: "Is there anything we haven't touched on that you feel is important for me to know?" Most of the time this is considered a formula question by the interviewee, and the response will be "No." However, you are interested in the small percentage of time that this question opens the proverbial floodgates and much new (and often surprising) data are presented.

As you conclude the interview, there are other procedures to follow. Summarize and provide feedback on your overall impressions. Inform the interviewee about the subsequent steps to take and what you and other team members will do next. You may wish to ask the interviewee who you should talk with next. Set up future appointment times for follow-up interviews, thank the interviewee for his or her time, and shake hands.

WRITING THE INTERVIEW REPORT

Although the interview itself is complete, your work on the interview data is just beginning. You need to capture the essence of the interview through a written report. It is imperative that you write the interview report as soon as possible after the interview. This is another way you can assure quality of in-

Interviewee:	Sal Domask		Date:	March 3
Interviewer:	S. Cabbot		Subject:	Computer usage

Objectives of the interview: ⎰ Find out attitude about computer
usage; get user's estimate of usage;
Were objectives met? ⎱ find out opinion of newly proposed system

Objectives for follow-up interview:

Find out how Sal views support of systems department.
Find out opinions on who to talk to next.

Main Points of Interview:	Interviewer's Opinions:
✓ Sal said, "Computer is my friend."	Interested in learning more about how system can help with work.
✓ Uses computer "all the time."	Feels bored if not working with computer.
✓ Can't wait "until I get my hands on a new system."	Will be enthusiastic supporter/facilitator for new system.

terview data. The longer you wait to write up your interview, the more suspect the quality of your data becomes.

After this initial summary, go into more detail, noting main points of the interview and your own opinions. Figure 5.12 shows a sample interview report form that will aid you in capturing the interview essentials. It will help you in planning for your next interview as well.

Review the interview report with the respondent at a follow-up meeting. This helps clarify the meaning the interviewee had in mind and lets the interviewee know that you are interested enough to take the time to understand his or her point of view and perceptions.

JOINT APPLICATION DESIGN

No matter how adept you become as an interviewer, you will inevitably experience situations where one-on-one interviews do not seem to be as useful as you would like. Personal interviews are time-consuming, subject to error, and their data are prone to misinterpretation. An alternative approach to interviewing users one by one, called Joint Application Design (JAD), was developed by IBM. The motivation for using JAD is to cut the time (and hence the cost) required by personal interviews, to improve the quality of the results of information requirements assessment, and to create more user identification with new information systems as a result of the participative processes.

Although JAD can be substituted for personal interviews at any appropriate juncture during the systems development life cycle, Joint Application Design has usually been employed as a technique that allows you, as a systems analyst, to accomplish requirements analysis and to design the user interface jointly with users in a group setting. Sometimes a group decision support system (GDSS) can be used, but it is not mandatory. The many intricacies of this approach can only be learned in a paid seminar demonstrating proprietary methods. However, we can convey enough information about JAD here to make you aware of some of its benefits and drawbacks in comparison to one-on-one interviews.

Joint Application Design requires some specialized skills on the part of the analyst—and many skills and a firm commitment on the part of the organization and users who undertake to use this approach. However, in certain situations, JAD can be very effective and should be considered as an alternative to more traditional methods of systems analysis.

Conditions That Support the Use of JAD

The following list of conditions will help you decide when the use of JAD may be fruitful. Consider using Joint Application Design when:

1. User groups are restless and want something new, not a standard solution to a typical problem.
2. The organizational culture supports joint problem-solving behaviors among multiple levels of employees.
3. Analysts forecast that the number of ideas generated via one-on-one interviews will not be as plentiful as the number of ideas possible from an extended group exercise.
4. Organizational work flow permits the absence of key personnel during a two-to-four-day block of time.

Who Is Involved

Joint Application Design sessions include a variety of participants—analysts, users, executives, and so on—who will contribute differing backgrounds and skills to the sessions. Your primary concern here is that all project team members are committed to the JAD approach and become involved. Choose an executive sponsor, a senior person who will introduce and conclude the JAD session. Preferably, select an executive from the user group who has some sort of authority over the IS (information systems) people working on the project. This person will be an important, visible symbol of organizational commitment to the systems project.

At least one IS analyst should be present, but the analyst usually takes a passive role—unlike traditional interviewing where the analyst controls the interaction. As the project analyst, you should be present during JAD to listen to what users say and what they require. Additionally, you will want to give an expert opinion about any disproportionate costs of solutions proposed during the JAD session itself. Without this kind of immediate feedback, unrealistic solutions with excessive costs may creep into the proposal and prove costly to discourage later on.

From eight to a dozen users can be chosen from any rank to participate in JAD sessions. Try to select users above the clerical level who can articulate what information they need to perform their jobs, as well as what they desire in a new or improved computer system. Some of the ideas on sampling from Chapter 4 can be put to good use here, since your goal is to get a representative sample of users without forming such a large group that it becomes unwieldy during group interactions.

The session leader should not be an expert in systems analysis and design but rather someone who has excellent communication skills to facilitate appropriate interactions. Consider having a full-time training department member serve as session leader. Note that you do not want to use a session leader who reports to another person in the group. To avoid this possibility, an organization may want to retain an outside management consultant to serve as session leader. The point is to get a person who can bring the group's attention to bear on important systems issues, satisfactorily negotiate and resolve conflicts, and help group members reach consensus rather than rely on simple majority rule to make decisions.

Your JAD session should also include one or two observers who are analysts or technical experts from other functional areas to offer technical explanations and advice to the group during the sessions. Additionally, one scribe from the IS department should attend the JAD sessions to formally write down everything that is done. Ensure that the scribe publishes the record of JAD results rapidly once the group has met. Slow publication of results risks losing the time savings and momentum that are the prime motivations for using JAD in the first place. Consider selecting a second scribe from a user department as well. Then the responsibility for recording systems issues can be left to the IS scribe, and the scribe from the user group can note business-related content.

Planning for the JAD Session

One of the keys to a successful JAD workshop is laying the groundwork through advance study and planning. The session leader chosen will work with an executive sponsor to determine the scope of the project which JAD must cover. Sometimes the project requires more than one JAD workshop, but some of the benefits of JAD erode if too many independent sessions are planned. Following the definition of the project scope, participants will be selected, and the session leader will learn the application by doing some interviews with key users. The purpose of the interviews is to gather information to facilitate understanding of what is happening in the business.

Where to Hold JAD Meetings

If it is at all possible, we recommend holding the two-to-four-day sessions offsite, away from the organization, in comfortable surroundings. Some groups use executive centers or even group decision support facilities that are available at major universities. The idea is to minimize the daily distractions and responsibilities of the participants' regular work. The room itself should comfortably hold the twenty or so people invited. Minimal presentation support equipment includes two overhead projectors, a whiteboard, a flipchart, and easy access to a copier. Group decision support rooms will also provide networked microcomputers, a projection system, and software written to facilitate group interaction, while minimizing unproductive group behaviors.

Give adequate thought to the creature comforts of participants as well, since this will be an intense experience, quite different in nature from a typical day's work for most people. Plan for sufficient food, as well as ample refreshments during scheduled breaks before lunch and again in late afternoon.

Schedule your JAD session when all participants can commit to attending. Do not hold the sessions unless everyone who has been invited can actually attend. This is critical to the success of the sessions. Ensure that all participants receive an agenda before the meeting, and consider holding an orientation meeting for a half-day one week or so before the workshop so that those involved know what is expected of them. This allows you to move rapidly and act confidently once the actual meeting is convened.

Accomplishing a Structured Analysis of Project Activities

IBM recommends that the JAD sessions examine these points in the proposed systems project: planning, receiving, receipt processing/tracking, monitoring and assigning, processing, recording, sending, and evaluating. For each topic, the questions who, what, how, where, and why should also be asked and answered. Clearly, *ad hoc,* interactive systems such as decision support systems and other types of systems dependent on decision-maker style (including prototype systems) are not as easily analyzed with the structured approach of JAD.

As the analyst involved with the JAD sessions, you should receive the notes of the scribes and prepare a specifications document based on what happened at the meeting. Systematically present the management objectives as well as the scope and boundaries of the project. Specifics of the system, including details on screen and report layouts, should also be included. As a guide for what to include, use Chapter 13, which details the composition of a systems proposal. You can also look to the client organization for other guidelines to be followed in preparing this document.

Potential Benefits of Using JAD in Place of Traditional Interviewing

There are four major potential benefits that you, the users, and your systems analysis team should consider when you weigh the possibilities of using Joint Application Design. The first potential benefit is time savings over traditional one-on-one interviews. Some organizations have estimated that JAD sessions have provided a 15 percent time savings over the traditional approach. Hand-in-hand with time savings is the rapid development possible via JAD. Since user interviews are not accomplished serially over a period of weeks or months, the development can proceed much more quickly.

A third benefit to weigh is the possibility of improved ownership of the information system. As analysts, we are always striving to involve users in meaningful ways and to encourage users to take early ownership of the systems we are designing. Due to its interactive nature and high visibility, JAD helps users become involved early in systems projects and treats their feedback seriously. Working through a JAD session eventually helps reflect user ideas in the final design.

A final benefit of participating in JAD sessions is the creative development of designs. The interactive character of JAD has a great deal in common with brainstorming techniques that generate new ideas and new combinations of ideas because of the dynamic and stimulating environment. Designs can evolve through facilitated interactions, rather than in relative isolation.

Potential Drawbacks of Using JAD

There are three drawbacks or pitfalls that you should also weigh when making a decision on whether to do traditional one-on-one interviews or to use Joint Application Design. The first drawback is that JAD requires the commitment of a large block of time from all of the 18–20 participants. Since JAD requires a two-to-four-day commitment, it is not possible to do any other activities concurrently or to time-shift any activities, as is typically done in one-on-one interviewing.

A second pitfall occurs if preparation for the JAD sessions is inadequate in any regard or if the follow-up report and documentation of specifications is incomplete. In these instances, resulting designs could be less than satisfactory. Many variables need to come together correctly for JAD to be successful. Conversely, many things can go wrong. The success of designs resulting from JAD sessions is less predictable than that achieved through standard interviews.

Finally, the necessary organizational skills and organizational culture may not be sufficiently developed to enable the concerted effort required to be productive in a JAD setting. In the end you will have to make the judgment about whether the organization is truly committed to, and prepared for, this approach.

SUMMARY

This chapter has covered the process of interviewing, which is one method systems analysts use for collecting data on information requirements. Systems analysts listen for goals, feelings, opinions, and informal procedures in interviews with organizational decision makers. They also sell the system during interviews. Interviews are preplanned question-and-answer dialogues between two people.

There are five steps to be taken in preplanning the interview:

1. Read background material.
2. Establish interviewing objectives.
3. Decide who to interview.
4. Prepare the interviewee.
5. Decide on question types and structure.

Questions are of two basic types: open-ended or closed. Open-ended questions leave open all response options for the interviewee. Closed questions limit the possible options for response. Probes or follow-up questions can be either open-ended or closed, but they ask the respondent for a more detailed reply.

Interviews can be structured in three basic ways: pyramid, funnel, or diamond structure. Pyramid structures begin with detailed, closed questions and broaden to more generalized questions. Funnel-shaped structures begin with open-ended, general questions and then funnel down to more specific, closed questions. Diamond structures combine the strengths of the other two structures, but they take longer to conduct. There are trade-offs involved when deciding how structured to make interview questions and question sequences.

Interviews should be documented with audio recordings or notes. After the interview the interviewer should write a report listing the main points provided, as well as opinions about what was said. It is extremely important to document the interview soon after it has taken place.

To cut both the time and cost of personal interviews, analysts may want to consider Joint Application Design (JAD) as an alternative. Using JAD, analysts can both analyze requirements and design a user interface with users in a group setting. Careful assessment of the particular organizational setting will help the analyst judge whether JAD is a suitable alternative.

"Well, I did warn you that things weren't always smooth here at MRE. By now you've met many of our key employees and you are starting to understand the 'lay of the land.' Who would have thought that some innocent decisions about hardware, like whether to buy a COMTEX or Shiroma would cause such hostility? Well, live and learn, I always say. At least now you'll know what you're up against when you have to start recommending hardware!

"It's funny that not all questions are created equal. I myself favor asking open-ended questions, but when I have to answer them, it is not always easy. Have you been taking the opportunity to view people's offices when you've been in there to do your interviews? You can learn a lot more by using a structured observation method such as STROBE."

HYPERCASE QUESTIONS

1. Using the interview questions posed in HyperCase, give five examples of open-ended questions and five examples of closed questions. Explain why your examples are correctly classified as either open-ended or closed question types.

2. List three probing questions that are part of the HyperCase interviews. In particular what did you learn by following up on the questions you asked Snowden Evans?

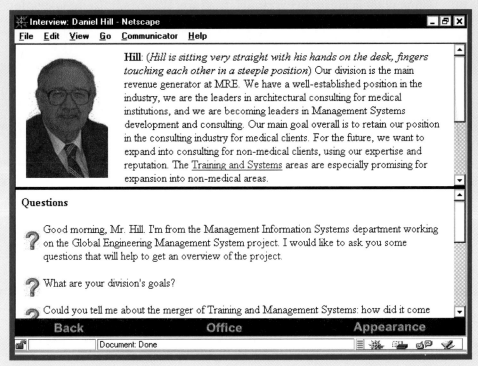

FIGURE 5.HC1
Pointing to a question in HyperCase will reveal an answer.

KEYWORDS AND PHRASES

interviewee opinions	leading questions
interviewee feelings	double-barreled questions
interviewee goals	pyramid structure
informal procedures	funnel structure
open-ended questions	diamond-shaped structure
closed questions	structured interviews
bipolar closed questions	unstructured interviews
probes	Joint Application Design (JAD)

REVIEW QUESTIONS

1. What kinds of information should be sought in interviews?
2. List the five steps in interview preparation.
3. Define what is meant by "open-ended" interview questions. Give eight benefits and five drawbacks of using them.
4. When are open-ended questions appropriate for use in interviewing?
5. Define what is meant by closed interview questions. Give six benefits and four drawbacks of using them.
6. When are closed questions appropriate for use in interviewing?
7. What is a probing question? What is the purpose of using a probing question in interviews?
8. What are leading questions? Why should they be avoided in interviews?
9. What are double-barreled questions? Why should they be avoided in interviews?
10. Define what is meant by pyramid structure. When is it useful to employ it in interviews?
11. Define what is meant by funnel structure. When is it useful to employ it in interviews?
12. Define what is meant by diamond-shaped structure. When is it useful to employ it in interviews?
13. What are the ten variables that become trade-offs between structured and unstructured interviews?
14. What are the four advantages and four disadvantages of making audio recordings of interviews?
15. What are the five advantages and four disadvantages of notetaking during interviews?
16. Why are you discouraged from using a laptop computer to record an interview which you are conducting?
17. Define the phrase "Joint Application Design."
18. List the situations that warrant use of JAD in place of personal organizational interviews.
19. List the potential benefits of using Joint Application Design.
20. List the three potential drawbacks of using JAD as an alternative to personal interviews.

PROBLEMS

1. While going over your interview schedule, you notice several questions that seem inadequate. Here are the original questions for the sales manager of Sampson Paper Products, whose company has expressed a desire to put some of its sales information on the Web and to al-

low managers to interactively comment on it in order to refine their sales projections. Rewrite the questions in a more appropriate manner.

   1. Your subordinates told me that you have a high level of computer anxiety. Is that true?
   2. I'm new to this. What did I leave out?
   3. What are your most used sources of information on sales figures and how frequently do you use them?
   4. Do you agree with other sales managers that putting some monthly sales on the Web and then doing trend analysis would be a major improvement?
   5. Isn't there a better way to project sales than the antiquated one you're using now?

2. As part of your systems analysis project to update the automated accounting functions for Chronos Corporation, a maker of digital watches, you will be interviewing Harry Straiter, the chief accountant. Write four to six interview objectives covering his use of information sources, information formats, decision-making frequency, desired qualities of information, and decision-making style.

   a. In a paragraph, write down how you will approach Harry to set up an interview.

   b. State which structure you will choose for this interview. Why?

   c. Harry has three subordinates who also use the system. Would you interview them also? Why or why not?

3. Here are five questions written by one of your systems analysis team members. Her interviewee is the local manager of LOWCO, an outlet of a national discount chain, who has asked you to work on a management information system to provide inventory information. Review these questions for your team member.

   1. When was the last time you thought seriously about your decision-making process?
   2. Who are the trouble makers in your store—I mean the ones who will show the most resistance to changes in the system that I have proposed?
   3. Are there any decisions you need more information about to make them?
   4. You don't have any major problems with the current inventory control system, do you?
   5. Tell me a little about the output you'd like to see.

   a. Rewrite each question to be more effective in eliciting information.

   b. Order your questions in either a pyramid-, funnel-, or diamond-shaped structure, and label the structure used.

   c. What guidelines can you give your team member for improving her interviewing questions for the future? Make a list of them.

4. Ever since you entered the door, your interviewee, Max Hugo, has been shuffling papers, looking at his watch, and lighting and snuffing out cigarettes. Based on what you know about interviews, you guess that Max is nervous because of the other work that he needs to do.

   a. In a paragraph, describe how you would deal with this situation so that the interview can be accomplished with Max's full attention. (Max cannot reschedule the interview for a different day.)

5. Write a series of six closed questions that cover the subject of decision-making style for the accountant described in problem 2.

6. Write a series of open-ended questions that cover the subject of decision-making style for the accountant described in problem 2.

7. Examine the interview structure presented in the sequencing of the following questions:
    1. How long have you been in this position?
    2. What are your key responsibilities?
    3. What reports do you receive?
    4. How do you view the goals of your department?
    5. How would you describe your decision-making process?
    6. How can that process best be supported?
    7. How frequently do you make those decisions?
    8. Who is consulted when you make a decision?
    9. What is the one decision you make that is essential to departmental functioning?

    a. What structure is being used? How can you tell?
    b. Restructure the interview by changing the sequence of the questions (you may omit some if necessary). Label the structure you have used.

8. This is the first interview report filed by one of your systems analysis team members:

    "In my opinion, the interview went very well. The subject allowed me to talk with him for an hour and a half. He told me the whole history of the business, which was very interesting. The subject also mentioned that things have not changed all that much since he has been with the firm, which is about 16 years. We are meeting again soon to finish the interview, since we did not have time to go into the questions I prepared."

    a. In two paragraphs, critique the interview report. Assume that you asked the team member to use the report form provided in Figure 5.12. What critical information is missing?
    b. What information is extraneous to the interview report?
    c. If what is reported actually occurred, what three suggestions do you have to help your teammate conduct a better interview next time?

GROUP PROJECTS

1. With your group members, role play a series of interviews with various end users at Maverick Transport (first introduced in the Chapter 4 Group Project). Each member of your group should choose one of the following roles: company president, information technology director, dispatcher, customer service agent, or truck driver. Those group members playing roles of Maverick Transport employees should attempt to briefly describe their job responsibilities, goals, and informational needs.

    Remaining group members should play the roles of systems analysts and devise interview questions for each employee. If there are enough people in your group, each analyst may be assigned to interview a different employee. Those playing the roles of systems analysts should work together to develop common questions that they will ask, as well as questions tailored to each individual employee. Be sure to include open-ended, closed, and probing questions in your interviews.

Maverick Transport is attempting to change from outdated and unreliable technology to more state-of-the-art, dependable technology. The company is seeking to move from dumb terminals attached to a mainframe because it wants to use PCs in some way and is also interested in investigating a satellite system for tracking freight and drivers. Additionally, the company is interested in pursuing ways to cut down on the immense storage requirements and difficult access of troublesome, handwritten, multipart forms that accompany each shipment.

2. Conduct all five interviews in a role-playing exercise. If there are more than ten people in your group, permit two or more analysts to ask questions.

3. Debrief from the interviews, using the forms provided in this chapter.

4. Formulate follow-up questions for second interviews, based on what you found out from the debriefing reports. Your group should produce a written list of follow-up questions for each employee interviewed.

5. With your group write a plan for a JAD session that takes the place of personal interviews. Include relevant participants, suggested setting, and so on.

SELECTED BIBLIOGRAPHY

Ackroyd, S., and J. A. Hughes. *Data Collecting in Context*, 2nd ed. New York: Longman, 1992.

Cash, C. J., and W. B. Stewart, Jr. *Interviewing Principles and Practices,* 4th ed. Dubuque, IA: Wm. C. Brown Company Publishers, 1986.

Deetz, S. *Transforming Communication, Transforming Business: Building Responsive and Responsible Workplaces.* Cresskill, NJ: Hampton Press, Inc., 1995.

Di Salvo, V. *Business and Professional Communication.* Columbus, OH: Charles E. Merrill Publishing Company, 1977.

Gane, C. *Rapid Systems Development.* New York: Rapid Systems Development, Inc., 1987.

Joint Application Design. GUIDE Publication GPP–147. Chicago: GUIDE International, 1986.

TELL ME MORE, I"LL LISTEN

"I've scheduled preliminary interviews with five key people. Since you've been so busy with Visible Analyst, I decided to do the first round of interviews myself," Anna tells Chip as they begin their morning meeting.

"That's fine with me," Chip says. "Just let me know when I can fill in. Who will you be talking to first? Dot?"

"No secret there, I guess," replies Anna. "She's critical to the success of the system. Her word is it when it comes to whether a project will fly or not."

"Who else?" asks Chip.

"I'll see who Dot refers me to, but I set up appointments with Mike Crowe, the maintenance expert; Cher Ware, the software specialist; and Paige Prynter, CPU's financial analyst."

"Don't forget Hy Perteks," says Chip.

"Right. The Information Center will be important to our project," says Anna. "Let me call and see when he's available."

After a brief phone conversation with Hy, Anna turns once again to Chip.

"He'll meet with me later today," Anna confirms.

"I can't wait to hear what they're thinking about the new system," says Chip. "Good luck."

INTERVIEWS WITH CPU STAFF MEMBERS

Interview One

Respondent: Dorothy (Dot) Matricks, manager, microcomputer systems
Interviewer: Anna Liszt
Location: Dorothy's office

Anna: *(Extending her hand as she enters Dorothy's office)* Hello, Dorothy. It's good to see you once again. I think we last saw each other when they had the reception for the new president.

Dot: *(Rising from her desk, shakes hands with Anna)* Please, call me Dot. And I remember that reception, too. It was fun. Please, have a seat *(she indicates a chair beside her desk)* while I call Pat to put a hold on my phone calls. I didn't know at the time we'd be working together. But *(she continues with a laugh)*, it seems sooner or later computer people find each other. I've heard through the grapevine that your group is contemplating helping us out of our quagmire here.

Anna: I'm not sure it's a "quagmire," but the administration has requested that the systems and programming group help you to manage your micros with a system of your own.

Dot: *(Sits back in her chair with a chuckle)* I couldn't be more delighted. That means that my efforts to get some help—or should I say my unabashed pleading—has not fallen on deaf ears. Tell me more.

Allen Schmidt,
Julie E. Kendall, and
Kenneth E. Kendall

Anna: I thought I'd keep this first interview short, about a half an hour to forty-five minutes *(glancing at her watch).* My overall objective is to find out about micro usage on campus currently, from your perspective. Later we can get into the system you use to manage the micros and its strengths and weaknesses.

Dot: It's easy enough to give an overview, since it's something I often communicate to people. Let me begin with a little history so you can understand where I'm coming from. We started getting involved with micros in the early Eighties. We thought we were very high-tech to be buying them as fast as they were produced.

Anna: Yes. Not many schools or even businesses had a plan for implementing microcomputer systems.

Dot: Don't be misled by the haze of history. We purchased some micros early, mostly for the accounting area. But we didn't have a plan, except that we reacted to demand. The beginning was slow, but once hardware and software became available, we grew explosively. Once a marketing professor saw what accounting was doing, he or she would say, "What's new for me? We don't want to deal with the mainframe unless we have to." And so we grew and grew. We now have about 1,620 micros with three or four pieces of equipment attached to each one. Do you believe there is a total of more than 6,000 tagged items in our inventory? By the end of next fall, 200 more micros will be added. You have probably noticed that we have a mix of brands. IBM is used primarily in the business courses, and Apple Macs are used in the art department. Science areas like to use both IBMs and Apples, it seems. Many of our computers are IBM compatibles.

Anna: *(Nodding as she absorbs Dot's response)* That's a lot for anyone to manage. But you seem to be up-to-date on what you have in inventory. What system are you using now to keep track of it all?

Dot: I've been here since the beginning, and I honestly believe we've done better than most, but still the database system we use is inadequate. Again, my analysis is that just like we outgrew our Apple IIs, we have outgrown our management system. But we are reluctant to fiddle with it too much.

Anna: Why?

Dot: Well, I guess it's because something is better than nothing, even if something is antiquated. We try to be resourceful. It all started in the late Eighties. I, and the few other people who were assigned to the micros (on a part-time basis, back then), began to realize that something had to be done to prevent chaos. People were asking us for things, and we couldn't lay our hands on them. At the same time, computers were breaking down, and we did not know who had the service contract on them, if they had ever been serviced, and so on. We sensed disaster in the making. From our old mainframe experience, we started trying to organize what we had in a logical way. We all agreed to get a system running with a little off-the-shelf database package (which was not user-friendly, may I be the first to point out). We had very much of a family atmosphere at the time.

Anna: What functions did the package perform?

Dot: It was very basic information, which is what we desperately needed at the time. It sounds simple now, but we took some time and we were thrilled to have inventory information, including the type of equipment, the manufacturer, initial cost, room number where equipment was located, serial number, and equipment purchase date. Even that took extensive updating.

Anna: Is it the same system you run today?

Dot: Yes and no. Same software, but we've been through three updates.

Anna: What other improvements were made?

Dot: After using the system for a couple of years, we knew what we wanted. We added fields to capture the memory size on each micro, and graphics boards were installed in the machines.

Anna: And is this the same system you are using now?

Dot: Yes. Yes it is. We can print a number of reports and some summary information. But don't get the wrong impression. The system as it stands is clearly inadequate. You won't get much argument on that point from anyone you interview. But we did what we could with what we had at the time. In fact, there still a few members of the original group here. I will admit that it's been interesting to watch the micros grow. It makes me feel like I had a hand in helping develop a very important area.

Anna: What do you see as the strengths of the current system?

Dot: Since I was in it from the start, I find it fairly easy to use. And it's flexible enough to produce a variety of reports. It's brought us quite far and it does provide the elementary information required to manage the micros.

Anna: Earlier you alluded to some limitations of the system. What are the specific weaknesses you were speaking about?

Dot: *(Reflecting before she speaks)* In a way they are not weaknesses of the system per se, but they are changes in the types of micros we are seeing that the system was not far-sighted enough to accommodate. For instance, the number of internal boards and disk drives has increased markedly. A few machines have modems, some have different graphics boards, some older EGA, a large number of VGA, and all the newer micros have SVGA graphics. Many have single hard drives, and some have only one hard drive. We will use a few of the older 5 1/4-inch disks, but most use 3 1/2. We have no information on file regarding the components, and we are asked many questions each week, such as "Where can I find a machine with SVGA graphics and a CD-ROM player?" Another problem is that we do not have a concise report of which peripherals are connected to the machines, so we do not have a handle on what type of keyboard, printer, mouse, or external zip drive unit each micro uses. Memory is also a mixed bag. Some machines have 4 megabytes, some have 8 meg, and some have 16 or more meg of memory installed. You can imagine what it is like to try and find the right memory to run a particular software package. Sometimes we run the software and run into problems.

Anna: How *do* you track what software is installed on which machine?

Dot: Well, unfortunately, we don't have a good grasp of that. We started to track it, but as I mentioned, the whole micro area is growing so fast.

We spend so much time putting out brush fires that we're losing the battle to keep track of the information we have.

Anna: Are there similar problems with maintaining the equipment?

Dot: You're getting the idea, now. We fix whatever we can as soon as possible. Some of the machines are shipped out on warranty. We don't even dream of preventive maintenance, even though we are agreed that it is important.

Anna: Really, I am interested in what you are dreaming about for the new system. What would you like it to accomplish?

Dot: That's easy for me to summarize. All of the weaknesses I've outlined should be addressed. I'd like it to have a dossier about each machine—its internal components, the peripherals attached to it. I would also like to have good cost and repair information maintained. As changes occur, we need to keep the files up-to-date.

Anna: Anything specifically related to software?

Dot: Software cross-referencing is a must.

Anna: One of the items I picked up on during our conversation today has been your dissatisfaction with the capability of the old system to keep pace with the micros' growth. How would any future plans affect the system we develop?

Dot: Certainly we will be adding significant numbers of machines every year. The requests for machines far exceed the budget for several years. We expect that new technology will be adding new components, such as optical disks, that must be added to the system. Also, the use of laptop and notebook micros that actually leave the premises with users will probably grow. Perhaps they will be checked out by individuals for teaching remote classes, research, curriculum development, and the like.

Anna: *(Glancing at her notes)* We've covered quite a bit, I think I am beginning to understand what the old system does and doesn't do, what you'd like to see in the new system, and what you project for growth in the coming years. Is there anything else that you think is important for me to know that I haven't asked?

Dot: It's an oversight of mine, but I should mention that we also have micros on our four satellite campuses in outlying areas. Those machines and all they entail need to be included in our system plans.

Anna: I know there are several people who can help with this project. Is there anyone in particular you would recommend that I talk to?

Dot: There are several people that you will want to seek out. They will be very useful to us. Mike Crowe is our maintenance expert. He's been here almost as long as I have. You will enjoy him very much. His counterpart in software is Cher Ware. She's easy to talk with. Don't forget to touch base with Paige Prynter. She's in charge of financial information about the micros. She'll have what you need in that area. And Hy Perteks runs the Information Center for us. Certainly you will want to see him before you're done.

Anna: Yes. In fact, they are already on my schedule. We must be thinking alike. As I summarize our interview for the systems team, I may have some follow-up questions for you.

Dot: I'm delighted to be a part of this. Call me anytime.

Anna: *(Standing up and extending her hand to Dot)* Thanks very much for your time. The information you provided gave me a solid start. I will be back in touch.

Dot: *(Shaking hands and standing)* Let me know how I can help. My door is always open.

Interview Two

Respondent: Mike Crowe, maintenance expert, microcomputers
Interviewer: Anna Liszt
Location: Mike's workroom, at a workbench

Anna: *(Entering his workroom and extending her hand)* Hello, Mike. I'm Anna from systems and programming. The administration asked my team to develop a system to keep track of maintenance costs, preventive maintenance, and other information about the micros. Dot said you'd be a good person to talk to.

Mike: *(Shakes hands heartily. Clears a spot for Anna to sit beside the workbench)* Hello Anna. What do you need to know?

Anna: I'd like to ask you some questions regarding the maintenance of the microcomputers.

Mike: *(Looks around a room strewn with open micros, cables, parts that defy description, tools, and general clutter)* As you can see, we're constantly working on the machines that have problems. Some of these are breakdowns, but a lot of the work is upgrading machines to include new capabilities. These things on the workbench are getting memory expansion; those over there are having graphics accelerator boards installed. Really sharp images, with high speed SVGA resolution. The micros stacked in boxes behind me are to be installed in Room 472. They'll be linked using Zipnet software and a Maxus XZ server with 32 meg of RAM. A T1 line is connected to the backbone and soon all the computer lab rooms will have really fast SLIP server access and Internet speed.

Anna: Tell me about your preventive maintenance program.

Mike: *(Laughs)* When we have time. We would like to periodically blow the dust off every machine, keyboard, and printer, and vacuum the CPUs. The disk drives should also be cleaned once in a while. Often we simply don't have the time to accomplish this work.

Anna: How many people are working on maintenance?

Mike: There's me, my assistant, and quite a few students who work part-time for me.

Anna: How do you know when to perform the periodic maintenance?

Mike: Well, we don't have any exact way to do that. Normally we go from room to room, as we have time. When a room is completed, we write it on a list. Let me show you the clipboard we use. We just keep it hanging on the wall. Since the students do a lot of the preventive maintenance, I'm not directly involved in each room. I spot-check their work. You know how kids are, though. Sometimes they forget to write which rooms they've completed, and I have to get after 'em. But I rely on them. They're good for the most part.

Anna: What aspects of maintenance would you like the new system to help you with?

Mike: I've seen some systems at other places, and they can get pretty fancy. I don't think I need anything that complicated. I would like to know which machines are still under warranty. That's a big one. Right now, if a machine breaks down I have to look through stacks of information to find out the warranty period and when we bought the thing.

Anna: *(Nodding as she makes a note)* What else would be useful?

Mike: I'd like to know which machines are lemons. Which are constantly breaking down, I mean. I'd take those right out of the high usage areas. Knowing how often we had to repair the machine would be useful. It would be great to have a list of machines showing which ones need preventive maintenance the most. This would probably cut down on the number sent in for repairs.

Anna: Do all of the machines have the same preventive maintenance interval?

Mike: No. *(Mike's portable pager sounds. In response, he goes to the phone and has a short conversation about a microcomputer problem.)* Now, where were we? Oh, yes. The interval between maintenance. There is different timing for each machine. It would be good to keep that information on file somewhere.

Anna: Is there anything else you would like to add that I haven't covered?

Mike: Let me say it again, loud and clear. We need warranty information. Also, it would be good to get a report saying which machine needs preventive maintenance and when. Putting it in order of room numbers where the machines are located would make it easy to find the things.

Anna: *(Standing and extending her hand to shake Mike's)* Thanks for your time, Mike. May I get back to you with any further questions and also have you review my interview summary?

Mike: *(Standing and shaking hands)* Sure. Just have the office page me and leave your number. If you build me a system like the one I just described, I'll put it to good use.

Interview Three

> Respondent: Cher Ware, software specialist, microcomputer systems
> Interviewer: Anna Liszt
> Location: Cher's office

Anna: *(Entering the open office and extending her hand to the woman perched on an old sofa to one side of the office)* How do you do? I'm Anna from systems and programming. Dot mentioned that you would be an important person to talk to about building a new system for managing the micros. I'd like to ask you some questions about the systems you have for managing software for the micros.

Cher: *(Gesturing to a spot on the sofa next to her and shaking hands with Anna)* Sure. I was expecting you. Dot told me all about you. She keeps us going. She is order itself. I'm happy to talk to you because I know that we need a system for managing our software. It's not like I haven't been trying to keep a grasp on all this, but we've had a fantastic explosion of software. It's growing like "The Thing that Ate Sacramento." I feel like we're living in a science fiction flick half the time. The software is clearly trying to gobble up our database capacity. Just to track it takes a lot.

Anna: *(Laughing)* Well, what are some of the basics about "The Thing," the software that's in use here at CPU?

Cher: Well, it started around the early part of the Eighties. Or was it 1985? I lose track. The Seventies were the best for me personally, but the millennium should be good too. What was your question?

Anna: How many software packages did you have in the Eighties?

Cher: Early on, there were only a few. Some simple packages. A word processor, a database, a spreadsheet. Boy, when you think of how things have changed!

Anna: Can you contrast that to the number of packages that are in use now?

Cher: A humongous variety now. Lots and lots of versions of each of them, too. You don't see plain vanilla packages anymore, either. There are several word processors, several database, spreadsheet, and graphics packages. Then we have software for the science and math programs. Mac packages for the art department. And they're pretty jazzy, too. Not to mention the grammar checkers for the English profs. And everybody wants Internet software—not only access to the Web like browsers and e-mail, but the kind you use to create Web pages and that cool animation stuff. You know, I don't actually know how many packages there are.

Anna: How does the current system work for managing software?

Cher: It's a simple database system that was developed years ago. We never expected to see the growth that we have. Almost since the beginning, our system hasn't been able to maintain all of the information that we need. Information is also missing. Let me say it better. Not all of the software packages have been captured by our system. Many times a professor gets software for class or research and forgets to tell us about it. I wish that I wasn't the last person on earth to know about nifty updates and new packages. If there was just one process for registering software with us that everyone had to follow, life would be rosier.

Anna: What process is followed when your office receives a new piece of software?

Cher: We inventory it, inform the professor that it has arrived, and key the information into the database. Then it is delivered to the lab or the prof that requested it.

Anna: What happens to the older version of the software, if there is one?

Cher: Chaos city. I mean we are talking nightmare time. Golden oldies should be deleted from the hard disks and scratched. But that's not the case. Often we have several versions of the same software in several different labs and campuses, even though we try not to let it happen. WonderWord is a good example. We have WonderWord 4.1, 5.0, and 5.1. The same is true of our DOS versions. But really, sometimes there's a good reason for having multiple versions, since not all of the equipment in all of the labs is upgraded to run new software.

Anna: Do site licenses add further complications?

Cher: You guessed it. Recently, we've been getting site licenses for some of the most commonly used software. Some of it is used on a LAN where there are many workstations and only one copy of the software. If there is no site license, then we need to know how many copies of a particular package we have and on which machines they're located.

Anna: How do you determine which machines or labs will have a new package installed?

Cher: We like to think we have that under control. The normal situation is to use the labs that are designated for that application. For example, DrAwsome is installed in Room 320, the art department's lab. It is an awesome package, by the way. Excelerator is installed in the information sciences lab. Some packages, like WonderWord, are installed in several labs. There are some exceptions to this, though. For instance, some of the scientific software now requires high-quality SVGA graphics and 8 MB of RAM. Typically, scientific packages would be installed in the science- and math-complex labs, but only the machines in the information sciences lab have the SVGA monitors and enough memory in them. So that's where the new scientific packages wind up.

Anna: Describe the problems you encounter when locating a machine for installation of new software.

Cher: Sometimes we have requirements for graphics and printers and don't really know which machines have the specific configuration needed. That kind of information is not maintained by either our system or the hardware system. Sometimes the machines don't have enough main memory, especially the older ones. Sometimes the hard disks are simply full. We usually investigate these cases, though. Lots of times students put their own games and stuff on machines. We take them off when it's noticed.

Anna: Explain what happens when you receive a request for the location of a particular software package.

Cher: We have a sorted listing of software by its name, which also contains the room number. We can't trust it completely, though, since it's often outdated and incomplete. Not all software is registered with our area, as I mentioned earlier. For example, last week a professor asked me where he could use the language "C++." We informed him of the labs where it was supposed to be located, and later he called to tell us that he found it close to his office, on machines that weren't supposed to have "C++."

Anna: Do you currently keep financial information pertaining to software?

Cher: Not on the same database. I know this is critical information that should be maintained, though. It would be extremely useful to know the total costs of each software package and category, such as word processors. It would also be great to have total cost available for an upgrade. The upgrades seem to happen so often that we can hardly install all of the packages and provide training before a new release is announced.

Anna: From what you've said today, I can see that you have an incredibly complex operation. You've been very helpful explaining how the software is managed and giving me ideas about what you would like to see the new system do. Is there anything that we have not covered that you would like to mention?

Cher: Well, talking to you reminded me of a lot of things I hadn't thought about for a while. I hope the new system can help out, especially in getting all software registered with our office. We'd also like to be able to tie into the hardware system to determine which machines will actually run the software we have.

Anna: *(Rises and extends her hand to shake Cher's)* I will be back in touch with you as the project continues. We should be able to help out. I'll ask you to review an interview summary in a few days. Thanks very much for your time.

Cher: *(Shaking hands and rising as Anna leaves)* My pleasure. We have a lot of fun here, even though it's crazy. I'm happy to help any way I can.

Interview Four

Respondent: Paige Prynter, financial analyst
Interviewer: Anna Liszt
Location: Paige's office

Anna: *(Knocking on Paige's door. As Paige opens the door she extends her hand to shake Paige's.)* Hello Ms. Prynter. I'm Anna Liszt from systems and programming.

Paige: *(Shaking hands, then showing Anna to a chair opposite her desk)* I've been expecting you. Please have a seat. Dot told me you would be contacting me.

Anna: The administration has asked my group to help build a system to manage the microcomputers, and I am doing a series of interviews with key people who will use the information provided by the system.

Paige: The system is sorely needed. What do you need to know from me?

Anna: I'd like to ask you some questions about the financial needs regarding microcomputers used at CPU. More specifically, what types of reports are you currently receiving?

Paige: We get a report listing the cost of all the microcomputers and a total. That is about the extent of our financial information right now.

Anna: Would it be useful to have subtotals added to the reports?

Paige: Yes. That would be extremely useful for costs on each type of machine.

Anna: Do you receive financial information on software?

Paige: You've touched on an issue that is controversial these days. We receive absolutely no computerized information on software. And, of course, the software has just snowballed. We have no idea of the total amount invested. What we scrape by with are outdated requisitions for software. We desperately need more information about software purchases in order to formulate better controls and put together reasonable budgets. We need subtotals by product and by category of software, such as word processing.

Anna: How do site licenses fit into the picture?

Paige: We would like to have the figure for the site license as a total and then not have to calculate the amount for each copy.

Anna: Your current needs are clearly pressing. But is there anything you would add to the system for the future?

Paige: Yes. We would like to input the cost of an upgrade to a particular software package and have the computer tell us how much it would cost for all of the currently installed software. We also need subtotals by product for both hardware and software, along with totals. It would also be useful to have totals for each of the satellite campuses.

Anna: You've answered all of the questions I have right now. Is there anything you would like to add?

Paige: Yes. We need to take an accurate inventory of the hardware periodically. Machines have an annoying habit of moving from one room to another over the course of a semester. But we need to know what we have and precisely where it is. You can imagine how time-consuming the inventory process is. Automating it would be highly desirable.

Anna: May I get back to you with a summary of our interview and also any further questions I might have?

Paige: Certainly. Just set up an appointment ahead of time again, and I will be glad to speak with you.

Anna: *(Rising and extending her hand to shake Paige's)* Thank you very much for your time. Your input will be valuable in helping to put together the new system.

Paige: *(Shaking Anna's hand and rising from her desk)* I hope that the new system will provide us with the vital information we need. I don't like to complain, but it's been a long time in coming. Please close the door behind you.

Interview Five

Respondent: Hy Perteks, director, Information Center
Interviewer: Anna Liszt
Location: Hy's office in the Information Center

Anna: *(Walking past several students and faculty working on micros to get to Hy's open door; pausing at the entrance)* Hello, Hy. I'm Anna.

Hy: *(Getting up from a crowded desk to welcome her and extending his hand to shake Anna's)* I remember you. We were at that conference together about two years ago. Please come in and pull up a chair. I got your message, and Dot said you'd be by, too.

Anna: *(Sitting down in a chair by the side of Hy's desk)* She probably told you that the administration has asked my group to help with designing a system to manage the micros. I've been doing a series of interviews with key people, and it's time for me to find out about the needs you are experiencing here in the Information Center.

Hy: What we need so badly I can taste it is a centralized bank of information on the micros and the software we have.

Anna: Who is served by the Information Center?

Hy: Our clients come from every level of the university. We serve administrators, both on the managerial and support staff levels, and we also serve the needs of faculty for teaching and research. Our clients are pretty evenly split between those groups, with maybe a little lean toward the faculty.

Anna: What services do you provide them?

Hy: We do a lot of training. A lot. Every so often we offer classes in popular software packages. You've probably gotten some of our flyers announcing those classes. We answer (or try to answer) tons of technical questions as well. They usually are specific as to how to perform advanced tasks with the software. A third category of service we perform is helping users to adapt software to their particular application. We also help in figuring out which software would be most effective in solving their problems.

Anna: It seems that the staff here has to be fairly well-versed in many different areas. Do you have an expert in each software package?

Hy: No, although I personally am familiar with the basics of all the packages. I receive training in the operation of the software and work on small projects just to familiarize myself with new programs. When the nitty-gritty detailed technical questions arise, I dive into the manuals and other reference materials we have here in the IC library. But I'm not alone. I often call on specialists who are on the faculty to help with particularly thorny problems. At times I even call software vendors for help.

Anna: How often do you add new software packages?

Hy: More often than you would believe. We do upgrades, as well as altogether new software. For example, we recently purchased a math word processor and are scheduling classes for training. We are being absolutely deluged with requests from the math and science faculty. They are so tickled that the package is here and running. There's never a dull moment. That's why I love the job.

Anna: What are some of the problems you are experiencing that might be dealt with more effectively via an improved microcomputer system?

Hy: I know there's a lot that can be done that we haven't, just because no one has taken the time. For one, we need to know what version of software a person is using. You wouldn't believe how critical this is in determining the solution to a technical question, such as how to create a macro or transfer files from one package to another. Lots of times the users just aren't sure of what version they're using. And we'd also like to know the phone numbers of software providers so we can quickly phone for assistance. Sometimes it's difficult to find an expert around the university for a particular program. I meet a lot of interesting people searching for help, though.

Anna: Other people have mentioned the need to know which software is located on which machine in which room. Is this important to you?

Hy: You bet. We get requests for training, or someone wants to use software that isn't in the Information Center. If it's an oddball package, we don't know where it's located without lots of calling around.

Anna: You've told me a good deal in a short time. Is there anything else that you'd like to add that we haven't covered?

Hy: I know I talk a lot. But I mean well. Really, I think we've covered all the bases. Let me just add that I would like to have a sense of how many people would be interested in training on software that we have now. I'd also like to know which software people want us to purchase. We can't get everything, but if they don't ask, I'll never know. That's a tall order, though. I'm not sure how to get that without surveying the entire university.

Anna: *(Rising and extending her hand to shake Hy's)* We'll try to include as much of what you've said as we can. Thanks for your time. May I get back to you with follow-up questions if they are needed?

Hy: *(Shaking her hand and rising to accompany her to the door)* No problem. Service is what we're here for. If you end up using a micro package as part of the solution, I can get involved even more.

Exercises

E-1. Assume that Chip conducted all of the initial interviews rather than Anna. In small groups, role-play the part of Chip and the interviewees. Assign students to analyze and comment on the differences in the results.

E-2. Analyze the five interviews. In a paragraph, discuss what type of structure each interview had.

E-3. List each interview, 1–5, and then write a paragraph for each one, discussing ways that Anna might improve on her interviews for next time.

E-4. Analyze the questions used in the five interviews. In a paragraph, discuss the question types used and whether they were appropriate for getting needed information.

6
USING QUESTIONNAIRES

KINDS OF INFORMATION SOUGHT

Questionnaires are an information-gathering technique that allows systems analysts to study attitudes, beliefs, behaviors, and characteristics of several key people in the organization who may be affected by the current and proposed systems, as shown in Figure 6.1. Attitudes are what people in the organization say they want (in a new system, for instance); beliefs are what people think is actually true; behavior is what organizational members do; and characteristics are properties of people or things.

Responses gained through questionnaires (also called surveys) using closed questions can be quantified. Responses to questionnaires using open-ended questions are analyzed and interpreted in other ways. Answers to questions on attitudes and beliefs are notably sensitive to the wording chosen by the systems analyst.

Through the use of questionnaires, the analyst may be seeking to quantify what was found in interviews. Additionally, questionnaires may be used to determine how widespread or limited a sentiment expressed in an interview really is. Conversely, questionnaires can be used to survey a large sample of system users in order to sense problems or raise important issues before interviews are scheduled.

Throughout this chapter, we will compare and contrast questionnaires with interviews, which were covered in Chapter 5. There are many similarities between the two techniques, and perhaps the ideal would be to use them in conjunction with each other, either following up unclear questionnaire responses with an interview or designing the questionnaire based on what is discovered in the interview. However, each technique has its own specific functions, and it is not always necessary or desirable to use both.

PLANNING FOR THE USE OF QUESTIONNAIRES

At first glance questionnaires may seem to be a quick way to gather massive amounts of data about how users assess the current system, about what problems they are experiencing with their work, and about what people expect

149

FIGURE 6.1
Kinds of information sought
when using questionnaires.

from a new or modified system. While it is true that you can gather lots of information through questionnaires without spending time in face-to-face interviews, developing a useful questionnaire takes extensive planning time in its own right.

You must first decide what you are attempting to gain through using a survey. For instance, if you want to know what percentage of users prefer a help desk as a means of learning about new software packages, then a questionnaire might be the right technique. If you want to do an in-depth analysis of a manager's decision-making process, then an interview is a better choice.

Here are some guidelines to help you decide whether use of questionnaires is appropriate. Consider using questionnaires if:

1. The people you need to question are widely dispersed (different branches of the same corporation).
2. A large number of people are involved in the systems project, and it is meaningful to know what proportion of a given group (for example, management) approves or disapproves of a particular feature of the proposed system.
3. You are doing an exploratory study and want to gauge overall opinion before the systems project is given any specific direction.
4. You wish to be certain that any problems with the current system are identified and addressed in follow-up interviews.

Once you have determined that you have good cause to use a questionnaire and have pinpointed the objectives to be fulfilled through its use, you can begin formulating questions.

Writing Questions

The biggest difference between the questions used for most interviews and those used on questionnaires is that interviewing permits interaction between the questions and their meanings. In an interview the analyst has an opportunity to refine a question, define a muddy term, change the course of questioning, respond to a puzzled look, and generally control the context.

Little of this is possible on a questionnaire. What this means for the analyst is that questions must be transparently clear, the flow of the questionnaire cogent, the respondent's questions anticipated, and the administration of the questionnaire planned in detail. (A respondent is the person who responds to or answers the questionnaire.)

The basic question types used on the questionnaire are open-ended and closed, as discussed for interviewing. Due to the constraints placed on questionnaires, some additional discussion of question types is warranted.

OPEN-ENDED QUESTIONS. Recall that open-ended questions (or statements) are those that leave all possible response options open to the respondent. For example, open-ended questions on a questionnaire might read, "Describe any problems you are currently experiencing with output reports," or "In your opinion, how helpful are the user manuals for the current system's accounting package?"

When you write open-ended questions for a questionnaire, anticipate what kind of response you will get. It is important that responses you receive are capable of correct interpretation. Otherwise, many resources will have been wasted in the development, administration, and interpretation of a useless questionnaire.

For instance, if you ask a question such as "How do you feel about the system?" the responses are apt to be too broad for accurate interpretation or comparison. So even when you write an open-ended question, it must be narrow enough to guide respondents to answer in a specific way. (Examples of open-ended questions can be found in Figure 6.2.)

For instance, if you really want to gather feelings toward the current system, you might couch your questions in the context of satisfaction versus dissatisfaction with the system. Furthermore, you might suggest some system features to prompt respondents in recalling which features are of interest.

Open-ended questions are particularly well-suited to situations in which you want to get at organizational members' opinions about some aspect of the system, whether product or process. In such cases you will want to use open-ended questions when it is impossible to list effectively all of the possible responses to the question.

Additionally, open-ended questions are useful in exploratory situations. These occur when the systems analyst is not able (because of diversity of opinion or far-flung employees) to determine precisely what problems plague the current system. Responses to the open-ended questions will then be used to focus on cited problems more narrowly, via interviews with a handful of key decision makers.

CLOSED QUESTIONS. Recall that closed questions (or statements) are those that limit or close the response options available to the respondent. For example, in Figure 6.3 the statement in question 23 ("Below are the six software packages currently available in the Information Center. Please check the package you personally use most frequently") is closed. Notice that respondents are not asked *why* the package is preferred; nor are they asked to select more than one, even if that is a more representative response.

Closed questions should be used when the systems analyst is able to list effectively all of the possible responses to the question and when all the listed responses are mutually exclusive, so that choosing one precludes choosing any of the others.

FIGURE 6.2
Open-ended questions used for questionnaires.

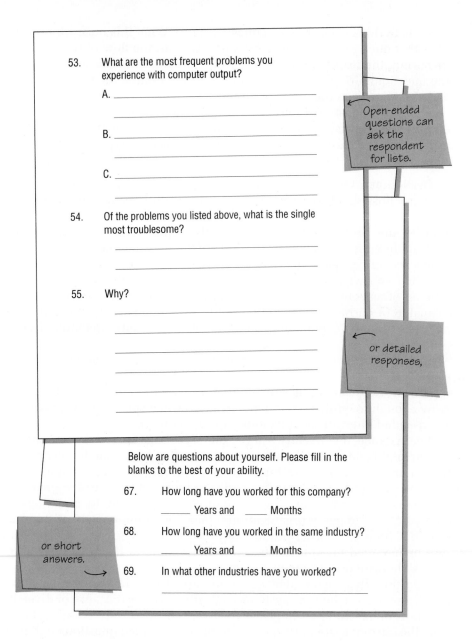

53. What are the most frequent problems you experience with computer output?

A. _____

_____

B. _____

_____

C. _____

Open-ended questions can ask the respondent for lists.

54. Of the problems you listed above, what is the single most troublesome?

_____

_____

55. Why?

_____

_____

_____

_____

_____

_____

or detailed responses,

Below are questions about yourself. Please fill in the blanks to the best of your ability.

67. How long have you worked for this company?

_____ Years and _____ Months

68. How long have you worked in the same industry?

_____ Years and _____ Months

or short answers.

69. In what other industries have you worked?

_____

Use closed questions when you want to survey a large sample of people. The reason for this becomes obvious when you start imagining how the data you are collecting will look. If you use only open-ended questions for hundreds of people, correct analysis and interpretation of their responses becomes impossible without the aid of a computerized content analysis program.

There are trade-offs involved in choosing either open-ended or closed questions for use on questionnaires. Figure 6.4 summarizes these trade-offs. Notice that responses to open-ended questions can help analysts gain rich, exploratory insights, as well as breadth and depth on a topic. While open-ended questions can be written easily, responses to them are difficult and time-consuming to analyze.

When we refer to the writing of closed questions with either ordered or unordered answers, we often refer to the process as scaling. The use of scales in surveys is discussed in detail in a later section.

FIGURE 6.3
Closed questions on questionnaires can help ensure
responses.

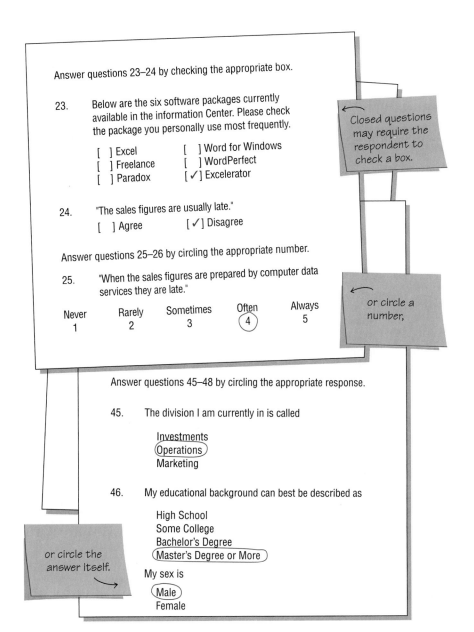

Answer questions 23–24 by checking the appropriate box.

23. Below are the six software packages currently
     available in the information Center. Please check
     the package you personally use most frequently.

     [ ] Excel   [ ] Word for Windows
     [ ] Freelance   [ ] WordPerfect
     [ ] Paradox   [✓] Excelerator

24. "The sales figures are usually late."
     [ ] Agree   [✓] Disagree

Answer questions 25–26 by circling the appropriate number.

25. "When the sales figures are prepared by computer data
     services they are late."

     Never   Rarely   Sometimes   Often   Always
       1   2   3   (4)   5

Closed questions may require the respondent to check a box.

or circle a number,

Answer questions 45–48 by circling the appropriate response.

45. The division I am currently in is called

     Investments
     (Operations)
     Marketing

46. My educational background can best be described as

     High School
     Some College
     Bachelor's Degree
     (Master's Degree or More)

My sex is
     (Male)
     Female

or circle the answer itself.

CHOICE OF WORDS. Just as with interviews, the language of questionnaires is an extremely important aspect of their effectiveness. Even if the
systems analyst has a standard set of questions concerning system development, it is wise to write them to reflect the business's own terminology.

Respondents appreciate the efforts of someone who bothers to write a
questionnaire reflecting their own language usage. For instance, if the business uses the term *supervisors* instead of *managers,* or *units* rather than *departments,* incorporating the preferred terms into the questionnaire helps respondents relate to the meaning of the questions. Responses will be easier to
interpret accurately, and respondents will be more enthusiastic overall.

In order to double-check whether language used on the questionnaire
is that of the respondents, try some sample questions on a pilot group. Ask
them to pay particular attention to the appropriateness of the wording and to
change any words that do not ring true.

Open-ended		Closed
Slow	Speed of Completion	Fast
High	Exploratory Nature	Low
High	Breadth and Depth	Low
Easy	Ease of Preparation	Difficult
Difficult	Ease of Analysis	Easy

Here are some guidelines to use when choosing language for your questionnaire:

1. Use the language of respondents whenever possible. Keep wording simple.
2. Work at being specific rather than vague in wording. However, avoid overly specific questions as well.
3. Keep questions short.
4. Do not patronize respondents by talking down to them through low-level language choices.
5. Avoid bias in wording. This also means avoiding objectionable questions.
6. Target questions to the right respondents (that is, those who are capable of responding). Don't assume too much knowledge.
7. Ensure that questions are technically accurate before including them.
8. Use software to check whether the reading level is appropriate for the respondents.

USING SCALES IN QUESTIONNAIRES

Scaling is the process of assigning numbers or other symbols to an attribute or characteristic for the purpose of measuring that attribute or characteristic. Scales are often arbitrary and may not be unique. For example, temperature is measured in a number of ways; the two most common are the Fahrenheit scale (where water freezes at 32 degrees and boils at 212 degrees) and the Celsius scale (where freezing occurs at 0 degrees and boiling at 100 degrees).

Scaling Fundamentals

REASONS FOR SCALING. The systems analyst may want to design scales either (1) to measure the attitudes or characteristics of the people answering the questionnaire or (2) to have the respondents judge the subjects of the questionnaire. Let's look at how each of these types of scales can be applied. For our purposes each will use the same set of questions about a number of sample monthly statement printouts for the Never Fail Bank of America.

If the analyst wants to measure attitudes or characteristics of the respondents, the responses can be combined or grouped to reflect that information. A number of people might fall into a group that doesn't want to change the monthly printouts at any cost, another group may want cleaner output, while a third group might want to add features such as sorting checks by number and category. Here we are trying to measure the differences among respondents, and it doesn't matter how each one of the sample printouts was rated. Other examples of measuring characteristics or attitudes will be discussed later in this chapter.

If the systems analyst was interested in how each of the sample monthly statements fared, the respondents would serve as judges. In this case, it wouldn't matter how much respondents differ in their attitudes.

MEASUREMENT. There are four different forms of measurement scales, each form offering different degrees of accuracy. The form of measurement also dictates how to analyze the data collected. The four forms of measurement are:

1. Nominal
2. Ordinal
3. Interval
4. Ratio

Nominal scales are used to classify things. A question such as:

> What type of program do you use the most?
>
> 1 = A WORD PROCESSOR
>
> 2 = A SPREADSHEET
>
> 3 = A DATABASE
>
> 4 = A GRAPHING PROGRAM

uses a nominal scale. Obviously, nominal scales are the weakest of the forms of measurement. Generally, all the analyst can do with them is obtain totals for each classification.

Ordinal scales, like nominal scales, allow classification. The difference, however, is that the ordinal scale also implies rank ordering. In this example, a systems analyst asks an end user to circle one of the numbers:

> The support staff of the Technical Support Group is:
>
> 1. EXTREMELY HELPFUL
>
> 2. VERY HELPFUL
>
> 3. MODERATELY HELPFUL
>
> 4. NOT VERY HELPFUL
>
> 5. NOT HELPFUL AT ALL

Ordinal scales are useful because one class is greater or less than another class. On the other hand, no assumption can be made that the difference between choices 1 and 2 is the same as the difference between choices 3 and 4.

Interval scales possess the characteristic that the intervals between each of the numbers are equal. Due to this characteristic, mathematical operations can be performed on the questionnaire data, resulting in a more complete analysis. Examples of interval scales are the Fahrenheit and Celsius scales, which measure temperature.

The foregoing example of the information center is definitely not that of an interval scale, but by anchoring the scale on either end, the analyst *may* want to make the assumption that the respondent perceives the intervals to be equal:

How useful is the support given by the Technical Support Group?

NOT USEFUL   *EXTREMELY*
AT ALL   *USEFUL*
1   2   3   4   5

If the systems analyst makes this assumption, more quantitative analysis is possible.

Ratio scales are similar to interval scales insofar as the intervals between numbers are assumed to be equal. Ratio scales, however, have an absolute zero. An example of a ratio scale is length as measured by a ruler. Another example is the following:

Approximately how many hours do you spend on the computer daily?

0   2   4   6   8

Ratio scales will be used less often by the systems analyst.

As a guideline, a systems analyst should use:

1. A ratio scale when the intervals are equal and there is an absolute zero.
2. An interval scale when it can be assumed that the intervals are equal but that there is no absolute zero.
3. An ordinal scale when it is impossible to assume that the intervals are equal but when the classes can be ranked.
4. A nominal scale if the systems analyst wants to classify things but if they cannot be ranked.

VALIDITY AND RELIABILITY. There are two measures of performance in constructing scales: validity and reliability. The systems analyst should be aware of these concerns.

Validity is the degree to which the question measures what the analyst intends to measure. For example, if the purpose of the questionnaire is to determine whether the organization is ready for a major change in computer operations, do the questions measure this?

Reliability measures consistency. If the questionnaire was administered once and then again under the same conditions and if the same results were obtained both times, the instrument is said to have external consistency. If the questionnaire contains subparts and these parts have equivalent results, the instrument is said to have internal consistency. Both external and internal consistency are important.

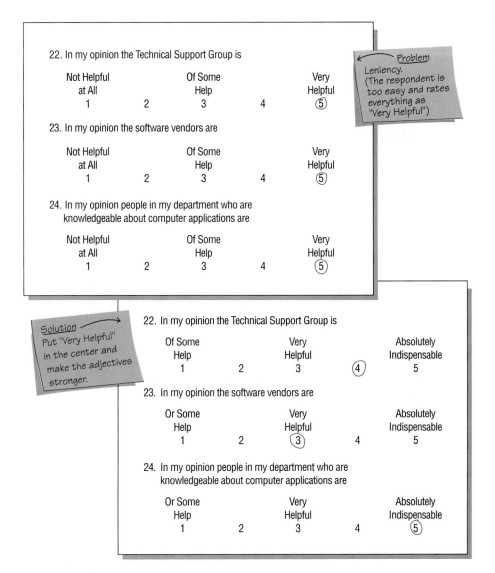

FIGURE 6.5
Correcting the problem of respondent's leniency.

Constructing Scales

The actual construction of scales is a serious task. Careless construction of scales can result in one of the following problems:

1. Leniency
2. Central tendency
3. Halo effect

Leniency is a problem caused by respondents who are easy raters. A systems analyst can avoid the problem of leniency by moving the "average" category to the left (or right) of center, as shown in Figure 6.5.

Central tendency is a problem that occurs when respondents rate everything as average. The analyst can improve the scale either (1) by making the differences smaller at the two ends, (2) by adjusting the strength of the descriptors, or (3) by creating a scale with more points. An example of correcting for central tendency can be found in Figure 6.6.

FIGURE 6.6
Correcting the problem of respondent's central tendency.

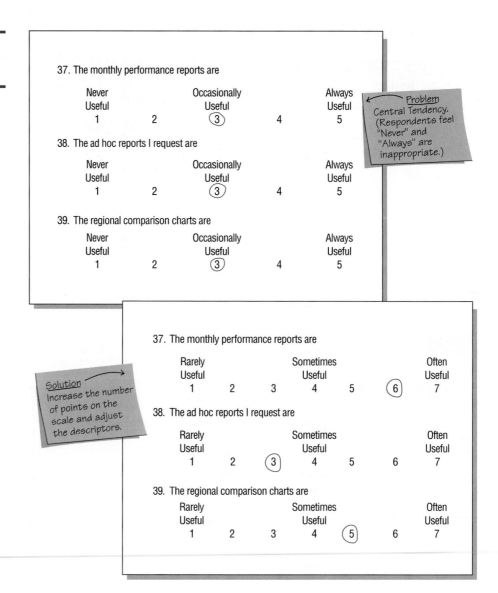

The halo effect is a problem that arises when the impression formed in one question carries into the next question. For example, if you are rating an employee about whom you have a very favorable impression, you may give a high rating in every category or trait, regardless of whether or not it is a strong point of the employee's. The solution is to place one trait and several employees on each page, rather than one employee and several traits on a page. An example of correcting for the halo effect can be found in Figure 6.7.

DESIGNING AND ADMINISTERING THE QUESTIONNAIRE

Designing the Questionnaire

Many of the same principles that are relevant to the design of forms for data input (as covered in Chapter 16) are important here as well. Although the intent of the questionnaire is to gather information on attitudes, beliefs, behavior, and characteristics whose impact may substantially alter users'

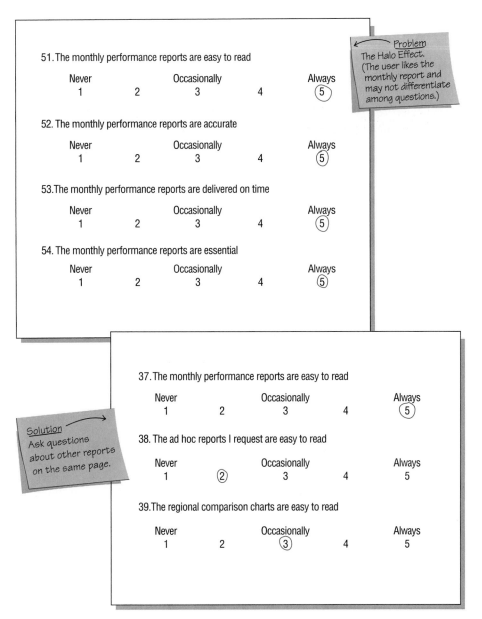

FIGURE 6.7
Correcting the problem of respondent's answering everything favorably due to a halo effect.

work, respondents are not always motivated to respond. Remember that organizational members as a whole tend to receive too many surveys, which are often ill-conceived and trivial.

A well-designed, relevant questionnaire can help overcome some of this resistance to respond. This section discusses the stylistic considerations that can help improve the response rate to questionnaires. It also presents the guidelines for ordering the content for the best results.

QUESTIONNAIRE FORMAT

Allow ample white space. The most important consideration in designing the questionnaire format is to allow enough white space so that the respondent is drawn into the form. White space refers to blank space surrounding printed matter on a page. A questionnaire that is squeezed together without

The Unbearable Questionnaire

"I'm going to go into a depression or at least a slump if someone doesn't figure this out soon," say Penny Stox, office manager for Carbon, Carbon & Rippy, a large brokerage firm. Penny is sitting across a conference table from you and two of her most productive account executives, By Lowe and Sal Hy. All of you are mulling over the responses to a questionnaire that has been distributed among the firm's account executives, which is shown in Figure 6.C1.

"We need a crystal ball to understand these," By and Sal call out together.

"Maybe this reflects some sort of optimistic cycle, or something," Penny says as she reads more of the responses. "Who designed this gem, anyway?"

"Rich Kleintz," By and Sal call out in unison.

"Well, as you can see, it's not telling us anything," Penny exclaims.

Penny and her staff are dissatisfied with the responses they have received on the unbearable questionnaire, and they feel that the responses are unrealistic reflections of the amount of information account executives want. In a paragraph state why this is occurring. On a separate sheet, change the scaling of the questions in order to avoid these problems.

Circle the appropriate number for each source of information described.

1. Industry Reports

Less		About The Same		More
1	2	3	4	(5)

2. Trend Analysis

Less		About The Same		More
1	2	3	4	(5)

2. Computer Generated Graphs

Less		About The Same		More
1	2	3	4	(5)

4. Investment Advisory Services

Less		About The Same		More
1	2	3	4	(5)

We need to change this questionnaire -Penny

5. Point and Figure Charts

Less		About The Same		More
1	2	3	4	(5)

6. Computerized Portfolio Analysis

Less		About The Same		More
1	2	3	4	(5)

7. Hot Tips

Less		About The Same		More
1	2	3	4	(5)

FIGURE 6.C1
Questionnaire developed for the brokerage firm of Carbon, Carbon, & Rippy by Rich Kleintz.

benefit of adequate white space is not as likely to be completed, even though it will take less paper to print. To further increase the response rate, use only white or off-white paper for questionnaires.

Allow adequate space for responses. Above and beyond allowing white space to set off the printed material, allow adequate space for responses as well. If you expect respondents to write a paragraph in response to an open-ended question, you must leave three to five blank lines for them to do so.

Ask respondents to circle their answers. Another good practice for capturing a response correctly is to request that respondents circle their answers (or numbers if you are employing a scale). Figure 6.8 shows what can happen if respondents aren't encouraged to circle numbers. In this example the analyst would have a difficult time trying to determine if the respondent meant to choose a 3 or 4.

Sometimes it is permissible to have respondents check a box [ ] created by a pair of brackets or check a space ( ) created with a pair of parentheses. However, care must be taken to allow enough space for people who make large checkmarks. Data tabulation and analysis become difficult if respondents inadvertently check through several boxes.

Use objectives to help determine format. Before you design the questionnaire, you need to articulate your objectives. For instance, if your objective is to poll as many organizational members as possible concerning an identified list of problems in the current system, it is probably best to use a response form that is machine readable. This will affect how you design the questionnaire and what kinds of instructions you will include.

Alternatively, if you desire written responses, you need to calculate the amount of space that will be needed for the length of response you want, and then you will have to be sure to include that space on the form or on a separate answer sheet. You might need to plan for both numerical and written responses.

You may also wish to assign someone other than the respondents to enter the responses on the questionnaire. Although doing so presents a greater possibility of errors in interpretation, it does prevent the kind of mechanical

In this section, please circle the number that best suggests your opinion about each topic. Remember to circle only ONE number for each question.

10. Monthly reports of sales figures for our division reach me in time to make decisions

Never	Seldom	Sometimes	Usually	Always
1	2	3	4	5

11. I use the display screen to view monthly sales figures

Never	Seldom	Sometimes	Usually	Always
1	2	3	4	5

12. Monthly sales reports are valuable to me in making decisions

Never	Seldom	Sometimes	Usually	Always
1	2	3	4	5

13. There are several errors in the monthly reports that must be corrected before they are useful

Never	Seldom	Sometimes	Usually	Always
1	2	3	4	5

14. I think the monthly sales reports are irrelevant to most of those who receive them

Never	Seldom	Sometimes	Usually	Always
1	2	3	4	5

data-entry errors that inexperienced respondents might make. Additionally, keep in mind that questionnaire sheets on which respondents can write directly are often easier for them to complete correctly than are machine-readable response forms.

Be consistent in style. Organize the questionnaire consistently throughout. Put instructions in the same place in relation to question subsections, so respondents always know where to find instructions.

Be consistent, as shown in Figure 6.9. If you use shaded boxes, use them in the same way from question to question. Following this format consistently allows respondents to get through the questionnaire quickly and reduces the chance of error.

Another major part of designing the questionnaire is deciding the order in which questions should appear. You will often need the input of a pilot group to help decide the most appropriate question order.

ORDER OF QUESTIONS. There is not one best way to order questions on the questionnaire. Once again, as you order questions, you must think about your objectives in using the questionnaire and then determine the function of each question in helping you to achieve your objectives. It is also important to see the questionnaire through the respondent's eyes. If you are without the help of a pilot group, always ask yourself how respondents will feel about the order and placement of particular questions, as well as whether this is indeed how you want them to react.

Questions of importance to respondents go first. The first questions should deal with subjects that respondents view as being important. This approach makes for an intriguing start to the questionnaire, and it is a technique to get people quickly involved. Respondents should feel that by answering each question and completing the form, they can cause a change or have some impact. For example, if organizational members are keen on rating potential software packages for the proposed system, begin with questions on this subject.

This technique is quite different from the typical novice's approach, which is to begin by asking for demographic information such as job title, years with the company, number of subordinates, male or female, and years in school. Some people will find this style boringly similar to other forms they routinely fill out, whereas others may actually find it threatening, especially if you stressed confidentiality earlier but are now requesting data that will clearly allow identification of the respondent.

Cluster items of similar content together. When you build a frame of reference for respondents, take advantage of it by placing questions related to each other close together on the questionnaire. For example, all questions dealing with end-user computing might be grouped together in one subheaded section of the questionnaire.

Some researchers have suggested that data are cleaner if questions appear randomly; however, this approach is not recommended here. Randomization in this case merely tries the patience of respondents who are likely to prefer being able to see for themselves that questionnaire construction is logical.

Employ respondents' associational tendencies. This consideration is similar to the guideline for clustering questions on similar topics. However, it goes even further by reminding the analyst to anticipate the kinds of associations that respondents make and then to use these associations in ordering questions.

For instance, if you ask, "How many subordinates do you have?" you will probably want to continue in that vein and ask about other formal organizational relationships as well. Furthermore, the respondent may associate the formal organizational structure with the informal. If that is the case, it is appropriate to include questions about the informal relationships in the same section of the questionnaire. Figure 6.10 shows an associational ordering of questions.

Bring up less controversial items first. In your preliminary assessment of what is happening in the business, you will have run into some issues that are, for one reason or another, divisive to particular groups. If you be-

FIGURE 6.10
Using an associational ordering of questions to enable
respondents to think about
unrelated subjects.

Below are questions about data entry procedures. Please answer the questions in the space provided.

21. List the methods you feel are appropriate for correcting erroneous entries.

22. List the methods that currently are in use to prevent data entry errors.

23. Which of the methods you listed are effective? Why?

24. Which of the methods you listed are ineffective? Why?

25. What controls would you like to see added to improve the quality of data entry?

lieve that those issues still must be examined, try to put less controversial items before divisive or inflammatory items in a questionnaire.

For example, if you realize that computerization of manual tasks has long been a sore point with some employees but if you want to find out how widespread this sentiment is, the questions should still be asked, but they should follow less upsetting ones.

Since your overall objective is to gather data on attitudes, beliefs, behaviors, and characteristics, you expect and seek some diversity among respondents; otherwise, a questionnaire would be extraneous. However, you want respondents to feel as unthreatened by and interested in the questions being asked as possible, without getting overwrought about a particular issue.

Administering the Questionnaire

RESPONDENTS. Deciding who will receive the questionnaire is done in conjunction with the task of setting up objectives for its results. Sampling, which was covered in Chapter 4, helps the systems analyst to determine what sort of representation is necessary—and hence what kind of respondents should receive the questionnaire.

Recipients are often chosen as representative because of their rank, length of service with the company, job duties, or special interest in the current or proposed system. Be sure to include enough respondents to allow for a reasonable sample in the event that some questionnaires are not returned or some response sheets are incorrectly completed and thus must be discarded.

METHODS OF ADMINISTERING THE QUESTIONNAIRE. The systems analyst has several options for administering the questionnaire, and the choice of administration method is often determined by the existing business situation. Options for administering the questionnaire include:

1. Convening all concerned respondents together at one time.
2. Personally handing out blank questionnaires and taking back completed ones.
3. Allowing respondents to self-administer the questionnaire at work and drop it in a centrally located box.
4. Mailing questionnaires to employees in branch or satellite sites and supplying a deadline, instructions, and return postage.
5. Administering the questionnaire electronically.

Each of these five methods has advantages and disadvantages. Collecting questionnaire data from a group gathered in one place at one time is helpful because there is no wait time (except whatever time it takes to complete the form) involved before getting back the data. Additionally, the analyst is better able to control the data collection situation by guaranteeing that everyone receives the same instructions and that 100 percent of the forms will be returned.

A disadvantage of group data collection is that not all employees in the sample will be free at the scheduled time. Additionally, there may be some resentment at being asked to focus on the task of filling out the questionnaire when other work seems more pressing. Peer pressure in this context can work for or against the completion of the questionnaire. If key respondents seem favorable, the majority will catch on and react in the same way, and vice versa.

The systems analyst can also guarantee a good response rate by personally handing out and collecting questionnaires, but analyst time becomes a problem when a large or widely dispersed group is sampled. Also, respondents may be skeptical that even though the questionnaire stressed confidentiality, the analyst is all too aware of who is turning in which form.

Allowing respondents to self-administer the questionnaire is done frequently. Response rates with this method are a little lower than with the other methods, since people may forget about the form, lose it, or purposely ignore it. However, self-administration allows people to feel that their anonymity is assured and may result in less guarded answers from some respondents.

One way to increase the response rate on self-administered forms is to set up a central drop box at an employee's desk and ask him or her to cross off the names of respondents who return a form. That way, a particular person is not associated with a particular response form, but there is still subtle pressure to return the form.

The response rate for mailing, the fourth method of questionnaire administration, is notably poorer. Mailing a questionnaire does not involve the respondent in a personal way with the survey. However, it is often important to include remote organizational members just because they are not as involved with life at headquarters and will likely have a different perspective on current and prospective computer systems that should be taken into account.

Administering the questionnaire electronically is one way to quickly reach current system users. Costs of duplication are minimized. In addition responses can be made at the convenience of the respondent, then they can be collected and stored electronically. Research has not definitively determined response rates for electronic surveys, so some caution is warranted. Also, respondents may question the confidentiality of responses that are given electronically. An additional concern is the possibility that the analyst could miss potential users who do not currently have access to a computer system.

SUMMARY

By using questionnaires, systems analysts can gather data on attitudes, beliefs, behaviors, and characteristics from key people in the organization. Questionnaires are useful if: people in the organization are widely dispersed, many people are involved with the systems project, exploratory work is necessary before recommending alternatives, or there is a need for problem sensing before interviews are conducted.

Once objectives for the questionnaire are articulated, the analyst can begin writing either open-ended or closed questions. Choice of wording is extremely important and should reflect the language of the organizational members. Ideally, the questions should be simple, specific, short, free of bias, not patronizing, technically accurate, addressed to those who are knowledgeable, and at an appropriate reading level.

Scaling is the process of assigning numbers or other symbols to an attribute or characteristic. The systems analyst may want to use scales either to measure the attitudes or characteristics of respondents or to have respondents act as judges for the subject of the questionnaire.

The four forms of measurement are nominal, ordinal, interval, and ratio scales. The form of measurement is often dictated by the data, and the analysis of data is in turn dictated to some degree by the form of measurement.

Systems analysts need to be concerned with validity and reliability. Validity means that the questionnaire measures what the systems analyst intended to measure. Reliability means that the results are consistent.

Analysts should be careful to avoid problems such as leniency, central tendency, and the halo effect when constructing scales.

Consistent control of the questionnaire format and style can result in a better response rate. Additionally, the meaningful ordering and clustering of questions is important for helping respondents understand the questionnaire. Surveys can be administered in a variety of ways, including (but not limited to) electronically or with the analyst present in a group of users.

KEYWORDS AND PHRASES

questionnaire	interval scale
survey respondents	ratio scale
open-ended questions	validity
closed questions	reliability
scaling	leniency
nominal scale	central tendency
ordinal scale	halo effect

Order in the Courts

"I love my work," Tennys says, beginning the interview with a volley. "It's a lot like a game. I keep my eye on the ball and never look back," he continues. Tennyson "Tennys" Courts is a manager for Global Health Spas, Inc., which has popular health and recreation spas worldwide.

"Now that I've finished my M.B.A., I feel like I'm on top of the world with Global," Courts continues. "I think I can really help this outfit shape up with its computers and health spas."

Tennys is attempting to help your systems group, which is developing a system to be used by all 80 out-

lets (where currently each group handles its paperwork in its own way). "Can I bounce this off you?" he asks Terri Towell, a member of your team of systems analysts. "It's a questionnaire I designed for distribution to all spa managers."

Ever the good sport, Terri tells Tennys that she'd love to take a look at the form. But back in the office, Terri puts the ball in your court. Systematically critique Tennys' technique as depicted in Figure 6.C2, and explain to him point by point what it needs to be a matchless questionnaire with a winning form.

QUESTIONNAIRE FOR ALL MANAGERS OF HEALTH SPAS

URGENTFILL OUT IMMEDIATELY AND RETURN PERSONALLY TO YOUR DIVISION MANAGER. YOUR NEXT PAYCHECK WILL BE WITHHELD UNTIL IT IS CONFIRMED THAT YOU HAVE TURNED THIS IN.

In ten words or less, what complaints have you lodged about the current computer system in the last six months to a year? Are there others who feel the same way in your outlet as you do? Who? List their names and positions.

1.   2.
3.   4.
5.
7.

Terri
Please help me improve this form.
Tennys

What is the biggest problem you have when communicating your information requirements to headquarters? Describe it briefly.

How much computer down time did you experience last year?

1 - 2 - 3 - 4 - 5 - 6 - 7 - 8 - 9 - 10 -

Is there any computer equipment you never use?

Description   Serial Number

Do you want it removed? Agree   Neutral   Disagree

In your opinion, what's next as far as computers and Global Spas are concerned?

Thanks for filling this out • • • • • • • • • • • • • •

FIGURE 6.C2
Questionnaire developed for managers of Global Health Spas by Tennys Courts.

REVIEW QUESTIONS

1. What kinds of information is the systems analyst seeking through the use of questionnaires or surveys?
2. List four situations that make the use of questionnaires appropriate.
3. What are the two basic question types used on questionnaires?
4. List two reasons why a systems analyst would use a closed question on a questionnaire.
5. List two reasons why a systems analyst would use an open-ended question on a questionnaire.

"You've probably noticed by now that not everyone enjoys filling out questionnaires at MRE. We seem to get more questionnaires than most organizations. But I think it's because many of the employees, especially those from the old Training Unit, value the contributions of questionnaire data in our work with clients. When you examine the questionnaire that Snowden distributed, you'll probably want not only to look at the results, but also to critique it from a methods standpoint. I always feel strongly that we can improve our internal performance so that eventually we can better serve our clients. The next time we construct a questionnaire, we want to be able to improve three things: the reliability of the data, the validity of the data, and the response rate that we get."

HyperCase Questions

1. What evidence of questionnaires have you found at MRE? Be specific about what you have found and where.

2. Critique the questionnaire that Snowden circulated. What can be done to it to improve its reliability, validity, and response rate? Provide three practical suggestions.

3. Write a short questionnaire to follow up on some aspects of the merger between Management Systems and the Training Unit at MRE that are still puzzling you. Be sure to observe all the guidelines for good questionnaire design.

6. What are the seven guidelines for choosing language for the questionnaire?
7. Define what is meant by *scaling*.
8. What are two kinds of information that can be gained by the use of scales on questionnaires?
9. What are nominal scales used for?
10. What is the difference between nominal and ordinal scales?
11. Give an example of an interval scale.
12. When should the analyst use interval scales?
13. Describe the difference between interval and ratio scales.
14. Define reliability as it refers to the construction of scales.
15. Define validity as it refers to the construction of scales.
16. List three problems that can occur because of careless construction of scales.
17. What are four actions that can be taken to ensure that the questionnaire format is conducive to a good response rate?
18. Which questions should be placed first on the questionnaire?
19. Why should questions on similar topics be clustered together?
20. What is an appropriate placement of controversial questions?
21. List five methods for administering the questionnaire.

PROBLEMS

1. Cab Wheeler is a newly hired systems analyst with your group. Cab has always felt that questionnaires are a waste. Now that you will be doing a systems project for MegaTrucks, Inc., a national trucking firm with branches and employees in 130 cities, you want to use a questionnaire to elicit some opinions about the current and proposed systems.
   a. Based on what you know about Cab and MegaTrucks, give three persuasive reasons why he should use a survey for this study.
   b. Given your careful arguments, Cab has agreed to use a questionnaire but strongly urges that all questions be open-ended so as not to constrain the respondents. In a paragraph, persuade Cab that closed questions are useful as well. Be sure to point out trade-offs involved with each question type.

2. "Everytime we get a consultant in here, they pass out some goofy questionnaire that has no meaning to us at all. Why don't they bother to personalize it, at least a little?" You are discussing the possibility of beginning a systems project with Pohattan Power Company (PPC) of Far Meltway, N.J.
   a. What steps will you follow to personalize a standardized questionnaire?
   b. What are the advantages of adapting a questionnaire to a particular organization? What are the disadvantages?

3. A sample question from the draft of the Pohattan Power Company questionnaire reads:
   I have been with the company:
   20–upwards years
   10–15 years upwards
   5–10 years upwards
   less than a year
   Check one that most applies
   a. What kind of a scale is the question's author using?
   b. What errors have been made in the construction of the question, and what might be the possible responses?
   c. Rewrite the question to achieve clearer results.
   d. Where should the question you've written appear on the questionnaire?

4. Also included on the PPC questionnaire is this question: When a residential customer calls, I always direct them to our Web site to get an answer.

Sometimes	Never	Always	Usually
1	2	3	4

   a. What type of scale is this intended to be?
   b. Rewrite the question and possible responses to achieve better results.

5. Another question used on the PPC draft questionnaire reads: My satisfaction with access time to the customer database is:

Displeased				Satisfaction
0%	5%	25%	50%	100%

FIGURE 6.EX1
Questionnaire developed by
Di Wooly.

Hi! All Employees

What's new? According to the grapevine, hear we're in for a new computer. Here's some questions for you to think about.

a. How long have you used the old computer? _____

b. How often does it go down? _____

c. Who repairs it for you? _____

d. When was the last time you suggested a new improvement to the computer system and it was put into use? What was it? _____

e. When was the last time you suggested a new improvement to the computer system and nobody used it? What was it? _____

f. Do you use a VDT or printer or both? _____

g. How fast do you type? _____

h. How many people need to access the database regularly at your branch? Is there anyone not using the computer now who would like to? _____

    a. What kind of scale does the question's author intend to use?

    b. Is the intended scale appropriate for the question? Why or why not?

    c. Rewrite the question to achieve clearer results.

6. Figure 6.EX1 is a questionnaire designed by an employee of Green Toe Textiles, which specializes in manufacturing men's socks. Di Wooly wrote the questionnaire because, as the office manager at headquarters in Juniper, Tennessee, she is concerned with the proposed purchase and implementation of a new computer system.

    a. Provide a one-sentence critique for each question given.

    b. In a paragraph, critique the layout and style in terms of white space used, room for responses, ease of responding, and so on.

7. Based on what you surmise Ms. Wooly is trying to get at through the questionnaire, rewrite and reorder the questions (use both open-ended and closed questions) so that they follow good practice and result in useful information for the systems analysts.

    a. Indicate next to each question that you write whether it is open-ended or closed, and write a sentence indicating why you have written the question this way.

8. Frieda Forall, head of nursing, is insistent that employees at her for-profit hospital should complete questionnaires about the proposed computer system at home, on their own time, not the hospital's.

    a. Write a paragraph to convince Frieda that administering the questionnaire in a way other than self-administration off the premises would garner better results and be a worthwhile use of employees' time.

    b. Nurse Forall is wavering in her position on self-administration but as yet remains unconvinced. List some incentives that can motivate managers to administer a questionnaire properly the first time.

GROUP PROJECTS

1. Using the interview data you gained from the group exercise on Maverick Transport in Chapter 5, meet with your group to brainstorm the design of a questionnaire for the hundreds of truck drivers which Maverick Transport employs. Recall Maverick is interested in implementing a satellite system for tracking freight and drivers. There are other systems

that may impact the drivers as well. As your group constructs the questionnaire, consider the drivers' likely level of education and any time constraints the drivers are under for completing such a form.

2. Using the interview data you gained from the group exercise on Maverick Transport in Chapter 5, your group should meet to design a questionnaire for surveying the company's 20 programmers (15 of whom have been hired in the past year) about their skills, ideas for new or enhanced systems, and so on. As your group constructs the programmer survey, consider what you have learned about users in the other interviews, as well as what vision the director of information technology holds for the company.

SELECTED BIBLIOGRAPHY

Babbie, E. R. *Survey Research Methods.* Belmont, CA: Wadsworth Publishing Company, Inc., 1973.

Dillman, D. A. *Mail and Telephone Surveys.* New York: John Wiley & Sons, 1978.

Emory, C. W. *Business Research Methods,* 3rd ed. Homewood, IL: Richard D. Irwin, Inc., 1985.

Hessler, R. M. *Social Research Methods.* New York: West Publishing Company, 1992.

Sudman, S., and N. M. Bradburn. *Asking Questions: A Practical Guide to Questionnaire Design.* San Francisco: Jossey-Bass Publishers, 1988.

THE QUEST CONTINUES . . .

Anna sits at her desk, reviewing the interview summaries and the memos that were gathered during the summer. There are several stacks of papers neatly filed in expansion folders.

"We have so much information," she remarks to Chip. "Yet I sense that we are only working with the tip of the iceberg. I don't have a solid feeling for the difficulties of faculty members and research staff. Are they experiencing some of the problems that came out in the memos and interviews? Are there additional problems that we haven't heard about?"

Chip looks up from his work of trying to extract key points for defining the problems. "I wonder if we should do more interviews, or perhaps gather more documents," he says.

"That would be a good idea, but how many interviews should we conduct and who should we interview?" Anna replies. "Suppose we interview several staff members and base the new system on the results. We could interview the wrong people and design a system to satisfy only their needs, missing key problems that the majority of faculty and staff need to have solved."

"I see what you mean," Chip answers. "Perhaps we should design a questionnaire and survey the faculty and research staff. Most of them would return the survey if it was easy to complete, especially people with major concerns."

"Great idea!" Anna says. "How should we decide which questions to include on the survey?"

"Let's speak with some key people and base the survey on the results. A good starting point would be Hy Perteks, since he is always talking with the faculty and staff. I'll give him a call and arrange a meeting," Chip says.

Chip arranged the meeting for the following morning, it would be held in a conference room adjacent to the Information Center.

"Thanks for meeting with us on such short notice," Chip opens. "We're thinking about surveying the faculty and research staff to obtain additional information that will help us define the system concerns."

"I think it's a tremendous idea," Hy replies. "I would also like some information that would give me a clue as to what type of software should be available in the Information Center and the type of training we should provide."

"What type of software information do you think we should obtain?" asks Anna.

"Certainly the major package types used," Hy answers. "Word processing software is extremely popular. We should find out which package each user likes and, equally important, which *version* of the package. I know that some are using WordPerfect while others are using Word and Ami Pro. I have a few folks using some minor word processing software that they are comfortable with. Database software also varies. Many are using Access, while others are involved with Paradox, dBase, or FoxPro. Same for spreadsheets, with Lotus, Excel, and Quattro Pro being the most popular."

"Another consideration would be what type of specialized software is being used by groups of faculty members," muses Hy. "Many of the people

Allen Schmidt,
Julie E. Kendall, and
Kenneth E. Kendall

in the math department are using Exp, a math word processor. Others are using various software packages for a number of courses. For instance, the information science people are using Visible Analyst Workbench, while a few are using Excelerator. I've also heard that we're getting some biology and astronomy software. And the art department is moving strongly into the Mac arena for full-color production. Some of the faculty are getting heavily into Web site software."

"Other than software packages and versions, what types of information should we capture?" asks Chip.

"I would like to know what level of expertise each person has," responds Hy. "No doubt, some are beginners while others have a good knowledge but have not mastered all of the features of a particular package. Some are experts, without question. They know the software inside and out. I'm interested in the beginners and intermediate users, since we should be providing different training for them. And I would really like to know who the experts are. Then I could contact them and ask if they would be willing to conduct a training session or serve as a resource if someone has a problem with an advanced feature of the software."

"Is there anything else you feel we should find out about in the survey?" asks Chip.

"The only other thing that I worry about are problems that result in a faculty or staff member not using the software," Hy replies.

"What do you mean?" asks Chip.

"Well, suppose a person has the software but it is installed incorrectly or displays a message, such as 'Not enough memory to run,' or 'This feature isn't installed,'" replies Hy. "I've had some inquiries about this matter recently. One person said that they couldn't use Access except for simple tasks since they always got a message saying that the wizards weren't installed. It turned out that the system was not configured correctly to run over a network. It was a simple matter to fix the problem, but it had been going on for a long time! Other such problems must exist, and I'd like to know what they are. This will make our whole staff more productive and comfortable with using microcomputers."

"Do you know of a representative faculty or staff member who we should interview?" Anna inquires.

"Yes, there's a faculty member in math, Rhoda Booke, who has consistently shown interest in hardware and software issues. I've helped her a number of times, and she's always friendly and grateful."

"Thanks once again for all your help," says Chip. "We'll get back to you later with the results of the survey."

Anna arranges a meeting with Rhoda and explains the nature of the project and why she was selected as a faculty representative. The meeting was held in a small conference room in the math department.

"Thanks for meeting with us," says Anna after introductions had been made. "We'd like to have the faculty perspective on problems encountered with microcomputers and the associated software. Our goal is to provide the faculty with the best possible resources with the least number of problems."

"I'm really glad to be a part of the project," exclaims Rhoda. "I've been using software for about five years, and what a learning experience it has been! Thank goodness that Hy is available as a resource person. I've taken hours of his time, and it's been well worth the effort. I feel much more productive, and the students are using software that helps them grasp the material more thoroughly than simply doing math exercises and reading the text."

"That's good news. But are there some difficulties that you've been experiencing?" asks Chip.

"Well, becoming familiar with the software is a major hurdle. I spent a good portion of last summer, when I wasn't working on my book, learning how to use some of the classroom software for both algebra and calculus. The stuff's great, but I got stuck several times and had to call for help. It's necessary to understand the software in order to prepare lesson plans and explain to the students how to use it."

"How about problems with installing the software or hardware?" Anna asks.

"Oh, yes!" exclaims Rhoda. "I tried to install the software, and it went smoothly until the part where the screen asked what type of monitor was being used—either EGA, VGA, or SVGA. I didn't even know what those letters meant," laughs Rhoda.

"Then there were setup problems," Rhoda continues. "I needed to figure out what to install on the network and what to include on the local hard drive. What a learning experience that was. Some of the computers in the student lab gave us 'Not enough memory' error messages, and we learned that they had been installed with minimum main memory. I've heard that the physics faculty had the same problem."

"Are there any other concerns you have or feel that we should include on our survey to the faculty and research staff?" Chip asks.

"It would be useful to know who is using the same software in different departments and what software is supplied by which vendor. Perhaps if we have many packages from one vendor, we could get a larger discount for software. The department software budget is already overwhelmed with requests," Rhoda says.

"Thanks for all your help," Anna says. "If you think of any additional questions we should include on the survey, please do not hesitate to call us."

Back in their office, the analysts start compiling a list of the issues to be contained on the survey.

"We certainly need to ask about the software in use and about training needs," remarks Anna. "We should also address the problems that are occurring."

"Agreed," replies Chip. "I feel that we should include questions on software packages, vendors, versions, level of expertise, and training concerns. What I'm not so sure about is how to obtain information on problems the faculty and staff are encountering. How should we approach these issues?"

"Well," replies Anna, "we should focus on matters with which they are familiar. We might ask questions about the type of problems that are occurring—but certainly not technical ones that they wouldn't find to be of interest. For example, we should not ask, 'How much main memory is available on your machine?' because they may not know or care. They probably would not be familiar with the Windows files or network access rights for the software either. And the survey should not ask any questions that we could easily look up answers to, such as 'Who is the vendor for the software?'"

"I see," replies Chip. "Let's divide the questions into categories. Some would be closed questions and some would be open-ended. Then there's the matter of which structure to use. . . ."

Exercises

E-1. Based on the dialogue among Chip, Anna, Hy, and Rhoda, make a detailed list of concerns raised about hardware and software for faculty microcomputing.

E-2. From the list of concerns, select the issues that would best be phrased as closed questions.

E-3. From the list of concerns, select the issues that would best be phrased as open-ended questions.

E-4. On the basis of problems 2 and 3, design a questionnaire to be sent to the faculty and research staff.

E-5. Pilot your questionnaire by having other students in class fill it out. On the basis of their feedback and your capability to analyze the data you receive, revise your questionnaire.

OBSERVING DECISION-MAKER BEHAVIOR AND THE OFFICE ENVIRONMENT

KINDS OF INFORMATION SOUGHT

Observing the decision maker and the decision maker's physical environment are important information-gathering techniques for the systems analyst. Through observing activities of decision makers, the analyst seeks to gain insight about what is actually done, not just what is documented or explained. Additionally, through observation of the decision maker, the analyst attempts to see firsthand the relationships that exist between decision makers and other organizational members.

By observing the office environment, the systems analyst seeks the symbolic meaning of the work context for decision makers. The analyst examines physical elements of the decision maker's workspace for their influence on decision-making behavior. Furthermore, through observation of the physical elements over which the decision maker has control (clothing, desk position, and so on), the analyst works to understand what messages the decision maker is sending. Finally, through observation, the analyst works to comprehend the influence of the decision maker on others in the organization. All of these kinds of information are summarized in Figure 7.1.

OBSERVING A DECISION MAKER'S BEHAVIOR

Systems analysts use observation for many reasons. One reason is to gain information about decision makers and their environments that is unavailable through any other method. Observing also helps to confirm or negate and reverse what has been found through interviewing, questionnaires, and other methods.

Observation must be structured and systematic if the findings are to be interpretable. Thus, it is of utmost importance that the systems analyst know *what* is being observed. Great care and thought must go into what and who will be observed, as well as when, where, why, and how. It is not enough simply to be aware of the need for observation.

FIGURE 7.1
Kinds of information sought
when observing decision-
maker behavior and the office
environment.

Many observational schemes are available, each with its own objectives. Analysts are encouraged to draw from research as well as from their own experience to devise observational schemes that are workable.

Observing a Typical Manager's Decision-Making Activities

Managers' workdays have been described as a series of interruptions punctuated by short bursts of work. In other words, pinning down what a manager "does" is a slippery proposition even under the best of circumstances. In order for the systems analyst to grasp adequately how managers characterize their work, interviews and questionnaires are used, as discussed in Chapters 5 and 6. However, observation allows the analyst to see firsthand how managers gather, process, share, and use information to get work done.

The following steps aid in observing a manager's typical decision-making activities:

1. Decide what is to be observed (activities).
2. Decide at what level of concreteness activities are to be observed (that is, will the analyst observe that "The manager freely shared information with subordinates" or make a much more concrete observation such as "Manager sends a copy of the same memo to three subordinates"?). Determining the level of concreteness of observation will also dictate the amount of inference in each observation and subsequently the amount of interpretation needed once observations are made.
3. Create categories that adequately capture key activities.
4. Prepare appropriate scales, checklists, or other materials for observation.
5. Decide when to observe.

Deciding when to observe is covered in the next subsection.

Time and Event Sampling

Each approach to when to observe has its own advantages and trade-offs. Time sampling allows the analyst to set up specific intervals at which to observe managers' activities. For example, time sampling might specify ob-

	Time Sampling	**Event Sampling**
Advantages	• Cuts down on bias with randomization of observations • Allows a representative view of frequent activities	• Allows observation of behavior as it unfolds • Allows observation of an event designated as important
Disadvantages	• Gathers data in a fragmented fashion that doesn't allow time for a decision to unfold • Misses infrequent but important decisions	• Takes a great deal of analyst's time • Misses a representative sample of frequent decisions

FIGURE 7.2
Advantages and disadvantages of time versus event sampling.

serving a decision maker during five randomly chosen ten-minute intervals throughout seven eight-hour days. The advantages of time sampling include cutting down on the bias that might otherwise enter into observations made "just anytime." Time sampling also allows for a representative view of activities that occur fairly frequently.

The drawbacks of time sampling include gathering observational data in a piecemeal fashion that may not allow sufficient time for an event such as a decision to unfold in its entirety. A second problem with using time sampling to gather observational data is that rare or infrequent but important events (for example, a strategic decision on a five-year investment in a new management information system) may not be represented in the time that is sampled. Yet the decision is important and will have an impact.

Event sampling addresses both of these concerns by purposefully sampling entire events such as "a board meeting" or "a user training session," rather than sampling time periods randomly. Event sampling provides for observation of an integral behavior in its natural context. A drawback of event sampling is that it may not be possible to achieve a representative sample of frequent occurrences.

In light of the pros and cons of both approaches, analysts who are interested in observation are encouraged to combine time and event sampling when deciding on the what, when, why, and how of decision-maker activities. A comparison and contrast of time versus event sampling is given in Figure 7.2.

As discussed in Chapter 2, decision making occurs on the operational, managerial, and strategic levels of the organization. The preceding discussion assumed that decision makers at all levels of the organization will interact with the information system and hence should be observed.

Observing a Decision Maker's Body Language

The systems analyst subconsciously observes body language during the interviews and other interactions. This discussion is intended to bring that awareness to the conscious level, where it can be recognized and used by the analyst. Understanding body language enables the analyst to better understand the information requirements of the decision maker by adding dimension to what is being said. Nevertheless, although it is important to observe decision makers' body language, precise interpretation of it, movement for movement, is immensely difficult and also varies across cultures.

FIGURE 7.3
A sample adjective-pairs sheet
for observing a decision
maker.

Name of Observer _Kendall, K_
Decision Maker _D. Side_
Date Observed _10/24/1997_
Observed From _8 a.m. to 8:30 a.m._

From each pair, circle the one adjective that best describes the
decision maker during the time you were observing.

1. (Assertive) / Unassertive

2. Calm / (Excited)

3. (Credible) / Not Believable

4. (Outgoing) / Inward-looking

5. (Talkative) / Silent

6. (Articulate) / Inarticulate

7. Authoritative / (Uninformed)

8. (Self-started) / Unmotivated

9. (Goal-oriented) / Unfocused

10. (Problem Solver) / Problem Maker

Adjective Pairs and Categories. Adjective pairs have become a popular way to record behavior. An example of decision-making behavior described in adjective pairs is: decisive/indecisive, confident/not confident, assertive/unassertive, and so on, as depicted in Figure 7.3.

Category systems for recording decision-making behavior were discussed briefly before. The analyst determines activity categories before observations are undertaken. An example of a concrete category is "Accesses database personally." Examples of a category system that asks for more analyst inference in recording observation are "Uses internal sources of data" or "Shows initiative in accessing data." Forms listing categories are then copied in sufficient number and taken along to be completed as the analyst observes. A sample form illustrating the category system is shown in Figure 7.4.

The Analyst's Playscript. Systems analysts can also use a technique called playscripting to record observed behavior. With this technique the "actor" is the decision maker who is observed "acting" or making decisions. In setting up a playscript, the actor is listed in the left-hand column and all of his or her actions are listed in the right-hand column, as shown in Figure 7.5. All activities are recorded with action verbs so that a decision maker would be described as "talking," "sampling," "corresponding," and "deciding."

Playscript is an organized and systematic approach that demands that the analyst be able to understand and articulate the *action* taken by each observed decision maker. This approach eventually assists the systems analyst in determining what information is required for major and/or frequent decisions made by the observed people. For instance, from the quality assurance manager example in the playscript, it becomes clear that even though this

FIGURE 7.4
A sample observation form
employing categories of
decision-maker behavior.

Name of Observer __Kim McCabe__
Decision Maker __A.K. Stratton__
Date Observed __6 / 10 /1997__
Observed From __8:30__ to __12:00__
(Start time to end time)

Each time the decision maker is observed engaging anew in the behavior listed, put 1 mark in the box beside the appropriate category. Mark only when you actually observe the decision maker in action. Fill out the first column ONLY when you are in the presence of the decision maker you are observing.

Behavior	Number of Times Behavior Occurs	Total	Percentage of Total
Instructs Subordinates	///	3	5
Instructs Peers	//	2	4
Instructs Superiors	/	1	2
Questions Subordinates	//	2	4
Questions Peers	///	3	5
Questions Superiors	/	1	2
Reprimands Subordinates	——	0	0
Reprimands Peers	——	0	0
Reprimands Superiors	——	0	0
Opens Mail	⧸⧸⧸⧸	5	9
Answers Phone	⧸⧸⧸⧸ //	7	13
Makes Phone Call	⧸⧸⧸⧸ ⧸⧸⧸⧸	10	18
Reads External Information	⧸⧸⧸⧸ ⧸⧸⧸⧸ ///	13	23
Reads Internal Information	///	3	5
Processes Own Information	//	2	4
Asks Others to Process Information	///	4	7
		56 ≈	100%

decision maker is on the middle management level, he or she still requires a fair amount of external information to perform the required activities of this specific job.

OBSERVING THE PHYSICAL ENVIRONMENT

Observing the activities of decision makers is just one way to assess their information requirements. Observing the physical environment in which decision makers work also reveals much about their information requirements. Most often, this means systematically examining the offices of decision makers since offices constitute their primary workplace. Decision makers influence and are in turn influenced by their physical environments.

Structured Observation of the Environment

Film critics sometimes use a structured form of criticism called *mise-en-scène* analysis to systematically assess what is in a single shot of the film—looking at editing, camera angle, set decor, and the actors and their

Playscript Analysis	Company: Solid Steel Shelving Analyst: L. Bracket	Scenario: Quality Assurance Date: 9/3/1997

Decision Maker (Actor)	Information-Related Activity (Script)
Quality Assurance Manager	Asks shop floor supervisor for the day's production report
Shop Floor Supervisor	Prints out daily computerized production report
	Discusses recurring problems in production runs with quality assurance (QA) manager
Quality Assurance Manager	Reads production report
	Compares current report with other reports from the same week
	Inputs data from daily production run into QA model on micro
	Observes on-screen results of QA model
	Calls steel suppliers to discuss deviations from quality standards
Shop Floor Supervisor	Attends meeting on new quality specifications with quality assurance manager and vice president of production
Quality Assurance Manager	Drafts letter to inform suppliers on new quality specifications agreed upon in meeting
	Sends draft to vice president via e-mail
Vice President of Production	Reads drafted letter
	Returns corrections and comments via e-mail
Quality Assurance Manager	Reads corrected letter on e-mail
	Rewrites letter to reflect changes

costumes to find out how they are shaping the meaning of the film as intended by the director. Sometimes the film's *mise-en-scène* will contradict what is said in the dialogue. For information requirements analysis, the systems analyst can take on a role similar to that of the film critic. It often is possible to observe the particulars of the surroundings that will confirm or negate the organizational narrative (or dialogue) that is found through interviews or questionnaires.

The method for *STR*uctured *OB*servation of the *E*nvironment is referred to as STROBE. It is systematic because (1) it provides a standard methodology and standard classification for the analysis of those organizational elements that influence decision making; (2) it allows other systems analysts to apply the same analytic framework to the same organization; and (3) it limits analysis to the organization as it exists during the current stage in its life cycle.

Filmic Elements	Organizational Elements
Set location	Office location
People positioned within a frame	Decision maker's placement in an office (i.e., desk placement)
Stationary objects	File cabinets, bookshelves, and equipment for storing information
Props (movable objects)	Calculators, PCs, and other items used for processing information
External objects (brought in from other scenes)	Trade journals, newspapers, and items used for external information
Lighting and color	Office lighting and color
Costumes	Clothing worn by decision makers

FIGURE 7.6
The analogy between filmic elements for observation and elements of STROBE.

A correspondence exists between the elements of analysis for film criticism and those used in the STROBE assessment of a decision maker's information requirements. This correspondence makes it possible for the systems analyst to remember easily the analogy, as pictured in Figure 7.6. A more detailed discussion of each of these elements follows.

STROBE ELEMENTS. There are seven concrete elements that are easily observable by the systems analyst. These elements can reveal much about the way a decision maker gathers, processes, stores, and shares information, as well as about the decision maker's credibility in the workplace. The seven observable elements are described in the following paragraphs.

Office location. One of the first elements a systems analyst should observe is the location of a particular decision maker's office with respect to other offices. Accessible offices tend to increase interaction frequency and informal messages, while inaccessible offices tend to decrease the interaction frequency and increase task-oriented messages. Offices distributed along the perimeter of the building usually result in a report or memo being held up in one of the offices, while office clusters encourage information sharing. It is also likely that the people whose offices are separated from others may tend to view the organization differently and so drift further apart from other organization members in their objectives.

Placement of the decision maker's desk. Placement of a desk in the office can provide clues to the exercise of power by the decision maker. Executives who enclose a visitor in a tight space with their back to the wall, while allowing themselves a lot of room, put themselves into the strongest possible power position. An executive who positions his or her desk facing the wall with a chair at the side for a visitor is probably encouraging participation and equal exchanges. The systems analyst should notice the arrangement of the office furniture and in particular the placement of the desk.

Stationary office equipment. File cabinets, bookshelves, and other large equipment for storing items are all included in the category of stationary office equipment. If there is no such equipment, it is likely that the decision maker stores very few items of information personally. If there is an

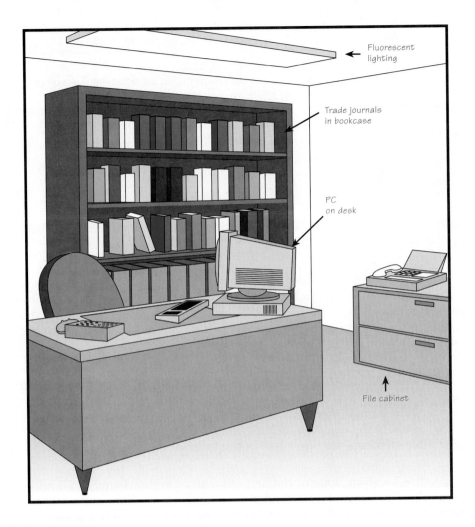

abundance of such equipment, it is presumed that the decision maker stores and values much information.

Props. The term *props* (an abbreviation of the stage/film term properties) refers to all of the small equipment used to process information. This includes calculators, PCs, pens, pencils, and rulers. The presence of calculators and PCs suggests that a decision maker who possesses such equipment is more likely to use it personally than one who must leave the room to use it.

Trade journals and newspapers. A systems analyst needs to know what type of information is used by the decision maker. Observation of the type of publications stored in the office can reveal whether the decision maker is looking for external information (found in trade journals, newspaper clippings about other companies in the industry, and so on) or relies more on internal information (company reports, intra-office correspondence, policy handbooks).

Office lighting and color. Lighting and color play an important role in how a decision maker gathers information. An office lighted with warm, incandescent lighting indicates a tendency toward more personal communica-

Characteristics of Decision Makers	Corresponding Elements in the Physical Environment
Gathers information informally	Warm, incandescent lighting and colors
Seeks extraorganizational information	Trade journals present in office
Processes data personally	Calculators, PCs present in office
Stores information personally	Equipment/files present in office
Exercises power in decision making	Desk placed for power
Exhibits credibility in decision making	Wears authoritative clothing
Shares information with others	Office easily accessible

FIGURE 7.8
A summary of decision-maker characteristics that correspond to observable elements in the physical environment.

tion. An executive in a warmly lit office will gather more information informally, while another organizational member working in a brightly lit, brightly colored office may gather information through more formal memos and official reports. Figure 7.7 shows a decision maker's office equipment, props, trade journals, office lighting, and color.

Clothing worn by decision makers. Much has been written about the clothing worn by executives and others in authority. The systems analyst can gain an understanding of the credibility exhibited by managers in the organization by observing the clothing they wear on the job. The formal three-piece suit for a male or the skirted suit for a female represents the maximum authority according to some researchers who have studied perceptions of executive appearance. Casual dressing by leaders tends to open the door for more participative decision making, but such attire often results in some loss of credibility in the organization if the predominant culture values traditional, conservative clothing.

Through the use of STROBE, the systems analyst can gain a better understanding of how managers gather, process, store, and use information. A summary of the characteristics exhibited by decision makers and the corresponding observable elements is shown in Figure 7.8. The following subsection examines options available to the systems analyst for recording and documenting observations.

APPLICATION ALTERNATIVES. Analysts may choose among many application strategies when using the STROBE approach. These strategies vary from very structured (such as taking photographs for later analysis) to unstructured. Four strategies are described in the following paragraphs.

Analysis of photographs. Photographing the environments of decision makers and then analyzing the photographs for elements of STROBE is most closely allied with the original use of *mise-en-scène* for film criticism. Interestingly, this application has parallels in much earlier management work, since at the turn of the century, Frank Gilbreth used film in his famous time-motion studies, analyzing frame-by-frame what motions were necessary to complete a task.

Don't Bank on Their Self-Image

or

Not Everything Is Reflected in a Mirror

"I don't want any power here," demurs Dr. Drew Charles, medical director of the regional blood center where your systems group has just begun a project. "I'm up to my neck in work just keeping the regional physicians informed so they follow good bloodbanking practices," he says, as he shields his eyes from the bright sunlight streaming into his office. He clicks off the monitor connected to his PC and turns his attention to you and the interview.

Dr. Charles is dressed in a conservative, dark wool suit and is wearing a red-striped silk necktie. He continues, "In fact, I don't make decisions. I'm here purely in a positive support role." He pulls out the organizational chart shown below to illustrate his point. "It is as clear as a fracture. The administrator is the expert on all administrative matters. I am the medical consultant only."

Dr. Charles' office is stacked high not only with medical journals such as *Transfusion* but also with *BYTE* magazine and *Business Week.* Each is opened to a different page, as if the doctor were in the process of devouring each new morsel of information. However, the overflow journals are not stored meticulously on metal bookshelves as expected. In sharp contrast to the gleaming, new equipment you saw being used in the donor rooms, the journals are piled a foot high on an old blood-donating bed that has been long retired from its intended use.

Next, you decide to interview the chief administrator, Craig Bunker, to whom Dr. Charles has alluded. Fifteen minutes after the scheduled start of your appointment, Bunker's secretary, Dawn Upshaw, finally allows you to enter his office. Bunker, who has just finished a phone call, is dressed in a light-blue sport coat, checkered slacks, light-blue shirt, and a necktie. "How are you doing? I've just been checking around to see how everything's perking along," Bunker says by way of introduction. He is outgoing and very friendly.

As you glance around the room, you notice that there are no filing cabinets, nor is there a PC such as the one Dr. Charles was using. There are lots of photos of Craig Bunker's family, but the only item resembling a book or magazine is the center's newsletter, *Bloodline.* As the interview begins in earnest, Bunker cheerfully launches into stories about the Pennsylvania Blood Center, where he held the position of assistant administrator six years ago.

Finally, you descend the stairs to the damp basement level of the Heath Lambert Mansion. The bloodmobiles have just returned, and processed blood has been shipped to area hospitals. You decide to talk with Sang Kim, a bloodmobile driver; Jenny McLaughlin, the distribution manager; and Roberta Martin, a lab technician who works the night shift.

Roberta begins, "I don't know what we'd do without the doctor." But in the same vein, Sang feeds the conversation by remarking, "Yeah, he helped us by thinking up a better driving schedule last week."

Jenny adds, "Dr. Charles is invaluable in setting the inventory levels for each hospital, and if it wasn't for him, we wouldn't have word processing yet, let alone our new computer."

As one of the systems analysis team members assigned to the blood center project, develop an anecdotal checklist using STROBE to help you systematically interpret the observations you made about the offices of Dr. Charles and Craig Bunker. Consider any disparities between a decision maker's clothing, what a decision maker states, and what is said by others; between office location and what is stated; and between office equipment and policies stated. Additionally, in a paragraph, suggest possible follow-up interviews and/or observations to help settle any unresolved questions.

FIGURE 7.C1
Organization chart of the regional blood center.

Photographic applications of STROBE have some distinct advantages. One is that a document is made that can be referred to repeatedly. This can be extremely helpful when organizational visits must be limited due to time, distance, or expense.

A second advantage is that the photographer can focus specifically on pertinent elements of STROBE and thereby exclude extraneous elements. Additionally, using photography for STROBE allows a side-by-side comparison of organizations, since the limitations of time and space are overcome by photography. A fourth advantage is that a photograph can supply detail that is easily overlooked during personal contact, when the systems analyst is not only observing but is also conducting an interview or investigating hard data. A fifth advantage is that a photograph can be scanned into a Web document for use by all team members if the organization so agrees to this use.

There are also drawbacks to using photography for implementing STROBE. First and foremost may be the problem of deciding what to photograph. In contrast to the human eye, photographs are very limited as to what they can aim at and "take in."

The second drawback is that photography, although it may prove unobtrusive in the long term, is initially obtrusive. The systems analyst will face problems of decision makers who wind up posing, as well as intentionally or unintentionally changing their environments in an attempt to make them somehow more acceptable to the analyst.

Checklist/Likert scale approach. A second application of STROBE is a less-structured technique than photography—a checklist/Likert scale approach. Researchers developed five-point Likert-type scales relating to seven decision-maker characteristics that were observable through physical elements in decision makers' organizational environments, as shown in Figure 7.9.

In the original study using this scale to assess sixteen blood administrators and medical directors from the United States and Canada, researchers found convergent and discriminant validity of the information gained through the STROBE scales and of the information gained through interviewing and behavioral scales. The same Likert-type scales are recommended to systems analysts, who can use them as an application of STROBE in conjunction with more traditional methods.

Anecdotal list (with symbols). A third, and even less-structured way to implement STROBE is through the use of an anecdotal checklist with meaningful shorthand symbols. This approach to STROBE was useful in ascertaining the information requirements for four key decision makers in a midwestern blood center.

As can be seen in Figure 7.10, five shorthand symbols were used by the systems analysts to evaluate how observation of the elements of STROBE compared with the organizational narrative generated through interviews. The five symbols are:

1. A checkmark that means the narrative is confirmed.
2. An "X" that means the narrative is reversed.
3. An oval or eye-shaped symbol that serves as a cue for the systems analyst to look further.

STROBE Scales for Observing the Physical Environment

1. Office lighting, walls, paintings, and graphics are warm-toned, creating an informal arena for information exchange.

   Fluorescent lights, cool-colored walls, no decorations   *Incandescent lights, warm-colored wall, warm graphics*

   1   2   3   4   5

2. Office contains various forms of information brought from outside the organization, including trade journals, association newsletters, and business newspapers.

   No outside sources of information   *Four or more journals or newspapers*

   1   2   3   4   5

3. Aids for processing of information are present in the office and are easily accessible.

   No calculators or PCs visible   *Calculator or PCs accessible without leaving a chair*

   1   2   3   4   5

4. Office houses many pieces of equipment used for storing information.

   No storage cabinets in office   *Four or more file cabinets or shelves*

   1   2   3   4   5

5. Desk is placed to maximize territory for administrator and limit visitor space.

   Desk placed against wall   *Desk used as barrier with little space for visitor*

   1   2   3   4   5

6. Wears authoritative business suits rather than casual or sporty clothing.

   Wears casual or sporty clothing   *Wears conservative business suits*

   1   2   3   4   5

7. Administrator's office is easily accessible.

   Office located on separate floor from subordinates   *Office within 50 feet of subordinates*

   1   2   3   4   5

4. A square that means observation of the elements of STROBE modifies the narrative.

5. A circle that means the narrative is supplemented by what is observed.

When STROBE is implemented in this manner, the first step is to determine key organizational themes growing out of interviews. Next, the elements of STROBE are systematically observed, and then a matrix is constructed that lists major ideas from the organizational narrative about information gathering, processing, storing, and sharing on one axis and elements of STROBE on the other. When narrative and observations are compared, one of the five appropriate symbols is then used to characterize the relationship between the narrative and the relevant element observed. The analyst thus creates a table that first documents and then aids in the analysis of observations.

Anecdotal List with Symbols for Applying STROBE

Narrative Portrayed by Organization Members	Office Location and Equipment	Office Lighting Color and Graphics	Clothing of the Decision Maker
Information is readily flowing on all levels	Negate	Supplement	Supplement
Adams says, "I figure out the percentages myself"	Negate	Supplement	Supplement
Vinnie says, "I like to read up on these things"	Confirm	Supplement	Supplement
Ed says, "The right hand doesn't always know what the left hand is doing"	Cue to look further	Supplement	Supplement
Adams says, "Our company doesn't change much"	Supplement	Confirm	Supplement
The operations staff works all night sometimes	Supplement	Cue to look further	Supplement
Vinnie says, "We do things the way Mr. Adams wants to"	Supplement	Supplement	Modify
Julie says, "Stanley doesn't seem to care sometimes"	Supplement	Supplement	Confirm
	Supplement	Supplement	Supplement
	Supplement	Supplement	Supplement
	Supplement	Supplement	Supplement
	Supplement	Supplement	Supplement

Key

✓ Confirm the narrative
✕ Negate or reverse the narrative
◈ Cue to look further
▢ Modify the narrative
● Supplement the narrative

FIGURE 7.10
An anecdotal list with symbols for use in applying STROBE.

Observation/narrative comparison. The fourth way to implement STROBE is also the least structured method. Although filmgoers rarely attend a film with a *mise-en-scène* checklist in hand, few of its elements fail to make at least a subconscious impact on them. As long as the systems analyst is *aware* of the elements of *mise-en-scène* and as long as they are consciously observed, valuable insights can be gained, even without the aid of a checklist. Examining the organization from a heightened awareness of the elements of STROBE creates a base for making structured observations. These observations can be used later in assessing information requirements.

SUMMARY

Analysts use observation as an information-gathering technique. Through observation they gain insight into what is actually done; see firsthand the relationships among decision makers in the organization; understand the influence of the physical setting on the decision maker; interpret the messages sent by the decision maker through clothing and office arrangement; and comprehend the influence of the decision maker on others.

Using time or event sampling, the analyst observes typical decision-maker activities and body language. There are numerous systems for recording such observations, including category systems, checklists, scales, field notes, and playscripts.

In addition to observing a decision maker's behavior, the systems analyst should observe the decision maker's surroundings. A method for *STRuctured OBservation of the Environment* is called STROBE. A systems analyst uses STROBE in the same way that a film critic uses a method called *mise-en-scène* analysis to analyze a shot in a film.

Several concrete elements in the decision maker's environment can be observed and interpreted. These elements include (1) office location; (2) placement of the decision maker's desk; (3) stationary office equipment; (4) props, such as calculators and PCs; (5) trade journals and newspapers; (6) office lighting and color; and (7) clothing worn by the decision maker. STROBE can be used to gain a better understanding of how decision makers actually gather, process, store, and share information.

There are a number of alternatives for applying STROBE in an organization. These include analysis of photographs that can be mounted on a team Web site, using a checklist based on Likert scales, adopting an anecdotal list with symbols, and simply writing up an observation/narrative comparison. Each method has certain advantages as well as drawbacks that the analyst needs to weigh when choosing one alternative over the other.

KEYWORDS AND PHRASES

systematic observation	placement of decision maker's
time sampling	desk
event sampling	stationary office equipment
decision maker's body language	props
adjective pairs	trade journals and newspapers
category systems	clothing worn by decision
analyst's playscript	makers
STROBE	office lighting and color
office location	

REVIEW QUESTIONS

1. List three reasons why observation is useful to the systems analyst in the organization.
2. Why is it important that observation of decision makers be structured and systematic?
3. List five steps to help the analyst observe the decision maker's typical activities.
4. What are the advantages of using time sampling of observations?
5. What are the disadvantages of using event sampling of observations?

6. Compare the use of adjective pairs versus the analyst's playscript.

7. What three attributes make STROBE a systematic approach to observing the decision maker's physical environment?

8. List the seven concrete elements of the decision maker's physical environment that can be observed by the systems analyst using STROBE.

9. What are four different application strategies for using STROBE?

PROBLEMS

1. "I think I'll be able to remember most everything he does," says Ceci Awll. Ceci is about to interview Biff Welldon, vice president of strategic planning of OK Corral, a steak restaurant chain with 130 stores. "I mean, I've got a good memory. I think it's much more important to listen to what he says than to observe what he does anyway." As one of your systems analysis team members, Ceci has been talking with you about the desirability of writing down her observations of Biff's office and activities during the interview.

   a. In a paragraph, persuade Ceci that listening is not enough in interviews and that observing and recording those observations is also important.

   b. Ceci seems to have accepted your idea that observation is important but still doesn't know *what* to observe. Make a list of items and behaviors to observe, and in a sentence beside each behavior, indicate what information Ceci should hope to gain through observation of it.

   c. Ceci is uncomfortable writing down observations during her interviews. In a paragraph, suggest two methods for recording observations that do not require that they be used as the observation occurs. Now recommend *one* of the methods, and in a sentence or two, justify why you feel it would be a good method for Ceci in particular to try.

2. "We're a progressive company—always looking to be ahead of the power curve. We'll give anything a whirl if it'll put us ahead of the competition, and that includes every one of us to a man," says I. B. Daring, an executive with Michigan Manufacturing (2M). You are interviewing Daring as a preliminary step in a systems project, one in which his subordinates have expressed interest. As you listen to I. B., you look around his office to see that most of the information he has stored on shelves can be classified as internal procedures manuals. Additionally, you notice a PC on a back table of I. B.'s office. The monitor's screen is covered with dust, and the manuals stacked beside the PC are still encased in their original shrink-wrap. Even though you know that 2M uses an intranet, no cables are visible going to or from I.B.'s PC. You look up behind I. B.'s massive mahogany desk to see on the wall five framed oil portraits of 2M's founders, all clustered around a gold plaque bearing the corporate slogan, which states, "Make sure you're right, then go ahead."

   a. What is the organizational narrative or storyline as portrayed by I. B. Daring? Rephrase it in your own words.

   b. List the elements of STROBE that you have observed during your interview with I. B.

   c. Next to each element of STROBE that you have observed, write a sentence on how you would interpret it.

"We're proud of our building here in Tennessee. In fact we used the architectural firm of I. M. Paid to carry the same theme, blending into the local landscape while still reaching out to our clients, throughout all of the branches. We get lots of people coming through just to admire the building once they catch on to where it is exactly. In fact, by Tennessee standards we get so many sightseers that it might as well be the pyramids! Well, you can see for yourself as you go through. The East Atrium is my favorite place: plenty of light, lots of louvered blinds to filter it. But it has always fascinated me that the building and its furnishings might tell a story quite different from the one its occupants tell.

"Sometimes employees complain that the offices all look the same. But the public rooms are spectacular. Even the lunchroom is inviting. Most people can't say that about their cafeterias at work. You'll notice that everyone personalizes their office, anyway. So even if the offices were of the "cookie cutter" kind, their occupants' personalities seem to take over as soon as they have been here awhile. What have you seen? Was there anything that surprised you so far?"

HYPERCASE QUESTIONS

1. Use STROBE to compare and contrast Snowden Evans' and Ketcham's offices. What sort of conclusion about each person's use of information technology can you draw from your observations? How compatible do

FIGURE 7.HC1
There are hidden clues in HyperCase. Use STROBE.

Evans and Ketcham seem in terms of the systems they use? What other clues to their storage, use, and sharing of information can you discover based on your observations of their offices?

2. Carefully examine Kathy Blandford's office. Use STROBE to confirm, reverse, or negate what you have learned during your interview with her. List anything you found out about Ms. Blandford from observing her office that you did not know from the interview.

3. Carefully examine the contents of the MRE reception area using STROBE. What inferences can you make about the organization? List them. What interview questions would you like to ask, based on your observations of the reception area? Make a list of people you would like to interview and the questions you would ask each of them.

4. Describe in a paragraph the process you would go through in applying STROBE to observing an MRE office setting. List all elements in the MRE offices that seem important to understanding the users' decision-making behavior.

d. Construct a matrix with the organizational storyline down the left-hand side of the page and the elements of STROBE across the top. Using the symbols from the "anecdotal list" application of STROBE, indicate the relationship between the organizational storyline as portrayed by I. B. and each element you have observed (that is, indicate whether each element of STROBE confirms, reverses, causes you to look further, modifies, or supplements the narrative).

e. Based on your observations of STROBE and your interview, state in a paragraph what problems you are able to anticipate in getting a new system approved by I. B. and others. In a sentence or two, discuss how your diagnosis might have been different if you had just talked to I. B. over the phone or if you had read his written comments on a systems proposal.

GROUP PROJECTS

1. Arrange to visit a local organization that is expanding or otherwise enhancing its information systems. To allow your group to practice the various observation methods described in this chapter, assign one of the following techniques to each group member: time sampling, event sampling, observing decision makers' body language, developing the analyst's playscript, and using STROBE. Many of these strategies can be employed during one-on-one interviews, while some require formal organizational meetings. Try to accomplish several objectives during your visit to the organization by scheduling it at an appropriate time, one that permits all team members to try their assigned method of observation. Using multiple methods such as interviewing and observation (often simultaneously) is the only cost-effective way to get a true, timely picture of the organization's information requirements.

2. The members of your group should meet and discuss their findings. Were there any surprises? Did the information garnered through observation confirm, reverse, or negate what was learned in interviews? Were any of the findings from the observational methods in direct conflict with each other? Work with your group to develop a list of ways to address any puzzling information (for example, by doing follow-up interviews).

SELECTED BIBLIOGRAPHY

Edwards, A., and R. Talbot. *The Hard-Pressed Researcher.* New York: Longman, 1994.

Kendall, K. E., and J. E. Kendall. "Observing Organizational Environments: A Systematic Approach for Information Analysts." *Management Information Systems Quarterly,* Vol. 5, No. 1, 1981, pp. 43–55.

Kendall, K. E., and J. E. Kendall. "STROBE: A Structured Approach to the Observation of the Decision-Making Environment." *Information & Management,* Vol. 7, No. 1, 1984, pp. 1–11.

Kendall, K. E., and J. E. Kendall. "Structured Observation of the Decision-Making Environment: A Validity and Reliability Assessment." *Decision Sciences,* Vol. 15, No. 1, 1984, pp. 107–118.

Runkel, P. J., and J. E. McGrath. *Research on Human Behavior: A Systematic Guide to Method.* New York: Holt, Rinehart and Winston, Inc., 1972.

Shultis, R. L. "'Playscript'—A New Tool Accountants Need." *NAA Bulletin,* Vol. 45, No. 12, August 1964, pp. 3–10.

Weick, K. E. "Systematic Observational Methods." In G. Lindzey and E. Aronson (eds.), *The Handbook of Social Psychology,* 2nd ed., Vol II. Reading, MA: Addison-Wesley Publishing Company, 1968.

SEEING IS BELIEVING

"Chip, I know the interviews took a long time, but they were worth it," Anna says defensively as Chip enters her office with a worried look on his face.

"I'm sure of *that*," Chip says. "You really made a good impression on them. People have stopped me in the hall and said they're glad we're working on the new system. I'm not worried about the interviews themselves. But I was concerned that we didn't have time to discuss observations before you did them."

"Rest assured, I was all eyes," Anna laughs. "I used a technique called STROBE (*STR*uctured *OB*servation of the *E*nvironment) to systematically see our decision maker's habitats. You'll be interested in these notes I wrote up for each person I interviewed," says Anna, as she hands Chip her written, organized observations from each interview.

Observations of Decision Makers' Offices

Decision maker	Dot Matricks
Office location	An enclosed office in the Administrative Data Processing area. The door is usually open. Large windows with a beautiful view are located opposite the door.
Placement of desk	Center of the room with a chair across the desk from Dot and another chair at the side of the desk.
Stationary equipment	There are two large bookcases containing a variety of books. One is ceiling height and another is desk height.
Decorations	On the lower bookcase are pictures of Dot's children. There are several pictures on the walls. One is a farm scene from the last century with a horse and buggy and two riders trotting up a dirt road.
Props	A mainframe/microcomputer work station, turned on with a sign-on screen displayed. A stack of reports is on the left side. Several pens and a printer calculator are above the reports. A laptop computer is in the shorter bookcase.
Trade journals and newspapers	Several copies of *Computerworld* and the *Journal of Management Systems* are on top of the bookcase. The latest *Computerworld* issue is on the desk.

*Allen Schmidt,
Julie E. Kendall, and
Kenneth E. Kendall*

Office lighting/color	Brightly lit, warm tan walls with a brown accent stripe.
Clothing	A dress, authoritatively jacketed with a navy blazer.

Decision maker	Mike Crowe
Office location	Workroom near the mainframe computer complex. A desk is in a cubicle partitioned at one end of the room.
Placement of desk	Against the wall. A chair is at the side of the desk and is piled high with technical manuals.
Stationary equipment	A file cabinet and a half-size bookcase. A long, low workbench covered with micros and parts.
Decorations	Posters of a magnified microchip showing the circuitry. Several posters of railroad trains.
Props	The bookcase is stacked high with papers, magazines, manuals, software packages, and diskettes. An Pentium 120 is on the desk. Displayed on it are several open windows overlapping each other.
Trade journals and newspapers	There are numerous catalogues for parts and a stack of *PC Tech Journals* in evidence.
Office lighting/color	The office is well lit with large overhead fluorescent lights as well as desk and work-area lighting.
Clothing	Dark slacks, a lightly striped shirt, and a dark tie accenting the shirt stripes.

Decision maker	Cher Ware
Office location	Within Administrative Data Processing. Cubicle, near the center of the microcomputer area.
Placement of desk	Facing a wall of the cubicle with a chair behind the desk and at the side of the desk. An old sofa is against another wall.
Stationary equipment	A bookcase and a file cabinet. The bookcase contains a variety of books referencing microcomputer software and hardware.
Decorations	Posters of mountain scenery, tranquil lakes, a forest, and one that says "Flower Power."
Props	The desk is rather cluttered with paper, pencils, coffee cups, and the like. A PC is on the desk, with a word processing screen and some partially keyed text displayed.

Trade journals and newspapers	Several internal reports. The latest copy of *Word-Perfect* magazine is stacked next to two micro-computer magazines. Each is folded back, exposing a product review page.
Office lighting/color	The cubical has burgundy walls and is warmly lit with ceiling and desk lighting.
Clothing	A flowered pastel blouse and a denim skirt.

Decision maker	Paige Prynter
Office location	Administration building, an enclosed office. Located near other decision makers. The office door is normally closed. Thin vertical windows are part of the wall to the hallway.
Placement of desk	Close to the door. Expansive space behind the desk. Chair of visitor is against the wall and directly across the desk from Paige's chair.
Stationary equipment	A file cabinet is in the corner. There is a bookcase containing bound sets of books neatly organized.
Decorations	A framed print of an English landscape is on the wall.
Props	A terminal sits on the desk. It is turned off. A gold pen set is the only other object on the desk.
Trade journals and newspapers	A copy of the *Wall Street Journal* and some educational journals are visible on a small bookcase. No journals or reports are on the desk.
Office lighting/color	Lighting is fluorescent. The colors of the office are grey and mauve.
Clothing	Skirted suit with white blouse.

Decision maker	Hy Perteks
Office location	In the Information Center. A faculty and staff resource room with microcomputer and several mainframe workstations. The office is partitioned off at one end of the room.
Placement of desk	The desk has its side against the partition wall with a chair to the side of it. The space behind and in front of the desk are fairly balanced.
Stationary equipment	There are two desk-height bookcases and several four-drawer file cabinets.

Decorations	The walls are covered with numerous posters and with artwork that his children have created. The posters are of astronomical objects, distant countries, and interesting surrealistic-looking computer artwork, some depicting fractals.
Props	The desk has a Pentium MMX displaying a Web site. There are pens and a metal printer-spacing ruler on the desk. Several smoke-colored boxes of diskettes are on a shelf.
Trade journals and newspapers	Several issues of *PC Magazine* and a *Macintosh* journal are on the bookcase. The latest issue of *Byte* is on the desk.
Office lighting/color	The office is well lit with desk and overhead fluorescent lamps. The colors are a warm off-white.
Clothing	A sports jacket with a pale yellow shirt and dark tie. Dress slacks that coordinate with his jacket.

Exercises

E-1. Based on Anna's written observation of Dot's office and clothing, use STROBE to analyze Dot as a decision maker. In two paragraphs, compare and contrast what you learned in Dot's interview (Chapter 5) and what you learned via STROBE.

E-2. After examining Anna's written observations about Mike Crowe's office, use STROBE to analyze Mike as a decision maker. What differences (if any) did you see between Mike in his interview (Chapter 5) and Mike in Anna's observations? Use two paragraphs to answer.

E-3. Use STROBE to analyze Anna's written observations about Cher Ware and Paige Prynter. Use two paragraphs to compare and contrast the decision-making style of each person as it is revealed by their offices and clothing.

E-4. Use STROBE to analyze Anna's written observations about Hy Perteks. Now compare your analysis with Hy's interview in Chapter 5. Use two paragraphs to discuss whether STROBE confirms, negates, reverses, or serves as a cue to look further in Hy's narrative. (Include any further questions you would ask Hy to clarify your interpretation.)

8

PROTOTYPING

KINDS OF INFORMATION SOUGHT

Prototyping of information systems is a worthwhile technique for quickly gathering specific information about users' information requirements. As will become evident in the second section of this chapter, there are four basic approaches to prototyping. Generally speaking, effective prototyping should come early in the systems development life cycle, during the requirements determination phase. However, prototyping is a complex technique that requires knowledge of the entire systems development life cycle before it is successfully accomplished.

Prototyping is included at this point in the text to underscore its importance as an information-gathering technique. When using prototyping in this way, the systems analyst is seeking initial reactions from users and management to the prototype, user suggestions about changing or cleaning up the prototyped system, possible innovations for it, and revision plans detailing which parts of the system need to be done first or which branches of an organization to prototype next. Figure 8.1 shows the four kinds of information that analysts seek during prototyping.

INITIAL USER REACTIONS

As the systems analyst presenting a prototype of the information system, you are keenly interested in the reactions of users and management to the prototype. You want to know in detail how they react to working with the prototype and how good the fit is between their needs and the prototyped features of the system. Reactions are gathered through observation, interviews, and feedback sheets (possibly questionnaires) designed to elicit each person's opinion about the prototype as he or she interacts with it. Through such user reactions, the analyst discovers many perspectives on the prototype, including whether users seem happy with it and whether there will be difficulty in selling or implementing the system.

FIGURE 8.1
Kinds of information sought
when prototyping.

User Suggestions

The analyst is also interested in user and management suggestions about refining or changing the prototype that has been presented. Suggestions are garnered from those experiencing the prototype as they work with it for a specified period. The time that users spend with the prototype is usually dependent on their dedication to and interest in the systems project.

Suggestions are the product of users' interaction with the prototype as well as their reflection on that interaction. The suggestions obtained from users should point the analyst toward ways of refining, changing, or "cleaning up" the prototype so that it better suits users' needs.

Innovations

Innovations for the prototype (which, if successful, will be part of the finished system) are part of the information sought by the systems analysis team. Innovations are new system capabilities that have not been thought of prior to the time when users began to interact with the prototype. These innovations go beyond the current prototyped features by adding something new and innovative.

Revision Plans

Prototypes preview the future system. Revision plans help identify priorities for what should be prototyped next. In situations where many branches of an organization are involved, revision plans help to determine which branches to prototype next.

Information gathered in the prototyping phase allows the analyst to set priorities and redirect plans inexpensively, with a minimum of disruption. Because of this feature, prototyping and planning go hand in hand.

APPROACHES TO PROTOTYPING

Kinds of Prototypes

The word *prototype* is used in many different ways. Rather than attempting to synthesize all of these uses into one definition or trying to mandate one correct approach to the somewhat controversial topic of prototyping, we will illustrate how each of several conceptions of prototyping may be usefully applied in a particular situation.

FIGURE 8.2
A patched-up prototype
works but is neither efficient
nor elegant.

PATCHED-UP PROTOTYPE. The first kind of prototyping has to do with constructing a system that works but is patched up or patched together. In engineering this approach is referred to as breadboarding—creating a patched-together, working model of an (otherwise microscopic) integrated circuit.

An example in information systems is a working model that has all the necessary features but is inefficient. In this instance of prototyping, users can interact with the system, getting accustomed to the interface and types of output available. However, the retrieval and storage of information may be inefficient, since programs were written rapidly with the objective of being workable rather than efficient. A patched-up prototype may be envisioned as something like the illustration shown in Figure 8.2.

Another example of a patched-up prototype is an information system that has all the proposed features but is really a basic model that will eventually be enhanced.

NONOPERATIONAL PROTOTYPE. The second conception of a prototype is that of a nonworking scale model which is set up to test certain aspects of the design. An example of this approach is a full-scale model of an automobile which is used in wind tunnel tests. The size and shape of the auto are precise, but the car is not operational. In this case only features of the automobile essential to wind tunnel testing are included.

A nonworking scale model of an information system might be produced when the coding required by the applications is too extensive to prototype but when a useful idea of the system can be gained through the prototyping of the input and output only. This kind of prototype is shown conceptually in Figure 8.3. In this instance processing, because of undue cost and time, would not be prototyped. However, some decisions on the utility of the system could still be made based on prototyped input and output.

FIRST-OF-A-SERIES PROTOTYPE. A third conception of prototyping involves creating a first full-scale model of a system, often called a pilot. An example is prototyping the first airplane of a series. The prototype is completely operational and is a realization of what the designer hopes will be a series of airplanes with identical features.

This type of prototyping is useful when many installations of the same information system are planned. The full-scale working model allows users to experience realistic interaction with the new system, yet it minimizes the cost of overcoming any problems that it presents. This sort of prototype is depicted in Figure 8.4.

FIGURE 8.3
A nonoperational prototype
may seek users' opinions on
the interfaces (input and output).

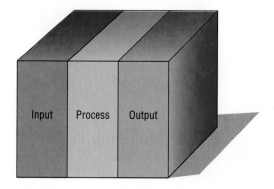

For example, when a retail grocery chain intends to use EDI (electronic data interchange) to check in suppliers' shipments in a number of outlets, a full-scale model might be installed in one store in order to work through any problems before the system is implemented in all the others.

Another example is found in banking installations for electronic funds transfer. A full-scale prototype is installed in one or two locations first, and if successful, duplicates are installed at all locations based on customer usage patterns and other key factors.

SELECTED FEATURES PROTOTYPE. A fourth conception of prototyping concerns building an operational model that includes some, but not all, of the features that the final system will have. An analogy would be a new retail shopping mall that opens before the construction of all shops is complete.

In a newly opened retail mall, essential functions such as being able to purchase some goods, eating in a fast-food restaurant, and parking nearby are possible, although not all space is occupied and not all goods that will ultimately be for sale are available when the complex first opens. Nonetheless, from initial contact with the retail complex, it is possible to gain a good understanding of what future visits will be like.

When prototyping information systems in this way, some, but not all, essential features are included. For example, a system menu may appear onscreen that lists six features: add a record, update a record, delete a record, search a record for a keyword, list a record, or scan a record. However, in the prototyped system, only three of the six may be available for use, so that the user may add a record (feature 1), delete a record (feature 3), and list a record (feature 5), as illustrated in Figure 8.5.

FIGURE 8.4
A first-of-a-series prototype is
a working model that will be
used elsewhere if it is successful.

FIGURE 8.5
A selected features prototype
allows the system to be put
into place, while other features can be added at a later
date.

When this kind of prototyping is done, the system is accomplished in modules, so that if the features that are prototyped are evaluated as successful, they can be incorporated into the larger, final system without undertaking immense work in interfacing. Prototypes done in this manner are part of the actual system. They are *not* just a mock-up as in the first definition of prototyping considered previously.

Prototyping as an Alternative to the Systems Development Life Cycle

Some analysts argue that prototyping should be considered as an alternative to the systems development life cycle (SDLC). Recall that the SDLC, introduced in Chapter 1, is a logical, systematic approach to follow in the development of information systems.

Complaints about going through the SDLC center around two main concerns, which are interrelated. The first concern is the extended time required to go through the development life cycle. As the investment of analyst time increases, the cost of the delivered system rises proportionately.

The second concern about using the SDLC is that user requirements change over time. During the long interval between the time that user requirements are analyzed and the time that the finished system is delivered, user requirements are evolving. Thus, because of the extended development cycle, the resulting system may be criticized for inadequately addressing current user information requirements.

It is apparent that the concerns are interrelated, since they both pivot on the time required to complete the SDLC and the problem of falling out of touch with user requirements during subsequent development phases. If a system is developed in isolation from users (after initial requirements analysis is completed), it will not meet their expectations.

A corollary of the problem of keeping up with user information requirements is the suggestion that users cannot really know what they do or do not want until they see something tangible. And in the traditional SDLC, it often is too late to change an unwanted system once it is delivered.

To overcome these problems, some analysts propose that prototyping be used as an alternative to the systems development life cycle. When prototyping is used in this way, the analyst effectively shortens the time between ascertainment of information requirements and delivery of a workable system. Additionally, using prototyping instead of the traditional systems development life cycle might overcome some of the problems of accurately identifying user information requirements.

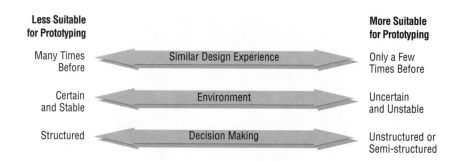

FIGURE 8.6
Certain factors determine whether a system is more or less suitable for prototyping.

With a prototype, users can actually see what is possible and how their requirements translate into hardware and software. Any of the four kinds of prototyping discussed earlier might be used.

Drawbacks to supplanting the systems development life cycle with prototyping include prematurely shaping a system before the problem or opportunity being addressed is thoroughly understood. Also, using prototyping as an alternative may result in producing a system which is accepted by specific groups of users but which is inadequate for overall system needs.

The approach we advocate here is to use prototyping as a part of the traditional systems development life cycle. In this view prototyping is considered as an additional, specialized method for ascertaining users' information requirements.

DEVELOPING A PROTOTYPE

In this section guidelines for developing a prototype are advanced. The term *prototyping* is taken in the sense of the last definition that was discussed—that is, a selected-features prototype that will include some but not all features, one that, if successful, will eventually be part of the larger, final system that is delivered.

When deciding whether to include prototyping as a part of the systems development life cycle, the systems analyst needs to consider what kind of problem is being solved and in what way the system presents the solution. Different types of systems and their suitability for prototyping are depicted in Figure 8.6. A straightforward payroll or inventory system which solves a highly structured problem in a traditional manner is not a good candidate for prototyping, because the outcome of the system as a solution is well-known and predictable.

Rather, consider the novelty and complexity of the problem and its solution. A novel and complex system that addresses unstructured or semistructured problems in a nontraditional way is a perfect candidate for prototyping. Decision support systems, which are the subject of Chapter 12, are personalized information systems that support users in semistructured decision making. As such, DSSs are well-suited to prototyping.

The systems analyst must also evaluate the environmental context for the system when deciding whether to prototype. If the system will exist in an environment that is stable for long periods, prototyping may be unnecessary. However, if the environment for the system changes rapidly, then prototyping should be seriously considered. By their nature prototypes are evolutionary and can absorb many revisions.

The prototype system is actually an operational portion of the eventual system that you will build. It is not a complete system, since you will

Customer File

Customer's Name:
Address:

Phone:
Comments:

Customer File

Customer's Name:
Company:
Department:
Street Address:
City and State: Zip:
Office Phone: Extension:
Fax: Last Visit:
Comments:

strive to build it quickly; only some essential functions will be included in the model. However, it is important to envision and then build the prototype as part of the actual system with which the user will interact. It must incorporate enough representative functions to allow users to understand that they are interacting with a real system.

Prototyping is a superb way to elicit feedback about the proposed system and about how readily it is fulfilling the information needs of its users, as depicted in Figure 8.7. The first step of prototyping is to estimate the costs involved in building a module of the system. If costs of programmers' and analysts' time, as well as equipment costs, are within the budget, then building of the prototype can proceed. Prototyping is an excellent way to facilitate the integration of the information system into the larger system of the organization.

Source © 1996 Ted Goff from The Cartoon Bank, Inc. All Rights Reserved.

Guidelines for Developing a Prototype

Once the decision to prototype has been made, there are four main guidelines that must be observed when integrating prototyping into the requirements determination phase of the systems development life cycle:

1. Work in manageable modules.
2. Build the prototype rapidly.
3. Modify the prototype in successive iterations.
4. Stress the user interface.

As you can see, the guidelines suggest ways of proceeding with the prototype that are necessarily interrelated. Each guideline is explained in the following subsections.

WORKING IN MANAGEABLE MODULES. When prototyping some of the features of a system into a workable model, it is imperative that the analyst work in manageable modules. One of the distinct advantages of prototyping is that it is not necessary or desirable to build an entire working system for prototype purposes.

A manageable module is one that allows users to interact with its key features yet can be built separately from other system modules. Module features that are deemed less important are purposely left out of the initial prototype.

BUILDING THE PROTOTYPE RAPIDLY. Speed is essential to the successful prototyping of an information system. Recall that one of the complaints voiced against following the traditional systems development life cycle is that the interval between requirements determination and delivery of a complete system is far too long to effectively address evolving user needs.

Analysts can use prototyping to shorten this gap by using traditional information-gathering techniques to pinpoint salient information require-

CONSULTING OPPORTUNITY 8.1

Is Prototyping King?

"As you know, we're an enthusiastic group. We're not a dynasty yet, but we're working on it," Paul Le Gon tells you. Paul (introduced in Consulting Opportunity 2.2), at 24 years of age, is the "boy king" of Pyramid, Inc., a small but successful, independent book publishing firm that specializes in paperback books outside of the publishing mainstream. As a systems analyst, you have been hired by Pyramid, Inc., to help develop a computerized warehouse inventory and distribution information system.

"We're hiring lots of workers," Paul continues, as if to convince you of the vastness of Pyramid's undertaking. "And we feel Pyramid is positioned perfectly as far as our markets in the north, south, east, and west are concerned.

"My assistant, Ceil Toom, and I have been slaving away, thinking about the new system. And we've concluded that what we really need is a prototype. As a matter of fact, we've tunneled through a lot of material. Our fascination with the whole idea has really pyramided."

As you formulate a response to Paul, you think back over the few weeks you've worked with Pyramid, Inc. You feel that the business problems that its information system must resolve are very straightforward. You also know that the people in the company are on a limited budget and cannot afford to spend like kings. Actually, the entire project is quite small.

Ceil, building on what Paul has said, tells you, "We don't mean to be too wrapped up with it, but we feel prototyping represents the new world. And that's where we all want to be. We know we need a prototype. Have we convinced you?"

Based on Paul and Ceil's enthusiasm for prototyping and what you know about Pyramid's needs, would you support construction of a prototype? Why or why not? Formulate your decision and response in a letter to Paul Le Gon and Ceil Toom. Present a justification for your decision based on overall criteria that should be met in order to justify prototyping.

ments and then they can quickly make decisions that bring forth a working model. In effect the user sees and uses the system very early in the systems development life cycle instead of waiting for a finished system to gain hands-on experience.

After a brief analysis of information requirements using traditional methods, such as interviewing, observing, and researching archival data, the analyst constructs working models for the prototype. The prototype should take less than a week to put together; two or three days is preferable and possible. Remember that in order to build a prototype this quickly, you must use special tools, such as an existing database management system, as well as software that allows generalized input and output, interactive systems, and so on. All these tools permit speed of construction that is impossible with traditional programming.

It is important to emphasize that at this stage in the life cycle, the analyst is still gathering information about what users need and want from the information system. The prototype becomes a valuable extension of traditional requirements determination. The analyst assesses user feedback about the prototype in order to get a better picture of overall information needs.

Putting together an operational prototype both rapidly and early in the systems development life cycle allows the analyst to gain valuable insight into how the remainder of the project should go. By showing users very early in the process how parts of the system actually perform, rapid prototyping guards against overcommitting resources to a project that may eventually become unworkable.

MODIFYING THE PROTOTYPE. A third guideline for developing the prototype is that its construction must support modifications. Making the prototype modifiable means creating it in modules that are not highly interdependent. If this guideline is observed, less resistance is encountered when modifications in the prototype are necessary.

The prototype is generally modified several times, going through several iterations. Changes in the prototype should move the system closer to what users say is important. Each modification necessitates another evaluation by users.

As with the initial development, modifications must be accomplished swiftly, usually in a day or two, in order to keep the momentum of the project going. However, the exact timing of modifications depends on how dedicated users are to interacting with modified prototypes. Systems analysts must encourage users to do their share by evaluating changes rapidly.

The prototype is not a finished system. Entering the prototyping phase with the idea that the prototype will require modification is a helpful attitude that demonstrates to users how necessary their feedback is if the system is to improve.

STRESSING THE USER INTERFACE. The user's interface with the prototype (and eventually the system) is very important. Since what you are really trying to achieve with the prototype is to get users to further articulate their information requirements, they must be able to interact easily with the system's prototype. For many users the interface *is* the system. It should not be a stumbling block.

For example, at this stage the goal of the analyst is to design an interface that both allows the user to interact with the system with a minimum of training and allows a maximum of user control over represented functions. Although many aspects of the system will remain undeveloped in the prototype, the user interface must be well developed enough to enable users to pick up the system quickly and not be put off. On-line, interactive systems using GUI interfaces are ideally suited to prototypes. Chapter 18 describes in detail the considerations that are important in designing the user interface.

Many of the intricacies of interfaces must be streamlined or ignored altogether in the prototyping phase. However, if prototype interfaces are not what users need or want or if systems analysts find that the interfaces do not adequately allow system access, then they, too, are candidates for modification.

Disadvantages of Prototyping

As with any information-gathering technique, there are several disadvantages to prototyping. The first is that it can be quite difficult to manage prototyping as a project within the larger systems effort. The second disadvantage is that users and analysts may adopt a prototype as a completed system when it is in fact inadequate and was never intended to serve as a finished system.

The analyst needs to weigh these disadvantages against the known advantages when deciding whether to prototype, when to prototype, and how much of the system to prototype.

MANAGING THE PROJECT. All of the systems analysts' management skills that you learned in Chapter 3 come into play again as your systems analysis team constructs and modifies a prototype. All of the possible problems that project management is subject to are relevant here.

CONSULTING OPPORTUNITY 8.2

Clearing the Way for Customer Links

World's Trend (see Chapter 9 for a detailed corporate description) is building a Web site on which to sell clearance merchandise usually sold through the Web and through its catalog operation. As a newly-hired Web consultant, Lincoln Cerf finds himself in a very cold, wintry city, fighting his way through several inches of snow to meet with one of the system team members, Mary Maye, at World's Trend headquarters.

Mary welcomes Lincoln, saying "At least the weather doesn't seem to effect our Web sales! They're brisk no matter what." Lincoln groans appreciatively at her weak attempt at humor, smiles, and says, "I gathered from your e-mail last week that you are trying to determine the type of information that needs to be displayed on our clearance Web site." Mary replies, "Yes, I'm trying to get it organized in the best possible way. Our customers are all so busy. I know photos of all of our merchandise can take a long time to appear on the page if a customer is accessing the Web via a slower modem from home."

Mary continues by saying, "Linc, I'm not even that concerned about how to design our clearance site at this time. I am worried, though, about how much information we need to include on a page. For example, when items are on clearance, not all colors and sizes are available. Which do you think is better—to include some basic information and let the customer click a button to ask for more information, or to be as complete as possible on one page? If I use the linking method, then I could fit more items on the screen . . . but it might be too orderly. Customers like the look and feel of a sale where merchandise is kind of jumbled together."

Linc continues her line of thought, saying, "Yeah, I wonder how customers want the information organized. Have you actually watched them use the Web? I mean, do they look for shoes when they buy a suit? If so, should shoes appear on the suit page or be linked in some way?"

Mary comments, "Those are my questions, too. Then I wonder if we should just try this for men's clothes first, before we implement the same approach for women's clothing. What if their approaches to shopping on the Web are different?"

As a third member of the World's Trend Web site development group, respond in a brief written report to Lincoln and Mary about whether you should use a prototype to elicit recommendations from potential customers about the proposed Web site. What type of prototype is appropriate? Consider each form of prototype and explain why each type would apply (or would not apply) to this problem. Devote a paragraph to each explanation.

Although several iterations of the prototype may be necessary, extending the prototype indefinitely also creates problems. It is important that the systems analysis team devise and then carry out a plan regarding how feedback on the prototype will be collected, analyzed, and interpreted. Set up specific time periods during which you and management decision makers will use feedback to evaluate how well the prototype is performing. Even though the prototype is prized for its evolutionary nature, the analyst cannot permit prototyping to overtake other phases in the systems development life cycle.

Elicit feedback from users periodically, not just once, and ask them if previous suggestions for improvements or changes have been acted upon satisfactorily. Feedback is directed to the members of the systems analysis team for their reaction and possible modification of the prototype to better fit user needs. Recall that modifications to the prototype should be managed on a tight schedule of only a day or two each throughout the successive iterations.

ADOPTING AN INCOMPLETE SYSTEM AS COMPLETE. A second major disadvantage of prototyping is that if a system is needed badly and welcomed readily, the prototype may be accepted in its unfinished state and pressed into service without the necessary refinements. While superficially, this may seem to be an appealing way to short-cut the development effort, it works to the business' and team's disadvantage.

Users will develop interaction patterns with the prototype system that are not compatible with what will actually occur with the complete system. Additionally, a prototype will not perform all necessary functions. Eventually, when users discover the deficiencies, user backlash may develop if the prototype has been mistakenly adopted and integrated into the business as if it were a complete system.

Advantages of Prototyping

Prototyping is not necessary or appropriate in every systems project, as we have seen. However, the advantages should also be given consideration when deciding whether to prototype. The three major advantages of prototyping are: the potential for changing the system early in its development, the opportunity to stop development on a system that is not working, and the possibility of developing a system that more closely addresses users' needs and expectations. All three advantages are interrelated.

CHANGING THE SYSTEM EARLY IN ITS DEVELOPMENT. Successful prototyping depends on early and frequent user feedback, which can be used to help modify the system and make it more responsive to actual needs. As with any systems effort, early changes are less expensive than changes made late in the project's development.

Since the prototype can be changed many times and since flexibility and adaptation are at the heart of prototyping, the feedback that calls for a change in the system is often the action taken. Feedback will help tell you if changes are warranted in the input, process, or output areas, or if all three need adjustment.

When changing a prototype, analysts do not need to worry about wasting many man-hours of their efforts and those of programmers who have developed a full-blown system only to find that it needs modifications. Although the prototype represents an investment of time and money, it is always considerably less expensive than a completed system. Concomitantly, system problems and oversights are much easier to trace and detect in a prototype with limited features and limited interfaces than they are in a complex system.

SCRAPPING UNDESIRABLE SYSTEMS. A second advantage of using prototyping as an information-gathering technique is the possibility of scrapping a system that is just not what users and analysts had hoped it would be. Once again, the issue of time and money arises. A prototype represents much less of an investment than a completely developed system.

Permanently removing the prototype system from use is done when it becomes apparent that the system is not useful and does not fulfill the information requirements (and other objectives) that have been set. Although scrapping the prototype is a difficult decision to make, it is infinitely better than putting increasing sums of time and money into a project that is plainly unworkable.

DESIGNING A SYSTEM FOR USERS' NEEDS AND EXPECTATIONS. A third advantage of prototyping is that the system being developed should be a better fit with users' needs and expectations. Many studies of failed information

CONSULTING OPPORTUNITY 8.3

To Hatch a Fish

"Just be a little patient. I think we need to add a few more features before we turn it over to them. Otherwise, this whole prototype will sink, not swim," says Sam Monroe, a member of your systems analysis team. All four members of the team are sitting together in a hurriedly called meeting, and they are discussing the prototype that they are developing for an information system to help managers monitor and control water temperature, number of fish released, and other factors at a large, commercial fish hatchery.

"They've got plenty to do already. Why, the system began with four features and we're already up to nine. I feel like we're swimming upstream on this one. They don't need all that. They don't even want it," argues Belle Uga, a second member of the systems analysis team. "I don't mean to carp, but just give them the basics. We've got enough to tackle as it is."

"I think Monroe is more on target," volunteers Wally Ide, a third member of the team, baiting Belle a little. "We have to show them our very best. Even if it means being a few weeks later in hatching our prototype than we promised."

"Okay," Belle says warily, "but I want the two of you to tell the managers at the hatchery why we aren't delivering the prototype. I don't want to. And I'm not sure they'll let you off the hook that easily."

Monroe replies, "Well, I guess we could, but we probably shouldn't make a big deal out of being later than we wanted. I don't want to rock the boat."

Wally chimes in, "Yeah. Why point out our mistakes to everyone? Besides, when they see the prototype, they'll forget any complaints they had. They'll love it."

Belle finds a memo in her notebook from their last meeting with the hatchery managers and reads it aloud. "Agenda for meeting of September 22. 'Prototyping—the importance of rapid development, putting together the user analyst team, getting quick feedback for modification . . .'" Belle's voice trails off, omitting the last few agenda items. In the wake of her comments, Monroe and Ide look unhappily at each other.

Monroe speaks first. "I guess we did make a try to get everyone primed for receiving a prototype quickly. And to be involved from day one." Noting your silence up until now, Monroe continues, "But still waters run deep. What do you think we should do next?" he asks you.

As the fourth member of the systems analysis team, what actions do you think should be taken? In a one-or two-paragraph e-mail message to your teammates, answer the following questions: Should more features be added to the hatchery system prototype before giving it to the hatchery managers to experiment with? How important is the rapid development of the prototype? What are the tradeoffs involved in adding more features to the prototype versus getting a more basic prototype to the client when it was promised? Complete your message with a recommendation.

systems indict the long interval between requirements determination and the presentation of the finished system; these systems failed precisely because it is common for systems analysts to develop systems while sequestered away from users during this critical period.

It is a better practice to interact with users throughout the systems development life cycle. If your team makes a commitment to ongoing user involvement in all phases of the project, then the prototype can be used as an interactive tool that shapes the final system to accurately reflect users' requirements.

Users who take early ownership of the information system work harder to ensure its success. One way to foster early user support is to involve users actively in prototyping.

If your evaluation of the prototype indicates that the system is functioning well and within the guidelines that have been set, the decision should be to keep the prototype going and continue expanding it to include other functions as planned. This, then, is considered an operational prototype. The decision is made to keep the prototype functioning if the prototype is within the budget set for programmers' and analysts' time, if users find the system worthwhile, and if it is meeting the information require-

FIGURE 8.8
Disadvantages and advantages
of prototyping.

Disadvantages to Prototyping	Advantages to Prototyping
• Difficult to manage prototyping as a project within a larger systems effort • Users and analysts may adopt a prototype as a completed system when it is inadequate	• Potential exists for changing the system early in its development • Opportunity exists to stop development on a system that is not working • May address user needs and expectations more closely

ments and objectives that have been set. A list comparing disadvantages and advantages of prototyping is given in Figure 8.8.

USERS' ROLE IN PROTOTYPING

The users' role in prototyping can be summed up in two words: honest involvement. Without user involvement there is little reason to prototype. The precise behaviors necessary for interacting with a prototype can vary, but it is clear that the user is pivotal to the prototyping process. Realizing the importance of the user to the success of the process, the members of the systems analysis team must encourage and welcome input and guard against their own natural resistance to changing the prototype.

Interaction with the Prototype

There are three main ways a user can be of help in prototyping:

1. Experimenting with the prototype
2. Giving open reactions to the prototype
3. Suggesting additions to and/or deletions from the prototype

All of the foregoing stem from the users' initial and successive interactions with the prototype.

EXPERIMENTING WITH THE PROTOTYPE. Users should be free to experiment with the prototype. In contrast to a mere list of systems features, the prototype allows users the reality of hands-on interaction. Mounting a prototype on an interactive Web site is one way to facilitate this interaction. Limited functionality along with the capability to send comments to the systems team can be included.

Users need to be encouraged to experiment with the prototype. The final system will be delivered with documentation stating how the system is to be used, and this in effect constrains experimentation. But in the prototyping stage, the user is free from all but minimal instruction on how to use the system. When this is the case, experimentation becomes necessary to make the prototype work.

Analysts need to be present at least part of the time when experimentation is occurring. They can then observe users' interactions with the system, and they are bound to see interactions they never planned. A form for observing user experimentation with the prototype is shown in Figure 8.9. Some of the variables you should observe include user reactions to the prototype, user suggestions for changing or expanding the prototype, user inno-

Prototype Evaluation Form				
Observer Name		Date		
System or Project Name		Company or Location		
Program Name or Number		Version		
	User 1	User 2	User 3	User 4
User Name				
Period Observed				
User Reactions				
User Suggestions				
Innovations				
Revision Plans				

FIGURE 8.9
An important step in prototyping is to properly record user reactions, user suggestions, innovations, and revision plans.

vations for using the system in completely new ways, and any revision plans for the prototype that aid in setting priorities. When revising the prototype, analysts should circulate their recorded observations among team members so that everyone is fully informed.

GIVING OPEN REACTIONS TO THE PROTOTYPE. Another aspect of the users' role in prototyping requires that they give open reactions to the prototype. Unfortunately, this is not something that occurs on demand. Rather, making users secure enough to give an open reaction is part of the relationship between analysts and users that your team works to build.

Additionally, if users feel wary about commenting on or criticizing what may be a pet project of organizational superiors or peers, it is unlikely that open reactions to the prototype will be forthcoming. Providing a private (relatively unsupervised) period for users to interact with and respond to the prototype is one way to insulate them from unwanted organizational influences. An exclusive Web site set up for users and analysts can also help in this regard.

SUGGESTING CHANGES TO THE PROTOTYPE. A third aspect of the users' role in prototyping is their willingness to suggest additions to and/or deletions from the features being tried. The analysts' role is to elicit such suggestions by assuring users that the feedback they provide is taken seriously, by observing users as they interact with the system, and by conducting short, specific interviews with users concerning their experiences with the prototype.

Although users will be asked to articulate suggestions and innovations for the prototype, in the end it is the analyst's responsibility to weigh this feedback and translate it into workable changes where necessary. Users need

This Prototype Is All Wet

"It can be changed. It's not a finished product, remember," affirms Sandy Beach, a systems analyst for RainFall, a large manufacturer of fiberglass bathtub and shower enclosures for bathrooms. Beach is anxiously reassuring Will Lather, a production scheduler for RainFall, who is poring over the first hard-copy output produced for him by the prototype of the new information system.

"Well, it's okay," Lather says quietly. "I wouldn't want to bother you with anything. Let's see, . . . yes, *here* they are," he says as he finally locates the monthly report summarizing raw materials purchased, raw materials used, and raw materials in inventory.

Lather continues paging through the unwieldy computer printout. "This will be fine." Pausing at a report, he remarks, "I'll just have Miss Fawcett copy this part over for the people in Accounting." Turning a few more pages, he says, "And the guy in QA should really see this column of figures, although the rest of it isn't of much interest to him. I'll circle it and make a copy of it for him. Maybe I should phone part of this into the warehouse, too."

As Sandy prepares to leave, Lather bundles up the pages of the reports, commenting, "The new system will be a big help. I'll make sure everybody knows about it. Anything will be better than the 'old monster' anyway. I'm glad we've got something new."

Sandy leaves Will Lather's office feeling a little lost at sea. Thinking it over, he starts wondering why Accounting, QA, and the warehouse aren't getting what Will thinks they should. Beach phones a few people,

and he confirms that what Lather has told him is true. They need the reports and they're not getting them.

Later in the week, Sandy approaches Lather about rerouting the output as well as changing some of the features of the system. These modifications would allow Lather to get onscreen answers regarding "what-if" scenarios about changes in the prices suppliers are charging; changes in the quality rating of the raw materials available from suppliers (or both); as well as allow him to see what would happen if a shipment was late.

Lather is visibly upset with Sandy's suggestions for altering the prototype and its output. "Oh, don't do it on my account. It's okay really. I don't mind taking the responsibility for routing information to people. I'm always showering them with stuff anyway. Really, this is working pretty well. I would hate to have you take it away from us at this point. Let's just leave it in place."

Sandy is pleased that Lather seems so satisfied with the prototyped output, but he is concerned about Lather's unwillingness to change the prototype, since he has been encouraging users to think of it as an evolving product, not a finished one.

Write a brief report to Sandy listing changes to the prototype prompted by Will's reactions. In a paragraph, discuss ways that Sandy can calm Lather's fears about having the prototype "taken away." Discuss in a paragraph some actions that can be taken *before* a prototype is tried out to prepare users for its evolutionary nature.

---

to be encouraged to brainstorm about possibilities and to be reminded that their input during the prototyping phase helps determine whether to save, scrap, or modify the system. In other words users should never be resigned to accepting in the prototype stage something less than what they want. Systems analysts must remember to stress to users and management alike that prototyping is the most appropriate time for system changes.

In order to facilitate the prototyping process, the analyst must clearly communicate the purposes of prototyping to users, along with the idea that prototyping is valuable only when users are meaningfully involved.

Prototyping and the "Year 2000 Crisis"

It seems so easy to type in a year as 97 or 98 instead of entering 1997 or 1999. It also saves a lot of valuable space in a database and everything fits better on a computer screen.

This was the standard way of thinking in the early days of computing and is still the case even now. Banks encouraged the practice by putting 19__ on checks so their customers wouldn't have to write in the 19.

In the late 1990s programmers started to question whether this was a good idea. After all, what happens in the year 2000. Will users want to see the 00 appear on the screen or report?

When we calculated a person's age in 1996, we took $1996 - 1975 = 21$. That is, if you were born in 1975 you turned 21 on your birthday in 1996. If we only stored the last 2 digits, the calculation was $96 - 75 = 21$ years old.

Let's try the same in the year 2000. Take $2000 - 1979$ and the answer is also 21, but take $00 - 79$ and the answer is -79 or minus 79 years old. This is part of the year 2000 crisis as well.

Prototyping can help determine problems such as this. When you develop a prototype, make sure you encourage users to give constructive criticism. In this way some problems, like the year 2000 crisis, may be averted.

SUMMARY

Prototyping is an information-gathering technique useful for supplementing the traditional systems development life cycle. When systems analysts use prototyping, they are seeking user reactions, suggestions, innovations, and revision plans in order to make improvements to the prototype and thereby modify system plans with a minimum of expense and disruption. Systems that support semistructured decision making (as decision support systems do) are prime candidates for prototyping.

The term *prototyping* carries several different meanings, four of which are commonly used. The first definition of prototyping is that of constructing a patched-up prototype. A second definition of prototyping is a nonoperational prototype that is used to test certain features of the design. A third conception of prototyping is creating the first-of-a-series prototype that is fully operational. This kind of prototype is useful when many installations of the same information system (under similar conditions) are planned. The fourth kind of prototyping is a selected features prototype that has some, but not all, of the essential system features. It uses self-contained modules as building blocks, so that if prototyped features are successful, they can be kept and incorporated into the larger, finished system.

The four major guidelines for developing a prototype are to: (1) work in manageable modules, (2) build the prototype rapidly, (3) modify the prototype, and (4) stress the user interface.

One disadvantage of prototypes is that managing the prototyping process is difficult because of the rapidity of the process and its many iterations. A second disadvantage is that an incomplete prototype may be pressed into service as if it were a complete system.

Although prototyping is not always necessary or desirable, it should be noted that there are three main, interrelated advantages to using it: (1) the potential for changing the system early in its development, (2) the opportunity to stop development on a system that is not working, and (3) the possibility of developing a system that more closely addresses users' needs and expectations.

Users have a distinct role to play in the prototyping process. Their main concern must be to interact with the prototype through experimentation. Systems analysts must work systematically to elicit and evaluate users reactions to the prototype. Sometimes this can be accomplished by mounting the prototype on an interactive Web site that permits users to see limited functionality and to enter comments for the systems team. Analysts then work to incorporate worthwhile user suggestions and innovations into subsequent modifications.

"Thank goodness it's the time of year when everything is new. I love spring; it's the most exhilarating time here at MRE. The trees are so green, with leaves in so many different shades. So many new projects to do, too; so many new clients to meet. It's really exciting. It reminds me of prototyping. Or what I know about prototyping, anyway. It's something new and fresh, a quick way to find out what's happening.

"In fact, I believe that we have a few prototypes already going on here. The best thing about them is that they can change. I don't know anyone who's really been satisfied with a first pass at a prototype. But it is fun to be involved with something that is happening fast, and something that will change."

HYPERCASE QUESTIONS

1. Locate the prototype currently proposed for use in one of MRE's departments. Suggest a few modifications that would make this prototype even more responsive to the unit's needs.

2. Using a word processor, construct a nonoperational prototype for a Training Unit Project Reporting System. If you have a hypertext program available, attempt to create partial functionality by making the menus functional. *Hint:* See sample screens in Chapters 15 and 16 to help you in your design.

FIGURE 8.HC1
One of the many prototype screens found in HyperCase.

KEYWORDS AND PHRASES

prototype
patched-up prototype
nonoperational prototype
first-of-a-series prototype
selected features prototype
working in manageable modules

building the prototype rapidly
modifying the prototype
stressing the user interface
user involvement with
 prototyping

REVIEW QUESTIONS

1. What four kinds of information is the analyst seeking through prototyping?
2. What is meant by the term "patched-up prototype"?
3. Define a prototype that is a "nonworking scale model."
4. Give an example of a prototype that is a "first full-scale model."
5. Define what is meant by a prototype that is a model with some, but not all, essential features.
6. List the advantages and disadvanges of using prototyping to *replace* the traditional systems development life cycle.
7. Describe how prototyping can be used to augment the traditional systems development life cycle.
8. What are the criteria for deciding whether a system should be prototyped?
9. List four guidelines that the analyst should observe in developing a prototype.
10. What are the two main problems identified with prototyping?
11. List the three main advantages in using prototyping.
12. How can a prototype mounted on an interactive Web site facilitate the prototyping process? Answer in a paragraph.
13. What are three ways that a user can be of help in the prototyping process?

PROBLEMS

1. As part of a larger systems project, Clone Bank of Clone, Colorado, wants your help in setting up a new monthly reporting form for its checking and savings account customers. The president and vice presidents are very attuned to what customers in the community are saying. They feel that their customers want a checking account summary that looks like the one offered by the other three banks in town. However, they are unwilling to commit to that form without a formal summary of customer feedback that supports their decision. Feedback will not be used to change the prototype form in any way. They want you to send a prototype of one form to one group and to send the old form to another group.

   a. In a paragraph, discuss why it probably is not worthwhile to prototype the new form under these circumstances.

   b. In a second paragraph, discuss a situation under which it would be advisable to prototype a new form.

2. C. N. Itall has been a systems analyst for Tun-L-Vision Corporation for many years. When you came on board as part of the systems analysis team and suggested prototyping as part of the SDLC for a current project, C. N.

said, "Sure, but you can't pay any attention to what users say. They have no idea what they want. I'll prototype, but I'm not 'observing' any users."

a. As tactfully as possible, so as not to upset C. N. Itall, make a list of the reasons that support the importance of observing user reactions, suggestions, and innovations in the prototyping process.

b. In a paragraph, describe what might happen if part of a system is prototyped and no user feedback about it is incorporated into the successive system.

3. "Every time I think I've captured user information requirements, they've already changed. It's like trying to hit a moving target. Half the time, I don't think they even know what they want themselves," exclaims Flo Chart, a systems analyst for 2 Good 2 Be True, a company that surveys product use for the marketing divisions of several manufacturing companies.

a. In a paragraph, explain to Flo Chart how prototyping can help her to better define users' information requirements.

b. In a paragraph, comment on Flo's observation: "Half the time, I don't think they even know what they want themselves." Be sure to explain how prototyping can actually help users better understand and articulate their own information requirements.

c. Suggest how an interactive Web site featuring a prototype might address Flo's concerns about capturing user information requirements. Use a paragraph.

4. Harold, a district manager for the multi-outlet chain of Sprocket's Gifts, thinks that building a prototype can mean only one thing: a nonworking scale model. He also believes that this is too cumbersome a way to prototype information systems and thus is reluctant to do so.

a. Briefly (in two or three paragraphs) compare and contrast the other three kinds of prototyping that are possible, so that Harold has an understanding of what prototyping can mean.

b. Harold has an option of implementing one system, trying it, and then having it installed in five other Sprocket locations if it is successful. Name a type of prototyping that would fit well with this approach, and in a paragraph defend your choice.

5. "I've got the idea of the century!" proclaims Bea Kwicke, a new systems analyst with your systems group. "Let's skip all of this SDLC garbage and just prototype everything. Our projects will go a lot more quickly, we'll save time and money, and all of the users will feel as if we're paying attention to them instead of going away for months on end and not talking to them."

a. List the reasons that you (as a member of the same team as Bea) would give her to dissuade her from trying to scrap the SDLC and prototype every project.

b. Bea is pretty disappointed with what you have said. In order to encourage her, use a paragraph to explain the situations that you feel would lend themselves to prototyping.

6. The following remark was overheard at a meeting between managers and a systems analysis team at the Fence-Me-In fencing company: "You told us the prototype would be finished three weeks ago. We're still waiting for it!"

a. In a paragraph, comment on the importance of rapid delivery of a portion of a prototyped information system.

b. List three elements of the prototyping process that must be controlled in order to assure prompt delivery of the prototype.

c. What are some elements of the prototyping process that are difficult to manage? List them.

7. Nordic Designs, a chain of stores specializing in contemporary furniture from Scandinavia, has been circulating a corporate newsletter that brags about the prototype of its shipping information system. The newsletter story proclaims, "Our shipping information system prototype was put into service as soon as it was delivered. With absolutely no changes necessary, managers say it's the perfect solution to tracking furniture shipments. Watch for the prototype in your store soon."

a. How has the writer of the story apparently misunderstood the concept of prototyping? Explain in a paragraph.

b. List the problems faced by designers of prototypes if users expect that "absolutely no changes are necessary."

GROUP PROJECTS

1. Divide your group into two smaller subgroups. Have Group 1 follow the processes specified in this chapter for creating prototypes. Using a CASE tool or a word processor, Group 1 should devise two nonworking prototype screens using the information collected in the interviews with Maverick Transport employees accomplished in the group exercise in Chapter 5. Make any assumptions necessary to create two screens for truck dispatchers. Group 2 (playing the roles of dispatchers) should react to the prototype screens and provide feedback about desired additions and deletions.

2. The members of Group 1 should revise the prototype screens based on the user comments they received. Those in Group 2 should respond with comments about how well their initial concerns were addressed with the refined prototypes.

3. As a united group, write a paragraph discussing your experiences with prototyping for ascertaining information requirements.

SELECTED BIBLIOGRAPHY

Alavi, M. "An Assessment of the Prototyping Approach to Information Systems Development." *Communications of the ACM,* Vol. 27, No. 6, June 1984, pp. 556–63.

Avison, D., and D. N. Wilson. "Controls for Effective Prototyping." *Journal of Management Systems,* Vol. 3, No 1, 1991.

Davis, G. B., and M. H. Olson. *Management Information Systems: Conceptual Foundations, Structure, and Development,* 2nd ed. New York: McGraw-Hill Book Company, 1985.

Dearnley, P., and P. Mayhew. "In Favour of System Prototypes and Their Integration into the Systems Development Cycle." *The Computer Journal,* Vol. 26, February 1983, pp. 36–42.

Gremillion, L. L., and P. Pyburn. "Breaking the Systems Development Bottleneck." *Harvard Business Review,* March–April 1983, pp. 130–37.

Harrison, T. S. "Techniques and Issues in Rapid Prototyping." *Journal of Systems Management.* Vol. 36, No. 6, June 1985, pp. 8–13.

Naumann, J. D., and A. M. Jenkins. "Prototyping: The New Paradigm for Systems Development." *Management Information Systems Quarterly,* September 1982, pp. 29–44.

Sano, D. *Designing Large-Scale Web Sites.* New York: John Wiley & Sons, Inc., 1996.

"We need to get a feel for some of the output needed by the users," Anna comments. "It will help to firm up some of our ideas on the information they require."

"Agreed," replies Chip. "It will also help us determine the necessary input. From that we can design corresponding data entry screens. Let's create prototype reports and screens and get some user feedback. Why don't we use Microsoft Access to quickly create screens and reports? I'm quite familiar with the software."

Anna starts by developing the PREVENTIVE MAINTENANCE REPORT prototype. Based on interview results, she sets to work creating the report she feels Mike Crowe will need.

"This report should be used to predict when machines should have preventive maintenance," Anna thinks. "It seems to me that Mike would need to know *which* machine needs work performed as well as *when* the work should be scheduled. Now let's see, what information would identify the machine clearly? The inventory number, brand name, and model would identify the machine. I imagine that the room and campus should be included to quickly locate the machine. A calculated maintenance date would tell Mike when the work should be completed. What sequence should the report be in? Probably the most useful would be by location."

The PREVENTIVE MAINTENANCE REPORT prototype showing the completed report is shown in Figure E8.1. Notice that Xxxxxxx's and generic dates are used to indicate where data should be printed. Realistic Campus and Room Locations as well as Inventory Numbers are included. This is necessary for Access to accomplish group printing.

The report prototype is soon finished. After printing the final copy, Anna takes the report to both Mike Crowe and Dot Matricks. Mike Crowe is enthusiastic about the project and wants to know when the report will be in production. Dot is similarly impressed.

Several changes come up. Mike wants an area to write in the Completion Date of the preventive maintenance so the report can be used to reenter the dates into the computer. Dot wants the report number assigned by data control to appear at the top of the form for reference purposes. She also suggests that the report title be changed to WEEKLY PREVENTIVE MAINTENANCE REPORT. The next step is to modify the prototype report to reflect the recommended changes and then to have both Mike and Dot review the result.

The report is easily modified and printed. Dot is pleased with the final result. "This is really a fine method for designing the system," she comments. "It's so nice to feel that we are a part of the development process and that our opinions count. I'm starting to feel quite confident that the final system will be just what we've always wanted."

Mike has similar praise, observing, "This will make our work so much smoother. It eliminates the guesswork about which machines need to be maintained. And sequencing them by room is a fine idea. We won't have to spend so much time returning to rooms to work on machines."

Chip makes a note about each of these modifications on the Prototype Evaluation Form shown in Figure E8-2. This form gets Chip organized and documents the prototyping process.

Allen Schmidt,
Julie E. Kendall, and
Kenneth E. Kendall

221

Campus Location	Room Location	Inventory Number	Brand Name	Model	Last Preventive Maintenance Date	Done
Central Administration	11111	84004782	Xxxxxxxxxxxxxxx	Xxxxxxxxxxxxxxxxxxx	1/1/99	_____
Central Administration	11111	90875039	Xxxxxxxxxxxxxx	Xxxxxxxxxxxxxxx	1/1/99	_____
Central Administration	11111	93955411	Xxxxxxxxxxxxxxx	Xxxxxxxxxxxxxxxxxxx	1/1/99	_____
Central Administration	11111	99381373	Xxxxxxxxxxxxxx	Xxxxxxxxxxxxxxxxxxx	1/1/99	_____
Central Administration	22222	10220129	Xxxxxxxxxxxxx	Xxxxxxxxxxxxxxxxx	1/1/99	_____
Central Administration	99999	22838234	Xxxxxxxxxxxxx	Xxxxxxxxxxxxxx	1/1/99	_____
Central Administration	99999	24720952	Xxxxxxxxxxxxx	Xxxxxxxxxxxxxxxxx	1/1/99	_____
Central Administration	99999	33453403	Xxxxxxxxxxxxx	Xxxxxxxxxxxxxx	1/1/99	_____
Central Administration	99999	34044449	Xxxxxxxxxxx	Xxxxxxxxxxxxxxxxx	1/1/99	_____
Central Administration	99999	40030303	Xxxxxxxxxxxxxxx	Xxxxxxxxxxxxxxxxxxxxx	1/1/99	_____
Central Administration	99999	47403948	Xxxxxxxxxxxxx	Xxxxxxxxxxxxxx	1/1/99	_____
Central Administration	99999	56620548	Xxxxxxxxxxxxx	Xxxxxxxxxxxxxx	1/1/99	_____
Central Computer	22222	34589349	Xxxxxxxxxxxx	Xxxxxxxxxxxxxxxxx	1/1/99	_____
Central Computer	22222	38376910	Xxxxxxxxxxx	Xxxxxxxxxxxxxxxxx	1/1/99	_____
Central Computer	22222	94842282	Xxxxxxxxxxxxxx	Xxxxxxxxxxxxxxxxxxx	1/1/99	_____
Central Computer	99999	339393	Xxxxxxxxxxxxx	Xxxxxxxxxxxxxx	1/1/99	_____
Central Zoology	22222	11398423	Xxxxxxxxxxxxxx	Xxxxxxxxxxxxxxxxxxx	1/1/99	_____
Central Zoology	22222	28387465	Xxxxxxxxxxxxxx	Xxxxxxxxxxxxxxxxxxx	1/1/99	_____
Central Zoology	99999	70722533	Xxxxxxxxxxxx	Xxxxxxxxxxxxxx	1/1/99	_____
Central Zoology	99999	99481102	Xxxxxxxxxxxxxx	Xxxxxxxxxxxxxxxxxxx	1/1/99	_____

Total microcomputers scheduled for preventive   25

FIGURE E8.1
Prototype for PREVENTIVE MAINTENANCE REPORT. This report needs to be
revised.

Chip and Anna next turned their attention to creating screen prototypes. "Since I like the hardware aspect of the system, why don't I start
working on the ADD NEW MICROCOMPUTER screen design," offers Chip.

"Sounds good to me," Anna replies. "I'll focus on the software aspects."

Chip analyzes the results of detailed interviews with Dot and Mike. He
compiles a list of elements that each user would need when adding a microcom-

	User 1	User 2	User 3	User 4
Prototype Evaluation Form				
Observer Name Chip Puller			Date 1/06/1997	
System or Project Name Microcomputer System		Company or Location Central Pacific University		
Program Name or Number Prev. Maint.		Version 1		
User Name	Mike C.	Dot M.		
Period Observed	1/06/1997 AM	1/06/1997 AM		
User Reactions	Generally favorable, got excited about project	Excellent!		
User Suggestions	Add the date when maintenance was performed.	Place a form number on top for reference. Place word WEEKLY in title.		
Innovations				
Revision Plans	Modify on 1/08/1997. Review with Dot and Mike.			

FIGURE E8.2
Prototype evaluation form.

puter. Other elements, such as location and maintenance information, would update the MICROCOMPUTER MASTER later, after the machine was installed.

The ADD NEW MICROCOMPUTER prototype screen created with the Access form feature is shown in Figure E8.3. Placed on the top of the screen are the current date and time as well as a centered screen title. Field captions are placed on the screen, with the left characters aligned. Check boxes are included for several fields, as well as pull-down lists for the type of Monitor, Printer and Internet connections. A small Board Code table is included to add several internal boards for one microcomputer. An Add Record and Print button are included.

"Having the database tables defined sure helps to make quick prototypes," Chip comments. "It didn't take very long to complete the screen. Would you like to watch me test the prototype?"

"Sure," replies Anna. "This is my favorite part of prototyping."

Chip executes the screen design as Anna, Mike, and Dot watch. The pull-down list boxes and check boxes make it easy to enter accurate data.

"I really like this," Dot says. "May I try adding some data?"

"Be my guest," replies Chip. "Try to add both invalid and valid data. And notice the help messages that appear at the bottom of the screen to indicate what should be entered."

Dot is plainly enjoying herself as she enters data and tests the screen. Mike also spends time testing the screen. Both users state that they have a good understanding of the system and how it will operate when complete. Enthusiasm for the project is taking on a life of its own.

FIGURE E8.3

Prototype for the ADD NEW MICROCOMPUTER screen. Microsoft Access was used as the prototyping tool. Improvements can be made at this stage.

Anna returns to her desk and creates the ADD SOFTWARE RECORD screen design.

When Anna completes the screen design, she asks Cher to test the prototype. Cher keys information in, checks the pull-down list values, and views help messages.

"I really like the design of this screen and how it looks," remarks Cher. "However, it lacks some of the fields that would normally be included when a software package is entered, like the computer brand and model that the software runs on, the memory required, monitor, and the printer or plotter required. I would also like buttons to save the record and exit the screen."

"Those are all doable. I'll make the changes and get back to you," replies Anna, making some notes to herself.

Before Anna can put away her notes, Cher returns to Anna's office, with a worried look on her face. "You know, there may be something else to change on the new trial screens. I've been reading about the Year 2000." Anna looks up at her expectantly, "And?"

Cher continues, "It could mean trouble for us. I think all of the screens you showed me just had a 2-digit year." "Like '97,' rather than '1997.'"

Anna immediately grasps what has happened and calls Chip in to listen to Cher. Before nodding to Cher to continue, she, Anna tells Chip, "We've got some work to do. Cher will tell you."

As Cher explains, Chip and Anna listen intently. When she is finished, Anna says, "Don't worry. We know what the problem is. We still have some time, but thanks for mentioning it right away."

After Cher departs, Chip turns to Anna with a sheepish grin and says, "That's what prototypes are for, right?"

FIGURE E8.4
Prototype for the ADD SOFTWARE RECORD screen. Microsoft Access was used as the prototyping tool. This screen can be improved.

A short time later, Cher again tests the ADD SOFTWARE RECORD screen. It includes all of the features that she requires. The completed screen design is shown in Figure E8.4. Notice that there is a line separating the software information from the hardware entries.

Anna and Chip continued to work on prototypes by designing, obtaining user feedback, and modifying the design to accommodate user changes. Now that the work is complete, they have a solid sense of the requirements of the system.

Exercises*

Critique the report and screen prototypes for the problems below (E1–E10). Pay particular attention to whether Chip and Anna have resolved the "Year 2000 Problem." If they have not, indicate a solution wherever it is relevant in an exercise. Record the changes on a copy of the Prototype Evaluation Form (see Figure E8.2). If you have Microsoft® Access, modify the report and screen prototypes with the suggested changes. Print the final prototypes.

Use the following guidelines to help in your analysis:
1. *Alignment of fields on reports.* Are the fields aligned correctly? Are report column headers aligned correctly over the columns? If the report has captions to the left of data fields, are they aligned correctly (usually on the left)?

---

* Exercises preceded by a disk icon require the program Visible Analyst Workbench or another CASE tool. A disk is provided free of charge to any professor adopting this book. The examples on the disk may be imported into Visible Analyst Workbench and then used by students.

Campus	Room Location	Inventor Number	Brand Name	Model	Present
Central Administration	11111	84004782	Xxxxxxxxxx	Xxxxxxxxxxxxxxxx	_____
Central Administration	11111	90875039	Xxxxxxxxxx	Xxxxxxxxxxxxxxx	_____
Central Administration	11111	93955411	Xxxxxxxxxx	Xxxxxxxxxxxxxxxx	_____
Central Administration	11111	99381373	Xxxxxxxxxx	Xxxxxxxxxxxxxxxx	
	Total number of machines in room is		4		
Central Administration	22222	10220129	Xxxxxxxxxx	Xxxxxxxxxxxxxxxx	_____
	Total number of machines in room is		1		
Central Administration	99999	22838234	Xxxxxxxxxx	Xxxxxxxxxxxxxxx	_____
Central Administration	99999	24720952	Xxxxxxxxxx	Xxxxxxxxxxxxxxxx	_____
Central Administration	99999	33453403	Xxxxxxxxxx	Xxxxxxxxxxxxxxx	_____
Central Administration	99999	34044449	Xxxxxxxxxx	Xxxxxxxxxxxxxxxx	_____
Central Administration	99999	40030303	Xxxxxxxxxx	Xxxxxxxxxxxxxxxx	_____
Central Administration	99999	47403948	Xxxxxxxxxx	Xxxxxxxxxxxxxxx	_____
Central Administration	99999	56620548	Xxxxxxxxxx	Xxxxxxxxxxxxxxxx	_____
	Total number of machines in room is		7		
Central Computer Science	22222	34589349	Xxxxxxxxxx	Xxxxxxxxxxxxxxxx	_____
Central Computer Science	22222	38376910	Xxxxxxxxxx	Xxxxxxxxxxxxxxxx	_____
Central Computer Science	22222	94842282	Xxxxxxxxxx	Xxxxxxxxxxxxxxxx	_____
	Total number of machines in room is		3		
Central Computer Science	99999	339393	Xxxxxxxxxx	Xxxxxxxxxxxxxxxx	_____
	Total number of machines in room is		1		
Central Zoology	22222	11398423	Xxxxxxxxxx	Xxxxxxxxxxxxxxxx	_____
Central Zoology	22222	28387465	Xxxxxxxxxx	Xxxxxxxxxxxxxxxx	_____
	Total number of machines in room is		2		
Central Zoology	99999	70722533	Xxxxxxxxxx	Xxxxxxxxxxxxxxx	_____
Central Zoology	99999	99481102	Xxxxxxxxxx	Xxxxxxxxxxxxxxxx	_____
	Total number of machines in room is		2		

FIGURE E8.5
Prototype for the HARDWARE INVENTORY LISTING. Many improvements can be made to this report.

2.   *Report content.* Does the report contain all the necessary data? Are appropriate and useful totals and subtotals present? Are there extra totals or data that should not be on the report? Are codes or the meaning of the codes printed on the report (codes should be avoided since they may not clearly present the user with information)?

3.   *Check the visual appearance of the report.* Does it look pleasing? Are repeating fields group printed (that is, the data should print only once, at the beginning of the group)? Are there enough blank lines between groups to easily identify them?

4.   *Screen data and caption alignment.* Are the captions correctly aligned on the screens? Are the data fields correctly aligned? Is the data *within* a field correctly aligned?

5.   *Screen visual appearance.* Does the screen have a pleasing appearance? Is there enough vertical spacing between fields? Is there enough horizontal spacing between columns? Are the fields logically grouped together? Are features, such as buttons and check boxes, grouped together?

Title	Version	Operating System	Site License	Number of Copies	Unit Cost	Software Cost
ABC Flowcharter	6.0	Windows 95	No	20	$100.00	$2,000.00
Corel Draw!	7	Windows 95	No	16	$200.00	$3,200.00
Eudora Pro	3	Windows 3.X	No	60	$60.00	$3,600.00
Excelerator	1.8	DOS 3.X	No	40	$250.00	$10,000.00
Excelerator	1.9	DOS 3.X	No	40	$250.00	$10,000.00
Excelerator	2.0	Windows 3.X	No	40	$250.00	$10,000.00
Lotus Organizer 97		Windows 95	No	12	$70.00	$840.00
Perfect Presentations	2.0	Windows 3.X	Yes		$999.99	$999.99
Perfect Presentations	3.0	Windows 3.X	No	30	$39.99	$1,199.70
Photo Delux		Windows 95	No	10	$90.00	$900.00
Visible Analyst	6	Windows 95	No	60	$50.00	$3,000.00
Win Fax	Pro	Windows 3.X	No	5	$88.00	$440.00
Word Perfect	6.1	Windows 3.X	Yes		$999.99	$999.99
Word Perfect	7	Windows 95	Yes		$999.99	$999.99
WordPerfect	6.0	Windows 3.X	Yes		$999.99	$999.99
WordPerfect Suite	7	Windows 95	No	400	$39.00	$15,600.00

Total Software Cost $64,779.66

FIGURE E8.6
Prototype for the SOFTWARE INVESTMENT REPORT. A number of changes can be made to improve this report.

6.   *Does the screen contain all the necessary functional elements?* Look for missing buttons that would help the user work smoothly with the screen; also look for missing data, extra unnecessary data, or for fields that should be replaced with a check box or drop-down list.

E-1.   The HARDWARE INVENTORY LISTING is shown in Figure E8.5. It shows all microcomputers, sorted by campus and room.

E-2.   The SOFTWARE INVESTMENT REPORT is illustrated in Figure E8.6. It is used to calculate the total amount invested in software.

E-3.   One page of the INSTALLED MICROCOMPUTER REPORT is shown in Figure E8.7. It shows the information for a single machine. (The full report would be many pages long.)

E-4.   Figure E8.8 shows the prototype for the MICROCOMPUTER PROBLEM REPORT. It should list all machines sorted by the total cost of repairs and include the number of repairs (some machines do not have a high cost, since they are still under warranty). This prototype is used to calculate the total cost of repairs for the entire university, as well as to identify the problem machines.

E-5.   The NEW SOFTWARE INSTALLED REPORT is illustrated in Figure E8.9. It shows the number of machines with each software package that are installed in each room of each campus.

Campus Description		Central Administration			
Room Location	11111	Brand Name	Xxxxxxxxxxxxxx	Memory Size	16
		Model	Xxxxxxxxxxxxxxxx	Hard drive	1600
		Inventory Number	90875039	Second Fixed	0
		Monitor Code	SVGA	Disk size	3.5
		Printer Code	20201	Secondary	3.5
		CD ROM Drive	8X	Zip Drive	No
		Internet	1	Tape Backup Unit	No
		Internal Board Names		Network	Yes
		Network Board			
Room Location	22222	Brand Name	Xxxxxxxxxxxxxx	Memory Size	16
		Model	Xxxxxxxxxxxxxxxxxx	Hard drive	1600
		Inventory Number	10220129	Second Fixed	0
		Monitor Code	SVGA	Disk size	3.5
		Printer Code	20201	Secondary	3.5
		CD ROM Drive	8X	Zip Drive	No
		Internet	1	Tape Backup Unit	No
		Internal Board Names		Network	Yes
		FAX Modem			

FIGURE E8.7
Prototype for the INSTALLED MICROCOMPUTER REPORT. Many improvements
can be made to this report.

Inventory Number	Brand Name	Model	Cost of Repairs	Warranty
40030303	Xxxxxxxxxxxxxx	Xxxxxxxxxxxxxxxx	$955.25	Yes
34589349	Xxxxxxxxxxxx	Xxxxxxxxxxxxxxxx	$720.00	Yes
56620548	Xxxxxxxxxxxxxx	Xxxxxxxxxxxxxxxx	$487.22	Yes
84004782	Xxxxxxxxxxxxxx	Xxxxxxxxxxxxxxxx	$376.90	Yes
24720952	Xxxxxxxxxxxxxx	Xxxxxxxxxxxxxxxx	$290.00	Yes
93955411	Xxxxxxxxxxxxxx	Xxxxxxxxxxxxxxxx	$242.55	Yes
33453403	Xxxxxxxxxxxxxx	Xxxxxxxxxxxxxxxx	$155.50	Yes
99381373	Xxxxxxxxxxxxxx	Xxxxxxxxxxxxxxxx	$40.00	Yes
10220129	Xxxxxxxxxxxxxx	Xxxxxxxxxxxxxxxx	$20.00	Yes

FIGURE E8.8
Prototype for the MICROCOMPUTER PROBLEM REPORT. Users might ask for
changes to this report based on this prototype.

Software Category Code   CASE

Title	Version	Operating System	Publisher	Brand/ Model	Campus Code Room	Number of Copies
Excelerator	1.8	3	Intersolv	Xxxxxxxxxxxxxxx Xxxxxxxxxxxxxxxxx	1018 22222	40
Excelerator	2.0	W	Intersolv	Xxxxxxxxxxxxxxx Xxxxxxxxxxxxxxxxx	1018 22222	40
Visible Analyst	6	9	Visible Systems	Xxxxxxxxxxxx Xxxxxxxxxxxxxxxxx	1001 99999	60
Visible Analyst	6	9	Visible Systems	Xxxxxxxxxxxx Xxxxxxxxxxxxxxxxx	1007 22222	60
Visible Analyst	6	9	Visible Systems	Xxxxxxxxxxxxx Xxxxxxxxxxxxxxxxx	1001 99999	60
Visible Analyst	6	9	Visible Systems	Xxxxxxxxxxxxx Xxxxxxxxxxxxxxxxx	1007 99999	60
Visible Analyst	6	9	Visible Systems	Xxxxxxxxxxxxx Xxxxxxxxxxxxxxxxx	1001 22222	60
Visible Analyst	6	9	Visible Systems	Xxxxxxxxxxxxxxx Xxxxxxxxxxxxxxxxx	1001 99999	60
Visible Analyst	6	9	Visible Systems	Xxxxxxxxxxxxxxx Xxxxxxxxxxxxxxxxx	1001 11111	60
Visible Analyst	6	9	Visible Systems	Xxxxxxxxxxxxxxx Xxxxxxxxxxxxxxxxx	1018 22222	60

Software Category Code   GRPH

Title	Version	Operating System	Publisher	Brand/ Model	Campus Code Room Location	Number of
ABC Flowcharter	6.0	9	Micrografx	Xxxxxxxxxxxxx Xxxxxxxxxxxxxxxxx	1001 99999	20
ABC Flowcharter	6.0	9	Micrografx	Xxxxxxxxxxxxx Xxxxxxxxxxxxxxxxx	1001 99999	20
ABC Flowcharter	6.0	9	Micrografx	Xxxxxxxxxxxxxxx Xxxxxxxxxxxxxxxxx	1018 99999	20

FIGURE E8.9
Prototype for the NEW SOFTWARE INSTALLED REPORT. Modifications can improve this.

⊟ **E-6.** The first page of the SOFTWARE CROSS REFERENCE REPORT is shown in Figure E8.10. It lists all locations for each version of each software package.

⊟ **E-7.** Figure E8.11 illustrates the DELETED MICROCOMPUTER RECORD screen. The entry area is the Hardware Inventory Number field. The other fields are for display only, to identify the machine. The users would like the ability to print each record before they delete it. They also want to scroll to the next and previous

| Title: | ABC Flowcharter | | | Publisher: | Micrografx |
| Version: | 6.0 | | | Operating System code: | 9 |

Campus	Room	Hardware Number	Brand	Model
Central Administration	99999	24720952	Xxxxxxxxxxxxxx	Xxxxxxxxxxxxxxxxxx
Central Administration	99999	33453403	Xxxxxxxxxxxxxx	Xxxxxxxxxxxxxx
Central Zoology	22222	11398423	Xxxxxxxxxxxxxx	Xxxxxxxxxxxxxxxxxxxx

| Title: | Corel Draw! | | | Publisher: | Corel |
| Version: | 7 | | | Operating System: | 9 |

Campus	Room	Hardware Number	Brand	Model
Central Zoology	22222	28387465	Xxxxxxxxxxxxxx	Xxxxxxxxxxxxxxxxxxxx

| Title: | Eudora Pro | | | Publisher: | Eudora |
| Version: | 3 | | | Operating System: | W |

Campus	Room	Hardware Number	Brand	Model

| Title: | Excelerator | | | Publisher: | Intersolv |
| Version: | 1.8 | | | Operating System: | 3 |

Campus	Room	Hardware Number	Brand	Model

| Version: | 1.9 | | | Operating System: | 3 |

Campus	Room	Hardware Number	Brand	Model
Central Zoology	22222	11398423	Xxxxxxxxxxxxxx	Xxxxxxxxxxxxxxxxxxxx

| Version: | 2.0 | | | Operating System: | W |

Campus	Room	Hardware Number	Brand	Model
Central Zoology	22222	11398423	Xxxxxxxxxxxxxx	Xxxxxxxxxxxxxxxxxxxx

| Title: | Lotus Organizer 97 | | | Publisher: | Lotus |
| Version: | | | | Operating System: | Windows 95 |

Campus	Room	Hardware Number	Brand	Model
Central Administration	99999	33453403	Xxxxxxxxxxxxxx	Xxxxxxxxxxxxxx

FIGURE E8.10

Prototype for the SOFTWARE CROSS REFERENCE REPORT. Many improvements can be made to this report.

records. *Hint:* Examine the fields shown in the HARDWARE IN-VENTORY LISTING report.

🖫 **E-8.** Mike Crowe needs a screen to enable him to change maintenance information about microcomputers. Sometimes these are routine changes, such as the LAST PREVENTIVE MAINTENANCE DATE or the NUMBER OF REPAIRS, but other changes may occur only sporadically, such as the expiration of a warranty. The HARD-WARE INVENTORY NUMBER is entered, and the matching MI-CROCOMPUTER RECORD is found. The BRAND and MODEL are displayed for feedback. The operator may then change the WAR-

FIGURE E8.11
Prototype for the DELETE MICROCOMPUTER RECORD SCREEN. Changes can improve it.

RANTY, MAINTENANCE INTERVAL, NUMBER OF REPAIRS, LAST PREVENTIVE MAINTENANCE DATE, and TOTAL COST OF REPAIRS fields. Mike would like to easily print the screen information, as well as undo any changes. The screen is illustrated in Figure E8.12.

E-9.   The SOFTWARE LOCATION INQUIRY screen is shown in Figure E8.13. The TITLE, VERSION NUMBER, and OPERATING SYSTEM are entered. The output portion of the screen should show the CAMPUS LOCATION, ROOM LOCATION, HARDWARE INVENTORY NUMBER, BRAND NAME, and MODEL. Buttons allow the user to move to the next record, the previous record, and to close and exit the screen.

E-10.   Figure E8.14 illustrates the HARDWARE CHARACTERISTIC INQUIRY screen design. The operator enters a BRAND NAME and CD ROM DRIVE type. The MONITOR and PRINTER CODE fields have drop-down lists to select the appropriate codes. The display portion of the inquiry screen consists of CAMPUS, ROOM, and INVENTORY NUMBER.

FIGURE E8.12
Prototype for the UPDATE MAINTENANCE INFORMATION SCREEN. Modifications can make the screen better.

FIGURE E8.13
Prototype for the SOFTWARE LOCATION INQUIRY SCREEN. Many improvements can be made.

FIGURE E8.14
Prototype for the HARDWARE CHARACTERISTIC SCREEN. Modifications will improve the screen.

USING DATA FLOW DIAGRAMS

The systems analyst needs to make use of the conceptual freedom afforded by data flow diagrams (DFD), which graphically characterize data processes and flows in a business system. In their original state data flow diagrams depict the broadest possible overview of system inputs, processes, and outputs, which correspond to those of the general systems model discussed in Chapter 2. A series of layered data flow diagrams may also be used to represent and analyze detailed procedures within the larger system.

THE DATA FLOW APPROACH
TO REQUIREMENTS DETERMINATION

When systems analysts attempt to understand the information requirements of users, they must be able to conceptualize how data moves through the organization, the processes or transformation that the data undergoes, and what the outputs are. Although interviews and the investigation of hard data provide a verbal narrative of the system, a visual depiction can crystallize this information in a useful way.

Through a structured analysis technique called data flow diagrams (DFD), the systems analyst can put together a graphical representation of data processes throughout the organization. The data flow approach emphasizes the logic underlying the system. By using combinations of only four symbols, the systems analyst can create a pictorial depiction of processes that will eventually provide solid system documentation.

Advantages of the Data Flow Approach

The data flow approach has four chief advantages over narrative explanations of the way data moves through the system. The advantages are:

1. Freedom from committing to the technical implementation of the system too early.

2. Further understanding of the interrelatedness of systems and subsystems.

3. Communicating current system knowledge to users through data flow diagrams.

4. Analysis of a proposed system to determine if the necessary data and processes have been defined.

Perhaps the biggest advantage lies in the conceptual freedom found in the use of the four symbols (which are covered in the upcoming subsection on DFD conventions). (You will recognize three of the symbols from Chapter 2.) None of the symbols specifies the physical aspects of implementation. For instance, although an analyst will signify that data are stored at a particular point, the data flow approach does not dictate specifying the medium for storage. This allows the systems analyst to conceptualize necessary data flows and to avoid committing too quickly to their technical realization.

The data flow approach has the additional advantage of serving as a useful exercise for systems analysts, enabling them to better understand the interrelatedness of the system and its subsystems. Recall that in Chapter 2 we stressed the importance of being able to differentiate the system from its environment by locating its boundaries. It requires discipline and true understanding to conceptualize the system in a broad overview and then explode it into its functional subsystems.

A third advantage of the data flow approach is that it can be used as a tool to interact with users. An interesting use of DFDs is to show them to users as incomplete representations of the analyst's understanding of the system. Users can then be asked to comment on the accuracy of the analyst's conceptualization, and the analyst can incorporate changes that more accurately reflect the system from the users' perspectives.

Although many texts tout the ease of communicating to users through data flow diagrams, this benefit does not occur automatically. If you want to use DFDs for interaction, you must assume responsibility for educating users about their purposes. Necessary background must be provided to users before data flow diagrams will be meaningful rather than confusing.

The last advantage of using data flow diagrams is that they allow analysts to describe each component used in the diagram. Analysis can then be performed to ensure that all necessary output may be obtained from the input data and that processing logic is reflected in the diagram. Detecting and correcting errors and design flaws of this nature in the earlier stages of the systems development life cycle is far less costly than in the later phases of programming, testing, and implementation.

Conventions Used in Data Flow Diagrams

Four basic symbols are used to chart data movement on data flow diagrams. They are a double square, an arrow, a rectangle with rounded corners, and an open-ended rectangle (closed on the left side and open-ended on the right), as shown in Figure 9.1. An entire system and numerous subsystems can be depicted graphically with these four symbols in combination.[1]

The double square is used to depict an external entity (another department, a business, a person, or a machine) that can send data to or receive data

---

[1] Diagramming symbols used for data flow diagrams are based on work by C. Gane and T. Sarson. *Structured Systems Analysis and Design Tools and Techniques* (Englewood Cliffs, N.J.: Prentice Hall, Inc., 1979).

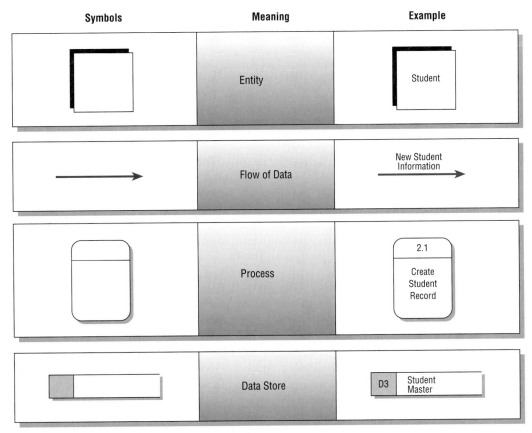

Symbols	Meaning	Example
	Entity	Student
→	Flow of Data	New Student Information →
	Process	2.1 Create Student Record
	Data Store	D3 Student Master

FIGURE 9.1
The four basic symbols used in data flow diagrams, their meanings, and examples.

from the system. The external entity or entity, is also called a source or destination of data, and it is considered to be external to the system being described. Each entity is labeled with an appropriate name. Although it interacts with the system, it is considered as outside of the boundaries of the system. Entities should be named with a noun. The same entity may be used more than once on a given data flow diagram to avoid crossing data flow lines.

The arrow shows movement of data from one point to another, with the head of the arrow pointing toward the data's destination. Data flows occurring simultaneously can be depicted doing just that through the use of parallel arrows. Since an arrow represents data about a person, place, or thing, it too should be described with a noun.

A rectangle with rounded corners is used to show the occurrence of a transforming process. Processes always denote a change in or transformation of data; hence, the data flow leaving a process is *always* labeled differently from the one entering it. Processes represent work being performed within the system and should be named using one of the following formats. A clear name makes it easier to understand what the process is accomplishing.

1. Assign the name of the whole system when naming a high-level process. An example is INVENTORY CONTROL SYSTEM.
2. To name a major subsystem, use a name such as INVENTORY REPORTING SUBSYSTEM.

3. Use a verb-adjective-noun format for detailed processes. The verb describes the type of activity, for example, COMPUTE, VERIFY, PREPARE, PRINT, or ADD. The noun indicates what the major outcome of the process is, for instance, REPORT or RECORD. The adjective illustrates which specific output, such as BACKORDERED or INVENTORY, is produced. Examples of complete process names are: COMPUTE SALES TAX, VERIFY CUSTOMER ACCOUNT STATUS, PREPARE SHIPPING INVOICE, PRINT BACKORDERED REPORT, and ADD INVENTORY RECORD.

A process must also be given a unique identifying number indicating its level within the diagram. This organization is discussed later in this chapter. Several data flows may go into and out of each process. Examine processes with a single flow in and out for missing data flows.

The last basic symbol used in data flow diagrams represents a data store and is an open-ended rectangle. This is drawn with two parallel lines, which are closed by a short line on the left side and open-ended on the right. These symbols are drawn only wide enough to allow identifying lettering between the parallel lines. In logical data flow diagrams, the type of physical storage (for example, tape, diskette, etc.) is not specified. At this point the data store symbol is simply showing a depository for data that allows addition and retrieval of data.

The data store may represent a manual store, such as a filing cabinet, or a computerized file or database. Since data stores represent a person, place, or thing, they are named with a noun. Temporary data stores, such as scratch paper or a temporary computer file, are not included on the data flow diagram. Neither are any blank forms or blank diskettes included, even though they may be necessary for a business activity. Give each data store a unique reference number, such as D1, D2, D3, and so on, to identify its level as described in the following section.

DEVELOPING DATA FLOW DIAGRAMS

Data flow diagrams can and should be drawn systematically. Figure 9.2 summarizes the steps involved in successfully completing data flow diagrams. First, the systems analyst needs to conceptualize data flows from a top-down perspective.

To begin a data flow diagram, collapse the organization's system narrative into a list with the four categories of external entity, data flow, process, and data store. This list in turn helps determine the boundaries of the system you will be describing. Once a basic list of data elements has been compiled, begin drawing a context diagram.

Creating the Context Diagram

With a top-down approach to diagramming data movement, the diagrams move from general to specific. While the first diagram helps the systems analyst grasp basic data movement, its general nature limits its usefulness. The initial context diagram should be an overview, one including basic inputs, the general system, and outputs. This will be the most general diagram— really a bird's-eye view of data movement in the system and the broadest possible conceptualization of the system.

The context diagram is the highest level in a data flow diagram and contains only one process, representing the entire system. The process is given the number zero. All external entities are shown on the context dia-

FIGURE 9.2
Steps in developing data flow
diagrams.

**Developing Data Flow Diagrams
Using A Top-Down Approach**

1   Make a list of business activities and use it to determine various
    • External Entities
    • Data Flows
    • Processes
    • Data Stores

2   Create a context diagram which shows external entities and data
    flows to and from the system. Do not show any detailed processes
    or data stores.

3   Draw Diagram 0, the next level. Show processes, but keep them
    general. Show data stores at this level.

4   Create a child diagram for each of the processes in Diagram 0.

5   Check for errors and make sure the labels you assign to each
    process and data flow are meaningful.

6   Develop a physical data flow diagram from the logical data flow
    diagram. Distinguish between manual and automated processes,
    describe actual files and reports by name, and add controls to
    indicate when processes are complete or errors occur.

7   Partition the physical data flow diagram by separating or grouping
    parts of the diagram in order to facilitate programming and
    implementation.

gram, as well as major data flow to and from them. The diagram does not contain any data stores and is fairly simple to create, once the external entities and the data flow to and from them are known to analysts from interviews with users and as a result of document analysis.

Drawing Diagram 0 (The Next Level)

More detail than the context diagram permits is achievable by "exploding the diagrams." Inputs and outputs specified in the first diagram remain constant in all subsequent diagrams. However, the rest of the original diagram is exploded into close-ups involving three to nine processes and showing data stores and new lower-level data flows. The effect is that of taking a magnifying glass to view the original data flow diagram. Each exploded diagram should use only a single sheet of paper. By exploding DFDs into subprocesses, the systems analyst begins to fill in the details about data movement. The handling of exceptions is ignored for the first two or three levels of data flow diagramming.

Diagram 0 is the explosion of the context diagram and may include up to nine processes. Including more processes at this level will result in a cluttered diagram that is difficult to understand. Each process is numbered with an integer, generally starting from the upper left-hand corner of the diagram and work-

FIGURE 9.3
Context diagrams (above) can
be "exploded" into Diagram 0
(below). Note the greater detail in Diagram 0.

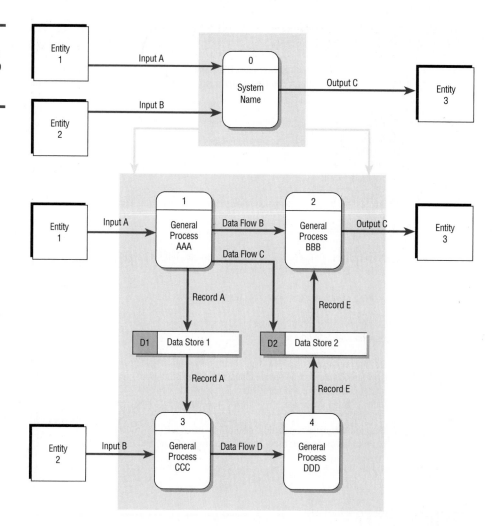

ing toward the lower right-hand corner. The major data stores of the system (representing master files) and all external entities are included on Diagram 0. Figure 9.3 schematically illustrates both the context diagram and Diagram 0.

Since a data flow diagram is two-dimensional (rather than linear), you may start at any point and work forward or backward through the diagram. If you are unsure of what you would include at any point, take a different external entity, process, or data store, and then start drawing the flow from it. You may:

1. Start with the data flow from an entity on the input side. Ask questions such as: "What happens to the data entering the system?" "Is it stored?" "Is it input for several processes?"

2. Work backwards from an output data flow. Examine the output fields on a document or screen. (This approach is easier if prototypes have been created.) For each field on the output, ask: "Where does it come from?" *or* "Is it calculated or stored on a file?" For example, when the output is a PAYCHECK, the EMPLOYEE NAME and ADDRESS would be located on an EMPLOYEE file, the HOURS WORKED would be on a TIME RECORD, and the GROSS PAY and DEDUCTIONS would be calculated. Each file and record would be connected to the process that produces the paycheck.

CONSULTING OPPORTUNITY 9.1

Go with the Flow

"Let's see. We've got a clerk adding up the day's receipts from the cash register tape by calculator. After she adds them initially, she separates them into separate departments, including juvenile, maternity, and infants. Then she gives her departmental subtotals and total on scratch paper to me," says Luis Asperilla.

Pamela Coburn, a systems analyst who is working with a group of 26 franchise clothing stores called Bonton's, is talking to the South Street store's manager, Luis, and she is trying to understand the data flows within the store. Luis continues the narrative. "Then I recheck the day's receipts, looking for any discrepancies. Next, I enter the day's breakdown of the day's receipts, their departments, and the total day's receipts into the ledger, and I fill out the deposit for the bank. All daily receipt information is stored in one place, in the ledger in my office."

Pamela asks, "Do you keep a copy anywhere?" Luis pauses, then replies, "Well, there is a weekly report that summarizes all of the weekly information for the head of franchising in New York. They enter it into their computers and we get sent a printout at the end of the month. So if I wait five weeks, I do in effect get a copy back. Except that I keep each printout and reconcile it against my own monthly summary that I do by hand. You'd be surprised at how often there is a mistake in what they send back. Then I write them a letter and try to get it corrected so my six-month inventories come out right. I keep copies of all correspondence to New York in a file drawer. I'm always writing to them on something they've screwed up. And I need a copy to prove I sent in a correction."

Luis continues, "Computers in New York seem worth it, I suppose, but I think they introduce an awful lot of errors if you don't use common sense when you enter the numbers in. But the ledger book does get heavy to pull down from the shelf by the end of the year."

"I keep a lot of what happens in the store in my head, too," Luis adds thoughtfully. "It's so hard to write everything down, because we get so busy. Like which customers are allowed layaway privileges and information like that. I keep a few notes in my desk. I think you'll find that I'm really organized compared to the other managers in town."

Draw a data flow diagram of Luis' description of the store's data flows. What are some of the specific physical barriers to implementation that Pamela can overcome by representing the store's data flow in a data flow diagram? Describe them in a paragraph.

---

3. Examine the data flow to or from a data store. Ask: "What processes put data into the store?" *or* "What processes use the data?" Note that a data store used in the system you are working on may be produced by a different system. Thus, from your vantage point, there may not be any data flow into the data store.

4. Analyze a well-defined process. Look at what input data the process needs and what output it produces. Then connect the input and output to the appropriate data stores and entities.

5. Take note of any fuzzy areas where you are unsure of what should be included or of what input or output is required. Awareness of problem areas will help you formulate a list of questions for follow-up interviews with key users.

Creating Child Diagrams (More Detailed Levels)

Each process on Diagram 0 may in turn be exploded to create a more detailed child diagram. The process on Diagram 0 that is exploded is called the *parent process,* and the diagram that results is called the *child diagram.* The primary rule for creating child diagrams, vertical balancing, dictates that a child diagram cannot produce output or receive input that the parent process does not also produce or receive. All data flow into or out of the parent process must be shown flowing into or out of the child diagram.

The child diagram is given the same number as its parent process in Diagram 0. For example, process 3 would explode to Diagram 3. The processes on the child diagram are numbered using the parent process number, a decimal point, and a unique number for each child process. On Diagram 3, the processes would be numbered 3.1, 3.2, 3.3, and so on. This convention allows the analyst to trace a series of processes through many levels of explosion. If Diagram 0 depicts processes 1, 2, and 3, then the child diagrams 1, 2, and 3 are all on the same level.

Entities are usually not shown on the child diagrams below Diagram 0. Data flow that matches the parent flow is called an *interface data flow* and is shown as an arrow from or into a blank area of the child diagram. If the parent process has data flow connecting to a data store, the child diagram may include the data store as well. Additionally, this lower-level diagram may contain data stores not shown on the parent process. For example, a file containing a table of information, such as a tax table, or a file linking two processes on the child diagram may be included. Minor data flow, such as an error line, may be included on a child diagram but not on the parent.

Processes may or may not be exploded, depending on their level of complexity. When a process is not exploded, it is said to be functionally primitive and is called a *primitive process.* Logic is written to describe these processes and will be discussed in detail in Chapter 11. Figure 9.4 illustrates detailed levels within a child data flow diagram.

Checking the Diagrams for Errors

Numerous errors may occur when drawing data flow diagrams. Some of the more common mistakes are shown in Figure 9.5.

It is useful to see how mistakes can come about in a data flow diagram. Figure 9.6 is an example of a data flow diagram that, if implemented, would produce an employee paycheck with many flaws. Several common errors made when drawing data flow diagrams are:

1. Forgetting to include a data flow or pointing an arrowhead in the wrong direction. An example is a drawn process showing all of its data flow as input or as output. Each process transforms data and must receive input and produce output. Usually this type of error occurs when the analyst has forgotten to include a data flow or placed an arrowhead pointing in the wrong direction. Process 1 in Figure 9.6 contains only input because the GROSS PAY arrow is pointing in the wrong direction. This error also affects Process 2, CALCULATE WITHHOLDING AMOUNT, which is additionally missing a data flow representing input for the withholding rates and the number of dependents.

2. Connecting data stores and external entities directly to each other. Data stores and entities may not be connected to each other; data stores and external entities must connect only with a process. A file does not interface with another file without the help of a program or a person moving the data, so EMPLOYEE MASTER in Figure 9.6 cannot directly produce the CHECK RECONCILIATION file. External entities do not directly work with files. For example, you would not want a customer rummaging around in the customer master file. Thus, in Figure 9.6 the EMPLOYEE does not create the EMPLOYEE TIME FILE. If two external entities are directly connected, it indicates that they wish to communicate with each other. This connection is not included on the data flow diagram unless the system is facilitating the communication. Producing a

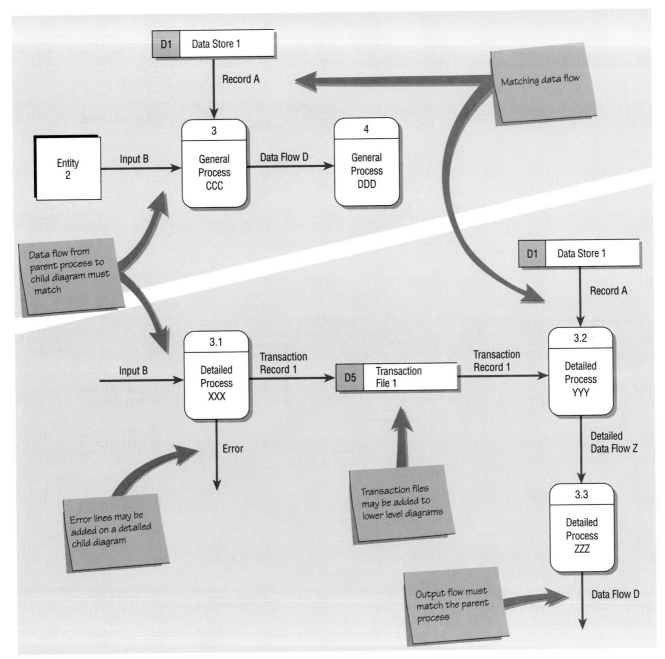

FIGURE 9.4
Differences between the parent diagram (above) and the child diagram (below).

report is an instance of this sort of communication. However, a process must still be interposed between the entities to produce the report.

3. Incorrectly labeling processes and/or data flow. Inspect the data flow diagram to ensure that each object or data flow is properly labeled. A process should indicate the system name or use the verb-adjective-noun format. Each data flow should be described with a noun.

4. Including more than nine processes on a data flow diagram. This creates a cluttered diagram that is confusing to read and hinders rather

FIGURE 9.5
Don't break the rules when
drawing data flow diagrams.

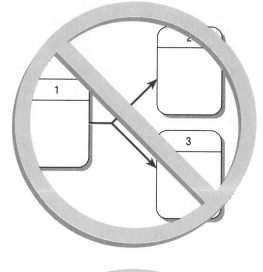

Data flows should
not split into two
or more different
data flows.

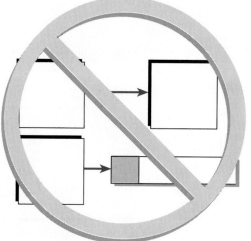

All data flows must
EITHER originate
or terminate at
a process.

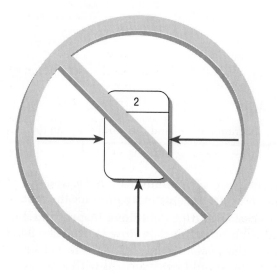

Processes need to have
at least one input data
flow and one output
data flow.

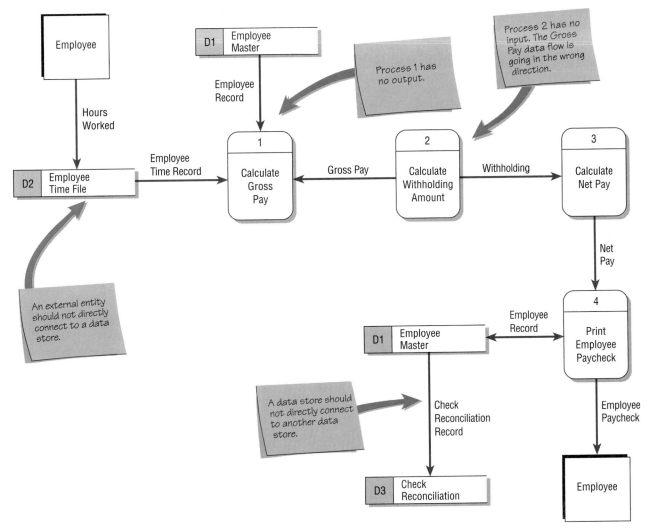

FIGURE 9.6
Typical errors that can occur in a data flow diagram (payroll example).

then enhances communication. If more than nine processes are involved in a system, group some of the processes that work together into a subsystem and place them in a child diagram.

5. Omitting data flow. Examine your diagram for linear flow, that is, data flow where each process has only one input and one output. Except in the case of very detailed child data flow diagrams, linear data flow is somewhat rare. Its presence usually indicates that the diagram has missing data flow. For instance, in Figure 9.6 the process CALCULATE WITHHOLDING AMOUNT needs the number of dependents that an employee has and the WITHHOLDING RATES as input. In addition NET PAY cannot be calculated solely from the WITHHOLDING, and the EMPLOYEE PAYCHECK cannot be created from the NET PAY alone. It also needs to include an EMPLOYEE NAME and the current and year-to-date payroll and WITHHOLDING AMOUNT figures.

FIGURE 9.7
The correct data flow diagram for the payroll example.

6. Creating unbalanced decomposition in child diagrams. Each child diagram should have the same input and output data flow as the parent process. An exception to this rule is minor output, such as error lines, which are included only on the child diagram. The data flow diagram in Figure 9.7 is correctly drawn. Note that although the data flow is not linear, you can clearly follow a path directly from the source entity to the destination entity.

FIGURE 9.8
Features common of logical
and physical data flow diagrams.

Design Feature	Logical	Physical
What the model depicts	How the business operates	How the system will be implemented (or how the current system operates)
What the processes represent	Business activities	Programs, program modules, and manual procedures
What the data stores represent	Collections of data, regardless of how the data is stored	Physical files and databases, manual files
Type of data stores	Show data stores representing permanent data collections	Master files, transaction files. Any processes that operate at two different times must be connected by a data store.
System controls	Show business controls	Show controls for validating input data, for obtaining a record (record found status), for ensuring successful completion of a process, and for system security (example: journal records)

LOGICAL AND PHYSICAL DATA FLOW DIAGRAMS

Data flow diagrams are categorized as either logical or physical. A logical data flow diagram focuses on the business and how the business operates. It is not concerned with how the system will be constructed. Instead, it describes the business events that take place and the data required and produced by each event. Conversely, a physical data flow diagram shows how the system will be implemented, including the hardware, software, files, and people involved in the system. The chart shown in Figure 9.8 contrasts the features of logical and physical models. Notice that the logical model reflects the business, while the physical model depicts the system.

Ideally, systems are developed by analyzing the current system (the current logical DFD), then adding features that the new system should include (the proposed logical DFD). Finally, the best methods for implementing the new system should be developed (the physical DFD).

Developing a logical data flow diagram for the current system affords you a clear understanding of how the current system operates and thus a good starting point for developing the logical model of the current system. This time-consuming step is often omitted in order to go straight to the proposed logical DFD.

One argument in favor of taking the time to construct the logical data flow diagram of the current system is that it can be used to create the logical data flow diagram of the new system. Processes that will be unnecessary in the new system may be dropped, and new features, activities, output, input, and stored data may be added. This approach provides a means of ensuring that the essential features of the old system are retained in the new system. Additionally, using the logical model for the current system as a basis for the

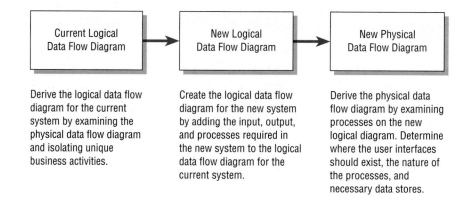

FIGURE 9.9
The progression of models
from logical to physical.

Derive the logical data flow diagram for the current system by examining the physical data flow diagram and isolating unique business activities.

Create the logical data flow diagram for the new system by adding the input, output, and processes required in the new system to the logical data flow diagram for the current system.

Derive the physical data flow diagram by examining processes on the new logical diagram. Determine where the user interfaces should exist, the nature of the processes, and necessary data stores.

proposed system provides for a gradual transition to the design of the new system. After the logical model for the new system has been developed, it may be used to create a physical data flow diagram for the new system. The progression of these models is illustrated in Figure 9.9.

Figure 9.10 shows a logical data flow diagram and a physical data flow diagram for a grocery store cashier. The CUSTOMER brings the ITEMS to the register; PRICES for all ITEMS are LOOKED UP and then totaled; next, PAYMENT is given to the cashier; finally, the CUSTOMER is given a RECEIPT. The logical data flow diagram illustrates the processes involved without going into detail about the physical implementation of activities. The physical data flow diagram shows that a bar code—the UPC BAR CODE found on most grocery store items—is used. In addition the physical data flow diagram mentions manual processes such as scanning, explains that a temporary file is used to keep a subtotal of items, and indicates that the PAYMENT could be made by CASH, CHECK, or DEBIT CARD. Finally, it refers to the receipt by its name, CASH REGISTER RECEIPT.

Developing Logical Data Flow Diagrams

First, construct a logical data flow diagram for the current system. There are a number of advantages to using a logical model, including:

1. Better communication with users.
2. More stable systems.
3. Better understanding of the business by analysts.
4. Flexibility and maintenance.
5. Elimination of redundancies and easier creation of the physical model.

A logical model is easier to use when communicating with users of the system because it is centered on business activities. Users will thus be familiar with the essential activities and many of the information requirements of each activity.

Systems formed using a logical data flow diagram are often more stable than those that are not because they are based on business events and not on a particular technology or method of implementation. Logical data flow diagrams represent features of a system that would exist no matter what the physical means of doing business are. For example, activities such as applying for a video store membership card, checking out a video tape, and returning the tape would all occur whether the video store had an automated, manual, or hybrid system. A logical data flow diagram has a business emphasis and helps the an-

Logical Data Flow Diagram

Physical Data Flow Diagram

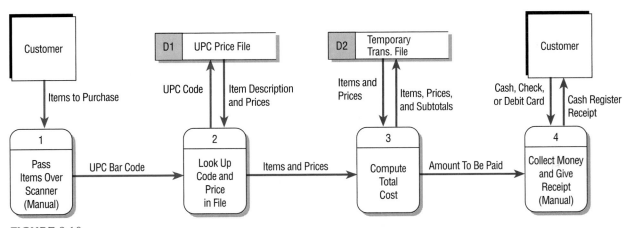

FIGURE 9.10
The physical data flow diagram (below) shows certain details not found on the logical data flow diagram (above).

alyst to understand the business being studied, to grasp why procedures are performed, and to determine the expected result of performing a task.

The new system will be more flexible and easier to maintain if its design is based on a logical model. Business functions are not subject to frequent change. Physical aspects of the system change more frequently than do business functions.

Examining a logical model may help you to create a better system by eliminating redundancies and inefficient methods that exist in the current system. Additionally, the logical model is easy to create and simpler to use because it does not often contain data stores other than master files or a database.

FIGURE 9.11
Physical data flow diagrams
contain many items not found
in logical data flow diagrams.

Contents of Physical Data Flow Diagrams

- Manual processes
- Processes for adding, deleting, changing, and updating records
- Data entry and verifying processes
- Validation processes for ensuring accurate data input
- Sequencing processes to rearrange the order of records
- Processes to produce every unique system output
- Intermediate data stores
- Actual file names used to store data
- Controls to signify completion of tasks or error conditions

Developing Physical Data Flow Diagrams

When the logical model of the new system is complete, it may be used to create a physical data flow diagram for the new system. The physical data flow diagram shows how the system will be constructed. Just as logical data flow diagrams have certain advantages, physical data flow diagrams have others, including:

1. Clarifying which processes are manual and which are automated.
2. Describing processes in more detail than do logical DFDs.
3. Sequencing processes that have to be done in a particular order.
4. Identifying temporary data stores.
5. Specifying actual names of files and printouts.
6. Adding controls to ensure the processes are done properly.

Figure 9.11 lists the contents of physical data flow diagrams. Notice that the list includes manual processes such as opening mail orders, creating a batch of forms for keying, visually inspecting a form, and so on. Also included are processes for adding, deleting, changing, and updating records. Each master file should link to one corresponding process for each of these tasks. Data entry processes such as keying (either batch or on-line) and verifying are also part of physical data flow diagrams.

Since much of the work performed in a system involves validation, such processes for ensuring accurate input should be included. It is estimated that 50–90 percent of program code is related to validation. Sequencing processes such as sorting and merging may also be included. Processes to produce every unique system output should be added, since each report or screen should be produced by a separate process.

Physical data flow diagrams also have intermediate data stores—often, a transaction file. Transaction or master files or a database are required to link any two processes that operate at different times. For example, a program may be used to process customer orders on a minute-by-minute basis. The information that this program generates may then have to be stored in a monthly file for sending customer bills and in an annual file for producing an annual sales summary report. Also part of physical data flow diagrams are physical data stores. These are designated by the actual names of the files or database (for example, CUSTOMER MASTER FILE rather than the label CUSTOMERS used on a logical data flow diagram), and they may be further described by including the data set name, number of records, and other key attributes.

Controls are also included in physical data flow diagrams. Among them are: editing input data, "record found" status when accessing a file or database, security and backup controls such as a journal record, and batch update controls to ensure that files produced by one process are correctly transmitted to the next process. Make distinctions in the physical data flow diagram between which processes are manual and which are automated.

Manual processes should be documented with written procedures that instruct employees on how to accomplish the tasks at hand. Automated procedures require computer programs, either written in-house or purchased from a vendor. Processes that are automated should be described in the diagram either as on-line or batch, and timing information may also be included. For example, an edit program must be run before an update program. Updates must be performed before producing a summary report. Note that because of such considerations, a physical data flow diagram may appear more linear than a logical model.

Intermediate data stores often consist of transaction files used to store data between processes. Since most processes that require access to a given set of data are unlikely to execute at the same instant in time, transaction files must hold the data from one process to the next. An easily understood example of this concept is found in the everyday experience of grocery shopping. The activities are:

1. Selecting items from shelves.
2. Checking out and paying the bill.
3. Transporting the groceries home.
4. Preparing a meal.
5. Eating the meal.

Each of these five activities would be represented by a separate process on a physical data flow diagram, and each one occurs at a different time. For example, you would not typically transport the groceries home and eat them at the same time. Therefore, a "transaction data store" is required to link each task. When you are selecting items, the transaction data store is the shopping cart. After the next process (checking out), the cart is unnecessary. The transaction data store linking checking out and transporting the groceries home is the shopping bag (cheaper than letting you take the cart home!). Bags are an inefficient way of storing the groceries once they are home, so cupboards and a refrigerator are used as a transaction data store between the activity of transporting the goods home and preparing the meal. Finally, a plate, bowl, and cup constitute the link between preparing and eating the meal.

Create the physical data flow diagram for a system by analyzing its output and input. Determine which data fields or elements need to be keyed. These are called *base elements* and must be stored in a file. Elements that are not keyed but are rather the result of a calculation or logical operation are called *derived elements.* When examining the output, determine whether the information must immediately be displayed or made available to numerous users. The processes that produce such output are usually on-line. Processes that involve a high volume of transactions, such as billing or check processing, or a large number of records that need to be summarized are usually batch processes, meaning that the documents are keyed as a group, edited as a group, or printed as a group. Printed reports are usually produced by batch processes, and screens tend to be on-line processes.

Analyze the output data flows and ask the question, "Is the information output coming from base elements on input flows or from calculations?" Often, determining this is easier after you have an understanding of the project data dictionary, which is discussed in Chapter 10. Regardless, create a process for each distinct output. If the stored information necessary for the report or screen is located in several files, show each file as an input data flow. If the output data needs to appear in a specific sequence, check to see if the files need to be sorted or indexed to match the sequence. Sorting is usually included on a lower-level child diagram as a separate process. Also, analyze the input. In a lower-level diagram, include processes for keying, input record validation, and verification. Finally, be sure to add processes for updating master files with input data.

Sometimes it is not clear how many processes to place in one diagram and when to create a child diagram. One suggestion is to examine each process and count the number of data flows entering and leaving it. If the total is greater than four, the process is a good candidate for a child diagram. Physical data flow diagrams will be illustrated in the example later in this chapter.

PARTITIONING DATA FLOW DIAGRAMS

Partitioning is the process of examining a data flow diagram and determining how it should be divided into collections of manual procedures and collections of computer programs. Analyze each process to determine whether it should be a manual or automated procedure. Group automated procedures into a series of computer programs. A dashed line is often drawn around a process or group of processes that should be placed into a single computer program.

A process performed by people rather than by computers is a manual process. Filling out or inspecting forms, picking order items, and so on are examples of manual processes. Written procedures should be developed for training new employees and developing operational consistency, so that each person performs a given procedure in the same way.

Automated processes use computer technology for performing the work even if such processes include some human activity, such as keying or verifying input data. These processes become either a batch or an on-line program as the system is developed. To determine whether a process is to be batch or on-line, examine the data flow into and out of the process. If the data flow both into and out of the process is composed entirely of stored information generated and accessed by the computer, thus requiring no human intervention, the process is a batch process. Using a transaction or master file to produce a report is an example of a batch process.

If some of the input or output is entered or examined by people, the process may be either batch or on-line. For example, keying new customer information could be performed as a batch by a data entry department or on-line by the users. The data flow that links a manual process or an external entity to an automated process represents a person–computer interaction that requires a user interface, a means for an individual to work with the information technology. Typically, this interface is on-line, and it may consist of a screen, a report, or a hand-held optical scanner like those commonly used in retail stores.

Batch processes are usually used when programs process a high volume of data. For example, a large amount of data may need to be entered when processing a mailbag containing customer orders in a mail-order company. Batch processes are also used when a large amount of data must be read and summarized—or otherwise processed—to produce output. An example is reading an entire file of a bank's customers to determine overdrawn accounts.

Another consideration the analyst must address in the physical data flow diagram is whether several batch processes should be combined into one computer program or job stream. A *job stream* is several programs written separately but running back-to-back. On-line programs are usually reserved for low-volume transactions or inquiries or cases in which an employee is working directly with a customer, such as a telephone inquiry about the current status of a bank account.

To develop a collection or group of computer programs and manual procedures, you should examine each process and ask questions about the nature of the work being done. An element of experimentation or play may enter the design process at this time, as you think about each process in the data flow diagram and see if it could be both batch and on-line. Reflect on which option would be better for the user community. Describe the processes as manual, batch, or on-line.

There are six reasons for partitioning data flow diagrams:

1. *Different user groups.* Are the processes performed by several different user groups, often at different physical locations within the company? If so, they should be partitioned into different computer programs. An example is the need to process customer returns and customer payments in a department store. Both processes involve obtaining financial information that is used to adjust customer accounts (subtracting from the amount the customer owes), but they are performed by different user groups at different locations. The counter handling items returned by customers is usually located at a desk near the store entrance. The payment counter is located somewhere in the interior of the store (for security) and is staffed by security personnel. Each group needs a different screen for recording the particulars of the transaction—either a credit screen or a payment screen.

2. *Timing.* Examine the timing of the processes. If two processes execute at different times, they cannot be grouped into one program.

3. *Similar tasks.* If two processes perform similar tasks and both are batch processes, they may be grouped into one computer program. For example, in a monthly run to adjust customer balances, both return item credits and customer payments are subtracted from the customer balance due. These two adjustment processes may readily be combined into one program.

4. *Efficiency.* Several batch processes may be combined into one program for efficient processing. For example, if a series of reports needs to use the same large input files, producing them from the same batch program may save considerable computer run time.

5. *Consistency of data.* Processes may be combined into one program for consistency of data. For example, an accounts receivable report needs to be printed periodically to show the amount due from each customer. The same figures must also be included on bills sent to the customers. If these two distinct outputs were produced in separate computer runs and if the customer master file was updated between the runs, then the

FilmMagic

Summary of Business Activities
Customer Rental System

1. Customers apply for a video rental card. They fill out a form and provide a means of verifying their identity. They are issued a video rental card.

2. Customers rent videos by giving the clerk their video rental card and the video cassettes or video games. The clerk totals the amount of the rental, which is received from the customers. The customer is given a receipt with the due date on it. A record is created for each item rented.

3. Customers return video cassettes or video games. If the video is returned late, a note and the amount of the late fee is made on their record.

4. If a customer has a late fee, he or she is required to pay the amount the next time they rent an item.

5. The company has several special policies designed to provide a competitive edge in the video rental market. Once a month, the customer rental records are reviewed for customers who have rented more than the bonus level, currently set at $50. Bonus customers are sent a letter thanking them for their business as well as issuing them several free rental coupons (depending on the amount of rental for the month).

6. Once a year, the customer records are examined for persons who have rented more than a yearly bonus level (currently set at $250). A letter, free rental coupons, and a certificate for a free video (if they have rented over two times the bonus level) are sent to the customer.

bills would have different data. The result is an unreliable, inconsistent system.

6. *Security.* Processes may be partitioned into different programs for security reasons. An example is a system with a process for adding a new customer and a process for changing customer financial information. Each process should have a separate program because, whereas only one person (or several in a large organization) should have password access to the program that changes customer financial data, many persons may be needed and authorized to add new customer records.

A DATA FLOW DIAGRAM EXAMPLE

The corporation in our example is FilmMagic, a video rental chain founded by three people with expertise in the video rental business. The plan is to have a series of stores scattered strategically around a metropolitan area. The company has also adopted a unique policy of giving free rentals and videos to its high-volume customers in an attempt to gain a large market share.

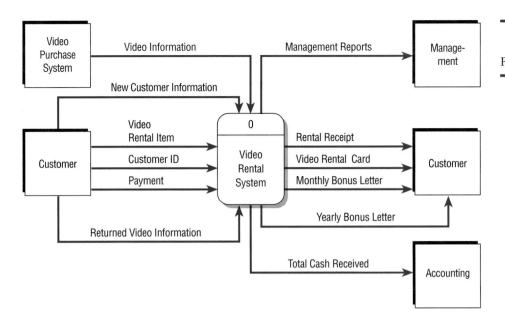

FIGURE 9.13
Context level diagram for the
FilmMagic video rental stores.

According to one of the company's owners, "If the airlines can have frequent flyer programs, our video stores can have a recurrent rental program." Consequently, a monthly customer bonus program will be part of the system.

Creating the Context Diagram

A summary of the business activities obtained from interviews with the owners of FilmMagic is illustrated in Figure 9.12. The context-level data flow diagram, representing an overview of the entire system, appears in Figure 9.13. Since the system must keep track of the number of videos a customer has rented, the external CUSTOMER has the most data flow to and from it. Note that the context diagram is relatively simple.

Drawing Diagram 0

Diagram 0, shown in Figure 9.14, depicts the major activities for the FilmMagic video rental system. Note that there is one process for each major activity. Each process is analyzed to determine the data required and the output produced. Process 1, RENT VIDEO ITEMS, summarizes the main function of the system and is thus a complex process. Notice the many input and output data flows.

To correctly draw the data flow diagram, questions must be asked such as, "What information is needed to rent a video?" A VIDEO RENTAL ITEM (which may be either a video cassette or a video game), a PAYMENT, and a CUSTOMER ID (a rental card) are required from the CUSTOMER. The VIDEO RENTAL ITEM is used to find matching information about the video, such as the price and description. The process creates a CASH TRANSACTION, which will eventually produce information about the total cash received. The CUSTOMER RECORD is obtained and updated with the total amount of the rental. A double-headed arrow indicates that the CUSTOMER RECORD is obtained from and replaced in the same file location. The RENTAL RECEIPT and video are given to the CUSTOMER. RENTAL INFORMATION such as the date and the item rented is produced for later use to generate MANAGEMENT REPORTS.

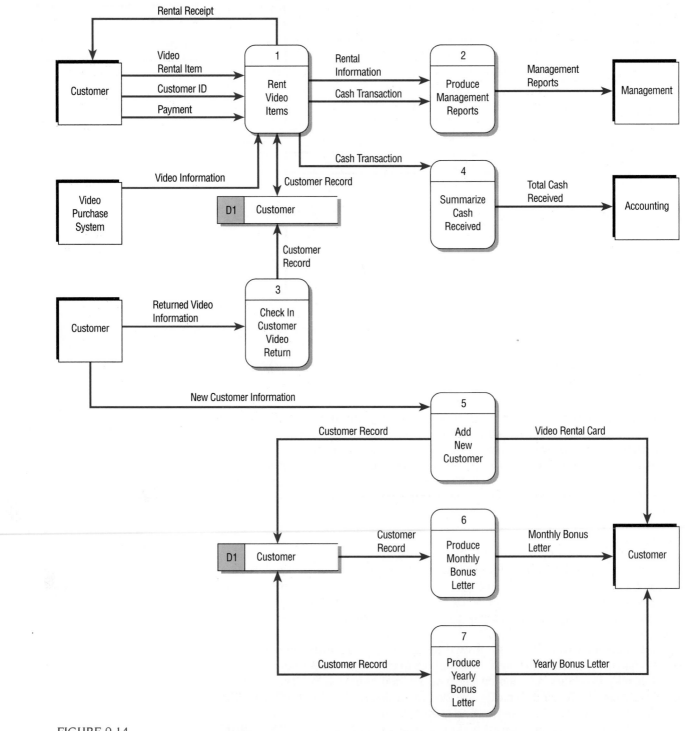

FIGURE 9.14
Diagram 0 for the FilmMagic video rental system shows seven major processes. This
logical DFD tells us what the system does, what is stored, who or what provides the
inputs, and who receives the output.

The other processes are simpler, with less input and output. Process 3, CHECK IN CUSTOMER VIDEO RETURN, updates the CUSTOMER data store indicating that items are no longer checked out. New customers must be added to the CUSTOMER data store before a video may be checked out. Process 5, ADD NEW CUSTOMER, takes NEW CUSTOMER INFORMATION and issues the customer a VIDEO RENTAL CARD. The card must be presented each time a customer wishes to check out a video.

Processes 2 and 4 produce useful information for managing the business and making decisions, such as when to lower the price of videos that are in demand and when to advertise to draw more customers, thereby increasing cash flow. Processes 6 and 7 use CUSTOMER data store information to PRODUCE MONTHLY and YEARLY CUSTOMER BONUS LETTERS. Notice that the names of the data flows going out of the processes are different, indicating that something has transformed input data to produce output. All processes start with a verb such as RENT, PRODUCE, CHECK IN, SUMMARIZE, or ADD.

Creating a Child Diagram

Figure 9.15 is the child diagram of process 1, RENT VIDEO ITEMS, in the FilmMagic example. The input data flow VIDEO INFORMATION is connected only to the process GET VIDEO RECORD. The source of this input is a blank area in the drawing. This incomplete interface flow matches the flow into process 1 on Diagram 0. The same is true for VIDEO RENTAL, PAYMENT, and CUSTOMER ID.

The CUSTOMER RECORD is also an interface data flow, but it is connected on Diagram 1 to the CUSTOMER data store, since data stores in the parent diagram may also be included on the child diagram. The output data flows CASH TRANSACTION and RENTAL RECEIPT are interface flows that match the parent process output. The flow NOT FOUND ERROR is not depicted in the parent process since an error line is considered a minor output.

Child diagram processes are more detailed, illustrating the logic required to produce the output. The process GET VIDEO RECORD uses VIDEO RENTAL, which indicates what video the customer wishes to rent, to find the matching VIDEO INFORMATION (title, price, and so on). Process 1.5, FIND CUSTOMER RECORD, uses the CUSTOMER ID on the video rental card to locate the CUSTOMER record. The CUSTOMER NAME AND ADDRESS are printed on the RENTAL RECEIPT printed from process 1.4.

CREATING A PHYSICAL DATA FLOW DIAGRAM

Figure 9.16 is the physical data flow diagram corresponding to the FilmMagic logical Diagram 0 data flow diagram. Notice that the data flow names have been changed to reflect the method of implementation. The customer now supplies a VIDEO RENTAL BAR CODE and a CUSTOMER ID BAR CODE to process 1, RENT VIDEO ITEMS. The entity VIDEO PURCHASE SYSTEM has been replaced with a VIDEO MASTER FILE, since files are used to communicate between systems. There are now two transaction files: CASH TRANSACTIONS and the RENTAL TRANSACTION FILE. The RENTAL TRANSACTION FILE is used to store information from the time the videos are rented until they are returned. The CASH TRANSACTIONS file is necessary since videos are rented throughout the day and the CASH RECEIVED REPORT is produced once a week. When customers return a video, data is entered using the RETURNED VIDEO SCREEN (to determine

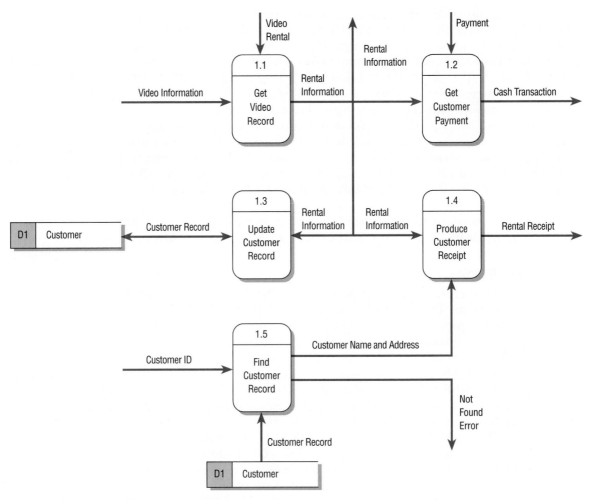

FIGURE 9.15
The child diagram for process 1 shows more detail than does Diagram 0. Process 1.1
is GET VIDEO RECORD. The logical DFD tells us what is accomplished but not how
to do it.

any late charges which is accomplished in process 3, CHECK IN CUS-
TOMER VIDEO RETURN) and this step then updates the RENTAL TRANS-
ACTION FILE. New customers fill out the NEW CUSTOMER FORM,
whereas on the logical data flow diagram this step is simply called NEW
CUSTOMER INFORMATION.

An example of a physical child data flow diagram is Diagram 1 of the
FilmMagic example, which is illustrated in Figure 9.17. Notice that there are
processes for scanning bar codes, displaying screens, locating records, and
creating and updating files. The sequence of activities is important here,
since the emphasis is on how the system will work and in what order events
happen.

Partitioning the Data Flow Diagram

Figure 9.18 illustrates partitioning for the FilmMagic physical data flow diagram. Notice the use of dotted lines to indicate which processes should be in
separate programs. The process RENT VIDEO ITEMS operates on a minute-

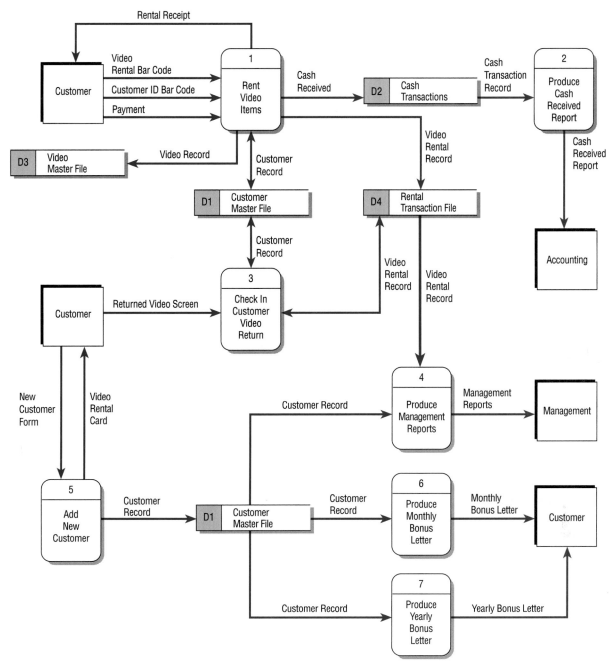

FIGURE 9.16
This physical data flow diagram corresponds to logical Diagram 0. Note the subtle differences. CUSTOMER ID is now CUSTOMER ID BAR CODE, emphasizing physical implementation.

by-minute basis. The process CHECK IN CUSTOMER VIDEO RETURN also operates on a minute-by-minute basis. However, returns are handled at a time later than the rental process, and both procedures should thus be in separate programs.

The PRODUCE CASH RECEIVED REPORT process is weekly and therefore must also be in a separate program. Since the CASH TRANSAC-

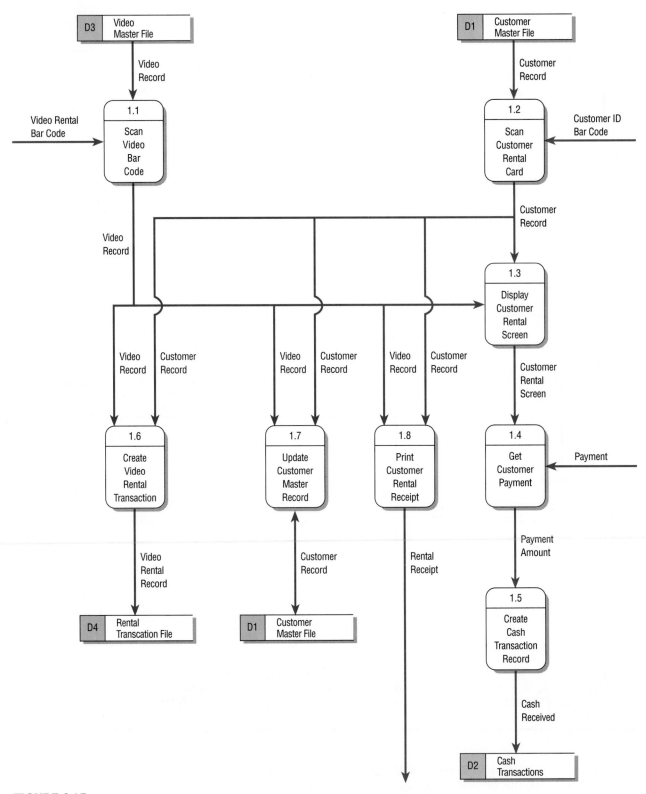

FIGURE 9.17
This physical child data flow diagram shows details about real world implementation. The logical diagram process 1.1 was GET VIDEO RECORD, but the physical diagram process 1.1 tells us how (SCAN VIDEO BAR CODE).

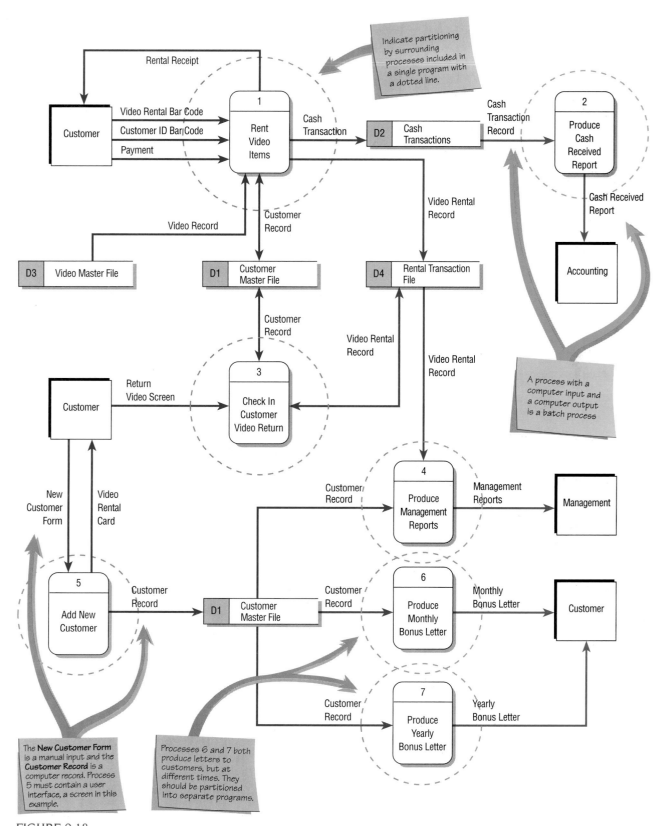

FIGURE 9.18
Partitioning the FilmMagic physical data flow diagram. Partitioning takes the physical DFD and makes programming and implementation manageable.

261

FIGURE 9.19
A summary of business activi-
ties for World's Trend Catalog
Division.

World's Trend
1000 International Lane
Cornwall, CT 06050

World's Trend is a mail order supplier of high quality, fashionable clothing. Customers place
orders either by telephone, faxing, or mailing in order form included with each catalog.

List of Business Activities

1. Add new customers to the customer master file. When customers are added to the master
    file, they are assigned a customer number, which is used when placing subsequent orders.

2. Perform inquiries to let customers know the current selling price of an item and the quantity
    available for sale.

3. Process customer orders by verifying that all order information is accurate and that a
    record exists for the customer placing the order. If a customer record does not exist, it is
    added to the master file. As orders are entered, customer and item master record fields are
    updated.

4. If a customer orders more of an item than is currently available in stock, backordered item
    information is sent to the inventory control department. When backordered items are
    received from World's Trend suppliers, they are shipped to the customers.

5. Orders are sent to the warehouse where they are filled.

6. A shipping statement is attached to the filled order. Mailing labels are prepared and the
    order is shipped to the customer.

7. Order information is used to produce a billing statement for all customers charging their
    goods to their World's Trend account.

8. Order information is used to produce an Accounts Receivable report for the Accounting
    department.

TION RECORD that goes into this process and the CASH RECEIVED RE-
PORT that comes out of the process are both computer information, the
process should be implemented as a batch program. The same is true for
process 4, PRODUCE MANAGEMENT REPORTS; for process 6, PRODUCE
MONTHLY BONUS LETTER; and for process 7, PRODUCE YEARLY
BONUS LETTER.

Process 5, ADD NEW CUSTOMER, could be either batch or on-line.
Since the customer is probably waiting for the video rental card on the other
side of a counter, an on-line process would provide the best customer service.

A SECOND DATA FLOW DIAGRAM EXAMPLE

Often, a person's first exposure to data flow diagrams seems confusing because there are so many new concepts and definitions. This next example is
intended to illustrate the development of a data flow diagram by selectively
looking at each of the components we explored earlier in this chapter. The

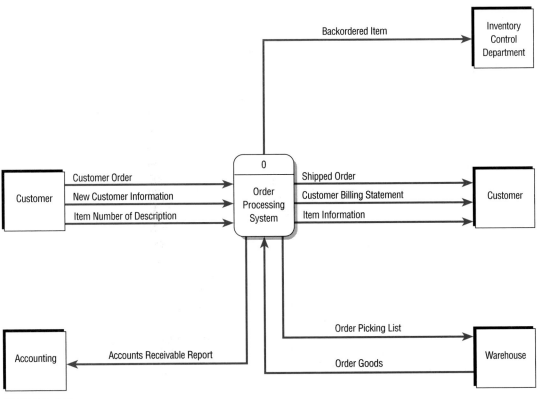

FIGURE 9.20
A context-level data flow diagram for the order processing system at World's Trend.

example, called "World's Trend Catalog Division," will also be used to illustrate concepts covered in Chapters 10 and 11.

A list of business activities for World's Trend can be found in Figure 9.19. You could develop this list using information obtained through interviews, investigation, and observation. The list can be used to identify external entities like CUSTOMER, ACCOUNTING, and WAREHOUSE, as well as data flows such as ACCOUNTS RECEIVABLE REPORT and CUSTOMER BILLING STATEMENT. Later (when developing level 0 and child diagrams), the list can be used to define processes, data flows, and data stores.

Once this list of activities is developed, create a context diagram as shown in Figure 9.20. This diagram shows the ORDER PROCESSING SYSTEM in the middle (no processes are described in detail in the context level diagram) and five external entities (the two entities called CUSTOMER are really one and the same). The data flows that come from and go to the external entities are shown as well (for example, CUSTOMER ORDER and ORDER PICKING LIST).

Next, go back to the activity list and make a new list of as many processes and data stores as you can find. You can add more later, but start making the list now. If you think you have enough information, draw a level 0 diagram such as the one found in Figure 9.21. Call this Diagram 0 and keep the processes general so as not to overcomplicate the diagram. Later, you can add detail. When you are finished drawing the seven processes, draw data flows between them and to the external entities (the same external entities shown in the context diagram). If you feel there needs to be a data store such

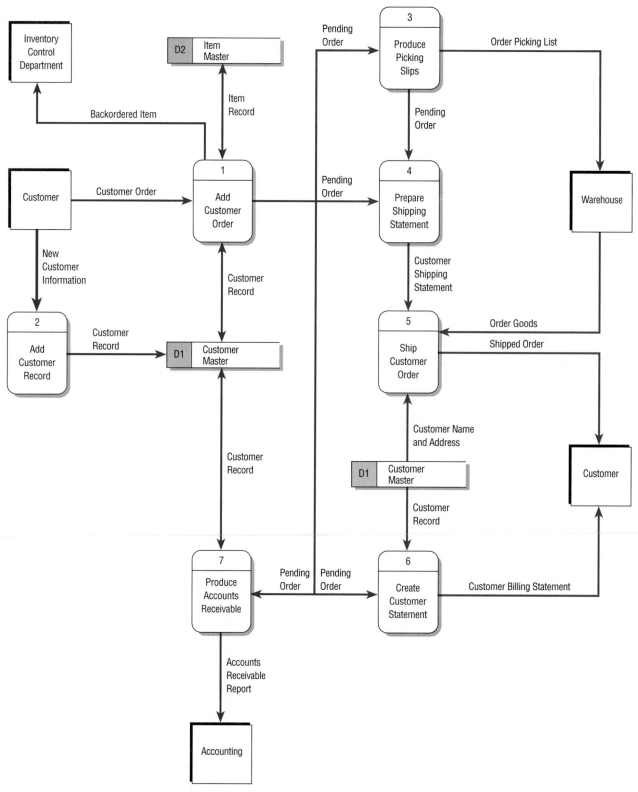

FIGURE 9.21
Diagram 0, of the order processing system for World's Trend Catalog Division.

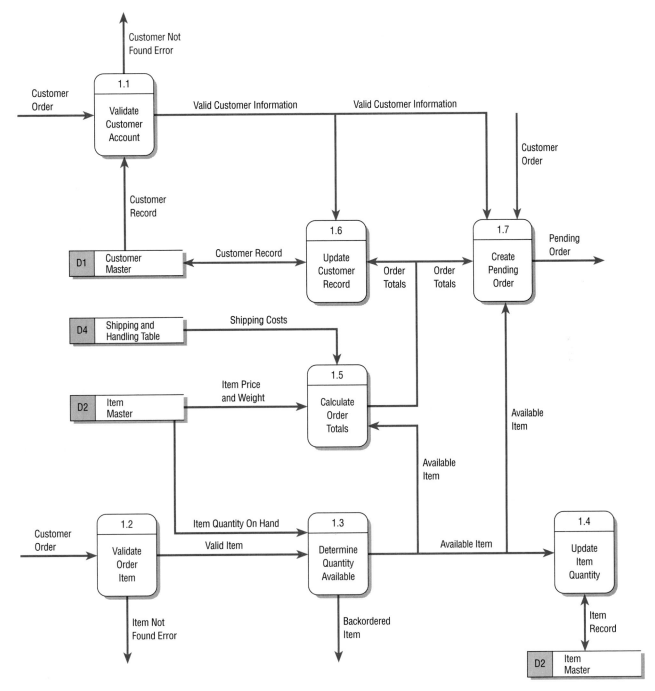

FIGURE 9.22
Diagram 1, of the order processing system for World's Trend Catalog Division.

as ITEM MASTER or CUSTOMER MASTER, draw those in and connect them to processes using data flows. Now take the time to number the processes and data stores. Pay particular attention to making the labels meaningful. Check for errors and correct them before moving on.

At this point try to draw a child diagram (sometimes also called a level 1 diagram) like the one in Figure 9.22. Number your child diagrams Diagram 1,

FIGURE 9.23
A physical data flow child diagram for World's Trend Catalog Division.

Diagram 2, and so on, in accordance with the number you assigned to each process in the level 0 diagram. When you draw Diagram 1, make a list of subprocesses first. A process such as ADD CUSTOMER ORDER can have subprocesses (in this case, there are seven). Connect these subprocesses to one another and also to data stores when appropriate. Subprocesses do not have to be connected to external entities, since we can always refer to the parent (or level 0) data flow diagram to identify these entities. Label the subprocesses 1.1, 1.2, 1.3, and so on. Take the time to check for errors and make sure the labels make sense.

If you want to go beyond the logical model and draw a physical model as well, look at Figure 9.23, which is an example of a physical data flow child diagram of process 3, PRODUCE PICKING SLIPS. When you label a physical model, take care to describe the process in great detail. For example, subprocess 3.3 in a logical model could simply be SORT ORDER ITEM, but in the physical model, a better label is SORT ORDER ITEM BY LOCATION WITHIN CUSTOMER. When you write a label for a data store, refer to the actual file or database, such as CUSTOMER MASTER FILE or SORTED ORDER ITEM FILE. When you describe data flows, describe the actual form, report, or screen. For example, when you print a slip for order picking, call the data flow ORDER PICKING SLIP.

Finally, take the physical data flow diagram and suggest partitioning, combining or separating the processes. As stated earlier, there are many reasons for partitioning: identifying distinct processes for different user groups, separating processes that need to be performed at different times, grouping similar tasks, grouping processes for efficiency, combining processes for consistency, or separating them for security. Figure 9.24 shows that partitioning is useful in the case of World's Trend Catalog Division. You would first group processes 1 and 2 because it would make sense to add new customers at the same time their first order was placed. You would then put processes 3 and 4 in two separate partitions. Although both are batch processes, they must be done at different times from one another and thus cannot be grouped into a single program.

This completes the process of developing a data flow diagram from the top down, first drawing a companion physical data flow diagram to accompany the logical data flow diagram, then partitioning the data flow diagram by grouping or separating the processes. The World's Trend example will be used again in Chapters 10 and 11.

USING DATA FLOW DIAGRAMS

Data flow diagrams are useful throughout the analysis and design process. Use original, unexploded data flow diagrams early when ascertaining information requirements. At this stage they can help provide an overview of data movement through the system, lending a visual perspective unavailable in narrative data.

Tradeoffs are involved in deciding how far the data streams should be exploded. Time may be wasted and understandability sacrificed if data flow diagrams are overly complex. On the other hand, if the data flow diagrams are underexploded, errors of omission could eventually occur that might affect the system that is being developed.

If data flow diagrams are used as a tool to solicit more specific information requirements from users, they should not be highly exploded or finalized in any medium before users have had a chance to walk through them

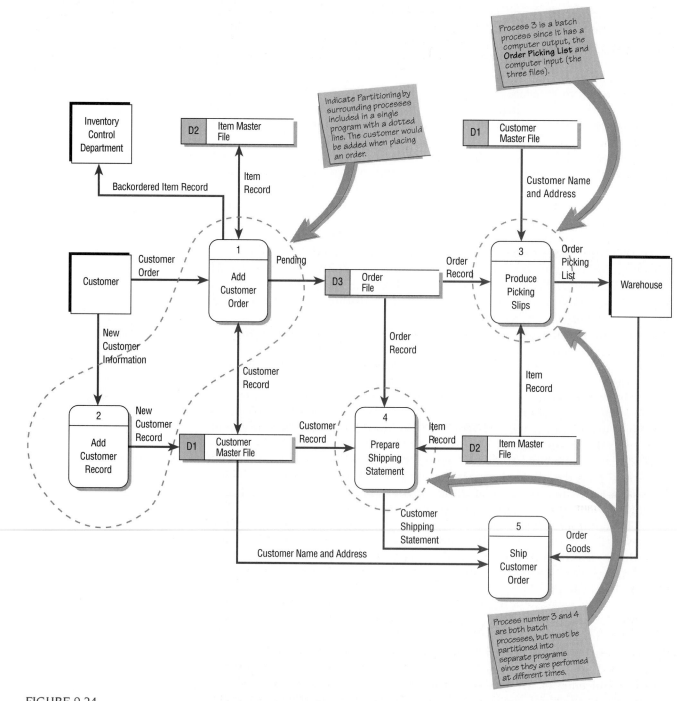

FIGURE 9.24
Partitioning the data flow diagram (Showing part of Diagram 0).

with the systems analyst. Changes need to be incorporated after getting users' input. Overly exploded diagrams may not be helpful to users. And if data flow diagrams are too complex before presentation to users, the systems analyst is more likely to defend the representation than to welcome any user corrections.

After exploding the original data flow diagrams, use them as a tool
for further interaction with users. At this stage the data flow diagram
shows your own conceptualization of the business data streams. Educate key users about the conventions used in data flow diagrams, then
go through the successive levels with them. Ask for changes that they
may suggest to clarify processes or to make the diagrams more accurate in
some way.

After user modifications are added, users and the systems analysis
team approve the data flow diagrams as accurate reflections of the organization's data flows. The data flow diagrams can then be finalized and drawn
using a CASE tool, as shown in Figure 9.25.

Once their content is clarified, the data flow diagrams need to be redrawn and relabeled in a meaningful way. The systems analyst might be
quite competent at sketching through the logic of the data stream for data
flow diagrams, but to make the diagrams truly communicative, meaningful
labels for all data components are also required. Labels should not be
generic, since then they do not tell us enough about the situation at hand.
All general systems models bear the configuration of input, process, and output, so labels for a data flow diagram need to be more specific than that.

Consider effective naming as a top priority, so that someone unfamiliar
with the system will be able to pick up a data flow diagram and, with a little
training, understand what it depicts. Make labels as specific yet concise as
possible. Try to avoid using the same term to mean two different things. Conversely, consolidate terms wherever possible, using only a few terms for the
data item. Part of the reason data flow diagrams are effective is that they are
consistent from page to page (recall the requirement that inputs and outputs
remain constant between diagrams). The same sort of consistency should be
evident in labeling.

There's No Business Like Flow Business

The phone at Merman's rings, and Annie Oaklea, head of costume inventory, picks it up and answers a query by saying, "Let me take a look at my inventory cards. Sorry, it looks as if there are only two male bear suits in inventory—with extragrowly expressions at that. We've had a great run on bear. When do you need them? Perhaps one will be returned. No, can't do it, sorry. Would you like these two sent, regardless? The name of your establishment? Theatre in the Square? Right. Delightful company! I see by our account card that you've rented from us before. And how long will you be needing the costumes?"

Figure 9.C1 is a data flow diagram that sets the stage for processing of costume rentals from Merman's. It shows rentals like the one Annie is doing for Theatre in the Square.

After conversing for another few moments about shop policy on alterations, Annie concludes her conversation by saying, "You are very lucky to get the

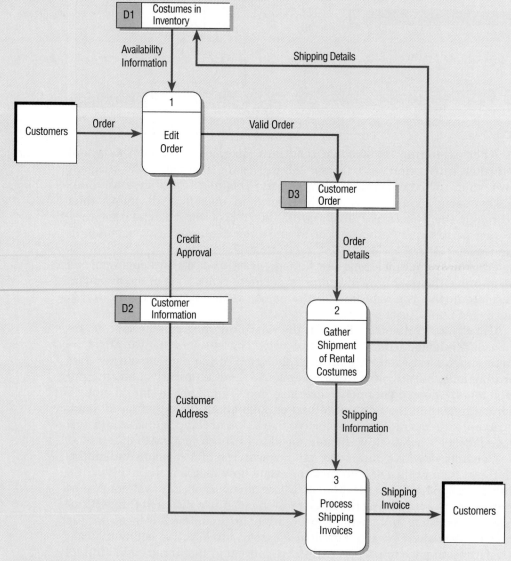

FIGURE 9.C1
A data flow diagram for Merman's Costume Rentals.

bears on such short notice. I've got another company reserving them for the first week in July. I'll put you down for the bear suits, and they'll be taken to you directly by our courier. As always, prompt return will save enormous trouble for us all."

Merman's costume rental enterprise is located in London's world-famous West End theatre district. When a theatre or television production company lacks the resources (either time or expertise) to construct a costume in its own shop, the cry goes up to "Ring up Merman's!" and it proceeds to rent what it needs with a minimum of fuss.

The shop (more aptly visualized as a warehouse) goes on for three floors full of costume racks, holding thousands of costumes hung together by historical period, then grouped as to whether they are for men or women, and then by costume size.[1] Most theatre companies are able to locate precisely what they need through Annie's capable assistance.

Now tailor-make the *rental return* portion of the data flow diagram given earlier. Remember that timely returns are critical for keeping the spotlight on costumes rented from Merman's.

---

[1] Western Costume Company in Hollywood, California, is said to have more than 1 million costumes worth about $40 million.

Finally, remember that data flow diagrams are used to document the system. Assume that data flow diagrams will be around longer than the people who drew them—this is, of course, always true if an external consultant is drawing them. Data flow diagrams can be used for documenting high or low levels of analysis and helping to substantiate the logic underlying the data flows of the organizations.

SUMMARY

In order to better understand the logical movement of data throughout a business, the systems analyst draws data flow diagrams (DFDs). Data flow diagrams are structured analysis and design tools that allow the analyst to comprehend the system and subsystems visually as a set of interrelated data flows.

Graphical representations of data movement storage and transformation are drawn with the use of four symbols: a rounded rectangle to depict data processing or transformations; a double square to show an outside data entity (source or receiver of data); an arrow to depict data flow; and an open-ended rectangle to show a data store.

The systems analyst extracts data processes, sources, stores, and flows from early organizational narrative and uses a top-down approach to first draw a context diagram of the system within the larger picture. Then a level 0 logical data flow diagram is drawn. Processes are shown and data stores are added. Next, the analyst creates a child diagram for each of the processes in Diagram 0. Inputs and outputs remain constant, but the data stores and sources change. Exploding the original data flow diagram allows the systems analyst to focus on ever more detailed depictions of data movement within the system. The analyst then develops a physical data flow diagram from the logical data flow diagram, partitioning it to facilitate programming. Each process is analyzed to determine whether it should be a manual or automated procedure. Automated procedures are subsequently grouped into a series of computer programs, designated as either batch or on-line. Six con-

"You take a very interesting approach to the problems we have here at MRE. I've seen you sketching diagrams of our operation almost since the day you walked in the door. I'm actually getting used to seeing you doodling away now. What did you call those? Oh, yes. Context diagrams. And flow charts? Oh, no. Data flow diagrams. That's it, isn't it?"

HYPERCASE QUESTIONS

1. Find the data flow diagrams already drawn in MRE. Make a list of those you found and add a column to show where in the organization you found them.

2. Draw a context diagram modeling the Training Unit Project Development process, one that is based on case interviews with relevant Training Unit staff. Then draw a level 0 diagram detailing the process.

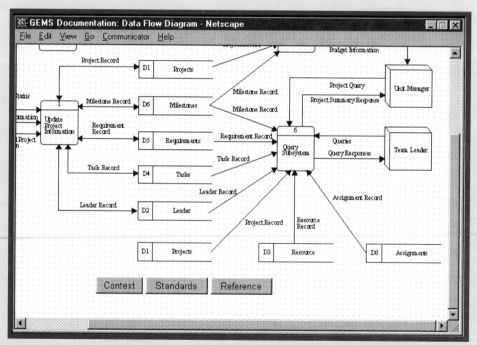

FIGURE 9.HC1
In HyperCase you can click on elements in a data flow diagram.

siderations for partitioning data flow diagrams include whether: there are processes performed by different user groups, processes execute at the same times, processes perform similar tasks, batch processes can be combined for efficient processing, processes may be combined into one program for consistency of data, or processes may be partitioned into different programs for security reasons.

The advantages of data flow diagrams include the simplicity of notation; using them to gain clearer information from users; allowing the systems analyst to conceptualize necessary data flows without being tied to a particular physical implementation; allowing analysts to better conceptualize the interrelatedness of the system and its subsystems, and analyzing a proposed system to determine if the necessary data and processes have been defined.

KEYWORDS AND PHRASES

data-oriented systems	parent process
data flow diagrams	child diagram
context diagram	vertical balancing
base elements	interface data flow
derived elements	functionally primitive
level 0 diagram	primitive process
external entity	logical model
(source or destination)	physical model
transforming process	physical data stores
data store	batch processes
exploding	on-line processes
top-down approach	transaction data store

REVIEW QUESTIONS

1. What is one of the main methods available for the analyst to use in analyzing data oriented systems?
2. What are the four advantages of using a data flow approach over narrative explanations of data movement?
3. What are the four data items that can be symbolized on a data flow diagram?
4. What is a context diagram? Contrast it to a level 0 DFD.
5. Define the top-down approach as it relates to drawing data flow diagrams.
6. Describe what "exploding" data flow diagrams means.
7. What are the tradeoffs involved in deciding how far data streams should be exploded?
8. Why is labeling data flow diagrams so important? What can effective labels on data flow diagrams accomplish for those unfamiliar with the system?
9. What is the difference between a logically and physically oriented data flow diagram?
10. List three reasons for creating a logically oriented data flow diagram.
11. List five characteristics found on a physical data flow diagram that are not on a logical data flow diagram.
12. When are transaction files required in the system design?
13. What is partitioning and how is it used?
14. How can an analyst determine when a user interface is required?
15. List three ways of determining partitioning on a data flow diagram.
16. List three ways to use completed data flow diagrams.

PROBLEMS

1. Pamela Coburn, a systems analyst, has worked for some time with Luis Asperilla, the manager of the South Street Bonton's clothing store, observing him in action during the day and talking with him whenever business slows. Pamela is feeling fairly sure of the store's processes

now and wants to capture what she's learned on paper. (Consulting Opportunity 9.1 provides the background Pamela has gained.)

    a. Draw a context diagram for Bonton's.

    b. Draw a level 0 data flow diagram of data movement at Bonton's on South Street, as Pamela might.

    c. Explode one of the processes from your first-level diagram into more detail, adding data stores and data flows. Make reasonable assumptions about the operation of a retail clothing store, if necessary, to finish the diagrams.

    d. In a paragraph, write a description of the process you exploded in problem 1, part c. What assumptions, if any, did you have to make in order to draw the second-level diagram?

2. In two paragraphs, defend the statement that "An advantage of logical data flow diagrams is that they free the systems analyst from premature commitment to technical implementation of the system." Use an example to support what you write.

3. Up to this point, you seem to have had excellent rapport with Kathy Kline, one of the managers who will use the system you are proposing. However, when you showed her the data flow diagrams you drew, she did not understand them.

    a. In a paragraph, write down in general terms how to explain to a user what a data flow diagram is. Be sure to include a list of symbols and what they mean.

    b. It takes some effort to educate users about data flow diagrams. Is it worthwhile to share them with users? Why or why not? Defend your response in a paragraph.

4. One common experience that students in every college and university share is enrolling in a college course.

    a. Draw a first-level data flow diagram of data movement for enrollment in a college course. Use a single sheet and label each data item clearly.

    b. Explode one of the processes in your original data flow diagram into subprocesses, adding data flows and data stores.

    c. List the parts of the enrollment process that are "hidden" to the outside observer and about which you have had to make assumptions to complete a second-level diagram.

5. Figure 9.EX1 is a level 1 data flow diagram of data movement in a Niagara Falls tour agency called Marilyn's Tours. Read it over, checking for any inaccuracies.

    a. List and number the errors that you have found in the diagram.

    b. Redraw and label the data flow diagram of Marilyn's so that it is correct. Be sure that your new diagram employs symbols properly in order to cut down on repetitions and duplications where possible.

6. Perfect Pizza wants to install a system to record orders for pizza and Buffalo chicken wings. When regular customers call Perfect Pizza on the phone, they are asked their phone number. When the number is typed into a computer, the name, address, and last order date is automatically brought up on the screen. Once the order is taken, the total, including tax and delivery, is calculated. Then the order is given to the cook. A receipt is printed. Occasionally, special offers (coupons) are printed so the customer can get a discount. Drivers who make

FIGURE 9.EX1
A hand-sketched data flow diagram for Marilyn's Tours.

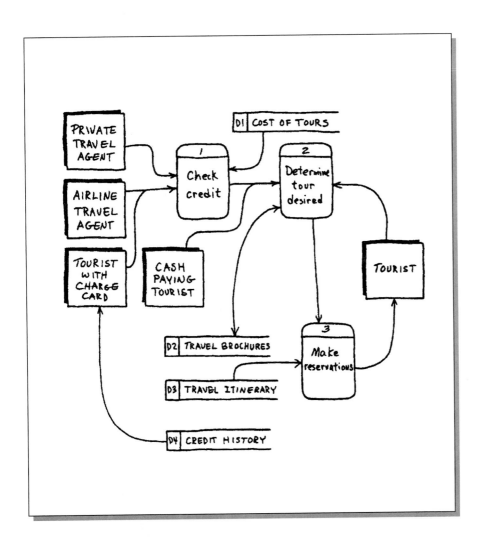

deliveries give customers a copy of the receipt and a coupon (if any). Weekly totals are kept for comparison with last year's performance. Write a summary of business activities for taking an order at Perfect Pizza.

7. Draw a context diagram for Perfect Pizza (problem 6).

8. Explode the context-level diagram in problem 7 showing all the major processes. Call this Diagram 0. It should be a logical data flow diagram.

9. Draw a logical child diagram for Diagram 0 in problem 8 for the process that adds a new customer if he or she is not in the database currently (has never ordered from Perfect Pizza before).

10. Draw a physical data flow diagram for problem 8.

11. Draw a physical data flow diagram for problem 9.

12. Partition the physical data flow diagram in problem 8, grouping and separating processes as you deem appropriate. Explain why you partitioned the data flow diagram in this manner. (Remember that you do not have to partition the entire diagram, only the parts that make sense to partition.)

13. **a.** Draw a logical child diagram for process 6 in Figure 9.21.
    b. Draw a physical child diagram for process 6 in Figure 9.21.

14. Draw a physical data flow diagram for process 1.1 in Figure 9.22.

15. Create a context diagram for a real estate agent trying to create a system that matches up buyers with potential houses.

16. Draw a logical data flow diagram showing general processes for problem 15. Call it Diagram 0.

17. Create a context diagram for billing in a dental office. External entities include the patients and insurance companies.

18. Draw a logical data flow diagram showing general processes for problem 17. Call it Diagram 0.

19. Create a data flow diagram for the following situation:

Technical Temporaries

Technical Temporaries is a company that specializes in placing employees in businesses for short periods of time. The company specializes in "temporaries" who have a high degree of proficiency in working with PC software, such as word processing and spreadsheets, as well as other technical areas. Each employee must pass proficiency tests for areas in which they wish to be certified. The system described below is responsible for matching employees with short term openings that are available.

List of Business Activities

a. Businesses telephone the company to request temporaries to fill specific positions. The requests are used to create a Temporary Employment Request record. If the business requesting the temporary employee is not on the Employer Master file, a record is created for it.

b. Employees are selected to fill the temporary positions based on employee qualifications and availability. The Temporary Employee Master and the Temporary Employment Request files are used to list all qualified candidates.

c. Contracts are sent to the selected temporaries. Information is printed from the Employee Master, Employer Master, and Temporary Employment Request files.

d. Returned contracts are used to update the Employee Master file. The Temporary Employment Request file is updated with scheduling and personnel information.

e. Monthly schedules are printed for each employee. They contain information from the Employee Master, the Employer Master, and the Temporary Employment Request files, and they are sequenced by employment date for each employee.

f. Notification is sent to the business requesting the temporary employees confirming the date and qualifications of the workers as well as their names.

20. Create a physical child data flow diagram for the following situation: The Fastbase Corporation develops PC database software products that are sold for both the domestic and international market. Customers receiving the products are sent a set of additional fonts if they return a warranty registration card that is included with the software and documentation. The diagram represents a batch process and is the child of process 5, ADD CUSTOMER REGISTRATION. The following tasks are included:

a. Inspect the Warranty Registration Card received from the customer to ensure that the information is complete and accurate. Incomplete cards are placed in a reject box.

b. Data entry operators key the Warranty Registration Card, thus creating a Warranty Registration File.

c. A different data entry operator verifies the keyed data by reentering the Warranty Registration Card information. The data entry terminal compares the data previously keyed with the entry made by the second operator. Discrepancies are displayed.

d. The Warranty Registration File is input to a batch edit program. Each record is checked for accuracy. Errors are printed on a Warranty Validation Report, and valid records are placed on a Valid Warranty Registration File.

e. The Valid Warranty Registration File is used as input, along with the Customer Master File, into the Customer Warranty Update Program. Records are added or updated, depending on whether the customer already exists on the Customer Master File.

f. The Valid Warranty Registration File is used to print a series of mailing labels for sending the font software to the customer.

21. Use the principles of partitioning to determine which of the processes in problem 20 should be included in separate programs.

22. Create a physical child data flow diagram for the following situation: The local Personal Computer Users Group (PCUG) holds meetings once a month with informative speakers, door prizes, and sessions for special interest groups. A laptop computer is taken to the meetings, and it is used to add the names of new members to the group. The diagram represents an on-line process and is the child of process 1, ADD NEW MEMBERS. The following tasks are included:

a. Key the new member information.

b. Validate the information. Errors are displayed on the screen.

c. When all the information is valid, a confirmation screen is displayed. The operator visually confirms that the data are correct and either accepts the transaction or cancels it.

d. Accepted transactions add new members to the Membership Master file, which is stored on the laptop hard drive.

e. Accepted transactions are written to a Membership Journal file, which is stored on a diskette.

GROUP PROJECTS

1. Meet with your group to develop a context diagram for Maverick Transport (first introduced in Chapter 5). Use any data you have subsequently generated with your group about Maverick Transport. (*Hint:* Concentrate on one of the company's functional areas rather than try to model the entire organization.)

2. Using the context diagram developed in problem 1, develop with your group a level 0 logical data flow diagram for Maverick Transport. Make any assumptions necessary to draw it. List them.

3. With your group, choose one key process and explode it into a logical child diagram. Make any assumptions necessary to draw it. List follow-

up questions and suggest other methods to get more information about processes which are still unclear to you.

4. Use the work your group has done to date to create a physical data flow diagram of a portion of the new system you are proposing for Maverick Transport.

SELECTED BIBLIOGRAPHY

Colter, M. "A Comparative Examination of Systems Analysis Techniques." *Management Information Systems Quarterly,* June 1984, Vol. 8, No. 1, pp. 51–66.

Davis, G. B., and M. H. Olson. *Management Information Systems, Conceptual Foundations, Structure and Development,* 2nd ed. New York: McGraw-Hill Book Company, 1985.

Gane, C., and T. Sarson. *Structured Systems Analysis and Design Tools and Techniques.* Englewood Cliffs, NJ: Prentice-Hall, Inc., 1979.

Gore, M., and J. Stubbe. *Elements of Systems Analysis,* 3rd ed. Dubuque, IA: William C. Brown Co., 1983.

Leeson, M. *Systems Analysis and Design.* Chicago, IL: Science Research Associates, Inc., 1985.

Lucas, H. *Information Systems Concepts for Management,* 3rd ed. New York: McGraw-Hill Book Company, 1986.

McFadden, F. R., and J. A. Hoffer. *Data Base Management.* Menlo Park, CA: The Benjamin/Cummings Publishing Company, 1985.

Martin, J. *Strategic Data-Planning Methodologies.* Englewood Cliffs, NJ: Prentice-Hall, Inc., 1982.

Senn, J. A. *Analysis and Design of Information Systems.* New York: McGraw-Hill Book Company, 1984.

Sprague, R. H., and E. D. Carlson. *Building Effective Decision Support Systems.* Englewood Cliffs, NJ: Prentice-Hall, Inc., 1982.

JUST FLOWING ALONG

After the results of interviews, questionnaires, and prototyping are gathered and analyzed, Anna and Chip move to the next step—modeling the system. Their strategy is to create a layered set of data flow diagrams and then describe the components.

Modeling starts with analyzing the context diagram of the current microcomputer system. This diagram is simple to create and is the foundation for successive levels because it describes the external entities and the major data flow.

"Shall we create a physical data flow diagram of the current system?" asks Chip.

Anna replies, "No, it's fairly simple to understand, and we wouldn't gain any significant new knowledge of how the system operates. Let's start by creating a logical model of the current system."

The logical data flow diagrams are completed within a few days. Anna and Chip hold an afternoon meeting to review the diagrams and give each other feedback. "These look good," remarks Chip. "We can clearly see the business events that comprise the current system."

Anna replies, "Yes, let's take the current logical data flow diagrams and add all the requirements and desired features of the new system. We can also eliminate any of the unnecessary features that wouldn't be implemented in the new system."

Anna takes the context level diagram (shown in Chapter 2) and adds many of the reports, inquiries, and other information included in the new system. The finished context level diagram is shown in Figure E9.1. Notice that there are many new data flows. The maintenance department will receive reports that currently are not available. There is a report, for example, that helps to automate the installation of new microcomputers, the INSTALLATION LISTING, and another report intended for management that shows which software is located on which machines, the SOFTWARE CROSS-REFERENCE REPORT.

Chip reviews the finished diagram, commenting, "This is more art than science. It looks like all of the requirements of the new system are included. But this is far more complex than I originally thought it would be."

Anna replies, "Let's expand this to Diagram 0 for the new system. This will be a logical data flow diagram since we want to focus on the business needs. Perhaps it would be best if we work in a team for this diagram."

After working for several hours that afternoon and a good portion of the next morning, they complete the diagram. It is reviewed and modified with some minor changes. The finished Diagram 0 is shown in Figures E9.2 and E9.3. Since this is a logical diagram, it shows no keying or validation operations; nor does it show any temporary data stores or transaction files. Timing is not a consideration (an example is the ADD NEW MICROCOMPUTER process, where it appears that orders are updated and reports simultaneously produced).

"This finally looks right," muses Chip. "All the major processes, data flow, and data stores are accounted for. And the overall diagram doesn't look too complicated."

*Allen Schmidt,
Julie E. Kendall, and
Kenneth E. Kendall*

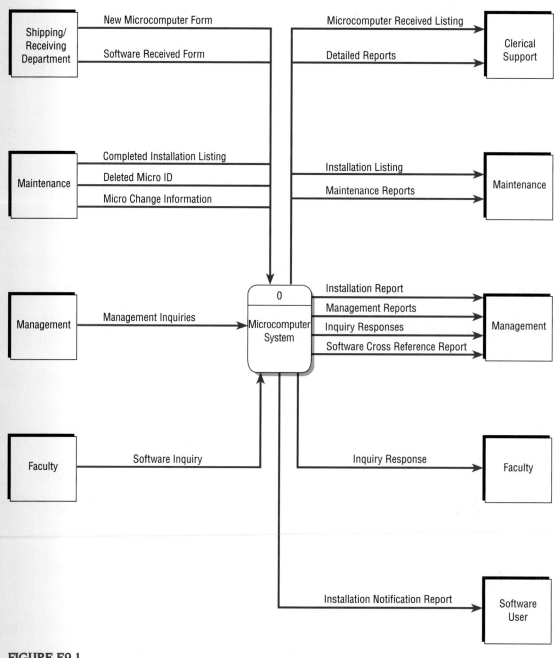

FIGURE E9.1
Context level data flow diagram, Proposed System.

"Putting all of the inquiries into one subsystem and all the reports into another helped. Remember how complex the original diagram was?" asks Anna.

"I sure do," Chip replies. "I started to think we were tackling too much at once with this system. At least it's more manageable now. Since this is finished, what's the next step?"

"We need to decide how to implement the data flow diagram into a series of steps, which are shown on the physical data flow diagram." Anna

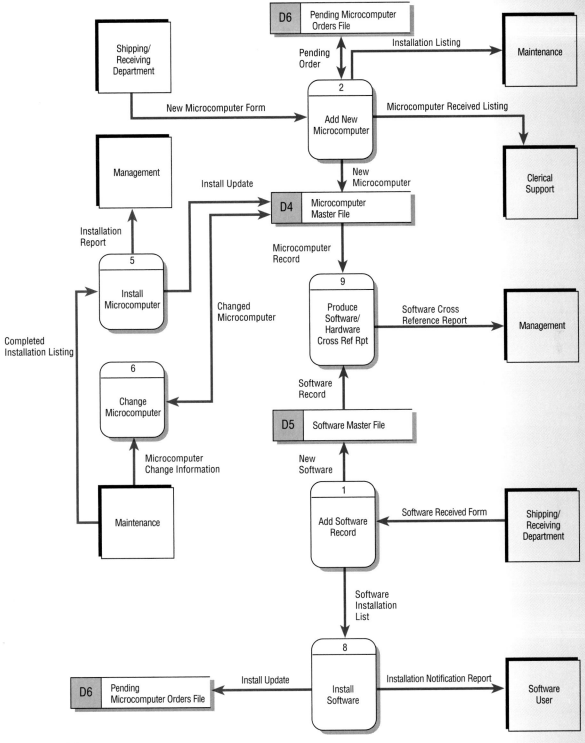

FIGURE E9.2
Diagram 0: Proposed Microcomputer System (part 1).

FIGURE E9.3
Diagram 0: Proposed Micro-computer System (part 2).

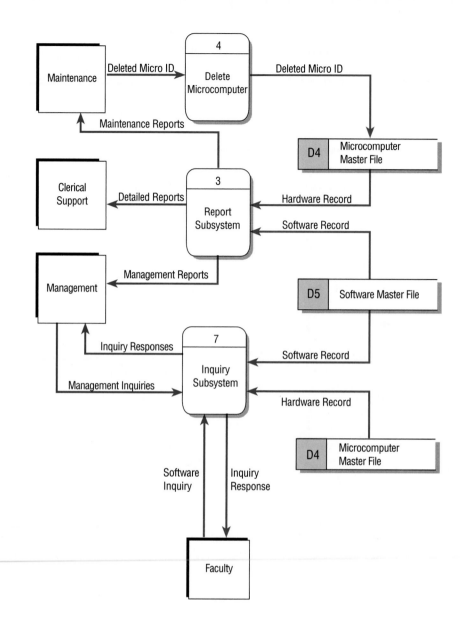

says. "This logical data flow diagram shows the business tasks—or *what* should be accomplished. Now we need to show *how* the system will work. Keying, validation, information on whether programs are on-line or batch, and transaction files need to be added."

Chip and Anna divide up the work by major tasks to be accomplished. Chip starts working on the ADD MICROCOMPUTER process.

When Chip draws the diagrams, he sees that he is drawing a level 0 diagram and then exploding it into many level 1 diagrams. Just as a parent may have many children, there may be many level 1 diagrams for a specific level 0 diagram. For this reason some analysts refer to these as parent and child diagrams.

Chip and Anna decide to abbreviate level 0 diagram as Diagram 0. The details are shown on a child diagram, Diagram 2. The external entities do not appear on the diagram, since they are only shown on the context diagram and Diagram 0, the context diagram explosion.

Figure E9.4 is the finished version of Diagram 2, a batch process for adding new microcomputers. The NEW MICROCOMPUTER FORM is an in-

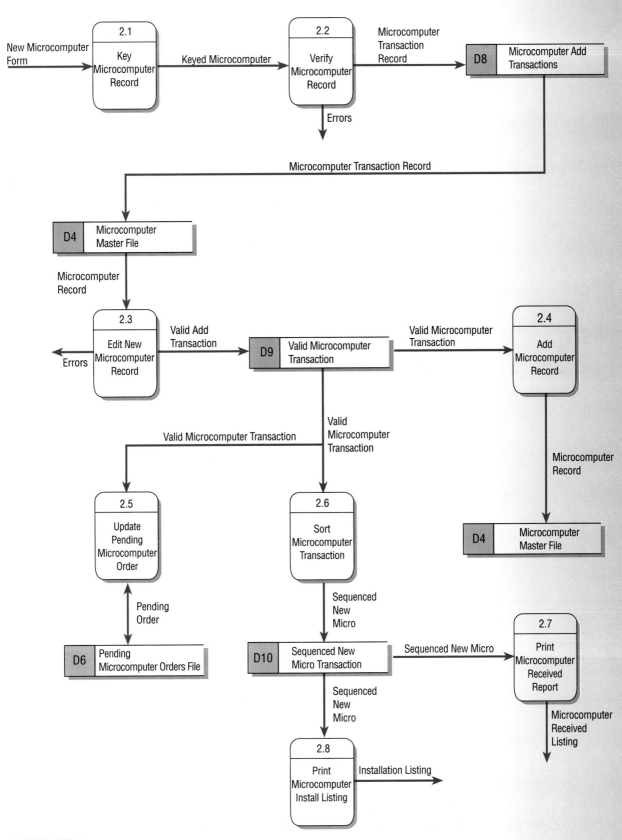

FIGURE E9.4
Diagram 2: Proposed Microcomputer System.

put interface flow that matches the parent diagram. The MICROCOMPUTER RECEIVED LISTING and INSTALLATION LISTING are output interface flows. Notice that several transaction files are needed to hold data between each process that runs at a different time. Errors are also shown, as a minor interface flow, which need not be present on the parent diagram. Keying, validation, and sorting processes are included, since they are necessary for implementation of the design.

Chip has some difficulty creating the diagram. The starting point is the input flow, NEW MICROCOMPUTER FORM. This has to be keyed, and since this is a batch process, the forms should be rekeyed by a separate operator to catch any keying errors. The results are stored on a transaction file.

Chip is unsure what activities will take place next so he decides to work backward from the MICROCOMPUTER MASTER FILE data store. The records must be added to the master file. This means an update program is necessary. "Would the input to the ADD MICROCOMPUTER RECORD process be the keyed transactions?" Chip wonders to himself. "No. The data must be edited to ensure validity. The edit program should check all records for syntax errors and confirm that a record for the same microcomputer does not already exist on the master file."

"Should the edit and update activities be accomplished in the same process?" Chip wonders. After he gives it some thought, the answer becomes clear. "We need to have a file of the new transactions for printing the IN-STALLATION LISTING and the MICROCOMPUTER RECEIVED LISTING. It makes sense to separate the programs and create a VALID MICROCOM-PUTER TRANSACTION file out of the edit program."

Chip then decides to work backward from the INSTALLATION LIST-ING interface flow. "It needs to be printed, but what is the sequence of the prototype report? Ah, here it is!" he exclaims softly. Since the INSTALLA-TION LISTING needs to be in sequence by the manufacturer and model, it needs to be sorted. A sort process was added with the MICROCOMPUTER TRANSACTION RECORD as input. This same sequence was needed for the MICROCOMPUTER RECEIVED LISTING. "All done," thinks Chip. "One more review and . . . whoops, forgot about updating the PENDING MICRO-COMPUTER ORDERS FILE data store." One last change, and then the diagram was completed.

Anna reviews the diagram for omissions and errors. "I can see that you've put a great deal of thought into this," she exclaims. "It's really well designed. I've been working on Diagram 1, an explosion of process 1, ADD SOFTWARE RECORD. Perhaps you would like to review the finished result."

"Sure," replies Chip. "I'll check it for omissions and errors."

Diagram 1 is shown in Figure E9.5. Since this is an on-line process, there are no key and verify operations. Instead, NEW SOFTWARE INFOR-MATION is keyed and edited by the same program. Errors are reported on the screen and corrected by the operator. After all errors have been corrected, the operator has a chance to sight-verify the data. If correct, the operator presses a key to accept the data; otherwise the transaction may be canceled or corrected.

Confirmed data is added to the SOFTWARE MASTER file and is used to create a SOFTWARE LOG RECORD. This record contains all of the keyed information as well as the date, time, and user ID of the person entering the transaction. In the ADD SOFTWARE diagram, this record is used to create the SOFTWARE INSTALLATION LIST as well as to provide a backup of all new transactions and an audit trail of entries.

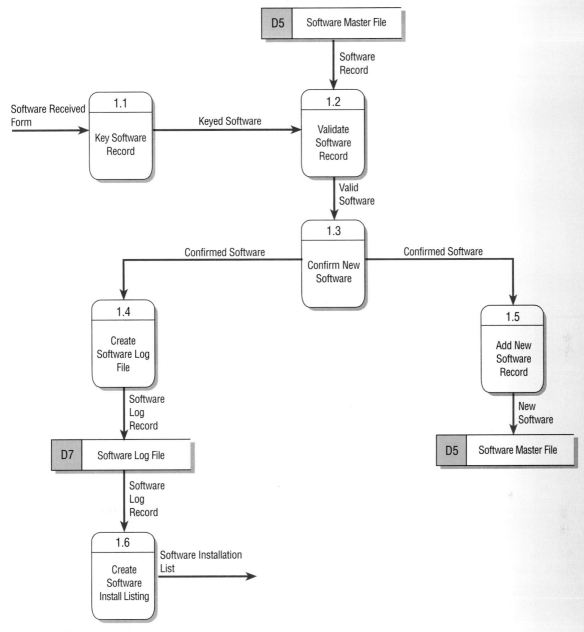

FIGURE E9.5
Diagram 1: Proposed Microcomputer System.

Since Chip and Anna are using Visible Analyst to create the data flow diagrams, all the components of the diagram may be described in the Visible Analyst repository. Chip starts by working on the ADD MICROCOMPUTER data flow diagram.

The description for process 2.5, UPDATE PENDING MICROCOM-PUTER ORDER is shown in Figure E9.6. The **Label** area contains the text that appears on the diagram. The Process Description entry is one of the most important entry areas. In the example shown, Chip outlines the detailed logic for updating the PENDING MICROCOMPUTER ORDER file.

A second description screen, which is shown in Figure E9.7, shows the diagram that the process is located on.

Similarly, Chip describes process 1 from the parent data flow diagram. This process is printed using the Report Query feature of Visible Analyst, and it is illustrated in Figure E9.8. Notice that when a repository entity is printed, the information from several screens is included on one easy-to-read report.

FIGURE E9.7

Process description screen,
UPDATE PENDING MICRO-
COMPUTER ORDER, second
screen.

2/6/97   11:47 PM

```
                              Detailed Listing - - Alphabetically
        Date: 2/6/97                Project :  CPU                      Page:  1
        Time: 11:46PM

                              Detailed Listing -- Alphabetically
_____

Add New Microcomputer                          Process
                Description:
                    Add a new microcomputer to the Microcomputer Master File.
                    Update Pending Microcomputer file and produce reports.
                Process #: 2
                Process Description:
                    Enter and validate data from the New Microcomputer Form. Update
                    the matching record on the Pending Microcomputer Orders file.
                    Produce the Microcomputer Received Report and the Installation
                     Listing.
                    Add a new record to the Microcomputer Master File.

                Notes:
                    It is expected that about 50 new records will be added per month.
                Location:
                    Microcomputer System - Diagram 0 (0)
                        Input Flows:
                            New Microcomputer Form
                        Output Flows:
                            Microcomputer Received Listing
                            Installation Report
                            Pending Order
                            Installation Listing
                            New Microcomputer
                Date Last Altered: 2/6/97 Date Created: 2/4/97
```

FIGURE E9.8
Printout for process 2.

Anna describes the SOFTWARE MASTER data store, shown in Figure E9.9. This data store has the structure of the record stored in the SOFTWARE RECORD, which is indicated in the **Composition** area. The **Notes** area contains details of the index elements or key fields, and the approximate size of the file in records.

The NEW MICROCOMPUTER FORM data flow designed by Chip is shown in Figure E9.10. The **Alias** area contains the name of the computer screen that will be used to enter the data from the form. This data flow has the NEW MICROCOMPUTER FORM RECORD in its **Composition** field. This record contains the details, such as structures and elements, that are the details of the NEW MICROCOMPUTER FORM. The **Notes** area contains some of the details of how the form is represented on a screen. A second screen, illustrated in Figure E9.11, indicates the diagrams that contain the data flow.

It takes time to enter descriptions for all of the objects, but once the entries are complete, Visible Analyst will provide analysis of the design. The Analyze feature for Data Flow Diagram provides several important features for validating the data flow diagram, the explosion diagrams, and the connections.

FIGURE E9.9
Data store description screen, SOFTWARE MASTER.

Define Item — 1 of 2

Label: Software Master File

Entry Type: Data Store

Description: Contains a record for each unique software package.

Alias: Software Master Table

Composition: Software Record

Notes: This is a database table. The primary key is Software Inventory Number, with a secondary key of Title, Version Number and Operating System.

The file contains approximately 1924 records.

Long Name:

SQL Info | Delete | Next | Save | Search | Jump | File | << | >> | ?
History | Erase | Prior | Exit | Expand | Back | Qcomp | Search Criteria

FIGURE E9.10
Data flow description screen, NEW MICROCOMPUTER.

Define Item — 1 of 2

Label: New Microcomputer Form

Entry Type: Data Flow

Description: A paper form that contains information about a new microcomputer that has been received. Used to add new hardware to the Microcomputer Master

Alias: New Microcomputer Screen

Composition: New Microcomputer Form Record

Notes: Some of the areas on the form will be converted into drop down lists and check boxes on the New Microcomputer Screen.

Long Name:

SQL Info | Delete | Next | Save | Search | Jump | File | << | >> | ?
History | Erase | Prior | Exit | Expand | Back | Qcomp | Search Criteria

FIGURE E9.11
Second data flow description screen, NEW MICROCOMPUTER.

When a specified data flow diagram is analyzed, the resultant report may reveal that any of the following data flow diagram syntax errors exist in that DFD:

1. The data flow diagram must have at least one process and must not have any freestanding objects or objects connected to themselves.
2. A process must receive at least one data flow and create at least one data flow. Processes with all input or all output should not occur.
3. A data store should be connected to at least one process.
4. External entities should not be connected to each other. Although they communicate independently, that communication is not part of the system being designed.

Visible Analyst does not show the following errors or check the standards set by Chip and Anna for the project:

1. Data flow names into and out of a process should change (with exceptions).
2. Linear flow (several processes with only one input and output) is rarely found. Except in very low-level processes, it is a warning sign that some of the processes may be missing input or output flow.
3. External entities should not be connected directly to data stores. For example, you would not let an employee rummage through the Employee master file!
4. Process names should contain a verb describing the work being performed (with exceptions, such as INQUIRY SUBSYSTEM). Data flow names should be nouns.

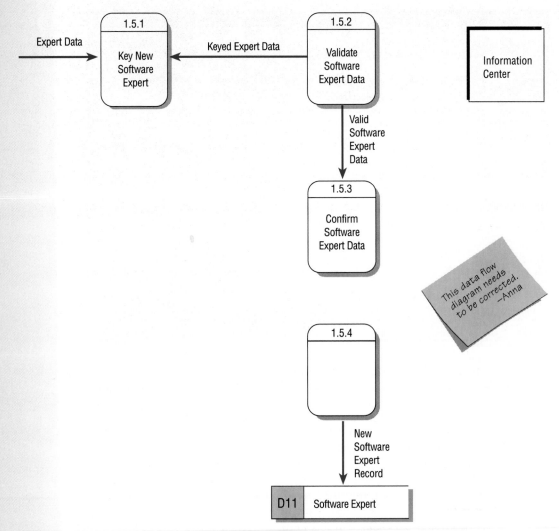

FIGURE E9.12
Data flow diagram with errors.

Chip and Anna both use Visible Analyst to verify that the data flow diagram syntax is correct. Figure E9.12 shows a data flow diagram that has syntactical errors. The analysis report is shown in Figure E9.13. Notice that a descriptive error message is given for each error, with the diagram object that relates to the problem indicated with quotation marks.

Visible Analyst will also check that the levels balance among data flow diagram processes and the child diagrams. Inputs and outputs that do not match are shown.

*Exercises**

⊟ **E-1.** Use Visible Analyst to view the context diagram for the Proposed Microcomputer System. Experiment with the **Zoom** settings of

* Exercises preceded by a disk icon require the program Visible Analyst Workbench or another CASE tool. A disk is provided free of charge to any professor adopting this book. The examples on the disk may be imported into Visible Analyst Workbench and then used by students.

```
2/6/97    11:28 PM

                        DFD Analysis Errors [Project 'CPU']

Error:        Process labeled 'Key New Software Expert' is an input only Process.
Error:        Process labeled 'Validate Software Expert Data' is an output only Process.
Error:        Process labeled 'Confirm Software Expert Data' is an input only Process.
Error:        External Entity labeled 'Information Center' is dangling.
Error:        There are 1 unnamed Process(es).
Error:        Net output Data Flow 'New Software Expert Record' is not shown attached
              to parent Process.
Error:        Net input Data Flow 'Expert Data' is not shown attached to parent Process.
Error:        Output Data Flow 'New Software' on parent is not shown.
Error:        Input Data Flow 'Confirmed Software' on parent is not shown.
```

FIGURE E9.13
Data flow diagram error report.

the **View** menu to change from a global to a detailed view of the diagram. Double click on the central process to examine the Repository entry for it. Click Exit to return to the diagram. Right click on the central process to display the object menu for the central process. Use the Explode option to display Diagram 0, representing the details of the central process. Maximize the window and double click on some of the data stores and data flows to examine their repository entries. Press Exit to return to the diagram. Zoom to 100 percent and scroll around the screen to view different regions of the diagram; then print the diagram using a landscape orientation. Click FILE, NEST, and PARENT to return to the context level diagram. Maximize the window.

E-2. Modify Diagram 0 of the Proposed Microcomputer System. Add process 10, UPDATE SOFTWARE RECORD. You will have to move the Management external entity lower in the diagram; place it to the left of process 7, Inquiry Subsystem. Create a Repository entry for the process and then press **Exit** to return to the diagram. Print the diagram using a landscape orientation.

Input:	1.	Software Change Data, from Clerical Support
	2.	Software Delete ID, from Management
Output:	1.	Software Record, an update from the Software Master data store

E-3. Explode to Diagram 10, UPDATE SOFTWARE RECORD. Maximize the window and create the diagram illustrated in Figure E9.14. Connect to the SOFTWARE MASTER FILE using a double-headed arrow. (*Hint:* Right click on the data flow, select Change Item, then select Change Type, and Terminator Type, Double Filled.) Print the final diagram.

E-4. Modify Diagram 8, INSTALL SOFTWARE. Add the following processes, describing each in the Repository. Zoom to 100 percent

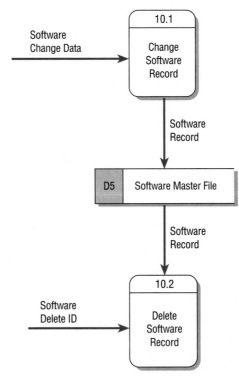

FIGURE E9.14
Data flow diagram, UPDATE SOFTWARE RECORD.

and scroll around the screen, checking your diagram for a professional appearance. Print the final result.

Process:		8.2 Install Microcomputer Software
Description:		Manual process, place software on machine
Input:	1.	Microcomputer Location, from process 8.1
	2.	Software Title and Version, from process 8.1
Output:	1.	Installed software form
Process:		8.3 Create Installed Software Transaction
Description:		Batch data entry process for creating installed software transactions, including validation
Input:	1.	Installed software form
Output:	1.	Installed Software transaction, to Installed Software data store
Process:		8.4 Update Software Master
Description:		Random update of the SOFTWARE MASTER FILE data store with update information
Input:	1.	Installed Software Transaction
Output:	1.	Software Master, update

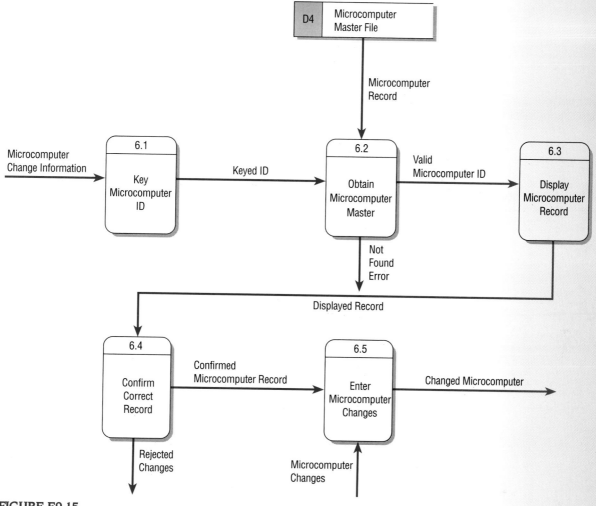

FIGURE E9.15
Data flow diagram, CHANGE MICROCOMPUTER RECORD.

Process:		8.5 Produce Installation Notification
Description:		Produce an installation notification informing users onto which machines the software has been installed
Input:	1.	Installed Software Transaction
	2.	Software Master, from the SOFTWARE MASTER FILE data store
	3.	Hardware Master, from the MICROCOMPUTER MASTER FILE data store
Output:	1.	Installation Notification listing, an interface flow

E-5. Modify Diagram 6, CHANGE MICROCOMPUTER RECORD, which is shown in Figure E9.15. This is an interactive, on-line program to change microcomputer information. Add the following three processes. Create Repository entries for each of the processes as well as the data flow. When completed, zoom to 100 percent and change any data flow arrows that are not straight and move data flow labels for a professional-looking graph. Print the diagram using landscape orientation.

    a. Process 6.6, VALIDATE CHANGES. This process edits each change field for validity. The input is the KEYED CHANGES. The output fields are CHANGE ERRORS (interface flow) and VALID CHANGES (to process 6.7).

    b. Process 6.7, CONFIRM CHANGES. This is a visual confirmation of the changes. The operator has a chance to reject the changes or accept them. Input is the VALID CHANGES. The output fields are REJECTED CHANGES (interface flow) and CONFIRMED CHANGES (to process 6.8).

    c. Process 6.8, REWRITE MICROCOMPUTER MASTER. This is a rewrite of the Microcomputer Master record with the changes on the record. Input is the CONFIRMED CHANGES. Output flow is the MICROCOMPUTER MASTER record, to the MICROCOMPUTER MASTER FILE data store.

🖫 **E-6.** Create the explosion data flow diagram for process 4, DELETE MICROCOMPUTER. The following table summarizes input, process, and output. Describe each process and data flow in the Repository. When completed, zoom to 100 percent, move any data flow lines that are not aligned correctly, move the data flow labels for a professional-looking graph, and print the diagram.

Process:	4.1	Key Delete ID
Description:		The microcomputer ID is keyed interactively
Input:	1.	Deleted Micro ID
Output:	1.	Keyed Delete
Process:	4.2	Obtain Microcomputer Record
Description:		Microcomputer Master record is read to ensure that it exists
Input:	1.	Keyed Delete (interface)
	2.	Microcomputer record, from the Microcomputer Master data store
Output:	1.	Not Found Error (interface)
	2.	Valid Microcomputer record
Process:	4.3	Confirm Microcomputer Deletion
Description:		The microcomputer information is displayed on the screen for operator confirmation or rejection
Input:	1.	Valid Microcomputer record
Output:	1.	Rejected Deletion (interface)
	2.	Confirmed Deletion
Process:	4.4	Delete Microcomputer Record
Description:		The microcomputer record is *logically* (not physically) deleted from the Microcomputer master file by rewriting the record with an I for inactive in the Record Code field

FIGURE E9.16
Repository report inquiry screen used to create a summary listing report.

| Input: | 1. | Confirmed Deletion |
| Output: | 2. | Deleted Microcomputer, a double-headed arrow to the Microcomputer Master data store |

⊟ **E-7.** Run the data flow diagram analysis feature (select Diagram and Analyze). Print the report for each of the data flow diagrams described in previous problems. Examine the diagrams and note the problems detected.

FIGURE E9.17
Repository report inquiry screen used to create a diagram location matrix report.

⊟ **E-8.** Run the syntax checking report (select Repository and Syntax Check) to produce the syntax check report for the diagrams. Examine and interpret the information provided.

⊟ **E-9.** Create an Undescribed Repository Entities report for the diagrams produced in previous problems. Select Repository and Reports and make the selections illustrated in Figure E9.16. Print the report and make a note of the corrections that need to be made for the design material to be complete.

⊟ **E-10.** Create a matrix showing all the data stores for all diagrams. Select Repository and Reports and make the selections illustrated in Figure E9.17. Preview the report and examine the output. Write a short paragraph stating what the diagram is illustrating and how it would be useful to the analyst.

10

ANALYZING SYSTEMS USING DATA DICTIONARIES

After successive levels of data flow diagrams are complete, systems analysts use them to help catalog the data processes, flows, stores, structures, and elements in a data dictionary. Of particular importance are the names used to characterize data items. When given an opportunity to name components of data-oriented systems, the systems analyst needs to work at making the name meaningful yet exclusive of other existing data component names. This chapter covers the data dictionary, which is another method to aid in the analysis of data-oriented systems.

THE DATA DICTIONARY

The data dictionary is a specialized application of the kinds of dictionaries used as references in everyday life. The data dictionary is a reference work of data about data (that is, *metadata*), one that is compiled by systems analysts to guide them through analysis and design. As a document, the data dictionary collects and coordinates specific data terms, and it confirms what each term means to different people in the organization. The data-flow diagrams covered in Chapter 9 are an excellent starting point for collecting data dictionary entries.

Systems analysts must be aware of and catalog different terms that refer to the same data item. This awareness helps them avoid duplication of effort, allows better communication between organizational departments sharing a database, and makes maintenance more straightforward. The data dictionary can also serve as a consistent standard for data elements.

Automated data dictionaries (also part of the CASE tools mentioned earlier) are valuable for their capacity to cross-reference data items, thereby allowing necessary program changes to all programs sharing a common element. This feature supplants changing programs on a haphazard basis, or it prevents waiting until the program won't run because a change has not been implemented across all programs sharing the updated item. Clearly, automated data dictionaries become important for large systems that produce several thousand data elements requiring cataloging and cross-referencing.

Need for Understanding the Data Dictionary

Many database management systems now come equipped with an automated data dictionary. These dictionaries can be either elaborate or simple. Some computerized data dictionaries automatically catalog data items when programming is done; others simply provide a template to prompt the person filling in the dictionary to do so in a uniform manner for every entry.

Despite the existence of automated data dictionaries, understanding what data composes a data dictionary, the conventions used in data dictionaries, and how a data dictionary is developed are issues that remain pertinent for the systems analyst during the systems effort. Small systems with up to 1,000 entries can still be kept effectively in a manual data dictionary. Understanding the process of compiling a data dictionary can aid the systems analyst in conceptualizing the system and how it works. The upcoming sections allow the systems analyst to see the rationale behind what exists in automated data dictionaries as well as manual ones.

In addition to providing documentation and eliminating redundancy, the data dictionary may be used to:

1. Validate the data-flow diagram for completeness and accuracy.
2. Provide a starting point for developing screens and reports.
3. Determine the contents of data stored in files.
4. Develop the logic for data-flow diagram processes.

THE DATA REPOSITORY

While the data dictionary contains information about data and procedures, a larger collection of project information is called a repository. The repository concept is one of the many impacts of CASE tools and may contain the following:

1. Information about the data maintained by the system, including data flow, data stores, record structures, and elements.
2. Procedural logic.
3. Screen and report design.
4. Data relationships, such as how one data structure is linked to another.
5. Project requirements and final system deliverables.
6. Project management information, such as delivery schedules, achievements, issues that need resolving, and project users.

The data dictionary is created by examining and describing the contents of the data flow, data stores, and processes, as illustrated by Figure 10.1. Each data store and data flow should be defined and then expanded to include the details of the elements it contains. The logic of each process should be described using the data flowing into or out of the process. Omissions and other design errors should be noted and resolved.

The four data dictionary categories—data flows, data structures, data elements, and data stores—should be developed to promote understanding of the data of the system. Procedural logic will be presented in Chapter 11.

To illustrate how data dictionary entries are created, we will refer to an example for World's Trend Catalog Division. This company sells clothing and other items by mail order.

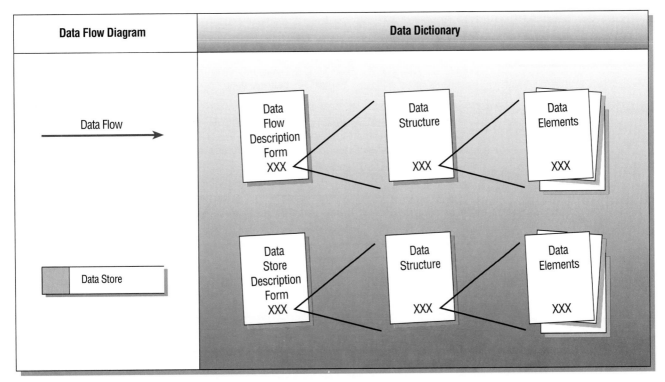

Data Flow Diagram	Data Dictionary

FIGURE 10.1
How data dictionaries relate to data flow diagrams.

The World's Trend order form shown in Figure 10.2 gives some clues about what to enter into a data dictionary. First, you need to capture and store the name, address, and telephone number of the person placing the order. Then you need to address the details of the order: the item description, size, color, price, quantity, and so on. The customer's method of payment must also be determined. Once you have done this, these data may be stored for future use. This example will be used throughout this chapter to illustrate each part of the data dictionary.

Defining the Data Flow

Data flow is usually the first component to be defined. System inputs and outputs are determined from interviewing, observing users, and analyzing documents and other existing systems. The information captured for each data flow may be summarized using a form containing the following information:

1. ID, an optional identification number. Sometimes the ID is coded using a scheme to identify the system and the application within the system.
2. A unique descriptive name for this data flow. This name is the text that should appear on the diagram and be referenced in all descriptions using the data flow.
3. A general description of the data flow.
4. The source of the data flow. This could be an external entity, a process, or a data flow coming from a data store.

FIGURE 10.2
An order form from World's
Trend Catalog Division.

World's Trend
1000 International Lane
Cornwall, CT 06050
Customer Order

Please print clearly. See reverse side for item size codes. If the payment is made using a bank credit card,
please include the credit card number and expiration date. Use charts on the reverse side for size codes
and to determine postage. Connecticut residents must include sales tax.

Name (First, Middle, Last)					
Gilbert Sullivan					

Street			Apartment		
115 Buttercup Lane					

City		State	Zip		Country
Penzance		PA	17057		

Customer number (if known)		Catalog no.	Order Date (MM/DD/YYYY)	Telephone (Incl. Area Code)
09288		9401A	03/12/1997	(215) 747-2837

Quantity	Item Number	Item Description	Size	Color	Price	Item Total
1	12343	Jogging Suit	M	BL	35.50	35.50
4	54224	Cushion impact socks/pair	M	WH	4.25	17.00
1	10617	Running shorts	M	BL	12.25	12.25
1	10617	Running shorts	M	GR	12.25	12.25

Method of Payment			Merchandise Total	77.00
☐ Check	☑ Charge	☐ Money Order		

Fill in for credit card purchase only					Tax (CT Only)	
☑ World's Trend	☐ AmExpress	☐ Discover	☐ MC	☐ Visa	Shipping and Handling	9.80

Credit Card Number - Not required for World's Trend Charges Expiration Date-MM/YYYY	Order Total	86.80

Form Number 0001 03/1997

5. The destination of the data flow (same items listed under the source).

6. An indication of whether the data flow is a record entering or leaving a file, or a record containing a report, form, or screen. If the data flow contains data that are used between processes, it is designated as *internal.*

7. The name of the data structure describing the elements found in this data flow. For a simple data flow, this could be one or several elements.

8. The volume per unit of time. This could be records per day or any other unit of time.

9. An area for further comments and notations about the data flow.

Once again we can use our World's Trend Catalog Division example from Chapter 9 to illustrate a completed form. Figure 10.3 is an example of the data flow description representing the screen used to add a new CUSTOMER

Data Flow Description

ID _____
Name __Customer Order_____
Description__Contains customer order information and is used to update the
____customer master and item files and to produce an order record._____
_____

Source	Destination
Customer	Process 1

Type of Data Flow

☐ File   ☑ Screen   ☐ Report   ☐ Form   ☐ Internal

Data Structure Traveling with the Flow	Volume/Time
Order Information	10/hour

Comments __An order record information for one customer order. The order__
____may be received by mail, FAX or by the customer telephoning the order__
____processing department directly._____

ORDER and to update the customer and item files. Notice that the external entity CUSTOMER is the input and that PROCESS 1 is the destination, providing linkage back to the data flow diagram. The checked box for "Screen" indicates that the flow represents an input screen. The detailed description of the data flow would not appear on this form, but it would appear as a data structure.

Data flow for all input and output should be described first, followed by the intermediate data flow and the data flow to and from data stores. The detail of each data flow is described using a data structure, a group of elements sometimes called fields. A simple data flow may be described using a single element, for example, a customer number used by an inquiry program to find the matching customer record. An example of an electronic form is shown in Figure 10.4. Visible Analyst was used to create the form.

Describing Data Structures

Data structures are usually described using algebraic notation. This method allows the analyst to produce a view of the elements that make up the data structure, along with information about those elements. For instance, the analyst will denote whether there are many of the same element within the data structure (a repeating group) or whether two elements may exist mutually exclusive of each other. The algebraic notation uses the following symbols:

1. An equal sign (=) means "is composed of."
2. A plus sign (+) means "and."
3. Braces { } indicate repetitive elements, also called repeating groups or tables. There may be one repeating element or several within the group.

The repeating group may have conditions, such as a fixed number of repetitions or upper and lower limits for the number of repetitions.

4. Brackets [ ] represent an either/or situation. Either one element may be present or another, but not both. The elements listed between the brackets are mutually exclusive.

5. Parentheses ( ) represent an optional element. Optional elements may be left blank on entry screens and may contain spaces or zeros for numeric fields on file structures.

Figure 10.5 is an example of the data structure for adding a customer order at World's Trend Catalog Division. Each NEW CUSTOMER SCREEN consists of the entries found on the right side of the equal signs. Some of the entries are elements, but others, such as CUSTOMER NAME, ADDRESS, and TELEPHONE, are groups of elements or structural records. For example, CUSTOMER NAME is made up of FIRST NAME, MIDDLE INITIAL, and LAST NAME. Each structural record must be further defined until the entire set is broken down into its component elements. Notice that following the definition for the customer order screen are definitions for each structural record. Even a field as simple as the TELEPHONE NUMBER is defined as a structure so that the area code may be processed individually.

Structural records and elements that are used within many different systems are given a nonsystem specific name, such as street, city, and zip, that does not reflect the functional area within which they are used. This allows the analyst to define these records once and use them in many different applications. For example, a city may be a customer city, supplier city, or employee city. Notice the use of parentheses to indicate that (MIDDLE INITIAL), (APARTMENT), and (ZIP EXPANSION) are optional ORDER information (but not more than one). Indicate the OR condition by enclosing the options in square brackets and separating them with the symbol |.

FIGURE 10.5
Data structure example for
adding a customer order at
World's Trend Catalog
Division.

Customer Order =	Customer Number + Customer Name + Address + Telephone + Catalog Number + Order Date + {Available Order Items} + Merchandise Total + (Tax) + Shipping and Handling + Order Total + Method of Payment + (Credit Card Type) + (Credit Card Number) + (Expiration Date)
Customer Name =	First Name + (Middle Initial) + Last Name
Address =	Street + (Apartment) + City + State + Zip + (Zip Expansion) + (Country)
Telephone =	Area Code + Local Number
Available Order Items =	Quantity Ordered + Item Number + Item Description + Size + Color + Price + Item Total
Method of Payment =	[Check ¦ Charge ¦ Money Order]
Credit Card Type =	[World's Trend ¦ Amer. Express ¦ Discover ¦ MasterCard ¦ Visa]

Logical and Physical Data Structures

When data structures are first defined, only the data elements that the user would see, such as a name, address, and balance due, are included. This stage is the logical design, showing what data the business needs for its day-to-day operations. Using the logical design as a basis, the analyst then designs the physical data structures. These include additional elements necessary for implementing the system. Examples of physical design elements are:

1. Key fields used to locate records in a file. An example is an item number, which is not required for a business to function but is necessary for identifying and locating computer records.

FIGURE 10.6
Physical elements added to a
data structure.

Customer Billing Statement = Current Date +
Customer Number +
Customer Name +
Address +
$^5_1${Order Line} +
(Previous Payment Amount) +
Total Amount Owed +
(Comment)

Order Line = Order Number +
Order Date +
Order Total

2. Codes to identify the status of master records, such as whether an employee is active (currently employed) or inactive. Such codes can be maintained on files that produce tax information.

3. Transaction codes are used to identify types of records when a file contains different record types. An example is a credit file containing records for returned items as well as records of payments.

4. Repeating group entries containing a count of how many items are in the group.

5. Limits on the number of items in a repeated group.

Figure 10.6 is an example of the data structure for a Customer Billing Statement, one showing that the Order Line is both a repeating item and a structural record. The Order Line limits are from 1 to 5, indicating that the customer may order from one to five items on this screen. Additional items would appear on subsequent orders.

The repeating group notation may have several other formats. If the group repeats a fixed number of times, that number is placed next to the opening brace, as in 12 {Monthly Sales}, where there are always 12 months in the year. If no number is indicated, the group repeats indefinitely. An example is a file containing an indefinite number of records, such as Customer Master File = {Customer Records}.

The number of entries in repeating groups may also depend on a condition, such as an entry on the Customer Master Record for each item ordered. This condition could be stored in the data dictionary as {Items Purchased} 5, where 5 is the number of items.

Data Elements

Each data element should be defined once in the data dictionary and may also be entered previously on an element description form, such as the one illustrated in Figure 10.7. Characteristics commonly included on the element description form are:

1. Element ID. This optional entry allows the analyst to build automated data dictionary entries.

Element Description Form

ID _____

Name _Customer Number_____

Alias _Client Number_____

Alias _Receivable Account Number_____

Description ___Uniquely identifies a customer who has made any business
_____transaction within the last five years._____

Element Characteristics

Length ____6_____ Dec. Pt. _____ ☐ Alphabetic

Input Format __9 (6)_____ ☐ Alphanumeric

Output Format __9 (6)_____ ☐ Date

Default Value _____ ☑ Numeric

☑ Continuous or ☐ Discrete ☐ Base or ☑ Derived

Validation Criteria

Continuous	Discrete	
Upper Limit _<999999_	Value	Meaning
Lower Limit _>0_		

Comments ___The customer number must pass a modulus-11 check digit test.
___It is derived because it is computer generated and a check digit is added.__

FIGURE 10.7
An element description form
example from World's Trend
Catalog Division.

2. The name of the element. This should be descriptive, unique, and based on what the element is commonly called in most programs or by the major user of the element.

3. Aliases, which are synonyms or other names for the element. These are names used by different users within different systems. For example, a CUSTOMER NUMBER may also be called a RECEIVABLE ACCOUNT NUMBER or a CLIENT NUMBER.

4. A short description of the element.

5. Whether the element is base or derived. A base element is one that is initially keyed into the system, such as a customer name, address, or city. Base elements must be stored on files. Derived elements are created by processes as the result of calculations or logic. An example is the total amount that a customer owes or an employee's gross pay. Analysis of base and derived elements differs, and this difference provides a means of determining areas of the system that may need further work.

6. The length of an element. This should be the *stored* length of the item. The on-screen and printed lengths of the item may differ from this value, but the programs responsible for displaying the item on the screen or printing it in a report will insert any additional formatting

characters required. An important consideration is how long to make an element. Some elements have standard lengths. In the United States, for example, lengths for state name abbreviations, zip codes, and telephone numbers are all standard. For other elements, the lengths may vary, and the analyst and user community must jointly decide the final length based on the following considerations:

a. Numeric amount lengths should be determined by figuring the largest number the amount will probably contain and then allowing reasonable room for expansion. Lengths designated for totals should be large enough to accommodate the sum of the numbers accumulated in them.

b. Name and address fields may be given lengths based on the following table. For example, a last name field of 11 characters will accommodate 98 percent of the last names in the United States.

Field	Length	Percent of data that will fit (U.S.)
Last Name	11	98
First Name	18	95
Company Name	20	95
Street	18	90
City	17	99

c. For other fields, it is often useful to examine or sample historical data found within the organization to determine a suitable field length. For example, scanning a list of item descriptions would allow the analyst to find the largest description as well as a reasonable average length.

7. The type of data: numeric, date, alphabetic, or alphanumeric. Alphanumeric fields may contain a mixture of letters, numbers, and special characters. If the element is a date, its format—for example, MMDDYYYY—must be determined. If the element is numeric, its storage type should be determined. There are three standard formats: zoned decimal, packed decimal, and binary. The zoned decimal format is used for printing and displaying data. The packed decimal format is commonly used to save space on file layouts and for elements that require a high level of arithmetic to be performed on them. The binary format is suitable for the same purposes as packed decimal format but is less commonly used.

8. Input and output formats should be included, using special coding symbols to indicate how the data should be presented. These symbols and their use are illustrated in Figure 10.8. Each symbol represents one character or digit. If the same character repeats several times, the character followed by a number in parentheses indicating how many times the character repeats is substituted for the group. For example, XXXXXXXX would represent as X(8).

9. Validation criteria for ensuring that accurate data are captured by the system. Elements are either discrete, meaning they have certain fixed values, or continuous, with a smooth range of values. Here are common editing criteria:

a. A range of values is suitable for elements that contain continuous data. For example, in the United States a student grade point aver-

Formatting Character	Meaning
X	May enter or display / print any character
9	Enter or display only numbers
Z	Display leading zeros as spaces
,	Insert commas into a numeric display
.	Insert a period into a numeric display
/	Insert slashes into a numeric display
-	Insert a hyphen into a numeric display
V	Indicate a decimal position (when the decimal point is not included)

FIGURE 10.8
Format character codes.

age may be from 0.00 through 4.00. If there is only an upper or lower bound to the data, a limit is used instead of a range.

b. A list of values is indicated if the data are discrete. Examples are codes representing the colors of items for sale in World's Trends' catalog.

c. A table of codes is suitable if the list of values is extensive (for example, state abbreviations, telephone country codes, or U.S. telephone area codes).

d. For key or index elements, a check digit is often included.

10. Any default value the element may have. The default value is displayed on entry screens and is used to reduce the amount of keying that the operator may have to do. Usually, several fields within each system have default values.

11. An additional comment or remarks area. This might be used to indicate the format of the date, special validation that is required, the check digit method used (explained in Chapter 19), and so on.

An example of a Visible Analyst data element description form can be found in Figure 10.9. As shown on the form, the CUSTOMER NUMBER may be called CLIENT NUMBER elsewhere in the system (perhaps old code written with this alias needs to be updated). The form is also useful because we can tell from it that the element is a numeric variable with a length of six characters. This variable can be as large as 999999 but cannot be less than zero.

Another kind of data element is an alphabetic element. In the case shown in Figure 10.10, the element is a discrete variable assigned certain codes. At World's Trend Catalog Division, codes are used to describe colors: BL for blue, WH for white, and GR for green. When this element is implemented, a table will be needed in order for users to look up the meanings of these codes. (Coding will be discussed further in Chapter 19.)

Data Stores

All base elements must be stored within the system. Derived elements, such as the employee year-to-date gross pay, may also be stored in the system. Data stores are created for each different data entity being stored. That is, when data-flow base elements are grouped together to form a structural record, a data store is created for each unique structural record.

Since a given data flow may only show part of the collective data that a structural record contains, you may have to examine many different data

FIGURE 10.9
Visible Analyst Workbench (VAW) screens showing an element description. Two pages are required to define an element.

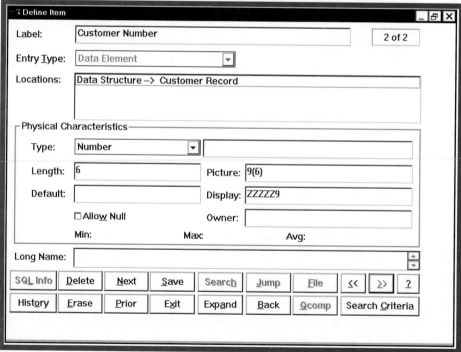

flow structures to arrive at a complete data store description. For example, when adding a customer, you may initially include only information known when the record is first created. Running balances, transaction dates, and other information added to the CUSTOMER data store only after business has progressed would be on different data flows.

FIGURE 10.10
An example of an alphabetic
element description form
from World's Trend Catalog
Division.

Element Description Form

ID _____

Name _Color._____

Alias _____

Alias _____

Description _____

_____

Element Characteristics

Length ___2_____ Dec. Pt. _____ ☑ Alphabetic

Input Format _x (2)_____ ☐ Alphanumeric

Output Format _x (2)_____ ☐ Date

Default Value _____ ☐ Numeric

☐ Continuous or ☑ Discrete ☐ Base or ☐ Derived

Validation Criteria

Continuous	Discrete	
Upper	Value	Meaning
Limit _____	BL	Blue
	WH	White
Lower		
Limit _____	GR	Green

Comments _____

_____

_____

_____

_____

Figure 10.11 is a typical form used to describe a data store. The information included on the form is:

1. The Data Store ID. This is often a mandatory entry to prevent the analyst from storing redundant information. An example would be D1 for the CUSTOMER MASTER FILE.

2. The Data Store Name, which is descriptive and unique.

3. An Alias for the file, such as CLIENT MASTER FILE for the CUSTOMER MASTER FILE.

4. A short description of the data store.

5. The file type, either manual or computerized.

6. If the file is computerized, the file format designates whether the file is a database file or has the format of a traditional flat file. (File formats are detailed in Chapter 17.)

7. The maximum and average number of records on the file, as well as the growth per year. This information helps the analyst to predict the amount of disk space required for the application and is necessary for hardware acquisition planning.

8. The data set name specifies the file name, if known. In the initial design stages, this item may be left blank. An electronic form produced using Visible Analyst is shown in Figure 10.12. This example shows

FIGURE 10.11
A data store form example
for World's Trend Catalog
Division.

Data Store Description Form

ID _D1_

Name _Customer Master File_

Alias _Client Master File_

Description _Contains a record for each customer._

Data Store Characteristics

File Type ☑ Computer ☐ Manual

File Format ☑ Database ☐ Indexed ☐ Sequential ☐ Direct

Record Size (Characters): _200_ Block Size: _4000_

Number of Records: Maximum _45,000_ Average _42,000_

Percent Growth per Year: _6_ %

Data Set Name _Customer.MST_

Copy Member _Custmast_

Data Structure _Customer Record_

Primary Key _Customer Number_

Secondary Keys _Customer Name_

Zip

Year-to-Date Amount Purchased

Comments _The Customer Master file records are copied to a history file and_
purged if the customer has not purchased an item within the past
5 years. A customer may be retained even if he or she has not made a
purchase by requesting a catalog.

that the CUSTOMER MASTER file is stored on a computer in the form of a database with a maximum number of 45,000 records. (Records and the keys used to sort the database will be explained in Chapter 17.)

9. The data structure should use a name found in the data dictionary, providing a link to the elements for this data store. Primary and secondary keys must be elements (or a combination of elements) found within the data structure. In the example, the CUSTOMER NUMBER is the primary key and should be unique. The CUSTOMER NAME, ZIP, and YEAR-TO-DATE AMOUNT PURCHASED are secondary keys used to control record sequencing on reports and, to directly locate records. (Keys will be discussed in Chapter 17.)

CREATING THE DATA DICTIONARY

Data dictionary entries may be created after the data-flow diagram has been completed, or they may be constructed as the data-flow diagram is being developed. The use of algebraic notation and structural records allows the analyst to develop the data dictionary and the data-flow diagrams using a top-down approach. For instance, the analyst may create a data-flow Diagram 0 after the first few interviews and, at the same time, make the preliminary data dictionary entries. Typically, these consist of the data flow names found on the data-flow diagram and their corresponding data structures. After several additional interviews have been conducted to learn the details of the system, the

Define Item — □ ⊟ ✕

Label:	Customer Master	1 of 2
Entry Type:	Data Store	
Description:	Contains a record for each customer.	
Alias:	Client Master File	
Composition:	Customer Record	

Notes: The Customer Master file records are copied to a history file and purged if the customer has not purchased an item within the past 5 years. A customer may be retained even if they have not made a purchase by requesting a catalog.

Long Name: |

SQL Info	Delete	Next	Save	Search	Jump	File	<<	>>	?
History	Erase	Prior	Exit	Expand	Back	Qcomp	Search Criteria		

analyst will expand the data-flow diagram and create the child diagrams. The data dictionary is then modified to include the new structural records and elements gleaned from further interviews, observation, and document analysis.

Each level of a data-flow diagram should use data appropriate for the level. Diagram 0 should include only forms, screens, reports, and records. As child diagrams are created, the data flow into and out of the processes becomes more and more detailed, including structural records and elements. Thus, each data-flow diagram has data appropriate for the level of detail it is depicting. The data dictionary is needed because you would not want to show records and screens on a detailed child data-flow diagram, nor scores of elements on a high-level data-flow diagram.

Figure 10.13 illustrates a portion of two data-flow diagram levels and corresponding data dictionary entries for producing an employee paycheck. Process 5, found on Diagram 0, is an overview of the production of an EMPLOYEE PAYCHECK. The corresponding data dictionary entry for EMPLOYEE RECORD shows the EMPLOYEE NUMBER and four structural records, the view of the data obtained early in the analysis. Similarly, TIMEFILE RECORD and the EMPLOYEE PAYCHECK are also defined as series of structures.

If prototypes or sample documents are available, the complete data dictionary and set of data-flow diagrams may be developed. If you have not previously obtained complete information, use the preliminary documentation to formulate questions such as "How is the payroll produced?" and "What fields are found on the paycheck?" for a second series of interviews with systems users. After each interview, the emerging system is documented by creating child diagrams and completing the corresponding data structures (process 5.3, for example). This procedure is repeated until all data structures are completely defined.

As mentioned in Chapter 9, data-flow diagrams must be balanced vertically between the parent process and the child diagram, yet each diagram

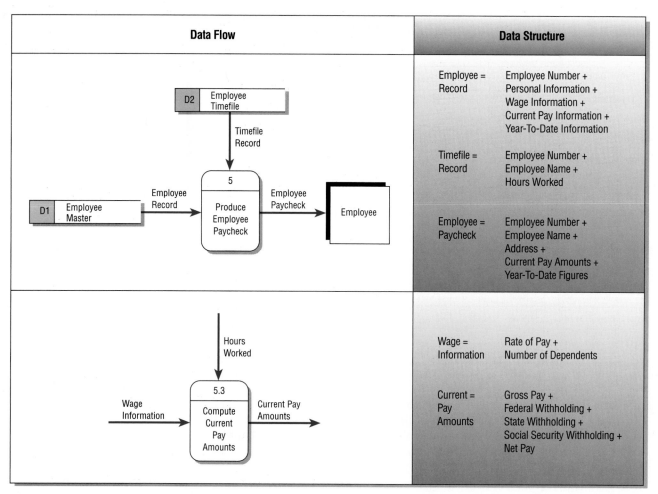

Data Flow	Data Structure

Data Flow

D2 Employee Timefile

Timefile Record

5 Produce Employee Paycheck

D1 Employee Master

Employee Record

Employee Paycheck

Employee

Hours Worked

5.3 Compute Current Pay Amounts

Wage Information

Current Pay Amounts

Data Structure

Employee = Record   Employee Number +
Personal Information +
Wage Information +
Current Pay Information +
Year-To-Date Information

Timefile = Record   Employee Number +
Employee Name +
Hours Worked

Employee = Paycheck   Employee Number +
Employee Name +
Address +
Current Pay Amounts +
Year-To-Date Figures

Wage = Information   Rate of Pay +
Number of Dependents

Current = Pay Amounts   Gross Pay +
Federal Withholding +
State Withholding +
Social Security Withholding +
Net Pay

FIGURE 10.13
Two data flow diagrams and corresponding data dictionary entries for producing an employee paycheck.

should use meaningful names for its level of data flow. Balancing data-flow diagram levels is accomplished by using the data dictionary structures. Names do not have to match between the parent process and a corresponding child diagram. What is important is that the data flow names on the child data-flow diagram are contained as elements or structural records within the data flow on the parent process. Returning to the example, WAGE INFORMATION (input into process 5.3, COMPUTE CURRENT PAY AMOUNTS) is a structural record contained within the EMPLOYEE RECORD (input to process 5). Similarly, GROSS PAY (output from process 5.3.4 a lower level process not shown in the figure) is contained within the structural record CURRENT PAY AMOUNTS (output from the parent process 5.3, COMPUTE CURRENT PAY AMOUNTS).

Analyzing Input and Output

An important step in creating the data dictionary is to identify and categorize system input and output data flow. Input and output analysis forms, such as the one example shown in Figure 10.14, may be used to organize the

Input and Output Analysis Form

Input/Output Name   Customer Billing Statement
User Contact   Susan Han

File Type   ☑ Output   ☐ Input
File Format   ☑ Report   ☐ Screen   ☐ Undetermined

Sequencing Element(s)   Zip Code (Page Sequence)
Order Number

Element Name	Length	B/D	Edit Criteria
Current Date	6	B	(System Supplied)
Customer Number	6	D	(Includes Check digit)
Customer First Name	20	B	Not Spaces
Customer Last Name	15	B	Not Spaces
Customer Middle Initial	1	B	A Through Z or Space
Street	20	B	Not Spaces
Apartment	20	B	Not Spaces
City	20	B	Not Spaces
State	2	B	Valid State Abbr.
Zip	9	B	Numeric, Last 4 Opt.
Order Number	6	D	> 0
Order Date	8	B	MM/DD/YYYY
Order Total	9	D	Format: 9 (7) V99
Previous Payment Amount	5	D	Format: 9 (7) V99
Total Amount Owed	9	D	Format; 9 (7) V99
Comment	60	B	

Comments   Print one page for each customer. If there are more items
than will fit on a page, continue on a second page.

FIGURE 10.14
An input/output analysis
form example for World's
Trend Catalog Division.

information obtained from interviews and document analysis. Notice that this form contains the following commonly included fields:

1. A descriptive name for the input or output. If the data flow is on a logical diagram, the name should identify what the data are (for example, CUSTOMER INFORMATION). However, if the analyst is working on the physical design or if the user has explicitly stated the nature of the input or output, the name should include that information regarding the format. Examples are CUSTOMER BILLING STATEMENT and CUSTOMER DETAILS INQUIRY.
2. The user contact responsible for further details clarification, design feedback, and final approval.
3. Whether the data is input or output.
4. The format of the data flow. In the logical design stage, this may be undetermined.
5. Elements indicating the sequence of the data on a report or on a screen (perhaps in columns).
6. A list of elements, including their names, lengths, and whether they are base or derived, and their editing criteria.

Once the form has been completed, each element should be analyzed to determine whether the element repeats, whether it is optional, or whether it is

CONSULTING OPPORTUNITY 10.1

Want to Make It Big in the Theatre? Improve Your Diction(ary)!

As you enter the door of Merman's, Annie Oaklea greets you warmly, saying, "I'm delighted with the work you have done on the data flow diagrams. I would like you to keep playing the role of systems analyst for Merman's and see if you can eventually get a new information system for our costume inventory sewn up. Unfortunately, some of the terms you're using don't come off very well in the language of Shakespeare. Bit of a translation problem, I suspect."

Clinging to Annie's initial praise, you are undaunted

by her exit line. You determine that a data dictionary based on the rental and return data flow diagrams would make a big hit.

Begin by writing entries for a manual system in as much detail as possible. Prepare two data process entries, two data flow entries, two data store entries, one data structure entry, and four data element entries using the formats in this chapter. Portraying interrelated data items with preciseness will result in rave reviews. (Refer to Consulting Opportunity 9.2.)

mutually exclusive of another element. Elements that fall into a group or that regularly combine with several other elements in many structures should be placed together into a structural record.

These considerations can be seen in the completed Input and Output Analysis Form for World's Trend Catalog Division. In this example of a CUSTOMER BILLING STATEMENT, the CUSTOMER FIRST NAME, the CUSTOMER LAST NAME, and CUSTOMER MIDDLE INITIAL should be grouped together in a structural record.

Developing Data Stores

Another activity in creating the data dictionary is developing data stores. Up to now, we have determined what data needs to flow from one process to another. This information is described in data structures. The information, however, may be stored in numerous places, and in each place the data store may be different. Whereas, data flows represent data in motion, data stores represent data at rest.

For example, when an order arrives at World's Trend, it contains information of a temporary nature—that is, the information needed to fill that particular order. Meanwhile, some of the information on the order form might be stored permanently. Examples of the latter include information about customers (so catalogs can be sent to them) and information about items (because these items will appear on many other customer's orders). Figure 10.15 shows that from a series of customer orders, information can be captured and stored into two data stores called CUSTOMER MASTER FILE and the ITEM MASTER FILE. An example of these data stores can be found in Figure 10.16.

Data stores contain information of a permanent or semipermanent nature. An ITEM NUMBER, DESCRIPTION, and ITEM COST are examples of information that is relatively permanent. So is the TAX RATE. But when the ITEM COST is multiplied by the TAX RATE, the TAX CHARGED is calculated (or derived). Derived values do not have to be stored in a data store. When developing data stores, it is acceptable to start with some information and then add more information to the data store when you analyze more data flows and realize more information needs to be added.

FIGURE 10.15
Information that comes from
customer orders may find its
way into different data stores.

**Customer
Orders**

Order

XXX

XXXX

Order

XXX

XXXX

Customer
Master File

Item
Master File

Order

XXX

XXXX

Order

XXX

XXXX

When data stores are created for only one report or screen, we can refer to them as "user views," because they represent the way that the user wants to see the information. A systems designer has to determine whether to set up individual files representing user views or set up a database representing many user views instead. The trade-offs associated with these two approaches are discussed in Chapter 17.

USING THE DATA DICTIONARY

The ideal data dictionary is automated, interactive, on-line, and evolutionary. As the systems analyst learns about the organization's systems, data items are added to the data dictionary. On the other hand, the data dictionary is not an end in itself and must never become so. To avoid becoming sidetracked with the building of a complete data dictionary, the systems analyst should view it as an activity that parallels systems analysis and design.

To have maximum power, the data dictionary should be tied into a number of systems programs so that when an item is updated or deleted from the data dictionary, it is automatically updated or deleted from the

FIGURE 10.16
Data stores derived from a
pending order at World's
Trend Catalog Division.

Customer Master =	Customer Number + Customer Name + Address + Telephone + Corporate Credit Card Number + Expiration Date
Item Master =	Item Number + Price + Quantity On Hand
Order Record =	Customer Number + Catalog Number + Order Date + {Available Order Items} + Merchandise Total + (Tax) + Shipping and Handling + Order Total + Method of Payment + (Credit Card Type) + (Credit Card Number) + (Expiration Date)
Available Order Items =	Item Number + Quantity Ordered + Quantity Shipped + Current Price
Method of Payment =	[Check ¦ Charge ¦ Money Order]
Credit Card Type =	[World's Trend ¦ Amer. Express ¦ Discover ¦ MasterCard ¦ Visa]

database. The data dictionary becomes only an historic curiosity if it is not kept current. Automated data dictionaries allow dramatic improvements in the upkeep of documentation. In doing so, they also change the work of the systems analyst.

The data dictionary may also be used to create screens, reports, and forms. For example, examine the data structure for the World's Trend ORDER PICKING SLIP in Figure 10.17. Since the necessary elements and their lengths have been defined, the process of creating physical documents consists of arranging the elements in a pleasing and functional way using design guidelines and common sense. Repeating groups become columns and structural records are grouped together on the screen, report, or form. The report layout for the World's Trends ORDER PICKING SLIP is shown in Figure 10.18. Notice that FIRST NAME and LAST NAME are grouped together in NAME and that QUANTITY (PICKED and ORDERED), SECTION, SHELF NUMBER, ITEM NUMBER, ITEM DESCRIPTION, SIZE, and COLOR form a series of columns, because they are the repeating elements.

The data structure and elements for a data store are commonly used to generate corresponding computer source language code, which is then in-

FIGURE 10.17
Data structure for an order
picking slip at World's Trend
Catalog Division.

Order Picking Slip =	Order Number +
	Order Date +
	Customer Number +
	Customer Name +
	Customer Address +
	Customer Telephone +
	{Order Item Selection} +
	Number of Items
Order Item Selection =	Item Number +
	Item Description +
	Size Description +
	Color Description +
	Warehouse Section +
	Shelf Number +
	Quantity Ordered +
	Quantity Picked
Customer Name =	First Name +
	(Middle Initial) +
	Last Name
Address =	Street +
	(Apartment) +
	City +
	State +
	Zip +
	(Zip Expansion) +
	(Country)
Telephone =	Area code +
	Local Number

corporated into computer programs. The data dictionary may be used in conjunction with a data flow diagram to analyze the system design, detecting flaws and areas that need clarification. Some considerations are:

1. All base elements on an output data flow must be present on an input data flow to the process producing the output. Base elements are keyed and should never be created by a process.

2. A derived element must be created by a process and should be output from at least one process into which it is not input.

3. The elements that are present on a data flow coming into or going out of a data store must be contained within the data store.

Even though the trend is toward on-line automated data dictionaries, it is important to appreciate the importance of compiling even a manual data dictionary that is common to the organization. If begun early, a data dictionary can save many hours of time in the analysis and design phases. The data dictionary is the one common source in the organization for answering

FIGURE 10.18
Order picking slip created from the data dictionary.

questions and settling disputes about any aspect of data definition. A current data dictionary can serve as an excellent reference for maintenance efforts on unfamiliar systems. Automated data dictionaries can serve as references for both people and programs.

SUMMARY

Using a top-down approach, the systems analyst uses data-flow diagrams to begin compiling a data dictionary, which is a reference work containing data about data, or *metadata,* on all data processes, stores, flows, structures, and logical and physical elements within the system being studied. One way to begin is by including all data items from data-flow diagrams.

A larger collection of project information is called a repository. CASE tools permit the analyst to create a repository that may include information about data flow, stores, record structures, and elements; about procedural logic screen and report design; about data relationships; about project requirements and final system deliverables; and about project management information.

Each entry in the data dictionary contains: the item name, an English description, aliases, related data elements, the range, the length, encoding, and necessary editing information. The data dictionary is useful in all phases of analysis, design, and ultimately documentation, since it is the authoritative source on how a data element is used and defined in the system. Many large systems feature computerized data dictionaries, which cross-reference all programs in the database using a particular data element.

KEYWORDS AND PHRASES

data dictionary	repeating item
data structure	base element
data element	derived element
repository	zoned decimal
system deliverables	packed decimal
structural record	binary formats
physical data structures	repeating groups

REVIEW QUESTIONS

1. Define what is meant by the term *data dictionary*. Define *metadata*.
2. What are four reasons for compiling a complete data dictionary?
3. What are the chief differences between automated and manual data dictionaries?
4. What information is contained in the data repository?
5. What is a structural record?
6. List the eight specific categories that each entry in the data dictionary should contain. Briefly give the definition of each category.
7. What are the basic differences among data dictionary entries prepared for data stores, data structures, and data elements?
8. Why are structural records used?
9. What is the difference between logical and physical data structures?
10. Describe the difference between base and derived elements.
11. How do the data dictionary entries relate to levels within a set of data flow diagrams?
12. List the four steps to take in compiling a data dictionary.
13. Why shouldn't compiling the data dictionary be viewed as an end in itself?
14. What are the main benefits of using a data dictionary?

PROBLEMS

1. Based on Figure 9.EX1 in Chapter 9, Joe, one of your systems analysis team members made the following entry for the manual data dictionary used by Marilyn's Tours:

   DATA ELEMENT = TOURIST* * * * PAYMENT
   ALIAS = TOURIST PAY
   CHARACTERS = 12–24
   RANGE = $5.00–$1,000
   VARIABLES = $5.00, $10.00, $15.00 up to $1,000, and anything in between in dollars and cents.
   TO CALCULATE = TOTAL COST OF ALL TOURS, ANY APPLICABLE N.Y. STATE TAX, minus any RESERVATION DEPOSITS made.

   a. Is this truly a data element? Why or why not?
   b. Rewrite the data dictionary entry for TOURIST PAYMENT, reclassifying it if necessary. Use the proper form for the classification you choose.

"You're really doing very well. Snowden says you've given him all sorts of new ideas for running the new department. That's saying quite a lot, when you consider that he has a lot of his own ideas. By now I hope you've had a chance to speak with everyone that you would like to: certainly Snowden himself, Tom Ketcham, Daniel Hill, and Mr. Hyatt.

"Mr. Hyatt is an elusive soul, isn't he? I guess I didn't meet him until well into my third year. I hope you get to find out about him much sooner. Oh, but when you do get to see him, he cuts quite a figure, doesn't he? And those crazy airplanes. I've almost been conked on the head by one in the parking lot. But how can you get angry, when it's The Boss who's flying it? He's also got a secret—or should I say private—oriental garden off of his office suite. No, you'll never see it on the building plans. You have to get to know him very well before he'll show you that. But I would wager it's the only one like it in Tennessee—and maybe in the whole U.S. He fell in love with the wonderful gardens he saw in Southeast Asia as a young man. But it goes deeper than that. Mr. Hyatt knows the value of contemplation and meditation. If he has an opinion, you can be sure it has been well thought through."

HYPERCASE QUESTIONS

1. Briefly list the data elements that you have found on three different reports produced at MRE.

2. Based upon your interviews with Snowden Evans and others, list the data elements that you believe you should add to the Management

FIGURE 10.HCI
In HyperCase you can look at the data dictonary kept at MRE.

Unit's project reporting systems to better capture important data on project status, project deadlines, and budget estimates.

3. Create a data dictionary entry for a new data store, a new data flow, and a new data process that you are suggesting based on your response to question 2.

4. Suggest a list of new data elements that might be helpful to Jimmie Hyatt but are clearly not being made available to him currently.

2. Pamela, the systems analyst, has made significant progress in understanding the data movement at Bonton's clothing store. In order to share what she has done with other members of her team as well as the head of franchising in New York, she is manually composing a data dictionary.

   a. Write an entry in Pamela's data dictionary for one of the data flows that you depicted in your data flow diagram in problem 1 in Chapter 9. Be as complete as possible.

   b. Write an entry in Pamela's data dictionary for one of the data stores that you depicted in your data flow diagram in problem 1 in Chapter 9. Be as complete as possible.

3. Cecile, the manager of the bookstore that your systems analysis team has been working with to build a computerized inventory system, feels as if one of your team members is making a nuisance of himself by asking her extremely detailed questions about data items used in the system. For example, he asks, "Cecile, how much space, in characters, does listing of an ISBN number take?"

   a. What are the problems created by going directly to the manager with questions concerning data dictionary entries? Use a paragraph to list the problems you can see with your team member's approach.

   b. In a paragraph, explain to your team member how he can better gather information for the data dictionary.

4. The Motion Manufacturing Company assembles bicycles, tricycles, scooters, rollerblades, and other outdoor sports equipment. Each outdoor product is built using many parts, which vary from product to product. Interviews with the head parts clerk have resulted in a list of elements for the Product-Part Listing, showing which parts are used in the manufacture of each product. A prototype of the Product-Part Listing is illustrated in Figure 10.EX1. Create a data structure dictionary entry for the Product-Part Listing. The head parts clerk has informed us that there are never more than 50 different parts for each product.

5. Analyze the elements found on the Product-Part Listing and create the data structure for the Product Master File and the Part Master File data stores.

PRODUCT NUMBER	PRODUCT DESCRIPTION	CREATION DATE	PRODUCT COST	NUMBER OF PARTS	PART NUMBER	PART DESCRIPTION NUMBER	PART QUANTITY	WAREHOUSE LOCATION
999999	XXXXXXXXXXXXXXXXXXX	Z9-ZZZ-9999	ZZ,ZZ9.99	Z9	9999999	XXXXXXXXXXXXXXX	ZZ9	ZZZZ9
					9999999	XXXXXXXXXXXXXXX	ZZ9	ZZZZ9
					9999999	XXXXXXXXXXXXXXX	ZZ9	ZZZZ9
					9999999	XXXXXXXXXXXXXXX	ZZ9	ZZZZ9
					9999999	XXXXXXXXXXXXXXX	ZZ9	ZZZZ9
					9999999	XXXXXXXXXXXXXXX	ZZ9	ZZZZ9
					9999999	XXXXXXXXXXXXXXX	ZZ9	ZZZZ9
					9999999	XXXXXXXXXXXXXXX	ZZ9	ZZZZ9
999999	XXXXXXXXXXXXXXXXXXX	Z9-ZZZ-9999	ZZ,ZZ9.99	Z9	9999999	XXXXXXXXXXXXXXX	ZZ9	ZZZZ9
					9999999	XXXXXXXXXXXXXXX	ZZ9	ZZZZ9
					9999999	XXXXXXXXXXXXXXX	ZZ9	ZZZZ9
					9999999	XXXXXXXXXXXXXXX	ZZ9	ZZZZ9
					9999999	XXXXXXXXXXXXXXX	ZZ9	ZZZZ9
					9999999	XXXXXXXXXXXXXXX	ZZ9	ZZZZ9

TOTAL NUMBER OF PRODUCTS ZZZZ9

FIGURE 10.EX1
A prototype of the Product-Part Listing.

6. Which of the elements on the Product-Part Listing are derived elements?

7. The Caribbean Cruise Company arranges cruise vacations of varying lengths at several locations. When customers call to check on the availability of a cruise, a Cruise Availability Inquiry, illustrated in Figure 10.EX2, is used to supply them with information. Create the data dictionary structure for the Cruise Availability Inquiry.

8. List the master files that would be necessary to implement the Cruise Availability Inquiry.

```
MM/DD/YYYY                          CRUISE AVAILABILITY                   HH:MM
ENTER STARTING DATE Z9-ZZZ-9999


- - - - - - - - - - - - - - - - - - - - - - - - - - - - - - - - - - - - - -


CRUISE INFORMATION:
CRUISE SHIP            XXXXXXXXXXXXXXXXXXX
LOCATION              XXXXXXXXXXXXXXXXXX
STARTING DATE         Z9-ZZZ-9999              ENDING DATE Z9-ZZZ-9999
NUMBER OF DAYS        ZZ9
COST                 ZZ,ZZZ.99
DISCOUNTS ACCEPTED    XXXXXXXXXXXX    XXXXXXXXXXXX    XXXXXXXXXXXX
OPENINGS REMAINING  ZZZZ9


XXXXXXXXXXXXXXXXXXXXXXXXXXXX COMMENTS XXXXXXXXXXXXXXXXXXXXXXXXXXXXXXXXXXXXX
F1 – HELP, F3 – MENU, F8 – NEXT CRUISE, F7 – PREVIOUS CRUISE, F10 – PORTS LIST
XXXXXXXXXXXXXXXXXXXXXXXXXX FEEDBACK MESSAGE XXXXXXXXXXXXXXXXXXXXXXXXXXXXXXXXX
```

FIGURE 10.EX2
A VDT screen showing cruise availability

9. The following ports of call are available for the Caribbean Cruise Company:

Kingston	Port-au-Prince	Nassau
Montego Bay	St. Thomas	Freeport
Santo Domingo	Hamilton	Point-à-Pitre
San Juan	Port of Spain	St. Lucia

Create the PORT OF CALL element. Examine the data to determine the length and format of the element. *ex. pg. 309*

GROUP PROJECTS

1. Meet with your group and use a CASE tool or a manual procedure to develop data dictionary entries for a process, data flow, data store, and data structure based on the data flow diagrams you completed for Maverick Transport in the Chapter 9 group exercises. As a group, agree on any assumptions necessary to make complete entries for each data element.

2. Your group should develop a list of methods to help you make complete data dictionary entries for this exercise as well as for future projects. For example, study existing reports, base them on new or existing data flow diagrams, and so on.

SELECTED BIBLIOGRAPHY

Colter, M. "A Comparative Examination of Systems Analysts Techniques." *Management Information Systems Quarterly,* June 1984, Vol. 8, No. 1, pp. 51–66.

Davis, G. B., and M. H. Olson. *Management Information Systems, Conceptual Foundations, Structure, and Development,* 2nd ed. New York: McGraw-Hill Book Company, 1985.

Gane, C., and T. Sarson. *Structured Systems Analysis and Design Tools and Techniques.* Englewood Cliffs, NJ: Prentice-Hall, 1979.

Gore, M., and J. Stubbe. *Elements of Systems Analysis,* 3rd ed. Dubuque, IA: William C. Brown Co., 1983.

Leeson, M. *Systems Analysis and Design.* Chicago, IL: Science Research Associates, Inc., 1985.

Lucas, H. *Information Systems Concepts for Management,* 3rd ed. New York: McGraw-Hill Book Company, 1986.

McFadden, F. R., and J. A. Hoffer. *Data Base Management.* Menlo Park, CA: The Benjamin/Cummings Publishing Company, 1985.

Martin, J. *Strategic Data-Planning Methodologies.* Englewood Cliffs, NJ: Prentice-Hall, 1982.

Schmidt, A. *Working with Visible Analyst Workbench for Windows.* Upper Saddle River, NJ: Prentice-Hall, 1996.

Semprevivo, P. C. *Systems Analysis and Design: Definition, Process, and Design.* Chicago, IL: Science Research Associates, Inc., 1982.

Senn, J. A. *Analysis and Design of Information Systems.* New York: McGraw-Hill Book Company, 1984.

Sprague, R. H., and E. D. Carlson. *Building Effective Decision Support Systems.* Englewood Cliffs, NJ: Prentice-Hall, 1982.

DEFINING WHAT YOU MEAN

"We can use the data flow diagrams we completed to create data dictionary entries for all data flow and data stores," Chip says to Anna at their next meeting. Each of these components has a Composition entry in the repository. The records created for the Microcomputer System are thus linked directly to the data flow diagram components that describe data.

Anna and Chip meet to divide the work of creating records and elements. "I'll develop the data dictionary for the software portion of the system," Anna says.

"Good thing I enjoy doing the hardware," Chip kids her good-naturedly.

Records, or data structures, are created first. They may contain elements, the basic building blocks of the data structure, and they may also contain other records within them called structural records. Program code may be easily generated using the dictionary (professional version of Visible Analyst only). Visible Analyst also maintains relationships among graph components, records, and elements that may be used for analysis and reporting.

Using information from interviews and the prototype screens, Anna started to create the Software records. Since the output of a system will determine what data needs to be both stored and obtained via data entry screens, the starting point was the output data flow SOFTWARE INSTALLATION LIST. This prototype identifies some of the elements that should be stored within the Software Master file:

SOFTWARE INVENTORY NUMBER   DISKETTE SIZE
VERSION NUMBER   HARDWARE INVENTORY
NUMBER OF DISKETTES   NUMBER
CAMPUS LOCATION   ROOM LOCATION
TITLE

Other output prototype reports and screens were also examined. Additional elements were obtained from the ADD SOFTWARE prototype screen.

The final element list is shown in Figure E10.1. These elements were arranged into a logical sequence for the SOFTWARE MASTER file. The following standards for arranging elements within a record were used:

1. The major key element that uniquely identified the record. An example is the SOFTWARE INVENTORY NUMBER.

2. Descriptive information, such as TITLE, VERSION NUMBER, and PUBLISHER.

3. Information that is periodically updated, for example, the NUMBER OF COPIES.

4. Any repeating elements, such as HARDWARE INVENTORY NUMBER, denoting the machines on which the software has been installed.

Allen Schmidt,
Julie E. Kendall, and
Kenneth E. Kendall

```
Date:     21-Feb-97
Time:     17:06
                    Software Elements

          Active Software Code
          Computer Type
          Employee Number
          Expert Teach Course
          Media Code
          Memory Required
          Minimum Processor
          Monitor Required
          Number of Copies
          Number of Diskettes
          Operating System
          Printer Required
          Publisher
          Site License
          Software Category
          Software Cost
          Software Inventory Number
          Title
          Version Number
```

FIGURE E10.1
Software element list.

Next, the SOFTWARE MASTER file record was created using the Visible Analyst Repository. The description screen for creating a record is shown in Figure E10.2. Notice the entry area for an Alias, or a different name for the record, used by a different user group. Since each user may refer to the same record by a different name, all such names should be documented, resulting in enriched communication among users.

Each element or structural record needs to be defined as part of the whole record, and it is entered in the Composition area. If the element or structural record is a repeating group, the name is enclosed within curly brackets ({}) and the number of times it repeats is placed in front of the name. If the data is a key, a code is put in brackets ([]) in front of the name. The symbol [pk] represents a primary key. The symbol [akn] represents an alternate key, where n defines each different key or group of fields that, when combined, make a secondary key. When a group of fields make up a secondary key, that key is called a concatenated key.

Examine the SOFTWARE MASTER file. It contains a primary key of SOFTWARE INVENTORY NUMBER and a concatenated secondary key of TITLE, OPERATING SYSTEM and VERSION NUMBER.

Visible Analyst allows you to easily describe each structural record or element composing the larger record. Anna places the cursor in each name in the Composition area and presses the Jump button. Futher record and element screens are displayed and detailed information is entered.

"This is great!" Anna thinks to herself. "It's so easy to enter the details, and by using this method I won't accidentally forget to describe an element."

Chip is also impressed with the simplicity of creating the data dictionary. Following a process similar to Anna's, he creates a record description for the MICROCOMPUTER MASTER file. It contains a table of five internal boards and two structural records, PERIPHERAL EQUIPMENT and MAIN-

FIGURE E10.2
Record description screen, SOFTWARE MASTER file.

TENANCE INFORMATION, illustrated in Figure E10.3. The Composition area for entering Element or Record names is a scroll region, meaning that more lines may be keyed than will fit in the screen area. As entries are added to the bottom of the region, top entries scroll out of the area.

As elements are added to the record, Chip decides to describe each in detail. The Element description screen for the HARDWARE INVENTORY NUMBER is shown in Figure E10.4. Observe the areas for entering element attributes. Several aliases may be included along with a definition. A **Notes** area contains any other useful information about the element. Chip and Anna employ this area to enter further edit criteria and other useful notation. The description for the HARDWARE INVENTORY NUMBER details how this HARDWARE INVENTORY NUMBER is used to physically keep track of the machines.

Pressing the >> button displays a second screen for the HARDWARE INVENTORY NUMBER, illustrated in Figure E10.5. It contains an area showing which structures the element is contained within, as well as an area for the type of data, the length, and the picture used to describe how the data is formatted. Each such picture is a coded entry, similar to those used in programming languages. Examples of some of the codes are:

9   Represents numeric data: Only numbers may be entered when prototyping.
A   Alphabetic: Only alphabetic characters may be entered.
X   Alphanumeric: Any characters may be entered.
Z   Zero suppression: Replace leading zeros with spaces.
$ Dollar sign: Replace leading zeros with a dollar sign.

FIGURE E10.3
MICROCOMPUTER MASTER record description screen.

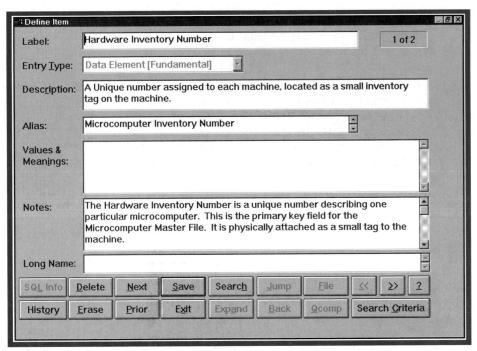

FIGURE E10.4
Element description screen, HARDWARE INVENTORY NUMBER.

FIGURE E10.5
HARDWARE INVENTORY NUMBER, element characteristics screen.

Chip is careful to include complete entries for these areas, including any default values and whether the entry may be null or not.

Anna and Chip repeat this process for all elements found on each record. This is a time-consuming but worthwhile effort. After the first few records are created, it becomes easier to create the remaining record structures. Visible Analyst has a search feature that provides lists of the elements contained within the design.

"I think that we've designed a complete set of elements," Chip says at a checkpoint meeting.

"Yes," replies Anna. "There are reports that will show us the details of the data structures and help us to spot duplications and omissions. Let's put Visible Analyst to work producing record layouts for us."

The Reports feature was used to print record layouts for all master files. Figure E10.6 is the output for the MICROCOMPUTER MASTER FILE. Notice that all the information from both screens is included, along with the data flow diagrams that the data store is contained within and the input and output data flow to and from the data store.

RECORD AND ELEMENT ANALYSIS

"Now let's really put the power of Visible Analyst to use," Anna says. "Let's see how well we've really designed our data."

"What do you mean?" Chip asks.

"I've been studying the analysis features contained within Visible Analyst, and there's a wealth of options for checking our design for consistency and correctness," Anna replies. "The first step is to use the Reports feature to produce a summary report of the elements we've added. Then we can examine the list for duplications and redundancy."

Microcomputer Master File   Data Store
    Description:
        Contains information about each installed microcomputer.
    Data Store #: D4
    Composition:
        Microcomputer Master

    Notes:
        The primary key is the Hardware Inventory Number with
            secondary keys of Brand Number, Serial Number, and a
            concatenated key of Campus Location and Room Location.
        There are approximately 4368 records on the file.
    Location:
        Microcomputer System - Diagram 0 (0)
            Input Flows:
                Install Update
            Input Flows:
                Changed Microcomputer
                Install Update
                New Microcomputer
            Output Flows:
                Microcomputer Record
            Output Flows:
                Hardware Record
            Input Flows:
                Deleted Micro ID
            Output Flows:
                Hardware Record
        Add New Microcomputer (2)
            Output Flows:
                Microcomputer Record
            Input Flows:
                Microcomputer Record
        Change Microcomputer (6)
            Output Flows:
                Microcomputer Record
        Report Subsystem (3)
            Output Flows:
                Hardware Record
                Hardware Record
                Hardware Record
                Hardware Record
        Date Last Altered: 9/3/97   Date Created: 2/4/97

FIGURE E10.6
MICROCOMPUTER MASTER, data store print.

Date: 9/3/97   Project: CPU   Page: 1
Time: 8:02 AM
                    Summary Listing -- Alphabetically
                  All Data Element Entries -- Data Flow Diagrams

    Active Software Code   Data Element
        Description:
            Code to determine if software is currently in use.
    Board Code   Data Element
        Description:
            Code used to indicate the type of internal microcomputer board.
    Board Name   Data Element
        Description:
            The name of an internal microcomputer board. Used as a
            match for the board code.
    Brand Name   Data Element
        Description:
            The name of the microcomputer brand.
    Brand Subtotal   Data Element
    Campus Code   Data Element
    Campus Description   Data Element
        Description:
            The description of a Central Pacific University campus building.
            This field matches the Campus Code.
    Campus Location   Data Element
        Description:
            Campus where microcomputer is located.
    Campus Name   Data Element
        Description:
            The campus name that matches the campus code.
    Category of Software   Data Element
        Description:
            A coded entry for the type of software. Stored as an Access table.
    CD ROM Drive   Data Element
        Description:
            A code for the CD ROM drive for the computer.
    Class Length   Data Element
        Description:
            The length of a software training class, in days.
    Class Name   Data Element
        Description:
            The name of a software training class.
    Computer Brand   Data Element
        Description:
            The brand of computer necessary to run the software.
    Computer Model   Data Element
        Description:
            The specific model of computer necessary to run software.
    Computer Type Code   Data Element
        Description:
            A coded entry for the type of computer.
    Cost for all packages   Data Element

FIGURE E10.7
Element summary report.

```
Date: 9/3/97          Project:  CPU          Page:  1
Time: 8:09 AM
          Summary Listing -- Alphabetically
     All Data Element Entries with No Location References -- Data Flow
        Diagrams
_____

  Category of Software            Data Element
     Description:
        A coded entry for the type of software.  Stored as an Access table.
  Course Instructor               Data Element
     Description:
        Name of the instructor for a microcomputer software course.
  Course Level                    Data Element
     Description:
        Difficulty Level: B Beginning, I Intermediate, A Advanced,
           P Profes
  Department Name                 Data Element
     Description:
        University Department Name.
  Disk Size                       Data Element
     Description:
        The size of the diskette with the original software package.
  Grand Total Micro Investment    Data Element
     Description:
        The grand total amount invested in hardware or software.
  Hardware Number                 Data Element
     Description:
        A unique number assigned to each machine, located on machine.
  Hardware Subtotal               Data Element
     Description:
        Total for all hardware in selected group
  Last Prevent. Maintenance Date  Data Element
```

FIGURE E10.8
No Location References report.

Figure E10.7 is an example of a portion of the element summary report. Examine the contents carefully and look for redundancy, or elements defined more than once. These may be easy to spot since the list is sorted by element name. The elements HARDWARE INVENTORY NUMBER and HARDWARE NUMBER, and SOFTWARE INVENTORY NUMBER and SOFTWARE NUM, appear to be duplicate elements. Other duplicates, such as ROOM LOCATION and LOCATION, are harder to spot.

"Next we should use the **No Location References** option, which shows all the elements that are not included on any record.

Figure E10.8 shows a portion of the report produced for elements that are not included anywhere.

"This is terrific!" exclaims Chip. "This **No Location References** shows design work that needs to be completed. We should produce this for all the design components."

The elements were either added to other structures or deleted as duplicates. Producing the No Location References report a second time revealed no further isolated elements.

```
Date: 9/3/97              Project:  CPU              Page:  1
Time: 11:27 AM
                    Summary Listing -- Alphabetically


    Campus Code                        Data Element
    Cost for all packages              Data Element
    Course Number                      Data Element
       Description:
           A unique number that identifies a course offered by the
             training staff or a software expert.
    Course Training Level Code         Data Element
       Description:
           A code to determine the level of training.
    Course Training Level Description  Data Element
       Description:
           The description for the training level code.
    Date Ordered                       Data Element
       Description:
           The date that a microcomputer was ordered.
    Delete Software Expert             Data Element
    Email Address                      Data Element
    Employee Number                    Data Element
       Description:
           A number that uniquely identifies an Employee.
    Expert First Name                  Data Element
       Description:
           The first name of a software expert.
    Expert Last Name                   Data Element
       Description:
           The last name of a software expert.
    First Name                         Data Element
    Fixed Disk Capacity                Data Element
       Description:
           The size of a fixed disk (hard drive).
    Grand Total                        Data Element
    Hardware Problem Update            Data Element
    Installed Boards                   Data Element
       Description:
           Board Name that is installed in a Microcomputer.
    Internet connection                Data Element
    Internet connection name           Data Element
    Last Name                          Data Element
    Last Preventive Maintenance        Data Element
```

FIGURE E10.9
Elements Without Pictures report.

"Well, I guess that wraps up the data portion of the system design," Chip says.

"Guess again," replies Anna. "We've only begun to analyze. The **Report Query** feature will provide us with a lot of design information, both for analysis and for documentation."

```
Date: 9/3/97           Project: CPU          Page:  1
Time: 11:35 AM
                  Summary Listing -- Alphabetically


     Campus Code                      Data Element
     Cost for all packages            Data Element
     Course Number                    Data Element
        Description:
           A unique number that identifies a course offered by the
              training staff or a software expert.
     Course Training Level Code       Data Element
        Description:
           A code to determine the level of training.
     Course Training Level Description    Data Element
        Description:
           The description for the training level code.
     Date Ordered                     Data Element
        Description:
           The date that a microcomputer was ordered.
     Delete Software Expert           Data Element
     Email Address                    Data Element
     Employee Number                  Data Element
        Description:
           A number that uniquely identifies an Employee.
     Expert First Name                Data Element
        Description:
           The first name of a software expert.
     Expert Last Name                 Data Element
        Description:
           The last name of a software expert.
```

FIGURE E10.10
Undefined Elements report.

The analysts select a report called Def Entities without Composition as their first choice. The report shows entries that are a data store or data structure and do have a Composition entry. The output shows that there are no records in error. The next report query is Elements without pictures, and it shows all elements that do not have pictures defined for them. A portion of this report is illustrated in Figure E10.9. A last report that Chip and Anna created is called Undefined Elements, indicating all elements that have not been defined—that is, they exist in the Repository as a name only, but with no physical characteristics. A portion of the report is illustrated in Figure E10.10.

"I'm really impressed with this analysis," Chip says. "Since correcting the errors in our design, I've come to realize how easy it is to feel confident that the design has been completed when there are discrepancies and omissions still needing our attention."

"We're not finished yet. There are some useful matrices that will provide documentation for any changes that may be made in the future. Let's produce the Data Elements vs. Data Structures matrix, which shows records and their elements," Anna suggests.

The Report feature has the ability to produce reports as well as matrices in a grid representation. The first matrix produced is the Data Elements

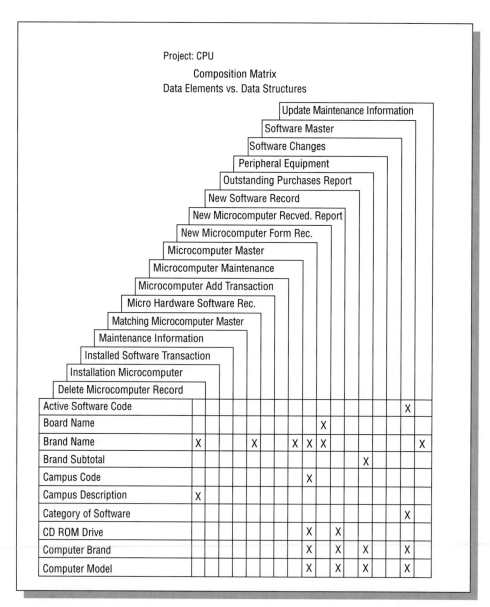

FIGURE E10.11
Data Elements vs. Data Structures Matrix report.

vs. Data Structures, illustrated in Figure E10.11. It shows all elements and the data structures that they are contained within. This matrix is used to access the impact of changing an element by showing which corresponding data structures must be changed.

The next matrix created is the Diagram Location Matrix, showing all data stores and the diagrams that they are located on. This is useful if a change needs to be made to the data store, because it will indicate where programs and documentation need to be changed. A portion of this matrix is illustrated in Figure E10.12.

A final grid is the Composition Matrix, showing all Data Elements and the Data Stores that they are contained within. A portion of this matrix is il-

Date: 9/3/1997   Project: CPU
Time: 11:55 AM
                    Diagram Location Matrix
                   Data Stores vs. Diagrams

	Add New Microcomputer	Add New Software Expert	Add Software Record	Change Microcomputer	Microcomputer System - Diagram 0	Report Subsystem
Campus Names						X
Installed Software						
Microcomputer Add Transactions	X					
Microcomputer Master File	X			X	X	X
Monitor Names						X
Pending Microcomputer Orders File	X					
Printer Names						X
Sequenced New Micro Transaction	X					
Software Expert		X				
Software Log File			X			
Software Master File			X		X	X
Valid Microcomputer Transaction	X					

FIGURE E10.12
Diagram Location Matrix report.

lustrated in Figure E10.13. This gives Chip and Anna a picture of which elements may be stored redundantly, that is, in several data stores rather than one.

"There are many other reports and matrices that would be useful for us to produce," Anna says. "Some of these should be used later for documentation and tracking any proposed changes. I'm really pleased with what we've accomplished."

Exercises*

🖫 **E-1.**   Use Visible Analyst to view the Microcomputer Master File Data Store. Jump to the data structure and browse the elements and structural records.

🖫 **E-2.**   Print the Software Master File record using the Report feature.

---

* Exercises preceded by a disk icon require the program Visible Analyst Workbench or another CASE tool. A disk is provided free of charge to any professor adopting this book. The examples on the disk may be imported into Visible Analyst and then used by students.

Composition Matrix
Data Elements vs. Data Stores

Data Element	Microcomputer Master File	Software Master File
Active Software Code		X
Board Code		
Board Name		
Brand Name	X	
Brand Subtotal		
Campus Location	X	
Category of Software		X
CD ROM Drive	X	
Computer Brand		X
Computer Model		X
Cost		
Cost Of Repairs	X	
Date Ordered		
Date Purchased	X	
Disk Drive A	X	
Disk Drive B	X	
Diskette Size		X
Fixed Disk	X	
Fixed Disk 2	X	
Hardware Inventory Number	X	X
Internal Boards	X	
Internet Connection	X	

FIGURE E10.13
Composition Matrix report.

🖫 **E-3.**   Use the Jump command to move to the Software Record Structure. Delete the following elements:

ACTIVE SOFTWARE CODE
INSTALLATION MICRO
SOFTWARE EXPERT

🖫 **E-4.**   Modify the Software Changes record, supplying changes to the Software Master record. The modifications are:
   a. Add a [pk], for primary key, in front of the Software Inventory Number.
   b. Add the following elements: Computer Brand, Computer Model, Memory Required, Monitor Required, Printer Required, Diskette Size, Site License, and Number of Copies.

🖫 **E-5.** Modify the Microcomputer Add Transaction record, which contains new microcomputer records to be placed on the Microcomputer Master data store.
    a. Insert the Brand Name and Model above the Serial Number.
    b. Place the Campus Location and Room Location after the Serial Number.
    c. Add the following elements at the bottom of the list: Fixed Disk, Fixed Disk 2, Disk Drive A, and Disk Drive B.
    d. Delete the Internal Boards element, which will be determined after the microcomputer installation.

🖫 **E-6.** Modify the Installed Software Transaction, which is used to update the Software Master and to produce the Software Installation Listing. Delete the Title and Version Number, since they may be obtained from the Software Master and are redundant keying. Add the Hardware Inventory Number, specifying the installation microcomputer. Delete the Campus Location and Room Location, since these are elements of the installation microcomputer.

🖫 **E-7.** View the alias entry for the Software Master Table.

🖫 **E-8.** Modify the INSTALLED SOFTWARE data store. Add the Composition record INSTALLED SOFTWARE TRANSACTION. The index elements are SOFTWARE INVENTORY NUMBER and HARDWARE INVENTORY NUMBER.

🖫 **E-9.** Define the data store SOFTWARE LOG FILE. This file is used to store information on the new software records plus the date, time, and user-ID of the person entering the record. Index elements are SOFTWARE INVENTORY NUMBER, TITLE, VERSION (a concatenated key), and SOFTWARE CATEGORY.

🖫 **E-10.** Define the data store PENDING MICROCOMPUTER ORDERS FILE. This file is created when a purchase order is made for ordering new microcomputers, and it is updated by the Microcomputer system. Place a comment in the **Notes** area stating that the average number of records is 100. Index elements are PURCHASE ORDER NUMBER and a concatenated key consisting of BRAND NAME and MODEL.

🖫 **E-11.** View the entry for the Software Record data flow. Press Jump with the cursor in the Composition area and examine the Software Master record. Press Back to return to the data flow description screen.

🖫 **E-12.** Modify the SOFTWARE UPGRADE INFORMATION data flow. The **Composition** record is SOFTWARE UPGRADE INFORMATION.

🖫 **E-13.** Modify the SOFTWARE CROSS-REFERENCE REPORT data flow. The **Composition** record is SOFTWARE CROSS-REFERENCE REPORT.

🖫 **E-14.** Modify the data flow entity for INSTALL UPDATE. This flow updates the Microcomputer Master record with installation information. Its data structure is INSTALL UPDATE RECORD. Include a comment that it processes about 50 records per month in updating the Microcomputer Master File.

🖫 **E-15.** Use the INSTALL UPDATE data flow to jump to (and create) the INSTALL UPDATE RECORD. Provide a definition based on information supplied in the previous problem. Enter the following elements:

HARDWARE INVENTORY NUMBER (primary key)
CAMPUS LOCATION
ROOM
INTERNAL BOARDS (Occurs 5 times)
FIXED DISK 2
MOUSE
PRINTER
MAINTENANCE INTERVAL
DATE INSTALLED

🖫 **E-16.** Create the data flow description for the SOFTWARE INSTALLATION LIST. This flow contains information on specific software packages and the machines on which the software should be installed. The Composition should include the SOFTWARE INSTALLATION LISTING, a data structure.

🖫 **E-17.** Use the SOFTWARE INSTALL LIST to jump to (and therefore create) the SOFTWARE INSTALLATION LISTING. The elements on the listing are:

Name

SOFTWARE INVENTORY NUMBER
TITLE
VERSION NUMBER
NUMBER OF DISKETTES
DISKETTE SIZE
HARDWARE INVENTORY NUMBER
CAMPUS LOCATION
ROOM LOCATION

🖫 **E-18.** Modify and print the element HARDWARE SUBTOTAL. Change the Type to Numeric, the Length to 6,2 and the Picture to Z, ZZZ, ZZ9.99.

🖫 **E-19.** Modify and print the MONITOR NAME element, the result of a table lookup using a monitor code. The Type to should be Character, the Length to 30 and the Picture to X(30).

🖫 **E-20.** Modify and print the DEPARTMENT NAME element. Create an Alias of Staff Department Name. In the Notes area, enter the comment: Table of codes: Department Table. The Type to should be Character, the Length to 25 and the Picture to X(25).

🖫 **E-21.** Create the following element descriptions. Use the values supplied in the table. Create any alternate names and definitions based on your understanding of the element.

Name	Purchase Order Number	Problem Description
Type	Character	Character
Length	7	70
Picture	9999999	X(70)

Name	Total Microcomputer Cost	Next Preventive Maintenance Date
Type	Numeric	Date
Length	7,2	8
Picture	Z, ZZZ, ZZ9.99	Z9/99/9999
Notes		The Next Preventive Maintenance Date is calculated by adding the Maintenance Interval to the Last Preventive Maintenance Date.

Name	Phone Number	Repair Status
Type	Character	Character
Length	7	1
Picture	999-9999	X
Notes		Table of codes: Repair Table
Default		C

E-22. Use the Repository Reports feature to produce the following reports and matrices. The selection criteria from the Repository Reports dialogue box are listed, separated with a slash (/). Explain in a paragraph where the information produced may be effectively used.

    a. Data Flow/Cross Reference Listing/Data Element/Entire Project

    b. Data Flow/Cross Reference Listing/Data Structure/Entire Project

    c. Record Contains Element (One Level) matrix

    d. Data FLow/Single Entry Listing/Software Master— Normalized

    e. Data Flow/Diagram Location Matrix/Data Stores vs. Diagrams

    f. Data Flow/Composition Matrix/Data Elements vs. Data Flows

    g. Data Flow/Composition Matrix/Data Elements vs. Data Structures

    h. Data Flow/Composition Matrix/Data Element vs. Data Stores

E-23. Use the Report Query feature to produce the following reports. Explain in a sentence what information the report is providing you with.

    a. The Undefined Elements report.

    b. The Elements Without Pictures report.

    c. The Coded Elements report.

    d. The Any Item WIth Components report.

E-24. Print a summary report for all data flow components that do not have a description. (Hint, click the No Descriptive Info. radio button)

CHAPTER 10: ANALYZING SYSTEMS USING DATA DICTIONARIES

⊞ **E-25.** Print a summary report for all data flow components that are not on a diagram. (Hint, click the No Location References radio button).

⊞ **E-26.** Print a detailed report for all elements. Include only the physical information and the values and meanings. (Hint, click the Fields button, then the Invert button and select the fields that you want printed.) Why would this report be useful to the analyst?

DESCRIBING PROCESS SPECIFICATIONS AND STRUCTURED DECISIONS

METHODS AVAILABLE

The systems analyst approaching process specifications and structured decisions has many options for documenting and analyzing them. In Chapters 9 and 10, you noted processes such as VERIFY AND COMPUTE FEES, but you did not explain the logic necessary to execute these tasks. The methods available for documenting and analyzing the logic of decisions include structured English, decision tables, and decision trees. It is important to be able to recognize logic and structured decisions that occur in a business and how they are distinguishable from semistructured decisions. Then it is critical to recognize that structured decisions lend themselves particularly well to analysis with systematic methods that promote completeness, accuracy, and communication.

Decision analysis focuses on the logic of the decisions that are made, or need to be made, within the organization in order to carry out the objectives of the firm. This chapter covers the methods of structured English, decision tables, and decision trees that are used to analyze decisions and describe process logic, and in doing so it complements the material on data flow diagrams from Chapter 9 and on the data dictionary from Chapter 10.

OVERVIEW OF PROCESS SPECIFICATIONS

In order to determine the information requirements of a decision analysis strategy, the systems analyst must first determine the organization's objectives, using a top-down approach. The systems analyst must understand the principles of organizations (as covered in Chapter 2) and have a working knowledge of data-gathering techniques (as presented in Chapters 4 through 8). The top-down approach is critical because all decisions in the organization should be related, at least indirectly, to the broad objectives of the entire organization.

Process specifications—sometimes called *minispecs,* since they are a small portion of the total project specifications—are created for primitive processes on a data-flow diagram as well as for some higher-level processes that explode to a child diagram. These specifications explain the decision-making logic and formulas that will transform process input data into output. Each derived element must have process logic to show how it is produced from the base elements or other previously created derived elements that are input to the primitive process.

The three goals of producing process specifications are:

1. To reduce the ambiguity of the process. This goal compels the analyst to learn details about how the process works. Any vague areas should be noted, written down, and consolidated for all process specifications. These observations form a basis and provide the questions for a follow-up interview with the user community.
2. To obtain a precise description of what is accomplished, which is usually included in a packet of specifications for the programmer.
3. To validate the system design. This goal includes ensuring that a process has all the input data flow necessary for producing the output. Additionally, all input and output must be represented on the data flow diagram.

You will find many situations where process specifications are not created. Sometimes the process is very simple, or the computer code already exists. This eventuality would be noted in the process description, and no further design would be required. Categories of processes that generally *do not* require specifications are:

1. Processes that represent physical input or output, such as read, write, and so on. These processes usually require only simple logic.
2. Processes that represent simple data validation, which is usually fairly easy to accomplish. The edit criteria are included in the data dictionary and incorporated into the computer source code. Process specifications may be produced for complex editing.
3. Processes that use prewritten code. These are generally included in a system as subprograms and functions.

Subprograms are computer programs that are written, tested, and stored on the computer system. They usually perform a general system function, such as validating a date or a check digit. These general purpose subprograms are written and documented only once but form a series of building blocks that may be used within many systems throughout the organization. Thus, these subprograms appear as processes on many data-flow diagrams. Functions are similar to subprograms but are coded differently. For example, a function library may be purchased for use in the C-programming language or in a database environment.

Process Specification Format

Process specifications link the process to the data-flow diagram and hence the data dictionary, as illustrated in Figure 11.1. Each process specification should be entered on a separate form or into a CASE tool screen such as the

Data Flow Diagram	Process Specification and Logic

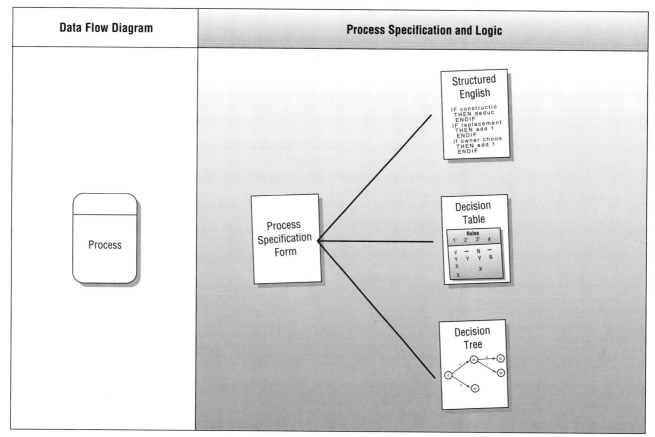

FIGURE 11.1
How process specifications relate to the data-flow diagram.

one used for Visible Analyst and shown in the CPU case at the end of this chapter. Enter the following information:

1. The process number, which must match the process ID on the data-flow diagram. This specification allows an analyst to work on or review any process and easily locate the data-flow diagram containing the process.
2. The process name, which again must be the same as the name displayed within the process symbol on the data-flow diagram.
3. A brief description of what the process accomplishes.
4. A list of data input flow, using the names found on the data-flow diagram. Data names used in the formula or logic should match those in the data dictionary to ensure consistency and good communication.
5. The output data flow, also using data-flow diagram and data dictionary names.
6. An indication of the type of process: batch, on-line, or manual. All on-line processes require screen designs, and all manual processes should have well-defined procedures for employees performing the process tasks.
7. If the process uses prewritten code, include the name of the subprogram or function containing that code.

FIGURE 11.2
An example of a completed
Process Specification form for
determining whether an item
is available.

Process Specification Form

Number __1.3__

Name ___Determine Quantity Available___

Description ___Determine if an item is available for sale, if it is not available, create a backordered item record. Determine the quantity available.___

Input Data Flow
Valid item from Process 1.2
Quantity on Hand from Item Record

Output Data Flow
Available Item (Item Number + Quantity Sold) to Process 1.4 & 1.5
Backordered item to Inventory Control

Type of Process			Subprogram/Function Name
☑ Online	☐ Batch	☐ Manual	

Process Logic:
IF the <u>Order Item Quantity</u> is greater than <u>Quantity On Hand</u>
    Then Move <u>Order Item Quantity</u> to <u>Available Item Quantity</u>
        Move <u>Order Item Number</u> to <u>Available Item Number</u>
ELSE
    Subtract <u>Quantity on Hand</u> from <u>Order Item Quantity</u>
        giving <u>Quantity Backordered</u>
    Move <u>Quantity Backordered</u> to <u>Backordered Item Record</u>
    <u>Move Item Number</u> to <u>Backordered Item Record</u>
    DO write <u>Backordered Record</u>
    Move <u>Quantity on Hand</u> to <u>Available Item Quantity</u>
    Move <u>Order Item Number</u> to <u>Available Item Number</u>
ENDIF

Refer to: Name: _____

☐ Structured English   ☐ Decision Table   ☐ Decision Tree

Unresolved Issues: Should the amount that is on order for this item be taken into account? Would this, combined with the expected arrival date of goods on order, change how the quantity available is calculated?

8. A description of the process logic that states policy and business rules in everyday language, not computer language pseudocode.

9. If there is not enough room on the form for a complete structured English description or if there is a decision table or tree depicting the logic, include the corresponding table or tree name.

10. List any unresolved issues, incomplete portions of logic, or other concerns. These issues form the basis of the questions used for follow-up interviews.

The above items should be entered to complete a process specification form, which includes a process number and/or name from the data-flow diagram, as well as the eight other items shown in the World's Trend example (Figure 11.2). Notice that completing this form thoroughly facilitates linking the process to the data-flow diagram and the data dictionary. When using an electronic form, such as the Visible Analyst screens shown in Figure 11.3, the description will not fit on one page. This disadvantage is offset by the fact that it permits the user to electronically search for key words.

FIGURE 11.4
Analyzing a rate document
to determine actions and
conditions.

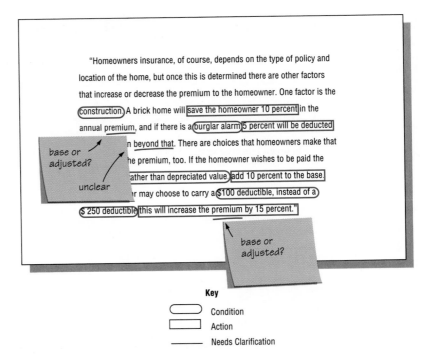

Key

⬭ Condition

▭ Action

— Needs Clarification

Information Required for Structured Decisions

Conditions, condition alternatives, actions, and action rules must be known in order to design systems for structured decisions. The analyst first determines the conditions—that is, an occurrence that might affect the outcome of something else. In the next step, the systems analyst defines the condition alternatives as specified by the decision maker; these alternatives can be as simple as "yes" or "no," or they can be more descriptive, such as "less than $50," "between $50 and $100," and "greater than $100."

Next, actions are identified. These can include any instruction that needs to be carried out as a result of one or more of the above conditions. Instructions to somehow manipulate or total numbers, print reports, or even disallow the transaction in question all involve examples of potential actions. They are tied to the conditions by the action rules, which are directions to execute the required actions in order.

Examples of action rules are provided below from a rate document supplied to insurance agents from the Fortress Insurance Corporation:

> Homeowners insurance, of course, depends on the type of policy and the location of the home, but once this is determined there are other factors that increase or decrease the premium to the homeowner. One factor is the construction. A brick home will save the homeowner 10 percent in the annual premium, and if there is a burglar alarm, 5 percent will be deducted from the premium beyond that. There are choices that homeowners make that will increase the premium, too. If the homeowner wishes to be paid the replacement, rather than depreciated value, add 10 percent to the base. The homeowner may choose to carry a $100 deductible, instead of a $250 deductible; this will increase the premium by 15 percent.

This statement may seem clear at first, but a careful examination reveals ambiguities that need resolution before decision analysis is completed.

Number	Conditions	Condition Alternatives	Actions	Action Rule
1	Construction	Brick	Deduct 10% of Base* from Subtotal	Do This First
		Other	—	—
2	Home Has Burglar Alarm	Yes	Deduct 5% of Adjusted Subtotal	Do This After Number 4
		No	—	—
3	Replacement Option is Chosen	Yes	Add 10% of Base* to Subtotal	Do This After Number 1
		No	—	—
4	Deductible	$100 Option	Add 15% of Subtotal to Subtotal	Do This After Number 3
		Standard $250	—	—

* Base is the original premium based on amount the home is insured for and the location of the home.

In Figure 11.4, this rate document was analyzed to determine the actions and conditions. A box was drawn around each action, and each condition was circled. (Boxes and circles will be used again later in the decision tree.) After this is done, questionable terms, ambiguities, unclear adjectives, and instances of "however" and "but" will be underlined.

Problems occurred because (1) the "base" is not defined; (2) it isn't clear what the phrase "beyond that" refers to; (3) when the "premium" is modified, it is not clear if the deduction or increase is applied to the original premium or the adjusted premium, nor is it clear in what order this is done. To clear up these details, an interview was conducted and Figure 11.5 was drawn to organize the decision process. Notice that the alternatives are clearly specified; the actions are more specific; "base" is defined; and the action rules are described and ordered.

In the following sections, three alternatives for decision analysis of structured decisions will be explored. First, we will discuss structured English, then decision tables, and finally decision trees.

STRUCTURED ENGLISH

When the process logic involves formulas or iteration or when structured decisions are not complex, an appropriate technique for analyzing the decision process is the use of structured English. As the name implies, structured English is based on (1) structured logic, or instructions organized into nested and grouped procedures; and (2) simple English statements such as add, multiply, move, and so on.

The previous Fortress Insurance Corporation example provides us with a good use for structured English, and it can be transformed into structured English, as shown in Figure 11.6, by putting the decision rules into their proper sequence and using the convention of IF-THEN-ELSE statements throughout.

Once this example is written in structured English, one can see that it is a rather simple sequential decision. Structured English can be more complex if blocks of instructions are nested within other blocks of instructions, as shown in Figure 11.7.

Kit Chen Kaboodle, Inc.

"I don't want to get anyone stirred up, but I think we need to sift through our unfilled order policies," says Kit Chen. "I wouldn't want to put a strain on our customers. As you know already, Kit Chen Kaboodle is a mail-order cookware business specializing in 'klassy kitsch for kitchens,' like our latest catalog says. I mean, we've got everything you need to do gourmet cooking and entertaining: nutmeg grinders, potato whisks, egg separators, turkey basters, placemats with cats on 'em, ice cube trays in shamrock shapes, and more.

"Here's how we've been handling unfilled orders. We search our unfilled orders file once a week. If the order was filled this week, we delete the record, and the rest is gravy. If we haven't written to the customer in four weeks, we send 'em this cute card with a chef peeking into the oven, saying, 'Not ready yet.' (It's a notification that their item is still on backorder.)

"If the backorder date changed to greater than forty-five days from now, we send out a notice. But if the merchandise is seasonal (like Halloween treat bags, Christmas cookie cutters, or Valentine's Day cake molds) and the backorder date is thirty days or more, we send out a notice with a chef glaring at his egg timer.

"If the backorder date changed at all and we haven't sent out a card within two weeks, we send out a card with a chef checking his recipe. If the merchandise is no longer available, we send a notice (complete with chef crying in the corner) and delete the record.

"Thanks for listening to all of this. I think we've got the right ingredients for a good policy; we just need to blend them together and cook up something special."

Since you are the systems analyst that Kit hired, go through the narrative of how Kit Chen Kaboodle, Inc., handles unfilled orders, drawing boxes around each action she mentions and circling each condition brought up. Make notes of any ambiguities you would like to clarify in a later interview.

Writing Structured English

In order to write structured English, it is advisable to use the following conventions:

1. Express all logic in terms of sequential structures, decision structures, case structures, or iterations (see Figure 11.8 for examples of these).
2. Use and capitalize accepted keywords such as IF, THEN, ELSE, DO, DO WHILE, DO UNTIL, and PERFORM.
3. Indent blocks of statements to show their hierarchy (nesting) clearly.
4. When words or phrases have been defined in a data dictionary (as in Chapter 10), underline those words or phrases to signify that they have a specialized, reserved meaning.
5. Be careful when using "and" and "or," and avoid confusion when distinguishing between "greater than" and "greater than or equal to" and like relationships. Clarify the logical statements now rather than wait until the program coding stage.

A STRUCTURED ENGLISH EXAMPLE. The following example demonstrates how a spoken procedure for processing medical claims is transformed into structured English:

We process all of our claims in this manner. First we determine whether the claimant has ever sent in a claim before; if not, we set up a new record. The claim totals for the year are then updated. Next we determine if a claimant has policy *A* or policy *B,* which differ in de-

FIGURE 11.6
Using structured English for
analyzing the decision
process for a simple sequential decision.

Calculate Base Premium
IF constuction is brick
 THEN deduct 10 percent of base to total
ENDIF
IF replacement option is chosen
 THEN add 10 percent of base to subtotal
ENDIF
If owner chooses $100 deductible
 THEN add 15 percent of subtotal
ENDIF
IF home has burglar alarm
 THEN deduct 5 percent of adjusted subtotal
ENDIF

ductibles and co-payments (the percentage of the claim claimants pay themselves). For both policies, we check to see if the deductible has been met ($100 for plan *A* and $50 for plan *B*). If the deductible has not been met, we apply the claim to the deductible. Another step adjusts for the co-payment; we subtract the percentage the claimant pays (40 percent for plan *A* and 60 percent for plan *B*) from the claim. Then

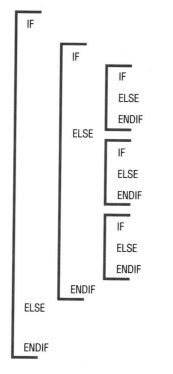

FIGURE 11.7
Proper use of structured
English will involve nesting blocks of instructions
within others.

FIGURE 11.8
Examples of logic expressed
in a sequential structure, a decision structure, a case structure, and an iteration.

Structured English Type	Example

Sequential Structure
  A block of instructions where no
  branching occurs
	Action #1
	Action #2
	Action #3

Decision Structure
  Only IF a condition Is true,
  complete the following
  statements; otherwise jump to the
  ELSE
	IF Condition A is True
	  THEN implement Action A
	ELSE implement Action B
	ENDIF

Case Structure
  A special type of decision
  structure where the cases are
  mutually exclusive (if one occurs
  the others cannot)
	IF Case #1 implement Action #1
	ELSE IF Case #2
	       Implement Action #2
	ELSE IF Case #3]
	       Implement Action #3
	ELSE IF Case #4
	       Implement Action #4
	ELSE print error
	ENDIF

Iteration
  Blocks of statements that are
  repeated until done
	DO WHILE there are customers.
	Action #1
	ENDDO

we issue a check if there is money coming to the claimant, print a summary of the transaction, and update our accounts. We do this until all claims for that day are processed.

In examining the foregoing statements, one notices some simple sequence structures, particularly at the beginning and end. There are a couple of decision structures, and it is most appropriate to nest them, first by determining which plan (*A* or *B*) to use and then by subtracting the correct deductibles and co-payments. The last sentence points to an iteration: Either DO UNTIL all the claims are processed or DO WHILE there are claims remaining.

Realizing that it is possible to nest the decision structures according to policy plans, we can write the structured English for the foregoing example (see Figure 11.9). As one begins to work on the structured English, one finds that some logic and relationships that seemed clear at one time are actually ambiguous. For example, do we add the claim to the year-to-date (YTD) claim before or after updating the deductible? Is it possible that an error can occur if something other than plan *A* or *B* is stored in the claimant's record? We subtract 40 percent of what from the claim? These ambiguities need to be clarified at this point.

Besides the obvious advantage of clarifying the logic and relationships found in human languages, structured English has another important advantage: It is a communication tool. Structured English can be taught to and hence understood by others in the organization, so if communication is important, structured English is a viable alternative for decision analysis.

Kneading Structure

Kit Chen has risen to the occasion and answered your questions concerning the policy for hand-ling unfilled orders at Kit Chen Kaboodle, Inc. (with a minimum of yolking around). Based on those answers and any assumptions you

need to make, pour Kit's narrative (from Consulting Opportunity 11.1) into a new mold by rewriting the recipe for handling unfilled orders in structured English.

Data Dictionary and Process Specifications

All computer programs may be coded using the three basic constructs: sequence, selection (IF . . . THEN . . . ELSE and the case structure), and iteration or looping. The data dictionary indicates which of these constructs must be included in the process specifications.

If the data dictionary for the input and output data flow contains a series of fields without any iteration—{ }—or selection—[ ]—the process specification will contain a simple sequence of statements, such as MOVE,

```
DO WHILE there are claims remaining
    IF claimant has not sent in a claim
        Set up new claimant record
    ELSE continue
    Add claim to YTD Claim
    IF claimant has policy–plan A
        THEN IF deductible of $100.00 has not been met
            THEN subtract deductible–not–met from claim
            Update deductible
        ELSE continue
        ENDIF
        Subtract co-payment of 40% of claim from claim
    ELSE IF claimant has policy–plan B.
        THEN IF deductible of $50.00 has not been met
            THEN subtract deductible–not–met from claim
            Update deductible
        ELSE continue
        ENDIF
        Subtract co-payment of 60% of claim from claim
    ELSE continue
    ELSE write plan–error–message
    ENDIF
    ENDIF
    IF claim is greater than zero
        Print check
    ENDIF
    Print summary for claimant
    Update accounts
ENDDO
```

FIGURE 11.9
Structured English for the medical-claim processing system. Underlining signifies that the terms have been defined in the data dictionary.

FIGURE 11.10
Data structure for a shipping
statement for World's Trend.

Shipping Statement =	Order Number +
	Order Date +
	Customer Number +
	Customer Name +
	Customer Address +
	$^5_1${Order Item Lines} +
	Number of Items +
	Merchandise Total +
	(Tax) +
	Shipping and Handling +
	Order Total +
Customer Name =	First Name +
	(Middle Initial) +
	Last Name +
Address =	Street +
	(Apartment) +
	City +
	State +
	Zip +
	(Zip Expansion) +
	(Country) +
Order Item Lines =	Item Number +
	Quantity Ordered +
	Quantity Backordered +
	Item Description +
	Size Description +
	Color Description +
	Unit Price +
	Extended Amount +

ADD, SUBTRACT, and so on. Refer to the example of a data dictionary for the SHIPPING STATEMENT, illustrated in Figure 11.10. Notice that the data dictionary for the SHIPPING STATEMENT has the ORDER NUMBER, ORDER DATE, and CUSTOMER NUMBER as simple sequential fields. The corresponding logic, shown in lines 3 through 5 in the corresponding structured English in Figure 11.11, consists of simple move statements.

A data structure with optional elements contained in parentheses or either/or elements contained within brackets will have a corresponding IF . . . THEN . . . ELSE statement in the process specification. Also, if an amount, such as QUANTITY BACKORDERED, is greater than zero, the underlying logic will be IF . . . THEN . . . ELSE. Iteration, indicated by braces on a data structure, must have a corresponding DO WHILE, DO UNTIL, or PERFORM UNTIL to control looping on the process specification. The data structure for the Order Items lines allows up to five items in the loop. Lines 8 through 17 show the statements contained within

Structured English

Format the shipping statement. After each line of the statement has been formatted, write the shipping line.

1. GET Order Record
2. GET Customer Record
3. Move Order Number to shipping statement
4. Move Order Date to shipping statement
5. Move Customer Number to shipping statement
6. DO format Customer Name (leave only one space between First/Middle/Last)
7. DO format Customer Address lines
8. DO WHILE there are items for the order
9.   GET Item Record
10.   DO Format Item Line
11.   Multiply Unit Price by Quantity Ordered giving Extended Amount
12.   Move Extended Amount to Order Item line
13.   Add Extended Amount to Merchandise Total
14.   IF Quantity Backordered is greater than zero
15.   Move Quantity Backordered to Order Item line
16.   ENDIF
17. ENDDO
18. Move Merchandise Total to shipping statement
19. Move 0 to Tax
20. IF State is equal to CT
21.   Multiply Merchandise Total by Tax Rate giving Tax
22. ENDIF
23. Move Tax to shipping statement
24. DO calculate Shipping and Handling
25. Move Shipping and Handling to shipping statement
26. Add Merchandise Total, Tax and Shipping and Handling giving Order Total
27. Move Order Total to shipping statement

the DO WHILE through the END DO necessary to produce the multiple Order Items.

DECISION TABLES

A decision table is a table of rows and columns, separated into four quadrants, as shown in Figure 11.12. The upper left quadrant contains the condition(s); the upper right quadrant contains the condition alternatives. The lower half of the table contains the actions to be taken on the left side and the rules for executing the actions on the right. When a decision table is used to determine which action needs to be taken, the logic moves clockwise beginning from the upper left.

Suppose a store wanted to illustrate its policy on noncash customer purchases. The company could do so using a simple decision table as shown in Figure 11.13. Each of the three conditions (sale under $50, pays by check,

FIGURE 11.12
The standard format used for
presenting a decision table.

Conditions and Actions	Rules
Conditions	Condition Alternatives
Actions	Action Entries

and uses credit cards) has only two alternatives. The two alternatives are *Y* (yes, it is true) or *N* (no, it is not true). Four actions are possible:

1. Ring up the sale.
2. Look up the credit card number in a book before ringing up the sale.
3. Call the supervisor for approval.
4. Call the bank for credit card authorization.

The final ingredient that makes the decision table worthwhile is the set of rules for each of the actions. Rules are the combinations of the condition alternatives that precipitate an action.

For example, rule 3 says:

	IF
N	the total sale is NOT under $50.00
	and
Y	the customer paid by check and had two forms of ID
	and
N	the customer did not use a credit card
	THEN
X	call the supervisor for approval.

The foregoing example featured a problem with four sets of rules and four possible actions, but this is only a coincidence. The next example demonstrates that decision tables often become large and involved.

FIGURE 11.13
Using a decision table for illustrating a store's policy of customer checkout with four sets of rules and four possible actions.

Conditions and Actions	Rules			
	1	2	3	4
Under $50	Y	Y	N	N
Pays by check with 2 forms of ID	Y	N	Y	N
Uses credit card	N	Y	N	Y
Ring up sale	X			
Look up credit card in book		X		
Call supervisor for approval			X	
Call bank for credit authorization				X

Developing Decision Tables

In order to build decision tables, the analyst needs to determine the maximum size of the table, eliminate any impossible situations, inconsistencies, or redundancies, and simplify the table as much as possible. The following steps provide the analyst with a systematic method for developing decision tables:

1. Determine the number of conditions that may affect the decision. Combine rows that overlap—for example, conditions that are mutually exclusive. the number of conditions becomes the number of rows in the top half of the decision table.

2. Determine the number of possible actions that can be taken. This becomes the number of rows in the lower half of the decision table.

3. Determine the number of condition alternatives for each condition. In the simplest form of decision table, there would be two alternatives (*Y* or *N*) for each condition. In an extended-entry table, there may be many alternatives for each condition.

4. Calculate the maximum number of columns in the decision table by multiplying the number of alternatives for each condition. If there were four conditions and two alternatives (*Y* or *N*) for each of the conditions, there would be sixteen possibilities as follows:

Condition 1:	2 alternatives
Condition 2: ×	2 alternatives
Condition 3: ×	2 alternatives
Condition 4: ×	2 alternatives
	16 possibilities

5. Fill in the condition alternatives. Start with the first condition and divide the number of columns by the number of alternatives for that condition. In the foregoing example, there are sixteen columns and two alternatives (*Y* or *N*), so sixteen divided by two is eight. Then choose one of the alternatives, say *Y,* and write it in the first eight columns. Finish by writing *N* in the remaining eight columns as follows:

    Condition 1:   Y Y Y Y Y Y Y Y N N N N N N N N

    Repeat this for each condition, using a subset of the table:

    Condition 1:   Y Y Y Y Y Y Y Y N N N N N N N N
    Condition 2:   Y Y Y Y N N N N
    Condition 3:   Y Y N N
    Condition 4:   Y N

    and continue the pattern for each condition:

    Condition 1:   Y Y Y Y Y Y Y Y N N N N N N N N
    Condition 2:   Y Y Y Y N N N N Y Y Y Y N N N N
    Condition 3:   Y Y N N Y Y N N Y Y N N Y Y N N
    Condition 4:   Y N Y N Y N Y N Y N Y N Y N Y N

6. Complete the table by inserting an X where rules suggest certain actions.

7. Combine rules where it is apparent that an alternative does not make a difference in the outcome; for example:

Condition 1: Y Y
Condition 2: Y N
───────────────
Action 1: X X

can be expressed as:

Condition 1: Y
Condition 2: —
───────────────
Action 1: X

The dash [—] signifies that Condition 2 can be either *Y* or *N*, and the action will still be taken.

8. Check the table for any impossible situations, contradictions, and redundancies. These will be discussed in more detail later.

9. Rearrange the conditions and actions (or even rules) if this makes the decision table more understandable.

A DECISION TABLE EXAMPLE. Figure 11.14 is an illustration of a decision table developed using the steps previously outlined. In this example, a company is trying to maintain a meaningful mailing list of customers. The objective is to send out only the catalogs from which customers will buy merchandise.

The company realizes that certain loyal customers order from every catalog and some people on the mailing list never order. These ordering patterns are easy to observe, but deciding which catalogs to send customers who order only from selected catalogs is more difficult. Once these decisions are made, a decision table is constructed for three conditions (C1: customer ordered from Fall catalog; C2: customer ordered from Christmas catalog; and C3: customer ordered from specialty catalog), each having two alternatives (*Y* or *N*). Three actions can be taken (A1: send out this year's Christmas catalog; A2: send out the new specialty catalog; and A3: send out both catalogs). The resulting decision table has six rows (three conditions and three actions) and eight columns (two alternatives × two alternatives × two alternatives).

The decision table is now examined to see if it can be reduced. There are no mutually exclusive conditions, so it is not possible to get by with

FIGURE 11.14
Constructing a decision table for deciding which catalog to send to customers who order only from selected catalogs.

Conditions and Actions	Rules							
	1	2	3	4	5	6	7	8
Customer ordered from Fall catalog	Y	Y	Y	Y	N	N	N	N
Customer ordered from Christmas catalog	Y	Y	N	N	Y	Y	N	N
Customer ordered from special catalog	Y	N	Y	N	Y	N	Y	N
Send out this year's Christmas catalog		X		X		X		X
Send out special catalog			X				X	
Send out both catalogs	X				X			

Saving a Cent on Citron Car Rental

"We feel lucky to be this popular. I think customers feel we have so many options to offer that they ought to rent an auto from us," says Ricardo Limon, who manages several outlets for Citron Car Rental. "Our slogan is, 'You'll never feel squeezed at Citron.' We have five sizes of cars that we list as A through E.

A Subcompact
B Compact
C Midsize
D Full-size
E Luxury

Standard transmission is available only for A, B, and C. Automatic transmission is available for every size car.

"If a customer reserves a subcompact (A) and finds on arriving that we don't have one, that customer gets a free upgrade to the next-sized car, in this case a compact (B). Customers also get a free upgrade from their reserved car size if their company has an account with us. There's a discount for membership in any of the frequent flyer clubs run by cooperating airlines, too. When customers step up to the counter, they tell us what size car they reserved, and then we check to see if we have it in the lot ready to go. They usually bring up any discounts, and we ask them if they want insurance and how long they will use the car. Then we calculate their rate and write out a slip for them to sign right there."

Ricardo has asked you to computerize the billing process for Citron, so that customers can get their car quickly and still be billed correctly. Draw a decision table that represents the conditions, condition alternatives, actions, and action rules you gained from Ricardo's narrative that will guide an automated billing process.

fewer than three condition rows. No rules allow the combination of actions. It is possible, however, to combine some of the rules as shown in Figure 11.15. For instance, rules 2, 4, 6, and 8 can be combined since they all have two things in common:

Conditions and Actions				Rules				
	1	2	3	4	5	6	7	8
Customer ordered from Fall catalog	Y	Y	Y	Y	N	N	N	N
Customer ordered from Christmas catalog	Y	Y	N	N	Y	Y	N	N
Customer ordered from specialty catalog	Y	N	Y	N	Y	N	Y	N
Send out this year's Christmas catalog		X		X		X		X
Send out specialty catalog			X				X	
Send out both catalogs	X				X			

Conditions and Actions		Rules	
	1'	2'	3'
Customer ordered from Fall catalog	—	—	—
Customer ordered from Christmas catalog	Y	—	N
Customer ordered from specialty catalog	Y	N	Y
Send out this year's Christmas catalog		X	
Send out specialty catalog			X
Send out both catalogs	X		

FIGURE 11.15
Combining rules to simplify the customer-catalog decision table.

FIGURE 11.16
Adding a rule to the customer-catalog decision table changes the entire table.

Conditions and Actions	Rules			
	1'	2'	3'	4'
Customer ordered from Fall catalog	—	—	—	—
Customer ordered from Christmas catalog	Y	—	N	—
Customer ordered from specialty catalog	Y	N	Y	—
Ordered $50 or more	Y	Y	Y	N
Send out this year's Christmas catalog		X		
Send out specialty catalog			X	
Send out both catalogs	X			
Do not send out any catalog				X

1. They instruct us to send out this year's Christmas catalog.
2. The alternative for condition 3 is always *N*.

It doesn't matter what the alternatives are for the first two conditions, so it is possible to insert dashes [—] in place of the *Y* or *N*.

The remaining rules—1, 3, 5, and 7—cannot be reduced to a single rule because two different actions remain. Instead, rules 1 and 5 may be combined; likewise, rules 3 and 7 can be combined.

Checking for Completeness and Accuracy

Checking over your decision tables for completeness and accuracy is essential. Four main problems can occur in developing decision tables: incompleteness, impossible situations, contradictions, and redundancy.

Assuring that all conditions, condition alternatives, actions, and action rules are complete is of utmost importance. Suppose an important condition had been left out of the catalog store problem discussed earlier: if a customer ordered less than $50. The whole decision table would change because a new condition, a new set of alternatives, new action, and one or more new action rules would have to be added. Suppose the rule is: IF the customer did not order more than $50, THEN do not send any catalogs. A new rule 4 would be added to the decision table, as shown in Figure 11.16.

When building decision tables as outlined in the foregoing steps, it is sometimes possible to set up impossible situations. An example of this is

FIGURE 11.17
Checking the decision table for impossible situations is important.

Conditions and Actions	Rules			
	1	2	3	4
Salary > $50,000/year	Y	Y	N	N
Salary < $2,000/month	Y	N	Y	N
Action 1				
Action 2				

This is an impossible situation.

Conditions and Actions	Rules						
	1	2	3	4	5	6	7
Condition 1	Y	Y	Y	Y	Y	N	N
Condition 2	Y	Y	Y	N	N	Y	N
Condition 3	—	N	—	—	—	N	Y
Action 1	X			X	X		
Action 2			X			X	
Action 3		X					X

Contradiction ⎿_____⏌ ⎿_____⏌ Redundancy

FIGURE 11.18
Checking the decision table for inadvertent contradictions and redundancy is important.

shown in Figure 11.17. Rule 1 is not feasible, since a person cannot earn greater than $50,000 per year and less than $2,000 per month at the same time. The other three rules are valid. The problem went unnoticed because the first condition was measured in years and the second condition in months.

Contradictions occur when rules suggest different actions but satisfy the same conditions. The fault could lie with the way the analyst constructed the table or with the information the analyst received. Contradictions often occur if dashes [—] are incorrectly inserted into the table. Redundancy occurs when identical sets of alternatives require the exact same action. Figure 11.18 is an illustration of a contradiction and a redundancy. The analyst has to determine what is correct and resolve the contradiction or redundancy.

More Advanced Decision Tables

Decision tables can become very burdensome because they grow rapidly as the number of conditions and alternatives increases. A table with only seven conditions with yes or no alternatives would have 128 columns. One way to reduce the complexity of unwieldy decision tables is to use extended entries or the ELSE rule, or to construct multiple tables.

Notice in the following Y or N table that the conditions are mutually exclusive.

C1: Did not order	Y	N	N	N
C2: Ordered once	N	Y	N	N
C3: Ordered twice	N	N	Y	N
C4: Ordered more than twice	N	N	N	Y

Therefore, they can be written in extended-entry form as follows:

C1: Number of times customer ordered   0 1 2 >2

The number of required columns and rows decreases while the understandability increases. Instead of using four rows for the number of times a customer orders, only one row is needed.

An example of a structured inventory ordering policy is shown in Figure 11.19. The cost of an item can be less than $10, between $10 and $50 inclusive, or greater than $50. In addition, the order quantity can be

FIGURE 11.19
Using extended-entry tables
reduces the possibility of redundancy and contradiction.

Conditions and Actions	Rules 1	2	3	4	5	6
Cost of the Item		Less than $10	Between $10 and $50 Inclusive	Greater than $50	Less than or Equal to $50	Greater than $50
Order Quantity	Less than 50 Units	Betweeen 50 and 100 Units Inclusive	Between 50 and 100 Units Inclusive	Between 50 and 100 Units Inclusive	Over 100 Units	Over 100 Units
Order Immediately			X			
Wait Until Regular Order is Placed	X	X				
Check With Supervisor				X	X	
Send to Purchasing for Bid						X

less than 50 units per order, between 50 and 100 units, or over 100 units. The decision table only has two condition rows, and the alternatives are written in words in the upper right-hand quadrant. By using extended-entry tables, the probability of redundancy and contradiction becomes smaller.

FIGURE 11.20
The ELSE rule can be used to
eliminate repetitious rules requiring the same action.

Conditions and Actions	Rules 1	2	3	4	ELSE
Cost of the Item A cost < $10 B $10 ≤ cost ≤ $50 C cost > $50	–	A	B	C	
Order Quantity D quantity < 50 E 50 ≤ quantity ≤ 100 F quantity > 100	D	E	E	F	
Order Immediately			X		
Wair Until Regular Order is Placed	X	X			
Send to Purchasing for Bid				X	
Check with Supervisor					X

DECISION TABLE 1.0

CONDITIONS AND TRANSACTION	1	2	3	4	5
C1:					
C2:					
C3:					
A1:					
PERFORM TABLE 1.1					X
A5:					
A6:					

DECISION TABLE 1.0

CONDITIONS AND TRANSACTION	1	2	3	4	5
C4:					
C5:					
C6:					
A2:					
A3:					
A4:					
RETURN					X

FIGURE 11.21
Use PERFORM to transfer to
another decision table and
RETURN to come back.

Another useful technique in building decision tables is to use the ELSE column. This technique is useful in helping to eliminate many repetitious rules requiring the exact same action. It is also useful in preventing errors of omission. Figure 11.20 shows how the automatic inventory ordering policy can take advantage of the ELSE rule.

Multiple tables are used to control the size of the table. A structured approach to building decision tables would avoid the use of GOTOs (jumping to another table) and instead use the instruction PERFORM. The PERFORM action allows an orderly transfer from the original to another table and then a return to the original table. Figure 11.21 shows how transfer is made between tables using PERFORM.

Decision tables are an important tool in the analysis of structured decisions. One major advantage of using decision tables over other methods is that tables help the analyst ensure completeness. When using decision tables, it is also easy to check for possible errors, such as impossible situations, contradictions, and redundancy. Decision table processors, which take the table as input and provide computer program code as output, are also available.

DECISION TREES

Decision trees are used when complex branching occurs in a structured decision process. Trees are also useful when it is essential to keep a string of decisions in a particular sequence. Although the decision tree derives its name from natural trees, decision trees are most often drawn on their side, with the root of the tree on the left-hand side of the paper; from there, the tree branches out to the right. This orientation allows the analyst to write on the branches in order to describe conditions and actions.

Unlike the decision tree used in management science, the analyst's tree does not contain probabilities and outcomes, because in systems analysis trees are used mainly for identifying and organizing conditions and actions in a completely structured decision process.

Drawing Decision Trees

It is useful to distinguish between conditions and actions when drawing decision trees. This distinction is especially relevant when conditions and actions take place over a period of time and their sequence is important. For this purpose, use a square node to indicate an action and a circle to represent a condition, as shown in Figure 11.22. Using notation makes the decision tree more readable, as does numbering the circles and squares sequentially. Think of a circle as signifying IF, while the square means THEN.

When decision tables were discussed in an earlier section, a point-of-sale example was used to determine the purchase approval actions for a department store. Conditions included the amount of the sale (under $50) and whether the customer paid by check or credit card. The four actions possible were to ring up the sale, look up the credit card in a book, call the supervisor for approval, or call the bank for credit card authorization. Figure 11.23 illustrates how this example can be drawn as a decision tree. In drawing the tree:

1. Identify all conditions and actions and their order and timing (if they are critical).
2. Begin building the tree from left to right while making sure you are complete in listing all possible alternatives before moving over to the right.

This simple tree is symmetrical, and the four actions at the end are unique. A more complex example follows to demonstrate both that the tree does not have to be balanced and that identical actions may appear more than once.

FIGURE 11.22
Conventions for drawing a decision tree where circles can be thought of as meaning IF and squares meaning THEN.

PART 3:
THE ANALYSIS
PROCESS

362

A Tree for Free

"I know you've got a plane to catch, but let me try to explain it once again to you, sir," pleads Glen Curtiss, a marketing manager for Premium Airlines. Curtiss has been attempting (unsuccessfully) to explain the airline's new policy for accumulating miles for awards (such as upgrades to first class, free flights, etc.) to a member of Premium's "Flying for Prizes" club.

Curtiss takes another pass at getting the policy off the ground, saying, "You see, sir, the traveler (that's you, Mr. Icarus) will be awarded the miles actually flown. If the actual mileage for the leg was less than 500 miles, the traveler will get 500 miles credit. If the trip was made on a Saturday, the actual mileage will be multiplied by 2. If the trip was made on a Tuesday, the

multiplication factor is 1.5. If this is the ninth leg traveled during the calendar month, the mileage is doubled no matter what day, and if it is the seventeenth leg traveled, the mileage is tripled.

"I hope that clears it up for you, Mr. Icarus. Enjoy your flight, and thanks for flying Premium."

Icarus, whose desire to board the Premium plane has all but melted away during Curtiss' long explanation, fades into the sea of people wading through the security lanes, without so much as a peep in reply.

Develop a decision tree for Premium Airlines' new policy for accumulating award miles, so that the policy becomes clearer, is easier to grasp visually, and hence is easier to explain.

A COMPLEX DECISION TREE EXAMPLE. A systems analyst was hired to help Festival-on-the-Lake, a very popular theatre festival, fill requests for tickets. Here is part of an interview with the box office manager:

When patrons request seats for a play, we try to fill their request, but often the seat they would like on their first performance date preference is sold out. On our order form, we ask the patron to choose three performance dates in order of preference, to indicate whether they prefer orchestra or balcony, and finally, to select the price of the seat they would like. We have three prices—$25, $20, and $15—and each price is available in both orchestra and balcony.

Since we fill most of our ticket orders by mail, we have to assume a number of things and try to come as close as possible to the desires of the patron.

If orchestra is not available, we assign balcony and vice versa, but if the first night selected is unavailable in the price requested either in orchestra or balcony, we look at the second night. If the second

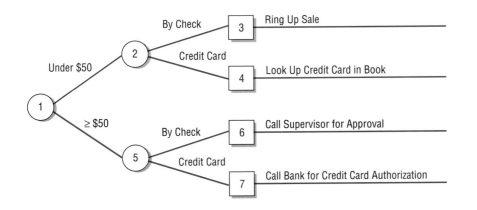

FIGURE 11.23
Drawing a decision tree to show the noncash purchase approval actions for a department store.

CHAPTER 11:
DESCRIBING PROCESS
SPECIFICATIONS
AND STRUCTURED DECISIONS

night is unavailable, we look for options on the third. If the third night is unavailable, we select the next lower price and repeat the process. If the patron originally selected the lowest price, we must issue a notice that the ticket request could not be filled.

The foregoing interview suggests the use of a decision tree for two reasons: (1) The process is accomplished in stages ("First we try this, and if it doesn't work, we try this"); and (2) the logic is asymmetrical, lending itself to decision trees rather than decision tables.

The steps in building the decision tree are as follows:

1. Identify the conditions:
    1st choice of dates
    2nd choice of dates
    3rd choice of dates
    1st price preference
    2nd price preference
    3rd price preference
    orchestra preference
    balcony preference
2. Identify the condition alternatives:
    available
    not available
3. Identify the actions:
    assign seats
    issue tickets
    check 1st choice of dates
    check 2nd choice of dates
    check 3rd choice of dates
    repeat process for next lower price category
    check location preference
    issue sold out notice
4. Identify action rules (in order):
    start with ideal choice
    assign seats if available
    issue tickets if assigned
    check alternate location (orchestra/balcony)
    look at next choice of dates
    look at next price category
    issue notice if order is unfilled

The decision tree for the theatre festival is found in Figure 11.24. Actions are represented by the square nodes, and conditions are depicted by the circles. Notation of this sort keeps the processes clearer: The circles represent IF, and the squares represent THEN.

In building the tree, focus on the first action that should be taken, place it on the extreme left side, and then build from left to right with conditions or further actions. In the theatre example, choose ideal price and location on first choice of dates. If this ideal choice is available, two actions are taken: (1) The seat is assigned; and (2) tickets are issued. If the ideal choice is not available, the action taken is to check on availability of the alternate location

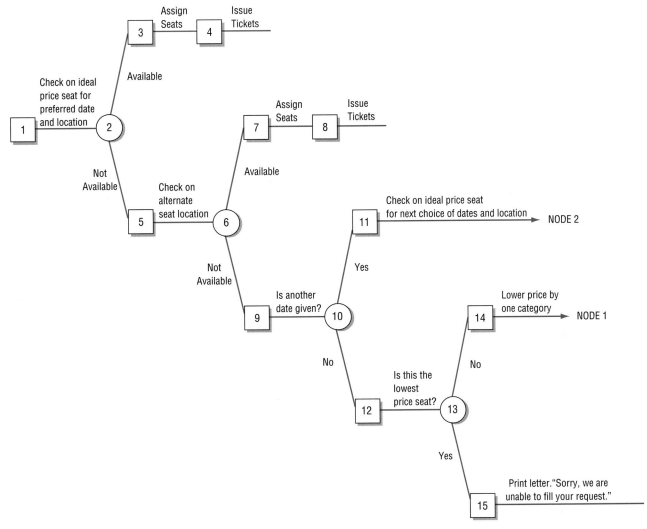

FIGURE 11.24
Building a decision tree for a process accomplished in stages whose logic is asymmetrical.

(orchestra or balcony). If this is not available, the second choice of dates is examined, and so forth.

One caution about decision trees bears mentioning. The tree takes up considerable space, and consequently a minimum amount of description on conditions and actions is written on the tree. Instructions such as "Assign Seats" are not spelled out in enough detail at this point. The systems analyst needs to be aware of the implications of this brief statement: In this case, reserve the seats chosen, so they cannot be assigned to more than one patron; and then match the seat numbers with the patron, so they can be mailed. Furthermore, data requirements are not specified on the tree; only the conditions and actions are specified.

The decision tree has three main advantages over a decision table. First, it takes advantage of the sequential structure of decision tree branches, so the order of checking conditions and executing actions is immediately noticeable.

Second, conditions and actions of decision trees are found on some branches but not on others; this contrasts with decision tables, where they are all part of the same table. Those conditions and actions that are critical are connected directly to other conditions and actions, while those conditions that do not matter are absent. In other words, the tree does not have to be symmetrical.

Third, compared to decision tables, decision trees are more readily understood by others in the organization. Consequently, they are more appropriate as a communication tool.

CHOOSING A STRUCTURED DECISION ANALYSIS TECHNIQUE

We have examined the three techniques for analysis of structured decisions: structured English, decision tables, and decision trees. Although they need not be used exclusively, it is customary to choose one analysis technique for a decision rather than employing all three. The following guidelines provide you with a way to choose one of the three techniques for a particular case:

1. Use structured English when
   a. There are many repetitious actions.
      OR
   b. Communication to end users is important.
2. Use decision tables when
   a. Complex combinations of conditions, actions, and rules are found.
      OR
   b. You require a method that effectively avoids impossible situations, redundancies, and contradictions.
3. Use decision trees when
   a. The sequence of conditions and actions is critical.
      OR
   b. When not every condition is relevant to every action (the branches are different).

PHYSICAL AND LOGICAL PROCESS SPECIFICATIONS

The remaining sections in this chapter are advanced topics that may be explored further if you wish. The first topic shows how a data-flow diagram can be transformed into process specifications. The second section explains how process specifications can, in turn, be used to balance (and correct) a data-flow diagram.

Each data-flow diagram process expands to a child diagram, a structure chart (discussed in Chapter 20), or process specifications (as structured English). If the process is primitive, the specifications show the logic, arithmetic, or algorithm for transforming the input into output. These specifications are a portion of the logical model—the business rules—which would exist regardless of the type of system used to implement the business. Business rules often form the basis for creating procedural language when using code generators.

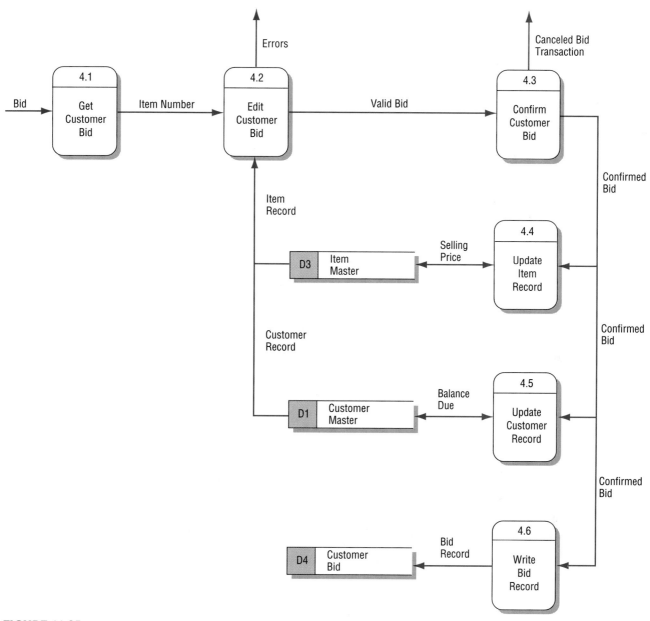

FIGURE 11.25
Data-flow diagram explosion of process 4, RECORD CUSTOMER BID.

For example, we observe that an auction house has a computer system to keep track of successful customer bids (process 4) and to produce a payment statement for the person supplying the auctioned item (process 3).

If the process expands to a child diagram or a structure chart, the process specification describes the order and conditions under which the child diagram processes will execute. This control logic is a part of the physical model and would be created after the method of implementation (either batch or on-line) for the process has been determined. Figure 11.25 shows the auction system Diagram 4, an explosion of process 4, RECORD CUS-TOMER BID. Figure 11.26 illustrates the structured English format for

FIGURE 11.26
Structured English for a
process that explodes to a
child diagram.

Process Specification Form

Number ___4___

Name ___RECORD CUSTOMER BID___

Description ___Operators key the customer bid. If the entries are correct, the___
___Item Master and Customer Master files are updated.___
___A Bid Record is created.___

Input Cata Flow

Bid

Customer Record Balance Due

Item Record

Output Data Flow

Bid Record

Customer Record Balance Due

Item Record

Type of Process ☑ Online ☐ Batch ☐ Manual	Subprogram/Function Name

Process Logic:

DO Get Customer Bid Screen

DO Edit Customer Bid

    Until Valid Bid

    Or   Operator Cancel

IF Valid Bid

    DO Confirm Customer Bid (Visual confirm of the data)

    IF Confirmed

        Do Update Customer Record

        DO Update Inventory Record

        DO Write Bid Record

    ENDIF

ENDIF

Refer to: Name:_____

☐ Structured English   ☐ Decision Table   ☐ Decision Tree

Unresolved Issues:

---

process 4. Note that most of the logic involves IF and PERFORM statements, which are typical of controlling program modules.

Using Process Specifications: Horizontal Balancing

Process specifications, whether on paper or captured using a CASE tool, may be used for generating computer language source code and for analyzing the system design. Computer programs are indicated by partitioning on a data-flow diagram. All of the individual process specifications for a program are consolidated to become the processing details in a program specification packet.

    To attempt to write the specifications for a program without examining each process may lead to omissions and errors. Since process specifications are developed on a small scale, one process at a time, each one may be analyzed for complete and correct logic. When the analysis is finished and corrections are made for all processes within a program, the final program specifications should be complete and accurate.

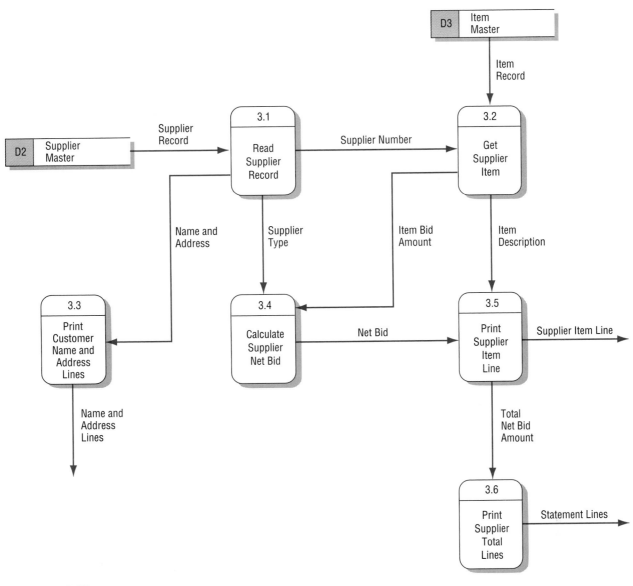

FIGURE 11.27
Diagram 3, Produce Supplier Payment Statement.

Horizontal Balancing

Process specifications may be used to analyze the data-flow diagram and data dictionary through a method called horizontal balancing. Horizontal balancing dictates that all output data-flow elements must be obtained from the input elements and process logic. Base elements on an output data flow must be present on the input flow, and derived elements on an output flow must be either present on an input data flow or created using the process specifications. Unresolved areas should be summarized into a series of interview questions. Be sure to pose these questions during follow-up interviews with key users.

Figure 11.27 illustrates Diagram 3, an explosion of the Auction System process 3, PRODUCE SUPPLIER PAYMENT STATEMENT. Figure 11.28 shows the corresponding data dictionary entries. Figure 11.29 is the struc-

FIGURE 11.28
Data dictionary entries for
producing the Supplier Sales
Receipt.

Supplier Sales Receipt =   Current Date +
                             Supplier Type +
                             Supplier Name +
                             Address +
                             {Supplier Item Line} +
                             Auction Surcharge +
                             Total Amount Paid to Supplier

Supplier Item Line =   Item Description +
                             (Item Bid Amount) +
                             (Net Bid) +
                             (Date Sold)

Supplier Record =   Supplier Number +
                             Supplier Type +
                             Supplier Name +
                             Address

Item Record =   Item Number +
                             Item Description +
                             (Item Bid Amount) +
                             (Amount Paid to Supplier) +
                             (Date Sold) +
                             Supplier Number

tured English for process 3.4, CALCULATE SUPPLIER NET BID, and for process 3.5, PRINT BID LINE. Figure 11.30 is the structured English for process 3.6, PRINT SUPPLIER TOTAL DUE LINE.

The output from process 3.4 is the NET BID for each item, a derived element. The logic for the process requires as input the SUPPLIER TYPE and ITEM BID AMOUNT, both used in the NET BID calculation. Checking the data flow diagram reveals that both these elements are input to process 3.4. However, only the NET BID is shown as output from the process. The AMOUNT PAID TO SUPPLIER, included in the structured English figure, is not shown on the data-flow diagram, nor is the ITEM MASTER data store. The YEAR-TO-DATE NET BID is not included in the data dictionary for the SUPPLIER RECORD, nor is it shown on the data-flow diagram. The data-flow diagram and data dictionary must be updated to include these missing components. Figure 11.31 shows Diagram 3 with the necessary corrections.

Examine the output from process 3.5. The SUPPLIER ITEM LINE contains four elements: ITEM DESCRIPTION, ITEM BID AMOUNT, NET BID, and DATE SOLD. The ITEM DESCRIPTION and NET BID are input to process 3.5, but DATE SOLD and ITEM BID AMOUNT, which are base elements, are not on any input flow. They must be added to the data-flow diagram. To avoid having three input flows (ITEM DESCRIPTION, ITEM BID AMOUNT, and DATE SOLD) traveling from process 3.2 to 3.3, the entire item record is passed between the two processes. The final process to be examined is 3.6. The structured English requires that

FIGURE 11.29
Structured English description for processes 3.4 and 3.5.

Structured English: Process 3.4 , CALCULATE SUPPLIER NET BID

BEGIN CASE
IF the Supplier Type is a charitable organization
    THEN Commission Rate = 10%
ELSE IF the Supplier Type is a government unit
    THEN Commission Rate = 15%
ELSE IF the Supplier Type is a bankruptcy
    THEN Commission Rate = 18%
ELSE IF the Supplier type is an estate
    THEN Commission Rate = 20%
ELSE Commission Rate = 25%
END CASE
Multiply Item Bid Amount by Commission Rate giving Commission
Subtract Commission from Item Bid Amount giving Net Bid
Move Net Bid to the Amount Paid in Supplier on the Item Record
Rewrite the Item Record
Add Net Bid to Year to Date Net Bid on the Supplier Record
Rewrite the Supplier Record

Structured English: Processes 3.5, PRINT BID LINE

Move Item Description to Supplier Item Line
Move Date Sold to Supplier Item Line
Move Item Bid Amount to Supplier Item Line
Move Net Bid to the Supplier Item Line
Write Supplier Item Line
Add Net Bid to Total Net Bid Amount

SUPPLIER TYPE and TOTAL NET BID AMOUNT be present as input flow. Since only the TOTAL NET BID AMOUNT is present, process 3.6 has missing input.

SUMMARY

Once the analyst identifies data flows and begins constructing a data dictionary, it is time to turn to process specification and decision analysis. The three methods for decision analysis and describing process logic discussed in this chapter are: structured English, decision tables, and decision trees.

    Process specifications (or minispecs) are created for primitive processes on a data-flow diagram, as well as for some higher-level processes that explode to a child diagram. These specifications explain the decision-making logic and formulas that will transform process input data into output. The three goals of process specification are: to reduce the ambiguity of

FIGURE 11.30
Structured English description for process 3.6.

Structured English: Process 3.6 , PRINT SUPPLIER TOTAL DUE LINE

Note: The Auction Surcharge is a one–time cost per auction to cover set-up costs

BEGIN CASE
IF the Supplier Type is a charitable organization
    THEN Auction Surcharge = $200
ELSE IF the Supplier Type is a governmental unit
    THEN Auction Surcharge = $500
ELSE IF the Supplier Type is a bankruptcy
    THEN Auction Surcharge = $400
ELSE IF the Supplier Type is an estate
    THEN Auction Surcharge = $300
ELSE Auction Surcharge = $500
END CASE
Multiply Item Bid Amount to Statement Line
Write Statement Line
Move Auction Surcharge to Statement Line
Write Statement Line
Subtract Auction Surcharge from Total Net Bid Amount giving Payment Total
Move Payment Total to Statement Line
Write Statement Line

---

the process, to obtain a precise description of what is accomplished, and to validate the system design.

A large part of a systems analyst's work will involve structured decisions—that is, decisions that can be automated if identified conditions occur. In order to do this, the analyst needs to define four variables in the decision being examined: conditions, condition alternatives, actions, and action rules.

One way to describe structured decisions is to use the method referred to as structured English, where logic is expressed in sequential structures, decision structures, case structures, or iterations. Structured English uses accepted keywords such as IF, THEN, ELSE, DO, DO WHILE, and DO UNTIL to describe the logic used, and it indents to indicate the hierarchical structure of the decision process.

Decision tables provide another way to examine, describe, and document decisions. Four quadrants (viewed clockwise from the upper left-hand corner) are used to: (1) describe the conditions; (2) identify possible decision alternatives (such as *Y* or *N*); (3) indicate which actions should be performed; and (4) describe the actions. Decision tables are advantageous since the rules for developing the table itself, as well as the rules for eliminating redundancy, contradictions, and impossible situations, are straightforward and manageable. The use of decision tables promotes completeness and accuracy in analyzing structured decisions.

The third method for decision analysis is the decision tree, consisting of nodes (a square for actions and a circle for conditions) and branches. Decision trees are appropriate when actions must be accomplished in a certain sequence. There is no requirement that the tree be symmetrical, so only those conditions and actions that are critical to the decisions at hand are found on a particular branch.

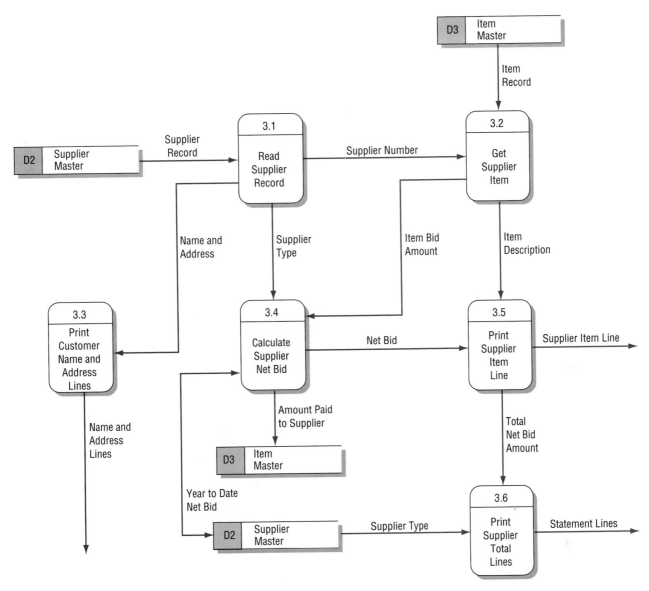

FIGURE 11.31
Corrected data-flow diagram, an explosion of process 3, Produce Supplier Payment Statement.

Each of the decision analysis methods has its own advantages and should be used accordingly. Structured English is useful when many actions are repeated and when communicating with others is important. Decision tables provide a complete analysis of complex situations while limiting the need for change attributable to impossible situations, redundancies, or contradictions. Decision trees are important when proper sequencing of conditions and actions is critical and when each condition is not relevant to each action.

Each data flow diagram process expands to a child diagram, a structure chart, or process specifications (as structured English). If the process is primitive, the specifications show the logic, arithmetic, or algorithm for trans-

"It's really great that you've been able to spend all of this time with us. One thing's for sure, we can use the help. And clearly, from your conversations with Snowden and others, you must realize we all believe that consultants have a role to play in helping companies change. Well, most of us believe it anyway.

"Sometimes structure is good for a person. Or even a company. As you know, Snowden is keen on any kind of structure. That's why some of the Training people can drive him wild sometimes. They're good at structuring things for their clients, but when it comes to organizing their own work, it's another story. Oh well, let me know if there's any way I can help you."

HyperCase Question

1. Assume you will create the specifications for an automated project tracking system for the Training employees. One of the system's functions will be to allow project members to update or add names, addresses, and phone/fax numbers of new clients. Using structured English, write a procedure for carrying out the process of entering a new client name, address, and phone/fax number. [*Hint:* The procedure should ask for a client name, check to see if the name is already in an existing client file, and let the user either validate and update the current client address and phone/fax (if necessary) or add a new client's address and phone/fax number to the client file.]

forming the input into output. These logical model specifications are part of the business rules (which are often used as the basis for creating procedural language when code generators are used).

If the process expands to a child diagram or a structure chart, the process specification describes the order and conditions under which the child diagram processes will execute. This control logic is part of the physical model.

Process specifications may be used to analyze the data-flow diagram and data dictionary through a method called horizontal balancing, which dictates that all output data-flow elements must be obtained from the input elements and process logic. Unresolved areas can be posed as questions in follow-up interviews.

KEYWORDS AND PHRASES

minispecs

structured decision

conditions

condition alternatives

actions

action rules

structured English

decision tables

impossible situations

redundancy

contradictions

incompleteness

decision trees

process specifications

horizontal balancing

REVIEW QUESTIONS

1. List three reasons for producing process specifications.
2. Define what is meant by a structured decision.
3. What four elements must be known in order for the systems analyst to design systems for structured decisions?
4. What are the two building blocks of structured English?
5. List five conventions that should be followed when using structured English.
6. What is the advantage of using structured English to communicate with people in the organization?
7. Which quadrant of the decision table is used for conditions? Which is used for condition alternatives?
8. What is the first step to take in developing a decision table?
9. List the four main problems that can occur in developing decision tables.
10. What is one way to reduce the complexity of unwieldy decision tables?
11. What is one of the major advantages of decision tables over other methods of decision analysis?
12. What are the main uses of decision trees in systems analysis?
13. List the four major steps in building decision trees.
14. What three advantages do decision trees have over decision tables?
15. In which two situations should you use structured English?
16. In which two situations do decision tables work best?
17. In which two situations are decision trees preferable?
18. How do data dictionary structures help in determining the type of structured English statements for a process?
19. What is horizontal balancing? Why is it desirable to balance each process?

PROBLEMS

1. Clyde Clerk is reviewing his firm's expense reimbursement policies with the new salesperson, Trav Farr. "Our reimbursement policies depend on the situation. You see, first we determine if it is a local trip. If it is, we only pay mileage of 18.5 cents a mile. If the trip was a one-day trip, we pay mileage and then check the times of departure and return. In order to be reimbursed for breakfast, you must leave by 7:00 A.M., lunch by 11:00 A.M., and have dinner by 5:00 P.M. To receive reimbursement for breakfast, you must return later than 10:00 A.M., lunch later than 2:00 P.M., and have dinner by 7:00 P.M. On a trip lasting more than one day, we allow hotel, taxi, and airfare, as well as meal allowances. The same times apply for meal expenses." Write structured English for Clyde's narrative of the reimbursement policies.

2. Draw a decision tree depicting the reimbursement policy given in problem 1.

3. Draw a decision table for the reimbursement policy given in problem 1.

4. A computer supplies firm called True Disk has set up accounts for countless businesses in Dosville. True Disk sends out invoices monthly and will give discounts if payments are made within ten days. The discounting policy is as follows: If the amount of the order for computer supplies is greater than $1,000, subtract 4 percent for the order; if the

amount is between $500 and $1,000, subtract a 2 percent discount; if the amount is less than $500, do not apply any discount. Any special order (computer furniture, for example) is exempt from all discounting.

Develop a decision table for True Disk discounting decisions, where the condition alternatives are limited to *Y* and *N*.

5. Develop an extended-entry decision table for the True Disk company discount policy described in problem 4.

6. Develop a decision tree for the True Disk company discount policy presented in problem 4.

7. Write structured English to solve the True Disk company situation in problem 4.

8. Premium Airlines has recently offered to settle claims for a class action suit, which was originated for alleged price fixing of tickets. The proposed settlement is stated as follows:

"Initially, Premium Airlines will make available to the settlement class a main fund of $25 million in coupons. If the number of valid claims submitted is 1.25 million or fewer, the value of each claim will be the result obtained by dividing $25 million by the total number of valid claims submitted. For example, if there are 500,000 valid claims, each person submitting a valid claim will receive a coupon with a value of $50.

"The denomination of each coupon distributed will be in a whole dollar amount not to exceed $50. Thus, if there are fewer than 500,000 valid claims, the value of each claim will be divided among two coupons or more. For example, if there are 250,000 valid claims, each person submitting a valid claim will receive two coupons, each having a face value of $50, for a total coupon value of $100.

"If the number of valid claims submitted is between 1.25 million and 1.5 million, Premium Airlines will make available a supplemental fund of coupons, with a potential value of $5 million. The supplemental fund will be made available to the extent necessary to provide one $20 coupon for each valid claim.

"If there are more than 1.5 million valid claims, the total amount of the main fund and the supplemental fund, $30 million, will be divided evenly to produce one coupon for each valid claim. The value of each such coupon will be $30 million divided by the total number of valid claims."

Draw a decision tree for the Premium Airlines settlement.

9. Write structured English for premium Airlines in problem 8.

10. "Well, it's sort of hard to describe," says Sharon, a counselor at Less Is More Nutrition Center. "I've never had to really tell anybody about the way we charge clients or anything, but here goes.

"When clients come into Less Is More, we check to see if they've ever used our service before. Unfortunately for them, I guess, we have a lot of repeat clients who keep bouncing back. Repeat clients get a reduced rate (pardon the pun) of $100 for the first visit if they return within a year of the end of their program.

"Everyone new pays an initial fee, which is $200 for a physical evaluation. The client may bring in a coupon at this time, and then we deduct $50 from the up-front fee. Half of our clients use our coupons and find out about us from them. But we just give our repeaters their $100 off—they can't use a coupon, too! Clients who transfer in from one of our centers in another city get $75 off their first payment fee, but

Conditions and Actions	Rules															
	1	2	3	4	5	6	7	8	9	10	11	12	13	14	15	16
Sufficient Quantity on Hand	Y	Y	Y	Y	Y	Y	Y	Y	N	N	N	N	N	N	N	N
Quantity Large Enough for Discount	Y	Y	Y	Y	N	N	N	N	Y	Y	Y	Y	Y	N	N	N
Wholesale Customer	Y	Y	N	N	Y	Y	N	N	Y	Y	N	N	Y	Y	N	N
Sales Tax Exemption Filed	Y	N	Y	N	Y	N	Y	N	Y	N	Y	N	Y	N	Y	N
Ship Items and Prepare Invoice	X	X	X	X	X	X	X	X								
Set up Backorder									X	X	X	X	X	X	X	X
Deduct Discount	X	X														
Add Sales Tax		X	X	X		X	X	X								

FIGURE 11.EX1
A decision table for a warehouse.

the coupon doesn't apply. Customers who pay cash get 10 percent off the $200, but they can't use a coupon with that."

Create a decision table with *Y* and *N* conditions for the client charge system at Less Is More Nutrition Center.

11. Reduce the decision table in Figure 11.EX1 to the minimum number of rules.

GROUP PROJECTS

1. Each group member (or each subgroup) should choose to become an "expert" and prepare to explain how and when to use one of the following structured decision techniques: structured English, decision tables, or decision trees. Each group member or subgroup should then make a case for the usefulness of its assigned decision analysis technique for studying the types of structured decisions made by the Maverick Transport company on dispatching particular trucks to particular destinations. Each group should make a presentation of its preferred technique.

2. After hearing each presentation, the group should reach a consensus on *which* technique is most appropriate for analyzing the dispatching decisions of Maverick Transport and *why* that technique is best in this instance.

SELECTED BIBLIOGRAPHY

Adam, E. E., Jr., and R. J. Ebert. *Production and Operations Management,* 3rd ed. Englewood Cliffs, NJ: Prentice-Hall, 1986.

Anderson, D. R., D. J. Sweeney, and T. A. Williams. *An Introduction to Management Science,* 8th ed. New York: West Publishing Company, 1997.

Awad, E. M. *Systems Analysis and Design,* 2nd ed. Homewood, IL: Richard D. Irwin, Inc., 1985.

Evans, J. R. *Applied Production and Operations Management,* 4th ed. Minneapolis/St. Paul: West Publishing Company, 1993.

Gane, C., and T. Sarson. *Structured Systems Analysis and Design Tools and Techniques.* Englewood Cliffs, NJ: Prentice-Hall, 1979.

Hartman, W., H. Matthes, and A. Proeme. *Management Information Systems Handbook.* New York: McGraw-Hill Book Company, 1968.

TABLING A DECISION

 After doing many follow-up interviews with Dot Matricks, Anna tells Chip, "I've determined the logic needed to update the PENDING MICROCOMPUTER ORDERS data store. Since many micros may be ordered on the same purchase order, as each microcomputer is entered, the matching record is located and one is subtracted from the number of outstanding micros per purchase order."

Anna shows Chip the Process repository screen print (depicted in Figure E11.1). "The name of the corresponding process, UPDATE PENDING MICROCOMPUTER ORDER (process 2.5), links the process specification to the data-flow diagram," she explains. Inputs and outputs are listed and should match the data-flow into or out of the process. "The VALID MICROCOMPUTER TRANSACTION record is input, and the updated PENDING ORDER is the output flow."

"That will be useful," Chip says. "Even though it took a while to untangle it all."

Anna points out, "The **Process Description** area contains the logic, shown in structured English."

When the logic is complete, Anna further enters a few notes on the nature of the process, the fact that it is a batch process, and also adds timing information.

Allen Schmidt,
Julie E. Kendall, and
Kenneth E. Kendall

FIGURE E11.1
Process Repository screen, UPDATE PENDING MICROCOMPUTER ORDER.

A decision table may be created for control or process logic. Before the decision table is keyed, it is a good idea to create it on paper and optimize the table. This way only the essential conditions and actions will be entered.

"I've been busy too," Chip assures Anna. "I've spoken with Cher Ware several times since you interviewed her. I've finally captured some of the logic for calculating the cost of a software upgrade.

"Cher indicated three different conditions affecting the cost. The site license provides unlimited copies and is used for popular software installed on many micros. An educational discount is provided by many publishers, and a discount for quantity is usually available," Chip says.

"First I determined the values for the conditions and the number of combinations," Chip continues. He set out the three conditions and their values as follows:

Condition	Values	Number of Values
SITE LICENSE	Y/N	2
EDUCATIONAL DISCOUNT	Y/N	2
DISCOUNT FOR QUANTITY	Y/N	2

"The total number of combinations is found by multiplying the number of values for each of the conditions, $2 \times 2 \times 2 = 8$. The next step is to decide which conditions should be first." Chip continues, "I reason that a SITE LICENSE would not have a discount for quantity or an additional educational discount, since the actual site license cost already reflects this kind of discount. Therefore the SITE LICENSE should be the first condition. Each of the two other conditions would not have any particular advantage over the other, so the order is unimportant.

"Since the total number of conditions is eight and the SITE LICENSE condition has two possible values, the repeat factor would be 8/2 or 4." Chip continues by noting that the first row of the decision table would be:

Condition	1	2	3	4	5	6	7	8
SITE LICENSE	Y	Y	Y	Y	N	N	N	N

"The next condition is EDUCATIONAL DISCOUNT, which also has two values. Dividing these two into the previous factor of four yields $4/2 = 2$ for the next repeat factor." Chip notes that the decision table now expands to:

Condition	1	2	3	4	5	6	7	8
SITE LICENSE	Y	Y	Y	Y	N	N	N	N
EDUCATIONAL DISCOUNT	Y	Y	N	N	Y	Y	N	N

Chip continues, "The last condition, DISCOUNT FOR QUANTITY, also has two values, and dividing these two into the previous repeat factor of two gives $2/2 = 1$, which should always be the repeat factor for the last row of the conditions." He notes that the completed condition entry is:

Condition	1	2	3	4	5	6	7	8
SITE LICENSE	Y	Y	Y	Y	N	N	N	N
EDUCATIONAL DISCOUNT	Y	Y	N	N	Y	Y	N	N
DISCOUNT FOR QUANTITY	Y	N	Y	N	Y	N	Y	N

Chip points out that when the actions are included, the completed decision table is:

Condition	1	2	3	4	5	6	7	8
SITE LICENSE	Y	Y	Y	Y	N	N	N	N
EDUCATIONAL DISCOUNT	Y	Y	N	N	Y	Y	N	N
DISCOUNT FOR QUANTITY	Y	N	Y	N	Y	N	Y	N

Actions	1	2	3	4	5	6	7	8
COST = SITE LICENSE COST	X	X	X	X				
COST = EDUCATIONAL COST × COPIES						X		
COST = DISCOUNT COST × COPIES							X	
COST = UPGRADE COST × COPIES								X
COST = (EDUC COST − DISC) × COPIES					X			

"I have proceeded to reduce some of the redundant actions, specifically those occurring when a SITE LICENSE has been obtained," Chip continues. "Since the actions are the same for SITE LICENSE values of Y, the educational and quantity discounts are meaningless to the condition and don't have to be considered. Rules 1 through 4 may be reduced to one rule." Chip concludes by noting that the final optimized decision table is:

Condition	1	2	3	4	5
SITE LICENSE	Y	N	N	N	N
EDUCATIONAL DISCOUNT	—	Y	Y	N	N
DISCOUNT FOR QUANTITY	—	Y	N	Y	N

Actions	1	2	3	4	5
COST = SITE LICENSE COST	X				
COST = EDUCATIONAL COST × COPIES			X		
COST = DISCOUNT COST × COPIES				X	
COST = UPGRADE COST × COPIES					X
COST = (EDUC COST − DISC) × COPIES		X			

The final decision table is shown in Figure E11.2 and contains the optimized decision table. There are three conditions: whether a site license, an educational discount, or a quantity discount is available. The top left quadrant contains the conditions. Directly below it are the actions. The condition alternatives are in the upper right quadrant, and the action entries are in the lower right quadrant. The actions show how the UPGRADE COST is determined for each condition, indicated by an **X** in the rule columns.

Exercises*

🖫 **E-1.**   Use Visible Analyst to view the Process repository entry for UP-DATE PENDING MICRO ORDER.

---

* Exercises preceded by a disk icon require the program Visible Analyst Workbench or another CASE tool. A disk is provided free of charge to any professor adopting this book. The examples on the disk may be imported into Visible Analyst Workbench and then used by students.

Conditions and Actions	1	2	3	4	5
Site License	Y	N	N	N	N
Educational Discount		Y	Y	N	N
Discount for Quantity		Y	N	Y	N
Upgrade cost = Site License Cost	X				
Upgrade cost = Educational Cost * Number of Copies			X		
Upgrade cost = Discount Cost * Number of Copies				X	
Upgrade cost = Cost Per Copy * Number of Copies					X
Upgrade cost = (Educational Cost - Discount) *Number of Copies		X			

FIGURE E11.2
Decision Table, UPGRADE COST

E-2. Modify and print the ACCUMULATIVE HARDWARE SUBTO-TALS Process entry. Add the **Process Description** "Accumulate the hardware subtotals. These include the number of machines for each hardware brand."

E-3. Modify and print the CONFIRM MICROCOMPUTER DELETION Process entry. Add the following Description:

Use the Mircrocomputer Record to format the Deletion Confirmation Screen (refer to the Delete Microcomputer Prototype Screen).

Prompt the user to press the **OK** button to confirm the deletion, otherwise press the **Cancel** button to cancel the deletion.

If the operator presses **OK** to delete the record, delete the record and display a "Record Deleted' message, otherwise display a 'Deletion Canceled' message.

E-4. Create Process specifications for process 6.6, VALIDATE MICRO-COMPUTER CHANGES. The Description for the process is:

Validate the changes to the MICROCOMPUTER MASTER. Include a note to use the edit criteria established for each element. Provide the following additional editing criteria:

The ROOM LOCATION must be valid for a particular campus.

The MONITOR must not be a lower grade than the graphics board. An example of this error would be a SVGA (higher resolution) graphics board paired with a VGA (lower resolution) monitor.

There must not be a second fixed disk without the first one.

The LAST PREVENTIVE MAINTENANCE DATE must not be greater than the current date.

The DATE PURCHASED must not be greater than the LAST PREVENTIVE MAINTENANCE DATE or greater than the current date.

The MODEL must conform to the type supported by the BRAND name.

No changes may be made to an inactive record.

Conditions and Actions	1	2	3	4	5
Matching Software Record Found	Y	Y	Y	Y	N
Version of Software Found	Y	Y	Y	N	
Matching Microcomputer Record Found	Y	Y	N		
Campus Code Found In Table	Y	N			
Display 'No Matching Software Record' Error Message					X
Display 'Version Not Available' Error Message				X	
Display 'Machine Not Found' Error Message			X		
Display 'Campus Code Not Found' Error Message		X			
Display Location Information	X				

FIGURE E11.3
Decision Table, FIND SOFTWARE LOCATION.

🖫 **E-5.** Create process specifications for process 1.4, CREATE SOFTWARE LOG FILE. Use the data flow diagram examples to determine inputs and outputs. Process details are:

Format the SOFTWARE LOG RECORD from the following information:

The confirmed NEW SOFTWARE RECORD elements.

The following system elements: System date, System time, User ID, Network ID.

When the record has been formatted, write to the SOFTWARE LOG FILE.

🖫 **E-6.** Produce process specifications for process 9.7.2, FIND MATCHING HARDWARE RECORD. This is part of a program producing a report showing all microcomputers on which each software package would be located. Use Visible Analyst to view data-flow diagram 9.7. Use structured English to depict the following logic:

For each SOFTWARE RECORD, loop while there is a matching hardware inventory number. Within the loop, accomplish the following tasks:

Randomly read the MICROCOMPUTER MASTER file.

If a record is found, format the MATCHING MICROCOMPUTER RECORD information.

If no record is found, format a NO MATCHING error line.

Furthermore, if the found MICROCOMPUTER RECORD is inactive, indicating that it has been removed from service, format an INACTIVE MATCHING MICROCOMPUTER error line.

🖫 **E-7.** Use paper or any word processor that supports tables to create the CALCULATE SOFTWARE UPGRADE COST decision table, shown in Figure E11.2.

🖫 **E-8.** Create the FIND SOFTWARE LOCATION decision table, representing the logic for an inquiry program for displaying all locations for a given SOFTWARE TITLE and VERSION. The conditions have been created and optimized, resulting in five rules, illustrated in Figure E11.3. Enter the actions that need to be entered and an X in the column related to the conditions. If you are using a word processor, print the final decision table. The conditions and actions are represented by the following logic:

The SOFTWARE MASTER file is located for the specified TITLE. If the matching record is not found, an error message is displayed. Since there may be several versions, the VERSION NUMBER on the record is checked for a match to the version entered. If the requested version is not found, further records are read using the alternate index. If all records are read and the version number is not found, an error message VERSION NOT AVAILABLE is displayed.

Once the correct software has been located, a matching MICRO-COMPUTER MASTER record is obtained. If the MICROCOMPUTER MASTER is not found, the error message MACHINE NOT FOUND is displayed. For each matching machine, the CAMPUS TABLE is searched for the CAMPUS LOCATION code. If the code is not found, the message CAMPUS CODE NOT FOUND is displayed.

If no errors occur, the requested information is displayed.

⊟ **E-9.** Create a decision table for a batch update of the MICROCOMPUTER MASTER FILE. There are three types of updates: Add, Delete, and Change.

The MICROCOMPUTER MASTER record must be read. If the transaction is an Add and the master is not found, format and write the new microcomputer master record. Print a valid transaction line on an UPDATE REPORT. For a Change or Delete transaction, print a CHANGE ERROR LINE or a DELETE ERROR LINE if the master record is not found.

If the master record is found, check the active code. If the record is inactive and the transaction is an Add, format and rewrite the new microcomputer master record. Print a valid transaction line on an UPDATE REPORT. For a Change or Delete transaction, print a CHANGE ERROR LINE or a DELETE ERROR LINE.

If the MICROCOMPUTER MASTER RECORD is active and the transaction is an Add, print an ADD ERROR LINE. For a Change transaction, format the changes and rewrite the MICROCOM-PUTER MASTER RECORD. Print the VALID TRANSACTION LINE. For a Delete transaction, change the ACTIVE CODE to inactive and rewrite the MICROCOMPUTER MASTER RECORD. Print the VALID TRANSACTION LINE.

12

ANALYZING SEMISTRUCTURED DECISION SUPPORT SYSTEMS

METHODS AVAILABLE

Three major concerns arise when analyzing semistructured decision support systems. The systems analyst needs to know (1) whether decision makers are primarily analytic or heuristic; (2) how decisions are made in the three problem-solving phases of intelligence, design, and choice; and (3) the multiple-criteria methods that are useful in solving semistructured problems.

Decision support systems (DSS) can function in many ways. They can organize information for decision situations, interact with decision makers, expand the decision makers' horizons, present information for decision makers' understanding, add structure to decisions, and use multiple-criteria decision-making models. Multiple-criteria models include tradeoff processes, weighting methods, and sequential elimination methods, which are all well suited to handling the complexity and semistructured nature of many problems supported through DSS. This chapter covers what the systems analyst needs to know about analytic and heuristic decision makers, about the three phases of problem solving supported by DSS, and about the multiple-criteria methods needed to solve semistructured problems.

DECISION SUPPORT SYSTEMS

Decision support systems possess many characteristics that differentiate them from other, more traditional management information systems. End users of DSS, by virtue of the types of problems they address and the learning they undergo, also possess special characteristics that need to be considered.

Characteristics of a Decision Support System

First and foremost, a decision support system is a way to organize information intended for use in decision making. It involves the use of a database for a specific decision-making purpose. A DSS does not just automate transformations performed on data; neither does it simply provide output in the form of reports. Rather, a decision support system supports the decision-making process through the presentation of information that is designed for the decision maker's problem-solving approach and application needs. It neither displaces judgment nor makes a decision for the user.

A DSS allows the decision maker to interact with it in a natural manner by virtue of the careful design of the user interface. A useful DSS will challenge and eventually change a decision maker. By contrast, a management information system (MIS) provides output but no real impetus for change in the person receiving it. Interacting with a DSS will prove to be new and challenging for most decision makers and will provide new perspectives on the decision-making process that are attractive and understandable yet innovative. By furnishing a new way to see problems and opportunities, a DSS eventually changes the user's decision-making process and, along with it, the user.

Decision support systems are designed to help support decisions involving complex problems that are formulated as semistructured. Because such problems remain resistant to complete computerization, a solution per se is not the goal of the DSS; instead a DSS supports the decision process that leads to a solution.

A DSS may be constructed to support one-time decisions, those that are infrequent, or those that occur routinely. The type of problem or opportunity best addressed through use of a DSS is one both that ultimately requires human judgment—either because humans feel it is inappropriate to relinquish their judgment or because the problem cannot be fully automated—and is complex enough to benefit from the time savings to be gained through partial automation. Medical decisions involving differential diagnosis are a good example of such problems.

A decision support system is typically designed for either a particular decision maker or a group of decision makers. This high degree of individualization allows the system designer to customize important system features to adapt to the type of representations (graphs, tables, charts, and so on) and interface that the user understands best.

Rather than building a specific DSS "from scratch," a systems analyst can use a package of interrelated hardware and software called a DSS generator (DSSG). There has been considerable growth in the sales of DSSGs because they can lessen the time and cost associated with building a case-specific DSS. Hardware and software designated as DSS tools aid in the building of both specific DSSs and DSS generators.

A decision support system is best conceptualized as a process instead of a product. Figure 12.1 contrasts the product orientation of the traditional MIS with the process-oriented DSS. Notice that the focus of the DSS is on the decision maker's interaction with the system and not on the output generated. As discussed in Chapter 2, processes are ways to transform inputs into outputs. In the instance of a DSS, the process works to transform the user—the decision maker—by changing and improving upon his or her decision-making performance.

What this process orientation means is that DSSs are evolutionary in nature. Decision support systems change as the needs of the end user change, and the decision maker changes by interacting with the DSS process.

Decision Support System Users

Decision making in organizations occurs on three main levels: the strategic, the managerial, and the operational, as discussed in Chapter 2. Many of the decisions required on the operational level can be successfully and thor-

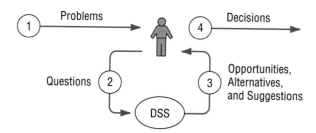

FIGURE 12.1
Decision support systems
have a process orientation
focusing on the decision
maker's interaction with
the system.

oughly automated. The same can be said for many routine managerial decisions. However, when problems and opportunities cannot be totally structured and when human judgment and experience are required to make a decision, traditional management information systems are often considered inadequate for the task. It is in developing the solution of semistructured, complex problems that a DSS can be of use. This kind of problem most often occurs on the strategic and managerial levels.

Although the use of a decision support system is not limited to middle- and upper-level managers or chief executive officers, these individuals are most often the primary users. They bring with them differing decision-making styles, differing needs, and differing levels of sophistication. The DSS designer therefore needs to take specific decision-making attributes into consideration so that it is possible for the user to interact successfully with the DSS. If the end user is too busy or too threatened by the prospect of interacting with the DSS, a technical go-between or assistant may be used to interact with the computer. In this way, the decision maker is free to analyze and react to the process, not to the mechanics of it.

Since DSSs are designed specifically for a user or a group of users (as in group DSS, commonly abbreviated GDSS), systems analysts need to be acutely aware of how a decision maker's style might influence DSS design. In the following sections, we discuss several concepts pertinent to decision support systems, including decision making under risk; decision-making style; and how decisions can be classified as structured, unstructured, and semistructured.

DECISION-MAKING CONCEPTS RELEVANT TO DSS

Many concepts help inform us about the relationship between decision making and decision support systems, including theories about certainty, uncertainty, and risk; and how they help shape a decision maker's style as either analytic or heuristic. The three problem-solving phases of intelligence, choice, and design as they are supported by decision support systems are also of interest here.

Decision Making under Risk

Classical decision-making theory usually assumes that decisions are made under three sets of conditions: certainty, uncertainty, and risk. Certainty means that we know everything in advance of making our decision. A common management science model that assumes conditions of certainty is linear programming, where the resources, rates of consumption, constraints, and profits are all assumed to be known and correct. Uncertainty implies just the opposite; we know nothing about the probabilities or the consequences of our decisions.

Between the two extremes of certainty and uncertainty lies the huge set of conditions called risk. Decisions made under risk assume that we are somewhat knowledgeable about our alternatives (controllable variables), about what we cannot control but only estimate (environmental variables), and about what the outcomes will be (dependent variables). Not only can we estimate the environmental variables, but we can also estimate the probability that they will occur. This information can be 100 percent accurate, partially accurate, or false; but we still attempt to base the decision on the information we have. Most business decisions are made under risk.

AN EXAMPLE OF UNCERTAINTY, CERTAINTY, AND RISK. To help understand these three sets of conditions, suppose you had to decide whether to carry an umbrella into work one morning. There is only one circumstance that represents complete certainty; it is raining now. If you open the door, look outside, and it is raining, you know you must use an umbrella or you will get drenched. If the sun is out now, it still might rain in the afternoon.

Risk implies that we have an idea about the alternatives, probabilities, and outcomes. If we listen to the weather forecast on television and the forecaster says there is a 40 percent chance of rain, we can use that information to make our decision about whether to carry an umbrella.

To understand conditions of complete uncertainty, visualize being locked in a room without windows or visitors. Furthermore, your television cable company is having service problems, your radio's batteries are corroded, and your newspaper has been lost en route. In this situation, all of your sources of information about the outside weather would be gone.

But is this uncertainty? If all of your sources of information were taken away, wouldn't you still be able to make a decision under risk? Most everyone would be able to do so, because most people would realize where they were and what time of year it was. In other words, we know from experience what the probability of rain is in our location at this time of year. This example suggests that experience, as well as information, helps us to make decisions.

The relationship among certainty, uncertainty, and risk, along with the resources of information and experience, is shown in Figure 12.2. Some individuals rely more heavily on information, while others prefer to base their decisions on experience. The next subsection builds upon this relationship as it discusses decision-making style.

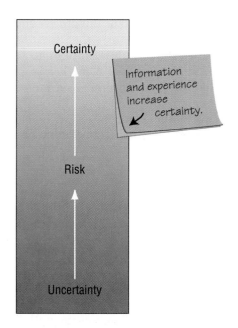

Decision-Making Style

The way in which information is gathered, processed, and used, together with the manner in which decisions are communicated and implemented, forms the parameters of decision-making style. Decision makers are often characterized as being either analytic or heuristic.

ANALYTIC DECISION MAKING. An analytic decision maker relies on information that is systematically acquired and systematically evaluated to narrow alternatives and make a choice that is information based. As shown in Figure 12.3, analytic decision makers learn by analyzing a particular situation. They are methodical, using step-by-step procedures to make decisions. Analytic decision makers value quantitative information and the models that generate and use it.

Additionally, decision makers with an analytic style use mathematics to model problems and algorithms to solve them. An analytic decision maker seeks optimal—rather than completely satisfying—solutions, being content with answers which satisfy most but not all requirements. Analytic decision makers use decision techniques such as graphing, probability mod-

Analytic Decision Maker	**Heuristic Decision Maker**
• Learns by analyzing	• Learns by acting
• Uses step-by-step procedure	• Uses trial and error
• Values quantitative information and models	• Values experience
• Builds mathematical models and algorithms	• Relies on common sense
• Seeks optimal solution	• Seeks satisficing solution

FIGURE 12.3
Decision makers can be characterized as either analytic or heuristic by examining the information they use and how they make their decisions.

els, and mathematical techniques to ensure a sound decision-making process. These methods, however, require that the information employed is: (1) available, (2) reasonable, (3) complete, and (4) accurate.

An example of an analytic decision maker is a manager who, when faced with a problem, employs a computerized management science model to resolve conflicts in an optimal way. To accomplish this goal, the manager determines an objective function and constraints, builds mathematical relationships, gathers information for the model, and solves the problem.

HEURISTIC DECISION MAKING. A decision maker who uses heuristics is making decisions with the aid of some guidelines (or rules of thumb), although they may not always be applied consistently or systematically. They seek a satisficing, not an optimal, solution. Heuristics are generally experience-based.

Heuristic decision makers learn by acting. They use trial and error to find a solution. Because of this, they value experience, relying on common sense to guide them.

An example is a manager deciding heuristically from which company to purchase raw materials. Based on past experience, the manager knows that materials shipped from the East Coast tend to arrive at the plant on time. Formulating that experience as a heuristic, or rule of thumb, the manager decides to try and pick a supplier of raw materials from the East Coast.

The decision-making style of managers relates back to the openness and closedness of organizational systems. If information in the business is free-flowing, the opportunities for the use of decision aids and systematic analysis may be greater. If timely information is difficult to acquire, the organization may be encouraging managers (albeit unwillingly) toward a more heuristic style.

IMPLICATIONS FOR DEVELOPMENT OF DECISION SUPPORT SYSTEMS. Analytic decision makers are systematic in their evaluation of alternatives in a decision situation. A DSS for an analytic decision maker should include several mathematical and graphical models that allow desired comparisons. It is also important to make supporting evidence for alternatives available through the DSS.

Heuristic decision makers are somewhat systematic in their approach to decision making, but they use rules of thumb for guidelines instead of carefully reasoning through each alternative each time it is presented. A decision support system supporting a heuristic thinker might present summary information on alternatives rather than detail pros and cons in copious output. A DSS for heuristic decision makers might also display past decisions and their outcomes in support of the preference for experience-based data. Further discussions of DSS output are featured in Chapter 15, which deals with output design.

Problem-Solving Phases

Decision making (or problem solving) is a process and is conceived of in phases rather than in steps. In phases, the occurrence of behavior swells and tapers off, with some overlap between each phase. In stepped behavior, one

Walking into Open Arms

"I helped start Open Arms four years ago, after I earned my MBA," says Maria Ewing-Barton, the 36-year-old administrator of a health-care referral service. "When the County Medical Society realized that the health-care services here in Laramie weren't being fully utilized, a group of us thought about what we could do to fill the gap. We aim to match up patients with appropriate health-care providers. For various reasons (transiency, poverty, newly transferred to the city), patients have no regular contact with a health-care provider. I see anywhere from five to twenty patients a day. Some have chronic illnesses, such as alcoholism; some have a common cold. I assess what level of treatment is relevant and what funding is possible, and then I decide what the next step for the patient will be. For example, should they see a private physician today or schedule an appointment with an eye doctor sometime in the future? I called you in to help me strengthen and justify the decision-making process I go through in making referrals, maybe through the creation of a DSS.

"I'd like to have a lot of information at my fingertips so that I can make decisions quickly. Although most cases are not life or death, some are serious. Also, I don't have much time to spend with each patient. I want to be sure I can justify my referral decisions, since some local doctors think I'm usurping their decision-making power. Most of the people in health care here trust my judgment, but the occasional physician is still skeptical of my qualifications. They resent the fact that my training is in management, not health care. As an upshot, I have to be very methodical in defending my referral decisions to them.

"I keep statistics on the patients we've referred, and I read everything I can get my hands on in the medical and health-care administration journals, although they don't bear directly on what we do. I also talk to other administrators to keep current on the services their facilities are offering. What's frustrating is that the services available change so often. It seems as if local hospitals are only concerned with marketing their profitable specialties.

"I've been playing with the data I've accumulated, looking for patterns and trying to create some sort of model for the way Open Arms is working. As you can see, I have an old PC computer here in my office, and I've spent many evenings entering data to help formulate reasonable models of Open Arms. Although accurate records are important, I want to do more with the data than merely store it.

"Quite frankly, a large part of my decision on whether to refer is based on how I size up a person initially. I know it's important to be objective, but with so little time to make a decision, I usually go with my heart and not my head. Eventually, I would like to rely on the numbers I generate with my PC to match patients with health-care providers. Then I can justify my decisions when necessary. It's a way to make more effective matches, too, that are fairer to everyone."

What type of decision maker is Maria? Which of her characteristics lead to this viewpoint? Describe what you think is Maria's typical decision-making process regarding patient referrals.

---

step occurs independently of the next and is completed before the next step is carried out.

The three phases of problem solving are intelligence, design, and choice (Simon, 1965). The decision maker begins with the intelligence phase, with design and choice following in phased succession. Let's examine each phase as it relates to decision-maker behavior.

INTELLIGENCE. Intelligence is awareness of a problem or opportunity. In this phase, the decision maker searches the external and internal business environments, checking for decisions that need to be made, problems that need to be solved, or opportunities that need to be examined. Intelligence means an active awareness of changes in environments that call for action.

Intelligence translates to vigilance: continual searching and scanning. The intelligence phase provides the impetus for the other two phases and always precedes them.

DESIGN. In the design phase, the decision maker formulates a problem and analyzes several alternative solutions. The design phase allows the decision maker to generate and analyze alternatives for their potential applicability.

CHOICE. In the choice phase, the decision maker chooses a solution to the problem or an opportunity identified in the intelligence phase. This choice follows from the foregoing analysis in the design phase and is reinforced by information gained in the choice phase. It also includes implementation of the decision maker's choice. Other authors have added separate phases for implementation and evaluation.

SEMISTRUCTURED DECISIONS

Many people conceive of decisions as existing on a continuum from structured to unstructured. Structured decisions are those where all or most of the variables are known and can be totally programmed. Decisions that are structured are routine and require little human judgment once the variables are programmed. Analysis of structured decisions is covered extensively in Chapter 11.

Unstructured decisions are those that are currently resistant to computerization and depend primarily on intuition. Semistructured decisions are those that are partially programmable but still require human judgment. Decision support systems are most powerful when addressing semistructured decisions, since a DSS supports the decision maker in all phases of decision making but does not mandate one final answer.

It is hypothesized that all decisions may contain "deep structure"—that is, structure that is present but not yet apparent. If this is true, then eventually all decisions could be treated as semistructured, and the usefulness of a DSS would be substantially broader.

An argument used in support of the presence of deep structure is that the game of tic-tac-toe appears to be unstructured to a five-year-old child. While the child is learning to play the game, it isn't clear which move is the best, and the game itself seems suspenseful and exciting. As the child grows up, however, it soon becomes apparent that there is indeed a structure. If certain rules are applied, the outcome can be maximized by guaranteeing at least a tie.

However, tic-tac-toe is not like a business situation. First, the rules for tic-tac-toe are simple: Place an X in one of the spaces and wait until your opponent responds. Second, the objective is simple: Tie, or perhaps win, by placing three Xs (or Os) in a row if your opponent makes an error. The only factor that makes the game unstructured is the decision skill of the decision maker. That is, the average child doesn't yet possess the analytical skills or experience needed to win the game.

Dimensions of Semistructured Decisions

Decisions are called semistructured or unstructured for a number of reasons. It is useful to visualize the dimensions of structured decisions as a cube, as illustrated in Figure 12.4. The three dimensions are:

1. The degree of decision-making skill required.
2. The degree of problem complexity.
3. The number of decision criteria considered.

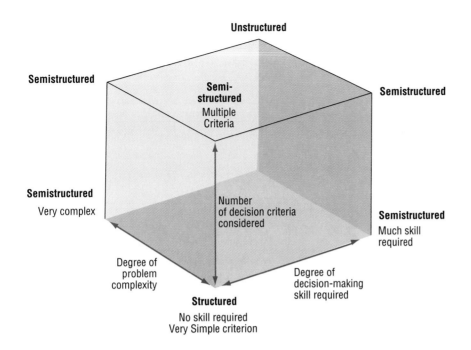

In the tic-tac-toe example, the five-year-old child would not see the game as structured even though there was a single criterion and very simple rules, because the child's decision-making skill has not been sufficiently developed.

DEGREE OF DECISION-MAKING SKILL REQUIRED. The degree of decision-making skill relates back to the concepts of analytic and heuristic decision makers. Decision-making skill is measured in the analytic and experience-based maturity of the decision maker. A DSS could help upgrade decision-making skill by providing easy-to-comprehend models (for the analytic thinker) or analogies (for the heuristic thinker).

THE DEGREE OF PROBLEM COMPLEXITY. If a problem is highly complex, it seems semistructured or even unstructured. A DSS can help in this regard by encouraging the decision maker to define the boundary of the system, and he or she would accomplish this goal by clearly defining the problem and limiting the number of variables. In addition, the DSS should provide support in helping the decision maker systematically eliminate some alternatives. Decision support systems are needed to organize information, track variables, and present the problems, alternatives, and choices in a manner easily understandable to the manager.

NUMBER OF CRITERIA CONSIDERED. A manager concerned with a single decision criterion is dealing with a structured problem, but most real-world problems have multiple, conflicting goals and multiple decision criteria. Consequently, they are by nature semistructured. An example of a decision maker dealing with multiple conflicting objectives is a production manager deciding on a production schedule whose objectives include keeping costs to a minimum, maximizing customer satisfaction by meeting the delivery schedule, keeping quality high, and minimizing idle time. The production

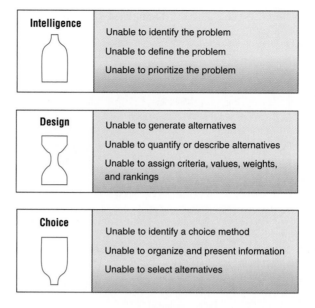

manager cannot optimize one of these objectives unless other objectives are sacrificed.

A decision involving multiple criteria may include choosing a software package that is powerful, has clear documentation, and is user-friendly but inexpensive. Since it is unlikely that any single product fulfills all of the requirements, the decision maker must assign importance (rank or weight) to each criterion. Decision support systems are invaluable in helping decision makers handle multiple criteria. A more extensive discussion of multiple-objective and multiple-criteria models follows in a later section of this chapter.

Semistructured Decisions in Intelligence, Design, and Choice

No matter what the decision is, the decision has to go through each of the three phases (intelligence, design, and choice) in the decision-making process. Semistructured decisions are made in each of the phases of decision making. Sometimes the decision is easy and other times it is very cumbersome, but rarely do we encounter a problem in which every decision-making phase is equally difficult.

Figure 12.5 identifies some of the bottlenecks that occur in each of the three phases of the decision-making process. Bottlenecks in the intelligence phase occur because the decision maker is unable to identify a problem, define it, or set priorities for tackling the problem. During the design phase, bottlenecks can occur because the decision maker cannot generate feasible alternatives, assign values and/or outcomes to the alternatives, or establish performance criteria to compare alternatives. The choice phase can present bottlenecks, too, when the decision maker is unable to choose a decision method, organize and present information, or select an alternative. The following discussion focuses on how decision support systems can alleviate bottlenecks and thus assist the decision maker.

INTELLIGENCE PHASE DECISION SUPPORT SYSTEMS. Decision making is often difficult because the problem itself is difficult to identify. Problems are noticed only if appropriate performance measures are put in place to highlight

The Proof Is in the Pizza

"I really enjoy my current position," says 53-year-old Hal Lupino. He is the district manager for the Calliope chain of seven Nebraska pizza palaces, which his father and uncle founded and still run. There are four stores in Lincoln (where the business started), two in Omaha, and one in Grand Island. They have expanded from small take-out places to sit-down restaurants that feature a giant, electronically controlled calliope that plays music while pizza eaters dine. However, the main attraction of the chain is still a secret family pizza recipe.

"Some people think I'm too old to be a district manager, but I have the best of both worlds in this job," Hal continues. "I've got a lot of decision-making power, with Dad and Uncle Reg getting up in years. But I still talk with lots of customers, too. The stores' profits have been increasing since 1964. We added the last store in Lincoln in 1994.

"'Everyone, inside and out, has been sort of pressuring us to expand again. My son is an MBA student and he recommended you to help me set up a DSS to support location decisions.

"My thinking is that we should make the most of the delivery network we already have set up, since it's so darn expensive to move the ingredients we need. With the rotten luck the farmers are having and the fact that there are more sand dunes than people in western Nebraska, I think expansion there is out. My gut reaction is that competition is too fierce to get anything else going in Omaha.

"But I'll let managers and customers be my guide on where to locate next. I'm a people person. Why not ask someone a question rather than read a report about it? My father and uncle are different, though. Those guys love numbers. So if I don't give them some numbers to back up my decisions, I'll have a hard time getting them implemented. I've been humoring them by passing out questionnaires on new locations to our customers. Someday I'll have my secretary tally what they wrote. I've been reading their open-ended comments though; they're more interesting to me.

"I keep notes about what I hear from customers and managers on the bulk napkins we buy for the restaurants. They go in here (he indicates an in-basket piled with napkins) when I've read them. Otherwise, I keep 'em in my folder. I don't throw much away, but finding a key comment is a tough task.

"I guess I'm a slow-poke when it comes to making a decision. I go over and over what I've seen in the markets we serve and review all my experience in the business and all the talks with our customers. I keep going back to our last location decision when we opened the new store in Lincoln. If the proof is in the pudding, then Lincoln may just be the spot for the new one, too."

How can a decision support system make Hal a better decision maker? In particular, what features of his style could it support? What features of his style might a decision support system change?

---

them. Suppose a clothing store set a goal of selling $30,000 worth of merchandise in a week and always exceeded that goal; no problem would be identified. But what if more information revealed that for the square footage leased, the store needs to make a minimum of $35,000 per week to stay in business? Without the additional information, the problem goes unnoticed. An effective DSS, therefore, must contain mechanisms for recognizing problems.

Once a problem is identified, it needs to be defined. A DSS could help the decision maker determine the scope of the problem to minimize the complexity of the decision. A store manager might choose to limit the problem to strategic pricing or strategic advertising. Other possible approaches, such as firing employees or changing the merchandise mix, would not be considered.

The final step in the intelligence phase is to assign a priority to the problem. The problem may be of an immediate nature, or it may be a future opportunity that could be pursued if other, more pressing problems are addressed first. For example, an opportunity to expand may look very attractive initially, but it may be delayed because of more pressing problems in the original store. Decision support systems are needed for problem and project selection.

CHAPTER 12:
ANALYZING SEMISTRUCTURED
DECISION SUPPORT SYSTEMS

DESIGN PHASE DECISION SUPPORT SYSTEMS. In a relationship that parallels the one just discussed, alternatives need to be identified. A decision support system can aid in generating alternatives that might not have occurred to the decision maker. Experience-based DSSs can compare the current situation with similar scenarios and guide the manager through the maze of alternatives. Some alternative situations that the clothing manager could investigate include varying the types and amounts of advertising or changing the prices of certain merchandise items to attract more customers.

Next the alternatives need to be quantified or described. A decision maker could retrieve data from a database, collect new data, and manipulate data. A more heuristic decision maker might take an extra-organizational approach, build analogies, and seek opinions or consider various scenarios. The clothing store manager could gather quantitative information on, for example, costs and the effectiveness of advertising, the competitor's pricing, and price elasticity. The manager could also gather information from employees and customers. This information could be compiled and summarized for decision-making purposes.

Once alternatives are generated and organized, performance criteria need to be established. Then the decision maker can assign values, risks, weights, and/or a rank to each alternative. The clothing store manager may set weekly sales volume as one criterion but may also want to include weekly costs, as well as intangibles, such as customer satisfaction and employee morale. Spreadsheets are excellent ways to list various alternatives, and graphs provide vivid visuals to limit the number of alternatives being considered.

Decision support systems can represent possible choices to decision makers in ways that may not conform to their typical way of seeing the world. For example, if a problem solver is not accustomed to considering other alternatives, the DSS can suggest them. In essence, the DSS can expand the field of vision for the decision maker.

The interaction between the DSS and the decision maker is strong in this phase. It is entirely feasible to build a DSS that will work through several "what-if" scenarios with numerous variables, something that is too complex for lone decision makers to do. In this way, a DSS enhances the design phase by greatly expanding the number of possible actions that can be considered in detail, as well as by suggesting new alternatives that the decision maker might otherwise overlook.

CHOICE PHASE DECISION SUPPORT SYSTEMS. Choosing a solution is obviously important, and in semistructured decisions the choice must be left up to the judgment of the decision maker who is supported by the DSS. First, the DSS can be of help by reminding the decision maker of what methods of choice are appropriate for the problem. This means the DSS can include suggestions for analytic techniques (which management science models to rely on) or heuristic techniques (how best to display information when making a choice). For example, our store manager may want to approach the problem on a simple cost-benefit basis, since the approaches being considered do not involve a great many intangibles (unlike the approaches to firing employees or changing store hours). By helping present methods for selection of alternatives a DSS can support the choice phase.

The decision support system can also help the decision maker organize and present the information. For one decision maker, this might mean defining variables and formulating constraints that make up a management sci-

CONSULTING OPPORTUNITY 12.3

The History of Scheduling

"I like my work here at the university," Stuart Dent admits. At age 22, he is younger than many of the students and staff he deals with in his job of scheduling classes for the approximately 27,000 students who attend regular semester sessions. "I've been here two years, ever since I graduated in art history," Stu Dent continues.

"The person who had the job before me generated a whole stack of computer reports that showed each department's course schedule, availability of faculty, how often courses needed to be offered, what day they were offered on last, student preferences for course days, and availability of rooms. All that was a jumble, so I called you in to help. I know you teach a DSS course on campus.

"I want to schedule each required course at a time that is satisfactory to both faculty and students. I think the larger picture is important. Courses that occur in a cycle (for example, many graduate-level courses) should be offered when promised. I want to eliminate double-bind situations where a student is unable to take a course because its prerequisite hasn't ever been offered.

"I guess I'm pretty idealistic. I like thinking about historical trends and trying to characterize them. I asked my co-workers about the scheduling problem, but they keep sending me to the mountain of computer reports made by the guy who had my job before me. I'm so sick of their advice that I've 'joined the enemy' and decided to actually do something for the students. I've been interviewing a handful of students from each college on campus.

"I've also reviewed my own scheduling hassles as a student, in case they offer a key. Here are some of the charts I've sketched to summarize information from my experiences and the interviews, but as you can see, it's slow going.

"Although the old computer reports seem virtually useless, I've been careful to inventory them and maintain them. In fact, I labeled them and put them on a shelf here in my office. I know the value of history. The tapes I have of student interviews contain enough 'horror stories' about five-year undergrads being standard because of poor scheduling that they may be potentially damaging to the administration. I've duplicated them, and both sets of tapes are at home.

"I want to make my decisions quickly, since scheduling for each semester is done well in advance and must be done twice a year. The students accept me and respect that I'm trying to do a good job. But Cyril, my boss, likes numbers, and I know he'll never go along with my suggestions for scheduling unless I back up my intuition with some quantitative data. The people I work with think I'm overwhelmed by the volume of data this department generates. They're doing what they always do and ignoring me until I sort everything out. But I'm confident in my ability to make good decisions."

In what ways can a decision support system help Stu? Describe how it can help in the intelligence, design, and choice phases of his decision making.

---

ence model. For another manager, this may mean selecting the type of graph (line, bar, or pie chart), the scale, or the range of data to be considered. For our clothing store example, the manager might prefer to see the information displayed on a personal computer's spreadsheet.

Finally, the decision support system needs to be able to handle multiple-criteria decision problems. The DSS would ideally carry out cumbersome manipulations but leave the decision up to the personal judgment of the decision maker. Since our store manager preferred information in the form of a spreadsheet, a trade-off or weighting technique might be appropriate. Due to the increasing importance of making decisions based on multiple criteria, the subject is covered in more detail in the next section.

MULTIPLE-CRITERIA DECISION MAKING

Even in problems with complete information, a limited number of variables can be semistructured. These problems have numerous, often conflicting objectives, and they are of much interest to the DSS designer. In modeling these decisions as realistically as possible, researchers have developed numerous approaches to evaluating multiple-objective or multiple-criteria problems.

Multiple-criteria approaches allow decision makers to set their own priorities, and most allow the decision maker to perform sensitivity analysis by asking "what-if" types of questions. These methods include the trade-off process, weighting methods, the conjunctive constraints approach, Analytic Hierarchy Processing and goal programming. When included in DSS or MIS, multiple-criteria decision-making models give the decision maker a more powerful way to evaluate alternatives in the design phase of decision making.

Using a Trade-off Process

The trade-off approach is often referred to as a favorite of the statesman Benjamin Franklin. When he had a difficult problem to solve, he said that he drew a line to divide a sheet of paper into two columns. On one side, he wrote all of the reasons pro, and on the other all of the reasons con. Then he would begin to cross out any pros that were equal to any cons. Sometimes it would take two pros to equal a con, or vice versa.

The designer of decision support systems can use an updated version of this method in designing a decision support system. An example of this approach is depicted in Figure 12.6. Here we have two alternatives available to the decision maker, in this case a rent or buy decision. The advantages of each alternative are listed in columns *A* and *C* of the spreadsheet. In columns *B* and *D,* a number 1 is entered to indicate that the advantage is still a consideration.

As the decision maker analyzes the problem, any advantages in the *A* column are compared with advantages in column *C*. If the advantages are considered equal, the 1s are changed to 0s. Sometimes the decision maker may want to zero out a group of advantages, perhaps three on one side and

FIGURE 12.6
Using a trade-off approach to compare two alternatives with the help of a decision support system.

	A	B	C	D
1	RENTAL		PURCHASE	
2				
3	NO CAPITAL IS TIED UP	1	TAX ADVANTAGES	1
4	NO FINANCING REQUIRED	1	OWN SYSTEM OUTRIGHT	1
5	EASY TO CHANGE SYSTEMS	1	FULL CONTROL	1
6	MAINTENANCE INCLUDED	1	SAVES 20,000 OVER 6 YEARS	1
7	KNOW RENTAL COMPANY WELL	1		
8	INSURANCE INCLUDED	1		
9				
10				
11				
12		6		4
13				
14				
15				
16				
17				
18				
19				
20				

	A	B	C	D
1	RENTAL		PURCHASE	
2				
3	NO CAPITAL IS TIED UP	1	TAX ADVANTAGES	0
4	NO FINANCING REQUIRED	1	OWN SYSTEM OUTRIGHT	0
5	EASY TO CHANGE SYSTEMS	0	FULL CONTROL	0
6	MAINTENANCE INCLUDED	0	SAVES 20,000 OVER 6 YEARS	0
7	KNOW RENTAL COMPANY WELL	0		
8	INSURANCE INCLUDED	1		
9				
10				
11				
12		3		0
13				
14				
15				
16				
17				
18				
19				
20				

FIGURE 12.7
Zeroing out advantages that are equal to each other in order to decide on an alternative.

two on the other. The process continues until either column *B* or *D* totals 0, as in Figure 12.7. The trade-off approach has obvious limitations, but it still must not be overlooked as a decision aid for solving difficult problems.

Using Weighting Methods

Students encounter a weighting method in every course they take when their grade is computed. Various components of the course are worth a certain percentage—for instance, 20 percent each for the first and second ex-

Source: Arnie Levin © 1997
The *Cartoon Bank.*
All Rights Reserved.

	A	B	C	D	E
1	%	ATTRIBUTES	DATAQUIX	BIGBASE	FLEXI FILE
2					
3	.20	FAST RESPONSE TIME	10	6	5
4	.05	MANY OUTPUT OPTIONS	6	4	7
5	.25	EASY TO USE	5	8	7
6	.20	EASY ERROR RECOVERY	10	7	6
7	.05	FLEXIBILITY	10	8	10
8	.10	GOOD DOCUMENTATION	8	9	10
9	.05	HOT LINE SUPPORT	8	10	5
10	.10	ABLE TO HANDLE BIG FILES	2	10	5
11					
12					
13					
14					
15		TOTALS	7.45	7.60	6.55
16					
17					
18					
19					
20					

ams, 20 percent for the term paper, and 40 percent for the final examination. Numerical scores for each component are then multiplied by the percentages, and the final grade is calculated.

A spreadsheet example of a weighting approach is depicted in Figure 12.8. Here a purchase decision is needed regarding three database packages appropriate for a business. Each of the attributes is assigned a value by the decision maker. After examining the software packages, the decision maker assigns a grade to each attribute for each package—in this case, a grade of 1 to 10. The total score is then calculated in the last row of the spreadsheet, and the decision maker chooses the package with the highest total score. The decision maker has the opportunity to change some of the values for attributes, or even the scores assigned to each package in case "what-if" analysis is desired.

Using Sequential Elimination by Lexicography

Sometimes decision makers feel weighting methods disguise the best features of an alternative by taking a weighted average of all attributes. One method that features the importance of individual attributes is sequential elimination by lexicography. This method is less demanding than weighting because the attributes are simply ranked in order of importance rather than assigned weights. Intra-attribute values are still specified as in weighting.

An example of lexicography is found in Figure 12.9. A matrix of attributes and alternatives is entered into a spreadsheet. The spreadsheet is sorted, first by attribute from top (most important) to bottom (least important). Next, the alternatives are sorted row by row. Only those alternatives that have the highest possible score (in this case 10) for the first attribute are considered further. In other words, only 5, 6, 3, and 4 are potential answers.

FIGURE 12.9
Using sequential elimination by lexicography, which ranks the importance of individual attributes.

	A	B	C	D	E	F	G	H
1	ATTRIBUTE	RANK	CAR 5	CAR 6	CAR 3	CAR 4	CAR 2	CAR 1
2								
3	PRICE	1	10	10	10	10	5	4
4	MILEAGE	2	10	8	5	10	3	2
5	SAFETY	3	5	3	8	3	10	10
6	RESALE	4	7	9	10	5	5	10
7	COMFORT	5	10	3	2	10	2	3

The data is sorted by rank (1 is most important).

FIGURE 12.10
Narrowing alternatives through the use of sequential elimination by lexicography.

	A	B	C	D	E	F	G	H
1	ATTRIBUTE	RANK	CAR 5	CAR 4	CAR 6	CAR 3	CAR 2	CAR 1
2								
3	PRICE	1	10	10	10	10	5	4
4	MILEAGE	2	10	10	8	5	3	2
5	SAFETY	3	5	3	3	8	10	10
6	RESALE	4	7	5	9	10	5	10
7	COMFORT	5	10	10	3	2	2	3

Car 5 is chosen after the first three attributes are considered.

FIGURE 12.11
An example of a spreadsheet
approach to using sequential
elimination by conjunctive
constraints.

	A	B	C	D	E	F	G	H	I
1	ATTRIBUTE		STANDARD	CAR 1		CAR 2		CAR 3	
2									
3	PRICE	<	13000	11500	T	12600	T	12900	T
4	MILEAGE	>	18	25	T	19	T	21	T
5	SAFETY	>=	5	7	T	6	T	5	T
6	RESALE	>	.20	.10	F	.25	T	.25	T
7	COMFORT	>=	5	3	F	5	T	5	T
8	FEATURES	>=	4	8	T	9	T	4	T
9									
10									
11									
12	"AND"				F		T		T
13									
14									
15									
16									
17									
18									
19									
20									

The constraints are not tight enough. Two alternatives still remain.

Then the second attribute is considered, and only 5 and 4 are considered further, as shown in Figure 12.10.

The final result is that alternative 5 is best because the score for the third attribute is higher for alternative 5 than for alternative 4. Once again, the decision maker can perform sensitivity analysis and rerun the sorting procedure to see if the answer changes.

Using Sequential Elimination by Conjunctive Constraints

Another sequential elimination technique is conjunctive constraints. As its name implies, the decision maker sets constraints, or standards, and then proceeds to eliminate all alternatives that do not satisfy the set of all constraints. If the constraints are set too tight, all of the alternatives are eliminated, but if they are not tight enough, many alternatives still remain. To use this method, the decision maker is required to employ an interactive approach.

Figure 12.11 shows a spreadsheet approach to sequential elimination by conjunctive constraints. In this example, the decision maker is trying to choose the most appropriate company vehicle. The attributes are listed in column A, the direction of constraints are placed in column B, and the value of the constraints in column C. Columns D, F, and H are used to contain any numerical values, and columns E, G, and I are used to show if the relationship is true or false. At the bottom of the spreadsheet, an "AND" condition is set up so that all of the constraints must be met for the relationship at the bottom to be true.

At first, many alternatives may be feasible, so the decision maker then proceeds to change the values in column C until only one alternative remains. In the example shown in Figure 12.12, the decision maker changes

	A	B	C	D	E	F	G	H	I
1	ATTRIBUTE		STANDARD	CAR 1		CAR 2		CAR 3	
2									
3	PRICE	<	13000	11500	T	12600	T	12900	T
4	MILEAGE	>	20	25	T	19	F	21	T
5	SAFETY	>=	5	7	T	6	T	5	T
6	RESALE	>	.20	.10	F	.25	T	.25	T
7	COMFORT	>=	5	3	F	5	T	5	T
8	FEATURES	>=	4	8	T	9	T	4	T
9									
10									
11									
12	"AND"				F		F		T
13									
14									
15									
16									
17									
18									
19									
20									

When the mileage is changed to 20 mpg, the number of alternatives is reduced to one.

the mileage from 18 to 20 miles per gallon, leaving car 3 as the only remaining alternative.

The usefulness of this approach becomes apparent when you realize that a person often trades off attributes by interactively relaxing or tightening one or more constraints. This explains why people are willing to spend a little more money than they said initially, even though they rank price as the most important constraint.

Using Goal Programming

A discussion of multiple-criteria decision making is not complete without a discussion of goal programming, which has been widely applied to numerous problems in profit and nonprofit organizations. Goal programming, an example of which is featured in Figure 12.13, is similar in construct to linear programming, and therefore it has the same assumptions and limitations.

A goal-programming model contains decision variables, deviational variables, priorities, and sometimes weights. Consequently, the decision maker must not only set goals for each of the goal equations in the problem but also choose priorities for minimizing the deviational variables. Goal programming is a valuable technique when the information required is readily available and the decision maker is knowledgeable and confident about goals and priorities. In addition, the decision maker must be skilled at formulating goal equations—not a simple task.

Using Analytic Hierarchy Processing

Another method for solving multiple-criteria problems is Analytic Hierarchy Processing (AHP). This process requires decision makers to make judgments regarding the relative importance of each of the criteria and then to in-

FIGURE 12.13
A goal-programming model
for supporting the decision on
allocating money for radio
and television advertising.

PRIORITY 1   Do not exceed the total budget of $200,000
PRIORITY 2   Meet or exceed the contract of at least 40 TV spots
PRIORITY 3   Schedule at least 100 total (TV and radio) spots
PRIORITY 4   Keep the radio advertisements to 60 or less

Minimize $P_1 d_1^+ = P_2 d_2^- + P_3 d_3^- + P_4 d_4^+$

s.t. Budget $400\,x_1 + 200\,x_2 + d_1^- + d_1^+ = 200{,}000$
      TV Spots $x_1 + + d_2^- + d_2^+ = 40$
      Total Spots $x_1 + + d_3^- + d_3^+ = 100$
      Radio Spots $ x_2 + d_4^- + d_4^+ = 60$

Where x_1 is the number of television spots
x_2 is the number of radio spots

Priorities are taken in order, starting with P_1. The d^+ means that the number on the
right-hand side will not be exceeded if the priority can be met. The d^- means that the
number on the right-hand side will not be underachieved. Since there are multiple,
conflicting goals, not all of the priorities will be met.

dicate their preference regarding the importance of each of the criteria for each alternative.

Take once again our example about purchasing a car. Figure 12.14 shows a hierarchy tree for the decision. Since the overall goal is choosing the best car (our alternatives), we indicate that their are six branches (our criteria): price, mileage, safety, resale, comfort, and features (our attributes). Underneath each branch, you can see each of our three cars listed. Each one of the cars in our original example has a number associated with it, but that does not have to be the case.

We could have described safety as good (5), above average (6), and much better than average (7). Or we could have described comfort in words such as poor (3) and adequate (5). One advantage that AHP has over goal programming is that the decision maker does not have to quantify the attributes.

The steps for AHP are simple:

1. Decide which car is preferred over another car and by how much. (In our example, compare A to B; A to C; and B to C.) This is called pairwise comparison, because two alternatives are compared at a time.
2. Do this for each of the criteria (in our example there are six criteria).
3. Rate each of the criteria according to its importance.

To begin our example, step one requires us to compare each car on the first criterion. Suppose we look at safety first (note that we do not know how important safety is at this point). We compare car A to car B; car A to car C; and

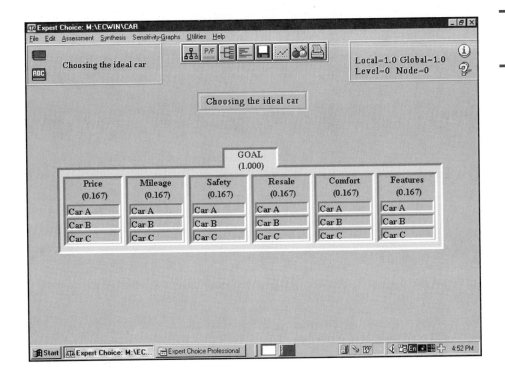

FIGURE 12.14
An AHP screen from Expert
Choice.

car B to car C. AHP uses a system as follows to convert verbal judgment into numbers:

Verbal Judgment	Numerical Preference
Extremely preferred	9
Very strongly to extremely preferred	8
Very strongly preferred	7
Strongly to very strongly preferred	6
Strongly preferred	5
Moderately to strongly preferred	4
Moderately preferred	3
Equally to moderately preferred	2
Equally preferred	1

So if our decision maker judges each of the cars on safety, then one possible judgment is: "I *moderately prefer* car A to car B, I *very strongly prefer* car A to car C, and I *moderately to strongly prefer* car B to car C." The AHP model would assign preferences to each statement (i.e., a 3 to *moderately prefer,* a 7 to *very strongly prefer,* and a 4 to *moderately to strongly prefer*). The AHP model creates a matrix such as this:

	Safety		
	Car A	Car B	Car C
Car A		3	7
Car B			4
Car C			

CHAPTER 2:
UNDERSTANDING
ORGANIZATIONAL STYLE
AND ITS IMPACT ON
INFORMATION SYSTEMS

405

Shelving Your Concerns

"I never know what to do. Sometimes one supplier's quality is good, but its cost is too high. Then I've got one who isn't that reliable, but when it can deal, its price makes it a steal. I'm just drawn to some suppliers like a magnet. It's rough to know how to decide. I mean, we literally go through tons of steel to make our shelves, and I've got to decide who to buy it from. We're the largest manufacturer of adjustable and nonadjustable shelving for retailers. Sometimes I think we could conquer the world with wall-to-wall shelves," says Abel Gance, director of purchasing for Gaul's Shelving.

"I've been trying to figure out a system for rating our steel suppliers, but most of my data just winds up sitting on a shelf because we're so busy with other stuff." Abel hands you the following breakdown of how he's been rating the suppliers (see the chart below).

What sort of approach would you recommend for Abel in determining which supplier to purchase steel from? Could you quantify the responses Mr. Gance gave you regarding the criteria? What type of multiple-criteria approach would you recommend? Why?

Supplier	Quality of Product	Cost of Items	Reliable Service	Merchandise Out-of-Stock	Return Policy
Bona Parts	Above average	Very high	Always reliable	Sometimes	Excellent
Waterloo	Average	Low	Seldom reliable	Often	Satisfactory
Corsica Corp.	Above average	Average	Often reliable	Never	Poor
Josephine's Supplies	Below average	Low	Often reliable	Never	Satisfactory
Wellington General Stores	Above average	Average	Always reliable	Sometimes	Excellent

Then it normalizes and computes a priority vector showing the relative priority of cars A, B, and C. The priority vector for the entries above would be:

$$.656$$
$$.265$$
$$.080$$

which add up to 1.0 (forgiving the rounding error, of course). This would seem to indicate that car A is preferred (with a priority of .656). Once this is done for each of the six criteria and then each of the criteria themselves are compared on importance, the AHP model makes its final calculation and lists the choice, again displaying relative weights that add up to 1.0

Rather than go through all of the calculations, we suggest that you get a copy of Expert Choice or some other AHP-based decision tool and try it out. Some AHP-based tools are found in Figure 12.15. Most of these tools are available on a trial basis from their respective Web sites. You will see that the actual software does much more than help make a decision. These tools are also helpful in performing sensitivity analysis, which will help the deci-

Product	Company	Web Site
Analytica	Decisioneering	www.decisioneering.com
DecideRight	Avantos Performing Systems	www.Avantos.com
Decision Grid	Softkit Technologies	www.softkit.com
Expert Choice	ExpertChoice	www.expertchoice.com

FIGURE 12.15
Selected software packages that use either AHP or similar multicriteria techniques.

sion maker examine "what-if" scenarios and sleep better at night after making a crucial decision.

One of the disadvantages of using AHP models comes from the pairwise method used to evaluate alternatives. It is easy sometimes to say car A is better than B; car B is better than car C; and car C is better than car A. But this doesn't make sense. The principle of transitivity has been violated. There are ways to check for consistency using AHP models, but mistakes can happen.

Expert Systems, Neural Nets, and Other Decision Tools

Other decision models available to managers include expert systems and neural nets. Expert systems are rule-based reasoning systems developed around an expert in the field. Gathering expertise is called knowledge acquisition and is the most difficult part of rule set specification. From this point on, you can assume that software tools are widely available in all price categories.

Neural nets are developed by solving a number of problems of one type and letting the software get feedback on the decisions, observing what was involved in successful decisions. This process is referred to as training the neural net. Some widely available neural nets and expert systems are described in Figure 12.16.

Both of these models are mentioned in the realm of artificial intelligence. What makes them decision support systems? Typically it takes a human decision maker to do problem identification, knowledge acquisition, and sensitivity analysis. Rarely are these decisions left solely to the computer. The complexity of the problems solved allows these techniques to be part of the decision support system world.

Product	Company	Web Site	Description
Braincel	Promised Land Technologies	www.palisade.com	Neural Net add-in for Excel spreadsheets
Exsys	Exsys	www.exsys.com	Expert System
Neuralyst	Chesire Engineering	www.palisade.com	Neural Net add-in for Excel or Lotus 1-2-3 spreadsheets

FIGURE 12.16
Selected expert system and neural net software for the personal computer.

Company	Products	Web Site	Rating System	Sample Web Sites
Firefly Network, Inc.	Firefly catalog navigator Community navigator, Passport office	www.firefly.net	Numeric 1–7	www.my.yahoo.com www.barnesandnoble.com www.filmfinder.com
LikeMinds, Inc.	Preference Server	www.likeminds.com	Alphanumeric A–F	www.cinemax.com www.moviecritic.com
Net Perceptions Inc.	Group Lens Recommendation Engine	www.netperceptions.com	Numeric 1–5 or 1–13 and implicit (i.e., reading time)	www.amazon.com www.moviefinder.com
Wise Wire Corp.	WiseWire.com	www.wisewire-corp.com	Number 1–10	www.wisewire.com

FIGURE 12.17
Selected recommendation systems using numeric and alphanumeric ranking systems.

Recommendation Systems

Recommendation systems are software and database systems that allow decision makers to reduce the number of alternatives by ranking or counting or some other method. A restaurant guide, such as *Zagat's,* is an example of a recommendation system. It surveys diners and reports the results both online and in a book. A widely-used term for the process is *collaborative filtering.*

More sophisticated recommendation systems are being developed all of the time. Figure 12.17 lists a number of systems that allow users to rate the alternatives using a numeric system (such as 1 to 7) or an alphanumeric system (A–F, such as grades). Users can get collaborative filtering of books, cars, current films, and so on.

A recommendation system does not depend on numeric weights. This system counts the number of occurrences, such as how many people bookmarked a certain Web site or how many users mentioned an author. A list of some of these systems can be found in Figure 12.18.

Getting External Information from the Web

There are times when decision makers want to filter their own information rather than depend on recommendation systems. We can classify this information as news—news about the economy, industry, competition, and so on. But the Web is dynamic, and it is difficult to predict how executives will get their information in the years ahead. Figure 12.19 lists a sampling of various types of services a decision maker can use to obtain external information about the things like the economy, customers, or trends.

Company	Source of Information	Aggregation Scheme	Recommended as
PHOAKS	Mined from use-net postings	One person one vote (per URL)	Mention of a URL
ReferralWeb	Mined from public data sources	Assemble referral chain to desired person	Mention of a person or a document
Siteseer	Mined from existing bookmark folders	Frequency of mention in overlapping folders	Mention of a URL

FIGURE 12.18
Selected recommendation systems that use methods other than numeric weighting or ranking.

Push technologies (the first group) have enormous potential. Executives can configure one of these products to receive news from the Internet directly on their personal computers. A version of these push products can also serve as a screen saver, where news crawls across the screen much like a stock ticker. Personalized home pages can be set up to search for specific

Type of Service	Product	Web Site
Push technologies	BackWeb	www.backweb.com
	Marimba Castanet	www.marimba.com
	PointCast	www.pointcast.com
	Webcaster	www.microsoft.com/ie/ie40
	Netcaster	www.netscape.com/communicator
Personalized home pages	My Yahoo!	www.my.yahoo.com
	Personal Front Page	www.msnbc.com
On-line Newspapers	CNN Interactive	www.cnn.com
	London Times	www.the-times.co.uk
	New York Times	www.nytimes.com
	USA Today	www.usatoday.com
Intelligent Agents	Farcast	www.farcast.com
	Headliner	www.headliner.com
	Press Agent	www.agentware.com

FIGURE 12.19
Selected sources for external information available on the Web.

CHAPTER 12:
ANALYZING SEMISTRUCTURED
DECISION SUPPORT SYSTEMS

409

FIGURE 12.20
Screen from ProModel's
Process Model software.

information. On-line newspapers are good for browsing, since the user has control over a broad search. Finally, intelligent agents get to know your personality, learn your behavior, and track the topics they think you want to keep up to date on.

Process Simulation Models

Simulations, sometimes called a method of last resort, are making a comeback. New tools for decision makers are called ServiceModel and ProModel, both by the ProModel Corporation. ServiceModel is a full-scale simulation for service system modeling and analysis, and it is used by airports, banks, restaurants, and so on. With this tool, a decision maker can draw an office layout, model employee interaction and machine utilization, observe animation showing the movement and bottlenecks in the office, and analyze detailed reports and graphs.

Figure 12.20 is a screen from ServiceModel. It depicts bank customers being served in a single-server queue. ProModel does much the same thing in a manufacturing environment.

SUMMARY

Decision support systems (DSS) are a special class of information systems that emphasize the process of decision making and changing DSS users through their interaction with the system. Decision support systems are well suited for addressing semistructured problems where human judgment is still desired or required. Decision support systems do not come up with one solution for users; rather they support the decision-making process by helping the user explore alternatives and consider their ramifications through different modeling techniques.

"So many decisions are made here. You'd be surprised at the types of things even the administrative assistants like me are asked to decide. And at the spur of the moment, not after long hours of analysis. And they are not trivial questions by any means. It seems as if the computers could help us decide most things, if we would just plan for it. But it's all of these ad hoc decisions we make that could use some support. I think Snowden would be all for it. I can certainly see the benefits."

HyperCase Questions

1. Where might a decision support system (DSS) fit in at MRE?
2. Who (which MRE employees) would be most likely to benefit from a DSS? Defend your choices.
3. Identify three semistructured decisions that are being made in the Management Systems and Training Unit. Choose one to support with a DSS. Explain your choice.

Users of DSS or group decision support systems (GDSS) come from all three management levels of the organization; however, semistructured decisions are most often required on the middle managerial and strategic levels. Users of a DSS are eventually changed through the process of interacting with the system.

The decision-making style of users can be categorized as either analytic or heuristic. Analytic decision makers tend to break down problems into quantitative components and use mathematical models to make a decision, while heuristic decision makers rely on experience. Decision support systems can be designed with the decision maker's predominant style in mind, so that analytical thinkers are supplied with quantitative models and heuristic decision makers are provided with summary information and memory aids that allow them to recall how they used heuristics in the past.

Semistructured decisions are those where human judgment is still required or considered desirable. Some decisions are considered to be semistructured because the decision maker doesn't possess the decision-making skills to make the decision. Also, if a problem is too complex, it is classified as semistructured. Finally, a problem could be called semistructured if multiple criteria must be addressed. Decision support systems are especially well suited to help solve semistructured problems.

In all problem solving, decision makers go through three phases: intelligence, choice, and design. In the intelligence phase, the decision maker is scanning external and internal business environments for potential problems and opportunities. The design phase consists of articulating the problem or opportunity by discovering and creating alternatives, evaluating them, and examining their implications. The choice phase is comprised of choosing an alternative from among those that have been considered and determining the reasons and rationales for the adoption of that solution. Decision support systems should be designed to support decisions in all three phases of problem solving.

A complete decision support system should be able to support multiple-criteria decision making. The decision maker using this kind of DSS has a large repertoire of methods available, including a trade-off process, a weighting method, sequential elimination by lexicography, sequential elimination by conjunctive constraints, goal programming, and analytic hierarchy processing.

Decision makers can also use expert systems and neural nets to solve problems. They can also seek advice from recommendation systems, which poll user preferences and arrive at results by either numerical weighting or by occurrence. Executives seek external information, and there are many different ways to obtain that information from the Web. These methods include push technologies, personalized home pages, on-line newspapers, and intelligent agents. Finally, simulation is being recognized as a tool for analyzing process flows in organizations.

KEYWORDS AND PHRASES

decision support system (DSS)
decision support system
  generator (DSSG)
group decision support
  system (GDSS)
decision making under certainty
decision making under
  uncertainty
decision making under risk
analytic decision making
heuristic decision making
intelligence phase
design phase
choice phase
semistructured decision
deep structure
decision-making skill
problem complexity
multiple criteria

trade-off process
weighting methods
sequential elimination
  by lexicography
sequential elimination
  by conjunctive constraints
goal programming
Analytic Hierarchy
  Processing (AHP)
pairwise comparison
expert systems
neural nets
recommendation systems
collaborative filtering
push technologies
personalized home pages
on-line newspapers
intelligent agents (re: the Web)
process simulations

REVIEW QUESTIONS

1. List the functions of decision support systems.
2. Define a decision support system and compare it to a management information system.
3. What is a DSS generator?
4. What type of problem or opportunity is best addressed through the use of a decision support system?
5. Why is a decision support system best conceptualized as a process rather than as a product?
6. How does a decision support system change its user?
7. Define the concept of decision making under certainty.
8. Define the concept of decision making under uncertainty.
9. Define the concept of decision making under risk.
10. Describe the characteristics of an analytic decision maker.
11. Describe the characteristics of a heuristic decision maker.

12. What are some features that a decision support system for an analytic decision maker should include?
13. What are some features that a decision support system for a heuristic decision maker should include?
14. Define what is meant by the intelligence phase of problem solving. How can a DSS support the intelligence phase?
15. Define what is meant by the design phase of problem solving. How can a DSS support the design phase?
16. Define what is meant by the choice phase of problem solving. How can a DSS support the choice phase?
17. What is meant by characterizing a decision as structured?
18. What is meant by characterizing a decision as semistructured?
19. Define the concept of deep structure in decisions.
20. What does decision-making skill mean? How can a DSS help in upgrading decision-making skill?
21. What does degree of problem complexity mean? How can a DSS decrease problem complexity?
22. List three multiple-criteria approaches to decision making.
23. Define what is meant by the term *weighting method* as it applies to decision making.
24. Define sequential elimination by lexicography.
25. Define sequential elimination by conjunctive constraints.
26. List the elements that compose a goal-programming model. Why is goal programming of limited use as a standard DSS tool?
27. What does AHP stand for?
28. List the three steps in AHP.
29. Define pairwise comparison.
30. Does AHP have any advantages over goal programming?
31. What is a disadvantage of AHP?
32. What are recommendation systems?
33. What is the difference between the numerical weighting recommendations and the other types of recommendation systems?
34. How can decision makers get external information from the Web?
35. What is the difference between push technologies, personalized home pages, on-line newspapers, and intelligent agents?
36. How do simulation models help the decision maker?

PROBLEMS

1. While you are working on a large information systems project for a pharmaceutical company, Bob, a newly hired production supervisor, mentions to you that he heard about decision support systems in an MBA class. He would like to have you work on one for him as a sort of subsystem of the larger project. As a production supervisor, Bob reports to a production manager, but he makes routine decisions about production schedules, has input into the purchasing of ingredients, and manages line workers. He feels a DSS would be helpful in supporting these functions.

   a. In a paragraph, deny Bob's request for a decision support system. Provide reasons for not pursuing a DSS that would support Bob's decision-making functions.

   b. What changes in Bob's decision-making situation might make a DSS appropriate? Respond in a paragraph.

2. Mary Wren is owner of five Wren's Auto Supply Stores, a chain that sells all manner of auto parts to wholesale and retail customers. She currently uses a small computer rigged up by a friend who was interested in electronics to help her decide what to stock in each of the stores, which are located in five population centers. When her father was alive, he visited each store and based his orders on what managers said was selling well. Mary still visits stores, but she also inputs sales figures into a computer model that displays buying trends for each store. The model also has "what-if" capabilities so that Mary can experiment with different scenarios, such as falling oil prices, increasing length of original car ownership, and increasing popularity of customizing kits. Mary does not rely solely on the computer to make her ordering decisions; she also uses her own observations about what is selling well to make ordering decisions for each store.

   a. Would you characterize the ordering decisions Mary must make for her five auto supply stores as semistructured? Why or why not? What are some of the variables involved? Respond in two paragraphs.

   b. What features of the information system that Mary is using would support the assertion that it is more of a decision support system than a traditional management information system? List them.

   c. How is Mary's decision process improved upon by the DSS she is using? (Compare it to the way her father made decisions.) Respond in a paragraph.

3. After watching customer patterns for the first few weeks in her new business, Anita knows that most of her customers arrive in the early morning (before 9:30 A.M.) or in the late afternoon (between 3:30 P.M. and 5:00 P.M.). Based on this information, she has decided to close her fabric shop at 5:30 P.M.

   a. Is Anita making her decision under conditions of certainty, uncertainty, or risk? Explain in two sentences.

   b. Is her information most likely based on information or experience? Explain in two sentences.

4. "If this doesn't work, I can do something else. I just keep experimenting with different glazes for the figurines I sculpt. If they don't look pretty when they come out of the kiln, or if they blow up, or if no one buys them, I can try something else. Live and learn," says Emmy Potts, a sculptor who has a growing business selling custom-made ceramics.

   a. Would you characterize Emmy as an analytic or heuristic decision maker?

   b. Write a paragraph supporting your choice in 4a.

   c. Emmy wants a system to keep track of her reactions (and her customers' reactions) to different glazes and ceramics molds for the eventual purpose of ordering supplies and deciding what pieces to make (that is, what pieces will sell even though they are not commissioned). What features would you incorporate into a decision support system for Emmy? List the features and write a sentence giving the reason for each one.

5. Emmy's husband, Buddy, is retiring from his position as a district manager for a chain of hardware stores. For several years, he has been doing market research for the stores. He is systematic in the way he approaches problems and has long used mathematical formulas to project sales and so on. Al-

though her business has been doing well in the last year and a half, Emmy is getting too bogged down in backlogged orders to use the decision support system you built for her. Buddy has agreed to take over the management aspects of her shop so that she can concentrate on artistic aspects.

a. How would you characterize Buddy as a decision maker? Explain in a paragraph.

b. What features could you include in a DSS to support Buddy's decision-making style? List them and write a sentence supporting each feature.

6. Louis, a systems analyst, has designed and implemented a decision support system for Scott Weidenfeed, owner of Grass That Grows, a huge suburban lawn care service. Part of the system is designed to flag any unusual problems that are reported by the numerous lawn crews. Some problems are of critical importance (detection of Dutch Elm disease, for example), since they will affect much of the community and must be addressed as soon as they are recognized. Resolving them will mean deciding on reassignment of crews from regular lawn care, authorizing the extra expense to the company in terms of chemicals needed, and so on.

a. Which of the three phases of problem solving is this part of the DSS supporting? Explain in a paragraph.

b. Extend the lawn care example and describe in two paragraphs how the decision support system might support the two phases of problem solving that you did not list in 6a. Make any assumption necessary about the company.

7. Howie Johnson is the president of the regional data-processing association. He is trying to choose a hotel to host the regional convention for the association.

a. Make a list of eight to ten criteria for a good convention hotel.

b. Choose a multiple-criteria decision method for selecting a hotel.

c. In a paragraph, defend the method you chose.

8. Jo Pshop wants to determine how to sequence orders that are coming into her specialized invitation shop (invitations for weddings, parties, etc.). Business has been heavy lately, and sequencing of jobs is critical. Her choices are:

1. First come, first served.

2. Shortest processing time (the easiest jobs are done first).

3. Due date (do them in the order promised).

Since her decision is semistructured, you have suggested a trade-off approach. List some criteria and explain how this technique would work.

9. Cary Farr has the job of choosing one of five shipping companies that he will use for his business. This is the information he has gathered on the shipping companies' attributes:

	Cost	Damage	Percentage on Time	Complaints	Courteous
All American	2	4	5	3	1
United Truckers	4	3	2	3	4
Rapido Lines	1	1	3	4	3
Carefree Shippers	3	4	5	5	5
We-Do-It-All	4	3	4	3	3

The numbers are estimates based on the following scale:

1	2	3	4	5

much
worse than
average

average

much
better than
average

Cary gives the order of importance for each criterion as follows:

> Least cost (most important)
> Least damage
> Largest percentage on time
> Fewest complaints
> Most courteous (least important)

Help Cary by choosing a shipping company. Solve this problem using sequential elimination by lexicography.

10. Solve problem 9 using sequential elimination by lexicography, given the following order of importance:

> Least damage (most important)
> Largest percentage on time
> Fewest complaints
> Least cost
> Most courteous (least important)

11. Assume that in problem 9, weights were assigned for each of the criteria as follows:

Cost	.4
Damage	.2
Percentage on time	.2
Complaints	.1
Courteous	.1
	1.0

Solve using the weighting method.

12. Solve problem 9 using sequential elimination by conjunctive constraints given the following constraints (remember, 3 = average, 5 = much better than average).

Cost	Must be average or better
Damage	Must be average or better
Percentage on time	Does not matter
Complaints	Must be better than average
Courteous	Must be average or better

13. For problem 9, draw a tree structure for AHP. Label all criteria and alternatives.

14. Using pairwise comparison, show how all five shipping companies would be compared using the courtesy criteria from problem 9. Use the preference ratings (1 to 9) found in the Analytic Hierarchy Processing section of this chapter. Draw the resulting matrix.

SELECTED BIBLIOGRAPHY

Alter, S. *Decision Support Systems: Current Practices and Continuing Challenges.* Reading, MA: Addison-Wesley, 1980.

Bennett, J. L. (ed.), *Building Decision Support Systems.* Reading, MA: Addison-Wesley, 1982.

Davis, G. B., and M. H. Olson. *Management Information Systems, Conceptual Foundations, Structure, and Development,* 2nd ed. New York: McGraw-Hill Book Company, 1985.

Dhar, V., and R. Stein. *Intelligent Support Methods: The Science of Knowledge Work.* Upper Saddle River, NJ: Prentice Hall, 1997.

Keen, P. W., and M. S. Scott Morton. *Decision Support Systems: An Organizational Perspective.* Reading, MA: Addison-Wesley, 1978.

Kendall, K. E., and B. A. Schuldt. "Case Progression Decision Support System Improves Drug and Criminal Investigator Effectiveness," *Omega,* Vol. 21, No. 3, 1993, pp. 319–328.

Kendall, K. E., and B. A. Schuldt. "Decentralizing Decision Support Systems: A Field Experiment with Drug and Criminal Investigators," *Decision Support Systems,* Vol. 9, 1993, pp. 259–268.

Sauter, V. L. *Decision Support Systems: An Applied Managerial Approach.* New York: John Wiley & Sons, Inc., 1997.

Simon, H. *The Shape of Automation for Men and Management.* New York: Harper & Row, 1965.

Sprague, R. H., Jr., and E. D. Carlson. *Building Effective Decision Support Systems.* Englewood Cliffs, NJ: Prentice Hall, 1982.

Sprague, R. H., Jr., and B. C. McNurlin. *Information Systems Management in Practice.* Englewood Cliffs, NJ: Prentice Hall, 1986.

Turban, E. *Decision Support and Expert Systems: Management Support Systems.* New York: Macmillan Publishing Company, 1993.

Watson, H., and R. Sprague (eds.). *Decision Support Systems: Putting Theory into Practice,* 3rd ed. Englewood Cliffs, NJ: Prentice Hall, 1993.

AWAITING A WEIGHTY DECISION

"Now that the data flow diagrams, data dictionary, and process logic have been clearly defined, we should spend some time looking at the physical design alternatives for the new microcomputer system," says Chip. "We need to look at which of the several different designs is the best for Dot, Mike, Cher, Paige, and Hy."

"Yes," Anna replies, "and since this is not a problem of economics, we have no cost-benefit figures that would make the choice of the new system obvious. I suggest that we use a weighted method for determining which solution will be the best for the user group."

"That's an excellent idea!" exclaims Chip. "We already have a problem definition with weights assigned by the users. We should list the objectives for each problem and then analyze each alternative, determining the quality of the solution for the users."

Chip and Anna created three alternative solutions:

1. A mainframe batch solution, which uses the data entry department for entering all system input. Updates are periodically performed. This alternative has a lower development cost and takes advantage of the rapid keying ability of the data-entry operators.

2. An on-line mainframe solution, with terminals installed in the user areas. This alternative has increased reliability since keyed data would immediately update master files. Inquiries would reflect changes made seconds ago.

3. A microcomputer solution using a local area network to provide access to a centralized database. This provides a high degree of reliability and quick response time. Each user could use the microcomputer for other tasks.

The microcomputer system has ten criteria that must be addressed. These objectives are summarized in Figure E12.1.

"Of the ten system objectives, the highest priority is to provide software and hardware cross-reference information," asserts Chip. "Let's start with this issue and examine how each of the solutions would satisfy it."

"The batch solution would print a report listing each machine and the software installed on it," says Anna. "The on-line system could also provide a similar report or have an inquiry screen to display the information. The microcomputer solution could also have reports or inquiries."

"Why don't we each determine a performance weight, using a scale from one to ten, on how the three solutions compare. Then we can average them together," Chip suggests.

Anna agrees, and the resulting performance weights for the first criterion are:

1. Batch solution scores a 7, a lower score than the others since it lacks the reliability of the up-to-date inquiry information that the on-line and

Allen Schmidt,
Julie E. Kendall, and
Kenneth E. Kendall

microcomputer solutions provided. Any recent changes would be reflected on the screens but not on the report, which would be printed only after a batch of updates was processed.

2. On-line solution scores a 10.
3. Microcomputer solution scores a 10.

Anna and Chip continue to analyze the quality of each of the three alternatives for the remaining issues. The results are shown in Figure E12.2, which depicts each of the ten system objectives and the weight or importance assigned to the objectives by the users.

Each solution has a brief narrative explaining how the solution will achieve the objective and a performance weight indicating the quality of the solution. The weight for each objective is then multiplied by the performance to determine a score for each solution fragment. The resulting scores are finally summed to provide an overall measure for the solution.

Exercises

E-1. Calculate the total score for solution 2, the mainframe on-line solution.

E-2. Calculate the final score for solution 3, the microcomputer local area network.

E-3. Which solution should be designed and implemented to solve the users' problems? Describe the system in a paragraph. If some of the performances were incorrectly estimated by a small amount, would a different solution be chosen? Explain your reasoning in a paragraph.

Objectives	Weight
Provide software/hardware cross-reference.	10
Maintain complete microcomputer information.	9
Automate software installation procedure.	8
Provide software upgrade installation machine information.	7
Provide preventive and other maintenance information.	7
Maintain up-to-date accurate software information.	6
Provide complete cost information for microcomputer inventory.	5
Provide information on the cost to upgrade software.	5
Design a process for performing accurate and efficient physical microcomputer inventory.	3
Maintain and provide training and software expert information.	2

FIGURE E12.1
Microcomputer system objectives.

MICROCOMPUTER SYSTEM PROPOSAL:
SYSTEM ALTERNATIVES

Objectives	Weight	SOLUTION 1 Mainframe Batch	Performance	SOLUTION 2 Mainframe On line	Performance	SOLUTION 3 Microcomputer LAN	Performance
Provide softwear/hardware cross-reference.	10	Print cross-reference report after batch update	7	Software location inquiry screen. Provide a cross–reference report when requested.	10	Software location inquiry screen. Provide a cross-reference report when requested.	10
Maintain complete microcomputer information	9	Send forms to data entry, key and verify. Batch update of indexed files.	5	Screens to add, delete, and change microcomputer information. Immediate update.	9	Screens to add, delete, and change microcomputer information. Screens to change maintenance data.	10
Automate software installation procedure.	8	Produce a fist of all machines that must contain the upgrade software. Update files using data entry.	5	Use inquiry screens to determine which machines should contain the software. Automatically update master files.	9	Inquiry screens to determine installation machines. Update files automatically with overrides for exceptions.	10
Provide complete cost information for microcomputer hardware.	5	Produce reports providing cost detail and summary information.	7	Provide detail and summary cost reports. Include cost information on inquiry screens.	9	Provide detail and summary cost reports. Include cost and summary information on inquiry screens.	10
Provide information on the cost to upgrade software.	5	Produce report to show upgrade cost for all software.	4	On-line selection of package to be upgraded. Cost figures calculated based on number of upgrades.	10	On-line selection of package to be upgraded. Cost figures calculated based on number of upgrades. User may calculate individual departmental costs.	10
Design a process for performing accurate and efficient physical microcomputer inventory.	3	Inventory forms printed. Physical inventory competed and report used for data entry.	7	Physical inventory listing printed and used as a turn-around document. On-line update of changes.	9	Physical inventory listing printed. On-site entry of changes using local microcomputer	10
Maintain and provide training and software expert information.	2	Batch add of software expert and training information.	5	On-line update of software expert and training courses. Inquiry screens to locate experts. Training listing printed.	9	On-line update of software expert and training courses. Inquiry screens provide expert information. Training listings printed.	10
Provide software upgrade installation machine information.	7	List all machines containing the software to be upgraded. Send changes to data entry.	6	Print report of all machines containing software. Note any installation exceptions and use screens to modify upgrade records.	8	A single screen to automatically upgrade all records. Use a micro-computer in the installation room to immediately update any upgrade exceptions.	10
Provide preventive and other maintenance information.	7	Reports showing which machines require preventive maintenance. Update records via data entry.	7	Reports sorted by location for all machines requiring preventive maintenance. On-line update reflecting work completed.	8	Reports sorted by location for all machines requiring preventive maintenance. On-site creation of records using local microcomputer.	10
Maintain up to-date accurate software information.	6	Weekly batch update of all additions, changes, and deletes.	4	On-line add, delete, and change programs. Automatic deletion of old versions when software is upgraded.	10	Screens for additions, deletions, and changes.	9

FIGURE E12.2
Three microcomputer system alternatives. Weight is the user-assigned weight, indicating importance of the objective. Performance is the performance weight, indicating the quality of the solution.

PREPARING THE SYSTEMS PROPOSAL

METHODS AVAILABLE

The systems proposal is a distillation of all that the systems analyst has learned about the business and about what is needed to improve its performance. In order to address information requirements adequately, the systems analyst must use systematic methods for acquiring hardware and software, must identify and forecast future costs and benefits, and must perform cost-benefit analysis. All of these methods are used in preparing systems proposal material.

Information needs of users drive the selection of computer hardware, data storage media, and any prepackaged software. The hardware and software system that is eventually proposed is the analyst's response to users' information needs. This chapter provides the methods that are needed to project future needs systematically and then to weigh current hardware and software alternatives. Forecasting, guidelines for hardware and software acquisition, and cost-benefit analysis are also considered.

ASCERTAINING HARDWARE AND SOFTWARE NEEDS

In this section, we cover the process of estimating the present and future workloads of a business and the process involved in evaluating the ability of computer hardware and software to handle workloads adequately. Figure 13.1 shows the steps the systems analyst takes in ascertaining hardware and software needs. First, all current computer hardware must be inventoried to discover what is on hand and what is usable. Then current and future system workloads must be estimated. Following this, an evaluation of available hardware and software is undertaken.

The systems analyst needs to work along with users to determine what hardware will be needed. Hardware determinations can come only in conjunction with determining information requirements. Knowledge of the organizational structure (as discussed in Chapter 2) can also be helpful in

FIGURE 13.1
Steps in choosing hardware
and software.

**Steps in Acquiring Computer
Hardware and Software**

Inventory
Computer
Hardware

↓

Estimate
Workloads

↓

Evaluate
Hardware

Evaluate
Software

↓

Choose
the Vendor

↓

Acquire the
Computer
Equipment

hardware decisions. Only when systems analysts, users, and management have a good grasp of what kinds of tasks must be accomplished can hardware options be considered.

Inventorying Computer Hardware

Begin by inventorying what computer hardware is already available in the organization. As will become apparent, some of the hardware options involve expanding or recycling current hardware, so it is important to know what is on hand.

If an updated computer hardware inventory is unavailable, the systems analyst needs to set up one quickly and carry through on it. You need to know:

1. The type of equipment—model number, manufacturer.
2. The status of the equipment operation—on order, operating, in storage, in need of repair.
3. The estimated age of the equipment.
4. The projected life of the equipment.
5. The physical location of the equipment.
6. The department or person considered responsible for the equipment.
7. The financial arrangement for the equipment—owned, leased, or rented.

Figure 13.2 provides an example of a hardware inventory form that can be given to the relevant people. It should be easy to fill out and should explicitly request that peripherals, such as disk drives and VDTs, be enumerated separately.

	First Computer	Second Computer	Third Computer

1. Equipment
  a. CPU/type/
    manufacturer/model
  b. Storage/type/
    manufacturer/model
  c. Input/type/
    manufacturer/model
  d. Output/type/
    manufacturer/model
  e. Communications/type/
    manufacturer/model			

2. Status
  On order
  Fully operational
  In need of repair
  In storage			

3. Estimated Age of Equipment			
4. Projected Life			
5. Located			

6. Name of Individual or Department
Responsible for Equipment
  Purchase
  Operation
  Maintenance			

7. Financial Agreement
  Owned
  Rented
  Leased			

FIGURE 13.2
Using a form for taking inventory of equipment currently available in the organization.

Ascertaining the current hardware available will aid in a sounder decision-making process when hardware decisions are finally made, since much of the guesswork about what exists will be eliminated. Through your earlier interviewing, questionnaires, and research of archival data, you will already know the number of people available for data processing as well as their skills and capabilities. Use this information to project how well the staffing needs for new hardware can be met.

Estimating Workloads

The next step in ascertaining hardware needs is to estimate workloads. This means that systems analysts formulate numbers that represent both current and projected workloads for the system, so that any hardware obtained will possess the capability to handle current and future workloads.

If estimates are accomplished properly, the business should not have to replace hardware solely due to unforeseen growth in system use. (However,

FIGURE 13.3
Comparisons of workloads between existing and proposed
systems.

	Existing System	Proposed System
Task	Monthly summary of shipments to distribution warehouses	Same
Method	Manual	Computer
Personnel	Distribution Manager	Computer Operator
Cost/Hour	$20.00	$10.00

When and How	Daily:
	  files shipping receipts
	  for each warehouse
	Monthly:
	  summarizes daily records
	  using calculator and
	  prepares report
		Daily:
		  runs program that totals
		  shipments and writes to
		  disk
		Monthly:
		  runs program that
		  summarizes and prints
		  reports

Human Time Requirements	Daily: 20 minutes Monthly: 8 hours	Daily: 4 minutes Monthly: 20 minutes
Computer Time Requirements	None	Daily: 4 minutes Monthly: 20 minutes

other events, such as superior technological innovations, may dictate hardware replacement if the business wants to maintain its competitive edge.)

Out of necessity, workloads are sampled rather than actually put
through several computer systems. The guidelines given on sampling in
Chapter 4 can be of use here, since in workload sampling the systems analyst is taking a sample of necessary tasks and the computer resources required to complete them.

Figure 13.3 is a comparison of the times required by an existing and a
proposed information system that are supposed to handle a given workload.
Notice that the company is currently using a manual system to prepare a
monthly summary of shipments to its distribution warehouses, and a computer system is being suggested. The workload comparison looks at the cost
per hour of each system, when and how each process is done, how much human time is required, and how much computer time is needed.

Evaluating Computer Hardware

Evaluating computer hardware is the shared responsibility of management,
users, and systems analysts. Although vendors will be supplying details
about their particular offerings, analysts need to oversee the evaluation
process personally since they will have the best interests of the business at
heart. Additionally, systems analysts may have to educate users and management about the general advantages and disadvantages of hardware before
they can capably evaluate it.

Based on the current inventory of computer equipment and adequate estimates of current and forecasted workloads, the next step in the process is to consider the kinds of equipment available that appear to meet projected needs. Information from vendors on possible systems and system configurations becomes more pertinent at this stage and should be reviewed with management and users.

Additionally, workloads can be simulated and run on different systems, including those already used in the organization. This process is referred to as benchmarking.

Criteria that the systems analysts and users should use to evaluate performance of different systems hardware include:

1. The time required for average transactions (including how long it takes to input data and how long it takes to receive output).
2. The total volume capacity of the system (how much can be processed at the same time before a problem arises).
3. The idle time of the central processing unit.
4. The size of the memory provided.

Some criteria will be shown in formal demonstrations; some cannot be simulated and must be gleaned from manufacturers' specifications. It is important to be clear about the required and desired functions before getting too wrapped up in vendors' claims during demonstrations.

Once functional requirements are known and the current products available are comprehended and compared with what already exists in the organization, decisions are made by the systems analysts in conjunction with users and management about whether obtaining new hardware is necessary. Options can be thought of as existing on a continuum from using only equipment already available in the business all the way to obtaining entirely new equipment. In between are options to make minor or major modifications to the existing computer system.

COMPUTER SIZE AND USE. The rapid advance of technology dictates that the systems analyst research types of computers available at the particular time that the systems proposal is being written. Computer sizes range all the way from the smallest notebook-sized microcomputers to room-sized supercomputers. Each has different attributes that should be considered when deciding how to implement a computer system.

Acquisition of Computer Equipment

The three main options for acquisition of computer hardware include buying, leasing, or renting it. There are advantages and disadvantages that ought to be weighed for each of the decisions, as shown in Figure 13.4. Some of the more influential factors to consider in deciding which option is best for a particular installation include initial versus long-term costs; whether the business can afford to tie up capital in computer equipment; and whether the business desires full control of and responsibility for the computer equipment.

Buying implies that the business itself will own the equipment. One of the main determinants of whether to buy is the projected life of the system.

FIGURE 13.4
Comparing the advantages
and disadvantages of buying,
leasing, and renting computer
equipment.

	Advantages	**Disadvantages**
Buying	• Cheaper than leasing or renting over the long run • Ability to change system • Provides tax advantages of accelerated depreciation • Full control	• Initial cost is high • Risk of obsolescence • Risk of being stuck if choice was wrong • Full responsibility
Leasing	• No capital is tied up • No financing is required • Leases are lower than rental payments	• Company doesn't own the system when lease expires • Usually a heavy penalty for terminating the lease • Leases are more expensive than buying
Renting	• No capital is tied up • No financing is required • Easy to change systems • Maintenance and insurance are usually included	• Company doesn't own the computer • Cost is very high because vendor assumes the risk (most expensive option)

If the system will be used longer than four to five years (with all other factors held constant), the decision is usually made to buy. Notice in the example in Figure 13.5 that the cost of purchase after six years is dramatically lower than that of leasing or renting. As systems become smaller and distributed systems become increasingly popular, more businesses are deciding to purchase equipment.

Leasing, rather than buying, computer hardware is another possibility. Leasing equipment from the vendor or a third-party leasing company is more practical when the projected life of the system is less than four years. Additionally, if significant change in technology is imminent, leasing is a better choice. Leasing also allows the business to put its money elsewhere, where it can be working for the company rather than be tied up in capital equipment. Over a long period, however, leasing is not an economical way to acquire computer power.

FIGURE 13.5
Comparison of alternatives for
computer acquisition.

Rental

Monthly rental x 36 months	$170
Total cost over 3 years	$6,120

Lease

Monthly lease x 36 months	$150
Subtotal	5,400
Initial payment	500
Total cost over 3 years	$5,900

Purchase

Purchase price	$6,000
Scrap value	− 500
Total cost over 3 years	$5,500

FIGURE 13.6
Guidelines for vendor
selection.

Vendor Selection Criteria

- Hardware Support
    - Full line of hardware
    - Quality products
    - Warranty
- Software Support
    - Complete software needs
    - Custom programming
    - Warranty
- Installation and Training
    - Commitment to schedule
    - In-house training
    - Technical assistance
- Maintenance
    - Routine maintenance procedures
    - Specified response time in emergencies
    - Equipment loan while repair is being done

Rental of computer hardware is the third main option for computer acquisition. One of the main advantages of renting is that none of the company's capital is tied up. Hence, no financing is required. Also, renting computer hardware makes it easier to change system hardware. Finally, maintenance and insurance are usually included in rental agreements. However, because of the high costs involved and the fact that the company will not own the rented equipment, rental should be contemplated only as a short-term move to handle nonrecurring or limited computer needs or technologically volatile times.

EVALUATION OF VENDOR SUPPORT FOR COMPUTER HARDWARE. There are several key areas that ought to be evaluated when weighing the support services available to businesses from vendors. Most vendors offer testing of hardware upon delivery and a 90-day warranty covering any factory defects, but you must ascertain what else the vendor has to offer. Vendors of comparable quality frequently distinguish themselves from others by the range of support services they offer.

A list of key criteria that ought to be checked when evaluating vendor support is provided in Figure 13.6. Most of the extra vendor support services listed there are negotiated separately from hardware lease or purchase contracts.

Support services include routine and preventive maintenance of hardware; specified response time (within six hours, next working day, etc.) in case of emergency equipment breakdowns; loan of equipment in the event that hardware must be permanently replaced or off-site repair is required; and in-house training, or off-site group seminars for users. Remember that it may be more difficult to obtain training for unique hardware that is not widely used by other organizations. While the possibility of a customized installation may be attractive, the prospects for its long-term support may be diminished. Peruse the support services documents accompanying the purchase or lease of equipment and remember to involve appropriate legal staff before signing contracts for equipment or services.

FIGURE 13.7
The cost of software as a percentage of total hardware and
software cost is rising.

Total Hardware and Software Costs

Unfortunately, evaluating computer hardware is not as straightforward as simply comparing costs and choosing the least expensive option. Some other eventualities commonly brought up by users and management include (1) the possibility of adding on to the system if the need comes up later; (2) the possibility of interfacing with equipment from other vendors if the system needs to grow; (3) the benefits of buying more memory than is projected as necessary, with the expectation that business will eventually "grow into it"; and (4) the corporate stability of the vendor.

Adding on to the existing system is often the spur for systems projects. Installing a system with add-on capability is a worthwhile way to proceed. Although it takes a little extra planning, it is cheaper and more flexible than the third approach—that is, obtaining excess memory and carrying it in inventory for a number of years.

Competition among vendors has made the idea of producing hardware that is compatible with a competitor's important for vendors' survival. However, before becoming convinced that buying cheaper compatibles is the way to endow your system with add-on capability, do enough research to feel confident that the original vendor is a stable corporate entity.

Software Evaluation

Packaged software, rather than application programs specifically written for an installation, are becoming more readily available and certainly should be given careful consideration. Many hours of valuable programmer time can be saved if packaged software is deemed suitable for part or all of the system and if extensive customizing isn't necessary. The bar chart in Figure 13.7 shows the cost of software (projected as ever-increasing) as part of total hardware and software costs.

Once again, you will be dealing with vendors who may have their own best interests at heart. You must be willing to evaluate software along with users and not be unduly influenced by vendors' sales pitches. Specifically, there are six main categories on which to grade software, as shown in Figure 13.8: performance effectiveness, performance efficiency, ease of use, flexibility, quality of documentation, and manufacturer support.

FIGURE 13.8
Guidelines for evaluating
software.

Software Evaluation

- Performance Effectiveness
  - Able to perform all required tasks
  - Able to perform all tasks that may be desired at some time in the future
  - Well-designed display screens
  - Adequate capacity
- Performance Efficiency
  - Fast response time
  - Efficient input
  - Efficient output
  - Efficient storage of data
  - Efficient back-up
- Ease of Use
  - Satisfactory user interface
  - Help menus available
  - ReadMe files for last minute changes
  - Flexible interface
  - Adequate feedback
  - Good error recovery
- Flexibility
  - Options for input
  - Options for output
  - Usable with other software
- Quality of Documentation
  - Good organization
  - Adequate online tutorial
  - Web site with FAQ
- Manufacturer Support
  - Tech support hot line
  - Newsletter/email
  - Web site with downloadable product updates

Evaluate packaged software based on a demonstration with test data from the business considering it and an examination of accompanying documentation. Vendors' descriptions alone will not suffice. Vendors typically certify that software is working when it leaves their supply house, but they will not guarantee that it will be error-free in every instance or that it will not "crash" when incorrect actions are taken by users. Obviously, they will not guarantee their packaged software if used in conjunction with faulty hardware.

The need for multiple copies or network versions of software (for use at several microcomputer workstations, for instance) means negotiating a multiple-use agreement with the vendor so that copyrights are not infringed through the creation of illegal copies. This often means the purchase of one software package at its regular price and the purchase of any additional copies at a reduced price.

It is also possible to negotiate a special vendor services contract covering support for purchased software. This might include extended technical assistance, emergency and preventive maintenance, free or reduced-price updates, additional copies of documentation, and special user training.

CONSULTING OPPORTUNITY 13.1

Veni, Vidi, Vendi—or I Came, I Saw, I Sold

"It's really some choice. I mean, no single package seems to have everything we want. Some of them come darn close, though," says Roman, an advertising executive for *Empire Magazine,* with whom you have been working on a systems project. Recently, the two of you have decided that packaged software would probably suit the advertising department's needs and stem its general decline.

"The last guy's demo we saw, you know, the one who worked for Data Coliseum, really had a well-rounded pitch. And I like their brochure. Full-color printing, on card stock. Classic," Roman asserts.

"And what about those people from Vesta Systems? They're really fired up. And their package was easy to use with a minimum of ceremony. Besides, they said they would train all twelve of us, on-site, at no charge. But look at their advertising. They just take things off their printers."

Roman fiddles in his chair as he continues his ad-hoc review of software and software vendors. "That one package from Mars, Inc., really sold me all on its own, though. I mean, it had a built-in calendar. And I

like the way the menus for the screen displays could all be chosen by Roman numerals. It was easy to follow. And the vendor isn't going to be hard to move on price. I think they're already in a price war."

"But, do you want to know my favorite?" Roman asks archly. "It's the one put out by Jupiter, Unlimited. I mean, it has everything, doesn't it? It costs a little extra coin, but it does what we need it to do, and the documentation is heavenly. They don't do any training of course—they think they're above it."

You are already plotting that in order to answer Roman's burning questions by your March 15 deadline, you need to evaluate the software systematically, as well as the vendors, and then render a decision. Evaluate each vendor and package based on what Roman has said so far (assume you can trust his opinions). What are Roman's apparent biases when evaluating software and vendors? What further information do you need about each company and its software before making a selection?

IDENTIFYING AND FORECASTING COSTS AND BENEFITS

Costs and benefits of the proposed computer system must always be considered together, since they are interrelated and often interdependent. Although the systems analyst is trying to propose a system that fulfills various information requirements, decisions to continue with the proposed system will be based on a costs and benefits analysis, not on information requirements. In many ways, benefits are measured by costs, as will become apparent in the next section.

Forecasting Costs and Benefits

Systems analysts are required to predict certain key variables before the proposal is submitted to the client. To some degree, a systems analyst will rely on a "what-if" analysis—for example, "What if labor costs rise only 5 percent per year for the next three years, rather than 10 percent?" However, the systems analyst should realize that you cannot rely on "what-if" analysis for everything if the proposal is to be credible, meaningful, and valuable.

The systems analyst has many forecasting models available. The main condition for choosing a model is the availability of historical data. If they are unavailable, the analyst must turn to one of the judgment methods: estimates from the salesforce, surveys to estimate customer demand, Delphi studies (a consensus forecast developed independently by a group of experts through a series of iterations), creating scenarios, or drawing historical analogies.

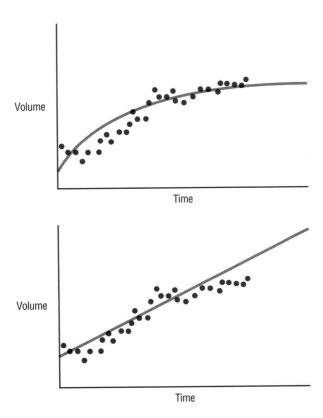

If historical data are available, the next differentiation between classes of techniques involves whether the forecast is conditional or unconditional. Conditional implies that there is an association among variables in the model or that such a causal relationship exists. Common methods in this group include correlation, regression, leading indicators, econometrics, and input-output models.

Unconditional forecasting means the analyst isn't required to find or identify any causal relationships. Consequently, systems analysts find that these methods are low-cost, easy-to-implement alternatives. Included in this group are graphical judgment, moving averages, and analysis of time series data. Since these methods are simple, reliable, and cost-effective, the remainder of the section focuses on them.

ESTIMATION OF TRENDS. Trends can be estimated in a number of different ways. The most widely used techniques are: (1) graphical judgment, (2) the method of least squares, and (3) the moving average method. A brief explanation of these techniques is in order.

Graphical judgment. The simplest way to identify a trend and forecast future trends is by graphical judgment. This is accomplished by simply looking at the graph and estimating by freehand an extension of a line or curve. An example of graphical judgment is illustrated in Figure 13.9.

The disadvantages of this method are obvious from looking at the graphs in the figure. The extension of the line or curve may depend too much on individual judgment and may not represent the real situation. The graphical judgment method is useful, however, because the ability to per-

FIGURE 13.10
The objective of the least
squares method is to find the
"best-fitting line."

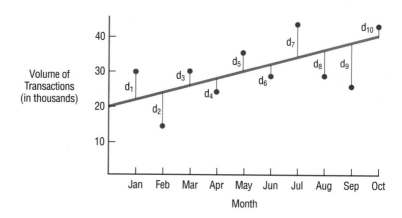

form sensitivity analysis ("what-if") has increased with the introduction of electronic spreadsheets.

The method of least squares. When a trend line is constructed, the actual data points will fall on either side of that line. The objective in estimating a trend using the least squares method is to find the "best-fitting line" by minimizing the sum of the deviations from a line. Once the best-fitting line is found, it can be graphed, and the line can then be extended to forecast what will happen.

The best-fitting line, or least square line, is developed from the data points (X_1, Y_1), (X_2, Y_2), . . . (X_N, Y_N), where the X coordinates signify the time periods and the Y coordinates represent the variable the systems analyst is trying to predict. The equation for the least square line is expressed in the form

$$Y = m * X + b$$

where the variable m represents the slope of the line and b represents the Y intercept, the point at which the line intercepts the Y axis.

An example of a least square line is drawn in Figure 13.10. In this illustration, the least square line is drawn to estimate a trend in transactions from January to October. The volume starts at 20,000 in January and rises an average of 2,000 units per month.

We recommend a more computationally efficient method to find the least square equation by calculating the center of gravity of the data by taking $x = X - \overline{X}$ and $y = Y - \overline{Y}$ and then calculating the least square line as

$$y = \left(\frac{\Sigma xy}{\Sigma x^2}\right) * x$$

finally substituting back the $X - \overline{X}$ for x and $Y - \overline{Y}$ for y.

Moving averages. The method of moving averages is useful because some seasonal, cyclical, or random patterns may be smoothed, leaving the trend pattern. The principle behind moving averages is to calculate the arithmetic mean or data from groups of periods, using the equation

$$\frac{Y_1 + Y_2 + \cdots + Y_N}{N}$$

1987	440	490
1988	500	470
1989	520	470
1990	550	458
1991	440	410
1992	340	400
1993	500	396
1994	460	
1995	310	
1996	390	
1997	320	

FIGURE 13.11
Calculating a five-year moving average.

and then to calculate the next arithmetic mean by discarding the oldest period's data and adding data from the next period

$$\frac{Y_2 + Y_3 + \cdots + Y_{N+1}}{N}$$

and in this manner say the average is moving.

Figure 13.11 shows one type of moving average. Here five years' data are averaged and the resulting figure is indicated. Notice that years 1987 through 1991 inclusive are averaged to represent 1989, then the years 1988 through 1992 are averaged to get a representative figure for 1990, and so on. When the results are graphed as in Figure 13.12, it is easily noticeable that the widely fluctuating data are smoothed.

The moving average method is useful for its smoothing ability, but at the same time it has many disadvantages. First, the data at the very beginning and end are lost. In the preceding example, we lost data for 1987 and 1988 at the be-

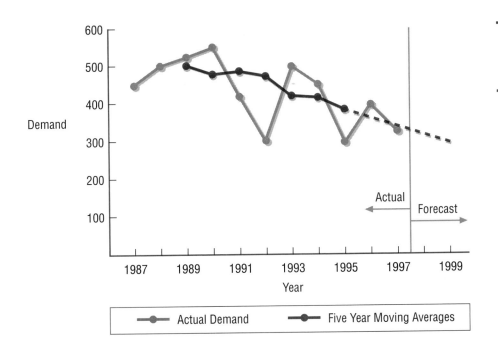

FIGURE 13.12
A five-year moving average smooths widely fluctuating data.

A systems analyst can have a difficult time estimating intangible costs and benefits. THE FAR SIDE. Copyright 1986 UNIVERSAL PRESS SYNDICATED. Reprinted with permission. All rights reserved.

Einstein discovers that time is actually money.

ginning and years 1996 and 1997 at the end. The trend line must be extended from 1995, rather than from 1997, as would have been the case in the least squares method. Furthermore, moving averages are more strongly affected by extreme values than the methods of graphical judgment and least squares.

Many worthwhile forecasting packages are available for microcomputers as well as for mainframes. The analyst should learn forecasting well, as it often provides information valuable in justifying the entire project.

Identifying Benefits and Costs

Benefits and costs can be thought of as either tangible or intangible. Both tangible and intangible benefits and costs must be taken into account when systems are considered.

TANGIBLE BENEFITS. Tangible benefits are advantages measurable in dollars that accrue to the organization through the use of the information system. Examples of tangible benefits are an increase in the speed of processing, access to otherwise inaccessible information, access to information on a more timely basis than was possible before, the advantage of the computer's superior calculating power, and decreases in the amount of employee time needed to complete specific tasks. And there are still others. Although measurement is not always easy, tangible benefits can actually be measured in terms of dollars, resources, or time saved.

The Birth of a System

"Yup, what little there is is all mine. I started in this business because I couldn't keep my hands off of the stuff. I loved tinkering with our electronic equipment, taking apart TVs and VCRs. Ask my wife, Carol. Then I started helping friends with their projects, and they thought I was pretty good. When I inherited some money, I opened this little shop selling and repairing TVs and VCRs and renting videotapes," says Roger Corman, owner of a video rental and repair store.

"Right now," Roger continues as he tours you around the small store, "we use a manual system for keeping track of rental videotapes. We make a a 3 × 5 card for each title we own and the name of the person renting the tape is recorded on this card.

"The cards were okay for a while, but now I need your help. I'm afraid that if things keep growing like they have, I'll need a computer soon. But I didn't get into this business overnight, and I want to be sure that the computer will pay for itself. I need proof. I've got to see it in black and white," Roger confides.

"I was interested enough to keep a log of demand for rental tapes for the past 27 months," Roger continues. "Here it is."

Hoping to catch up on some movies you've missed recently, you agree to do a small systems project for Roger in return for a fee and some free videotaped films. Using the methods you have learned so far, forecast the demand for tape rentals and for new titles.

Month	Number of Rentals	Number of Titles
January	1000	70
February	1200	100
March	1400	130
April	1800	140
May	2200	150
June	2000	160
July	1800	170
August	1800	180
September	2500	200
October	2800	220
November	3000	280
December	3500	260
January	4000	280
February	4600	300
March	4800	320
April	5200	340
May	5700	360
June	5000	380
July	4800	400
August	3500	260
September	4000	280
October	4600	300
November	4800	320
December	5200	340
January	5700	360
February	5000	380
March	4800	400

The Birth of a System II: The Sequel

"That's a good question. I can think of a million problems we have here. But just off the top of my head, here are the big ones," says Roger Corman during his second interview with you. "It's taking us time to keep up records. It's getting to be extremely difficult to sniff out tapes that aren't returned. I like detective flicks, but I'm no Sherlock Holmes. I usually have to track down tapes myself, and that takes me away from my repair service.

"What really gripes me about tapes that aren't returned on time is that they result in lost rentals, since most of my customers choose from the selections in stock that they can see on the shelves. And I don't have any information about the categories of tapes my customers prefer. But part of it is my fault, I guess, since I haven't bothered to set up a reservation system. I mean, there are probably more problems, but those are the ones I handle every day," says Roger.

You analyze the recording process and determine that employees can save two minutes for each tape rented and half a minute for each title in inventory per month. Mr. Corman himself gets involved with tracking down late tapes (about one for every 250 tapes rented), and you find he can save half an hour per month for each tape he has to track down if he uses the computer instead.

Assume that Mr. Corman can take out a small loan at 15 percent to purchase the computer and pay for development costs. The economy is reasonably good with an inflation rate of 5 percent. Your time, as well as Mr. Corman's time, can be valued at $20 per hour. His employees' time is worth $6 per hour.

You estimate that systems analysis will take 30 hours, system design 40 hours, and development and implementation 30 hours. Mr. Corman will be involved in answering questions for about 15 hours, and in addition, you will have to individually train two people and Mr. Corman for five hours each.

The microcomputer, printer, and software cost $4,000. After the system is up and running, you have advised Mr. Corman that he will need to earmark $20 per month for supplies and maintenance.

After discussing your analysis with Roger, he says, "I don't like giving you a lot of direction, but would you make a list for me? I'd like to screen all of this, so I can project what will happen. Give it your best shot, so I can take a close-up look."

From the foregoing data, prepare a list of tangible and intangible costs and benefits for Mr. Corman. You will be asked to analyze these costs in Consulting Opportunity 13.4.

INTANGIBLE BENEFITS. Some benefits that accrue to the organization from the use of the information system are difficult to measure but are important nonetheless. These are known as intangible benefits.

Intangible benefits include improving the decision-making process, enhancing accuracy, becoming more competitive in customer service, maintaining a good business image, and increasing job satisfaction for employees by eliminating tedious tasks. As you can judge from the list given, intangible benefits are extremely important and can have far-reaching implications for the business as it relates to people both outside and within the organization.

While intangible benefits of an information system are important factors which must be considered when deciding whether to proceed with a system, a system built solely for its intangible benefits will not be successful. You must discuss both tangible and intangible benefits in your proposal, since presenting both will allow decision makers in the business to make a well-informed decision about the proposed system.

TANGIBLE COSTS. The concepts of tangible and intangible costs present a conceptual parallel to the tangible and intangible benefits discussed already. Tangible costs are those that can be accurately projected by the systems analyst and the business' accounting personnel.

Included in tangible costs are the cost of equipment such as computers and terminals, the costs of resources, the cost of systems analysts' time, the cost of programmers' time, and other employees' salaries. These costs are typically well-established or can be found out quite easily and are the costs that will require a cash outlay of the business.

INTANGIBLE COSTS. Intangible costs are difficult to estimate and may not be known. They include losing a competitive edge, losing the reputation for being first with an innovation or the leader in a field, declining company image due to increased customer dissatisfaction, and ineffective decision making due to untimely or inaccessible information. As you can imagine, it is next to impossible to accurately project a dollar amount for intangible costs. In order to aid decision makers who want to weigh the proposed system and all of its implications, you must include intangible costs even though they are not quantifiable.

COMPARING COSTS AND BENEFITS

There are many well-known techniques for comparing the costs and benefits of the proposed system. They include break-even analysis, payback, cash-flow analysis, and present value. All of these techniques provide straightforward ways of yielding information to decision makers about the worthiness of the proposed system.

Break-Even Analysis

By comparing costs alone, the systems analyst can use this kind of analysis to determine the break-even capacity of the proposed information system. The point at which the total costs of the current system and of the proposed system intersect represents the break-even point—where it becomes profitable for the business to get the new information system.

Total costs include the costs that recur during operation of the system plus the developmental costs that occur only once (one-time costs of installing a new system)—that is, the tangible costs that were just discussed. Figure 13.13 is an example of break-even analysis on a small store that maintains inventory using a manual system. As volume rises, the costs of the manual system rise at an increasing rate. A new computer system would cost a substantial sum up front, but the incremental costs for higher volume would be rather small. The graph shows that the computer system would be cost-effective if the business sold about 600 units per week.

Break-even analysis is useful when a business is growing and volume is a key variable in costs. One disadvantage of break-even analysis is that benefits are assumed to remain the same, regardless of which system is in place. From our study of tangible and intangible benefits, we know this is clearly not the case.

Payback

Payback is a simple way to assess whether a business should invest in a proposed information system, one that is based on how long it will take for the benefits of the system to pay back the costs of developing it. Briefly, the payback method determines the number of years of operation that the information system needs to pay back the cost of investing in it. Figure 13.14 illustrates a system with a payback period of three and a half years.

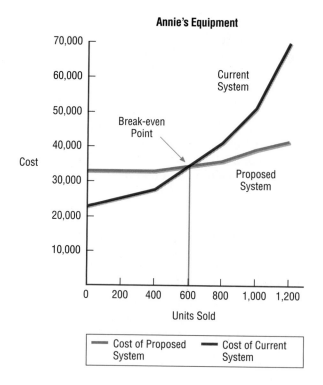

FIGURE 13.13
Break-even analysis for the proposed inventory system.

Payback can be determined in one of two ways—either by increasing revenues or increasing savings. A combination of the two methods can also be used. Since this is a popular way to assess alternative investments, businesses will typically have a set time period for payback assessments (three years, for example). This is something you can find out from the accounting personnel with whom you are working on the systems project.

If the proposed system has a projected payback of six years in a company that adheres to a three-year maximum payback on projects involving fast-changing technology, the system will be rejected. Payback that is made within the range used by the business but is still longer than typical (for example, four years instead of three) may not be rejected outright but may be subject to scrutiny through other methods.

Although the payback method offers a well-known and simple way to assess the worthiness of the information system, it has three drawbacks that limit its usefulness. One drawback is that it is strictly a short-term approach to investment and replacement decisions; the second is that it does not consider the importance of how repayments are timed; and the third is that the payback method does not consider the total returns from the proposed systems project that may go well beyond the payback year. Other forms of analysis should be used to augment the payback method and overcome some of these flaws.

Cash-flow Analysis

Cash-flow analysis examines the direction, size, and pattern of cash flow that is associated with the proposed information system. If you are proposing the replacement of an old information system with a new one and if the new information system will not be generating any additional cash for the

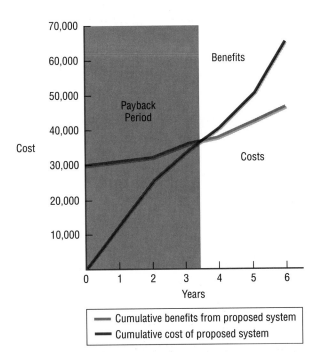

FIGURE 13.14
Payback analysis showing a
payback period of three and a
half years.

Year	Cost	Cumulative Costs	Benefits	Cumulative Benefits
0	30,000	30,000	0	0
1	1,000	31,000	12,000	12,000
2	2,000	33,000	12,000	24,000
3	2,000	35,000	8,000	32,000
4	3,000	38,000	8,000	40,000
5	4,000	42,000	10,000	50,000
6	4,000	46,000	15,000	65,000

business, only cash outlays are associated with the project. If this is the case, the new system cannot be justified on the basis of new revenues generated and must be examined closely for other tangible benefits if it is to be pursued further.

Figure 13.15 shows a small company that is providing a mailing service to other small companies in the city. Revenue projections are that only $5,000 will be generated in the first quarter, but after the second quarter, revenue will grow at a steady rate. Costs will be large in the first two quarters and then level off. Cash-flow analysis is used to determine when a company will begin to make a profit (in this case, it is in the third quarter, with a cash flow of $7,590) and when it will be "out of the red"—that is, when revenue has made up for the initial investment (in the first quarter of year two, when accumulated cash flow changes from a negative amount to a positive $10,720).

The proposed system should have increased revenues along with cash outlays. Then the size of the cash flow must be analyzed along with the patterns of cash flow associated with the purchase of the new system. You must ask when cash outlays and revenues will occur, not only for the initial purchase but also over the life of the information system.

FIGURE 13.15
Cash-flow analysis for the
computerized mail-addressing
system.

	Year 1 Quarter 1	Quarter 2	Quarter 3	Quarter 4	Year 2 Quarter 1
Revenue	5,000	20,000	24,960	31,270	39,020
Software					
Development	10,000	5,000			
Personnel	8,000	8,400	8,800	9,260	9,700
Training	3,000	6,000			
Equipment					
Lease	4,000	4,000	4,000	4,000	4,000
Supplies	1,000	2,000	2,370	2,990	3,730
Maintenance	0	2,000	2,200	2,420	2,660
Total Costs	26,000	27,400	17,370	18,670	20,090
Cash Flow	-21,000	-7,400	7,590	12,600	18,930
Cumulative Cash Flow	-21,000	-28,400	-20,810	-8,210	10,720

Present Value

Present value analysis helps the systems analyst to present to business decision makers the time value of the investment in the information system as well as the funds flow (as discussed in the previous section). Present value is a way to assess all of the economic outlays and revenues of the information system over its economic life and to compare costs today with future costs and today's benefits with future benefits.

In Figure 13.16, system costs total $272,000 over six years and benefits total $280,700. Therefore, we might conclude that benefits outweigh the costs. However, benefits only started to surpass costs after the fourth year, and dollars in the sixth year will not be equivalent to dollars in year one.

For instance, a dollar investment at 7 percent today will be worth $1.07 at the end of the year and will double in approximately ten years. The present value, therefore, is the cost or benefit measured in today's dollars and depends on the cost of money. The cost of money is the opportunity cost, or the rate that could be obtained if the money invested in the proposed system were invested in another (relatively safe) project.

The present value of $1.00 at a discount rate of i is calculated by determining the factor

$$\frac{1}{(1 + i)^n}$$

where n is the number of periods. Then the factor is multiplied by the dollar amount, yielding present value as shown in Figure 13.17. In this example,

FIGURE 13.16
Without considering present
value, the benefits appear to
outweigh the costs.

	Year						
	1	**2**	**3**	**4**	**5**	**6**	**Total**
Costs	40,000	42,000	44,100	46,300	48,600	51,000	272,000
Benefits	25,000	31,200	39,000	48,700	60,800	76,000	280,700

	Year						
	1	**2**	**3**	**4**	**5**	**6**	**Total**
Costs	40,000	42,000	44,100	46,300	48,600	51,000	
Multiplier	.89	.80	.71	.64	.57	.51	
Present Value of Costs	35,600	33,600	31,311	29,632	27,702	26,010	183,855
Benefits	25,000	31,200	39,000	48,700	60,800	76,000	
Multiplier	.89	.80	.71	.64	.57	.51	
Present Value of Benefits	22,250	24,960	27,960	31,168	34,656	38,760	179,484

FIGURE 13.17
Taking into account present value, the conclusion is that the costs are greater than the benefits. The discount rate, *i*, is assumed to be .12 in calculating the multipliers in this table.

the cost of money—the discount rate—is assumed to be 0.12 (12 percent) for the entire planning horizon. Multipliers are calculated for each period: $n = 1, n = 2, . . ., n = 6$. Present values of both costs and benefits are then calculated using these multipliers. When this is done, the total benefits (measured in today's dollars) are $179,484—less than the costs (also measured in today's dollars). The conclusion to be drawn is that the proposed system is not worthwhile if present value is considered.

Although this example, which used present value factors, is useful in explaining the concept, all electronic spreadsheets have a built-in present value function. The analyst can directly compute present value using this feature.

Guidelines for Analysis

The use of the methods discussed in the preceding subsections depends on the methods employed and accepted within the organization itself. However, for general guidelines it is safe to say:

1. Use break-even analysis if the project needs to be justified in terms of cost, not benefits, or if benefits do not substantially improve with the proposed system.
2. Use payback when the improved tangible benefits form a convincing argument for the proposed system.
3. Use cash-flow analysis when the project is expensive relative to the size of the company, or when the business would be significantly affected by a large drain (even if temporary) on funds.
4. Use present value when the payback period is long or when the cost of borrowing money is high.

Whichever method is chosen, it is important to remember that cost-benefit analysis be approached systematically, in a way that can be explained and justified to management, who will eventually decide whether to commit resources to the systems project. Next, we turn to the importance of comparing many systems alternatives.

The Birth of a System III: More Graphic Than Ever

"The list you made of tangible and intangible costs and benefits really helped," raved Roger. "You had to do some tight editing to make anything out of the melodrama I spun for you the other day. Before we produce a system, however, I'd like you to *analyze* the tangible costs and benefits you wrote for me. Even films have critics," Roger reminds you, as he slips back out of view and heads back to his repair bench.

Using one of the methods discussed in this chapter, perform the analysis Roger called for, and make a convincing case for the systems solution you preview. Use graphs to get the proper angle on the project, and put the debut of your analysis in its best light.

Examining Alternative Systems

Through the use of break-even, payback, cash-flow, and present value analyses, it is possible to compare alternatives for the information system. As was shown previously, it is important to use multiple analyses in order to adequately cover the shortcomings of each approach. Although you will consider several alternatives, the proposal itself will recommend only one. This means that you will have done comparative analyses about which system makes better economic sense before the proposal is written. Those analyses can be included to provide support for the system you are recommending.

Do not think there is only one "correct" system solution to help a business solve its problems and reach its goal. Different businesses call for different system attributes, and system analysts themselves differ about the best way to handle various business problems.

Based on your ascertainment of information requirements, the tangible costs and benefits of the system, and so on, compare the alternatives with which you are working. This might call for the use of one of the multiple-criteria methods described in Chapter 12. Be open-minded as you compare alternatives so that the system you are recommending can be said to fit within the business as its members experience it.

The key point is that you want to compare and contrast opinions in as fair a manner as possible, so that a true choice is offered to organizational decision makers. The closer their initial identification with and acceptance of the proposed system, the greater the likelihood of its continued use and acceptance once the system is in place. Continue including decision makers in the planning, even though you must in some ways expect to play the role of the systems expert now.

SUMMARY

Evaluating hardware and software, identifying and forecasting costs and benefits, and performing cost-benefit analysis are all necessary activities the systems analyst must accomplish in preparing material for the systems proposal. Information requirements help shape what software is purchased or written, as well as what hardware is needed to perform required data transformation functions.

Systems analysts must estimate workloads in order to adequately characterize current and projected workload capacity necessary for hardware. Sample workloads can then be run on the hardware under consideration.

"Sometimes the people who have been here for some time are surprised at how much we have actually grown. And yes, I do admit that it isn't easy to keep track of what each person is up to, or even what purchases each department has made in the way of hardware and software. We're working on it, though. Snowden would like to see more accountability for computer purchases. He wants to make sure that we know what we have, where it is, why we have it, who's using it, and if it's boosting MRE productivity or, as he so delicately puts it, 'to see whether it's just an expensive toy' that we can live without."

HYPERCASE QUESTIONS

1. Using the form provided in Chapter 13, complete a computer equipment inventory form for the Training and Management Systems Unit.

2. Using the "Software Evaluation" guidelines in Chapter 13, do a brief evaluation of GEMS, which is used by the Management Systems employees. In a paragraph, briefly critique this custom-made software by comparing it to off-the-shelf software such as Lotus' "Organizer," or Microsoft's "Project." (Both are mentioned in Chapter 3.)

3. List the intangible costs and benefits of GEMS as reported by employees of MRE.

4. Briefly describe the two alternatives Snowden is considering for the proposed project tracking and reporting system.

5. What organizational and political factors should Snowden consider in proposing his new system at MRE? (In a brief paragraph, discuss three central conflicts.)

Although computer equipment changes rapidly, the process used in evaluating hardware need not change too often. By inventorying equipment already on hand and on order, systems analysts will be able to better determine if new, modified, or current computer hardware is to be recommended.

Computer hardware can be acquired through purchase, lease, or rental. Vendors will supply support services such as preventive maintenance and user training that are typically negotiated separately.

Packaged software must also be evaluated by the systems analyst and pertinent users. Much programming time can be saved if such a package is usable without extensive customizing. Software needs to be evaluated on how well it performs desired functions, on its ease of use, on the adequacy of documentation, and on the support services vendors may offer.

Preparing a proposal means identifying all of the costs and benefits of a number of alternatives. The systems analyst has a number of methods available to forecast future costs, benefits, volumes of transactions, and economic variables that affect costs and benefits. Costs and benefits can be tangible (quantifiable) or intangible (nonquantifiable and resistant to direct comparison).

A systems analyst has many methods for analyzing costs and benefits. Break-even analysis examines the cost of the existing system versus the cost of the proposed system. The payback method determines the length of time it will take before the new system is profitable. Cash-flow analysis is appropriate when it is critical to know the amount of cash outlays, while present value takes into consideration the cost of borrowing money. These tools help the analyst examine the alternatives at hand and make a well-researched recommendation in the systems proposal.

KEYWORDS AND PHRASES

benchmarking
estimated workload
vendor support
forecasting
graphical judgment
method of least squares
moving averages
tangible benefits

intangible benefits
tangible costs
intangible costs
break-even analysis
payback
cash-flow analysis
present value

REVIEW QUESTIONS

1. List the elements that should be included on a computer hardware inventory form.
2. What is meant by the words *estimated workload*?
3. List four criteria for evaluating system hardware.
4. What are the three main options for the acquisition of computer hardware?
5. Under what conditions is rental of computer hardware appropriate?
6. List four extra support services that are negotiable with vendors of computer hardware.
7. List the six main categories on which to grade software.
8. Why is forecasting a useful tool for the systems analyst?
9. Define unconditional forecasting.
10. What is a disadvantage of graphical judgment?
11. What is the objective in estimating a trend using the least squares method?
12. Why is the method of moving averages a useful one?
13. Define tangible costs and benefits. Give an example of each one.
14. Define intangible costs and benefits. Give an example of each one.
15. List four techniques for comparing the costs and benefits of a proposed system.
16. When is break-even analysis useful?
17. What are the three drawbacks of using the payback method?
18. When is cash-flow analysis used?
19. Define present value analysis.
20. As a general guideline, when should present value analysis be used?

PROBLEMS

1. Delicato, Inc., a manufacturer of precise measuring instruments for scientific purposes, has presented you with a list of attributes that its managers think are probably important in selecting a vendor for computer

hardware and software. The criteria are not listed in order of importance.

1. Low price.
2. Precisely written software for engineering applications.
3. Vendor performs routine maintenance on hardware.
4. Training for Delicato employees.

a. Critique the list of attributes in a paragraph.

b. Using its initial input, help Delicato, Inc., draw up a more suitable list of criteria for selecting computer hardware and software vendors.

2. SoftWear Silhouettes is a rapidly growing mail-order house specializing in all-cotton clothing. Management is contemplating the purchase of microcomputers and software to help with supplier and customer accounts. Company offices are located in a small, isolated New England town, and the employees have little computer training.

a. Considering the company's situation, draw up a list of software attributes that SoftWear Silhouettes should emphasize in its choice of software.

b. List the variables that contributed to your response in part **a** above.

3. Below is ten years' demand for YarDarts, an outdoor game for the whole family that is part of the 65-game product line of Open Air, Ltd., a manufacturer specializing in outdoor games that can be played in a small area.

Year	Demand
1988	20,900
1989	31,200
1990	28,000
1991	41,200
1992	49,700
1993	46,400
1994	51,200
1995	52,300
1996	49,200
1997	57,600

a. Graph the demand data for YarDarts.

b. Forecast the demand for YarDarts for the next five years using the graphical judgment approach.

4. a. Determine the linear trend for YarDarts demand using the least squares method.

b. Estimate the demand for YarDarts for the next five years using the trend you determined.

5. a. Determine the linear trend for YarDarts using a three-year moving average.

b. Use least squares on the averages in part 3a to determine a linear trend.

c. Estimate demand for YarDarts for the next five years by extending the linear trend found in part 3b.

6. Does the data for YarDarts appear to have a cyclical variation? Explain.

7. Interglobal Paper Company has asked for your help in comparing its present computer system with a new one its board of directors would like to see implemented. Proposed system and present system costs are listed in the following table.

Year 1	Proposed System Costs	Present System Costs
Equipment Lease	$20,000	$11,500
Salaries	30,000	50,000
Overhead	4,000	3,000
Development	30,000	—
Year 2		
Equipment Lease	$20,000	$10,500
Salaries	33,000	55,000
Overhead	4,400	3,300
Development	12,000	—
Year 3		
Equipment Lease	$20,000	$10,500
Salaries	36,000	60,000
Overhead	4,900	3,600
Development	—	—
Year 4		
Equipment Lease	$20,000	$10,500
Salaries	39,000	66,000
Overhead	5,500	4,000
Development	—	—

a. Using break-even analysis, determine the year in which Interglobal Paper will break even.

b. Graph the costs and show the break-even point.

8. Below are system benefits for Interglobal Paper Company (from problem 7):

Year	Benefits
1	$55,000
2	75,000
3	80,000
4	85,000

a. Use the costs of Interglobal's proposed system from problem 7 to determine the payback period (use the payback method).

b. Graph the benefits versus the costs and indicate the payback period.

	Month				
	July	August	September	October	November
REVENUE	35,000	36,000	42,000	48,000	57,000
COSTS					
Office Remodeling	25,000	8,000			
Salaries	11,000	12,100	13,300	14,600	16,000
Training	6,000	6,000			
Equipment Lease	8,000	8,480	9,000	9,540	10,110
Supplies	3,000	3,150	3,300	3,460	3,630

9. Glenn's Electronics, a small company, has set up a computer service. The table above shows the revenue expected for the first five months of operation, in addition to the costs for office remodeling, and so on. Determine the cash flow and accumulated cash flow for the company. When is Glenn's expected to show a profit?

10. Alamo Foods of San Antonio wants to introduce a new computer system for its perishable products warehouse. The costs and benefits are listed below.

Years	Costs	Benefits
1	$33,000	$21,000
2	34,600	26,200
3	36,300	32,700
4	38,100	40,800
5	40,000	51,000
6	42,000	63,700

    a. Given a discount rate of 8 percent (.08), perform present value analysis on the data for Alamo Foods. (*Hint:* Use the formula

$$\frac{1}{(1 + i)^n}$$

to find the multipliers for years 1 to 6.)

    b. What is your recommendation for Alamo Foods?

11. **a.** Suppose the discount rate in problem 10 changes to 13 percent (.13). Perform present value analysis using the new discount rate.

    b. What is your recommendation to Alamo Foods now?

    c. Explain the difference between problem 10, part b, and problem 11, part b.

12. Solve problem 7 using an electronic spreadsheet program such as LOTUS or Excel.

13. Use a spreadsheet program to solve problem 9.

14. Solve problem 10 using a function for net present value—for example: @NPV (*x*, range) in LOTUS.

SELECTED BIBLIOGRAPHY

Alter, S. *Information Systems: A Management Perspective.* Menlo Park, CA: Benjamin/Cummings Publishing Company, Inc., 1996.

Buffa, E. S. *Modern Production/Operations Management,* 6th ed. New York: John Wiley & Sons, 1980.

Cleland, D. I., and W. R. King. *Systems Analysis and Project Management,* 2nd ed. New York: McGraw-Hill Book Company, 1975.

Lazzaro, V. "Outlining for Conducting and Implementing a Systems Study." In V. Lazarro (ed.), *Systems and Procedures: A Handbook for Business and Industry,* 2nd ed. Englewood Cliffs, NJ: Prentice Hall, 1968.

Levine, D. M., P. R. Ramsey, and M. L. Berenson. *Business Statistics for Quality and Productivity.* Englewood Cliffs, NJ: Prentice-Hall, Inc., 1995.

Lucas, H. *Information Systems Concepts for Management,* 3rd ed. New York: McGraw-Hill Book Company, 1986.

Meredith, J. R., and T. E. Gibbs. *The Management of Operations,* 2nd ed. New York: John Wiley & Sons, 1984.

Sumner, M. *Computers, Concepts and Uses.* Englewood Cliffs, NJ: Prentice Hall, 1985.

Voich, D., Jr., H. J. Mottice, and W. A. Shrode. *Information Systems for Operations and Management.* Cincinnati: South-Western Publishing Company, 1975.

PROPOSING TO GO FORTH

"Since we chose to design and implement the new microcomputer system using microcomputers linked with a local area network, we should work on preparing the systems proposal," Anna begins. She and Chip are meeting to plan the next phase of the design.

"Yes," replies Chip, "we need to make some hardware and software decisions as well as to ensure that the users are aware of the benefits the new system will provide."

"We should determine which software will be required to implement the system and the hardware requirements for each user of the system," notes Anna. "Why don't you work on the hardware portion, and I'll investigate software?"

"Sure," Chip replies. "I plan to meet with each of the users again. When I have all of the information, I'll produce a summary report."

Chip proceeds to work with each user to determine what equipment would be required. Some of his findings are:

Mike Crowe has a Pentium 166 microcomputer on the desk. This is more than adequate for serving the needs of the new system. Additional, necessary equipment is a portable microcomputer for creating transactions when performing physical inventory and preventive maintenance work.

Dot Matricks has a Pentium 120 combination mainframe/microcomputer workstation. This is adequate for the new system.

Hy Perteks has an older microcomputer on his desk. Recommend that it be replaced with Pentium MMX microcomputer.

Paige Prynter has a mainframe terminal. Recommend replacing the terminal with Pentium workstation. Purchase software to run terminal emulation on the workstation.

Cher Ware has an older 486 microcomputer. Recommend that it be upgraded with a Pentium MMX workstation.

Other equipment and supplies: a server microcomputer to manage the network. This should be a Pentium 166 or better, one fitted with communication boards. A higher-speed laser printer with font cartridges attached directly to the server and smaller personal laser printers attached to each microcomputer should be provided. Additionally, cable must be purchased to connect each of the users on the network.

Meanwhile, Anna is determining the software that would be needed to implement the system. Since each of the users would be receiving software developed by programmers, the major task was to decide what software would be needed for system development and to network the microcomputers. After researching software options, Anna made the following recommendations:

1. Development software to create the system. Three options are available:
   a. Use a microcomputer-based COBOL package, which would need to be purchased. The versions used in the classroom are the result of a

*Allen Schmidt,
Julie E. Kendall, and
Kenneth E. Kendall*

grant and are limited to educational use only. The advantage of COBOL is that it is currently being used by the programming staff and it is available in new object-oriented versions.

    b. Use a database package and write object-oriented code. Compile the database programs into executable code. Currently, Access is available in the student labs. Other database packages should be evaluated.

    c. Build a client-server solution. Visual Basic, Delphi, and Power-Builder software are very powerful, and they work with many different databases.

2. Network software is required to establish and make the local area network "user-friendly" with graphical interface screens.

Chip and Anna sit at a work table and examine each other's findings.

    "I suppose the next task is to obtain some cost figures for the hardware and software selection," Anna says. "What do you think is our best source of cost information?"

    "There are several sources of information," Chip replies. "One would be to examine trade journals for prices. There are many mail-order houses that would have posted prices. We should also call or visit dealers and obtain quotes, especially with educational discounts. The manufacturers may have special programs available. We'll check with the university purchasing officer, too. Once we have all the cost information, we can produce a document as part of the systems proposal."

Exercises*

    E-1. Use microcomputer periodicals in your library to investigate costs for each of the machines and peripheral devices to be purchased. Make a comparison list for each machine.

    E-2. Visit a local computer retail store and obtain cost information for each of the microcomputers listed in this episode. Include printers and, at a minimum, VGA-quality monitors. Make a comparison list for each machine.

    E-3. Investigate three different network costs. Include hardware, software, network boards, and 500 feet of cable to connect the machines. Write a list or use a spreadsheet to summarize your work.

    E-4. Scan trade journals and summarize your findings, comparing three different database packages, their features, and costs.

    E-5. Investigate the features and prices for microcomputer COBOL packages. Make a summary list of your findings.

    E-6. Investigate the features and prices for microcomputer database packages. Make a summary list of your findings.

    E-7. Investigate the features and prices for PowerBuilder, Visual Basic, and Delphi. Make a summary list of your findings.

    E-8. Use the World Wide Web to find out information about the features of three of the software packages mentioned above. Make a summary list of your findings.

    E-9. Using the information gathered in the problems above, calculate the total cost for three unique solutions.

* Exercises preceded by a disk icon require the program Visible Analyst Workbench or another CASE tool. A disk is provided free of charge to any professor adopting this book. The examples on the disk may be imported into Visible Analyst Workbench and then used by students.

14

WRITING
AND PRESENTING
THE SYSTEMS
PROPOSAL

METHODS AVAILABLE

The written proposal serves as a summary of the systems analyst's work in the business up to that point, and as such it is essential that great care is given to writing and presenting it. Through the use of three methods, the analyst can create a successful systems proposal. These methods are effectively organizing the content, writing in a professional style, and orally presenting the proposal in an informative way.

THE SYSTEMS PROPOSAL

Organizing the Systems Proposal

Once you have gathered the material to be included in your systems proposal, you need to piece it together in a logical and visually effective way. This means including ten main functional sections, using an effective writing style, using figures to supplement your writing, and attending to the visual details of the written proposal.

WHAT TO INCLUDE IN THE SYSTEMS PROPOSAL. There are ten main sections comprising the written systems proposal, as shown in Figure 14.1. Each part has a particular function, and the eventual proposal should be arranged in the following order:

1. Cover letter.
2. Title page of project.
3. Table of contents.
4. Executive summary (including recommendations).
5. Outline of systems study with appropriate documentation.
6. Detailed results of the systems study.
7. Systems alternatives (three or four possible solutions).

451

8. Systems analysts' recommendations.
9. Proposal summary.
10. Appendices (assorted documentation, summary of phases, correspondence, and so on).

Cover letter. A cover letter to management and the MIS task force should accompany the systems proposal. It should list the people who did the study and summarize the objectives of the study. The cover letter can also include information about the prearranged time and place for the oral presentation of the systems proposal. Keep the cover letter concise (one page maximum) and friendly, since its function is to reacquaint management with the systems project.

Title page. Include on the title page the name of the project, the names of the systems analysis team members, and the date the proposal is submitted. Keep the title page uncluttered in appearance.

Titling a project is more art than science. The proposal title must accurately express the content of the proposal, but it can also exhibit some imagination. Alliteration, using the same letter to begin each word ("The Simon Says System"), can work sometimes, but there are many other ideas that will serve as well, such as using the main title with a subtitle and separating them with a colon. If the project has developed an acronym that is recognized and respected in the organization, it can be used in the title. The main

FIGURE 14.1
Each systems proposal should contain ten main sections, each serving a unique function.

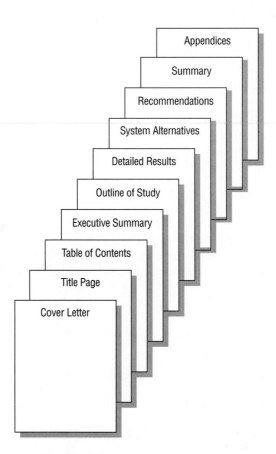

Appendices

Summary

Recommendations

System Alternatives

Detailed Results

Outline of Study

Executive Summary

Table of Contents

Title Page

Cover Letter

Making It Reel

"As you know from working with me the past few weeks, I'm a technical guy," admits Roger as you are about to leave his store after follow-up interviews one afternoon. "I can understand most anything about computers you want to throw at me. Your proposal can be as technical as you like."

Thinking that writing up the proposal might actually be enjoyable for a change, you look happily at Roger, who is relaxing with his feet up on his desk. As you open the door of the store to exit, Roger calls after you casually, "Of course, the proposal isn't really for me. Remember, I want it simple enough so I can explain it to the employees and to my banker."

As a systems analyst, you have been working with Roger Corman on developing a microcomputer-based system for tracking the rental of movies and other features on videotape. Based on the assignments you completed in Chapter 13 and what Roger has just told you about the expectations for the proposal, write a one-page executive summary to serve as the first page in the report. It should cogently summarize your recommendations in layman's terms. Use an appealing layout, and follow the guidelines for executive summaries.

point is that titling is important in getting your reader to open the proposal, and it should not be done as an afterthought.

Table of contents. The table of contents can be enormously useful to readers of long proposals. If the proposal is very short (less than ten pages), omit the table of contents, since it is superfluous in such a short document.

The time to produce a useful table of contents occurs much earlier in proposal preparation, when the analyst writes sections and subsections with expressive headings and subheadings to indicate the contents of each one. The more concise yet telling they are, the more useful will be the resulting table of contents.

Executive summary. Executive summaries are so well known in the business world that they have become a cliché that conjures up a harried businessperson who is only able to grasp the rudimentary elements of organizational functioning in such summaries. We can laugh at the cliché while still acknowledging that a well-written executive summary is critical to the systems proposal.

The executive summary, in 250 to 375 words, provides the who, what, when, where, why, and how of the proposal—just as would the first paragraph in a newspaper story. It goes right to the heart of the systems project, so that anyone reading it will have an accurate concept of what is going on. It should also include the recommendations of the systems analysts and desired management action, since some people will only have time to read the summary. The executive summary is difficult to write since it is content-laden yet concise. It should be written only after the remainder of the proposal is complete, since only then will the analyst have an adequate, overall picture of what is being proposed.

Outline of systems study. This section provides information about all of the methods used in the study and who or what was studied. Any questionnaires, interviews, sampling of archival data, observation, or prototyping used in the systems study should be discussed in this section.

CHAPTER 14:
WRITING
AND PRESENTING
THE SYSTEMS
PROPOSAL

453

Detailed results of systems study. This section details what the systems analyst has found out about the system through all of the methods described in the preceding section. Any conclusions about systems problems that have come to the fore through the study should be noted here. This includes kinds and rates of errors; current and projected work volume; and how work is being handled by the current system.

This section presents the problems that exist in the existing system. The material included here should raise the problems or suggest opportunities that call forth the alternatives presented in the next section.

Systems alternatives. In this portion of the proposal, the analyst presents two or three alternative solutions that directly address the aforementioned problems. Although more than three solutions are usually possible, preliminary analyses should leave you with the best two or three alternatives, which should be included here. The alternatives you should present should include one that recommends keeping the system the same.

Each alternative (even that of preserving the status quo) should be explored separately. Describe the costs and benefits of each situation. This is an excellent place to insert graphs clearly comparing the costs and benefits of each solution. Since there are usually tradeoffs involved in any solution, be sure to include the advantages and disadvantages of each one.

Each alternative must clearly indicate what management must do to implement it. This should be written as clearly as possible—for example, "Buy PCs for all middle managers"; "Purchase packaged software to manage inventory"; "Modify the existing system through funding in-house programming efforts"; and so on.

Systems analysts' recommendations. After the systems analysis team has weighed the alternatives, it will have a definite professional opinion about which solution is most workable. This section expresses the *recommended* solution. Include the reasons supporting the team's recommendation, so that it is easy to understand why it is being made. The recommendation should flow logically from the preceding analysis of alternative solutions.

Proposal summary. The proposal summary is a brief statement that mirrors the content of the executive summary. It should not quote the material from the executive summary verbatim, however. It gives the objectives of the study and the recommended solution. It also allows the analyst one more chance to stress the project's importance and feasibility along with the value of the recommendations. Conclude the proposal on a positive note.

Appendices. This is the last part of the systems proposal, and it can include any information that the systems analyst feels may be of interest to specific individuals, but that is not essential for understanding the systems study and what is being proposed. Appendices might include pertinent correspondence, a summary of phases completed in the study, detailed graphs for analysis purposes, or even previously done systems studies.

While it is important to be complete, do not overkill with large volumes of meaningless data in the appendices. If material is not impor-

An Inflammatory Appendage

A new member of your systems analysis team has just handed you a rough draft of the table of contents for the team's system proposal. Without even reading the rest of the proposal, you are getting worried. The page below is what you have read so far:

What are some of the items that are causing you to feel some pain? Based on what you can diagnose from the table of contents alone, what are some cuts you would make to the systems proposal? Consider your clients and the purposes of the systems proposal (*not* to anesthetize them) in making your revision.

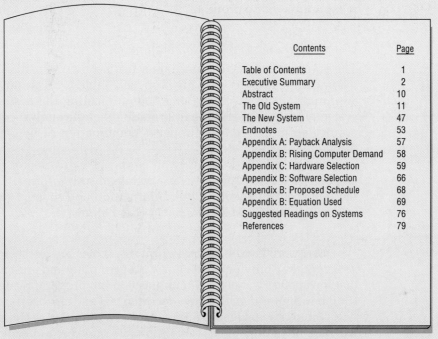

FIGURE 14.C1
A table of contents from the proposal.

tant enough to be in the body of the proposal, perhaps it should not be included at all.

It is difficult to provide useful heuristics about the appropriate length of the systems proposal. Keep in mind that the proposal's size is directly related to the size of the modification or system being proposed. A minor systems alteration should not evoke a 300-page tome.

Once the systems proposal is written, carefully select who should receive the report. Not everyone needs a copy or should get one. Personally hand the report to the people you have selected. This is a way to impress upon them your continuing enthusiasm for and involvement in the project. Your visibility is important for the acceptance and eventual success of the system.

CHAPTER 14:
WRITING
AND PRESENTING
THE SYSTEMS
PROPOSAL

455

Choosing a Writing Style

Although a business style of writing is most often appropriate for writing a systems proposal, your choice of a writing style will ultimately be determined by what you have already witnessed in the organization's own publications. If the people who compose your target audience favor a certain style, use it to write your proposal.

Keeping the people in your audience in mind means presenting information in a way that is easily comprehensible to them without being condescending. This requires finesse, since there should be enough detail for management to make informed decisions without being overwhelmed. Keep references to a minimum and do not use footnotes. Where appropriate, use examples, illustrations, diagrams, tables, figures, and graphs to support the main points of the proposal.

Using Figures for Effective Communication

The emphasis so far in this chapter has been on considering your audience when composing the systems proposal. Tables and graphs as well as words are important in capturing and communicating the basics of the proposed system. In fact, much of the information that the analyst collects can be communicated more readily through a combination of figures and words than through words alone.

Integrating figures into your proposal helps demonstrate that you are responsive to the different ways people absorb information. Figures within the report supplement written information and must always be interpreted in words. Tables and graphs never stand alone.

EFFECTIVE USE OF TABLES. Although tables are not technically termed *visual aids,* they provide a different way of grouping and presenting analyzed data that the analyst wants to communicate to the proposal reader. Tables are more similar to figures than they are to written text and are therefore discussed here.

Tables use labeled columns and rows to present statistical or alphabetical data in an organized way. Each table must be numbered according to the order in which it appears in the proposal and should be meaningfully titled. Figure 14.2 shows appropriate layout and labeling for a table.

Some guidelines for tables include:

1. Type only one table per page, and rather than relegate it to the end of the proposal, integrate it into the body of the proposal.
2. Try to fit the entire table vertically on a single page if possible.
3. Number and title the table at the top of the page. Make the title descriptive and meaningful.
4. Label each row and column. Use more than one line for a title if necessary.
5. Use a boxed table if room permits. Vertically ruled columns will enhance the readability.
6. Use an asterisk if necessary to explain detailed information contained in the table.

Several methods for comparing costs and benefits were presented in Chapter 13. Tabled results of those comparisons should appear in the systems proposal. If a break-even analysis is done, a table illustrating results of the

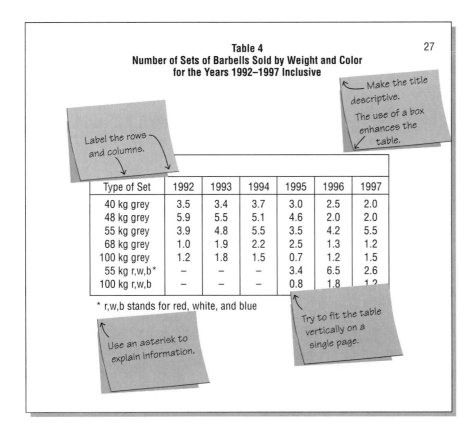

FIGURE 14.2
Guidelines for creating
effective tables.

analysis should be included. Payback can be shown in tables that serve as additional support for graphs. A short table comparing computer systems or options might also be included in the systems proposal.

EFFECTIVE USE OF GRAPHS. This section covers different kinds of graphs, including line graphs, column charts, bar charts, and pie charts. Line and column graphs and bar charts compare variables, while pie charts illustrate the composition of 100 percent of an entity.

The guidelines for including effective graphs in a proposal are:

1. Draw only one graph to a page unless you want to make a critical comparison between graphs.
2. Integrate the graph into the body of the proposal.
3. Give the graph a sequential figure number and a meaningful title.
4. Label each axis and any lines, columns, bars, or pieces of the pie on the graph.
5. Include a key to indicate differently colored lines, shaded bars, or crosshatched areas.

An example of how a graph would appear on a page in a systems proposal is shown in Figure 14.3. Our explanation of graphs will begin with the simplest type, called a line graph.

Line graphs. Line graphs are used primarily to show change over time. No other type of graph shows a trend more clearly than a line graph. Changes in a single variable or up to five variables can be illustrated in a single line graph.

CHAPTER 14:
WRITING
AND PRESENTING
THE SYSTEMS
PROPOSAL

457

FIGURE 14.3
Guidelines for drawing effective line graphs.

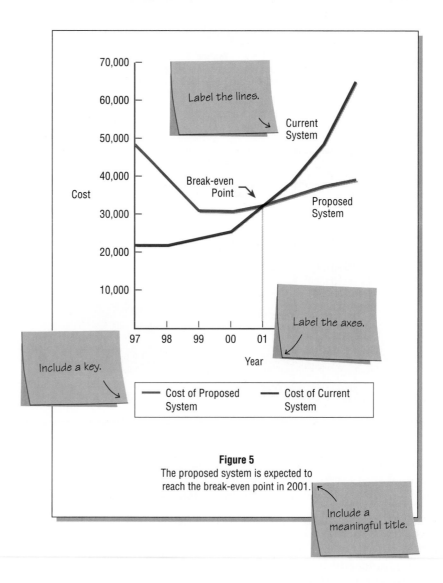

Figure 5
The proposed system is expected to
reach the break-even point in 2001.

There are times, however, when a line graph is used to show something other than time on the horizontal axis. This situation occurs when one has to estimate when two or more lines intersect, as shown in Figure 14.4. In this example, the current system is the least expensive until Annie's Equipment grows to approximately 24,000 units per year. Then Computer Data Services offers the least expensive option. Later we find that Syscom becomes the least expensive option if Annie's were to grow to over 28,000 units annually.

A dramatic method of visual comparison, in the same general family as line graphs, is the area chart. Figure 14.5 shows the growth of the video-cassette industry over the time period 1992–1997. In this area chart, the total gross receipts consist of both sales (the shaded area) and rentals (the colored area). The area chart is very useful when the difference between two variables expands greatly.

In Chapter 13, the importance of forecasting for justifying the systems project was stressed. Line graphs are excellent ways of showing proposal readers how demand on the computer system may change within a certain number of years or how demand for the products or services of a business may change within a specific time period.

FIGURE 14.4
Depicting each variable with
a different kind of line
on the line graph.

Line graphs are also useful for representing results of payback analysis or break-even analysis to decision makers. Graphic display of the payback period is an excellent way to portray the economic feasibility of the proposed system, as is a graph of break-even results.

Column charts. Other familiar kinds of graphs are column charts. Column charts can depict a comparison between two or more variables over time, but they are used more often to compare different variables at a particular point in time. Although they do not show trends as well as line graphs—nor can one easily estimate value between columns using them— many people find column charts easier to understand than line graphs.

A simple column chart is shown in Figure 14.6. In this example, the columns consist of diskettes. One way to attract the reader, particularly someone who disdains statistics and graphs, is to make the graph more human. A familiar icon, such as a diskette, can be useful in this regard.

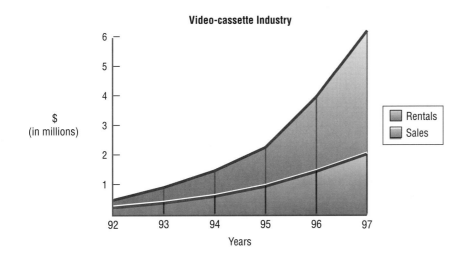

FIGURE 14.5
An area chart is a form of
line graph that may make
more of an impact.

CHAPTER 14:
WRITING
AND PRESENTING
THE SYSTEMS
PROPOSAL

459

FIGURE 14.6
A familiar icon such as a
diskette can be used to create
columns on a column chart.

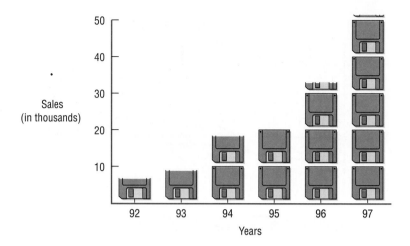

Figure 14.7 shows a column chart with more than one variable. When this occurs, draw the columns in different colors or shades to distinguish between the variables. Notice that there is space between each of the two classes (HQ and Troops A, B, C, D, and E) but no space between the two variables, "current strength" and "minimum required."

There are also special forms of column charts. A 100-percent stacked column chart is shown in Figure 14.8. This type of chart is used to show the relationship between two variables that make up 100 percent of an entity. Here, sporting goods sales are made up of competitive sporting equipment and individual achievement equipment. The chart depicts the competitive sporting equipment as shrinking as a percentage of total sales. (It does not show, however, the actual sales, which may indeed be growing even though the percentage is diminishing.)

Another special type of column chart is the deviation column chart. This type of chart is useful for emphasizing years that show a loss or pointing out the year in which the company intends to break even. Furthermore, the chart can be drawn to show the deviation from an average. An example

FIGURE 14.7
More than one variable can be
displayed on a column chart
by shading or coloring the column bars.

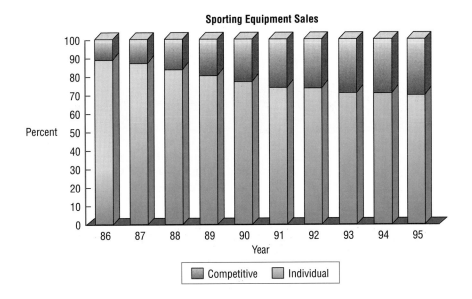

of a deviation column chart is shown in Figure 14.9, where the differences in above- and below-average months are emphasized.

Bar charts. Bar charts are similar to column charts, but they are never used to show a relationship over a period of years. Rather, they are used to show one or more variables within certain classes or categories during a specific time period.

The bars themselves may be organized in many different ways. They can be in alphabetical, numerical, geographical, or progressive order, or they can be sorted by magnitude. For instance, in a systems proposal, a bar chart would be useful in comparing the volumes of shipping invoices, customer accounts, and vendor invoices processed by the computer system during July, as shown in Figure 14.10. A bar chart is one of the most widely known forms of graphs and can make a comparison in a straightforward way.

There are special types of bar charts, just as there are special column charts. One example, shown in Figure 14.11, is a 100-percent subdivided bar

FIGURE 14.9
A deviation column chart can be more effective in showing which months have above-average transactions.

CHAPTER 14:
WRITING
AND PRESENTING
THE SYSTEMS
PROPOSAL

461

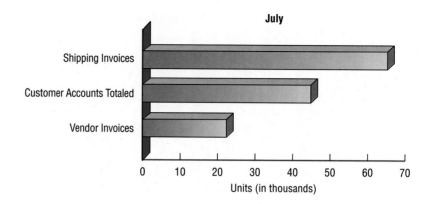

FIGURE 14.10
A bar chart is like a column chart, but it is mainly used to compare different items at a specific point in time.

chart. This is the equivalent of a 100-percent stacked column chart and is used to demonstrate what percentages of males and females rent certain categories of videotapes.

Pie charts. Another commonly used type of graph is the circle or pie chart. It is used to show how 100 percent of a commodity is divided at a particular point in time, as in Figure 14.12. The data display begins at 12 o'clock on the circle and works clockwise, placing the largest percentage (or wedge of pie) next to the second largest, all the way down to the smallest. Observe this convention unless you want to show dramatic contrasts in percentages by placing the largest and smallest percentages side by side. In this example, a pie chart is used to show the market share of three computer software companies. Computer Data Services has the largest share at approximately 45 percent of the total market, while Digitec has the second biggest share at 35 percent. Finally, Syscom has only 20 percent of the market. If for some reason we want to emphasize one aspect of the data—a company in this example—we can separate that piece of the pie from the remainder.

Pie charts are easier to read than 100-percent stacked column charts or 100-percent subdivided bar charts. Their main disadvantage is that they take up a lot of room on a page. If an analyst wanted to show more than six cate-

FIGURE 14.11
A 100-percent bar chart makes the items appear to be of equal importance so it is easier to analyze the percentages visually.

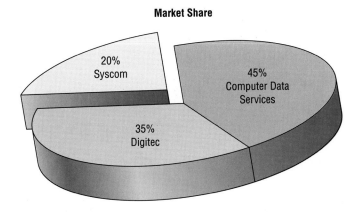

Market Share

20%
Syscom

45%
Computer Data
Services

35%
Digitec

FIGURE 14.12
A visually appealing way to
display how 100 percent of an
entity is divided up at a particular time is a pie chart.

gories, one of the previously mentioned 100-percent charts would be preferable to drawing six individual pie charts.

EFFECTIVE USE OF SCHEDULING CHARTS AND DIAGRAMS. In Chapter 3,
Gantt charts generated by project management software were recommended
for use in scheduling systems projects. Include a summary Gantt chart of the
kind shown in Figure 14.13 in the systems proposal. This chart graphically
shows when the project will be completed, and it also shows estimates of
time required for each analysis and design activity.

PERT diagrams, as discussed in Chapter 3, are another specialized kind
of graph for a more technical audience. It is possible to include a computer-
generated PERT diagram in the systems proposal appendix to illustrate
more precisely the work path that is planned for the systems analysis team.
Technical readers reviewing the proposal may use the PERT diagram you
provide to see if dates for critical activities conflict with other organizational
deadlines.

GUIDELINES FOR USING FIGURES IN THE SYSTEMS PROPOSAL. Figures (tables
and graphs) can communicate in a way that is not possible in words alone.
When preparing the systems proposal, remember to take advantage of the
graphs and tables that you are already using for planning purposes. The
following guidelines help enhance the systems proposal through the use of
figures:

1. Whenever possible, integrate the figure into the body of the proposal it-
    self. The figure may be placed on the page following its first reference.
    If your first thought is to relegate the figure to an appendix, it may not
    be important enough to include at all.
2. Always introduce figures in the text before they appear.
3. Always interpret figures in words; never leave them to stand on their
    own.
4. Title all figures, label each axis, and provide legends where necessary.
5. Use more that one figure if necessary, so that the point you make is
    clear and figures are uncluttered.

This has been a cursory glance at using tables and graphs to help you make
a point within the systems proposal. For a more detailed, in-depth discussion of the use of figures, see Chapter 15 on designing effective output.

CHAPTER 14:
WRITING
AND PRESENTING
THE SYSTEMS
PROPOSAL

463

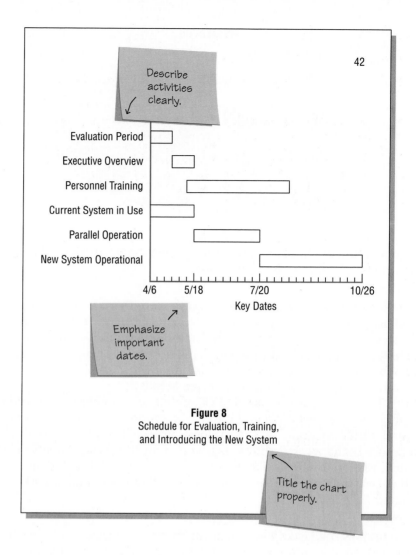

Figure 8
Schedule for Evaluation, Training, and Introducing the New System

Adopting a Unifying Proposal Style

VISUAL AND FORMATTING CONSIDERATIONS. Proposals are persuasive documents. All the best arguments for proceeding in a specific way are brought to the fore when writing the systems proposal. By the same token, the proposal must be visually persuasive. Content and style go hand in hand, and neglecting this relationship only defeats the proposal's purpose. Figure 14.14 shows how visual elements can be used to offset the written material.

Use of white space. White space distributed throughout the text of the systems proposal helps to set off ideas, assuring that they will be noticed. Write concisely so that white space can be used without bloating the proposal to an overly long document. Leave margins of one inch at the top, bottom, left, and right of each page. Leave one and a half inches if you intend to bind the left side. Double-space the entire report.

Use of headings and subheadings. Use of headings and subheadings is critical, especially if the proposal is long. Headings set apart each section and point the reader to a main section. If imaginatively written, headings

Should This Chart Be Barred?

"Gee, I'm glad they hired you guys. I know the Redwings will be better next season because of you. My job'll be a lot easier, too," says Andy Skors, ticket manager for the Kitchener, Ontario, hockey team, the Kitchener Redwings. Andy has been working with your systems analysis team on analyzing the systems requirements for computerizing ticket sales.

Recall that when we last heard from the systems analysis team, consisting of Hy Sticking (your leader), Rip Shinpadd, Fiona Wrink, and yourself, you were wrestling with whether to expedite the project and to set team productivity goals (in Consulting Opportunity 3.3).

Andy is talking with the team about what to include in the systems proposal to make it as persuasive as possible to the Redwings' management. "I know they're going to like this chart," Andy continues. "It's a little something I drew up after you asked me all those questions on past ticket sales, Rip."

Andy hands the bar chart to Rip, who looks at it and suppresses a slight smile. "As long as we have you here Andy, why don't you explain it for us?"

Like a player fresh out of the penalty box, Andy skates smoothly into his narrative of the graph. "Well, our ticket sales reached an all-time high in 1993. We were real crowd pleasers that year. Could've sold seats on the scoreboard if they let me. Unfortunately, ticket sales were at an all-time low in 1994. I mean, we're talking about a disaster. Tickets moved slower than a glacier. I had to convince the players to give tickets away when they made appearances at the shopping mall. Why, just look at this table, it's terrible.

"I think computerizing the ticket sales will help us pick out who our season supporters are. We've got to figure out who they are and get them back. Get them to stick with us. That would be a good goal to shoot for," Andy concludes.

As Andy's presentation finally winds down, Hy looks as if he thought the twenty-minute period would never end. Picking up on his signal, Fiona says, "Thanks for the data, Andy. We'll work on getting them into the report somehow."

As Fiona and Rip head out of the room with Andy, Hy realizes the bench has emptied, so he asks you, the fourth team member, to coach Andy on his bar chart by making a list of the problems you see in it. Hy would also like to sketch some alternate ways to graph the data on ticket sales so that a correct and persuasive graph of ticket sales can be included in the systems proposal.

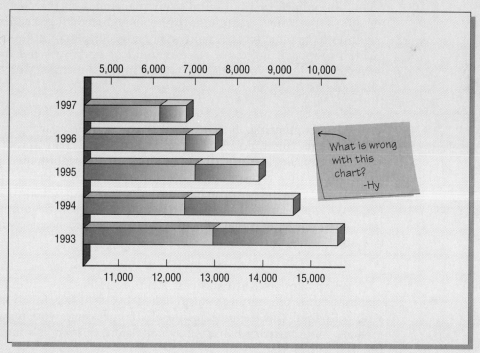

FIGURE 14.C2
An incorrectly drawn graph.

Status	Year	Average tickets sold per game	Season tickets sold per season
Best Year	1993	15,643	7,505
	1994	14,880	6,808
	1995	14,100	7,089
	1996	13,254	6,735
Worst Year	1997	12,690	6,351

help readers to follow the logic of the writing and to maintain their interest. Subheadings function in much the same way but refer to more specific points. When taken altogether, headings and subheadings should provide a useful and instructive outline of the entire proposal.

Headings can be set off in many ways to alert readers typographically to a change in sections. Common methods are using all capital letters, centering, indenting, underlining, bold and double-strike printing, or any combination of these methods.

Headings and subheadings should be distinguishable from each other, not only by content but also by placement on the page or by the use of one of the other treatments previously listed. For headings and subheadings to be effective, the analyst must be consistent in their use throughout the proposal. Follow a style manual or employ a personal style, but be consistent in its application to maximize the impact of headings and subheadings.

Page numbering. It is important to number every page, since page numbers are the quickest way for readers to find their places. Page numbers can be in four places: either in the right-hand corner of the page; alternating left and right-hand corners if material is printed back-to-back and bound; at the bottom of the page; or at the top of the page. Whichever position you choose, be consistent. Page numbers of proposal pages on which major headings occur should be listed in the table of contents.

References and appendices. Keeping references to external support materials to a minimum is appreciated by most organizational audiences who will read the systems proposal. If necessary, you may include references, double-spaced and in a consistent format, at the end of your report.

Proposal readers usually have diverse organizational interests. If the proposal seeks to address technical as well as other users, the addition of appendices that includes technical specifications may be wise. A separate,

Allow ample margins

1"

1 1/2"

number each page → 26

difference of each year between lease and buy, multiplied by its respective probability.

It would also be possible to use different capital gain or loss tax treatment for salvage value and different discounting rate, but again the small amount involved does not justify the additional complexity in calculation.

Use numerous subheads

Lease Term Analysis

Bakerloo Bros. presently leases a large number of notebook PCs on a three-month basis. The company could save substantially if it acquires longer lease contracts, because an investigation of the contracts shows a high percentage of contract extensions. Bakerloo Bros. is therefore paying a premium for a short-term lease when the notebook is being used for extended periods. Of the seven notebooks acquired in 1997 and currently being used, for example, six are on monthly extensions of three-month leases.

1"

The detailed analysis for term of lease can be found in Appendix 2. In addition to the break-even analysis, a graphical representation of the break-even point is provided.

RECOMMENDATIONS

After examining all of the options available for Bakerloo Bros., the following three options are recommended. The first option is to

1"

more detailed proposal addressing technical concerns is also an option, although time costs must be considered before too much custom tailoring is done on the proposal.

You should request times to present the systems proposal orally. These occasions are excellent opportunities to sell your ideas and the system, as well as to answer any questions that arise. Oral presentations help you to retain your visibility in the organization, and they are essential.

PRESENTING THE SYSTEMS PROPOSAL

The topic of the presentation is obviously the systems proposal itself (or some part of it). The next considerations include who will compose the audience for the presentation and how to organize, support, and deliver the oral presentation. All of these areas are interrelated, but for the sake of clarity we will begin by examining each separately.

CHAPTER 14:
WRITING
AND PRESENTING
THE SYSTEMS
PROPOSAL
467

Understanding the Audience

Just as the audience for the written proposal helps dictate writing style, level of detail, the type of figures, the audience for the oral presentation helps the speaker discover how formal to be, what to present, and what types of visual aids to include. It is imperative that you know *who* you will be addressing.

Organizing the Systems Proposal Presentation

Page through the data collected from the organization that is summarized in the written proposal. Find four to six main points that capsulize the proposal. In particular, check the executive summary, the recommendation sections, and the proposal summary. If the time allotted for the oral presentation is longer than half an hour, main points can be expanded to nine or more. However, for most brief oral presentations, four to six main points are all that can be absorbed by the listener.

Each main point of the oral report needs support to back up any assertions that are made. It is incorrect to assert a main point and not justify it. There are many options for supporting main points. They include examples, illustrations, quotations of testimony or authority, and statistics.

PLANNING THE INTRODUCTION AND CONCLUSION. Once main points and supporting points are worked out, an introduction and conclusion can be written. Notice that writing the introduction comes last, not first. That is because the introduction should preview the proposal's four to six main points, which are impossible to determine at the outset. The preview cues the audience to listen for what is coming up.

The introduction should also include a "hook," something that will get the audience intrigued with what is coming next. This should be a creative approach to the proposal that directly unites the audience's interests with the new material being presented. For example, an anecdote, an analogy, a quotation, poetry, or even a joke can open a presentation successfully, while avoiding a dull or trite beginning. If humor is used, it should be directly relevant to the topic and should make a point about what is coming up.

As noted before, the introduction and conclusion for an oral presentation are written in parallel. Recall that this approach is similar to the way the executive summary and proposal summary are handled for the written proposal. The reason for this is that conclusions should mirror introductions. Conclusions should review main points in a manner similar to the introduction's preview. The analyst shouldn't quote verbatim from the introduction, but the main ideas should be reiterated, and a closing thought (similar to the creative hook of the introduction) should be given. For instance, if you began with a metaphor (analogizing the growth of a system with the way a plant grows), return to the analogy for the close. The definite closure provided is reasonable and satisfying to the audience.

FIELDING QUESTIONS. Questions can be taken either during or after the presentation. Answering questions during the presentation itself makes for a more informal, relaxed meeting. However, if there is a serious challenge, it could derail the proposal prematurely. In order to maintain control and communicate your points effectively, it is permissible to request that questions be saved until the end.

Software Manufacturer	Product	Web Site
Lotus Corporation	Freelance	www.lotus.com/freelance/
Micrografx	Graphics Suite	http://www.micrografx.com/graphicssuite/
Corel (WordPerfect)	Corel Presentations	www.corel.com/
Microsoft	PowerPoint	www.microsoft.com/mspowerpoint/

FIGURE 14.15
Slide presentation packages permit users to choose a template style, format and insert text, and include graphics and video.

USING VISUALS. Visuals used in an oral presentation function in a way that is similar to the use of figures in the written proposal—they supplement and enliven material. Consider enlarging some of the key figures from the proposal for use in the presentation. Visuals should be as professional-looking as possible (if an artist is available to create visuals for you, all the better). All printing on visuals should be uniform and legible from anywhere in the audience. For this occasion, visuals should be prepared ahead of time, not drawn while you are speaking.

Use PC-based packages to produce visuals for your presentation and report. A list of selected PC packages can be found in Figure 14.15. Now there are services that make high-resolution slides and overheads from text and graphics produced on microcomputers. You can draw a diagram in Micrografx Designer™ or some other graphics package, transmit it via modem, and the service will produce and send out the 35 mm slide on the same day.

Practice using visuals so that any ineptness with the equipment doesn't become the focus of the audience's attention. Make sure that necessary display equipment will be available on the day of your presentation. Remember to look directly at the audience, not at the visual, when you speak.

TAKING A PC INTO THE PRESENTATION. One of the most effective visuals you can use is a VDT display powered by a portable PC. If you are building a microcomputer system, this is doubly true.

There are some logistics to be aware of when taking a PC into the proposal meeting. If possible, try to use a large-screen projector system so that everyone in the room is able to see the VDT display at the same time. If this is not possible, use of multiple PCs and accompanying VDTs should be considered. No more than five onlookers to a VDT screen is a useful heuristic.

Microcomputers are valuable for presenting the slide shows discussed previously, as well as spreadsheets with "what-if" capability. For example, "What if the interest rate drops dramatically? How will that affect the payback period?" A PC and a properly set up spreadsheet can let decision makers entertain numerous "what-if" scenarios during the meeting itself.

The system that you are proposing may involve PCs. In this instance, microcomputers can act as a prototype, and users and decision makers in the meeting will be provided with an early, concrete realization of the system to come. Do not hesitate to let people other than the presenters use the computer. In our experience, this has worked very well; even people lacking computer experience have found it appealing.

On the other hand, do not put the entire burden of your systems presentation on the microcomputer. Even if you take a PC into the presentation, you will still need to explain what you are doing. Also, things can and do go wrong. You must plan a backup method for presenting material just in case

CHAPTER 14:
WRITING
AND PRESENTING
THE SYSTEMS
PROPOSAL

469

Source: Robert Mankoff ©
1997 from the *Cartoon Bank.*
All Rights Reserved.

"Great graphics, Dave, but the answer is still no."

you encounter software or hardware problems that are not solvable on the spot.

Systems analysts can also make presentations go smoothly by using professional hypermedia programs such as HyperWriter by Ntergaid. Hypermedia allows the audience to explore certain areas more deeply. Hypermedia can also be used for tutorials and training later on.

Now that audiences, supporting materials, and visuals have been discussed, we turn to oral delivery of the systems proposal. This is where the systems presentation departs radically from the written systems proposal.

Using Presentation in Graphics Packages

One of the most exciting ways to present your systems proposal is to make a slide show using a presentation software package such as Freelance Graphics for Windows by Lotus. An easy-to-use, professional-looking template called SmartMasters includes an icon and a way to organize text on the slide (a bulleted list or other designation). Figure 14.16 is an example of a beginning slide for a presentation that the user is making to update the audience with new information.

Basically, you are asked to choose a look for your presentation from among several professionally designed templates. Notice that in our example, the user has chosen a notebook template that makes it look as if the information is displayed on a spiral-bound notebook page. Color can also be added to support this effect. The choice of a notebook template is appropriate to a rather informal, educational presentation.

The next step in creating a slide show is to select page layout from the multiple choices of professionally designed templates. In our example, a bulleted list with a chart has been chosen. The user could also have chosen a numbered list or one of many other format options. The next step is to fill in the content of the presentation for each slide. Notice that you can add a

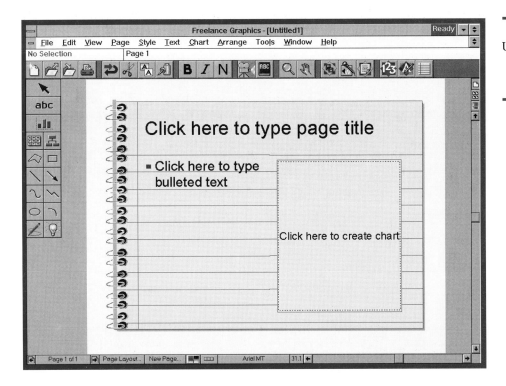

FIGURE 14.16
Use any of the thousands of library clip art available to enliven slide presentations and reinforce your key points.

graphic or clip art to the slide. If you use a program such as Charisma, you can even add a video clip to enhance your presentation.

In Figure 14.17 the user has chosen a different template and then included three different pieces of library clip art to reinforce the points being made in the text. Notice that a variety of interesting and engaging clipboard

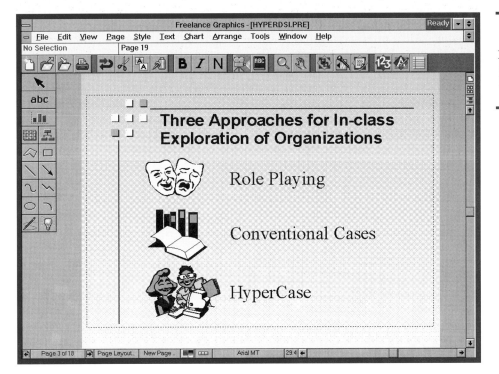

FIGURE 14.17
In this example, drawn using Lotus Corporation's Freelance Graphics, a key is included to help the audience distinguish among three treatments.

CHAPTER 14:
WRITING
AND PRESENTING
THE SYSTEMS
PROPOSAL

471

FIGURE 14.18
Rearrange the order of your
slide presentation to suit a
specific audience or to com-
press or expand the time it
takes to present your talk. The
lower right-hand corner of the
screen shows an option for
taking advantage of multimedia capabilities by including
sound in your slideshow.

art is available to users. Remember to choose images that help to creatively enliven what you are trying to communicate. If you have CD-ROM capability, your choices and the combinations you can create are virtually limitless, since the clip art library disks that are purchased with software can include over 12,000 images, symbols, and fonts.

Using the slide software presentation package to create your talk permits you to rearrange the order of your presentation, as shown in Figure 14.18. This becomes important if you want to tailor your presentation to suit different audiences. Additionally, you may want to add or delete slides to shorten or expand the time it takes to present your talk, depending on the time constraints for your meeting. A page of thumbnail views of the slides can be printed, copied, and distributed to audience members after your talk to serve as notes of your presentation. For legibility—and to leave room for additional audience members' notes—limit the number of slide images per page to half a dozen or so for thumbnail views. If views are too small, they will not be readable.

In the lower right-hand corner of this example, you can see that users have the option of taking advantage of multimedia capabilities by including sound in their slideshow. Again, use your creativity to employ sound in a memorable way. For example, launching a new project may call for the sound of a rocket blast-off countdown or the sound of the blast-off itself. Music and, in some cases, full-motion video can be used to highlight a presentation as well. Remember to include charts and graphs in your slideshow where appropriate. They are easy to do, and they make your point nicely, with meaningful graphics, when words just cannot say it all.

More powerful packages are available to create illustrations for your presentations to more technical audiences. The software package Micrografx Graphics Suite 2 offers Designer, a precision vector-oriented graphics package; Quick Silver a vector-oriented, interactive graphics package for the Web; and Picture Publisher for retouching photographs. Also included in the package is

FIGURE 14.19
A graphics package, such as
Micrgrafx FlowCharter, can
be used to quickly create
commonly used images
such as checklists, bar
charts, and timelines with
very little effort.

FlowCharter which allows the user to create living flowcharts and network diagrams that permit people to walk through business processes dynamically. Figure 14.19 illustrates the CoolSheets feature for developing bar charts, checklists, and timelines, using very colorful and expressive templates.

Figure 14.20 shows a screen from the Micrografx application Simply 3D. This application facilitates the creation of three dimensional images as

FIGURE 14.20
A graphics package like Micrografx Simply 3D can be
used to create and animate 3D
images for the Web or for
slideshow presentations. Here
the text Year 2000 is being
transformed from a wireframe
view to a final 3D image.

CHAPTER 14:
WRITING
AND PRESENTING
THE SYSTEMS
PROPOSAL

473

CONSULTING OPPORTUNITY 14.4

Fast Forward on the Systems Proposal

Entering Roger Corman's office, you ask him when he would like to schedule an oral presentation of the systems proposal. Corman replies, "Look, your presentation can be pretty informal for me. After talking to you for so many weeks, I feel like we've known each other a long time. If you're ready now, let's grab a cup of coffee and talk over your findings."

An hour later, Roger is enthusiastically discussing the finer points of your proposed system. "You know what would be great? We have all this video stuff here, so why not take advantage of it? It's hard to get time to talk to the employees together. Why don't you make a fifteen-minute tape of your presentation of the systems proposal and let employees watch it at their convenience? It will help convince them of the benefits of the system," Roger asserts persuasively.

Prepare an outline of your systems proposal talk that lists (four to six) main points along with their supporting points. Also indicate on the outline where visuals such as graphs will be shown. What are some changes to consider when presenting the system to potential users, rather than to decision makers? How does a taped presentation differ from a live one?

well as animated three dimensional displays that are highly dynamic. You can even embed a 3D scene into a common Word document to liven up your systems proposal. For use on Web pages or for exciting slideshows, Simply 3D enables the user to animate the image.

There are a few guidelines to follow when creating a slideshow. Though many of the design lessons you will learn in Chapters 15 and 16 will be helpful, some criteria are unique to this situation. When creating a slideshow, remember to:

1. Use the templates provided by most packages for a well-designed, consistent effect as well as to save time.
2. Use a combination of graphics and text to communicate. Data can be charted in many different ways for effective display. Fonts and font sizes should be chosen for readability and appropriateness.
3. Keep a clean look to each slide and guard against clutter. Include no more than five key points per slide.
4. Use color in a meaningful way. Provide a color key for complicated visuals such as charts.
5. Use clip art with text to add humor and to reinforce your points.
6. Use sound to help reinforce the points of your presentation. Judicious use of sound will help your audience recall your talk.
7. Take a multimedia approach to your presentation, integrating slides, video, and sound through hypermedia to communicate in a memorable way.

Using presentation software to create a slideshow results in an interesting, consistent, and easy-to-follow presentation with many potential uses. Save the slides you create on disk because they can be presented and used in many different ways. Presentation options include showing the slides on a single monitor; projecting them to a group through projection hardware and creating a multimedia show; or printing them out to create overhead transparencies or audience notes (four to eight per page). Many speakers like to use a combination approach, perhaps projecting their slideshow and then reinforcing it with an audience handout. You may want to include copies of the presentation charts you have created in the systems proposal document itself.

Principles of Delivery

Knowing who is in the audience will tell the analyst how formal to make the presentation. If the chief executive officer is included in the meeting, chances are it will be quite formal. If primary users, rather than executives, compose the audience, perhaps a less formal, workshop-type presentation will be more appropriate.

One of the best ways to gauge the formality of presentations is by observing many different organizational meetings prior to the systems proposal presentation. This helps in understanding implicit organizational expectations. Expectations are usually based on customs and culture and may dictate that every presenter must use an overhead projector, show professionally made 35mm slides, or provide an outline of his or her remarks. Although these customs may not be articulated by organizational members, observing them may determine whether a presentation is judged to be successful or not.

The rules for delivery, shown in Figure 14.21, are basic:

1. Project loud enough so that the audience can hear you.
2. Look at each person in the audience as you speak.
3. Make visuals large enough so that the audience can see them.
4. Use gestures that are natural to your conversational style.
5. Introduce and conclude your talk confidently.

The very thought of getting up in front of people can make presenters extremely nervous—in fact, the greatest fear of males is said to be public speaking (it's the second greatest fear of females). Four guidelines that can help presenters overcome anxiety are: (1) be yourself; (2) be prepared; (3) speak naturally (do not memorize or read); and (4) breathe deeply before your presentation. Each of these guidelines is discussed in the upcoming sections.

THE FIRST GUIDELINE: BE YOURSELF. "Be yourself" means that the persona of the speaker is very important in persuading an audience. Presenters need to develop themselves in all aspects of personality—intellectually, emotionally, spiritually. The ancient Greeks held to the idea that speakers had to earn the right to address the audience through development of a complete self.

Modern audiences may not seem as demanding, and yet a fully developed personality puts the presenter in an excellent position to cope with any contingencies of the speaking situation, such as challenging questioners, taking unfavorable stands, or something as mundane as overcoming faulty equipment. It is also a great source of insight when attempting to put a creative twist on uninspiring material.

THE SECOND GUIDELINE: BE PREPARED. Being prepared means that the more thoroughly the analyst knows his or her material, the easier it will be to deliver it. One excellent speaker we know goes on what she calls "automatic pilot." She admits to paralyzing stage fright, but she overcomes it by thoroughly knowing her main points. When presenting, she seemingly allows her subconscious to deliver her well-prepared talk. This translates into the necessity of adequate rehearsal time for presenters. Few, if any, speakers

CHAPTER 14:
WRITING
AND PRESENTING
THE SYSTEMS
PROPOSAL

475

FIGURE 14.21
Guidelines for the effective
oral delivery of the systems
proposal.

are so gifted as to be able to ad lib a talk. Being prepared gives speakers the confidence that they do indeed have something important to tell the audience members and that they will do anything (including overcoming anxiety) to communicate with them.

THE THIRD GUIDELINE: SPEAK NATURALLY. Speaking naturally, not memorizing or reading, may seem antithetical to being prepared, since a speaker reading from a prepared text has little chance of departing from his or her key points. However, reading destroys speaker credibility by taking away opportunities for vital eye contact. Memorizing a talk lessens chances for successfully adapting to a particular audience. And when a speaker loses his or her place in a memorized talk, it is nearly impossible to recover gracefully. Those who memorize their talks tend to concentrate on getting the presentation letter perfect rather than on communicating the content. Analysts who memorize or read their presentations are in danger of losing an audience's interest very rapidly.

Instead of reading or memorizing, know your five or six key points very well. Be confident that you have a message to deliver, and know what it is. Know what support materials accompany each main point, but do not write them out. If time is short, or if the audience is different from the one you had expected, you can change your supporting material on the spot and still communicate key points. The notes for your oral presentation should be limited to an easily readable listing of main points, perhaps with a symbol to indicate when to show a visual. Short notes prevent speakers from falling into the trap of reading if they become nervous.

THE FOURTH GUIDELINE: REMEMBER TO BREATHE. Reminding the presenter to breathe is meant to be only slightly facetious, since we breathe without even considering it. However, an excellent way to achieve a strong speaking voice is to become aware of the breathing process. Take long, deep breaths immediately before addressing the group. Allow yourself to breathe between sentences and during normal pauses in your speaking. It is physiologically impossible to breathe deeply and still be nervous.

SUMMARY

The systems analyst has three main steps to follow for putting together an effective systems proposal: effectively organizing the proposal content, writing the proposal in an appropriate business style, and orally presenting an informative systems proposal. Since the proposal is the embodiment of the work that has been done thus far and the proposed effort, it is a critical document for selling the system. To be effective, the proposal should be written in a clear and understandable manner, and its content should be divided into ten functional sections. It should have an appropriate title that catches the interest of readers and clearly portrays what is forthcoming. The proposal should feature an executive summary that offers a concise overview of the systems project and analysts' recommendations.

Visual considerations are important when putting together a proposal that communicates well. Use enough white space to set off text; be generous when including headings and subheadings; number all pages; and keep references and appendices to a minimum.

Much of what is important in the systems proposal can be enhanced through the correct use of figures, including tables and graphs. Graphs compare two or more variables over time or at a particular point in time. Figures are always accompanied with a written interpretation in the proposal. The graphs and tables used for planning prior to the proposal can be incorporated into it when relevant.

The oral presentation of the system is based on the written proposal and is another way of effectively selling the system. One option for presentation is to create a slideshow using presentation software. Also, graphics presentation packages and clip art can be used to enhance the visual presentation of the systems proposal. In order to give a strong oral presentation, the analyst should know four elements ahead of time: who will compose the audience; the topic (presumably the systems proposal or some part of it); time allotted for the presentation; and equipment available (including room setup). All four elements are interrelated, and each needs to be thought through and planned to ensure success.

CHAPTER 14:
WRITING
AND PRESENTING
THE SYSTEMS
PROPOSAL

477

"I know it's hard to get your feet wet, but you've been here long enough to know that we're all curious about what you've come up with so far. We're especially interested in what you think of us! Are we one big happy family or is this a zoo? Seriously, Snowden would like it very much if you gave a brief oral presentation of a preliminary proposal for a new automated project reporting system for the Training Group. Who should we include? Well, Mr. Torrey, Dan Hill, Tom Ketcham, and Snowden, of course, will want to be there. Let's see . . . I've got the executive calendar on the screen here. Everyone we need is free a week from Thursday at 3:00. You can bring your whole team along if you want. That room has multimedia capabilities, if you want to get fancy, but keep it to about 15 minutes at the most. Oh, one more thing, I'm sure Mr. Hyatt will want to come. Have fun!"

HYPERCASE QUESTIONS

1. Prepare an outline of the preliminary proposal for a new automated project reporting system for the Training Group. Include enough detail so that it would be possible to use your outline as speaking notes during a presentation.

2. Use a software package such as Freelance Graphics by Lotus Corporation to create a short (3–5 slides) slideshow to illustrate the preliminary proposal for the automated project reporting system you outlined in problem 1.

3. Have your teammates role play the parts of Warren Torrey, Dan Hill, Tom Ketcham, and Snowden Evans (the part of Mr. Hyatt is optional). Present your brief preliminary proposal for the new automated project reporting system to them. Use the slideshow you have created for problem 2.

4. Write a two-paragraph report based on feedback received on the preliminary proposal during the role playing in problem 3. What questions arose? What changes will you make?

KEYWORDS AND PHRASES

systems proposal	bar charts
executive summary	pie charts
analysts' recommendations	oral presentation
line graphs	visuals
column charts	principles of delivery

REVIEW QUESTIONS

1. What are the three steps the systems analyst must follow to put together an effective systems proposal?
2. List the ten main sections of the systems proposal.
3. Which sections of the systems proposal should include the solution the analyst thinks is *most* workable?

4. What relationships does a line graph depict?
5. What relationships does a column chart depict?
6. What relationships does a bar chart depict?
7. What relationships does a pie chart depict?
8. List the five guidelines for using figures effectively in the systems proposal.
9. What purpose do headings and subheadings serve in the written systems proposal?
10. What sort of support material should be included in an oral presentation of the systems proposal to executive audiences?
11. When should the introduction for an oral presentation of the systems proposal be written?
12. How can a microcomputer be used as a visual aid in an oral presentation of the systems proposal?
13. List the seven guidelines for creating a slideshow on your computer.
14. List the five rules for effective oral delivery of the systems proposal.

PROBLEMS

1. "I think it's only fair to write up *all* of the alternatives you've considered," says Lou Cite, a personnel supervisor for Day-Glow Paints. "After all, you've been working on this systems thing for a while now, and I think my boss and everyone else would be interested to see what you've found out." You are talking with Lou as you prepare to put together the final systems proposal that your team will be presenting to upper management.

   a. In a paragraph, explain to Lou why your proposal will not (and should not) contain all of the alternatives that your team has considered.

   b. In a paragraph, discuss the sorts of alternatives that should appear in the final systems proposal.

2. In going over the data you have collected for your proposal for Linder's Machine Parts of Duluth, Minnesota, you find a forecast of demand for parts for the next five years, as well as the forecast of the number of companies purchasing parts. You would like to include the data in your systems proposal to help support the need for a new system, and the numbers currently given in this narrative are: "The columns show that demand of 120,000 will increase to 130,000 in year 2, go up 20,000 in year 3, go up 40,000 in year 4, and level off in year 5. Although demand for parts will be going up, the total number of companies who will be buying will be 700 in year 1 and will be reduced by 50 companies each year through the next five years."

   a. Based on the narrative, draw a bar graph to depict demand over the next five years for Linder's Machine Parts.

   b. Based on the narrative, draw a column chart to depict demand over the next five years for Linder's Machine Parts.

   c. Based on the narrative, draw a bar graph to show the decline in total number of companies ordering machine parts from Linder's.

   d. Based on the narrative, draw a line graph to depict the increase in demand and the decrease in total number of companies purchasing parts together.

CHAPTER 14:
WRITING
AND PRESENTING
THE SYSTEMS
PROPOSAL

479

3. "I was thinking of how I'll handle my portion of the presentation to management," says Margaret, a member of your systems analysis team. "Even though some of them told us they 'haven't been keeping up with computers,' I think they need to know the technical aspects of our recommended system inside and out; otherwise they may not accept it. So I'll begin by defining basic terms like 'byte' and 'program code,' and then I'll turn the meeting into a short tutorial on computing. What do you think?"

   a. In a paragraph, critique Margaret's approach to the systems proposal presentation to the executive audience.

   b. In a paragraph, suggest a different way to approach the executive audience for the systems proposal presentation. Be sure to include types of support—as well as topics—that would be more appropriate than what Margaret has in mind.

SELECTED BIBLIOGRAPHY

Carey, P., and J. Carey. *Microsoft® PowerPoint®97 at a Glance.* Redmond, WA: Microsoft Press, 1997.

Deetz, S. *Transforming Communication, Transforming Business: Building Responsible and Responsive Workplaces.* Cresskill, NJ: Hampton Press, Inc., 1995.

Di Salvo, V. S. *Business and Professional Communication.* Columbus, OH: Charles E. Merrill Publishing Company, 1976.

Himstreet, W. C., and W. M. Baty. *Business Communication Principles and Methods,* 6th ed. Boston: Kent Publishing Company, 1981.

Humes, J. C. *The Sir Winston Method: The Five Secrets of Speaking the Language of Leadership.* New York: William Morrow and Company, Inc., 1991.

Lewis, P. V., and W. H. Baker. *Business Report Writing.* Columbus, OH: Grid, Inc., 1978.

Stefik, M., G. Foster, D. G. Bobrow, K. Kahn, S. Lanning, and L. Suchman. "Beyond the Chalkboard: Computer Support for Collaboration and Problem Solving in Meetings," *Communications of the ACM,* Vol. 30, No. 1, January 1987, pp. 32–47.

SHOW AND TELL

"That completes the list," Anna says. "I've contacted each user of the system as well as management. The presentation meeting for the proposed new microcomputer system is scheduled for 10 A.M. next Tuesday. We have most of the materials ready, so let's put the finishing touches on the documentation."

Chip looks up from the task of creating an executive summary. "It seems hard to believe that we're almost finished with the analysis stage. I'm a little apprehensive about the meeting. I hope everything goes well."

"I'm sure it will," Anna says reassuringly. "We've been thorough in our analysis, and the proposal seems to be coming along nicely too."

Chip completes the executive summary, shown in Figure E14.1. This is the document that gives an overview of the nature of the system and the recommended solution. After completing the executive summary, he proceeds to create the outline of the study. This document, shown in Figure E14.2, is another summary, since many of the persons reviewing the proposal have been involved in the interviews and prototypes. It provides a concise review of the methods that have been used in analyzing the needs of the microcomputer system.

Meanwhile, Anna was working on polishing the results section of the analysis, called the *problem definition.* Earlier in the analysis, she had taken information from the interviews, survey, and prototypes, and she produced ten concise points reflecting system needs. These points had been reviewed by the users and modified with minor changes to clarify them. Each user was then requested to rank the issues on relative importance, using a scale from one to ten. These final ranks were then averaged to become weights, indicating overall importance. The completed problem definition is shown in Figure E14.3.

Alternatives for the proposed system have already been created and evaluated (refer to Chapter 12). The recommended solution is a microcomputer local area network.

"We should include information showing how we are going to evaluate the installed system," Chip says. "How do you feel we should create evaluation criteria?"

"Well . . ." Anna replies thoughtfully, "perhaps we should restate the objectives in more concise terms. The original objectives were broadly stated, allowing us to be more flexible and creative in our choice of solutions. The new objectives would be measurable, describing deliverables: the specific screens, reports, and other products of systems development."

Chip and Anna work together to develop the measurable objectives. They start with the first objective and work down the list, point by point. Following are the broadly stated objectives:

1. Provide software/hardware cross-reference.
2. Maintain complete microcomputer information.
3. Automate software installation procedure.
4. Provide information on software upgrade installation by machine.

*Allen Schmidt,
Julie E. Kendall, and
Kenneth E. Kendall*

5. Provide preventive and other maintenance information.
6. Maintain up-to-date, accurate software information.
7. Provide complete cost information for microcomputer hardware.
8. Provide information on the cost to upgrade software.
9. Design a process for performing accurate and efficient physical microcomputer inventory.
10. Maintain and provide training and software expert information.

"How do you think we can restate item one—'Provide software/hardware cross-reference'—as a measurable objective?" asks Chip.

"Let's look at the data flow diagrams, data dictionary records, and prototypes to review how we plan to provide the cross-reference information,"

Microcomputer System Proposal
Executive Summary

The system for managing microcomputer hardware and software is inadequate for the current level of devices and software packages. The designers of the original system, installed in the early 1980s, could not foresee the rapid development of products culminating in the tremendous variety presently available.

Analysts Anna Liszt and Chip Puller have conducted extensive interviews with system users. Persons interviewed include Mike Crowe, Dot Matricks, Hy Perteks, Paige Prynter, and Cher Ware. The problems determined from these interviews include missing information and a lack of cross-referencing hardware and software information. As software and hardware demands escalate in the future, this lack of information will result in an increase in redundant information and a duplication of costly services.

We recommend a Microcomputer System with a local area network linking all parties involved in the system. Menu screens will allow users to select options to update hardware and software information. Reports will be periodically produced and a variety of inquiry screens made available.

Additional benefits include improved cost information, automating the preventive maintenance scheduling, ease of updating software versions, and improved techniques for performing physical device inventory.

Programs and data will be secured by requiring users to enter a user identification number and password. The user ID will further control who has access to the various system functions: update, report generation, or inquiry.

Training sessions will be conducted prior to final installation of the Microcomputer System. It is recommended that at least two persons should be trained for each system aspect.

The estimated completion date is August 19th. The estimated time for development is 8 person months at an expense of $50,000. Hardware expenditures should not exceed $15,000.

FIGURE E14.1
Executive summary.

Microcomputer System Proposal
Outline of Systems Study

The Microcomputer System has been thoroughly investigated using a series of interviews, examination of memos, a survey of the faculty and staff, and a series of prototype screens and reports.

The memos examined included a period from July through August. These provided initial information on the nature of the problems inherent in the current system.

A series of initial and follow-up interviews was conducted with the following individuals: Mike Crowe, Microcomputer Specialist; Dot Matricks, Manager of Microcomputer Systems; Hy Perteks, Information Center Director; Paige Prynter, Financial Analyst, and Cher Ware, Software Specialist.

The results of the interviews became the basis of a questionnaire administered to the faculty and research staff. This confirmed the rapid expansion of microcomputer hardware and software in almost every discipline as well as confirming the need for training.

Prototypes were designed to elicit feedback from system users. These were carefully constructed, demonstrated, and modified based on the comments of users.

FIGURE E14.2
Outline of a systems study.

responds Anna. "How about 'Provide a software inquiry listing the machine and its location for each copy of the software. Produce hardware/software cross-reference report on demand?'"

"Sounds good," says Chip, "The next one—'Maintain complete microcomputer information'—could be stated as 'Add maintenance, preventive maintenance, boards, cost, and peripheral information to the HARDWARE MASTER file. Create separate on-line programs for adding, deleting, changing, and modifying maintenance information.'"

Chip and Anna work together to restate the third objective—"Automate software installation procedure"—as "Create an on-line inquiry screen to determine the location of suitable microcomputers. Use the screen to choose locations. Print the location list. Provide automatic update of files after installation."

When the material has been completed and proofed, Chip starts to work on creating a microcomputer presentation of the project.

"This presentation software makes it easy to create a slide show," says Chip with a smile. "I feel that it will help to control the sequence of the presentation and make it easier for us to relax."

"I agree," replies Anna. "And I especially enjoy the pieces of clip art that you have included to liven it up a bit. I'll arrange to have one of the new computer projection units delivered to the conference room. They have an exceptionally bright image."

Tuesday morning finds Chip and Anna in the conference room. Copies of the proposal are neatly placed on the table in front of each seat. The pre-

Microcomputer System Proposal
Detailed Results – Problem Definition

The Microcomputer System has become inadequate to handle the current volume of microcomputers, their peripheral devices and software installed upon them. Additional information needs to be added to existing files and there is a lack of cross-referencing software packages installed upon machines.

The Microcomputer Maintenance department has difficulty determining which machines require preventive maintenance and a physical inventory of microcomputers and the peripheral devices is not regularly performed.

Cost information is not accurately maintained or reported.

Issues–Present Situation	Weight
1. There is a lack of information about which software is installed on any given microcomputer.	10
2. Incomplete information is maintained for each microcomputer.	9
3. The present system does not provide microcomputer capacity information used to determine which machine software may be installed upon.	8
4. There is no method of determining which machines contain software scheduling for an upgrade.	7
5. Preventive and other maintenance information is not acquired. There is no reliable method for predicting preventive maintenance dates.	7
6. Software information is missing and out of date, with redundant records for older versions.	6
7. Cost information is incomplete for microcomputers.	5
8. Software upgrade cost data is unavailable.	5
9. The process for performing physical microcomputer inventory is inaccurate and inefficient.	3
10. There is no method for maintaining training and software expert information.	2

FIGURE E14.3
Problem definition.

sentation equipment is connected and has been carefully tested to make sure that everything is working properly.

"I'm feeling a few butterflies in my stomach," murmurs Chip. "Even though I've spoken with all these people before, this is different somehow."

"I'm a little nervous myself," answers Anna. "It's normal to feel that way. But don't worry, we're well prepared and we'll take turns presenting different topics and features."

The users arrive and the presentation begins. Anna starts with opening remarks and an introductory summary. Chip takes a deep breath and walks to the front of the room. He gains confidence as he reviews some of the problems and displays the graphs showing the increase in software and hardware over the past ten years. The audience is listening intently, visibly interested in what he is saying.

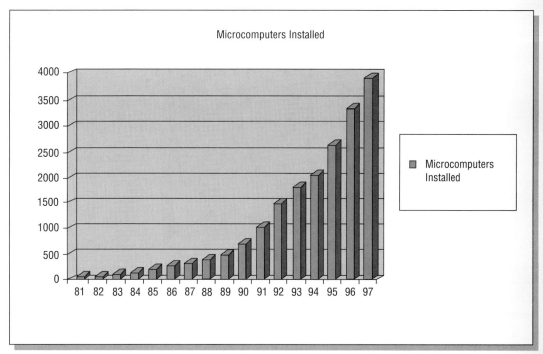

FIGURE E14.4
MICROCOMPUTER GROWTH, presentation graph.

The presentation lasts about an hour. User feedback is detailed and enthusiastic. Chip and Anna are delighted when the users unanimously approve their recommendation.

Exercises*

E-1. Rewrite the last seven broadly stated objectives as measurable objectives.

E-2. Create a cover letter based on the information presented in the CPU case.

E-3. Work in small groups to deliver a presentation of the CPU system to the class, based on information mentioned in Chapters 13 and 14 and on previous exercises.

E-4. Research presentation software packages. What are their features, advantages, and disadvantages. Summarize the information for three presentation packages.

E-5. Work as a small group to create a slideshow using presentation software that explains the features of presentation software. Have other students view the slide show and comment on it.

⊟ E-6. Use Access to view the MICROCOMPUTER GROWTH presentation graph (under the Reports tab), illustrated in Figure E14.4.

---

* Exercises preceded by a disk icon require the program Visible Analyst Workbench or another CASE tool. A disk is provided free of charge to any professor adopting this book. The examples on the disk may be imported into Visible Analyst Workbench and then used by students.

FIGURE E14.5
SOFTWARE GROWTH, presentation graph.

FIGURE E14.6
Microcomputer network configuration.

⊟ **E-7.** Use Access to view the SOFTWARE GROWTH presentation graph, illustrated in Figure E14.5.

⊟ **E-8.** Modify the database table, **Software Installed,** and print the SOFTWARE GROWTH chart report (under the Reports tab). Add diskette symbols to reflect the following total number of software packages for each of the following years:

Year	Cumulative Software Packages
1994	3,759
1995	4,276
1996	4,804
1997	5,309

⊟ **E-9.** Use Visible Analyst to modify the MICROCOMPUTER CONFIGU-RATION presentation graph shown in Figure E14.6. Include the portable microcomputer that Mike Crowe will use to update records from remote locations.

15

DESIGNING EFFECTIVE OUTPUT

OUTPUT DESIGN OBJECTIVES

Output is information delivered to users through the information system by way of intranets, extranets, or the World Wide Web. Some data require extensive processing before they become suitable output; other data are stored, and when they are retrieved, they are considered output with little or no processing. Output can take many forms: the traditional hard copy of printed reports, and soft copy such as computer screens, microforms, and audio output. Users rely on output in order to accomplish their tasks, and they often judge the merit of the system solely by its output. In order to create the most useful output possible, the systems analyst works closely with the user through an interactive process until the result is considered to be satisfactory.

Since useful output is essential to ensuring the use and acceptance of the information system, there are several objectives that the systems analyst tries to attain when designing output. As shown in Figure 15.1, there are six objectives for output:

1. Design output to serve the intended purpose.
2. Design output to fit the user.
3. Deliver the appropriate quantity of output.
4. Assure that the output is where it is needed.
5. Provide the output on time.
6. Choose the right output method.

Designing Output to Serve the Intended Purpose

All output should have a purpose. It is not enough to make a report, screen, or Web page available to users because it is technologically possible to do so. During the information requirements determination phase of analysis, the systems analyst finds out what purposes must be served. Output is then designed based on those purposes.

FIGURE 15.1
Six objectives for the design
of output.

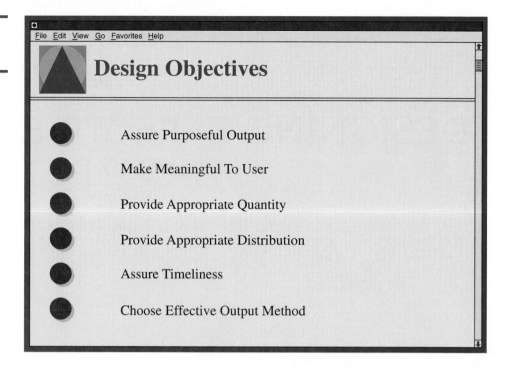

Design Objectives

- Assure Purposeful Output
- Make Meaningful To User
- Provide Appropriate Quantity
- Provide Appropriate Distribution
- Assure Timeliness
- Choose Effective Output Method

You will see that you have numerous opportunities to supply output simply because the application permits you to do so. However, remember the rule of purposiveness. If the output is not functional, it should not be created, since there are costs of time and materials associated with all output from the system.

Designing Output to Fit the User

With a large information system serving many users for many different purposes, it is often difficult to personalize output. On the basis of interviews, observations, cost considerations, and perhaps prototypes, it will be possible to design output that addresses what many, if not all, users need and prefer.

Generally speaking, it is more practical to create user-specific or user customizable output when designing it for a decision support system or other highly interactive applications such as those mounted on the Web. However, it is still possible to design output to fit a user's function in the organization, which leads us to the next objective.

Delivering the Appropriate Quantity of Output

More is not always better, especially where the amount of output is concerned. Part of the task of designing output is deciding what quantity of output is correct for users. You can see that this is a very difficult task, since information requirements are in continuing flux.

A useful heuristic is that the system must provide what each person needs to complete his or her work. However, this is still far from a total solution, since it may be appropriate to display a subset of that information at first and then provide a way for the user to access additional information easily. For example, rather than cluttering a screen with an entire year's sales, each of twelve screens or Web pages might provide a month's sales, with subsequent months and summary information available on separate screens or through hyperlinks, which are traceable as the user desires more information.

The problem of information overload is so prevalent as to have become a cliché, but it remains a valid concern. No one is served if excess information is given only to flaunt the capabilities of the system. Always keep the decision makers in mind when deciding about quantity of output. Often they will not need great amounts of output, especially if there is an easy way to access more.

Making Sure the Output Is Where It Is Needed

Output is printed on paper, displayed on screens, piped over speakers, made available on the Web, and stored on microforms. Output is often produced at one location (for example, in the data-processing department) and then distributed to the user.

The increase in on-line, screen-displayed output that is personally accessible has cut down somewhat on the problem of distribution, but appropriate distribution is still an important objective for the systems analyst. To be used and useful, output must be presented to the right user. No matter how well-designed reports are, if they are not seen by the pertinent decision makers, they have no value.

Providing the Output on Time

One of the most common complaints of users is that they do not receive information in time to make necessary decisions. The systems analysts' objectives for output are thus compounded. Not only do you have to be conscientious about who is receiving what output, you must also be concerned about the timing of output distribution.

Although timing isn't everything, it does play a large part in how useful output will be to decision makers. By this phase in the systems development life cycle, you have learned what output is necessary—and at what time—to drive each stage of the organization's processes. Many reports are required on a daily basis, some only monthly, others annually, others only by exception. Using well-publicized Web-based output can alleviate some problems with the timing of output distribution as well. Accurate timing of output can be critical to business operations.

Choosing the Right Output Method

As mentioned earlier, output can take many forms, including printed paper reports, information on screens, audio with digitized sounds that simulate the human voice, microforms, and Web documents. Choosing the right output method for each user is another objective in designing output.

For many people, the term output still conjures up the vision of stacks of paper computer printouts, but this situation is changing rapidly. With the movement to on-line systems, much output now appears on display screens, while giving users the option of printing it out with their own printer. The analyst needs to recognize the trade-offs involved in choosing an output method. Costs differ; for the user, there are also differences in the accessibility, flexibility, life span, distribution, storage and retrieval possibilities, transportability, and overall impact of the data. Choice of output methods is not trivial, nor is it usually a foregone conclusion.

FIGURE 15.2
A turnaround document for
Minigasco's data processing.

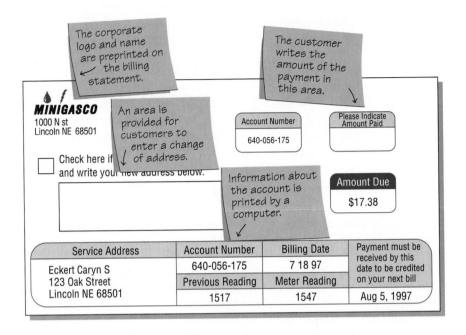

RELATING OUTPUT CONTENT TO OUTPUT METHOD

The content of output from information systems must be considered as interrelated to the output method. Whenever you design output, you need to think of how function influences form and how the intended purpose will influence the output method that you choose.

Output should be thought of in a general way, so that any information put out by the computer system that is useful to people in some way can be considered output. It is possible to conceptualize output as either external (going outside the business), such as information that appears on the Web, or internal (staying within the business), such as material available on an intranet.

External output is familiar to you through utility bills, advertisements, paychecks, annual reports, and myriad other communications that organizations have with their customers, vendors, suppliers, industry, and competitors. Some of this output, such as utility bills, is designed by the systems analyst to serve double duty as a turnaround document. Figure 15.2 is a gas bill that is a turnaround document for the gas company's data processing. In other words, the output for one stage of processing becomes the input for the next. When the customer returns the designated portion of the document, it is optically scanned and used as computer input.

External output differs from internal output not only in its distribution, but often in its design and appearance as well. Many external documents must include instructions to the recipient if they are to be used correctly. Additionally, many external outputs are placed on preprinted forms or Web sites bearing the company logo and corporate colors.

Internal outputs include various reports to decision makers. These range all the way from short summary reports to lengthy, detailed reports. An example of a summary report is a report summarizing monthly sales totals. A detailed report might give weekly sales by salesperson.

Other kinds of internal reports include historical reports that recount an occurrence and exception reports that are output only at the time an exception (a deviation from the expected) occurs. Examples of exception reports are a listing of all employees with no absences for the year; a listing of all salespeople who did *not* meet their monthly sales quota; or a report on consumer complaints made in the last six months.

In this section, different output technologies (the processes whereby output is produced) are covered. In addition, the factors involved in choosing a particular output method are discussed. The effects of different kinds of output on users are then considered. Directions are given for presenting output to users, and at the end of the chapter, guidelines for designing effective Web sites are given.

Choosing Output Technology

Producing different types of output requires different technologies. For printed computer output, the options include impact and nonimpact printers. For screen output, the options include attached or stand-alone cathode ray tubes or liquid crystal displays. Audio output can be amplified over a loudspeaker or listened to through small speakers on a PC. Microforms of output are created by specially equipped camera and film in microfiche and microfilm, and electronic output is created with special software tools. As you can see, the choices are numerous. Figure 15.3 is a comparison of output methods.

PRINTERS. Since printed reports are still the most common kind of output, it is logical to assume that in any large organization printers are ubiquitous. Although other types of output are gaining popularity, for the foreseeable future it is likely that businesses will still desire printed output or will want to design output that will look good if customers, suppliers, or vendors print it out using their own software and hardware.

As a systems analyst, it is up to you to keep current on the available output technology—through your experience, through trade publications, and by attending trade shows and professional meetings. Printers are changing so rapidly that any list of them is outdated the next year. For instance, the nation's largest manufacturer of computers has 70 printers in its printer line alone. However, it is possible to review some general features of printers that are currently available, as well as some trends in the technology.

The trend in printers for mainframe computer systems as well as for personal computers is toward increased flexibility. This translates into expanding the options for the location of the printing site itself; into accommodating different numbers of characters per page; into including numerous type styles and type fonts; into the changeable positioning of print on the page; into including more graphics capability (including the use of color); into producing quieter printing; into reducing the number of preprinted forms in inventory; into simplifying operator tasks; and into reducing the amount of overall operator intervention. Even when printers are dedicated to one particular use, vendors are stressing flexibility to facilitate that use.

Together with users, the systems analyst must determine the purpose for the printer. Once this is established, there are three key factors to keep in mind. They are the printer's:

1. Reliability.
2. Compatibility with software and hardware.
3. Manufacturer support.

Output Method	Advantages	Disadvantages
Printer	• Affordable for most organizations • Flexible in types of output, location, and capabilities • Handles large volumes of output • Reaches many inexpensively • Highly reliable with little down time	• May be noisy • Compatibility problems with computer software • May require special, expensive supplies • Still requires some operator intervention • Depending on model, may be slow
Specialty Printers (label makers, envelope printers, etc.)	• Can easily accomplish special tasks that would be difficult on a standard printer • Speeds up the job at hand	• Incurs additional cost of printer and specialty labels • Adds clutter to desks • Cannot be networked
Display Screen	• Interactive • Works in on-line, real time transmission through widely dispersed network • Quiet • Takes advantage of computer capabilities for movement within databases and files • Good for frequently accessed, ephemeral messages	• Requires cabling and setup space • Still may require printed documentation • Can be expensive if required for many users
Audio Output	• Good for individual user • Good for transient messages • Good where worker needs hands free • Good if output is highly repetitive	• Is expensive to develop • Needs dedicated room where output will not interfere with other tasks • Has limited application • Is not yet perfected
Microform	• Handles large volumes of information • Reduces space required for storage • Preserves fragile but frequently used materials • Avoids problems of paging through physically cumbersome reports	• Requires special software for easy accessibility • Needs special equipment for printing hard copy • Can be expensive initial investment
DVD and CD-ROM	• Has large capacity • Allows multimedia output • Has speedy retrieval • Is less vulnerable to damage	• Is expensive to develop • Is more difficult to update • Is more difficult to use on a network
Electronic Output (e-mail, faxes, and Web pages)	• Reduces Paper • Can be updated very easily • Eliminates "telephone tag" • Can be "broadcast" • Can be made interactive	• Has generally lower resolution • Is not conducive to formatting (e-mail) • Is difficult to convey context of messages (e-mail) • Web sites need diligent maintenance

FIGURE 15.3
A comparison of output methods.

Reliability means that the printer can be counted on to do what it was acquired to do over a period of time, with a tolerable amount of repairs. A reliable printer is extremely important when large volumes of materials (such as customer account bills) are being prepared to meet a particular deadline.

Compatibility of the printer with software and hardware is important when you consider that many times systems are modified or networked with

FIGURE 15.4
Creating labels is easy using
a Label Writer II printer
and software from CoStar
Corporation.

other smaller systems. Severe compatibility problems may result in systems not being used at all.

As with the purchase, rental, or leasing of computers themselves, manufacturer support of printers is typically negotiated separately from other agreements. However, it is important to make sure that manufacturers are willing to service printers on-site the same day problems occur or to provide reasonable equipment loans while a printer is being repaired.

SPECIALTY PRINTERS. Mailing labels are some of the most commonly used system output. A number of specialty printers dedicated to a single task have been developed to address this task. Specialty printers involve inexpensive, highly useful desktop technology. High-quality label printers such as CoStar's Label Writer have become immensely popular and accept text from most standard office applications.

Envelopes and mailing labels present another output design opportunity for the analyst. Notice in Figure 15.4 that with specialty technology you can design a desired layout form that will include a bar code and merge lines of text from a word processor or most other applications that the user would access routinely. Corporate logos or other meaningful icons can also be added to envelopes and labels. Since addresses and other information are captured directly from the original source, keying errors are prevented. Additionally, expensive printer resources are not tied up with a small job. Disadvantages of this technology include the possible proliferation of specialty printers and the resulting additional desktop clutter and difficulties in networking them.

SCREENS AS OUTPUT. Screens are an increasingly popular output technology. Once used mostly for data entry, screens are becoming a feasible technology for many other uses as well as their size and price decrease and as their compatability with other system components increases.

In addition to their initial equipment cost, screens require adequate and correct cabling that connect them to the system, as well as space for their proper positioning at workstations. Even though they resemble printers in this regard, screens have distinct advantages over printers because of their quietness and potential for interactive user participation. In the latter regard, screen output (depending, of course, on systems design) can afford flexibility in allowing the user to change output information in real time either through deletion, addition, or modification. Screens also permit the review of stored output through access to and the display of items from a relevant database. This permits individual decision makers to move away from storing redundant printouts.

Conversely, screens may provide an ideal output technology for information that is needed only once and that need never be stored. For example, output concerning whether all system terminals are currently in use is pertinent for a user trying to get on the system only in real time. In other words, screen output can be ephemeral, and this fleeting quality works to the user's advantage so that output is obtained, acted upon for a momentary decision, and never used again. In this instance, the message "All terminals are in use, please try the system later" would lead the user to quit the system and try again later in the workday. In Chapter 18, we discuss another potential drawback—the health concerns recently raised about the soundness of prolonged cathode ray terminal (CRT) use on the job.

AUDIO OUTPUT. In a way, audio output could be thought of as the exact opposite of printed output. Audio output is transient, whereas the printed word is permanent. Audio output is usually output for the benefit of one user, whereas printed output is often widely distributed.

Audio output is interpreted by the human ear as speech, although it is actually produced by discrete digital sounds that are then put together in such a way as to be perceived as continuous words. Telephone companies were among the first businesses to produce systems using audio output for customers.

In the production of audio output, the content for a particular application must be determined first; then a vocabulary is recorded and then translated into digital signals that are stored. When a user interfaces with the computer, an appropriate response is located in memory and sent over the audio output device for the user to hear.

The systems designer needs to be aware of the value of sound output. Programs such as Wired for Sound, by Aristosoft, Inc., are useful to the personal computer user because verbal confirmation sometimes allows a user to work more quickly and with more confidence. Sound also gives the user time cues (Talking Clock), verbal confirmation of typing (Talking Calculator), and verbal confirmation when deleting files (Talking Graveyard). Even a simple confirmation of "OK," "Cancel," or "Please load more paper" are sometimes useful.

Sound can also enhance a presentation. Public domain music and sound effects are readily available. Presentation packages like Microsoft PowerPoint allow users to insert sound, music and even videos. Sound files come in various formats, but one of the most common for the IBM compatible is the .WAV files that can be played in Microsoft Windows. These .WAV files can be obtained from various bulletin boards and are also available on CD-ROM.

Even speech synthesis has come to the personal computer, making it possible to proof a document or spreadsheet by listening to the words as well as by reading them on paper. A sound board and programs such as Monologue make it possible to accomplish these and other sound output options.

CONSULTING OPPORTUNITY 15.1

Your Cage or Mine?

"Why can't they get this right? It's driving me to distraction. The zoo in Colombia is writing to me about a tiger that has been on loan from our place since 1993. They should be writing to Tulsa," trumpets Ella Fant, waving a letter in the air. Ella is general curator in charge of the animal breeding program at the Gotham Zoo.

She is talking with members of the the zoo's five-person committee about the proposals before them. The committee meets every month to decide which animals to loan to other zoos and which animals to get on loan in order to breed them. The committee is composed of Ella Fant, the general curator; Ty Garr, the zoo's director; two zoo employees, Annie Malle and Mona Key; and a layman, Rex Lyon, who is a businessman in the community.

Ty Garr paces in front of the group and continues the meeting, saying, "We have the possibility of loaning out two of our gold lion tarmarins. And we have the opportunity to play matchmaker for two lesser pandas. Since three of you are new to the committee, I'll briefly discuss your responsibilities. As you know, Ella and I would pounce on any chance to lure animals in for the breeding program. Your duties are to assess the zoo's financial resources and to look at our zoo's immediate demands. You also must consider the season and our shipping capability, as well as that of the zoo's we're considering. The other zoos charge us nothing for the loan of their animals for the breeding program. We pay the shipping for any animal being loaned to us and then maintain them, and that gets expensive."

"We are linked, via the Internet, into a database of selected species with 164 other zoos," says Ella as she picks up the story from Ty. "My office has a computer equipped with a monitor. I can access the records of all captive animals in the system, including those from the two zoos we are negotiating with right now."

As the committee members work they begin asking questions. "I need to read some information, get some meat to sink my teeth into, before I'm ready to decide whether the loan of the lesser pandas is a good idea. Where are the data on the animals we're considering?" growls Rex.

Annie replies, "We have to go to Ella's office to get to it. Mostly, the other employees who need to know just use her computer. We've been waiting for other users for our computer so that we could justify getting more high-quality printers. Right now the one we're using is just for drafts, and the output doesn't copy very well."

Mona Key gets into the swing of the discussion and says, "Some information on the current state of the budget would be divine, too. I'll go bananas with new expenditures until we at least have a summary of what we're spending. I bet it's a bunch."

Ty answers, saying, "We don't mean to monkey around, but frankly we feel trapped. Costs of reproducing all of the financial data seem high to us. We'd rather put our money into reproducing rare and endangered species! Paperwork multiplies on its own."

The group laughs nervously together, but there is an air of expectancy in the room. The consensus is that the committee members need more internal information about the zoo's financial status and the prospective loan animals.

Ella, aware that the group cannot be tamed in the way the previous one was, suggests, "The old committee preferred to get their information informally, through chattering with us. Let's spend this first meeting discovering what kinds of documents you feel you need to do your work as a committee. Financial data is on a stand-alone PC that our financial director uses. It's his baby, of course."

What are some of the problems related to output that the committee is experiencing? What suggestions do you have for improving output to the committee? How can the budget constraints of the zoos be met while still allowing the committee to receive the output it needs to function? Comment on the adequacy of the output technology that is currently in use at the zoo. Suggest alternatives or modifications to output and output technology that would enhance what is being done. [*Hint:* Consider ways in which the committee can leverage its use of the Internet (say more use of the Web)] to get the output that it needs and that it needs to share. Analyze both internal and external output requirements.

Audio output is being used to "staff" toll-free catalog numbers 24 hours a day. By using a digital phone, consumers can call the number and, in response to instructions via audio output, enter the item number, quantity, price, and their credit card number. This means that stores are capturing sales that would otherwise be missed, since hiring actual employees might be too expensive to justify offering a 24-hour number.

MICROFORMS. Microforms, including microfilm and microfiche (a sheet of microfilm), are ways to store large volumes of information in approximately one percent of the space that the printed material would take. Microforms are ideal for large volumes of output such as cataloged parts or customer lists, and they can significantly reduce the physical space required for storage.

Special machines are needed to take magnetic computer tapes and create microfilm. Projector-like machines are then used to magnify the images so that they can be read. It is possible to purchase computer-assisted retrieval systems for microfilm that index and quickly retrieve desired material.

The drawbacks of using microfilmed output are the necessity of acquiring and maintaining new equipment as well as training users on it. A hard copy of microfilmed material is often needed, which means that copy equipment must also be acquired. As you can see, it is difficult to get away from creating a paper copy. Finally, without the benefits of a computer-aided retrieval system, accessing microfilmed documents can be time-consuming and frustrating.

The advantages of microforms are saving a great deal of space, maintaining required records without needing massive storage, preservation of frequently used but fragile materials, and avoiding the trouble of physically paging through voluminous reports.

CD-ROMs AND DVDs. With the demand for multimedia output growing, the display of material on CD-ROMs has become increasingly widespread. Once used almost exclusively for reference works because of their large storage capacity, CD-ROMs are being used to output any information that is voluminous and somewhat stable in content. For example, CD-ROM displays are used to supply parts numbers for auto manufacturers and to provide extended training courses for consultants.

Retrieval of CD-ROM output is faster than older methods, such as accessing paper and microforms. Additionally, CD-ROM disks are less vulnerable to damage from human handling than other output. CD-ROMs can include full-color text and graphics, as well as music and full motion video, so as an output medium they provide a designer maximum creativity. The drawback of designing content for CD-ROM output is that it is very time-consuming and therefore expensive.

The DVD (Digital Versatile Disk) is expected to replace the CD-ROM soon because a DVD has more capacity and a DVD drive can read CD-ROMs as well as DVDs. Not only will DVDs be used for output, but also they will be used for storage as in the DVD-RAM (random access memory).

ELECTRONIC OUTPUT. Many of the new systems you design will have the capability of sending electronic output in the form of e-mail, faxes, and bulletin board messages that can be sent from one computer to another without the need for hard copy. Many of the advances in electronic output are paving the way for what is often called the "information superhighway," "the Internet," or more simply "the Net." Part of the Internet is the World Wide Web (or simply the Web). Web sites feature Web pages that are newer forms of electronic output that are accessible to Internet users who have special software to view the hypertext-based Web pages. This special software is called a "browser." In an upcoming section we provide some key definitions of de-

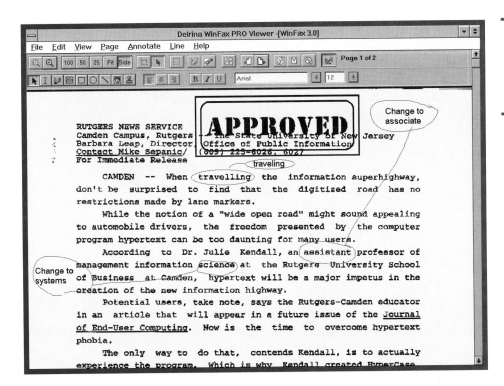

FIGURE 15.5
Users can annotate a fax and send it back to the sender without paper output using Symantec's (formerly Delrina) WinFax Pro.

sign terms that will be helpful in designing Web sites for the World Wide Web. While we leave it to you to trace out the far-reaching social implications of these shifts, in a very practical way, as an analyst, you are already involved with them.

Some of the advantages of electronic output can be realized by looking at the example in Figure 15.5, a fax sent via Symantec's (formerly Delrina) WinFax Pro. Notice that the recipient of the fax was able to electronically mark up the text with revisions and corrections, then fax it back to the source with the changes electronically included. No paper output was exchanged, and yet the revision process was facilitated. Part of your task when designing electronic output may be to help the organization develop guidelines about what constitutes a "legal" electronic signature for such signed documents.

Electronic mail (e-mail) is an exchange of messages between computers, which you can set up and run internally within the organization through an intranet, or which can be set up through communication companies or on-line services such as CompuServe or America OnLine (AOL). By designing e-mail systems, you can support communication throughout the organization, help reduce paper waste, cut down on the tiresome game of telephone tag, help users broadcast messages to many others, and provide a means for updating output very easily. A useful and flexible e-mail system can form the basis of support for workgroups. In Chapter 21, we cover groupware in detail.

The disadvantages of e-mail output include the difficulty in formatting control, the potential for abusing the system (for example, incorrectly using the "Reply" function and thereby broadcasting a message meant for a particular person), difficulties in developing useful protocols for handling "junk" e-mail, and the need to develop organizational policies for acceptable usage. Printed output can use fonts very effectively, and it can denote the serious

Source: Arnie Levin © 1995 from The New Yorker *Collection. All Rights Reserved.*

"You are entitled to one call, one fax, or one e-mail."

nature of a memo or report or convey a casual style to encourage informality. This is becoming easier now that user-friendly communication software such as Eudora Pro are available. Such software permits you to attach a word processing document or graphics file (which is complete and intact, just the way you designed it) to an e-mail message.

The most popular function on the Internet is international e-mail, which is very fast and low in cost in comparison to many other e-mail systems. (The Internet can be thought of as a "network of networks," since at last count over 11,000 networks were connected to it.) In addition to e-mail, an almost overwhelming amount of information may also be accessed on the Internet through the hypertext-based organization of the Net, called the World Wide Web. Offerings include several hundred libraries worldwide; bulletin boards; and free, high-quality downloadable software. Though a network provider can help you facilitate physically connecting the organization to the Internet, doing so requires careful planning (in addition to administrative paperwork), planning that allows you to envision how the existing LAN structure, as well as the organizational culture, can support this important change. After the organization is connected, a systems designer may help it make use of information services such as Listservs, Gopher, and a variety of relevant Web sites; or he or she may assist the organization in designing its own Web site.

FACTORS TO CONSIDER WHEN CHOOSING OUTPUT TECHNOLOGY. As you can determine from this brief discussion of output technology, there are several factors to consider when choosing it. Although the technology changes rapidly, certain usage factors remain fairly constant in relation to technological breakthroughs. These factors, some of which present trade-offs, must be considered. They include:

1. Who will use (see) the output (requisite quality)?
2. How many people need the output?
3. Where is the output needed (distribution/logistics)?
4. What is the purpose of the output?
5. What is the speed with which output is needed?
6. How frequently will the output be accessed?
7. How long will (or must) the output be stored?
8. Under what special regulations is the output produced, stored, and distributed?
9. What are the initial and ongoing costs of maintenance and supplies?
10. What are the environmental requirements (noise absorption, controlled temperature, space for equipment, and cabling) for output technologies?

Examining each factor separately will allow you to see the interrelationships and how they may be traded off for one another in a particular system.

Who will use (see) the output? Discovering who will use the output is important because job requirements help dictate what output method is appropriate. For example, when district managers must be away from their desks for extended periods, they need printed output that can travel with them or technology that can access appropriate Web sites and databases as they visit the managers in their region. Screen output or interactive Web documents are excellent for people such as truck dispatchers who are deskbound for long periods.

Also, different standards apply depending on whether a recipient of output is internal or external to the business. External recipients of output (clients and customers, vendors and suppliers, shareholders and regulatory agencies) and users within the business will require different output. Clients, vendors, and suppliers can be part of several extranets, which are networks of computers built by the organization, providing applications, processing, and information to users on the network. These networks are not necessarily part of the Internet, although they can be. If users have difficulty accessing electronic output, because they do not have the equipment, it is sometimes worthwhile for the company to provide the necessary software or hardware to keep the client involved. Alternatively, you can provide printed output for clients or develop another common interface (such as a touch-tone phone), whereas screen, Web documents, audio, or print output all might be viable options for internal use.

Knowing who will be using the output should also help you determine the requisite quality of output. Internal users may not require letterhead; they may just need draft-quality laser printing on standard white paper. Therefore, while a low-end laser printer will serve as a satisfactory output method for much internal work, a letter-quality laser printer is necessary for most external contacts. Special forms such as computerized turnaround documents (output that becomes input when turned around or sent back by customers) will be covered in an upcoming subsection.

How many people need the output? Choice of output technology is also influenced by how many users need the output. If many people need output, Web-based documents or printed copies are probably justified. If only one user needs the output, a screen, microform, or even audio may be more suitable.

If many users in the business need different output at different times for short periods and they need it quickly, then Web documents or screens connected to on-line terminals that are able to access database contents are a viable option.

Where is the output needed (distribution/logistics)? Another factor influencing choice of output technology is the physical destination of the output. Information that will remain close to its point of origin, that will be used by a few users within the business, and that may be stored or referred to frequently can safely be printed or mounted on an intranet. An abundance of information that must be transmitted to users at great distances in branch operations may be better distributed electronically, via the Web or extranets, with the recipient deciding whether to customize and print output, display it on screens, or store it. One example of such information is documentation for an application.

Sometimes federal or state regulations dictate that a printed form remain on file at a particular location for a specified period of time. In those instances, it is the responsibility of the systems analyst to see that the regulation is observed for any new or modified output that is designed.

What is the purpose of the output? The purpose of the output is another factor to consider when choosing output technology. If the output is intended to be a report whose purpose is to attract shareholders to the business by allowing them to peruse corporate finances at their leisure, then well-designed, printed output such as an annual report is desirable. A variety of media may be used too, so that the annual report is available on the Web as well as in printed form. If the purpose of the output is to provide fifteen-minute updates on stock market quotations and if the material is highly encoded and changeable, then screen displays, Web pages, or even audio is preferable.

What is the speed with which output is needed? As we go down through the three levels of strategic, middle, and operations management within the organization, we find decision makers at the lowest level of operations management need output rapidly so that they can quickly adjust to events such as a stopped assembly line, raw materials that have not arrived on time, or a worker who is absent unexpectedly. On-line, on-screen output may be useful here.

As we ascend up the management levels, we observe that strategic managers are much less likely to need output rapidly. They are more in need of output for a specific time period, which helps in forecasting business cycles and trends.

Additionally, particular businesses are more likely to need rapid output of the sort which is often provided on screen through on-line systems. A case in point is an intensive care unit; here a nurse continually surveys a heart-attack victim's pulse using a monitor connected to a video display terminal. In contrast, a doctor reads the printout from an EKG during a healthy patient's routine physical examination. The first is literally a life-or-death situation; the second presumably is not. In the intensive care unit, reaction time to output is everything. Therefore, real-time output is needed. In the second situation, there is likely a time lapse between the completion of the EKG and the reading of the results, with no criticality involved. Fortunately, most technological decisions on output are not life-or-death, but this example does point up the burden on the systems analyst to make reasonable choices.

How frequently will the output be accessed? The more frequently output is accessed, the more important is its display on screens connected to Local Area Networks or the Web. Infrequently accessed output which is needed by only a few users is well-suited to microforms such as microfiche or microfilm. For example, university librarians at U.S. schools make observations about the frequency of use when deciding to microfilm daily newspapers from foreign countries.

Output that is accessed frequently is a good candidate for incorporation into Web-based or other on-line systems or networks, with display on screens. Adopting this type of technology allows users easy access and alleviates physical wear and tear that causes frequently handled printed output to deteriorate.

How long will (or must) the output be stored? As just noted, output printed on paper deteriorates rapidly with age. Output preserved on microforms and microfilms is not as prone to succumb to environmental disturbances such as light, humidity, and human handling. Therefore, in order to store output for long periods, it may be necessary to microfilm it.

The business in question may be subject to governmental regulations on local, state, or federal levels, regulations that dictate how long output must be kept on file. As long as the corporation is willing to maintain it and it is nonproprietary, archival information, it can be maintained in Web documents as part of the organization's Web site. Organizations themselves also enact policies about how long output must be retained. For example, some universities require professors to retain student work (output) for a full semester after a final grade for the student has been recorded. While student papers may take a lot of storage space, the short retention period does not justify the cost of microfilming them.

Under what special regulations is the output produced stored, and distributed? The appropriate format for some output is actually regulated by the government. For example, an employee's W-2 form must be printed; its final form cannot be a screen or microform output. Each business exists within a different complex of regulations under which it produces output. To that extent, appropriate technology for some functions may be dictated by law.

However, much of this regulation is industry-dependent. For example, a regional blood system is required by federal law to keep a medical history of a blood donor—as well as his or her name—on file. The exact output form is not specified, but the content is strictly spelled out. Other governmental regulations may require the printing and storing of output on standardized forms. The analyst must be aware of these regulations and make sure the business is in compliance.

A *Right Way, a Wrong Way, and a Subway*

"So far so good. Sure, there have been some complaints, but any new subway will have those. The 'free ride' gimmick has helped attract some people who never would have ridden otherwise. I think there are more people than ever before interested in riding the subway," says Bart Rayl. "What we need is an accurate fix on what ridership has been so far so we can make some adjustments on our fare decisions and scheduling of trains."

Rayl is an operations manager for S.W.I.F.T., the newly built subway for Western Ipswich and Fremont Transport that serves a major northeastern city in the United States. He is speaking with Benton Turnstile, who reports to him as operations supervisor of S.W.I.F.T. The subway system is in its first month of operation, offering limited lines. Marketing people have been giving free rides on the subway in order to increase public awareness of S.W.I.F.T.

"I think that's a good idea," says Turnstile. "It's not just a token effort. We'll show them we're really on the right track. I'll get back to you with ridership information soon," he says.

A month later, Rayl and Turnstile meet to compare the projected ridership with the new data. Turnstile proudly presents a two-inch-high stack of computer printouts to Rayl. Rayl looks a little surprised but proceeds to go through it with Turnstile. "What all is in here?" Rayl asks, fingering the top page of the stack hesitantly.

"Well," says Turnstile, training his eyes on the printout, "It's a list of all of the tickets that were sold from the computerized machines. So it tells us how many tickets were bought and what kinds of tickets were bought. The guys from Systems That Think, Inc., told me that this report would be the most helpful for us, just like it was for the operations people in Buffalo and Pittsburgh," says Turnstile, turning quickly to the next page.

"Maybe, but remember those subway systems began with really limited service. We're bigger. And what about the sales from the three manned ticket booths in the Main Street Terminal?" asks Rayl.

"The clerks in the booth can get information summarizing ticket sales on-screen any time they want it. But it's not included here. Remember we projected only 10 percent of our sales would be from the booths anyway. Let's go with our original idea, and add that to the printout," suggests Turnstile.

Rayl replies, "But I've been observing riders. Half of them seem to be afraid of the computerized ticket machines. Others start using them, get frustrated reading the directions, or don't know what to do with the ticket that comes out, and they wind up at the ticket booth blowing off steam. Furthermore, they can't understand the routine information posted on the kiosks, which is all in graphics. They wind up asking clerks what train goes where." Rayl pushes the printout holding the ticket sales to one side of the conference table and says, "I don't have much confidence in this report. I feel as if we're sitting here trying to operate the most sophisticated subway system in the U.S. by peering down a tunnel instead of at the information as we should be. I think we need to think seriously about capturing journey information on magnetically-stripped cards like New York City is doing. Every time you insert the card to take a ride, the information is stored."

What are some of the specific problems with the output that the systems consultants and Benton Turnstile gave to Bart Rayl? Evaluate the media that are being used for output, as well as the timing of its distribution. Comment on the external output that users of the computerized ticket machines are apparently receiving. Suggest some changes in output to help Rayl get the information he needs to make decisions on fares and scheduling of trains and to help users of the subway system get the information they need. What are some decisions facing organizations like the New York Transit Authority if they collect and store input concerning an individual's destinations each time a trip is taken? What changes would S.W.I.F.T. have to make to its output and its tickets if it adopted this technology?

What are the initial and ongoing costs of maintenance and supplies? The initial costs of purchasing or leasing equipment must be considered as yet another factor that enters into the choice of output technology. Most vendors will help you estimate the initial purchase or lease costs of computer hardware, including the cost of printers and monitors, the cost of access to on-line service providers (Internet access), or the costs of building intranets and extranets. However, many vendors do not provide information about how much it costs to keep a printer working (paper, toner, photoelectric unit, repairs, and maintenance). So it falls to the analyst to research the costs of operating different output technologies or of maintaining a corporate Web site over time.

Beyond that, the systems analyst may need to gather cost information about other, less-used alternatives, such as audio output and microforms. Both may cost substantially more than traditional output methods, but their costs can decrease with use so that in the long run, the user would be better off financially with an audio system. As you have seen, original and maintenance costs are far from the only factors influencing the choice of output method.

What are the environmental requirements (noise absorption, controlled temperature, space for equipment, and cabling) for output technologies? As noted earlier, printers require a dry, cool environment to operate properly. Monitors for screen-displayed output require space for setup and cabling to connect them to the database being accessed. Audio output requires a relatively quiet place that allows the user to make sense of digitized sounds. Web access requires reliable phone lines, or preferably lines that meet ISDN (Integrated Services Digital Network) standards.

Output technologies themselves actually create environmental disturbances. The systems analyst must be careful with the choice of technology because of this factor. Audio output requires a quiet environment if it is to be heard, and it should not be audible to employees (or customers) who are not using it. This means that the analyst should not specify audio output for a work situation where many employees are engaged in a variety of tasks unrelated to the output. For example, grocery store managers using microprocessor-based audio output attached to scanners at checkstands have found that cashiers working side-by-side with many other checkers often turn down the volume on their speakers (which name aloud each item scanned and its price) to avoid irritation and errors. Unfortunately, this defeats the audio double-check.

Conversely, some output technologies are prized for their unobtrusiveness. Libraries that emphasize silence in the workplace make extensive use of display screens for Web documents and for the display of other networked database information, while printers might be scarce. This choice is much quieter than having a patron physically check the stacks for a book.

REALIZING HOW OUTPUT BIAS AFFECTS USERS

Whatever form it takes, output is not just a neutral product that is subsequently analyzed and acted upon by decision makers. Output affects users in many different ways. The significance of this fact for the systems analyst is that great thought and care must be put into designing the output in order to avoid biasing it.

Recognizing Bias in the Way Output Is Used

It is a common error to assume that once the systems analyst has signed off of a system project, his or her impact is ended. Actually, the analyst's influence is long-lasting. Much of the information on which organizational members base their decisions is determined by what analysts perceive is important to the business.

Bias is present in everything that humans create. This is not to judge bias as bad but to make the point that it is inseparable from what we (and consequently our systems) produce. The concerns of systems analysts are to avoid unnecessarily biasing output and to make users aware of the possible biases in the output they receive.

There are three main ways in which presentations of output are unintentionally biased:

1. How information is sorted.
2. Setting of acceptable limits.
3. Choice of graphics.

Each source of bias is discussed separately in the following subsections.

INTRODUCING BIAS WHEN INFORMATION IS SORTED. Bias is introduced to output when the analyst makes choices about how information is sorted for a report. Common sorts include alphabetical, chronological, and cost.

Information presented alphabetically may overemphasize the items that begin with the letters A and B, since users tend to pay more attention to information presented first. For example, if past suppliers are listed alphabetically, companies such as "Aardvark Printers," "Advent Supplies," and "Barkley Office Equipment" are shown to the purchasing manager first.

Bias is also unintentionally introduced into reports that are arranged chronologically. Once again, users' attention is drawn to the events listed first, which are those things that occurred first. So in reviewing the use of computing time, any MIS manager who uses output presented chronologically may be biased toward examining usage for January, February, and March and slighting the figures for November and December.

A third type of sorting—by cost—may also bias the output. Presenting information by cost alone (or by any single factor) can be extremely misleading. Providing a context for cost—such as listing benefits, the time period during which cost was assessed, or other variables considered—are ways to correct for this particular bias. Customizable sorting designed by the user can move away from analysts' biases but may unfortunately magnify biases of the user creating the sorts.

INTRODUCING BIAS BY SETTING LIMITS. A second major source of bias in output is the predefinition of limits for particular values being reported. Many reports are generated on an exception basis only, which means that when limits on values are set beforehand, only exceptions to those values will be output. Exception reports make the decision maker aware of deviations from satisfactory values. There are four general problems with setting limits that may bias output:

1. Limit set too low.
2. Limit set too high.
3. Range of exceptions output too narrow.
4. Range of exceptions output too wide.

Limits that are set too low for exception reports can bias the user's perception. For example, an insurance company that generates exception reports on all accounts one week overdue has probably set too low a limit on overdue payments. The decision maker receiving the output will be over-

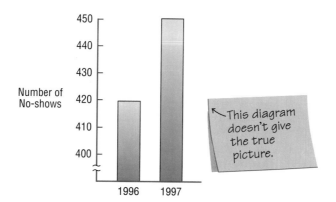

FIGURE 15.6
A misleading graph that
might bias the user.

whelmed with "exceptions" that are not really cause for concern. The one-week overdue exception report leads to the user's misperception that there are a great many overdue accounts. A more appropriate limit for generating an exception report would be accounts thirty days overdue.

Users can also be biased by output that is printed in an exception report when too high a limit is to be met before information is included. For example, a quality assurance manager for a large manufacturer receives an exception report if more than 10 lots of rubber hoses out of 100 that are produced are defective according to specifications such as tensile strength. Typically, the manager can expect 3 lots to be defective. However, the limit is too high to be of any tangible value because the problem could have been detected earlier as the defective rate began to rise. For the information to be useful, limits on allowable defects must be tightened. The resultant bias of setting too high a limit is that a false sense of security is generated. In fact, there is little, if any, timely output when allowances are set at unrealistically high limits.

A third way that setting limits can introduce bias is if the range of information output in an exception report is set too narrowly. For example, if the marketing department of a food manufacturer generates reports on the number of consumers between the ages of eight and ten who send in for offers from the back of cereal boxes, they may not be generating much useful information. A too narrowly defined range may mean losing the very information that you were originally attempting to pinpoint.

Conversely, setting too wide a range for information output on an exception report can also bias users. For example, if the gas company generates an exception report on its high-volume residential users but employs a range of all residential customers using between 6 and 2,600 cubic feet of gas per month, the output will be overwhelming. The range of usage is too broad to get a grasp of high usage; rather, the report includes just about all of the gas company's residential customers. Output generated within too broad a range can bias the user into magnifying the existence of "exceptions" or problems.

INTRODUCING BIAS THROUGH GRAPHICS. Output is subject to a third type of presentation bias, which is brought about by the analyst's choice of graphics for output display. Bias can occur in the selection of the graphic size, its color, the scale used, and even the type of graphic.

Graphic size must be proportional, so that the user is not biased as to the importance of the variables that are presented. For example, Figure 15.6 shows a column chart comparing the number of no-shows for hotel bookings in 1996 with no-shows for hotel bookings in 1997. Notice that the vertical axis is broken, and it appears that the number of no-shows for 1997 is twice as much as the number of no-shows in 1996, although the number of no-shows has actually gone up only slightly.

Choice of graphic color is also important because it, too, may unduly bias the user. The analyst needs to be aware that any colored output naturally claims more user attention than black-and-white printed or displayed output. Certain colors may be assigned meanings within business, and those should not be changed by the analyst without good cause. For instance, red might be used to indicate a problem, such as a budget that is "in the red," as part of an exception report. Some colors are not easily legible (see Chapter 16 on input design for specifics on screen color), so they should be avoided. Otherwise, users will be biased against even reading information or related graphics. Notice that Web graphics are included in Web pages. Care must be taken to view color combinations with many different browsers, since not all browsers can handle all colors, and strange combinations occur when millions of colors are viewed as only 256 colors.

The scale of graphics used for output can also potentially bias the user. Most users perceive that the larger the item, the greater its importance. For example, if a pictograph shows a small icon of a ship, which represents overseas trade, in one year and, on the same graph, shows a larger icon, which represents the same amount of shipping a year later, it may bias the user's interpretation by suggesting that overseas trade has grown, when only the year has changed. Size of graphics also becomes an issue when users attempt to load huge graphics files quickly.

Users also perceive that when more of an item is displayed, it is more important. Graphic output that always shows an icon symbolizing 10 units that are produced is automatically interpreted as meaning "30 units were produced" if three icons are shown. Users might thus be biased if the icon were used in a cluster of three on a newly developed output screen to denote that the user was seeing a production report.

The type of graphic chosen for output is also a potential source of bias for users. A pie chart is inappropriate if percentages of a whole are not the point. Bar and column charts can overexaggerate differences between variables. As discussed in Chapter 14, if more that two variables are to be shown over time, it is more appropriate to depict them on a line chart than on a bar chart. A poor choice of graph along with an inappropriate presentation can bias the user as to the meaning of the output. Graphics for oral presentation were covered in Chapter 14, and a more detailed discussion concerning choice of graphics is presented in a later section of this chapter on designing graphics for a decision support system.

Avoiding Bias in the Design of Output

There are specific strategies that systems analysts can use to avoid biasing the output they design:

1. Be aware of the sources of bias.
2. Create an interactive design of output that includes users and a variety of differently-configured systems during the testing of Web document appearance.
3. Work with users so that they are informed of the output's biases and can recognize the implications of customizing their displays.

4. Create output that is flexible and that allows users to modify limits and ranges.

5. Train users to rely on multiple output for conducting "reality tests" on system output.

All of these (except the first) focus on the relationship between the systems analyst and the user as it involves output. Systems analysts must recognize the potential impact of output and be aware of the possible ways in which output is unintentionally biased.

Interactive design of output means that output cannot be successfully designed in a vacuum. Rather, the systems analyst must actively solicit user feedback regarding output. The design process will require several iterations before users feel output is useful. Unavoidably, users will incorporate their own biases into output, but they will also be clearer about how to interpret output that they helped design, or which they customized.

The third way to avoid unintentional bias is to work with users so that they are informed of the output's biases. This is done in training sessions, as well as in the documentation. Output (especially screens) can include information about the way the information has been generated, thus pinpointing potential biases included in the report.

Biased output can also be avoided (or at least made explicit) if users are able to modify the limits and ranges set for output. This approach is especially suited to on-line, interactive systems. The drawback is that there may be a lack of consistency in output that could lead to problems if future comparisons are necessary. Flexibility in output may also lead to communication problems among users who, for example, may be using different ranges of values to spot problems.

A fifth way to help avoid unintentional bias in output is to train users to conduct "reality tests" on the output they receive. This includes comparing output with their own experience and expectations (asking whether what they are reading make sense in a practical way) and using multiple output from different sources (daily and monthly reports, observation and speaking with others in the business, and so on) to arrive at an understanding of what is actually happening in the organization. Such checks prevent an overreliance on any one source of output and help correct for bias by introducing other perspectives.

DESIGNING PRINTED OUTPUT

Using the information gained through the information requirements determination phase and having decided to use printed output, the systems analyst is ready to begin its physical design. The source of information to be included in reports is the data dictionary, the compilation of which was covered in Chapter 10. Recall that the data dictionary includes names of data elements as well as the required field length of each entry.

Guidelines for Printed Report Design

Figure 15.7 is an output report that is intended for divisional managers of a food wholesaler that supplies a number of franchise grocery stores. We will focus on different aspects of the report as we cover the tools, conventions, and functional and stylistic design attributes of printed output reports.

Franchise Store Information
Ranked by Earnings in Dollars
For the Month Ending MM/DD/YYYY

F NO	Store Names	D I V	Dist	Rank	Sales Dollar 1,000's	Gross Profit 1,000's	%	Other Income 1,000's	%	Allacated Expenses 1,000's	%	Earnings Dollars	%
C 5112	Front Royal, VA	20	23	51	126	5	3.93	2	1.8	5	4.0	2,144	1.7
S 4311	Rockville, MD	40	41	52	144	6	4.27	0	0.3	4	3.1	2,062	1.4
R 3021	Middleburg, VA	20	22	53	95	4	4.29	2	1.9	4	4.0	2,057	2.2
S 5021	Culpeper, VA	20	26	54	219	8	3.78	3	1.5	10	4.4	2,005	0.9
R 2820	Waldorf, MD	40	42	55	72	3	4.69	1	1.2	2	3.3	1,903	2.6
C 4424	Fairfax-Lee Hgwy	20	22	56	131	5	4.16	2	1.3	5	4.0	1,869	1.4
C 4423	Baileys X-Roads	20	22	57	98	5	4.70	2	1.7	5	4.6	1,727	1.8
S 3821	Herndon, VA	20	23	58	221	7	3.35	4	1.7	9	4.2	1,703	0.8
C 7126	Frederick, MD	30	32	59	125	5	4.04	2	1.6	5	4.3	1,615	1.3
S 8029	Centreville, VA	20	27	60	175	7	3.73	3	1.9	8	4.7	1,593	0.9
R 5029	Minnieville, VA	20	34	61	34	2	5.28	1	3.3	1	4.0	1,572	4.7
S 7520	Mount Vernon	20	24	62	90	5	5.22	2	1.7	5	5.2	1,558	1.7
C 4712	D.C. M Street	40	44	63	235	10	4.35	4	1.8	13	5.5	1,489	0.6
S 4716	Annandale	20	25	64	126	6	4.52	0	0.1	4	3.5	1,457	1.2
S 7922	Vienna, VA	20	25	65	177	9	4.86	2	1.2	9	5.3	1,447	0.8
R 4491	Great Falls	20	24	66	86	4	4.39	2	1.9	4	4.7	1,364	1.6
R 3926	Harper's Ferry	30	33	67	68	3	4.80	0	0.3	2	3.1	1,325	1.9
C 2422	Falls Church	20	27	68	144	6	4.06	2	1.4	7	4.6	1,322	.9
R 3024	Clifton, VA	20	23	69	53	3	5.17	1	1.6	2	4.3	1,273	2.4
C 4511	Silver Spring, MD	20	42	70	121	5	4.06	1	1.2	5	4.3	1,237	1.0
R 5120	Olney, MD	30	31	71	43	2	4.60	1	.2.	2	4.0	1,217	2.8
C 4527	D.C Connecticut Ave	40	45	72	110	5	4.28	0	0.2	4	3.4	1,200	1.1
C 4526	Pennsylvania Ave	40	42	73	134	6	4.55	0	0.2	5	4.0	1,073	0.8
S 2923	Manassas	20	25	74	198	7	3.54	0	0.1	6	3.1	1,057	0.5
	City Stores				6,025	255	4.23	67	1.1	190	3.2	69,987	1.2
	Suburban Stores				3,402	171	5.03	54	1.6	133	3.9	35,020	1.0
	Rural Stores				2,018	92	4.56	27	1.3	47	2.3	43,223	2.1
	Total (All Stores in Region)				11,445	518	4.52	148	1.3	370	3.2	148,230	1.3

FIGURE 15.7
A printed output report for divisional managers of a food wholesaler.

REPORT DESIGN CONVENTIONS. Conventions to follow when designing a form include the type of data (alphabetic, special, or numeric) that will appear in each position; showing the size of the form being prepared; and showing the way to indicate a continuation of data on consecutive layout forms. Most form design software that analysts' now use features standard conventions for designing forms on-screen. Additionally, they feature familiar drag and drop interfaces that allow you both to select attributes such as an address "block" with a mouse click and then to drop it on the screen where you want to position it on your form. You will be using "WYSIWYG" or "What You See Is What You Get," so it makes the design of forms a very visual exercise.

Constant information is information that remains the same whenever the report is printed. The title of the report and all of the column headings are written in as constant information. *Variable information* is information that can vary each time the report is printed out. In our example, the sales figures in thousands of dollars will change, and hence it is indicated as variable information.

Your software design tool will also have conventions to permit you to easily signify whether you will be using alphabetic or numeric characters in a field. Additionally, form design software permits you to easily mark information that must be repeated in the same position in a column.

PAPER QUALITY, TYPE, AND SIZE. Output can be printed on innumerable kinds of paper. The overriding constraint is usually cost. Paper that is treated in any special way—either preprinted, inked in color, multipart with carbon interleaves, or carbonless transfer—is more expensive than plain paper.

However, the kind of paper used has a predictable effect on the user, so investing in special papers may be justified. For example, using bond to print letters of appreciation to employees would be a way of showing that the letter has special content and differs in importance from everyday internal memos. Other examples are the use of security paper for checks and check envelopes, as well as documents that must bear official, inalterable seals or even holograms, such as passports, birth certificates, and many others.

Paper also differs as to its weight, depending on the rag (cotton) content. More cotton means better quality, durability, and a higher price, but a business may still want particular correspondence to be printed on cotton bond in order to present a more distinguished image. Common lengths for reports in the United States,—whether they appear on preprinted forms or computer printouts—are 3 1/2, 3 2/3, 5 1/2, 6, 7 1/2, and 11 inches.

SPECIAL OUTPUT FORMS. The variety of special output forms is seemingly endless, since virtually any color ink or paper can be used. Many options on positioning of headings and logotypes are open. The systems analyst lays out the content of the report on-screen using a template, in the same manner as on the computer-prepared report.

Preprinted forms are used for many purposes—for example, they may be sent to customers as turnaround documents. Preprinted forms can easily convey a distinctive corporate image through the use of corporate colors and design. Using innovative shapes, colors, and layouts are also dramatic ways of drawing users attention to the report that is contained on the preprinted form.

The chief drawback of preprinted forms is their cost. They are extremely expensive in comparison to computer-generated report forms, sometimes costing three times as much. Also, more forms must be kept in inventory. However, the expense may be justified, especially in instances where creating interest is of competitive importance. The advent of Web-based forms has alleviated some of the inventory costs, since when the output form is created as a Web document, it is not stocked in inventory per se; rather it is maintained on the company's Web site.

DESIGN CONSIDERATION. In designing the printed report, the systems analyst incorporates both functional and stylistic or aesthetic considerations so that the report supplies the user with necessary information in a readable format. Since function and form reinforce each other, one should not be emphasized at the expense of the other.

Functional attributes. The functional attributes of a printed report include (1) the heading or title of the report, (2) the page number, (3) the date of preparation, (4) the column headings, (5) the grouping of related data items together, and (6) the use of control breaks. Each of these serves a distinctive purpose for the user.

The heading or the title of the report immediately orients users to what it is they are reading. The title should be descriptive, yet concise. It is often redundant to include the word "report" in the title.

CONSULTING OPPORTUNITY 15.3

Is Your Work a Grind?

"I want everything I can get my hands on. And the tighter the information is packed, the better. Forget that stuff you hear about information overload. It's not in my vocabulary. I want it all. And not in a bunch of pretty looking, half-page reports either. All together, packed on one sheet that I can take into a meeting in case I need to look something up. And I need it every week," proclaims Stephen Links, vice president of a large, family-owned sausage company.

During an interview, Links has been grilling Paul Plishka, who is part of the systems analysis team that is busy designing an information system for Links Meats. Although Paul is hesitant about what Links has told him, he proceeds to design a printed report that includes all of the important items the team has settled on during the analysis phase.

However, when a prototype of the new report, designed to his specifications, is handed to Stephen, there appears to be a change of heart. Links says in no uncertain terms that he can't find what he needs.

"This stuff looks terrible. It looks like scraps. My kindergartner makes better reports in crayon. Look at this: It's all ground up together. I can't find anything. Where's the summary of the number of pork items sold in each outlet? Where is the total volume of items sold for *all* outlets? How about the information on our own shop downtown?" says Links, slicing at the report.

The report clearly needs to be redesigned. Design a report (or reports) that better suits Stephen Links. What tack can the analyst take in suggesting more reports with a less-crowded format? Comment on the difficulty of implementing user suggestions that go against your design training. What are the trade-offs involved (as far as information overload goes) in generating numerous reports as opposed to generating one large report containing all of the information that Stephen wanted? Devise a heuristic concerning the display of report information on one report in contrast to the generation of numerous reports. Consider advocating a Web-based solution that would permit hyperlinks to all of the information Stephen desires. How feasible is this?

Each page should be numbered so that the user has an easy point of reference when discussing output with others or when locating important figures. Also, if pages of output become separated, page numbers are invaluable in reconstructing the document.

Include the date when the report was prepared on each printout. Sometimes this helps users estimate the value of the output. Often, the more timely the output, the more valuable it is.

Column heading serve to further orient the user as to the report contents. Each data item must have a heading. Headings should be short and descriptive. It is permissible to use abbreviations if they are common to users and meaningful to them. Check that abbreviations are not used elsewhere in the organization with a meaning different from that intended in the report.

Data items that are related to one another should be grouped together on the report. This facilitates understanding for the user, and in many instances it fulfills their expectations of where items should appear. In our sample worksheet, store name and store number are grouped together because divisional managers use them interchangeably in referring to stores.

Use control breaks (which are breaks in data where summaries occur) to help readability. Separate these breaks from the rest of the data with additional lines of space. For example, if 200 franchise grocery stores are grouped by division, the report might feature a control break at the end of each division.

Stylistic/aesthetic attributes. There are several stylistic or aesthetic considerations for the systems analyst to observe when designing a printed report. If printed output is unappealing and difficult to read, it will not be used effectively or may not be used at all. The upshot is uninformed decision makers and a waste of computer time, as well as other organizational resources.

Printed reports should be well organized, reflecting the way that the eye sees. In this culture, that means the report should read from top to bottom and left to right. As mentioned before, related data items should be grouped together. The aesthetics of Web site and Web page design are covered in an upcoming subsection.

Additional blank spaces between columns also contribute to the readability of a report. Users should be able to locate key figures easily on a page; adding blank spaces will facilitate this.

As with the systems proposal report discussed in Chapter 14, printed output reports require ample margins on the right and left, as well as on the top and bottom. These serve to focus the user's attention on the material centered on the page and to make reading easier. Since the point of creating output is to make it usable, the importance of organization, readability, and ease of use cannot be overstated.

Other stylistic elements that can be used to distinguish printed output are the use of color coding, organizational logos, or preprinted forms that feature these items. Graphics are also a possibility for printed output. They are covered in the subsections on designing output for decision support systems. Show users a prototype of the output report (either on the Web, if that is where it is to reside, or in printed form) so they can make changes. The mock-up should look as realistic as possible.

Steps in Designing Output Reports with a Computer-Aided Software Tool

The following is a step-by-step guide for preparing screen-based prototypes of output reports:

1. Determine the need for the report.
2. Determine the users.
3. Determine the data items to be included.
4. Estimate the overall size of the report.
5. Title the report.
6. Number the pages of the report.
7. Include the preparation date on the report.
8. Label each column of data appropriately.
9. Define variable data, indicating on the screen whether each space or field is to be used for an alphabetic, special, or numeric character.
10. Indicate the positioning of blank lines used to help organize information.
11. Review prototype reports (use screens for Web-based documents and use hard copy output for printed reports) with users and programmers for feasibility, usefulness, readability, understandability, and aesthetic appeal.

Your expertise as a systems analyst enters in when you are required to design printed reports that bring content and form together in a meaningful way. Printed output is the embodiment of your belief about what users need to know to make decisions. There is a trade-off involved between wanting

Source: Arnie Levin © 1997 from The Cartoon Bank. All Rights Reserved.

"Hold on a second, my printer's going nuts."

decision makers to have all available information and designing a useful report that does not overwhelm them with extraneous details.

DESIGNING SCREEN OUTPUT

Chapter 16 covers designing screens for input, and the same guidelines also apply here for designing screen output, although the contents will change. Notice that screen output differs from printed output in a number of ways. It is ephemeral—that is, a screen display is not "permanent" in the same way that printouts are—it can be more specifically targeted to the user, it is available on a more flexible schedule, it is *not* portable in the same way, and sometimes it can be changed through direct interaction.

Additionally, users must be instructed on which keys to press when they want to continue reading further screens, when they want to know how to end the display, and when they want to know how to interact with the display (if possible). Access to screen displays may be controlled through the use of a password, whereas distribution of printed output is controlled by other means.

Guidelines for Screen Design

There are four guidelines to facilitate the design of screens. To summarize, they are to:

1. Keep the screen simple.
2. Keep the screen presentation consistent.
3. Facilitate user movement among screens.
4. Create an attractive screen.

Two examples of output screens are shown in Figures 15.8 and 15.9. Notice the difference between the readability of the two screens. On the first, the district number is listed in every instance for the voting register. The readability of the screen is improved when the district number is listed only

Voter Registration Records
New Rochelle Office

Dist.	Number	Street	Last Name	First	Party	Last
69	11413	Bonny Meadow Lane	Petrie	Laura	D	11/1997
69	11413	Bonny Meadow Lane	Petrie	Robert	D	11/1995
69	11414	Bonny Meadow Lane	Helper	Jerry	D	11/1995
69	11414	Bonny Meadow Lane	Helper	Millicent	D	06/1996
69	11415	Bonny Meadow Lane	Brady	Alan	R	11/1995
69	11416	Bonny Meadow Lane	Sorel	Buddy	D	11/1993
69	11416	Bonny Meadow Lane	Sorel	Pickles	D	11/1993
69	11417	Bonny Meadow Lane	Coolie	Melvin	R	06/1997
69	11418	Bonny Meadow Lane	Rogers	Sally	D	11/1996
69	11341	Elm Street	Cleaver	June	R	06/1997
69	11341	Elm Street	Cleaver	Ward	R	06/1997

Press the PGDN key to continue

F1 = Help	F2 = Return to the Main Menu	F3 = Change Party
F4 = Change Name	F5 = Add a Voter	F6 = Change Last Voted

Voter Registration Records
New Rochelle Office
District Number 69

Street	Number	Last Name	First	Party	Last
Bonny Meadow Lane	11413	Petrie	Laura	D	11/1997
			Robert	D	11/1995
	11414	Helper	Jerry	D	11/1995
			Millicent	D	06/1996
	11415	Brady	Alan	R	11/1995
	11416	Sorel	Buddy	D	11/1993
			Pickles	D	11/1993
	11417	Coolie	Melvin	R	06/1997
	11418	Rogers	Sally	D	11/1996
Elm Street	11341	Cleaver	June	R	06/1997
			Ward	R	06/1997

Press the PGDN key to continue

F1 = Help	F2 = Return to the Main Menu	F3 = Change Party
F4 = Change Name	F5 = Add a Voter	F6 = Change Last Voted

once, thus eliminating repeating information. This section concentrates on how this kind of graphical and tabular output is created for on-screen display. Chapter 16 covers specific information on how to achieve the four guidelines.

A Screen Design Example. Just as form design software tools are used to plan for printed output, the same tools can be used to plan screens and communicate that detail to programmers. Basically, the same conventions of notation are followed for screen layout as for printed output layout. Differences in screen design include the necessity of putting instructions on screen for changing screens, moving between screens, and terminating the display of output.

Figure 15.10 is an example of screen layout that is being prepared for outputting tabular reports for use by the shipping department of a stuffed animal manufacturer called New Zoo. The shipping department is currently using a manual system to keep track of shipments, but with the growth in outlets it has experienced in the past year, this approach is no longer practical. The shipping department would like a running summary of shipping activity so that any problems can be handled quickly, especially during the heavy shipping season in September.

Notice that the screen is generally divided into three parts. The top gives the title or heading of the screen report, "NEW ZOO ORDER STATUS." Just as the columns were all given headings on the paper printout, so too are they given headings on the screen. Note, too, that the screen reads from top to bottom and from left to right.

Continuing our analysis of this example, the columns are written in exactly as they are to appear on the screen. RETAILER, ORDER #, ORDER DATE, and ORDER STATUS are all columns that will appear on the screen.

FIGURE 15.10
An electronic form used for planning a screen layout.

New Zoo Order Status

Retailer	Order #	Order Date	Order Status
XXXXXXXXXXXXXXXXXXX	999999	MM/DD/YYYY	XXXXXXXXXXXXXXXXXXXX
XXXXXXXXXXXXXXXXXXX	999999	MM/DD/YYYY	XXXXXXXXXXXXXXXXXXXX
XXXXXXXXXXXXXXXXXXX	999999	MM/DD/YYYY	XXXXXXXXXXXXXXXXXXXX
XXXXXXXXXXXXXXXXXXX	999999	MM/DD/YYYY	XXXXXXXXXXXXXXXXXXXX
XXXXXXXXXXXXXXXXXXX	999999	MM/DD/YYYY	XXXXXXXXXXXXXXXXXXXX
XXXXXXXXXXXXXXXXXXX	999999	MM/DD/YYYY	XXXXXXXXXXXXXXXXXXXX
XXXXXXXXXXXXXXXXXXX	999999	MM/DD/YYYY	XXXXXXXXXXXXXXXXXXXX
XXXXXXXXXXXXXXXXXXX	999999	MM/DD/YYYY	XXXXXXXXXXXXXXXXXXXX
XXXXXXXXXXXXXXXXXXX	999999	MM/DD/YYYY	XXXXXXXXXXXXXXXXXXXX
XXXXXXXXXXXXXXXXXXX	999999	MM/DD/YYYY	XXXXXXXXXXXXXXXXXXXX
XXXXXXXXXXXXXXXXXXX	999999	MM/DD/YYYY	XXXXXXXXXXXXXXXXXXXX
XXXXXXXXXXXXXXXXXXX	999999	MM/DD/YYYY	XXXXXXXXXXXXXXXXXXXX
XXXXXXXXXXXXXXXXXXX	999999	MM/DD/YYYY	XXXXXXXXXXXXXXXXXXXX
XXXXXXXXXXXXXXXXXXX	999999	MM/DD/YYYY	XXXXXXXXXXXXXXXXXXXX
XXXXXXXXXXXXXXXXXXX	999999	MM/DD/YYYY	XXXXXXXXXXXXXXXXXXXX
XXXXXXXXXXXXXXXXXXX	999999	MM/DD/YYYY	XXXXXXXXXXXXXXXXXXXX
XXXXXXXXXXXXXXXXXXX	999999	MM/DD/YYYY	XXXXXXXXXXXXXXXXXXXX

Press any key to see the rest of the the list; ESC to end; ? for help
For more detail place cursor over the order number and hit the Enter key.

FIGURE 15.11
The resulting screen shows
how the information actu-
ally appears.

New Zoo Order Status

Retailer	Order #	Order Date	Order Status
Animals Unlimited	933401	09/05/1997	Shipped On 09/29
	934567	09/11/1997	Shipped On 09/21
	934613	09/13/1997	Shipped On 09/21
	934691	09/14/1997	Shipped On 09/21
Bear Bizarre	933603	09/02/1997	Partially Shipped
	933668	09/08/1997	Scheduled For 10/03
	934552	09/18/1997	Scheduled For 10/03
	934683	09/18/1997	Shipped On 09/28
Cuddles Co.	933414	09/12/1997	Shipped On 09/18
	933422	09/14/1997	Shipped On 09/21
	934339	09/16/1997	Shipped On 09/26
	934387	09/18/1997	Shipped On 09/21
	934476	09/25/1997	Backordered
Stuffed Stuff	934341	09/14/1997	Shipped On 09/26
	934591	09/18/1997	Partially Shipped
	934633	09/26/1997	Backordered
	934664	09/29/1997	Partially Shipped

Press any key to see the rest of the the list; ESC to end; ? for help
For more detail place cursor over the order number and hit the Enter key.

In the RETAILER column, notice that the output is designated as alphabetic characters, whereas ORDER # is shown as numeric, with the use of 9s. ORDER STATUS is also noted as alphabetic characters.

Notice that the two bottom lines of the screen are used for instructions to the user. When the user positions the cursor over any ORDER # and hits ENTER, he or she will automatically bring up another screen that gives more detailed information about that particular retailer's shipment.

When the screen is in a preliminary design phase, before it is finalized, it is wise to show a prototype screen to users and get their feedback about changes or improvements that they would like to see. This interactive process continues until users feel satisfied that the output provides what they need to see in a usable format. Just as with printed output, good screen layouts cannot be created in isolation. Systems analysts need the feedback of users to design worthwhile screens. Once approved by users, the screen layout can be finalized.

The screen produced from the screen design display is pictured in Figure 15.11. Notice that the screen is uncluttered, yet it gives a basic summary of the shipping status. The display orients users as to what they are looking at with the use of a heading. Instructions at the bottom of the screen provide users with several options, including continuing the present display, ending the display, getting help, or getting more detail.

Output screens within an application should display information consistently from screen to screen. Figure 15.12 shows the screen that results when the user positions the cursor over the ORDER # for a particular retailer. The new screen presents more details on Bear Bizarre. In the body of the screen, the user can see the retailer's order number, complete address, the order date, and the status. Additionally, a detailed breakdown of the shipment and a detailed status of each part of the shipment are given. A contact name

FIGURE 15.12
If users want more details regarding the shipping status,
they can call up a separate
screen.

Order #		Retailer	Order Date		Order Status
933603		Bear Bizarre	09/02/1997		Partially Shipped
		1001 Karhu Lane			
		Bern, Virginia 22024			

Units	Pkg	Description	Price	Amount	Detailed Status
12	Each	Floppy Bears	20.00	240.00	Backordered Due 10/15
6	Each	Growlers	25.00	150.00	Backordered Due 10/15
2	Each	Special Edition	70.00	140.00	Shipped 09/02
1	Box	Celebrity Mix	150.00	150.00	Shipped 09/02
12	Each	Santa Bears	10.00	120.00	Backordered Due 10/30
				800.00	

Contact	Account Balance	Credit Rating	Last Order	Shipped
Ms. Ursula Major	0.00	Excellent	08/21/1994	On-time
703-484-2327				

Press any key to see the rest of the list;   ESC to end;   ? for help

and phone number are supplied, along with the account balance, credit rating, and shipment history. Notice that the bottom portion of the screen ad-
vises the user of options, including more details, ending the display, or getting help.

Rather than crowding all retailer information onto one screen, the analyst has made it possible for the user to bring up a particular retailer if a
problem or question arises. If, for example, the summary screen indicates
that an order was only "partially shipped," the user can check further on the
order by calling up a detailed retailer screen and then following up with appropriate action. So far, we have been discussing general tabular output for
information system screen displays. Although there is much overlap, some
aspects of interaction with displays, as well as how the decision maker uses
them, change as we turn to designing tabular output specifically for decision
support systems.

Tabular Output for Decision Support Systems

In Chapter 12, information systems that were designed to support decision
makers in semistructured decision systems, called decision support systems
(DSS), were introduced. A DSS helps the decision maker to make a decision
through interaction with the system. The DSS often uses screen output with
a mouse or keyboard interface in order to accomplish that interaction. Output designed for decision support systems is thus characterized by modifia-
bility and flexibility, which are not as important in output from a traditional
MIS.

Figure 15.13 shows a screen for the Nebraska State Patrol Manpower
Planning DSS (based an earlier work with Merrill Warkentin). The screen is
from a Lotus spreadsheet, so the rows are numbered in the left margin, and

```
040:                                                              CMD MENU
Help   Update   Results   Print    Graph     Quit
Incidents       Variables        Parameters      Decision      Quit
                O         P       Q        R       S      T      U      V
21   Number of Calls (by Type) recorded by the Incident Reporting System
22   May 1997
23
24                      ============= TROOP =================    State
25   Type of Call        HQ      A       B       C       D       E     Totals
26   ================   --------------------------------------------------
27   Accidents           79      67      73      52      53      45     369
28   Criminal complaints 47      47      49      41      37      43     264
29   Motorist assists    36      13       6      32      34      22     143
30   Traffic violations  29      18      22      20      12      12     113
31   Relays               7       8      11       9      18       4      57
32   REDDI calls         44      16      12      49      34      22     177
33   Other hway emergencies 25   18       7      19      22      51     142
34   Other requests      47       4      19      38      42       4     154
35      HISTORICAL       --------------------------------------------------
36   Total number of calls 314   191     199     260     252     203    1419
37   # Troopers & Sergeants 51    33      44      38      30      30     226
38   Average Response Time 27.0  20.6    26.4    20.4    45.2    30.0    28.5
39
40               PgDn for additional Incident Reporting data
```

the columns are indicated by the letters Q to V in the fourth row. There are also two menu-command rows at the top of the screen. Data are entered by viewing the output screen, placing the cursor over the cell the decision maker wants to change, and typing in a new value.

The performance measures for response time of the State Patrol troops are shown in Figure 15.14. Once again, the rows are numbered and the columns are indicated by letters. The response times are listed in a matrix by type of call and troop. Notice the instruction at the bottom of the screen that tells the user to page down for more information.

Graphical Output for Decision Support Systems

All throughout the analysis process, the systems analyst has been using graphs: to organize information through the use of data flow diagrams; to schedule activities with PERT charts; and to inform management about recommendations on the proposed information system. In Chapter 14, we covered the use of line graphs, as well as bar, column, and pie charts in the written and oral systems proposal. Refer to that chapter for details on the effects of different kinds of graphs on decision makers.

We now turn briefly to designing graphical output for decision makers using decision support systems. Extensive growth in the use of graphical output for decision support systems is expected in the next few years. There are already numerous graphics packages on the software market. Graphical output can aid decision makers by showing them a trend or concept quickly, with analysis to follow. Note, however, that graphical output is not considered to be a replacement for tabular output, but it serves to supplement it.

FIGURE 15.14
A DSS screen showing the
weighted average response
time of the Nebraska State
Patrol troops.

```
020:                                                                    READY


                O           P       Q       R       S       T       U       V
    1   Response Times (by troop area) from the Incident Reporting System
    2   May 1997
    3
    4                       ============= TROOP =================
    5   Average Response to     HQ      A       B       C       D       E     State
    6   =================   ------------------------------------------------
    7   Accidents           32.6    13.0    36.5    16.3    38.8    18.0    26.6
    8   Criminal complaints  19.6    14.2    17.3    12.9    32.7    40.7    22.4
    9   Motorist assists     19.5    12.8    10.8    17.1    19.8    35.3    20.5
   10   Traffic violations   24.7    18.9    11.3    30.7    47.7    37.1    26.0
   11   Relays               52.7    35.3    66.4    19.3    62.8    42.0    50.1
   12   REDDI calls          13.3    25.4    18.5    24.4    72.6    25.0    30.7
   13   Other hway emergencies 20.2   61.8    18.1    33.1    45.9    31.0    35.0
   14   Other requests       44.7    22.7    18.4    19.9    54.1     0.0    36.2
   15   ---------------                                           ------
   16   Average Response Time 27.0    20.6    26.4    20.4    45.2    30.0    28.5
   17
   18
   19
   20                    PgDn for additional Incident Reporting data
```

As with the presentation of tabular output, graphical output needs to be accurate and easy to understand and to use if it is to be effective in communicating information to users. As discussed in an earlier section in this chapter, decision makers using the graphs need to know the assumptions (biases) under which the graphs are being constructed so that they can adjust to or compensate for them.

In designing graphical output, the systems analyst must determine (1) the purpose of the graph, (2) the kind of data that needs to be displayed, (3) its audience, and (4) the effects on the audience of different kinds of graphical output. In the instance of a decision support system, the purposes of graphical displays are to support any of the three phases of problem solving: intelligence, design, or choice. The data to display will vary, and the user is often a lone decision maker.

The Nebraska State Patrol Manpower Planning Decision Support System also allows the decision maker to graph response times, as in Figure 15.15. Here current response times, forecasted response times, and minimum requirements are graphed as differently shaded bars.

Graphical output can be enormously useful to decision makers if they are trained in how to interpret it and when to use it. Without the training, it is doubtful that graphs mean much. This is in contrast to the assumed ability of the decision maker to use tabular output, which is the most common kind of report.

In a good decision support system, the output should be able to call up a variety of user views as well as a library of possible commands. In addition, the user needs to be able to call up a workspace and move data from one model or database to another workspace and back to others. All of these functions can be accomplished by using Windows, as is discussed in Chapter 18.

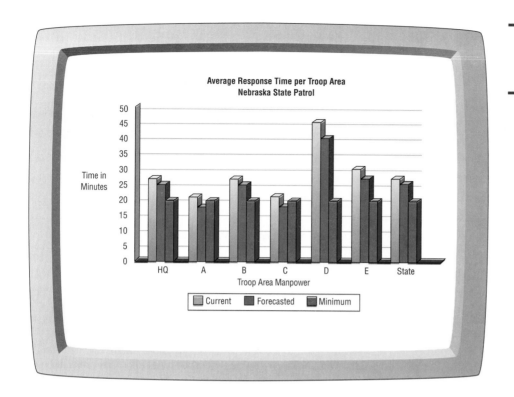

DESIGNING A WEB SITE

Your can use some of the design principles from designing screens when you design a Web site. Remember, though, the key word here is "site." The first documents displayed on the Internet using the http protocol were called "home pages," but it became apparent very quickly that companies, universities, governments, and people were not going to be displaying just one page. The term "Web site" replaced the words "home page," indicating that the array of pages would have to be organized, coordinated, designed, developed, and maintained in an orderly process.

In addition to the general design elements discussed earlier in this chapter, there are specific guidelines appropriate for the design of professional quality Web sites. Web terms are defined in Figure 15.16. The following subsections address each of them.

General Guidelines for Designing Web Sites

USE PROFESSIONAL TOOLS. Use software called a Web editor like Microsoft's FrontPage or Adobe Page Mill. These tools are definitely worth the price. You will be more creative and you'll get the Web site finished much faster. There is no need to work directly with HTML (Hypertext Markup Language) anymore.

STUDY OTHER WEB SITES. Look at Web sites you think are engaging. Analyze what design elements are being used, and see how they are functioning. Then try to emulate what you see by creating prototype pages. (If you are really ambitious, you can usually print out the HTML and try to do similar things on your page.)

Web Terms	Meaning
bookmark	A stored address of a Web page. (In Microsoft Internet Explorer bookmarks are called "favorites.") You can jump to a page by clicking on its bookmark.
browser	Software that allows you to read Web pages, copy, save, and print these pages. They also allow you to navigate the Web by following links, going backward and forward, and jumping to favorite Web pages you have bookmarked. Popular browsers are Netscape Communicator and Microsoft Internet Explorer.
FAQ	Stands for "Frequently Asked Questions." Web sites often have a page devoted to these so the company sales force or tech support are not inundated with the same questions over and over again and users can have 24 hour access to answers.
FTP	"File Transfer Protocol" is currently the most common way to move files between computer systems.
GIF	"Graphic Interchange Format" A popular compressed image format best suited for artwork.
Java	An object-oriented language that allows dynamic applications to be run on the Internet. Non-programmers can use software packages such as Symantec's *Visual Café for Java.*
JPEG	"Joint Photographic Expert Group" developed and gave the acronym of its name to title this popular compressed image format best suited for photographs. The quality or the image can be adjusted by the designer.
HTML	"Hypertext Markup Language" is the language behind the appearance of documents on the Web. It is actually a set of conventions that mark the portions of a document, telling a browser what distinctive format should appear on each portion of a page.
http://	"Hypertext Transfer Protocol" is used to move Web pages between computers. For example from a Web site on a computer in another country to your personal computer.
hyperlink	In a hypertext system words, phrases or images that are underlined or emphasized in some way (often with a different color). When the user clicks on one of them with the mouse, another document is displayed. HTML has features that allow authors to insert hyperlinks in their documents and hyperlinks can point to a local page or another URL. Often links will change color, to indicate that the user has already clicked on them before.
plug-ins	Additional software (often developed by a third party) that can be used with another program; for example, RealNetworks' Real Player or Macromedia Flash are used as plug-ins in Web browsers to play CD-quality streaming audio or video and view vector-based animation while you are visiting the Web site.
URL	"Uniform Resource Locator" is the address of a document or program on the Internet. Familiar extensions are .com for commercial, .edu for educational institution, .gov for government, and .org for organization.
VRML	"Virtual Reality Markup Language" A language similar to HTML that allows users to browse in 3D.
Webmaster	The person responsible for maintaining the Web site.
www	"World Wide Web" A global hypertext system that uses the Internet. Now we refer to it as just "the Web"

FIGURE 15.16
Web vocabulary terms.

USE THE RESOURCES THAT THE WEB HAS TO OFFER. Look at Web sites that give hints on design. One such site is `www.clever.net/gomer/tips.htm`

EXAMINE THE WEB SITES OF PROFESSIONAL DESIGNERS. Some of the design houses are listed in Figure 15.17, along with some of the often-visited and praised Web sites they developed.

As you look at these pages ask yourself, "What works? What doesn't work? In what ways can users interact with the site? For example, does the site have hot links to e-mail addresses, interactive forms to fill in, consumer surveys, games, quizzes, chat rooms and so on?"

USE THE TOOLS YOU'VE LEARNED. Figure 15.18 provides a form that has been used successfully by Web designers to systematically evaluate Web pages. You might want to use copies of the form to help you compare and contrast the many Web sites you will visit as you go about learning Web page design.

CONSULT THE BOOKS. Something that can add to your expertise in this new field is to read a book or books about Web design. Note that the following books do not cover much on HTML anymore. Some books on Web site design are

Fahey, M. J., and J. Brown. *Web Publishers Design Guide,* Scottsdale, AZ: Coriolis Group, 1995.

Horton, W. K., *et al. The Web-page Design Cookbook: All the Ingredients You Need to Create 5-star Web Pages.* New York: John Wiley, 1996.

Weinman, L. *Designing Web Graphics 2: How to Prepare Images and Media for the Web,* 2nd ed., NRP, 1997.

LOOK AT SOME POOR EXAMPLES OF WEB PAGES, TOO. Critique them and remember to avoid those mistakes. One site intentionally created to give a bad impression is `www.earth.com/bad-style/`.

CREATE TEMPLATES OF YOUR OWN. If you adopt a standard looking page for most of the pages you create, you'll get the Web site up and running faster and it will look good consistently.

FIGURE 15.17
Selected Web site
designer houses.

Design House	Its Web Address	Sites It Designed
Archetype	www.cmdesigns.com	www.sundancefilm.com/
Avalanche systems	www.avsi.com	www.superbowl.com www.faoschwarz.com www.elektra.com
Organic Online	www.organic.com	www.yahoo.com/ www.macromedia.com/ www.levi.com
Vivid Studios	www.vivid.com	www.sony.com www.aidsquilt.org

USE PLUG-INS, AUDIO, AND VIDEO VERY SPARINGLY. It is wonderful to have features that the professional pages have, but remember that everyone looking at your site doesn't have every new plug-in. Don't discourage visitors to your page.

PLAN AHEAD. Good Web sites are well thought out. Pay attention to

1. Structure.
2. Content.
3. Text.
4. Graphics.
5. Presentation.
6. Navigation.
7. Promotion.

Each of these are described in more detail below.

Structure. Planning a Web site is one of the most important steps in developing a professional Web site. Web pages should be designed according to content. Each page within the overall Web structure should have a distinct message or other related information. The home page should link to all other pages. Sometimes it is useful to examine professional pages to analyze them for content and features. Figure 15.19 is a screen capture from the ABC News Web site. The purpose for the site (up to the minute news) and the Web medium work exceptionally well together. This tragic breaking story was available on the ABC site well before local news could confirm it. In this outstanding site, notice that there is great attention to detail. There are words, graphics, photos, and icons. Additionally, there are many kinds of links: to audio, to pages with greater depth, to many other news stories. Java applets are used to display feature stories, to launch a news crawl on your desktop, and to help the user check the weather.

The planning of a Web site takes a considerable amount of thought. Webmasters must consider loading times and limit the amount of material squeezed on to each page. Providing a main page that links to more detailed pages is the best strategy. Links include pointers to other pages in the Web

FIGURE 15.18
A Web site evaluation form.

Web Site Critique

Analyst's Name _____

Date Visited: __ / __ / __

Time Visited: _____

URL Visited _____

	Needs Improvement				Excellent
DESIGN					
Overall Appearance	1	2	3	4	5
Use of Graphics	1	2	3	4	5
Use of Color	1	2	3	4	5
Use of Sound/Video (multimedia)	1	2	3	4	5
Use of New Technology and Products	1	2	3	4	5
CONTENT & INTERACTIVITY					
Content	1	2	3	4	5
Navigability	1	2	3	4	5
Site Management and Communications	1	2	3	4	5

SCORE		/40

COMMENTS:

site, pointers to images (composed of GIF or JPEG files) on the local Web site, pointers to return to the Web site home page, and links to other Web sites. In order to keep track of the links the Webmaster draws a sitemap, using tree-like diagrams to show the variety of links that sprout forth from each page.

A Webmaster can benefit from using one of the many Web site diagramming and mapping tools available. Micrografx has a product called ABC WebCharter and Visio Corporation has a Web charting option built into their Visio products. Although helpful for development, these tools become even more important when maintaining a Web site. Given the dynamic nature of the Web, Web sites that may be linked to your Web site may move at any time, requiring the Webmaster to update the links.

In Figure 15.20 a map of a section of the ABC News Web site is shown in a window from the package ABC WebCharter (the similarity in names is coincidental, there is no relation to ABC News). In this example we explored the Web site down to two levels on linked pages. If we want to explore further, we could click on a URL that has a question mark and the software (referred to as a wizard) will explore that page further. If no links are found, the question mark is removed. Images, such as GIFs and JPEGs are indicated with a color icon and broken links are indicated by an X. After the site is explored, a diagram is drawn using ABC FlowCharter. This diagram, or sitemap, can be displayed on the wall where it serves as a visual reference for identifying and updating the Web site links.

Find a book that discusses Web site structure. One such book is *Large-Scale Web Sites* by Darrell Sand, which is published by Netscape Communications Corporation.

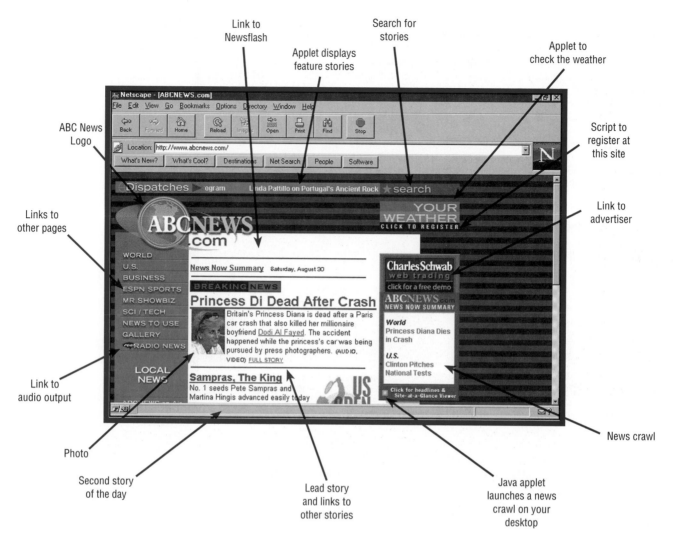

FIGURE 15.19
The ABC News Web site makes the most of frames, hot spots, hyperlinks and Java applets.

Content. Content is critical. Without anything to say, your Web site will fail. A 12-year-old friend of ours, wise beyond his age, confided to us, "I could make my own Web site. But what's the point? I have nothing to say!" Exciting animation, movies, and sounds are fun, but you have to include appropriate content to keep the reader interested.

Web pages should be designed according to content. Each page within the overall Web structure should have a distinct message or other related information. The home page should link to all other pages.

Provide something important to Web site viewers, some timely advice, important information, a free offer, or any activity that you can provide which is interactive and moves users away from a browsing mode and into an interactive one.

FIGURE 15.20
Using a package such as
Micrografx ABC WebCharter
facilitates exploration of web
sites such as this one from
ABC News.

Use a metaphor or use images that provide a metaphor for your site. This can be a theme, such as a store front, with additional pages having various metaphors related to the storefront, such as a deli. Avoid the overuse of cartoons, and don't be too repetitive.

Remember to adjust the content for the intended audience. If you're selling products or services, you want to write in a style that's distinctly different from the tone you take when writing technical support manuals.

Every web site should include a FAQ page. FAQ means "frequently asked questions." By having answers readily available, 24 hours a day, you will save valuable employee time and also save user time as well. A FAQ page also demonstrates to users of your site that you are in concert with them and possess a good feel for what they would like to know.

Text. Place meaningful words in the first sentence appearing on your Web page. Let people know that they have indeed navigated to the right Web site.

Write text in a way so that people can find Web pages when using keyword searches. This is especially important for the headings, subheadings, and the first paragraph. It helps to repeat the same key words a few times in your many pages.

Graphics.

1. Use one of the two most commonly used image formats, either JPEG (which is an acronym for the group that created the software, "Joint Photographic Expert Group") or GIF (which stands for "Graphic Inter-

change Format") files. JPEGs are best for photographs. GIFs are best for artwork images.

2. Create a few professional-looking graphics for use on your pages. They create a much better impression than several poor-quality graphics.

3. Keep the background simple and make sure users can read (and print-out) the text clearly. When using a background pattern, make sure that you can see the text clearly on top of it. Many viewers will be using the page at 256 colors, and as a result, it may be hard to read the text.

4. Examine your Web site on a variety of monitors and low-end graphics boards. Scenes and text that look great on a high-end video display may not look good to others with poorer-quality equipment. Also the amount of material that displays on a 13-inch monitor and a 21-inch monitor differs depending on the resolution.

5. Save JPEG images, a type of compressed file format for graphics, at the highest quality possible. Since JPEG is a compression, the files can be saved as low, medium, or high quality images.

6. Use horizontal rules (lines, images, or icons) to break apart sections of your Web pages in a meaningful way.

7. Use colorful bullets for lists, and consider using hot buttons for links to other pages or sites.

8. Keep graphics images small.

9. Although JPEG images are rectangular, the image itself doesn't have to be. The trick is to make the image a transparent GIF or even place it on a more interesting patterned background.

10. Use a package like Microsoft Image Composer (this is included with FrontPage) to tilt your image.

Presentation.

1. Provide an entry screen (also called a home page) that introduces the visitor to the Web site. The entry screen must be designed to load quickly. A useful rule-of-thumb is to design a page that will load in 14 seconds while assuming that a user has a 14,000 baud modem. (Although you may be designing the page on a workstation at the university, a visitor to your Web site may be accessing it from home.) The entry screen should contain a number of choices, much like a menu. An easy way to accomplish this is to design a set of buttons and position them on the left side of the screen. These buttons can be linked to other pages on the same Web site or even linked to different Web sites. An example of this is shown in Figure 15.21, an entry screen that contains a large image and some content, but then directs the visitor to journey

FIGURE 15.21
When using software such as Symantec's VisualPage a Web page designer can see what a page looks like in a browser and the HTML Code (see bottom of screen) at the same time.

elsewhere in the site. This page was constructed using Symantec's VisualPage, which allows the designer to see HTML code (at the bottom of the screen) at the same time they see what the page would look like in a browser.

2. Keep the number of graphics to a reasonable minimum. It takes additional download time to transfer a graphics intensive site.

3. Use large and colorful fonts for headings.

4. Use interesting images and buttons for links. Sometimes a row of images is called an image map, and Web designers like to refer to "hot spots" that act as links to other pages. Tables are useful, too. Frames are very effective and widely used, but frames make it a bit more difficult for visitors to bookmark your site and print the information they want. Figure 15.21 shows how a captured frame looks when a user prints it out. While the pertinent information inside of the frame prints out, other information does not. Frames can disrupt users' work and cause extra steps to be taken; hence many programmers and users find them to be very controversial.

5. Use the same graphics image on several Web pages. This will improve consistency, and the pages will load much faster because the computer stores the image in a cache so it doesn't have to load again.

6. Avoid overusing animation, sound, and other elements that might make the site too jumpy or cluttered. Do not put everything possible on a page. The space should be functional and interesting. Avoid busy animation or blinking text that is not serving a specific function.

7. Provide an area on the left side of the Web page for buttons (or icons) that link to other pages in the Web site. Alternatively you can place a menu bar at the bottom of the page. A visitor will expect to see naviga-

tional links in one of these two places. Wherever you place them, make sure they are located consistently from one page to another.

8. Make sure your initial page on your Web site loads quickly. Keep the page relatively short, the images small and simple, and keep photos to a minimum. You can always link to other local pages.

9. Use color, fonts, images, and animation wisely. You will draw people into your site if it is inviting and features interactive uses. Change the site occasionally. Many users check the same pages frequently, especially if you teach them to anticipate exciting changes on a regular basis. Remember, however, not to overdo the number of colors, fonts, or animated GIFs—less is sometimes more. Recall that simplicity and functionality are cornerstones of good design of any kind.

10. Add one or two Java applets if possible. For nonprogrammers, one of the best tools to use is Symantec Visual Cafe Pro. An example of Visual Cafe Pro can be found in Figure 15.22.

Navigation. Is it fun for you to follow links on the Web? The answer most likely is: It depends. When you discover a Web site that loads easily, has meaningful links, allows you to easily return to the places you want to go back to, then chances are you think it is fun. Fun is not just play; it can be an important part of work, too. Recent research shows that fun can have a powerful effect on making computer training effective. If on the other hand, you (1) can't decide which button or "hot spot" to push, and (2) are afraid to choose the wrong one because you might get into the wrong page that takes a long time to load, then navigation is more painful than fun. An example is visiting a software company's page to find out information about the features

FIGURE 15.22
Development of Java applets using Symantec's Visual Cafe Pro.

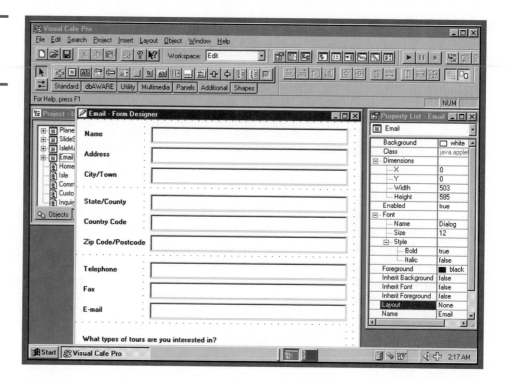

A *Field Day*

"The thing of it is, I get impatient," says Seymour Fields, who is owner of a chain of fifteen highly successful florist shops/indoor floral markets, called "Fields," which are located in three Midwestern cities. "See this thing here?" He taps his PC and screen irritatedly. "We do all of the payroll, all of the accounting with these things. But I don't use it like I should. I actually feel a little guilty about it. See?" he makes a streak on the screen with his finger. "It's even got dust on it. But I'm a practical person. If it's sitting here, taking up space, I want to use it. Or smell it, or at least enjoy looking at it, like flowers, right? Or weed it out, that's what I say. The one time I tried something with it, it was a real disaster. Well look, I can show you if I still remember how." Seymour proceeds to try to boot a program, but can't seem to get it working.

Clay Potts, a systems analyst, has been working on a systems project for the entire Fields' chain. Part of the original proposal was to provide Seymour and his vice presidents with a group decision support system that would help them devise a strategy for which European markets to go to in order to purchase fresh flowers; which outlets to ship particular kinds of flowers to; and how much general merchandise such as planters,

vases, note cards, and knickknacks to stock in each outlet.

Seymour continues. "But I can tell you what we disliked about the program I worked with. Too many darn layers, too much foliage, or whatever you call it, to go through. Even with a screen in front of me, it was like paging through a thick report. What do you call that?"

"Menus?" Potts suggests helpfully. "The main point is, you didn't like having to go through lots of information to get to the display you needed."

Seymour Fields looks happily at Potts and says, "You've got it. I want to see more fields on each screen."

How should Potts design screen output so that Fields and his group can get what they want on each screen while observing the guidelines for good screen design? Remember that the group members are busy and that they are infrequent computer users. Design a hyperlinked page that would work well in a DSS for the vice presidents. What should be included in the first display and what should be stored in hyperlinks? List elements for each and explain why you have decided upon this strategy.

---

of the latest version of a product. You have choices such as products, download, FAQ, and tech support. Which button will lead to the answers you're looking for?

If a page is lengthy, provide links to information lower on the page and links back to the top. This acts as a short table of contents. Do not cram too much information onto one long lengthy page. Neither should you create pages that have only a solitary image on them that says "click here."

Promotion. Promote your site. Don't assume that search engines will find you right away. Submit and resubmit your site every few months to various search engines. You can also purchase software to make this process easier. Use e-mail to promote your site, but have a specific reason for doing so, or others will consider it junk e-mail or spam.

Encourage your readers to bookmark your Web site. If you link to and suggest that they go to the "best movie review page in the world" or the "get music for free" Web site, don't assume they'll be coming back to your site in the near future. You will encourage them to revisit if they bookmark your site (bookmarks are called "favorites" on Microsoft Explorer).

Make it clear who is maintaining the Web site (the Webmaster) by including their name, title, and e-mail address on the page. After building several Web sites ourselves and talking frequently to those who design pages and do their upkeep, we cannot stress enough the importance of almost perpetual *maintenance* of the Web site. This is a newly added responsibility in the corporate world, one that takes some time and patience. However, your efforts toward maintenance will be rewarded. Remember that the Web is dynamic and that sites appear and disappear at alarming rates. The Webmaster is maintaining not only corporate information, but also—and maybe even more importantly—they are maintaining the hyperlinks to other documents and pages. Once your users have your site bookmarked, your maintenance efforts must be an essential part of the plan to keep them coming back.

SUMMARY

Output is any useful information or data delivered by the information system or decision support system to the user. Output can take virtually any form, including print, screen, audio, microforms, CD-ROM or DVD, electronic, and Web-based documents.

The systems analyst has six main objectives in designing output. They are to design output to serve the intended purpose, to fit the user, to deliver the right quantity of output, to deliver it to the right place, to provide output on time, and to choose the right output method.

It is important that the analyst realize that output content is related to output method. Output of different technologies affects users in different ways. Output technologies also differ in their speed, cost, portability, flexibility, and storage and retrieval possibilities. All of these factors must be considered when deciding among print, on-screen, audio, microforms, electronic, or Web-based output, or a combination of these output methods.

The presentation of output can bias users in their interpretation of it. Analysts must be aware of the sources of bias, must interact with users to design and customize output, must inform users of the possibilities of bias in output, must create flexible and modifiable output, and must train users to use multiple output to help verify the accuracy of any particular report.

Printed reports are designed with the use of computer-aided software design tools that feature form design templates and drag and drop interfaces. The data dictionary serves as the source for necessary data on each report. Mock-ups or prototypes of reports and screens are shown to users before the report or Web-page design is completed, and any necessary changes are then made. The systems analyst uses newly-designed screens to communicate physical design to the programmer.

Display screens, which are an especially important form of output for decision support systems as well as for traditional information systems, are also designed using on-screen templates. Once again, aesthetics and usefulness are important when creating a well-designed screen. It is important to produce prototypes of screens and Web documents that allow users to make changes where desired.

On-screen graphical output is becoming increasingly popular, especially for decision support systems. The systems analyst must consider the effect of graphs on users, the kind of data to be displayed, the purpose of the graphs, and their intended audience. Many software packages devoted to graphics are available. It is essential that decision makers receive training in how to interpret graphs if graphs are to be useful to them.

"I'd say the reception you received (or should I say that your team received) for your proposal presentation was quite warm. How did you like meeting Mr. Hyatt? What? He didn't come? Oh *(laughing)*, he's his own man. Anyway, don't worry about that too much. The reports I got from Snowden were encouraging. In fact, now he wants to see some preliminary designs from you all. Can you have something on his desk (or screen) in two weeks? He'll be in Singapore on business next week, but then when he recovers from the jet lag, he'll be looking for those designs. Thanks."

HYPERCASE QUESTIONS

1. Consider the reports from the Training Unit. What are Snowden's complaints about these reports. Explain in a paragraph.

2. Using either a layout paper form or a CASE tool, design a prototype output screen based on the Training Unit's reports that will summarize the following information for Snowden:

   Number of accepted projects in the training unit.
   Number of projects currently being reevaluated.
   Training subjects areas for which a consultant is being requested.

3. Design an additional output screen that you believe will support Snowden in the kind of decision making he does frequently.

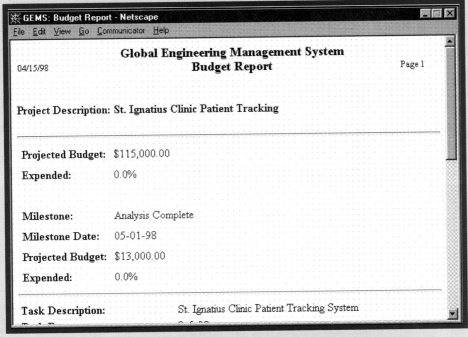

FIGURE 15.HC1
You have the ability to view and critique output screens in HyperCase.

Continued

4. Show your screens to three classmates. Get written feedback from them about how to improve the output screens you have designed.

5. Redesign the screens to capture the improvements suggested by your classmates. In a paragraph, explain how you have addressed each of their concerns.

KEYWORDS AND PHRASES

external output
internal output
output design
display screen
audio output
microforms
CD-ROM
DVD
electronic output
e-mail
electronic bulletin boards
browser
The World Wide Web (www)
Web site

output bias
constant information
variable information
Web pages
bookmark
FAQ (Frequently Asked
  Questions)
Java
hyperlink
plug-ins
URL (Uniform Resource Locator)
Webmaster
hypertext

REVIEW QUESTIONS

1. List six objectives the analyst pursues in designing system output.
2. Contrast external output with internal output produced by the system.
3. What are three situations that point to printers as the best choice for output technology?
4. Give two instances that indicate that on-screen output is the best solution for the choice of output technology.
5. Cite two instances in which microforms would be a worthwhile choice for output.
6. List potential electronic output methods.
7. What are the drawbacks of electronic and Web-based output?
8. List ten factors that must be considered when choosing output technology.
9. What output type is best if frequent updates are a necessity?
10. What kind of output is desirable if many readers will be reading, storing, and reviewing output over a period of years?
11. What are two of the drawbacks to audio output?
12. List three main ways in which presentations of output are unintentionally biased.
13. What are five ways the analyst can avoid biasing output?
14. What is the difference between constant and variable information presented on a report?
15. Why is it important to show users a prototype output report or screen?

16. List six functional elements of printed reports.
17. List five stylistic/aesthetic elements of printed reports.
18. In what ways do screens, printed output, and Web-based documents differ?
19. List four guidelines to facilitate the design of good screen output.
20. What differentiates output for a DSS from that of a more traditional MIS?
21. What are the four primary considerations the analyst has when designing graphical output for decision support systems?
22. What is the difference between an Internet and an intranet?
23. List 10 guidelines for creating good Web sites.
24. List the 10 guidelines for using graphics in designing Web sites.
25. What are 10 ideas for ways to improve the presentation of corporate Web sites that you design?
26. Give two hints for improving navigation of your Web sites for users.
27. In what ways can you encourage companies to promote their Web sites that you have developed?
28. What are some differences among the most popular browsers? List them.

PROBLEMS

1. "I'm sure they won't mind if we start sending them the report on these oversized computer sheets. All this time we've been condensing it, re-typing it, and sending it to our biggest accounts, but we just can't now. We're so understaffed, we don't have the time," says Otto Breth. "I'll just write a comment on here telling them how to respond to this, and then we can send it out."

   a. What potential problems do you see in casually changing external output? List them.

   b. Discuss in a paragraph how internal and external output can differ in appearance and function.

2. "I don't need to see it very often, but when I do, I have to be able to get at it quickly. I think we lost the last contract because the information I needed was buried in a stack of paper on someone's desk somewhere," says Luke Alover, an architect describing the company's problems to one of the analysts assigned to the new systems project. "What I need is in-stant information about how much a building of that square footage cost the last time we bid it; what the basic materials such as steel, glass, and concrete now cost from our three top suppliers; who our likely competi-tion on this type of building might be; and who composes the committee that will be making the final decision on who gets the bid. But right now, it's in a hundred reports somewhere. I have to look all over for it."

   a. Given the limited details you have here, use a paragraph to suggest an output method for Luke's use that will solve some of his current problems. In a second paragraph, explain your reasons for choosing the output method you did. (*Hint:* Be sure to relate output method to output content in your answer.)

   b. Luke's current thinking is that no paper record of the output dis-cussed above need be kept. In a paragraph, discuss what factors should be weighed before screen output is used to the exclusion of printed reports.

   c. Make a list of five to seven questions concerning the output's function in the organization that you would ask Luke and others before decid-ing to do away with any printed reports currently being used.

3. Here are several situations calling for decisions about output content, output methodology, distribution, and so on. For each situation, note the appropriate output decision.

   a. A large, well-regarded supplier of key raw materials to your company's production process requires a year-end summary report of totals purchased from it. Output method?

   b. Internal "brainstorming" memos are circulated through the staff regarding plans for a company picnic/fundraiser. Output method?

   c. A summary report of the financial situation is needed by a key decision maker who will use it when presenting a proposal to potential external backers. Output method?

   d. A listing of the current night's hotel room reservations is needed for front desk personnel. Output method?

   e. A listing of the current night's hotel room reservations is needed by the local police. Output method?

   f. A real-time count of people passing through the gates of Wallaby World (an Australian theme park) will be used by parking lot patrols. Output method?

   g. An inventory system must register an item each time it has been scanned by a wand. Output method?

   h. A summary report of merit pay increases allotted to each of 120 employees will be used by 22 supervisors during a joint supervisors' meeting and subsequently when explaining merit pay increases to the supervisors' own departmental employees. Output method?

   i. Competitive information is needed by three strategic planners in the organization, but it is industrially sensitive if widely distributed. Output method?

   j. Historical files of actual documents filed are kept for a period of seven years, as mandated by federal regulations. Output method?

4. "I think I see now where that guy was coming from, but he had me going for a minute there," say Miss deLimit. She is discussing a prototype of screen output, one designed by the systems analyst, that she has just seen. I mean, I never considered it a problem before if even as much as 20 percent of the total class size couldn't be fit into a class. We know our classes are in demand, and since we can't hire more faculty to cover the areas we need, the adjustment has to come in the student demand. He's got it highlighted as a problem if only 5 percent of the students who want a class can't get in. But that's okay. Now that I know what he means, I'll just ignore it when the computer beeps.

   a. In a sentence or two, describe the problem Miss deLimit is experiencing with the screen output.

   b. Is her solution to "ignore the beeps" a reasonable one given that output is in the prototype stage?

   c. In a paragraph, explain how the screen output for this particular problem can be changed so that it better reflects the rules of the system Miss deLimit is using.

5. Here is a log sheet for a patient information system used by nurses at a convalescent home to record patient visitors and activities during their shifts. Design a printed report using form design software that provides a summary for the charge nurse of each shift and a report for the activities

Date	Patient	Visitors	Relationship	Activities
2/14	Clarke	2	Mother, father	Walked about halls, attended chapel, meals in cafeteria
	Coffey	6	Co-workers	Played games, party in room
	Martine	0	—	meals in room
	Laury	4	Husband and friends	Games in sunroom, watched TV
	Finney	2	Parents	Conversation, meals in cafeteria
	Cartwright	1	Sister	Conversation, crafts room
	Goldstein	2	Sister, brother	Conversation, games out of room, whirlpool

coordinator at the end of a week. Be sure to use proper conventions to indicate constant and variable data, and so on. These reports will be used to determine staffing patterns and future activities offerings.

6. Design a screen for problem 5, using form design software. Make any assumptions about system capability necessary, and follow screen design conventions for on-screen instructions. (*Hint:* You can use more than one screen if you wish.)

    a. In a paragraph, discuss why you designed each report as you did in problems 5 and 6. What are the major differences in your approach to each one? Can the printed reports be successfully transplanted to the screen without changes? Why or why not?

7. Clancy Corporation manufactures uniforms for police departments worldwide. Its uniforms are chosen by many groups because of their low cost and simple, yet dignified design. You are helping to design a DSS for Clancy Corp., and it has asked for tabular output that will help it in making various decisions about what designers to use, about where to market its uniforms, and about what changes to make to uniforms to keep them looking up to date. Here are some of the data the company would like to

Style Name	Example Buyer	Designers
Full military	(NYPD)	Claudio, Rialtto, Melvin Mine
Half military	(LAPD)	Rialtto, Calvetti, Duran, Melvin Mine
Formal dress	Australian Armed Forces	Claudio, Dundee, Melvin Mine
Casual dress	("Miami Vice")	Johnson, Melvin Mine

see in tables, including: uniform style names; example of a buyer group for each style; and which designers design which uniform styles.

    a. Prepare an example of on-screen tabular output that incorporates the foregoing data about Clancy's. Follow proper conventions for on-screen tabular output. Use codes and a key where appropriate.

8. Clancy's is also interested in graphical output for its DSS. It wants to see a graphical comparison of how many of each style of uniform is being sold each year.

    a. Choose an appropriate graph style and design and an on-screen graph that incorporates the following data:

    1993 full military (57 percent of all sales)
    1994 full military (59 percent of all sales)
    1995 casual dress (62 percent of all sales)
    1996 casual dress (55 percent of all sales)
    1997 casual dress (40 percent) and half military (22 percent)
    Be sure to follow proper screen design conventions. Use codes and a key if necessary.

    b. Chose a second method of graphing that might allow the decision makers at Clancy's to see a trend in the purchase of particular uniform styles over time. Draw an on-screen graph for use as part of the output for Clancy's DSS. Be sure to follow proper screen design conventions. Use codes and a key if necessary.

    c. In a paragraph, discuss the differences in the two on-screen graphs you have chosen. Defend your choices.

9. Use the Internet at your campus to view well designed and poorly designed Web sites. Comment on what makes the sites good or bad, using the critique form given earlier in the chapter to compare and contrast them.

10. Propose a Web site for Clancy's, the uniform company described in problems 7 and 8. Sketch by hand, or use form design software to create a prototype of a Clancy's home page. Indicate hyperlinks, and include a sketch of one hyperlink document. Remember to include graphics, icons, and even sound or other media if it is appropriate. In a paragraph, describe who the intended users of the Web site are, and state why it makes sense for Clancy's to have a Web presence.

GROUP PROJECTS

1. Brainstorm with your team members about what types of output are most appropriate for a variety of employees of Maverick Transport. Include a list of environments or decision making situations and type of output. In a paragraph, discuss why the group suggested particular options for output.

2. Have each group member design an output screen or form for the output situations you listed in problem 1. (Use either a CASE tool or paper layout form to complete each screen or form.)

3. Share each output screen or form among your team members. Using the feedback gathered, improve the screens or forms you have designed.

4. Design a Web site, either on paper or using software that you are familiar with, for Maverick Transport. Although you may sketch documents or graphics for hyperlinks on paper, create a prototype home page for

Maverick, indicating hyperlinks where appropriate. Obtain feedback from other groups in your class, and modify your design accordingly. In a paragraph, discuss how designing a Web site is different from designing screens for other on-line systems.

SELECTED BIBLIOGRAPHY

Davenport, T. H. "Saving IT's Soul: Human-Centered Information Management." *Harvard Business Review,* March–April, 1994, pp. 119–131.

Davis, G. B., and H. M. Olson. *Management Information Systems, Conceptual Foundations, Structure, and Development,* 2nd ed. New York: McGraw-Hill Book Company, 1985.

Fahey, M. J. and J. Brown. *Web Publishers Design Guide.* Scottsdale, AZ: Coriolis Group, 1995.

Horton, W. K. *et al. The Web-page Design Cookbook: All the Ingredients You Need to Create 5-star Web Pages.* New York: John Wiley, 1996.

Jarvenpaa, S. L., and G. W. Dickson. "Myth vs. Facts About Graphics in Decision Making," *Spectrum,* vol. 3, no 1., February 1986, pp. 1–3.

Laudon, K. C., and J. P. Laudon. *Management Information Systems,* 4th ed. Upper Saddle River, NJ: Prentice-Hall, Inc., 1996.

McCombie, K. "Connecting Your Enterprise LAN to the Internet," *Internet World,* June 1994.

Merholz, Peter. "10 Hottest Web Designers & Design Houses" *the Net,* vol. 2, issue 1 (No. 6, 1996), p. 46.

Pfaffenberger, B., and D. Wall. *Que's Computer & Internet Dictionary,* 6th ed. Indianapolis, IN: Que Corporation, 1995.

Quarterman, J. S. "What Can Businesses Get Out of Internet." *Computerworld,* February 22, 1993.

Senn, J. A. *Analysis and Design of Information Systems,* 2nd ed. New York: McGraw-Hill Book Company, 1987.

Weinman, L. *Designing Web Graphics 2: How to Prepare Images and Media for the Web,* 2nd ed., NRP, 1997.

Whitten, J. L., L. D. Bentley, and V. M. Barlow. *Systems Analysis and Design,* 3rd ed. Barr Ridge, IL: Irwin, 1994.

REPORTING ON OUTPUTS

"Let's create output specifications and then work backward through the data flow to determine the corresponding input data," says Anna during her next meeting with Chip.

"Of course," Chip agrees.

Output was separated into two categories: reports and screens. Reports were further defined as external reports, such as the User Software Notification, or internal reports like the Hardware Inventory Listing. Each report was further classified as a detailed, exception, or summary report.

Based on conversations with Paige Prynter, the analysts believe that the HARDWARE INVESTMENT REPORT has the highest priority. It is needed as soon as possible because the budget process will soon reach a critical phase and there are many requests for new hardware.

The process used for creating the HARDWARE INVESTMENT REPORT is similar to the process for creating all reports. Chip examines the data flow diagrams for the new system and locates the data flow labeled HARDWARE INVESTMENT REPORT. Double clicking on the data flow line brings up the repository entry for this report, illustrated in Figure E15.1, HARDWARE INVESTMENT REPORT. It contains a definition giving information about the type of report and an Alias. The **Composition** area provides a list of all the elements on the report. The **Notes** area provides additional information necessary for creating the report.

FIGURE E15.1
HARDWARE INVESTMENT REPORT data flow screen.

Allen Schmidt,
Julie E. Kendall, and
Kenneth E. Kendall

1/12/98	Hardware Investment Report			Page 1 of 1
Brand Name	Model		Number of Machines	Total Invested
Xxxxxxxxxxxx	Xxxxxxxxxxxxxxxxx		3	$29,997.00
		Brand Subtotal	3	$29,997.00
Xxxxxxxxxxxxxx	Xxxxxxxxxxxxxxxxx		4	$39,996.00
Xxxxxxxxxxxxxx	Xxxxxxxxxxxxxxxxxxx		2	$19,998.00
		Brand Subtotal	6	$59,994.00
Xxxxxxxxxxxxxxxx	Xxxxxxxxxxxxxxxxx		3	$29,997.00
Xxxxxxxxxxxxxxxx	Xxxxxxxxxxxxxxxxxxxx		8	$79,992.00
		Brand Subtotal	11	$109,989.00
		Grand Total	20	$199,980.00

FIGURE E15.2
HARDWARE INVESTMENT REPORT sample output.

"I'm really glad that we took the time to document the prototype reports and screens when creating the data flow diagrams," remarks Chip. "And I can easily identify the elements required to produce the report."

Chip places the cursor in a composition element and presses the **Jump** key to display the details for each element.

"This is great," exclaims Chip. "It was a good idea to define all the elements as we learned about them."

Chip then proceeds to create a sample report using Access. After the first draft, Chip uses the Print Preview feature to preview the report.

"Hmmm," murmurs Chip, "Some of the fields need re-arranging and the horizontal spacing needs some work."

The report design is modified and reviewed again. By the third try, the report was in its final form. The next step is crucial—Chip asks Paige to review the report and make any changes she likes. Chip asks, "Are there any additional columns or other data missing that would make for a more useful report? Is all the data on the report necessary?"

Paige studies the output for a few minutes and remarks, "Subtotals for each BRAND, including the NUMBER OF MACHINES and grand totals, are necessary. We receive requests for different types of machines, and knowing how many of each machine may help determine what is purchased."

Chip returns to his microcomputer and makes the necessary changes. The final HARDWARE INVESTMENT REPORT sample is shown in Figure E15.2. This is again reviewed by Paige, and she signs off on the layout as complete.

The logic for this summary report is outlined in a process specification. The MICROCOMPUTER MASTER file is sorted by MODEL within BRAND. Records are read from the MICROCOMPUTER MASTER file, and totals for each BRAND and MODEL are accumulated. When either BRAND or MODEL changes, a report line is printed. When a change in BRAND occurs, BRAND SUBTOTALS are printed. GRAND TOTALS are printed after all records are processed.

Anna spends some time speaking with Cher Ware about her report needs. Several printed reports were outlined when Cher asks the question, "Will I get reports on the screen, ones that I can quickly view, that have the latest information?"

The discussion that followed resulted in the creation of several screen reports.

"How would you like to view the software categories?", asks Anna. "Would you like to see all the software on one large scrolling screen?"

"Well, I would like to have some way of finding one category, and then displaying all the software available for that category," replies Cher. "And it would be useful to be able to move to subsequent and previous categories."

Anna works with the Visible Analyst repository for the SOFTWARE BY CATEGORY data flow, shown in Figure E15.3. She enters the contents of the screen and makes some notes about what additional things are required for a successful program.

Anna creates the SOFTWARE BY CATEGORY screen by creating an Access form, shown in Figure E15.4. There is a button for finding records, as well as buttons to move to the previous and next categories. In the lower area of the screen is an area to display multiple software packages for the category. The Operating System field is stored as a code on the corresponding database table, and is converted to the code description on the screen.

Anna shows both Chip and Cher the completed screen. "I'm impressed," exclaims Cher. "This is exactly what I need!"

At that moment, Hy Perteks saunters in. "What's going on?", he asks. After viewing the screen, he remarks, "I've been involved in the intranet project underway. Is their any chance of getting some information posted to a web page?"

FIGURE E15.3
SOFTWARE BY CATEGORY data flow screen.

FIGURE E15.4
SOFTWARE BY CATEGORY, Access screen.

"What do you have in mind," inquires Chip.

"Well, I have been giving it some thought," replies Hy. "I envision that it would be useful for the faculty and staff to be able to look up information about the software courses that we are planning to offer. Later we could add an intranet form for them to enroll in the courses."

"I've heard a lot about the intranet," remarks Chip. "This would be a fun project to work on!"

"Count me in on it," replies Anna. "I've been creating some personal home pages myself. What would you like on the page?"

"I would like to create a main page that lists the courses, followed by other pages that list the level, such as beginning or intermediate for the course and the dates that the courses start," replies Hy.

Chip and Anna set to work on the web page. The fields were identified and grouped onto the TRAINING CLASSES OFFERED data flow, illustrated in Figure E15.5. Note that the web address is included as an Alias. Anna creates the final intranet web page, illustrated in Figure E15.6. Chip and Hy review the page.

"I think that it needs some small modifications," remarks Chip. "For example, why not use the university colors of Blue and White?"

"It would add some pizzazz if we include an image for the mascot," adds Hy. "And the university motto."

"I'll get right on it," replies Anna. "These are really good suggestions."

The final intranet screen is finished and approved by Hy.

"I'll put out an e-mail to all the faculty and staff on the listserve," remarks Hy. "Thanks for including my e-mail address. It should help to facilitate registering for courses and answering any questions. I feel that we are really making progress!"

FIGURE E15.5
TRAINING CLASSES OFFERED data flow screen.

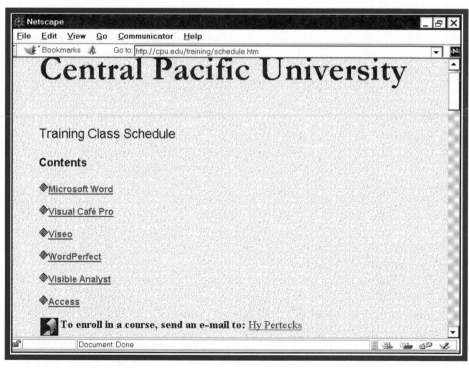

FIGURE E15.6
An intranet Web page for Central Pacific University.

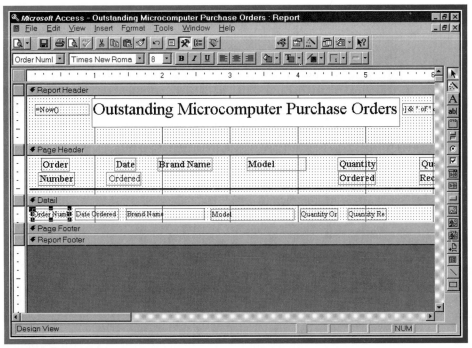

FIGURE E15.7
Modifications can be made to the reports and screens residing in an Access
database.

The following exercises may be done by designing the report or screen
using Printer or Screen layout forms or they may be created using any word
processor that you are familiar with. The fields and other related information for the reports are contained in Visible Analyst data flow repository entries. The names for the data flow are listed for each exercise.

Corresponding reports and screens (called forms in Access) have been
created. All the information is present in the Access database, you only
have to modify the existing reports and screens to produce the final versions. Modifications are made by clicking on the desired report or screen
and then clicking the Design button. The following modifications may be
made. The Page Header contains column headings. The Detail area contains
the print fields for the report. Refer to Figure E15.7, which shows the design layout for the OUTSTANDING MICROCOMPUTER PURCHASE OR-
DERS report.

Click in a field to select it. Click on several fields while holding the
shift key to select them.

Drag a selected field (or fields) to move them.

Click on one of the small boxes surrounding the field to change the
field size.

Select several fields and click **Format** and either:

Align - to align all fields with the top, left, etc. field.

Size - to make fields equal to the widest, tallest, etc. field.

Horizontal Spacing - to make horizontal spacing equal, or increase
or decrease the spacing.

Vertical Spacing - to make vertical spacing equal, or increase or decrease the spacing.

*Exercises**

⌑ **E-1.** Use Access to view the HARDWARE INVESTMENT Report.

⌑ **E-2.** Chip, Dot, and Mike participated in several brainstorming sessions resulting in the outlining of several reports. Design (or modify using Access) the HARDWARE MASTER REPORT. This is a large report, and you will have to be careful to include all the data in the report area. You may want to have several detail lines for each record. Print the completed report.

⌑ **E-3.** After meeting with Cher Ware and Hy Perteks to discuss reporting needs, Anna has identified the fields for the partially completed the NEW SOFTWARE INSTALLED report. Design (or modify) the report to include the elements found in the data flow repository entry. Is the report a summary or detailed report? In a paragraph, outline the logic that you feel the report-producing program must use.

⌑ **E-4.** Both Dot and Mike need to know when new microcomputers have been received. Create the NEW MICROCOMPUTER RECEIVED REPORT. The data flow MICROCOMPUTER RECEIVED REPORT contains the necessary elements.

⌑ **E-5.** Design the SOFTWARE MASTER REPORT, containing pertinent information that helps Cher and Hy to easily locate the various copies of any software package. The elements necessary to produce the report are located on the SOFTWARE MASTER REPORT data flow.

The TITLE, VERSION, OPERATING SYSTEM NAME, PUBLISHER, CATEGORY, and the FIRST and LAST NAME of the software expert should be group printed. Totals are to be included for each Title/Operating System/Version combination. Print the completed report design.

⌑ **E-6.** Design the HARDWARE INVENTORY LISTING, showing the software available in at each room within each campus. The Campus field should be the CAMPUS DESCRIPTION, not the code representing the campus.

⌑ **E-7.** Design the INSTALLED MICROCOMPUTER REPORT, showing microcomputers that have been installed in each room. Use the CAMPUS DESCRIPTION, and group print by CAMPUS DESCRIPTION and ROOM LOCATION. The Installed boards is a repeating group, with up to five entries per microcomputer.

⌑ **E-8.** Use Access to view the SOFTWARE BY CATEGORY screen report. Press the **Find** Button and locate CASE toolset. Press the **Next** and **Previous** buttons to view next and previous Software Categories.

⌑ **E-9.** Design the SOFTWARE BY MACHINE screen report. Refer to the data flow repository entry for elements.

⌑ **E-10.** Design the MICROCOMPUTER PROBLEM REPORT. This report shows all microcomputers that have a large number of repairs or a large repair cost. Refer to the repository description for the data flow for the elements or modify the Access report.

⌑ **E-11.** Design or modify the INSTALLATION REPORT. Refer to the repository entry for the data flow for the elements. This report

---

* Exercises preceded by a disk icon require the program Visible Analyst Workbench or another CASE tool. A disk is provided free of charge to any professor adopting this book. The examples on the disk may be imported into Visible Analyst Workbench and then used by students.

shows which machines have been recently received and are available for installation.

E-12. Design the NEW MICROCOMPUTER RECEIVED report. Refer to the repository description for the data flow for the elements or modify the Access report. This summary report shows the number of machines of each brand and model. These machines need to be unpacked, and have component boards and other hardware installed before they may be installed in rooms.

E-13. Design or modify the PREVENTIVE MAINTENANCE REPORT. Refer to the repository entry for the data flow for the elements. This report shows which machines need to have preventive maintenance performed on them.

E-14. Design the SOFTWARE CROSS REFERENCE report. Refer to the repository description for the data flow for the elements or modify the Access report. This report shows the machines that each software package is installed on. The TITLE, VERSION, OPERATING SYSTEM MEANING and PUBLISHER are group printed. The detail lines under the group contain data showing the machine and the installation campus and room.

E-15. Design or modify the OUTSTANDING MICROCOMPUTER PURCHASE ORDERS report. Refer to the repository entry for the data flow for the elements. This would be produced for all PURCHASE ORDER records that have a purchase order code of M101, representing microcomputers, with the further condition that the QUANTITY ORDERED on the record must be greater than QUANTITY RECEIVED. In a paragraph, state whether this is a summary, exception, or detailed report. Explain.

E-16. Design the SOFTWARE INVESTMENT report. Refer to the repository description for the data flow for the elements or modify the Access report.

## 16

DESIGNING EFFECTIVE INPUT

INPUT DESIGN OBJECTIVES

The quality of system input determines the quality of system output. It is vital that input forms, screens, and interactive Web documents be designed with this critical relationship in mind. By insisting on well-designed input, the systems analyst is acknowledging that poor input calls into question the trustworthiness of the entire system.

Well-designed input forms, screens, and interactive Web fill-in forms should meet the objectives of effectiveness, accuracy, ease of use, consistency, simplicity, and attractiveness, as depicted in Figure 16.1. All of these objectives are attainable through the use of basic design principles, through the knowledge of what is needed as input for the system, and through an understanding of how users respond to different elements of forms and screens.

Effectiveness means that input forms, input screens, and fill-in forms on the Web all serve specific purposes in the information system, while accuracy refers to design that assures proper completion. Ease of use means that forms and screens are straightforward and require no extra time to decipher. Consistency in this case means that all input forms, whether they are input screens or fill-in forms on the Web, group data similarly from one application to the next; while simplicity refers to keeping those same designs purposely uncluttered in a manner that focuses the user's attention. Attractiveness implies that users will enjoy using, or even be drawn to using, input forms, input screens, and fill-in Web forms through their appealing design.

GOOD FORM DESIGN

Although an in-house forms specialist may be available, the systems analyst should be capable of designing a complete and useful form. It is also important to be able to recognize poorly designed, overlapping, or unnecessary forms that are wasting the organization's resources and therefore should be eliminated.

549

FIGURE 16.1
Six objectives for the design
of input.

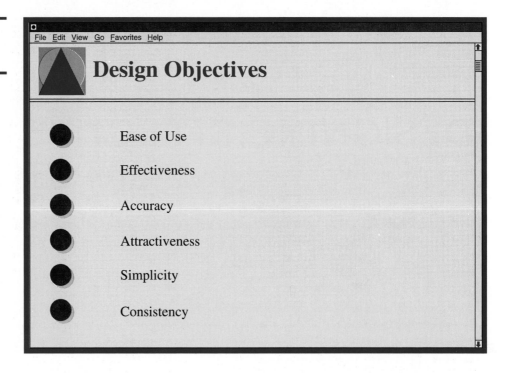

Forms are important instruments for steering the course of work. By definition, they are preprinted or duplicated papers that require people to fill in responses in a standardized way. Forms elicit and capture information required by organizational members that will often be input to the computer. Through this process, forms often serve as source documents for data entry personnel.

Four guidelines for form design should be observed in order to design useful forms:

1. Make forms easy to fill out.
2. Ensure that forms meet the purpose for which they are designed.
3. Design forms to assure accurate completion.
4. Keep forms attractive.

There are a number of ways to achieve each guideline for form design. Each of the four guidelines is considered separately in the following subsections.

Making Forms Easy to Fill In

To reduce error, speed completion, and facilitate the entry of data, it is essential that forms be easy to fill in. This guideline is based on more than well-placed empathy for the user. The cost of the forms is minimal compared to the cost of the time employees spend filling them in manually and then entering data into the information system. Sometimes it is possible to eliminate the process of transcripting data that is entered on a form into the system by using electronic submission, which often features data keyed in by the users themselves.

FORM FLOW. Designing a form with proper flow can minimize the time and effort expended by employees in form completion. Forms should flow

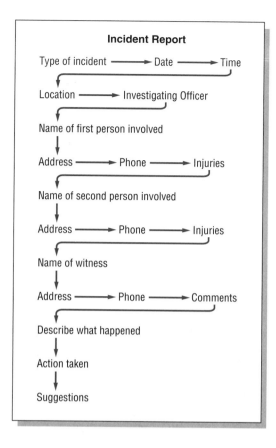

FIGURE 16.2
Good form flow makes the
form easy to use.

from left to right and top to bottom, as shown in the police incident report depicted in Figure 16.2.

The flow of the incident report works because it is based on the way people in the Western culture read a page. The incident report is designed so that the attending officer first fills in the date, then the time, then continues on to the bottom of the form, which elicits suggestions on further handling of the situation.

Illogical flow takes extra time and is frustrating. A form that requires people to go directly to the bottom of the form and then skip back up to the top for completion exhibits poor flow.

SEVEN SECTIONS OF A FORM. A second technique that makes it easy for people to fill out forms correctly is logical grouping of information. The seven main sections of a strong form are:

1. Heading.
2. Identification and access.
3. Instructions.
4. Body.
5. Signature and verification.
6. Totals.
7. Comments.

Ideally, these sections should appear on a page grouped as they are in Figure 16.3. Notice that the seven sections cover the basic information re-

FIGURE 16.3
Seven sections found in well-
designed forms.

Heading	Identification and Access
Instructions	
Body	
Signature and Verification	Totals
Comments	

quired on most forms. The top quarter of the form is devoted to three sections: the heading, the identification and access section, and the instructions section.

The heading section usually includes the name and address of the business originating the form. The identification and access section includes codes that may be used to file the report and gain access to it at a later date. (In Chapter 17, we discuss in detail how to access specially keyed information in a database.) This information is very important when an organization is required to keep the document for a specified number of years. The instructions section tells how the form should be filled out and where it should be routed when complete.

The middle of the form is its body, which composes approximately half of the form. This is the part of the form that requires the most detail and development from the person completing it. The body is the part of the form most likely to contain explicit, variable data. For example, on a parts requisition form, this section might include data such as the firm ordering the part, part number, quantity ordered, and price.

The bottom quarter of the form is composed of three sections: signature and verification, totals, and comments. By requiring a signature in this part of the form, the designer is echoing the design of other familiar documents, such as letters. Requiring ending totals and a summary of comments is a logical way to provide closure for the person filling out the form.

FIGURE 16.4
Major captioning
alternatives.

First Name _____   Last Name _____

Title _____   Telephone ( ) _____ –

_____   _____
First Name   Last Name

_____   _____
Title   Telephone

First Name   Last Name

Title   Telephone
                                               _____ – _____

Check off method of travel:
☐ Airplane
☐ Train
☐ Company Car
☐ Personal Car

Photo Lab ☐   Printing Department ☐   Maintenance ☐   Supplies ☐

Quantity	Unit	Item Description	User Cost	Expanded Cost
			Subtotal	
			Sales Tax	
			Total	

Line caption

Below line caption

Boxed caption

Vertical check off

Horizontal check off

Table caption

CAPTIONING. Clear captioning is another technique that can make easy work of filling out a form. Captions tell the person completing the form what to put on a blank line, space, or box. Several options for captioning, are shown in Figure 16.4. Two types of line captions, two types of check-off captions and examples of a boxed caption and table caption are shown.

The advantage of putting the caption below the line is that there is more room on the line itself for data. The disadvantage is that it is sometimes unclear which line is associated with the caption: the line above or below the caption. The person filling out the form may realize that the wrong line has been used and will subsequently have to complete a new form.

Line captions can be to the left of blanks and on the same line, or they can be printed below the line where data will be entered.

Another way to caption is to provide a box for data instead of a line. Captions can be placed inside, above, or below the box. Boxes on forms help people enter data in the correct place, and they also make reading the form easier for the form's recipient. The caption should use a small type point size, so that it does not dominate the entry area. Small vertical "tick marks" may be included in the box if the data is intended for entry into a computer system. If there is not enough room on a record for the data, the person filling out the form, rather than the data entry operator, has the freedom to determine how the data should be abbreviated. Captions may also include small clarification notes to help the user correctly enter the information, such as Date (MM/DD/YYYY) or Name (Last, First, Middle Initial).

Whatever styles of line caption are chosen, it is important to employ them consistently. For instance, it is confusing to fill out a form that has both above- and below-line captions.

Check-off captions are superior when response options are necessarily restricted. Notice the list of travel methods shown for the vertical check-off example in the previous figure. If employee expenses for business travel are reimbursed only for those travel methods listed, a check-off system is more expedient that a blank line. This method has the added advantage of reminding the person who is verifying the data to look for an airline ticket stub or other receipt.

A horizontal check-off caption is also superior to a line caption when information required is routine and constant. An example is a form that would request services from one of the following departments: Photo Lab, Printing Department, Maintenance, or Supplies. The departments routinely provide services to others in the organization and are not likely to change quickly.

Table captions work well in the body of a form where details are required. When an employee properly fills out a form with table captions, he or she is creating a table for the next person receiving the form, thereby helping to organize data coherently.

A combination of captions can also be used effectively. For example, table captions can be used to specify categories such as quantity, and line captions can be used to indicate where the subtotal, sales tax, and total should be typed. Since different captions serve different purposes, it is generally necessary to employ several caption styles in each form.

Meeting the Intended Purpose

Forms are created to serve one or more purposes in the recording, processing, storing, and retrieving of information for businesses. Sometimes it is desirable to provide different information to different departments or users yet still to share some basic information. This situation is where specialty forms are useful.

One example of a specialty form can be found in Figure 16.5, a three-part form with each part serving a specific purpose. This form is a purchase invoice for Annie's Equipment, a gymnastic and exercise equipment retailer. The form is actually a three-part preprinted form with two pull-out carbon sheets.

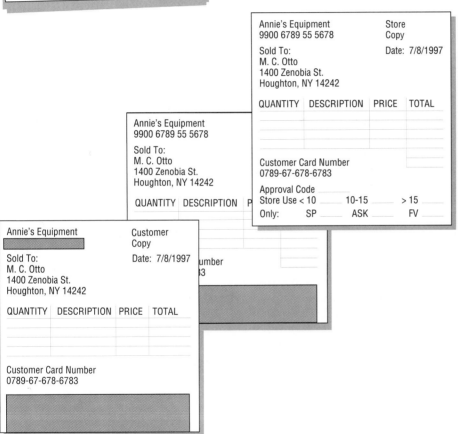

FIGURE 16.5
A three-part specialty form.

By virtue of its functional design, the invoice serves accounting and salespeople in the store, the bank that processes customers' credit-card charges, and the customer. The top copy of the invoice is the store's copy. Notice that it requires the most detailed information of the three copies. The store copy includes the store number as well as the customer card number and the approval code for the charge. All of the information is used by a data entry person to ensure proper billing.

Some of the unique entries required on the store copy are used to track the productivity of Annie's eight salespeople. Since these data might be bothersome to anyone outside of the store, instructions for the proper completion of the bottom blanks are not printed, but rather they are provided orally.

The bottom of the store copy requires the salesperson to check off how much time was necessary to make the sale: less than 10 minutes, 10 to 15 minutes, or more than 15 minutes. It also requires the salesperson (SP) to initial the form, check off whether the customer asked (ASK) for them by name, and whether it was the customer's first visit (FV) to Annie's.

The second copy of the three-part invoice is routed to the bank holding the customer's credit-card account. Notice that the bank still needs store and customer account numbers, but the sales performance data are omitted through the use of a short carbon. Wherever the carbon is cut or blocked out, nothing will be printed.

The customer copy of the invoice is the simplest. It copies essential information that satisfies the customer's needs, such as date, description of equipment purchased, price paid, and credit card used. However, the customer copy uses a specially shaded box to block out Annie's store number, which would be unnecessary for the customer. Sales performance data are also omitted from the customer copy.

The term *specialty form* can also refer solely to the way forms are prepared by the stationer. Examples of stationers' specialty forms are multiple-part forms that are used to create instant triplicates of data, continuous-feed forms that run through the printer without intervention, and perforated forms that leave a stub behind as a record when they are separated. Use of such forms must be judicious; they are costly, and users can quickly be strangled with the red tape generated by meaningless multiple-part forms.

Assuring Accurate Completion

Error rates typically associated with collecting data will drop sharply when forms are designed to assure accurate completion. Design is important in making people do the right thing with the form, whether it is the first or four-hundredth time they are using it. When service employees such as gas meter readers or inventory takers use hand-held devices to scan or otherwise key in data at the appropriate site, then the extra step of transcription during data entry is avoided. Hand-held devices are plugged back into larger computer systems to which they can upload the data that the service worker has stored. No further transcription of what has occurred in the field is necessary.

The Bakerloo Brothers employee expense voucher, shown in Figure 16.6, goes a long way toward securing accurate form completion. Many of the form design techniques we have discussed are utilized in this sample expense voucher. The form design implements the correct flow: top to bottom, and left to right. It also observes the idea of seven main sections or information categories. Additionally, the employee expense voucher uses a combination of clear captions and instructions.

Since Bakerloo Brothers employees are reimbursed only for actual expenses, getting a correct total expenditure is essential. The form design provides an internal double check with column totals and row totals expected to sum to the same number. If the row and column totals don't sum to the same number, the employee filling out the form knows there is a problem and can correct it on the spot. An error is prevented, and the employee can be reimbursed the amount due; both outcomes are attributable to a suitable form design.

Bakerloo Brothers

EMPLOYEE EXPENSE VOUCHER
Claimant: Make No Entries
In Shaded Areas

Full Name of Employee _____

Department _____ Room Number _____

Social Security Number

Voucher Number

Action Taken On:

LIST EXPENSES FOR EACH DAY SEPARATELY. ATTACH RECEIPTS FOR ALL EXPENSES EXCEPT MEALS, TAXIS, AND MISCELLANEOUS ITEMS LESS THAN $3.00. ITEMIZE ALL MISCELLANEOUS EXPENSES.

Date / /	Place City, State	Meal Expenses	Lodging Expenses	Automobile		Miscellaneous		Taxi Cost	Total Cost
				Miles	Cost	Description	Cost		
Totals									

I certify that all the above information is correct

_____   _____
Signature of Claimant   Date

_____   _____
Approved by   Date

Form BB-104 8.85

FIGURE 16.6
A form that encourages accurate completion.

Keeping Forms Attractive

Although attractiveness of forms is dealt with last, its order of appearance is not meant to diminish its importance. Rather, it is addressed last because making forms appealing is accomplished by applying the techniques discussed in the preceding subsections. Aesthetic forms draw people into them and encourage completion. This means that people who fill out the forms will be more satisfied and that the forms will be completed.

Forms should look uncluttered. They should appear organized and logical after they are filled in. Providing enough space for printed or manually-prepared responses will help in this regard. Computer printer entries require a minimum of 1/6-inch spacing between lines, and handwritten entries require approximately 1/4-inch. Forms designed for completion by either hand or printer should allow about 1/3-inch intervals between lines. A use-

This Form May Be Hazardous to Your Health

Figure 16.C1 is a printed medical history form that Dr. Mike Robe, a family practitioner, has his receptionist give to all new patients. All patients must fill it out before they see the doctor.

The receptionist is getting back many incomplete and/or confusing responses. This makes it difficult for Dr. Robe to review the forms and understand why the new patient is there. Additionally, the poor responses make it time-consuming for the receptionist to enter new patients into the files.

Redesign the form on 8 1/2" × 11" paper so that pertinent new patient data can be collected in a logical and inoffensive way. Make sure the form is

---

Medical History Form

Name _____ Employer _____ Age _____

Address _____ Zip _____ Phone _____ Office _____

Insurer _____ Is this [ ] your policy [ ] your spouse's policy

Blue Cross [ ]   State Physician's Service [ ]   Other [ ]   (state) _____

- -

Have you ever had surgery?   Yes_____   No_____   If so, when?_____

Describe the surgery_____

Have you ever been hospitaziled?   Yes_____   No_____   If so, when?_____

Why? _____

Complete the following...

	I have had	Family history
Diabetes	☐	☐
Heart trouble	☐	☐
Cancer	☐	☐
Seizure	☐	☐
Fainting	☐	☐

What have you been immunized for?

Family: _____ _____ _____
        Spouse or next of kin   Relationship   Address

Date of last exam ____/____ Who refered you? _____

Why are you seeing the doctor today?

Are you currently having pain? _____ Constant _____ Sporadic _____

How long does it last? _____ Please give us your soc. sec. #_____

IMPORTANT! We need your correct insurance carrier number _____

FIGURE 16.C1
Your help in improving this form is greatly appreciated.

self-explanatory to new patients. It should also be easy for Dr. Robe to read and easy for the receptionist to enter into the patient database, which is sorted by patient name and social security number. The office uses PCs connected by a LAN. How would you redesign the form so it can be electronically submitted by the receptionist? Which office procedures would you have to change?

ful heuristic for gauging the appropriate length of lines is allowing for five handwritten or eight printed characters per inch. Allowing ample room invites completion.

To be attractive, forms should elicit information in the expected order: Convention dictates asking for name, street address, city, state, and zip or postal code (and country, if necessary). Proper layout and flow contribute to a form's attractiveness.

Using different fonts for type within the same form can help make it appealing to fill in. Separating categories and subcategories with thick and thin lines can also encourage interest in the form. Type fonts and line weights are useful design elements for capturing attention and making people feel secure that they are filling in the form correctly.

Computer-Assisted Form Design

Numerous form design packages are available for PCs. One of the best packages at the time of this writing is called FormFlow by JetForm. FormFlow runs in the Windows environment with a familiar graphical user interface. Some of the features of FormFlow are given in Figure 16.7.

FormFlow was used to draw the Job Application form in Figure 16.8. Notice the floating toolbar. Company logos can be imported, bar codes can be used, and photos can be stored as well. Judicious use of these features allows forms to be designed with great precision.

Controlling Business Forms

Controlling business forms is an important task. Businesses often have a forms specialist who controls forms, but sometimes this job falls to the systems analyst, who sets up and implements forms control.

The basic duties for controlling forms include making sure that each form in use fulfills its specific purpose and that the specified purpose is integral to organizational functioning; preventing duplication of the information that is collected and of the forms that collect it; designing effective forms; deciding on how to get forms reproduced in the most economical way; and establishing stock control and inventory procedures that make forms available (when needed) at the lowest possible cost. A unique form number and revision date (month/year) should be included on each form, regardless of whether it is completed and submitted manually or electronically.

Even if a form specialist is available, control of paperwork is still an area that must be double-checked by the systems analyst. Improvement and change in information systems is highly dependent on managerial information activities, many of which derive from data originally captured on forms.

FIGURE 16.7
Software for electronic form
design has many dynamic
features.

Features of Electronic Form Design Software
• Gives the ability to design paper forms, electronic forms, or Web-based forms using one, integrated package
• Allows forms design using forms templates
• Enables forms design by cutting and pasting familiar shapes and objects
• Facilitates electronic form completion through use of a companion data entry software package
• Permits customization of electronic form completion with the capability to customize menus, toolbars, keyboards, and macros
• Supports integration with popular databases
• Enables the sending and broadcasting of electronic forms
• Permits sequential routing of forms
• Assists tracking of routed forms
• Encourages automatic delivery and processing (push technology for forms)
• Allows the development of roles databases (that show relationships between people and types of information)
• Establishes security protection for electronic forms

GOOD SCREEN AND WEB FORMS DESIGN

Much of what we have already said about good form design is transferable to screen design and eventually to the good design of Web sites and their pages. Once again, the user must remain foremost in the analyst's thoughts during the design of display screens.

There are differences, however, and systems analysts should strive to realize the unique qualities of screen displays rather than to blindly adopt the conventions of paper forms. One big difference is the constant presence of a cursor (a block of light or other pointer) on the screen, which orients the user to the current data-entry position. As data are entered on screen, the cursor moves one character ahead, pointing the way.

Another major difference among electronic, Web, and static forms is the fact that designers can include context-sensitive help in any electronic fill-in form. This practice can reduce the need for instructions being displayed for each line, thus reducing the clutter of the form and cutting down on calls to Technical Support. Using a Web-based approach also permits the designer to take advantage of hyperlinks, thus ensuring that the forms are filled out correctly by providing users with hyperlinked examples of correctly completed forms to the Web form.

In this section, we present guidelines for effective screen design. These are presented in order to aid the attainment of the overall input design goals of effectiveness, accuracy, ease of use, simplicity, consistency, and attractiveness.

FIGURE 16.8
Designing forms using Form-
Flow by JetForm.

The four guidelines for screen design are important but not exhaustive. As noted in Chapter 15, they include:

1. Keep the screen simple.
2. Keep the screen presentation consistent.
3. Facilitate user movement among screens.
4. Create an attractive screen.

In the next subsections, we develop each of these guidelines, and we present many design techniques for observing the four guidelines.

Keeping the Screen Simple

The first guideline for good screen design is to keep the screen display simple. The display screen should show only that which is necessary for the particular action being undertaken.

THREE SCREEN SECTIONS. Figure 16.9 shows a division of the screen into three sections; this method is useful because it simplifies interactions with screens. The top of the screen features a "heading" section, part of which is written into the software to describe to the user where he or she is in the package. The rest of the heading might consist of the file name created by the user.

The middle section is called the "body" of the screen. This can be used for data entry and is organized from left to right and top to bottom, since people in Western cultures move their eyes on a page in this way. Captions and instructions should be supplied in this section to help the user enter the pertinent data in the right place.

Field definitions showing how much data are allowable in each field of the screen's body should also be supplied to the user. This can be accom-

FIGURE 16.9
Three sections of a VDT
screen.

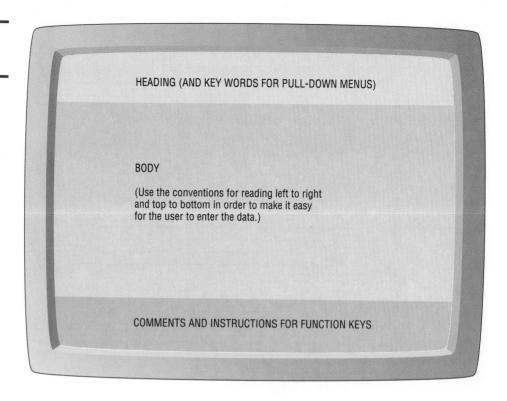

HEADING (AND KEY WORDS FOR PULL-DOWN MENUS)

BODY

(Use the conventions for reading left to right
and top to bottom in order to make it easy
for the user to enter the data.)

COMMENTS AND INSTRUCTIONS FOR FUNCTION KEYS

plished through several different design features: color; inverse video to highlight the precise length of each field; on-screen boxes within which data must fit; brackets, braces, or ampersands to denote the beginnings and endings of fields; or instructions to the user to type directly over a display of distinctive symbols (such as periods) that will then be automatically replaced with data. Sounds such as "beeps" can be included on Web and other interactive fill-in forms to warn users that they are entering numerics rather than alphabetics. Additionally, the computer can "beep" or make a sound when the user has reached the end of a field but doesn't notice—and so continues typing without entering anything in.

Context-sensitive help can also be made available by having the user click the right mouse button within the body section of the screen.

The third section of the screen is the "Comments and Instructions" section. This section may display a short menu of commands that remind the user of basics such as how to change screens or functions, save the file, or terminate entry. Inclusion of such basics can make inexperienced users feel infinitely more secure about their ability to operate the computer without causing a fatal error. Instructions in the third section could also list acceptable code choices the user needs for completing data entry—or ways to get "help."

Figure 16.10 shows a display screen of a check register program used by a women's clothing store. The basic check register screen is simple, following the three basic sections suggested. The heading contains the title "Check Register"; the body asks for specific variable data—"Check Number," "Date," and so on—to be entered by the user; and the comments section provides a list of "Classification Codes" to aid the operator in correctly classifying the expense for later analysis.

FIGURE 16.10
A screen with classification
codes at the bottom.

Check Register

Check Number

Date   /   /

Paid to

For

Amount

Classification

Classification Codes

ADS	Advertising	PAY	Payroll
CUST	Customer (refund)	POST	Postage
MAIN	Maintenance	RENT	Rent
MERC	Merchandise	SERV	Services
MISC	Miscellaneous	SUPP	Supplies
INS	Insurance	TAX	Taxes

USING WINDOWS OR HYPERLINKS. Another way to keep the screen display simple is to list a few basic commands that, when used, will overlay windows to partially or totally fill the current screen with new information. Users can minimize or maximize the size of windows as needed. In this way, users start with a simple, well-designed screen whose complexity they can customize and control through the use of multiple windows. Hyperlinks on a Web-based fill-in form serves a similar purpose.

Figure 16.11 shows an alternative screen display of the check register program along with the window of classification codes the user has asked for. The basic check register screen is simple; it is designed in a format that is familiar through other check forms. By typing a "?" the user is able to access the necessary classification codes.

Making this window available facilitates quick and correct entry, since the user need not remember the infrequently used codes or leave the screen to check a hardcopy list for them before completing data entry. Additionally, the bookkeeping software can be programmed to accept only the classification codes listed on the screen, automatically producing the window if the code entered was incorrect. This helps prevent errors that might have occurred if all classification codes were accepted by the system.

Windows and hyperlinks have almost limitless applications. For instance, they may allow users to stop data entry and jump to or pull down another menu choice; to get visual help showing how the data entry process should proceed; to calculate a value on-screen and then return to data entry to enter the sum calculated; to set an alarm clock for an appointment reminder; or to perform a number of other possible actions.

Since multiple windows are possible, any or all of the preceding functions could appear in varying sizes—or as hyperlinked graphics, images,

FIGURE 16.11
A window can keep the
screen simple.

Check Register

Check Number

Date   /   /

Paid to

For

Amount

Classification

Classification Codes	
ADS	Advertising
CUST	Customer (refund)
MAIN	Maintenance
MERC	Merchandise
MISC	Miscellaneous
INS	Insurance
PAY	Payroll
POST	Postage
RENT	Rent
SERV	Services
SUPP	Supplies
TAX	Taxes

Type ? to see classification codes

icons, or words on a screen at the same time. Clicking the right mouse button might bring up more window options. Entering another command or pressing a predefined key might allow the operator to clear the windowed information from the screen and return to the original display.

One of the main disadvantages of windows is that they allow the user to overcomplicate a simple screen. By including too many windowing operations, the designer may be inviting the creation of a chaotic-looking screen that subsequently results in a user who is lost and frustrated by all the clutter. Windows and hyperlinks must be used judiciously so that they will support the purpose of the user, not hinder it.

Keeping the Screen Consistent

The second guideline for good screen design is to keep the screen display consistent. If users are working from paper forms, screens should follow what is shown on paper. Screens can be kept consistent by locating information in the same area each time a new screen is accessed. Also, information that logically belongs together should be consistently grouped together: Name and address go together, not name and zip code.

The check register depicted earlier helps users input data correctly because it requests data that is consistent with familiar paper checks. For example, "Date," "Paid to," and "Amount" are all expected to be found on a check.

When the user accesses the next screen in order to input the next check, "Check Number," "Date," and "Paid to" are all in the same place as on the previous screen. Keeping the data entry fields in the same place for every screen helps maintain consistency. Recalling and using the three sections of a screen presented previously will also help designers keep screens consistent.

Facilitating Movement

The third guideline for good screen design is to make it easy to move from one screen to another. Web-based forms facilitate movement with the use of hyperlinks to other relevant screens. Another common method for movement is to have users feel as if they are physically moving to a new screen. There are at least three ways this illusion of physical movement among screens is developed.

SCROLLING. An example of effective scrolling is shown in Figure 16.12, which depicts employee records with name, address, and city displayed on the first screen. This example is from an Excel spreadsheet. The screen designer used the command "freeze pane" to ensure that row 1 and columns A and B will always be displayed no matter which way the user scrolls, as shown in Figure 16.13.

Another method mimicking physical movement from screen to screen is to employ keys already assigned on the computer keyboard. PC keyboards have keys labeled "Pg Up" for page up and "Pg Dn" for page down, which in effect take the user to a new page (screen display). This is an extremely easy way for inexperienced users to change screens, although it does take up additional keyboard space and forces users to take their hands off the alphabetic keyboard to use the keypad. These are commonly employed on Web sites as well, with the inclusion of commands such as "Go To Top of Page" or a "Back" command that allows the user to return to the immediately previous screen that he or she was in.

CALLING UP MORE DETAIL. Another general approach to movement between screens allows users to call up another screen quickly by using cursor

FIGURE 16.12
The first screen shows columns A to D. To see more, the user must scroll.

FIGURE 16.13
After scrolling, the user still
sees columns A and B and
also sees columns F to I.

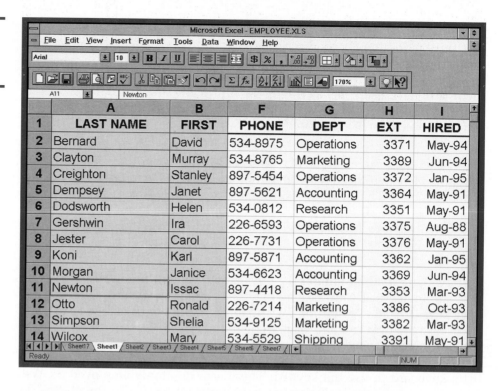

positioning along with a specific command. For example, Figure 16.14 exhibits a screen devoted to employee travel expenses records. In order for the budget manager to call up a specific employee meal expense, he or she just positions the cursor over the button labeled "Meal . . ." and clicks the mouse.

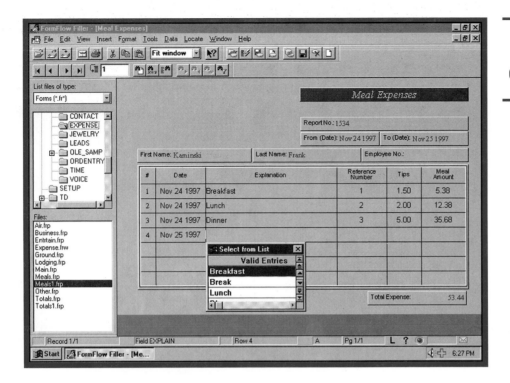

That command brings up the next screen of detailed employee meal expenses, as shown in Figure 16.15. The screens could be effectviely hyperlinked as well. The manager sees a breakdown of employee meal expenses.

ON-SCREEN DIALOG. Displaying prompts facilitates a special kind of user movement between screens. Prompts are extremely useful in applications such as telemarketing. The initial screen used by Summerfest volunteers at public station DETV for their Summerfest fund drive is shown in Figure 16.16. Volunteer phone answerers are facing this first screen when the phone rings. The left side of the screen shows the dialog (prompts) that the volunteer should use. The right-hand side of the screen shows default (most likely) responses for each question.

The phone answerer begins a call by asking if the person is calling to contribute. If the answer is "yes," the default response (the Enter key, for instance) is pressed, and the volunteer continues the dialog with the second question. The volunteer types the caller's last name into the database that contains active contributors.

The next question should confirm what the caller has said about contributing. If the person never before contributed to DETV, a window is pulled up on the screen (or a hyperlink can be used for Web-based fill-in forms) as shown in Figure 16.17. The prompt reminds the volunteer to ask for and enter the caller's address, then to inquire about the existence of an apartment number.

Alternatively, if the caller responds that he or she has contributed before, a different window is called up, as shown in Figure 16.18, or a hyperlink can be followed. This screen provides the caller's last-known address, then prompts the volunteer to ask if it is still correct. The dialog proceeds until the contribution amount and method of payment are finalized. All

FIGURE 16.16
First screen for public broadcasting station DETV's Summerfest drive.

throughout the contribution process, the volunteer has used split-screen dialog prompts and defaults to move from screen to screen in order to procure
and enter the correct data.

An interesting method of creating the feel of physically moving from
screen to screen is direct manipulation (a graphical user interface that will

FIGURE 16.17
Window displayed if the
caller has not contributed to
DETV before.

FIGURE 16.18
Window displayed if the
caller has contributed to
DETV before.

Educational Television Summerfest Drive

Suggested Dialog	Default	Response

Hello this is DETV summerfest.
Are you calling to contribute?   Y

Thank you. What is your last
name, please?   [ ]

Have you contributed to DETV
before?

Our records show that you live at:

8126 N. Seneca Road
Lewiston, NY 15342

Is this still correct?   Y

be discussed in detail in Chapter 18). An example is designing a cursor to look like a human hand—in other words, an on-screen icon. This on-screen hand would be used to push forward to a new screen or back to a previous one by use of a mouse in a way that is analogous to pushing a piece of paper upward or downward on a desk. This also works on Web-based fill-in forms. Remember you have standard features such as a "Back" button and a "Home" button that can be invoked when designing a Web form.

Designing an Attractive Screen

The fourth guideline for good screen design is to create an attractive screen for the user. If users find screens appealing, they are likely to be more productive, to need less supervision, and to make fewer errors. Some of the design principles used for forms apply here, too, and some aesthetic principles have already come up in a slightly different context.

Screens should draw users into them and hold their attention. This is accomplished with the use of plenty of open area surrounding data-entry fields, so that the screen achieves an uncluttered appearance. You would never crowd a form; similarly you should never crowd a screen. You are far better off using multiple screen windows or hyperlinks than jamming everything onto one screen or page. By creating screens that are easy to grasp at first glance, you appeal to both inexperienced and experienced users.

Use logical flow in the plan to your screens. Organize screen material to take advantage of the way people function so that they can easily find their way around the screen. Also, consistently partition information into the three smaller sections detailed earlier.

If the screen is necessarily complex, appeal is heightened by separating information categories with lines composed of periods, dashes, ampersands, exclamation points, or boxes. The check register screen shown in Figure

FIGURE 16.19
A check register screen that
shows balanced design.

Check Register

Check Number	
Date	/ /
Paid to	
For	
Amount	
Classification	

Classification Codes

ADS	Advertising	PAY	Payroll
CUST	Customer (refund)	POST	Postage
MAIN	Maintenance	RENT	Rent
MERC	Merchandise	SERV	Services
MISC	Miscellaneous	SUPP	Supplies
INS	Insurance	TAX	Taxes

16.19 uses boxes to define data-entry fields. Note that the boxes are left-justified, which results in an orderly look for the screen.

Thickness of separation lines between subcategories can also be varied to add further distinctions. This helps the user to see quickly both the purpose of the screen and what data items are required.

With the advent of Graphical User Interfaces (GUIs), it is possible to make input screens very attractive. By using color or shaded boxes and creating three-dimensional boxes and arrows, you can make forms user-friendly and fun to use. Figure 16.20 shows an example of an order entry screen that is effective. These features are also available for Web-based fill-in forms.

INVERSE VIDEO AND BLINKING CURSORS. Other techniques can also effectively enhance the attractiveness of screens, but only if they are used sparingly. They include inverse video, blinking cursor or fields, and type fonts in various styles and sizes.

When you are considering the use of these techniques, simplicity is still the watchword. Design the basic screen that will include basic information first. Then, if greater differentiation is still needed, the basics can be embellished. Fortunately, additional enhancements may not be as costly for screen design as they are for forms.

Inverse video swaps the foreground color for the background color. This is an excellent way to highlight an important field, but employing it can cause users to be so overwhelmed with the brightness of the inverse that they ignore other fields.

Blinking video displays, when used for a cursor, are one way to alert an inexperienced user to its location. Blinking can also be used for error control by calling attention to a field that was skipped. However, some users find

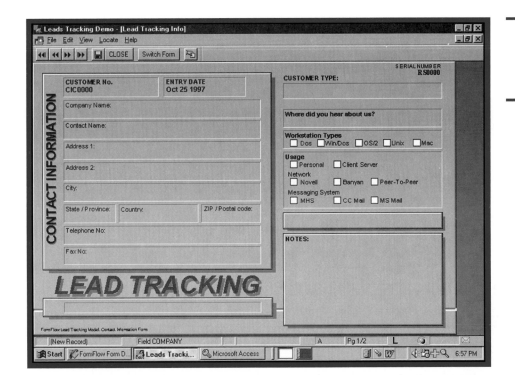

FIGURE 16.20
You can design an attractive data entry screen with a 3-dimensional effect using JetForm's FormFlow.

blinking video annoying, imagining that the computer is impatiently awaiting the next entry.

USING DIFFERENT TYPE FONTS. State-of-the-art computer systems and software allow type fonts of different styles and sizes. Type fonts are another way to make screens attractive to users. Different styles enhance differentiation among categories. For instance, thick, sans serif type styles can be used to denote main categories and to give screens a modern look. Larger type can indicate captions for data-entry fields. Thinner type with serifs can be used to designate subcategories on the same screen and can provide a more conservative look.

When contemplating the use of different type styles and sizes, ask yourself if they truly assist the user in understanding and liking the screen. If they draw undue attention to the art of screen design or if they serve as a distraction, leave them out. Be aware that not all Web pages are viewed identically by different browsers. Test your forms with a variety of combinations to see if the resultant color combinations will be pleasing or distressing to the majority of users.

Differences in Mainframe and Microcomputer Screen Design

Mainframe and microcomputer design have much in common, but there are some critical differences between them. A mainframe computer is designed to work with many terminals, whereas a microcomputer is a self-contained processing unit and terminal. To increase mainframe efficiency, screens are sent as a whole rather than as a series of individual keystrokes. Conversely, a microcomputer is designed to respond to any keystroke.

When using a PC, the user may be prompted to press a certain key, and the program responds by displaying information. For example, most spreadsheet programs allow the user to press a slash (/) to bring up a menu of options. A microcomputer program may pause for the user to examine the screen, which displays the message "Press any key to continue." When the user presses a key, the program continues.

A mainframe computer operates differently. The data entered on the screen is stored at the terminal and not transmitted to the mainframe until the user presses one of several keys designated as transmission keys. These keys (on an IBM mainframe) are called AID keys, for **A**ttention **ID**entifier, and they include the Enter key, the Clear key, function keys 1 to 24 (PF1–24), and three **P**rogram **A**ttention keys called PA1 through PA3. When one of these keys is pressed, the screen data, along with whichever of the keys has been pressed, is transmitted to the mainframe. By utilizing AID keys, the mainframe does not have to respond to each terminal keystroke, and each user thus benefits from improved response time. (Response time is the time that elapses between the moment the user presses an AID key and the appearance of a new screen generated by the computer.)

Another technique used in mainframe systems is to transmit only the data fields on a screen that have been altered—that is, those fields in which the user has entered new data or changed existing data. Clearly defining the screen fields ensures that only the minimal number of characters are transmitted from each terminal to the central computer, and response time again is thereby improved.

ATTRIBUTES. The data fields on a screen are defined using a field attribute character. The attribute character occupies one screen position, immediately preceding the data field, and it always appears as a blank (invisible) character on the screen. Figure 16.21 illustrates a screen used to enter new item information with the attribute characters indicated by small rectangles. Notice that these rectangles are located before, and sometimes after, each screen data field.

Attribute characters control the characteristics of the screen field to the right of them and include the following qualities:

1. Protection.
2. Intensity.
3. Shift and extended attributes.

These are described in the following subsections.

Protection. Protection determines whether the user may enter data into the screen field or not. There are three types of protection: unprotected, which allows any users to enter data; protected, used for output display information such as an operator message; and auto skip, used for captions, titles, and other screen features that do not change. The cursor will only be placed in unprotected areas of the screen.

On the ADD NEW ITEM screen, there is a protected attribute in front of the date, the time, the operator message (indicating the function key assignments), and the feedback message line. As the program processes input data, different information will be sent to these fields, but the user will not be allowed to key any data into them.

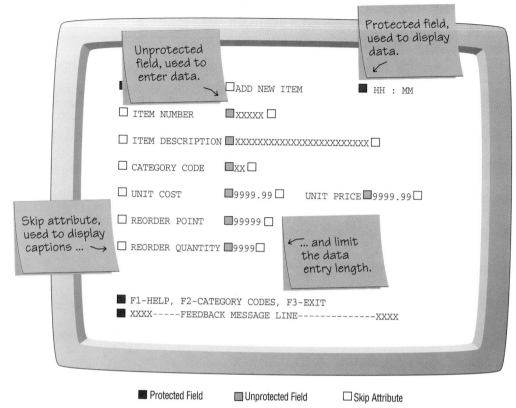

FIGURE 16.21
A screen showing attribute characters.

The title ADD NEW ITEM and the captions—ITEM NUMBER, ITEM DESCRIPTION, CATEGORY CODE, and so on—all have the skip attribute, since these displays do not change on the ADD NEW ITEM screen.

The Xs representing where the ITEM NUMBER, ITEM DESCRIPTION, and CATEGORY CODE—as well as the 9s representing areas where numeric data is to be entered—are all designated as unprotected. After each unprotected screen field, there is another auto skip attribute character. This is used to control the number of characters the user may enter for each screen field. As each character is entered, the cursor advances to the right. When the auto skip attribute character is reached, the cursor "jumps" to the next unprotected screen field. When the last entry field is completed, the cursor wraps around to the first screen field.

Intensity. Intensity is how bright a screen field will appear. Three choices are available: normal, generally used both for displaying captions, titles, date, time, and other fixed information and for entering data; bright, or high-intensity, often used to display error messages and to highlight an error in a field; and invisible, usually reserved for passwords. A combination of protected or unprotected and normal or bright intensities provides different screen colors for data and captions: usually white, green, blue, and red.

Shift and extended attributes. The shift attribute limits data fields to numeric or alphanumeric entries when data is keyed. If a screen field uses the

Squeezin' Isn't Pleasin'

The Audiology Department in a large veteran's hospital is using a PC and monitor so that audiology technicians can enter data directly into the patient records system. After talking with Earl Lobes, one of the technicians, you determine that the screen design is a major problem.

"We used a form at one time, and that was decent," said Mr. Lobes. "But the screen doesn't make sense. I guess they had to squeeze everything on there, and that ruined it."

You have been asked to redesign the screen (Figure 16.C2) to capture the same information, but to simplify it, and by doing so, to reduce the errors that have been plaguing the technicians. You realize that squeezing isn't the only problem with the screen.

Explain your reasons for changing the screen as you did. You may use more than one screen if you think it is necessary.

AUDIOLOGICAL EXAMINATION REPORT

Patient last name   First   middle initial
Examining Station   Date of exam
Patient number   Social Security number
First exam   Claim number

AIR CONDUCTION

Right ear   Left ear

| 500 | 1000 | 2000 | 4000 | 6000 | | 500 | 1000 | 2000 | 4000 | 6000 |
| □ | □ | □ | □ | □ | | □ | □ | □ | □ | □ |

BONE CONDUCTION

Right ear   Left ear

| 500 | 1000 | 2000 | 4000 | 6000 | | 500 | 1000 | 2000 | 4000 | 6000 |
| □ | □ | □ | □ | □ | | □ | □ | □ | □ | □ |

SPEECH AUDIOMETRY SECT.   Comments [
SPEECH RECEP. THRESHOLD
Right Ear [ ]
Left Ear [ ]   Referred by [   ]
RIGHT EAR DISCR.   Reason for referral
% [ ] Masking [ ]   Examining Audiologist
LEFT EAR DISCRIM. Exam. Audiologist's No.
% [ ] Masking [ ]   Next Appt.

FIGURE 16.C2
This screen can be designed to be more user-friendly.

numeric shift attribute, data entered as 123 in an 8-character field will be both right-justified in the field and padded with zeros on the left after the Enter key has been pressed, resulting in 00000123. This attribute is frequently used for numeric data-entry fields. Extended attributes may be included, which provide for reverse video, underline, extra color, and blinking.

ATTRIBUTE CHARACTER CONSIDERATIONS. When designing mainframe terminal screens for entering data, the attribute character must be taken into consideration. At least one space must be reserved between captions and data-entry areas for the attribute character. Normally, dates are entered without any slashes, spaces, or hyphens separating the month, the day, and the year. The reason for not entering a slash, for example, is that either the operator would have to key the slash or the program would have to display the slash. Having the operator key the slash slows the data entry process and may lead to the inconsistent entry of dates. Some users might enter dates with slashes while other users might forget to enter the slashes.

If the program displays the slashes and the entire date entry field is unprotected, the operator may accidentally overtype the slashes. If the slashes are placed on the screen as protected entry fields, there must be an attribute byte before and after each of the slashes to protect them. The field would have the following attribute character format: **u**MM**s/u**DD**s/u**YYYY**s** where **u** represents the unprotected attribute character necessary for entering a month, day, or year, and **s** represents the auto skip attribute for jumping the cursor over the slashes. The data would appear to be spread out across the screen and would display as MM/DD/YYYY.

This consideration is also taken into account when designing entry fields for other fields that have editing characters in them, such as a standard U.S. telephone number—(nnn)nnn–nnnn. Social security numbers are another case in point. Finally, including a fixed screen location for the placement of the decimal point in amount fields is a common example of the need for attribute characters.

SCREEN CODE GENERATION. Screens may be designed using a number of CASE tools. Visible Analyst Workbench screens may be used to generate COBOL and other language code. A commonly used IBM mainframe screen programming language is CICS (Customer Information Control System, sometimes pronounced "kicks"). CICS code makes extensive use of attribute character control and is one of the most efficient means for sending and receiving mainframe screens. Many of the powerful CASE code generators, such as Texas Instruments' IEF (Information Engineering Facility) and Knowledgeware's IEW (Information Engineering Workbench), generate CICS code. Excelerator may be linked through an additional interface product to Micro Focus, which will generate CICS code for an Excelerator screen. This code may be tested and executed on a microcomputer and then ported to the mainframe.

Micro Focus has a powerful toolset called Dialog System 3270. This code generation software will take a mainframe CICS screen and automatically generate Windows, OS/2, or one of several other screen formats which function as entry or display screens. This provides great flexibility when creating systems. A program may run on a mainframe, a microcomputer, or other system, and you can get it to do so without rewriting program code. This flexibility is often used in a client/server architecture, where the database may reside on the mainframe and the screen interface may exist on a PC or as a mainframe program.

Figure 16.22 is an example of a mainframe CICS screen for adding customer payments. A CUSTOMER NUMBER is entered, and customer information (NAME, STREET, BALANCE DUE, and so on) is displayed using data from the CUSTOMER MASTER file. An INVOICE NUMBER, CHECK NUMBER, and PAYMENT AMOUNT are entered on the lower

FIGURE 16.22
Mainframe screen for adding
customer payments.

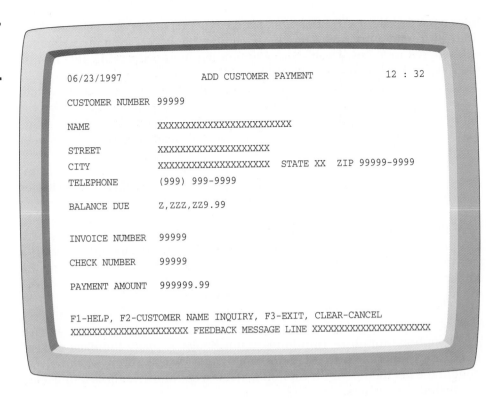

portion of the screen. Figure 16.23 is an example of the corresponding Windows or OS/2 screen that is generated using the Micro Focus Dialog System. Notice that all entry or protected display fields are surrounded by rectangles, the standard entry field for a graphical user interface screen. Captions do not have a rectangle, since they do not change as various payments are

FIGURE 16.23
Windows or OS/2 screen
that corresponds to the
mainframe screen.

FIGURE 16.24
Icons from Microsoft
Excel 7.0.

entered. Protection, color, and so on are all translated onto the graphical screen.

Using Icons in Screen Design

Icons are pictorial, on-screen representations symbolizing computer actions that users may select using a mouse, keyboard, lightpen, or joystick. Icons serve functions similar to those of words and may replace them in many menus, since their meaning is more quickly grasped than words. Icons designed for the spreadsheet for Excel 7.0 shown in Figure 16.24.

There are some guidelines for the design of effective icons. Shapes should be readily recognizable, so that the user is not required to master a new vocabulary. Numerous icons are already known to most users. Use of standard icons can quickly tap into this reservoir of common meaning. A user may point to a file cabinet, "pull out" a file folder icon, "grab" a piece of paper icon, and "throw it" in the wastebasket icon. By employing standard icons, designers and users all save time.

Icons for a particular application should be limited to around twenty recognizable shapes so that icon vocabulary is not overwhelming and a worthwhile coding scheme can still be realized.

Use icons consistently throughout applications where they will appear together. This ensures continuity and understandability. Standardizing icon usage can be taken even further. Some software houses are developing their own corporate icon systems so that when different application packages are purchased from them, the user can count on employing familiar icons. Researchers are also attempting to invent a standardized icon system.

Generally, icons are useful if they are meaningful. New environments for PCs and Web-based applications use many more icons than even a few years ago. Their chief advantage so far has been to attract inexperienced users and to get them excited about the computer's potential. Experienced users may become annoyed with the pseudo-simplicity and cuteness of icons or become impatient with the way in which icons tend to mask what the computer is actually doing. However, it is conceivable that experienced users prefer command language (discussed in Chapter 18) more out of habit than out of any real dislike for icons.

What's That Thing Supposed to Be?

Art Istik flips off his monitor with a loud click. "I've just about had it," he says, turning impatiently to his colleague. Looking at Art with mock sympathy, Sim Ball says, "New system is too much for you, isn't it?" Art replies, "No, it's not. But I'll tell you what's really wrong. It's these silly pictures."

Art clicks on his newly installed microcomputer, rebooting a database management program that appears on his VDT. The first screen shows icons shaped like a Sherlock Holmes cap, some kind of tree, a pair of socks, an apple, a door, and a rabbit. Sim, leaning over Art's shoulder, takes one look at the screen and laughs uncontrollably.

Art says sarcastically, "I knew you would be able to help." Sim manages to stop laughing long enough to point to the pair-of-socks icon and demands, "What's that thing supposed to be?"

Art replies, "I have no idea. All I know is that this database management package is from some West Coast company called 'Organic Outputs.' The software is called 'DATAPIX: The icon-based database' by a guy

named Drew Ikahn. Maybe we ought to call him up. His idea of a good screen is way out. No way can I learn all these crazy pictures." Sim returns to his desk, saying, "Yeah, but at least it's entertaining."

As a last resort, Art turns to the DATAPIX user's manual, which provides translations for the unconventional icons.

Based on Art Istik's and Sim Ball's comments (and laughter), describe what you feel is amiss with the DATAPIX icons (see Figure 16.C3). To what do Art and Sim seem to attribute some of the problems with their database management program? Applying some of the information you learned about using icons effectively, redraw the DATAPIX icons to improve them. What icons have become universally recognizable with the widespread use of Windows? Draw three of them, and write the meaning for each of them next to their name. In a paragraph, discuss the importance of standardizing icons. Add a paragraph voicing your opinion about whether it is possible or desirable to create one universal icon "dictionary" for use with all applications.

Icon		Meaning
Apple		**Create** a file (as in Adam and Eve)
Door		**Enter** data (as you would a door)
Sherlock's Cap		**Find** (after Holmes' famous investigative powers)
Pair of Socks		**Sort** (as in laundry)
Tree		**Print** (a gentle reminder that printing destroys the trees)
Rabbit		**Copy** a file (for making multiple copies)

FIGURE 16.C3
These DATAPIX icons can be improved.

Graphical User Interface Design

A Graphical User Interface (GUI, pronounced "gooey") uses a Windows, OS/2, Macintosh, or other graphics screen for entering and displaying data. While these screens have traditional data entry and display fields, several additional features are also included in the screen design. These are illus-

FIGURE 16.25
Illustration of GUI
components.

trated in Figure 16.25. The screen shown is used to add a customer order and has been designed to illustrate many of the GUI features.

Rectangles, as mentioned previously, are used to outline data entry and display fields. A check box is used to indicate a new customer. Check boxes contain an X or are empty, corresponding to whether the user selected or did not select the option; they are used for nonexclusive choices, where one or more of the options may be checked. An alternative notation is to use a square button with a check mark (√) to indicate that the option has been selected. Note that check box text is usually placed to the right of the box.

A circle, called a radio button, is used to select exclusive choices: Either one or the other option can be chosen, but not both. An example of this device is shown by the buttons located under the caption SELECT CUS-TOMER TYPE. The customer is either a REGULAR CUSTOMER or a HIGH-VOLUME CUSTOMER, but not both. The selected button has a darkened center. Choices are again listed to the right of the button.

A list box is one which displays several options that may be selected with the mouse. A drop-down list box is used when there is little room available on the screen. (In the figure, a drop-down list box is used for se-lecting the method of payment.) A single rectangle exists with an arrow pointing down toward a line, located on the right side of the rectangle. Se-lecting this arrow causes a list box to be displayed. In the ADD CUSTOMER ORDER example, the method of payment may be chosen from this list. The scroll bars on the right side of the list box are used if there are more choices than will display within the box. Once a choice has been made, it is dis-played in the drop-down selection rectangle, and the list box disappears. As illustrated, the previous credit card choice in this example was MasterCard.

A command button performs an action when the user selects it with the mouse. CALCULATE TOTAL, ADD ORDER, and OK are examples of com-mand buttons. The text is centered inside the button, which has a rectangular shape. If there is a default action, such as the OK button, the text is generally surrounded with a dashed line. The button may also be shaded to indicate that it is the default. The user may press the Enter key to select the default button.

Several other symbols are often used on GUI screens to send important messages to the user. Each should be within a rectangular window and should clearly spell out the message. An "i" within a circle represents "information" and alerts the user with a message. The information symbol in Figure 16.25 is used to alert the user to the fact that the customer is already on file. An exclamation point within a circle indicates a warning message, and a stop sign is used for a critical error or other action message.

Tab Control Dialog Boxes

Tab control dialog boxes are another part of graphical user interfaces and another way to get users organized and into system material efficiently. Figure 16.26 provides an example of a tab control dialog box. Guidelines for designing the control dialog boxes include:

1. Create a separate tab for each unique feature. (For example, a tab to select color; another to select text, background, grid, or other font characteristics.)
2. Place the most commonly used tabs in front and display them first.
3. Consider including three basic buttons in your design: OK, Cancel, and Help.

Using Color in Screen Design

Color is an appealing and proven way to facilitate computer input. Appropriate use of color on display screens allows you to contrast foreground and background; to highlight important fields on forms; to feature errors; to specially code input; and to call attention to many other special attributes.

Highly contrasting colors should be used for foreground and background. This helps users grasp what is presented quickly without straining. Also, background color will affect perception of foreground color. For example, dark green may look like a different color if taken off a white background and placed on a yellow one. Specifically, the top five most legible combinations of foreground lettering on background are (starting with the most legible combination):

1. Black on yellow.
2. Green on white.
3. Blue on white.
4. White on blue.
5. Yellow on black.

The least legible are red on green and blue on red. As can be gathered from these possible foreground and background combinations, bright colors should be used for foregrounds, with less bright colors for the background. Strongly contrasting colors should be assigned first to fields that must be differentiated; then other colors can be assigned.

FIGURE 16.26
A dialog tab control box from Micrografx Designer showing drop-down boxes, radio buttons, and check boxes. Good design includes push buttons for "OK," "Close," and "?" or "Help."

Use color to highlight important fields on screens. Fields that are important can be colored differently from the rest. Alternatively, important fields and data can be programmed in a color that is brighter than those that are less important. Fields that are used often should be colored differently from other fields. When creating Web-based forms, hyperlinks are usually color-coded to show users that a hypertext path can be taken. Hyperlinks can be made to change color after a user has clicked on them once with the mouse. This color coding prevents users from pursuing previously-used hyperlinks and thus helps organize their search and save them valuable time.

Like colors can mean similar situations, so that the red end of the spectrum (red, pink, fuchsia) might, for example, indicate dangerous or error situations. As is shown in Figure 16.27, red may mean that entering data at the time of its display will permanently alter a file.

On this screen the column depicting June's sales data for all car salespeople is red on a white background, which means it is ready to be updated. The programmer has also highlighted headings for the rows and columns in blue so that the user can easily distinguish them from other material. In this instance, blue means "headings." It is important to assign only one meaning to each color.

Color can assist in the special coding of input and should be used in addition to a well-formatted screen. Color coding is of great help in assisting users with searching and counting tasks. Alphanumeric blocks, groups, or columns are usefully distinguished through the use of color. If displays are

FIGURE 16.27
Color enhancement of a computer display screen.

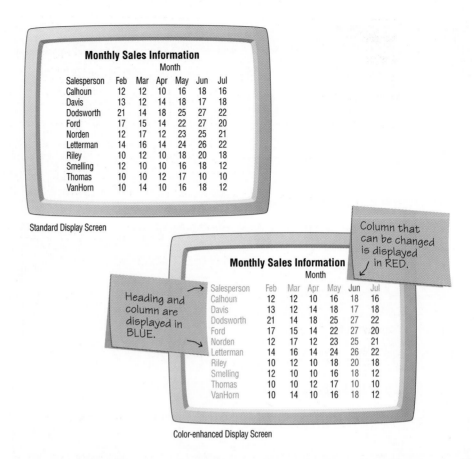

high-density, it is wise to use a double coding strategy, one employing both color and shape or color and patterns. Many applications now permit users to customize colors.

As with any enhancement, screen designers need to question the added value of using color. Use of color can be overdone; a useful heuristic is no more than four colors for new users, and only up to seven for experienced ones. Irrelevant colors distract users and detract from their performance. However, there are numerous instances where color has been shown to facilitate use in very specific ways. Color should be considered an important way to contrast foreground and background, to highlight important fields and data, to point out errors, and to allow special coding of input.

INTRANET AND INTERNET PAGE DESIGN

In Chapter 15, the rudiments of designing Web sites were discussed. There are more hints about designing a good Internet or intranet fill-in form that should be noted, now that you have learned some of the elementary aspects of input form and screen design. Figure 16.28 shows a fill-in form order screen that shows many elements of good design for the Web. Guidelines include:

1. Use a variety of text boxes, push buttons, drop-down menus, check boxes, and radio buttons to serve specific functions and to create interest in the form. For example, a text box can be used to capture pieces of information about a Web-site visitor.

FIGURE 16.28
A fill-in form order screen
from the Dell computer
store Web site.

2. Provide clear instructions, since Web users may not be familiar with the terminology or the computer, and users are likely to be international rather than local.

3. Include radio buttons when users must choose one answer in a bipolar, close-ended question, the responses to which could be either "Yes" or "No"; "Agree" or "Disagree"; "True" or "False"; but not both.

4. Employ check boxes to allow users to show whether a test condition is either true or untrue. For example, "This is the first time I have visited this site."

5. Demonstrate a logical entry sequence for fill-in forms, especially since the users may have to scroll down to a region of the page that is not visible at the top.

6. Prepare two basic buttons on every Web fill-in form: "Submit" "Clear Form."

7. Provide a scrolling text box at times when you are uncertain about how much space users will need to respond to a question, or about what language, structure, or form users will use to enter data.

SUMMARY

This chapter has covered elements of input design for forms, screens, and Web fill-in forms. Well-designed input should meet the goals of effectiveness, accuracy, ease of use, simplicity, consistency, and attractiveness. Knowledge of many different design elements will allow the systems analyst to reach these goals.

The four guidelines for well-designed input forms are:

1. Forms must be easy to fill out.
2. Forms must meet the purpose for which they are designed.

3. Forms must be designed to assure accurate completion.
4. Forms must be attractive.

Design of useful forms, screens, and Web fill-in forms overlaps in many important ways, but there are some distinctions. Screens display a cursor which continually orients the user. Screens often provide assistance with input, whereas with the exception of preprinted instructions, it may be difficult to get additional assistance with a form. Web-based documents have additional capabilities such as embedded hyperlinks and context-sensitive help functions.

The four guidelines for well-designed screens are:

1. Screens must be kept simple.
2. Screens must be consistent from screen to screen.
3. Screen design must facilitate movement between screens.
4. Screens must be attractive.

Many different design elements allow the systems analyst to meet these guidelines.

The proper flow of paper forms, screens and fill-in forms on the Web are important. Forms should group information logically into seven categories, and screens should be divided into three main sections. Captions on forms and screens can be varied, as can type fonts and the weights of lines dividing subcategories of information. Multiple-part forms are another way to ensure that forms meet their intended purposes. Designers can use windows, prompts, dialog boxes, and defaults on-screen to assure the effectiveness of design. There are many similarities, but some critical differences, between screen design for mainframe systems and screen design for microcomputers. To increase efficiency, mainframe screens are sent as a whole rather than as a series of individual keystrokes.

Data fields on a mainframe screen are defined using a field attribute character, which controls the qualities of protection, intensity, shift, and extended attributes. The attribute character must be considered when designing mainframe terminal screens.

Screens can be designed using a number of CASE tools. A commonly used IBM mainframe screen programming language is CICS (Customer Information Control System). Many of the powerful CASE code generators generate CICS code. Icons, color, and graphical user interfaces can also be used to enhance user understanding of input screens.

Web fill-in forms should be constructed with the following seven guidelines in mind, as well as those in Chapter 15:

1. Use a variety of text boxes, push buttons, drop-down menus, check boxes, and radio buttons
2. Provide clear instructions,

"Isn't Spring the most beautiful season here? The architect really captured the essence of the landscape, didn't he? I mean, you can't go anywhere in the building without seeing another beautiful vista through those huge windows. When Snowden came back, he looked at your output screens. The good news is that he thinks they'll work. The project is blossoming, just like the flowers and trees. When Snowden returns from Finland, would you have some input screens ready to demonstrate? He doesn't want things to slow down just because he's out of the country. By the way, the Singapore trip was very successful. Maybe MRE will be worldwide someday."

HYPERCASE QUESTIONS

1. Using either a paper layout form or software such as JetForm's Form-Flow, design a prototype paper form that captures client information for the Training Unit.

2. Test your form on three classmates by having each of them fill it out. Ask them for a written critique of the form.

3. Redesign your input form to reflect your classmates' comments.

4. Using either a paper layout form or a CASE tool design a prototype screen form that captures client information for the Training Unit.

FIGURE 16.HCI
Take a look at some of the input screens in HyperCase. You may want to redesign some of the electronic forms.

Continued

5. Test your input screen on three classmates by having each of them try it out. Ask them for a written critique of the screen's design.

6. Redesign the input screen based on the comments you receive. In a paragraph, explain how you have addressed each comment.

3. Include radio buttons when users must choose one answer in a bipolar,

4. Employ check boxes to allow users to show whether a test condition is either true or untrue.

5. Demonstrate a logical entry sequence for fill-in forms.

6. Prepare two basic buttons on every Web fill-in form: "Submit" and "Clear Form."

7. Provide a scrolling text box at times when you are uncertain about how much space users will need to respond to a question.

KEYWORDS AND PHRASES

form flow	inverse video
seven sections of a form	blinking cursor
three screen sections	response time
line captions	attribute characters
box captions	CICS
table caption	check box
horizontal check-off captions	radio buttons
vertical check-off captions	drop-down list
specialty forms	list box
control of business forms	command button
cursor	tab control dialog box
windows for screens	on-screen color
facilitating screen movement	screen color combinations
scrolling on screen	Internet/intranet fill-in forms
on-screen dialog	text boxes
on-screen icons	prompt

REVIEW QUESTIONS

1. What are the design objectives for paper input forms, input screens, or Web-based fill-in forms?
2. List the four guidelines for good form design.
3. What is proper form flow?
4. What are the seven sections of a good form?
5. List four types of captioning for use on forms.
6. What is a specialty form? What are some disadvantages of using specialty forms?
7. List the guidelines for the spacing of handwritten forms and printed forms.
8. What are the basic duties involved in controlling forms?
9. List the four guidelines for good screen design.
10. What are the three sections useful for simplifying a screen?

11. What are the advantages of using on-screen windows?
12. What are the disadvantages of using on-screen windows?
13. List two ways screens can be kept consistent.
14. Give three ways to facilitate movement between screens.
15. What are the differences between mainframe and microcomputer screen design?
16. What is an attribute character? Where is it used?
17. What screen characteristics are stored in an attribute character?
18. List four graphical interface design elements. Alongside each one, describe when it would be appropriate to incorporate each of them in a screen design or on a Web-based fill-in form.
19. Define what is meant by on-screen icons. When are icons generally useful for screen design? For the design of Web-based fill-in forms?
20. List the five most legible foreground and background color combinations for VDT use.
21. What three buttons should be included with a tab control dialog box?
22. What are four situations where color may be useful for screen and Web fill-in form design?
23. List seven design guidelines for a Web-based fill-in form.

PROBLEMS

1. Here are captions used for a state census form:

Name
....
Occupation
....
Address
....
                          Zip code
....
Number of people in household?
....
Age of head of household
....

   a. Redo the *captions* so that the state census bureau can capture the same information requested on the old form without confusing respondents.
   b. Redesign the form so it exhibits proper flow. (*Hint:* Make sure to provide an access and identification section so that the information can be stored in the state's computers.)
   c. Redesign the form so it can be filled in by citizens who visit the state's Web site. What changes were necessary in moving from a paper form to one that will be electronically submitted?

2. Elkhorn College needs to keep better track of the books checked out from its Buck Memorial Library.
   a. Design and draw a form on 4-1/4 by 5-1/2 inch-long paper to use for checking out library books. Label the seven sections of a form that you included.
   b. Design and draw a representation of a screen to accomplish the same thing. Label the three sections of a screen that you included.

3. Refer to Figure 16.24 which shows the icons from Excel 7.0, the spread-sheet program from Microsoft, and try to explain what each of the icons mean. Propose new icons if the actual ones are confusing.

4. Take a look at Figure 16.EX1. These are icons from Freelance Graphics, a presentation package from Lotus Development Corporation. Try to guess what the icons mean. Does the light bulb have the same meaning as the lightbulb in the Microsoft application in problem 3? Explain. Suggest other icons that are better.

5. Speedy Spuds is a fast-food place offering all manner of potatoes. The manager has a 30-second rule for serving customers. Servers say they could achieve this if the form they must fill out and give to the kitchen crew were simplified. The information from the completed form is keyed into the computer system at the end of the day, when the data entry person needs to enter the kind of potato purchased, additional toppings purchased, the quantity, and the price charged. The current form is difficult for servers to scan and fill out quickly.

   a. Design and draw a form (you choose the size, but be sensible) that lists possible potatoes and toppings in a manner that is easy for servers and kitchen crew to scan and can also be used as input for the inventory/reorder system that is on the extranet connecting Speedy Spuds and Idaho potato growers. (*Hint:* Remember to ob-serve *all* of the guidelines for good form design.)

   b. Design and draw a representation of a display screen that can be used by the servers/clerks to fill in the information captured on the form.

   c. Design a display screen based on the screen you designed in part b. This time, it should function as a screen that shows a kitchen crew member what to prepare for each Spuds order. List three changes to the existing screen that you made in order to adapt it to function as an output screen.

6. Sherry's Meats, a regional meat wholesaler/retailer, needs to collect up-to-date information on how much of each meat product it has in each store. It will then use that information to schedule deliveries from its central warehouse. Currently, customers entering the store fill out a detailed form specifying their individual orders. The form lists over 150 items; it includes meat and meat products available in different amounts. At the end of the day, between 250 and 400 customer orders are tabulated and deducted from the store's inventory. Then the office worker in each store phones in an order for the next day. Store employees have a difficult time tabulating sales because of the mistakes customers make in filling out their forms.

   a. It is not possible to have the solitary office worker in each store fill out the numerous customer order forms. Change the form (3-1/2 inches by 6 inches *either* horizontal *or* vertical) and draw it so that it is easier for customers to fill out correctly and for office workers to tabulate.

   b. Design and draw a specialty form of the same size that will meet the needs of Sherry's customers, office workers, and warehouse workers.

   c. Design and draw two different forms of the same size to meet the purposes in part b, since Sherry's carries both pork and beef products. (*Hint:* Think about ways to make forms easy to distinguish visually.)

   d. Design a fill-in form for on-screen display. When a customer submits an order, it is entered into Sherry's inventory system by any person who is serving customers at the counter. This information will be captured and sent to the central warehouse computer to help control inventory.

   e. In a paragraph, describe the drawbacks of having lots of different people at different locations enter data. In a paragraph, list steps you can take as the designer to ensure that the fill-in form is designed to ensure accuracy of entry.

7. R. George's, a fashionable clothing store that also has a mail-order business, would like to keep track of the customers coming into the store in order to expand its mailing list.

   a. Design and draw a simple form that can be printed on 3 × 5-inch cards and given to in-store customers to fill out. (*Hint:* The form must be aesthetically appealing to encourage R. George's upscale clientele to complete it.)

   b. Design and draw a representation of a display screen that captures in-store customer information from the cards in part a.

   c. Design and draw an on-screen tab control dialog box that can be used with the screen in part b, one that allows a comparison between in-store customer information and a listing of customers who hold R. George's credit cards.

   d. Design and draw a second on-screen tab control dialog box that compares in-store customers with mail-order customers.

8. Zero Corp. likes what you have achieved for it in forms control, but it would like to set up an in-house forms specialist to continue your work. Compose a concise job description for an in-house forms specialist that lists four of his or her most important job responsibilities. Remember to include Web-based forms as part of this employee's responsibilities.

FIGURE 16.EX2
Icons from Lotus Develop-
ment Corporation's Organizer.

9. Figure 16.EX2 depicts the icons from the Personal Information Manager (PIM) that we discussed in Chapter 3, called Organizer. See if you
can guess what each of the icons mean. Why do you think that good
icon design is important? Explain in a paragraph why you think (or do
not think) that these icons conform to the principles of good design.

10. Design a system of on-screen icons with readily recognizable shapes
that allows account executives in brokerage houses to determine at a
glance what actions (if any) need to be taken on a client's account.
(*Hint:* Use color coding as well as icons to facilitate quick identification
of extreme conditions.)

   a. Draw icons that correspond to:
      i. Transaction completed on the same day.
      ii. Account needs updating.
      iii. Client has requested information.
      iv. Account in error.
      v. Account inactive for two months.
      vi. Account closed.

   b. Recently, an up-and-coming discount brokerage house expressed an
   interest in developing its own portfolio management software that
   clients could use at home on their PCs to make trades, get real-time
   stock quotes, and so on. The software should be an improvement
   over the high-quality software competitors that are already offering
   it. Design two input screens that make data entry easy for the client.
   The first screen should allow users to enter stock symbols for the
   stocks they want to track on a daily basis. The second screen should
   allow the client to use an icon-based system to design a customized
   report showing stock price trends in a variety of graphs or text.

   c. Suggest two other input screens that should be included in this new
   portfolio management software.

11. My Belle Cosmetics is a large business that has sales well ahead of any
other regional cosmetics firm. As an organization, it is very sensitive to
color, since it introduces new color lines in its products every fall and
spring. The company has recently begun using technology to electroni-

cally show in-store customers how they appear in different shades of cosmetics without requiring them to actually apply the cosmetics. The company is also considering developing color display screens for its executive offices to aid in decision making.

    a. Design and draw a representation of a display screen that can be used by sales clerks at a counter to try many shades of lipstick and makeup on an individual customer very quickly and with a high degree of accuracy. Input from customers should be their hair color, the color of their favorite clothing, their typical environmental lighting (fluorescent, incandescent, outdoor, and so on).

    b. Design and draw a representation of a display screen which is equivalent to the one in part a but which vividly demonstrates to decision makers in My Belle how color improves the understandability of the screen.

12. The Home Finders Reality Corporation specializes in locating homes for prospective buyers. Home information is stored in a database and is to be displayed on an inquiry screen. Design a GUI interface, Web-based screen to enter the following data fields, which are used to select and display homes matching the criteria. Keep in mind the features that are available for a GUI screen. The screen elements (which are not in any particular sequence) are:

    a. Minimum size (in square feet).

    b. Maximum size (optional, in square feet).

    c. Minimum number of bedrooms.

    d. Minimum number of bathrooms.

    e. Garage size (optional, number of cars).

    f. School district (a limited number of school districts are available for each area).

    g. Swimming pool (yes/no, optional).

    h. Setting (either city, suburban, or rural).

    i. Fireplace (yes/no, optional).

    j. Energy efficient (yes/no).

    k. Describe the hyperlinks necessary to achieve this type of interaction.

13. Use index cards to design a tab control dialog box, one that changes the following database screen settings. Use one card for each tab. Be sure to group each tab by function.

    a. Change the background color.

    b. Change the font.

    c. Change the object border to a raised look.

    d. Set the foreground color.

    e. Change the object border to a sunken look.

    f. Set the border color.

    g. Change the font size.

    h. Set the text to bold.

    i. Change the object border to a flat look.

    j. Set the text to underline.

    k. Change the object background color.

14. Design an Internet home page for the Home Finders Reality Corporation screen created in problem 12.

GROUP PROJECTS

1. Maverick Transport is considering updating its mainframe screens. With your team, brainstorm about what should appear on input screens of mainframe terminal operators who are entering delivery load data as loads are approved. Fields will include date of delivery, contents, weight, special requirements (for example, whether contents are perishable), and so on.

2. Each team member should design an appropriate input screen using either a CASE tool or paper and pencil. Share your results with your team members.

3. Make a list of other input screens that Maverick Transport should develop. Remember to include dispatcher screens as well as screens to be accessed by customers and drivers. Indicate which should be microcomputer screens PIM displays on mainframe screens.

4. Design a Web-based screen that will allow Maverick Transport customers to track the progress of a shipment. Brainstorm with team members for a list of elements, or perform an interview with a local trucking company to find out its requirements. List what hyperlinks will be essential.

SELECTED BIBLIOGRAPHY

Dahlboom, B., and L. Mathiassen. *Computers in Context.* Cambridge, MA: NCC Blackwell, 1993.

Gibbs, M. "Forms Design and Control." In V. Lazarro (ed.), *Systems and Procedures: A Handbook for Business and Industry,* 2nd ed. Englewood Cliffs, NJ: Prentice Hall, 1968.

Ives, B. "Graphical User Interfaces for Business Information Systems." *Management Information Systems Quarterly* (Special Issue), December 1982, pp. 15–48.

Reisner, P. "Human Factors Studies of Data Base Query Languages: A Survey and Assessment." *Computing Surveys,* Vol. 4, No. 1, 1981.

FORMING SCREENS AND SCREENING FORMS

Pooling information from the output design and reviewing their progress, Chip and Anna proceeded to the next stage, the design of input. "Forms and screens must be designed to easily and accurately capture input information," remarks Anna.

Chip replies, "Special attention should be placed on creating input screens that are easy to use and require minimal operator entry."

Chip loads Visible Analyst and examines Diagram 0. "Perhaps the first form that we should create is the NEW MICROCOMPUTER RECORD, flowing from the SHIPPING/RECEIVING DEPARTMENT into process 2, ADD NEW MICROCOMPUTER." Chip double-clicks on the data flow representing the form to bring up its repository record. It's **Composition** area contains a data structure called NEW MICROCOMPUTER FORM RECORD. "I decided to create a separate structure for the form, since the elements are used both on the form and on the matching screen," muses Chip. He clicks in the area and presses the **Jump** button. The elements contained on the form are included in the structure's **Composition** area, illustrated in Figure E16.1. Notice that the **Notes** area contains information about which fields should be implemented as drop-down lists and check boxes.

Chip goes to work at designing the form. It is zoned to group logically related elements, which are arranged in a manner that would allow the user to easily complete the form. Since a prototype of the data-entry screen was previously approved, the task of designing the form is considerably simplified.

Label:	New Microcomputer Form Record	1 of 2
Entry Type:	Data Structure
Description:	Contains the elements required to add a new microcomputer.
Alias:	
Composition:	Hardware Inventory Number + Brand Name + Model + Serial Number +
Notes:	Monitor, Printer and Modem entry fields should be drop down lists. Zip Drive Connected, Tape Backup Unit, Network and Warranty should be check boxes. Boards should be selected from a drop down list, with multiple boards
Long Name:	

SQL Info | Delete | Next | Save | Search | Jump | File | << | >> | ?
History | Erase | Prior | Exit | Expand | Back | Qcomp | Search Criteria

FIGURE E16.1
NEW MICROCOMPUTER FORM RECORD data structure screen showing elements.

Allen Schmidt,
Julie E. Kendall, and
Kenneth E. Kendall

Add New Microcomputer Form

Complete for every microcomputer received. Inventory number is located on the tag supplied by Maintenance. Second Fixed Disk and Second Diskette Drive are optional entries. If the replacement cost is equal to the Purchase Cost, leave it blank.

Inventory Number		Serial Number

Brand Name

Model

Date Purchased (mm/dd/yyyy)	Purchase Cost

Memory (MB)	Replacement Cost

Drives

Hard Drive (MB)	Second Hard Drive		Diskette Size	Second Diskette Size
			☐ 3$\frac{1}{2}$ inch ☐ 5$\frac{1}{4}$ inch	☐ 3$\frac{1}{2}$ inch ☐ 5$\frac{1}{4}$ inch

Connections

CD Rom ☐ 2X ☐ 4X ☐ 8X ☐ 10X ☐ 12X ☐ 16X		☐ Zip Drive	☐ Tape Backup Unit
Internet ☐ Modem 28.8 ☐ 36.6 ☐ T1 ☐ Other		☐ Network	☐ Warranty

Peripherals

Monitor		Printer

Installed Boards

Form MS001-02 *Revised 7/97*

FIGURE E16.2
ADD NEW MICROCOMPUTER form.

Chip schedules a meeting with Dot to review the form. She looks thoughtfully at the document for a few minutes and remarks, "This looks very good. I can see you've considered our viewpoint when designing the form. The only change I would recommend is to separate the initial information we have when the microcomputer is received from the data that is supplied as we make decisions on which printer and monitor to attach."

Chip revises the form with the suggested changes and obtains final approval from Dot. The completed form is shown in Figure E16.2. Notice the

FIGURE E16.3
The ADD NEW MICROCOMPUTER Access screen.

zoning and the use of tick marks indicating the number of characters to be keyed. These help the user decide how to abbreviate data that would not fit within the file or database field length.

With the form complete, Chip starts working on modifying the screen used to enter the form data. The screen design matched the form, with fields on the screen in the same order and rough placement as on the form. The ADD NEW MICROCOMPUTER entry screen is shown in Figure E16.3.

One of the considerations of the entry screen is ease of entering data, and another is accuracy. Another consideration is the availability of help. New employees would not be familiar with the operation of the system or with what is required for a particular field entry. To achieve these goals, Chip included pull-down lists for the MONITOR, PRINTER, INTERNET CONNECTION, and MICROCOMPUTER BOARDS. "I like the way these pull-down lists work," he remarks to Anna. "The users can easily select the codes that should be stored in the database."

"Why have the users select codes," replies Anna. "There must be a way for them to select descriptive code meanings, such as the name of the printer, and have the computer store the codes."

"That's an excellent idea," exclaims Chip. A short time later, the modifications have been implemented.

Anna reviews the screen and remarks, "This looks terrific! I like the grouping of the check boxes and descriptive information contained in the drop-down lists."

"Watch this screen in action," replies Chip. "I've added a button for the users to press when they have entered all the data and made all the selections. They can also print the completed form."

"What about help?" asks Anna.

FIGURE E16.4
Pull-down lists on the ADD NEW MICROCOMPUTER Access screen.

"I've thought about that also," answers Chip. "As the cursor moves from field to field, the status line on the bottom of the screen displays one line of help appropriate for that field. I can also add tool-tip help, a small box of help options that appears when the mouse cursor remains over one entry area for a short amount of time." Notice that the pull-down lists have meaningful names in the data areas. There is room for three microcomputer boards in the BOARD CODE entry area. Scroll bars provide additional entry areas if needed. Help is displayed in the status line on the bottom of the screen. An example of selecting monitor types from a pull-down list is illustrated in Figure E16.4.

Dot reviews the completed screen and enters some test data. "I'm really impressed!" she exclaims. "This is much smoother than I ever expected. When can we expect the rest of the system?" Chip smiles with appreciation and remarks that great progress is being made. "I do hope that the rest of the system is as clear to use and easy to operate!" Dot says appreciatively.

Meanwhile Anna is meeting with Hy Perteks, who is desperately seeking help. "I'm swamped with requests for help on software packages! Is there any way to design a portion of the system for maintaining information on the available software experts?" asks Hy. "I have names written on scraps of paper and I keep misplacing them. Often I find out who these experts are only after someone else finds them first."

Anna asks some questions about what information would be required and how Hy would like to maintain and display the records. Hy replies, "There is so much expertise available, but the only way I have of locating the person's information is by using their name as an index. And I confess, I'm awful at remembering the correct spelling of the first name, let alone the last name." Anna assures him that there will be an easy-to-use system available soon.

FIGURE E16.5
The CHANGE SOFTWARE EXPERT Access screen

Back at her desk, Anna thinks about the problem. "The ADD screen would be easy to create, but what about the CHANGE screen?" She wonders, "How can I?" then thinks, "Ah ha!" and snaps her fingers. The design becomes clear. There would be a screen with two distinct regions on it. The first region would contain the last and first name of the Software Expert. Included with the screen is a **Find** button as well as buttons for scrolling back and forth through records. If the users made a mistake entering data, there is an **Undo** button, and there is also a button to save the changes. The completed screen is illustrated in Figure E16.5.

Anna tests the **Find** button. "Check this out," says Anna, glancing over at Chip. Clicking the **Find** button displays a **Find** dialog box. Anna selects **Any Part of Field** for a **Match** choice. She enters rock in the **Find What** area and clicks the **Find First** button. Refer to the screen shown in Figure E16.6.

"Great looking screen," grins Chip. "I want to be here when you show it to Hy."

The problem of deleting Software Course records for software that is no longer in use required a different approach. Anna reasoned that this would be easy if she used the **Find** feature to locate a record and then used a **Find Next** button to locate the next record that matched the criteria. There would also be buttons that allowed her to move to the next or previous records.

After the record is located, the DELETE SOFTWARE COURSE program would display pertinent information. All codes on the file, such as the COURSE LEVEL and OPERATING SYSTEM would be replaced with the full code meaning. None of the data would be able to be modified at this time. The operator would have the opportunity to review the record and then choose to either delete or not delete the record. When the delete button is

FIGURE E16.6
The CHANGE EXPERT Access screen, name selection.

pressed, a dialog box is displayed asking the users if they really want to delete the record. They may choose to cancel the delete at that time. The final screen is shown in Figure E16.7.

Hy is delighted with the prototype screens. As he tests each of them, he remarks, "You don't know how easy it's going to be for me to answer help requests. This is fabulous!" He pauses for a long moment and then asks, "I have a lot of requests about providing periodically scheduled training courses. Do you think that we could work on a system to register for courses?"

Anna purses her lips for a moment and remarks, "Did you ever hear of a project having scope creep—always adding little things and the project never ends!? However, the University does have an intranet initiative going, and it is looking for volunteers. Perhaps we can design a Web page for registering courses."

"That's great!" replies Hy. "More than I ever hoped for."

Anna starts to design the Web page, including the users' first and last names as well as their Internet addresses and office phones. Additional areas are used to enter the campus where they are located, the software they use, and their class level. Chip reviews the form and remarks, "Rather than have them enter the Campus and Software, why not have them select them from a pull-down list?"

"Good idea," replies Anna. "And I think that the level of training should be a radio button." The completed intranet Web page is illustrated in Figures E16.8 and E16.9. Notice that there are buttons to submit the query or reset it to spaces and pull-down list default values. There is also a link to e-mail questions to the Training Officer.

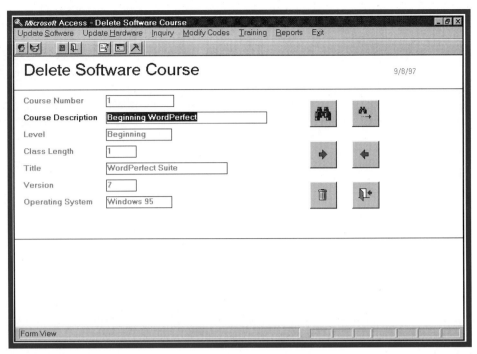

FIGURE E16.7
The DELETE SOFTWARE COURSE, Access screen.

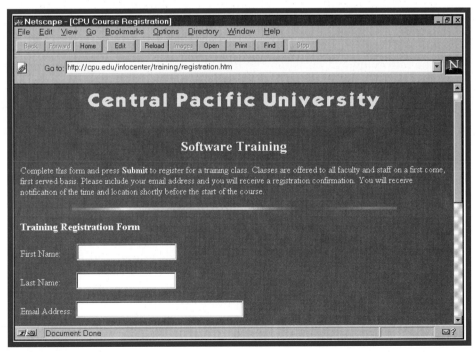

FIGURE E16.8
An intranet Web form for Training Registration.

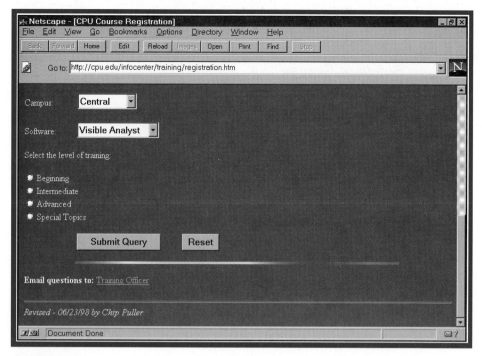

FIGURE E16.9
Drop-down lists and radio buttons on the Training Registration intranet form.

Hy is thrilled. "This is better than I ever imagined. I feel that we are really providing effective training registration, and I know that my phone will not be ringing as much. I've got another great idea. . . ."

The following exercises may be done by designing the report or screen using Printer or Screen layout forms, or they may be created using any word processor that you are familiar with. The fields and other related information for the reports are contained in Visible Analyst data flow repository entries. The names for the data flow are listed for each exercise.

Corresponding reports and screens (called forms in Access) have been created. All the information is present in the Access database; you only have to modify the existing reports and screens to produce the final versions. Modifications are made by clicking on the desired report or screen and then clicking the **Design** button. The following modifications may be made. The Page Header contains column headings. The Detail area contains the print fields for the report. Refer to Figure E15.7

Click in a field to select it. Click on several fields while holding the Shift key to select them.

Drag a selected field (or fields) to move them.

Click on one of the small boxes surrounding the field to change the field size.

Select several fields and click **Format** and either:

Align—to align all fields with the top, left, and so on, field.

Size—to make fields equal to the widest, tallest, and so on, field.

Horizontal Spacing—to make horizontal spacing equal, or to increase or decrease the spacing.

Vertical Spacing—to make vertical spacing equal, or to increase or decrease the spacing.

💾 **E-1.** Cher Ware has remarked several times that a good form would make the task of adding new software much easier. It would also provide permanent paper documentation for software additions.

Design a form to add software to the SOFTWARE MASTER file. Open Diagram 0 in Visible Analyst and double click on the SOFTWARE RECEIVED FORM data flow to view the Repository entry for the data flow. Click on the NEW SOFTWARE RECORD in the **Composition** area and press the **Jump** button to view the data structure containing the elements that are required on the form. **Jump** to each element to determine the length of the screen field. You may also use the **Repository Reports** and **Single Entry Listing** to print a list of elements for the form.

💾 **E-2.** Design the ADD SOFTWARE RECORD screen, either on paper or by modifying the Access screen. Use the fields created in Exercise E-1. The Visible Analyst data structure name is NEW SOFTWARE RECORD.

💾 **E-3.** Hy Perteks would like a form to fill out as he learns about new Software Experts. Use the Visible Analyst ADD SOFTWARE EXPERT Data Structure to determine the fields required for the form.

💾 **E-4.** Create the ADD SOFTWARE EXPERT screen, either on paper, using a word processor, or by modifying the Access form. Test the ADD SOFTWARE EXPERT screen, using the drop-down lists and observing the status bar on the bottom of the screen.

💾 **E-5.** Design or modify the Access form for the DELETE SOFTWARE EXPERT screen. Which fields are drop-down lists? Use the Visible Analyst DELETE SOFTWARE EXPERT data structure.

💾 **E-6.** Design or modify the Access form for the DELETE MICROCOMPUTER RECORD screen. The Visible Analyst structure is called DELETE MICROCOMPUTER RECORD.

💾 **E-7.** Cher Ware and Anna spent the better part of a morning working out the details on the software portion of the system. Plagued by the problem of providing consistent software upgrades for all machines, Cher would like an easy method of upgrading. A few older versions of software may also be retained for special needs.

Part of the solution is to produce a report, sorted by location, of all machines containing the software to be upgraded. As the new software is installed, a check mark is placed on the report after each machine.

Design the UPGRADE SOFTWARE screen design. Add a **Find** button to locate the title and to provide a field that can be used to enter the new VERSION NUMBER. The update program will display a line for each machine containing the old version of the installed software. These lines are sorted by CAMPUS LOCATION and ROOM LOCATION.

Columns are CAMPUS LOCATION, ROOM LOCATION, INVENTORY NUMBER, BRAND NAME, MODEL, UPGRADE, and RETAIN OLD VERSION. The UPGRADE column contains a check box that is to be checked if the software is to be upgraded. The RE-

---

* Exercises preceded by a disk icon require the program Visible Analyst Workbench or another CASE tool. A disk is provided free of charge to any professor adopting this book. The examples on the disk may be imported into Visible Analyst Workbench and then used by students.

TAIN OLD VERSION is also a check box, unchecked by default. The users would check the box for a specific machine that must retain the old and new versions of the software.

Look in the Visible Analyst SOFTWARE UPGRADE data structure for the elements contained on the screen.

E-8. Explain why the UPGRADE SOFTWARE screen would display machines rather than have Cher enter the machine IDs. In a paragraph, discuss why the screen displays records in a CAMPUS/ROOM sequence.

E-9. Design the CHANGE SOFTWARE screen. This screen allows Cher Ware to modify data that has been incorrectly entered, as well as information that routinely changes, such as SOFTWARE EXPERT and NUMBER OF COPIES. The SOFTWARE INVENTORY NUMBER is the primary key and may not be changed. The other SOFTWARE MASTER fields that should be included on the screen are found in the Visible Analyst SOFTWARE CHANGES data structure. Use these fields to design the screen. A limited screen, CHANGE SOFTWARE RECORD has been created in Access. Use the Access **Field List** to add fields to the screen. Include the following buttons: Find, Find Next, Previous Record, Next Record, Save Record and Cancel Changes.

E-10. Hy Perteks is concerned that old courses for obsolete versions of software are cluttering the disks. Create and print the Delete Software Course screen.

Entry fields are the SOFTWARE TITLE, OPERATING SYSTEM, and VERSION NUMBER. The program displays a line for each course taught for the software version. The first column contains an entry field with a D (for Delete) presented as a default. Placing a space in the field will prevent the record from being deleted. The other columns for each line are: COURSE TITLE, LEVEL, and CLASS LENGTH. Add a meaningful operator message.

E-11. Design the UPDATE MAINTENANCE INFORMATION screen. It contains entry fields that allow Mike Crowe to change maintenance information as computers are repaired or as routine maintenance is performed on them. The Visible Analyst data structure is UPDATE MAINTENANCE INFORMATION.

## 17

DESIGNING THE FILE OR DATABASE

DESIGN OBJECTIVES

Data storage is considered by some to be the heart of an information system. The general objectives in the design of data storage organization are shown in Figure 17.1.

First, the data has to be available when the user wants to use it. Second, the data must be accurate and consistent (it must possess integrity). Beyond this, the objectives of database design include efficient storage of data as well as efficient updating and retrieval. Finally, it is necessary that information retrieval be purposeful. The information obtained from the stored data must be in a form useful for managing, planning, controlling, or decision making.

CONVENTIONAL FILES AND DATABASES

There are two approaches to the storage of data in a computer-based system. The first method is to store the data in individual files, each unique to a particular application. Figure 17.2 illustrates an organization with a number of information systems using conventional, separate files: SALES-FILE, which contains historical sales information; CURRENT-ACTIVITY, which is updated often; and PERSONNEL-FILE, which contains addresses, titles, and so on.

Notice that the NUM and NAME exist in each file. Besides the extra effort needed to input the NAME three times, a name change (because of a change in marital status, for instance) would require updating three separate files.

The second approach to the storage of data in a computer-based system involves building a database. A database is a formally defined and centrally controlled store of data intended for use in many different applications. Figure 17.3 shows that different users in different departments within the orga-

FIGURE 17.1
Five objectives for the design
of data storage.

File Edit View Go Favorites Help

Design Objectives

- Purposeful Information Retrieval

- Efficient Data Storage

- Data Availability

- Efficient Updating and Retrieval

- Data Integrity

FIGURE 17.2
The use of separate files
means that the same data often are stored in more than
one place.

CURRENT-ACTIVITY

NUM	NAME	AREA	1997

SALES-FILE

NUM	NAME	1995	1996	1997

PERSONNEL-FILE

NUM	DEPT	NAME	ADDRESS	PHONE	HIRED	SALARY	TITLE

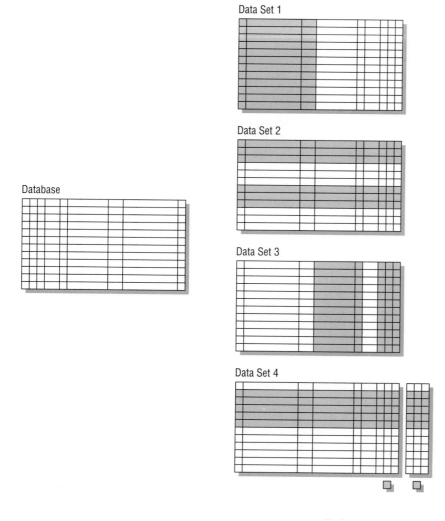

Data Set 1

Data Set 2

Database

Data Set 3

Data Set 4

FIGURE 17.3
The database approach allows
different users to share the
same database yet access
different data sets.

nization can share the same database. A user may select a portion of the database as shown in data set 1, or certain rows in data set 2. data set 3 contains selected columns, and data set 4 uses some rows to calculate totals. These data sets are overlapping, indicating that data that were redundant in conventional files are only stored once in the database.

Conventional Files

Conventional files will remain a practical way to store data for some (but not all) applications. A file can be designed and built quite rapidly, and any concerns about data availability and security are minimized. When file designs are carefully thought out, all the necessary information can be included, and the risk of unintentionally omitting data will be low. If the user is personally involved with organizing the file, there will be few problems with understanding how to access the data.

An analyst rarely encounters a situation in which there are no existing applications. Chances are that separate files are already in service. If development time is an important consideration, the systems analyst cannot take on the problem of redoing data storage in order to achieve a database approach. The obvious solution given time constraints is to limit the scope of the project by designing another, separate file for the new application.

Processing speed is another advantage of using files. It is possible to choose the optimal technique for the file processing of a single application, but it is impossible to come up with an optimal design for many different tasks. Consequently, if the systems analyst is faced with designing a system for one specific application when processing efficiency is of the utmost concern, the best approach may be to design an individual file for that purpose.

The use of individual files has many consequences. One major problem is the lack of potential for files to evolve. Files are often designed only with immediate needs in mind. When it becomes important to query the system for a combination of some of the attributes, these attributes may be contained in separate files or may not even exist. Redesigning files often implies that programs that access the files must be rewritten accordingly. This translates into expensive programmers time for file and program development and maintenance.

A system using conventional files implies that stored data will be redundant. Furthermore, updating files is more time-consuming. Data integrity is a concern, since a change in one file will also require modification of the same data in other files. Seldom-used files may be neglected when it is time for updating.

DATABASES

Databases are not merely a collection of files. Instead, a database is a central source of data meant to be shared by many users for a variety of applications. The heart of a database is the DBMS (database management system), which allows the creation, modification, and updating of the database; the retrieval of data; and the generation of reports. The person who ensures that the database meets its objectives is called the database administrator.

The effectiveness objectives of the database include:

1. Ensuring that data can be shared among users for a variety of applications.
2. Maintaining data that are both accurate and consistent.
3. Ensuring that all data required for current and future applications will be readily available.
4. Allowing the database to evolve and the needs of the users grow.
5. Allowing users to construct their personal view of the data without concern for the way the data are physically stored.

The foregoing list of objectives provides us with a reminder of the advantages and disadvantages of the database approach. First, the sharing of the data means that data need to be stored only once. This in turn helps achieve data integrity, since changes to data are accomplished more easily and reliably if the data appear once rather than in many different files.

When a user needs particular data, a well-designed database anticipates the need for such data (or perhaps it has already been used for another application). Consequently, the data have a better chance of being available in a database than in a conventional file system. A well-designed database can also be more flexible than separate files—that is, a database can evolve as the needs of users and applications change.

Finally, the database approach has the advantage of allowing users to have their own view of the data. Users need not be concerned with the actual structure of the database or its physical storage.

CONSULTING OPPORTUNITY 17.1

Hitch Your Cleaning Cart to a Star

The Marc Schnieder Janitorial Supply Company has asked for your assistance in cleaning up its data storage. As soon as you begin asking Marc Schnieder detailed questions about his database, his face gets flushed. "We don't really have a database as you describe it," he says with some embarrassment. "I've always wanted to clean up our records, but I couldn't find a capable person to head the effort."

After talking with Mr. Schnieder, you walk down the hall to the closet-sized office of Stan Lessink, the chief programmer. Stan fills you in on the historical development of the current information system. "The Marc Schnieder Janitorial Supply Company is a rags-to-riches story," Stan remarks. "Mr.Schnieder's first job was as a janitor in a bowling alley. He saved enough money to buy some products and started selling them to other alleys. Soon he decided to expand the janitorial supply business. He found out that as his business grew, he had more product lines and types of customers. Salespeople in the company are assigned to different major product lines (stores, offices, and so on); some are in-house sales; and some specialize in heavy equipment, such as floor strippers and waxers. Records were kept in separate files."

"The problem is that we have no way to compare the profits of each division. We would like to set up incentive programs for salespeople and provide better balance in allocating salespeople to each product line," states Mr. Schnieder.

When you talk with Stan, however, he adds, "Each division has its own incentive system. Commissions vary. I don't see how we can have a common system. Besides, I can get our reports out quickly because our files are set up the way we want them. We have never issued a paycheck late."

Describe how you would go about analyzing the data storage needs of the Marc Schnieder Janitorial Supply Company. Would you trash the old system or just polish it up a bit? Discuss the implications of your decision.

The first disadvantage of the database approach is that all of the data are stored in one place. Therefore, data are more vulnerable to catastrophes and require complete backup. There is a risk that the database administrator becomes the only one privileged or skilled enough to go near the data. The bureaucratic procedures required to modify or even update the database can seem insurmountable.

Other disadvantages come about when attempting to achieve two efficiency objectives for the management of the data resource:

1. Keeping the time required to insert, update, delete, and retrieve data to a tolerable amount.

2. Keeping the cost of storing the data to a reasonable amount.

Remember that a database cannot be optimized for retrieving data for a specific application, since it may be shared by many users for various applications. Furthermore, additional software for the DBMS is required, and occasionally a larger computer is required.

The database approach is a concept that is becoming increasingly important. The use of relational databases (covered later in this chapter) on networked PCs means that the concept is becoming understandable to many users. Many users are extracting parts of the central database from mainframes and downloading them onto personal computers. These smaller databases are then used to generate reports or answer queries specific to the end user.

Relational databases for PCs have improved dramatically over the last few years. The competition among database software vendors is keen, so that most standard PC databases are extremely flexible a feature which aids in

FIGURE 17.4
Reality, data, and metadata.

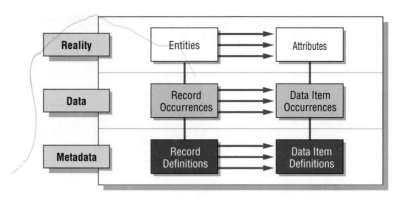

the design of reports and labels. They allow the end user to read in databases from other software programs. All have good query capability. Some are more user-friendly than others.

One major technological change has been the design of database software that takes advantage of the Graphical User Interface (GUI). With the advent of programs such as Microsoft Access, users can drag and drop fields between two or more tables. Developing relational databases with these tools has been made relatively easy.

DATA CONCEPTS

It is important to understand how data are represented before considering the use of files or the database approach. In this section critical definitions are covered, including the abstraction of data from the real world to the storage of data in files.

Reality, Data, and Metadata

The real world itself will be referred to as reality. Data collected about people, places, or events in reality will eventually be stored in the file or database. In order to understand the form and structure of the data, information about the data itself is required. The information that describes data is referred to as metadata.

The relationship between reality, data, and metadata is pictured in Figure 17.4. Within the realm of reality, there are entities and attributes; within the realm of actual data, there are record occurrences and data item occurrences; within the realm of metadata, there are record definitions and data item definitions. The meanings of these terms are discussed in the following subsections.

ENTITIES. Any object or event about which someone chooses to collect data is an entity. An entity may be a person, place, or thing—for example, a salesperson, a city, or a product. Any entity can also be an event or unit of time such as a machine breakdown, a sale, or a month or year.

RELATIONSHIPS. Relationships are associations between entities (sometimes they are referred to as data associations). Figure 17.5 is an entity-relationship (E-R) diagram that shows various types of relationships.

The first type of relationship is a one-to-one relationship (designated as 1:1). The diagram shows that there is only one PRODUCT PACKAGE for

Examples of E-R Diagrams   **Relationships**

Product —— has —— Product Package

Employee —— is assigned to —— Office

One-to-one (1:1)

Physician —— treats —— Patient

Employee —— belongs to —— Department

One-to-many (1:M) or Many-to-one (M:1)

Student —— takes —— Courses

Salesperson —— serves —— City

Many-to-many (M:N)

FIGURE 17.5
Entity-relationship diagrams can show one-to-one, one-to-many, many-to-one, or many-to-many associations.

Symbol	Official explanation	What it really means
	Entity	(a class of persons, places, or things)
	Associative entity	(used to join two entities)
	Attributive entity	(used for repeating groups)
	To 1 relationship	(exactly one)
	To many relationship	(one or more)
	To 0 or 1 relationship	(only zero or one)
	To 0 or more relationship	(can be zero, one, or more)
	To more than 1 relationship	(greater than one)

FIGURE 17.6
The entity-relationship symbols and their meaning.

each PRODUCT. The second one-to-one relationship shows that each EM-PLOYEE has a unique OFFICE. Notice that all of these entities can be described further (a PRODUCT PRICE would not be an entity, nor would a phone extension).

Another type of relationship is a one-to-many (1:M) or a many-to-one association. As shown in the figure, a PHYSICIAN in a health-maintenance organization is assigned many PATIENTS, but a PATIENT is assigned only one PHYSICIAN. Another example shows that an EMPLOYEE is a member of only one DEPARTMENT, but each DEPARTMENT has many EMPLOYEE(s).

Finally, a many-to-many relationship (designated as M:N) describes the possibility that entities may have many associations in either direction. For example, a STUDENT can have many COURSES, while at the same time a COURSE may have many STUDENT(s) enrolled in it. The second example shows that a SALESPERSON can call on many cities, and a CITY can be a sales area for many SALESPERSON(s).

The standard symbols for Crow's Foot notation, the official explanation of the symbols, and what they actually mean are all given in Figure 17.6. Notice that the symbol for an entity is a rectangle. An entity is defined as a class

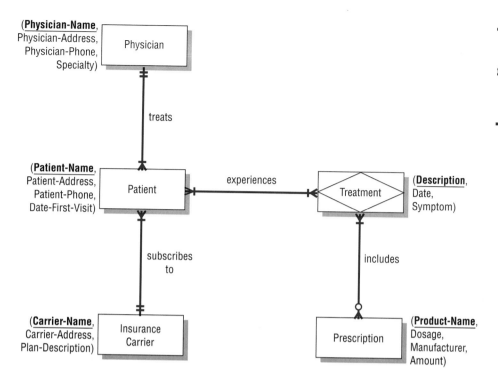

(**Physician-Name**,
Physician-Address,
Physician-Phone,
Specialty)

Physician

treats

(**Patient-Name**,
Patient-Address,
Patient-Phone,
Date-First-Visit)

Patient

experiences

Treatment

(**Description**,
Date,
Symptom)

subscribes
to

includes

(**Carrier-Name**,
Carrier-Address,
Plan-Description)

Insurance
Carrier

Prescription

(**Product-Name**,
Dosage,
Manufacturer,
Amount)

FIGURE 17.7
The entity-relationship diagram for patient treatment. Attributes can be listed alongside the entities. In each case,
the key is underlined.

of a person, place, or thing. The rectangle with the diamond inside stands for
an associative entity, which is used to join two entities. A rectangle with an
oval in it stands for an attributive entity, which is used for repeating groups.

The other notations necessary to draw E-R diagrams are the connections, of which there are five different types. In the lower portion of this preceding figure, the meaning of the notation is explained. When a straight line
connects two plain entities and the end of the lines are marked with two
short marks (||), a one-to-one relationship exists. Following that you will
notice a crow's foot with a short mark (|); when this notation links entities,
it indicates a relationship of one-to-one or one-to-many (to one or more). En-
tities linked with a straight line plus a short line (|) and a zero (but which
looks more like a circle or ○) are depicting a relationship of one-to-zero or
one-to-one (only zero or one). A fourth type of link for relating entities is
drawn with a straight line marked on the end with a zero (○) followed by a
crow's foot. This shows a zero-to-zero, zero-to-one, or zero-to-more relationship. Finally, a straight line with a crow's foot at the end linking entities depicts a relationship to more than (greater than) one.

The relationships in words can be written along the top or the side of
each connecting line. In practice, you see the relationship in one direction,
although you can write relationships on both sides of the line, each representing the point of view of the entity. (See Chapter 2 for more details about
drawing E-R diagrams.)

AN ENTITY-RELATIONSHIP EXAMPLE. An entity-relationship diagram containing many entities, many different types of relations, and numerous attributes is featured in Figure 17.7. In this E-R diagram we are concerned
about a billing system, and in particular with the prescription part of the system. (For simplicity, we will assume office visits are handled differently and
are outside the scope of this system.)

The entities are therefore PRESCRIPTIONS, PHYSICIANS, PATIENTS, and the INSURANCE CARRIER. The entity TREATMENTS is not important for the billing system, but it is part of the E-R diagram because it is used to bridge the gap between PRESCRIPTION and PATIENT. We therefore drew it as an associative entity in the figure.

Here, a PHYSICIAN treats many PATIENT(s) (1:M), who each subscribe to an individual INSURANCE CARRIER. Of course, the PATIENT is only one of many patients that subscribe to that particular INSURANCE CARRIER (M:1).

To complete the PHYSICIAN's records, the physician needs to keep information about the treatments a PATIENT has. Many PATIENT(s) experience many TREATMENT(s), making this a many-to-many (M:N) relationship. TREATMENT is represented as an associative entity because it is not important in our billing system by itself. TREATMENT(s) can include the taking of PRESCRIPTION(s), and likewise this is a M:N relationship because many treatments may call for combinations of pharmaceuticals, and many drugs may work for many treatments.

Some detail is then filled in for the attributes. The attributes are listed next to each of the entities, and the key is underlined. For example, the entity PRESCRIPTION has a PRODUCT-NAME, DOSAGE, MANUFACTURER, and AMOUNT. Ideally, it would be beneficial to design a database in this fashion, using entity-relationship diagrams and then filling in the details concerning attributes. This is a desirable, top-down approach, but it is sometimes very difficult to achieve.

ATTRIBUTES. An attribute is some characteristic of an entity. There can be many attributes for each entity. For example, a patient (entity) can have many attributes, such as last name, first name, street address, city, state, and so on. The date of the patient's last visit, as well as the prescription details, are also attributes. When the data dictionary was constructed in Chapter 10, the smallest particular described was called a data element. When files and databases are discussed, these data elements are generally referred to as data items. Data items are in fact the smallest units in a file or database. The words *data item* are also used interchangeably with the word attribute.

Data items can have values. These values can be of fixed or variable length; they can be alphabetic, numeric, special characters, or alphanumeric. Examples of data items and their values can be found in Figure 17.8.

Sometimes a data item is also referred to as a field. A field, however represents something physical, not logical. Therefore, many data items can be packed into a field; the field can be read and converted to a number of data items. A common example of this is to store the date in a single field as MM/DD/YYYY. In order to sort the file in order by date, three separate data items are extracted from the field and sorted first by YYYY, then by MM, and finally by DD.

RECORDS. A record is a collection of data items that have something in common with the entity described. Figure 17.9 is an illustration of a record with many related data items. The record shown is for an order placed with a mail-order company. The ORDER-#, LAST NAME, INITIAL, STREET ADDRESS, CITY, STATE, and CREDIT CARD are all attributes. Most records are of fixed length, so there is no need to determine the length of the record each time.

Entity	Data Item	Value
Salesperson	Salesperson Number Salesperson Name Company Name Address Sales	87254 Kaytell Music Unlimited 45 Arpeum Circle $20,765
Package	Width Height Length Weight Mailing Address Return Address	2 16 16 3 765 Dulcinea Drive P.O. Box 341 Spring Valley, MN
Order	Product(s) Description(s) Quantity Ordered Last Name of Person Who Placed the Order First Initial Street Address City State Zip Code Credit Card Number Date Order Was Placed Amount Status	B521 "My Fair Lady" compact disc 1 Kiley R. 765 Dulcinea Drive La Mancha CA 93407 65-8798-87 05/01/1997 $6.99 Backordered

FIGURE 17.8
Typical values assigned to data items may be numbers, alphabetic characters, special characters, and combinations of all three.

Under certain circumstances (for instance, when space is at a premium), variable-length records are used. A variable-length record is used as an alternative to reserving a large amount of space for the longest possible record—for example, the maximum number of visits a patient has made to a physician. Each visit would contain many data items that would be part of the patient's full record (or file folder in a manual system). Later in this chapter, normalization of a relation is discussed. Normalization is a process that eliminates repeating groups found in variable-length records.

KEYS. A key is one of the data items in a record that is used to identify a record. When a key uniquely identifies a record, it is called a primary key. For example, <u>ORDER-#</u> can be a primary key because only one number is as-

FIGURE 17.9
A record has a primary key and may have many attributes.

Data Item	Value	
Salesperson Number	N	5
Salesperson Name	A	20
Company Name	A	26
Address	A	36
Sales	N	9.2
Width	N	2
Height	N	2
Length	N	2
Weight	N	2
Mailing Address	A	36
Return Address	A	36
Product(s)	A	4
Description(s)	A	30
Quantity Ordered	N	2
Last Name of Person Who Placed the Order	A	24
First Initial	A	1
Street Address	A	28
City	A	12
State	A	2
Zip Code	N	9
Credit Card Number	N	10
Date Order Was Placed	D	8 MM/DD/YYYY
Amount	$	7.2
Status	A	22

Fields
N Numeric
A Alphanumeric or text
D Date MM/DD/YYYY
$ Currency
M Memo

Special formats for fields may be specified.

7.2 means that the field takes up 7 digits, two of which are right of the decimal.

signed to each customer order. In this way, the primary key identifies the real-world entity (customer order).

A key is called a secondary key if it cannot uniquely identify a record. Secondary keys can be used to select a group of records that belong to a set (for example, orders that come from the state of Virginia).

When it is not possible to identify a record uniquely by using one of the data items found in a record, a key can be constructed by choosing two or more data items and combining them. This is called a concatenated key. When a data item is used as a key in a record, the description is underlined. Therefore, in the ORDER RECORD (ORDER-#, LAST NAME, INITIAL, STREET ADDRESS, CITY, STATE, CREDIT CARD) the key is ORDER-#. If an attribute is a key in another file, it should be underlined with a dashed line.

METADATA. Metadata is data about the data in the file or database. Metadata describes the name given and the length assigned each data item. Metadata also describes the length and composition of each of the records.

Figure 17.10 is an example of metadata for a database for some generic software. The length of each data item is indicated according to a convention whereby 5.2 means that 5 spaces are reserved for the number, two of which are to the right of the decimal point. The letter N signifies "numeric," and the A stands for "alphanumeric." The D stands for "date" and is automatically in the form MM/DD/YYYY. Some programs, such as Microsoft Access use plain English for metadata, so words such as "text," "currency," and "number" are used. Access provides a default of 50 characters as the field length for names, which is fine when working with small systems. However, if you are working with a large database for a bank or a utility company, for example, you do not want to devote that much space to that field. Otherwise, the database would become quite large and filled with wasted space. That is when you can use metadata to plan ahead and design a more efficient database.

File Organization

A file contains groups of records used to provide information for operations, planning, management, and decision making. The types of files used are discussed first, followed by a description of the many ways conventional files can be organized.

FILE TYPES. Files can be used for storing data for an indefinite period of time, or they can be used to store data temporarily for a specific purpose. Master files and table files are used to store data for a long period. The temporary files are usually called transaction files, work files, or report files.

Master files. Master files contain records for a group of entities. The attributes may be updated often, but the records themselves are relatively permanent. These files tend to have large records containing all the information about a data entity. Each record usually contains a primary key and several secondary keys. Often, master files are stored as indexed or indexed-sequential files. While the analyst is free to arrange the data elements within a master file in any order, a standard arrangement is usually to place the primary key field first, followed by descriptive elements and, finally, by elements that reflect the business and change frequently with business activities. This procedure allows analysts or other operational people to identify records easily when a file is listed with a print utility.

Descriptive information is data that does not change with business events, such as an item description, customer name, address, or employee department. These elements are usually changed by maintenance programs using direct access methods. Generally, these elements contain alternate keys or indexes, and the data are in display format.

Business information elements are those that periodically change with business events, such as year-to-year gross pay, grade point average, customer account balance, and the customer date-of-last-purchase. These elements are changed by update programs, which usually read both files and sequentially match records for efficiency. The record elements are modified only when the data is in error by correcting programs using random update methods. Often the dollar amount fields are in a compressed data format called packed decimal to save room on files and to speed up program execution time.

If the master file is stored using conventional file methods, an expansion area is reserved at the end of each record. This provides room for adding new fields to the record as business needs change. If the file is part of a database structure, expansion area is not required. Examples of a master file include patient records, customer records, a personnel file, or a parts inventory file.

Table files. A table file contains data used to calculate more data or performance measures. One example is a table of postage rates which is used to determine the shipping costs of a package. Another example is a tax table. Table files usually are read only by a program.

Transaction files. A transaction file is used to enter changes that update the master file and produce reports. Suppose a newspaper subscriber master file needs to be updated; the transaction file would contain the subscriber number, a transaction code such as E for extending the subscription, C for canceling the subscription, or A for address change. Then only information relevant to the updating needs to be entered—that is, the length of renewal if E, and the address if A. No additional information would be needed if the subscription was canceled. The rest of the information already exists in the master file. As a result, transaction files are usually kept to a minimum length. Transaction files may contain several different types of records, such as the three used for updating the newspaper subscription master, with a code on the transaction file indicating the type of transaction.

Work files. A program can sometimes run more efficiently if a work file is used. A common example of a work file is a file that is resorted so that records may be accessed more quickly.

Report files. When it is necessary to run a program but when no printer is available (or a printer is busy printing other jobs), a report file is used. Sending the output to a file rather than a printer is called spooling. Later, when the device is ready, the document can be printed. Report files are very useful, because users can take files to other computer systems and output to specialty devices such as plotters, laser printers, microfiche units, and even computerized typesetting machines.

SEQUENTIAL ORGANIZATION. When records are physically in order in a file, the file is said to be a sequential file. When a sequential file is updated, it is necessary to go through the entire file. Since records cannot be inserted in the middle of the file, a sequential file is usually copied over during the updating process.

Figure 17.11 illustrates a file of current orders for a mail-order company that sells compact discs. The file contains twelve records and is stored sequentially according to the ORDER-#. If we want to look up order 13432, we would start at the beginning and read through the file until we arrived at order 13432.

Sequential master files are used when the hardware requires it (remember that a magnetic tape is a sequential device) or when the normal access requires that most of the records be accessed. In other words, when we need to read or update only a few records, it is inefficient to use a sequential structure, but when many records need to be read or modified, sequential organization would make sense. Sequential organization is normally used for all types of files except master files.

LINKED LISTS. When files are stored on direct-access devices such as a disk, the options are expanded. Records can be sorted logically, rather than physically, using linked lists. Linked lists are achieved by using a set of pointers to direct you to the next logical record located anywhere in the file.

	ORDER-#	LAST NAME	I	STREET-ADDRESS	CITY	ST	CREDIT-CARD
1	10784	MacRae	G	2314 Curly Circle	Lincoln	NE	45-4654-76
2	10796	Jones	S	34 Dream Lane	Oklahoma City	OK	45-9876-74
3	11821	Preston	R	1008 Madison Ave.	River City	IA	34-7642-64
4	11845	Channing	C	454 Harmonia St.	New York	NY	34-0876-87
5	11872	Kiley	R	765 Dulcinea Drive	La Mancha	CA	65-8798-87
6	11976	Verdon	G	7564 K Street	Chicago	IL	67-8453-18
7	11998	Rivera	C	4342 West Street	Chicago	IL	12-2312-54
8	12765	Orbach	J	1345 Michigan Ave.	Chicago	IL	23-4545-65
9	12769	Steele	T	3498 Burton Lane	Finnian	NJ	65-7687-09
10	12965	Crawford	M	1986 Barnum Cir.	London	NH	23-0098-23
11	13432	Cullum	J	354 River Road	Shenandoah	VT	45-8734-33
12	13542	Mostel	Z	65 Fiddler Street	Anatevka	ND	34-6723-98

FIGURE 17.11
A sequential file sorted by ORDER-#.

Figure 17.12 shows the compact disc ordering file with an additional attribute used to store the pointer. Since the file is already stored in sequential order according to ORDER-#, the pointer is used to point to records in logical (alphabetical) order by LAST NAME. This example shows an obvious advantage of using linked lists: Files can be sorted logically in many different ways by using a variety of pointers.

HASHED FILE ORGANIZATION. Direct-access devices also permit access to a given record by going directly to its address. Since it is not feasible to reserve a physical address for each possible record, a method called hashing is used. Hashing is the process of calculating an address from the record key.

Suppose that there were 500 employees in an organization and we wanted to use the social security number as a key. It would be inefficient to reserve 999,999,999 addresses, one for each social security number. Therefore, we could take the social security number and use it to derive the address of the record.

There are many hashing techniques. A common one is to divide the original number by a prime number that approximates the storage locations and then to use the remainder as the address, as follows: Begin with the so-

ORDER FILE   START = 4

	ORDER-#	LAST NAME	I	STREET-ADDRESS	CITY	ST	CREDIT-CARD	POINTER
1	10784	MacRae	G	2314 Curly Circle	Lincoln	NE	45-4654-76	6
2	10796	Jones	S	34 Dream Lane	Oklahoma City	OK	45-9876-74	4
3	11821	Preston	R	1008 Madison Ave.	River City	IA	34-7642-64	9
4	11845	Channing	C	454 Harmonia St.	New York	NY	34-0876-87	1
5	11872	Kiley	R	765 Dulcinea Drive	La Mancha	CA	65-8798-87	5
6	11976	Verdon	G	7564 K Street	Chicago	IL	67-8453-18	END
7	11998	Rivera	C	4342 West Street	Chicago	IL	12-2312-54	10
8	12765	Orbach	J	1345 Michigan Ave.	Chicago	IL	23-4545-65	8
9	12769	Steele	T	3498 Burton Lane	Finnian	NJ	65-7687-09	11
10	12965	Crawford	M	1986 Barnum Cir.	London	NH	23-0098-23	2
11	13432	Cullum	J	354 River Road	Shenandoah	VT	45-8734-33	3
12	13542	Mostel	Z	65 Fiddler Street	Anatevka	ND	34-6723-98	7

FIGURE 17.12
A linked list uses pointers to designate the logical order of the records.

FIGURE 17.13
Inverted lists can have
many indices.

LAST-NAME INDEX

Channing	4
Crawford	10
Cullum	11
Jones	2
Kiley	5
MacRae	1
Mostel	12
Orbach	8
Preston	3
Rivera	7
Steele	9
Verdon	6

CITY INDEX

Anatevka			12
Chicago	6	7	8
Finnian			9
La Mancha			5
Lincoln			1
London			10
New York			4
Oklahoma City			2
River City			3
Shenandoah			11

CREDIT-CARD INDEX

12-2312-54	7
23-0098-23	10
23-4545-65	8
34-0876-87	4
34-6723-98	12
34-7642-64	3
45-4654-76	1
45-8734-33	11
45-9876-74	2
65-7687-09	9
65-8798-87	5
67-8453-18	6

STATUS INDEX

Backordered	5	8	9	12
In Process	3	4	10	11
Shipped 5/12	1	6	7	
Shipped 5/14	2			

ORDER FILE

	ORDER-#	LAST NAME	I	STREET-ADDRESS	CITY	ST	CREDIT-CARD	STATUS
1	10784	MacRae	G	2314 Curly Circle	Lincoln	NE	45-4654-76	Shipped 5/12
2	10796	Jones	S	34 Dream Lane	Oklahoma City	OK	45-9876-74	Shipped 5/14
3	11821	Preston	R	1008 Madison Ave.	River City	IA	34-7642-64	In process
4	11845	Channing	C	454 Harmonia St.	New York	NY	34-0876-87	In process
5	11872	Kiley	R	765 Dulcinea Drive	La Mancha	CA	65-8798-87	Backordered
6	11976	Verdon	G	7564 K Street	Chicago	IL	67-8453-18	Shipped 5/12
7	11998	Rivera	C	4342 West Street	Chicago	IL	12-2312-54	Shipped 5/12
8	12765	Orbach	J	1345 Michigan Ave.	Chicago	IL	23-4545-65	Backordered
9	12769	Steele	T	3498 Burton Lane	Finnian	NJ	65-7687-09	Backordered
10	12965	Crawford	M	1986 Barnum Cir.	London	NH	23-0098-23	In process
11	13432	Cullum	J	354 River Road	Shenandoah	VT	45-8734-33	In process
12	13542	Mostel	Z	65 Fiddler Street	Anatevka	ND	34-6723-98	Backordered

cial security number 053-46-8942. Then divide by 509, yielding 105047. Note that 105047 multiplied by 509 does not equal the original number; it equals 53468923 instead. The difference between the original number, 53468942, and the dividend, 53468923, is the remainder, and it equals 19. The storage location of the record for an employee whose social security number is 053-46-8942 would thus be 19.

A problem arises, however, when a person with a different social security number (say, 472-38-4086) has the same remainder. When this occurs, the second person's record has to be placed in a special overflow area.

INDEXED ORGANIZATION. An index is different from a pointer, since it is stored in a file that is separate from the data file. Figure 17.13 shows that four separate index files are generated on the ORDER FILE for compact discs.

The numerous index files have practical applications. If we want to list the details of the order placed by "Cullum," we can look up "Cullum" in the

LAST-NAME INDEX file and go directly to record 11. The CITY INDEX could be used for a mailing list; the STATUS INDEX could be used to write notices to people with backordered items; and so on.

When the number of index files increases, it is possible to use index files for storing much of the data. The amount of information in the index files can be quite large. In this case, the structure is referred to as an inverted list.

Inverted lists are most appropriate when used to find information on a specific combination of keys. For example, a query such as "Who in Chicago still has an item that is backordered?" could be answered efficiently. Inverted lists, however, are difficult to maintain. Hence, inverted lists are more appropriate for a file that is rarely updated.

INDEXED-SEQUENTIAL ORGANIZATION. A widely used method of file organization is called indexed-sequential organization, or ISAM (for indexed-sequential access method). In an ISAM file, the records are arranged in blocks. The records within blocks are stored in order physically, but the blocks of records may be in any order. Therefore, an index is needed to locate the blocks of records.

A newer organizational format used for mainframe computers is the VSAM (virtual storage access method), a more modern and efficient method for handling indexed-sequential files. Indexed-sequential files allow programs to read records directly (that is, randomly) without reading other records in the file. Records written using an indexed-sequential method are placed in sequence within the file. When organized in this way, records may be deleted or rewritten without reading other records as well. When a record is rewritten, it is physically placed on the disk in the same location from which the original record was obtained.

Database Organization

LOGICAL AND PHYSICAL VIEWS OF DATA. A database, unlike a file, is intended to be shared by many users. It is clear that the users all see the data in different ways. We refer to the way a user pictures and describes the data as a user view. However, the problem is that different users have different user views. These views are examined by the systems analyst, and an overall logical model of the database needs to be developed. Finally, the logical model of the database must be transformed into a corresponding physical database design. Physical design is involved with how data are stored and related, as well as how they are accessed.

In database literature, the views are referred to as *schema*. Figure 17.14 shows how the user reports and user views (user schema) are related to the logical model (conceptual schema) and physical design (internal schema).

There are three main types of logically structured databases: hierarchical, network, and relational.

Hierarchical data structures. Hierarchical data structures imply that an entity can have no more than one owning entity. Therefore, it is a structure made up of many one-to-many or one-to-one associations. Other associations such as many-to-one or many-to-many are not allowed.

Hierarchical structures are sometimes called trees because the subordinates connected to the owning entities resemble the branches of a tree, but they are usually drawn upside down as shown in Figure 17.15.

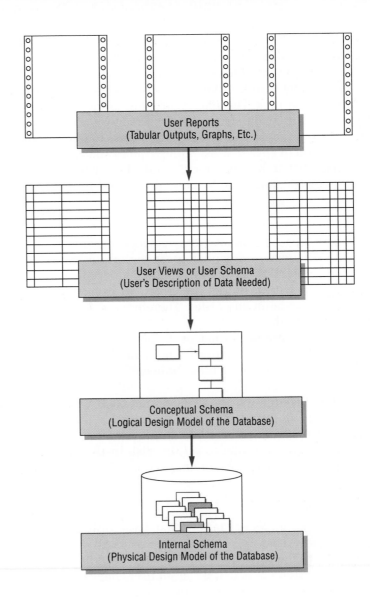

FIGURE 17.14
Database design includes synthesizing user reports, user views, and logical and physical designs.

User Reports
(Tabular Outputs, Graphs, Etc.)

User Views or User Schema
(User's Description of Data Needed)

Conceptual Schema
(Logical Design Model of the Database)

Internal Schema
(Physical Design Model of the Database)

FIGURE 17.15
Retrieving data in a hierarchical data structure is accomplished by following the branches.

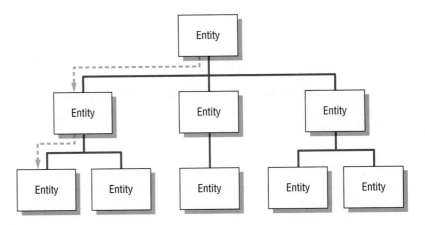

Entity

Entity

Entity

Entity

Entity

Entity

Entity

Entity

Entity

Entity

ITEM

B235	Guys and Dolls		8.99				

CUSTOMER

10784	MacRae	G	2314 Curly Circle	Lincoln	NE	45-4654-76	Shipped 5/12
10796	Jones	S	34 Dream Lane	Oklahoma City	OK	45-9876-74	Shipped 5/4
11872	Kiley	R	765 Dulcinea Drive	La Mancha	CA	65-8798-87	In process

B521	My Fair Lady		6.99				

11821	Preston	R	1008 Madison Ave.	River City	IA	34-7642-64	In process

B894	42nd Street		10.99				

11845	Channing	C	454 Harmonia St.	New York	NY	34-0876-87	Backordered
11872	Kiley	R	765 Dulcinea Drive	La Mancha	CA	65-8798-87	Shipped 5/12

B992	A Chorus Line		10.99				

10784	MacRae	G	2314 Curly Circle	Lincoln	NE	45-4654-76	Shipped 5/12

FIGURE 17.16
In a hierarchical data structure, the CUSTOMERs are represented as the subordinates to the ITEM.

Sometimes it is very easy to retrieve information from a hierarchical database. As an example, consider the hierarchical structure in Figure 17.16. In this example, each compact disc (ITEM) has one or more subordinates (CUSTOMERS). If we wanted to see who ordered the CD "42nd Street," we would go to the owning entity B894 only and look at each subordinate (in this case, 11845 and 11872) to find the names "Channing" and "Kiley."

Sometimes, however, operations may become difficult. For example, if we found an error in the credit-card number of "G. MacRae," we would have to search through each owning entity to ensure that we find every occurrence of "G. MacRae." Notice also that we cannot add a new customer until a specific item is chosen. This is one of the disadvantages of the hierarchical structure.

Network data structures. A network structure allows any entity to have any number of subordinates or superiors. A network structure is shown in Figure 17.17. Entities are connected using network links, which are data items common to both of the connected entities. Some of the problems inherent in hierarchical structures can be alleviated using the network structure, but the network structure is more complex.

An example of the compact disc ordering database using a network structure is shown in Figure 17.18. The entities (ITEM-DESCRIPTION and ORDER-DETAILS) are connected by network links (STATUS-LINK). Updating a record (such as correcting a person's credit-card number) is easier than in the hierarchical structure, because the order record (10784 for "MacRae") appears only once. It is also possible to insert records for customers who have not yet placed orders (for instance, if they wish to be on a catalog mailing list). The appropriate ITEM-DESCRIPTION can be added at a later date, when the order is placed.

FIGURE 17.17
Network structures allow the
entity to have any number of
subordinates or superiors, and
entities are connected by common links.

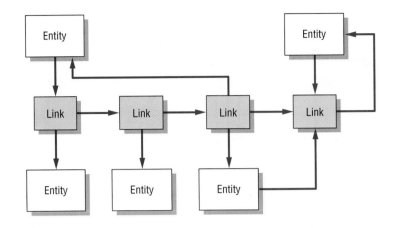

Relational data structures. A relational structure consists of one or more two-dimensional tables, which are referred to as relations. The rows of the table represent the records, and the columns contain attributes.

The compact disc ordering database is depicted as a relational structure in Figure 17.19. Here, three tables are needed to (1) describe the items and keep track of the current price of compact discs (ITEM-PRICE), (2) describe the details of the order (ORDER), and (3) identify the status of the order (ITEM-STATUS).

FIGURE 17.18
The STATUS-LINK is used in this example to link the ITEM-DESCRIPTION to the ORDER-DETAILS in this network data structure.

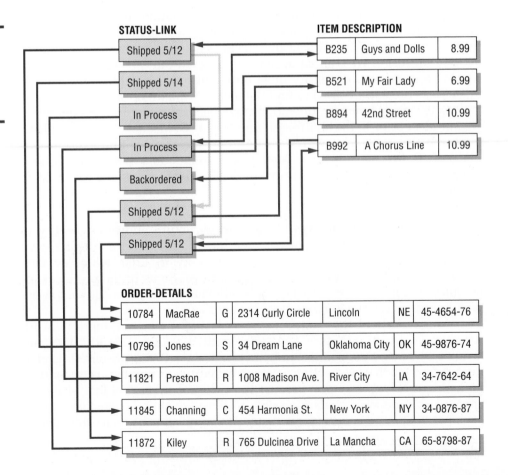

ITEM-PRICE

ITEM-#	TITLE	PRICE
B235	Guys and Dolls	8.99
B521	My Fair Lady	6.99
B894	42nd Street	10.99
B992	A Chorus Line	10.99

FIGURE 17.19
In a relational data structure,
data are stored in many tables.

ORDER

ORDER-#	LAST NAME	I	STREET-ADDRESS	CITY	ST	CHARGE-ACCT
10784	MacRae	G	2314 Curly Circle	Lincoln	NE	45-4654-76
10796	Jones	S	34 Dream Lane	Oklahoma City	OK	44-9876-74
11821	Preston	R	1008 Madison Ave.	River City	IA	34-7642-64
11845	Channing	C	454 Harmonia St.	New York	NY	34-0876-87
11872	Kiley	R	765 Dulcinea Drive	La Mancha	CA	65-8798-87

ITEM-PRICE

ITEM-#	ORDER-#	STATUS
B235	10784	Shipped 5/12
B235	19796	Shipped 5/14
B235	11872	In Process
B521	11821	In Process
B894	11845	Backordered
B894	11872	Shipped 5/12
B992	10784	Shipped 5/12

To determine the price of an item, we need to know the item number to be able to find it in the relation ITEM-PRICE. To update "G. MacRae's" credit-card number, we can search the ORDER relation for MacRae and correct it only once, even though he ordered many compact discs. To find out the status of part of an order, however, we must know the ITEM-# and ORDER-#, and then we must locate that information in the relation ITEM-STATUS.

Maintaining the tables in a relational structure is usually quite simple when compared to maintaining a hierarchical or network structure. One of the primary advantages of relational structures is that ad-hoc queries are efficiently handled.

When relational structures are discussed in the database literature, different terminology is often used. A file is called a relation, a record is usually referred to as a tuple, and the attribute value set is called a domain.

In order for relational structures to be useful and manageable, the relational tables must first be "normalized." Normalization is detailed in the following section.

NORMALIZATION

Normalization is the transformation of complex user views and data stores to a set of smaller, stable data structures. In addition to being simpler and more stable, normalized data structures are more easily maintained.

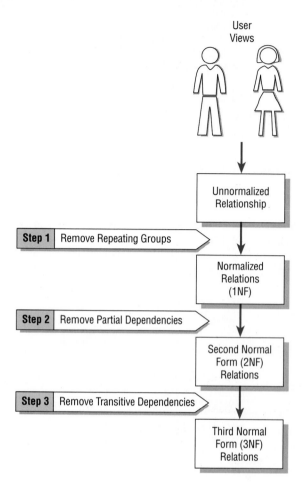

FIGURE 17.20
Normalization of a relation
is accomplished in three
major steps.

User
Views

Unnormalized
Relationship

Step 1 Remove Repeating Groups

Normalized
Relations
(1NF)

Step 2 Remove Partial Dependencies

Second Normal
Form (2NF)
Relations

Step 3 Remove Transitive Dependencies

Third Normal
Form (3NF)
Relations

The Three Steps of Normalization

Beginning with either a user view or a data store developed for a data dictionary (see Chapter 10), the analyst normalizes a data structure in three steps, as shown in Figure 17.20. Each step involves an important procedure, one that simplifies the data structure.

The relation derived from the user view or data store will most likely be unnormalized. The first stage of the process includes removing all repeating groups and identifying the primary key. In order to do this, the relation needs to be broken up into two or more relations. At this point, the relations may already be of the third normal form, but more likely more steps will be needed to transform the relations to the third normal form.

The second step ensures that all nonkey attributes are fully dependent on the primary key. All partial dependencies are removed and placed in another relation.

The third step removes any transitive dependencies. A transitive dependency is one in which nonkey attributes are dependent on other nonkey attributes.

A Normalization Example

Figure 17.21 is a user view for the Al S. Well Hydraulic Equipment Company. The report shows (1) the SALESPERSON-NUMBER, (2) the SALES-PERSON-NAME, and (3) the SALES-AREA. The body of the report shows

Al S. Well
Hydraulic Equipment Company
Spring Valley, Minnesota

Salesperson #: 3462
Name: Waters
Sales Area: West

CUSTOMER NUMBER	CUSTOMER NAME	WAREHOUSE NUMBER	WAREHOUSE LOCATION	SALES
18765	Delta Services	4	Fargo	13,540
18830	M. Levy and Sons	3	Bismarck	10,600

the (4) CUSTOMER-NUMBER and (5) CUSTOMER-NAME. Next is (6) the WAREHOUSE-NUMBER that will service the customer, followed by (7) the WAREHOUSE-LOCATION, which is the city in which the company is located. The final information contained in the user view is (8) the SALES-AMOUNT. The rows (one for each customer) on the user view show that items 4 through 8 form a repeating group.

If the analyst was using a data flow/data dictionary approach, the same information in the user view would appear in a data structure. Figure 17.22 shows how the data structure would appear at the data dictionary stage of analysis. The repeating group is also indicated in the data structure by an asterisk (*) and indentation.

Before proceeding, note the data associations of the data elements in Figure 17.23. This type of illustration is called a bubble diagram or data model diagram. Each entity is enclosed in an ellipse, and arrows are used to show the relationships. Although it is possible to draw these relationships with an E-R diagram, sometimes it is easier to use the simpler bubble diagram to model the data.

In this example, there is only one SALESPERSON-NUMBER assigned to each SALESPERSON-NAME, and that person will cover only one SALES-

SALESPERSON-NUMBER
SALESPERSON-NAME
SALES-AREA
CUSTOMER-NUMBER* (1-)
    CUSTOMER-NAME
    WAREHOUSE-NUMBER
    WAREHOUSE-LOCATION
    SALES-AMOUNT

FIGURE 17.22
The analyst would find a data
structure (from a data dictionary) useful in developing
a database.

FIGURE 17.23
Drawing data model diagrams
for data associations sometimes helps analysts ap-
preciate the complexity
of data storage.

AREA, but each SALES-AREA may be assigned to many salespeople: hence, the double arrow notation from SALES-AREA to SALESPERSON-NUMBER. For each SALESPERSON-NUMBER, there may be many CUSTOMER-NUMBER(s).

Furthermore, there would be a one-to-one correspondence between CUSTOMER-NUMBER and CUSTOMER-NAME; the same is true for WARE-HOUSE-NUMBER and WAREHOUSE-LOCATION. CUSTOMER-NUMBER will have only one WAREHOUSE-NUMBER and WAREHOUSE-LOCATION, but each WAREHOUSE-NUMBER or WAREHOUSE-LOCATION may service many CUSTOMER-NUMBER(s). Finally, in order to determine the SALES-AMOUNT for one salesperson's calls to a particular company, it is necessary to know both the SALESPERSON-NUMBER and the CUSTOMER-NUMBER.

The main objective of the normalization process is to simplify all of the complex data items that are often found in users views. For example, if the analyst were to take the user view discussed above and attempt to make a relational table out of it, the table would look like Figure 17.24. Since this is a relation based on our initial user view, we will refer to it as SALES-REPORT.

SALES-REPORT is an unnormalized relation, since it has repeating groups. It is also important to observe that a single attribute such as

SALESPERSON NUMBER	SALESPERSON NAME	SALES AREA	CUSTOMER NUMBER	CUSTOMER NAME	WAREHOUSE NUMBER	WAREHOUSE LOCATION	SALES AMOUNT
3462	Waters	West	18765	Delta Systems	4	Fargo	13540
			18830	A. Levy and Sons	3	Bismarck	10600
			19242	Ranier Company	3	Bismarck	9700
3593	Dryne	East	18841	R. W. Flood Inc.	2	Superior	11560
			18899	Seward Systems	2	Superior	2590
			19565	Stodola's Inc.	1	Plymouth	8800
etc.							

FIGURE 17.24
If the data were listed in an unnormalized table, there could be repeating groups.

SALESPERSON-NUMBER cannot serve as the key. The reason for this is clear when one examines the relationships between SALESPERSON-NUMBER and the other attributes in Figure 17.25. Although there is a one-to-one correspondence between SALESPERSON-NUMBER and two attributes (SALESPERSON-NAME and SALES-AREA), there is a one-to-many relationship between SALESPERSON-NUMBER and the other five attributes (CUSTOMER-NUMBER, CUSTOMER-NAME, WAREHOUSE-NUMBER, WAREHOUSE-LOCATION, and SALES-AMOUNT).

SALES-REPORT can be expressed in the following shorthand notation:

SALES REPORT   (SALESPERSON-NUMBER,
                    SALESPERSON-NAME, SALES-AREA,
                    (CUSTOMER-NUMBER,
                    CUSTOMER-NAME,
                    WAREHOUSE-NUMBER,
                    WAREHOUSE-LOCATION,
                    SALES-AMOUNT))

where the inner set of parentheses represent the repeated group.

FIRST NORMAL FORM (1NF). The first step in normalizing a relation is to remove the repeating groups. In our example, the unnormalized relation SALES-REPORT will be broken up into two separate relations. These new relations will be named SALESPERSON and SALESPERSON-CUSTOMER.

Figure 17.26 shows how the original, unnormalized relation SALES-REPORT is normalized by separating the relation into two new relations. Notice that the relation SALESPERSON contains the primary key SALESPERSON-NUMBER and all of the attributes that were not repeating (SALESPERSON-NAME and SALES-AREA).

The second relation, SALESPERSON-CUSTOMER, contains the primary key from the relation SALESPERSON (the primary key of SALESPERSON is SALESPERSON-NUMBER) as well as all of the attributes that were part of the repeating group (CUSTOMER-NUMBER, CUSTOMER-NAME, WAREHOUSE-NUMBER, WAREHOUSE-LOCATION, and SALES-AMOUNT). However, knowing the SALESPERSON-NUMBER does not automatically mean you will know the CUSTOMER-NAME, SALES-AMOUNT, WAREHOUSE-LOCATION, and so on. In this relation, one must use a concatenated key (both SALESPERSON-NUMBER and CUSTOMER-NUMBER)

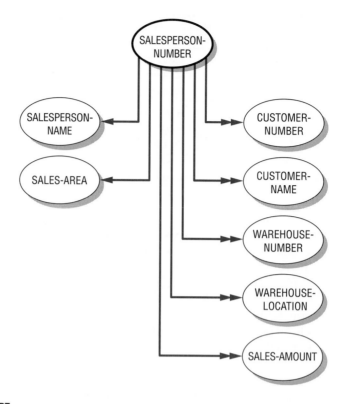

FIGURE 17.25
A data model diagram shows that in the unnormalized relation, the SALESPERSON-NUMBER has a one-to-many association with some attributes.

FIGURE 17.26
The original unnormalized relation SALES-REPORT is separated into two relations, SALESPERSON (3NF) and SALESPERSON-CUSTOMER (1NF).

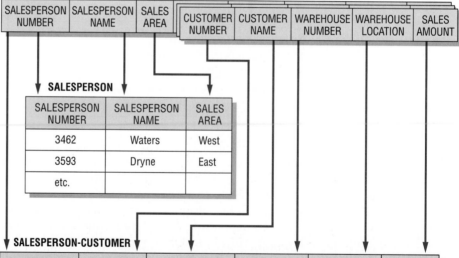

SALESPERSON

SALESPERSON NUMBER	SALESPERSON NAME	SALES AREA
3462	Waters	West
3593	Dryne	East
etc.		

SALESPERSON-CUSTOMER

SALESPERSON NUMBER	CUSTOMER NUMBER	CUSTOMER NAME	WAREHOUSE NUMBER	WAREHOUSE LOCATION	SALES AMOUNT
3462	18765	Delta Systems	4	Fargo	13540
3462	18830	A. Levy and Sons	3	Bismarck	10600
3462	19242	Ranier Company	3	Bismarck	9700
3593	18841	R. W. Flood Inc.	2	Superior	11560
3593	18899	Seward Systems	2	Superior	2590
3593	19565	Stodola's Inc.	1	Plymouth	8800
etc.					

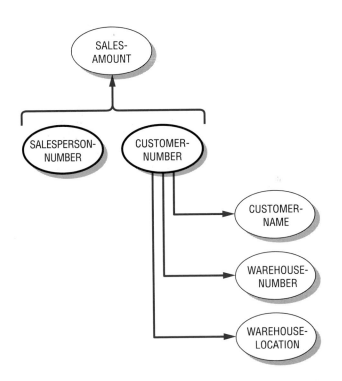

FIGURE 17.27
A data model diagram shows
that three attributes are dependent on CUSTOMER-
NUMBER, so the relation is
not yet normalized. Both
SALESPERSON-NUMBER
and CUSTOMER-NUMBER
are required to look up
SALES-AMOUNT.

to access the rest of the information. It is possible to write the relations in shorthand notation as follows:

SALESPERSON   (<u>SALESPERSON-NUMBER</u>, SALESPERSON-NAME, SALES-AREA)

and

SALESPERSON-CUSTOMER   (<u>SALESPERSON-NUMBER</u>,
<u>CUSTOMER-NUMBER</u>,
CUSTOMER-NAME,
WAREHOUSE-NUMBER,
WAREHOUSE-LOCATION,
SALES-AMOUNT)

The relation SALESPERSON-CUSTOMER is a first normal relation, but it is not in its ideal form. Problems stem from the fact that some of the attributes are not functionally dependent on the primary key—that is, <u>SALESPERSON-NUMBER</u>, <u>CUSTOMER-NUMBER</u>. In other words, some of the nonkey attributes are dependent only on CUSTOMER NUMBER, and not on the concatenated key. The data model diagram in Figure 17.27 shows that SALES-AMOUNT is dependent on both <u>SALESPERSON-NUMBER</u> and <u>CUSTOMER-NUMBER</u>, but the other three attributes are dependent only on <u>CUSTOMER-NUMBER</u>.

SECOND NORMAL FORM (2NF). In the second normal form, all of the attributes will be functionally dependent on the primary key. Therefore, the next step is to remove all of the partially dependent attributes and

FIGURE 17.28
The relation SALESPERSON-
CUSTOMER is separated into
a relation called
CUSTOMER-WAREHOUSE
(2NF) and a relation called
SALES (1NF).

SALESPERSON-CUSTOMER

SALESPERSON NUMBER	CUSTOMER NUMBER	CUSTOMER NAME	WAREHOUSE NUMBER	WAREHOUSE LOCATION	SALES AMOUNT

CUSTOMER-WAREHOUSE

CUSTOMER NUMBER	CUSTOMER NAME	WAREHOUSE NUMBER	WAREHOUSE LOCATION
18765	Delta Systems	4	Fargo
18830	A. Levy and Sons	3	Bismarck
19242	Ranier Company	3	Bismarck
18841	R. W. Flood Inc.	2	Superior
18899	Seward Systems	2	Superior
19565	Stodola's Inc.	1	Plymouth
etc.			

SALES

SALESPERSON NUMBER	CUSTOMER NUMBER	SALES AMOUNT
3462	18765	13540
3462	18830	10600
3462	19242	9700
3593	18841	11560
3593	18899	2590
3593	19565	8800
etc.		

place them in another relation. Figure 17.28 shows how the relation SALESPERSON-CUSTOMER is split into two new relations: SALES and CUSTOMER-WAREHOUSE. These relations can also be expressed as:

SALES   (SALESPERSON-NUMBER, CUSTOMER-NUMBER, SALES-AMOUNT)

and

CUSTOMER-WAREHOUSE   (CUSTOMER-NUMBER, CUSTOMER-NAME, WAREHOUSE-NUMBER, WAREHOUSE-LOCATION)

The relation CUSTOMER-WAREHOUSE is in the second normal form. It can still be simplified further because there are additional dependencies within the relation. Some of the nonkey attributes are dependent not only on the primary key, but also on a nonkey attribute. This dependency is referred to as a transitive dependency.

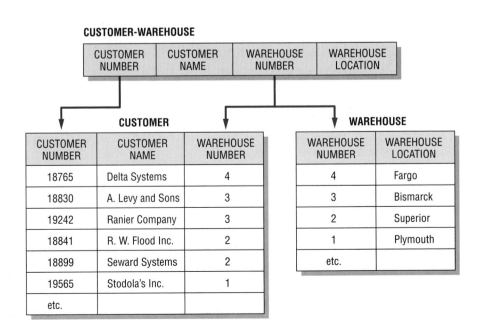

Figure 17.29 shows the dependencies within the relation CUSTOMER-WAREHOUSE. In order for the relation to be a second normal form, all of the attributes must be dependent on the primary key <u>CUSTOMER-NUMBER</u>, as shown in the diagram. However, WAREHOUSE-LOCATION is obviously dependent on WAREHOUSE-NUMBER also. To simplify this relation, another step is required.

THIRD NORMAL FORM (3NF). A normalized relation is third normal if all of the nonkey attributes are fully functionally dependent on the primary key and there are no transitive (nonkey) dependencies. In a manner similar to the previous steps, it is possible to break apart the relation CUSTOMER-WAREHOUSE into two relations, as shown in Figure 17.30.

FIGURE 17.30
The relation CUSTOMER-WAREHOUSE is separated into two relations called CUSTOMER (1NF) and WAREHOUSE (1NF).

CUSTOMER-WAREHOUSE

CUSTOMER NUMBER	CUSTOMER NAME	WAREHOUSE NUMBER	WAREHOUSE LOCATION

CUSTOMER

CUSTOMER NUMBER	CUSTOMER NAME	WAREHOUSE NUMBER
18765	Delta Systems	4
18830	A. Levy and Sons	3
19242	Ranier Company	3
18841	R. W. Flood Inc.	2
18899	Seward Systems	2
19565	Stodola's Inc.	1
etc.		

WAREHOUSE

WAREHOUSE NUMBER	WAREHOUSE LOCATION
4	Fargo
3	Bismarck
2	Superior
1	Plymouth
etc.	

The two new relations are called CUSTOMER and WAREHOUSE and can be written as follows:

CUSTOMER   (<u>CUSTOMER-NUMBER</u>, CUSTOMER-NAME, <u>WAREHOUSE-NUMBER</u>)

and

WAREHOUSE   (<u>WAREHOUSE-NUMBER</u>, WAREHOUSE-LOCATION)

The primary key for the relation CUSTOMER is <u>CUSTOMER-NUMBER</u>, and the primary key for the relation WAREHOUSE is <u>WAREHOUSE-NUMBER</u>.

In addition to these primary keys, we can identify WAREHOUSE-NUMBER to be a foreign key in the relation CUSTOMER. A foreign key is any attribute that is nonkey in one relation but a primary key in another relation. We designated WAREHOUSE-NUMBER as a foreign key in the previous notation and in the figures by underscoring it with a dashed line:_ _ _ _ _ _ _ _ _ _ _.

Finally, the original, unnormalized relation SALES-REPORT has been transformed into four third normal (3NF) relations. In reviewing the relations shown in Figure 17.31, one can see that the single relation SALES-REPORT was transformed into the following four relations:

SALESPERSON   (<u>SALESPERSON-NUMBER</u>, SALESPERSON-NAME, SALES-AREA)

SALES   (<u>SALESPERSON-NUMBER</u>, <u>CUSTOMER-NUMBER</u>, SALES-AMOUNT)

CUSTOMER   (<u>CUSTOMER-NUMBER</u>, CUSTOMER-NAME, <u>WAREHOUSE-NUMBER</u>)

and

WAREHOUSE   (<u>WAREHOUSE-NUMBER</u>, WAREHOUSE-LOCATION)

The third normal form is adequate for most database design problems. The simplification gained from transforming an unnormalized relation into a set of 3NF relations is a tremendous benefit when it comes time to insert, delete, and update information in the database.

An entity-relationship diagram for the database is shown in Figure 17.32. One SALESPERSON serves many CUSTOMER(s) who generate SALES and receive their items from one WAREHOUSE (the closest WAREHOUSE to their location). Take the time to notice how the entities and attributes relate to the database.

Using the Entity-Relationship Diagram to Determine Record Keys

The entity-relationship diagram may be used to determine the keys required for a record or a database relation. The first step is to construct the entity-relationship diagram and label a unique (primary) key for each data entity.

SALESPERSON

SALESPERSON NUMBER	SALESPERSON NAME	SALES AREA
3462	Waters	West
3593	Dryne	East
etc.		

SALES

SALESPERSON NUMBER	CUSTOMER NUMBER	SALES AMOUNT
3462	18765	13540
3462	18830	10600
3462	19242	9700
3593	18841	11560
3593	18899	2590
3593	19565	8800
etc.		

FIGURE 17.31
The complete database consists of four 1NF relations called SALESPERSON, SALES, CUSTOMER, and WAREHOUSE.

CUSTOMER

CUSTOMER NUMBER	CUSTOMER NAME	WAREHOUSE NUMBER
18765	Delta Systems	4
18830	A. Levy and Sons	3
19242	Ranier Company	3
18841	R. W. Flood Inc.	2
18899	Seward Systems	2
19565	Stodola's Inc.	1
etc.		

WAREHOUSE

WAREHOUSE NUMBER	WAREHOUSE LOCATION
4	Fargo
3	Bismarck
2	Superior
1	Plymouth
etc.	

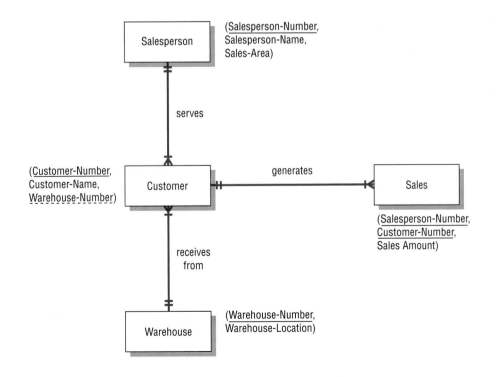

FIGURE 17.32
An entity-relationship diagram for the Al S. Well Hydraulic Company database.

FIGURE 17.33
An entity-relationship diagram for customer orders.

Figure 17.33 shows an entity-relationship diagram for a customer order system. There are three data entities: CUSTOMER, with a prime key of CUSTOMER-NUMBER; ORDER, with a primary key of ORDER-NUMBER; and ITEM, with ITEM-NUMBER as the prime key. One CUSTOMER may place many orders, but each ORDER can be placed by one CUSTOMER only, so the relationship is one-to-many. Each ORDER may contain many ITEMS, and each ITEM may be contained within many ORDERS, so the ORDER-ITEM relationship is many-to-many.

A foreign key, however, is a data field on a given file which is the primary key of a different master file. For example, a DEPARTMENT-NUMBER indicating a student's major may exist on the STUDENT MASTER file. DEPARTMENT-NUMBER could also be the unique key for the DEPARTMENT MASTER file.

One-to-Many Relationship

A database file cannot contain a repeating group or table, but a traditional indexed-sequential file may have one. The file on the "many" end may have foreign keys stored in a table on the file at the "one" end. For example, the CUSTOMER MASTER FILE may be designed to contain a table of outstanding order numbers. The disadvantage of using such a table is that all the table entries may be filled with order numbers, and the analyst is then faced with the decision of having to expand the table (which is expensive and time-consuming) or lose some of the data in the table.

Many-to-Many Relationship

When the relationship is many-to-many, three files are necessary: one for each data entity and one for the relationship. The ORDERS and ITEMS entities in our example have a many-to-many relationship. The primary key of each data entity is stored as a foreign key of the relational file. The relational file may simply contain the primary keys for each data entity or may contain additional data, such as the grade received for a course or the quantity of an item ordered. Refer to the file layout illustrated in Figure 17.34. The ORDER ITEM FILE contains information about which order contains which items and provides a link between the ORDER FILE and the ITEM MASTER FILE.

The relationship file should be indexed on each foreign key—one for each of the files in the relationship—and may have a primary key consisting of a combination of the two foreign keys. To find many records from a second file given the first file, directly read the relational file for the desired key. Locate the matching record in the second "many" file. Continue to loop through the relational file until the desired key is no longer found. For example, to find records in the ITEM MASTER for a specific record in the ORDER MASTER FILE, directly read the ORDER-ITEM FILE using the ORDER-NUMBER as the

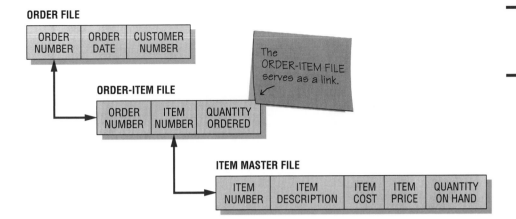

ORDER FILE

ORDER NUMBER	ORDER DATE	CUSTOMER NUMBER

The ORDER-ITEM FILE serves as a link.

ORDER-ITEM FILE

ORDER NUMBER	ITEM NUMBER	QUANTITY ORDERED

ITEM MASTER FILE

ITEM NUMBER	ITEM DESCRIPTION	ITEM COST	ITEM PRICE	QUANTITY ON HAND

FIGURE 17.34
When the relationship is
many-to-many, three files
are necessary.

index. Records are logically sequenced based on the data in the index, so all records for the same ORDER-NUMBER are grouped together. For each ORDER ITEM record that matches the desired ORDER-NUMBER, directly read the ITEM MASTER FILE using the ITEM-NUMBER as an index.

The logic is the same for the reverse situation—for example, finding all the orders for a backordered item that has been received. Use the desired ITEM-NUMBER to directly read the ORDER-ITEM FILE. The ORDER ITEM INDEX is set to the ITEM-NUMBER. For all matching ORDER ITEM records, use the ORDER-NUMBER to directly read the ORDER FILE. Finally, directly read the CUSTOMER MASTER FILE to obtain the CUSTOMER-NAME and ADDRESS using the CUSTOMER-NUMBER on the ORDER FILE.

With indexed-sequential files, one of the files may contain a table of keys for the other file, eliminating the need for a relational file. Refer to the example illustrated in Figure 17.35. The ORDER-KEY FILE has a table of order item information. Each element in the table contains an ITEM-NUMBER and the QUANTITY-ORDERED. The remaining information about all items is found in the ITEM MASTER FILE, which is organized sequentially by ITEM-NUMBER. The disadvantage of this method is that it is difficult and time-consuming to find the orders that match a specific item number. Many conventional file systems utilize tables on master file records.

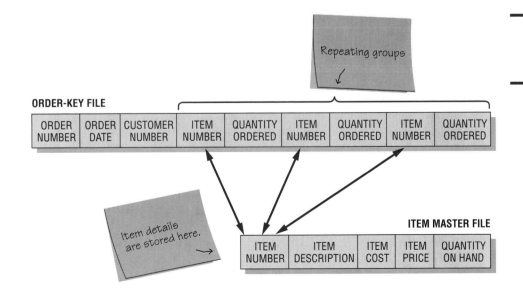

Repeating groups

ORDER-KEY FILE

ORDER NUMBER	ORDER DATE	CUSTOMER NUMBER	ITEM NUMBER	QUANTITY ORDERED	ITEM NUMBER	QUANTITY ORDERED	ITEM NUMBER	QUANTITY ORDERED

Item details are stored here.

ITEM MASTER FILE

ITEM NUMBER	ITEM DESCRIPTION	ITEM COST	ITEM PRICE	QUANTITY ON HAND

FIGURE 17.35
With indexed-sequential
files, one of the files may
contain a table of keys.

FIGURE 17.36
Example of a poorly designed
item master file.

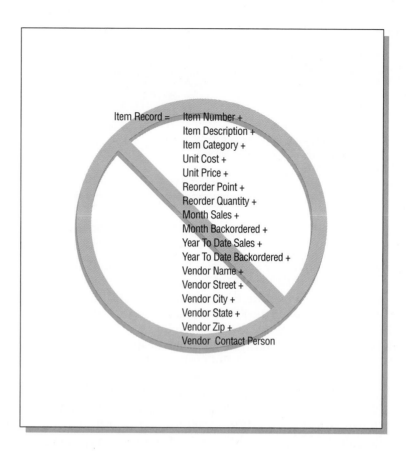

Item Record = Item Number +
Item Description +
Item Category +
Unit Cost +
Unit Price +
Reorder Point +
Reorder Quantity +
Month Sales +
Month Backordered +
Year To Date Sales +
Year To Date Backordered +
Vendor Name +
Vendor Street +
Vendor City +
Vendor State +
Vendor Zip +
Vendor Contact Person

GUIDELINES FOR FILE/DATABASE RELATION DESIGN

The following guidelines should be taken into account when designing master files or database relations:

1. Each separate data entity should create a master file. Do not combine two distinct entities on one file. For example, items are purchased from vendors. The ITEM MASTER FILE should contain only item information and the VENDOR MASTER FILE should contain only vendor information. Figure 17.36 illustrates the data dictionary for a poorly designed ITEM MASTER FILE, which includes information about the vendor. There may be many items purchased from one vendor, and the VENDOR NAME and ADDRESS in this arrangement would be stored on many records. If a vendor changes its address, multiple item records would have to be modified. If some were modified and others were not, the system would produce inconsistent results, such as purchase orders for one item going to the old address and other purchase orders being sent to the new address. Figure 17.37 illustrates the data dictionary for the improved ITEM MASTER FILE and VENDOR MASTER FILE.

2. A specific data field should exist only on one master file. For example, the CUSTOMER NAME should exist only on the CUSTOMER MASTER FILE, not on the ORDER FILE or any other master file. The exceptions to this guideline are the key or index fields, which may be on as many files as necessary. If a report or screen needs information from many

FIGURE 17.37
The improved item and vendor master files.

```
Item Record =        Item Number +
                     Item Description +
                     Item Category +
                     Unit Cost +
                     Unit Price +
                     Reorder Point +
                     Reorder Quantity +
                     Month Sales +
                     Month Backordered +
                     Year To Date Sales +
                     Year To Date Backordered +
                     Vendor Number

Vendor Record =      Vendor Number +
                     Vendor Name +
                     Vendor Street +
                     Vendor City +
                     Vendor State +
                     Vendor Zip +
                     Vendor  Contact Person
```

files, the indexes should provide the linkage for obtaining the required records.

3. Each master file or database relation should have programs to **C**reate, **R**ead, **U**pdate, and **D**elete (abbreviated CRUD) the records. Ideally, only one program should add new records, and one program should delete specified records. Data records may be changed—for instance, to change an address or correct an incorrect customer balance—by one program or several, depending on the data. These file maintenance programs are responsible for infrequent, unpredictable changes to the data.

Usually many update programs are responsible for changing data fields in the course of normal business activities. For example, a customer master file may have a CURRENT BALANCE field that is increased by the ORDER TO-TAL within the order processing program and decreased by a PAYMENT AMOUNT or an AMOUNT RETURNED (using output by two additional programs).

MAKING USE OF THE DATABASE

Steps in Retrieving and Presenting Data

There are eight steps in the retrieval and presentation of data:

1. Choose a relation from the database.
2. Join two relations together.
3. Project columns from the relation.
4. Select rows from the relation.
5. Derive new attributes.

6. Index or sort rows.
7. Calculate totals and performance measures.
8. Present data.

The first and last steps are mandatory, but the six steps inbetween are optional, depending on how data are to be used. Figure 17.38 is a visual guide to the steps, which are described in the following section.

FIGURE 17.38
Data are retrieved and presented in eight distinct steps.

Choose a relation(s) from the database

Join the relations together

Project columns from the relation

Select rows from the relation

Derive new attributes

Index or sort rows

Calculate totals and performance measures

Present data

CUSTOMER

CUSTOMER NUMBER	CUSTOMER NAME	WAREHOUSE NUMBER
18765	Delta Systems	4
18830	A. Levy and Sons	3
19242	Ranier Company	3
18841	R. W. Flood Inc.	2
18899	Seward Systems	2
19565	Stodola's Inc.	1
etc.		

WAREHOUSE

WAREHOUSE NUMBER	WAREHOUSE LOCATION
4	Fargo
3	Bismarck
2	Superior
1	Plymouth
etc.	

Join

CUSTOMER-WAREHOUSE-LOCATION

CUSTOMER NUMBER	CUSTOMER NAME	WAREHOUSE NUMBER	WAREHOUSE LOCATION
18765	Delta Systems	4	Fargo
18830	A. Levy and Sons	3	Bismarck
19242	Ranier Company	3	Bismarck
18841	R. W. Flood Inc.	2	Superior
18899	Seward Systems	2	Superior
19565	Stodola's Inc.	1	Plymouth
etc.			

FIGURE 17.39
The operation join takes two relations and puts them together to form a single relation.

CHOOSE A RELATION FROM THE DATABASE. The first and obvious step is to choose a relation from the database. A good way to accomplish this is to keep a directory of user views as a memory aid. Even if the user wants an ad-hoc query, it is useful to have similar views available.

JOIN TWO RELATIONS TOGETHER. The operation join is intended to take two relations and put them together to make a larger relation. In order for two relations to be joined, they must have a common attribute. For instance, take two relations from our example:

CUSTOMER   (<u>CUSTOMER-NUMBER</u>, CUSTOMER-NAME,
                   <u>WAREHOUSE-NUMBER</u>)

and

WAREHOUSE   (<u>WAREHOUSE-NUMBER</u>,
                      WAREHOUSE-LOCATION)

FIGURE 17.40
Relations can be joined subject to certain conditions.

SALES

SALESPERSON NUMBER	CUSTOMER NUMBER	SALES AMOUNT
3462	18765	13540
3462	18830	10600
3462	19242	9700
3593	18841	11560
3593	18899	2590
3593	19565	8800
etc.		

QUOTA

AWARD LEVEL	AMOUNT
Certificate	9000
Medal	12000

Join

SALES-QUOTA

SALESPERSON NUMBER	CUSTOMER NUMBER	SALES AMOUNT	AWARD LEVEL	AMOUNT
3462	18765	13540	Certificate	9000
3462	18765	13540	Medal	12000
3462	18830	10600	Certificate	9000
3462	18830	10600	Medal	12000
3462	19242	9700	Certificate	9000
3593	18841	11560	Certificate	12000
etc.				

Suppose we join these relations over WAREHOUSE-NUMBER to get a new relation, CUSTOMER-WAREHOUSE-LOCATION. The joining of these relations is illustrated in Figure 17.39. Also note that the new relation is not 3NF.

The operation join may also go one step further—that is, it may combine files for rows that have an attribute that meets a certain condition. Figure 17.40 shows an example in which two relations, SALES and QUOTA, are joined by satisfying the condition that a salesperson has met or exceeded predetermined quotas.

Join is an important operation because it can take many 3NF relations and combine them to make a more useful relation. Together with the operations below it, join is a powerful operation.

PROJECT COLUMNS FROM THE RELATON. Projection is the process of building a smaller relation by choosing only relevant attributes from an existing relation. In other words, projection is the extraction of certain columns from a relational table.

An example of projection is featured in Figure 17.41. The relation:

CUSTOMER-WAREHOUSE-LOCATION   (<u>CUSTOMER-NUMBER</u>,
CUSTOMER-NAME,
<u>WAREHOUSE-NUMBER</u>),
WAREHOUSE-LOCATION

CUSTOMER-WAREHOUSE-LOCATION

CUSTOMER NUMBER	CUSTOMER NAME	WAREHOUSE NUMBER	WAREHOUSE LOCATION
18765	Delta Systems	4	Fargo
18830	A. Levy and Sons	3	Bismarck
19242	Ranier Company	3	Bismarck
18841	R. W. Flood Inc.	2	Superior
18899	Seward Systems	2	Superior
19565	Stodola's Inc.	1	Plymouth
etc.			

Projection

CUSTOMER-LOCATION

CUSTOMER NUMBER	WAREHOUSE LOCATION
18765	Fargo
18830	Bismarck
19242	Bismarck
18841	Superior
18899	Superior
19565	Plymouth
etc.	

is projected over CUSTOMER-NUMBER and WAREHOUSE-LOCATION, and during the projection process, duplicate records are removed.

SELECT ROWS FROM THE RELATION. The operation referred to as selection is similar to projection, but instead of extracting columns it extracts rows. Selection creates a new (smaller) relation by extracting records that contain an attribute meeting a certain condition.

Figure 17.42 illustrates how the selection operation works. Selection is performed on the relation PERSONNEL to extract salaried employees only. There is no need to remove duplicate records here as there was in the previous illustration of projection.

Selection may also be performed for a more complex set of conditions—for example, select all of the employees who are salaried *and* who make more than $40,000 annually, or select employees who are hourly *and* make more than $15.00 per hour. Selection is an important operation for ad-hoc queries.

DERIVE NEW ATTRIBUTES. The fifth step involves the manipulation of the existing data plus some additional parameters (if necessary) to derive new data. New columns are created for the resulting relation. An example of de-

PERSONNEL

NUMBER	EMPLOYEE NAME	DEPARTMENT	S/H	GROSS
72845	Waters	Outside Sales	S	48960
72888	Dryne	Outside Sales	S	37200
73712	Fawcett	Distribution	H	23500
80345	Well, Jr.	Marketing	S	65000
84672	Piper	Maintenance	H	20560
89760	Acquia	Accounting	H	18755
etc.				

Selection

SALARIED-EMPLOYEES

NUMBER	EMPLOYEE NAME	DEPARTMENT	S/H	GROSS
72845	Waters	Outside Sales	S	48960
72888	Dryne	Outside Sales	S	37200
80345	Well, Jr.	Marketing	S	65000
etc.				

rivation of new attributes can be found in Figure 17.43. Here, two new attributes are determined: (1) GIRTH (by multiplying the sum of width and height by 2 and adding it to length), and (2) SHIPPING-WEIGHT (which depends on the girth).

INDEX OR SORT ROWS. People require data to be organized in a certain order so they can either locate items in a list more easily or group and subtotal items more easily. Two options for ordering data are available: indexing and sorting.

Indexing is the logical ordering of rows in a relation according to some key. As discussed in the previous section, the logical pointer takes up space, and listing the relation by using an index is slower than if the relation were in the proper physical order. The index, however, takes up far less space than a duplicate file.

Sorting is the physical ordering of a relation. The result of physical sorting is a sequential file as discussed earlier in the chapter. Figure 17.44 illustrates indexing and sorting of the relation PERSONNEL by employee name in alphabetical order.

CALCULATE TOTALS AND PERFORMANCE MEASURES. Once the appropriate subset of data is defined and the rows of the relation are ordered in the required manner, totals and performance measures can be calculated. Figure 17.45 shows how calculation is performed.

PACKAGE NUMBER	WIDTH	HEIGHT	LENGTH	WEIGHT
A3456	4	3	26	4
A3457	12	12	20	10
A3458	10	20	34	20
A3459	15	15	22	18
A3460	10	10	40	40
A3461	10	20	34	22
A3462	5	10	15	30
A3463	8	14	44	35

Some Examples: GIRTH = 2 (WIDTH + HEIGHT) + LENGTH

Derivation

IF GIRTH > 84 AND WEIGHT < 25
THEN SHIPPING WEIGHT = WEIGHT
ELSE SHIPPING WEIGHT = WEIGHT

PACKAGE NUMBER	WIDTH	HEIGHT	LENGTH	WEIGHT
A3456	4	3	26	4
A3457	12	12	20	10
A3458	10	20	34	20
A3459	15	15	22	18
A3460	10	10	40	40
A3461	10	20	34	22
A3462	5	10	15	30
A3463	8	14	44	35

GIRTH	SHIPPING WEIGHT
50	4
68	10
94	25
82	18
80	40
90	25
45	30
88	35

PRESENT DATA TO THE USER. The final step in the retrieval of data is presentation. Presentation of the data abstracted from the database can take many forms. Sometimes the data will be presented in tabular form, sometimes in graphs, and other times as a single-word answer on a screen. Output design, as covered in Chapter 15, provides a more detailed look at presentation objectives, forms, and methods.

SUMMARY

How to store data is often an important decision in the design of an information system. There are two approaches to storing data. The first approach is to store data in individual files, one file for each application. The second approach is to develop a database that can be shared by many users for a variety of applications as the need arises. Dramatic improvements have been made in the design of database software to take advantage of the graphical user interface.

The conventional file approach may at times be a more efficient approach since the file can be application-specific. On the other hand, the

FIGURE 17.44
Sort orders the records (rows)
in the relation so that records
can be displayed in order
and can be grouped for
subtotals. Here the PERSON-
NEL relation is sorted
alphabetically according
to EMPLOYEE NAME.

PERSONNEL

NUMBER	EMPLOYEE NAME	DEPARTMENT	S/H	GROSS
72845	Waters	Outside Sales	S	48960
72888	Dryne	Outside Sales	S	37200
73712	Fawcett	Distribution	H	23500
80345	Well, Jr.	Marketing	S	65000
84672	Piper	Maintenance	H	20560
89760	Acquia	Accounting	H	18755

Sort

EMPLOYEES-BY-NAME

NUMBER	EMPLOYEE NAME	DEPARTMENT	S/H	GROSS
89760	Acquia	Accounting	H	18755
72888	Dryne	Outside Sales	S	37200
73712	Fawcett	Distribution	H	23500
84672	Piper	Maintenance	H	20560
72845	Waters	Outside Sales	S	48960
80345	Well, Jr.	Marketing	S	65000

database approach may be more appropriate because the same data need to be entered, stored, and updated only once.

An understanding of data storage requires a grasp of three realms: reality, data, and metadata. An entity is any object or event for which we are willing to collect and store data. Attributes are the actual characteristics of these entities. Data items can have values and can be organized into records that can be accessed by a key. Metadata describes the data and can contain restrictions about the value of a data item (such as numeric only).

Examples of conventional files include master files, table files, transaction files, work files, and report files. They can have a sequential organization, linked lists, hashed file organization, indexed organization, or indexed-sequential organization. A more modern and efficient way to handle indexed-sequential files is the VSAM. Databases can have hierarchical, network, or relational structures.

Normalization is the process that takes user views and transforms them into less complex structures called normalized relations. There are three steps in the normalization process. First, all repeating groups are removed. Second, all partial dependencies are removed. Finally, the transitive dependencies are taken out. After these three steps are completed, the result is the creation of numerous relations that are of third normal form (3NF).

SHIPPING-WEIGHT

PACKAGE NUMBER	WIDTH	HEIGHT	LENGTH	WEIGHT	GIRTH	SHIPPING WEIGHT
A3456	4	3	26	4	50	4
A3457	12	12	20	10	68	10
A3458	10	20	34	20	94	25
A3459	15	15	22	18	82	18
A3460	10	10	40	40	80	40
A3461	10	20	34	22	90	25
A3462	5	10	15	30	45	30
A3463	8	14	44	35	88	35

Calculation

Some Examples:

Total girth and shipping weight → 597 | 187

Number of packages that weighed less than 25 pounds but were shipped at the 25 pound rate → 2

Total number of packages shipped → 8

Percentage of packages that weighed less than 25 pounds but were shipped at the 25 pound rate → 25

FIGURE 17.45
Calculation provides subtotals, totals, and other performance measures.

The entity-relationship diagram may be used to determine the keys required for a record or a database relation. The three guidelines to follow when designing master files or database relations are: (1) each separate data entity should create a master file (do not combine two distinct entities on one file); (2) a specific data field should exist only on one master file; and (3) each master file or database relation should have programs to create, read, update, and delete.

The process of retrieving data may involve as many as eight steps: (1) a relation or relations are chosen and (2) joined; (3) projection and (4) selection are performed on the relation to extract the relevant rows and columns; (5) new attributes may be derived; (6) rows are sorted or indexed; (7) totals and performance measures are calculated; and finally (8) the results are presented to the user.

KEYWORDS AND PHRASES

data storage
conventional file
database
database management
  system (DBMS)

logical view
physical view
hierarchical data structure
network data structure
relational data structure

"I hear very good things about your team from the people in Management Systems. You even got some hard-earned praise from Training people. You know, Tom Ketcham isn't easy to please these days. Even *he* is seeing some possibilities. I think you'll pull us together yet. Unless we all go off in different directions again . . . I'm just teasing you. I told you to think about whether we are a family, a zoo, or a war zone. Now's the time to start designing systems for us that fit us. You've been here long enough now to form those opinions. I hope they're favorable. I think our famous Southern hospitality should help influence you, don't you? I was so busy persuading you that we're worth the effort that I almost forgot to tell you: Tom and Snowden have agreed to think about moving toward a database of some sort. Would you have this ready in the next two weeks? Tom is at a conference in Minneapolis, but when he returns you should have some database ideas worked up for Snowden and him to discuss it. Keep at it."

HyperCase Questions

1. Assume your team members have used the Training Unit Client Characteristics Report to design a database table to store the relevant information contained on this report, with the following result:

Table name: CLIENT TABLE

COLUMN NAME	DESCRIPTION
CLIENT ID (primary key)	Mnemonic made up by users like STHSP for State Hospital
CLIENT NAME	The actual, full client name
ADDRESS	The client's address
CONTACTS	The names of contact persons
PHONE NUMBER	The phone numbers of contact persons
CLASS	The type of institution (VA hospital, clinic, other, etc.)
STAFF-SIZE	Size of client staff (number)
TRAINING LEVEL	Minimum required expertise level of the staff (as defined by the class)
EQUIP-QTY	The number of medical machines that the client has
EQUIP TYPE	The type of medical machines (e.g., x-ray, MRI, CAT)
EQUIP MODEL-YR	The model and year of each medical machine

2. Apply normalization to the table your team has developed to remove repeating groups. Display your results.

3. Remove transitive dependencies from your table, and show your resulting database table.

database administrator
reality, data, and metadata
data item
entity
relationship
attribute
record
key
primary key
secondary key
concatenated key
master file
table file
transaction file
work file
report file
sequential organization
linked list
hashed file organization
indexed organization
indexed-sequential organization
indexed-sequential access
  method (ISAM)
virtual storage access
  method (VSAM)

normalization
unnormalized relation
repeating groups
transitive dependencies
data model diagram
bubble diagram
first normal form (1NF)
second normal form (2NF)
third normal form (3NF)
CRUD (Create, Read, Update,
  and Delete)
retrieval
steps in information retrieval
  choose
  join
  project
  select
  derive
  index or sort
  calculate
  present
partial dependencies
entity-relationship (ER) diagram
data elements
special characters

REVIEW QUESTIONS

1. What are the advantages of organizing data storage as separate files?
2. What are the advantages of organizing data storage using a database approach?
3. What are the effectiveness measures of database design?
4. What are the efficiency measures of database design? Why do they conflict with each other?
5. List some examples of entities and their attributes.
6. Define the term *metadata*. What is its purpose?
7. List file types of commonly used conventional files. Which of these are temporary files?
8. What is a linked list?
9. What often occurs when a hashed file organization is used?
10. What is an inverted list? When is it valuable to have an inverted list?
11. Name the three main types of database organization.
12. Define the term *normalization*.
13. What is removed when a relation is converted to the first normal form?
14. What is removed when a relation is converted from 1NF to 2NF?
15. What is removed when a relation is converted from 2NF to 3NF?
16. List the eight steps for retrieving, presorting, and presenting data.
17. What does join do? What is projection? What is selection?
18. State the differences between "sort" and "index."
19. List two ways of storing a many-to-many relationship and the differences between the two methods.

PROBLEMS

1. Given the following file of renters:

Record #	Last Name	Apartment Number	Rent	Lease Expires
41	Warkentin	102	550	4/30
42	Buffington	204	600	4/30
43	Schuldt	103	550	4/30
44	Tang	209	600	5/31
45	Cho	203	550	5/31
46	Yoo	203	550	6/30
47	Pyle	101	500	6/30

   a. Develop a linked list by apartment number in ascending order.
   b. Develop a linked list according to last name in ascending order.

2. Develop an inverted file. Develop an index for each of the attributes.

3. The following is an example of a grade report for two students at the University of Southern New Jersey:

USNJ Grade Report
Spring Semester 1997

Name: I. M. Smarte   *Major: MIS*
Student: 053-6929-24   *Status: Senior*

Course Number		Course Title	Professor	Professor's Department	Grade
MIS	403	Systems Analysis	Kendall, K.	DESC	A
MIS	411	Conceptual Foundations	Kendall, J.	DESC	A
MIS	420	Human Factors in IS	Kendall, J.	DESC	B
CIS	412	Database Design	Sibley, E.	CIS	A
DESC	353	Management Models	Kelly, D.	DESC	A

USNJ Grade Report
Spring Semester 1997

Name: E.Z. Grayed   *Major: MIS*
Student: 472-6124-59   *Status: Senior*

Course Number		Course Title	Professor	Professor's Department	Grade
MIS	403	Systems Analysis	Kendall, K.	DESC	B
MIS	411	Conceptual Foundations	Kendall, J.	DESC	A

   Draw a hierarchical data structure for this user view. Focus on each individual course and follow the approach used in Figure 17.15.

4. Draw a network data structure for the user view in problem 3. Use grade as a link and follow the approach in Figure 17.17.

5. Draw a data model diagram with associations for the user view in problem 3.

6. Convert the user view in problem 3 to a 3NF relation. Show each step along the way.

7. Draw an entity-relationship diagram for the following:

   Many students play many different sports. One person, called the head coach, assumes the role of coaching all of these sports. Each of the entities have a number and a name. (Make any assumptions necessary to complete a reasonable diagram. List your assumptions.)

8. The entity-relationship diagram you drew in problem 7 represents the data entities that are needed to implement a system for tracking students and the sports teams that they play. List the files that are needed to implement the system, along with primary, secondary, and foreign keys that are required to link the files.

9. Draw an entity-relationship diagram for the following situation:

   A commercial bakery makes many different products. These include breads, desserts, specialty cakes, and many other baked goods. Ingredients such as flour, spices, milk, and so on are purchased from vendors. Sometimes an ingredient is purchased from a single vendor, and other times an ingredient is purchased from many vendors. The bakery has commercial customers, such as schools and restaurants, that regularly place orders for baked goods. Each baked good has a specialist that oversees the setup of the bake operation and inspects the finished product.

10. List the files and keys that are needed to implement the commercial bakery system.

SELECTED BIBLIOGRAPHY

Avison, D. E. *Information Systems Development: A Database Approach,* 2nd ed. London: Blackwell Scientific Publications, 1992.

Avison, D. E., and G. Fitzgerald. *Information Systems Development: Methodologies, Techniques and Tools,* 2nd ed. New York: McGraw Hill, 1995.

Everest, G. C. *Database Management: Objectives, System Functions, and Administration.* New York: McGraw-Hill Book Company, 1985.

Gane, C., and T. Sarson. *Structured Systems Analysis: Tools and Techniques.* Englewood Cliffs, NJ: Prentice-Hall, 1979.

McFadden, F., and J. A. Hoffer. *Modern Database Management,* 4th ed. Redwood City, CA: The Benjamin/Cummings Publishing Company, Inc., 1994.

Sanders, G. L. *Data Modeling.* New York: Boyd & Fraser Publishing Company, an International Thomson Publishing Company book, 1995.

BACK TO DATA BASICS

After numerous interviews, prototypes, data flow diagrams, and data dictionary entries had been completed, Anna and Chip both start work on the entity-relationship model. "I'll be responsible for creating the Access table relationships," Anna promises. Chip volunteers to complete an entity-relationship diagram. "Let's compare the two diagrams for accuracy and consistency when we're done," Anna suggests, and so they did.

Figure E17.1 shows the entity-relationship diagram for the microcomputer system. Visible Analyst calls each of the rectangles an *entity*. This is distinct from an external entity, which represents a source or recipient of information on a data flow diagram. The entity represents a file of information stored within the system, one corresponding to a data store on the data flow diagram. Each of the diamond rectangles represents a relationship between the data entities. A rectangle with an oval in it represents an entity that cannot exist without the connecting entity, such as a table of codes.

"I've created the entity-relationship diagram, starting with the simplest portions of the system," Chip tells Anna. "The first data entities created are SOFTWARE and HARDWARE. The relationship is that software is installed on the hardware. Next I determined the cardinality of the relationship. Since

FIGURE E17.1
Unnormalized entity-relationship diagram for the Microcomputer System.

Allen Schmidt,
Julie E. Kendall, and
Kenneth E. Kendall

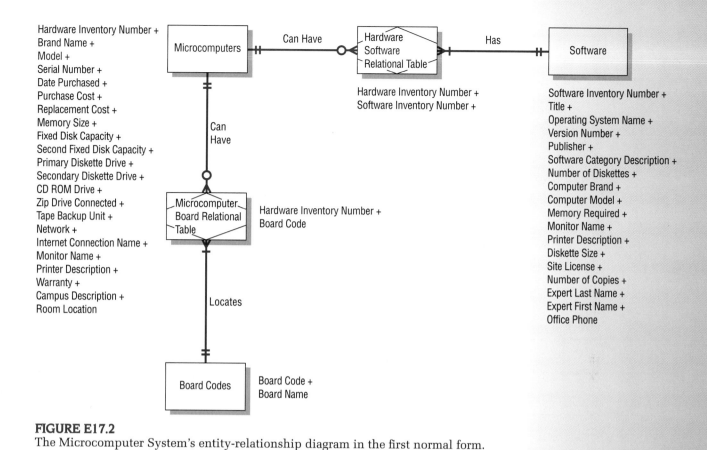

Hardware Inventory Number +
Brand Name +
Model +
Serial Number +
Date Purchased +
Purchase Cost +
Replacement Cost +
Memory Size +
Fixed Disk Capacity +
Second Fixed Disk Capacity +
Primary Diskette Drive +
Secondary Diskette Drive +
CD ROM Drive +
Zip Drive Connected +
Tape Backup Unit +
Network +
Internet Connection Name +
Monitor Name +
Printer Description +
Warranty +
Campus Description +
Room Location

Microcomputers

Can Have

Hardware
Software
Relational Table

Has

Software

Hardware Inventory Number +
Software Inventory Number +

Software Inventory Number +
Title +
Operating System Name +
Version Number +
Publisher +
Software Category Description +
Number of Diskettes +
Computer Brand +
Computer Model +
Memory Required +
Monitor Name +
Printer Description +
Diskette Size +
Site License +
Number of Copies +
Expert Last Name +
Expert First Name +
Office Phone

Can
Have

Microcomputer
Board Relational
Table

Hardware Inventory Number +
Board Code

Locates

Board Codes

Board Code +
Board Name

FIGURE E17.2
The Microcomputer System's entity-relationship diagram in the first normal form.

one software package could be installed on many microcomputers, this relationship is one-to-many. Each microcomputer may also have many different software packages installed on it, so that it also provides a one-to-many relationship. Since there is a one-to-many relationship for each of the data entities, the full relationship between them becomes many-to-many." The unnormalized entity-relationship diagram is shown in Figure E17.1, along with the data dictionary entries for the tables.

Chip continues by saying, "This first view is far from normalized. Notice that the BOARD CODE and SOFTWARE INVENTORY NUMBER are repeating elements on the HARDWARE entity. I will have to create several entities for each of them." A while later Chip reviews his work with Anna. The BOARD CODES have become a separate entity, linked by a relational entity, and the SOFTWARE INVENTORY NUMBER has been removed and placed in a relational entity. Refer to the entity-relationship diagram illustrated in Figure E17.2. "This places the data in the first normal form," remarks Chip. "And there are no elements that are dependent on only a part of the key, so the data is also in the second normal form. However, there are elements that are not part of the entity that is represented on the diagram, and they will have to be removed. For example, look at the MONITOR NAME and PRINTER DESCRIPTION. These elements are not a part of the microcomputer but are connected to it. They should have their own entity. This makes it easier to change the spelling of, say, a printer. Rather than having to change the spelling of the printer on many of the MICROCOMPUTER records, it would only have to be changed once."

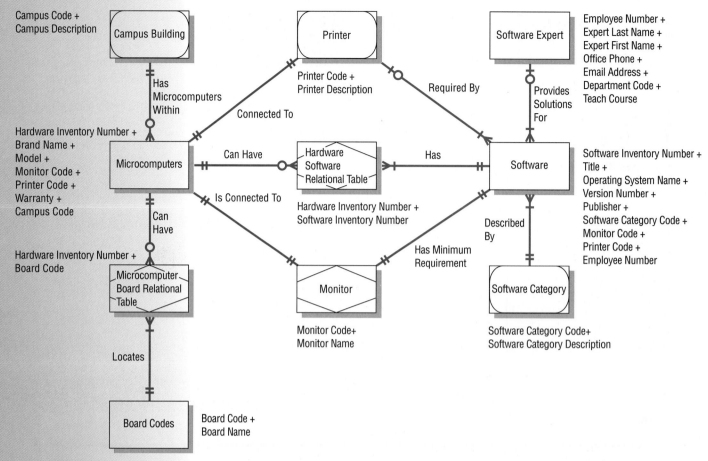

Campus Code +
Campus Description

Campus Building

Printer

Software Expert

Employee Number +
Expert Last Name +
Expert First Name +
Office Phone +
Email Address +
Department Code +
Teach Course

Has
Microcomputers
Within

Printer Code +
Printer Description

Required By

Provides
Solutions
For

Hardware Inventory Number +
Brand Name +
Model +
Monitor Code +
Printer Code +
Warranty +
Campus Code

Microcomputers

Connected To

Can Have

Hardware
Software
Relational Table

Has

Software

Software Inventory Number +
Title +
Operating System Name +
Version Number +
Publisher +
Software Category Code +
Monitor Code +
Printer Code +
Employee Number

Is Connected To

Hardware Inventory Number +
Software Inventory Number

Can
Have

Described
By

Hardware Inventory Number +
Board Code

Microcomputer
Board Relational
Table

Monitor

Has Minimum
Requirement

Software Category

Software Category Code+
Software Category Description

Monitor Code+
Monitor Name

Locates

Board Codes

Board Code +
Board Name

FIGURE E17.3
Final entity-relationship diagram for the Microcomputer System.

Anna agrees, remarking "That's really a good assessment of the situation. It will make implementing the Access tables easier."

Chip continues to work on the entity-relationship diagram. After a few hours he exclaims, "I think that it's done. Would you take a look at the final version." The final version is shown in Figure E17.3. All the entities and relationships have been described in the repository. Figure E17.4 shows the first repository screen for the entity MICROCOMPUTERS. Notice that the Composition area contains the final elements for keeping track of Microcomputers and that the keys are indicated using the notation [Pk] for the primary key and [Akn] for an alternate key, where n represents any unique number. Foreign keys are lower in the list and are indicated using the notation [Fk]. The second screen is illustrated in Figure E17.5 and contains information about the relationships that the MICROCOMPUTERS entity has with other entities, including the cardinality. This screen also contains the locations of the entity.

The PROVIDES SOLUTIONS FOR relationship, linking SOFTWARE EXPERT and SOFTWARE, is shown in Figure E17.6, and it has a definition as well as the entities that are linked at either end of the relationship. Cardinality is included for each end of the relationship.

FIGURE E17.4
Entity description screen for MICROCOMPUTERS, first repository screen.

FIGURE E17.5
MICROCOMPUTERS entity, second repository screen.

FIGURE E17.6
PROVIDES SOLUTIONS FOR relationship screen.

Anna reviews the final version and exclaims, "This looks great! You are right in moving the PRINTER and MONITOR to their own entities. I see that the CAMPUS BUILDING has been moved to its own entity. Good idea, since the building is not a part of the microcomputer. And the SOFTWARE EXPERT is definitely not a part of the software entity. How about the SOFTWARE CATEGORY?"

"I moved the SOFTWARE CATEGORY into its own entity to save room on the master files when they are constructed. It is really a table of codes, and we can store a small code, rather than a lengthy description. Why don't you double check the various keys on the diagram. Each related entity, on the many end, should have a foreign key that matches the primary key of the entity on the one end."

Anna examines the diagram for a while and remarks, "This looks good to me, but why don't you run some of the Visible Analyst analysis reports for the entity-relationship diagram?"

"That's an excellent idea!" exclaims Chip. The first step in the diagram is to run the Visible Analyst syntax check for the final entity-relationship diagram. This option checks for entities and relationships that have not been named, and it produces no errors when Chip runs it. Next Chip runs the Normalization analysis option. This displays a series of warning error messages, illustrated in Figure E17.7. These inform Chip that some of the relationships have a one-to-one cardinality, which is acceptable. The other warning messages let Chip know that the SOFTWARE CATEGORY and CAMPUS BUILDING do not have identifying relationships. This means that the record keys have not been defined in the repository.

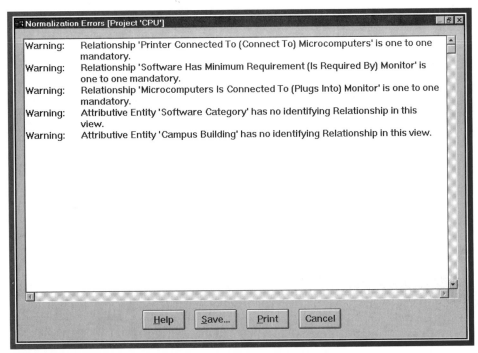

FIGURE E17.7
Normalization Errors output screen, showing warning messages.

The next analysis that Chip runs is Key Analysis. This option performs syntax and normalization analysis as well as reporting problems with primary and foreign keys. The analysis report, which shows that the SOFTWARE CATEGORY has no primary key and that the entity PRINTER has no identifying relationship, is illustrated in Figure E17.8 The final analysis report that Chip runs is the Model Balancing report, which is shown in Figure E17.9. This report produces some of the errors detected by previous reports, but it additionally shows all elements that are contained in the Composition area of the entities and are not used by a data flow diagram process.

After spending time examining both the diagram as well as the repository entries and analysis reports, both Anna and Chip are satisfied that the relationships between the data have been accurately portrayed. Next they decided how to design the files or database from the diagrams. A critical choice had to be made: whether to use files or a database. "I think a series of indexed files and COBOL language is best," Chip says.

Anna says, "The system should be implemented using Access, since a database structure would easily accommodate the many relationships."

The HARDWARE/SOFTWARE relationship is analyzed first. Since there is a many-to-many relationship between these two data entities, it may be implemented in one of two forms:

1. Use three indexed files, which is the database solution. These are:
   a. HARDWARE MASTER.
   b. SOFTWARE MASTER.
   c. a hardware/software relationship file. This would contain the key fields for the HARDWARE and SOFTWARE master file for all software installed on all machines.

FIGURE E17.8
Key Analysis Errors output screen.

FIGURE E17.9
Data Flow Diagram/Entity-Relationship Diagram Balancing Errors screen.

2. While the preceding database solution could also be used when designing a COBOL-indexed file structure, a better alternative would be to use a repeating group on one of the files, which references the other master file. This is easier for accomplishing file maintenance and producing information. The files would be:

a. a HARDWARE MASTER file.
b. a SOFTWARE MASTER file with a repeating group or table of HARDWARE INVENTORY NUMBERS, the key field of the MICRO-COMPUTER MASTER on which the software would be installed. This table could also be included on the HARDWARE MASTER file, which references the SOFTWARE INVENTORY NUMBER for each software package installed on the machine.

"I finally see your way of thinking," Chip says. After a lengthy discussion, they decide to go ahead with the database solution. It will be easier for the programmers to design, code, implement, and maintain the system. Furthermore, the file structures will be easy to modify as the system evolves. "I guess that it's my turn to work on the relationships," says Anna as she takes a copy of the entity-relationship diagram. "I'll modify the Access tables from the prototyping sessions." Anna starts by setting up the primary keys for each of the tables. When the tables were in their final form, she began creating the relationships between them. The Access Relationships diagram is illustrated in Figure E17.10. Rectangles on the diagram represent the database tables and correspond to the various entity types found on the entity-relationship diagram. Notice that the cardinality is represented by 1 and infinity symbols. The primary key fields are listed as the first field of each rectangle; they are also displayed in boldface type. Foreign keys are

FIGURE E17.10
Microsoft Access Relationships diagram

| | DD2 SOFTWARE MASTER | | |
	DD1 MICROCOMPUTER MASTER		
Board Codes			
Campus Building			
Component Board		X	X
Hardware Software Relational Table		X	X
Microcomputer Board Relational Table		X	X
Microcomputer Maintenance		X	X
Microcomputers		X	X
Monitor		X	X
Peripheral Equipment		X	X
Printer			
Rooms			
Software		X	X
Software Category			
Software Expert			
Software Hardware Relation		X	X
Vendor			

FIGURE E17.11
Entities vs. Data Stores Matrix.

shown attached to the other end of the relationship line, if the foreign key is visible in the table rectangle. Keys are dragged from one table to another to establish a relationship, and a dialog box appears to determine properties of the relationship. For example, the property called Enforce Referential Integrity means that you cannot create a record in the many end of the table without first creating it in the one end (containing the primary key).

"I would like to produce some documentation for the system," remarks Anna. "It would help when we need to modify the design, as well as the Access objects and code." There are several matrices found in the Repository Reports feature that are useful to produce. The first is the Entities vs. Data Stores Matrix, which is illustrated in Figure E17.11. It shows the entities found on all the entity-relationship diagrams and data stores that contain similar elements. This is useful for mapping the entity-relationship diagram into a data flow diagram.

The Composition Matrix is produced next. It provides a cross-reference grid of elements and the entities that they are contained within. This matrix is useful for determining what entities will need to be modified (or what tables in Access) if the element size or any other characteristic of the element changes. A portion of this matrix is illustrated in Figure E17.12. A last matrix that is useful in assessing changes to the entire system is the Diagram Location Matrix. This shows the entities and the diagrams that they are contained within. Figure E17.13 is an example of this matrix. Notice that it also shows how more entities are added as the diagram becomes more normalized, a process resulting from pulling elements off entities into new ones.

Exercises*

🖫 **E-1.** Use Visible Analyst to view the unnormalized and first normal form entity-relationship diagrams for the Microcomputer System.

🖫 **E-2.** Use Visible Analyst to view the entity-relationship diagram for the Microcomputer System.

🖫 **E-3.** Add the VENDOR entity to the diagram. The vendor warrants the microcomputers, and the relationship between VENDOR and MICROCOMPUTERS is that one VENDOR can warrant many MICROCOMPUTERS.

🖫 **E-4.** Add the MAINTENANCE entity to the diagram. Maintenance repairs are performed on microcomputers, and the relationship between MAINTENANCE and MICROCOMPUTERS is such that one MICROCOMPUTER may have many MAINTENANCE records.

🖫 **E-5.** Describe the SOFTWARE CATEGORY entity in the repository. Include the elements found on the entity-relationship diagram below SOFTWARE CATEGORY in the **Composition** area.

🖫 **E-6.** Describe the MAINTENANCE entity in the repository. The elements are
   a. MAINTENANCE ORDER NUMBER
   b. HARDWARE INVENTORY NUMBER
   c. MAINTENANCE DATE
   d. TYPE OF MAINTENANCE
   e. COST OF MAINTENANCE
   f. MAINTENANCE COVERED BY WARRANTY

🖫 **E-7.** Describe the VENDOR entity. The elements are
   a. VENDOR NUMBER
   b. VENDOR NAME
   c. STREET
   d. CITY
   e. STATE
   f. ZIP CODE
   g. TELEPHONE NUMBER
   h. DATE LAST ORDER SENT
   i. TOTAL AMOUNT PURCHASED FROM VENDOR
   j. TOTAL NUMBER OF ORDERS SENT TO VENDOR

---

* Exercises preceded by a disk icon require the program Visible Analyst Workbench or another CASE tool. A disk is provided free of charge to any professor adopting this book. The examples on the disk may be imported into Visible Analyst Workbench and then used by students.

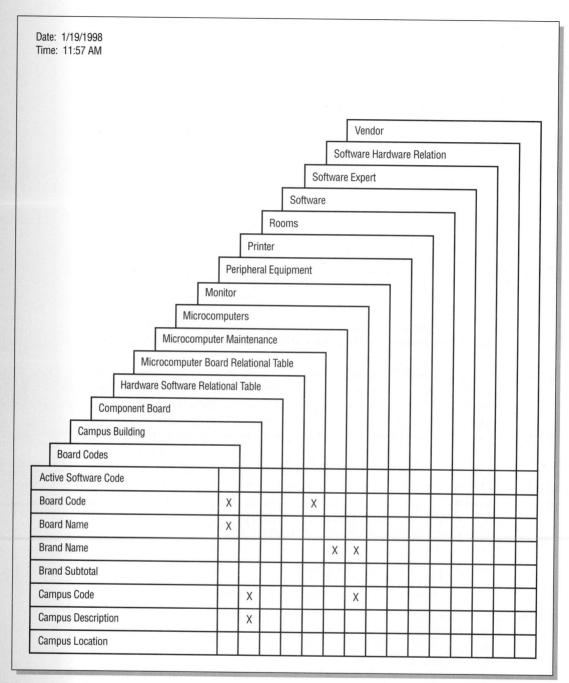

Date: 1/19/1998
Time: 11:57 AM

FIGURE E17.12
Data Elements vs. Entities Composition Matrix.

☐ **E-8.** Produce the following reports using Visible Analyst:

    a. Open the Microcomputer System entity-relationship diagram; then syntax check the diagram (Diagram/Analyze/Syntax Check).

    b. Run the Normalization analysis report for the Microcomputer System entity-relationship diagram (Diagram/Analyze/Normalization).

| | Microcomputer System-Unnormalized | | |
| | Microcomputer System-First Normal Form | | |
	Microcomputer System		
Board Codes	X	X	
Campus Building	X		
Component Board			
Hardware Software Relational Table	X	X	
Microcomputer Board Relational Table	X	X	
Microcomputer Maintenance			
Microcomputers	X	X	X
Monitor	X		
Peripheral Equipment			
Printer	X		
Rooms			
Software	X	X	X
Software Category	X		
Software Expert	X		
Software Hardware Relation			
Vendor			

FIGURE E17.13
Diagram Location Matrix.

c. The Key Analysis report.
d. The Key Synchronization Report.
e. The Model Balancing Report.
f. The Entities vs. Data Stores Matrix.
g. The Composition Matrix.
h. The Diagram Location Matrix.

E-9. Explain in a paragraph why you think a table would be acceptable on a record in an indexed file system written in COBOL.

E-10. Explain in a paragraph the relationship between a foreign key and a primary key and why it is necessary to have them on separate entities when there is a relationship between the entities.

18

DESIGNING
THE USER INTERFACE

USER INTERFACE OBJECTIVES

The interface *is* the system for most users. However well or poorly designed, it stands as the representation of the system, and, by reflection, your competence as a systems analyst.

Your goal must be to design interfaces that help users and businesses get the information they need in and out of the system by addressing the following objectives:

1. Effectiveness as achieved through the design of interfaces that allow users to access the system in a way that is congruent with their individual needs.

2. Efficiency as demonstrated through interfaces that both increase the speed of data entry and reduce errors.

3. User consideration as demonstrated in the design of suitable interfaces and by providing appropriate feedback to users from the system.

4. Productivity as measured by ergonomically sound principles of design for user interfaces and workspaces.

With these goals in mind, we move to more detailed discussions of how each of the objectives, as shown in Figure 18.1, can be met.

TYPES OF USER INTERFACE

In this section, several different kinds of user interface are described, including natural-language interfaces, question-and-answer interfaces, menus, form-fill interfaces, command-language interfaces, and graphical user interfaces (GUIs) and the Web (also called the World Wide Web or www). The user interface has two main components: presentation language, which is the computer-to-human part of the transaction, and action language, which characterizes the human-to-computer portion. Together, both concepts cover the form and content of the term *user interface*.

663

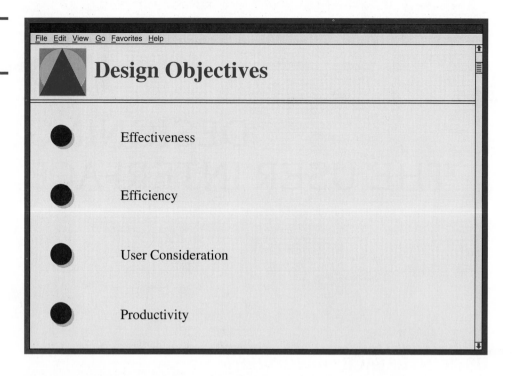

FIGURE 18.1
The four user interface objectives.

Natural-Language Interfaces

Natural-language interfaces are perhaps the dream and ideal of inexperienced users, since they permit users to interact with the computer in their everyday or "natural" language. No special skills are required of the user, who interfaces with the computer using natural language.

The screen depicted in Figure 18.2 lists three natural-language questions from three different applications. Notice that interaction with each seems very easy. For instance, the first sentence—which says, "List all of the salespeople who met their quotas this month"—seems straightforward.

The subtleties and irregularities residing in the ambiguities of English produce an extremely exacting and complex programming problem. However, attempts at natural-language interfacing for particular applications where any other type of interface is nonfeasible (say in the case of a user who is disabled) are meeting with some success, although these interfaces are typically expensive. Implementation problems and extraordinary demand on computing resources have so far kept natural-language interfaces to a minimum. However, the demand exists, and so many programmers and researchers are working diligently on natural-language interfaces. It is a growth area, and it therefore merits your continued monitoring.

Question-and-Answer Interfaces

In this kind of interface, the computer displays a question to the user on the screen. In order to interact, the user enters an answer (via a keyboard stroke or a mouse click), and the computer then acts on that input information in a preprogrammed manner, typically by moving to the next question.

Many management science applications use a question-and-answer interface. A goal programming example is shown in Figure 18.3. As with most question-and-answer interfaces, the computer system directs the questioning sequence. The user responds to what is asked. For instance, in respond-

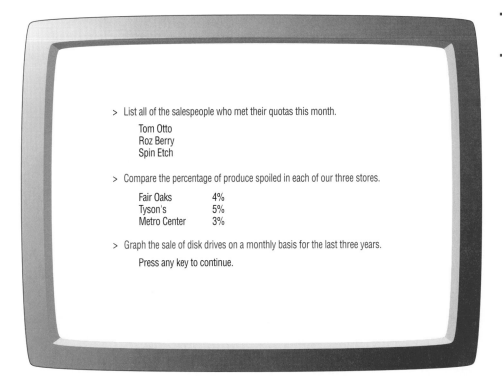

FIGURE 18.2
Natural-language interfaces.

ing to the phrase "Now enter the number of constraints," the user types in an appropriate number.

Another type of question-and-answer interface, called a dialog box, is shown in Figure 18.4. This acts as a question-and-answer interface within another application, in this case a PERT chart for a systems analysis project

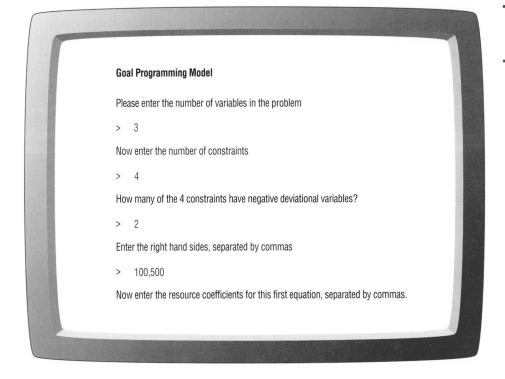

FIGURE 18.3
Question-and-answer
interface.

FIGURE 18.4
A dialog box: one type of
question-and-answer
interface.

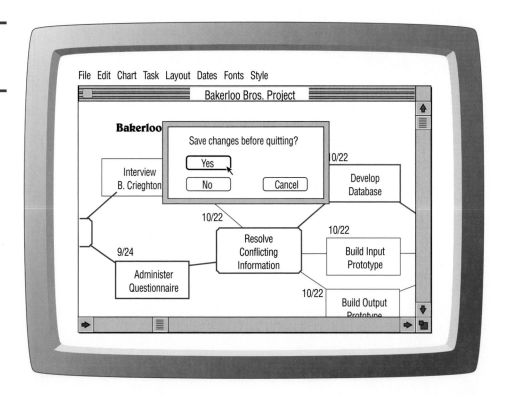

for the Bakerloo Brothers. Notice that the rectangle for YES is highlighted, indicating it is the most likely answer for this situation. The main interface for this application need not necessarily be question-and-answer. Rather, by incorporating a dialog box, the programmer has included an easy-to-use interface within a more complicated one.

Programmers attempt to phrase questions for display in a question-and-answer interface in a concise and understandable manner, but they also need to anticipate the kinds of answers that both the user will input and the system will accept. Greater latitude for user response translates directly into an increase in the complexity of the programming required.

When interfaces are designed, a decision is made on how much flexibility to allow the user in responding to questions. Users require instruction about how much flexibility they are being afforded. For instance, users must know if typing "Y" or clicking on a "Y" in a highlighted box are acceptable replacements for typing "Yes" as a response.

It is possible to include additional help or prompting to remind the user of acceptable responses, and many programmers do. This is important because if users expend too much additional effort in searching for responses or remembering how to respond, they could be dissatisfied and not want to use the system.

Experience suggests that as users become more proficient with the system, they may become impatient with detailed, repetitive questions. They might prefer an option allowing responses to short, abbreviated versions of the questions.

Users unfamiliar with particular applications or not knowledgeable about a topic may find question-and-answer interfaces most comfortable, quickly gaining confidence through their success. However, system designers need to guard against lulling an overly confident new user into expecting system capabilities above what are actually present.

Menus

This interface appropriately borrows its name from the list of dishes that can be selected in a restaurant. Similarly, a menu interface provides the user with an on-screen list of available selections.

In responding to the menu, a user is limited to the options displayed. The user need not know the system but *does* need to know what task should be accomplished. For example, with a typical word-processing menu, users can choose "edit," "copy," or "print" options. However, to best utilize the menu, users must know which task they desire to perform.

Menus as an interface are not hardware-dependent. Variations abound. Menus can be set up to use keyboard entry, lightpen, or mouse. Selections can be identified with a number, letter, or a keyword, or users can click on a selection with a mouse.

An example of a menu-driven program is shown in Figure 18.5. The user has a menu of seven different actions that may be taken on personnel files. In order to choose selection "5) Add an employee to this file," the user has only to type a 5. This takes the user to a new screen, which is ready for entry of new employee data.

Consistency is important in designing a menu interface. In order to access a menu selection, a user may be required to press the Enter key, or the computer may turn directly to the desired program when only a single key must be hit. For example, if the menu offers only the numbers 0 through 9, it is possible to use only one key stroke without hitting Enter. If more numbers are required, for example, Enter is needed to distinguish whether the user intends to enter 1, 10, or 100.

Menus can also be put aside until the user wants to employ them. Figure 18.6 shows how a pull-down menu is used while constructing a PERT diagram for a systems analysis project being completed for the Bakerloo

Personnel File

1) Locate an employee record by last name

2) Locate an employee record by social security number

3) Print employees in alphabetical order

4) Print employees first by department, then in alphabetical order

5) Add an employee to this file

6) Remove an employee from this file

7) Quit

FIGURE 18.5
A menu using numbers to select an action.

FIGURE 18.6
A pull-down menu is there
when the user needs it.

Brothers. The user puts the pointer on the word "Dates" and pulls it down. Then the user puts the arrow on "Calendar," selecting the option to display the project on a conventional monthly calendar.

Menus can be nested within one another to lead a user through options in a program. Nested menus have some advantages. They allow the screen to appear less cluttered, which is consistent with good screen design. Nested menus also allow users to avoid seeing menu options in which they have no interest, so irrelevant user information is reduced. Additionally, nested menus can move users quickly through the program.

When mainframe terminals are used, the menu is widely used to control the system. Pull-down menus and icons are generally used when the operator is using a PC.

Although generally a boon to the inexperienced user, menus can present some problems for those who are experienced. Experienced users may grow impatient at picking their way through successive menus every time a program is used. One way to overcome this would be to give users an option of entering all necessary menus in a single-line command entry. This makes the system amenable to both experienced and inexperienced users.

Form-Fill Interfaces (Input/Output Forms)

Form-fill interfaces consist of on-screen forms or web-based forms displaying fields containing data items or parameters that need to be communicated to the user. The form often is a facsimile of the paper form already familiar to the user. This interface technique is also known as a form-based method and input/output forms.

Figure 18.7 is an example from a product called FormFlow by JetForm. In this program, the end user can go from field to field by pressing the Tab key or using the mouse.

CONSULTING OPPORTUNITY 18.1

I'd Rather Do It Myself

"I can get Mickey to download any data I need from the Web or our server to my PC," DeWitt Miwaye, an upper-level manager for Yumtime Foods (a Midwest food wholesaler) tells you. "Getting data is no problem. What I don't want are a lot of reports. I'd rather play with the data myself."

Miwaye goes on to tell you that as an executive, he doesn't use his PC as often as he'd like—maybe only three times a month. But he has some very specific ideas about what he'd like to do with it.

"I'd like to be able to make some comparisons myself. I could compare the turnover rate for all twelve of

our warehouses. And I'd like to see how effectively the capacity of each of our warehouses is being used. Sometimes I'd like to be able to graph the comparisons, or see a chart of them over time."

In three paragraphs, compare three different types of interfaces that Miwaye could use. Then recommend one interface for his use that takes into account his infrequent use of the PC, his enjoyment in working with raw data, and his desire to see data displayed in a variety of ways.

On-screen forms are set up to show what information should be input and where. Blank fields requiring information can be highlighted with inverse or flashing characters. The cursor is moved by the user from field to field by a single stroke of the arrow key, for instance. This arrangement allows movement one field backward or one field forward by hitting the arrow key. Web-based forms afford the opportunity to include hyperlinks to examples of correctly filled-out forms or to further help and examples.

Form input for screens can be simplified by supplying default values for fields and then allowing users to modify default information if necessary. For example, a database management system designed to show a form for in-

FIGURE 18.7
An example of the form-fill interface.

putting checks may supply the next sequential check number as a default when a new check form is exhibited. If checks are missing, the user changes the check number to reflect the actual check being input.

A powerful use of input/output forms is shown in Figure 18.8. In this example, the programmer has set up a form for users in the State Motor Vehicle Division. But the form is more helpful than the typical input/output form, because it allows users who possess only a minimum of data to fill in the form partially. The computer will then take the data supplied (last name begins with McK, no valid license) and search the appropriate database to find information that completes the records already begun. The computer fills in the form with two names, McKinley and McKinnon. Notice that the computer does not pull up the record for McNeil, even though he fits the requirement of no valid driver's license. This is because McNeil does not fit the "McK" requirement the user previously stipulated.

Input for on-screen fields can be alphanumerically restricted, so that users can enter only numbers in a field requesting a social security number, or they can input only letters where a person's name is required. If numbers are input where only letters are allowed, the computer may alert the user that the field was filled out incorrectly. No matter what type of enforcement is employed to ensure that the form is filled out properly, users should be considered.

The chief advantage of the input/output form interface is that the printed version of the filled-in form provides excellent documentation. It shows field labels as well as the context for entries. Web-based documents can be sent directly to billing if a transaction is involved, or they can go directly to a consumer database if a survey is being submitted. Web-based forms push the responsibility for accuracy to the user and make the form available for completion and submission on a 24-hour, worldwide basis.

There are few disadvantages to input/output forms. The main drawback is similar to the "experienced user" problem discussed for question-and-answer interfaces and menus. Experienced users may become impatient with input/output forms and may want ways to enter data that are more efficient.

Command-Language Interfaces

A command-language interface allows the user to control the application with a series of keystrokes, commands, phrases, or some sequence of these three methods. It is a popular interface that is more refined than those previously discussed.

Two application examples of command language are shown in Figure 18.9. The first example shows the user who asks to use a file containing data on all salespeople and then asks the computer to display all last names, then first names, for all salespeople whose current sales (CURSALES) are greater than their quota. In the second example, the user asks to use a file called GROCER. Then the user directs the computer to calculate the spoilage (SPOILS) by subtracting produce sold from produce bought. After this is done, the user asks to go back to the top of the file and to print out (LIST) the file.

Contrast the comprehension difficulty of the command language with that of the natural-language interface. The command language has no inherent meaning for the user, and that fact makes it quite dissimilar to the other interfaces discussed so far.

FIGURE 18.8
Input/output interface for
locating records in a state
motor vehicle database.

State Motor Vehicle Division

Name (Last)	Moving Violation	Parking Citation	Valid License	Insurance Confirmation
Mck.			No	

VEHICLE DATABASE

NAME (LAST)	MOVING VIOLATION	PARKING VIOLATION	VALID LICENSE	INSURANCE CONFIRMATION
McKenzie	Yes	No	Yes	Yes
McKibben	No	No	Yes	Yes
McKinley	Yes	No	No	Yes
McKinnon	No	No	No	Yes
McMaster	Yes	No	Yes	Yes
McMichael	Yes	Yes	Yes	Yes
McNeil	No	No	No	Yes

This query searches the database ...

... and locates these two records.

State Motor Vehicle Division

Name (Last)	Moving Violation	Parking Citation	Valid License	Insurance Confirmation
McKinley	Yes	No	No	Yes
McKinnon	No	No	No	Yes

FIGURE 18.9
Command-language
interfaces.

USE SALESPPL

DISPLAY ALL LNAME, FNAME FOR CURSALES > QUOTA

USE GROCER

REPLACE ALL SPOILS WITH PBOUGHT - PSOLD

GOTO TOP

LIST

Command languages manipulate the computer as a tool by allowing the user to control the dialog. Therefore, command language affords the user more flexibility and control. When the user gives a command to the computer using command language, it is executed by the system immediately. Then the user may proceed to give it another command.

FIGURE 18.10
One common feature of GUI interfaces is "drag-and-drop." This business form is being created by dragging template symbols onto the screen using Visio Professional.

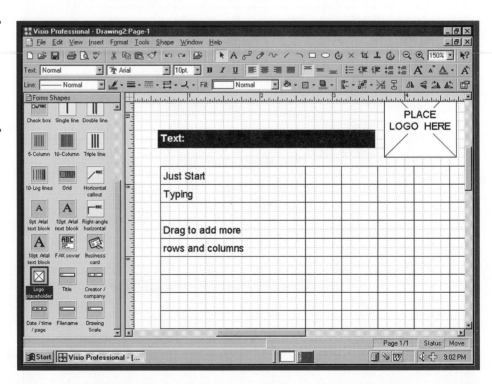

Don't Slow Me Down

"I've seen 'em all," Carrie Moore tells you. "I was here when they got their first computer. I guess I've sort of made a career of this," she says cheerfully, pointing to the large stack of medical insurance claim forms she has been entering into the computer system. As a systems analyst, you are interviewing Carrie, a data-entry operator for HealthPlus (a large, medical insurance company), about changes being contemplated in the computer system.

"I'm really fast compared to the others," she states as she nods toward the six other operators in the room. "I know, because we have little contests all the time to see who's the fastest, with the fewest errors. See that chart on the wall? That shows how much we enter, and how fast. The gold stars show who's the best each week."

"I don't really mind if you change computers—like I say, 'I've seen 'em all.'" She resumes typing on her keyboard as she continues the interview. "But whatever you do, don't slow me down. One of the things I'm most proud of is, I can still beat the other operators. They're good too, though," Carrie adds.

Based on this partial interview with Carrie Moore, what type of user interface will you design for her and the other operators? Assume that the new system will still require massive amounts of data entry from a variety of medical insurance forms sent in by claimants.

Compare and contrast interfaces such as natural language, question-and-answer, menus, input/output forms, and Web-based form-fill documents. Then choose and defend one alternative. What qualities possessed by Carrie and the other operators—and the data they will be entering—shaped your choice? Make a list of them. Is there more than one feasible choice? Why or why not? Respond in a paragraph.

Command languages require memorization of syntax rules that may prove to be obstacles for inexperienced users (however, anyone can learn them with practice). Other interfaces resemble human exchanges more closely and are therefore more easily understood by users unaware of how a computer functions. Experienced users tend to prefer command languages, possibly because of the faster completion time they allow.

Graphical User Interfaces (GUIs)

Graphical User Interfaces (GUIs) allow direct manipulation of the graphical representation on the screen, which can be accomplished with keyboard input, a joystick, or a mouse. Direct manipulation requires more system sophistication than the interfaces discussed previously.

An example of the drag-and-drop feature of a GUI interface (sometimes simply called a drag-and-drop interface) is shown in Figure 18.10. In this screen from Visio Professional by Visio Corporation, the symbols arrayed on the left are called templates. In order to draw with this interface, users drag and drop a master shape into their drawing. By creating entity-relationship diagrams or other specialized drawings, this kind of interface makes the work of the analyst much easier. Visio comes with many more stencils for drawing data flow diagrams, program flow charts, network diagrams, object-oriented diagrams—and it even has templates for designing office spaces.

The key to GUI is the constant feedback on task accomplishment that it provides. Continuous feedback on the manipulated object means that changes or reversals in operations can be made quickly, without incurring error messages. The concept of feedback for users is discussed thoroughly in an upcoming section, "Feedback for Users."

An imaginative use of a graphical user interface utilizing icons is shown in Figure 18.11. The top screen shows the layout of the city of Lake-

FIGURE 18.11
A GUI interface is used for assigning drivers to routes.

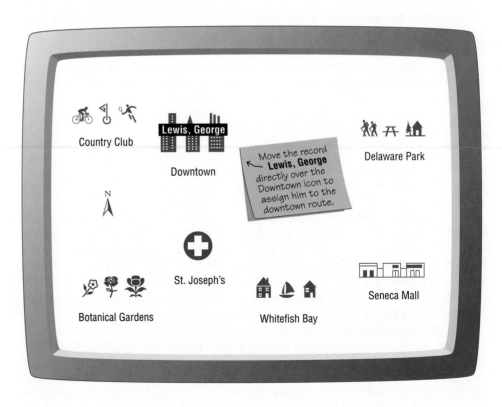

wood, along with a pull-down menu listing available delivery drivers. All possible routes, such as "Country Club" and "Botanical Gardens," are shown as icons.

In order to assign one of the drivers—in this case, "Lewis, George,"—to the downtown delivery route, the scheduler moves Lewis's record, via arrow keys or a mouse, directly over the downtown icon. Lewis is then assigned to the downtown route. This is a quick, visual way to assign drivers to routes, which does not demand that a user have longstanding familiarity with the geographical layout of the city, the routes, or the drivers.

Icons are used extensively when running on a PC. By double-clicking the left mouse button rapidly, the user selects an icon to run the corresponding program. Icons are often arranged within larger windows, called program groups or folders. When a program group icon is selected, the window opens up, displaying the group icons. The analyst should design program groups with the same care used to design full-screen or pull-down menus.

The creation of GUI interfaces poses a challenge, since an appropriate model of reality or an acceptable conceptual model of the representation must be invented. This requires combining several skills in a way that stretches the capabilities of most systems analysts and programmers. Designing GUI interfaces for use on intranets, extranets, and even more pressingly, on the Web requires even more careful planning (see Chapter 16 on Web-site design). By and large, the users of Web-sites are unknown to the developer, so a design must be clear-cut. Choice of icons, language, and hyperlinks becomes an entire set of decisions and assumptions about what kinds of users we are hoping to attract. In fact, the Web is creating change so rapidly, that Strom (1997, p. 25) quotes one software developer as saying, "Application developers who aren't using the Web as their primary end-user interface will be in the same position as scribes after the invention of the printing press." This is definitely something to reflect on as you go about conceptualizing new projects.

DIALOG AND DESKTOPS

Guidelines for Dialog Design

Dialog is the communication between the computer and a person. Well-designed dialog makes it easier for people to use a computer and leads to less frustration with the computer system. There are several key points for designing good dialog. Some of them were mentioned in Chapter 16. They include:

1. Meaningful communication, so that the computer understands what people are entering and people understand what the computer is presenting or requesting.
2. Minimal user action.
3. Standard operation and consistency.

COMMUNICATION. The system should present information clearly to the user. This means presenting an appropriate title on each screen, minimizing the use of abbreviations, and providing clear user feedback. Inquiry programs should display code meanings as well as data in an edited format—for example, displaying slashes between the month, day, and year in a date field or commas and decimal points in an amount field. User instructions should be supplied (usually on one line only) regarding details, such as available function key assignments. Displaying the instruction line using inverse video helps to draw the user's attention to the instructions. In a graphical interface, the cursor may change shape depending on the work being performed.

Easy-to-use help screens should be provided. Many PC help screens have additional topics that may be directly selected using highlighted text displayed on the first help screen. These hyperlinks are usually in a different color, which makes them stand out in contrast to the rest of the help text. They are usually selected using a mouse. Many of the newer GUI interfaces also incorporate tool tip help, displaying a small help message identifying the function of a command button when the cursor is placed over it.

The other side of communication is that the computer should "understand what the user has entered." This means that all data entered on the screen should be edited for validity.

MINIMAL USER ACTION. Keying is often the slowest part of a computer system, and good dialog will minimize the number of keystrokes required. You can accomplish this in a number of different ways:

1. Keying codes instead of whole words on entry screens. Codes are also keyed when using a command-language interface. An example is entering DIR, for Directory, to obtain a list of files on a personal computer, or CD for Change Directory. On a GUI screen, the codes may be entered by selecting them from a pull-down list of available codes. To enhance communication, the pull-down lists should contain the names of the codes, even though codes are stored on the files.

2. Only entering data that is not already stored on files. For example, when changing or deleting item records, only the item number should be entered. The computer responds by displaying descriptive information that is currently stored on the item file. When entering an order for customers, the customer number is entered and the name and address is displayed, allowing the operator to sight-verify that the customer number has been entered correctly.

3. Supplying the editing characters (for example, slashes as date field separators) by means of software for personal computers. Users should not have to enter formatting characters such as leading zeros, commas, or a decimal point when entering a dollar amount; nor should they have to enter slashes or hyphens when entering a date. (On a mainframe terminal, these characters are omitted.)

4. Using default values for fields on entry screens. Defaults are used when a user enters the same value in a screen field for the majority of the records being processed. The values are displayed, and the user may press the Enter key to accept the default or overtype the default value with a new one. For example, an inventory control clerk may use a screen to generate purchase orders for items that are low in stock. The screen would display the reorder quantity from the item record as a default purchase quantity. Under typical circumstances, the user would simply press Enter to accept this quantity, but if the item were a popular sale item, the operator might choose to enter a higher amount to increase the quantity purchased.

FIGURE 18.12
Example of a pull-down menu
with shortcut keys.

If the software must be flexible enough to accommodate different user situations, it should be designed so that the preset defaults may be changed. The new defaults should display each time the software is invoked. An example would be changing the screen colors, which should not have to be manually reset each time the screen is used.

GUI interfaces may contain check boxes and radio buttons that are selected when a dialog box opens. Provide context sensitive menus that appear when an object is clicked with the right mouse button. These menus contain options specific for the object under the mouse.

5. Designing an inquiry (or change or delete) program so that the user needs to enter only the first few characters of a name or item description. The program displays a list of all matching names, and when the operator chooses one, the matching record is displayed.

6. Providing keystrokes for selecting pull-down menu options. Often, these options are selected using a mouse, followed by some keying. This requires users to move their hand from the keyboard to the mouse and back to the keyboard. As users become familiar with the system, keystrokes often provide a faster method for manipulating the pull-down menus, since both hands remain on the keyboard. On a PC, this usually involves pressing a function key or the Alt key followed by a letter, as illustrated in the Ecco screen shown in Figure 18.12. Notice that the menu choices are along the top, and by pressing Alt and the letter C, the user has pulled down a menu that permits adding items to the calendar itself, as well as to the way it is displayed. On this screen, the user has hit Alt "S" for "Sidebar Shows" and then Alt "T" for "Three Months." This resulted in the three months being displayed on the left-hand side of the screen.

Any combination of these six approaches can help the analyst decrease the number of keystrokes required by the user, thereby speeding up data entry and minimizing errors.

STANDARD OPERATION AND CONSISTENCY. The system should be consistent throughout its set of different screens and in the mechanisms for controlling the operation of the screens throughout different applications. Consistency makes it easier for the users to learn how to use new portions of the system once they are familiar with one component. You can achieve consistency by:

1. Locating titles, date, time, and operator and feedback messages in the same places on all screens.

2. Exiting each program by the same key or menu option. It would be a poor design that used function key 4 (F4) to exit the ADD CUSTOMER program and function key 6 (F6) to exit the CHANGE CUSTOMER program.

3. Canceling a transaction in a consistent way, usually by using the CLEAR key on a mainframe and the ESCAPE key on a PC.

4. Obtaining help in a standardized way. The industry standard for help is function key 1 (F1), and most microcomputer software developers are adopting this convention.

5. Standardizing the color used for all screens. Error messages are typically displayed in red. Remember to keep the background screen color the same for all applications.

6. Standardizing the use of icons for similar operations when using a graphical user interface. For example, a small piece of paper with a bent upper corner often represents a document.

An example of good GUI design is the tab control dialog box shown in Figure 18.13. Currently, the user is choosing printer options, and he or she is in the "Paper" tab, but he or she also has the choice of six other tabs, including "Fonts," "Graphics," and so on. This screen shows selections that a user has made by clicking on the left or right arrows on the horizontal sliding bar that runs beneath the envelope sizes, "Com-10 Env, Monarch E, DL Env, C5 Env," and so on. The darkened area indicates that the user has chosen to print a C5 envelope. Notice that the designer of this interface has used option buttons for both "Layout" and "Orientation." The user has clicked on a choice of "Portrait" for orientation. A drop-down menu is also used to select the paper source. In this instance, the user has chosen "AutoSelect Tray." The designer has also used push buttons at the very bottom of the screen that allow users to enter "OK," "Cancel," or "Apply" in regard to the options they have just chosen.

Other User Interfaces

Other user interfaces, while less common that those discussed previously, are growing in popularity. These interfaces include pointing devices such as the stylus, touch-sensitive screens, and speech recognition and synthesis. Each of these interfaces has its own special attributes that uniquely suit it to particular applications.

The stylus (a pointed stick that resembles a pen) is becoming popular because of new handwriting recognition software and personal digital assis-

FIGURE 18.13
Tab control dialog box.

tants (PDAs). The 3COM (US Robotics) Palm Pilot has been a success because it does a limited number of things very well and sells for a low price. It includes a calendar, an address book, a to-do list, and a memo pad. Data entry is also facilitated with a docking cradle so you can synchronize data with your PC. The Interlink Electronics VersaPad allows for stylus interface directly to PCs.

Touch-sensitive screens allow a user to use a finger (or object) to activate the screen when it comes close to the screen surface. Coming close to the screen breaks a grid of light beams within or just over the screen's surface.

Touch-sensitive screens are useful in public information displays such as maps of cities and their sights, which are posted in hotel lobbies. They can also be used to explain dioramas in museums and to locate camping facilities in state parks. Touch-sensitive screens require no special expertise from users, and the screen is self-contained, requiring no special input device that might be broken or stolen.

Voice recognition has long been the dream of scientists and science fiction writers alike. It is intuitively appealing, since it seems to approximate human communication. With voice recognition, the user speaks to the com-

That's Not a Light Bulb

From your preliminary analysis, it appears that many reductions in error will be realized if sales clerks at Bright's Electric (which sells electrical parts, bulbs, and fixtures to wholesale customers) adopt an on-line system. The new system would allow sales clerks to withdraw a part from inventory (and thereby update inventory), return a part to inventory, check on the inventory status, and check on whether a part is backordered. Currently, in order to update inventory, sales clerks fill out a three-part form by hand. The customer gets one, inventory keeps one, and at the end of the day the originals are deposited in the front office.

The next morning, the first thing the lone office worker does is enter the data from the forms into the computer. Errors occur when she enters the wrong part numbers or quantities. Additional time is consumed when inventory workers hunt for a part that they think might be in stock—but which is not. Updated inventory sheets are available to the sales clerks around noon, but by that time they have already taken from inventory twice the number of parts that will be taken out after noon. Clearly, a well-designed on-line system would help reduce these errors and also help with inventory control.

The owner, Mr. Bright, has entertained the idea of an on-line system and dropped it several times over the last five years. The chief reason is that the sales clerks, who would be the heaviest users of the system, do not think the systems analysts they've talked to can fulfill their needs.

M. T. Sockette, the sales clerk who has been with Bright's the longest is the most vocal, telling you, "We know the parts, we know our customers. What we could do with a computer here would be great. But the guys they've brought in here to get it going! I mean, they say things like, 'You can step right up and type one 60-watt General Electric light bulb into the computer.'"

"To us, that's not a light bulb, it's a GE60WSB. All of us know the part numbers here. We pride ourselves on it. Typing in all that junk will take all day."

After talking to Mr. Bright, you decide to implement an on-line system. You have talked to M. T. and the others and reassured them that the system will use the part numbers they're familiar with, and it will save them time. Although skeptical, they have been persuaded by you to give it a try.

What type of user interface will you design for the sales clerks? Before you come to your solution, do a careful analysis in three paragraphs that compares and contrasts natural language, question-and-answer, menus, input/output forms, command language, and Web-based form-fill documents for their suitability as user interfaces at Bright's. Then choose one interface and explain in a paragraph why you find this one most appropriate based on what you know about Bright's sales clerks and their current system. Draw a prototype of a screen that will be part of your solution. Describe in a paragraph how you will test it with the sales clerks.

puter, and the system is able to recognize an individual's vocal signals, convert them, and store the input. Voice recognition inventory systems are already in operation.

An advantage of voice recognition systems is that their use can speed data entry enormously, while freeing the user's hands for other tasks. Speech input adds still another dimension to the PC. It is now possible to add equipment and software that allows a personal computer user to speak commands such as "Open File" or "Save File" to avoid using the keyboard or mouse. The obvious advantages of this technology are increased accuracy and greater speed than what conventional mouse movements afford, as well as the avoidance of repetitive stress injuries, such as carpal tunnel syndrome, which can debilitate the wrist and hand.

The two main developments in speech recognition are (1) continuous speech systems, which allow for the input of regular text in word processors and (2) speaker independence, so any number of people can enter commands or words at a given workstation.

Dragon Systems products include dictation systems, command systems, and text to speech systems. Dragon Naturally Speaking by Dragon Sys-

FIGURE 18.14
Feedback is used
in many ways.

Feedback Is Needed to Tell the User That:
• The computer has accepted the input • The input is in the correct form • The input is not in the correct form • There will be a delay in the processing • The request has been completed • The computer is unable to complete the request • More detailed feedback is available (and how to get it)

tems, Inc. is the first large vocabulary continuous speech and recognition product for the PC. (The current version has an active vocabulary starting at 30,000 words and expanding up to 235,000 words.) The vocabulary is not merely a spelling list, but includes speaker-independent acoustic and language usage information, which means more accurate recognition. It is now possible for the user to talk naturally, using words they normally would use in conversation and for those words to then be recognized by the software.

When evaluating the interfaces you have chosen, there are some standards to keep in mind:

1. The necessary training period for users should be acceptably short.

2. Users early in their training should be able to enter commands without thinking about them or without referring to a help menu or manual. Keeping interfaces consistent throughout applications can help in this regard.

3. The interface should be "seamless," so that errors are few and those that do occur are not occurring because of poor design.

4. The time that users and the system need to bounce back from errors should be short.

5. Infrequent users should be able to relearn the system quickly.

There are many different interfaces available, and it is important to realize that an effective interface goes a long way toward successfully involving users. Users should want to use the system. In the next section, we discuss the importance of providing feedback for users in order to support and sustain their involvement with the system.

FEEDBACK FOR USERS

All systems require feedback, in order to monitor and change behavior, as was discussed in Chapter 2. Feedback usually compares current behavior with predetermined goals and gives back information describing the gap between actual and intended performance.

Since humans themselves are complex systems, they require feedback from others to meet psychological needs. Feedback also increases human confidence. How much feedback is required is an individual characteristic.

When users interface with machines, they still need feedback about how their work is progressing. As designers of user interfaces, systems analysts need to be aware of the human need for feedback and build it into the system. When we discuss feedback for users, we typically refer to feedback from on-line systems—typically text. However, note that standardized icons can often be used to supply feedback. For example, displaying an hourglass while the

Waiting to Be Fed

"Yeah, we were sold a package all right. This one right here. Don't get me wrong, it gets the work done. We just don't know when."

You are talking with Owen Itt, who is telling you about the sales unit's recent purchase of new software for its PCs that allows input of sales data for each of its sixteen salespeople, provides output comparison data for them, and projects future sales based on past sales records.

"But we've had some odd experiences with this program," Owen continues. "It seems slow or something. For instance, we're never sure when it's done. I type in a command to get a file and nothing happens. About half a minute later (if I'm lucky), the screen I want might come up. But I'm never sure. If I ask it to save sales data, I just get a whirring sound. If it works, I'm re-turned to where I was before. If it doesn't save data, I'm still returned to where I was before. It's confusing. And I never know what to do. There's nothing on the screen that tells me what to do next. See the manual that came with this? It's dog-eared because we have to keep thumbing through trying to figure out what to do next."

Based on what you've heard in the interview, take this opportunity to supplement the program by designing some on-screen feedback for Owen and his sales team. The feedback should address all of Owen's concerns, while following the guidelines for giving feedback to users and the guidelines for good screen design. Draw a prototype of the screen or screens you think are necessary to address the problems he lists above.

system is processing encourages the user to wait for some time, rather than repeatedly hitting keys to try and invoke another screen or response.

Feedback to the user from the system is necessary in seven distinct situations, as shown in Figure 18.14. Feedback that is ill-timed or too plentiful is not helpful since we can process only a limited amount of information. Each of the seven situations where feedback is appropriate is explained in the upcoming subsections.

ACKNOWLEDGING ACCEPTANCE OF INPUT. The first situation in which users need feedback is to learn that the computer has accepted the input. For example, when a user enters a name on a line, the computer provides feedback to the user by advancing the cursor one character at a time when the letters are entered correctly.

RECOGNIZING THAT INPUT IS IN THE CORRECT FORM. Users need feedback to tell them that the input is in the correct form. For example, a user inputs a command, and the on-screen computer feedback is "READY" as the program progresses to a new point. A poor example of feedback that tells the user that input is in the correct form would be the message, "INPUT OK," since this takes extra space, is cryptic, and does nothing to encourage input of more data.

NOTIFYING THAT INPUT IS NOT IN THE CORRECT FORM. Feedback is necessary to warn users that input is not in the correct form. When data are incorrect, one way to inform the user is to generate a window that briefly describes the problem with the input and tells how the user can correct it, as shown in Figure 18.15.

Notice that the message concerning an error in inputting the length of subscription is polite and concise but not cryptic, so that even inexperienced users will be able to understand it. The subscription length entered is wrong, but the feedback given does not dwell on the fact that the user made

FIGURE 18.15
Feedback informs the user
that input was not in the correct form and lists options.

a mistake. Rather, it offers options (13, 26, or 52 weeks) so that the error can be corrected easily.

So far we have been discussing visual feedback in text or iconic form, but many systems have audio feedback capabilities as well. When a user inputs data in the incorrect form, as shown previously for subscription length, the system might beep instead of providing a window. Beeping, buzzing, or ringing that is set off by common data-entry errors causes users to become disgruntled or frustrated. Additionally, audio feedback alone is not descriptive, so it is not as helpful to users as on-screen directions. Use audio feedback sparingly, perhaps to denote urgent situations. This also applies to the design of Web sites, which may be viewed in an open office, where sounds carry and a co-worker's workstation speakers are within earshot of several other people.

EXPLAINING A DELAY IN PROCESSING. One of the most important kinds of feedback informs the user that there will be a delay in processing his or her request. Delays longer than 10 seconds or so require feedback so that the user knows the system is still working.

Figure 18.16 shows a screen providing feedback in a window for a user who has just requested a printout of the newspaper's subscription list. The screen displays a sentence reassuring the user that the request is being processed, as well as a sign in the upper-right-hand corner instructing the user to "WAIT" until the current command has been executed. The screen also provides a way to stop the operation if necessary.

One PC system uses an icon for feeding back information on processing delays. The icon is in the familiar shape of a wristwatch and serves as visual reassurance that the system is working. Sometimes during delays, while new software is being installed, a short tutorial on the new application is run, which is meant to be more of a distraction than feedback about installation.

FIGURE 18.16
Feedback tells the user that
there will be a delay while
printing is being done.

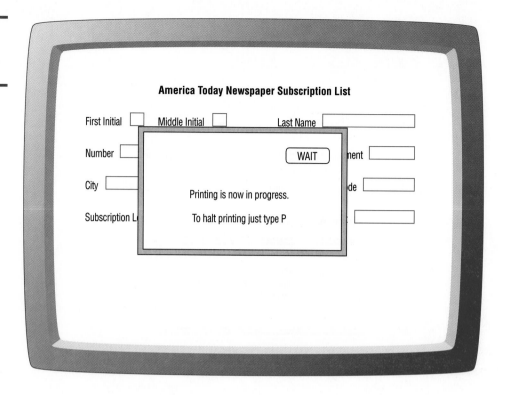

America Today Newspaper Subscription List

First Initial ☐   Middle Initial ☐   Last Name ☐

Number ☐   WAIT   ...ment ☐

City ☐   Printing is now in progress.   ...de ☐

Subscription L...   To halt printing just type P

Timing feedback of this sort is critical. Too slow a system response could cause the user to input commands that impede or disrupt processing, and too quick a response may make users feel as if the pace of their work is being propelled by the system.

ACKNOWLEDGING THAT A REQUEST IS COMPLETED. Users need to know when their request has been completed and new requests may be input. Figure 18.17 shows a screen where the user has requested preparation of an index by name. When the indexing is finished, the system replies with "DONE." The user then knows it is safe to proceed.

Often a specific feedback message is displayed when an action has been completed by a user, such as "EMPLOYEE RECORD HAS BEEN ADDED," "CUSTOMER RECORD HAS BEEN CHANGED," or "ITEM NUMBER 12345 HAS BEEN DELETED."

NOTIFYING THAT A REQUEST WAS NOT COMPLETED. Feedback is also needed to let the user know that the computer is unable to complete a request. Notice that in the last figure the system has displayed the message, "UNABLE TO PROCESS REQUEST. CHECK REQUEST AGAIN," in response to the user's request to locate subscribers by zip code. The user can then go back and check to see if the request has been input correctly rather than continue to enter commands that cannot be executed.

OFFERING THE USER MORE DETAILED FEEDBACK. Users need to be reassured that more detailed feedback is available, and they should be shown how they can get it. Notice that in the last figure the system has displayed a message instructing the user to type "ASSIST" for more information. When designing

FIGURE 18.17
Feedback tells when input is
accepted, whether processing
is completed or not, and how
to ask for further assistance.

Within the figure:

> USE NAMEFILE
READY

> INDEX ON NAMES
DONE

> LOCATE ALL FOR ZIP >68500 AND <68588
UNABLE TO PROCESS REQUEST. CHECK REQUEST AGAIN.
FOR MORE INFORMATION TYPE "ASSIST"

Web interfaces, hyperlinks can be embedded to allow the user to jump to the relevant help screens or to view more information. Hyperlinks are typically highlighted with underlining and/or they are italicized—or they may appear in a different color. Hyperlinks can be graphics, text, or icons,

Other commands, such as INSTRUCT, EXPLAIN, and MORE, may also be employed. Or the user may type a question mark or point to an appropriate icon to get more feedback. Using the command HELP or having users hit the Escape key as ways to obtain further information has been questioned, since users may feel helpless or caught in a trap from which they must escape. However, both conventions are in use, and their familiarity to users may overcome these concerns.

Feedback is essential to all humans. Even when interfacing with machines, people still require it. Plan to provide feedback for users so that they are aware of whether their input is being accepted; whether input is or is not in the correct form; whether processing is going on; whether requests can or cannot be processed; and whether more detailed information is available and how to get it.

It is well worth the systems analyst's time to provide user feedback. If used correctly, feedback can both be a powerful reinforcer of users' learning processes and serve to improve their performance with the system and increase their motivation to produce.

A VARIETY OF HELP OPTIONS. Feedback on personal computers has developed over the years. "Help" originally started as a response to the user who pressed a function key such as F1; the GUI alternative is the pull-down help menu. But this approach was cumbersome, because end users had to navigate through a table of contents or search using an index. Next came context-sensitive help. End users could simply click on the right mouse button, and topics or explanations about the current screen or area of the screen would be revealed. Sometimes software manufacturers call these cue cards. The third type of help on personal computers occurs when the end user places the arrow over an icon and leaves it there for a couple of seconds. At this point, some programs pop up a balloon similar to those found in comic strips. This balloon explains a little bit about the icon.

The fourth type of help are wizards, which ask the end user a series of questions and then take an action accordingly. Wizards have been used in narrowing a search in an encyclopedia such as Encarta, in designing a chart in Freelance or PowerPoint, or in choosing a style for a word-processing memo.

Besides building help into the software, software manufacturers offer help lines (most customer service telephone lines are not toll-free, however). Some manufacturers offer a fax-back system. An end user can request a catalog of various help documents to be sent by fax and then can order from the catalog by entering the item number with a touch tone phone.

Finally, software forums exist on CompuServe and America OnLine; they also exist as bulletin boards on the Net, which are maintained by the software company itself that wishes to capture Web-site visitors. An end user will often get information from the software manufacturer's technical support staff, but sometimes the end user can also get valuable information from other users of the product. This type of support is, of course, unofficial, and the information thus obtained may be true, partially true, or may even lead the user astray. The principles regarding the use of software forums are the same for those mentioned in Chapter 20, where FOLKLORE and recommendation systems are discussed. Read this section before you accept what is said on bulletin boards. Beware!

Besides informal help on software, vendor Web sites are extremely useful for updating drivers, viewers, and the software itself. Most computer magazines have some sort of "driver watch" or "bug report" that monitors the bulletin boards and Web sites for useful programs that can be downloaded. Programs such as Oil Change will forage vendor Web sites for the latest updates, inform the user of them, assist with the downloads, and actually upgrade user applications.

DESIGNING QUERIES

Query Types

The questions we pose concerning data from our database are referred to as queries. There are six basic query types. Each query involves three items: an entity, an attribute, and a value. In each case, two of these are given, and the intent of the query is to find the remaining item.

QUERY TYPE 1. In the first type of query, the entity and one of the entity's attributes are given. The purpose of the query is to find the value. The query can be expressed as:

What is the value of a specified attribute for a particular entity?

Sometimes it is more convenient to use notation to help formulate the query. This query can be written as:

$$V \longleftarrow (E, A)$$

where *V* stands for the value, *E* for entity, *A* for attribute, and the variables in parenthesis are given.

The following question:

What did employee number 73712 make in year 1997?

can be stated more specifically as:

What is the value of the attribute YEAR-97 for the entity EMPLOYEE-NUMBER 73712?

Basic query type 1 is illustrated in Figure 18.18. The record containing employee number 73712 was found, and the answer to the query was $27,100.

QUERY TYPE 2. The intent of query type 2 is to find an entity or entities when an attribute and value are given. Query type 2 can be stated as follows:

What entity has a specified value for a particular attribute?

Since values can also be numeric, it is possible to search for a value equal to, greater than, less than, not equal to, greater than or equal to, and so on. An example of this type of query is:

What employee(s) earned more than $50,000 in 1997?

or more specifically:

What entities (EMPLOYEE-NUMBER) have the value > 50,000 for the attribute YEAR-97?

The notation for query type 2 is:

$$E \longleftarrow (V, A)$$

Figure 18.19 illustrates query type 2. In this case, three employees made more than $50,000, so the response turned out to be a listing of the employee numbers for the three employees.

QUERY TYPE 3. The purpose of query type 3 is to determine which attribute(s) fits the description provided when the entity and value are given. It can be stated as:

What attribute(s) has a specified value for a particular entity?

This query is useful when there are many similar attributes that have the same property. The example below has similar attributes (specific years) that contain the annual salaries for the employees of the company:

What years did employee #72845 make over $50,000?

or more precisely,

What attributes {YEAR-94, YEAR-95, YEAR-96, YEAR-97} have a value > 50,000 for the entity EMPLOYEE-NUMBER = 72845?

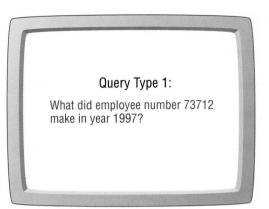

Query Type 1:

What did employee number 73712
make in year 1997?

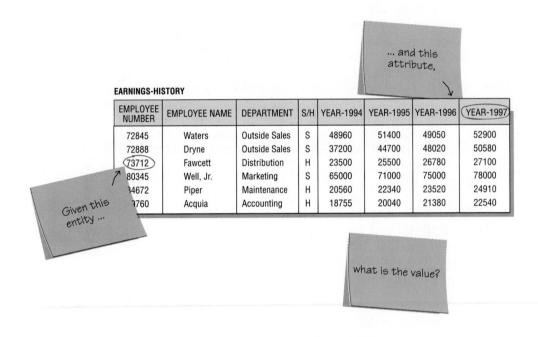

... and this attribute,

EARNINGS-HISTORY

EMPLOYEE NUMBER	EMPLOYEE NAME	DEPARTMENT	S/H	YEAR-1994	YEAR-1995	YEAR-1996	YEAR-1997
72845	Waters	Outside Sales	S	48960	51400	49050	52900
72888	Dryne	Outside Sales	S	37200	44700	48020	50580
73712	Fawcett	Distribution	H	23500	25500	26780	27100
80345	Well, Jr.	Marketing	S	65000	71000	75000	78000
84672	Piper	Maintenance	H	20560	22340	23520	24910
9760	Acquia	Accounting	H	18755	20040	21380	22540

Given this entity ...

what is the value?

Response:
$27,100

FIGURE 18.18
Query type 1 finds the value of an attribute for a given entity.

FIGURE 18.19
Query type 2 finds the entities
that satisfy a specific value for
a particular attribute.

Query Type 2:

What employee(s) earned more
than $50,000 in 1997?

Given a value
GT 50000 ...

... for this
attribute,

EARNINGS-HISTORY

EMPLOYEE NUMBER	EMPLOYEE NAME	DEPARTMENT	S/H	YEAR-1994	YEAR-1995	YEAR-1996	YEAR-1997
72845	Waters	Outside Sales	S	48960	51400	49050	52900
72888	Dryne	Outside Sales	S	37200	44700	48020	50580
73712	Fawcett	Distribution	H	23500	25500	26780	27100
80345	Well, Jr.	Marketing	S	65000	71000	75000	78000
84672	Piper	Maintenance	H	20560	22340	23520	24910
89760	Acquia	Accounting	H	18755	20040	21380	22540

what are the
entities?

Response:

Employee numbers:

72845
72888
80345

where the optional list in braces { } is the set of eligible attributes.

The notation for query type 3 is:

$$A \longleftarrow (V, E)$$

An illustration of query type 3 is given in Figure 18.20. In this example, Waters (#72845) made over $50,000 for two years. These years are listed in the response. Query type 3 is rarer than either type 1 or type 2 due to the requirement of having similar attributes exhibiting the same properties.

QUERY TYPE 4. This query is similar to query type 1. The difference is that the values of all attributes are desired. Query 4 can be expressed as:

List all the values for all of the attributes for a particular entity.

Examples of query 4 include:

List all the details in the earnings history file for employee number 72888.

or

List all of the information regarding the inventory status on part HV-5678.

The notation for query type 4:

$$\text{all } V \longleftarrow (E, \text{ all } A)$$

An illustration of query type 4 is shown in Figure 18.21. The response for this query was simply the record for the employee named Dryne (#72888).

QUERY TYPE 5. The fifth type is another global query, but it is similar in form to query type 2. Query type 5 can be stated as:

List all entities that have a specified value for all attributes.

An example of query type 5 is:

List all of the employees whose earnings exceeded $50,000 in any of the years available.

The notation for query type 5 is:

$$\text{all } E \longleftarrow (V, \text{ all } A)$$

An example of query type 5 is shown in Figure 18.22.

QUERY TYPE 6. The sixth query type is similar to query type 3. The difference is that query type 6 requests a listing of the attributes for all entities rather than one particular entity. Query type 6 can be stated as:

List all the attributes that have a specified value for all entities.

Query Type 3:

What year(s) did employee
number 72845 make
over $50,000?

... and a value
GT 50000,

EARNINGS-HISTORY

EMPLOYEE NUMBER	EMPLOYEE NAME	DEPARTMENT	S/H	YEAR-1994	YEAR-1995	YEAR-1996	YEAR-1997
72845	Waters	Outside Sales	S	48960	51400	49050	52900
72888	Dryne	Outside Sales	S	37200	44700	48020	50580
73712	Fawcett	Distribution	H	23500	25500	26780	27100
0345	Well, Jr.	Marketing	S	65000	71000	75000	78000
672	Piper	Maintenance	H	20560	22340	23520	24910
0	Acquia	Accounting	H	18755	20040	21380	22540

Given this entity ...

what are the
attributes?

Response:

Year-1995
Year-1997

FIGURE 18.20
Query type 3 finds the attributes when the entity and value are given.

FIGURE 18.21
Query type 4 lists all the
values for all attributes
of a particular entity.

Query Type 4:

List all of the details
for employee number 72888.

... for ALL
attributes,

EARNINGS-HISTORY

EMPLOYEE NUMBER	EMPLOYEE NAME	DEPARTMENT	S/H	YEAR-1994	YEAR-1995	YEAR-1996	YEAR-1997
72845	Waters	Outside Sales	S	48960	51400	49050	52900
72888	Dryne	Outside Sales	S	37200	44700	48020	50580
73712	Fawcett	Distribution	H	23500	25500	26780	27100
0345	Well, Jr.	Marketing	S	65000	71000	75000	78000
672	Piper	Maintenance	H	20560	22340	23520	24910
60	Acquia	Accounting	H	18755	20040	21380	22540

Given this
entity ...

list ALL of
the values.

Response:

72888 Dryne Outside Sales S 37200 44700 48020 50580

FIGURE 18.22
Query type 5 lists all of the
entities that satisfy a value for
all attributes described.

Query Type 5:

List all of the employees
whose earnings exceeded $50,000
in any of the years available.

Given a value
GT 50000 ...

... for ALL
attributes,

EARNINGS-HISTORY

EMPLOYEE NUMBER	EMPLOYEE NAME	DEPARTMENT	S/H	YEAR-1994	YEAR-1995	YEAR-1996	YEAR-1997
72845	Waters	Outside Sales	S	48960	51400	49050	52900
72888	Dryne	Outside Sales	S	37200	44700	48020	50580
73712	Fawcett	Distribution	H	23500	25500	26780	27100
80345	Well, Jr.	Marketing	S	65000	71000	75000	78000
84672	Piper	Maintenance	H	20560	22340	23520	24910
89760	Acquia	Accounting	H	18755	20040	21380	22540

list ALL of the
entities.

Response:

Employee numbers:

72845
72888
80345

The following is an example of query type 6:

List all of the years for which earnings exceeded $20,000 for all employees in the company.

The notation for query type 6 is:

$$\text{all } A \longleftarrow (V, \text{ all } E)$$

An illustration of query type 6 can be found in Figure 18.23. As with query type 3, query type 6 is not used as much as other types.

BUILDING MORE COMPLEX QUERIES. The preceding six query types are only building blocks for more complex queries. Expressions referred to as Boolean expressions can be formed for queries. One example of a Boolean expression is:

List all of the customers who have zip codes greater than or equal to 60001 and less than 70000 and who have ordered more than $500 from our catalogs or have ordered at least 5 times in the past year.

One of the difficulties with this statement is that is difficult to determine which operator (for example, AND) belongs with which condition; it is also difficult to determine the sequence in which the parts of the expression should be carried out. The following may help to clarify this problem:

LIST ALL CUSTOMERS HAVING (ZIP-CODE GE 60001 AND ZIP-CODE LT 70000) AND (AMOUNT-ORDERED GT 500 OR TIMES-ORDERED GE 5)

Now some of the confusion is eliminated. The first improvement is that the operators are expressed more clearly as GE, GT, LT than as English phrases, such as "at least." Second, the attributes are given distinct names, such as AMOUNT-ORDERED and TIMES-ORDERED. In the earlier sentence, these attributes were both referred to as "have ordered." Finally, parentheses are used to indicate the order in which the logic is to be performed. Whatever is in parentheses is done first. Figure 18.24 shows how a more complex query is performed on a relation.

Operators are generally performed in a predetermined order of precedence. Arithmetic operators are usually performed first (exponentiation, then either multiplication or division, and then addition or subtraction). Next, comparative operators are performed. These include GT (greater than), LT (less than), and others. Finally, the Boolean operators are performed (first AND and then OR). Within the same level, the order generally goes from left to right. The precedence is summarized in Figure 18.25.

Query Methods

QUERY BY EXAMPLE. Query by example (called QBE) is a simple, yet powerful method for implementing queries in database systems, such as Paradox and Access. The database fields are selected and displayed in a grid, and requested query values are either entered in the field area or below the field. The query should be able to select both rows from the table that match conditions as well as specific columns (fields). Complex conditions may be set

FIGURE 18.23
Query type 6 lists all of
the attributes that have
a specified value for
all entities.

Query Type 6:

List all of the years for
which earnings exceeded
$20,000 for all employees.

... given a value
GT 20000,

EARNINGS-HISTORY

EMPLOYEE NUMBER	EMPLOYEE NAME	DEPARTMENT	S/H	YEAR-1994	YEAR-1995	YEAR-1996	YEAR-1997
72845	Waters	Outside Sales	S	48960	51400	49050	52900
72888	Dryne	Outside Sales	S	37200	44700	48020	50580
73712	Fawcett	Distribution	H	23500	25500	26780	27100
80345	Well, Jr.	Marketing	S	65000	71000	75000	78000
84672	Piper	Maintenance	H	20560	22340	23520	24910
89760	Acquia	Accounting	H	18755	20040	21380	22540

For ALL
entities ...

list ALL of the
attributes.

Response:

Year-1995
Year-1996
Year-1997

FIGURE 18.24
Complex queries can be created using Boolean logic.

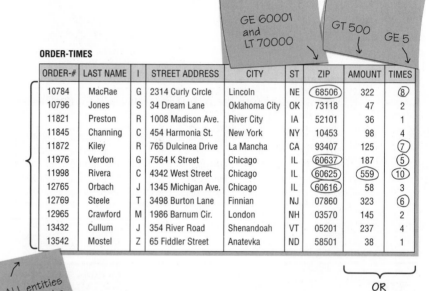

Query:

List all customers who have
zip codes greater or equal to
60001 and less than 70000 AND
(have either ordered more than
$500 from catalogs OR have
ordered at least 5 times
in the past year).

GE 60001
and
LT 70000

GT 500   GE 5

ORDER-TIMES

ORDER-#	LAST NAME	I	STREET ADDRESS	CITY	ST	ZIP	AMOUNT	TIMES
10784	MacRae	G	2314 Curly Circle	Lincoln	NE	68506	322	8
10796	Jones	S	34 Dream Lane	Oklahoma City	OK	73118	47	2
11821	Preston	R	1008 Madison Ave.	River City	IA	52101	36	1
11845	Channing	C	454 Harmonia St.	New York	NY	10453	98	4
11872	Kiley	R	765 Dulcinea Drive	La Mancha	CA	93407	125	7
11976	Verdon	G	7564 K Street	Chicago	IL	60637	187	5
11998	Rivera	C	4342 West Street	Chicago	IL	60625	559	10
12765	Orbach	J	1345 Michigan Ave.	Chicago	IL	60616	58	3
12769	Steele	T	3498 Burton Lane	Finnian	NJ	07860	323	6
12965	Crawford	M	1986 Barnum Cir.	London	NH	03570	145	2
13432	Cullum	J	354 River Road	Shenandoah	VT	05201	237	4
13542	Mostel	Z	65 Fiddler Street	Anatevka	ND	58501	38	1

OR

AND

List ALL entities
that satisfy the
conditions.

Response:
10784
11976
11998

Type	Level	Symbol
Arithmetic Operators	1 2 3	** * / + −
Comparative Operators	4	GT LT EQ NE GE LE
Boolean Operators	5 6	AND OR

FIGURE 18.25
Arithmetic, comparative, and Boolean operators are processed in a hierarchical order of precedence unless parentheses are used.

to select records, and the user may easily specify the columns to be sorted. Figure 18.26 is an example of query by example using Microsoft® Access. The query design screen is divided into two portions. The top portion contains the tables selected for the query and their relationships. The bottom portion contains the query selection grid. Fields from the database tables are dragged to the grid.

The first two rows contain the field and the table that the field is located in. The next row contains sorting information. In this example, the results will be sorted by CUSTOMER NAME. A check mark in the Show box (fourth row down) indicates that the field is to be displayed in the results. Notice that the CUSTOMER NUMBER, CUSTOMER NAME, and STATUS CODE MEANING are selected for the resulting display (other fields are displayed as well, but they do not show in the screen). Notice that the ACCOUNT STATUS CODE and ACCOUNT TYPE CODE are not checked and therefore will not be in the final results. In the Criteria rows, there is a 1 in the ACCOUNT STATUS CODE (indicating an active record) and a C and D (selecting a General Customer or a Discount Customer) in the ACCOUNT

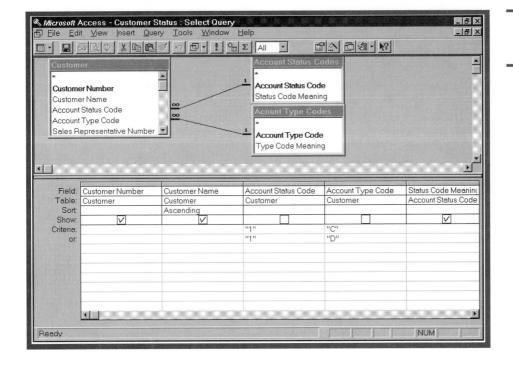

FIGURE 18.26
Query by example using Microsoft® Access.

FIGURE 18.27
Customer Status Query By
Example results, stored
in a table.

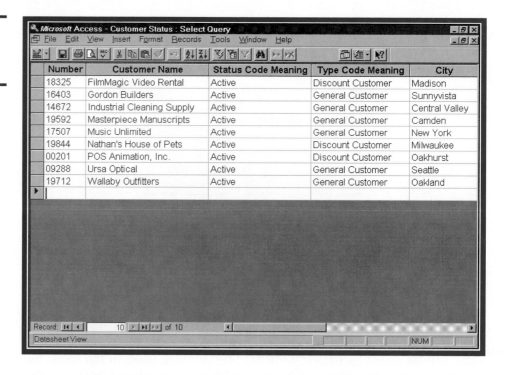

TYPE CODE columns. Two conditions in the same row indicate an AND
condition, and two conditions in different rows represent the OR conditions. This query specifies that the user should select both an Active Customer and either a General or Discount Customer.

The results of a query are displayed in a table, illustrated in Figure
18.27. Notice that the ACCOUNT STATUS CODE and ACCOUNT TYPE

FIGURE 18.28
Parameter Query
design screen.

FIGURE 18.29
Parameter Query entry
dialog box.

CODE do not display. They are not checked and are included in the query for selection purposes only. Instead, the code meanings are displayed, which are more useful to the user. The customer names are sequenced alphabetically.

One of the problems encountered when designing queries is that either the user must modify the query parameters or the same conditions are selected each time the query is executed. A solution to this problem is to use a parameter query. This type of query allows the user to enter the conditions in a dialog box each time the query is run. Figure 18.28 illustrates a parameter query. Notice that the criteria has the message "Enter a partial Customer Name" included inside brackets. Preceding the message is the word "Like," and following the message is an ampersand, indicating that an exact match is not required. When the query is executed, a dialog box opens with the query message on the top. Refer to Figure 18.29. The value "ma" is entered and used to select the name. The results are displayed in Figure 18.30. Notice that only customers whose names begin with the letters "ma" are selected and displayed.

STRUCTURED QUERY LANGUAGE (SQL). Structured Query Language (called SQL) is another popular way to implement queries. It uses a series of keywords and commands to select the rows and columns that should

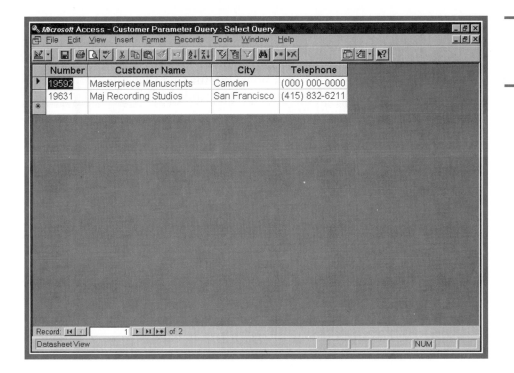

```
SELECT DISTINCTROW
        Customer.[Customer Number],
        Customer.[Customer Name],
        Customer.City,
        Customer.Telephone
FROM Customer
WHERE (((Customer.[Customer Name])
Like ([Enter a partial Customer Name] & "*")));
```

be displayed in the resulting table. Figure 18.31 illustrates the SQL code that is equivalent to the parameter query shown above. The SELECT DISTINCTROW keyword determines which rows are to be selected. The WHERE keyword specifies the condition that the CUSTOMER NAME should be used to select the data entered in the LIKE parameter.

Figure 18.32 is an example of the SQL code used to produce the results that match query by example. Notice both that there are additional keywords that include the relationship between the tables (INNER JOIN) and that the AND and OR logic is included in parenthesis to permit the correct evaluation of the conditions. The ORDER BY parameter indicates the sorting sequence of the resulting table.

SEARCHING ON THE WEB

It is impossible to discuss queries without talking about searching the Web or Internet. There are many search engines, Internet directories, and subject trees that all work in much the same fashion. Typically, a spider or robot will be sent out across the Web to discover Web sites that fit certain criteria or

FIGURE 18.32
Structured Query Language
commands for Customer Status query.

```
SELECT DISTINCTROW
        Customer.[Customer Number],
        Customer.[Customer Name],
        [Account Status Codes].[Status Code Meaning],
        [Acount Type Codes].[Type Code Meaning],
        Customer.City,
        Customer.Telephone
FROM [Acount Type Codes]
INNER JOIN ([Account Status Codes]
INNER JOIN Customer
ON [Account Status Codes].[Account Status Code]
        = Customer.[Account Status Code])
ON [Acount Type Codes].[Account Type Code]
        = Customer.[Account Type Code]
WHERE (((Customer.[Account Status Code])="1")
        AND ((Customer.[Account Type Code])="C"))
        OR
        (((Customer.[Account Status Code])="1")
        AND ((Customer.[Account Type Code])="D"))
ORDER BY Customer.[Customer Name];
```

keywords. These spiders and 'bots (short for "robots") bring URLs (addresses) back and store them in a database.

Search engines refer to the database when answering a query. Some popular search engines are:

HotBot	www.hotbot.com
Infoseek	www.infoseek.com
Excite	www.excite.com
Yahoo!	www.yahoo.com
AltaVista	www.altavista.digital.com
Four11	www.four11.com

As the book was written, HotBot and Infoseek offered the most exciting developments in searches, but it is impossible to tell which search engine is best because (1) these companies bring out updated versions with new features often and (2) the interface of one search engine might be more suitable for you than another. Also there are specific engines such as Four11, which is used as an on-line directory for finding people on the Internet.

In addition to the search engines listed above, there are meta-search engines such as Quarterdeck's WebCompass and Symantec's Internet Fast Find, off-line browsers such as Traveling Software's WebEx, and programs that manage your bookmarks such as Starfish's Internet Utilities. All of these can be helpful, and their features will likely be incorporated into new versions of the latest Web browsers.

Guidelines for Searching the Web

You can improve your chances of finding what you want by following some of these strategies:

1. Decide whether you really want to search or surf. If you know what information you want, use a search engine, such as Infoseek, that will find specific sites. If you want to browse, use a Web directory service such as Yahoo!

2. Think of your key terms before you sit down at the computer. It is usually better to plan than react.

3. Construct your search questions logically. Are you searching for "decision" AND "support" rather than "decision" OR "support" (you will get very different results)? Do you want to find all sites that have the words "decision," "support," and "systems"; or are you looking for a phrase "decision support systems"? You must let the search engine know your intentions. What happens when you enter "DSS"? (You get an avalanche of information about direct satellite systems and little about decision support systems.)

4. Use a search engine that saves your searches.

5. Use a search engine that informs you of changes in the Web sites you select.

6. Remember that the search engine business is very competitive. Check on the search engines periodically. You will find that some search engines that did not possess a feature in an earlier version have subsequently brought out an improved update. This new version could easily surpass the previous leader.

DATA MINING

The concept of data mining came from the desire to use the database for a more selective targeting of customers. Early approaches to direct mail included using ZIP code information as a way to determine what a family's income might be (assuming that a family has to generate sufficient income to afford to live in the prestigious Beverly Hills ZIP code 90210 or some other affluent neighborhood). It was a way (not perfect, of course) to limit the number of catalogs sent out.

Data mining takes this one step further. Assuming that past behavior is a good predictor for future purchases, a large amount of data is gathered on a particular person from, for example, credit card purchases. The company can tell what stores we shop in, what we have purchased, how much we paid for an item, and when and how frequently we travel. Data are also entered, stored, and used for a variety of purposes when we fill out warranties; when we apply for a driver's license; when we respond to a free offer, or when we apply for a membership card at a video rental store. Moreover, companies share this data and oftentimes make money on the sale of it as well. Figure 18.33 illustrates the data mining concept.

American Express has been a leader in data mining for marketing purposes. American Express will send you discount coupons for new stores or entertainment when it sends you a credit card bill after it determines you have shopped in similar stores or attended similar events. General Motors offers a MasterCard that allows customers to build up bonus points toward the purchase of a new car and then attempts to send out information about new vehicles at the most likely time that a consumer would be interested in purchasing a new car. The process of data mining includes using powerful supercomputers that process very large databases—or data warehouses—using techniques such as neural nets (see Chapter 12).

The data mining approach is not without problems, however. First, the costs may be too high to justify data mining, something that may only be discovered after huge setup costs have been accrued. Second, data mining has to be coordinated so that various departments or subsidiaries do not all try to reach the customer at the same time. Additionally, customers may feel that their privacy has been invaded and resent the offers that are coming their way. Finally, customers may feel that profiles created solely on the basis of their credit card purchases present a highly distorted image of who they are.

Several years ago, some disturbing civil rights issues arose when it was discovered that police authorities in England were observing citizens in their neighborhoods, making inferences about the people from their observed behavior, and storing those inferences in secret databases. Other police had access to those records, and the inferences were just that, since they were never seen or subject to review by the "suspected" citizen, and they were never validated by other types of data. Erroneous profiles were created, stored, acted upon—and not deleted. Even in a democracy, data mining has applications beyond benign marketing attempts to reach us with the latest product.

Analysts should take responsibility for considering the ethical aspects of any data mining projects that are proposed. Questions about the length of the time period that profile material is kept, the confidentiality of it, the pri-

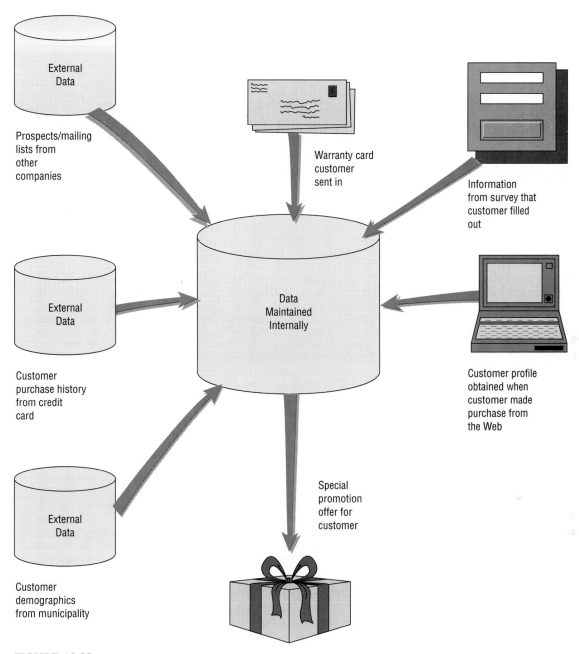

FIGURE 18.33
Data mining collects personal information about customers in an effort to be more specific in interpreting and anticipating their preferences.

vacy safeguards included, and the uses to which inferences are put should all be asked and considered with the client. The opportunities for abuse are apparent and must be guarded against. For consumers, data mining is another push technology—and if consumers do not want be pushed, the data mining efforts will backfire.

Losing Prospects

"Market share can be a real problem." So says Ryan Taylor, Director of Marketing Systems for a large East Coast health insurer. "One of the greatest challenges we face is how to identify good leads for our salespeople. With over 50% market share we must eliminate the names of most of the prospects we buy before populating our marketing database. It is critical that we get this right because our marketing database is a critical part of our company's arsenal of strategic information tools."

Ryan explains to Chandler, one of your systems analysis team members, "A marketing database, or MDB for short, is a powerful, relational database that is the heart of marketing systems. Our marketing database is used to provide information for all of marketing's systems. These include productivity tools, like our Sales Force Automation and our Mass Mailing Systems, which are designed to aid our salespeople in managing the sales cycle. They also include analytical tools, like our Geographic Information Systems (GIS) or Graphical Query Language tools (GQL), which are designed to provide decision support."

"But the primary function of a marketing database is to track information on our customers and prospects. We currently track geographic information, demographic information, and psychographic information. Or, as I like to say it, where they live, who they are, and how they think."

"The simplest marketing databases can be made up of just three files: Prospect Profile >>> Customer Profile >>> Purchase and Payment History."

"Once you have designed your marketing database, the next challenge is deciding how to populate it. We currently purchase our prospect information from a list vendor. Because our company's marketing strategy is based on mass marketing, we buy every business in our area. Because of this volume, we pay less than a dime for each prospect. If, however, a company is practicing product differentiation, their prospect base will likely be more defined. This company would likely pay a premium for more detailed data that has been carefully validated," explains Ryan.

"We face a real challenge. If I had a dollar for every time a rep complained to me about the address on a prospect being wrong, I could retire and move to Florida," Ryan quips. "I'm expected to identify which prospects are bad. That's not too hard if you only have a thousand of them, but what do you do when you have over a quarter of a million?"

Ryan continues, "Because we use this data frequently for large mailings, it is very important for us to ensure that the names and addresses on that file are as accurate as possible. For example, they should conform to postal standards and should not be duplicates."

"We achieve this through a technique called 'data hygiene.' How's that for a geeky term? Data hygiene is usually accomplished with specialized software, which is used to determine the validity of an address. This software matches the database address to its own internal database of valid streets and number ranges in a given city or zip code."

Ryan resumes, "One of the other data challenges that is faced by marketers is eliminating duplicate records in the marketing database. There are two types of duplicates we look for: internal duplicates, which are the existence of multiple records of the same customer or prospect, and external duplicates, which represents our inability to eliminate customers from our prospect data."

"Internal duplicates create reporting problems and increase mailing costs. External duplicates are even worse; they are both costly and embarrassing," Ryan explains. "One of the most embarrassing things for a sales representative is to have them make a prospecting call only to find out that the business is already our customer. The customer is generally left feeling like they are nothing more than a number in one of our computers. It creates a poor impression while wasting valuable time and resources."

In two paragraphs, describe some techniques that Ryan could use to help identify internal and external duplicates in his company's marketing database. Describe how you would build a marketing database to minimize duplicates (use a paragraph). Are there operational methods that might cut down on this problem? List them. Who else in the organization could help with this process? Provide a brief list. In a paragraph, recommend methods to Chandler and your other systems analysis team members that can be used to help enlist and secure the assistance of other relevant organizational members.

PRODUCTIVITY AND ERGONOMICS DESIGN

Users might avoid using a system or become dissatisfied with it simply because the systems analyst has not bothered to visualize what it would be like to sit at a workstation and enter data into the system day in and day out. The powerful influence of the workstation on user involvement with the system must be considered. Continued use as well as user productivity, comfort, and satisfaction with the system are all related to how ergonomically well-designed the workspace is. (*Ergonomics* refers to the application of biological and engineering data to the problems related to people and to the machines they use in work.)

Systems analysts can skillfully utilize their knowledge about the influence of well-designed workstations to support the behavior they want from users—that is, the productive use of the system. An example from a typical university computer room serves to underscore how workstation design determines the use of computers.

Universities often allow free use of PCs or workstations, but one or two workstations will usually have time restrictions posted. These workstations can be used by individuals who only have to make minor changes to a computer program. The concept is similar to a grocery store express lane, but instead of "eight items or less," the posted sign in the computer room about the restricted workstation states "five minutes or less." Policing this limit, however, is difficult. This is where the design takes over. Rather than monitoring usage of the workstation and cutting off users after five minutes, designers solve the problem by making users stand, rather than sit. Because no chairs are provided for the express workstations, there is rarely a problem with the five-minute rule. Comfortable seating is just one of the variables in getting users to use the system.

Sometimes what exists in the user workspace will not be under your control as a systems analyst. However, if the opportunity arises, you should be able to recommend ergonomically sound workstation designs. The user's office/workstation should be viewed as an improvable context that must be adapted to the individual if you want the system to be used. The workspace variables important to consider include: room color and lighting; screen displays, user keyboards, and mice; computer desks and user seating.

Computer Room Color and Lighting

Computer rooms should be painted in muted colors with flat paints that neither assault the senses of their inhabitants nor give off a glare. Some colors and decoration schemes produce negative effects on users. Painting every wall in a light, bright color (brighter than the brightest possible computer displays) should be avoided, since it increases glare on computer displays. Decorating computer rooms in several different colors should also be avoided. Too many wall colors distract users from their tasks and can be confusing.

Rooms where computers or terminals are used should not be lit by fluorescent light, which is too bright for computer display use and has an almost imperceptible, yet continuous, flicker. It is better to provide incandescent lamps that produce more natural light or lamps that use halogen bulbs (although these can become very hot). Rooms with computer displays should be about half as bright as rooms in typical offices, where people process paperwork.

Do not allow displays to be placed where direct window light can hit the screen, because this creates tremendous glare. Ideally, users should be furnished with adjustable task lights at their workstations.

FIGURE 18.34
Position of the display screen
and the desk height are key
factors in user satisfaction
and productivity.

Screen Displays, Keyboards, and Mice

The design of efficient and effective screen displays was covered in the preceding chapter, along with the design of user input and the use of screen color and icons. But there are some remaining ergonomic specifications and health considerations that also figure into the use of screen displays (also called monitors).

Researchers have found that the following guidelines will enhance the comfort of users who are viewing a display. Generally, flexibility and adjustability for individual preferences are the watchwords. The more control given users over the features of their displays the better.

1. Displays should be within comfortable sightlines, as pictured in Figure 18.34. That means setting displays at an angle 10 to 15 degrees from the vertical, away from the user. The user should look slightly downward; the screen should be 5 to 35 degrees from the horizontal.

2. Displays should be perceived as continuous images. This means no glare, no flickering of images, or no bleeding of characters into one another.

3. Displays should provide sharp contrast, with adjustable brightness and crisp image resolution.

Since the main form of data entry for most users is using a keyboard in front of a display, it becomes extremely important that displays are properly configured. Ideally the refresh rate should be at least 85 Hz. A subtle flicker will cause eyestrain. In addition to the refresh rate, the colors, brightness, and screen geometry must be set up properly.

Excellent tools are available to adjust monitors. For example, Display-Mate for Windows from Sonera Technologies (www.displaymate.com) uses a number of test patterns to optimize your display. You can use DisplayMate test screens to adjust the size of the screen, using the pincushion, trapezoid, hourglass, and tilt controls own your monitor so your lines are indeed

Hey, Look Me Over—Reprise

You have been called back to take another look at Merman's Costumes. Here is part of the database created for Annie Oaklea of Merman's (whom you last worked with in Consulting Opportunities 9.2 and 10.1). The database contains information, such as the cost of the rental, date checked out, date due back, and the number of days the costume has been rented since the beginning of the year (YTD DAYS OUT) (see Figure 18.C1).

Analyzing Annie's typical day in the costume rental business, you realize that there are several requests that she must make of the database so that she can make decisions on when to replace frequently used costumes—or even when to buy more costumes of a

particular type. She also needs to remember to keep in the good graces of customers she has previously turned down for a particular costume rental, she needs to know when to recall an overdue costume, and so on.

Formulate several queries that will help her get the information she needs from the database. (*Hint:* Make any assumptions necessary about the types of information she needs to make decisions, and use as many of the different query types discussed in this chapter as you can.) In a paragraph describe how Annie's queries would be different if she were working with a Web-based or hyperlinked system.

COSTUME-RENTAL

COSTUME NUMBER	DESCRIPTION	SUIT NUMBER	COLOR	COST OF	DATE CHECKED OUT	DUE DATE	YTD DAYS OUT	TYPE OF COSTUME	REQUESTS TURNED DOWN
0003	Lady MacBeth F, SM	01	Blue	15.00	10/15	11/30	150	Standard	2
1342	Bear F, MED	01	Dk. Brown	12.50	10/24	11/09	26	Standard	0
1344	Bear F, MED	02	Dk. Brown	12.50	10/24	11/09	115	Standard	0
1347	Bear F, LG	01	Black	12.50	10/24	11/09	22	Standard	0
1348	Bear F, LG	02	Black	12.50	11/01	11/08	10	Standard	0
1400	Goldilocks F, MED	01	Light Blue	7.00	10/24	11/09	140	Standard	0
1402	Goldilocks F, MED	02	Light Blue	7.00	10/28	11/09	10	Standard	0
1852	Hamlet M, MED	01	Dark Green	15.00	11/02	11/23	115	Standard	3
1853	Ophelia F, SM	01	Light Blue	15.00	11/02	11/23	22	Standard	0
4715	Prince M, LG	01	White/purple	10.00	11/04	11/21	145	Standard	5
4730	Frog M, SM	01	Green	7.00	11/04	11/21	175	Standard	2
7822	Jester M, MED	01	Multi	7.50	11/10	12/08	12	Standard	0
7824	Jester M, MED	02	Multi	7.50	11/09	11/15	10	Standard	0
7823	Executioner M, LG	01	Black	7.00	11/19	12/05	21	Standard	0
8645	Dr. Spock N, LG	01	Orange	18.00	09/07	09/12	150	Trendy	4
9000	Pantomime F,LG	01	Red	7.00	08/25	09/15	56	Standard	0
9001	Pantomime M, MED	01	Blue	7.00	08/25	09/15	72	Standard	0
9121	Juggler M, MED	01	Multi	7.00	11/05	11/19	14	Standard	0
9156	Napoleon M, SM	01	Blue/white	15.00	10/26	11/23	56	Standard	1

FIGURE 18.C1
A portion of the database from Merman's costume rental shop.

straight and your circles round. You can also eliminate distracting Moiré patterns and calibrate the color and intensity. All of these adjustments make for a better visual working environment.

Concerns have been voiced about possible health risks for users, some of whom have complained of physical symptoms ranging from headaches, eyestrain, and backaches to problem pregnancies and the early onset of cataracts. Studies of the effects of the extremely low-frequency radiation of cathode ray tubes (CRTs) have been controversial to date. CRTs use the same technology as television tubes. A stream of electrons are usually beamed from three guns (or one, as in Trinitron tubes) at a layer of phosphors. The glowing phosphors are what we see.

There are alternatives to CRTs. Liquid crystal displays (LCDs) have a thin layer of material that can either block or transmit light. Since they are thin and light, they are used in notebooks. Expect LCDs to show up on desktops, replacing large CRTs. Another alternative, Field Emission Displays (FEDs), have a layer of phosphors similar to CRTs but have hundreds of tiny electron transmitters behind each pixel rather than three large electronic guns. Use of LCDs and FEDs should cut down on some of the health concerns traditionally associated with CRTs.

User keyboards for computer interface should be as flexible and adjustable as possible. Detachability and light weight allow changes in sitting position for users, who need a break from doing data entry in a continuous pose. Remote mice, wireless mice, egg-shaped mice, and foot pedal controls are examples of designs developed to reduce health problems associated with overuse of hand and wrist muscles.

Workspace Furnishings

Workspace furnishings include the desks or stands on which computers and keyboards rest. Many times computers are put into existing furniture setups. While an old typing table might work in a pinch, because it is 26 inches high, putting a keyboard on an already existing desktop is not a good idea. The standard desktop height of 29 inches is too high for continuous keyboard use, because that height causes back, neck, and arm strain. If users have both a desk and a computer table, the desk should be 29 inches high, and the computer table should be 26 inches high. Both can be joined into an L-shaped configuration for ease of access.

As we saw in the example at the beginning of this section, user seating is important enough to influence whether systems are used—and with what satisfaction. Getting the correct chair can also increase user comfort and productivity. Well-designed seating often looks as if it had been sculpted around a person. Users' chairs should be armless with firm upper- and lower-back support (preferably adjustable for the individual), and a firm seat cushion should provide back support. Chairs with five casters provide excellent balance and mobility.

Seating height should be adjustable for the individual, but clearly it should preserve the prescribed relationship between the user's gaze and the display, as well as preserve the relationship among the user's posture, keyboard, and mouse (or other input device). In order to get users to use the system, well-designed workstations are essential.

SUMMARY

We have focused on system users, their interface with the computer, their need for feedback, the design of database queries, and the design of user workstations in this chapter. The success of the systems you design depends on user involvement and acceptance. Therefore, thinking about users in systematic and empathic ways is of utmost importance—and not a peripheral issue for systems analysts.

A variety of user interfaces and input devices were covered in this chapter. Some interfaces are particularly well-suited to inexperienced users, such as natural-language, question-and-answer, menus, form-fill and Web-based form-fill, graphical user interfaces (especially on Web pages), the

"I have no problem with using a mouse, or any other rodent you throw my way. Really, though, whatever Snowden needs is what I try to do. But everyone is different. I've seen people here go out of their way to avoid using a computer altogether. Other people would prefer not to talk with a human. In fact, they would be as happy as a puppy chewing on a new bedroom slipper if they could use command language to interact. I have a hunch they would prefer not talking to people at all. But that's just an impression. Most of the folks we have here are open to new things. Otherwise they wouldn't be here at MRE. We do pride ourselves on our creativity. I have you signed up for a meeting with people from the Training group, including Tom Ketchem, Melissa Smith, and Kathy Blandford. You can invite anyone else you think should be included. Snowden may sit in as well, if he has time. That's why he asked me to relay the message, I guess. They'll be very curious to see what kind of interface you are suggesting for them on the new project reporting system."

HYPERCASE QUESTIONS

1. Write a short proposal describing what type of user interface would be appropriate for the users of the project reporting system who are in the Training group. Include reasons for your decision.

2. Design a user interface using a CASE tool, such as Visible Analyst a software package such as Access, or paper layout forms. What are the key features that address the needs of the people in the Training group?

FIGURE 18 HC.1
In HyperCase, you can see how users process information in order to create a more effective user interface.

3. Demonstrate your interface to a group of students who can role play as members of the Training group. Ask for reactions.

4. Redesign the interface based on the feedback you have received. Write a paragraph to say how your new design addresses any comments you have received.

mouse, lightpens, the stylus, touch-sensitive screens, and voice recognition systems. Command language is better suited to experienced users. Some authors believe that the Web itself is the single most important interface for the future work of applications designers.

Combinations of interfaces can be extremely effective. For example, using pull-down menus with graphical user interfaces or employing nested menus within question-and-answer interfaces yields interesting combinations. Each interface poses a different level of challenge for programmers, with natural language being the most difficult to program. The Web has posed new challenges for designers, since the user is not known. Web design takes advantage of hyperlinks to allow users to take numerous paths as they interact with the Web site.

Users' need for feedback from the system was also stressed. System feedback is necessary to let users know if their input is being accepted; if input is or is not in the correct form; if processing is going on; if requests can or cannot be processed; and if more detailed information is available and how to get it. Feedback is most often visual, with text, graphics, or icons being used. Audio feedback can also be effective.

Queries are designed to allow users to extract meaningful data from the database. There are six basic types of queries, and they can be combined using Boolean logic to form more complex queries.

Some of the principles about data queries you learned can be used in Web searches. Internet search tools are called search engines. Users can be more effective if searches are carefully planned and logically structured.

Data mining involves using a database for the more selective targeting of customers. Assuming past behavior is a good predictor for future purchases, companies collect data about a person from past credit card purchases, driver's license applications, warranty cards, and so on. Data mining can be powerful, but it may be costly, and it needs to be coordinated and may infringe on consumer privacy or even a person's civil rights.

Finally, we considered both how users' workspaces influence their willingness to use the system and how workstations can be improved through the implementation of relevant ergonomic principles. There are specific productivity and comfort guidelines on the construction and positioning of displays, keyboards, computer stands, and users seating, but generally all of them should be flexible enough to permit adjustment for individual use.

KEYWORDS AND PHRASES

natural-language interfaces
dialog box
question-and-answer interfaces

stylus
touch-sensitive screen
speech recognition and synthesis

menus	continuous speech systems
pull-down menus	speaker independence
nested menus	feedback for users
form-fill (input/output form) interfaces	queries
	Boolean operators
Web form-fill interfaces	SQL
command-language interfaces	ergonomics
graphical user interface (GUI)	Web searching
templates	search engine
feedback	data mining
cue cards	data warehousing
wizards	ergonomic specifications

REVIEW QUESTIONS

1. What are the four objectives for designing user interfaces?
2. Define natural-language interfaces. What is their major drawback?
3. Explain what is meant by question-and-answer interfaces. What kind of users are they best suited to?
4. Describe how users use on-screen menus.
5. What is a nested menu? What are its advantages?
6. Define on-screen input/output forms. What is their chief advantage?
7. What are the advantages of Web-based fill-in forms?
8. What are the drawbacks of Web-based form-fill interfaces?
9. Explain what command-language interfaces are. What types of users are they best suited to?
10. Define graphical user interfaces. What is the key difficulty they present for programmers?
11. For what type of user is a GUI interface particularly effective?
12. What are the three guidelines for designing good screen dialog?
13. What are the roles of icons, graphics, and color in providing feedback?
14. List six ways for achieving the goal of minimal operator action when designing a user interface.
15. List five standards that can aid in evaluating user interfaces.
16. What are the seven situations that require feedback for users?
17. What is an acceptable way of telling the user that input was accepted?
18. When a user is informed that his or her input is not in the correct form, what additional feedback should be given at the same time?
19. Why is it unacceptable to notify the user that input is not correct solely through the use of beeping or buzzing?
20. When a request is not completed, what feedback should be provided to the user?
21. What are hypertext links? Where should they be used?
22. List in shorthand notation the six basic query types.
23. List six guidelines for searching the Web.
24. What is the purpose of data mining?
25. What sort of information is "mined for" in data mining?
26. Describe four problems with data mining.
27. Give three guidelines for setting up computer displays for user productivity and comfort.
28. What is the preferred height for computer desks? Why is the height important?

PROBLEMS

1. Design a nested menus interface for a check-in and check-out hotel-reservation system. Use numbers to select a menu item. Show how each menu would look on a standard PC display.

2. Design a form-fill interface for the inventory control of a musical CD and tape wholesale company that could be used on a PC display screen.

3. Design a Web-based form-fill interface to accomplish the same task as in problem 2 above.
   a. What difficulties did you encounter? Discuss them in a paragraph.
   b. Of the two designs you did, which would you say is better suited to the task? Why? List three reasons for your choice.

4. Design a command-language interface that a travel agent would use to book seats for an airline.
   a. Show what it would look like on a standard display screen.
   b. Make a list of commands needed to book an airline seat, and write down what each command means.

5. Design a graphical user interface for an executive desktop. Use icons for file cabinets, wastebasket, telephone, and so on. Show how they would appear on the computer display.

6. Design a screen that provides appropriate feedback for a user whose command cannot be executed.

7. Design a screen for a payroll software package that displays information telling the user how to get more detailed feedback.

8. Design a Web-based screen that displays an acceptable way to tell users that their input was accepted.

9. Write six different queries for the file in problem 1 in Chapter 17.

10. Write six different queries for the 3NF relation in problem 6 in Chapter 17.

11. Design a search that will find potential competitors of a company like World's Trend on the Web. Assume you are the customer.

12. Search for World's Trend's potential competitors on the Web. (Remember you won't find World's Trend itself on the Web. It is a fictional company.) Make a list of those you've found.

13. Design a data mining project for World's Trend. What information is needed? Suggest some projects you can undertake with data mining to improve marketing efforts at World's Trend.

14. Taking the data from your search for competitors in problem 12 above, make a brief list of Web site innovations they are using that could be of use to World's Trend in its data mining project (see problem 13 above).

15. Draw up a set of ethical guidelines or create a policy to help analysts evaluate the appropriate uses for data mining (you may also have to define what uses are not appropriate in order to do this). Discuss in a paragraph some precautions that should be taken by the analyst to protect the consumer privacy that may be at stake in data mining projects.

GROUP PROJECTS

1. With your group members, create a pull-down menu for an employment agency that matches professional candidates to position openings. Include a list of keystrokes that would directly invoke the menu options using the ALT-X format. The menu has the following options:

Add employee	Add employer	Add position
Change employee	Change employer	Change position
Delete employee	Delete employer	Delete position

Employee inquiry	Match employee to opening
Position inquiry	Print open positions report
Employer inquiry	Print successful matches report

2. In a paragraph, describe the problems your group faced in creating this menu.

3. The drag-and-drop feature is used in GUI interfaces and allows the user to move sentences around in a word processing package. As a group, suggest how drag-and-drop can be used to its fullest potential in the following applications:
   a. Project management software (Chapter 3)
   b. Relational database program (Chapter 17)
   c. Screen or forms designer (Chapter 16)
   d. Presentation package (Chapter 14)
   e. Spreadsheet program (Chapter 12)
   f. CASE tool for drawing data flow diagrams (Chapter 9)
   g. Fax program (Chapter 15)
   h. File management program (Chapter 18)
   i. Personal information manager (PIM) (Chapter 3)
   j. Illustration in a drawing package (Chapter 14)
   k. CASE tool for developing data dictionaries (Chapter 10)
   l. Decision tree drawing program (Chapter 11)
   m. Web site for collecting consumer opinions on new products (Chapter 15)
   n. Organizing bookmarks for Web sites

   For each solution your group designs, draw the screen and show movement by using an arrow.

4. Ask all the members of your group to request a search based on their hobbies or leisure activities. If there are four people in your group, there will be four unique searches to perform. Now go ahead and do all of the searches. Compare your results. Does the person who is involved with the hobby have an advantage over the people who know less about the hobby? Explain.

SELECTED BIBLIOGRAPHY

Benbesat, I., and R. G. Schroeder. "An Experimental Investigation of Some MIS Design Variables." *Management Information Systems Quarterly,* Vol. 2, No. 2, 1978, pp. 43–54.

Bennett, J. L. *Building Decision Support Systems.* Reading, MA: Addison-Wesley Publishing Company, 1983.

Davis, G. B., and M. H. Olson. *Management Information Systems: Conceptual Foundations, Structure, and Development.* New York: McGraw-Hill Book Company, 1985.

Dietsch, D. "Ergo, Ergonomics." *A+*, Vol. 3, Issue 6, 1985.

Gane, C., and T. Sarson. *Structured Systems Analysis: Tools and Techniques.* Englewood Cliffs, NJ: Prentice Hall, 1979.

Kleiner, A. (ed.). "The Health Hazards of Computers." *Whole Earth Review,* No. 48, 1985, pp. 80–93.

Large, P. *The Micro Revolution Revisited.* London: Franses Pinter (Publishers), 1984.

Laudon, K. C., and J. P. Laudon. *Management Information Systems,* 4th ed. New York: Macmillan Publishing Company, 1996.

Newman, W. M., and M. G. Lamming. *Interactive System Design.* Reading, MA: Addison-Wesley Publishing Company, 1995.

Sano, D. *Designing Large-Scale Web Sites; A Visual Design Methodology.* New York: John Wiley & Sons, Inc., 1996.

Strom, D. "Net Management Via Web: Another Pretty Interface?" *PC Week,* Vol. 14, No. 32A, 1997, p. 25.

UP TO THE USERS

"Let's take our prototypes and some new screens, reports, and forms to create the final user interface," Anna says to Chip. "It's about time, isn't it?" replies Chip. He was all too aware of the importance of designing a good interface.

After talking awhile, they set up the following screen dialog guidelines:

1. Well-designed screens should:

    Communicate actions and intentions clearly to users.
    Show options available to operators. Examples would be:
    > MAKE CORRECTIONS OR PRESS ESC TO CANCEL
    > ENTER HARDWARE INVENTORY NUMBER OR PRESS F10 TO
    >   EXIT
    > PRESS ENTER KEY
    > PRESS ENTER TO CONFIRM DELETE, ESC TO CANCEL
    > Buttons that say OK or CANCEL
    Standardize use of any abbreviations.
    Avoid the use of codes, substituting the code meaning.
    Provide help screens for complicated portions of the dialog.
    Provide tooltip help for toolbar icons.

2. Feedback should be provided to the users. This includes:

    Titles to show the current screen.
    Actions successfully completed messages, such as:
    > RECORD HAS BEEN ADDED
    > RECORD HAS BEEN CHANGED
    Error messages. Examples are:
    > INVALID DATE
    > CHECKDIGIT IS INVALID
    > SOFTWARE IS NOT ON FILE
    An invalid data dialog box, with an OK button on a graphical user interface screen.
    Processing delay messages similar to:
    > PLEASE WAIT—REPORT IS BEING PRODUCED
    An hourglass turning upside down on a graphical user interface.

3. There should be consistency in the design, including:

    Location of the OPERATOR MESSAGE line—line 23 on every screen.
    Location of the FEEDBACK MESSAGE line—chosen as line 24.
    Date, time, system name, and screen reference number should appear in heading lines.
    Consistent exit of all screens—for example, through the use of the same function key.
    Standard use of keys, such as PgDn and PgUp, to display a next or previous screen within a multiple-screen display.
    A consistent method of canceling an operation—for example, through the use of the Escape key (Esc).
    Standardized use of color and high-intensity display—for example, all error messages would appear in red.

*Allen Schmidt,
Julie E. Kendall, and
Kenneth E. Kendall*

Standardized use of icons on a GUI screen.
Standardized pull-down menus on a GUI screen.

4. Minimum operator actions should be required to use the system. Some examples are:

The use of **Y** and **N** as Yes and No replies. The use of the plus and minus signs on the number pad as a substitute for **Y** and **N**.

When changing or deleting records, only the record key need be specified. The system would obtain the record and display pertinent information.

When names are required as key entries, only the first few letters of the name need be entered. The program should find all matching record key names and present them for selection by the operator.

Data-entry screens should allow the entry of codes.

All numeric entries may omit leading zeros, commas, or a decimal point.

As each data field is completed, the cursor should advance to the next entry field.

After each option is completed, the same screen, with blank entry areas, should be redisplayed until the Exit key is pressed.

When an option is exited, the previous menu is to be displayed.

Drop-down list boxes should be used whenever possible on GUI screens.

Check boxes and radio buttons should be used to make selections whenever possible.

Default buttons should be outlined so the user can press the Enter key to press them.

5. Data entering the system should be validated. Guidelines are:

Specific fields should be verified according to edit criteria.

As errors are detected, operators should be given a chance either to correct the error or to cancel the transaction.

When no errors have been detected in a transaction, the screen should be presented to the operator for visual confirmation. The operator should have the opportunity either to accept the screen or to make corrections to the data entered.

Since the system is to be written using Access, Chip and Anna need to decide whether to use a menu screen or pull-down menus to control the system. The advantage of using a menu is that all the options may be written as independent objects and linked under the menu screen. Such a procedure also allows the flexibility of easy expansion as the system evolves. After Anna and Chip conferred with the users, a consensus was obtained that a menu screen was indeed the best choice. Hy Perteks and Mike Crowe were strongly in favor of the menu screen, but others wanted to use pull-down menus. Dot was strongly in favor of the pull-down menu-controlled system since it was easy for new employees to learn. She also wanted a button bar for the most commonly used features.

Upon examining the many screens and reports (over 30 in all), Chip and Anna decided to split the menu into several functions. "But how do we divide these various functions into a set of menus?" asked Chip.

"Why don't we use a decomposition diagram to organize the functions into a hierarchy," replied Anna. Chip and Anna began working on the dia-

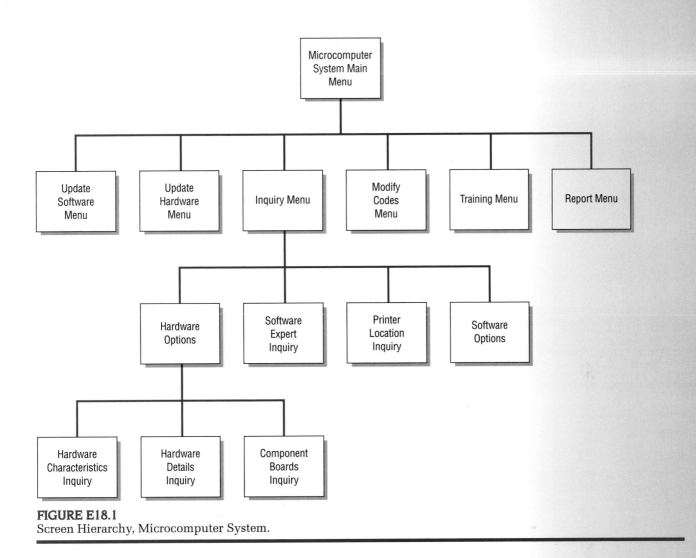

FIGURE E18.1
Screen Hierarchy, Microcomputer System.

gram. The menu interactions will be represented in a hierarchical structure, with options shown as rectangles and the overall menu represented by the rectangle on the top. Each secondary menu will be shown beneath the primary menu, with screen programs at the lowest level. The main menu will have six main choices, Update Software, Update Hardware, Inquiry, Modify Codes, Training, and Reports, as illustrated in Figure E18.1. Each of these options is further subdivided into smaller menus or individual functions. The Inquiry menu is subdivided into two smaller menus, Software Options and Hardware Options, as well as options for running the Software Expert Inquiry and the Printer Location Inquiry.

The rectangles on the functional decomposition diagram are implemented using a series of pull-down menu lists, which are shown in Figure E18.2. Notice that the Inquiry menu has functions corresponding to the rectangles on the decomposition diagram illustrated in the first figure in this episode. A row of buttons for common functions is included below the menus. The menu functions are included as a set of buttons in the main area of the screen, and these buttons may be clicked to run corresponding programs. It was decided that the Add Microcomputer, Add Software Package, and Change Microcomputer programs would be run directly from the

FIGURE E18.2
Microcomputer System Main Menu.

main menu. Clicking the other buttons causes selection dialog boxes to display, with choices for selecting programs. Figure E18.3 shows the dialog box for the **Reports. . .** option. All the reports are listed, with **Print Preview, Print,** and **Close Form** buttons for selecting actions.

"Here's what I think the guidelines for the update programs should be," Anna tells Chip. "The key focus is on accuracy, with comprehensive editing for each data field. Add programs will display an entry screen and allow either hardware or software records to be created. After all entries are complete, a user should double-check the data and press the Add Software Record button. Any data that are already on the system should be implemented using drop-down lists. (Refer to Figure E18.4.) There are also buttons to undo changes, move to different records, print the record, save the changes, and exit the screen. A record could be added only if the primary key for the record does not already exist."

"Delete screens must have a simple, primary key entry, such as the COURSE DESCRIPTION in the DELETE SOFTWARE COURSE screen," Anna continues. The DELETE SOFTWARE COURSE screen is illustrated in Figure E18.5. "The use of a **Find** button (the binoculars) helps to locate the desired record. The corresponding record is read and the information is displayed. Users press the **Delete** button and are prompted to confirm the delete. If the user clicks **Cancel,** the delete action is canceled. How does all this sound?" she asks Chip.

"So far, so good," he replies. "Anything on change screens?"

"Yes. Change screens have a primary key for the record entered and the matching record read. Record information is to be displayed that allows the operator to overtype the data with changes. All changes are to be validated

FIGURE E18.3
A Dialog Box for the Microcomputer System Report Menu.

FIGURE E18.4
ADD SOFTWARE RECORD screen showing command buttons and drop-down lists.

FIGURE E18.5
DELETE SOFTWARE COURSE screen.

with full editing. When all change fields are valid, the user must press a button to save the changes. Is that clear enough for the user?" Anna asks.

"I think it's very good," Chip acknowledges.

Chip is responsible for the inquiry portion of the system. The focus on these programs is speed. A short entry is obtained from the user, and the corresponding records are read. Information is formatted for maximum communication and displayed. "I've met with various users," he tells Anna. "Here's a list of inquiry programs." Each of the inquiry screens is designed, along with the database files needed and possible errors that could occur.

"The first screen I designed was the HARDWARE INQUIRY," Chip continues. "I used the description of the screen that we had put into the Visible Analyst repository after the prototypes had been created." The repository screen is shown in Figure E18.6. Notice that the **Notes** area contains information about how the screen should operate. An INVENTORY NUMBER or partial INVENTORY NUMBER should be entered. The first matching record is read (in the case of a partial INVENTORY NUMBER), and the user can scroll to the next record or to previous records.

"I produced a rough layout and met with Dot to obtain feedback on the design. After pointing out some minor corrections, she mentioned that the maintenance details should be included, providing complete information for each microcomputer."

The program logic is to use the HARDWARE INVENTORY NUMBER as the entry field of a Parameter Value dialog box, (illustrated in Figure E18.7), with the starting number of 3 entered. The record is located in the database. If it is not found, a message is displayed. Once the record is located, the matching board records are read. Board records contain a code for the type of board, and the BOARD CODE TABLE is searched for the matching code.

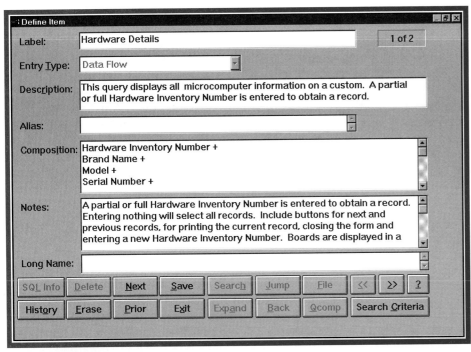

FIGURE E18.6
HARDWARE DETAILS Visible Analyst repository screen.

FIGURE E18.7
HARDWARE INVENTORY NUMBER Parameter Value dialog box.

The meaning of the code is formatted on the screen. The resulting screen is displayed in Figure E18.8. Notice that there are buttons for printing the current record on the form and closing the form. The **New Inventory Number** button redisplays the Parameter Entry dialog box, and it allows the user to choose a new record.

"I selected the SOFTWARE LOCATION inquiry as the next screen to develop," Chip tells Anna. "After talking at length with Cher, I produced the details and documented them in the Visible Analyst repository [illustrated in Figure E18.9]. The entry field is a partial software TITLE, entered in a Parameter Value dialog box. The first record matching the partial title is displayed, and since there are different operating systems and versions of the software, the user can click buttons to advance to the next (or previous) record. Five columns of information are displayed: HARDWARE INVENTORY NUMBER, BRAND NAME, MODEL, CAMPUS, and ROOM. This allows Cher to quickly locate a machine containing the desired software. She seems to be happy with this idea so far," Chip adds.

The Parameter Value dialog box is illustrated in Figure E18.10, and the SOFTWARE LOCATION inquiry screen is shown in Figure E18.11. The program locates the SOFTWARE MASTER file using the alternate key TITLE. If the matching record is not found, an error message is displayed. Since there may be several versions, the **Next Record** button may be pressed until the correct OPERATING SYSTEM and VERSION NUMBER are obtained.

Once the correct software has been obtained, the relational file is used to find the matching SOFTWARE INVENTORY NUMBER. This relational file contains the SOFTWARE INVENTORY NUMBER and the matching HARDWARE INVENTORY NUMBER, which is used to locate the matching record in the MICROCOMPUTER MASTER file. For each matching machine, the

FIGURE E18.8
HARDWARE INVENTORY NUMBER Access inquiry screen.

FIGURE E18.9
Visible Analyst repository screen for the SOFTWARE LOCATION inquiry.

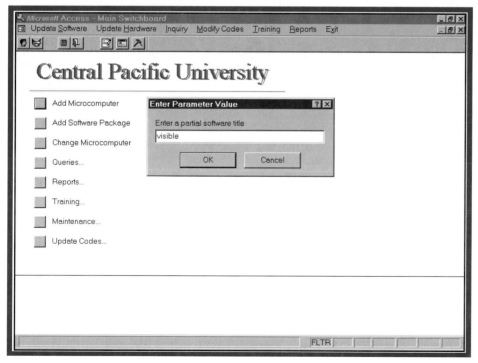

FIGURE E18.10
SOFTWARE LOCATION Parameter Value Entry dialog box.

FIGURE E18.11
SOFTWARE LOCATION INQUIRY screen.

CAMPUS table is used to locate the CAMPUS LOCATION code and to display the matching CAMPUS DESCRIPTION. The area for displaying the machines containing the software is a scroll region, since it may contain more machines than will fit on a single screen.

"I think we've got a good start on designing our user interfaces," Anna comments. Chip nods in agreement.

Exercises*

☐ **E-1.** Use Access to view the menu options for the Microcomputer System.

E-2. Examine the HARDWARE INQUIRY shown in Figures E18.5 and E18.6. Explain the inquiry **type** using the value, entity, and attribute (V, E, A) notation.

E-3. In a paragraph explain why a data-entry screen should emphasize accuracy while an inquiry screen emphasizes how fast results may be displayed.

☐ **E-4.** Modify and print the hierarchy chart representing the Hardware Update menu. Add rectangles to represent the following menu options.

> CHANGE MICROCOMPUTER
> DELETE MICROCOMPUTER RECORD
> UPDATE INSTALLED MICROCOMPUTER

---

* Exercises preceded by a disk icon require the program Visible Analyst Workbench or another CASE tool. A disk is provided free of charge to any professor adopting this book. The examples on the disk may be imported into Visible Analyst and then used by students.

⊞ **E-5.** Use the Functional Decomposition feature of Visible Analyst to draw a hierarchy chart representing the options found on the UPDATE SOFTWARE menu. Start with the top rectangle representing the UPDATE SOFTWARE menu.

ADD SOFTWARE PACKAGE
CHANGE SOFTWARE RECORD
DELETE SOFTWARE RECORD
UPGRADE SOFTWARE PACKAGE

E-6. Chip and Anna realize that the menu that has been designed is for the users involved in the installation and maintenance of microcomputer hardware and software. This menu would not be suitable for general faculty and staff members, since they should not have the ability to update the records. Design a menu, either on paper or using software that you are familiar with, that would provide the general user with the ability to perform inquiries and reports.

E-7. Discuss in a paragraph why the users would need to move to another screen (by pressing the Next Record button) to display the correct record for the SOFTWARE LOCATION inquiry.

⊞ **E-8.** Design the SOFTWARE DETAILS inquiry screen. The entry field is SOFTWARE INVENTORY NUMBER, and all Software information, with the exception of Expert and Machines Installed On, should be displayed. Refer to the Visible Analyst **Software Details** data flow repository entry.

⊞ **E-9.** When scheduling classrooms for student use, Cher Ware needs to know all the software packages in a given room. She would like to enter the CAMPUS LOCATION and the ROOM on an inquiry screen. The display fields would be TITLE, VERSION, SITE LICENSE, and NUMBER OF COPIES.

Design the **Software by Room** inquiry, which is described as a data flow in the Visible Analyst repository.

⊞ **E-10.** Mike Crowe needs to know which component boards are installed in each machine. Use Visible Analyst to view the data flow entry for **Component Boards** and to design the COMPONENT BOARD inquiry. The input field is the HARDWARE INVENTORY NUMBER. Output fields are BRAND NAME, MODEL, and a scroll region for BOARDS. The logic is to randomly read the MICROCOMPUTER MASTER using the HARDWARE INVENTORY NUMBER. If the record is not found, display an error message to that effect. Find the matching BOARD records. Write the notation using value, entity, and attribute (V, E, A) for the type of inquiry.

E-11. Every so often, Hy Perteks receives a request for help concerning a given software package. Staff members and students need to perform advanced options or transfer data to and from different packages, and they are having difficulties. Hy would like to enter the software TITLE and VERSION NUMBER. The resulting display would show the SOFTWARE EXPERT NAME and his or her CAMPUS LOCATION and ROOM NUMBER. Design the screen for the LOCATE SOFTWARE EXPERT inquiry. Describe the logic and files needed to produce the inquiry. Write the notation for this inquiry using value, entity, and attribute (V, E, A). The details for this inquiry are included in the Visible Analyst **Software Expert** data flow repository entry.

E-12. In a follow-up interview with Cher Ware, it was determined that she needs to know what machines are available to install any software package, given the package's graphics requirements. Produce an inquiry that would allow Cher to enter the monitor code and, optionally, a graphics board and campus location for the software. Four columns should be displayed:

HARDWARE INVENTORY NUMBER
CAMPUS LOCATION
ROOM LOCATION
GRAPHICS BOARD

Refer to the Visible Analyst **Monitor Required** data flow. Write a paragraph describing the logic involved in obtaining the results. Include the type of inquiry using value, entity, and attribute (V, E, A) notation.

E-13. Both Cher and Hy expressed an interest in finding machines of a specified brand connected to different printers. Sometimes the engineering students need a plotter, whereas other situations demand a laser or postscript printer.

Design an inquiry that would have the PRINTER and BRAND NAME of the microcomputer as input fields. Output would be two columns: CAMPUS LOCATION (full name, not a code) and ROOM LOCATION. Refer to the Visible Analyst **Printer Location** data flow.

Briefly describe the logic used in producing the output. Would this inquiry need a scroll region to display all the information? Why or why not? Use a paragraph to describe the type of inquiry using value, entity, and attribute (V, E, A) notation.

E-14. Hy receives a number of requests for training classes. He would like to plan training and place the upcoming classes on the intranet so that faculty would have an adequate amount of lead time to schedule a class. Design the SOFTWARE TRAINING CLASSES inquiry. The details may be found in the Visible Analyst data flow repository entry called **Software Training Classes**.

ACCURATE DATA-ENTRY PROCEDURES

Do you have a website?

Join the Borders.com Friends & Associates Program today and start earning commissions by providing your visitors with a vast selection of different books, CDs, videos and DVDs—all without having to worry about stocking inventory or building a title database.

Add Value
With millions of titles in stock, premium and original content, a well-developed community, and dedicated customer service, Borders.com offers visitors the ultimate online shopping experience.

Earn Commissions
Get paid up to a 7% commission on applicable books, CDs, videos and DVDs sold through links from your site to Borders.com.

Friends & Associates Program

Find out more about our program by going directly to http://go.borders.com/associates/index.xcv, or email us at associates@borders.com.

the system accurately is of the utmost
that the quality of data input determines
e systems analyst can support accurate
of three broad objectives, as shown in
ng, effective and efficient data capture
hrough validation.

rement of how consistently correct the
Effectively coded data facilitates accu-
he sheer quantity of data and thus the
n.

iciently, data entry is meeting predeter-
give the relationship between the time
data items entered. Efficient data entry
uickly and easily decipherable by data-
ms. Effective coding, effective and effi-
ssuring data quality through validation
ves covered in this chapter.

tered more accurately and efficiently is through the knowledgeable employment of various codes. The process of putting ambiguous or cumbersome data into short, easily entered digits or letters is called coding (not to be confused with program coding).

Coding aids the systems analyst in reaching the objective of efficiency, since data that are coded require less time to enter—and this thus reduces the number of items entered. Coding can also help in the appropriate sorting of data at a later point in the data transformation process. Additionally, coded data can save valuable memory and storage space. In sum, coding is a way of being eloquent but succinct in capturing data. Besides providing

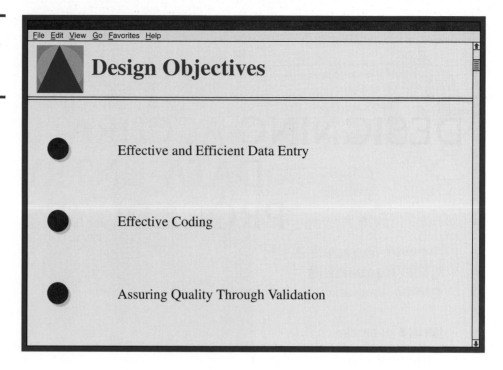

File Edit View Go Favorites Help

Design Objectives

● Effective and Efficient Data Entry

● Effective Coding

● Assuring Quality Through Validation

accuracy and efficiency, codes should have a purpose. Specific types of codes allow us to treat data in a particular manner. Purposes for coding include:

1. Keeping track of something.
2. Classifying information.
3. Concealing information.
4. Revealing information.
5. Requesting appropriate action.

Each of these purposes for coding is discussed in the following subsections, along with some example of codes.

Keeping Track of Something

Sometimes we want merely to identify a person, place, or thing in order to keep track of it. For example, a shop that manufactures custom-made upholstered furniture needs to assign a job number to a project. The salesperson needs to know the name and address of the customer, but the job shop manager or the workers who assemble the furniture need not know who the customer is. Consequently, an arbitrary number is assigned to the job. The number can be either random or sequential, as described in the following subsection.

SIMPLE SEQUENCE CODES. The simple sequence code is a number that is assigned to something if it needs to be numbered. It therefore has no relation to the data itself. Figure 19.2 shows how a furniture manufacturer's orders are assigned an order number. This is an easy reference number so the company can keep track of the order in process. It is more efficient to enter job

The Time Bomb

As you enter the IS groups' coffee room at Premium Airlines headquarters in Philadelphia, two of your systems teammates barely acknowledge your presence as they continue a lively discussion about a problem they're experiencing. Wanting to help out, you finally ask, "What's up guys?"

Kara Sell looks up briefly, gesturing for you to join them at the table. As you sit down next to her, Kara continues her conversation. "When we first started entering information about the date in our 'Flying for Prizes' mileage club, nobody ever imagined that there would *be* a year 2000 problem!"

Fresh from college and new to the team, Miles Garner is sitting across from you at the table. Miles asks, "What is a year 2000 problem anyway?"

After you and Kara exchange looks of slight surprise, Kara patiently explains. "The year 2000 problem refers to the crisis we will have with our database when the year 2000 comes around. When we entered data, we used a two-digit code for the year. For 1993 we entered 93; for 1994 we entered 94."

Miles replies quickly, "Well, I was still in school then. That's what we always did. But why does it matter that you entered '93 or '94? That was the right year, right?"

Kara tries to clarify her concern by giving an example. "Well, someone born in 1970 is 27 in the year 1997."

Miles interrupts. "Of course."

Kara continues. "That is, 97 − 70 = 27. But when the year 2000 comes, that person is 00 − 70 or −70 years old."

Replying swiftly, Miles counters, "Can't you just add 100 years when the year 2000 comes, so 100 + 00 −70 = 30? Wouldn't that solve it?"

You know from working with Kara for many years that she has been thinking about this for some time, as she tells Miles, "Well, that may work for awhile, but don't forget that we reward people who have been in our mileage program for five years. If someone joins in 1998, it will work, but what about our customers in the year 2000? In five years, that calculation would lead to 100 + 05 − 00 = 105 years."

Before you have a chance to contribute your own suggestion, Miles eagerly says, "Maybe we can fix that, too."

Kara looks up at the door as Douglas McDonnell, a long-time team member, enters. It's apparent he has been listening to the discussion from the hall and already has formulated a comment. After pouring himself a cup of coffee, he addresses Miles, saying, "I know you'll solve the year 2000 problem if you think about it long enough, but I am more concerned about the 1999 problem. Whenever our data entry people didn't know a person's date of birth, we instructed them to enter in a code of "99"—and our software recognized this as 'year unknown.' This was a common practice in computing for many, many years—and it made a lot of sense at the time. I am afraid that decision is going to explode in our faces."

How would you solve the year 2000 problem? (*Hint:* For more background on Premium Airlines, see Consulting Opportunity 11.4.) Suggest to your systems team in three paragraphs how you could solve it. Draw a data entry screen (or screens) for keeping track of customer frequent flier miles, birth dates, length of time in the program, and any other relevant data that shows your solution will work. Would your proposed solution to the year 2000 problem fix the 1999 problem as well? Respond in a paragraph. If not, propose what you would do in another paragraph-long response.

"5676" than "That brown and black rocking chair with the leather seat for Arthur Hook, Jr."

Using a sequence code rather than a random number has some advantages. First, it eliminates the possibility of assigning the same number. Second, it gives users an approximation of when the order was received.

Sequence codes should be used when order-of-processing requires knowledge of the sequence in which items enter the system or the order in which events unfold. An example is found in the situation of a bank running a special promotion that makes it important to know when a person applied for a special, low-interest home loan, since (all other things being equal) the special mortgage loans will be granted on a first-come, first-served basis. In this case, assigning a correct sequence code to each applicant is important.

FIGURE 19.2
Using a simple sequence code
to indicate the sequence in
which orders enter a custom
furniture shop.

Order #	Product	Customer
5676	Rocking Chair/with Leather	Arthur Hook, Jr.
5677	Dining Room Chair/Upholstered	Millie Monice
5678	Love Seat/Upholstered	J. & D. Pare
5679	Child's Rocking Chair/Decals	Lucinda Morely

ALPHABETIC DERIVATION CODES. There are times when it is undesirable to use sequence codes. The most obvious instance is when you do *not* wish to have someone read the code to figure out how many numbers have been assigned. Another situation in which sequence codes may not be useful is when a more complex code is desirable to avoid a costly mistake. One possible error would be to add a payment to account 223 when you meant to add it to account 224, because you entered an incorrect digit.

The alphabetic derivation code is a commonly used approach in identifying an account number. The example in Figure 19.3 comes from a mailing label for a magazine. The code becomes the account number. The first five digits come from the first five digits of the subscriber's zip code; the next three are the first three consonants in the subscriber's name; the next four numbers are from the street address; and the last three make up the code for the magazine. The main purpose of this code is to identify an account. Notice that the expiration date is not part of the account number, because that number can change more frequently than the other data.

Classifying Information

Coding affords the ability to distinguish among classes of items. Classifications are necessary for many purposes—for example, reflecting what parts of a medical insurance plan an employee carries or showing which student has completed the core requirements of his or her coursework.

To be useful, classes must be mutually exclusive. For example, if a student is in class F, meaning freshman, having completed 0 to 36 credit hours, he or she should not also be classifiable as a sophomore (S). Overlapping classes would be F = 0–36 credit hours and S = 32–64 credit hours, and so on. Data are unclear and not as readily interpretable when coding classes are not mutually exclusive.

FIGURE 19.3
Identifying the account of a
magazine subscriber with an
alphabetic derivation code.

Code	Explanation of Code
68506KND7533TVG	99999XXX9999XXX └── Abbreviation of magazine └── Four digits of street address └── First three consonants in last name └── First five digits of zip code

Code	Tax Deductible Item
I	Interest Payments
M	Medical Payments
T	Taxes
C	Contributions
D	Dues
S	Supplies

FIGURE 19.4
Grouping tax-deductible items
through the use of a one-letter
classification code.

CLASSIFICATION CODES. Classification codes are used to distinguish one group of data with special characteristics from another. Classification codes can consist of either a single letter or a number. They are a shorthand way of describing a person, place, thing, or happening.

Classification codes are listed in manuals or posted so that users can locate them easily. Many times, users become so familiar with frequently used codes that they memorize them. A user classifies an item, then enters its code directly into the terminal of an on-line system or onto a source document of a batch system.

An example of classification coding is the way you may wish to group tax-deductible items for the purpose of completing your income taxes. Figure 19.4 shows how codes are developed for items such as interest, medical payments, contributions, and so on. The coding system is simple: Take the first letter of each of the categories. Contributions are C; interest payments are I; supplies are S.

All goes well until we get to other categories (such as computer items, insurance payments, and subscriptions) that begin with the same letters we used previously. Figure 19.5 demonstrates what happens in this case. The coding was stretched so that we could use the P for "comPuter"; the N for "iNsurance"; and the B for "suBscriptions." Obviously, this is far from being

Code	Tax Deductible Item
I	Interest Payments
M	Medical Payments
T	Taxes
C	Contributions
D	Dues
S	Supplies
S	Subscriptions
C	Computer
I	Insurance
M	Miscellaneous
B	Subscriptions
P	Computer
N	Insurance
X	Miscellaneous

These duplicate codes ...

... are corrected by "forcing" the codes to fit.

FIGURE 19.5
Problems in using a one-letter
classification code occur
when categories share the
same letter.

FIGURE 19.6
Using a block sequence
code to group similar
software packages.

Code	Name of Software Package	Type
100	Netscape	Browser
101	Internet Explorer	
102	Lynx	
•	•	
•	•	
•	•	
200	Access	Database
201	Paradox	
202	Oracle	
•	•	
•	•	
•	•	
300	Word for Windows	Word Processing
301	Wordperfect	
•	•	
•	•	
•	•	
400	Astound	Presentation
401	Micrograf Designer	
402	PowerPoint	
•	•	
•	•	
•	•	

perfect. One way to avoid the confusion of this type is to allow for codes longer than one letter. This will be discussed later in this chapter, under the subheading of mnemonic codes.

BLOCK SEQUENCE CODES. Earlier, we discussed sequence codes. The block sequence code is an extension of the sequence code. Figure 19.6 shows how a business assigns numbers to microcomputer software. Main categories of software are browser packages, database packages, word-processing packages, and presentation packages. These were assigned sequential numbers in the following "blocks" or ranges: browser 100–199, database 200–299, and so forth. The advantage of the block sequence code is that the data are grouped according to common characteristics, while still taking advantage of the simplicity of assigning the next available number (within the block, of course) to the next item needing identification.

Concealing Information

Codes may be used to conceal or disguise information we do not wish others to know. There are many reasons why a business may want to do this. For example, a corporation may not want information in a personnel file to be accessed by data-entry workers. A store may want its salespeople to know the wholesale price to show them how low a price they can negotiate, but they may encode it on price tickets to prevent customers from finding that out. A restaurant may want to capture information about the service without letting the customer know the name of the server. The following subsection describes an example of concealing information through codes.

Code	Meaning	Example of Price Ticket
B	1	
L	2	GOLDEN'S ——— Store Name
E	3	202-395-40 ——— Style Code
A	4	BIMC ——— Coded Markdown Price
C	5	
H	6	Size 12 ——— Size of Garment
M	7	$25.00 ——— Customer Price
I	8	
N	9	Regular Price of Dress = $25.00
D	0	Markdown Ticket Encoded BIMC = $18.75

FIGURE 19.7
Encoding markdown prices
with a cipher code is a way of
concealing price information
from customers.

CIPHER CODES. Perhaps the simplest coding method is the direct substitution of one letter for another, one number for another, or one letter for a number. A popular type of puzzle called a cryptogram is an example of letter substitution. Figure 19.7 is an example of a cipher code taken from a Buffalo, New York, department store that coded all markdown prices with the words BLEACH MIND. No one really remembered why whose words were chosen, but all the employees knew them by heart, and so the cipher code was successful. Notice in this figure that an item with a retail price of $25.00 would have a markdown price of BIMC, or $18.75 when decoded letter by letter.

Revealing Information

Sometimes it is desirable to reveal information through a code. In a clothing store, information about the department, product, color, and size is printed along with the price on the ticket for each item. This helps the salespeople and stockpeople locate the place for the merchandise.

Another reason for revealing information through codes is to make the data entry more meaningful. A familiar part number, name, or description supports more accurate data entry. The examples of codes in the following subsection explain how these concepts can be realized.

SIGNIFICANT-DIGIT SUBSET CODES. When it is possible to describe a product by virtue of its membership in many subgroups, we can use a significant-digit subset code to help describe it. The clothing-store price ticket example in Figure 19.8 is an example of an effective significant-digit code.

To the casual observer or customer, the item description appears to be one long number. To one of the salespeople, however, the number is made up of a few smaller numbers, each one having a meaning of its own. The first three digits represent the department, the next three the product, the next two the color, and the last two the size.

Significant-digit subset codes may consist of either information that actually describes the product (for example, the number 10 means size 10) or numbers that are arbitrarily assigned (for instance, 202 is assigned to mean the maternity department). In this case, the advantage of using a significant-digit subset code is that it makes it possible to locate items that belong to a

FIGURE 19.8
Using a significant-digit subset code helps employees
locate items belonging to a
particular department.

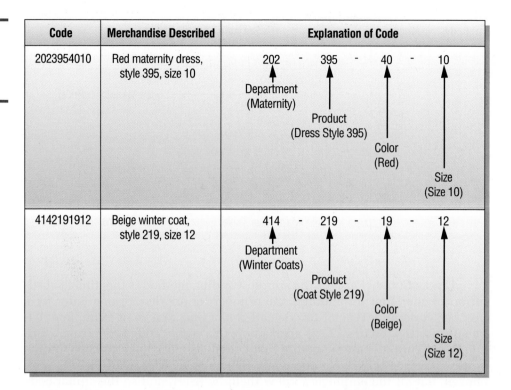

Code	Merchandise Described	Explanation of Code
2023954010	Red maternity dress, style 395, size 10	202 — 395 — 40 — 10 Department (Maternity) Product (Dress Style 395) Color (Red) Size (Size 10)
4142191912	Beige winter coat, style 219, size 12	414 — 219 — 19 — 12 Department (Winter Coats) Product (Coat Style 219) Color (Beige) Size (Size 12)

certain group or class. For example, if the store's manager decided to mark down all winter merchandise for an upcoming sale, salespeople could locate all items belonging to departments 310 through 449, the block of codes used to designate "winter" in general.

MNEMONIC CODES. A mnemonic (pronounced nî-môn′-ĭk) is a memory aid. Any code that helps either the data-entry person remember how to enter the data or the end user remember how to use the information can be considered a mnemonic. Using a combination of letters and symbols affords a strikingly clear way to code a product so that the code is easily seen and understood.

The city hospital codes used by the Buffalo regional blood center are mnemonic, as shown in Figure 19.9. The simple codes were invented precisely because the blood-bank administrators and systems analysts wanted to ensure that hospital codes were easy to memorize and recall. Mnemonic codes for the hospitals helped lessen the possibility of blood being shipped to the wrong hospital.

FIGURE 19.9
Mnemonic codes function as
memory aids by using a meaningful combination of letters
and numbers.

Code	City Hospitals
BGH	Buffalo General Hospital
ROS	Roswell Park Memorial Institute
KEN	Kenmore Mercy
DEA	Deaconess Hospital
SIS	Sisters of Charity
STF	Saint Francis Hospital
STJ	Saint Joseph's Hospital
OLV	Our Lady of Victory Hospital

Code	Function
1	Delivered
2	Sold
3	Spoiled
4	Lost or Stolen
5	Returned
6	Transferred Out
7	Transferred In
8	Journal Entry (Add)
9	Journal Entry (Subtract)

FIGURE 19.10
Function codes compactly
capture functions that the
computer must perform.

Requesting Appropriate Action

Codes are often needed to instruct either the computer or the decision maker about what action to take. Such codes are generally referred to as "function codes" and they typically take the form of either sequence or mnemonic codes.

FUNCTION CODES. The functions that the analyst or programmer desires the computer to perform with data are captured in function codes. Spelling out precisely what activities are to be accomplished is translated into a short numerical or alphanumeric code.

Figure 19.10 shows examples of a function code for updating inventory. Suppose you managed a dairy department and a case of yogurt spoiled, you would use the code 3 to indicate this event. Of course, data required for input vary depending on what function is needed. For example, appending or updating a record would require only the record key and function code, whereas adding a new record would require all data elements to be input, including the function code.

General Guidelines for Coding

In the previous subsections, we examined the purposes for using different types of codes when entering and storing data. Next, we examine a few heuristics for establishing a coding system. These rules are highlighted in Figure 19.11.

BE CONCISE. Codes should be concise. Overly long codes mean more keystrokes and consequently more errors. Long codes also mean that storing the information in a database will require more memory.

In Establishing a Coding System the Analyst Should:
• Keep codes concise
• Keep codes stable
• Make codes that are unique
• Allow codes to be sortable
• Avoid confusing codes
• Keep codes uniform
• Allow for modification of codes
• Make codes meaningful

FIGURE 19.11
There are eight general
guidelines for establishing
a coding system.

CONSULTING OPPORTUNITY 19.2

It's a Wilderness in Here

"I can't stand this. I've been looking for this (he swings a coonskin cap by its tail above his head) for the last forty-five minutes," complains Davey, one of the new warehouse workers for Crockett's, a large catalog-sales firm. "The catalog slip calls it a Coo m5–9w/tl. Good thing you told me Coo stands for coonskin. Then, of course, I thought about caps and looked over here. I found it here in this bin labeled BOYS/CAP. Wouldn't it be easier if the catalog matched the bins? To me, this invoice says, 'Cookware, metallic, 5–9-piece set with Teflon.' I've been stranded in the cookware sets the whole time."

Daniel, Davey's co-worker, barely listens to him as he hurriedly pulls items out of bins to fill another order. "You'll get used to it. They've got to have it this way so the computers can understand the bill later. Mostly, I look at the catalog page number on the invoice, then I look it up in the book and sort of translate it to back here . . . unless I remember it from finding it before," Daniel explains.

Davey persists, saying, "But computers are smart. And we have to fill so many orders. We should tell the people up in billing the names we've got on our bins."

Daniel replies cynically, "Oh, sure. They're dying to know what we think." Then he continues in a quieter tone. "You know, we used to have it like that. But when they got all the new computers and went to 24-hour phone orders, it all changed. Said the operators had to know more about what they were selling. So they changed their codes to be more like a story."

Davey, surprised at Daniel's revelation, asks, "What's the story for the one I was working on?"

Inspecting the code on the cap's invoice, Daniel replies, "The one you were working on was 'Coo m5–9w/tl.' After looking it up real fast on her computer the operator can tell the customer, 'It's a coonskin cap (Coo) for boys (m for male) ages 5–9 with a real tail (w/tl).' We can't see the forest for the trees because of their codes, but you know Crockett's—they've got to make the sale."

How important is it that the warehouse bins and invoices are encoded inconsistently? Respond in a paragraph. What are some of the problems created when a code appears to be mnemonic but employees are never given an appropriate "key" to decode it? Discuss your response in two paragraphs. What changes would you make to invoice/warehouse coding for Crockett's? Document your changes, identify the type of code you would use, and use the code in an example of a product that Crockett's might sell. Remember to decipher it as well.

Short codes are easier to remember and easier to enter. If codes must be long, they should be broken up into subcodes. For example, 5678923453127 could be broken up with hyphens as follows: 5678-923-453-127. This is a much more manageable approach and takes advantage of the way people are known to process information in short chunks.

KEEP THE CODES STABLE. Stability means that the identification code for a customer should not change each time new data are received. Earlier, we presented an alphabetic derivation code for a magazine subscription list. The expiration date was not part of the subscriber identification code because this was likely to change.

Don't change the code abbreviations in a mnemonic system. Once you have chosen the code abbreviations, do not try to revise them since this makes it extremely difficult for data-entry personnel to adapt.

ASSURE THAT CODES ARE UNIQUE. In order for codes to work, they must be unique. Make a note of all codes used in the system in order to assure that you are not assigning the same code number or name to the same items. Code numbers and names are an essential part of the entries in data dictionaries, as discussed in Chapter 10.

Incorrect Sorting Using MMM-DD-YYYY	Incorrect Sorting Using MM-DD-YYYY	Incorrect Sorting (Year 2000 Problem) YY-MM-DD	Correct Sorting Using YYYY-MM-DD
Dec-25-1998	06-04-1998	00-06-11	1997-06-12
Dec-31-1997	06-11-2000	97-06-12	1997-12-31
Jul-04-1999	06-12-1997	97-12-31	1998-06-04
Jun-04-1998	07-04-1999	98-06-04	1998-10-24
Jun-11-2000	10-24-1998	98-10-24	1998-12-25
Jun-12-1997	12-25-1998	98-12-25	1999-07-04
Oct-24-1998	12-31-1997	99-07-04	2000-06-11

FIGURE 19.12
Plan ahead in order to be able to do something useful with data that have been entered. In this example, the person creating the codes did not realize the data would have to be sorted.

ALLOW CODES TO BE SORTABLE. If you are going to manipulate the data usefully, the codes must be sortable. For example, if you were to perform a text search on the months of the year in ascending order, the "J" months would be out of order (January, July, then June). Dictionaries are sorted in this way, one letter at a time from right to left. So if you sorted MMMD-DYYYY where the MMM stood for the abbreviation for the month, DD for the day, and YYYY for the year, the result would be in error.

Figure 19.12 shows what would happen if a text search were performed on different forms of the date. The third column shows a problem that is part of the "Year 2000 crisis" that caused some alarm and even made the cover of *TIME* magazine.

One of the lessons learned is to make sure that you can do what you intend to do with the codes you create. Numerical codes are much easier to sort than alphanumerics; therefore, consider converting to numerics wherever practical.

AVOID CONFUSING CODES. Try to avoid using coding characters that look or sound alike. The characters O (the letter oh) and 0 (the number zero) are easily confused, as are the letter I and the number 1, and the letter Z and the number 2. Therefore, codes such as B1C and 280Z are unsatisfactory.

One example of a potentially confusing code is the Canadian Postal Code, as shown in Figure 19.13. The code format is X9X 9X9, where X stands for a letter and 9 stands for a number. One advantage to using letters in the code is to allow more data in a six-digit code (there are twenty-six letters, but only ten numbers). Since the code is used on a regular basis by Canadians, the code makes perfectly good sense to them. To foreigners send-

Code Format for Canadian Postal Code X9X 9X9			
Handwritten Code	**Actual Code**	**City, Providence**	**Problem**
L8S 4M4	L8S 4M4	Hamilton, Ontario	S looks like a 5
T3A ZE5	T3A 2E5	Calgary, Alberta	2 looks like a Z
			5 looks like an S
L0S IJ0	L0S 1J0	Niagra-on-the-Lake, Ontario	Zero and Oh look alike
			S looks like a 5
			1 looks like an I

FIGURE 19.13
Combining look-alike characters in codes can result in errors.

ing mail to Canada, however, it may be difficult to tell if the second-to-the-last symbol is a Z or a 2.

KEEP THE CODES UNIFORM. Codes need to follow readily perceived forms most of the time. Codes used together, such as BUF-234 and KU-3456, are poor because the first contains three letters and three numbers, while the second has only two letters followed by four numbers.

When you are required to add dates, try to avoid using the codes MMDDYYYY in one application, YYYYDDMM in a second, and MMDD19YY in a third. It is important to keep codes uniform among as well as within programs.

In the past, uniformity meant that all codes be kept the same length. With the introduction of on-line systems, the length is not as important as it once was. In a batch system, cards were keypunched and data generally had to be kept in distinct columns on the card. If most codes were four characters in length, a three-character code would require a blank. With on-line systems, the Enter key is hit after data entry is verified by the operator as correct, so it doesn't make much difference if the code is three or four characters long.

ALLOW FOR MODIFICATION OF CODES. Adaptability is a key feature of a good code. The analyst must keep in mind that the system will evolve over time, and the coding system should be able to encompass change. The number of customers should grow, customers will change names, and suppliers will modify the way they number their products. The analyst needs to be able to forecast the predictable and anticipate a wide range of future needs when designing codes.

MAKE CODES MEANINGFUL. Unless the analyst wants to hide information intentionally, codes should be meaningful. Effective codes not only contain information, they also make sense to the people using them. Meaningful codes are easier to understand, work with, and recall. The job of data entry becomes more interesting when working with meaningful codes instead of just entering a series of meaningless numbers.

EFFECTIVE AND EFFICIENT DATA CAPTURE

In order to assure the quality of data entered into the system, it is important to capture data effectively. Data capture has received increasingly more attention as the point in information processing at which excellent productivity gains can be made. Great progress in improving data capture has been made in the past three decades, as we have moved from a multiple-step, slow, and error-prone system such as keypunching to sophisticated, optical character recognition, bar codes, and point-of-sale terminals.

Deciding What to Capture

The decision about what to capture precedes user interaction with the system. Indeed, it is vital in making the eventual interface worthwhile, for the adage "Garbage in, garbage out" is still true.

Decisions about what data to capture for system input are made among systems analysts and systems users. Much of what will be captured is specific to the particular business. Capturing data, inputting it, storing it, and

CONSULTING OPPORTUNITY 19.3

Catching a Summer Code

Vickie takes her fingers off her keyboard and bends over her workstation to verify the letters on the invoices stacked in front of her. "What on earth?" Vickie says aloud as she further scrutinizes the letters that encode cities where orders are to be shipped.

Shelly Overseer, her supervisor, who usually sits a couple of workstations away, is passing by and sees Vickie's consternation. "What's the matter? Did the sales rep forget to write in the city code again?"

Vickie swings around in her chair to face Shelly. "No, there are codes here. But they're weird. We usually use a three-letter code, right? Like CIN for Cincinnati, SEA for Seattle, MIN for Minneapolis, BUF for Buffalo. But they're all *five*-letter codes here."

"Look," Vickie says, lifting the invoice to show Shelly. "CINNC, SEATT, MINNE. It'll take me all day to enter these. No kidding, it's really slowing me down. Maybe there's a mistake. Can't I just use the standard?"

Shelly backs away from Vickie's workstation as if the problem were contagious. Excusing herself apologetically, Shelly says, "It's the part-timers. They are learning sales now, and management was worried that they'd get messed up on their cities. I think it has something to do with mixing up Newark and New Orleans on the last orders. So a committee decided to

make the cities more recognizable by having them add two letters. Those kids can't learn everything we know overnight, even though they try. But it's just until August 19, until the part-timers go back to school."

As Vickie glumly turns back to her keyboard, Shelly puts her hand sympathetically on Vickie's shoulder and says, "I know it's a strain and it's making you feel miserable, but don't worry. You'll get over it. It's just a summer code."

What general guidelines of coding has management overlooked in its decision to use a summer code for cities? Make a list of them. What is the effect on full-time data-entry personnel of changing codes for the ease of temporary help? Respond in two paragraphs. What future impact could the temporary change in codes have on sorting and retrieving data entered during the summer period? Take two paragraphs to discuss these implications. What changes can you suggest so that the part-timers don't get mixed up on codes in the short term? In a memo to the supervisor of this work group, make a list of 5–7 changes in the data capture or data-entry procedures that can be made to accommodate short-term hires without disrupting normal business. In a paragraph, indicate how can this goal be accomplished without marring the productivity of data-entry personnel.

retrieving it are all costly endeavors, mostly due to the labor costs involved. With all these factors in mind, determining what to capture becomes an important decision.

There are two types of data to enter: data that *change* or *vary* with every transaction, and data that concisely *differentiate* the particular item being processed from all other items.

An example of changeable data is the quantity of supplies purchased each time an advertising firm places an order with the office supply wholesaler. Since quantities change depending on the number of employees at the advertising firm and on how many accounts they are servicing, quantity data must be entered each time an order is placed.

An example of differentiation data would be the inclusion on a patient record of the patient's social security number and the first three letters of his or her last name. In this way, the patient is uniquely differentiated from other patients in the same system.

Letting the Computer Do the Rest

When considering what data to capture for each transaction and what data to leave to the system to enter, the systems analyst must take advantage of what computers do best. In the preceding example of the advertising agency ordering office supplies, it is not necessary for the operator entering the sta-

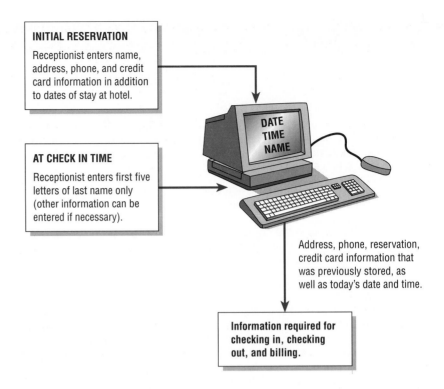

FIGURE 19.14
Automatically recording date and time in a hotel reservation system eliminates unnecessary data entry.

INITIAL RESERVATION
Receptionist enters name, address, phone, and credit card information in addition to dates of stay at hotel.

AT CHECK IN TIME
Receptionist enters first five letters of last name only (other information can be entered if necessary).

DATE
TIME
NAME

Address, phone, reservation, credit card information that was previously stored, as well as today's date and time.

Information required for checking in, checking out, and billing.

tionery order to reenter each item description each time an order is received. The computer can store and access this data easily.

Computers can automatically handle repetitive tasks, such as (1) recording the time of the transaction, (2) calculating new values from input, and (3) storing and retrieving data on demand. By employing the best features of computers, efficient data capture design avoids needless data entry. This, in turn, alleviates much human error and boredom.

Software can be written to indicate automatically the date of data entry so that the person inputting data does not have to bother with this for every transaction processed. Alternatively, the computer program can be written to ask the user to enter today's date. Once entered, the system proceeds to use that date on all transactions processed in that data-entry session.

Part of a display screen for hotel reservations and guest check-ins is shown in Figure 19.14. Notice that when a reservation is made initially, the guest's name and credit card number are entered. When the guest checks in, the desk clerk calls up the record without having to entirely reenter name or number. The system also automatically records date and time, saving further data entry.

As you can see, it is not necessary to enter data for each transaction that can be easily retrieved by the computer from storage. A prime example is that of the on-line computer library center used by over 4,000 libraries in the United States. Using thirteen mainframes hooked up to numerous mini- and microcomputers, OCLC was built upon the idea that each item bought by a library should only have to be cataloged once for all time. Once an item is entered, cataloging information goes into the huge OCLC database and is shared with participating libraries. In this case, implementation of the simple concept of entering data only once has saved enormous data-entry time.

The calculating power of the computer should also be taken into account when deciding what *not* to reenter. Computers are adept at long calculations, using data already entered.

For example, the person doing data entry may enter the flight numbers and account number of an air trip taken by a customer belonging to a frequent-flyer incentive program. The computer then calculates the number of miles accrued for each flight, adds it to the miles already in the customer's account, and updates the total miles accrued to the account. The computer may also flag an account that, by virtue of the large number of miles flown, is now eligible for a prize. Although all of this information may print out on the customer's updated account sheet, the only new data entered were the flight numbers of the flights flown.

Although users will have suggestions about what data are unnecessary, these decisions should not be made at the time of entry. Rather, the decision is best made by the systems analyst in conjunction with users at an earlier stage in the process. Through your prior analyses, you will possess the larger picture of what is being input to the system and for what purpose. When analyses are complete, unnecessary input becomes apparent—as do redundancies.

Avoiding Bottlenecks and Extra Steps

A bottleneck in data entry is an apt allusion to the physical appearance of a bottle. Data are poured rapidly into the wide mouth of the system only to be slowed in its "neck" because of an artificially created instance of insufficient processing for the volume or detail of the data being entered. One way a bottleneck can be avoided is by ensuring that there is enough capacity to handle the data that are being entered.

Ways to avoid extra steps are determined not only at the time of analysis, but also when users begin to interact with the system. The fewer steps involved in inputting data, the fewer chances there are for the introduction of errors. So beyond the obvious consideration of saved labor, avoiding extra steps is also a way to preserve the quality of data. Once again, use of an on-line, real-time system that captures customer data without necessitating the completion of a form is an excellent example of saving steps in data entry.

Starting with a Good Form

Effective data capture is achievable only if prior thought is given to what the source document should contain. The data-entry operator inputs data from the source document (usually some kind of form); this document is the source of a large amount of all system data. On-line systems (or special data-entry methods such as bar codes) may circumvent the need for a source document, but often some kind of paper form, such as a receipt is created anyway.

With effective forms, it is not necessary to reenter information that the computer has already stored or data such as time or date of entry that the computer can determine automatically. Chapter 15 discussed in detail how a form or source document should be designed to maximize its usefulness for capturing data and to minimize the time users need to spend entering data from it.

Choosing a Data-Entry Method

Several efficient data-entry methods are available, and choosing one of them is shaped by many factors, including the need for speed, accuracy, and operator training; the cost of the data-entry method (whether it is materials- or labor-intensive); and the methods currently in use in the organization.

FIGURE 19.15
Optical character recognition
(OCR) of special-character
source documents facilitates
data entry.

```
ABCDEFGHIJKLMN
OPQRSTUVWXYZ ,.
$/*- 1234567890
```

KEYBOARDS. Key boarding is the oldest method of data entry, and certainly it is the one with which organizational members are the most familiar. Some improvements have been made over the years to standardize keyboards, such as built-in numerical keypads that can be programmed with macros to reduce the number of keystrokes required, a better mouse (one that is shaped to the contours of the hand), and so on. Software permits researchers to analyze how many keystrokes are needed to enter certain types of data.

OPTICAL CHARACTER RECOGNITION. Optical character recognition (OCR) lets a user read input from a source document with an optical scanner rather than off the magnetic media we have been discussing so far. Using OCR devices can speed data input from 50 to 75 percent over some keying methods.

What is needed is a source document that can be optically scanned when it is filled out, either through special block printing or by hand, as shown in Figure 19.15. How the source document is filled in depends on the requirements of the particular hardware and software.

The increased speed of OCR comes through not having to encode or key in data from source documents. It eliminates many of the time-consuming and error-fraught steps of other input devices. In doing so, OCR demands few employee skills and commensurately less training. This results in fewer errors and less time spent by employees in redundant efforts, and it decentralizes responsibility for quality data directly to the unit that is generating it. Optical character recognition, which has become available to all, has one additional, highly practical use: the transformation of faxes into documents that can be edited.

OTHER METHODS OF DATA ENTRY. Other methods of data entry are also becoming more widely employed. Most of these methods reduce labor costs by requiring few operator skills or little training, they move data entry closer to the source of data, and they eliminate the need for a source document. In doing so, they have become fast and highly reliable data-entry methods. The data-entry methods discussed in the following sections include magnetic ink character recognition, mark-sense forms, punch-out forms, bar codes, and data strips.

Magnetic ink character recognition (MICR). Magnetic ink characters are found on the bottom of bank checks and some credit card bills. This method is akin to OCR in that special characters are read, but its use is limited. Data entry through magnetic ink character recognition (MICR) is done through a machine that reads and interprets a single line of material encoded with ink that is made up of magnetic particles.

FIGURE 19.16
A mark-sense form for data entry that is filled out in pencil and read by a scanner speeds data entry.

DIRECTIONS FOR MARKING

Use #2 or #2½ pencil only DO NOT use ink or ballpoint.
Make heavy black marks that fill the circle completely.
Erase cleanly any answer you wish to change–make no stray marks.

Examples of PROPER marks   Examples of IMPROPER marks

1. What levels of people do you <u>primarily</u> serve in your work?
   managers
   supervisors; foremen
   other salaried
   hourly
   volunteers

2. Total size of the organization you serve:
   less than 1,000   15,000-25,000
   1,000-5,000   more than 25,000
   5,000-15,000

   5. A Most Significant Part
   4. A Major Part
   3. A Substantial Part
   2. A Smaller Part
   1. A Minor Part
   0. Does Not Apply

3. What training and development techniques do you use? (please mark each technique)
   lecture with or without media
   films
   videotape closed-circuit TV
   discussions (cases, issues, etc.)
   role playing
   behavior modeling
   simulation; advanced gaming
   on-the-job training
   job rotation
   internships; assistantships
   organization development techniques
   Other

Some advantages of using MICR are (1) it is reliable, high-speed, and not susceptible to accepting stray marks (since they are not encoded magnetically); (2) if it is required on all withdrawal checks, it serves as a security measure against bad checks; and (3) data-entry personnel can see the numbers making up the code if it is necessary to verify it.

Mark-sense forms. Mark-sense forms allow data entry through the use of a scanner that senses where marks have been made by lead pencil on special forms. A common usage is for scoring answer sheets for survey questionnaires, as shown in Figure 19.16. Little training of entry personnel is necessary, and a high volume of forms can be processed quickly.

FIGURE 19.17
An example of a punch-out
form for capturing and entering small amounts of data
efficiently.

OFFICIAL BALLOT

Punch Out
One Only

Ray Zortax ☐

Lauren Orrder ☐

May Ralchoice ☐

The drawbacks of mark-sense forms include the fact that while the readers can determine whether a mark has been made, they cannot interpret the mark in the way that optical character readers do. Stray marks on forms can thus be entered as incorrect data. Additionally, choices are limited to the answers provided on the mark-sense form; forms have difficulty in capturing alphanumeric data because of the space required for a complete set of letters and numbers; and it is easy for those filling out mark-sense forms to get confused and put a mark in an incorrect position.

Punch-out forms. Punch-out forms are a quick and convenient way of capturing and entering limited data. Figure 19.17 shows an example of a punch-out form used for balloting purposes, where voters use a stylus to make a hole or deep indentation by the name of their chosen candidate. Punch-out forms are used for balloting purposes when votes must be tallied quickly.

Bar codes. Bar codes typically appear on product labels, but they also appear on patient identification bracelets in hospitals and in almost any context in which a person or object needs to be checked into and out of any kind of inventory system. Bar codes can be thought of as "metacodes," or codes encoding codes, since they appear as a series of narrow and wide bands on a label which encodes numbers or letters. These symbols in turn have access to product data stored in computer memory. A beam of light from a scanner or lightpen is drawn across the bands on the label either to confirm or record data about the product being scanned.

A bar-coded label, such as the one shown in Figure 19.18, includes coding for a particular grocery product: the manufacturer identification number, the product identification number, a code to verify the scan's accuracy, and codes to mark the beginning and end of the scan.

Bar coding affords an extraordinarily high degree of accuracy for data entry. It saves labor costs for retailers because each item does not have to be individually price-marked. Additionally, bar coding allows the automatic capturing of data that can be used for reordering, more accurate inventory tracking, and the forecasting of future needs. Sale prices or other changes in the meaning of the bar codes are entered into the central processor, thus saving the trouble of marking down numerous items.

One new use of bar coding is the tracking of an individual's credit card purchases for the purpose of building a consumer profile, which can then, in turn, be used to refine marketing to that individual or type of consumer. New

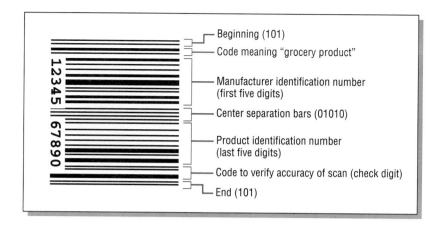

FIGURE 19.18
Bar coding, as shown in this label for a grocery product, affords highly accurate data entry. Used with the permission of the Uniform Code Council, Dayton, Ohio.

input devices are constantly being developed. Of course, it has been possible to transfer photographic images for some time now using systems like the Kodak Photo CD process, but using a digital camera eliminates the middle step of users needing to digitize their own photographs.

USING INTELLIGENT TERMINALS. Intelligent terminals can be considered a step above dumb terminals and a step below intelligent workstations and portable microcomputers in their capabilities. In many instances, intelligent terminals eliminate the need for a source document.

The biggest advantage of using intelligent terminals is that, through the use of a microprocessor, they are able to relieve the CPU of many of the burdens of editing, controlling, transforming, and storing data, processes which the dumb terminals require. Dumb terminals rely on the CPU for all data manipulation, including editing, updating, and so on.

The configuration for intelligent terminals is a microprocessor, display screen, and a keyboard. The intelligent terminal has access to the CPU through a network and can be either on-line or deferred on-line. In an on-line intelligent terminal, all of the steps in entry, processing, verifying, and output are done immediately with the customer present. The closer data entry is to the source of the data, the more accurate it is likely to be. A well-known example of an on-line intelligent terminal is the airline ticketing system.

Deferred on-line intelligent terminals allow data to be entered and verified immediately, but processing is batched and done later (which is less expensive). Electronic cash registers combine these attributes, with both input and output capabilities at point-of-sale terminals.

ASSURING DATA QUALITY THROUGH INPUT VALIDATION

So far, we have discussed assuring the effective capturing of data onto source documents and its efficient entry into the system through various input devices. Although these are necessary conditions for assuring quality data, they alone are not sufficient.

Errors cannot be ruled out entirely, and the critical importance of catching errors during input, *prior* to processing and storage, cannot be overemphasized. The snarl of problems created by incorrect input can be a

Source: *Gahan Wilson © 1993*
from The New Yorker *Collection.*
All Rights Reserved.

"*Garbage in, garbage out!*"

nightmare, not the least of which is that many problems take a long time to surface. The systems analyst must assume that errors in data *will* occur and must work with users to design input validation tests to prevent erroneous data from being processed and stored, since initial errors that go undiscovered for long periods are expensive and time-consuming to correct.

You cannot imagine everything that will go awry with input, but you must cover the kinds of errors that give rise to the largest percentage of problems. A summary of potential problems that must be considered when validating input are given in Figure 19.19.

Validating Input Transactions

Validating input transactions is largely done through software, which is the programmer's responsibility, but it is important that the systems analyst know what common problems might invalidate a transaction. Businesses committed to quality will include validity checks as part of their routine software.

Three main problems can occur with input transactions: submitting the wrong data to the system, the submitting of data by an unauthorized person, or asking the system to perform an unacceptable function.

SUBMITTING THE WRONG DATA. An example of submitting the wrong data to the system would be the attempt to input a patient's social security number into a hospital's payroll system. This error is usually an accidental one; however, it should be flagged before data are processed.

This Type of Validation:	Can Prevent These Problems
Validating Input Transactions	Submitting the wrong data Data submitted by an unauthorized person Asking the system to perform an unacceptable function
Validating Input Data	Missing data Incorrect field length Data have unacceptable composition Data are out of range Data are invalid Data do not match with stored data

FIGURE 19.19
Validating input is important
to ensure that most potential problems with data are
eliminated early.

SUBMITTING OF DATA BY AN UNAUTHORIZED PERSON. The system should also be able to discover if otherwise correct data are submitted by an unauthorized person. For instance, only the supervising pharmacist should be able to enter inventory totals for controlled substances in the pharmacy. Invalidation of transactions submitted by an unauthorized individual applies to privacy and security concerns surrounding payroll systems and employee evaluation records that determine pay levels, promotions, or discipline; files containing trade secrets; and files holding classified information, such as national defense data.

ASKING THE SYSTEM TO PERFORM AN UNACCEPTABLE FUNCTION. The third error that invalidates input transactions is asking the system to perform an unacceptable function. For instance, it would be logical for a human resources manager to update the existing record of a current employee; however, it would be invalid to ask the system to create a new file rather than merely to update an existing record.

Validating Input Data

It is essential that the input data itself, along with the transactions requested, are valid. Several tests can be incorporated into software to assure this. We will consider seven possible ways to validate input.

TEST FOR MISSING DATA. The first kind of validity test examines data to see if there are any missing items. For some situations, *all* data items must be present. For example, a social security file for paying out retirement or disability benefits would be invalid if it did not include the payee's social security number.

Additionally, the record should include both the key data that distinguishes one record from all others and the function code telling the computer what to do with the data. The systems analyst needs to interact with users to determine what data items are essential and to find out whether exceptional cases ever occur that would allow data to be considered valid even if some data items were missing.

TEST FOR CORRECT FIELD LENGTH. A second kind of validity test checks input to assure that it is of the correct length for the field. For example, if the Omaha, Nebraska, weather station reports into the national weather service computer but mistakenly provides a two-letter city code (OM) instead of the

To Enter or Not to Enter: That Is the Question

"I've just taken on the presidency of Elsinore Industries," says Rose N. Krantz. "We're actually part of a small cottage industry that manufactures toy villages for children seven years and up. Our tiny hamlets consist of various kits that will build what children want from interlocking plastic cubes—essentials like city hall, the police station, the gas station, a hot dog stand, and so on. Each kit has a unique part number from 200 to 800 (not every number is used, however). The wholesale price varies from $54.95 for the city hall to $1.79 for a hot dog stand.

"But I've been melancholy over what I've found out since signing on at Elsinore. 'Something is rotten' here, to quote a famous playwright. In fact, the invoicing system was so out of control that I've been working around the clock with our bookkeeper, Gilda Stern," Krantz soliloquizes.

"I would like you to help straighten things out," Rose continues. "We ship to 12 distribution warehouses around the country. Each invoice we write out includes the warehouse number (1–12), its street address, and the zip code. We also put on each invoice the date we fill the order, code numbers for the hamlet kits they or-der, a description of each kit, the price per item, and the quantity of each kit ordered. Of course, we also include the subtotals of kit charges, shipping charges, and the total that the warehouse owes us. No sales tax is added, since they resell what we send them to toy stores in all 50 states. I want you to help us design a computerized order-entry system that will be part of the invoicing system for Elsinore Industries."

For your design of a data-entry system for Elsinore, take into consideration all of the objectives for data entry discussed throughout this chapter. Draw any screens necessary to illustrate your design. How can you make the order entry system efficient? Respond in a paragraph. Specify what data can be stored and retrieved—and what data must be entered anew for each order. How can unnecessary work be avoided? Write a paragraph to explain why the system you propose is more efficient than the old one. How can data accuracy be assured? List three strategies that will work with the type of data that are being entered for Elsinore Industries.

---

national three-letter city code (OMA), the input data might be deemed invalid and hence would not be processed.

TEST FOR CLASS OR COMPOSITION. This type of validity test checks to see that data fields that are supposed to be exclusively composed of numbers do not include letters, and vice versa. For example, a credit card account number for American Express should not include any letters. Using a composition test, the program should not accept an American Express account number that includes both letters and numbers.

TEST FOR RANGE OR REASONABLENESS. These validity tests are really a common-sense measure of input that answers the question of whether data fall within an acceptable range or whether they are reasonable within predetermined parameters. For instance, if a user was trying to verify a proposed shipment date, the range test would neither permit a shipping date on the thirty-second day of October nor accept shipment in the thirteenth month, the respective ranges being 1 to 31 days and 1 to 12 months.

A reasonableness test ascertains whether the item makes sense for the transaction. For example, entering an age of 120 years would not be reasonable when adding a new employee to the payroll.

TEST FOR INVALID VALUES. Checking input for invalid values works if there are only a few valid values. This test is not feasible for situations in which values are neither restricted nor predictable. This kind of test is useful for checking responses where data are divided into a limited number of classes. For example, a brokerage firm divides accounts into three classes only: class 1 = active account; class 2 = inactive account; class 3 = closed account. If data are assigned to any other class through an error, the values are invalid.

TEST FOR COMPARISON WITH STORED DATA. The next test for validity of input data that we will consider is one comparing it with data that the computer has already stored. For example, a newly entered part number can be compared with the complete parts inventory in order to assure that the number exists and is being entered correctly.

SETTING UP SELF-VALIDATING CODES. Another method for assuring the accuracy of data, particularly identification numbers, is to use a check digit in the code itself. This procedure involves beginning with an original numerical code, performing some mathematics to arrive at a derived check digit, and then adding the check digit to the original code. The mathematical process involves multiplying each of the digits in the original code by some predetermined weights, summing these results, and then dividing this sum by a modulus number. The modulus number is needed because the sum usually is a large number, and we need to reduce the result to a single digit. Finally, the remainder is subtracted from the modulus number, giving us the check digit.

Figure 19.20 shows how a five-digit part number for a radiator hose (54823) is converted to a six-digit number containing a check digit. In this example, the weights chosen were the "1-3-1" system; in other words, the weights alternate between 1 and 3. After the digits 5, 4, 8, 2, and 3 were multiplied by 1, 3, 1, 3, and 1, they became 5, 12, 8, 6, and 3. These new digits sum to 34. Next, 34 is divided by the chosen modulus number, 10, with the result of 3 and a remainder of 4. The remainder, 4, is subtracted from the modulus number, 10, giving a check digit of 6. The digit 6 is now tacked onto the end of the original number, giving us the official product code for the radiator hose (548236).

Using check digits. The check digit system works in the following way. Suppose we had the part number 53411. This number has to be typed into the system, and while that is being done, different types of errors can occur. One possible error is the single digit miskey. For example, the clerk types in 54411 instead of 53411. Only the digit in the thousand place is incorrect, but this error may result in the wrong part being shipped.

A second type of error is transposed digits. It commonly occurs that the intended number 53411 gets typed in as number 54311 instead, just because two keys are pressed in reverse order. Transposition errors are also difficult for humans to detect.

These errors are avoidable through the use of a check digit because each of these numbers—the correct one and the error—would have a different check digit number, as shown in Figure 19.21. Now if part number 53411 was modified to 534118 (including the check digit 8) and either of the two errors just described occurred, the mistake would be caught. If the second digit was miskeyed as a 4, the computer would not accept 544118 as a valid number, since the check digit for 54411 would be 5, not 8. Similarly, if the second and third digits were transposed, as in 543118, the computer would also reject the number because the check digit for 54311 would be 6, not 8.

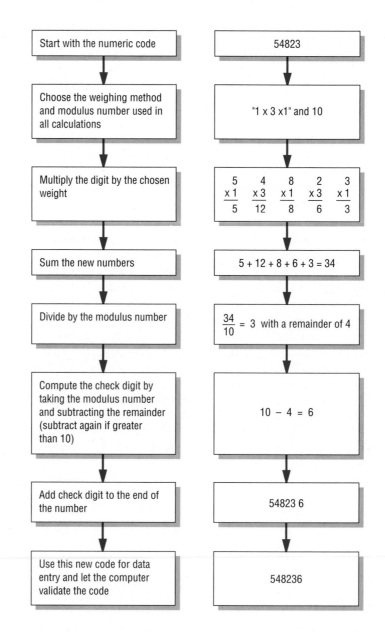

Start with the numeric code	54823
Choose the weighing method and modulus number used in all calculations	"1 x 3 x1" and 10
Multiply the digit by the chosen weight	5 4 8 2 3 / x 1 x 3 x 1 x 3 x 1 / 5 12 8 6 3
Sum the new numbers	5 + 12 + 8 + 6 + 3 = 34
Divide by the modulus number	$\frac{34}{10} = 3$ with a remainder of 4
Compute the check digit by taking the modulus number and subtracting the remainder (subtract again if greater than 10)	10 − 4 = 6
Add check digit to the end of the number	54823 6
Use this new code for data entry and let the computer validate the code	548236

FIGURE 19.21
Avoiding common data-entry errors through the use of a check digit.

Status	Original Code	Check Digit	New Code
Correct	5 3 4 1 1	8	534118
Single Digit Miskey	5④4 11	5	544115
Transpose	5④③1 1	6	543116

Do You Validate Parking?

"What are we going to do, Mercedes?" Edsel asks wearily. Together, Mercedes and Edsel are reviewing the latest billing printout for their firm, Denton & Denton Parking Garages. They have been purchasing batch billing services from a small, local computer services company since they acquired three parking garages in a medium-sized metropolitan area. Denton & Denton Parking Garages rents daily, monthly, and yearly parking places to corporations and individuals.

Mercedes replies, "I'm not sure what our next move is. But the billing is all wrong. Maybe we should try to talk to the computer people."

"They said they could figure out how to compute these charges from looking at what the old owners did by hand before, and they said they didn't want to run the old and new systems in parallel," Edsel remarks, shaking his head. "But this isn't right. At least I can't figure it out. Maybe you can."

Mercedes accepts the notion of chasing the suspect output and starts looking at the report in detail. "Well, for one thing, they don't realize we get cars from all over in here. Wherever we've got a car with plates that aren't in-state, it seems as if the computer stops figuring. Look, our plates start with a number and then a letter, right? Well this one from New York begins with three letters. The computer can't handle it," she says.

Edsel catches on and starts to think about the business as he looks at the printout. "Yeah, and look here. This person doesn't have a yearly account number, just a monthly one, so no bill came out," he says. "We've got monthlies, too, and the computer doesn't know it?"

"And look at this. It still made daily charges for the three days in November when we told them right out there weren't any vacancies for daily customers. It isn't reasonable," Mercedes asserts.

Edsel continues paging through the printout, but Mercedes stops him, saying, "But don't look any further. I'm calling the computer people so we can get this straightened out."

How would you characterize the problems being encountered with the current garage billing system? Use a paragraph to formulate a response. What are some tests for validity of data that could be included in the software for a revised billing system for the parking garages? List them. What could the programmer/analysts for the computer services company have done differently so that the customer was not faced with correcting the poor-quality output? Use three paragraphs to do a critical analysis of what was done—and what *should* have been done.

The systems analyst chooses the weights and the modulus number, but once chosen, they must not change. Some examples of weighting methods and modulus numbers can be found in Figure 19.22.

The check digit system is not foolproof. It is conceivable that two part numbers (732463 and 732413, for example) may have the same check digit. A single miskey in the second digit from the right would not be detected in that case.

The check digit system also has a cost. The added space taken up by the check digit must be considered, as well as the added computation involved in calculating and verifying the check digit. The check digit approach is useful when the original codes are five or more digits, when codes are simple numerics with no meaning, and when the cost of making miskey and transposition errors is high.

The seven tests for checking on validity of input can go a long way toward protecting the system from the entry and storage of erroneous data. Always assume that errors in input are more likely than not to occur. It is your responsibility to understand which errors will invalidate data and how to use the computer to guard against those errors—and thus to limit their intrusion into system data.

CHAPTER 19:
DESIGNING ACCURATE
DATA-ENTRY PROCEDURES

FIGURE 19.22
Examples of weighting methods and modulus numbers.

Check Digit Method	Calculations for Check Digit to be Added to the Original Number 29645
Modulus 10 "2-1-2"	2 9 6 4 5 x2 x1 x2 x1 x2 10 4 + 9 + 12 + 4 + 10 = 39/10 = 3 remainder (9) Check digit equals 1 Code with check digit is 296451.
Modulus 10 "3-1-3"	2 9 6 4 5 x3 x1 x3 x1 x3 10 6 + 9 + 18 + 4 + 15 = 52/10 = 5 remainder (2) Check digit equals 8 Code with check digit is 296458.
Modulus 11 "Arithmetic"	2 9 6 4 5 x6 x5 x4 x3 x2 11 12 + 45 + 24 + 12 + 10 = 103/11 = 9 remainder (4) Check digit equals 7 Code with check digit is 296457.
Modulus 10 "Geometric"	2 9 6 4 5 x32 x16 x8 x4 x2 11 64+144 + 48 + 16 + 10 = 282/11 = 25 remainder (7) Check digit equals 4 Code with check digit is 296454.

ACCURACY, CODES, AND THE GRAPHICAL USER INTERFACE

In systems that utilize a graphical user interface (GUI), codes are often stored either as a function or as a separate table in the database. There is a trade-off on creating too many tables, since the software must find matching records from each table, and this may lead to slow access. If the codes are relatively stable and rarely change, they may be stored as a database function. If the codes change frequently, they are stored on a table so that they may be easily updated.

A table of codes used in a CUSTOMER system is illustrated in Figure 19.23. This table represents customer account types and has been created using Microsoft® Access. Notice that there are only two fields, the code and the code meaning. The meaning is used on all reports and inquiry screens. In entry screens for tables that store the code, the table of codes is linked, using a drop-down list.

Figure 19.24 shows how a drop-down list is used to select the codes for adding or changing a record in the CUSTOMER table. Notice that the code is stored, but the drop-down list displays both the code and the code meaning. This helps to ensure accuracy, since the user does not have to guess at the meaning of the code and there is no chance of typing an invalid code.

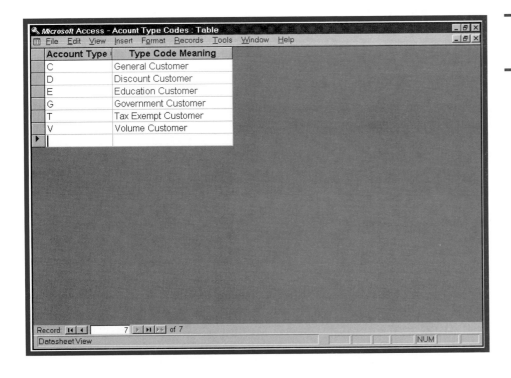

FIGURE 19.23
A table of codes representing
customer account types.

SUMMARY

Assuring the quality of the data input to the information system is critical to
assuring quality output. The quality of data entered can be improved
through the attainment of the three major data-entry objectives: effective
coding, effective and efficient data capture, and the validation of data.

FIGURE 19.24
Using a drop-down list for
adding or changing a record
in the customer table.

"Sometimes I think I'm the luckiest person on Earth. Even though I've been here five years, I still enjoy the people I meet and what I do. Yes, I know Snowden's demanding. You've experienced some of that, haven't you? He, for one, loves codes. I, for another, think that they are a pain. I always forget them or try to make up new ones or something. But some of the physicians think they're great. Must be all of those Latin abbreviations they studied in their med school classes. I hear that your most pressing assignment this week has to do with actually getting the information into the project reporting system. The Training Unit wants your ideas, and they want them fast. Good luck with it. Oh, and when Snowden gets back from Thailand, I'm certain he'll want to take a peek at what your team has been up to."

HᴘᴇʀCᴀsᴇ Qᴜᴇsᴛɪᴏɴs

1. Using a CASE tool, a software package such as Access or a paper layout form, design a data-entry procedure for the proposed project reporting system for the Training Unit. Assume we are particularly concerned about the consulting physicians staff, who don't want to spend a great deal of time keying in large amounts of data when using the system.

2. Test your data-entry procedure on three teammates. Ask for feedback concerning the appropriateness of the procedure, given the type of users the system will have.

3. Redesign the data-entry procedure to include the feedback you have received. Explain in a paragraph how your changes reflect the comments you were given.

One of the best ways to speed data entry is through effective use of coding, which puts data into short sequences of digits and/or letters. Both simple sequence codes and alphabetic derivation codes can be used to follow the progress of a given item through a system. Classification codes and block sequence codes are useful for distinguishing classes of items from each other. Codes such as the cipher code are also useful because they can conceal information that is sensitive or is restricted to personnel within the business.

Revealing information is also a worthwhile use of codes since it can enable business employees to locate items in stock and can also make data entry more meaningful. Significant-digit subset codes use subgroups of digits to describe a product. Mnemonic codes also reveal information by serving as memory aids that can help a data-entry operator enter data correctly or help the end user in using information. Codes that are useful for informing computers or people about what functions to perform or what actions to take are called function codes; they circumvent having to spell out in detail what actions are necessary.

Another part of assuring effective data entry is attention to the input devices being used. A well-designed, effective form that serves as a source document (where needed) is the first step. Data can be input through many different methods, each with varying speed and reliability. Keyboards have been redesigned for efficiency and improved ergonomics. Optical character recognition (OCR) allows the reading of input data through the use of special software, which eliminates some steps and also requires fewer employee skills.

Other data-entry methods include magnetic ink character recognition (MICR), which is used by banks to encode customer account numbers; mark-sense which are forms used for high-volume data entry; and punch-out forms which are used on ballots. Bar codes (applied to products or human identification and then scanned) also speed data entry and improve data accuracy and reliability. New input technologies such as digital cameras are falling in price, and they expand the ease of use and the range of functions available. Intelligent terminals are input devices (often microprocessor-based) with a screen display and keyboard, and they can be networked to the CPU. They permit transactions to be entered and completed in real time.

Along with appropriate coding, data capture, and input devices, accurate data entry can be enhanced through the use of input validation. The systems analyst must assume that errors in data *will* occur and must work with users to design input validation tests to prevent erroneous data from being processed and stored, since initial errors that go undiscovered for long periods are expensive and time-consuming to correct.

Input transactions should be checked to assure that the transaction requested is acceptable, authorized, and correct. Input data can be validated through the inclusion in the software of several types of tests that check for missing data, length of data item, range and reasonableness of data, and invalid values for data. Input data can also be compared with stored data for validation purposes. Once numerical data are input, they can be checked and corrected automatically through the use of check digits.

KEYWORDS AND PHRASES

coding	magnetic ink character recognition (MICR)
simple sequence code	
alphabetic derivation code	mark sense
classification code	punch outs
block sequence code	bar codes
cipher code	intelligent terminals
significant-digit subset code	validating input
mnemonic code	test for missing data
function code	test for correct field length
changeable	test for class or composition
differentiated	test for range or reasonableness
redundancy in input data	test for invalid values
bottlenecks	test for comparison with stored data
keyboarding	
optical character recognition (OCR)	self-validating codes
	check digits

REVIEW QUESTIONS

1. What are the three primary objectives of data entry?
2. List the five general purposes for coding data.
3. Define the term *simple sequence code.*
4. When is an alphabetic derivation code useful?

5. Explain what is accomplished with a classification code.
6. Define the term *block sequence code.*
7. What is the simplest type of code for concealing information?
8. What are the benefits of using a significant-digit subset code?
9. What is the purpose of using a mnemonic code for data?
10. Define the term *function code.*
11. List the eight general guidelines for proper coding.
12. What is changeable data?
13. What is differentiation data?
14. What is one specific way to reduce the redundancy of data being entered?
15. Define the term *bottleneck* as it applies to data entry.
16. What three repetitive functions of data entry can be done more efficiently by the computer than by the data-entry operator?
17. List seven data-entry methods.
18. List the three main problems that can occur with input transactions.
19. What are the seven tests for validating input data?
20. Which test checks to see whether data fields are correctly filled in with either numbers or letters?
21. Which test would not permit a user to input a date such as October 32?
22. Which test assures data accuracy by the incorporation of a number in the code itself?

PROBLEMS

1. A small, private university specializing in graduate programs wants to keep track of when a particular student actually enrolls. Suggest a kind of code for this purpose and give an example of its use in the university that demonstrates its appropriateness.

2. The military has been using a simple sequence code to keep track of new recruits. However, there have been some upsetting mixups between recruit files because of similar-looking recruit numbers.

   a. In a paragraph, suggest a different coding scheme that will help uniquely identify each recruit, and explain how it will prevent mixups.

   b. The military is concerned that confidential information in its coding of new recruits (such as IQ score and rating of physical condition upon entering the service) *not* be revealed to clerks who do not have appropriate clearance, but it wants this information to be encoded on a recruit's identification number so that those conducting basic training are immediately aware of the type of recruit they are training. Suggest a type of code (or combination of codes) that can accomplish this task, and give an example.

3. A code used by an ice cream store to order its products is 12DRM215-220. This code is deciphered in this manner: 12 stands for the count of items in the box, DRM stands for DREAMCICLES (a particular kind of ice cream novelty), and 215-220 indicates the entire class of low-fat products carried by the distributor.

   a. What kind of code is this? Describe the purpose behind each part (12, DRM, 215-220) of the code.

   b. Construct a coded entry using the same format and logic for an ice cream novelty called Pigeon Bars, which come in a six-count package and are *not* low-fat.

c. Construct a coded entry using the same format and logic for an ice cream novelty called Airwhips, which come in a 24-count package and are low-fat.

4. The data-entry operators at Cataldo's Construction have been making errors when entering the codes for residential siding products, which are: U = stUcco, A = Aluminum, R = bRick, M = Masonite, EZ = EZ colorlok enameled masonite, N = Natural wood siding, AI = pAInted finish, SH = SHake SHingles. Only one code per address is permitted.

a. List the possible problems with the coding system that could be contributing to erroneous entries. (*Hint:* Are the classes mutually exclusive?)

b. Devise a mnemonic code that will help the operators understand what they are entering and subsequently help their accuracy.

c. How would you redesign the classes for siding materials? Respond in a paragraph.

5. This is a code for one product in an extensive cosmetic line: L02002Z621289. L means that it is a lipstick; 0 means it was introduced without matching nail polish; 2002 is a sequence code indicating in what order it was produced; Z is a classification code indicating that the product is hypoallergenic; and 621289 is the number of the plant (there are fifteen plants) where the product is produced.

a. Critique the code by listing the features that might lead to inaccurate data entry.

b. Designer Melvin Mine owns the cosmetic firm that uses this coding scheme. Always interested in new design, Melvin is willing to look at a more elegant code that encodes the *same* information in a better way. Redesign the coding scheme and provide a key for your work.

c. Write a sentence for each change you have suggested, indicating what data-entry problem (from part a) the change will eliminate.

6. Melvin Mine's cosmetic firm requires its salespeople to use lap-top PCs to enter orders from retail department stores (their biggest customers). This information is then relayed to warehouses, and orders are shipped on a first-come, first-served basis. Unfortunately, the stores are aware of this policy and are extremely competitive about which one of them will offer a new Melvin Mine product first. Many retailers have taken the low road and persuaded salespeople to falsify their order dates on sales forms by making them earlier than they actually were.

a. This problem is creating havoc at the warehouse. Disciplining any of the personnel involved is not feasible. How can the warehouse computer be used to certify when orders are actually placed? Explain in a paragraph.

b. Salespeople are complaining that they have to ignore their true job of selling so that they can key in order data. List the data items relating to sales of cosmetics to retailers that should be stored in and retrieved from the central computer rather than keyed in for every order.

c. Describe in a paragraph or two how bar coding might help solve the problem in part b.

7. List the best data-entry method and your reason for choosing it for each of the five situations listed below:

a. Turnaround document for a utility company that wants notification of change in the customer address.

b. Data retrieval allowed only if there is positive machine identification of the party requesting data.

c. Not enough trained personnel available to interpret long written responses; many forms submitted that capture answers to multiple-choice examinations; high reliability necessary; fast turnaround not required.

d. Warehouse set up for a discount CD operation; CD bins are labeled with price information, but individual CDs are not; and few skilled operators available to enter price data.

e. Poison control center that maintains a large database of poisons and antidotes; needs a way to enter data on poison taken; also enter weight, age, and general physical condition of the victim when a person calls the center's toll-free number for emergency advice.

8. One of your systems analysis team members surprises you by asserting that when a system uses a test for correct field length, it is redundant also to include a test for range or reasonableness. In a paragraph, give an example that demonstrates that your team member is mistaken on this one.

9. Several retailers have gotten together and begun issuing a "state" credit card that is good only in stores within their state. As a courtesy, sales clerks are permitted to transcribe the 15-digit account number by hand (after getting it from the accounting office) if the customer is not carrying his or her card. The only problem with accounts that retailers have noticed so far is that sometimes erroneous account numbers are accepted into the computer system, and a bill is issued to a nonexistent account.

   a. What sort of validity test would clear up the problem? How? Respond in a paragraph.

   b. Suggest an alternative data entry method that might alleviate this problem altogether.

10. The following are part numbers:

    38902
    38933
    39402
    35693
    35405
    39204

    Develop a check digit for the preceding part numbers using 1-3-1-3-1 multipliers and modulus 11. Use the method presented in this chapter. Why do some numbers have the same check digit?

11. Develop a check digit system for the preceding part numbers using 5-4-3-2-1 multipliers and modulus.

12. Why would a check digit system such as 1-1-1-1-1 not work as well as other methods? What errors would it miss?

GROUP PROJECTS

1. Along with your group members, read Consulting Opportunity 19.4, "To Enter or Not to Enter: That Is the Question," which was presented earlier in this chapter. Design an appropriate data entry system for

Elsinore Industries. Your group's design should emphasize efficiency and accuracy. Additionally, distinguish between data that are changeable and that which differentiate an item being entered from all others. Draw prototypes of any screen necessary to explain what you are recommending.

2. Divide your group into analysts and Elsinore Industries employees in order to role play. The analysts should present the new data entry system, complete with prototype screens. Ask for feedback on the design from Elsinore employees.

3. Write a brief paragraph describing how to improve the original data-entry design based on the comments received.

SELECTED BIBLIOGRAPHY

Davis, G. B., and M. H. Olson. *Management Information Systems, Conceptual Foundations, Structure, and Development,* 2nd ed. New York: Mc-Graw-Hill Book Company, 1985.

Galitz, W. O. *Human Factors in Office Automation.* Atlanta, GA: Life Office Automation Management Association, 1980.

Lamming, M. G., P. Brown, K. Carter, M. Eldridge, M. Flynn, G. Louie, P. Robinson, and A. Sellan. "The Design of a Human Memory Prosthesis," *Computer Journal,* Vol.37, 1994, pp. 153–163.

Miller, G. A. "The Magical Number Seven, Plus or Minus Two: Some Limits on Our Capability for Processing Information," *The Psychological Review,* Vol. 63, No. 2, March 1956, pp. 81–97.

Newman, W. N., and M. G. Lamming. *Interactive System Design.* Reading, MA: Addison-Wesley Publishing Company, 1995.

Owsowitz, S., and A. Sweetland. "Factors Affecting Coding Errors." *Rand Memorandum RM-4346-PR.* Santa Monica, CA: The Rand Corporation, 1965.

Robey, D., and W. Taggart. "Human Processing in Information and Decision Support Systems," *Management Information Systems Quarterly,* Vol. 6, No. 2, June 1982, pp. 61–73.

ENTERING NATURALLY

Tuesday afternoon finds Anna and Chip having their weekly analysis and design review session. Chip waves toward a large stack of documents that are neatly organized on a large table. "I can't believe that we're almost finished with the design of this system," he remarks. "It's been a long process, but I'll bet we've obtained enough user feedback to ensure a high-quality system. All that's left is the design of the data-entry procedures, and we'll be ready to start packaging the specs for the programmers."

"Yes," replies Anna. "The end is in sight. Let's start by examining the design of the input portion of the system." The data-flow diagram shown in Figure E19.1 represents a portion of two Add programs. The top diagram depicts adding new microcomputers using a batch process.

"Since this is to be performed by data entry, we should use key-to-diskette data entry," remarks Anna. "The microcomputers are usually ordered for an entire lab, so they often arrive in shipments of 20 or more. We can take advantage of the keying speed of the data-entry operators. The new microcomputer information is on easy-to-enter forms that will be keyed by one operator and then rekeyed by a different person to verify the data. The results will be stored on a transaction file for use by the edit and update programs."

"The Add Software process will have a different design," notes Chip. "Since software does not arrive in a batch, the add program is on-line. Instead of a key-and-verify operation, the operator will have to search-verify each transaction. After all data fields have been edited for accuracy, a message will appear on the bottom of the screen. It will prompt the operators to check the data on the screen for accuracy against the form and click the **Save Record** button if correct. The operators will have a chance to make changes if the data are keyed incorrectly. This method may not be keyed as fast as data entry, but the errors are corrected by the person seeing the data, which speeds up the actual updating of the files."

Regardless of the method for adding information, every data field must be edited for accuracy. As Chip noted, "In the long run, it's better to have complete editing for accuracy in the programs rather than to find that erroneous data have been stored on master files and printed on reports."

The strategy for field editing is to check the data in the following order:

1. Syntax—whether the data is numeric or alphabetic—and the length of the data. An example is the HARDWARE INVENTORY NUMBER, which must be eight characters in length and numeric.

2. The contents of the field, including range, limit, and values for the data. When validating the DATE PURCHASED, the month must be from 1 to 12. This check should occur only after the month has been verified as numeric.

3. Cross-reference checks between two or more data elements. For those who are to check the day portion of the DATE PURCHASED, a table of the number of days possible for each month will be used for an upper limit. This table could not be used if the month number was not between 1 and 12. Check digits are another example of a cross-reference edit.

Allen Schmidt,
Julie E. Kendall, and
Kenneth E. Kendall

FIGURE E19.1
Data flow diagram portions, Add programs.

4. External edits, such as reading a file to verify if the record to be added already exists in the file. Reading records is slower than editing, which is performed in main memory, and it should occur only after the data successfully pass all other edits.

Edit criteria have been entered on the Visible Analyst Element Repository screen as the elements were added to the design. These elements include simple editing criteria and table checking. The **Notes** area may be used to enter editing criteria. The HARDWARE INVENTORY NUMBER entry shown in Figure E19.2 includes a reference for using the modulus-11 method of verifying the check digit portion of the number. Furthermore, when adding a new microcomputer, the MICROCOMPUTER MASTER file must be read to ensure that a record does not already exist with the same HARDWARE INVENTORY NUMBER. Figure E19.3 shows the details for the HARDWARE INVENTORY NUMBER. Notice that the Picture is 9(8); here, the 9's indicate that the data should be numeric, and the number in parentheses indicates that the length is 8.

FIGURE E19.2
Element Repository screen showing edit criteria, HARDWARE INVENTORY
NUMBER.

FIGURE E19.3
Element characteristics in the repository, HARDWARE INVENTORY NUMBER.

Date: 4/13/1997   Project : CPU   Page: 1
Time: 11:48PM

Detailed Listing -- Alphabetically
All Data Element Entries - - Data Flow Diagram

Active Software Code   Data Element
    Description:
        Code to determine if software is currently in use.
    Values & Meanings:
        A - Active
        I - Inactive
    Data element attributes
        Storage Type: Character
        Length: 1
        Picture: X
        Default: 'A'
        Allow Null:

— -

Board Code   Data Element
    Description:
        Code used to indicate the type of internal microcomputer board.
    Data element attributes
        Storage Type: Character
        Length: 3
        Picture: XXX
        Display Format: XXX
        Allow Null:
    Notes:
        Table of codes: This code is stored in the Access Board Codes table.

— -

Board Name   Data Element
    Description:
        The name of an internal microcomputer board. Used as a match for
        the board code.
    Data element attributes
        Storage Type: Character
        Length: 20
        Picture: X(20)
        Display Format: X(20)
        Allow Null:
    Notes:
        This data is stored in an Access table.

FIGURE E19.4
Microcomputer Master File Elements repository report.

"I think these reports will be useful," Chip tells Anna. "The first report involves creating a final list of all the elements found both on the MICROCOMPUTER MASTER file and the structural records contained within the master. The report is produced using the Report feature and shows the elements, their length, pictures, and edit criteria in the **Notes** area." (This report is shown in Figure E19.4.) This report is used to create the edit criteria table, which became part of the program specifications. The table is shown in Figure E19.5.

Element Name	Numeric	Alphabetic	Length	Date	Limit	Range	Table	Check Digit	Cross Refer	File Check
Brand Name			>0				X			
Campus Location	X						X			
CD ROM Drive	X									
Cost of Repairs	X									
Date Purchased	X		8	X						
Disk Drive A							3			
Disk Drive B							3		4	
Fixed Disk	X					5				
Fixed Disk 2	X					5			6	
Hardware Inventory Number	X		8		1			X		X
Internal Boards							X			
Internet Connection							11			
Last Prevent Maintenance Date	X		8	X						
Maintenance Interval	X					7				
Memory Size	X				8					
Model			>0							
Monitor							X			
Network		X	1				9			
Number of Repairs	X									
Printer							X			
Purchase Cost	X				1					
Record Code		X	1				10			
Replacement Cost	X									
Room Location			>0							
Serial Number			>0							
Tape Backup Unit		X	1				9			
Warranty		X	1				9			
Zip Drive Connected		X	1				9			

Legend of codes:
1 Limit: Must be greater than 0
2 Date must be not greater than current date
3 Values are 3.5DD, 3.5HD, 5.25DD, 5.25HD
4 Disk drive A must exist
5 Value is either 0 or greater than 18
6 First fixed disk must exist
7 Range: 7 to 250
8 Limit: Greater than 255
9 Values are Y or N
10 Values are A or I
11 Values are 0, 1, or M

FIGURE E19.5
Microcomputer Master edit table.

Board Code   Data Element
                   Description:
                      Code used to indicate the type of internal microcomputer board.
                   Data element attributes
                      Storage Type: Character
                      Length: 3
                      Picture: XXX
                      Default: XXX
                      Allow Null:
                   Notes:
                      Table of codes: This code is stored in the Access Board Codes table.
                   Location:
                      Data Structure -->New Microcomputer Form Record
                      Data Flow -->Hardware Characteristics
                   Date Last Altered: 4/13/97 Date Created: 3/15/97

— -

Category of Software   Data Element
Description:
   A code entry for the type of software. Stored as an Access table.
Data element attributes
   Storage Type: Character
   Length: 4
   Picture: X(4)
   Display Format:
   Allow Null:
Notes:
   Table of codes: Software Category Codes
Date Last Altered: 4/13/97 Date Created: 2/20/97

— -

Department Code   Data Element
Description:
   A code for a department at Central Pacific University. Stored on an
   Access table.
Data element attributes
   Storage Type: Character
   Length: 3
   Picture: XXX
   Display Format: XXX
   Allow Null:

FIGURE E19.6
Visible Analyst report listing all coded elements.

Several of the elements have **Notes** areas referring to tables, as well as entries for the codes in the Values & Meanings area. An example is the INTERNAL BOARDS element. "I'll produce a list of all tables we'll require," Anna offers. This time the **Report Query** feature is used to produce the necessary information. A list of all elements containing **Notes** starting with the word "Table of codes" was printed, as shown in Figure E19.6. Included on

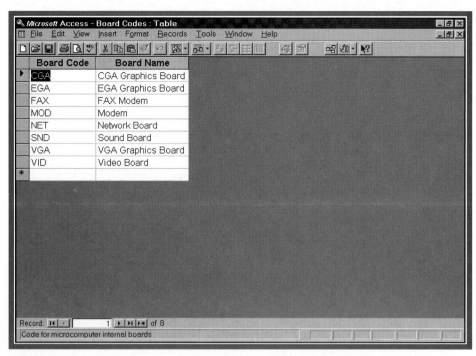

FIGURE E19.7
BOARD CODE TABLE defined using Access.

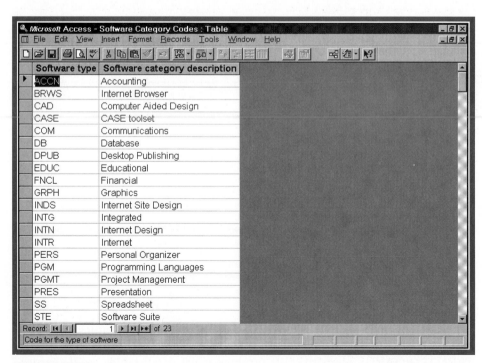

FIGURE E19.8
SOFTWARE CATEGORY code table.

the list is the Picture and Length, showing the syntax of the code. With this list, tables are created.

Each table is defined using Access tables. Chip and Anna each spend time working on the tables. A mnemonic code is chosen for BOARDS and MONITORS, since these two would be easy for maintenance personnel to work with. Mnemonic codes are also used to represent the SOFTWARE CATEGORY, since these will be easy for users to remember.

"There are a wide variety of printers available," remarks Chip. "I think a significant-digit coding scheme would be the best here. The first digit represents the type of printer—laser and so on. The next two digits are for manufacturer, and the last two a sequence number representing different model numbers."

Anna agrees. "That's good, Chip. That strategy can also be used for the campus buildings: the first digit for the campus location, and the remaining two digits representing individual buildings within the campus."

Chip designs the codes used for the BOARD TABLE. The Access screen is shown in Figure E19.7. Two columns are used to define codes. The left column contains the code, and the right column contains the meaning of the code. These entries may be modified, and new entries may be added, providing flexibility in the final system.

"Here's the SOFTWARE CATEGORY table that I created," says Anna. (The Access table is illustrated in Figure E19.8.) "This table may be easily updated as new software is developed and acquired by the university."

"That's a valuable component of the system," Chip comments. "It provides consistency for all codes and their meanings."

Chip and Anna finish their work the next morning at about 11:30. They glance around the room happily, frequently reexamining the final design. The months of analysis, design work, consultation with the users, and careful adherence to standards are finally complete.

"I feel really good about this project," says Anna.

Chip agrees, "I'm proud of the quality we put in."

Exercises*

E-1. Explain the difference between verifying input data in a batch data-entry situation and in an on-line program.

⊟ **E-2.** Modify and print the following elements with edit criteria in the **Notes** (or Values & Meanings for specific codes) area.

Element	Edit Criteria
a. SOFTWARE CATEGORY	Table of codes: Software Category Code
b. DISK DRIVE A	3.5DD, 3.5HD, 5.25DD, 5.25HD
c. COURSE TRAINING LEVEL CODE	B- Beginning; I - Intermediate; A - Advanced
d. INTERNET CONNECTION NAME	0 - No Internet; M - Modem; 1 - T1 Line
e. SOFTWARE MEDIA CODE	D - Diskette; C - CD ROM

---

* Exercises preceded by a disk icon require the program Visible Analyst Workbench or another CASE tool. A disk is provided free of charge to any professor adopting this book. The examples on the disk may be imported into Visible Analyst and then used by students.

| | f. | ZIP DRIVE CONNECTED | Y - Yes; N - No |
| | g. | OPERATING SYSTEM | W - Windows 3.X; |

M - Macintosh; O - OS/2;
9 - Windows 95;
N - Windows NT;
6 - DOS 6.X; 5 - DOS 5;
3 - DOS 3.X

E-3. Modify and print the following elements with edit criteria placed in the **Notes** area:

a. Element: SOFTWARE INVENTORY NUMBER

Notes: A modulus-11 check digit must be verified when entering the number. The ADD SOFT-WARE program creates the check digit.

The ADD SOFTWARE program should also check the SOFTWARE MASTER file to ensure that a record with the same inventory number does not already exist.

b. Element: DATE PURCHASED

Notes: Verify that the DATE PURCHASED is less than or equal to the current date.

c. Element: QUANTITY RECEIVED

Notes: Verify that the QUANTITY RECEIVED is less than or equal to the QUANTITY ORDERED.

d. Element: SOFTWARE UPGRADE VERSION

Notes: Ensure that the upgrade version is greater than the current version.

e. Element: FIXED DISK 2

Notes: FIXED DRIVE 2 may exist only if there is an entry for FIXED DISK.

E-4. View and print the Coded Elements Report Query.

E-5. Use Access to view the SOFTWARE CATEGORY CODES table.

E-6. Use Access to modify and print the BOARD CODES table. Add the following codes.

PCM	PCMCIA Fax Modem
XJK	XJACK Ethernet Modem
MAT	MATH CO-PROCESSOR CHIP
FAX	FAX BOARD

E-7. Use Access to modify and print the PRINTER CODES table. The format of this significant digit code is:

TMMSS where

T   is the type of printer

M   is the manufacturer

S   represents a sequence number, a higher number indicating an improved model

Values for the type of printer are:

0   Dot matrix
1   Daisy wheel
2   Ink jet
3   Thermal
4   Laser
5   Postscript
6   Plotter

Values for the manufacturer are:

01   IBM
02   Epson
03   Hewlett-Packard
04   Panasonic
05   Star Micronics
06   Okidata
07   Kodak
08   Texas Instruments

Add the following codes:

Code	Meaning
20301	Hewlett-Packard DeskJet PLUS
50801	Texas Instruments MicroLaser PS 17
40201	Epson Laser EPL-6000
40305	Hewlett-Packard LaserJet III
40401	Panasonic KX-p4420

E-8. Use Access to modify and print the MONITOR CODES table using the mnemonic form. Add the following entries:

Code	Meaning
VGA	VGA GRAPHICS MONITOR
EGA	ENHANCED GRAPHICS MONITOR
CGA	COLOR GRAPHICS MONITOR
MONO	MONOCHROME MONITOR-GREEN
ORAN	MONOCHROME MONITOR-ORANGE
HVGA	HIGH-RESOLUTION VGA MONITOR
PLSM	PLASMA MONITOR

E-9. After speaking with Dot Matricks and Mike Crowe, it has become apparent that the campus codes must be sortable for installing hardware and software, as well as for creating inventory sheets. Use Access to modify and print the CAMPUS LOCATION CODES table. The first digit represents the campus location. Values are:

1   Central Campus
2   Waterford Campus
3   Hillside Campus

The next three digits represent buildings within the campus, with the following building codes:

001	Administration	010	Environmental Studies
002	Admissions	011	Geology
003	Agricultural	012	Law
004	Astronomy	013	Library
005	Business	014	Mathematics
006	Chemical Engineering	015	Medicine
007	Computer Science	016	Physics
008	Education	017	Psychology
009	Engineering	018	Zoology

Use a combination (your choice) of campus and building codes to build the final table of codes. Include the meaning of the code.

20

QUALITY ASSURANCE THROUGH SOFTWARE ENGINEERING

APPROACHES TO QUALITY

Quality has long been a concern of businesses, as it should be for systems analysts in the analysis and design of information systems. It is too risky to undertake the entire analysis and design process without using a quality assurance approach. The three approaches to quality assurance through software engineering are: (1) securing total quality assurance by designing systems and software with a top-down, modular approach; (2) documenting software with appropriate tools; and (3) testing, maintaining, and auditing software.

Two thoughts guide quality assurance. The first is that the user of the information system is the single most important factor in establishing and evaluating its quality. The second is that it is far less costly to correct problems in their early stages than it is to wait until a problem is articulated through user complaints or crises.

We already have learned about the huge investment of labor and other business resources that are required to launch a system successfully. Using quality assurance throughout the process is a way to minimize risks and helps ensure that the resulting system is what is needed and wanted and that it will demonstrably improve some aspect of business performance. This chapter provides the analyst with three major approaches to quality.

THE TOTAL QUALITY MANAGEMENT APPROACH

Total quality management (TQM) is essential through all of the systems development steps. According to Dean and Evans (1994), the primary elements of TQM are meaningful only when occurring in an organizational context that supports a comprehensive quality effort. It is within this context that the elements of customer focus, strategic planning and leadership, continuous improvement, empowerment, and teamwork are united to change employees' behavior and, ultimately, the organization's course. Notice that the concept of quality has broadened over the years to reflect an organizational, rather than an exclusively production, approach. Instead of conceiving of quality as controlling the number of defective products produced, quality is now thought of as an evolutionary process toward perfection that is otherwise referred to as total quality management.

Systems analysts must be aware of the factors that are driving the interest in quality. It is important to realize that the increasing commitment of businesses to TQM fits extraordinarily well into the overall objectives for systems analysis and design.

Responsibility for Total Quality Management

Practically speaking, a large portion of the responsibility for the quality of information systems rests with systems users and management. Two things must happen for TQM to become a reality with systems projects. First, the full organizational support of management must exist—this is a departure from merely endorsing the newest management gimmick. This means establishing a context for management people to consider seriously how quality of information systems and information itself affects their work.

Early commitment to quality from the analyst and the business is necessary to achieve the goal of quality. This results in exerting an evenly paced effort toward quality throughout the systems development life cycle, and it stands in stark contrast to having to pour huge amounts of effort into ironing out problems at the end of the project.

Organizational support for quality in management information systems can be achieved by providing on-the-job time for IS quality circles, which consists of six to eight organizational peers specifically charged with considering both how to improve information systems and how to implement improvements.

Through work in IS quality circles or through other mechanisms already in place, management and users must develop guidelines for quality standards of information systems. Preferably, standards will be reshaped every time a new system or major modification is to be formally proposed by the systems analysis team.

Hammering out quality standards is not easy, but it is possible and it has been done. Part of the systems analyst's job is encouraging users to crystallize their expectations about information systems and their interactions with them.

Departmental quality standards must then be communicated through feedback to the systems analysis team. The team is often surprised at what has developed. Expectations typically are less complex than what experienced analysts know could be done with a system. Additionally, human issues that have been overlooked or underrated by the analyst team may be designated as extremely pressing in users' quality standards. Getting users involved in spelling out quality standards for IS will help the analyst avoid expensive mistakes in unwanted or unnecessary systems development.

Structured Walkthrough

One of the strongest quality management actions the systems analysis team can take is to routinely do structured walkthroughs. Structured walkthroughs are a way of using peer reviewers to monitor the system's programming and overall development, to point out problems, and to allow the programmer or analyst responsible for that portion of the system to make suitable changes.

Structured walkthroughs involve at least four people, including the person responsible for the part of the system or subsystem being reviewed (a programmer or analyst), a walkthrough coordinator, a programmer or analyst peer, and a peer who takes notes about suggestions.

Each person attending a walkthrough has a special role to play. The coordinator is there to ensure that the others adhere to any roles assigned to them and to assure that any activities scheduled are accomplished. The program author or analyst is there to listen, not to defend his or her thinking, rationalize a problem, or argue. The analyst or programmer peer is present to point out errors or potential problems, not to specify how the problems should be remedied. The note-taker records what is said so that the others present can interact without encumbrance.

Structured walkthroughs can be done whenever a portion of coding, a subsystem, or a system is finished. Just be sure that the subsystem under review is comprehensible outside of its larger context. Structured walkthroughs fit well within a total quality management approach when accomplished throughout the systems development life cycle. The time they take should be short—half an hour to an hour at most—which means that they must be well coordinated. Figure 20.1 shows a form that is useful in organizing the structured walkthrough as well as in reporting its results. Since walkthroughs take time, do not overuse them.

Use structured walkthroughs as a way to obtain (and then act on) valuable feedback from a perspective that you lack. As with all of the quality assurance measures, the point of walkthroughs is to evaluate the product systematically on an ongoing basis, rather than to wait until completion of the system.

Systems Design and Development

In this subsection we define the bottom-up and top-down design of systems as well as the modular approach to programming. We discuss the advantages of each one, as well as the precautions that should be observed when employing either a top-down or modular approach. We also discuss the appropriateness of the top-down and modular approaches for aiding in quality assurance of systems projects.

BOTTOM-UP DESIGN. Bottom-up design refers to identifying the processes that need computerization as they arise, analyzing them as systems and either coding the processes or purchasing packaged software to meet the immediate problem. The problems that require computerization are often on the lowest level of the organization. Problems on the lowest level of the organization are often structured and thereby the most ame-nable to computerization—and they are the most cost-effective. Hence, the name bottom-up refers to the bottom level on which computerization was first introduced. Businesses often take this approach to systems development by going out and acquiring, for example, software packages for accounting, a different package for production scheduling, and another one for marketing.

When in-house programming is done with a bottom-up approach, it is difficult to interface the subsystems so that they perform smoothly as a system. Interface bugs are enormously costly to correct, and many of them are not uncovered until programming is complete, when analysts are trying to meet a deadline in putting the system together. At this juncture, there is little time, budget, or user patience for the debugging of delicate interfaces that have been ignored.

Although each subsystem appears to get what it wants, when the overall system is considered, there are severe limitations to taking a bottom-up approach. One is that there is a duplication of effort in purchasing software and even in entering data. Another is that much worthless data are entered into the system. A third, and perhaps the most serious drawback of the bottom-up approach, is that overall organizational objectives are not considered and hence cannot be met.

TOP-DOWN DESIGN. It is easy to visualize what the top-down approach refers to; it means looking at the large picture of the system and then exploding it into smaller parts or subsystems, as shown in Figure 20.2. Top-down design allows the systems analyst to ascertain overall organizational objectives first, as well as to ascertain how they are best met in an overall system. Then the analyst moves to divide that system into subsystems and their requirements.

The Quality of MIS Is Not Strained

"Merle, come here and take a look at these end-of-the-week reports," Portia pleads. As one of the managers on the six-person IS task force/quality assurance committee, Portia has been examining for her marketing department the system output which has been produced by the prototype. The systems analysis team has asked her to review the output.

Merle Chant walks over to Portia's desk and takes a look at the prospectus she's holding. "Why, what's wrong? It looks okay to me. I think you're taking this task force deal too much to heart. We're supposed to get our other work done as well, you know." Merle turns to leave and returns to his desk slightly perturbed at being interrupted.

"Merle, have a little mercy. It is really silly to put up with these reports the way they are. I can't find anything I need, and then I'm supposed to tell everyone else in the department what part of the report to read. I, for one, am disappointed. This is slipshod. It doesn't make any sense to me. It's a rehash of the output we're getting now. Actually, it looks worse. I am going to bring this up at the next task force meeting," Portia proclaims insistently.

Merle turns to face her, saying, "Quality is their responsibility, Portia. If the system isn't giving us good reports, they'll fix it when it's all together. All you're doing is making waves. You're acting as if they actually value our input. I wouldn't give them the time of day, let alone do their work for them. They're so smart, let them figure out what we need."

Portia looks at Merle blankly, then starts getting a little angry. "We've been on the task force for four weeks. You've sat in on four meetings. We're the ones that know the business. The whole idea of TQM is to tell them what we need, what we're satisfied with. If we don't tell them what we need, then we can't complain. I'm bringing it up the next time we meet."

How effective do you think Merle will be in communicating his standards of quality to the systems analysis team and members of the MIS task force? Respond in a paragraph. If the systems analysts are able to perceive Merle's unwillingness to work with the task force on developing quality standards, what would you say to convince him of the importance of user involvement in TQM? Make a list of arguments supporting the use of TQM. How can the systems analysis team respond to the concerns Portia is bringing up? In a paragraph, devise a response.

Top-down design is compatible with the general systems thinking that was discussed in Chapter 2. When systems analysts employ a top-down approach, they are thinking about the interrelationships and interdependencies of subsystems as they fit into the existing organization. The top-down approach also provides desirable emphasis on synergy or the interfaces that systems and their subsystems require, which is lacking in the bottom-up approach.

The advantages of using a top-down approach to systems design include avoiding the chaos of attempting to design a system "all at once." As we have seen, planning and implementing an MIS is incredibly complex. Attempting to get all subsystems in place and running at once is agreeing to fail.

A second advantage of taking a top-down approach to design is that it enables separate systems analysis teams to work in parallel on different but necessary subsystems. This can save a great deal of time. The use of teams for subsystems design is particularly well suited to a total quality assurance approach.

A third advantage resides in the fact that it avoids a major problem associated with a bottom-up approach. That is, using a top-down approach prevents systems analysts from getting so mired in detail that they lose sight of what the system is supposed to do.

There are some pitfalls of top-down design that the systems analyst needs to be aware of. The first is the danger that the system will be divided

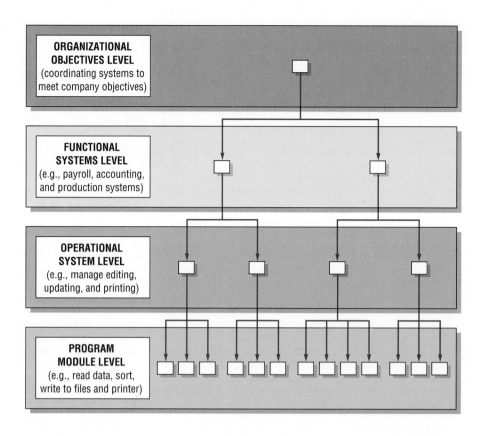

FIGURE 20.2
Using the top-down approach to first ascertain overall organizational objectives.

ORGANIZATIONAL OBJECTIVES LEVEL
(coordinating systems to meet company objectives)

FUNCTIONAL SYSTEMS LEVEL
(e.g., payroll, accounting, and production systems)

OPERATIONAL SYSTEM LEVEL
(e.g., manage editing, updating, and printing)

PROGRAM MODULE LEVEL
(e.g., read data, sort, write to files and printer)

into the "wrong" subsystems. Attention must be paid to overlapping needs and to the sharing of resources so that the partitioning of subsystems makes sense for the total systems picture. Furthermore, it is important that each subsystem address the correct problem.

A second danger is that once subsystem divisions are made, their interfaces may be neglected or ignored. Responsibility for interfaces needs to be detailed.

A third caution that accompanies the use of top-down design is that eventually subsystems must be reintegrated. Mechanisms for reintegration need to be put in place at the beginning. One suggestion is regular information trading between subsystem teams; another is using tools that permit flexibility if changes to interrelated subsystems are required.

Total quality management and the top-down approach to design can go hand in hand. The top-down approach provides the systems group with a ready-made division of users into task forces for subsystems. Task forces set up in this manner can then serve a dual function as quality circles for the management information system. The necessary structure for quality assurance is then in place, as is proper motivation for getting the subsystem to accomplish the departmental goals that are important to the users involved.

Modular Development

Once the top-down design approach is taken, the modular approach is useful in programming. This approach involves breaking the programming into logical, manageable portions, or modules. This kind of programming works well with top-down design because it emphasizes the interfaces between modules and does not neglect them until later in systems development. Ideally, each individual module should be functionally cohesive, so that it is charged with accomplishing only one function.

Modular program design has three main advantages. First, modules are easier to write and debug because they are virtually self-contained. Tracing an error in a module is less complicated, since a problem in one module should not cause problems in others.

A second advantage of modular design is that modules are easier to maintain. Modifications usually will be limited to a few modules and will not spread over an entire program.

A third advantage of modular design is that modules are easier to grasp, since they are self-contained subsystems. This means that a reader can pick up a code listing of a module and understand its function.

Some guidelines for modular programming include:

1. Keep each module to a manageable size (ideally including only one function).
2. Pay particular attention to the critical interfaces (the data and control variables that are passed to other modules).
3. Minimize the number of modules the user must modify when making changes.
4. Maintain the hierarchical relationships set up in the top-down phases.

Modularity in the Windows Environment

Modularity is becoming increasingly important. Microsoft developed two systems to link programs in its Windows environment. The first is called Dynamic Data Exchange (DDE), which shares code by using Dynamic Link Library (DLL) files. Using DDE, a user can store data in one program—perhaps a spreadsheet such as Excel—and then use that data in another program, such as a word-processing package like Word for Windows. The program that contains the original data is called the server, while the program that uses the data is called the client (another term for *client* host). The DDE link can be set up so that whenever the client's word-processing file is opened, the data are automatically updated and any changes made to the server spreadsheet file since the word-processing file was last opened will be reflected. (See Chapter 21 for an extended discussion of the client/server model.)

One of the most commonly used DLL files is COMMDLG.DLL, which contains Windows' File Open, File Save, Search, and Print dialog boxes. One advantage of using this file is that programs will have the same look and feel as other Windows programs. It also speeds development, because programmers do not have to write the code contained in common DLL files.

There is a big disadvantage in using a file such as COMMDLG.DLL, however: it is limited in features. Perhaps a systems designer thinks that it is important for the user to have the ability to create a subdirectory, or to move or rename files, when saving a file. Maybe it is important to search for a file when you try to open a file. In such cases, it becomes necessary to design your own File Open and File Save commands. The main disadvantage to using common DLL files is that these programs tend to use the least common denominator rather than take advantage of potentially powerful features; therefore, they appeal to the average user rather than the power user.

A second approach to linking programs in Windows is called Object Linking and Embedding (OLE). This method of connecting programs is su-

FIGURE 20.3
A structure diagram
encourages top-down
design using modules.

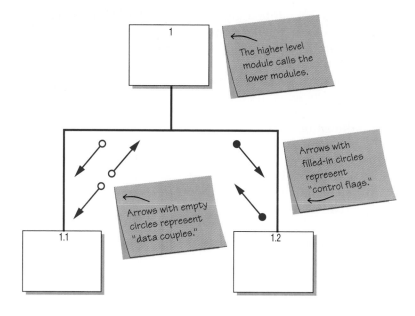

perior to DDE because it ties in application data and graphics. While DDE uses a cut-and-paste approach to linking data and does not retain formatting, OLE retains all of the properties of the originally created data. This object-oriented approach (see Chapter 22 for a discussion of object-oriented principles) allows the end user to remain in the client application and still edit the original data in the server application. With OLE, when an end user clicks on the embedded object, a toolbar pops up to allow visual editing.

Structure Charts

The recommended tool for designing a modular, top-down system is called a structure chart. A structure chart is simply a diagram consisting of rectangular boxes, which represent the modules, and connecting arrows.

Figure 20.3 shows three modules labeled 1, 1.1, and 1.2. As noted earlier with data-flow diagrams, the number to the right of the decimal point in 1.1 and 1.2 signifies that these modules are subsets of module 1.

Structure charts created using the program Visio can be seen in Figure 20.4. An alternative notation for the three modules is shown. These are labeled 000, 100, and 200 and are connected using right-angle lines. Higher-level modules are numbered by 100s or 1000s, while lower-level modules are numbered by 10s or 100s. This allows programmers to insert modules using a number between the adjacent module numbers. For example, a module inserted between modules 110 and 120 would receive number 115. If two modules were inserted, the numbers might be 114 and 117. These numbering schemes vary, depending on the organizational standards used.

Off to the sides of the connecting lines, two types of arrows are drawn. The arrows with the empty circles are called *data couples,* while the arrows with the filled-in circles are called *control flags* or *switches.* A switch is the same as a control flag except that it is limited to two values: either "yes" or "no." These arrows indicate that something is passed either down to the lower module or back up to the upper one.

Ideally, the analyst should keep this coupling to a minimum. The fewer data couples and control flags one has in the system, the easier it is to change

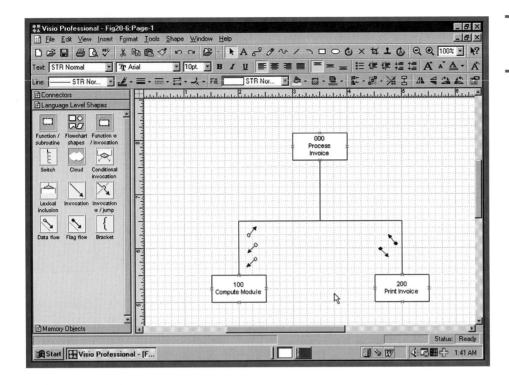

FIGURE 20.4
An alternative style for
structure charts.

the system. When these modules are actually programmed, it is important to pass the least number of data couples between modules.

Even more important, numerous control flags should be avoided. Control is designed to be passed from lower-level modules to those higher in the structure. However, on rare occasions, it will be necessary to pass control downward in the structure. Control flags govern which portion of a module is to be executed and are associated with IF . . . THEN . . . ELSE . . . and other similar types of statements. When control is passed downward, a low-level module is allowed to make a decision, and the result is a module that performs two different tasks. This violates the ideal of a functional module: It should perform only one task.

Figure 20.5 illustrates a portion of a structure chart for adding new employees. The program reads an EMPLOYEE TRANSACTION FILE and verifies that each record in the file contains only acceptable data. Separate reports are printed for both valid and invalid records, providing an audit trail of all transactions. The report containing invalid records is sent to the users for error correction. Records that are valid are placed on a valid transaction file, which is passed to a separate program for updating the Employee master file. Module 200, ADD NEW EMPLOYEE RECORD, represents the logic of adding one record. Since module 230 is used to print both reports, a control flag must be sent down to tell the module which report to print. The logic of module 230 is thus entirely controlled by an IF statement, which is illustrated in Figure 20.6.

Figure 20.7 shows the correct way to design the structure underneath module 200, ADD NEW EMPLOYEE RECORD. Here, each print function has been placed in a separate module, and control flags are only passed up the structure to the higher-level module.

The data that are passed through data couples must also be examined. It is best to pass only the data required to accomplish the function of the

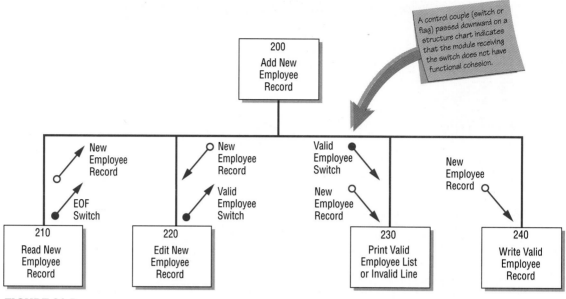

FIGURE 20.5
This structure chart illustrates control moving downward and also shows nonfunctional modules.

module. This approach is called "data coupling." Passing excessive data is called "stamp coupling," and while it is relatively harmless, it reduces the possibility of creating a reusable module. Figure 20.8 illustrates this concept. Here, the module EDIT NEW CUSTOMER passes the CUSTOMER RECORD to the EDIT CUSTOMER PHONE NUMBER module, where PHONE NUMBER, an element found within the CUSTOMER RECORD, is validated

FIGURE 20.6
Pseudocode for module 230
illustrating the effect of passing a switch downward.

```
Module 230 - Print Valid Employee List Or Invalid Line

IF VALID EMPLOYEE SWITCH = 'Y'
        Move EMPLOYEE NUMBER to VALID EMPLOYEE LIST
        Move EMPLOYEE NAME to VALID EMPLOYEE LIST
        Move EMPLOYEE JOB TITLE to VALID EMPLOYEE LIST
        Move EMPLOYEE DEPARTMENT to VALID EMPLOYEE LIST
        Move EMPLOYEE WORK PHONE NUMBER to VALID EMPLOYEE LIST
        Move EMPLOYEE DATE HIRED to VALID EMPLOYEE LIST
        DO PRINT VALID EMPLOYEE LIST
ELSE
        Move EMPLOYEE NUMBER to INVALID LINE
        Move EMPLOYEE NAME to INVALID LINE
        Move EMPLOYEE JOB TITLE to INVALID LINE
        Move EMPLOYEE DEPARTMENT to INVALID LINE
        Move EMPLOYEE WORK PHONE NUMBER to INVALID LINE
        Move EMPLOYEE DATE HIRED to INVALID LINE
        DO PRINT INVALID LINE
ENDIF
```

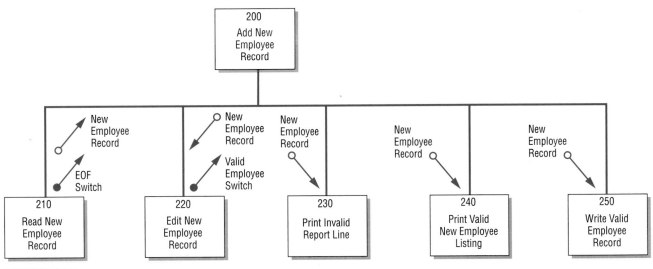

FIGURE 20.7
An improved structure chart showing control flowing upward.

and a control flag is passed back to the EDIT NEW CUSTOMER module. The TYPE OF ERROR (if any), one containing an error message such as "INVALID AREA CODE" or "PHONE NUMBER IS NOT NUMERIC," is also passed upward. The message may be either printed or displayed on a screen.

While such modules are fairly easy to create and modify every time a phone number from a different source record needs to be edited, a new module, similar to EDIT CUSTOMER PHONE NUMBER must be created. Furthermore, if the way the phone number is being validated changes, as occurs when a new area code or an international country code must be added, each of these lower-level modules must be modified.

Since the lower-level module does not require any of the other elements on the CUSTOMER RECORD, the solution is to pass only the PHONE NUMBER to the lower-level module. The name of the module in this scenario changes to EDIT PHONE NUMBER, and it may be used to edit *any* phone number: a customer phone number or an employee phone number. The modules on the right side of the figure illustrate this concept. When the rules for validating the phone number change, only EDIT PHONE NUMBER needs to be modified, regardless of how many programs utilize that module. Often these general-purpose modules are placed in a separately compiled program which is called either a subprogram, function, or procedure in various computer languages.

Another symbol used in structure charts is the loop, as shown in Figure 20.9. This symbol indicates that some procedures found in modules 2.1 and 2.2 are to be repeated until finished. In this example of organizing part numbers, the processes READ PART NUMBER and EDIT PART NUMBER are repeated until there are no more numbers. Then the numbers are sorted in module 2.3. In this example, the data couples are "raw input," "part numbers," and "sorted part numbers." Notice that some of these data couples occur twice, once going up to the main module 2 and once going down to the submodule. The control flags are "E-O-F flag" and "Edit flag."

Still another symbol used in structure charts is the small diamond. The diamond appears on the bottom of one of the rectangles, as shown in Figure

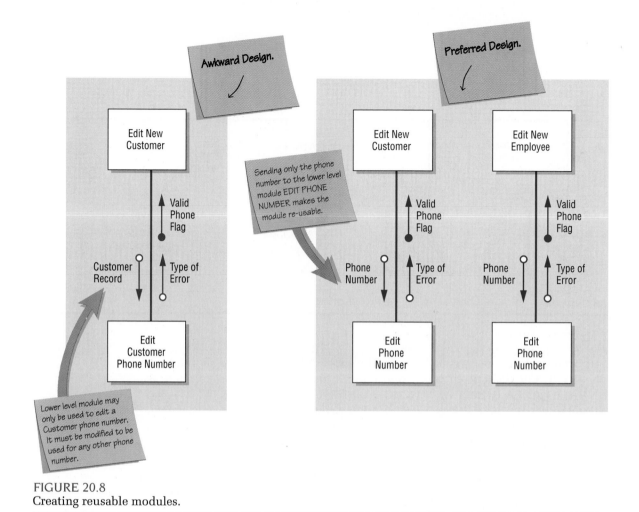

FIGURE 20.8
Creating reusable modules.

FIGURE 20.9
Iterations are depicted on structure charts by drawing a loop.

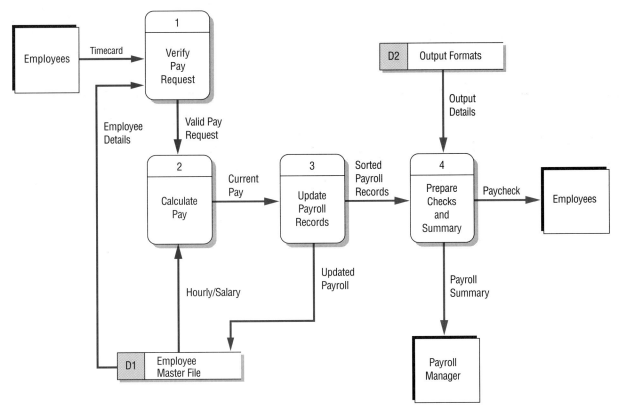

The diamond means that the module contains OR logic.

000
Update
Customer File

Some, but not all of the modules will be performed.

100
Sort by
Business Name

200
Sort by
Zip Code

300
Sort by
Area Code

20.10, and signifies that only some of the modules below the diamond will be performed. Notice that the diamond doesn't indicate which modules will be selected, nor does the loop indicate which modules will be repeated. They are meant to be general, not specific.

FIGURE 20.11
The data flow diagram for a payroll system is linear.

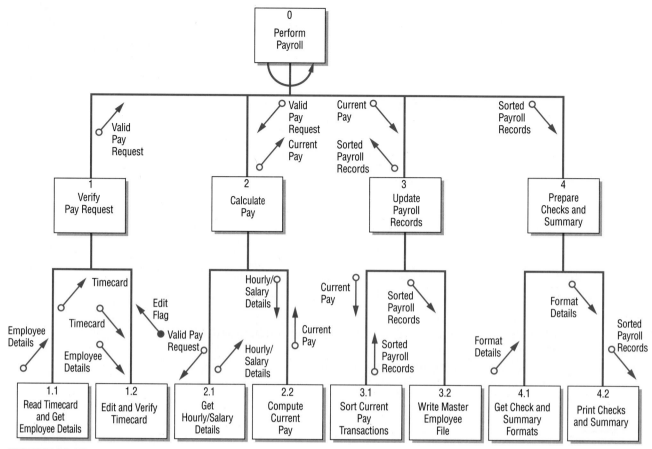

FIGURE 20.12
The structure chart for the payroll example shows hierarchy: data couples and control flags are kept to a minimum.

DRAWING A STRUCTURE CHART. Obviously, structure charts are meant to be drawn from the top down, but where does one start to find the processes that are to become the modules? Most likely, the best place to find this information is in the data-flow diagram (see Chapter 9).

Figure 20.11 is a data-flow diagram of a payroll system. The entities are the EMPLOYEES and the PAYROLL MANAGER. Four processes are drawn in the data-flow diagram:

1. Verify pay request.
2. Calculate pay.
3. Update payroll records.
4. Prepare checks and summary.

Notice that there are two data stores and many data flows. More importantly, observe that the data-flow diagram is laid out in a linear fashion. Now the data-flow diagram will be used to draw the hierarchical structure chart.

The structure chart is shown in Figure 20.12. The main process at the top of the chart is called PERFORM PAYROLL and represents the module that controls everything underneath. The modules on the second level bear the same names and perform the same processes shown in the data-flow diagram. Since

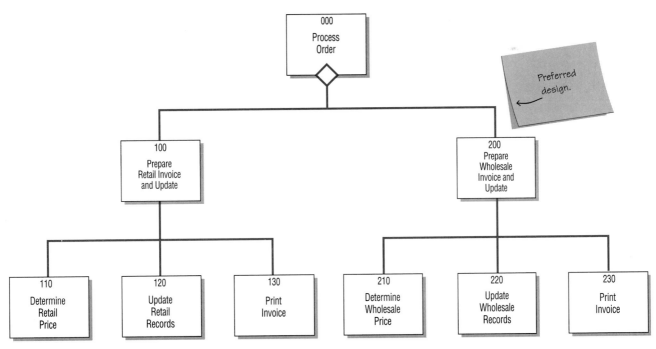

FIGURE 20.13
To prevent redundant decisions (or the passing of a control flag such as type of sale), the structure chart can be redrawn to make the decision at the top.

FIGURE 20.14
The data flow diagram for
newspaper subscriber transaction processing branches
out depending on the
transaction type.

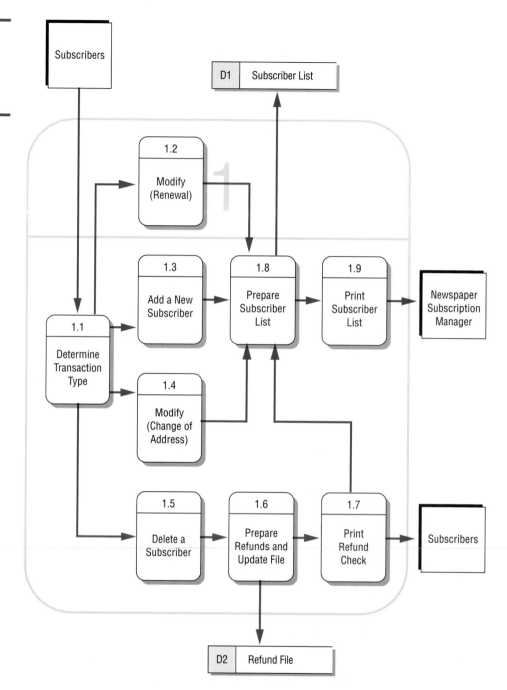

the data-flow diagram is intended to be a logical representation of the system, it is not unusual that the modules derived from the diagram are the same.

The modules on the second level will control the operations of the modules on the third level. These third-level modules accomplish separate functions such as "READ TIMECARD and get EMPLOYEE DETAILS," "EDIT and VERIFY TIMECARD," and so on. Each of these modules contains only one function, which is the ideal case.

The data flows on a data-flow diagram turn into the data couples found on a structure chart. Notice that the TIMECARD, VALID PAY REQUEST, and other data are present on both diagrams.

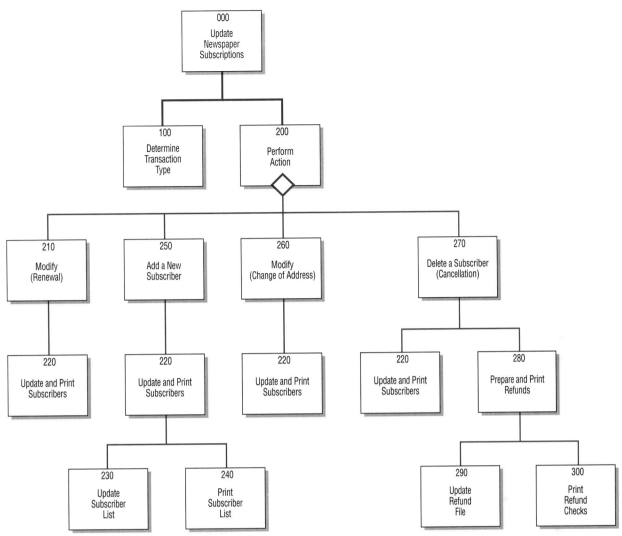

FIGURE 20.15
A structure chart for a transaction-centered system can branch out from a diamond and then later share the same module.

In this example, the data couples and control flags are kept to a minimum. The hierarchical structure makes the structure chart appear to be an inverted tree, but the symmetry is only a coincidence. This example is said to be "transform-centered," because all of the transactions follow the same path.

When all of the transactions do *not* follow the same path, the structure chart is said to be "transaction-centered." A simple example of a transaction-centered structure chart is shown in Figure 20.13. The two diagrams accomplish the same thing, but the top diagram is awkward because the same decision is made in two places. The bottom design is preferred because it can reduce the number of decisions (or alternatively, reduce the number of control flags that have to be passed between modules).

A data-flow diagram for a transaction-centered system is shown in Figure 20.14. Here, the major metropolitan newspaper company publishes a variety of newspapers such as the *Morning Star,* the *Daily Planet,* and the special *Weekend Nova.* Depending on the transaction the subscriber wants, a different set of actions will be taken. This sort of transaction-centered system is often drawn as a second-level data-flow diagram.

The resulting structure chart can be seen in Figure 20.15. It is important that the decision be made at a high level in the structure chart. One module simply determines the transaction type. Following this, one of the actions is performed. Notice that the module entitled "UPDATE AND PRINT SUBSCRIBERS" is common to all transactions.

This particular structure chart served the main objectives of drawing structure charts—that is:

1. To encourage a top-down design.
2. To support the concept of modules and identify the appropriate modules.
3. To identify and limit as much as possible the data couples and control flags that pass between modules.

When transforming a data flow diagram into a structure chart, there are several additional considerations to keep in mind. The data flow diagram will indicate the sequence of the modules in a structure chart. If one process provides input to another process, the corresponding modules must be performed in the same sequence. Figure 20.16 is a data flow diagram for preparing a student report card. Notice that process 1, READ GRADE RECORD, provides input to process 2, READ COURSE RECORD, and to process 3, READ STUDENT RECORD. The structure chart created for this diagram is illustrated in Figure 20.17. Notice that module 110, READ GRADE RECORD, must be executed first. Processes 2 and 3 must be executed next, but since they do not provide input to each other, the order of these modules (120 and 130) in the structure chart is unimportant and may be reversed without any effect on the final results. Processes 1 and 2 provide input to process 4, CALCULATE GRADE POINT AVERAGE (also known as module 140). Process 5, PRINT STUDENT REPORT CARD (module 150), receives data flow from all the other processes and must be the last module to be performed.

If a process explodes to a child data-flow diagram, the module corresponding to the parent process will have subordinate modules that correspond to the processes found on the child diagram. Process 5, PRINT STUDENT REPORT CARD, has four input data flows and one output and is therefore a good candidate for a child diagram. Figure 20.18 illustrates Diagram 5, the details of process 5. The processes on Diagram 5 translate to the modules subordinate to module 150, PRINT STUDENT REPORT CARD.

Types of Modules

Structure chart modules fall into one of three general categories: control, transformational (sometimes called worker), and functional or specialized. When producing a structure chart that is easy to develop and modify, one should take care not to mix the different types of modules.

Control modules are usually found near the top of the structure chart and contain the logic for performing the lower-level modules. The control modules may or may not be represented on the data flow diagram. The types of statements that are usually in control modules are IF, PERFORM, and DO. Detailed statements such as ADD and MOVE are usually kept to a minimum.

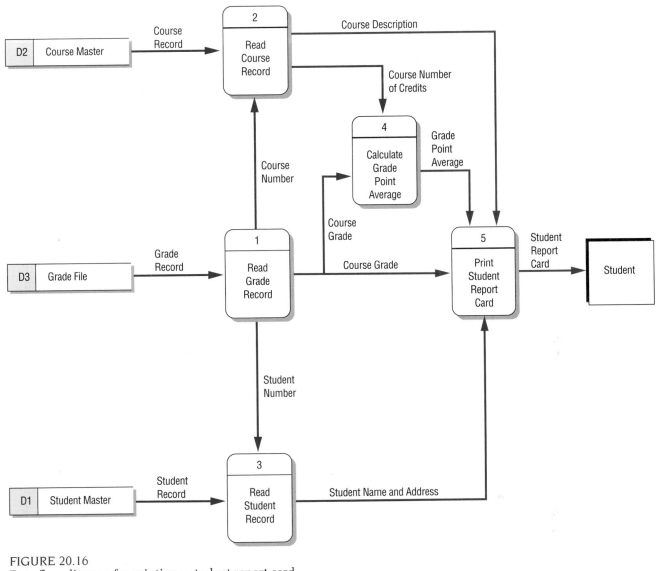

FIGURE 20.16
Data-flow diagram for printing a student report card.

Control logic is usually the most difficult to design, and therefore control modules should not be very large in size. If a control module has more than seven to nine subordinate modules, new control modules should be created that are subordinate to the original control module. The logic of a control module may be determined from a decision tree or decision table. A decision table with too many rules is split into several decision tables, with the first table performing the second table. Each decision table would create a resulting control module. (See Chapter 11 for more on decision trees and tables.)

Transformational modules are those created from a data-flow diagram. They usually perform only one task, although several secondary tasks may be associated with the primary task. For example, a module named "PRINT CUSTOMER TOTAL LINE" may format the total line, print the line, add to

FIGURE 20.17
A structure chart for producing student report cards.

the final totals, and finally set the customer totals to zero in preparation for accumulating the amounts of the next customer. Transformational modules usually have mixed statements, a few IF and PERFORM or DO statements, and many detailed statements such as MOVE, ADD, and so on. These modules are lower in the structure than control modules.

Functional or specialized modules are the lowest in the structure, with a rare subordinate module beneath them. They perform only one task, such as formatting, reading, calculating, writing, and so on. Some of these modules are found on a data-flow diagram, but others may have to be added, such as reading a record or printing an error line.

Figure 20.19 represents the structure chart for adding reservations for hotel guests. Modules 000, ADD GUEST RESERVATIONS, and 100, ADD ROOM RESERVATION, are control modules, representing the entire program (module 000), and they provide the control necessary for making one room reservation (module 100). Module 110, DISPLAY RESERVATION SCREEN, is a functional module responsible for displaying the initial reservation screen. Modules 120, GET VALID ROOM RESERVATION, and 160, CONFIRM ROOM RESERVATION, are lower-level control modules.

FIGURE 20.18
Child diagram for process 5, PRINT STUDENT REPORT CARD.

Module 120, GET VALID ROOM RESERVATION, is performed iteratively until the reservation data are valid or until the reservation operator cancels the transaction. This type of GET VALID. . . module relieves the 100 module of a fair amount of complex code. The modules subordinate to GET VALID ROOM RESERVATION are functional modules responsible for receiving the reservation screen, editing or validating the room reservation, and displaying an error screen if the input data are not valid. Since these modules are in a loop, control remains in this portion of the structure until the screen data are valid.

Module 160, CONFIRM ROOM RESERVATION, is also performed iteratively and allows the operator to sight-verify that the correct information has been entered. In this situation, the operator will inspect the screen and press a specified key (such as the Enter key if the data are correct or a different key) to modify or cancel the transaction. Again, the program will remain in these modules, looping until the operator accepts or cancels the reservation.

Module 190 is a transformational module that formats the RESERVATION RECORD and performs module 200 to write the RESERVATION RECORD. Modules 130, 140, 150, 170, 180, and 200 are functional modules,

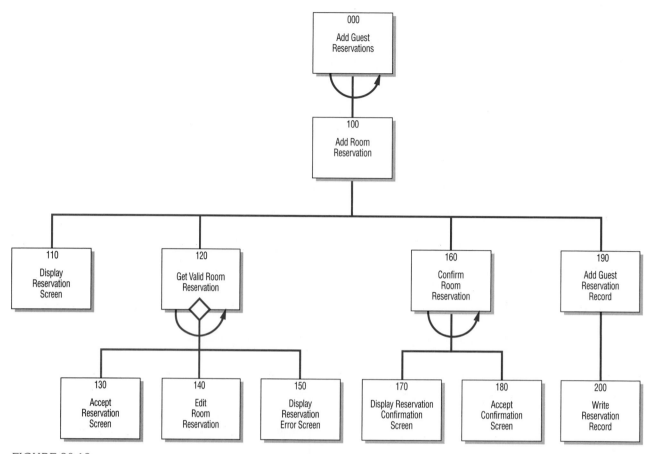

FIGURE 20.19
A structure chart for adding hotel guest reservations on-line.

performing only one task: accepting a screen, displaying a screen, or editing or writing a record. These modules are the easiest to code, debug, and maintain.

Module Subordination

A subordinate module is one lower on the structure chart called by another module higher in the structure. Each subordinate module should represent a task that is a part of the function of the higher-level module. Allowing the lower-level module to perform a task not required by the calling module is called improper subordination. In such a case, the lower module should be moved higher in the structure.

Figure 20.20 illustrates this concept using a structure chart for changing a customer master file. Examine module 120, READ CUSTOMER MASTER. It has the task of using the CUSTOMER NUMBER from the CHANGE TRANSACTION RECORD to directly obtain the matching CUSTOMER RECORD. If the record is not found, an error line is printed. Otherwise, the CUSTOMER MASTER is changed, and the record is rewritten. This should be a functional module, simply reading a record, but instead it has three subordinate modules. The question must be asked, "Does an error line have to be printed to accomplish reading the CUSTOMER MASTER?" Furthermore, "Does the new CUSTOMER MASTER RECORD have to be formatted and

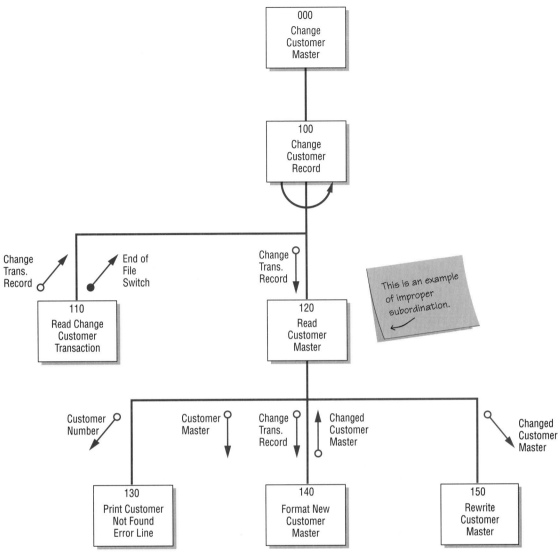

FIGURE 20.20
A structure chart illustrating the principle of improper subordination.

rewritten in order to read the CUSTOMER MASTER?" Since the answer to both questions is "No," modules 130, 140, and 150 should not be subordinate to READ CUSTOMER MASTER.

Figure 20.21 shows the corrected structure chart. Control statements are moved out of the READ CUSTOMER MASTER record and into the primary control module, CHANGE CUSTOMER RECORD. READ CUSTOMER MASTER becomes a functional module (module 120).

Even when a structure chart accomplishes all of the purposes for which it was drawn, the structure chart cannot stand alone as the sole design/documentation technique. First, it doesn't show the order in which the modules should be executed (a data flow diagram will accomplish this). Second, it doesn't show enough detail (Nassi-Shneiderman charts and pseudocode will accomplish this). The remainder of this chapter will discuss these more detailed design/documentation techniques for software development, using

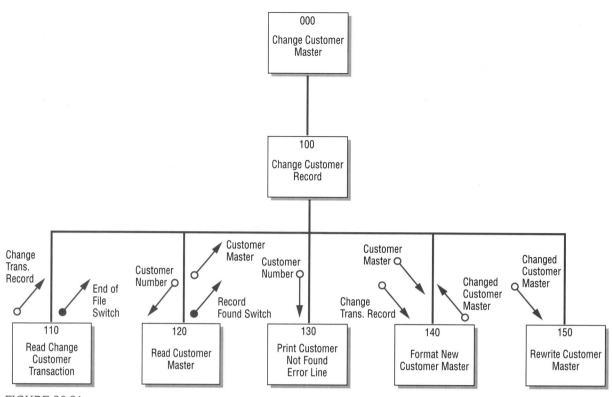

FIGURE 20.21
A corrected structure chart showing proper subordination.

the newspaper subscription problem presented earlier, which we will now view in more detail.

SOFTWARE ENGINEERING AND DOCUMENTATION

Planning and control are essential elements of every successful system. In developing software for the system, the systems analyst should know that planning takes place in the design before programming is even begun. We need techniques to help us set program objectives, so that our programs are complete. We also need design techniques to help us break apart the programming effort into manageable modules.

It is not satisfactory, however, to try to get by with just the planning stages. After programs are completed, they must be maintained, and maintenance efforts typically outweigh the effort expended on the original design and programming.

The techniques described in the upcoming section are meant not only to be used initially in the design of software, but also in its maintenance. Since most systems are not considered disposable, they will need to be maintained. The total quality assurance effort requires that programs be documented properly.

Software and procedures are documented so that they are encoded into a format that can be easily accessed. Access to procedures is necessary for new people learning the system and as a reminder to those who use the program infrequently. Documentation allows users, programmers, and analysts to "see" the system, its software, and procedures without having to interact with it.

Some documentation provides an overview of the system itself, while procedural documentation details what must be done to run software on the system, and program documentation details the program code that is used.

Turnover of information service personnel has traditionally been high in comparison to other departments, so chances are that the people who conceived of and installed the original system will not be the same ones who maintain it. Consistent, well-updated documentation will shorten the number of hours required for new people to learn the system before performing maintenance.

There are many reasons why systems and programs are undocumented or underdocumented; some of the problems reside with the systems and programs themselves, others with systems analysts and programmers.

Some legacy systems were written before the business standardized its documentation techniques, but they are still in use (*sans* documentation). Many other systems have tolerated major and minor modifications and patches over the years, but their documentation has not been modified to reflect them. Some systems featuring specialized programs were purchased for their important applications despite their lack of accompanying documentation.

Systems analysts may fail to document systems properly because they do not have the time or are not rewarded for time spent documenting. Some analysts do not document because they dread doing so or feel that it is not their real work. Furthermore, many analysts are reticent about documenting systems that are not their own, perhaps fearing reprisals if they include incorrect material about someone else's system. Documentation accomplished by means of a CASE tool during the analysis phases can address many of these problems.

There is no single standard design and documentation technique in use today. In this subsection, we discuss several different techniques that are currently in use. Each technique has its own advantages and disadvantages, because each one has unique properties.

Nassi-Shneiderman Charts

One structured approach for design and documentation is the Nassi-Shneiderman (N-S) chart. The main advantage of the N-S chart is that it adopts the philosophy of structured programming. Second, it uses a limited number of symbols so that the flowchart takes up less space and can be read by someone unfamiliar with symbols used in other types of flowcharts. Figure 20.22 shows the three basic symbols that are used in N-S charts.

The first symbol is a box, used to represent any process in the program. The second symbol is a column-splitting triangle that represents a decision. The most basic form of a decision—"true" or "false"—is modeled here, but any form of a decision including several condition alternatives can be depicted using this symbol. The third symbol is the box-within-a-box symbol that is used to show that an iteration takes place. The box-within-a-box also appears as an indentation on the whole chart.

In structured programming, a top-down approach is used. This means that the analyst would begin by drawing the major loops first and then indent to complete the inner loops later.

A newspaper subscription updating system is depicted in the N-S chart in Figure 20.23. The example shows that a process is repeated for every

FIGURE 20.22
The three basic symbols used
to draw Nassi-Shneiderman
charts.

FIGURE 20.23
Using a Nassi-Shneiderman
chart to depict a daily subscription updating service for
newspapers.

Getting a Leg Up

"I think it's magnificent," proclaims Glen. He's been taking a bird's-eye view of the decision tree you drew of Premium Airline's 'Flying for Prizes' policies. "This will help me straighten up and fly right when I'm explaining our program to everyone. You've put us on course, all right. Now if you can just get the computers to cooperate! No, I'm just kidding you. But you know, something else has come up since you've talked with the ticket agents. We've got new instructions on handling fliers' accounts.

"Basically, they say that we must update each 'Flying for Prizes' account on a daily basis, and we have to do this for each flier, for each leg they travel (an example of a leg is from Omaha to Chicago; another one

would be from Chicago to New York). If the miles flown in an account go over a multiple of 10,000, we must issue an award certificate. Then, each day, we need to print a summary of total miles flown (not for each person, just an aggregate of everybody's miles together). I hope you can computerize this for us. They've got pretty lofty expectations, but I guess it's good to aim high. Let us know if it's just pie in the sky, though."

Premium Airlines has asked you to help it with its Flying for Prizes system. Draw a Nassi-Shniederman chart that depicts the functions Glen has just described to you. Use the logic details given in Consulting Opportunity 11.4 to draw your diagram.

---

newspaper on a daily basis. Within each newspaper iteration, a number of operations, such as clearing newspaper totals, printing the date, and printing the newspaper name are performed. Then another loop is encountered; this loop is performed for every subscriber update. A search for the subscriber record is performed and, depending on whether the transaction is a (1) renewal, (2) new subscription, (3) cancellation, or (4) change of address, a different action is taken. Other tasks (such as updating totals and printing information) are performed, and the iterations are continued while there are subscribers and newspapers to update.

Nassi-Shneiderman charts must be complete and comprehensive in order to be understood. This is something of a disadvantage when compared to other methods, since the fear of being incomplete might prevent analysts and programmers from even starting an N-S chart. If changes to the system will be made regularly, N-S charts may not be appropriate. Since they must be entirely redrawn to accommodate change, N-S charts are not easily modified.

On the other hand, the benefits of using N-S charts are many. They provide analysts with a tool for aiding in the program design and development process because they are compatible with structured programming. The N-S chart is easy to read because no knowledge of complex symbols is required. It does not take up precious space either. In summary, the N-S chart can be a very valuable tool for the analyst, and it is supported by some CASE tools such as XperCASE.

Pseudocode

In Chapter 11, we introduced the concept of structured English as a technique of analyzing decisions. Pseudocode is similar to structured English because it is not a particular type of programming code, but it can be used as an intermediate step for developing program code. Pseudocode for the newspaper example is given in Figure 20.24.

The use of pseudocode is common in the industry, but lack of standardization will prevent it from being accepted by everyone. Since pseudocode is so close to program code, it is naturally favored by programmers, and consequently it is not as favored by business analysts. Pseudocode is frequently used to represent the logic of each module on a structure chart.

The data-flow diagram may be used to write the pseudocode logic. When used at a program level rather than at a system level, the data-flow diagram may incorporate several additional symbols. The asterisk (*), meaning "and," is used to indicate that both named data flows must be present. Refer to the portion of a data-flow diagram that is illustrated in Figure 20.25. If the input data flows are from different records, the presence of the "and" connector signifies that the process receiving the flow must perform some sort of file matching. This is either a sequential match, reading all the records from both files, or an indexed read of a second file using a key field obtained from the first file.

The plus sign enclosed in a circle (⊕) represents an exclusive "or" and indicates that one or the other data flow is present at any given time. Use of this symbol implies that the process receiving or producing the data flow must have a corresponding IF . . . THEN . . . ELSE statement. In the figure, process 1, EDIT EMPLOYEE CHANGES, must have an IF statement to determine if the change transaction is valid or not. Process 2, UPDATE EMPLOYEE RECORD, must have both the VALID EMPLOYEE TRANSACTION and the EMPLOYEE MASTER RECORD, and it must match the records somehow to produce the output.

Procedure Manuals

Procedure manuals are common organizational documents that most people have seen. They are the English component of documentation, although they may also contain program codes, flowcharts, and so on. Manuals are intended to communicate to those who use them. They may contain background comments, steps required to accomplish different transactions, instructions on how to recover from problems, and what to do next if something isn't working (troubleshooting). Many manuals are now available on-line, with hypertext capability that facilitates use.

A straightforward, standardized approach to creating user support documentation is desirable. A business will often make a person or even an entire department responsible for producing and maintaining manuals and other documents. It is essential that manuals are thought of as current, rather than historical, documents. To be useful, user documentation must be kept up to date. Use of the Web has revolutionized the speed with which assistance can be obtained by users. Many software developers are moving user support—complete with FAQ (Frequently Asked Questions), help desks, technical support, and fax-back service—to the Web. In addition, many software vendors include "read me" files with shipments of new software. These files serve a variety of purposes: to document changes, patches, or fixes for newly-discovered bugs in the application that have occurred too late in its development to be included in the accompanying user's manual.

Manuals should not contain overblown rhetoric touting the benefits of the application. Remember that the manual is not an advertisement.

A good printed manual will still be used repeatedly as a reference. As such, it needs to be organized in a logical way, with careful thought given to the circumstances that would call forth the use of the manual. On-line man-

```
Open Files
Summary.total = 0
Read the first newspaper.name
DO WHILE there are more newspaper.name(s)
    PRINT date
    PRINT newspaper.name
    Newspaper.total = 0
    Read first subscriber.record
    DO WHILE there are more subscriber.record(s)
        IF Action = Renewal
            THEN subs.length = subs.length + num.weeks
            IF address < > cur.address
                THEN PERFORM Address.change
            ELSE continue
        ELSE IF Action = New
            THEN PERFORM Address.change
            subs.length - num.weeks
        ELSE IF Action = Cancellation
            subs.length = 0
            PERFORM Refund
        ELSE IF Action = Address.change
            PERFORM Address.change
        ELSE PERFORM Action.error
        ENDIF
        Newspaper.total = Newspaper.total + 1
        PERFORM Print.subscriber
        Read another subscriber.record
    ENDDO
    PERFORM Print.newspaper
    Get next newspaper.name
ENDDO
Close Files
```

uals using a hypertext system assist users in accessing items that otherwise might be difficult to find.

Key sections of a manual should include an introduction, how to use the software, what to do if things go wrong, a technical reference section, an index, and information on how to contact the manufacturer. On-line manuals on Web sites should also include information on downloading updates and an FAQ page. The biggest complaints with procedure manuals are that: (1) they are poorly organized; (2) it is hard to find needed information in them; (3) the specific case in question does not appear in the manual; and (4) the manual is not written in plain English.

In addition to the manual's organization and clarity, careful thought should be given to the kinds of people who will be using the manual or accessing the Web site. In an upcoming section on testing, we discuss the importance of having users "test" systems manuals and prototype Web sites before they are finalized.

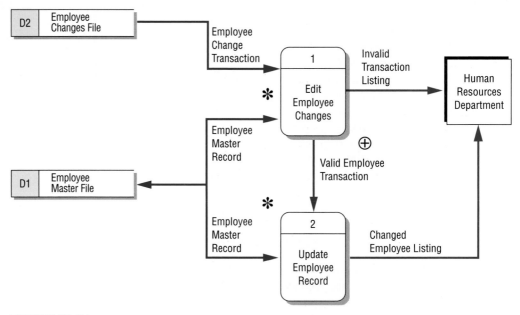

FIGURE 20.25
Use of "and" (*) and "or" (⊕) connectors to determine program logic.

The FOLKLORE Method

FOLKLORE is a system documentation technique that was created to supplement some of the techniques just covered. Even with the plethora of techniques available, many systems are inadequately documented or not documented at all. FOLKLORE gathers information that is often shared among users but is seldom written down.

FOLKLORE is a systematic technique, based on traditional methods used in gathering folklore about people and legends. This approach to systems documentation requires the analyst to interview users, investigate existing documentation in files, and observe the processing of information. The objective is to gather information corresponding to one of four categories: customs, tales, sayings, and art forms. Figure 20.26 suggests how each category relates to the documentation of information systems.

When documenting customs, the analyst (or other folklorist) tries to capture in writing what users are currently doing to get all programs to run without problems. An example of a custom is: "Normally, we take two days to update the monthly records because the task is quite large. We run commercial accounts on day one and save the others for the next day."

Tales are stories that users tell regarding how the systems worked. The accuracy of the tale, of course, depends on the user's memory and is at best an opinion about how the program worked. The following is an example of a tale:

The problem occurred again in 1985. This time the LIB409 job (monthly update) was run with only the "type 6" records in it. Because of this, there were no financial records in the LIBFIN file. When we tried to read the empty file, it was immediately closed, and the totals were consequently reported as zero. We were able to correct this problem by adding a "type 7" record and rerunning the job.

Tales normally have a beginning, a middle, and an end. In this instance, we have a story about a problem (the beginning), a description of the effects (the middle), and the solution (the end).

Sayings are brief statements representing generalizations or advice. We have many sayings in everyday life, such as "April showers bring May flowers" or "A stitch in time saves nine." In systems documentation, we have many sayings, such as, "Write-protect the original before you try to back it up," "Omit this section of code and the program will bomb," or "Always back up frequently." Users like to give advice, and the analyst should try to capture this advice and include it in the FOLKLORE documentation.

Gathering art forms is another important activity of traditional folklorists, and the systems analyst should understand its importance, too. Flowcharts, diagrams, and tables that users draw sometimes may be better or more useful than flowcharts drawn by the original system author. Analysts will often find such art posted on bulletin boards, or they may ask the users to clean out their files and retrieve any useful diagrams.

The FOLKLORE approach works because it can help fill the knowledge gap created when a program author leaves. Contributors to the FOLKLORE document do not have to document the entire system, only the parts they know about. Finally, it is fun for users to contribute, taking some of the burden from analysts. Recently, FOLKLORE was automated in Finland to aid in the documentation of a new system. Notice that the class of recommendation systems that was discussed in conjunction with decision support systems in Chapter 12 is very close to the FOKLORE conceptualization. These systems expand the idea of FOLKORE to include all kinds of recommendations, such as ratings of restaurants, movies, and so on. Through low or no-cost e-mail on the Net and later the Web, some initial barriers to gathering and sharing informal information have been overcome.

The danger of relying on FOLKLORE is that the information gathered from users may be correct, partially correct, or even incorrect. However, unless someone takes the time to redo program documentation entirely, the description of customs, tales, sayings, and art forms may be the only written information about how a set of programs works.

Write Is Right

"It's so easy to understand. I say if everybody uses Nassi-Shneiderman charts, we won't have trouble, you know, with things not being standardized," said Al Gorithm, a new programmer who will be working with your systems analysis team. Al is speaking to an informal meeting among three members of the systems analysis team, a six-person MIS task force from the advertising department, and two programmers who were all working to develop an information system for advertising personnel.

Philip, an advertising account executive and one of the members of the MIS task force, looks up in surprise. "What is this method called?" The two programmers reply at the same time, "Nassi-Shneiderman." Philip looks unimpressed and says, "That doesn't say anything to me."

Neeva Phail, one of the systems analysts, begins explaining. "It probably won't matter one way or the other what we use, if . . ."

Flo Chart, another systems analyst, breaks in saying, "I hate looking at Nassi-Shneiderman.

Pseudocode is much better." She looks hopefully at the programmers. "I'm sure we can agree on a better technique."

David, an older advertising executive, seems slightly upset, stating, "I learned about flowcharting from the first systems analysts we had years ago. Don't you people do that anymore? I think they work best."

What was at first a friendly meeting suddenly seems to have reached an impasse. The participants are looking warily at each other. As a systems analyst who has worked on many different projects with many different kinds of people, you realize that the group is looking to you to make some reasonable suggestions.

Based on what you know about the various documentation techniques, what technique or techniques would you propose to the members of the group? How will the technique(s) you proposed overcome some of the concerns they have voiced? What process will you use to decide on appropriate techniques?

Choosing a Design and Documentation Technique

The techniques discussed in this chapter are extremely valuable as design tools, memory aids, productivity tools—and as a means of reducing dependencies on key staff members. However, the systems analyst is faced with a difficult decision regarding which method to adopt. The following is a set of guidelines to help the analyst use the appropriate technique.

Choose a technique that:

1. Is compatible with existing documentation.
2. Is understood by others in the organization.
3. Allows you to return to working on the system after you have been away from it for a period of time.
4. Is suitable for the size of the system you are working on.
5. Allows for a structured design approach if that is considered to be more important than other factors.
6. Allows for easy modification.

CODE GENERATION AND DESIGN REENGINEERING

Code generation is the process of using software—often a lower or integrated CASE product—to create all or a part of a computer program. Many different code generators exist for both almost every popular computer language and every platform from the microcomputer to midrange and mainframe computers.

Full code generators require a formal methodology for entering all data, business rules, screen designs, and so on. Otherwise, much of the computer program code must be entered into the CASE toolset. Partial code generators generate only specific pieces of code that may be incorporated into a program being constructed by programmers. An example of partial code generation is a CASE tool's ability to generate record layouts and screen design layouts. With add-on products (such as a Microfocus interface module), Excelerator can generate COBOL paragraph names from a structure chart, as well as mainframe screen design code.

One advanced approach to code generation is a set of programs called XperCASE by Siemens AG Österreich. With this sophisticated set of tools, the systems analyst can not only generate program code, but also reengineer existing code. Reengineering (or reverse engineering) allows the analyst to take existing computer code, convert it to a standard structured tool such as a Nassi-Shneiderman chart, modify the logic, and output it as computer code in a different language. An example of reengineering occurs when an analyst begins with existing COBOL code, converts it to a Nassi-Shneiderman chart, adds new features, and outputs it in C++. Figure 20.27 is a segment of a COBOL program used to print a simple control break report.

The report generated in this example is a summary report. Therefore, each line in the report represents the total sales for a particular customer no matter how many times the customer has ordered from the company. The program logic goes as follows: the program reads a file of sales records, SALES-HISTORY-FILE, sorted by customer number, and it accumulates total sales for each customer. When a new customer number is detected, the program prints a line showing the current customer number and the total sales figure. Then the program moves on to the next customer and starts accumulating total sales for that customer. Once all the customer records are read and processed, the company total sales figures are printed.

Two modules are illustrated, 000-PREPARE-SALES-REPORT, which is responsible for producing the entire report, and 200-PRODUCE-SALES-LINE, which has the logic to read, accumulate, and print the customer total line when all the records have been read for a particular customer.

This program was reengineered using a product by Siemens of Vienna, Austria, called XperCASE in the United States. (XperCASE is called Easy-CASE in other parts of the world.) XperCASE uses Nassi-Shneiderman charts to depict program logic. Figure 20.28 is a Nassi-Shneiderman chart created from the COBOL paragraph 000-PREPARE-SALES-REPORT. Notice that the PERFORM UNTIL code has been translated into a sideways "L" shape, indicating iteration.

Figure 20.29 is the diagram created from paragraph 200-PRODUCE-SALES-LINE. Each PERFORM statement from the COBOL program, such as 210-READ-SALES-RECORD, is isolated in a rectangle with vertical bars at each end. IF . . . THEN . . . ELSE statements are transformed into the standard Nassi-Shneiderman format using angle lines to separate the IF actions from the ELSE actions. Refer to the block containing the IF logic to see if the new sales history customer number is greater than the old customer number (indicating that all of the records for the customer have been accumulated).

```
                PROCEDURE DIVISION.
        *
            000-PREPARE-SALES-REPORT.
        *

                OPEN INPUT    SALES-HISTORY-FILE
                OPEN OUTPUT  PRINT-FILE.
                PERFORM 100-FORMAT-HEADING-DATES.
                PERFORM 200-PRODUCE-SALES-LINE
                        UNTIL SALES-REC-EOF.
                PERFORM 300-PRINT-COMPANY-TOTAL-LINE.
                CLOSE SALES-HISTORY-FILE
                        PRINT-FILE.
                STOP RUN.
        *


        *
            200-PRODUCE-SALES-LINE.
        *

                PERFORM 210-READ-SALES-RECORD.
                IF FIRST-RECORD
                        MOVE SR-CUST-NO        TO-OLD-CUST-NO
                        MOVE 'N' TO FIRST-RECORD-SW
                ELSE
                        IF SR-CUST-NO GREATER THAN OLD-CUST-NO
                                PERFORM 230-PRINT-CUSTOMER-LINE.
                IF NOT SALES-REC-EOF
                        PERFORM 220-ACCUMULATE-CUSTOMER-TOTALS.
        *
```

Once the program code has been reverse engineered, the design may be modified, eliminating unused features and adding new features to the program. Figure 20.30 illustrates the Windows screen for inserting a new construct into the existing diagram. Notice the variety of statement structures that may be added, such as an IF-THEN-ELSE, a PARAGRAPH, or a PERFORM. The PERFORM option has an arrow pointing to the right, indicating that more options will appear once it is selected. Some examples are PERFORM BEFORE TEST, PERFORM OUTLINE, PERFORM INLINE, and PERFORM n TIMES.

Figure 20.31 illustrates the screen for editing existing portions of the diagram. Sections such as an IF-THEN-ELSE may be copied or moved to a new location, deleted, or enclosed (that is, surrounded by a new PERFORM UNTIL or other structure). Selecting Push down (Ctrl+D) moves the structure into a lower-level module within the diagram.

The diagram was modified to add another level of subtotals. The old version of the SALES REPORT contained only customer totals and a final total. Modifications were made to add an intermediate subtotal for each salesperson. If the salesperson number changes, lines are printed for both the customer and salesperson. If the salesperson number does not change but if the customer number does, a line is printed only for the customer. Figure 20.32

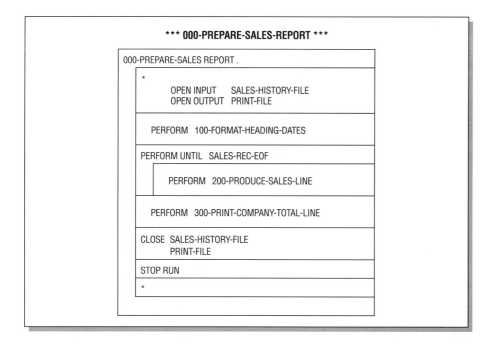

FIGURE 20.28
An XperCASE example of a Nassi-Shneiderman chart produced from the COBOL paragraph 000-PREPARE-SALES-REPORT.

illustrates the new Nassi-Shneiderman diagram with the salesperson IF logic and subtotals included.

The COBOL code for the updated Nassi-Shneiderman diagram was regenerated. Figure 20.33 shows the resulting program code for the 200 module, PRODUCE-SALES-LINE. Notice that the IF statement to check for a change in salesperson number has been generated, along with the two PERFORMs—230-PRINT-CUST-LINE and 235-PRINT-SLSPN-LINE. Another

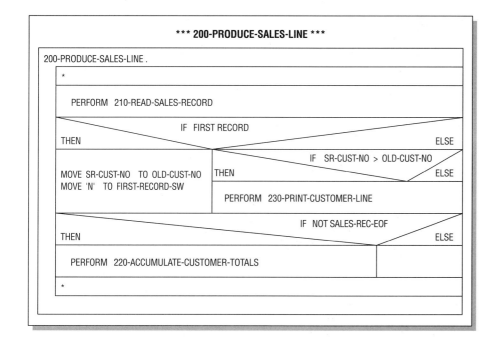

FIGURE 20.29
An XperCASE example of a Nassi-Shneiderman chart created from 200-PRODUCE-SALES-LINE.

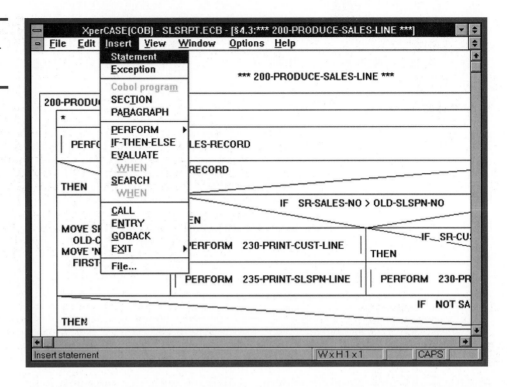

benefit of code regenerating is that the resulting code has been upgraded to the latest version of COBOL. The original code (shown earlier) was written using COBOL 74. The regenerated program is in the latest version, COBOL 85, and it contains statements, such as END-IF, that are not part of the older version of COBOL.

FIGURE 20.31
An XperCASE example of editing the Nassi-Shneiderman diagram.

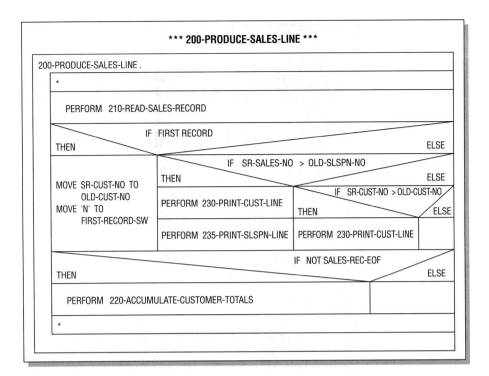

*** 200-PRODUCE-SALES-LINE ***

200-PRODUCE-SALES-LINE .

*

PERFORM 210-READ-SALES-RECORD

IF FIRST RECORD

THEN   ELSE

MOVE SR-CUST-NO TO OLD-CUST-NO
MOVE 'N' TO FIRST-RECORD-SW

IF SR-SALES-NO > OLD-SLSPN-NO
THEN   ELSE

PERFORM 230-PRINT-CUST-LINE

IF SR-CUST-NO > OLD-CUST-NO
THEN   ELSE

PERFORM 235-PRINT-SLSPN-LINE   PERFORM 230-PRINT-CUST-LINE

IF NOT SALES-REC-EOF

THEN   ELSE

PERFORM 220-ACCUMULATE-CUSTOMER-TOTALS

*

TESTING, MAINTENANCE, AND AUDITING

The Testing Process

All of the system's newly written or modified application programs—as well as new procedural manuals, new hardware, and all system interfaces—must be tested thoroughly. Haphazard, trial-and-error testing will not suffice.

Testing is done throughout systems development, not just at the end. It is meant to turn up heretofore unknown problems, not to demonstrate the perfection of programs, manuals, or equipment.

Although testing is tedious, it is an essential series of steps that helps assure the quality of the eventual system. It is far less disruptive to test beforehand than to have a poorly tested system fail after installation. Testing is accomplished on subsystems or program modules as work progresses. Testing is done on many different levels at various intervals. Before the system is put into production, all programs must be desk-checked, checked with test data, and checked to see if the modules work together with one another as planned.

The system as a working whole must also be tested. This includes testing the interfaces between subsystems, the correctness of output, and the usefulness and understandability of system documentation and output. Programmers, analysts, operators, and users all play different roles in the various aspects of testing, as shown in Figure 20.34. Testing of hardware is typically provided as a service by vendors of equipment who will run their own tests on equipment when it is delivered on-site.

PROGRAM TESTING WITH TEST DATA. Much of the responsibility for program testing resides with the original author(s) of each program. The systems analyst serves as an advisor and coordinator for program testing. In this capacity, the analyst works to ensure that correct testing techniques are im-

FIGURE 20.33
Portion of a COBOL program
showing regenerated Xper-
CASE code.

```
* --------------------------------------------------------
# XPER *
     200-PRODUCE-SALES-LINE.
  *
     PERFORM 210-READ-SALES-RECORD
     IF FIRST-RECORD
     THEN
         MOVE SR-CUST-NO TO
             OLD-CUST-NO
         MOVE 'N' TO
             FIRST-RECORD-SW
     ELSE
         IF SR-SALES-NO > OLD-SLSPN-NO
         THEN
             PERFORM 230-PRINT-CUST-LINE
             PERFORM 235-PRINT SLSPN-LINE
         ELSE
             IF SR-CUST-NO > OLD-CUST-NO
             THEN
                 PERFORM 230-PRINT-CUST-LINE
             END-IF
         END-IF
     END-IF
     IF NOT SALES-REC-EOF
     THEN
         PERFORM 220-ACCUMULATE-CUSTOMER-TOTALS
     END-IF
  *
             .
  *                                              # XPER P
* --------------------------------------------------------
# XPER )
```

plemented by programmers but probably does not personally carry out this level of checking.

At this stage, programmers must first desk check their programs to verify the way the system will work. In desk checking, the programmer follows each step in the program on paper to check whether the routine works as it is written.

Next, programmers must create both valid and invalid test data. These data are then run to see if base routines work and also to catch errors. If output from main modules is satisfactory, then you can add more test data in order to check other modules. Created test data should test possible minimum and maximum values, as well as all possible variations in format and codes. File output from test data must be carefully verified. It should never be assumed that data contained in a file are correct just because a file was created and accessed.

Throughout this process, the systems analyst checks output for errors, advising the programmer of any needed corrections. The analyst will usually not recommend or create test data for program testing but might point out to the programmer omissions of data types to be added in later tests.

LINK TESTING WITH TEST DATA. When programs pass desk checking and checking with test data, they must go through link testing, which is also referred to as string testing. Link testing checks to see if programs that are interdependent actually work together as planned.

A small amount of test data, usually designed by the systems analyst to test system specifications as well as programs, is used for link testing. It may take several passes through the system to test all combinations, because it is immensely difficult to unravel problems if you try to test everything all at once.

The analyst creates special test data that cover a variety of processing situations for link testing. First, typical test data are processed to see if the system can handle normal transactions—those that would make up the bulk of its load. If the system works with normal transactions, then variations are added, including invalid data used to ensure that the system can properly detect errors.

FULL SYSTEMS TESTING WITH TEST DATA. When link tests are satisfactorily concluded, the system as a complete entity must be tested. At this stage, operators and end users become actively involved in testing. Test data, created by the systems analysis team for the express purpose of testing system objectives, are used.

As can be expected, there are a number of factors to consider when systems testing with test data:

1. Examining whether operators have adequate documentation in procedure manuals (hard copy or on-line) to afford correct and efficient operation.
2. Checking whether procedure manuals are clear enough in communicating how data should be prepared for input.
3. Ascertaining if work flows necessitated by the new or modified system actually "flow."
4. Determining if output is correct and whether users understand that this is, in all likelihood, how output will look in its final form.

Remember to schedule adequate time for system testing. Unfortunately, this is a step that often gets dropped if system installation is lagging behind the target date.

Systems testing includes reaffirming the quality standards for system performance that were set up when initial system specifications were made. Everyone involved should once again agree on how to determine whether the system is doing what it is supposed to do. This will include measures of error, timeliness, ease of use, proper ordering of transactions, acceptable down time, understandable procedure manuals, and so on.

FULL SYSTEMS TESTING WITH LIVE DATA. When systems tests using test data prove satisfactory, it is a good idea to try the new system with several passes on what is called "live data"—data that have been successfully processed through the existing system. This step allows an accurate comparison of the new system's output with what you know to be correctly processed output, as well as a good feel for how actual data will be handled. Obviously, this step is not possible when creating entirely new outputs. As with test data, only small amounts of live data are used in this kind of system testing.

Testing is an important period for assessing how end users and operators actually interact with the system. Although much thought is given to user-system interaction (see Chapter 18), you can never fully predict the wide range of differences in the way users will actually interact with the system. It is not enough to interview users about how they are interacting with the system; you must observe them firsthand.

Items to watch for are ease of learning the system; the adjustment to ergonomic factors; and user reaction to system feedback, including what happens when an error message is received and what happens when the user is informed that the system is executing his or her commands. Be particularly sensitive to how users react to system response time and to the language of responses. Also listen to what users say about the system as they encounter it. Any real problems need to be addressed before the system is put into production, not just glossed over as adjustments to the system that users and operators "ought" to make on their own.

As mentioned earlier, procedure manuals also need to be tested. Although manuals can be proofread by support staff and checked for technical accuracy by the systems analysis team, the only real way to test them is to have users and operators try them, preferably during full systems testing with live data. Have them use accurate but not final versions of the manuals.

It is difficult to communicate procedures accurately. Difficulty is compounded when a systems analyst or programmer has been working with a system for a long time. Recalling your own early experiences with intimidating or frustrating new systems can help focus your thinking on producing readable and useful documentation. Remember that manuals need to be organized in different ways for users who will interact with the system in countless ways. Too much information will be just as much a deterrent to system use as too little. Use of Web-based documents can help in this regard. Users can jump to topics of interest and download and print what they want to keep. Consider user suggestions, and when possible, incorporate them into the final versions of Web pages, printed manuals, and other forms of documentation.

Cramming for Your Systems Test

"We're strapped for time. Just look at this projection," says Lou Scuntroll, the newest member of your systems analysis team, showing you the PERT diagram that the team has been using to project when the new system would be up and running. "We can't possibly make the July target date for testing with live data. We're running three weeks behind because of that slow equipment shipment."

As one of the systems analysts who has seen deadlines come and go on other projects, you try to remain calm and to size up the situation carefully before you speak. Slowly, you question Lou about the possibility of delaying testing.

Lou replies, "If we try to push the testing off until the first weeks of August, there are two key people from accounting who are going to be out on vacation." Lou is visibly upset at the possibility of missing the deadline.

Stan Dards, another junior member of your systems analysis team, enters Lou's office. "You two look terrible. Things are going okay, aren't they? I'm not reassigned to program a payroll application, am I?"

Lou looks up, obviously neither appreciating Stan's sense of humor nor what seems like his single-minded self-concern. "Good thing you came in when you did. We've got some big decisions to make about scheduling." Lou holds up the PERT diagram for Stan's inspection. Notice the July test date. "Notice that there is no way we can make it. Any bright ideas?"

Stan contemplates the chart momentarily, then states, "Something's got to go. Let's see here . . . maybe move testing of the accounting module to—"

Lou interrupts, saying bluntly, "Nope, already thought of that, but Stanford and Binet from accounting are out of town in August. Maybe we can skip that portion of the testing. They've been really cooperative. I don't think they'd object if we just 'do it for real' and test as we actually go into production."

"I think that's a good idea, Lou," Stan agrees, trying to make up for his earlier jokes. "We haven't had any real trouble with that, and the programmers sure are confident. That way we could stay on schedule with everything else. I vote for *not* testing the accounting portion, just sort of winging it when it starts up."

As the most senior member of the team present, what can you do to convince Lou and Stan about the importance of testing the accounting module with live data? What can systems analysts do in planning their time in order to allow adequate time for testing with test and live data? What are some of the possible problems the team members may encounter if they do not test the system completely with live data before putting the system into production? Realistically, are there steps in the system analysis and design process that can be collapsed in order to bring a delayed project in on time?

Maintenance Practices

Your objective as a systems analyst should be to install or modify systems that have a reasonable useful life. You want to create a system whose design is comprehensive and farsighted enough to serve current and projected user needs for several years to come. Part of your expertise should be used to project what those needs might be and then build flexibility and adaptability into the system. The better the system design, the easier it will be to maintain and the less money the business will have to spend on maintenance.

Reducing maintenance costs is a major concern, since software maintenance alone can devour upwards of 50 percent of the total data-processing budget for a business. Excessive maintenance costs reflect directly back on the system's designer, since approximately 70 percent of software errors have been attributed to inappropriate software design. From a systems perspective, it makes sense that detecting and correcting software design errors early on is less costly than letting errors remain unnoticed until maintenance is necessary.

Maintenance is performed most often to improve the existing software rather than to respond to a crisis or system failure. As users' requirements change, software and documentation should be changed as part of the maintenance work. Additionally, programs might be recoded to improve on the efficiency of the original program. Over half of all maintenance is comprised of such enhancement work.

Maintenance is also done to update software in response to the changing organization. This work is not as substantial as enhancing the software, but it must be done. Emergency and adaptive maintenance comprises less than half of all system maintenance.

Part of the systems analyst's job is to ensure that there are adequate channels and procedures in place to permit feedback about—and subsequent response to—maintenance needs. Users must be able to communicate problems and suggestions easily to those who will be maintaining the system. It is very discouraging (sometimes so much so that the system will fall into disuse) if the system is not properly maintained. One solution is to provide users e-mail access to technical support, as well as to allow them to download product updates or patches from the Web.

The systems analyst also needs to set up a classification scheme to allow users to designate the perceived importance of the maintenance being suggested or requested. Classifying requests enables maintenance programmers to understand how users themselves estimate the importance of their requests. This viewpoint, along with other factors, can then be taken into account when scheduling maintenance.

Auditing

Auditing is yet another way of assuring the quality of the information contained in the system. Broadly defined, auditing refers to having an expert who is not involved in setting up or using a system examine information in order to ascertain its reliability. Whether or not information is found to be reliable, the finding on its reliability is communicated to others for the purpose of making the system's information more useful to them.

For information systems, there are generally two kinds of auditors: internal and external. Whether both are necessary for the system you design depends on what kind of system it is. Internal auditors work for the same organization that owns the information system, whereas external (also called "independent") auditors are hired from the outside.

Basically, external auditors are used when the information system processes data that influences a company's financial statements. External auditors audit the system to assure the fairness of the financial statements being produced. They may also be brought in if there is something out of the ordinary occurring that involves company employees, such as suspected computer fraud or embezzlement.

Internal auditors study the controls used in the information system to make sure that they are adequate and that they are doing what they are purported to be doing. They also test the adequacy of security controls. Although they work for the same organization, internal auditors do not report to the people responsible for the system they are auditing. The work of internal auditors is often more in-depth than that of external auditors.

SUMMARY

The systems analyst uses three broad approaches to total quality management (TQM) for analyzing and designing information systems: designing systems and software with a top-down, modular approach; designing and

"This is a fascinating place to work. I'm sure you agree now that you've had a chance to observe us. Sometimes I think it must be fun to be an outsider . . . don't you feel like an anthropologist discovering a new culture? I remember when I first came here. Everything was so new, so strange. Why, even the language was different. It wasn't a 'customer'; it was a 'client.' And we didn't have 'departments'; we have 'units.' It's not an employee cafeteria; it's the 'canteen.' That goes for the way we work, too. We all have our different ways to approach things. I think I'm getting the hang of what Snowden expects, but every once in a while I make a mistake, too. For instance, if I can give him work on disk, he'd just as soon see it that way than get a printed report. That's why I have two computers on my desk, too! I always see you taking so many notes . . . I guess it makes sense, though. You're supposed to document what *we* do with our systems and information, as well as what your team is doing, aren't you?"

HYPERCASE QUESTIONS

1. Use the FOLKLORE method to complete the documentation of the Management Information Systems Unit GEMS system. Be sure to include customs, tales, sayings, and art forms.

2. In two paragraphs suggest a PC-based approach for capturing the elements of FOLKLORE so that it is not necessary to use a paper-based log. Make sure that your suggested solution can accommodate graphics as well as text.

FIGURE 20.HC1
In HyperCase, use FOLKLORE to document art forms that users have created or collected to make sense of their systems.

3. Design input and output screens for FOLKLORE that facilitate easy entry and provide prompting so that recall of FOLKLORE elements is immediate.

documenting systems and software using systematic methods; and testing systems and software so that they can be easily maintained and audited.

Users are critically important for establishing and evaluating the quality of several dimensions of management information systems and decision support systems. They can be involved in the entire evolution of systems through the establishment of MIS task forces or quality circles.

TQM can be successfully implemented by taking a top-down approach to design. This refers to looking at overall organizational objectives first, then decomposing them into manageable subsystem requirements. Modular development makes programming, debugging, and maintenance easier to accomplish. Programming in modules is well suited to taking a top-down approach.

Two systems that link programs in the Windows environment are DDE (Dynamic Data Exchange) which shares code by using Dynamic Link Library (DLL) files. Using DDE, a user can store data in one program and then use it in another. A second approach to linking programs in Windows is called OLE (for Object Linking and Embedding). This linking method is superior to DDE for linking application data and graphics, because of its object-oriented approach.

A recommended tool for designing a top-down, modular system is called a structure chart. Two types of arrows are used to indicate the kinds of parameters that are passed between the modules. The first is called a data couple; the second is called a control flag. Structure chart modules fall into one of three categories: control, transformational (sometimes called worker), and functional or specialized.

Part of total quality management is to see that programs and systems are properly designed, documented, and maintained. Some of the structured techniques that can aid the systems analyst are Nassi-Shneiderman charts, pseudocode, procedure manuals, and FOLKLORE. Pseudocode is frequently used to represent the logic of each module or structure chart. Pseudocode can be used for structured walkthroughs. Systems analysts must choose a technique both that fits in well with what was previously used in the organization and that allows flexibility and easy modification.

Code generation is the process of using software to create all or part of a computer program. Many code generators are now available commercially. Reengineering and reverse engineering refer to using software to analyze existing program code and to create CASE design elements from the code. CASE design may then be modified and used to generate new computer program code.

Testing of specific programs, subsystems, and total systems is essential to quality. Testing is done to turn up any existing problems with programs and their interfaces before the system is actually used. Typically, testing is done in a bottom-up fashion, with program codes being desk checked first. Following several intermediate test steps, testing of the full system with live data (actual data that has been successfully processed with the old system) is accomplished. This provides an opportunity to work out any problems that arise before the system is put into production.

System maintenance is an important consideration. Well-designed software can help reduce maintenance costs. Systems analysts need to set up channels for user feedback on maintenance needs, since systems that are not maintained will fall into disuse. Web sites can help in this regard by providing access to product updates and e-mail exchanges with technical staff.

Both internal and external auditors are used to determine the reliability of the system's information. They communicate their audit findings to others in order to improve the usefulness of the system's information.

KEYWORDS AND PHRASES

total quality management (TQM)
IS quality circles
structured walkthrough
bottom-up design
top-down design
modular development
dynamic data exchange (DDE)
dynamic link library (DLL)
object linking and
  embedding (OLE)
structure charts
transform centered
transaction centered
data couples
improper subordination
control flags (switches)
software documentation
software maintenance

stamp coupling
Nassi-Shneiderman charts
pseudocode
FOLKLORE method
code generation
code generators
reengineering (reverse
  engineering)
desk check
program testing with test data
link testing with test data
  (string testing)
full systems testing with
  test data
full systems testing with
  live data
internal auditor

REVIEW QUESTIONS

1. What are the three broad approaches available to the systems analyst for attaining quality in newly developed systems?
2. Who or what is the most important factor in establishing and evaluating the quality of information systems or decision support systems? Why?
3. Define the total quality management (TQM) approach as it applies to the analysis and design of information systems.
4. What is an IS quality circle?
5. Define what is meant by doing a structured walkthrough. Who should be involved? When should structured walkthroughs be done?
6. List the disadvantages to taking a bottom-up approach to design.
7. List the advantages of taking a top-down approach to design.
8. What are the three main disadvantages of taking a top-down approach to design?
9. Define modular development.
10. List four guidelines for correct modular programming.
11. How do structure charts help the analyst?
12. Name the two types of arrows used in structure charts.
13. Why do we want to keep the number of arrows to a minimum when using structure charts?
14. What are the two main types of structure charts?
15. Why should control flags be passed upward in a structure chart?

16. List two ways that the data flow diagram helps to build a structure chart.
17. List the three categories of modules. Why are they used in structure charts?
18. How can a Web site help in maintaining the system and its documentation?
19. Give two reasons that support the necessity of well-developed system and software documentation.
20. Give the two chief advantages of Nassi-Shneiderman charts.
21. Define *pseudocode.*
22. List the four biggest complaints users voice about procedure manuals.
23. In what four categories does the FOLKLORE documentation method collect information?
24. List six guidelines for choosing a design and documentation technique.
25. What are the advantages of using code generation and design reengineering for building systems?
26. Whose primary responsibility is it to test computer programs?
27. What is the difference between test data and live data?
28. What are the two types of systems auditors?

PROBLEMS

1. One of your systems analysis team members has been discouraging user input on quality standards, arguing that since you are the experts, you are really the only ones who know what constitutes a quality system. In a paragraph, explain to your team member why getting user input is critical to system quality. Use an example.
2. Draw a structure chart for the credit-reporting system in Figure 20.EX1.
3. Construct a structure chart for the payroll system in Figure 9.7 in Chapter 9.
4. Draw a Nassi-Shneiderman (N-S) chart to update your checkbook. Start with the balance the last time you balanced it. Subtract checks, electronic withdrawals, and any service charges. Add deposits and interest.
5. Write pseudocode for problem 5.
6. Bestmonth Lumber Company is setting up a monthly payroll report. The report has the following information:

Heading	(left)	department number
		run date
	(center)	company name
		title of report
	(right)	page number
Body		last name
		first name
		monthly gross
		federal taxes
		state taxes
		FICA taxes
		other deductions
		monthly net

7. Draw an N-S chart for problem 7.
8. Write pseudocode for the Citron Car rental policy provided in Consulting Opportunity 11.3 in Chapter 11.
9. Write a detailed table of contents for a procedure manual that explains to users how to log onto your school's computer network, as well as ex-

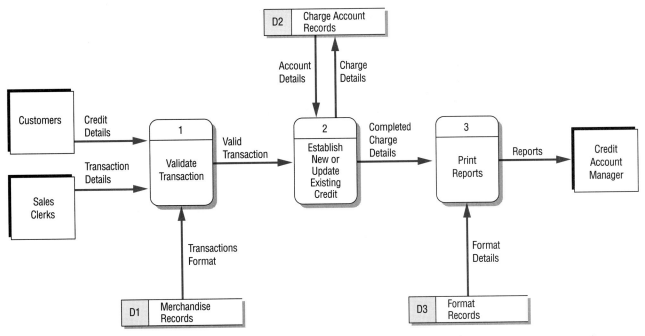

FIGURE 20.EX1
A data flow diagram for a credit reporting system.

plains network policies—who is an authorized user and so on. Make sure that the manual is written with the user in mind.

10. Your systems analysis team is close to completing a system for Meecham Feeds. Roger is quite confident that the programs that he has written for Meecham's inventory system will perform as necessary, since they are similar to programs he has done before. Your team has been very busy and would ideally like to begin full systems testing as soon as possible.

This is what two of your junior team members have proposed:

a. Skip desk checking of the programs (since similar programs were checked in other installations; Roger has agreed).

b. Do link testing with large amounts of data to prove that the system will work.

c. Do full systems testing with large amounts of live data to show the system is working.

Respond to each of the three steps in their proposed test schedule. Use a paragraph to explain your response.

11. Propose a revised testing plan for the Meecham Feeds problem (problem 10). Break down your plan into a sequence of detailed steps.

GROUP PROJECTS

1. Divide your group into two subgroups. One subgroup should interview the members of the other group about their experiences encountered in registering for a class. Questions should be designed to elicit information on customs, tales, sayings, and art forms that will help document the registration process at your school.

2. Reunite your group to develop a Web page for a short excerpt for a FOLKLORE manual that documents the process of registering for a class, one based on the folklore passed on in the interviews in problem 1. Remember to include examples of customs, tales, sayings, and art forms.

SELECTED BIBLIOGRAPHY

Dean, Jr., J. W., and J. R. Evans. *Total Quality.* Minneapolis/St. Paul: West Publishing Company, 1994.

Deming, W. E. *Management for Quality and Productivity.* Cambridge, MA: MIT Center for Advanced Engineering Study, 1981.

Katzan, H., Jr. *Systems Design and Documentation: An Introduction to the HIPO Method.* New York: Van Nostrand Reinhold Company, 1976.

Kendall, J. E., and P. Kerola. "A Foundation for the Use of Hypertext Based Documentation Techniques." *Journal of End User Computing,* Vol. 6, No. 1 Winter, 1994 pp. 4–14.

Kendall, K. E., and R. Losee. "Information System FOLKLORE: A New Technique for System Documentation." *Information & Management,* Vol. 10, No. 2, 1986 pp. 103–111.

Kendall, K. E., and S. Yoo. "Pseudocode-Box Diagrams: An Approach to More Understandable, Productive and Adaptable Software Design and Coding," *International Journal on Policy and Information,* Vol. 12, No. 1, June, 1988, pp. 39–51.

Lee, S. M., and M. J. Schniederjans. *Operations Management.* Boston: Houghton-Mifflin Company, 1994.

Porter, W. T., and W. E. Perry. *EDP Controls and Auditing,* 2nd ed. Belmont, CA: Wadsworth Publishing Company, Inc., 1977.

Shelly, G. B., and T. J. Cashman. *Business Systems Analysis and Design.* Fullerton, CA: Anaheim Publishing Company, 1975.

Yourdon, E. *Managing the Structured Techniques,* 2nd ed. Englewood Cliffs, NJ: Prentice Hall, 1977.

"Here they are, as promised," Chip and Anna say triumphantly as they hand over their specifications to Mack Roe, the project programmer.

"Thanks," Mack says. "I've got a lot of work ahead."

Mack's first task is to produce an overview of the programs that would work together. He uses Visible Analyst's Unstructured type of diagram to create system flowcharts of all the major programs that would operate together. The first system flow is the series of programs and manual processes depicting the installation of new microcomputers. The finished diagram is shown in Figure E20.1. Notice that all the programs and manual processes are centered in the drawing, identifying steps in the procedure.

NEW MICROCOMPUTER FORMS are sent to data entry, where they are keyed and verified. A VERIFICATION REPORT provides the first document in an audit trail of transactions. The MICROCOMPUTER ADD TRANSACTION is input into a validation program EDIT ADD TRANSACTIONS, ensuring that quality data enters the system. A second VALIDATION REPORT continues the audit trail, and a VALID ADD TRANSACTION file contains all records with no errors. This file is input to a program to add a new record to the MICROCOMPUTER MASTER file and a separate program to update the PENDING MICROCOMPUTER ORDER file.

VALID ADD TRANSACTIONS are sorted by MODEL within BRAND NAME for printing the MICROCOMPUTER RECEIVED REPORT and the MICROCOMPUTER INSTALLATION LISTING. This information will be used to determine which locations receive the machines.

Mack completes other system flowcharts for the remaining portions of the system. Next, the programs on each system flowchart are designed. Mack starts by creating a structure chart for each program and then for each module design. The PRODUCE SOFTWARE CROSS-REFERENCE REPORT structure chart is shown in Figure E20.2. The "C" in front of each module number refers to the CROSS-REFERENCE REPORT (a letter is required by Visible Analyst as the first character in a module name). This is the first draft that Mack uses in a structured walkthrough with Dee Ziner, a senior programmer.

Dee Ziner has several important suggestions for improving the structure. She says, "Module C130, PRINT ERROR LINE, is improperly subordinate to the calling module C120, READ HARDWARE RECORD. The question may be asked, 'Must the program print an error line in order to accomplish reading a HARDWARE RECORD?' Since the answer is 'No,' the module should be placed at the same level as C120, READ HARDWARE RECORD."

She continues discussing the situation with Mack, saying, "The same is true concerning module C160, PRINT SUBTOTAL LINES. This is not a function of accumulating hardware subtotals and should not be called from module C150, ACCUMULATE HARDWARE SUBTOTALS." Dee continues the walkthrough by asking the question, "May one SOFTWARE RECORD be located on many machines?" Mack responds that this is true, and another controlling module, PRINT SOFTWARE CROSS-REFERENCE LINES was included in the structure chart.

Allen Schmidt,
Julie E. Kendall, and
Kenneth E. Kendall

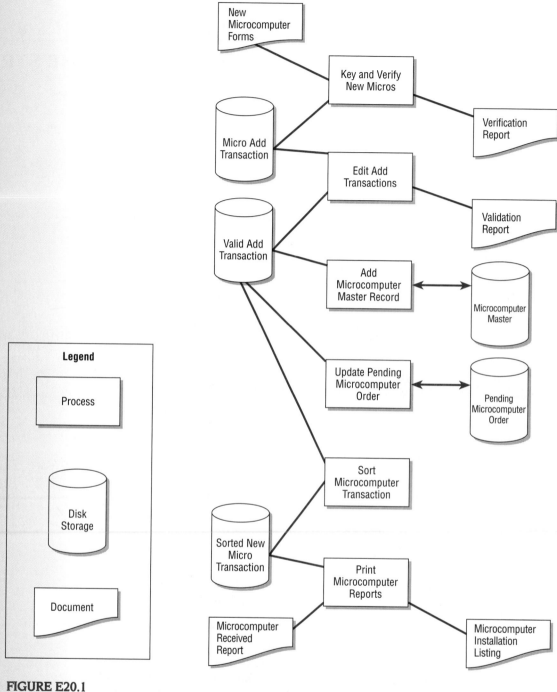

FIGURE E20.1
NEW MICROCOMPUTER system flowchart.

Mack proceeds to incorporate the changes to the structure chart. When the correct hierarchy is established, the coupling is added. Careful attention is given to pass minimal data and to only pass control *up* the structure chart. The final version is illustrated in Figure E20.3. Module C116 is new, using the SOFTWARE/HARDWARE RELATIONAL file to link one SOFTWARE RECORD to many HARDWARE RECORDS. The SOFTWARE INVENTORY

FIGURE E20.2
PRODUCE SOFTWARE CROSS-REFERENCE REPORT structure chart. The single asterisk (*) and the double asterisk (**) indicate the second and third occurence of module C140.

NUMBER is passed down to the module, and the relational file is randomly read. The HARDWARE INVENTORY NUMBER and control switch RELATION NOT FOUND are passed up the structure.

The final structure chart has a functional shape to it. A few control modules at the top of the structure, several worker modules in the middle, and a few specialist modules at the bottom provide a general fan-out, fan-in shape. The module names are all of the verb-adjective-noun form, describing what has been accomplished after the module has finished executing. For example, module C150 has the verb ACCUMULATE, describing the work accomplished by the module. SUBTOTALS, a noun, are being accumulated, and HARDWARE describes which subtotals are accumulated.

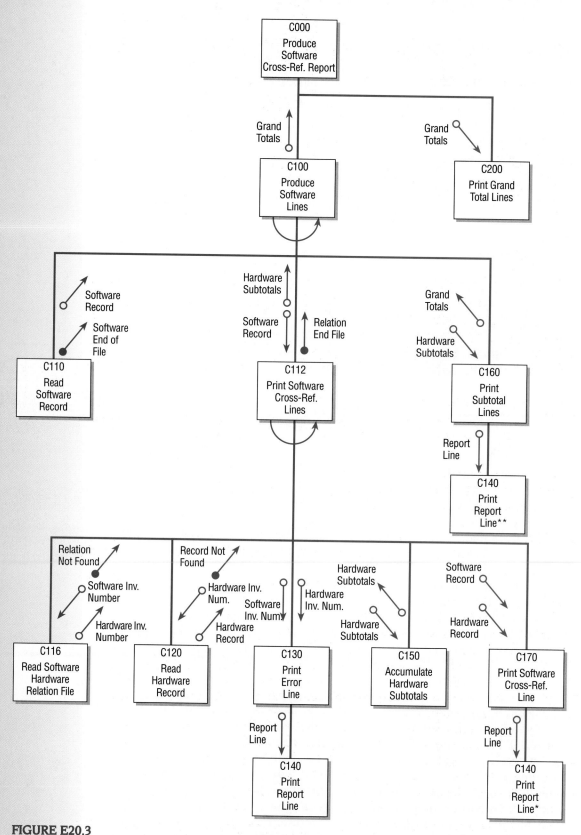

FIGURE E20.3
PRODUCE SOFTWARE CROSS-REFERENCE REPORT structure chart, with coupling.
The single asterisk (*) and the double asterisk (**) indicate the second and third
occurence of module C140.

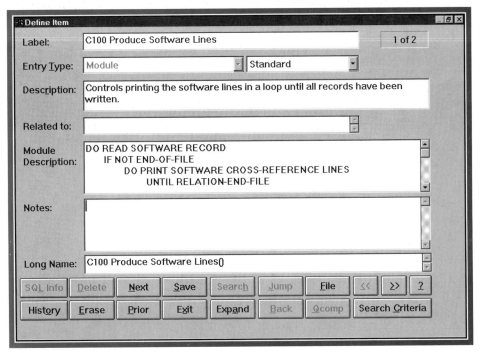

FIGURE E20.4
PRODUCE SOFTWARE LINES module repository screen.

Each of the modules on the structure chart were described in the repository. Figure E20.4 illustrates the screen describing the function for module C100, PRODUCE SOFTWARE LINES. Notice that the module description contains pseudocode depicting the logic of the module. Since PRODUCE SOFTWARE LINES is a control module, its logic should consist of looping and decision making, with minimal statements concerning processing details such as ADD or READ.

Each data and control couple on the structure chart may also be described in the repository. Figure E20.5 illustrates the repository screen for the SOFTWARE RECORD data couple. Notice that it has the entry SOFTWARE MASTER FILE in the **Related to** area. This provides a link to the repository entry that contains the details of elements contained in the SOFTWARE RECORD. The **Notes** area contains information about how the SOFTWARE RECORD is used on the structure chart. The RECORD NOT FOUND control couple is illustrated in Figure E20.6. Notice that the values for the switch are listed.

Test plans are completed for each program. These plans contain details about how to determine if the programs are working correctly, and they are sent to Mack and Dee, who will create the actual test data. Invalid and valid data are included on each test file used in batch programs. The same is true for interactive systems, except that the test data are written on forms imitating the screen design. After Mack has finished testing his programs and is satisfied that they are working correctly, he challenges Dee to find any errors in the programs. In turn, Dee has Mack test her programs in a round of friendly competition. They both realize that programmers may not always catch their own errors, since they are inti-

FIGURE E20.5
Repository screen for the SOFTWARE RECORD data couple.

FIGURE E20.6
RECORD NOT FOUND control couple repository screen.

mately familiar with their own programs and may not recognize subtle errors in logic.

Exercises*

💾 **E-1.** View the PRODUCE SOFTWARE CROSS-REF REP structure chart. Double click on the modules to view the repository entries for some of the modules.

💾 **E-2.** Modify the PRODUCE HARDWARE INVESTMENT RPT structure chart. Add the function PRINT INVESTMENT LINE in the empty rectangle provided. Subordinate to this module is PRINT HEADING LINES and WRITE REPORT LINE. Describe each function in the repository.

💾 **E-3.** Modify the CHANGE MICROCOMPUTER FILE structure chart. Include the Loop symbol and add the following modules subordinate to 160, CHANGE MICROCOMPUTER RECORD (also see below):

   A. DISPLAY CHANGE SCREEN
   B. ACCEPT MICROCOMPUTER CHANGES
   C. VALIDATE CHANGES
   D. DISPLAY ERROR MESSAGE
   E. CONFIRM CHANGES

The following modules should be subordinate to 220, PUT MICROCOMPUTER RECORD:

   A. FORMAT MICROCOMPUTER RECORD
   B. REWRITE MICROCOMPUTER RECORD

💾 **E-4.** Modify the ADD SOFTWARE RECORDS structure chart by adding a looping symbol and coupling for the connections. The following coupling should be placed on the connection line above each module (also see below):

   A. Module: DISPLAY ADD SOFTWARE SCREEN
      Passed Up: ADD SOFTWARE SCREEN
   B. Module: ACCEPT ADD SOFTWARE SCREEN
      Passed Up: EXIT INDICATOR (Control)
                     ADD SOFTWARE SCREEN DATA
   C. Module: VALIDATE ADD SOFTWARE DATA
      Passed Down: ADD SOFTWARE SCREEN DATA
      Passed Up: CANCEL TRANSACTION (Control)
                     VALID ADD SOFTWARE DATA
   D. Module: READ SOFTWARE RECORD
      Passed Down: SOFTWARE INVENTORY NUMBER
      Passed Up: RECORD FOUND (Control)
   E. Module: VALIDATE HARDWARE REQUIREMENTS
      Passed Down: ADD SOFTWARE SCREEN DATA
      Passed Up: VALID DATA (Control)
                     ERROR MESSAGE

---

* Exercises preceded by a disk icon require the program Visible Analyst Workbench or another CASE tool. A disk is provided free of charge to any professor adopting this book. The examples on the disk may be imported into Visible Analyst and then used by students.

F. Module: DISPLAY ERROR MESSAGE
    Passed Down: ERROR MESSAGE
G. Module: PUT NEW SOFTWARE RECORD
    Passed Down: VALID ADD SOFTWARE DATA
H. Module: FORMAT SOFTWARE RECORD
    Passed Down: VALID ADD SOFTWARE DATA
    Passed Up: FORMATTED SOFTWARE RECORD I.
    Module: WRITE SOFTWARE RECORD
    Passed Down: FORMATTED SOFTWARE RECORD

E-5. Create the PRINT PROBLEM MACHINE REPORT structure chart. An outline of the modules follows, with each subordinate module indented.

```
PRINT PROBLEM MACHINE REPORT
        PRINT PROBLEM MACHINE LINES
                READ MACHINE RECORD
                DETERMINE PROBLEM MACHINE
                PRINT PROBLEM MACHINE LINE
                        PRINT HEADING LINES
                        WRITE REPORT LINE
        PRINT FINAL REPORT LINES
                WRITE REPORT LINE
```

E-6. Create the CHANGE SOFTWARE RECORD structure chart. Modules of the program are shown with subordinate modules indented.

```
CHANGE SOFTWARE FILE
        CHANGE SOFTWARE RECORDS
                GET SOFTWARE RECORD
                        DISPLAY SOFTWARE ID SCREEN
                        ACCEPT SOFTWARE ID SCREEN
                        FIND SOFTWARE RECORD
                        DISPLAY ERROR LINE
                OBTAIN SOFTWARE CHANGES
                        DISPLAY CHANGE SCREEN
                        ACCEPT SOFTWARE CHANGES
                        VALIDATE CHANGES
                        DISPLAY ERROR LINE
                PUT SOFTWARE RECORD
                        FORMAT SOFTWARE RECORD
                        REWRITE SOFTWARE RECORD
```

E-7. Create the SOFTWARE DETAILS INQUIRY structure chart. Modules are listed with subordinate modules indented (see next page).

```
INQUIRE SOFTWARE DETAILS
        INQUIRE SOFTWARE RECORD
                GET SOFTWARE RECORD
                        DISPLAY SOFTWARE ID SCREEN
                        ACCEPT SOFTWARE ID SCREEN
                        FIND SOFTWARE RECORD
                        DISPLAY ERROR LINE
```

DISPLAY INQUIRY SCREEN
FORMAT SOFTWARE INQUIRY SCREEN
DISPLAY SOFTWARE INQUIRY SCREEN

⊟ **E-8.** View the ADD MICROCOMPUTER system flowchart.

⊟ **E-9.** Modify the ADD SOFTWARE system flow. Add the following program rectangles below the INSTALL SOFTWARE manual process. Include input and output files and reports specified for each program.

Program:	UPDATE SOFTWARE RELATIONAL FILE
Input:	UPDATE SOFTWARE INSTALLATION LIST, document
	UPDATE INSTALLED SOFTWARE SCREEN, display
Output:	SOFTWARE RELATIONAL FILE, disk
	INSTALLED SOFTWARE TRANSACTION, disk
Program:	PRINT USER NOTIFICATION REPORT
Input:	INSTALLED SOFTWARE TRANSACTION, disk
Output:	USER NOTIFICATION REPORT, report

⊟ **E-10.** Create the ADD STAFF system flowchart. There are two programs: ADD STAFF and PRINT NEW STAFF LIST. Input to the ADD STAFF program is a NEW STAFF listing and an ADD NEW STAFF entry screen. The STAFF MASTER file is updated and a NEW STAFF LOG FILE is produced. The NEW STAFF LOG FILE is input to the PRINT NEW STAFF LIST program, producing the report NEW STAFF LIST.

E-11. Design test data on paper to test the ADD MICROCOMPUTER program. Use Access to test the screen. Note any discrepancies.

E-12. Design test data and predicted results for the ADD SOFTWARE program. Use Access to test the screen and note whether the results conformed to your predictions.

E-13. Design test data and predicted results for the ADD TRAINING CLASS program. Use Access to test the screen and note whether the results conformed to your predictions.

E-14. Design test data on paper to test the CHANGE SOFTWARE EXPERT program. Use Access to test the screen. Note any discrepancies.

21

SUCCESSFULLY IMPLEMENTING THE INFORMATION SYSTEM

IMPLEMENTATION APPROACHES

The process of assuring that the information system is operational and then allowing users to take over its operation for use and evaluation is called implementation. The systems analyst has several approaches to implementation that should be considered as the changeover to the new system is being prepared. These include shifting more computer power to users through distributed processing; training users; converting from the old system; and evaluating the new one.

The first approach to implementation concerns the movement of computer power to individual users by setting up and shifting computer power and responsibility to groups throughout the business with the help of distributed computing.

The second approach to implementation is using different strategies for training users and personnel, including taking them on their own level, using a variety of training techniques, and making sure that each user understands any new role that he or she must take on because of the new information system.

Another approach to implementation is choosing a conversion strategy. The systems analyst needs to weigh the situation and propose a conversion plan that is appropriate for the particular organization and information system.

The fourth approach to implementation involves evaluating the new or modified information system. The analyst needs to formulate performance measures on which to evaluate the system. Evaluations come from users, management, and analysts themselves.

IMPLEMENTING DISTRIBUTED SYSTEMS

If the reliability of a telecommunications network is high, it is possible to have distributed systems for businesses, a setup which can be conceived of as an application of telecommunications. The concept of distributed systems is used in many different ways. Here, it will be taken in a broad sense

829

so that it includes workstations that can communicate with each other and data processors, as well as different hierarchical architectural configurations of data processors that communicate with each other and that have differing data-storage capabilities.

The information architecture model that will likely dominate networking in the next few years is that of the client/server. In this model, the processing functions are delegated either to "clients" (users) or to "servers," depending on which machines are most suitable for executing the work. In this type of architecture, the client portion of a network application will run on the client system, with the server part of the application running on the file server. With a client/server model, users interact with limited parts of the application, including the user interface, data input, database queries, and report generation. Functions such as controlling user access to centralized databases, retrieving or processing data, and other aspects (such as managing peripheral devices) are handled by the server.

Client/Server Technology

The client/server (C/S) model, client/server computing, client/server technology, and client/server architecture all refer to a design model that can be thought of as applications running on a local area network (LAN). In very basic terms, you can picture the client requesting—and the server executing or in some way fulfilling—the request. The computers on the network are programmed to perform work efficiently by dividing up processing tasks among clients and servers. Figure 21.1 shows how a client/server model might be configured with a LAN. Note that several "clients" are depicted as user workstations.

When you think of client/server, you should think of a system that accentuates the users as the center of the work, with their interaction with data being the key concept. Although there are two elements working—the client and the server—it is the intent of the C/S model that the user views it as one system. Indeed the hope is that the user is basically unaware of how the client/server network is performing its distributed processing, since it should have the look and feel of a unified system. In a peer-to-peer network, PCs can act as either the server or the client, depending on the requirements of the application.

CLIENTS AS PART OF THE C/S MODEL USING A LAN. When you see the term "client," you might be tempted to think of people or users—for example, we speak of "clients of our consulting practice." However, in the client/server model, the term "client" refers not to people but to networked machines which are typical points of entry to the client/server system that is used by humans. Therefore, "clients" could be networked desktop computers; a workstation or laptop computers; or any way in which the user can enter the system.

Using a graphical user interface (GUI), individuals typically interface directly only with the client part. Client workstations use smaller programs that stay resident in the client to do "front-end processing" (as opposed to the "back-end" processing mentioned below), including communicating with the user. If an application is called a "client-based application," it means that the application resides in a client computer and cannot be accessed by other users on the network. Note that client-based applications require separate installation on each workstation if the LAN has not purchased a site license.

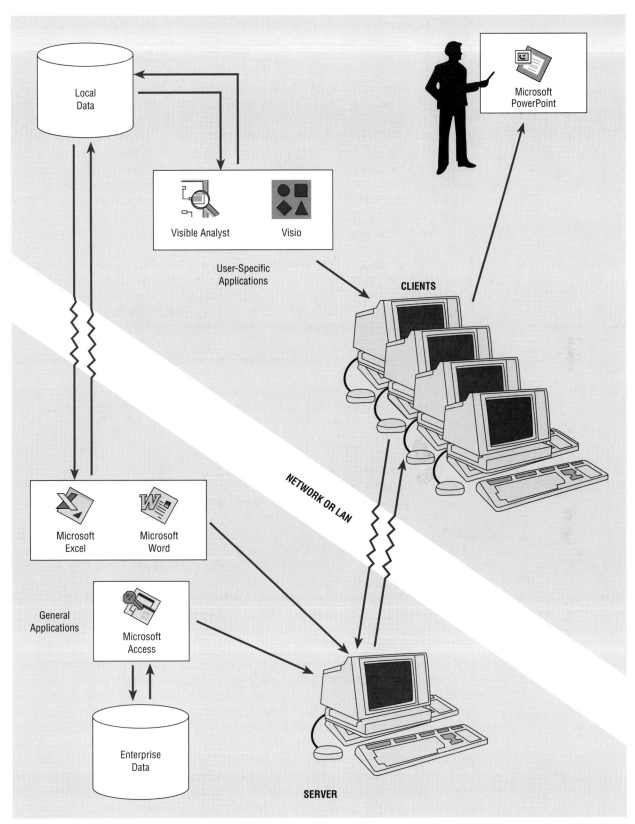

FIGURE 21.1
A client/server system configuration.

File server. File server is the term used to denote a computer on a LAN that stores on its hard disk the application programs and data files for all of the clients on the network. "Server-based" applications are types of client processing capabilities that permit the user to request network applications (programs stored on a network server rather than on a user's computer) from the server. Typically, "back-end" processing (things like a physical search of a database, for instance) will take place on a server. If a file server crashes, it would not affect client-based applications.

Designing a client/server network is a way to allocate resources in a LAN, so as to distribute computing power among the computers in the network. However, note it still makes sense to share some resources, which can be centralized in a file server. Client/server networks are proving to be a good, solid way to embody workgroup applications.

Print server. A print server on a LAN is accessible to all workstations. In contrast to a file server, a print server is a PC dedicated to receiving and (temporarily) storing files to be printed. The specialized software that the print server uses first enables it to store print jobs and then helps it to manage the distribution of printing tasks to printers hooked into the network.

See the section on designing Web sites in Chapter 15 for more information about Web applications. Note that although it sounds as if they are the same as print and file servers, Web servers are software, not a combination of software and hardware like the print servers and file servers discussed before.

WEIGHING THE ADVANTAGES AND DISADVANTAGES OF THE CLIENT/SERVER MODEL. Although many companies jumped right in and requested client/server systems, we have found from the experience of early adopters that C/S systems are not always the best solution to an organization's computing problems. Often, the systems designer is asked to endorse a client/server model that is already in the works. Just as with any other corporate computing proposal that you did not have an active part in creating, you must review the plan carefully. Will the organization's culture support a C/S model? What kinds of changes must be made in the informal culture and in the formal work procedures before C/S can be used to its full potential? What should your role as a systems analyst be in this situation?

Notice that although lower processing costs are cited as a benefit of the C/S model—and even though there is some anecdotal evidence to support this claim—there is very little actual data available to prove this. Certainly there are well-documented high start-up or switch-over costs associated with a movement to a C/S architecture. Applications for the client/server model must be written as two separate software components, each running on separate machines, but they must appear as if they are operating as one application. The client/server model is more expensive than other options, such as the X terminal model, which uses terminals to access remote computers. However, using the client/server model affords greater computer power and greater opportunity to customize applications.

Notice also that without the organizational support and structure required to realize the potential of putting "decision-making authority at user level and therefore closer to customers," this benefit is meaningless.

Types of Distributed Systems Networks

While networks can be characterized by their shape or topology, they are also discussed in terms of their geographic coverage and the kinds of services they offer. Standard types of networks include a wide-area network (WAN) and a local area network (LAN). Local area networks are standard for linking local computers and/or terminals within a department, building, or several buildings of an organization. Wide-area networks can serve users over several miles or across entire continents. There are four main types of distributed systems networks: hierarchical, star, ring, and bus. Each requires different hardware and software and has different capabilities.

Networking is now technically, economically, and operationally feasible for small offices as well, and it provides a solution that analysts should consider for small businesses. Network kits are sometimes called "networks in a box" since everything to set up a small network is provided for in one price (usually below $500). An example of one such kit includes adapters for PCs, an eight-port hub, and a good amount of cabling. Sometimes, worksheets to help you plan the network installation are also included in these bundles. Several vendors are offering easy-to-install network kits, including Lynksys, 3Com, Dayna, Hewlett-Packard, and NetGear.

Networking provides advantages for small businesses when one considers the possibility for the sharing of software and the improvement of group work. Also, small businesses may be able to invest in a better quality printer, CD-ROM drives, modems, or other peripherals because they need fewer of them when users can share resources over the network. Most of these exclude network operating system software, and this possibility allows the business flexibility in using whichever one fits the requirements of the small business.

HIERARCHICAL NETWORKS. In a basic hierarchical configuration, the host—a mainframe computer—controls all of the other nodes that include minicomputers and microcomputers. Notice that computers on the same level do not communicate with each other. With this arrangement, large-scale computing problems are handled by the mainframe, and lesser computing demands are handled on the correct level by either minicomputers or microcomputers.

STAR NETWORKS. Another popular configuration for distributed computing is the star network. A mainframe, PC, or workstation is designated the central node. As such, it communicates with the lesser nodes, but they cannot communicate directly with one another. A need for the microcomputers to communicate with each other would be met by one microcomputer sending data to the central node, which in turn would relay the data to a second microcomputer.

RING NETWORKS. Ring networks are another possibility for distributed computing. There is no central computer for a ring. Rather, its shape reminds us that all of the nodes are of equal computing power. With the use of a ring network, all microcomputers can communicate directly with one another, passing along all the messages they read to their correct destinations on the ring.

CHAPTER 21:
SUCCESSFULLY
IMPLEMENTING
THE INFORMATION
SYSTEM

833

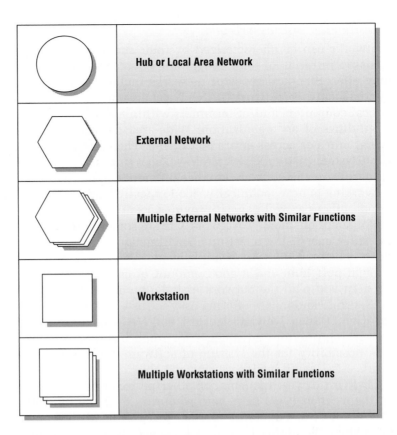

○	**Hub or Local Area Network**
⬡	**External Network**
⬡⬡	**Multiple External Networks with Similar Functions**
▢	**Workstation**
▢▢	**Multiple Workstations with Similar Functions**

BUS CONFIGURATIONS. Another type of network for distributed processing is the bus configuration. Bus configurations work well in close quarters, such as in a suite of offices where several different devices can be hooked together using a central cable. A bus configuration allows a great deal of change by permitting users to add or remove devices quite easily. In a bus configuration, the single, central cable serves as the only path.

Network Modeling

Since networking has become so important, the systems designer needs to consider network design. Whether a systems designer gets involved with decisions about token rings or Ethernet networks—or whether he or she worries about hardware like routers and bridges that must be in place when networks meet—the systems designer must always consider the logical design of networks. This is where network modeling enters in.

CASE tools such as Visible Analyst are not sufficient to help the systems designer with network modeling. It is possible to use some of a CASE tool's drawing capabilities, but forcing the data modeling tools to do network modeling just does not work. Therefore, we suggest using some sort of symbols (like the ones in Figure 21.2) to model the network. It is useful to have distinct symbols to distinguish among hubs, external networks, and workstations. It is also useful to adopt a convention for illustrating multiple networks and workstations.

Typically, a top-down approach is appropriate. The first step is to draw a network decomposition diagram that provides an overview of the system. Next, draw a hub connectivity diagram. Finally, explode the hub connectivity diagram to show the various workstations and how they are to be connected.

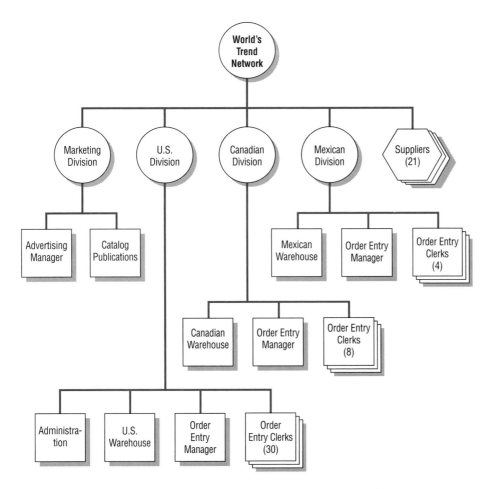

FIGURE 21.3
A network decomposition diagram for World's Trend.

DRAWING A NETWORK DECOMPOSITION DIAGRAM. We can illustrate drawing a network decomposition model by referring once again to the World's
Trend Catalog Division example from earlier chapters. Start by drawing a circle at the top and labeling it "World's Trend Network." Now draw a number
of circles on the level below, as shown in Figure 21.3. These circles represent hubs for the marketing division and each of the three order-entry and
distribution centers (the U.S. Division, the Canadian Division, and the Mexican Division).

We can extend this further by drawing another level. This time we can
draw in the workstations. For example, the Marketing Division has two
workstations connected to it, while the U.S. Division has 33 workstations on
its LAN (Administration, the U.S. Warehouse, the Order-Entry Manager, and
30 Order-Entry Clerks). This network is simplified for the purpose of providing a readily understandable example.

CREATING A HUB CONNECTIVITY DIAGRAM. The hub connectivity diagram
is useful for showing how the major hubs are connected. At World's Trend
(see Figure 21.4), there are four major hubs that are all connected to one another. In addition, there are external hubs (suppliers) that need to be notified
when inventory drops below a certain point, and so on. Each of the three
country divisions are connected to the 21 suppliers; however, the Marketing
Division does not need to be connected to suppliers.

CHAPTER 21:
SUCCESSFULLY
IMPLEMENTING
THE INFORMATION
SYSTEM

835

FIGURE 21.4
A hub connectivity diagram
for World's Trend.

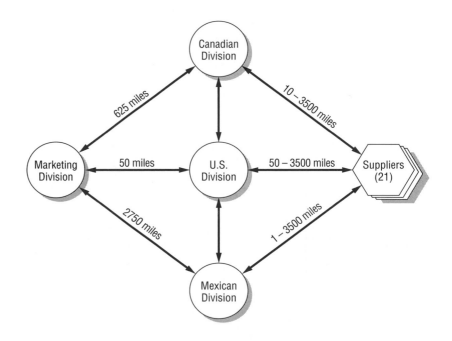

To produce an effective hub connectivity diagram, start by drawing all of the hubs. Then experiment (perhaps sketching it first on a sheet of paper) to see which links are necessary. Once this is done, you can redraw the diagram so it is attractive and communicates well to users.

EXPLODING THE HUB CONNECTIVITY DIAGRAM INTO A WORKSTATION CONNECTIVITY DIAGRAM. The purpose of network modeling is to show the connectivity of workstations in some detail. To do so, we explode the hub connectivity diagram. Figure 21.5 shows each of the 33 workstations for the U.S. Division and how they are to be connected.

Draw the diagrams for this level by examining the third level of the network decomposition diagram. Group items such as "Order-Entry Manager" and "Order-Entry Clerks" together, since you already recognize that they must be connected. Use a special symbol to show multiple workstations and indicate in parentheses the number of similar workstations. In our example, there are 30 order-entry clerks.

On the perimeter of the diagram, place workstations that must be connected to other hubs. In this way, it will be easier to represent these connections using arrows. Draw the external connections in a different color or use thicker arrows. External connections are usually long-distance. For example, Administration is connected to the Marketing Division, which is 50 miles away, and also to the Canadian and Mexican Divisions. The warehouse needs to communicate directly with the Canadian and Mexican warehouses in case it is possible to obtain the merchandise from another warehouse. Order-Entry Managers and Clerks do not have to be connected to anyone outside of their LAN.

Hub connectivity diagrams can be exploded to many levels. If doing so makes sense in your particular application, go ahead and draw it that way. There is no limit to the possible number of explosions.

Hub connectivity and workstation connectivity diagrams can be drawn using software packages as well. Although it may be difficult if you restrict

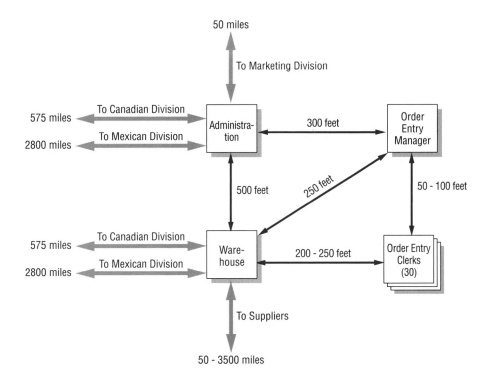

FIGURE 21.5
A workstation connectivity
diagram for World's Trend.

yourself to using CASE tool software, it is relatively simple if you use flexible drag-and-drop software, such as Visio. (See Figure 21.6.)

Visio even contains stencils that depict certain pieces of equipment if you wish to go into that much detail. Using specific stencils, an analyst could drag each symbol from the template to the piece of paper. Figure 21.7

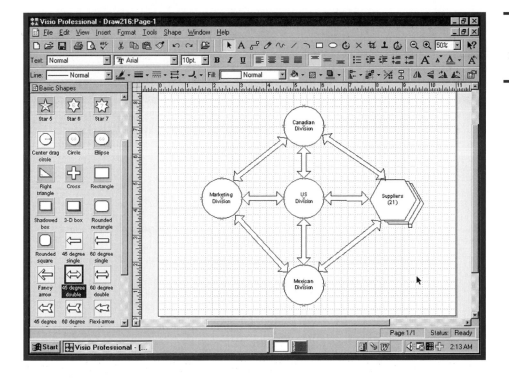

FIGURE 21.6
Analysts can draw hub connectivity diagrams using software like Visio Professional.

CHAPTER 21:
SUCCESSFULLY
IMPLEMENTING
THE INFORMATION
SYSTEM

837

FIGURE 21.7
A more detailed diagram of
two networks, drawn by selecting symbols from a template and dragging them to the
piece of paper. This diagram
was drawn using Visio Professional by Visio Corporation.

shows how two networks are set up for a software manufacturer. The top
part of the figure illustrates the program development sector's network of the
organization, while the bottom part shows the sales department's network.

Additional detail is shown by zooming in on the program development
network. In Figure 21.8, we can see that there are three PCs hooked up to a

FIGURE 21.8
A closer view of the network
shows what type of equip-
ment is connected to the program development group.

bus network that has a laser printer, a scanner, a modem for connection to laptop computers, and a server. Packages, such as Visio, are extremely useful to the systems analyst because they save time and enhance communication by using standard symbols.

Groupware

Writing applications either for an entire organization or a solitary decision maker has also begun to change dramatically. Because much of the organization's work is actually accomplished in groups or teams, there is now a powerful movement afoot to develop special software called "groupware" that supports people who work together in the organization. Groupware takes advantage of the potential synergies and power available from networked PCs in either local area networks (LANs), wide-area networks (WANs), or the Web. Groupware products can help group members to schedule and attend meetings, share data, create and analyze documents, communicate in unstructured ways with one another via e-mail, hold group conferences, do image management on the departmental level, and manage and monitor workflow.

We are still far from an integrated approach to groupware, which means that often developers will create a product which supports some combination but not all of the foregoing functions. At the heart of most groupware is a useful, easy-to-use, flexible e-mail system. If asked to develop workgroup applications, you should first assess whether there is currently a usable e-mail system in place, upon which to build other functions.

You can see from the wide range of possible capabilities that there is no standard definition for what comprises groupware. In fact, each software company seems to be putting forward a different vision of what kind of support groups need in order to function best.

The product that has defined groupware for many users is Lotus Notes, which Lotus corporate officers aptly refer to as "the Network GUI." Notes features a document-oriented database that has a wide range of options and far fewer restrictions than traditional databases. Group users working with Notes will find its fields can handle numerous fonts, text colors, scanned images, hypertext links to other documents in Notes, and even push buttons that are actually Notes macros. Using a simple, straightforward, "no-frills" interface, Notes helps novices get up and running quickly. All Notes databases use an identical interface, so that once a group member has learned one database, it is easy to use a new one.

Additionally, Notes has been called "mail-integrated" and provides flexible, wide-ranging mail capabilities that support the way group members work; it also lets them use mail in some novel way (for example, to send Notes messages to a database).

Many organizations experience difficulty in getting networked applications to run smoothly with adequate backups and security. In other words, many network applications purporting to be groupware do not deliver what has been promised because of both initial faulty development and subsequent poor implementation and backup. Lotus Notes has successfully addressed this pitfall by using a breakthrough replication technology that enables users to keep many copies of a database (whether they are on LANs or remote workstations) and to synchronize them by using background dial-up phone connections from time to time. Lotus Notes has been criticized as a very expensive, monolithic option for supporting group work, but it has attracted a large following.

CHAPTER 21:
SUCCESSFULLY
IMPLEMENTING
THE INFORMATION
SYSTEM

839

Advantages of Distributed Systems
• Allow data storage out of the way of on-line, real-time transactions
• Allow less expensive media for data storage when all data are not needed all of the time by all users
• Lower equipment cost since not all system parts need to perform all functions
• Lower equipment cost by permitting flexibility in choice of manufacturer
• Less expensive than large systems initially since expansion can be planned for without actually purchasing hardware

While most software companies agree to the importance of supporting group work, they differ in their visions of what groups and individuals need for support. For example, Novell currently offers groupware features such as e-mail, messaging, and calendaring in a networked environment. In the future, WordPerfect envisions supporting users by enabling them to pull together a report containing objects gathered from anywhere on the network, regardless of what systems were used to create them. Thus, a report could have text from the annual report, bar charts from last week's sales meeting, and scanned images of hand-drawn sketches that portray the latest departmental brainstorming session. In such a case, the computer would search out the various pieces, and the software would coordinate them for use in one document.

Another approach to developing groupware has been taken by Microsoft, which is giving rudimentary workgroup capability to products such as Windows for Workgroups and Windows NT. New graphical user interfaces dubbed Chicago and Cairo are also supposed to include an "object store" similar to the one currently available in Lotus Notes, so that Microsoft operating systems will have built-in workgroup capabilities. In the short term, Microsoft is working with smaller developers and consultants to develop workgroup application solutions. This bottom-up approach seems to be showing successful results as well. Different groupware offers different forms of support.

ADVANTAGES OF DISTRIBUTED SYSTEMS. Distributed systems allow the storage of data where they are not "in the way" of any on-line real-time transactions. For example, response time on inquiries might be improved if not all records need to be searched through before a response is made. Additionally, not all data are needed by all users all of the time, and so they can be stored in less expensive media at a different site and only accessed when needed.

Use of distributed systems can also lower equipment costs, since not all parts of the system need to be able to perform all functions. Some capabilities, such as processing and storage, can be shared.

Distributed systems can also help lower costs by permitting flexibility in the choice of manufacturer, since the whole focus of networks is on communicating between nodes and manufacturers make compatible components. This compatibility allows the user to shop for price as well as for function. Furthermore, distributed systems can be less expensive initially than large systems because it is feasible to plan for expansion without actually having to buy hardware at the time the system is implemented. Notice that developing corporate intranets is a proactive way to network organizational members, a way that can also serve as a means for cutting down on

Disadvantages of Distributed Systems
• Difficulty in achieving a reliable system • Security concerns increase commensurately when more individuals have access to the system • Analysts must emphasize the network and the interactions it provides and deemphasize the power of subsystems • Choosing the wrong level of computing to support (i.e., individual instead of department, department instead of branch)

FIGURE 21.10
There are four chief disadvantages to creating distributed systems.

problematical aspects of the Internet (such as aimless Web surfing during corporate time or possible security breakdowns caused by lack of firewalls) while at the same time supporting group work with useful applications. Extranets formed with suppliers and other important partners are also excellent ways of demonstrating that a business is outward looking and accessible. Advantages of distributed systems are given in Figure 21.9.

DISADVANTAGES OF DISTRIBUTED SYSTEMS. Distributed systems pose some unique problems that centralized computer systems do not. The analyst needs to weigh these problems against the advantages just presented and to raise them with the concerned business as well.

The first problem is that of network reliability. In order to make a network an asset rather than a liability, it must be possible to transmit, receive, process, and store data reliably. If there are too many problems with system reliability, the system will be abandoned.

Distributing greater computing power to individuals increases the threat to security because of widespread access. The need for secret passwords, secure computer rooms, and adequate security training of personnel are all concerns that multiply when distributed systems are implemented.

Systems analysts creating distributed systems need to focus on the network itself, or on the synergistic aspect of distributed systems. Their power resides in their ability to interact as user work groups share data. If the relationship between subsystems is ignored or deemphasized, you are creating more problems than you are solving. Disadvantages of distributed systems are listed in Figure 21.10.

TRAINING USERS

Systems analysts engage in an educational process with users that is called training. Throughout the systems development life cycle, the user has been involved, so that by now the analyst should possess an accurate assessment of the users who must be trained. As we have seen, information centers retain trainers of their own.

In the implementation of large projects, the analyst will often be managing the training rather than be personally involved in it. One of the most prized assets the analyst can bring to any training situation is the ability to see the system from the users viewpoint. The analyst must never forget what it is like to face a new system. Those recollections can help analysts empathize with users and facilitate their training.

CHAPTER 21:
SUCCESSFULLY
IMPLEMENTING
THE INFORMATION
SYSTEM

841

FIGURE 21.11
It may be possible to use
many different trainers in a
large systems project.

Possible Trainers	Who to Train	
	Primary Users	**Secondary Users**
Vendors		X
Systems Analysts	X	X
External Paid Trainers		X
In-House Trainers	X	
Other System Users	X	

The analyst has several options when considering which trainers to use.

The choice of trainer depends partially on who is being trained.

Training Strategies

Training strategies are determined by who is being trained and by who will train them. The analyst will want to ensure that anyone whose work is affected by the new information system is properly trained by the appropriate trainer.

WHO TO TRAIN. All people who will have secondary or primary use of the system must be trained. This includes everyone from data-entry personnel to those who will use output to make decisions without personally using a computer. The amount of training a system requires thus depends on how much someone's job will change because of the new system.

You must ensure that users of different skill levels and job interests are separated. It is certain trouble to include novices in the same training sessions as experts, since novices are quickly lost, and experts are rapidly bored with basics. Both groups are then lost.

PEOPLE WHO TRAIN USERS. For a large project, many different trainers may be used depending on how many users must be trained and who they are, as shown in Figure 21.11. Possible training sources include:

1. Vendors.
2. Systems analysts.
3. External paid trainers.
4. In-house trainers.
5. Other system users.

This list gives just a few of the options the analyst has in planning for and providing training.

Large vendors often provide off-site, one- or two-day training sessions on their equipment as part of the service benefits offered when corporations purchase expensive software. These sessions include both lectures and hands-on training in a focused environment.

Since systems analysts know the organization's people and the system, they can often provide good training. The use of analysts for training purposes depends on their availability, since they also are expected to oversee all of the implementation process.

External paid trainers are sometimes brought into the organization to help with training. They may have broad experience in teaching people how to use a variety of computers, but they may not give the hands-on training that is needed for some users. Additionally, they may not be able to custom-tailor their presentations enough to make them meaningful to users.

Full-time, in-house trainers are usually familiar with personnel and can tailor materials to their needs. One of the drawbacks of in-house trainers is that they may possess expertise in areas other than information systems, and they may therefore lack the depth of technical expertise that users require.

It is also possible to have any of these trainers train a small group of people from each functional area that will be using the new information system. They in turn can then be used to train the remaining users. This approach can work well if the original trainees still have access to materials and trainers as resources when they themselves are providing training. Otherwise, it might degenerate into a trial-and-error situation rather than a structured one.

Guidelines for Training

The analyst has four major guidelines for setting up training. They are: (1) establishing measurable objectives, (2) using appropriate training methods, (3) selecting suitable training sites, and (4) employing understandable training materials.

TRAINING OBJECTIVES. Who is being trained in large part dictates the training objectives. Training objectives for each group must be spelled out clearly. Well-defined objectives are of enormous help in letting trainees know what is expected of them. Additionally, objectives allow evaluation of training when it is complete. For example, operators must know such basics as turning on the machine, what to do when common errors occur, basic troubleshooting, and how to end an entry.

TRAINING METHODS. Each user and operator will need slightly different training. To some extent, their jobs determine what they need to know, and their personalities, experience, and background determine how they learn best. Some users learn best by seeing, others by hearing, still others by doing. Since it is usually not possible to customize training for an individual, a combination of methods is often the best way to proceed. That way, most users are reached through one method or another.

Methods for those who learn best by seeing include demonstrations of equipment and exposure to training manuals. Those who learn best by hearing will benefit from lectures about procedures, discussions, and question-and-answer sessions among trainers and trainees. Those who learn best by doing need hands-on experience with new equipment. For jobs such as that of computer operator hands-on experience is essential, whereas a quality assurance manager for a production line may only need to see output, learn how to interpret it, and know when it is scheduled to arrive.

CHAPTER 21:
SUCCESSFULLY
IMPLEMENTING
THE INFORMATION
SYSTEM

843

Elements	Relevant Factors
Training Objectives	Depend on requirements of user's job
Training Methods	Depend on user's job, personality, background, and experience; use combination of lecture, demonstration, hands-on, and study
Training Sites	Depend on training objectives, cost, availability; free vendor sites with operable equipment; in-house installation; rented facilities
Training Materials	Depend on user's needs; operating manuals, cases, prototypes of equipments and output; on-line tutorials

TRAINING SITES. Training takes place in many different locations, some of which are more conducive to learning than others. Large computer vendors provide special off-site locations where operable equipment is maintained free of charge. Their trainers offer hands-on experience as well as seminars in a setting that allows users to concentrate on learning the new system. One of the disadvantages of off-site training is that users are away from the organizational context within which they must eventually exist.

On-site training within the users' organization is also possible with several different kinds of trainers. The advantage is that users see the equipment placed as it will be when it is fully operational. A serious disadvantage is that trainees often feel guilty about not fulfilling their regular job duties if they remain on-site for training. Thus, full concentration on training may not be possible.

Off-site training sites are also available for a fee through consultants and vendors. These can be set up in places with rented meeting space, such as a hotel, or they may even be permanent facilities maintained by the trainers. These arrangements allow workers to be free from regular job demands, but they may not provide equipment for hands-on training.

TRAINING MATERIALS. In planning for the training of users, systems analysts must realize the importance of well-prepared training materials. These include training manuals; training cases, in which users are assigned to work through a case that incorporates most of the commonly encountered interactions with the system; and prototypes and mock-ups of output. Users of larger systems will sometimes be able to train on elaborate Web-based simulations or software that is identical to what is being written or purchased. Most packaged software provides on-line tutorials that illustrate basic functions, or vendors may maintain Web sites that feature pages devoted to FAQ (Frequently Asked Questions), the answers to which can be downloaded and printed. Changes to manuals can also be gleaned from many vendors' Web sites.

Because the user's understanding of the system depends on them, training materials must be clearly written. This means training materials should be well indexed, written for the correct audience with a minimum of jargon, and available to everyone who needs them. A summary of considerations for training objectives, methods, sites, and materials is provided in Figure 21.12.

CONSULTING OPPORTUNITY 21.1

You Can Lead a Fish to Water . . . But You Can't Make It Drink

Sam Monroe, Belle Uga, Wally Ide, and you make up a four-member systems analysis team that is developing an information system to help managers monitor and control water temperature, the number of fish released, and other factors at a large commercial fish hatchery. (They were last seen in Consulting Opportunity 8.2, when they asked you, as their fourth member, to help solve a problem involving the timely delivery of a system prototype.)

With your input, the team successfully turned the tide of the earlier dilemma, and the project has continued. Now you are discussing the training that you have begun to undertake for managers and other systems users. Due to some scheduling difficulties, you have decided to cut down on the number of different training sessions offered. This has resulted in primary and secondary users being in the same training sessions in some instances.

Laurie Hook, one of the operators who is being trained, has been in the same training "tank" with Wade Boot, one of the managers with whom you have been working. Both Laurie and Wade have come to the team privately with different concerns. Wade told you, "I'm mad that I have to type in my own data in the sessions. The Mississippi will freeze solid before I ever do that on my job. But I've got to know *when* to expect output and how to interpret it when it comes. I'm not spending time in training sessions if I can't get that."

Laurie, who shares training sessions with Wade, also complained to your group. "We should be getting more hands-on training. All we hear is a bunch of lectures. It's like school. Not only that, the managers in the group like to spin these 'fish stories' about what happened to them with the old system. It's boring. I want to know how to operate the thing. It's bait-and-switch, if you ask me. I'm not learning what you said I would, and besides, with all of those bosses in there, I feel like a fish out of water."

What problems are occurring with the training sessions? How can they be addressed, given the scheduling constraints mentioned? What basic advice on setting up training sessions did your team ignore?

CONVERSION

A third approach to implementation is physically converting the old information system to the new or modified one. There are many conversion strategies available to analysts, and there is also a contingency approach that takes into account several organizational variables in deciding which conversion strategy to use. These is no single best way to proceed with conversion. The importance of adequate planning and scheduling of conversion (which often takes many weeks), file backup, and adequate security cannot be overemphasized.

Conversion Strategies

The five strategies for converting from the old system to the new are given in Figure 21.13.

1. Direct changeover.
2. Parallel conversion.
3. Phased or gradual conversion.
4. Modular prototype conversion.
5. Distributed conversion.

Each of the five conversion approaches is described separately in the upcoming subsections.

CHAPTER 21:
SUCCESSFULLY
IMPLEMENTING
THE INFORMATION
SYSTEM

845

FIGURE 21.13
Five conversion strategies for
information systems.

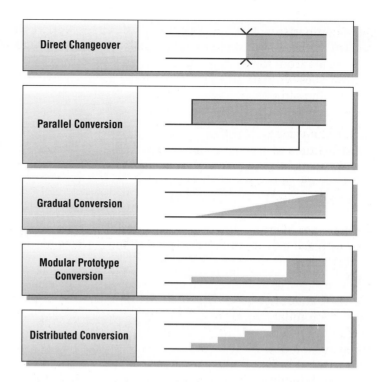

DIRECT CHANGEOVER. Conversion by direct changeover means that on a specified date, the old system is dropped and the new system is put into use. Direct changeover can only be successful if extensive testing is done beforehand, and it works best when some delays in processing can be tolerated. Sometimes, direct changeover is done in response to a government mandate. An advantage of direct changeover is that users have no possibility of using the old system rather than the new one. Adaptation is a necessity.

Direct changeover is considered a risky approach to conversion, and its disadvantages are numerous. For instance, long delays might ensue if errors occur, since there is no alternate way to accomplish processing. Additionally, users may resent being forced into using an unfamiliar system without recourse. Finally, there is no adequate way to compare new results with old.

PARALLEL CONVERSION. This refers to running the old system and the new system at the same time, in parallel. This is the most frequently used conversion approach, but its popularity may be in decline because it works best when a computerized system replaces a manual one. Both systems are run simultaneously for a specified period of time, and the reliability of results is examined. When the same results can be gained over time, the new system is put into use, and the old one is stopped.

The advantages of running both systems in parallel include the possibility of checking new data against old data in order to catch any errors in processing in the new system. Parallel processing also offers a feeling of security to users, who are not forced to make an abrupt change to the new system.

There are many disadvantages to parallel conversion. These include the cost of running two systems at the same time and the burden on employees of virtually doubling their workload during conversion. Another disadvantage is that unless the system being replaced is a manual one, it is difficult to make comparisons between outputs of the new system and the old one. Supposedly, the new system was created to improve on the old one. Therefore, outputs from the systems should differ. Finally, it is understandable that employees who are faced with a choice between two systems will continue to use the old one because of their familiarity with it.

GRADUAL CONVERSION. Gradual or phased conversion attempts to combine the best features of the earlier two plans, without incurring all of the risks. In this plan, the volume of transactions handled by the new system is gradually increased as the system is phased in. The advantages of this approach include allowing users to get involved with the system gradually and the possibility of detecting and recovering from errors without a lot of down time. Disadvantages of gradual conversion include taking too long to get the new system in place and its inappropriateness for conversion of small, uncomplicated systems.

MODULAR PROTOTYPE CONVERSION. This approach to conversion uses the building of modular, operational prototypes (as discussed in Chapter 8) to change from old systems to new in a gradual manner. As each module is modified and accepted, it is put into use. One advantage is that each module is thoroughly tested before being used. Another advantage is that users are familiar with each module as it becomes operational.

The fact that prototyping is often not feasible automatically rules out this approach for many conversions. Another disadvantage is that special attention must be paid to interfaces so that the modules being built actually work as a system.

DISTRIBUTED CONVERSION. This refers to a situation in which many installations of the same system are contemplated, as is the case in banking or in franchises such as restaurants or clothing stores. One entire conversion is done (with any of the four approaches considered already) at one site. When that conversion is successfully completed, other conversions are done for other sites.

An advantage of distributed conversion is that problems can be detected and contained rather than inflicted simultaneously on all sites. A disadvantage is that even when one conversion is successful, each site will have its own peculiarities to work through, and these must be handled accordingly.

A contingency approach to deciding on a conversion strategy is recommended—that is, the analyst considers many factors (including the wishes of clients) in choosing a conversion strategy. Obviously, no particular conversion approach is equally suitable for every system implementation.

Security

Security of computer facilities, stored data, and the information generated is part of a successful conversion. Recognition of the need for security is a natural outgrowth of the belief that information is a key organizational resource, as discussed in Chapter 1. With increasingly complex transactions and many innovative exchanges, the Web has brought heightened security concerns to the IS professional's world.

CHAPTER 21:
SUCCESSFULLY
IMPLEMENTING
THE INFORMATION
SYSTEM

847

It is useful to think of security of systems, data, and information on an imaginary continuum from totally secure to totally open. Although there is no such thing as a totally secure system, the actions analysts and users take are meant to move systems toward the secure end of the continuum by lessening the system's vulnerability. It should be noted that as more people in the organization gain greater computer power, gain access to the Web, or hook up with intranets and extranets, security becomes increasingly difficult and complex. Sometimes, organizations will hire a security consultant to work with the systems analyst when security is crucial to successful operations.

Security is the responsibility of all those who come into contact with the system and is only as good as the most lax behavior or policy in the organization. Security has three interrelated aspects: physical, logical, and behavioral. All three must work together if the quality of security is to remain high.

PHYSICAL SECURITY. Physical security refers to securing the computer facility, its equipment, and software through physical means. These can include controlling access to the computer room by means of machine-readable badges or a human sign-in/sign-out system; using closed-circuit television cameras to monitor computer areas; and backing up data frequently and storing backups in a fireproof, waterproof area.

Additionally, small computer equipment should be secured so that a typical user cannot move it, and it should be guaranteed uninterrupted power. Alarms that notify appropriate people of fire, flood, or unauthorized human intrusion must be in working order at all times.

Decisions about physical security should be made when the analyst is planning for computer facilities and equipment purchase. Obviously, physical security can be much tighter if anticipated in advance of actual installation and if computer rooms are specially equipped for security when they are constructed rather than outfitted as an afterthought.

LOGICAL SECURITY. Logical security refers to logical controls within software itself. The logical controls familiar to most users are passwords or authorization codes of some sort. When used, they permit the user with the correct password to enter the system or a particular part of a database.

However, passwords are treated cavalierly in many organizations. Employees have been overheard yelling a password across crowded offices, posting passwords by taping them to their terminals, and sharing personal passwords with authorized employees who have forgotten their own.

Special encryption software has been developed to protect commercial transactions on the Web, and business transactions are proliferating. However, Internet fraud is also up sharply, with few authorities trained in catching Internet criminals and a "Wild West, or Last Frontier" mentality clearly at play in many instances when authorities have been able to apprehend Web criminals.

One way for networks to cut down on the risk of exposure to security challenges from the outside world is to build what is called a firewall or a firewall system. Briefly, a firewall constructs a barricade between an internal organization's network and an external (inter)network, such as the Internet. The internal network is assumed to be trustworthy and secure, while the Internet is not. Firewalls are intended to prevent communication into or out of the network that has not been authorized, and which is not wanted. A fire-wall system is not a perfect remedy for organization/Internet security; it is an additional layer of security, which is now widely accepted. There is still no fully-integrated way to address security problems with internal and external networks, but they do deserve analysts' attention when they are planning any new or improved systems.

Logical and physical controls are important but clearly not enough to provide adequate security. Behavioral changes are also necessary.

BEHAVIORAL SECURITY. The behavioral expectations of an organization are encoded in its policy manuals and even on signs posted on bulletin boards, as we saw in Chapter 4. But the behavior that organization members internalize is also critical to the success of security efforts. (Note that one of the reasons that firewalls are not attack-proof is because many attacks to information systems come from within the organization.)

Security can begin with the screening of employees who will eventually have access to computers, data, and information in order to ensure that their interests are consistent with the organization's interests and that they fully understand the importance of carrying through on security procedures. Policies regarding security must be written, distributed, and updated so that employees are fully aware of expectations and responsibilities. Typically, this is where the systems analyst will first have contact with the behavioral aspects of security. Some organizations have written rules or policies prohibiting employees from surfing the Web during work hours—or even prohibiting Web surfing at all, if company equipment is involved. Other corporations use software locks to limit access to Web sites that are judged to be objectionable in the workplace, such as games, gambling, or pornographic sites.

Part of the behavioral facet of security is monitoring behavior at irregular intervals in order to ascertain that proper procedures are being followed and to correct any behaviors that may have eroded with time. Having the system log the number of unsuccessful sign-on attempts of users is one way to monitor whether unauthorized users are attempting to sign on to the system. Periodic and frequent inventorying of equipment and software is desirable. In addition, unusually long sessions or atypical after-hours access to the system should be examined.

Employees should clearly understand what is expected of them, what is prohibited, and the extent of their rights and responsibilities. You should disclose all monitoring that is being done or that is being contemplated, and you should supply the rationale behind it. This includes the use of video cameras, software monitoring, and so on.

Output generated by the system must be recognized for its potential to put the organization at risk in some circumstances. Controls for output include screens that can only be accessed via password; the classification of information (that is, to whom it can be distributed and when); and secure storage of printed and magnetically stored documents.

In some cases, provision for shredding documents that are classified or proprietary must be made. Shredding or pulverization services can be contracted from an outside firm that, for a fee, will shred magnetic media, typewriter and printer cartridges, and paper. A large corporation may shred upwards of 76,000 pounds of output in a variety of media annually.

CHAPTER 21:
SUCCESSFULLY
IMPLEMENTING
THE INFORMATION
SYSTEM

849

Other Conversion Considerations

Conversion also entails other details for the analyst, which include:

1. Ordering equipment (up to three months ahead of planned conversion).
2. Ordering any necessary materials that are externally supplied to the information system, such as toner cartridges, paper, preprinted forms, and magnetic media.
3. Appointing a manager to supervise or personally supervising the preparation of the installation site.
4. Planning, scheduling, and supervising programmers and data-entry personnel who must convert all relevant files and databases.

For many implementations, your chief role will be accurately estimating the time needed for each activity, appointing people to manage each subproject, and coordinating their work. For smaller projects, you will do much of the conversion work on your own. Many of the project management techniques learned in Chapter 3, such as Gantt charts, PERT, and successfully communicating with team members, are useful for planning and controlling implementation.

Organizational Metaphors and Their Relationship to Successful Systems

Be aware of organizational metaphors when you attempt to implement a system you have just developed. Our recent exploratory research has suggested that the success or failure of a system might have something to do with the metaphors used by organizational members.

When people in the organization describe the company as a zoo, you can infer that the atmosphere is chaotic; while if it is described as a machine, everything is working in an orderly fashion. When the predominant metaphor is war, journey, or jungle, the environment is chaotic, like the zoo. However, the war and journey metaphors are oriented toward an organization goal, while the zoo and jungle are not.

In addition to the machine, metaphors such as society, family, and the game, all signify order and rules. While the machine and game are goal oriented, the society and zoo do not stress the company's goal but instead allow the individuals in the corporation to set their own standards and rewards. Another metaphor, the organism, appears balanced between order and chaos, corporate and individual goals.

Our research suggests that the success or failure of a system may have something to do with the predominant metaphor. Figure 21.14 shows that a traditional MIS will tend to succeed when the predominant metaphor is society, machine, or family, but it might not succeed if the metaphor is war or jungle (two chaotic metaphors). Notice, however, that competitive systems will most likely succeed if the metaphor is war.

Positive metaphors appear to be the game, organism, and machine. Negative metaphors appear to be the jungle and the zoo. The others (journey, war, society, and family) show mixed success depending on the type of information system being developed. More research needs to be done in this area. In the meantime, the systems analyst should be aware that metaphors communicated in interviews could be meaningful and may

Success less likely with these metaphors	Type of Information System	Success more likely with these metaphors
War Jungle	Traditional MIS	Family Society Machine
War Journey	Decision Support Systems	Family Society Organism
Jungle Zoo	Expert Systems / AI	Game Organism Machine
Society Zoo	Cooperative Systems	Journey Game Organism
Zoo Family Society	Competitive Systems	War Game Organism
Journey Zoo	Executive Information Systems	Organism Game

FIGURE 21.14
Organizational metaphors may contribute to the success or failure of an information system.

even be a contributing factor toward the success of the information system implementation.

EVALUATION

Throughout the systems development life cycle, the analyst, management, and users have been evaluating the evolving information systems and networks in order to give feedback for their eventual improvement. Evaluation is also called for following system implementation.

Evaluation Techniques

In recognition of the fact that the ongoing evaluation of information systems and networks is important, many evaluation techniques have been devised. These techniques include cost-benefit analysis (as discussed in Chapter 13); models that attempt to estimate the value of a decision based on the effects of revised information using information theory; simulation or Bayesian statistics; user evaluations that emphasize implementation problems and user involvement; and information system utility approaches that examine the properties of information.

Each type of evaluation serves a different purpose and has inherent drawbacks. Cost-benefit analysis may be difficult to apply since information systems provide information about objectives for the first time, making it impossible to compare performance before and after implementation of the system or distributed network. The revised decision evaluation approach presents difficulty since all variables involved with the design, development, and implementation of the information system cannot be calculated or quantified. The user involvement approach yields some insight for new projects by providing a checklist of potentially dysfunctional behavior by various organizational members, but it stresses implementation over other aspects of IS design. The information system utility approach to evaluation can be more comprehensive than the others if it is expanded and systematically applied.

CHAPTER 21:
SUCCESSFULLY
IMPLEMENTING
THE INFORMATION
SYSTEM

851

The Sweet Smell of Success

Recall that in Consulting Opportunity 3.1, "The Sweetest Sound I've Ever Sipped," in Chapter 3, you met Felix Straw. Devise a systems solution that will address the problems discussed there. (*Hint:* The technology is important, but so are the way that people can use it.) Your solution should stress collaboration, flexibility, adaptability and access. Use network diagramming to illustrate your solution. In a few paragraphs, write a rationale for why your solution should be chosen.

The Information System Utility Approach

The information system utility approach for evaluating information systems can be a comprehensive and fruitful technique for measuring the success of a developed system. It also can serve as a guide in the development of any future projects the analyst might undertake.

Utilities of information include possession, form, place, and time. In order to evaluate the information system comprehensively, these utilities must be expanded to include actualization utility and goal utility. Then the utilities can be seen to address adequately the questions of who (possession), what (form), where (place), when (time), how (actualization), and why (goal). An example of this information utility approach can be seen in the evaluation of a blood inventory system in Figure 21.15.

POSSESSION UTILITY. Possession utility answers the question of who should receive output—in other words, who should be responsible for making decisions. Information has no value in the hands of someone who lacks the power to make improvements in the system or someone who lacks the ability to use the information productively.

FORM UTILITY. Form utility answers the question of what kind of output is distributed to the decision maker. The documents must be useful for a particular decision maker, in terms of the document's format and the jargon used. Acronyms and column headings must be meaningful to the user. Furthermore, information itself must be in an appropriate form. For example, the user should not have to divide one number by another to obtain a ratio. Instead, a ratio should be calculated and prominently displayed. At the other extreme is the presentation of too much irrelevant data. Information overload certainly decreases the value of an information system.

PLACE UTILITY. Place utility answers the question of where the information is distributed. Information must be delivered to the location where the decision is made. More detailed reports or previous management reports should be filed or stored to facilitate future access.

TIME UTILITY. Time utility answers the question of when information is delivered. Information must arrive before a decision is made. Late information has no utility. At the other extreme is the delivery of information too far in advance of the decision. Reports may become inaccurate or may be forgotten if delivered prematurely.

Information Systems Modules	Form Utility	Time Utility	Place Utility	Possession Utility	Actualization Utility	Goal Utility
Inventory Lists Good	Good. Acronyms used were the same as shipping codes. As systems grew, too much information was presented; this overload called for summary information.	Good. Reports were received at least one hour before scheduled shipments on a daily basis.	Good. Inventory lists were printed at the regional blood center. Lists were delivered to hospitals with the current shipments.	Good. The same people who originally kept manual records received these reports.	Good. Implementation was easy since hospitals found the inventory lists to be extremely useful.	Good. Information about the location of particular units was made available.
Management Summary Reports Good	Good. Summary report was designed to exact format specifications of manual summary reports developed by the blood administrator for city hospitals.	Good. Same as listings	Good. Summary reports were printed at the center where they were needed.	Good. Blood administrators who originally kept manual reports for city hospitals received summary information.	Good. Blood administrators participated in the design of the reports.	Good. Summary reports helped reduce outdating and prevent shortages.
Short-Term Forecasting Good	Good. A forecast was issued for each blood type.	Good. Forecasts were updated daily.	Good. Printed at blood center.	Good. Administrators concerned with distribution and collections received the report.	Good. Output design could have been more participative.	Good. Shortages were prevented by calling in more donors.
Heuristic Allocation Failure	Poor. The people who allocated blood mistrusted the mysterious numbers produced by the computer.	Good. Reports were provided one hour before allocation decisions were made.	Good. Printed at blood center.	Fair. Administrators responsible for daily blood allocation received the original.	Poor. Too many people were involved with the level of blood inventories to be able to participate in the design of the system. Hospitals were not prepared to participate with computer-based rationing of blood units.	Poor. Although consultants were concerned about reducing shipping costs, this was not an immediate goal of the blood region. Shipping costs were passed on to patients.
Decentralized Performance Measurement Good	Good. Peer review committee understood and accepted the reports.	Good. Monthly performance measures were available within one day after the month ended.	Good. Reports were mailed to the peer review committee.	Good. Performance reports were given to peer review committee and the regional blood administrator at the same time.	Fair. Trial period with peer committee was satisfactory, but the regional blood administrator was unwilling to participate. Consulting team was unable to convince blood administrator that outdating should be kept low.	Good. Goals were consistent with regional objectives. The blood administrator did not consider minimizing blood outdating to be a priority goal, even though it is national blood policy.
Bloodmobile Scheduling Partially Successful	Good. Tabular form included sufficient detail while computer-produced graph provided summary information as well.	Good. Feedback within one day.	Good. Computer terminal was in the same building so assistant administrator could make changes himself.	Good. Assistant administrator used system for one year. When he left, improving scheduling was not considered a priority item.	Fair. Trial period was successful, but when assistant administrator left, no one else had the knowledge to run the system. Perhaps the origination was not ready for the refinement in this module.	Fair. Goals of this module were overshadowed by more immediate goals.
Policy Planning Model Partially Successful	Good. The form was the same as the bloodmobile scheduling output.	Good. Immediate feedback.	Not applicable.	Results were published in blood management and health care journals.	Not applicable.	Good. Goals were long-range strategic planning alternatives.

FIGURE 21.15
Evaluating a blood inventory information and decision support system using the information system utility approach.

CONSULTING OPPORTUNITY 21.3

Mopping Up with the New System

"I don't know what happened. When the new system was installed, the systems analysts made a clean getaway as far as I can tell," says Marc Schnieder, waxing philosophic. Recall that he is owner of the Marc Schnieder Janitorial Supply Company. (You last met Marc in Consulting Opportunity 17.1, where you helped him with his data storage needs. In the interim, he has had a new information system installed.)

"The systems analysis team asked us some questions about how we liked the new system," Marc supplies eagerly. "We didn't really know how to tell them that the output wasn't as spotless as we'd like. I mean,

it's confusing, it isn't getting to the right people at the right time, or anything. We never really did get into the nitty gritty about the finished system with that consulting team. I feel as if we had to hire your group just to mop up after what they left."

After further discussions with Stan Lessink, the company's chief programmer, you realize that the team that did the initial installation had no evaluation mechanism. Suggest a suitable framework for evaluating the kinds of concerns that Mr. Schnieder raised about the system. What are the problems that can occur when a system is not evaluated systematically?

ACTUALIZATION UTILITY. Actualization utility involves how the information is introduced and used by the decision maker. First, the information system has value if it possesses the ability to be implemented. Second, actualization utility implies that an information system has value if it is maintained after its designers depart or if a one-time use of the information system obtains satisfactory and long-lasting results.

GOAL UTILITY. Goal utility answers the "why" of information systems by asking whether the output has value in helping the organization obtain its objectives. The goal of the information system must not only be in line with the goals of decision makers, but it must also reflect their priorities.

Evaluating the System

An information system can be evaluated as successful if it possesses all six utilities. If the system module is judged as "poor" in providing one of the utilities, the entire module will be destined to failure. A partial or "fair" attainment of a utility will result in a partially successful module. If the information system module is judged as "good" in providing every utility, the module is a success.

The information system utility approach of "who, what, when, where, why, and how" used to evaluate the regional blood inventory management information system resulted in the subjective judgments concerning the utility of the information system summarized in the table. As you can see, four of the modules were rated as "good" in each category of utility, and consequently these modules were considered successful. Two were evaluated as partially successful, and one module was judged a failure after the trial period. Explanations of each judgment made for the seven modules are also provided.

The information system utility approach is a workable and straightforward framework for evaluating large-scale information systems projects and ongoing efforts. It also can be usefully employed as a checklist to monitor the progress of systems under development. Furthermore, evaluation following implementation allows the analyst to acquire ideas about how to proceed with future systems projects.

SUMMARY

Implementation is the process of assuring that information systems and networks are operational and then involving well-trained users in their operation. In large systems projects, the primary role of the analyst is overseeing implementation by correctly estimating the time needed, then supervising the installation of equipment for information systems (which may be set up with a client/server approach over a local area network), training users, and converting files and databases to the new system.

Distributed systems take advantage of telecommunications technology and database management to interconnect people manipulating some of the same data in meaningful but different ways. As hardware and software are evaluated, the systems analyst also needs to consider the costs and benefits of employing a distributed system to fulfill user requirements.

One of the most popular ways to approach distributed systems is through the use of a client/server model. Standard types of organizational networks include the local area network (LAN) and the wide-area network (WAN). Using a top-down approach, analysts can use five symbols to help draw network decomposition and hub connectivity diagrams. Specialized software, called groupware, is written specifically to support groups or teams of workers with functional applications. Its purpose is to help group members to work together through networks.

Training users and personnel to interact with the information system is an important part of implementation, since typically they must be able to run the system without the intervention of the analyst. The analyst needs to consider who needs to be trained, who will train them, the objectives of training, the methods of instruction to be used, the sites, and the materials.

Conversion is also part of the implementation process. The analyst has several strategies for changing from the old information system to the new. The five conversion strategies include direct changeover, parallel conversion, phased or gradual conversion, modular prototype conversion, and distributed conversion. Taking a contingency approach to conversion strategies can help the analyst in choosing an appropriate strategy, one that suits different system and organizational variables.

Recent exploratory research suggests that systems analysts can improve the chances that newly implemented systems will be accepted if they develop systems with predominant organizational metaphors in mind. Nine main metaphors in use are: society, the family, machine, organism, journey, game, war, jungle, and zoo. For example, traditional MIS are more likely to succeed when metaphors such as the family, society, or machine are used, and they are less likely to succeed with organizational metaphors such as war and jungle.

After implementation, the new information system and the approach taken (perhaps client/server technology) should be evaluated. Many different evaluation approaches are available, including cost-benefit analysis, the revised decision evaluation approach, and user involvement evaluations.

The information system utility framework is a direct way to evaluate a new system based on the six utilities of possession, form, place, time, actualization, and goal. These utilities correspond to, and answer the questions of who, what, where, when, how, and why in order to evaluate the utilities

CHAPTER 21:
SUCCESSFULLY
IMPLEMENTING
THE INFORMATION
SYSTEM

855

of the information system. Utilities can also serve as a checklist for systems under development.

KEYWORDS AND PHRASES

distributed processing
LAN
client/server model
file server
print server
WAN
hierarchical network
star network
ring network
bus configuration
network modeling
network decomposition
hub connectivity
groupware
training objectives
training methods
training sites
training materials
direct changeover
parallel conversion
gradual or phased conversion
modular prototype conversion
distributed conversion

physical security
logical security
encryption software
behavioral security
firewall or firewall system
organizational metaphors
  zoo
  machine
  war
  journey
  jungle
  society
  family
  game
  organism
information system utility
  approach to evaluation
    possession utility
    form utility
    place utility
    time utility
    actualization utility
    goal utility

REVIEW QUESTIONS

1. List the four approaches to implementation.
2. Describe what is meant by *distributed system.*
3. What is a hierarchical network?
4. Draw a star network and label the nodes appropriately.
5. How does a ring network differ from a star network?
6. What is a bus configuration for distributed processing?
7. What is the client/server model?
8. Describe how a "client" is different from a user.
9. What is a peer-to-peer network? How does it differ from other client/server networks?
10. What is a file server?
11. What are the advantages of using a client/server approach?
12. What are the disadvantages of using a client/server approach?
13. What is the purpose of groupware?
14. Who should be trained to use the new or modified information system?
15. List the five possible sources of training for users of information systems.
16. Why is it important to have well-defined training objectives?
17. Some users learn best by seeing, others by hearing, still others by doing. Give an example of how each kind of learning can be incorporated into a training session.
18. State an advantage and a disadvantage of on-site training sessions.

"As you know, Snowden is determined to implement some kind of automated tracking for the Training people. But even after having you and your team here at MRE for all of this time, it isn't clear to me how this will ever come about. You've probably noticed by now that people like Tom Ketcham are pretty set in their ways. But so is Snowden, and he definitely has the upper hand. I'm not telling you anything you don't know already, am I? I think that when Snowden comes back from Poland, you should be ready to show him how we can implement an automated tracking system for the Training group. But it really has to be acceptable to the new users. After all, they're the ones who have to live with it. I'll pencil you in for a meeting with Snowden two weeks from today."

HYPERCASE QUESTIONS

1. Develop an *implementation plan* that would be useful to the Training group in changing to an automated project tracking system. Use a paragraph to explain your approach. Be sure that what you are doing also meets Snowden's expectations.

2. In two paragraphs, discuss what *conversion* approach is appropriate for adopting a new automated project tracking system for the Training group.

3. Provide an outline of steps you would take to train the users in the Training group so that they could use their new system. In a paragraph, discuss any obstacles you see to training the users in the Training group, and also list how you would overcome these problems.

19. List the attributes of well-executed training materials for users.
20. List the five conversion strategies for converting old information systems to new ones.
21. Define the terms physical, logical, and behavioral security and give an example of each one that illustrates the differences among them.
22. Define what encryption software means.
23. What is a firewall or firewall system?
24. List the nine organizational metaphors and the hypothesized success of each type of system given their presence.
25. List and describe the utilities of information systems that can be used to evaluate the information system.

PROBLEMS

1. Draw a local area network or some other configuration of distributed processing using the client/server approach to solve some of the data sharing problems that Bakerloo Brothers construction company is having. It wants to be able to allow teams of architects to work on blueprints at headquarters, to let the construction foreman enter last-minute changes to plans under construction from the field, and to permit clients

CHAPTER 21:
SUCCESSFULLY
IMPLEMENTING
THE INFORMATION
SYSTEM

857

to view plans from almost anywhere. Currently the company has a LAN for the architects who are in one city (Philadelphia) that lets them share some drawing tools and any updates that team members make with architects in other cities (New York, Terre Haute, Milwaukee, Lincoln, and Vancouver, BC). The foreman uses a laptop, cannot make any changes, and is not connected to a database. Clients view plans on screen displays, but sales representatives are not able to enter modifications to show them "what if" a wall was moved or a roof line altered. (*Hint:* List the problems that the company is encountering, analyze the symptoms, think of a solution, and then start drawing.) More than one network may be necessary, and not all problems will be amenable to a systems solution.

2. Cramtrack, the regional/commuter train system, is trying to train users of its newly installed computer system. In order for the users to get the proper training, the systems analysts involved with the project sent a memo to the heads of the four departments that include both primary and secondary users. The memo said in part, "Only people who feel as if they require training need to make reservations for off-site training; all others should learn the system as they work with it on the job." Only three of a possible forty-two users signed up. The analysts were satisfied that the memo effectively screened people who needed training from those who did not.

   a. In a paragraph, explain how the systems analysts got off the track in their approach to training.

   b. Outline the steps you would take to ensure that the right people at Cramtrack are trained.

   c. Suggest in a paragraph how the Web might be used to assist in training for Cramtrack.

3. A beautiful, full-color brochure arrived on Bill Cornwell's desk describing the Benny Company's off-site training program and facilities in glowing terms; it showed happy users at terminals and professional-looking trainers leaning over them with concerned looks. Bill ran excitedly into Roseann's office and told her, "We've got to use these people. This place looks terrific!" Ro was not persuaded by the brochure but didn't know what to say in defense of the on-site training for users that she had already authorized.

   a. In a few sentences, help Ro argue the usefulness of on-site training with in-house trainers in contrast to off-site training with externally hired trainers.

   b. If Bill does decide on Benny Company training, what should he do to verify that this is indeed the right place to train the company's information system users? Make a list of actions he should take.

4. "Just a little longer. I want to be sure this is working alright before I change over," says Buffy, the owner of three bathroom accessories boutiques called Tub 'n Stuff. Her accountant, who helped her set up a new accounting information system, is getting desperate to persuade Buffy to change over completely to the new system. Buffy has insisted on running the old and new systems in parallel for an entire year.

   a. Briefly describe the general problems involved in using a parallel conversion strategy for implementing a new information system.

b. In a paragraph, try to convince the owner of Tub 'n Stuff that a year of running a system in parallel is long enough. Suggest a way to end Tub 'n Stuff's dual systems that will provide enough reassurance to Buffy. (Assume that the new system is reliable.)

5. Ginny's Office Supplies Company recently had a new information system installed to help its managers with inventory. In speaking with managers, you notice that they seemed disgruntled with the system output, which is a series of screens that show current inventory, customer and supplier addresses, and so on. All screens need to be accessed through both several special commands and the use of a secret password. The managers had several opinions about the system but had no systematic way to evaluate it.

a. Devise a checklist or form that helps Ginny's managers evaluate the utilities of an information system.

b. Suggest a second way to evaluate the information system. Compare it with what you did in part a.

GROUP PROJECT

1. With your group members, prepare for your final exam by completing the crossword puzzle in Figure 21.EX1. The clues are found in Figure 21.EX2. Notice that there are hints regarding where to learn more about the material.

SELECTED BIBLIOGRAPHY

Baskerville, R. L. "An Analytical Survey of Information Systems Security Design Methods: Implications for Information Systems Development." *Computing Surveys,* 1994.

Carlyle, R. E. "Squeezing the Middle." *Datamation,* Vol. 32, No. 10, 1986, pp. 26–28.

Derfler, Jr., F. J., and Freed, L. *How Networks Work.* Emeryville, CA: Ziff-Davis Press, 1993.

FitzGerald, J., and T. S. Eason. *Fundamentals of Data Communication.* New York: John Wiley & Sons, Inc., 1978.

Ginzberg, M. J. "Key Recurrent Issues in the MIS Implementation Process." *Management Information Systems Quarterly,* Vol. 5, No. 2, 1981, pp. 47–59.

Gore, M., and J. Stubbe. *Elements of Systems Analysis.* Dubuque, IA: Wm. C. Brown Co. Publishers, 1983.

Jessup, L. M., and J. S. Valacich. *Group Support Systems.* New York: Macmillan, 1993.

Kendall, J. E. "Using Metaphors for Knowledge Elicitation During Expert Systems Development." *Proceedings of the First International Meeting of the Decision Sciences Institute.* Brussels, June 1991, pp. 153–155.

Kendall, J. E. "Using Metaphors to Enhance Intelligence in Information Systems: Rationale for an Alternative to Rule-Based Intelligence." In F. Vogt (ed.), *Information Processing 92, Volume III: Intelligent Systems and Personal Computers.* Amsterdam: Elsevier-North Holland, 1992, pp. 213–19.

Kendall, K. E. "Evaluation of a Regional Blood Distribution Information System." *International Journal of Physical Distribution and Materials Management,* Vol. 10, No. 7, 1980.

CHAPTER 21:
SUCCESSFULLY
IMPLEMENTING
THE INFORMATION
SYSTEM

859

FIGURE 21.EX1
A comprehensive crossword puzzle for systems analysts.

Kendall, J. E., and K. E. Kendall. "Metaphors and Methodologies: Living Beyond the Systems Machine." *MIS Quarterly,* Vol. 17, No. 2, June 1993, pp. 149–171.

Kendall, J. E., and K. E. Kendall. "Metaphors and Their Meaning for Information Systems Development." *European Journal of Information Systems,* Vol. 3, No. 1, 1994, pp. 37–47.

Labriola, D. "Remote Possibilities." *PC Magazine,* June 14, 1994.

Laudon, K. C., and J. Laudon. *Management Information Systems: Organization and Technology,* 4th ed. Upper Saddle River, NJ: Prentice Hall, 1996.

O'Hara, M. T., and R. T. Watson. "Automation, Business Process Reengineering and Client Server Technology: A Three Stage Model of Organizational Change." In V. Grover and W. J. Kittinger (eds.), *Business Process Change: Concepts, Methods and Technologies.* Harrisburg, PA: Idea Group Publishing, 1995, pp. 143–164.

Oppliger, R. "Internet Security: Firewalls and Beyond." *Communications of the ACM,* Vol. 40, No. 5, May 1997, pp. 92–102.

ACROSS

1 Always appears with ENNDO (Ch. 11)
2 File operation (Ch.17)
4 Type of file organization; Abbr. (Ch. 17)
7 Systems Analyst: Abbr.
9 Opposite of Output (Ch. 16)
11 Important person
12 Executive Information System: Abbr. (Ch. 1)
14 Systems Development Life Cycle: Abbr. (Ch. 1)
16 Expert System (Ch. 1)
18 _____ /CAM system
20 Like a beer
21 File operation (Ch. 17)
23 Opposite of East
25 Data gathering technique: Plural (Ch. 5)
27 Type of bar code (Ch. 19)
28 Overview in a DFD (Ch. 9)
30 Information Technology: Abbr.
31 Operating system: Abbr.
33 International Conference on Information Systems: Abbr.
37 Type of diagram: Abbr. (Chs. 2 and 17)
39 Project management technique (Ch. 3)
40 Big Blue
44 Foot: Abbr.
45 Not a renter (Ch. 13)
48 District Attorney: Abbr.
49 Warnier- _____ diagrams (Ch.20)
50 _____ Utility (Ch. 21)
51 Type of diagram: 2 wds. (Ch. 9)
52 Doesn't apply: Abbr.
53 Check digit method: Abbr. (Ch. 19)
55 Follow rules
57 Research and development: Abbr.
58 Educate users (Ch. 21)
60 Shape in a bubble diagram (Ch. 17)
62 Sylvester Stallone character
63 CAD/ _____ system
66 Vase
68 DFD symbol: 2 wds. (Ch. 9)
71 Quality approach: Abbr.
73 Symbol for gold in the periodic table of elements
74 Female deer
75 Mnemonic postal code for Pennsylvania (Ch. 19)
77 Mnemonic postal code for Illinois (Ch. 19)
78 Its symbol is a diamond (Ch. 17)
85 Method for documenting structured decisions (Ch. 11)
87 Direction of a data flow (Ch. 9)
89 _____ UNTIL or _____ WHILE (Ch. 11)
90 _____ Box: Abbr.
91 Code for arsenic in the periodic table of elements
93 Mnemonic postal code for Michigan (Ch. 19)
94 Noah's boat
96 A service on the Internet (Ch. 15)
98 Rapid development method (Ch 8)
102 Spanish for yes
103 Mnemonic postal code for New Mexico (Ch. 19)
104 Type of scale (Ch. 6)
105 _____ LSE _____ F in structured English (Ch. 11)
106 Type of data flow diagram (Ch. 9)
107 Good _____ gold
109 River that flows North
110 Mnemonic postal code for Montana (Ch. 19)
111 Mnemonic postal code for Massachusetts (Ch. 19)
112 Data _____ (Ch. 9)
113 The CPU case takes place in a computer _____
114 Mnemonic postal code for Washington (Ch. 19)
117 Los Angeles: Abbr.
119 Type of interface (Ch. 18)
120 Type of chart (Ch. 14)
121 To be or not to _____
122 Type of diagram: Abbr. (Ch. 20)
124 Electronic communication (Ch. 15)
126 Metaphor for a chaotic organization (Ch. 21)
128 Type of automated tool used by analysts (Ch. 1)
130 Information Center: Abbr. (Ch. 21)
131 Distortion of data (Chs. 4 and 15)
132 Part of the population (Ch. 4)
133 Type of type (Ch. 15)
134 Compact _____ (Ch. 15)

DOWN

1 _____ maker (Ch. 12)
2 Code for silicon in the periodic table of elements
3 Puccini wrote many of these
4 User _____ of data (Ch. 17)
5 Social security: Abbr.
6 Type of interface (Ch. 18)
8 An adverb
9 Symbol used in Windows (Ch. 18)
10 Validating computer code (Ch. 18)
11 Type of display (Ch. 15)
12 Data _____ , part of a data dictionary (Ch. 10)
13 Contains data (Ch. 17)
15 Data _____ (Ch. 10)
17 Street: Abbr.
19 Indefinite article
20 Artificial Intelligence: Abbr. (Ch. 1)
22 Data processing: Abbr. (Ch. 1)
23 Us
24 Describe a DFD process in greater detail (Ch. 9)
26 code for silicon in the periodic table of elements
29 Manufacturer of a CASE tool: Abbr. (Ch. 1)
32 Beginning
34 A word used in structured English (Ch. 11)
35 Method for structured observation (Ch. 7)
36 Cipher (Ch. 19)
38 Opposite of front
39 Symantec's WinFax _____ (Ch. 15)
41 Human computer
42 Mister: Abbr.
43 Control _____ (Ch. 20)
46 Custom or direction
47 Rural free delivery: Abbr
50 CompuServe command
54 _____ effect (Ch. 6)
56 Type of caption (Ch. 16)
59 Groove or depression
61 _____ programming (Ch. 12)
63 Code for cerium in the periodic table of elements
64 Systems _____ alyst (Ch. 1)
65 Mnemonic postal code for Montana (Ch. 19)
67 Before noon
69 U. S. agency that protects the environment: Abbr.
70 Rodent, but not a mouse
72 Operation performed on a database (Ch. 18)
74 _____ store (Ch. 10)
76 Boolean operator (Ch. 18)
77 Information Analyst: Abbr.
79 Edward: Abbr.
80 Type of data flow diagram (Ch. 9)
81 Type of system (Ch. 2)
82 Transformation of user views and data stores (Ch. 17)
83 Laser printer manufacturer
84 To break apart data flow diagrams (Ch. 9)
86 Check _____ (Ch. 19)
88 Operations Research: Abbr.
92 Earth
93 Type of code (Ch. 19)
95 Data item used to identify a record (Ch. 17)
97 Buddy or friend
98 Skillet
99 Digit
100 Decision _____ : Plural (Ch. 11)
101 Type of question (Ch. 5)
102 Society for Information Management: Abbr.
108 _____ what!
112 Kung _____
114 Worldwide _____ , electronic communication
115 _____ Pro, a word processing package
116 Type of system: Abbr. (Ch. 1)
118 Also known as: Abbr.
119 Rift
121 Type of chart (Ch. 14)
123 Mnemonic postal code for South Carolina (Ch. 19)
125 American Airlines: Abbr.
129 Edition: Abbr.

FIGURE 21.EX2
Clues for the crossword puzzle.

CHAPTER 21:
SUCCESSFULLY
IMPLEMENTING
THE INFORMATION
SYSTEM

861

Pfaffenberger, B., and D. Wall, *Que's Computer and Internet Dictionary,* 6th ed. Indianapolis, IN: Que Corporation, 1995.

Rigney, S. "Network in a Box." *PC Magazine,* Vol. 16, No. 16, September, 1997, pp. 167–170; 172; 174; 180; 184–186; 191–193; and 195.

Shaffer, G. "Coping With Change." *PC Magazine,* June 14, 1994.

Swanson, E. B. *Information System Implementation.* Homewood, IL: Richard D. Irwin, Inc., 1988.

Zmud, R. W., and J. F. Cox. "The Implementation Process: A Change Approach." *Management Information Systems Quarterly,* Vol. 3, No. 2, 1979, pp. 35–44.

SEMPER REDUNDATE

Mack Roe walks to Anna's desk where Chip is standing and says, "The last program has been tested and incorporated into the system test. The results indicate that the system is finally complete. Every program and subsystem is working as planned. The whole system checks out. Testing has been thorough and exacting, with all the problems and program bugs satisfactorily resolved. I've reviewed the deliverables, and each one has been developed into programs. I'll leave you two to install it and then celebrate."

"That's fantastic!" Anna replies as Mack leaves. "We've been anticipating this moment for a long time. We now have the task of installing the system. I've checked with Mike Crowe, and all the hardware has arrived and been installed. The microcomputers have been connected in a star configuration, and the network software has been installed. Why don't we make a list of the tasks to be completed?"

"Sure," answers Chip. "We'll need to train the users on the operation of the system. It would be good to provide some general training, followed by specific training for each user. We might want to train several people for each specific operation—the user and a backup person."

"That's all right with me," responds Anna. "But I don't think we should have a backup person for Paige Prynter. Somehow I don't feel that she would be fond of the idea."

"Speaking of back-up," says Chip, "what about creating back-ups of master and other system files? We should design an automated procedure for creating these copies."

"Yes," replies Anna. "We also need to be concerned with system security: Who may access the data and who has clearance to update various database elements?"

"I agree," remarks Chip. "Another consideration is converting the production files from the old system to the new format. We don't want to rekey all the records from the hardware and software master files."

"Why don't we have one of the programmers write a one-time program that will convert each file from the old format to the new?" suggests Anna. "The indexes could be automatically updated and additional fields initialized to spaces or zeros."

The programmers complete the file conversion programs within a short time. The new files are created and painstakingly verified for accuracy. This effort is rewarded with new master files that contain all of the necessary records loaded with correct information.

Training is scheduled to start in the Information Center. Hy Perteks is more than willing to reserve a block of time for installing the software and providing the training sessions. Chip and Anna alternated in providing instruction, each for portions of the system which they had created.

With the training sessions concluded, the last task is the conversion of the old system to the new. The phased method is selected as the best approach. First, the microcomputer hardware programs are installed. Records are updated with information for the additional elements included in the system design.

Allen Schmidt,
Julie E. Kendall, and
Kenneth E. Kendall

Next, the software update programs are installed. Again, updates to master file records are entered. When the records contain complete information, the inquiry screens are installed. Lastly, report and menu programs are added to the system.

"The installation is a great success," exults Chip. "Everything is working correctly, without a bug in the system. I guess we should knock on wood. Have you heard any comments from the users?"

"Yes," replies Anna. "They are happy and relieved to have their new system. Mike Crowe has already started to use the preventive maintenance feature and has his students help tackling one lab room at a time. Cher and Dot were running through the various screens and several times commented on how easy it is to perform tasks. I paid a visit to Paige Prynter, and she asked me what she should do with all her free time."

The analysts smile at each other. Chip says, "This has been a really great project to work on."

"It certainly has," answers Anna. "The best system we've ever created here at CPU."

"I've learned a lot about the university in my short time here, too. It's a great place to work," Chip muses.

"And as long as you remember our motto, you should do alright," Anna replies. "Semper redundate," she quotes to Chip.

"Yeah, I see it on all the letterhead. But I must admit, I never took Latin in school. What does the motto actually mean?" Chip asks.

"Always backup!" Anna says securely.

Exercises

E-1. Use a paragraph to speculate on why the star network configuration was used. Does the fact that users are in several different rooms play any part in the matter?

E-2. Describe procedures that should be designed to create automatic backup files. In your paragraph, be sure to consider the pros and cons of these procedures.

E-3. List security measures that should be taken to prevent unauthorized persons from using the microcomputer system.

E-4. Explain in a paragraph why a phased conversion would be used to install the microcomputer system.

OBJECT-ORIENTED SYSTEMS ANALYSIS AND DESIGN

Object-oriented (O-O) concepts arise from developments in modern programming languages. These O-O languages have new structures that are felt to improve program maintenance and make large parts of programs reusable. The consequent recycling of program parts should reduce the costs of development in computer-based systems. It has already proved very effective in the development of graphical user interfaces (GUIs) and databases. Because O-O languages have different constructs, computer systems must be specified in a way that maximizes the effective use of these constructs. This constraint has led to a number of new O-O systems analysis and design techniques. Given the possibility that much of the future programming workload could move to O-O programming, it is important for systems analysis and design students to become comfortable with O-O terminology and techniques.

In this chapter, we consider the essential concepts of the systems analysis and design techniques that are related to object-oriented programming technology. This activity will extend the analysis and design knowledge you have already developed into simple O-O skills. For example, O-O design notation combines aspects of both entity-relationship diagrams and data-flow diagrams. Furthermore, object specifications could employ flowcharts, structured English, decision tables, or any of the process specification notations that you have learned in earlier chapters as a point of departure.

Diverse approaches to O-O analysis and design have been published, perhaps best exemplified by Coad and Yourdon's "OOA-OOD" approach. We will use Coad and Yourdon's work for our consideration because it uses simple notation while retaining a very comprehensive O-O orientation, maintains a perspective on government standards, and uses the structured design presented in earlier chapters as its point of departure.

Object-oriented techniques are believed to be better than older approaches to handling the increasing pace of change in many of today's organizations. For example, many products are increasingly being made to order or manufactured in short-run batches as manufacturers concentrate on customer satisfaction and seek to penetrate niche markets. This trend means frequent changes to software bundled with these products. Also, many organizations are seeking to become more flexible through cross-functional teams, intercompany entrepreneurships, and virtual corporations. The constant shifting of people and responsibilities means an increasing need for rapid systems development and maintenance. O-O techniques are thought to work well in these kinds of situations where complicated information systems are undergoing continuous maintenance, adaptation, and redesign.

THE OBJECT-ORIENTED IDEA

Object-oriented analysis and design concepts were developed to support O-O programming technology. The development of this programming technology was not an instantaneous revolution, but rather it was the evolution of a collection of somewhat disconnected concepts that have been brought together to form a new paradigm for software engineering. For example, O-O programming draws its concept of encapsulation from the software engineering idea of data abstraction and its concept of inheritance from the database ideas of generalization and specialization.

Since O-O analysis and design is strongly related to O-O programming, we should briefly explore this O-O programming context *before* proceeding to O-O analysis and design. Six basic ideas characterize O-O programming: (1) objects, (2) classes, (3) messages, (4) encapsulation, (5) inheritance, and (6) polymorphism.

Objects

An object is a computer representation of some real-world thing or event. Figure 22.1 shows how a computer might represent your car. For example, if you own a Jeep Wrangler, the computer would store the name of the model (Jeep Wrangler), the vehicle ID number (#51Y62BG826341Y), and the motor type (6-Cyl). Objects can have both attributes (such as the model, VIN [Vehicle Identification Number], and motor type) and behaviors (such as "lights go on" and "lights go off").

Classes

A class is a category of similar objects. Objects are grouped into classes. Figure 22.2 shows how a group of objects representing automobiles might be formed into a class called "Automobile." A class defines the set of shared attributes and behaviors found in each object in the class. For example, every automobile will have attributes for Make/Model, VIN, and Engine. The programmer must define the classes in the program. When the program runs, objects can be created from the established class. The term "instantiate" is used when an object is created from a class. For example, a program could instantiate the Jeep Wrangler as an object from the class Automobile.

Messages

Information can be sent by one object to another. In Figure 22.3, an object (Kim) of the class "Operator" is sending a message to an object (Jeep) of the class "Automobile." The message is "Start Engine." These messages are not free-form in any sense; rather, the classes Operator and Automobile have been carefully programmed to send and receive a Start Engine message. The Operator class has been programmed to transmit a Start Engine message un-

Object

Jeep Wrangler	#51Y62BG826341Y	6-Cyl

der certain conditions. The Automobile class has been programmed to react to a Start Engine message in some way.

Encapsulation

Typically, the information about an object is encapsulated by its behavior. This means that an object maintains data about the real-world things it represents in a true sense. Typically an object must be "asked" or "told" to change its own data with a message—that is, it does not wait for such data from outside processes to change the nature of an object. In Figure 22.4, the John object (class Mechanic) sends a Pull Engine message to the Jeep object (class Automobile). The Automobile class reacts to this message with a behavior (also called a "method" or "procedure") that changes the Engine attribute to None. This method is named Pull Engine. We see that the Jeep object reacts to the message by changing one of its attributes to None.

It may seem trivial whether an attribute of an object is changed by directly altering its data or by sending a message to the object to trigger internal behavior that changes that data. But this difference is an extremely important characteristic of O-O programs. Encapsulated data can be protected in such a way that only the object itself can make such changes through its own behavior. This construct makes it easier to build objects that are very reliable and consistent because they have complete control over their own attributes. It also makes program maintenance and change much easier. For example, the Mechanic class is isolated completely from the internal details of the Automobile class. The Automobile class can be totally reprogrammed without changing anything in the Mechanic class, as long as the Automobile class continues to receive a Pull Engine message properly. This isolation

Class

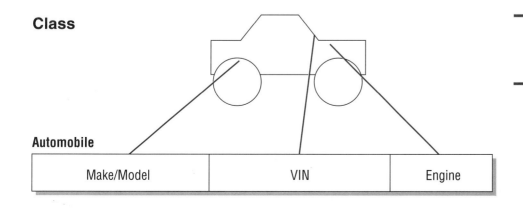

Automobile

Make/Model	VIN	Engine

Message

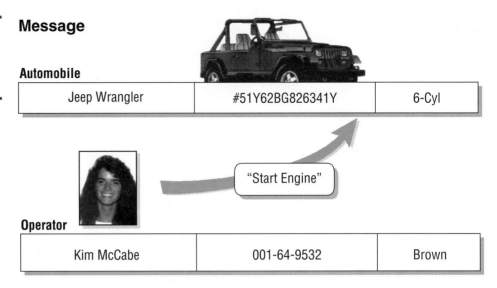

Automobile

Jeep Wrangler	#51Y62BG826341Y	6-Cyl

"Start Engine"

Operator

Kim McCabe	001-64-9532	Brown

FIGURE 22.3
Example of the information that can be sent by an object of one class to an object of another class.

makes it much easier to change one part of a program without causing problems to cascade out into other parts of the program.

Inheritance

Classes can have "children"—that is, one class can be created out of another class. The original—or parent class—is known as a "base class." The child class is called a "derived class." A derived class can be created in such a way that it will inherit all of the attributes and behaviors of the base class. In Figure 22.5, a derived class (Truck) is created such that it inherits all of the attributes of the base class Automobile. A derived class may have *additional* attributes and behaviors as well. For example, the class Truck not only has attributes for Make/Model, VIN, and Engine, but it also has attributes for Cargo Weight, Trailers, and Refridge. Automobile objects do not have these new attributes. Inheritance reduces programming labor by reusing old objects easily. The programmer only needs to declare that the Truck class in-

Encapsulation

Automobile

Jeep Wrangler	#51Y62BG826341Y	"None"

Start Engine	Stop Engine	Install Engine	Pull Engine

"Pull Engine"

Mechanic

John Lione	001-45-6630	Brown

FIGURE 22.4
Example illustrating how a message from one object causes another object from a different class to change one of its attributes.

Inheritance

Automobile

Make/Model	VIN	Engine

Truck: Inherit Automobile

Cargo Weight	Number of Trailers	Refridge
Make/Model	VIN	Engine

FIGURE 22.5
Example of inheritance of
parent class attributes by
a child class.

herits from the Automobile class and then to provide any additional details about new attributes or behaviors (shown in the solid-line box in the figure). All of the old attributes and behaviors of the Automobile class are automatically and implicitly part of the Truck class (these are shown in the dashed box) and require no new programming at all.

Some O-O programming languages provide multiple inheritance. In these special cases, a derived class can be created so that it inherits all of the attributes and behaviors of more than one base class. For example, if there were both a class called Automobile and a class called Bicycle, we could create a derived class called Motorcycle that inherits all of the attributes and behaviors of Automobile *and* all of the attributes and behaviors of Bicycle.

Polymorphism

The term polymorphism regards alternative behaviors among related derived classes. When several classes inherit both attributes and behaviors, there can be cases where the behavior of a derived class might be different from that of its base class or its sibling-derived classes. This means that a message may have different effects depending on exactly what class of object receives the message. In Figure 22.6, we see three classes: File, ASCII File, and Bitmap File. Both ASCII and Bitmap inherit all of the attributes of File *except* the Print behavior. A message to activate the Print behavior of an ob-

Polymorphism

File

| File Size | File Type | Date/Time | Print |

ASCII File: Inherit

| Delimiter | Rec Size | Print |

Bitmap File: Inherit File

| Color/Mono | Resolution | Print |

FIGURE 22.6
An example of polymorphism
among related classes.

FIGURE 22.7
The five layers of object-oriented analysis.

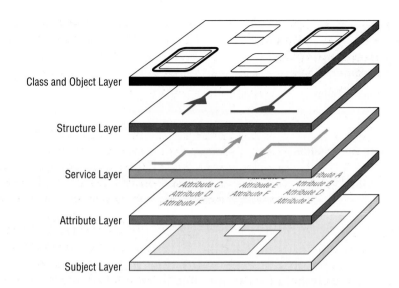

Class and Object Layer

Structure Layer

Service Layer

Attribute Layer

Subject Layer

ject of the generic parent File class might cause the File Size, File Type, and Date/Time attributes to be printed. The same message sent to an ASCII object might cause the text in the file to be sent to the printer. The same message sent to a Bitmap object might cause a graphic display program to execute.

OBJECT-ORIENTED ANALYSIS

The Coad and Yourdon approach to O-O analysis is based on a five-layer model. These layers consist of the (1) class/object layer, (2) structure layer, (3) service layer, (4) attribute layer, and (5) subject layer. We can visualize the entire process of analysis and design as being the development and assembly of these five layers into one laminated design package. Figure 22.7 illustrates how the five layers interlock. These layers add a three-dimensional structure to the analysis and design notation that gives further power in representing the complexity in flexible systems. Each of these layers will be discussed in more detail later in this chapter as we consider the activities of O-O analysis and design.

1. **THE CLASS/OBJECT LAYER.** This layer of the analysis and design denotes the classes and objects.
2. **THE STRUCTURE LAYER.** This layer captures various structures of classes and objects, such as one-to-many relationships and inheritance.
3. **THE SERVICE LAYER.** This layer denotes messages and object behaviors (services and methods).
4. **THE ATTRIBUTE LAYER.** This layer details the attributes of classes.
5. **THE SUBJECT LAYER.** This layer divides the design into implementation units or team assignments.

ANALYZING CLASSES AND OBJECTS

Coad and Yourdon distinguish Class, Object, and Class-&-Object in the following ways:

1. *Object:* An abstraction of something in a problem domain, reflecting the capabilities of a system to keep information about it, interact with

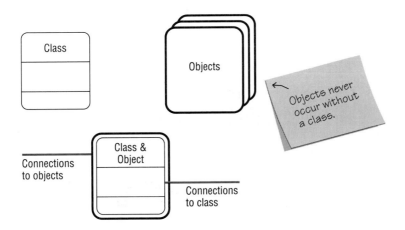

it, or both. An object represents an encapsulation of attribute values and their exclusive services. A synonym is "an instance."

2. *Class:* A description of one or more objects with a uniform set of attributes and services, including a description of how to create new objects in the class.

3. *Class-&-Object:* A term referring to both the class and the objects that are instantiated in the class.

There are five general types of objects that can be discovered during analysis. Objects often represent *tangible things* such as vehicles, devices, and books. Sometimes objects represent *roles* enacted by persons or organizations; roles include objects like customer, owner, or department. Objects may also be derived from *incidents* or events such as flight, accident, or meeting; incidents typically happen at a specific time. Other objects may denote *interactions* such as a sale or a marriage; interactions have a transaction or contract quality. Objects may also detail *specifications.* Specifications have standards or a definition quality and generally imply that other objects will represent instances of tangible things—for example, a class of object such as "insurance policy type" may have instances like "whole life," "term life," or "homeowners." Such a class of objects specifies qualities common to certain instances of another class of objects called "insurance policy."

The notation for Class, Objects, and Class-&-Object is shown in Figure 22.8. Classes are represented by rounded rectangular boxes (bubtangles) divided into three parts. The name of the class is shown in the upper division of the box. The other two divisions are used for the attribute and service layers. When a class appears without Objects, it can only be a base class, because the only reason for such an "objectless" class is to provide a means of grouping attributes and services that will be inherited by several other classes.

Objects that instantiate the Class are represented by a shaded box surrounded by the class (you will see an example of this later in this chapter). Since Objects instantiate a Class, it is not possible for Objects to exist independently of their class. Because of this dependence, some notation does not distinguish between classes and objects. Coad and Yourdon, however, provide the Class-&-Object notation in order to graphically distinguish between structures and messages that are intended for the Class (such as a "create a new instance object" message) from structures and messages intended for the Object (such as "pull engine").

Techniques for discovering objects are basically the same as those discussed in earlier chapters for discovering processes and data entities. However, there are certain criteria that we can use to help determine whether a new class of objects is justified:

1. There is a need to remember the object—that is, the object can be described in a definite sense, and its attributes are relevant to the problem.

2. There is a need for certain behaviors of the object—that is, even though an object has no attributes, there are services that it must provide or object states that must be recalled.

3. Typically, an object will have multiple attributes. Objects that have only one or two attributes suggest overanalyzed designs.

4. Typically, a class will have more than one object instantiation unless it is a base class.

5. Typically, attributes will always have a meaningful value for each object in a class. Objects that produce a NULL value for an attribute or for which an attribute is not applicable usually imply a generalization–specialization structure (described later in this chapter).

6. Typically, services will always behave in the same way for every object in a class. Services that vary dramatically for some objects in a class or that return without action for some objects also suggest a generalization–specification structure.

7. Objects should implement requirements that are derived from the problem setting, not the solution technology. The analysis portion of the O-O project should not become dependent on a particular implementation technology such as a specific computer system or a specific programming language. Objects that address such technical details should not appear until very late in the design stage. Technology-dependent objects suggest that the analysis process is faulty.

8. Objects should not duplicate attributes and services that could be derived from other objects in the system. For example, an object that stores the age of an employee is superfluous when a separate employee object exists that maintains a date-of-birth attribute. The age object can be eliminated by an age service that is a component of the employee object.

Kayjay World Example 1

Kayjay World is a small vacation theme park that operates a circular, six-train monorail system connecting a parking lot, a theme park, a hotel, and a concert hall/restaurant complex. There are four stations, each with a ticket booth and a boarding queue. Passengers obtain a ticket for one of the three possible destination stations and enter the boarding queue. The boarding queue is arranged in such a way that every seat on a train will be filled before any passenger can be left at a station. Trains consist of an engine and one to six passenger cars, each car carrying 50 passengers.

As shown in Figure 22.9, the rail system consists of 15 safety segments of track and a segment (S16) contains the barn. Each train in service occupies one of these segments. A train may not enter a segment that is occupied by another train. Each station counts as one segment, and each link between stations is divided into two or three segments. The barn is capable of storing

FIGURE 22.9
Diagram of the Kayjay World
monorail system.

all six trains with two access segments: one exit segment (S14) leading to the barn and yard, and one entrance segment (S15) departing from the barn and yard. There is only one junction switch, joining segment S10 to either segment S11 or S14. Segment S14 leads to the barn and thus is joined to the main circuit with the only system junction switch. The segment from the barn (S15) merges with the main track in a fixed junction and does not require a switch. When a train is on S13 and another is on S15—and both are thus competing for segment S1—the train on S15 is given priority.

The capacity manager initializes the system by ordering one train to leave the barn and thus be placed in service. At least one train remains in service until the capacity manager shuts down the system, ordering the last train out of service. However, when the excess capacity of every train in service falls below 50 percent and at least one train falls below 25 percent, another train leaves the barn and is placed in service. If the excess capacity of every train exceeds 50 percent, then one train is removed from service and sent to the barn. (This train accepts no new passengers beginning with station one and thus the remaining passengers disembark at station three.) A yard manager declares out-of-service trains in the barn and yard either "operable" or "inoperable." Operable trains are rotated back into service on a first-in, first-out basis. The yard manager switches inoperable trains out of the automatic system by removing them from the service queue. The inoperable trains then enter a manually switched maintenance yard. Although each train usually has four cars, if an engine fails during high season, the yard master may detach one or more of the inoperable train's cars, take an operable train into the service yard, and add one or more of the orphaned passenger cars to the operable train. An engine can pull six full cars, so the monorail can lose two engines and still operate at full capacity (1,200 passengers). However, this event raises the minimum capacity of the system from 200 to 300 passengers.

Based on the preceding problem description, we can sketch out a preliminary class and object analysis. At this early stage in this analysis, all of the objects are Class-&-Objects. As is typical of an early analysis, base classes will soon emerge from further analysis. Figure 22.10 is the initial outline of the Class-&-Object layer of the O-O design package.

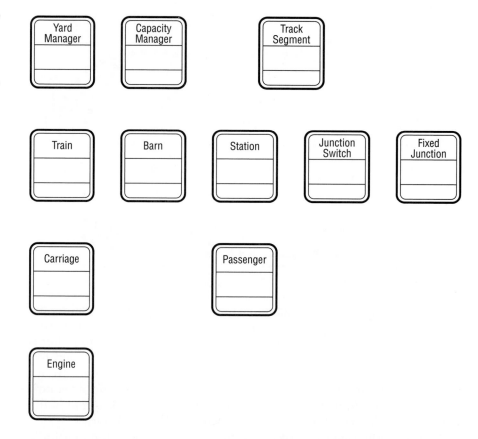

FIGURE 22.10
Initial outline of the Class-&-Object layer of Kayjay World's monorail system.

Analyzing Structures

There are two basic types of structures that might be imposed on classes and objects. These are the Generalization–Specialization structure (known as "Gen–Spec") and the Whole–Part structure.

1. GEN–SPEC STRUCTURES. Inheritance is created with Gen–Spec structures. These relationships between classes are sometimes called classification, subtype, or ISA (pronounced "ĭs-uh") relationships. Gen–Spec structures are denoted by a semicircle with its rounded edge toward the generalized class. These structures always connect class-to-class. They are typically of a hierarchical form. Figure 22.11 shows a Gen–Spec structure between Class-&-Objects in which the classes Bus and Motorcycle inherit all of the properties of the class Automobile.

2. WHOLE–PART STRUCTURES. These structures denote collections of different objects that compose another whole object. Such relationships between objects are sometimes called assemblies, aggregations, or HASA (pronounced "hăs-uh") relationships. Whole–Part structures are noted by a triangle pointing toward the "whole" object. These structures always connect object-to-object. Figure 22.12 shows a Whole–Part structure in which vehicle objects are shown to be composed of two other objects: Motor and Chassis.

Whole–Part structures also have cardinality, as represented by one-to-many or many-to-many. This concept was discussed in the section on entity-relationship models in Chapter 17. The notation "0,m" specifies that a

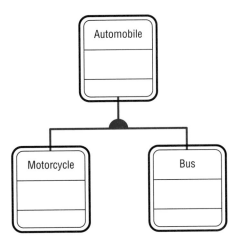

FIGURE 22.11
A Gen–Spec structure involving the relationship of the
classes Motorcycle and Bus to
the class Automobile.

Vehicle can have no motor (0) or one or more motors (m). The notation "0,1" specifies that a Motor can be part of no vehicle (0) or one vehicle (1), but never more than one. The "1,m" specifies that a Vehicle can have one (or more) Chassis, but never fewer than one. The "1" specifies that a Chassis is always related to one and only one Vehicle.

Kayjay World Example 2

We continue our work based on the problem description for Kayjay World given earlier by imposing a preliminary structure analysis—or structure layer—onto the Class-&-Object diagram. This structure analysis is shown in Figure 22.13. Note that the Barn, Station, Junction Switch, and Fixed Junction classes share similar functions with Track Segments. We can thus design a Gen–Spec structure between Track Segment and these other classes. This way, Station and the other classes inherit all of the attributes and services of a Track Segment.

We can also design several Whole–Part structures. For instance, a Station object may have Passenger objects. Similarly, a Train object may have Carriage objects and Passenger objects. We can also decide that the Yard Manager will have all of the Train assemblies and that the Capacity Manager will have all of the Track Segment objects.

The relationship between Carriage and Engine is a tricky one. A train engine is just a special kind of train carriage—a kind of carriage that has a

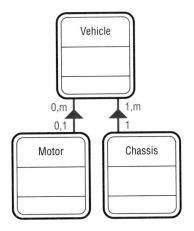

FIGURE 22.12
A Whole–Part structure illustrating the relationships of the
objects Motor and Chassis to
the object Vehicle.

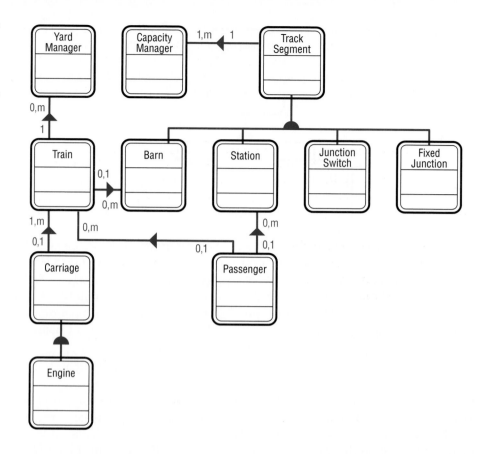

motor and very few seats. Also, it seems that the Barn object can have Train objects as part of it. This may create problems at implementation time because Train objects can then be part of both the Yard Manager and the Barn. But we will see how this seeming conflict can be sorted out during the design stage of the project.

Analyzing Attributes

The names of the attributes of a class are written in the center section of the class box in the design package. In Figure 22.14, the attributes Oname and Oaddress have been layered over the Owner object, and the attributes Model and Color have been layered over the Vehicle object. The basic idea of an attribute is unchanged from our earlier discussion of this topic in Chapter 17. However, three new related ideas are germane to our object-oriented perspective. First, attributes are always more prone to change than classes. If a structure or a set of classes seems to be getting cluttered because an object is changing from class to class, perhaps the Class-&-Object in question should simply become a set of attributes in another class.

FIGURE 22.14
Depiction of two classes and
their respective attributes.

876

Second, attributes should be kept as high as possible in Gen–Spec structures. This constraint reduces programming and maintenance because a change made in one Gen object will be automatically inherited by all of the Spec objects. Third, associations or relationships between objects (other than structures) should be detailed as instance connections rather than as foreign keys.

INSTANCE CONNECTIONS. The concept of primary and foreign keys was discussed earlier in Chapter 17. Rather than clutter up the design package with such implementation details, primary key attributes are not specified. Consequently, references between objects, such as associations or relationships, are denoted by a single line between objects with the same cardinality notation used in Whole–Part structures. Notice that instance connections always occur between objects, not classes. For example, an instance connection exists between owner and vehicle objects. The cardinality notes tell us that an owner may be related to zero, one, or more vehicles, but a vehicle must always be related to only one owner.

PRELIMINARY SPECIFICATION TEMPLATE. With the introduction of attributes, we need additional analysis details to support the layered diagram package. At this stage of the analysis, these details only regard descriptions of the attributes and constraints on their values. Coad and Yourdon recommend a specification template that provides an outline similar to a data dictionary. This template can then be expanded and modified as the analysis continues.

Kayjay World Example 3
The analysts for the Kayjay World project would next have to spend some time collecting information about the attributes of the monorail system's objects and the relationships between those objects, adding the attribute details and instance connections to the preliminary analysis. The attribute names and instance connections form the preliminary attribute layer of the O-O design package, as shown in Figure 22.15. We first spot the relationship between a Train and the Track Segment that it occupies. Also, carriages may be linked to other carriages when they form a train in a relationship called a self-association, represented with a line looping back to the same object. We continue by analyzing how passengers queue to buy tickets and board trains, so that each passenger is related to the preceding and the following passengers in the queue. We also note that Track Segments are related to other Track Segments because one segment follows a preceding segment and precedes a following segment. Fixed Junctions are branch segments related to a Track Segment joining the main line. There are many alternative ways to design branch track lines like the line going to the yard and the barn. One good way is to ensure that a Junction Switch has a branch line and that the line to the yard and barn belongs to the Junction Switch in a Whole–Part structure.

Now we can expand on the diagram of the attribute layer by creating a corresponding textual specification, as shown in Figure 22.16. This preliminary specification template contains more details about the attributes of the objects. It is called a template because it becomes the basic outline for the full specification that will be developed as the project continues.

FIGURE 22.15
Preliminary attribute layer
of the O-O design for
Kayjay World.

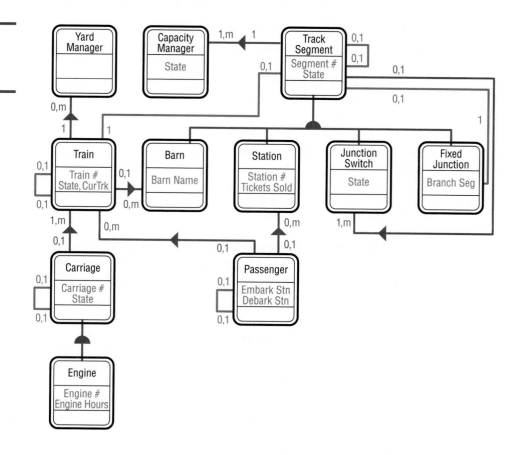

Analyzing Services

Services—also called methods or procedures—become part of objects in much the same way as attributes. Because services frequently involve changes in the state of an object, they are most commonly analyzed and designed using state diagrams. Consequently, service analysis consists of three activities: object state analysis, service specification, and message specification.

OBJECT STATE ANALYSIS. We can discover state changes most easily by finding those attributes in each object which affect the object's behavior. As we examine each attribute, we ask, "Will the object behavior change when this attribute's value is changed?" Where no attributes change the object behavior—yet when we know the object will behave differently under certain conditions—we should probably add a "state" attribute. For example, if we are analyzing a train carriage that will pick up and drop off passengers, we know that the train should behave differently in reaction to a "discharge passengers" message depending on whether the train is stopped at a station platform or careening down a straightaway track at 90 miles per hour. Figure 22.17 illustrates a state diagram for a state variable for such a train carriage. The arrow at the top of the State = Stopped box shows that the initial state when the object is created is always Stopped. The other arrows show possible state changes—for example, from Stopped to Running or Stopped to Unloading. Notice that there is no way to change states from Running to Unloading. This logically prevents the object from discharging passengers while in motion. State diagrams are added as needed to the specification templates to document such state attributes.

FIGURE 22.16
Preliminary specifications
template for the Kayjay
World monorail system.

Specification: Track Segment
    Attribute: Segment Number
    Attribute: State (Occupied/Free)
    Attribute: Next Segment
    Attribute: Previous Segment

Specification: Station
    Attribute: Station Number
    Attribute: Tickets Sold

Specification: Junction Switch
    Attribute: State (Normal/Branch); Normal means a connection to the Next Segment,
        Branch means a connection to Branch Segment

Specification: Fixed Junction
    Attribute: Branch Segment; The merging segment number

Specification: Barn
    Attribute: Barn Name

Specification: Train
    Attribute: Train Number
    Attribute: Service State (In/Out/Inop)

Specification: Carriage
    Attribute: Carriage Number
    Attribute: State (Operable/Inoperable)

Specification: Engine
    Attribute: Engine Number
    Attribute: Engine Hours

Specification: Passenger
    Attribute: Embarking Station
    Attribute: Destination Station

Specification: Capacity Manager
    Attribute: State (Operating/Closed)

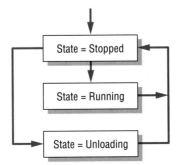

FIGURE 22.17
State diagram of a state
variable for train carriages
in the Kayjay World
monorail system.

FIGURE 22.18
Examples of complex services
depicted in the service layer
of the layered diagram.

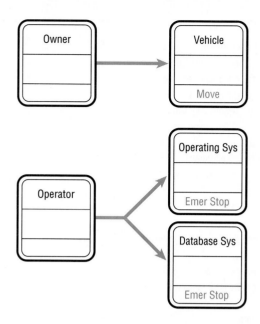

SERVICE SPECIFICATION. Services are categorized as either simple or complex. Simple services involve very few conditions or operations and often apply to every Class-&-Object in the system. These include such services as create-object, store-object, retrieve-object, connect-object (make an instance connection), access-object (get or set values for attributes), and delete-object. Simple services are implicit, sometimes specified once in the design and never mentioned again. Occasionally, very obvious simple services are not mentioned in the design at all but are instead left for the programmers to build as needed during implementation. Simple services may appear in the specification templates but are not mentioned in the layered diagram package.

Complex services involve loops, many operations, or compound conditions. These services typically apply to only one Class-&-Object. Complex services frequently entail "companion" or "private" services that are similar to subroutine modules. Private services are internal subroutines that only the object itself knows about and can trigger. Companion services are subroutines used by complex services that can also be triggered as distinct services by messages from other objects in the system. Complex services are always depicted in the service layer of the layered diagram package. The names of such services appear in the lower section of class boxes. Figure 22.18 shows three complex services: Move in the Vehicle object, Emer.Stop in the Operating Sys object, and Emer.Stop in the Database object.

We specify complex services more completely in the specification template. Almost any of the procedural specification tools discussed earlier in the chapters on Software Engineering (Chapter 20) and Structured Decision Systems (Chapter 11) can be used, such as program flowcharts, Warnier-Orr diagrams, decision tables, or structured English.

MESSAGE SPECIFICATION. Messages detail how one object's behavior can trigger behavior in another object—that is, messages are generated by one object with the intention of triggering a service in another object. Essentially, messages document the dependence of one process on another process in a different object. Messages exist solely to communicate between services and entail both control flow and data flow.

FIGURE 22.19
The basic outline for a
specification template.

Specification Template
Class-&-Object Name
Attributes
    Value Domain
External Input
External Output
State Diagram
Additional Constraints
Notes
Services
    input values
    output values
    structured English
    Warnier-Orr diagram
    decision chart
Error Codes
State Codes
Time Requirements
Memory Requirements

Messages regarding simple services are not documented in the layered diagram package because they are typically implicit in the simple services. Messages directed to classes, such as create-object or delete-object, are typically not diagrammed either. Consequently, most diagrammed messages end up being from object to object rather than from class to class or object to class.

Messages are shown as broad arrows in the service layer of the layered diagram package. In the lower portion of the figure, a single message is being sent from one object to two objects. Conversely, it may be the case that two services are needed independently by a single object. In this example, however, the Operator object generates a single message that triggers emergency shutdown behavior in both the Database and Operating Sys objects simultaneously.

Because messages detail complex services, they typically align with the sending service and the receiving service. However, even in moderately complex systems, there will be very few complex services and consequently very few messages in the diagram. This fact naturally tends to highlight the really important functions of the system.

Complex services that are not triggered by messages tend to be triggered by timed events or human interaction. A class without an incoming message but with a complex service will typically need some sort of human interface component.

Assembling the Specification Template

When we add service details to our O-O specification template, this portion of the analysis swells with detail. State diagrams, structured English, and flowcharts can be lengthy. The exact format of the specification can vary considerably from analysis to analysis. Figure 22.19 shows a basic specification template outline. We can add any important object details that need to be explicitly stated for the designers and programmers.

FIGURE 22.20
Layered diagram showing the
service layer of the Kayjay
World monorail system.

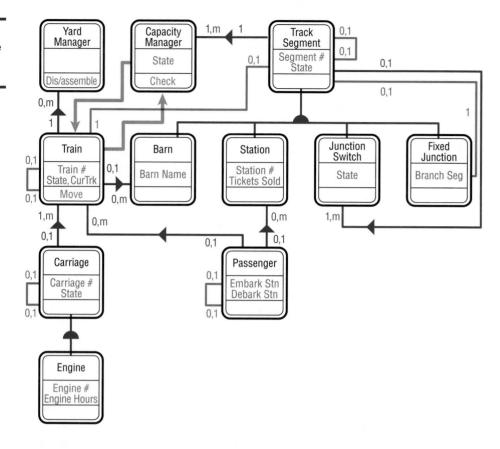

Kayjay World Example 4

Figure 22.20 shows the analysis of the Kayjay example with the Services layer added. There are three complex services among the objects: the Yard Manager's Assemble train/Disassemble train service, the Capacity Manager's Check service (Check determines whether to add or remove trains in the system), and the Move service in the Train object. Almost everything that happens in the system results from a train moving. Passengers might disembark because a train moves into a station. A junction switch may change states because a train moves out of service. It seems odd that in a traditional design we might have assumed that the Yard Manager or Capacity Manager was central to the design. But in this O-O approach, the Train is the center of the universe.

The Move service is triggered by the Capacity Manager when the train is moved into service. After that, the train Move service takes over. Each time a train moves, the Move service uses the opportunity to check the need to add or remove trains. Thus, the Move service triggers the Capacity Manager's capacity Check service. Notice that there is no message in the diagram that triggers the Yard Manager's Dis/assemble service. During the O-O design activities later in this chapter, we will learn that this "missing" trigger message implies that the Yard Manager class includes a human interface. This human interface allows an operator to manually trigger this service.

Figures 22.21*A* and 22.21*B* show the partial specification for the Train Class services. The Move service also triggers four private complex services

FIGURE 22.21A
Partial specification for the
Train class in the Kayjay
World system.

that do not appear in the layered diagram: One figures out where the train is, one handles setting the junction switch, one processes the train into the barn, and one handles the case of entering a fixed junction. In our example, we document two of these services using pseudocode. This partial specification also depicts the multiple inheritance from the List and Cell objects that arises in the first stages of O-O design activities. This is shown here because early prototyping of important objects and services during analysis is frequently useful for establishing feasibility and proof of concept. This early prototyping required the reuse of library classes that handled list and data structures. The List and Cell classes are discussed further in the Kayjay World example of problem domain component design. It is not unusual in O-O projects for analysis and design activities to merge temporarily under opportunistic circumstances, such as prototyping of our Train Move service.

FIGURE 22.21B
Partial specification for the
Train class in the Kayjay
World system.

```
Additional_Constraints:
Notes:        A train is a list of passengers. It is also related to the CARLIST
              object, which is a list of carriages.
Service: Create me
Service: Destroy me
Service: Access Train Number (read)
Service: Access Circuits completed (read, incr, zero)
Service: Access Service State (read, set states)
State Codes: Inoperable=0, Queued =1, Running=2, Barn-Destined=3, Station
             Debarking & Barn-Destined=4, Station Debarking & Running=5, Station
             Embarking=6
Return Codes: True=1, False=0
Error Codes: Success=0, Failure=-1
Train Service: enter station, debark & embark passengers
               enterStation (Station *) Service chart pseudocode
               Trigger "debark passengers" service
               IF train is "barnbound"
                       THEN enterStation service is complete
                ELSE
                       trigger "embark passengers" service
                       enterStation service is complete
Train Service: enter barn, join queue of ready trains (Service chart pseudocode not
               shown)
Train Service: set switch, check if train is occupying a switch–set proper track
               branch for next move opportunity (Service chart pseudocode not shown)
Train Service: get track, determine which track segment is under train (Service
               chart pseudocode not shown)
Train Service: find fixed junction, finds track segment that is next for a train
               entering a fixed junction (Service chart pseudocode not shown)
Train Service: move train, moves train to next segment when possible
               moveTrain ( ) Service chart pseudocode
               IF states are not ok
                       THEN return "fails" message
               trigger get track service
               IF get track fails
                       THEN return "fails" message
               trigger getNext (in list base class) service
               IF getNext is "none"
                       THEN trigger find fixed junction service
                               IF find junction fails
                               THEN setup next track with getHead (in list base class)
                               service
                       IF next track segment is not free
                               THEN return "error" message
                       IF next track is a barn
                               THEN trigger enter barn service
                               AND return "ok" message
                       occupy next track
                       set current track value
                       free previous track
                       IF next track is a station
                               THEN trigger enter station service
                       prepare for next move by doing
                               trigger setSwitch service
                               trigger check system capacity service
                       return "ok"
```

Analyzing Subjects

In the case of very large systems, we can use an additional layer in the O-O
layered diagram package to organize the work of analysis, design, and implementation. This layer provides a means of dividing a complex specification
into logical work units. A subject layer is only necessary in large projects involving many classes. The subjects are noted by layering a broad shaded line,
one that denotes the boundaries of a particular subject, onto the O-O diagram.
The name of the subject is noted in one corner of the subject box.

Usually, a subject will have an apparent "owner" class. This is a class
that is centrally connected to all of the classes and objects in the subject
space. Typically the subject is named after this class.

Market Changes

"They want the core of the customer service representative's user interface to be radically reprogrammed again!" fumes Alberto Santos, the Information Systems Development Director at Mandelbrot Mutual Funds. "Only eight months ago, we completed a two-year development project of the CSR System—the Customer Service Representative System. During that entire project, we endured a nightmare of moving requirements. Every month, those guys in the Marketing Department would invent some competitive new customer service feature, and within a week, the CSR group would be down here with vast changes to the CSR System specification. I thought we'd never finish that project! Now it looks like we will have to start a new reprogramming project on a system less than a year old. We had forecast this system for a seven-year lifespan! Now I think it may be going into eternal reconstruction."

Alberto is downloading on Jessica Coates, the senior application systems analyst responsible for the CSR system, and Fletcher Henderson, the programmer who wrote most of the user interface. "Calm down Al," flushes Jessica. "This is not the fault of the kids in Marketing or CSR. The nature of our business has been affected by fast-paced competition. Marketing doesn't invent these changes out of boredom. They are often responding to new, computer-based customer services offered by our competition. We have to stay ahead, or at least keep up, or we'll all be looking for a new job!"

"Al, Jessie, I think you better know that the situation may be worse than you think," Fletcher chips in. "The programmers have actually been making small changes in the CSR user interface for the past eight months anyway. The CSR users have been calling us directly and begging for help. They typically want just a small change to one isolated part of the system. However, this has created a high labor drain because we have to recertify the entire system. You know how the effects of a small change can ripple throughout a large program. We've billed the time to program maintenance on the grounds that we thought we were just fine-tuning the completed system. Although the changes have been gradual, in eight months we've pretty much rewritten about a quarter of the CSR user interface code already. The work has not been falling off. It's still pretty steady."

"So what you're telling me," says Alberto, nearly flaming, "is that we have system needs in this area that have been changing constantly while we tried to write specifications, tried to write program code, and tried to make a fixed solution work against a fluid problem. How can we afford to write programs if they will only last a few months without needing expensive maintenance?"

How can Alberto manage a systems development process that no longer has fixed or constant business processes as part of its goal set? Is there a way for Jessica to manage a specification and to control maintenance costs when programmers are constantly asked to tinker with isolated parts of a large program? Keep in mind that an important goal is to provide good support for the users' needs and the organization's business strategies.

Kayjay World Example 5

Because of the amount of work involved in designing the Train, perhaps we should decide to divide the project into two subjects: (1) the Train Subject, including the Yard Manager, Passengers, Trains, and their components; and (2) the Railroad Subject, including the Capacity Manager and all forms of Tracks. Figure 22.22 shows the analysis of Kayjay World with the subject layer added.

We could have named the subjects "Yard Manager" and "Capacity Manager," because one of these classes was at the top of each of the two respective subject structures. However, these names don't match the way the users described the two general subjects. We choose to be more consistent with the users' language and name the Subjects "Railroad" and "Train." We could then divide our analysis and design project (and perhaps later, implementation) between two teams: the Railroad Subject team and the Train Subject team.

FIGURE 22.22
Subject layer for the analysis
of the Kayjay World system.

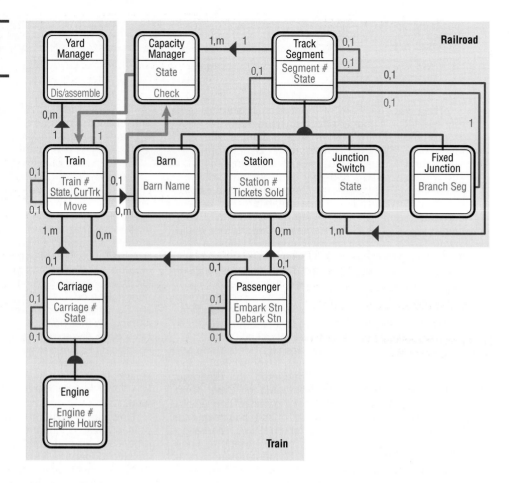

OBJECT-ORIENTED DESIGN

Design activities in the Coad and Yourdon approach carry the analysis tools forward into the complete set of specifications for implementation. Where the analysis is reasonably technology-independent, the design activities become increasingly oriented toward a particular O-O language and development environment.

O-O design activities are grouped into the four major components of the final system: the problem component, the human interface component, the data management component, and the task management component. Each of the five layers of the O-O design is expanded as needed across the four implementation components. Figure 22.23 shows how these elements interact to complete the system design.

All of the analysis documentation should carry directly into the design stage. Few new tools are needed at this point. The layered diagram package and the specification template remain the major components of the design. These documents are not supplemented or replaced, but instead are expanded to include the remaining implementation details during the design phase.

We frequently use prototypes (as discussed earlier in Chapter 8) during the design phase. Rough versions of the objects are created and tested in their roles within the four components. This means that frequently the design package is sent forward to the programmers with portions of the pro-

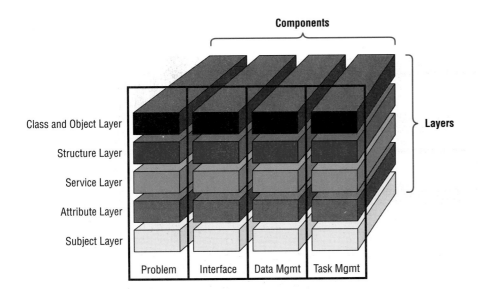

FIGURE 22.23
O-O design elements grouped
into components and layers.

gram code already written. Designers will often use the expected implementation language (such as C++ or SmallTalk) as the mechanism to write complete specifications for the classes. For example, the designer may find it easy to copy the C++ class definition from an operational prototype into the specification. This may prove to mean less work for the designer, and it eliminates duplicate efforts on the part of the designers and implementation programmers.

Designing the Problem Domain Component

The problem domain component (PDC) is the basic set of functional objects that arrive from the analysis stage. These objects directly solve the problems intended to be solved by the system we are building. The other components, such as human interface and data management, are incidental functions that must be added to the PDC in order to "get it working."

Consequently, the design for the PDC is mostly completed in the analysis stage. Only three activities are needed to complete the design of the PDC: reuse design, implementation structures, and language accommodation.

REUSE DESIGN. We may want to add new classes to the PDC in order to reuse objects. For example, there are commercial packages of highly generalized classes for objects. An experienced O-O programming organization usually owns a library of classes developed in-house for objects. These libraries and packages may contain classes that have attributes and services to objects similar to those required in our design. We can add these reusable classes to our design as base classes in a Gen–Spec structure. The derived classes in these Gen–Spec structures are the classes originally developed in the analysis stage.

IMPLEMENTATION STRUCTURES. We may want to add other structures to our design purely for implementation reasons. Also, we may want to use aggregation structures to create natural entry points for lists or queues—or a Gen–Spec structure to permit several classes of objects to share a protocol or data structure. These structures use the inheritance concept to make the programming task much easier.

LANGUAGE ACCOMMODATION. We may need to fix the design so that the structures can be built in the chosen programming language, since these languages may have different inheritance patterns. Some languages support multiple inheritance; others only support single inheritance; still others support *no* inheritance. In the more restrictive cases, the inheritance patterns in the design must be modified to allow for the capabilities of the implementation language.

Kayjay World Example 6

About this time in the project, we would probably begin to prototype the PDC using the planned program implementation language. For purposes of this example, we choose C++. We could use some of the C++ library classes for lists and queues as base classes for structures that connected tracks, connected passengers, and connected carriages. After some experimentation, we could settle on two base classes from a typical in-house library: List and Cell. The Cell class typically has all of the attributes and services needed for a doubly linked list data structure. The List class typically provides an "anchor" entry point for Cell-based lists and provides services such that the list could also be manipulated as a queue data structure.

Figure 22.24 illustrates a design for the List and Cell Gen–Spec structures. Every object that heads a list inherits the services and attributes of the List class from the library. Every object that is a member of a list inherits the services and attributes of the Cell class from the library. Notice that the List and Cell classes are never instantiated with objects of their own. They use Class symbols in the diagram rather than the Class-&-Object symbols used by all of the other classes. Track Segment is a specialization of both Cell, because it belongs to a list of track segments, and Passenger, which will belong to a list or queue of passengers. Likewise, Carriage belongs to a list of carriages in a train. Similarly, Station and Train are specializations of List because each may have a list of passengers. The Capacity Manager and Junction Switch have lists of tracks. The Yard Manager and Barn have lists of trains.

Train has multiple inheritance from both Cell and List. (This was also noted on the partial specification shown earlier.) It may be a member of a list or the head of a list—that is, it may be a member of a list of trains in the barn, for instance, and at the same time, the head of a list of on-board passengers. But there is a new Class-&-Object here as well: CarList. CarList is the head of a list and has an instance connection with Train: a one-to-one relationship. CarList is necessary because the Train object is actually the head of two lists: a list of passengers and a list of carriages. There is no easy way in C++ for Train to participate in two Gen–Spec structures with List. The only way to get a second Gen–Spec structure was to create the new Class-&-Object, CarList, and to connect it one-to-one with Train. Train is the head of a list of passengers and is directly related to one CarList, which is the head of a list of carriages.

Designing the Human Interface Component

In this activity, we create the menus, reports, and interactive screens that people will use to work with the system. The activities are basically the same as those we discussed earlier in Chapter 18 on Designing the User Interface. However, in the O-O design context, this phase culminates in a specification for new human interface component (HIC) classes that must be added to the design.

FIGURE 22.24
Design for the List and Cell
Gen–Spec structures for the
Kayjay World system.

Typically, we can lean heavily on library classes in the design of the HIC classes. This is one area where the reusability of O-O classes has proven to be very effective. Library classes usually provide generalizations of menus, windows, mouse control, icons, font control, and cut-and-paste utilities.

Prototypes are very useful during the HIC design for smoothing out just how the library classes will work with the PDC objects. As we described earlier in Chapter 8 on Prototyping, user interaction with the prototypes can provide extremely useful information about the effectiveness of the design.

Kayjay World Example 7

We generally employ interview information or user reflections to compile profiles of the users involved in the monorail system. Two examples built from Kayjay World user roles appear in Figure 22.25.

Based on these and other profiles, we could choose a touch-screen control interface based on a control panel metaphor. One reason for this choice is that the users lack the experience and education needed for more complex interfaces based on keyboards and menus. We might also have discovered that typical work environments were noisy and distracting, which could lead to errors unless the interface displays were large and clear.

Two major activities would follow: work on a command hierarchy (Figure 22.26) and work toward a crude prototype to determine what new classes would be needed from the C++ libraries. In this example, we need only add a single library class, ControlPanel, which provides all of the

FIGURE 22.25
Profiles of two users of the
Kayjay World monorail sys-
tem.

Kayjay World Monorail Control System User and Task Descriptions

1 I'm a Train Driver

1.1 Purpose: I control the deadman switch and emergency door and brake controls.
I also operate the radio and make announcements on the train's public address
system.

1.2 Characteristics

Age: I'm 20 years old.

Level of education: I'm a high school grad with 2 years of college.

Limitations: I don't have broad experience.

1.3 Critical Success Factors

I need to feel I am contributing.

I like to interact with people.

1.4 Skill level: Novice

1.5 Task scenario

Ride in front of train.

Monitor status indicators.

Operate deadman switch.

Make scripted announcements.

Follow emergency procedures.

2 I'm a Ticket Seller

2.1 Purpose: I explain the destinations to customers, collect cash or vouchers, and
issue tickets according to customers' requests.

2.2 Characteristics

Age: I'm 17 years old.

Level of education: I'm a high school student.

Limitations: I don't have broad experience.

2.3 Critical Success Factors

I need to feel I am contributing.

I like to interact with people.

2.4 Skill level: Novice

2.5 Task scenario

Customer arrives at window from queue, and I explain the three destinations.

I ask for destination & number in party.

I ask for the proper coupons or a cash amount.

If the coupons & cash are correct, I press the destination button and give
tickets to customer.

I tell the customer the next departure time and current train frequency (from
the video screen).

I direct customer to the boarding queue.

---

touch-screen management services. A prototype would show that most of
the HIC could be implemented as Menu objects derived from the Control-
Panel class.

The command hierarchy is carefully planned: The highest-level commands are directed to the lowest-level users. Ticket sales and status inquiries functions are most frequently used by young operators and station
managers. Further down the hierarchy are functions for the Station and Yard
Managers. At the very lowest level are sophisticated functions for assem-
bling trains for the system.

Now we can design and prototype the touch screens. Figure 22.27 depicts the prototype of the main control screen, and Figure 22.28 shows the
prototype of the main Yard Manager's screen.

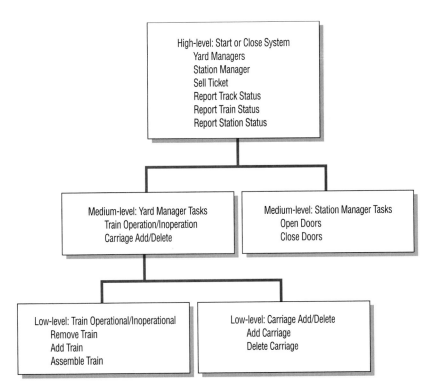

FIGURE 22.26
Command hierarchy for
the user interface design
for Kayjay World.

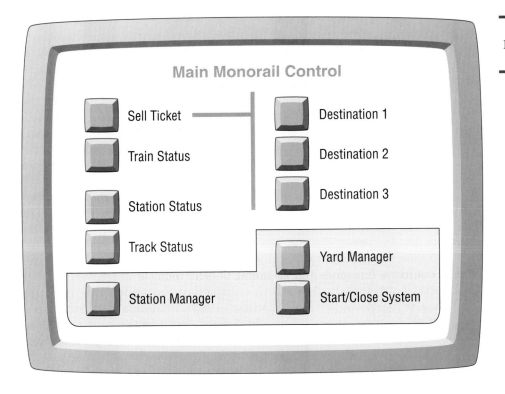

FIGURE 22.27
Main control touch screen for
the Kayjay World system.

FIGURE 22.28
Main screen for the Yard Manager of Kayjay World.

Designing Task and Data Management Components

These two components are very strongly linked to the implementation technology. Task management is heavily determined by the computing hardware configuration, and data management is heavily determined by the systems software available when the system is actually running.

The Task Management Component (TMC) is most important when the system is running on multiple processors or computers. A "task" is a collection of related services that should run together (perhaps on the same processor). Tasks are triggered by elapsed time or an event. The objects of the TMC obey task triggers, processor assignments, and priorities when services are invoked.

The TMC component typically appears as shown in Figure 22.29. This new TMC Subject is just added to the existing layered diagram package. The TMC component is then implemented by creating new Task objects as needed by the system.

The Data Management Component (DMC) typically regards the classes and objects needed to store and retrieve the other objects in the system. The DMC varies considerably depending on whether the underlying run-time technology is an object-oriented database, a relational database, or an ordinary "flat" file system. In an object-oriented database environment, the DMC is almost completely provided by the database. In a relational database or a flat-file environment, the DMC must provide storage services to the system.

There are three different ways to design the DMC. One approach is to build storage services into each Class-&-Object in the design. This usually involves a considerable amount of additional design programming.

An alternative is to create an ObjectServer Class-&-Object that provides all database services. This alternative involves a very complex object that

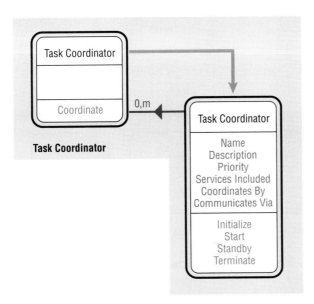

FIGURE 22.29
The task management
components of O-O
analysis and design.

knows how to store or retrieve all objects in the system. Any storage requests are made by means of messages to this single object. Figure 22.30 shows the design for an ObjectServer.

A third method is to create a Storable Class. This third approach is a combination of the previous two approaches. The Storable Class includes basic store-me and retrieve-me services in a generalized form. Every object in the system that must be stored or retrieved is then connected in a Gen–Spec structure to the Storable Class. This will usually work only in those cases where multiple inheritance is available in the implementation technology. Figure 22.31 shows a partial example of a Storable Class.

Kayjay World Example 8

The final steps in our example regard the design of the TMC and the DMC. The TMC is necessary because each train will process its object on the processor on-board each engine. This means that the services connected with moving a Train would form a natural task for these processors. We could also design three independent tasks that would run on the monorail system's central computer. One of them is the task associated with moving a train into the system. Another such task is the collection of routine mainte-

FIGURE 22.30
Design for an ObjectServer
Class-&-Object.

FIGURE 22.31
Partial example of a
Storable Class.

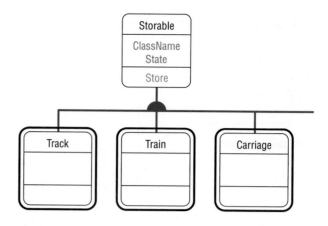

nance services. The third task running on the central computer is the task coordinator itself. The specifications for two of these task objects follow:

> **Task Name:** Coordinator
> > **Services:** Coordinate
> > **Processor:** Central
>
> **Task Name:** MoveTrain
> > **Description:** move train to next location
> > **Priority:** high
> > **Services:**
> > > train moves (train idle)
> > > switch branch or normal (empty train headed for barn
> > > > arrives at switch)
> > > occupy track (train moves)
> > > passenger embark & debark (trains stop at station)
> > **Coordinates by:** event (train idle)
> > **Communicates via:** input & output lines
> > **Processor:** Engine

In our example, we choose to use an ObjectServer approach to designing a DMC, since this could be easily implemented using the relational database already available to the monorail system computers. The ObjectServer will have to store and retrieve data about its own state and the state of the database as part of its processing. We must also design the relational table specifications for the objects Station, Junction Switch, Train, and Track, as well as the ObjectServer's own data (in a table named "StoreData"). We would likely have to prototype the ObjectServer, including the StoreData and Train tables, to make sure our design is feasible.

Prototyping would bring out some of the implementation problems more clearly. This design could be very difficult to implement for a variety of reasons. The C++ linked list structures and other object connections are probably all based on internal C++ pointers. These pointers would be meaningless when the object is stored in a database and deleted from the C++ memory heap. Consequently, the ObjectServer will have to both translate such references into relational foreign keys during storage and recreate the C++ linkages during retrieval. This is not a simple task, and it demonstrates the importance of an O-O database management system as part of the run-time package for an O-O design.

Below are a partial set of DMC specifications for the Kayjay World example:

Specification: ObjectServer
    Attribute: MetadataTable
    External_Input:
    External_Output:
    Object_State_Diagram:
    Additional_Constraints:
    Notes: Relational Database
    Service: Create me
    Service: Destroy me
    Service: Access MTableName
    Service: StoreObject
        Exit if unchanged
        If delete
            Switch on ClassName, each may
                delete inherited object rows
                delete object rows
                delete object
        If Update or Insert
            Switch on ClassName, each may
                Replace embedded pointers
                Add inherited pointers
                Insert or Update rows
                Set Storable State
    Service: RetrieveObject
        Switch on ClassName, each may
            Create Object
            Fetch & assign inherited rows
            Fetch & assign object row
            Set Storable State
    Service: Open
        For all TableNames in MTable
            Retrieve ClassName
            For all ObjIdNums in TableName
                RetrieveObject
    StateCodes: 0-unchanged since read, 1-newly created object, 2-updated since read, 3-deleted object

Table Specifications

Table: StoreData
Metadata for Monorail System

Column definitions

# Name	Type
1 ClassName	TEXT 25
Exact Class Name for object	
2 TableName	TEXT 20
Exact Database Table Name for Obj	
3 ColumnName	TEXT 20
Exact Database column name=Attrib	
4 AttribName	TEXT 25
Exact Attribute Name stored	

Table: Train
Table for storing train objects

Column definitions

# Name	Type
1 TrainNumber	INTEGER
2 Circuits	INTEGER
Circuits Complete	
3 State	INTEGER
Service State (Op, Inop, etc.)	
4 CurSeg	INTEGER
Current Track Segment Number	
5 CarList	INTEGER
ObjIdNum of related Car List	
6 Passengers	INTEGER
ObjIdNum of First Passenger	
7 ObjIdNum	INTEGER
ObjectIdNumber	

Table: Track
Table for storing track objects

Column definitions

# Name	Type
1 SegmentNumber	INTEGER
2 State	INTEGER
3 Us	INTEGER
ObjIdNumber of List of tracks	
4 PrevTrack	INTEGER
ObjIdNum of previous track	
5 NxtTrack	INTEGER
ObjIdNum of next track segment	
6 ObjIdNum	INTEGER
ObjectIdNumber	

Alternative Approaches and Notation

The O-O techniques presented here are based on one popular approach presented by Coad and Yourdon. There are many competing approaches which offer variations in the notation and types of analysis and design abstractions. The O-O community has searched for a unified methodology and notation. In 1997, two major proposals were placed before the Object Management Group as proposed standards for a visual modeling language for representing O-O systems. The Unified Modeling Language (UML) is one proposal submitted by a joint group of interested organizations, including Rational Software, Hewlett-Packard, Microsoft, Oracle, Texas Instruments, and Unisys. The OPEN (Object-Oriented Process, Environment, and Notation) Modeling Language (OML) is a competing proposal developed by an interested group of researchers, consultants and vendors. None of these techniques is easily comparable to the others. However, the notation can be translated directly. For example, in Figure 22.32, you will find the notation for inheritance used by UML and OML. They are mostly quite similar. The

Recycling the Programming Environment

"I feel like I'm writing the same code over and over again," says Benito Pérez, a programmer working on a new automated warehouse design. "I have written so many programs lately that dealt with robotic-type things that control themselves: automated mailroom trolleys, building surveillance robots, automatic pool cleaners, automatic lawnmowers, monorail trains, and now warehouse trolleys. These are all variations on a theme."

Lisa Bernoulli, the project manager, had heard this sort of complaint for years: "Oh come on, Ben, these things aren't really that close. How can you compare a mailroom robot, an automated warehouse, and a monorail train? I'll bet less than 10 percent of the code is the same."

"Look," says Benito, "all three involve machines that have to find a starting point, follow a circuitous route, make stops for loading and unloading, and eventually go to a stopping point. All three have to make decisions at branches in their routes. All three have to avoid colliding with things. I'm tired of redesigning code that is largely familiar to me."

"Hmmm," Lisa muses as she looks over the basic requirements for the warehouse system and remembers the monorail system she and Benito had worked on last year. The requirements regarded a small-lot electronics manufacturing firm that was automating its warehouse and product movement system. The warehouse contains incoming parts, work-in-progress, and finished goods. The automated warehouse uses a flatbed robot trolley. This robot is a four-wheel electric cart, similar to a golf cart, except that it has no seats. Flatbed robot trolleys have a flat, six-foot by four-foot cargo surface about three feet above ground level. These trolleys have a radio communications device that provides a real-time data link to a central warehouse computer. Flatbed trolleys have two sensors: a path sensor that detects a special type of paint and a motion sensor that detects movement. These trolleys follow painted paths around the factory floor. Special paint codes mark forks or branches in the paths, trolley start or stop points, and general location points.

The facility includes three loading dock stations and ten workstations. Each station has a video terminal or computer connected to the central computer. When products are needed or are ready to be collected from a workstation, the central computer is informed by the worker at the station. The central computer then dispatches trolleys accordingly. Each station has a drop point and a pickup point. Flatbed trolleys move about the factory picking up work at pickup points and dropping off work at drop points. The program that will run the trolleys must interact heavily with the existing job-scheduling program that helps schedule workstation tasks.

How similar are the trolleys to the monorail trains in the Kayjay World examples? How should Lisa go about reusing Benito Pérez's work on the monorail in their current task of creating a trolley object? Explain in two paragraghs.

---

important thing to realize here is that once you understand the principles of inheritance, a change in notation is not difficult.

Techniques for O-O analysis and design, which are much the same as O-O programming, are still somewhat in a developmental phase. Although it is not yet clear whether any single approach will become widely accepted, the techniques and notation that you have learned in this chapter certainly represent a good beginning for those interested in gaining further experience with the general concepts of object-oriented techniques.

SUMMARY

Object-oriented analysis and design techniques were developed in response to the increasing use of O-O programming languages. O-O designs can effectively specify such new O-O programming structures as inheritance and polymorphism. There are a number of diverse approaches to O-O analysis and design. In this chapter, we studied one such approach, which was devised by Peter Coad and Ed Yourdon.

FIGURE 22.32
Comparative inheritance design notation of different proposed O-O analysis and
design standards.

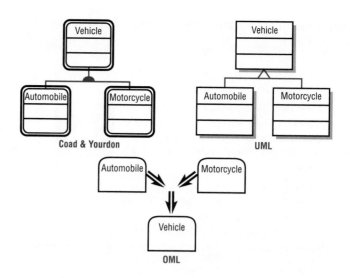

The basic concepts underlying object-oriented analysis are objects, classes, messages, encapsulation, inheritance, and polymorphism. An object is a computer representation of some real-world thing or event. Similar objects are grouped into categories called classes. A class is the system specification for a group of similar (or related) objects. Objects communicate with each other through messages. A message is sent by one object to another object and is intended to stimulate some particular, predefined behavior by the receiver. Because all of an object's internal data is buffered from other objects by internal predefined processes (the object's behavior), objects are said to encapsulate their data. The only way to change data held by an object is by sending a message to that object that will stimulate the object to make such an internal change. The inheritance concept refers to the ability to create new (derived) classes based in part on old (base) classes. Derived classes can inherit all or part of the structure and behavior of base classes and extend them with new structures and behaviors. Inheritance opens the way for polymorphic objects. Polymorphism permits a base class to take the form of any of its derived classes when the circumstances demand it. Furthermore, derived classes may substitute their own behavior in place of their base class's behavior in reaction to certain messages from other objects.

The Coad and Yourdon O-O model consists of five layers. Classes and objects are noted in the first layer. Second, a structure layer details relationships between classes or objects. Attributes of classes are noted in the third layer. A service layer details messages and object behaviors. Finally, a subject layer may be used to divide large models into project units.

Objects are computer representations of tangible things, roles, incidents, interactions, or specifications. Typically, objects embody a need to be recalled or remembered; a distinct set of several attributes, each with a meaningful value; siblings with exactly the same behavior; and independence from their implementation technology.

Structures link classes or objects. Classes may be linked together in a Gen–Spec structure for inheritance. Objects may also be linked together in a Whole–Part structure for aggregation. Aggregation involves objects that are composed or assembled from other objects.

Attributes are the data fields maintained by and related to a class. In addition, the attribute specification may include instance connections between objects. Instance connections represent some nonstructural relationship between two objects, such as the relationship between a vehicle object and an owner object.

Services are the behavior of objects and typically embody mechanisms by which the object can change its state. Simple services, such as those that merely set a data value, are generally not documented in the O-O model. Complex services that involve conditional processes or subroutines are documented in a specification template, which may also include attribute and state details. Services are typically triggered by messages created by other objects' services. Again, messages that trigger simple services are generally not detailed in the O-O model.

The entire O-O design package maps the five-layered O-O model onto four major system components. The problem domain component contains the basic set of functions that accomplish the system's primary goals or purposes. The human interface component includes menus, interactive screens, and reports that represent the exchanges between computers in the system and people using the system. The task management component collects various services together into tasks that occur at related times or are related to a particular processing unit. The data management component provides mechanisms for retrieving and storing objects, classes, and system states. The task and data management components are closely dependent on implementation technologies, such as the exact model and configuration of computer hardware and the exact vendor and version of database management programs, used in the system.

O-O analysis, design, and programming have been developed in response to the need for flexibility in computer-based information systems. Encapsulation, inheritance, and polymorphism are intended to provide complex systems with mechanisms for fast, easy, and reliable program maintenance and change. Although O-O development typically involves a more extensive (and expensive) analysis and design phase, this investment pays off in lower operating costs for systems that are likely to require high maintenance activity.

KEYWORDS AND PHRASES

object-oriented
instantiate
object
class
message
encapsulation
inheritance
base class
multiple inheritance
derived class
polymorphism
O-O analysis
subject
service layer
generalization–specialization
   structure (Gen–Spec)
classification
assemblies
cardinality

instance connections
whole–part structure
self association
object state analysis
problem component
specification template
simple services
human interface component
state diagrams
complex services
companion services
private services
Task Management
   Component (TMC)
Data Management
   Component (DMC)
object-oriented database
prototype

REVIEW QUESTIONS

1. What are the six basic ideas that characterize object-oriented programming?
2. Describe the difference between an Object and a Class.
3. How does encapsulation change the manner in which data are updated by programs?
4. What two types of classes are involved in any inheritance relationship?
5. Multiple inheritance means that there will be multiple occurrences of which type of class in the inheritance relationship?
6. Does polymorphism only occur where there is inheritance?
7. What are five general types of objects?
8. How can you tell from Coad and Yourdon's notation whether a class has been instantiated with objects?
9. What are eight criteria used to determine whether a new class is justified?
10. What are two basic types of structures that might be imposed on classes and objects?
11. What is the name of the notation used to denote a reference from one class to an unrelated class?
12. How can state changes be discovered easily in objects?
13. What are two categories of services?
14. How are messages denoted in the service layer of a Coad and Yourdon diagram?
15. What kind of project typically calls for the use of subject layers?
16. What four major components comprise the design activities?
17. What three activities take place in completing the problem domain component?
18. Which two design components are very strongly linked to implementation technology?
19. Define the term *TMC*.
20. What are three ways to design a Data Management Component?
21. Which approach to the design of the Data Management Component involves a very complex additional object?

PROBLEMS

1. The Kayjay World Station Master is typically a college student in his or her early twenties. The Station Master's duties include supervising the Ticket Seller and Platform Guards at their respective stations. The Station Master actually operates some train controls, including the "door open," "door close," and "boarding complete" switches. "I want a simple system," says Buffy Bronzebight, "one that I know will allow passengers to embark and debark safely. Confusion on the station platform is dangerous, and unexpected delays irritate the visitors. In the best of all worlds, the trains move regularly. Next best are delays you expect. You can announce them to the passengers, and then they don't get so mad. The worst delays are the unexpected ones. My job is pretty straightforward: When an arriving train comes to a complete halt, I press the 'door open' switch and allow train passengers to debark. After all passengers have debarked, I instruct the guards to allow the queued passengers to board the train. When all passengers have boarded or the train seats have filled, I instruct the guards to check the

platform for safety and press the 'door close' switch. I then check the train visually according to the safety procedure and press the 'boarding complete' switch so the train may leave."

Based on this information, write user and task descriptions for the Station Master.

2. The Kayjay World Capacity Manager is a full-time position typically held by an experienced person with a college degree, although this individual has only rarely been someone trained in computers or engineering. Sam Spindlefold has held this position for twelve years. "I monitor the operation of the monorail system and the barn," he says, "and watch over track conditions and station operations. It is my system: I'm in charge of starting and stopping the system and supervising all manual operations. I also have to be sure that the 'right' number of trains are operating. When the monorail was first installed, I spent three weeks with the contractor's engineers learning how it all worked. What matters most to me is that the system runs smoothly in bad conditions. Also, I should not be bothered with operational problems in typical conditions. I'm happy when the trains move smoothly around the system at peak hours and passengers are never delayed more than seven minutes when waiting for a train. I usually work the startup shift: I select 'startup system' from my screen. As soon as the Train Driver presses the deadman switch (kind of like a throttle), the first train launches from the barn. Although I rarely work a closedown shift, those people only have to select 'closedown system' from their screen. All empty trains exit the system. I dread 'alarm' conditions, such as a train failure or driver release of the deadman switch. In such cases, I may have to manually override controls by issuing radio instructions to Train Drivers or Station Managers, by having yard workers manually switch the junction, or by sending the gasoline-powered yard engine out to tow a disabled train."

Based on this information, write user and task descriptions for the Capacity Manager.

3. The Kayjay World Yard Manager is in charge of the operating condition of the trains, monitoring their operating performance, coupling trains and placing them in service, and uncoupling trains and removing them for maintenance. Yard Managers also remove or add rolling stock when new cars are purchased or old ones are junked. Yard Managers are often trained mechanics or machinists, and most are very experienced. Billy Leroy has been working at Kayjay World since it opened fifteen years ago. He says, "What I want most is a yard link that's easy to change and works all the time so's I can yank a train over to the yard fast and get another train out in its place fast. I don't want a complicated computer system that gets in my way when I need to assemble trains from yard stock. I want to turn the doggone computer control off if I need to. I spend most of my day fixing broken train parts. For example, say a train is sent to the barn with a jammed door. First I look for a quick fix. There usually isn't one, and I have to select commands from the computer menu that tells the system that the train is inoperable. Then I manually set two yard switches in the barn queue and yard and use manual controls to drive the train onto one yard siding. Next I have to uncouple the train and use a gasoline yard engine to pull the bad car onto the repair rack. I can then recouple the remaining cars and use the

computer menu to enter the new train configuration. Once again, I manually set two yard switches and return the short train to the barn queue, and then I use the computer menu to tell the system that the train is again operable."

Based on this information, write user and task descriptions for the Yard Manager.

4. Draw a prototype touch screen for the "Train Operational Control" portion of the Kayjay World Command hierarchy.

5. Complete the Kayjay World Example 8 TMC specifications by writing the ExitBarn and Maintenance task specifications. ExitBarn would move a train into the system. Maintenance would handle a number of miscellaneous tasks, chiefly those operating according to human input and control—that is, train enters barn queue because it is going out of service; start system (a clock-driven process each morning); close system (a clock-driven process each evening); a train breaks (becomes inoperative); a train gets fixed (becomes operative); a train gets assembled from cars and engines; a new car is added to the rolling stock; an old car gets junked.

6. Complete Kayjay World Example 8 DMC ObjectServer specifications by writing definitions for "Close" and "Backup" Services. Close would write all objects to the database as part of the shut-down process. Backup would capture a "snapshot" of the current objects in case of a computer crash.

7. Complete the Kayjay World Example 8 DMC Relational Database Table Specifications by writing the Station and JuncSwitch Objects table definitions. Work from the attribute definitions and don't forget to add any necessary referential attributes.

8. Complete the Kayjay World Example 4 Specification by designing a service logic flow diagram (or other procedural specification) for the "Enter Barn" train service.

9. Complete the Kayjay World Example 4 Specification by designing a service logic flow diagram (or other procedural specification) for the "Set Switch" train service.

10. Complete the Kayjay World Example 4 Specification by designing a service logic flow diagram (or other procedural specification) for the "Get Track" train service.

11. Complete the Kayjay World Example 4 Specification by designing a service logic flow diagram (or other procedural specification) for the "find fixed junction" train service.

SELECTED BIBLIOGRAPHY

Booch, G. *Object-Oriented Design with Applications,* 2nd ed. Redwood City, CA: Benjamin/Cummings, 1994.

Coad, P., and E. Yourdon. *Object-Oriented Analysis,* 2nd ed. Englewood Cliffs, NJ: Yourdon Press, 1991.

Coad, P., and E. Yourdon. *Object-Oriented Design.* Englewood Cliffs, NJ: Yourdon Press, 1991.

Embley, D., B. Kurtz, and S. Woodfield. *Object-Oriented Systems Analysis: A Model-Driven Approach.* Englewood Cliffs, NJ: Yourdon Press, 1992.

Firesmith, D., B. Henderson-Sellers, I. Graham, and M. Page-Jones. *OPEN Modeling Language (OML) Reference Manual Version 1.0.* Cary, North Carolina: OPEN Consortium, Knowledge Systems Corporation, December 8, 1996.

Rumbaugh, J., M. Blaha, W. Premerlani, F. Eddy, and W. Lorensen. *Object-Oriented Modeling and Design.* Englewood Cliffs, NJ: Prentice Hall, 1991.

Shlaer, S., and S. Mellor. *Object Lifecycles: Modeling the World in States.* Englewood Cliffs, NJ: Yourdon Press, 1992.

Shlaer, S., and S. Mellor. *Object-Oriented Systems Analysis: Modeling the World in Data.* Englewood Cliffs, NJ: Yourdon Press, 1988.

Unified Modeling Language Notation Guide ad/97–01–09. Santa Clara, CA: Rational Software Corporation, 1997.

INDEX

Page numbers followed by an italic *f* refer to figures.

Classes (continued)
new classes, criteria for, 872
Classification codes, 731–732
Class/object layer, O-O analysis, 871f
Client-based application, 830
Client/server model, 830–832
client in, 830
file server, 832
print server, 832
pros/cons of, 832
system configuration, 831f
Closedness, in organizations, 30
Closed questions
interviews, 115f–116
pros/cons of, 115–116, 152
questionnaires, 151–153f
Clothing, STROBE assessment, 185
Cluster sample, 82
COBOL code, generation of, 805–806, 808f
Code generation, 802–807
benefits of, 15–17
COBOL code, 805–806, 808f
example report, 803–806
full and partial generators, 803
meaning of, 802
software products for, 803, 805f–807f
Codes
data repository, 303
keying, and interface, 676
Coding, 727–738
advantages of, 727
alphabetic derivation codes, 730
block sequence codes, 732
cipher codes, 733
classification codes, 731–732
for classification of information, 730–732
for concealing information, 732–733
design guidelines, 735f–738
design objectives, 728f
function codes, 735
mnemonic codes, 734–735, 736
purposes of, 728
for requesting appropriate action, 735
for revealing information, 733–734
significant-digit subset codes, 733–734f
simple sequence codes, 728–729, 730f
for tracking purposes, 728–730
Collaborative filtering, 408
Color, input design, 579–582
Column charts
deviation column chart, 460–461f
100% column chart, 460, 461f
simple chart, 453–454f
systems proposal, 459–461
Command button, graphical user interface (GUI), 579
Command-language interface, 670–672f
operation of, 670, 672
Command languages, and syntax rules, 672
Communication
and CASE tools, 13–14
and team members, 67
Complex random sample, 81
Computer Aided Software Engineering. See CASE tools

Computer Assisted Reengineering (CARE), 17
Computer-based scheduling, 65–66
Computer supported collaborative work (CSCW). See Group decision support systems (GDSS)
Concatenated key, 614
Conclusion, presentations, 468
Conditional forecasting, 431
Consultants, systems analyst as, 5–6
Context diagram, 238–241, 240f, 255f, 263f
Context level data flow diagram, 32–33f
airline reservation system example, 32, 33f
symbols of, 32f
Context-sensitive help, 685–686
Continuous elements, 306
Continuous speech systems, 680
Control breaks, in printed report, 512, 513
Control flags, structure charts, 778, 779
Control modules, 788–789, 790, 792f
Convenience sample, 81
Conversion of system, 845–851
direct changeover, 845–846
distributed conversion, 847
gradual conversion, 847
modular conversion, 847
parallel conversion, 846–847
system analyst, role of, 850
CoolSheets, 472
Cost/benefit analysis, 434–442, 851
alternative methods, 442
break-even analysis, 437
cash-flow analysis, 438–439
general guidelines, 441
intangible benefits, 436
intangible costs, 437
limitations of, 851
payback, 437–438
present value, 440–441
tangible benefits, 434
tangible costs, 436–437
Cover letter, systems proposal, 452
Critical path, PERT diagrams, 62, 64–65
Crow's Foot notation, 33
Cue cards, 686
Culture, organizational, 42, 44

D

Data
attributes, 612
entities, 608
file organization, 615–619
keys, 613–614
metadata, 614–615
records, 612–613
relationships, 608–612
Database management system (DBMS), 606
Database organization, 619–623
files. See File organization
hierarchical data structures, 619–621, 620f, 621f
network data structures, 621–622f
relational data structures, 622–623f
Databases
data retrieval, steps in, 637–642, 638f

logical model, 619
objectives for use of, 606
pros/cons of, 606–608
relational databases, 607–608
views, 619
Data capture, 738–745
bottlenecks, avoiding, 741
and changeable data, 739
and computer capabilities, 739–741
data capture forms, 90–93
data entry methods, 741–745
and differentiation data, 739
effective source documents, 741
extra steps, avoiding, 741
initial decisions about, 738–739
Data coupling, 780
structure charts, 778
Data dictionary
and data flow diagram, 299f, 311–312, 312f
data stores, 314–315
functions of, 9, 297, 298
input/output data flows, 312–314
and process specifications, 351–353
repository. See Data repository
uses of, 315–318
Data elements, 304–307, 612
characteristics of, 304–307
element description form, 305f
Data entry
coding, 727–738
data capture, 738–745
data input validation, 745–751
and graphical user interface (GUI), 752
objectives of, 727
Data entry methods, 741–745
bar codes, 744–745
keyboard, 742
magnetic ink character recognition (MICR), 742–743
mark-sense forms, 743–744
optical character recognition (OCR), 742
punch-out forms, 744f
Data flow
data flow description form, 299, 301f
internal, 300
Data flow diagrams
advantages of, 235–236
child diagrams, 241–242, 243f, 258f, 265f, 266f
construction, examples of, 254–267
context diagram, 238–241, 240f, 255f, 263f
for data dictionary, 299f, 311–312, 312f
diagram 0, 239–241, 255–257, 256f, 257f, 264f
error checking, 242–247, 245f, 246f
exploding the diagrams, 239–241, 240f
functions of, 9
logical data flow diagrams, 247–249f
parent diagram, 241, 243f
partitioning of, 252–254, 257–262, 261f, 268f
physical data flow diagrams, 249f, 250–252, 259f
and process specifications, 343f, 366, 367f, 368f
structure charts, 783, 784f, 785, 787

HYPERCASE EXPERIENCES